The WESTERN HERITAGE

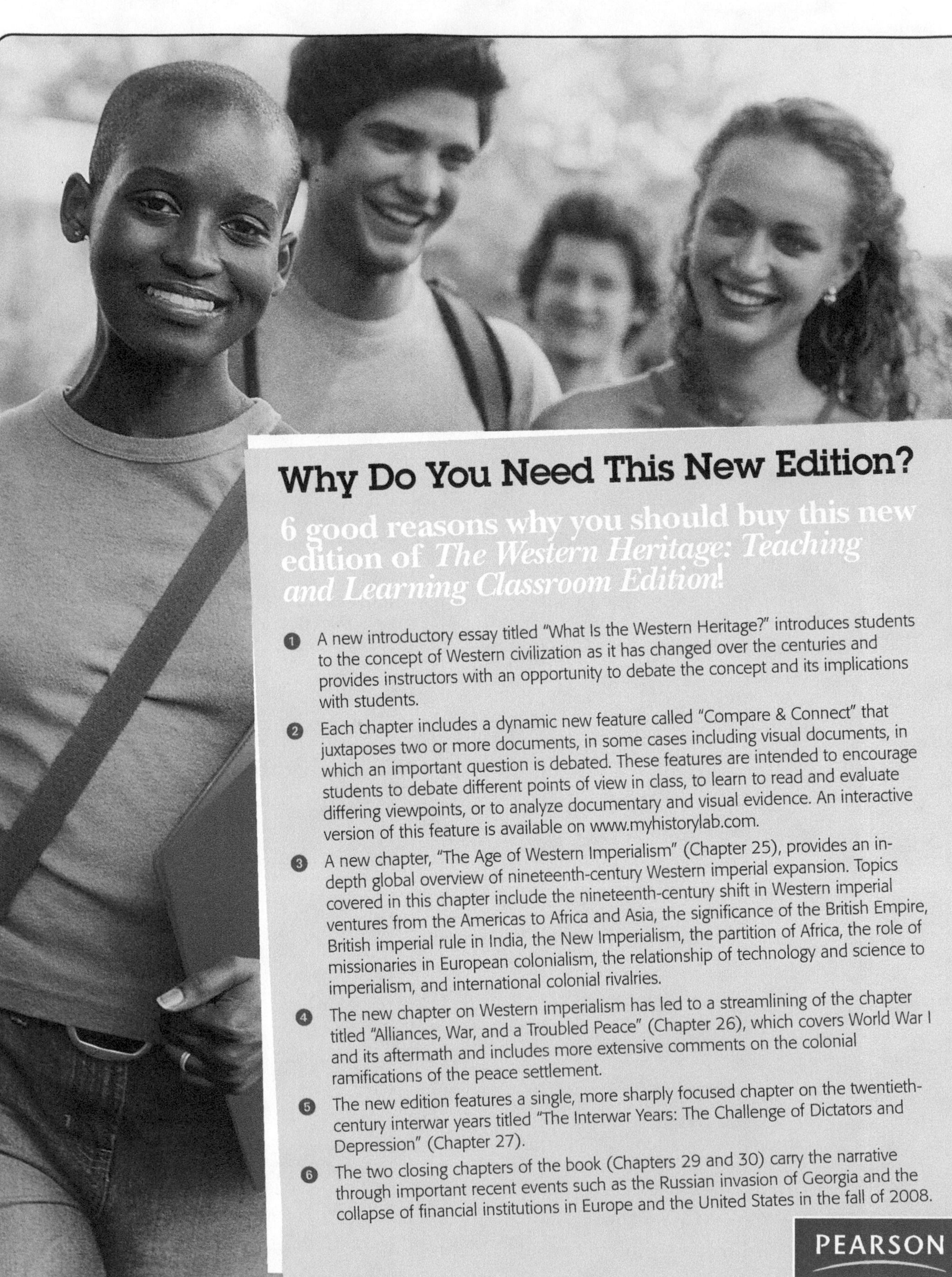
Why Do You Need This New Edition?
6 good reasons why you should buy this new edition of The Western Heritage: Teaching and Learning Classroom Edition!
1 A new introductory essay titled "What Is the Western Heritage?" introduces students to the concept of Western civilization as it has changed over the centuries and provides instructors with an opportunity to debate the concept and its implications with students.
2 Each chapter includes a dynamic new feature called "Compare & Connect" that juxtaposes two or more documents, in some cases including visual documents, in which an important question is debated. These features are intended to encourage students to debate different points of view in class, to learn to read and evaluate differing viewpoints, or to analyze documentary and visual evidence. An interactive version of this feature is available on www.myhistorylab.com.
3 A new chapter, "The Age of Western Imperialism" (Chapter 25), provides an in-depth global overview of nineteenth-century Western imperial expansion. Topics covered in this chapter include the nineteenth-century shift in Western imperial ventures from the Americas to Africa and Asia, the significance of the British Empire, British imperial rule in India, the New Imperialism, the partition of Africa, the role of missionaries in European colonialism, the relationship of technology and science to imperialism, and international colonial rivalries.
4 The new chapter on Western imperialism has led to a streamlining of the chapter titled "Alliances, War, and a Troubled Peace" (Chapter 26), which covers World War I and its aftermath and includes more extensive comments on the colonial ramifications of the peace settlement.
5 The new edition features a single, more sharply focused chapter on the twentieth-century interwar years titled "The Interwar Years: The Challenge of Dictators and Depression" (Chapter 27).
6 The two closing chapters of the book (Chapters 29 and 30) carry the narrative through important recent events such as the Russian invasion of Georgia and the collapse of financial institutions in Europe and the United States in the fall of 2008.
PEARSON

The Western Heritage

Teaching and Learning Classroom Edition

Brief Sixth Edition

Combined Volume

Donald Kagan
Yale University

Steven Ozment
Harvard University

Frank M. Turner
Yale University

Prentice Hall

Boston Columbus Indianapolis New York San Francisco Upper Saddle River
Amsterdam Cape Town Dubai London Madrid Milan Munich
Paris Montreal Toronto Delhi Mexico City Sao Paulo Sydney
Hong Kong Seoul Singapore Taipei Tokyo

VP, Editorial Director: Leah Jewell
Executive Editor: Charles Cavaliere
Editorial Project Manager: Rob DeGeorge
Production Project Manager: Lynn Savino Wendel
Editorial Assistant: Lauren Aylward
Director of Marketing: Brandy Dawson
Senior Managing Editor: Ann Marie McCarthy
Copy Editor: Martha Williams
Proofreader: Donna Mulder
Senior Operations Supervisor: Mary Ann Gloriande
Senior Art Director: Maria Lange
Text Designer: Jill Little
Cover Designer: John Christiana/Corrin Skidds
AV Project Manager: Mirella Signoretto
Manager, Visual Research: Beth Brenzel
Manager, Rights and Permissions: Zina Arabia
Image Permission Coordinator: Michelina Viscusi
Manager, Cover Visual Research & Permissions: Karen Sanatar
Cover Art: Karl Marx/Bettmann/Corbis
Media Director: Brian Hyland
Lead Media Project Manager: Sarah Kinney
Supplements Editor: Emsal Hasan
Composition, Full-Service Project Management: Rebecca Dunn, Prepare, Inc.
Printer/Binder: Courier Companies, Inc.
Cover Printer: Courier Companies, Inc.

This book was set in 10/13 Goudy Regular.

Credits and acknowledgments borrowed from other sources and reproduced, with permission, in this textbook appear on appropriate page within text.

Library of Congress Cataloging-in-Publication Data

Kagan, Donald.
The Western heritage/Donald Kagan, Steven Ozment, Frank M. Turner. —Teaching and learning classroom edition, Brief 6th ed.
p. cm.
"Combined volume."
Includes bibliographical references and index.
ISBN 978-0-205-72891-6 (combined)—ISBN 978-0-205-73210-4 (exam)—ISBN 978-0-205-72892-3 (volume one)—
ISBN 978-0-205-72893-0 (volume two)
1. Civilization, Western—History—Textbooks. I. Ozment, Steven E. II. Turner, Frank M. (Frank Miller), 1944 III. Title.
CB245.K28 2010b
909'.09821–dc22 2009014281

8 9 10 V092 16 15

Prentice Hall
is an imprint of

www.pearsonhighered.com

Student edition ISBN 10:0-205-72891-X
ISBN 13:978-0-205-72891-6
Examination Copy ISBN 10:0-205-73210-0
ISBN 13:978-0-205-73210-4

BRIEF CONTENTS

CONTENTS

PART 2 The Middle Ages, 476 C.E.–1300 C.E.

6 Late Antiquity and the Early Middle Ages: Creating a New European Society and Culture (476–1000) 148

7 The High Middle Ages: The Rise of European Empires and States (1000–1300) 176

8 Medieval Society: Hierarchies, Towns, Universities, and Families (1000–1300) 200

MAPS

PREFACE

Students undertaking the study of the Western heritage on the threshold of the second decade of the twenty-first century do so at a remarkable historical moment. In 2008, the United States elected its first African American president, a Democrat backed by larger Democratic congressional majorities pledged to undertaking major new policy directions at home and abroad. Both the Western and non-Western worlds confront a changing global economy that gave birth to a financial crisis with the most serious implications for economic stability since the 1930s. The August 2008 invasion of Georgia by Russian Federation troops signaled the possibility of a move from a period of relative quietude to one of military resurgence that may bring into question numerous strategic military assumptions that prevailed for almost two decades after the collapse of the Soviet Union. The United States and Western Europe, after several years of controversial military engagement in Iraq and Afghanistan, continue efforts to reshape foreign policy with an emphasis on diplomacy instead of preemptive warfare. Christians in the Northern and Southern Hemispheres continue to be sharply divided as they debate the character of their faith and its relationship to other faiths and the social questions of the day. A growing consensus of opinion recognizes the dangers posed by environmental change.

The authors of this volume continue to believe that the heritage of Western civilization remains a major point of departure for understanding and defining the challenges of this no longer new century. The unprecedented globalization of daily life that is a hallmark of our era has occurred largely through the spread of Western influences. From the sixteenth century onward, the West has exerted vast influences throughout the globe for both good and ill, and today's global citizens continue to live in the wake of that impact. It is the goal of this book to introduce its readers to the Western heritage, so that they may be better informed and more culturally sensitive citizens of the increasingly troubled and challenging global age. The events of recent years and the hostility that has arisen in many parts of the world to the power and influence of the West require new efforts to understand how the West sees itself and how other parts of the world see the West.

Since *The Western Heritage* first appeared, we have sought to provide our readers with a work that does justice to the richness and variety of Western civilization and its many complexities. We hope that such an understanding of the West will foster lively debate about its character, values, institutions, and global influence. Indeed, we believe such a critical outlook on their own culture has characterized the peoples of the West since the dawn of history. Through such debates we define ourselves and the values of our culture. Consequently, we welcome the debate and hope that *The Western Heritage: Teaching and Learning Classroom Edition*, Brief Sixth Edition, can help foster an informed discussion through its history of the West's strengths and weaknesses, and the controversies surrounding Western history. To further that debate, we have included a new introductory essay entitled "What Is the Western Heritage?" to introduce students to the concept of the West and to allow instructors and students to have a point of departure for debating this concept in their course of study.

We also believe that any book addressing the experience of the West must also look beyond its historical European borders. Students reading this book come from a wide variety of cultures and experiences. They live in a world of highly interconnected economies and instant communication between cultures. In this emerging multicultural society it seems both appropriate and necessary to recognize how Western civilization has throughout its history interacted with other cultures, both influencing and being influenced by them. For this reason, we have introduced to this edition a new chapter on the nineteenth-century European age of imperialism. Further examples of Western interaction with other parts of the world, such as with Islam, appear throughout the text.

In this edition as in past editions, our goal has been to present Western civilization fairly, accurately, and in a way that does justice to this great, diverse legacy of human enterprise. History has many facets, no single one of which can alone account for the others. Any attempt to tell the story of the West from a single overarching perspective, no matter how timely, is bound to neglect or suppress some important parts of this story. Like all other authors of introductory texts, we have had to make choices, but we have attempted to provide the broadest possible introduction to Western civilization.

Goals of the Text

Our primary goal has been to present a strong, clear, narrative account of the central developments in Western history. We have also sought to call attention to certain critical themes:

- The capacity of Western civilization, from the time of the Greeks to the present, to transform itself through self-criticism.
- The development in the West of political freedom, constitutional government, and concern for the rule of law and individual rights.
- The shifting relations among religion, society, and the state.
- The development of science and technology and their expanding impact on Western thought, social institutions, and everyday life.
- The major religious and intellectual currents that have shaped Western culture.

We believe that these themes have been fundamental in Western civilization, shaping the past and exerting a continuing influence on the present.

Flexible Presentation *The Western Heritage: Teaching and Learning Classroom Edition,* Brief Sixth Edition, is designed to accommodate a variety of approaches to a course in Western civilization, allowing teachers to stress what is most important to them. Some teachers will ask students to read all the chapters. Others will select among them to reinforce assigned readings and lectures. We believe the "Compare & Connect" and "Encountering the Past" features may also be adopted selectively by instructors for purposes of classroom presentation and debate and as the basis for short written assignments.

Integrated Social, Cultural, and Political History *The Western Heritage* provides one of the richest accounts of the social history of the West available today, with strong coverage of family life, the changing roles of women, and the place of the family in relation to broader economic, political, and social developments. This coverage reflects the explosive growth in social historical research in the past half-century, which has enriched virtually all areas of historical study.

We have also been told repeatedly by teachers that no matter what their own historical specialization, they believe that a political narrative gives students an effective tool to begin to understand the past. Consequently, we have sought to integrate such a strong political narrative with our treatment of the social, cultural, and intellectual factors in Western history.

We also believe that religious faith and religious institutions have been fundamental to the development of the West. No other survey text presents so full an account of the religious and intellectual development of the West. People may be political and social beings, but they are also reasoning and spiritual beings. What they think and believe are among the most important things we can know about them. Their ideas about God, society, law, gender, human nature, and the physical world have changed over the centuries and continue to change. We cannot fully grasp our own approach to the world without understanding the religious and intellectual currents of the past and how they influenced our thoughts and conceptual categories. We seek to recognize the impact of religion in the expansion of the West, including the settlement the Americas in the sixteenth century and the role of missionaries in nineteenth-century Western imperialism.

Clarity and Accessibility Good narrative history requires clear, vigorous prose. As with earlier editions, we have paid careful attention to our writing, subjecting every paragraph to critical scrutiny. Our goal has been to make the history of the West accessible to students without compromising vocabulary or conceptual level. We hope this effort will benefit both teachers and students.

The Brief Sixth Edition

New to This Edition

- We include a new introductory essay entitled "What Is the Western Heritage?" designed to introduce students to the concept of Western civilization as it has changed over the centuries and at the same to provide instructors the opportunity to debate this concept and its implications with their students.
- Each chapter includes a new feature entitled "**Compare & Connect**" that juxtaposes two or more documents in which an important question is debated or a comparison between a document and an illustration is presented. Each "Compare & Connect" feature contains three to five questions on each of the documents, one of which asks students to make connections between and among the viewpoints presented in the feature. These features are intended to encourage students to debate different points of view in class and to learn to read and evaluate differing viewpoints or to analyze documentary and visual evidence. An interactive version of this feature is available on www.myhistorylab.com.

- An entirely new chapter, "The Age of Western Imperialism" (Chapter 25), provides an in-depth global overview of nineteenth-century Western imperial expansion. Topics covered in this chapter include the nineteenth-century shift in Western imperial ventures from the Americas to Africa and Asia, the significance of the British Empire, British imperial rule in India, the New Imperialism, the partition of Africa, the role of missionaries in European colonialism, the relationship of technology and science to imperialism, and international colonial rivalries.
- The new chapter on imperialism has led to a streamlining of the chapter on World War I and its aftermath as well as more extensive comments on the colonial ramifications of the peace settlement (Chapter 26).
- A single, more sharply focused chapter on the twentieth-century interwar years (Chapter 27) has replaced two longer chapters on this period.
- The two closing chapters of the book (Chapters 29 and 30) carry the narrative through important recent events such as the Russian invasion of Georgia and the collapse of financial institutions in Europe and the United States in the fall of 2008.

Ongoing Features That Enliven Student Interest and Understanding

"Encountering the Past" Each chapter includes an essay on a significant issue of everyday life or popular culture. These essays explore a variety of subjects, including gladiatorial bouts and medieval games, smoking in early modern Europe, and the politics of rock music in the late twentieth century. These thirty essays, each of which includes an illustration and study questions, expand *The Western Heritage*'s rich coverage of social and cultural history.

Recent Scholarship As in previous editions, changes in this edition reflect our determination to incorporate the most recent developments in historical scholarship and the concerns of professional historians.

Maps and Illustrations To help students understand the relationship between geography and history, approximately half of the maps include relief features. One or two maps in each chapter feature interactive exercises that can be found in MyHistoryLab. All maps have been carefully edited for accuracy. The text also contains close to 500 color and black and white illustrations, many of which are new to the Brief Sixth Edition.

Pedagogical Features This edition retains the pedagogical features of previous editions, including glossary terms, chapter review questions, and questions accompanying all "Compare & Connect" and "Encountering the Past" features in the text. Each of these features is designed to make the text more accessible to students and to reinforce key concepts.

- **Summary** sections at the end of each chapter summarize the major themes of each chapter.
- **Chapter Review** questions help students focus on and interpret the broader themes of a chapter. These also can be used for class discussion and essay topics.
- **Chronologies** within each chapter help students organize a time sequence for key events.
- **Overview Tables** in each chapter summarize complex issues.
- **Quick Reviews,** found at key places in the margins of each chapter, encourage students to review important concepts.
- **Key Terms,** boldfaced in the text, are listed (with page reference) at the end of each chapter and defined in the book's glossary.
- **Suggested Readings** at the end of the book have been updated with new titles reflecting recent scholarship.
- **Map Explorations** and **Critical-Thinking Questions** prompt students to engage with maps, often in an interactive fashion. Each Map Exploration can be found at www.myhistorylab.com.

A Note on Dates and Transliterations This edition of *The Western Heritage* continues the practice of using B.C.E. (before the common era) and C.E. (common era) instead of B.C. (before Christ) and A.D. (anno Domini, the year of the Lord) to designate dates. We also follow the most accurate currently accepted English transliterations of Arabic words. For example, today *Koran* has been replaced by the more accurate

Qur'an; similarly *Muhammad* is preferable to *Mohammed* and *Muslim* to *Moslem.*

Ancillary Instructional Materials

The ancillary instructional materials that accompany *The Western Heritage: Teaching and Learning Classroom Edition,* Brief Sixth Edition, are designed to reinforce and enliven the richness of the past and inspire students with the excitement of studying the history of Western civilization.

For Instructors

Instructor's Manual The *Instructor's Manual* contains chapter summaries, key points and vital concepts, and information on audiovisual resources that can be used in developing and preparing lecture presentations. (ISBN 0-205-73241-0)

Test Item File The Test Item File includes over 1,500 multiple-choice, identification, map, and essay test questions. (ISBN 0-205-73240-2)

MyTest MyTest is a browser-based test management program. The program allows instructors to select items from the Test Item File in order to create tests. It also allows for online testing. (ISBN 0-205-73298-4)

The Instructor's Resource Center (www.pearsonhighered.com) Text-specific materials, such as the Instructor's Manual and the Test Item File, are available for downloading by adopters.

For Instructors and Students

myhistorylab MyHistoryLab (www.myhistorylab.com) MyHistoryLab provides students with an online package complete with the electronic textbook and numerous study aids. With several hundred primary sources, many of which are assignable and link to a gradebook, pre- and post-tests that link to a gradebook and result in individualized study plans, videos and images, as well as map activities with gradable quizzes, the site offers students a unique, interactive experience that brings history to life. The comprehensive site also includes a History Bookshelf with fifty of the most commonly assigned books in history classes and a History Toolkit with tutorials and helpful links. Other features include gradable assignments and chapter review materials as well as a Test Item File.

For Students

***The Primary Source: Documents in Western Civilization* DVD** This DVD-ROM offers a rich collection of textual and visual sources—many never before available to a wide audience—and serves as an indispensable tool for working with sources. Extensively developed with the guidance of historians and teachers, *Primary Source: Documents in Western Civilization* includes over 800 sources in Western civilization history—from cave art, to text documents, to satellite images of Earth from space. All sources are accompanied by headnotes and focus questions and are searchable by topic, region, or theme. In addition, a built-in tutorial guides students through the process of working with documents. The DVD can be bundled with *The Western Heritage: Teaching and Learning Classroom Edition,* Brief Sixth Edition, at no charge. Please contact your Pearson Arts and Sciences representative for ordering information. (ISBN 0-13-134407-2)

Two-volume print version of *Primary Source: Documents in Western Civilization* is also available:

Primary Sources in Western Civilization, Volume 1: *To 1700, Second Edition* (ISBN 0-13-175583-8)

Primary Sources in Western Civilization, Volume 2: *Since 1400, Second Edition* (ISBN 0-13-175584-6)

Please contact your Pearson Arts and Sciences representative for ordering information.

***Lives and Legacies: Biographies in Western Civilization,* Second Edition** Extensively revised, *Lives and Legacies* includes brief, focused biographies of sixty individuals whose lives provide insight into the key developments of Western civilization. Each biography includes an introduction, prereading questions, and suggestions for additional reading. Available in two volumes:

Lives and Legacies, Volume 1, Second Edition (ISBN 0-205-64915-7)

Lives and Legacies, Volume 2, Second Edition (ISBN 0-205-64914-9)

Western Civilization Study Site (www.ablongman.com/longmanwesterncivilization/) This course-based, open-access online companion provides both students and professors with links for further research as well as test questions in multiple choice, true/false, and fill-in-the-blank formats.

Penguin Classics Selected titles from the renowned Penguin Classics series can be bundled with *The Western Heritage: Teaching and Learning Classroom Edition*, Brief Sixth Edition, for a nominal charge. Please contact your Pearson Arts and Sciences sales representative for details.

Longman Atlas of Western Civilization This 52-page atlas features carefully selected historical maps that provide comprehensive coverage for the major historical periods. Contact your Pearson Arts and Sciences representative for details. (ISBN 0-321-21626-1)

***The Prentice Hall Atlas of Western Civilization,* Second Edition** Produced in collaboration with Dorling Kindersley, the leader in cartographic publishing, the updated second edition of *The Prentice Hall Atlas of Western Civilization* applies the most innovative cartographic techniques to present Western civilization in all of its complexity and diversity. Copies of the atlas can be bundled with *The Western Heritage: Teaching and Learning Classroom Edition*, Brief Sixth Edition, for a nominal charge. Contact your Pearson Arts and Sciences sales representative for details. (ISBN 0-13-604246-5)

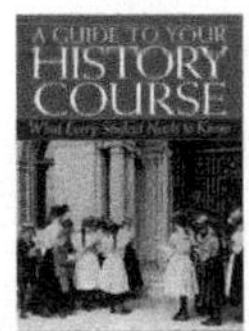

A Guide to Your History Course: What Every Student Needs to Know Written by Vincent A. Clark, this concise, spiral-bound guidebook orients students to the issues and problems they will face in the history classroom. Available at a discount when bundled with *The Western Heritage: Teaching and Learning Classroom Edition*, Brief Sixth Edition. (ISBN 0-13-185087-3)

***A Short Guide to Writing about History,* Seventh Edition** Written by Richard Marius, late of Harvard University, and Melvin E. Page, Eastern Tennessee State University, this engaging and practical text helps students get beyond merely compiling dates and facts. Covering both brief essays and the documented resource paper, the text explores the writing and researching processes, identifies different modes of historical writing, including argument, and concludes with guidelines for improving style. (ISBN 0-205-67370-8)

Interpretations of the Western World (www.pearsoncustom.com/custom-library/interpretations-of-the-western-world) The selections in this customizable database of secondary source readings are grouped together topically so instructors can assign readings that illustrate different points of view on a given historical debate.

ACKNOWLEDGMENTS

We are grateful to the scholars and teachers whose thoughtful and often detailed comments helped shape this revision:

Mark Baker, California State University, Bakersfield
Fred Baumgartner, Virginia Tech
Jane Bishop, The Citadel, The Military College of South Carolina
Eugene Boia, Cleveland State University
Kristen Burkholder, Oklahoma State University
Joseph Byrnes, Oklahoma State University
Anthony Cardoza, Loyola University, Chicago
Marcus Cox, The Citadel, The Military College of South Carolina
Delores Davison, Foothill College
Paul Deslandes, University of Vermont
Petra DeWitt, University of Missouri, Rolla
Richard Eller, Catawaba Valley Community College
Axel Fair-Schulz, State University of New York at Potsdam
Sean Field, University of Vermont
Shannon Fogg, Missouri S&T
Stephen Gibson, Ranken Technical College
Stephanie Hallock, Harford Community College
Michael Hickey, Bloomsburg University
Anthony Heideman, Range Community College
William Hudon, Bloomsburg University
Terry Jones, Oklahoma State University
Kevin Keating, Broward Community College
Michael Khodarkovsky, Loyola University, Chicago
Martha Kinney, Suffolk County Community College
Helena Krohn, Tidewater Community College
Eugene Larson, Los Angeles Pierce College
Karl Loewenstein, University of Wisconsin, Oshkosh
Arthur Lysiak, Bloomsburg University
William Martin, University of Utah
Lisa McClain, Boise State University
Daniel Miller, University of West Florida
Eva Mo, Meridian Junior College
Michelle Mouton, University of Wisconsin, Oshkosh
Tonia Sharlach Nash, Oklahoma State University
Charles Odahl, Boise State University
Mark Orsag, Doane College
Michael Pascale, SUNY at Suffolk, Farmingdale College
Neal Pease, University of Wisconsin, Milwaukee

Norman Raiford, Greenville Technical College
Pete Rottier, Cleveland State University
Thomas Rowland, University of Wisconsin at Oshkosh
Michael Rutz, University of Wisconsin, Oshkosh
Stephen Ruzicka, University of North Carolina at Greensboro
Mark Schumann, Eastern Michigan University
Patrick Speelman, The Citadel, The Military College of South Carolina
Frank W. Thackeray, Indiana University Southeast
Daniel Trifan, Missouri Western State University
Miriam Vivian, California State University, Bakersfield
Andrew Zimmerman, George Washington University

We would like to thank the dedicated people who helped produce this new edition. Our acquisitions editor, Charles Cavaliere; our development editor, Gerald Lombardi; our project manager, Rob DeGeorge; our production liaison, Lynn Savino Wendel; Maria Lange, who created the beautiful new design of this edition; Mary Ann Gloriande, our operations specialist; and Rebecca Dunn, production editor.

D.K.

S.O.

F.M.T.

Donald Kagan is Sterling Professor of History and Classics at Yale University, where he has taught since 1969. He received the A.B. degree in history from Brooklyn College, the M.A. in classics from Brown University, and the Ph.D. in history from Ohio State University. During 1958–1959 he studied at the American School of Classical Studies as a Fulbright Scholar. He has received three awards for undergraduate teaching at Cornell and Yale. He is the author of a history of Greek political thought, *The Great Dialogue* (1965); a four-volume history of the Peloponnesian war, *The Origins of the Peloponnesian War* (1969); *The Archidamian War* (1974); *The Peace of Nicias and the Sicilian Expedition* (1981); *The Fall of the Athenian Empire* (1987); a biography of Pericles, *Pericles of Athens and the Birth of Democracy* (1991); *On the Origins of War* (1995); and *The Peloponnesian War* (2003). He is coauthor, with Frederick W. Kagan, of *While America Sleeps* (2000). With Brian Tierney and L. Pearce Williams, he is the editor of *Great Issues in Western Civilization*, a collection of readings. He was awarded the National Humanities Medal for 2002 and was chosen by the National Endowment for the Humanities to deliver the Jefferson Lecture in 2004.

Steven Ozment is McLean Professor of Ancient and Modern History at Harvard University. He has taught Western Civilization at Yale, Stanford, and Harvard. He is the author of eleven books. *The Age of Reform, 1250–1550* (1980) won the Schaff Prize and was nominated for the 1981 National Book Award. Five of his books have been selections of the History Book Club: *Magdalena and Balthasar: An Intimate Portrait of Life in Sixteenth Century Europe* (1986); *Three Behaim Boys: Growing Up in Early Modern Germany* (1990); *Protestants: The Birth of a Revolution* (1992); *The Burgermeister's Daughter: Scandal in a Sixteenth Century German Town* (1996); and *Flesh and Spirit: Private Life in Early Modern Germany* (1999). His most recent publications are *Ancestors: The Loving Family of Old Europe* (2001); *A Mighty Fortress: A New History of the German People* (2004); and "Why We Study Western Civ," *The Public Interest 158* (2005).

Frank M. Turner is John Hay Whitney Professor of History at Yale University and Director of the Beinecke Rare Book and Manuscript Library at Yale University, where he served as University Provost from 1988 to 1992. He received his B.A. degree at the College of William and Mary and his Ph.D. from Yale. He has received the Yale College Award for Distinguished Undergraduate Teaching. He has directed a National Endowment for the Humanities Summer Institute. His scholarly research has received the support of fellowships from the National Endowment for the Humanities and the Guggenheim Foundation and the Woodrow Wilson Center. He is the author of *Between Science and Religion: The Reaction to Scientific Naturalism in Late Victorian England* (1974); *The Greek Heritage in Victorian Britain* (1981), which received the British Council Prize of the Conference on British Studies and the Yale Press Governors Award; *Contesting Cultural Authority: Essays in Victorian Intellectual Life* (1993); and *John Henry Newman: The Challenge to Evangelical Religion* (2002). He has also contributed numerous articles to journals and has served on the editorial advisory boards of *The Journal of Modern History, Isis,* and *Victorian Studies.* He edited *The Idea of a University* by John Henry Newman (1996); *Reflections on the Revolution in France* by Edmund Burke (2003); and *Apologia Pro Vita Sua* and *Six Sermons by John Henry Newman* (2008). Between 1996 and 2006, he served as a Trustee of Connecticut College and between 2004 and 2008 as a member of the Connecticut Humanities Council. In 2003, Professor Turner was appointed Director of the Beinecke Rare Book and Manuscript Library at Yale University.

WHAT IS THE WESTERN HERITAGE?

This book invites students and instructors to explore the Western Heritage. What is that heritage? The Western Heritage emerges from an evolved and evolving story of human actions and interactions, peaceful and violent, that arose in the eastern Mediterranean and then spread across the western Mediterranean into northern Europe and eventually to the American continents, and in their broadest impact, to the peoples of Africa and Asia as well.

The Western Heritage as a distinct portion of world history descends from the ancient Greeks. They saw their own political life based on open discussion of law and policy as different from that of Mesopotamia, Persia, and Egypt, where kings ruled without regard to public opinion. The Greeks invented the concept of citizenship, defining it as engagement in some form of self-government. Furthermore, through their literature and philosophy, the Greeks established the conviction, which became characteristic of the West, that reason can shape and analyze physical nature, politics, and morality.

The city of Rome, spreading its authority through military conquest across the Mediterranean world, embraced Greek literature and philosophy. Through their conquests and imposition of their law, the Romans created the Western world as a vast empire stretching from Egypt and Syria in the east to Britain in the west. Although the Roman Republic, governed by a Senate and popular political institutions, gave way after civil wars to the autocratic rule of the Roman Empire, the idea of a free republic of engaged citizens governed by public law and constitutional arrangements limiting political authority survived centuries of arbitrary rule by emperors. As in the rest of the world, the Greeks, the Romans, and virtually all other ancient peoples excluded women and slaves from political life and tolerated considerable social inequality.

In the early fourth century C.E., the Emperor Constantine reorganized the Roman Empire in two fundamental ways that reshaped the West. First, he moved the imperial capital from Rome to Constantinople (Istanbul), establishing separate emperors in the east and west. Thereafter, large portions of the western empire became subject to the rulers of Germanic tribes. In the confusion of these times, most of the texts embodying ancient philosophy, literature, and history became lost in the West, and for centuries Western Europeans were intellectually severed from that ancient heritage, which would later be recovered in a series of renaissances, or cultural rebirths, beginning in the eighth century.

Constantine's second fateful major reshaping of the West was his recognition of Christianity as the official religion of the empire. Christianity had grown out of the ancient monotheistic religion of the Hebrew people living in ancient Palestine. With the ministry of Jesus of Nazareth and the spread of his teachings by the Apostle Paul, Christianity had established itself as one of many religions in the empire. Because Christianity was monotheistic, Constantine's official embrace of it led to the eradication of pagan polytheism. Thereafter, the West became more or less coterminous with Latin Christianity, or that portion of the Christian Church acknowledging the Bishop of Rome as its head.

As the emperors' rule broke down, bishops became the effective political rulers in many parts of Western Europe. But the Christian Church in the West never governed without negotiation or conflict with secular rulers, and religious law never replaced secular law. Nor could secular rulers govern if they ignored the influence of the church. Hence, from the fourth century C.E. to the present day, rival claims to political and moral authority between ecclesiastical and political officials have characterized the West.

In the seventh century the Christian West faced a new challenge from the rise of Islam. This new monotheistic religion originating in the teachings of the prophet Muhammad arose on the Arabian Peninsula and spread through rapid conquests across North Africa and eventually into Spain, turning the Mediterranean into what one historian has termed "a Muslim lake." Between the eleventh and the thirteenth centuries, Christians attempted to reclaim the Holy Land from Muslim control in church-inspired military crusades that still resonate negatively in the Islamic world.

It was, however, in the Muslim world that most of the texts of ancient Greek and Latin learning survived and were studied, while intellectual life languished in the West. Commencing in the twelfth century, knowledge of those texts began to work its way back into Western Europe. By the fourteenth century European thinkers redefined themselves and their intellectual ambitions by recovering the literature and science

In his painting *The School of Athens*, the great Italian Renaissance painter Raphael portrayed the ancient Greek philosopher Plato and his student Aristotle engaged in debate. Plato, who points to the heavens, believed in a set of ideal truths that exists in its own realm distinct from the earth. Aristotle urged that all philosophy must be in touch with lived reality and confirms this position by pointing to the earth. Such debate has characterized the intellectual, political, and social experience of the West. Indeed, the very concept of "Western Civilization" has itself been subject to debate, criticism, and change over the centuries.

from the ancient world, reuniting Europe with its Graeco-Roman past.

From the twelfth through the eighteenth centuries, a new European political system slowly arose based on centralized monarchies characterized by large armies, navies, and bureaucracies loyal to the monarch and by the capacity to raise revenues. Whatever the personal ambitions of individual rulers, for the most part these monarchies recognized both the political role of local or national assemblies drawn from the propertied elites and the binding power of constitutional law on themselves. Also, in each of these monarchies, church officials and church law played important roles in public life. The monarchies, their military, and their expanding commercial economies became the basis for the extension of European and Western influence around the globe.

In the late fifteenth and early sixteenth centuries, two transforming events occurred. The first was the European discovery and conquest of the American continents, thus opening the Americas to Western institutions, religion, and economic exploitation. Over time the labor shortages of the Americas led to the forced migration of millions of Africans as slaves to the "New World." By the mid–seventeenth century, the West consequently embraced the entire transatlantic world and its multiracial societies.

Second, shortly after the American encounter, a religious schism erupted within Latin Christianity. Reformers rejecting both many medieval Christian doctrines as unbiblical and the primacy of the Pope in Rome established Protestant churches across much of northern Europe. As a consequence, for almost two centuries religious warfare between Protestants and Roman

Catholics overwhelmed the continent as monarchies chose to defend one side or the other. This religious turmoil meant that the Europeans who conquered and settled the Americas carried with them particularly energized religious convictions, with Roman Catholics dominating Latin America and English Protestants most of North America.

By the late eighteenth century, the idea of the West denoted a culture increasingly dominated by two new forces. First, science arising from a new understanding of nature achieved during the sixteenth and seventeenth centuries persuaded growing numbers of the educated elite that human beings can rationally master nature for ever-expanding productive purposes improving the health and well-being of humankind. From this era to the present, the West has been associated with advances in technology, medicine, and scientific research. Second, during the eighteenth century, a drive for economic improvement that vastly increased agricultural production and then industrial manufacturing transformed economic life, especially in Western Europe and later the United States. Both of these economic developments went hand in hand with urbanization and the movement of the industrial economy into cities where the new urban populations experienced major social dislocation.

During these decades certain Western European elites came to regard advances in agricultural and manufacturing economies that were based on science and tied to commercial expansion as "civilized" in contrast to cultures that lacked those characteristics. From these ideas emerged the concept of Western Civilization defined to suggest that peoples dwelling outside Europe or inside Europe east of the Elbe River were less than civilized. Whereas Europeans had once defined themselves against the rest of the world as free citizens and then later as Christians, they now defined themselves as "civilized." Europeans would carry this self-assured superiority into their nineteenth- and early-twentieth-century encounters with the peoples of Asia, Africa, and the Pacific.

During the last quarter of the eighteenth century, political revolution erupted across the transatlantic world. The British colonies of North America revolted. Then revolution occurred in France and spread across much of Europe. From 1791 through 1830, the Wars of Independence liberated Latin America from its European conquerors. These revolutions created bold new modes of political life, rooting the legitimacy of the state in some form of popular government and generally written constitutions. Thereafter, despite the presence of authoritarian governments on the European continent, the idea of the West, now including the new republics of the United States and Latin America, became associated with liberal democratic governments.

Furthermore, during the nineteenth century, most major European states came to identify themselves in terms of nationality—language, history, and ethnicity—rather than loyalty to a monarch. Nationalism eventually inflamed popular opinion and unloosed unprecedented political ambition by European governments.

These ambitions led to imperialism and the creation of new overseas European empires in the late nineteenth century. For the peoples living in European-administered Asian and African colonies, the idea and reality of the West embodied foreign domination and often disadvantageous involvement in a world economy. When in 1945 the close of World War II led to a sharp decline in European imperial authority, colonial peoples around the globe challenged that authority and gained independence. These former colonial peoples, however, often still suspected the West of seeking to control them. Hence, anticolonialism like colonialism before it redefined the West far from its borders.

Late-nineteenth-century nationalism and imperialism also unleashed with World War I in 1914 unprecedented military hostilities among European nations that spread around the globe, followed a quarter-century later by an even greater world war. As one result of World War I, revolution occurred in Russia with the establishment of the communist Soviet Union. During the interwar years a Fascist Party seized power in Italy and a Nazi Party took control of Germany. In response to these new authoritarian regimes, Western European powers and the United States identified themselves with liberal democratic constitutionalism, individual freedom, commercial capitalism, science and learning freely pursued, and religious liberty, all of which they defined as the Western Heritage. During the Cold War, conceived of as an East-West, democratic versus communist struggle that concluded with the collapse of the Soviet Union in 1991, the Western powers led by the United States continued to embrace those values in conscious opposition to the Soviet government, which since 1945 had also dominated much of Eastern Europe.

Since 1991, the West has again become redefined in the minds of many people as a world political and economic order dominated by the United States. Europe clearly remains the West, but political leadership has moved to North America. That American domination and recent American foreign policy have led throughout the West and elsewhere to much criticism of the United States.

Such self-criticism itself embodies one of the most important and persistent parts of the Western Heritage. From the Hebrew prophets and Socrates to the critics of European imperialism, American foreign policy, social inequality, and environmental devastation, voices in the West have again and again been raised to criticize often in the most strident manner the policies of Western governments and the thought, values, social conditions, and inequalities of Western societies.

Consequently, we study the Western Heritage not because the subject always or even primarily presents an admirable picture, but because the study of the Western Heritage like the study of all history calls us to an integrity of research, observation, and analysis that clarifies our minds and challenges our moral sensibilities. The challenge of history is the challenge of thinking, and it is to that challenge that his book invites its readers.

QUESTIONS

1. How have people in the West defined themselves in contrast with civilizations of the ancient East, and later in contrast with Islamic civilization, and still later in contrast with less economically developed regions of the world? Have people in the West historically viewed their own civilization to be superior to civilizations in other parts of the world? Why or why not?
2. How did the Emperor Constantine's adoption of Christianity as the official religion of the Roman Empire change the concept of the West? Is the presence of Christianity still a determining characteristic of the West?
3. How has the geographical location of what has been understood as the West changed over the centuries?
4. In the past two centuries Western nations established empires around the globe. How did these imperial ventures and the local resistance to them give rise to critical definitions of the West that contrasted with the definitions that had developed in Europe and the United States? How have those non-Western definitions of the West contributed to self-criticism within Western nations?
5. How useful is the concept of Western civilization in understanding today's global economy and global communications made possible by the Internet? Is the idea of Western civilization synonymous with the concept of modern civilization? Do you think the concept of the West will once again be redefined ten years from now?

To view a video of the authors discussing the Western heritage, go to www.myhistorylab.com

The WESTERN HERITAGE

1

The Birth of Civilization

This depiction of the Pharaoh Tutankahmun (r. 1336–1327 B.C.E.) and his queen comes from his tomb, which was discovered in the 1920s. "King Tut" died at the age of eighteen.

Robert Frerck/Odyssey Production/Woodfin Camp & Associates

How did Egyptian pharaohs use clothing, decoration, and ritual to emphasize their divine status?

For hundreds of thousands of years, human beings lived by hunting and gathering what nature spontaneously provided. Only some 10,000 years ago did they begin to cultivate plants, domesticate animals, and settle in permanent communities. About 5,000 years ago, the Sumerians, who lived near the confluence of the Tigris and Euphrates Rivers (a region Greek geographers called "Mesopotamia," i.e., "between-rivers"), and the Egyptians who dwelt in the Nile Valley pioneered civilization. By the fourteenth century B.C.E., *powerful empires had arisen and were struggling for dominance of the civilized world, but one of the region's smaller states probably had greater influence on the course of Western civilization. The modern West's major religions (Judaism, Christianity, and Islam) are rooted in the traditions of ancient Israel.*

EARLY HUMANS AND THEIR CULTURE

HOW DID life in the Neolithic Age differ from the Paleolithic?

Scientists estimate that creatures very much like humans appeared perhaps 3 to 5 million years ago, probably in Africa. Some 1 to 2 million years ago, erect and tool-using early humans spread over much of Africa, Europe, and Asia. Our own species, ***Homo sapiens***, probably emerged some 200,000 years ago, and the earliest remains of fully modern humans date to about 90,000 years ago.

Homo sapiens Our own species, which dates back roughly 200,000 years.

Humans, unlike other animals, are cultural beings. **Culture** may be defined as the ways of living built up by a group and passed on from one generation to another. It includes behavior such as courtship or child-rearing practices; material things such as tools, clothing, and shelter; and ideas, institutions, and beliefs. Because culture is learned and not inherited, it permits rapid adaptation to changing conditions, making possible the spread of humanity to almost all the lands of the globe.

culture Way of life invented by a group and passed on by teaching.

THE PALEOLITHIC AGE

Anthropologists designate early human cultures by their tools. The earliest period—the **Paleolithic** (from Greek, "old stone")—dates from the earliest use of stone tools some 1 million years ago to about 10,000 B.C.E. During this immensely long period, people were hunters, fishers, and gatherers, but not producers, of food. They learned to make and use increasingly sophisticated tools of stone and perishable materials like wood; they learned to make and control fire; and they acquired language and the ability to use it to pass on what they had learned.

Paleolithic Greek for "old stone"; the earliest period in cultural development that began with the first use of stone tools about a million years ago and continued until about 10,000 B.C.E.

These early humans, dependent on nature for food and vulnerable to wild beasts and natural disasters, may have developed responses to the world rooted in fear of the unknown—of the uncertainties of human life or the overpowering forces of nature. Evidence of religious faith and practice, as well as of magic, goes as far back as archaeology can take us. The sense that there is more to the world than meets the eye—in other words, the religious response to the world—seems to be as old as humankind.

The style of life and the level of technology of the Paleolithic period could support only a sparsely settled society. If hunters were too numerous, game would not suffice. In Paleolithic times, people were subject to the same natural and ecological constraints that today maintain a balance between wolves and deer in Alaska.

Evidence from Paleolithic art and from modern hunter-gatherer societies suggests that human life in the Paleolithic Age was probably characterized by a division of labor by sex. Men engaged in hunting, fishing, making tools and weapons, and fighting against other families, clans, and tribes. Women, less mobile because of childbearing, gathered nuts, berries, and wild grains, wove baskets, and made clothing. Women gathering food probably discovered how to plant and care for seeds. This knowledge eventually made possible the development of agriculture and animal husbandry.

The Neolithic Age

Only a few Paleolithic societies made the initial shift from hunting and gathering to agriculture. Anthropologists and archaeologists disagree as to why, but however it happened, some 10,000 years ago parts of what we now call the Near East began to change from a nomadic hunter-gatherer culture to a more settled agricultural one. This period is called the **Neolithic Age** (from Greek, "new stone"). Productive animals, such as sheep and goats, and food crops, such as wheat and barley, were first domesticated in the mountain foothills where they already lived or grew in the wild. Once domestication had taken place, people could move to areas where these plants and animals did not occur naturally, such as the river valleys of the Near East. The invention of pottery during the Neolithic Age enabled people to store surplus foods and liquids and to transport them, as well as to cook agricultural products that were difficult to eat or digest raw. Cloth was made from flax and wool. Crops required constant care from planting to harvest, so Neolithic farmers built permanent dwellings. Houses in a Neolithic village were normally all the same size and were built on the same plan, suggesting that most Neolithic villagers had about the same level of wealth and social status. A few items, such as stones and shells, were traded long distance, but Neolithic villages tended to be self-sufficient.

At Ain Ghazal, a Neolithic site in Jordan, several pits contained male and female statues made of clay modeled over a reed framework. Similar figures have been found at Jericho and other sites, all from the same period, about 8500–7000 B.C.E. They were probably used in religious rituals, perhaps connected with ancestor worship, as were plastered skulls, masks, carved heads, and other artifacts.

Archaeological Museum, Amman, Jordan, kingdom. Photograph © Erich Lessing, Art Resource, NY

What clues might such statues offer about the nature of Neolithic religion?

Two larger Neolithic settlements do not fit this village pattern. One was found at Çatal Höyük, in a fertile agricultural region about 150 miles south of Ankara, the capital of present-day Turkey. This was a large town covering over fifteen acres, with a population probably well over 6,000 people. The houses were clustered so closely that they had no doors, but were entered by ladders from the roofs. The agriculture, arts, and crafts of this town were astonishingly diversified and at a much higher level of attainment than other, smaller settlements of the period. The site of Jericho, an oasis around a spring near the Dead Sea, was occupied as early as 12,000 B.C.E. The inhabitants of Neolithic Jericho had a mixed agricultural, herding, and hunting economy and may have traded salt. These two sites show that the economy and the settlement patterns of the Neolithic period may be more complicated than many scholars have thought.

Throughout the Paleolithic Age, the human population had been small and relatively stable. The shift from food gathering to food production may not have been associated with an immediate change in population, but over time in the regions where agriculture and animal husbandry appeared, the number of human beings grew at an unprecedented rate. One reason for this is that farmers usually had larger families than hunters. When animals and plants were domesticated and brought to the river valleys, the relationship between human beings and nature was changed forever. People had learned to control nature, a vital prerequisite for the emergence of civilization. Some scholars refer to the dramatic changes in subsistence, settlement, technology, and population of this time as the Neolithic Revolution.

The Bronze Age and the Birth of Civilization

Neolithic agricultural villages and herding cultures gradually replaced Paleolithic culture in much of the world. Then another major shift occurred, first in the plains along the Tigris and Euphrates Rivers in the region the Greeks and Romans called Mesopotamia (modern Iraq), later in the valley of the Nile River in Egypt, and somewhat later in India and the Yellow River basin in China. This shift was associated initially with the growth of towns alongside villages, creating a hierarchy of larger and smaller settlements in the same region. Some towns then grew into much larger urban centers and often drew population into them, so that nearby villages and towns

Neolithic Age "New stone" age, dating back 10,000 years to when people living in some parts of the Middle East made advances in the production of stone tools and shifted from hunting and gathering to agriculture.

declined. The urban centers, or cities, usually had monumental buildings, such as temples and fortifications. These were vastly larger than individual houses and could be built only by the sustained effort of hundreds and even thousands of people over many years. Elaborate representational artwork appeared, sometimes made of rare and imported materials. New technologies, such as smelting and the manufacture of metal tools and weapons, were characteristic of urban life. Commodities, like pottery and textiles that had been made in individual houses in villages, were mass produced in cities, which also were characterized by social stratification—that is, the grouping of people into classes based on factors such as control of resources, family, religious or political authority, and personal wealth. The earliest writing is also associated with the growth of cities.

These attributes—urbanism; technological, industrial, and social change; long-distance trade; and new methods of symbolic communication—are defining characteristics of the form of human culture called **civilization**. At about the time the earliest civilizations were emerging, someone discovered how to combine tin and copper to make a stronger and more useful material—bronze. Archaeologists coined the term **Bronze Age** to refer to the period 3100 to 1200 B.C.E. in the Near East and eastern Mediterranean.

Ötzi is the nickname scientists have given to the remains of the oldest mummified human body yet discovered. This reconstruction shows his probable appearance and the clothing and weapons found on and with him.

Wieslav Smetek/Stern/Black Star

What light does the practice of mummification shed on Neolithic beliefs about the afterlife?

civilization Stage in the evolution of organized society that has among its characteristics urbanism, long-distance trade, writing systems, and accelerated technological and social development.

Bronze Age (3100–1200 B.C.E.) Began with the increasing importance of metal that also ended the Stone Ages.

EARLY CIVILIZATIONS TO ABOUT 1000 B.C.E.

WHY DID the first cities develop?

By 4000 B.C.E., people had settled in large numbers in the river-watered lowlands of Mesopotamia and Egypt. By about 3000 B.C.E., when the invention of writing gave birth to history, urban life and the organization of society into centralized states were well established in the valleys of the Tigris and Euphrates Rivers in Mesopotamia and of the Nile River in Egypt.

MESOPOTAMIAN CIVILIZATION

The first civilization appears to have arisen in Mesopotamia. The region is divided into two ecological zones, roughly north and south of modern Baghdad. In the south (Babylonia), irrigation is vital; in the north (later Assyria), agriculture is possible with rainfall and wells. The oldest Mesopotamian cities seem to have been founded by a people called the Sumerians during the fourth millennium B.C.E. in the land of Sumer, which is the southern half of Babylonia. By 3000 B.C.E., the Sumerian city of Uruk was the largest city in the world. (See Map 1–1.) Colonies of people from Uruk built cities and outposts in northern Syria and southern Anatolia.

QUICK REVIEW

The First Civilization

- Civilization first appeared in Babylonia
- First cities appeared in Sumer during fourth millenium B.C.E.
- Earliest urban center may have been at Uruk

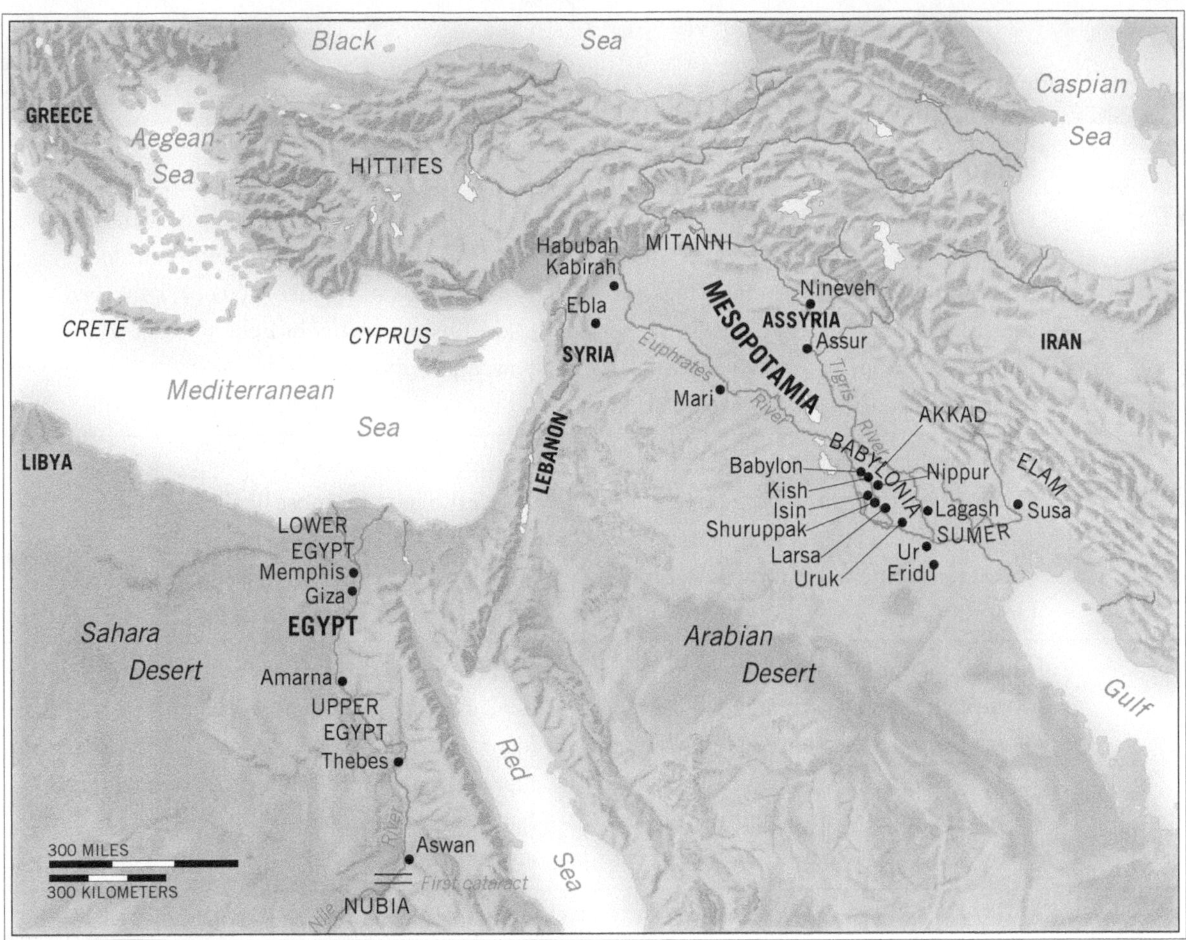

MAP 1–1 **The Ancient Near East** There were two ancient river-valley civilizations. Egypt was united into a single state, and Mesopotamia was long divided into a number of city-states.

Based on this map, what might explain why independent city-states were spread out in Mesopotamia while Egypt remained united in a single state?

From about 2800 to 2370 B.C.E., in what is called the Early Dynastic period, several Sumerian city-states, independent political units consisting of a major city and its surrounding territory, existed in southern Mesopotamia, arranged in north-south lines along the major watercourses. Among these cities were Uruk, Ur, Nippur, Shuruppak, and Lagash. Some of the city-states formed leagues among themselves that apparently had both political and religious significance. Quarrels over water and agricultural land led to incessant warfare, and in time, stronger towns and leagues conquered weaker ones and expanded to form kingdoms ruling several city-states.

Peoples who, unlike the Sumerians, mostly spoke Semitic languages (that is, languages in the same family as Arabic and Hebrew) occupied northern Mesopotamia and Syria. Many of these Semitic peoples absorbed aspects of Sumerian culture, especially writing. In northern Babylonia, the Mesopotamians believed the large city of Kish had the first kings in history. In the far east of this territory, not far from modern Baghdad, a people known as the Akkadians established their own kingdom at a capital city called Akkade, under their first king, Sargon, who had been a servant of the king of Kish.

Overview Mesopotamian and Egyptian Civilizations

	MESOPOTAMIA	EGYPT
GOVERNMENT	Different kinds of monarchies appeared in different times and places. Sumerian kings led armies; northern Assyrian kings were the chief priests; and, in the south, Babylonian kings and priests held separate offices.	*Nomarchs*, regional governors whose districts were called *nomes*, handled important local issues such as water management. However, Old Kingdom pharaohs held much of the power and resources.
LANGUAGE AND LITERATURE	Sumerians developed the world's first system of writing, *cuneiform*. Sumerian scribes had to learn several thousand characters; some stood for words, others for sounds.	Writing first appears in Egypt about 3000 B.C.E., the impetus most likely derived from Mesopotamian *cuneiform*. This writing system, *hieroglyphs*, was highly sophisticated, involving hundreds of picture signs.
RELIGION	The Mesopotamians were *polytheists*, worshipping many gods and goddesses, most of whom represented phenomena of nature (storms, earthquakes, etc.). The gods were grouped into families, heaven being organized like a community.	Egyptians had three different myths to explain the origin of the world, and each featured a different creator-god. Gods were represented in both human and animal form. Egyptians placed great trust in magic, oracles, and amulets to ward off evil.
SOCIETY	Parents usually arranged marriages. A marriage started out monogamous, but husbands could take a second wife. Women could own their own property and do business on their own.	Women's prime roles were connected with the management of the household. They could not hold office, go to scribal schools, or become artisans. Royal women often wielded considerable influence. In art, royal and nonroyal women are usually shown smaller than the male figures.
SLAVERY	The two main forms of slavery were chattel and debt slavery. Chattel slaves were bought and had no legal rights. Debt slaves, more common than chattel slaves, could not be sold, but they could redeem their freedom by paying off the loan.	Slaves did not become numerous in Egypt until the Middle Kingdom (about 2000 B.C.E.). Black Africans and Asians were captured in war and brought back as slaves. Slaves could be freed, but manumission was rare.

The Akkadians conquered all the Sumerian city-states and invaded southwestern Iran and northern Syria. This was the first empire in history, having a heartland, provinces, and an absolute ruler. Sargon's name became legendary as the first great conqueror of history. His grandson, Naram-Sin, ruled from the Persian Gulf to the Mediterranean Sea, with a standardized administration, unheard-of wealth and power, and a grand style that to later Mesopotamians was a high point of their history. External attack and internal weakness destroyed the Akkadian Empire, but several smaller states flourished independently, notably Lagash in Sumer, under its ruler Gudea.

About 2125 B.C.E., the Sumerian city of Ur rose to dominance, and the rulers of the Third Dynasty of Ur established an empire built on the foundation of the Akkadian Empire, but far smaller. In this period, Sumerian culture and literature flourished. Epic poems were composed, glorifying the deeds of the ancestors of the kings of Ur. A highly centralized administration kept detailed records of agriculture, animal husbandry, commerce, and other matters. After little more than a century of prominence, the kingdom of Ur disintegrated in the face of famine and invasion. From the east, the Elamites attacked the city of Ur and captured the king. From the north and west, a Semitic-speaking people, the Amorites, invaded Mesopotamia in large numbers, settling around the Sumerian cities and eventually founding their own dynasties in some of them, such as at Uruk, Babylon, Isin, and Larsa.

For some time after the fall of Ur, there was relative peace in Babylonia under the Amorite kings of Isin, who used Sumerian at their court and considered themselves the successors of the kings of Ur. Eventually, another Amorite dynasty at the city of Larsa contested control of Babylonia, and a period of warfare began. A powerful

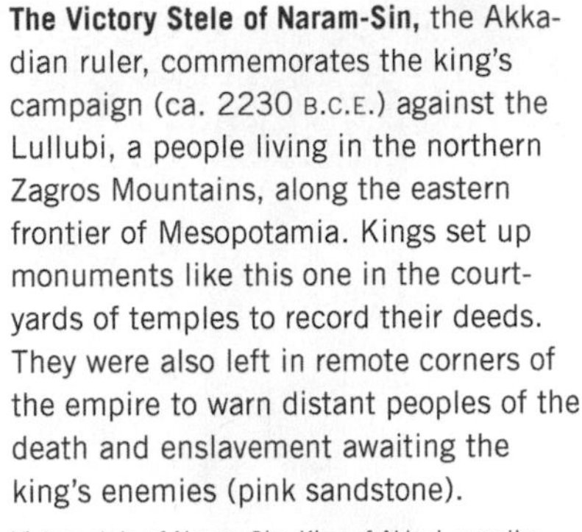

The Victory Stele of Naram-Sin, the Akkadian ruler, commemorates the king's campaign (ca. 2230 B.C.E.) against the Lullubi, a people living in the northern Zagros Mountains, along the eastern frontier of Mesopotamia. Kings set up monuments like this one in the courtyards of temples to record their deeds. They were also left in remote corners of the empire to warn distant peoples of the death and enslavement awaiting the king's enemies (pink sandstone).

Victory stele of Naram-Sin, King of Akkad, over the mountain-dwelling Lullubi, Mesopotamian, Akkadian Period, c. 2230 BC (pink sandstone). Louvre, Paris, France/The Bridgeman Art Library International Ltd.

What do such monuments tell us about how Akkadian kings wanted to be seen by their subjects?

The Royal Standard of Ur, a mosaic that dates from about 2750 B.C.E., shows officials from the Sumerian city of Ur celebrating a military victory as animals are brought in to be slaughtered for a feast.

British Museum, London, UK/Bridgeman Art Library

Why did Sumerian kings go to war? What was the most important job of a king? Warrior, judge, priest, administrator?

Code of Hammurabi

Stele of the Code of Laws of Hammurabi. c. 1792-1750 BCE. Diorite. 225 x 65 cm. Found at Susa. Photo: Ch. Larrieu. Reunion des Musées Nationaux et Ecoli du Louvre, Paris/ Art Resource, NY

How did the Code of Hammurabi reflect the social and political structure of Mesopotamia?

new dynasty at Babylon defeated Isin, Larsa, and other rivals and dominated Mesopotamia for nearly 300 years. Its high point was the reign of its most famous king, Hammurabi (r. ca. 1792–1750 B.C.E.), best known today for the collection of laws that bears his name. Hammurabi destroyed the great city of Mari on the Euphrates and created a kingdom embracing most of Mesopotamia.

The Code of Hammurabi reveals a society divided by class. There were nobles, commoners, and slaves, and the law did not treat all of them equally. In general, punishments were harsh, based literally on the principle of "an eye for an eye, a tooth for a tooth." Disputes over property and other complaints were heard in the first instance by local city assemblies of leading citizens and heads of families. Professional judges heard cases for a fee and held court near the city gate. In Mesopotamian trials, witnesses and written evidence had to be produced and a written verdict issued. False testimony was punishable by death. Cases of capital punishment could be appealed to the king. Hammurabi was closely concerned with the details of his kingdom, and his surviving letters often deal with minor local disputes.

About 1600 B.C.E., the Babylonian kingdom fell apart under the impact of invasions from the north by the Hittites, Hurrians, and Kassites, all non-Mesopotamian peoples.

Government From the earliest historical records, it is clear that the Sumerians were ruled by monarchs in some form. The type of rule varied at different times and places. In later Assyria, for example, the king served as chief priest; in Babylonia, the priesthood was separate from royalty. Royal princesses were sometimes appointed as priestesses of important gods.

The government and the temples cultivated large areas of land to support their staffs and retinue. Laborers of low social status who were given rations of raw foods and other commodities to sustain them and their families did some of the work on this land. Citizens leased some land for a share of the crop and a cash payment. The government and temples owned large herds of sheep, goats, cattle, and donkeys. The Sumerian city-states exported wool and textiles to buy metals, such as copper, that were not available in Mesopotamia. Families and private individuals often owned their own farmland or houses in the cities, which they bought and sold as they liked.

Writing and Mathematics Government, business, and scholarship required a good system of writing. The Sumerians invented the writing system now known as **cuneiform** (from the Latin *cuneus*, "wedge") because of the wedge-shaped marks they made by writing on clay tablets with a cut reed stylus. The Sumerian writing system used several thousand characters, some of which stood for words and some for sounds. Sumerian and Babylonian schools emphasized language and literature, accounting, legal practice, and mathematics, especially geometry, along with memorization of much abstract knowledge that had no relevance to everyday life. The ability to read and write was restricted to an elite who could afford to go to school. Success in school, however, and factors such as good family connections meant a literate Sumerian could find employment as a clerk, surveyor, teacher, diplomat, or administrator.

cuneiform Developed by the Sumerians as the very first writing system ever used, it used several thousand characters, some of which stood for words and some for sounds.

The Sumerians also began the development of mathematics. By the time of Hammurabi, the Mesopotamians were expert in many types of mathematics, including mathematical astronomy. The calendar the Mesopotamians used had twelve lunar months of thirty days each. To keep it in accordance with the solar year and the seasons, the Mesopotamians occasionally introduced a thirteenth month.

Religion The Sumerians and their successors worshipped many gods and goddesses. They were visualized in human form, with human needs and weaknesses. Most of the gods were identified with some natural phenomenon such as the sky, fresh water, or storms. They differed from humans in their greater power, sublime position in the universe, and immortality. The Mesopotamians believed the human race was created to serve the gods and to relieve the gods of the necessity of providing for themselves. The gods were considered universal, but also residing in specific places, usually one important god or goddess in each city. The Mesopotamians were religiously tolerant and readily accepted the possibility that different people might have different gods.

The Mesopotamians had a vague and gloomy picture of the afterworld. The winged spirits of the dead were recognizable as individuals. They were confined to a dusty, dark netherworld, doomed to perpetual hunger and thirst unless someone offered them food and drink. Some spirits escaped to haunt human beings. There was no preferential treatment in the afterlife for those who had led religious or virtuous lives—everyone was in equal misery. Mesopotamian religion focused on problems of this world and how to lead a good life before dying. (See "Encountering the Past: Divination in Ancient Mesopotamia," page 14.)

Religion played a large part in the literature and art of Mesopotamia. Epic poems told of the deeds of the gods, such as how the world was created and organized, of a great flood the gods sent to wipe out the human race, and of the hero-king Gilgamesh, who tried to escape death by going on a fantastic journey to find the sole survivor of the great flood. (See "Compare & Connect: The Great Flood," on pages 12–13.) There were also many literary and artistic works that were not religious in character, so we should not imagine religion dominated all aspects of the Mesopotamians' lives. Religious architecture took the form of great temple complexes in the major cities. The most imposing religious structure was the *ziggurat*, a tower in stages, sometimes with a small chamber on top.

QUICK REVIEW

Mesopotamian Religion

- Mesopotamians produced a large body of sacred literature
- *Ziggurat*: a huge terraced mound of mud-bricks topped by a temple
- Gods were grouped into families and heaven was organized like a human community

Society Hundreds of thousands of cuneiform texts from the early third millennium B.C.E. until the third century B.C.E. give us a detailed picture of how peoples in ancient Mesopotamia conducted their lives and of the social conditions in which they lived.

Categorizing the laws of Hammurabi according to the aspects of life with which they deal reveals much about Babylonian life in his time. The third largest category of laws deals with commerce, relating to such issues as contracts, debts, rates of interest, security, and default. Business documents of Hammurabi's time show how people invested their money in land, moneylending, government contracts, and international trade. Some of these laws regulate professionals, such as builders, judges, and surgeons. The second largest category of laws deals with land tenure, especially land given by the king to soldiers and marines in return for their service. The letters of Hammurabi that deal with land tenure show he was concerned to uphold the individual rights of landholders against powerful officials who tried to take their land from them. The largest category of laws relates to the family and its maintenance and protection, including marriage, inheritance, and adoption.

Parents usually arranged marriages, and betrothal was followed by the signing of a marriage contract. The bride usually left her own family to join her husband's. The husband-to-be could make a bridal payment, and the father of the bride-to-be provided a dowry for his daughter in money, land, or objects. A marriage started out monogamous, but a husband whose wife was childless or sickly could take a second wife. Sometimes husbands also sired children from domestic slave women. Women could possess their own property and do business on their own. Women divorced by their husbands without good cause could get their dowry back. A woman seeking divorce

COMPARE & CONNECT

THE GREAT FLOOD

Stories of a great deluge appeared in many cultures at various times in the ancient world. In the Mesopotamian world the earliest known story of a great flood sent by the gods to destroy mankind appeared in the Sumerian civilization. Later the story was included in the Gilgamesh epic in a Semitic language. The great flood of Noah's time appears in the book of Genesis in the Hebrew Bible.

QUESTIONS

1. In what ways is the story from the *Epic of Gilgamesh* similar to the Story of Noah in the Hebrew Bible?
2. How is the account of a great flood in the Story of Noah different from that in the *Epic of Gilgamesh?*
3. What is the significance of the similarities and differences between the two accounts?

I. THE BABYLONIAN STORY OF THE FLOOD

The passage that follows is part of the Babylonian Epic of Gilgamesh. *An earlier independent Babylonian story of the flood suggested that the gods sent a flood because there were too many people on the earth. A version of this story was later combined with the* Epic of Gilgamesh, *about a legendary king who became terrified of death when his best friend and companion died. After many adventures, Gilgamesh crossed the distant ocean and the "waters of death" to ask Utanapishtim, who, with his wife, was the only survivor of the great flood, the secret of eternal life. In response, Utanapishtim narrated the story of the great flood to show that his own immortality derived from a onetime event in the past, so Gilgamesh could not share his destiny.*

Six days and seven nights
The wind continued, the deluge and windstorm levelled the land.
When the seventh day arrived,
The windstorm and deluge left off their battle,
Which had struggled, like a woman in labor.
The sea grew calm, the tempest stilled, the deluge ceased.
I looked at the weather, stillness reigned,
And the whole human race had turned into clay.
The landscape was flat as a rooftop.
I opened the hatch, sunlight fell upon my face.
Falling to my knees, I sat down weeping,
Tears running down my face.
I looked at the edges of the world, the borders of the sea,
At twelve times sixty double leagues the periphery emerged.
The boat had come to rest on Mount Nimush,
Mount Nimush held the boat fast, not letting it move.
One day, a second day Mount Nimush held the boat fast, not letting it move.
A third day, a fourth day Mount Nimush held the boat fast, not letting it move.
A fifth day, a sixth day Mount Nimush held the boat fast, not letting it move.
When the seventh day arrived,
I brought out a dove and set it free.
The dove went off and returned,
No landing place came to its view, so it turned back.
I brought out a swallow and set it free,
The swallow went off and returned,
No landing space came to its view, so it turned back.
I brought out a raven and set it free.
The raven went off and saw the ebbing of the waters.
It ate, preened, left droppings, did not turn back.
I released all to the four directions,
I brought out an offering and offered it to the four directions.
I set up an incense burner on the summit of the mountain,
I arranged seven and seven cult vessels,
I heaped reeds, cedar, and myrtle in their bowls.
The gods smelled the savor,
The gods smelled the sweet savor,
The gods crowded round the sacrificer like flies.
As soon as the Belet-ili arrived,
She held up the great fly-ornaments that Anu had made in his ardor:
'O ye gods, as surely as I shall not forget these lapis pendants on my neck,
'I shall be mindful of these days and not forget, not ever!
'The gods should come to the incense burner,
'But Enlil should not come to the incense burner,
'For he, irrationally, brought on the flood,
'And marked my people for destruction!'
As soon as Enlil arrived,
He saw the boat, Enlil flew into a rage,
He was filled with fury at the gods:
'Who came through alive? No man was to survive destruction!'
Ninurta made ready to speak,
Said to the valiant Enlil:

The Flood Tablet (Tablet XI), which relates part of the *Epic of Gilgamesh.* The eleventh tablet describes the meeting of Gilgamesh and Utanapishtim who, along with his wife, survived a great flood that destroyed the rest of humankind.

What does the fact that the *Epic of Gilgamesh* was inscribed on a tablet tell us about its place in Mesopotamian culture?

'Who but Ea could contrive such a thing?
'For Ea alone knows every artifice.'
Ea made ready to speak,
Said to the valiant Enlil:
'You, O valiant one, are the wisest of the gods,
'How could you, irrationally, have brought on the flood?
'Punish the wrong-doer for his wrong-doing,
'Punish the transgressor for his transgression,
'But be lenient, lest he be cut off,
'Bear with him, lest he [. . .].
'Instead of your bringing on a flood,
'Let the lion rise up to diminish the human race!
'Instead of your bringing on a flood,
'Let the wolf rise up to diminish the human race!
'Instead of your bringing on a flood,
'Let famine rise up to wreak havoc in the land!
'Instead of your bringing on a flood,
'Let pestilence rise up to wreak havoc in the land!
'It was not I who disclosed the secret of the great gods,
'I made Atrahasis have a dream and so he heard the secret of the gods.
'Now then, make some plan for him.'
Then Enlil came up into the boat,
Leading me by the hand, he brought me up too.
He brought my wife up and had her kneel beside me.
He touched our brows, stood between us to bless us:
'Hitherto Utanapishtim has been a human being,
'Now Utanapishtim and his wife shall become like us gods.
'Utanapishtim shall dwell far distant at the source of the rivers.'

Source: "The Babylonian Story of the Flood" from *The Babylonian Epic of Gilgamesh*, in *The Epic of Gilgamesh*, trans. by Benjamin R. Foster. Copyright © 2001 by W.W. Norton & Company. Used by permission of W.W. Norton & Company, Inc.

II. NOAH'S FLOOD – GENESIS 7.11–9.11

In the six hundredth year of Noah's life, in the second month, on the seventeenth day of the month, on that day all the fountains of the great deep burst forth, and the windows of the heavens were opened. The rain fell on the earth forty days and forty nights. . . .

At the end of forty days Noah opened the window of the ark that he had made and sent out the raven; and it went to and fro until the waters were dried up from the earth. Then he sent out the dove from him, to see if the waters had subsided from the face of the ground; but the dove found no place to set its foot, and it returned to him to the ark, for the waters were still on the face of the whole earth. So he put out his hand and took it and brought it into the ark with him. He waited another seven days, and again he sent out the dove from the ark; and the dove came back to him in the evening, and there in its beak was a freshly plucked olive leaf; so Noah knew that the waters had subsided from the earth. Then he waited another seven days, and sent out the dove; and it did not return to him any more. . . .

Then God said to Noah and to his sons with him, "As for me, I am establishing my covenant with you and your descendants after you, and with every living creature that is with you, the birds, the domestic animals, and every animal of the earth with you, as many as came out of the ark. I establish my covenant with you, that never again shall all flesh be cut off by the waters of a flood, and never again shall there be a flood to destroy the earth."

ENCOUNTERING THE PAST

Divination in Ancient Mesopotamia

Mesopotamians believed the world was full of omens—events that, if properly interpreted, would enable them to predict the future. They did not view the future as a predestined, unalterable fate, but they assumed that if they knew what was going to happen, appropriate rituals and planning would enable them to head off unfavorable developments. Divination is the practice of foretelling the future by magical or occult means, and the Mesopotamians were pioneers of the art.

One of the earliest and most trusted divination methods involved the examination of the entrails of the animals offered at religious sacrifices. Deformities of organs were believed to be warnings from the gods. Clay models were made of these organs, and together with a report of the events they were believed to have predicted, these models were preserved in a kind of reference library for temple diviners.

Animal sacrifice was expensive and used most commonly by the state. Ordinary Mesopotamians relied on more economical methods to obtain the information they needed to plan for their futures. The seers who served them examined patterns made by the smoke of burning incense or oil poured onto water. Chance remarks of strangers, facial features, dreams, and birth defects were all considered significant. The movements of the heavenly bodies were believed to be extremely portentous for events on earth. Mesopotamian faith in astrology had the positive effect of gathering data that led to advances in astronomy. Any divergence from what were considered normal forms or patterns was considered a portent of disaster and called for prayers and magic to ward off suspected dangers.

Ancient Mesopotamians used astrology to predict the future. This calendar from the city of Uruk dates from the first millennium B.C.E. and is based on careful observation of the heavens.

Astrological calendar. From Uruk, Mesopotamia. Babylonian, 1st mill. B.C.E. Museum of Oriental Antiquities, Istanbul, Turkey. Photograph © Erich Lessing/Art Resource, NY

How did belief in the ability of humans to divine the future promote the study of astronomy in Mesopotamia?

HOW DID the Mesopotamians try to predict the future, and what did they do with the information they obtained?

could also recover her dowry if her husband could not convict her of wrongdoing. A married woman's place was thought to be in the home, but hundreds of letters between wives and husbands show them as equal partners in the ventures of life. Single women who were not part of families could set up in business on their own, often as tavern owners or moneylenders, or could be associated with temples, sometimes working as midwives and wet nurses, or taking care of orphaned children.

Slavery: Chattel Slaves and Debt Slaves There were two main types of slavery in Mesopotamia: chattel and debt slavery. Chattel slaves were bought like any other piece of property and had no legal rights. They were often non-Mesopotamians bought from slave merchants. Prisoners of war could also be enslaved. Chattel slaves were expensive luxuries during most of Mesopotamian history. They were used in domestic service rather than in production, such as fieldwork. A wealthy household might have five or six slaves, male and female.

Debt slavery was more common than chattel slavery. If debtors had pledged themselves or members of their families as surety for a loan, they became the slave of the creditor; their labor went to pay the interest on the loan. Debt slaves could not be sold but could redeem their freedom by paying off the loan. True chattel slavery did not become common until the Neo-Babylonian period (612–539 B.C.E.).

Although laws against fugitive slaves or slaves who denied their masters were harsh, Mesopotamian slavery appears enlightened compared with other slave systems in history. Slaves were generally of the same people as their masters. They had been enslaved because of misfortune from which their masters were not immune, and they generally labored alongside them. Slaves could engage in business and, with certain restrictions, hold property. They could marry free men or women, and the resulting children would normally be free. A slave who acquired the means could buy his or her freedom. Children of a slave by a master might be allowed to share his property after his death. Nevertheless, slaves were property, subject to an owner's will and had little legal protection.

Egyptian Civilization

As Mesopotamian civilization arose in the valley of the Tigris and Euphrates, another great civilization emerged in Egypt, centered on the Nile River. From its sources in Lake Victoria and the Ethiopian highlands, the Nile flows north some 4,000 miles to the Mediterranean. Ancient Egypt included the 750-mile stretch of smooth, navigable river from Aswan to the sea. South of Aswan the river's course is interrupted by several cataracts—rocky areas of rapids and whirlpools.

The Egyptians recognized two sets of geographical divisions in their country. **Upper** (southern) **Egypt** consisted of the narrow valley of the Nile. **Lower** (northern) **Egypt** referred to the broad triangular area, named by the Greeks after their letter "delta," formed by the Nile as it branches out to empty into the Mediterranean. They also made a distinction between what they termed the "black land," the dark fertile fields along the Nile, and the "red land," the desert cliffs and plateaus bordering the valley.

Upper Egypt Narrow valley extending 650 miles from Aswan to the border of Lower Egypt.

Lower Egypt The Nile's 100-mile deep, triangularly shaped delta.

The Nile alone made agriculture possible in Egypt's desert environment. Each year the rains of central Africa caused the river to rise over its floodplain, cresting in September and October. In places the plain extends several miles on either side; elsewhere the cliffs slope down to the water's edge. When the floodwaters receded, they left a rich layer of organically fertile silt. The construction and maintenance of canals, dams, and irrigation ditches to control the river's water, together with careful planning and organization of planting and harvesting, produced an agricultural prosperity unmatched in the ancient world.

The Nile served as the major highway connecting Upper and Lower Egypt. There was also a network of desert roads running north and south, as well as routes across the eastern desert to the Sinai and the Red Sea. Other tracks led to oases in the western desert. Thanks to geography and climate, Egypt was more isolated and enjoyed far more security than Mesopotamia. This security, along with the predictable flood calendar, gave

MAJOR PERIODS IN MESOPOTAMIAN AND EGYPTIAN HISTORY

MESOPOTAMIA	
ca. 3500 B.C.E.	Cities appear
ca. 2800–2370 B.C.E.	First Dynasties
2370–2205 B.C.E.	Sargon's empire
2125–2027 B.C.E.	III Dynasty of Ur
1792–1750 B.C.E.	Reign of Hammurabi
ca. 1600 B.C.E.	Fall of Amoritic Babylon
EGYPT	
ca. 3100–2700 B.C.E.	Early Dynastic Period (dynasties I–II)
ca. 2700–2200 B.C.E.	The Old Kingdom (dynasties III–VI)
2200–2025 B.C.E.	I Intermediate Period (dynasties VII–XI)
2025–1630 B.C.E.	The Middle Kingdom (dynasties XII–XIII)
1630–1550 B.C.E.	II Intermediate Period (dynasties XIV–XVII)
1550–1075 B.C.E.	The New Kingdom (dynasties XVIII–XX)

Egyptian civilization a more optimistic outlook than the civilizations of the Tigris and Euphrates, which were more prone to storms, flash floods, and invasions.

The 3,000-year span of ancient Egyptian history is traditionally divided into 31 royal dynasties, from the first, said to have been founded by Menes, the king who originally united Upper and Lower Egypt, to the last, established by Alexander the Great, who conquered Egypt in 332 B.C.E. (as we see in Chapter 3).

QUICK REVIEW

Egypt and the Nile

- Egyptian civilization developed along the Nile
- Predictable annual floods aided agriculture
- The Nile tied the people of Egypt together

The unification of Upper and Lower Egypt was vital, for it meant the entire river valley could benefit from an unimpeded distribution of resources. Three times in its history, Egypt experienced a century or more of political and social disintegration, known as Intermediate Periods. During these eras, rival dynasties often set up separate power bases in Upper and Lower Egypt until a strong leader reunified the land.

The Old Kingdom (2700–2200 B.C.E.) The Old Kingdom represents the culmination of the cultural and historical developments of the Early Dynastic period. For over four hundred years, Egypt enjoyed internal stability and great prosperity. During this period, the **pharaoh** was a king who was also a god. From his capital at Memphis, the god-king administered Egypt according to set principles, prime among them being *maat*, an ideal of order, justice, and truth. In return for the king's building and maintaining temples, the gods preserved the equilibrium of the state and ensured the king's continuing power, which was absolute. Since the king was obligated to act infallibly in a benign and beneficent manner, the welfare of the people of Egypt was automatically guaranteed and safeguarded.

pharaoh The god-king of ancient Egypt.

Nothing better illustrates the nature of Old Kingdom royal power than the pyramids built as pharaonic tombs. Beginning in the Early Dynastic period, kings constructed increasingly elaborate burial complexes in Upper Egypt. Djoser, a Third Dynasty king, was the first to erect a monumental six-step pyramid of hard stone. Subsequent pharaohs built other stepped pyramids until Snefru, the founder of the Fourth Dynasty, converted a stepped to a true pyramid over the course of putting up three monuments.

His son Khufu (Cheops in the Greek version of his name) chose the desert plateau of Giza, south of Memphis, as the site for the largest pyramid ever constructed. Its dimensions are prodigious: 481 feet high, 756 feet long on each side, and its base covering 13.1 acres. The pyramid is made of 2.3 million stone blocks averaging 2.5 tons each. It is also a geometrical wonder, deviating from absolutely level and square only by the most minute measurements using the latest modern devices. Khufu's successors, Khafre (Chephren) and Menkaure (Mycerinus), built equally perfect pyramids at Giza, and together, the three constitute one of the most extraordinary achievements in human history.

The pyramids are remarkable not only for the great technical skill they demonstrate, but also for the concentration of resources they represent. They are evidence that the pharaohs controlled vast wealth and had the power to focus and organize enormous human effort over the years it took to build each pyramid. They also provide a visible indication of the nature of the Egyptian state: The pyramids, like the pharaohs, tower above the land; the low tombs at their base, like the officials buried there, seem to huddle in relative unimportance.

Originally, the pyramids and their associated cult buildings contained statuary, offerings, and all the pharaoh needed for the afterlife. Despite great precautions and ingenious concealment methods, tomb robbers took nearly everything, leaving little for modern archeologists to recover. Several full-size wooden boats have been found, however, still in their own graves at the base of the pyramids, ready for the pharaoh's journeys in the next world. Recent excavations have uncovered remains of the large town built to house the thousands of pyramid builders, including the farmers who worked at Giza during the annual flooding of their fields.

Numerous officials, both members of the royal family and nonroyal men of ability, aided the god-kings. The highest office was the *vizier* (a modern term from Arabic). Central offices dealing with granaries, surveys, assessments, taxes, and salaries administered the land. Water management was local rather than on a national level. Upper and Lower Egypt were divided into ***nomes***, or districts, each governed by a *nomarch*, or governor, and his local officials. The kings could also appoint royal officials to oversee groups of *nomes* or to supervise pharaonic landholdings throughout Egypt.

nomes Egyptian districts ruled by regional governors who were called nomarchs.

QUICK REVIEW

The Pyramids

- Reveal the power and resources of Old Kingdom pharaohs
- Built as tombs for pharaohs
- Pyramids were originally filled with offerings to support pharaohs in the afterlife

The First Intermediate Period and Middle Kingdom (2200–1786 B.C.E.) Toward the end of the Old Kingdom, for a combination of political and economic reasons, absolute pharaonic power waned as the nomarchs and other officials became more independent and influential. About 2200 B.C.E., the Old Kingdom collapsed and gave way to the decentralization and disorder of the First Intermediate Period, which lasted until about 2052 B.C.E. Eventually, the kings of Dynasty 11, based in Thebes in Upper Egypt, defeated the rival Dynasty 10, based in a city south of Giza.

Amunemhet I, the founder of Dynasty 12 and the Middle Kingdom, probably began his career as a successful vizier under an Eleventh Dynasty king. After reuniting Upper and Lower Egypt, he turned his attention to making three important and long-lasting administrative changes. First, he moved his royal residence from Thebes to a brand-new town, just south of the old capital at Memphis, signaling a fresh start rooted in past glories. Second, he reorganized the nome structure by more clearly defining the nomarchs' duties to the state, granting them some local autonomy within the royal structure. Third, he established a co-regency system to smooth transitions from one reign to another.

Yet the events of the First Intermediate Period had irrevocably changed the nature of Egyptian kingship. Gone was the absolute, distant god-king; the king was now more directly concerned with his people. In art, instead of the supremely confident faces of the Old Kingdom pharaohs, the Middle Kingdom rulers seem thoughtful, careworn, and brooding.

Egypt's relations with its neighbors became more aggressive during the Middle Kingdom. To the south, royal fortresses were built to control Nubia and the growing trade in African resources. To the north and east, Syria and Palestine increasingly came under Egyptian influence, even as fortifications sought to prevent settlers from the Levant from moving into the Delta.

The Second Intermediate Period and the New Kingdom (1630–1075 B.C.E.) For some unknown reason, during Dynasty 13, the kingship changed hands rapidly and the western Delta established itself as an independent Dynasty 14, ushering in the Second Intermediate Period. The eastern Delta, with its expanding Asiatic populations, came under the control of the Hyksos (Dynasty 15) and minor Asiatic kings (Dynasty 16). Meanwhile, the Dynasty 13 kings left their northern capital and regrouped in Thebes (Dynasty 17).

Though much later sources describe the Hyksos ("chiefs of foreign lands" in Egyptian) as ruthless invaders from parts unknown, they were almost certainly Amorites from the Levant, part of the gradual infiltration of the Delta during the Middle Kingdom. After nearly a century of rule, the Hyksos were expelled, a process begun by Kamose, the last king of Dynasty 17, and completed by his brother Ahmose, the first king of Dynasty 18 and the founder of the New Kingdom.

The pyramids of Giza.

Peter Wilson © Dorling Kindersley

During Dynasty 18, Egypt pursued foreign expansion with renewed vigor. Military expeditions reached as far north as the Euphrates in Syria, with frequent campaigns in the Levant. To the south, major Egyptian temples were built in the Sudan, almost 1,300 miles from Memphis. Egypt's economic and political power was at its height.

Egypt's position was reflected in the unprecedented luxury and cosmopolitanism of the royal court and in the ambitious palace and temple projects undertaken throughout the country. Perhaps to foil tomb robbers, the Dynasty 18 pharaohs were the first to cut their tombs deep into the rock cliffs of a desolate valley in Thebes, known today as the Valley of the Kings. To date, only one intact royal tomb has been discovered there, that of the young Dynasty 18 king Tutankhamun, and even it had been disturbed shortly after his death. The thousands of goods buried with him, many of them marvels of craftsmanship, give an idea of Egypt's material wealth during this period.

Following the premature death of Tutankhamun in 1323 B.C.E., a military commander named Horemheb assumed the kingship, which passed in turn to his own army commander, Ramses I. The pharaohs Ramessides of Dynasty 19 undertook numerous monumental projects, among them Ramses II's rock-cut temples at Abu Simbel, south of the First Cataract, which had to be moved to a higher location when the Aswan High Dam was built in the 1960s. There and elsewhere, Ramses II left textual and pictorial accounts of his battle in 1285 B.C.E. against the Hittites at Kadesh on the Orontes in Syria. Sixteen years later, the Egyptians and Hittites signed a formal peace treaty, forging an alliance against an increasingly volatile political situation in the Mideast and eastern Mediterranean during the thirteenth century B.C.E.

Merneptah, one of the hundred offspring of Ramses II, held off a hostile Libyan attack, as well as incursions by the Sea Peoples, a loose coalition of Mediterranean raiders who seem to have provoked and taken advantage of unsettled conditions. One of Merneptah's inscriptions commemorating his military triumphs contains the first known mention of Israel.

Despite his efforts, by the end of Dynasty 20, Egypt's period of imperial glory had passed. The next thousand years witnessed a Third Intermediate Period, a Saite Renaissance, Persian domination, conquest by Alexander the Great, the Ptolemaic period, and finally, defeat at the hands of Rome in 30 B.C.E.

hieroglyphics ("sacred carving") Greek name for Egyptian writing. The writing was often used to engrave holy texts on monuments.

Language and Literature Writing first appears in Egypt about 3000 B.C.E. The writing system, dubbed **hieroglyphics** ("sacred carvings") by the Greeks, was highly sophisticated, involving hundreds of picture signs that remained relatively constant in the way they were rendered for over 3,000 years. A cursive version of hieroglyphics was used for business documents and literary texts, which were penned rapidly in black and red ink. The Egyptian language, part of the Afro-Asiatic (or Hamito-Semitic) family, evolved through several stages—Old, Middle, and Late Egyptian, Demotic, and Coptic—thus giving it a history of continuous recorded use well into the medieval period.

Egyptian literature includes narratives, myths, books of instruction in wisdom, letters, religious texts, and poetry, written on papyri, limestone flakes, and postherds. Unfortunately only a small fraction of this enormous literature has survived, and many texts are incomplete.

Religion: Gods and Temples Egyptian religion encompasses a multitude of concepts that often seem mutually contradictory to us. Three separate explanations for the origin of the universe were formulated, each based in the philosophical traditions of a venerable Egyptian city.

The Egyptian gods, or pantheon, similarly defy neat categorization, in part because of the common tendency to combine the character and function of one or more gods. Amun, one of the eight entities in the Hermopolitan cosmogony, provides a good example. Thebes, Amun's cult center, rose to prominence in the Middle Kingdom. In the New Kingdom, Amun was elevated above his seven cohorts and took on aspects of the sun god Re to become Amun-Re.

Not surprisingly in a nearly rainless land, solar cults and mythologies were highly developed. Much thought was devoted to conceptualizing what happened as the sun god made his perilous way through the underworld in the night hours between sunset and sunrise.

The Eighteenth Dynasty was one of several periods during which solar cults were in ascendancy. Early in his reign, Amunhotep IV promoted a single, previously minor aspect of the sun, the Aten ("disk") above Re himself and the rest of the gods. He declared that the Aten was the creator god who brought life to humankind and all living beings, with himself and his queen Nefertiti the sole mediators between the Aten and the people. For religious and political reasons still imperfectly understood, he went further, changing his name to Akhenaten ("the effective spirit of the Aten"), building a new capital called Akhetaten ("the horizon of the Aten") near Amarma north of Thebes, and chiseling out the name of Amun from inscriptions everywhere. Shortly after his death, Amarna was abandoned and partially razed. During the reigns of Akhenaten's successors, Tutankhamun (born Tutankhaten) and Horemheb, Amun was restored to his former position, and Akhenaten's monuments were defaced and even demolished.

In representations, Egyptian gods have human bodies, possess human or animal heads, and wear crowns, celestial disks, or thorns. The lone exception is the Aten, made nearly abstract by Akhenaten, who altered its image to a plain disk with solar rays ending in small hands holding the hieroglyphic sign for life to the nostrils of Akhenaten and Nefertiti. The gods were thought to reside in their cult centers, where, from the New Kingdom on, increasingly ostentatious temples were built, staffed by full-time priests. Though the ordinary person could not enter a temple precinct, great festivals took place for all to see. During Amun's major festival of Opet, the statue of the god traveled in a divine boat along the Nile, whose banks were thronged with spectators.

An elaborately decorated mummy coffin.

Peter Hayman © Dorling Kindersley

Worship and the Afterlife For most Egyptians, worship took place at small local shrines. They left offerings to the chosen gods, as well as votive inscriptions with simple prayers. Private houses often had niches containing busts for ancestor worship and statues of household deities. The Egyptians strongly believed in the power of magic, dreams, and oracles, and they possessed a wide variety of amulets to ward off evil.

The Egyptians thought the afterlife was full of dangers, which could be overcome by magical means, among them the spells in the *Book of the Dead.* The goals were to join and be identified with the gods, especially Osiris, or to sail in the "boat of millions." Originally only the king could hope to enjoy immortality with the gods, but gradually this became available to all. Since the Egyptians believed the preservation of the body was essential for continued existence in the afterlife, early on they developed mummification, a process that took seventy days by the New Kingdom. How lavishly tombs were prepared and decorated varied over the course of Egyptian history and in accordance with the wealth of a family.

Women in Egyptian Society It is difficult to assess the position of women in Egyptian society, because our pictorial and textual evidence comes almost entirely from male sources. Women's prime roles were connected with the management of the household. They could not hold office, go to scribal schools, or become artisans. Nevertheless, women could own and control property, sue for divorce, and, at least in theory, enjoy equal legal protection.

The Book of the Dead. The Egyptians believed in the possibility of life after death through the god Osiris. Aspects of each person's life had to be tested by forty-two assessor-gods before the person could be presented to Osiris. In the scene from a papyrus manuscript of the *Book of the Dead*, the deceased and his wife (on the left) watch the scales of justice weighing his heart (on the left side of the scales) against the feather of truth. The jackal-headed god Anubis also watches the scales, and the ibis-headed god Thoth keeps the record.

British Museum, London, UK/The Bridgeman Art Library International Ltd.

How did Egyptian beliefs about the afterlife differ from those of the Mesopotamians?

Royal women often wielded considerable influence, particularly in the Eighteenth Dynasty. The most remarkable was Hatshepsut, daughter of Thutmosis I and widow of Thutmosis II, who ruled as pharaoh for nearly twenty years. Many Egyptian queens held the title "god's wife of Amun," a power base of great importance.

Slaves Slaves did not become numerous in Egypt until the growth of Egyptian imperial power in the Middle Kingdom (2052–1786 B.C.E.). During that period, black Africans from Nubia to the south and Asians from the east were captured in war and brought back to Egypt as slaves. The great period of Egyptian imperial expansion, the New Kingdom (1550–1075 B.C.E.), vastly increased the number of slaves and captives in Egypt. Sometimes an entire people was enslaved, as the Bible says the Hebrews were.

Slaves in Egypt performed many tasks. They labored in the fields with the peasants, in the shops of artisans, and as domestic servants. Others worked as policemen and soldiers. Many slaves labored to erect the great temples, obelisks, and other huge monuments of Egypt's imperial age. Slaves could be freed in Egypt, but manumission seems to have been rare. Nonetheless, former slaves were not set apart and could expect to be assimilated into the mass of the population.

ANCIENT NEAR EASTERN EMPIRES

WHAT WERE the great empires of the ancient Near East?

In the time of Dynasty 18 in Egypt, new groups of peoples had established themselves in the Near East: the Kassites in Babylonia, the Hittites in Asia Minor, and the Mitannians in northern Syria and Mesopotamia. (See Map 1–2.) The Kassites and Mitanni-

MAP EXPLORATION

Interactive map: To explore this map further, go to www.myhistorylab.com

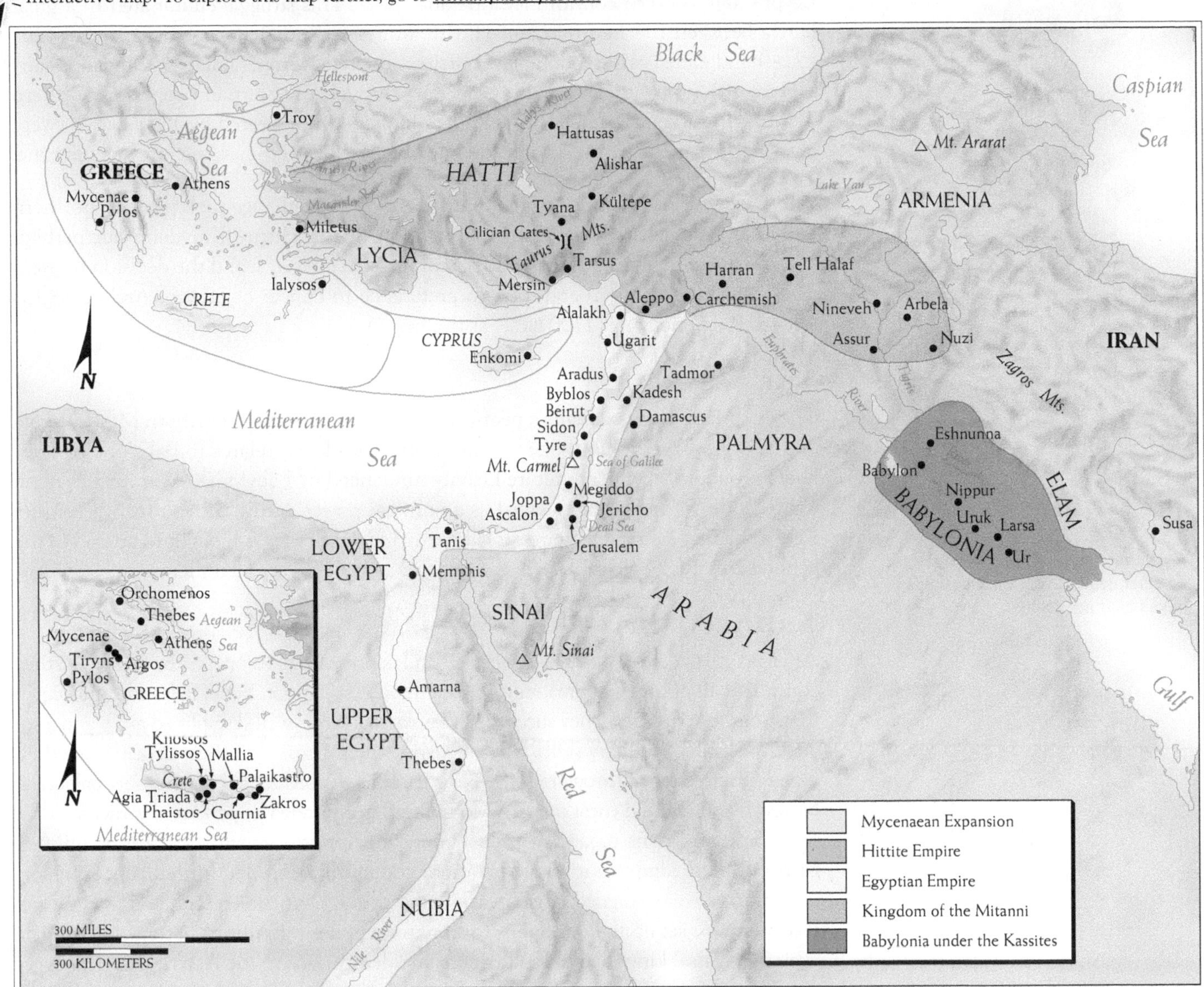

MAP 1–2 **The Near East and Greece about 1400 B.C.E.** About 1400 B.C.E., the Near East was divided among four empires. Egypt extended south to Nubia and north through Palestine and Phoenicia. The Kassites ruled in Mesopotamia, the Hittites in Asia Minor, and the Mitannians in Assyrian lands. In the Aegean, the Mycenaean kingdoms were at their height.

Based on the locations of the various states that had risen by the fifteenth century B.C.E., what were these new states dependent on, geographically, to succeed?

ans were warrior peoples who ruled as a minority over more civilized folk and absorbed their culture. The Hittites established a kingdom of their own and forged an empire that lasted some two hundred years.

The Hittites

The Hittites were an Indo-European people, speaking a language related to Greek and Sanskrit. By about 1500 B.C.E., they established a strong, centralized government with

Statue of Hatshepsut

"Statue of Hatshepsut." Red Granite. Dynasty 18, 1490–1480 B.C. (Egyptian). The Metropolitan Museum of Art, Rogers Fund and Edward S. Harkness Gift, 1929. (29.3.1)

Why were so many of the official statues and other depictions of Hatshepsut destroyed after her death?

a capital at Hattusas (near Ankara, the capital of modern Turkey). Between 1400 and 1200 B.C.E., they emerged as a leading military power in the Mideast and contested Egypt's ambitions to control Palestine and Syria. This struggle culminated in a great battle between the Egyptian and Hittite armies at Kadesh in northern Syria (1285 B.C.E.) and ended as a standoff. The Hittites adopted Mesopotamian writing and many aspects of Mesopotamian culture, especially through the Hurrian peoples of northern Syria and southern Anatolia. The Hittite kingdom disappeared by 1200 B.C.E., swept away in the general invasions and collapse of the Mideastern nation-states at that time.

The Discovery of Iron An important technological change took place in northern Anatolia, somewhat earlier than the creation of the Hittite Kingdom, but perhaps within its region. This was the discovery of how to smelt iron and the decision to use it to manufacture weapons and tools in preference to copper or bronze. Archaeologists refer to the period after 1100 B.C.E. as the Iron Age.

The Assyrians

The Assyrians were originally a people living in Assur, a city in northern Mesopotamia on the Tigris River. They spoke a Semitic language closely related to Babylonian. They had a proud, independent culture heavily influenced by Babylonia. Assur had been an early center for trade but emerged as a political power during the fourteenth century B.C.E. The first Assyrian empire spread north and west but was brought to an end in the general collapse of Near Eastern states at the end of the second millennium.

The Second Assyrian Empire

After 1000 B.C.E., the Assyrians began a second period of expansion, and by 665 B.C.E., they controlled all of Mesopotamia, much of southern Asia Minor, Syria, Palestine, and Egypt to its southern frontier. They succeeded, thanks to a large, well-disciplined army and a society that valued military skills. Some Assyrian kings boasted of their atrocities, so their names inspired terror throughout the Near East. They constructed magnificent palaces at Nineveh and Nimrud (near modern Mosul, Iraq), surrounded by parks and gardens.

The Assyrians organized their empire into provinces with governors, military garrisons, and administration for taxation, communications, and intelligence. Important officers were assigned large areas of land throughout the empire, and agricultural colonies were set up in key regions to store up supplies for military actions beyond the frontiers. Vassal kings had to send tribute and delegations to the Assyrian capital every year. Tens of thousands of people were forcibly displaced from their homes and resettled in other areas of the empire, partly to populate sparsely inhabited regions, partly to diminish resistance to Assyrian rule. People of the kingdom of Israel, which the Assyrians invaded and destroyed, were among them.

The empire became too large to govern efficiently. The last years of Assyria are obscure, but civil war apparently divided the country. The Medes, a powerful people from western and central Iran, had been expanding across the Iranian plateau. The Medes attacked Assyria and were joined by the Babylonians, who had always been restive under Assyrian rule, under the leadership of a general named Nebuchadnezzar. They eventually destroyed the Assyrian cities, including Nineveh in 612 B.C.E., so thoroughly that Assyria never recovered.

The Neo-Babylonians

The Medes did not follow up on their conquests, so Nebuchadnezzar took over much of the Assyrian Empire. Under him and his successors, Babylon grew into one of the greatest cities of the world. Nebuchadnezzar's dynasty did not last long, and the government passed to various men in rapid succession. The last independent king of Babylon

set up a second capital in the Arabian desert and tried to force the Babylonians to honor the Moon-god above all other gods. He allowed dishonest or incompetent speculators to lease huge areas of temple land for their personal profit. These policies proved unpopular—some said that the king was insane—and many Babylonians may have welcomed the Persian conquest that came in 539 B.C.E. After that, Babylonia began another, even more prosperous phase of its history as one of the most important provinces of another great Eastern empire, that of the Persians.

THE PERSIAN EMPIRE

WHAT WERE the Persian rulers' attitudes toward the cultures they ruled?

The great Persian Empire arose in the region now called Iran. (See Map 1–3.) The ancestors of the people who would rule it spoke a language from the Aryan branch of the family of Indo-European languages, related to the Greek spoken by the Hellenic peoples and the Latin of the Romans. The most important collections of tribes among them were the Medes and the Persians, peoples so similar in language and customs that the Greeks used both names interchangeably.

MAP EXPLORATION

Interactive map: To explore this map further, go to www.myhistorylab.com

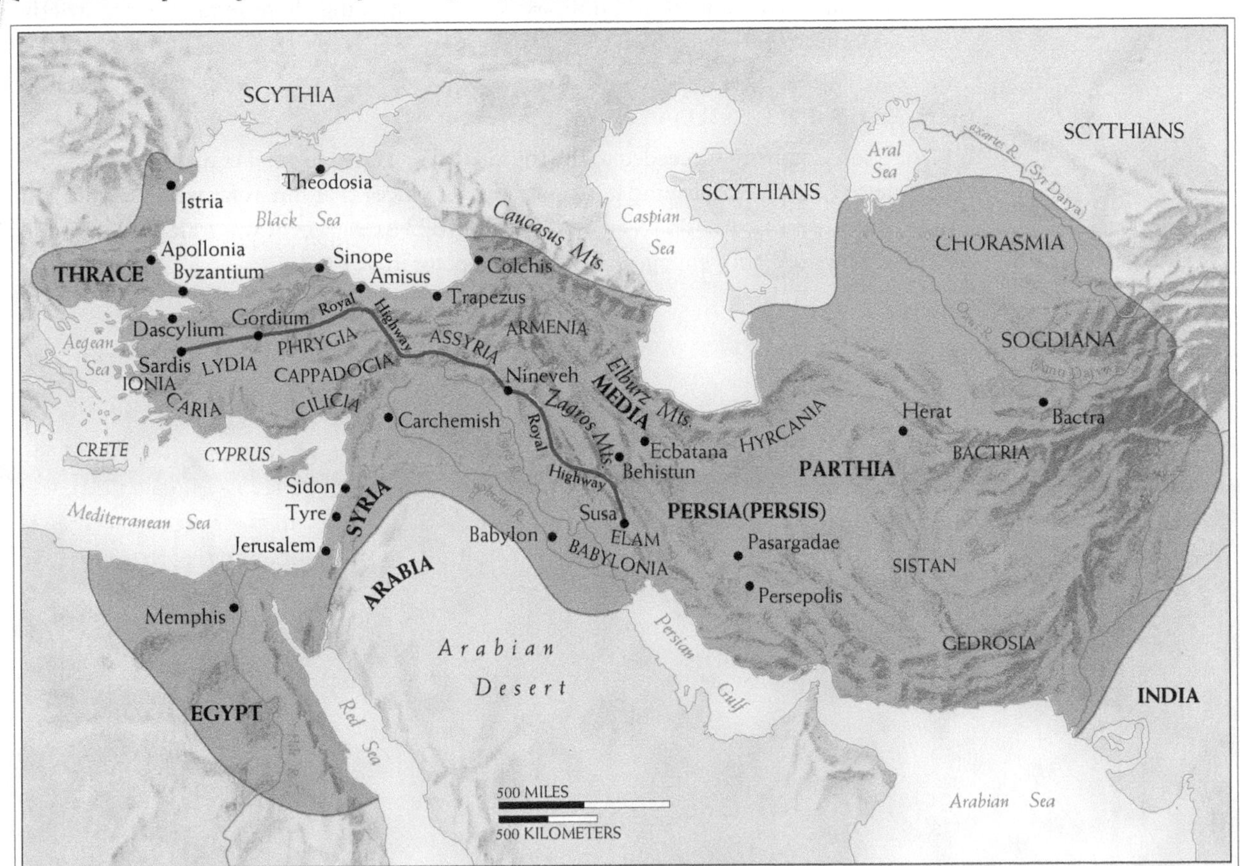

MAP 1–3 **The Achaemenid Persian Empire** The empire created by Cyrus had reached its fullest extent under Darius when Persia attacked Greece in 490 B.C.E. It extended from India to the Aegean, and even into Europe, encompassing the lands formerly ruled by Egyptians, Hittites. Babylonians, and Assyrians.

What strategies did the Persians use in their efforts to rule such a large and diverse empire?

Until the middle of the sixth century, the Persians were subordinate to the Medes, but when Cyrus II (called the Great) became King of the Persians (r. 559–530 B.C.E.), their positions were reversed. About 550 B.C.E., Cyrus captured the capital at Ecbatana and united the Medes and Persians under his own rule.

Cyrus the Great

Cyrus quickly expanded his power. The territory he inherited from the Medes touched on Lydia, ruled by the rich and powerful king Croesus. Croesus controlled western Asia Minor, having conquered the Greek cities of the coast about 560 B.C.E. Made confident by his victories, by alliances with Egypt and Babylon, and by what he thought was a favorable signal from the Greek oracle of Apollo at Delphi, he invaded Persian territory in 546 B.C.E. Cyrus achieved a decisive victory, capturing Croesus and his capital city of Sardis. By 539 B.C.E. he had conquered the Greek cities, and extended his power as far to the east as the Indus valley and modern Afghanistan. In that same year he captured Babylon.

Unlike the harsh Babylonian and Assyrian conquerors who preceded him, Cyrus pursued a policy of toleration and restoration. He did not impose the Persian religion but claimed to rule by the favor of the Babylonian god. Instead of deporting defeated peoples from their native lands and destroying their cities, he rebuilt their cities and allowed the exiles to return. This policy, followed by his successors, was effective but not as gentle as it might seem. Wherever they ruled, Cyrus and his successors demanded tribute from their subjects and military service, enforcing these requirements strictly and sometimes brutally.

Darius the Great

Cyrus's son Cambyses succeeded to the throne in 529 B.C.E. His great achievement was the conquest of Egypt, establishing it as a satrapy (province) that ran as far west as Lybia and as far south as Ethiopia. On Cambyses's death in 522 B.C.E., a civil war roiled much of the Persian Empire. Darius emerged as the new emperor in 521 B.C.E.

Darius. Persian nobles pay homage to King Darius in this relief from the treasury at the Persian capital of Persepolis. Darius is seated on the throne: his son and successor Xerxes stands behind him. Darius and Xerxes are carved in larger scale to indicate their royal status.

Courtesy of the Oriental Institute of the University of Chicago

What was the relationship between the Persian Empire and its subjects' kingdoms?

Darius's long and prosperous reign lasted until 486 B.C.E., during which he brought the empire to its greatest extent. To the east he added new conquests in northern India. In the west he sought to conquer the nomadic people called Scythians who roamed around the Black Sea. For this purpose he crossed into Europe over the Hellespont (Dardanelles) to the Danube River and beyond, taking possession of Thrace and Macedonia on the fringes of the Greek mainland. In 499 B.C.E., the Ionian Greeks of western Asia Minor rebelled, launching the wars between Greeks and Persians that would not end until two decades later. (See Chapter 2.)

Government and Administration

Like the Mesopotamian kingdoms, the Persian Empire was a hereditary monarchy that claimed divine sanction from the god **Ahura Mazda**. The ruler's title was *Shahanshah*, "king of kings." In theory all the land and the peoples in the empire belonged to him as absolute monarch, and he demanded tribute and service for the use of his property. In practice he depended on the advice and administrative service of aristocratic courtiers, ministers, and provincial governors, the satraps.

Ahura Mazda The chief deity of Zoroastrianism, the native religion of Persia. Ahura Mazda is the creator of the world, the source of light, and the embodiment of good.

The empire was divided into twenty-nine satrapies. The satraps were allowed considerable autonomy. They ruled over civil affairs and commanded the army in war, but the king exercised several means of control. In each satrapy he appointed a secretary and a military commander. He also chose inspectors called "the eyes and ears of the king" who traveled throughout the empire reporting on what they learned in each satrapy. Their travels and those of royal couriers were made swifter and easier by a system of excellent royal roads. Ruling over a vast empire whose people spoke countless different languages, the Persians did not try to impose their own, but instead adopted Aramaic, the most common language of Middle Eastern commerce, as the imperial tongue. This practical decision simplified both civil and military administration.

Medes and Persians made up the core of the army. Royal schools trained aristocratic Median and Persian boys as military officers and imperial administrators. The officers commanded not only the Iranian troops but also drafted large numbers of subject armies when needed.

Religion

Persia's religion was different from that of its neighbors and subjects. Its roots lay in the Indo-European traditions of the Vedic religion that Aryan peoples brought into India about 1500 B.C.E. Their religious practices included animal sacrifices and a reverence for fire. Although the religion was polytheistic, its chief god Ahura Mazda, the "Wise Lord," demanded an unusual emphasis on a stern ethical code. It took a new turn with the appearance of Zarathushtra, a Mede whom the Greeks called Zoroaster, perhaps as early as 1000 B.C.E., as tradition states, although some scholars place him about 600 B.C.E. He was a great religious prophet and teacher who changed the traditional Aryan worship.

Zarathushtra's reform made Ahura Mazda the only god, dismissing the others as demons not to be worshipped but fought. There would be no more polytheism and no sacrifices. Zarathushtra insisted that the people should reject the "Lie" (*druj*) and speak only the "Truth" (*asha*), portraying life as an unending struggle between two great forces, Ahura Mazda, the creator and only god, representing goodness and light, and Ahriman, a demon, representing darkness and evil.

Traditions and legends about Zarathustra as well as law, liturgy, and the teachings of the prophet are contained in the *Avesta*, the sacred book of the Persians. By the middle of the sixth century B.C.E., Zoroastrianism had become the chief religion of the Persians.

Art and Culture

Aramaic Semitic language spoken widely throughout the Middle East in antiquity.

The Persians learned much from the people they encountered and those they conquered, especially from Mesopotamia and Egypt, but they shaped it to fit comfortably on a Persian base. A good example is to be found in their system of writing. They adapted the **Aramaic** alphabet of the Semites to create a Persian alphabet and used the cuneiform symbols of Babylon to write the Old Persian language they spoke. They borrowed their calendar from Egypt. Persian art and architecture contain similar elements of talents and styles borrowed from other societies and blended with Persian traditions to serve Persian purposes.

PALESTINE

HOW WAS Hebrew monotheism different from Mesopotamian and Egyptian polytheism?

None of the powerful kingdoms of the ancient Near East had as much influence on the future of Western civilization as the small stretch of land between Syria and Egypt, the land called Palestine for much of its history. The three great religions of the modern world outside the Far East—Judaism, Christianity, and Islam—trace their origins, at least in part, to the people who arrived there a little before 1200 B.C.E. The book that recounts their experiences is the Hebrew Bible.

The Canaanites and the Phoenicians

Before the Israelites arrived in their promised land, it was inhabited by groups of people speaking a Semitic language called Canaanite. The Canaanites lived in walled cities and were farmers and seafarers. The Canaanites, like the other peoples of Syria-Palestine, worshipped many gods, especially gods of weather and fertility, whom they thought resided in the clouds atop the high mountains of northern Syria. The invading Israelites destroyed various Canaanite cities and holy places and may have forced some of the population to move north and west, though Canaanite and Israelite culture also intermingled.

Phoenicians Seafaring people (Canaanites and Syrians) who scattered trading colonies from one end of the Mediterranean to the other.

The **Phoenicians** were the descendants of the Canaanites and other peoples of Syria-Palestine, especially those who lived along the coast. They played an important role in Mediterranean trade, sailing to ports in Cyprus, Asia Minor, Greece, Italy, France, Spain, Egypt, and North Africa, as far as Gibraltar and possibly beyond. They founded colonies throughout the Mediterranean as far west as Spain. The most famous of these colonies was Carthage, near modern Tunis in North Africa. Sitting astride the trade routes, the Phoenician cities were important sites for the transmission of culture from east to west. The Greeks, who had long forgotten their older writing system of the Bronze Age, adopted a Phoenician version of the Canaanite alphabet that is the origin of our present alphabet.

The Israelites

The history of the Israelites must be pieced together from various sources. They are mentioned only rarely in the records of their neighbors, so we must rely chiefly on their own account, the Hebrew Bible. This is not a history in our sense, but a complicated collection of historical narrative, pieces of wisdom, poetry, law, and religious witness. Scholars of an earlier time tended to discard it as a historical source, but the most recent trend is to take it seriously while using it with caution.

According to tradition, the patriarch Abraham came from Ur and wandered west to tend his flocks in the land of the Canaanites. Some of his people settled there, and others wandered into Egypt. By the thirteenth century B.C.E., led by Moses, they had left Egypt and wandered in the desert until they reached and conquered Canaan. They established a united kingdom that reached its peak under David and Solomon in the tenth century B.C.E. The sons of Solomon could not maintain the unity of the kingdom, and it split into two parts: Israel in the north and Judah, with its capital at Jerusalem, in the south. The rise of the great empires brought disaster to the Israelites. The northern kingdom fell to the Assyrians in 722 B.C.E., and its people—the **ten lost tribes**—were scattered and lost forever. Only the kingdom of Judah remained. It is from this time that we may call the Israelites Jews.

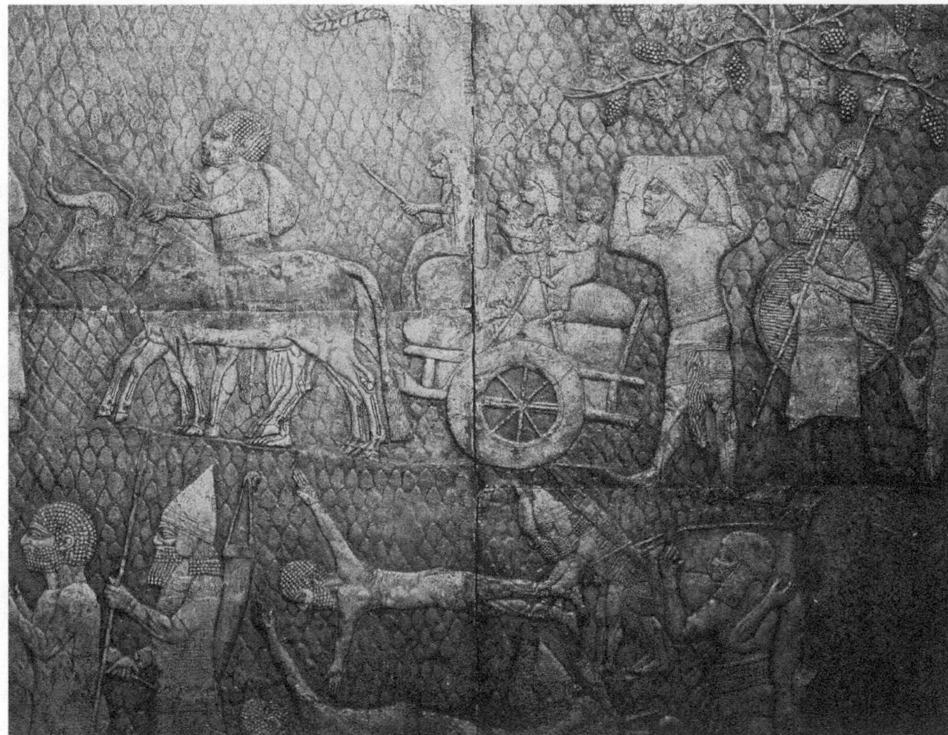

Exile of the Israelites. In 722 B.C.E. the northern part of Jewish Palestine, the kingdom of Israel, was conquered by the Assyrians. Its people were driven from their homeland and exiled all over the vast Assyrian Empire. This wall carving in low relief comes from the palace of the Assyrian king Sennacherib at Nineveh. It shows the Jews with their cattle and baggage going into exile.

Relief, Israel, 10th–6th Century: Judean exiles carrying provisions. Detail of the Assyrian conquest of the Jewish fortified town of Lachish (battle 701 B.C.). Part of a relief from the palace of Sennacherib at Niniveh, Mesopotamia (Iraq). British Museum, London, Great Britain. © Erich Lessing/Art Resource, NY.

What did the Assyrians hope to gain by exiling the Israelites?

In 586 B.C.E., Judah was defeated by the Neo-Babylonian king Nebuchadnezzar II. He destroyed the great temple built by Solomon and took thousands of hostages off to Babylon. When the Persians defeated Babylonia, they ended this Babylonian captivity of the Jews and allowed them to return to their homeland. After that, the area of the old kingdom of the Jews in Palestine was dominated by foreign peoples for some 2,500 years, until the establishment of the State of Israel in 1948 C.E.

ten lost tribes Israelites who were scattered and lost to history when the northern kingdom of Israel fell to the Assyrians in 722 B.C.E.

THE JEWISH RELIGION

The fate of the small nation of Israel would be of little interest were it not for its unique religious achievement. The great contribution of the Jews is the development of **monotheism**—the belief in one universal God, the creator and ruler of the universe. The Jewish God is neither a natural force nor like human beings or any other creatures; he is so elevated, that those who believe in him may not picture him in any form. The faith of the Jews is given special strength by their belief that God made a covenant with Abraham that his progeny would be a chosen people who would be rewarded for following God's commandments and the law he revealed to Moses.

monotheism Having faith in a single God.

Like the teachings of Zarathushtra in Iran, Jewish religious thought included a powerful ethical element. God is a severe, but just, judge. Ritual and sacrifice are not enough to achieve his approval. People must be righteous, and God himself appears to be bound to act righteously. The Jewish prophetic tradition was a powerful ethical force. The prophets constantly criticized any falling away from the law and the path of righteousness. They placed God in history, blaming the misfortunes of the Jews on God's righteous and necessary intervention to punish the people for their misdeeds. The prophets also promised the redemption of the Jews if they repented, however. The

prophetic tradition expected the redemption to come in the form of a Messiah who would restore the house of David. Christianity, emerging from this tradition, holds that Jesus of Nazareth was that Messiah.

Jewish religious ideas influenced the future development of the West, both directly and indirectly. The Jews' belief in an all-powerful creator (who is righteous himself and demands righteousness and obedience from humankind) and a universal God (who is the father and ruler of all peoples) is a critical part of the Western heritage.

GENERAL OUTLOOK OF MIDEASTERN CULTURES

WHAT SOCIAL and political contrasts existed between ancient Middle Eastern and Greek civilizations?

Our brief account of the history of the ancient Mideast so far reveals that its various peoples and cultures were different in many ways. Yet the distance between all of them and the emerging culture of the Greeks (Chapter 2) is striking. We can see this distance best by comparing the approach of the other cultures to several fundamental human problems with that of the Greeks: What is the relationship of humans to nature? To the gods? To each other? These questions involve attitudes toward religion, philosophy, science, law, politics, and government. Unlike the Greeks, the civilizations of the Mideast seem to have these features in common: Once established, they tended toward cultural uniformity and stability. Reason, though employed for practical and intellectual purposes, lacked independence from religion and the high status to challenge the most basic received ideas. The standard form of government was a monarchy; republics were unknown. Rulers were considered divine or the appointed spokesmen for divinity. Religious and political institutions and beliefs were thoroughly intertwined. Government was not subject to secular, reasoned analysis but rested on religious authority, tradition, and power. Individual freedom had no importance.

HUMANS AND NATURE

For the peoples of the Mideast, there was no simple separation between humans and nature or even between animate creatures and inanimate objects. Humanity was part of a natural continuum, and all things partook of life and spirit. These peoples imagined that gods more or less in the shape of humans ruled a world that was irregular and unpredictable, subject to divine whims. The gods were capricious because nature seemed capricious.

Humanity's function was merely to serve the gods. In a world ruled by powerful deities, human existence was precarious. Disasters that we would think human in origin, the Mesopotamians saw as the product of divine will. In such a universe, humans could not hope to understand nature, much less control it. At best, they could try by magic to use uncanny forces against others.

HUMANS AND THE GODS, LAW, AND JUSTICE

Human relationships to the gods were equally humble. There was no doubt that the gods could destroy human beings and might do so at any time for no good reason. Humans could—and, indeed, had to—try to win the gods over by prayers and sacrifices, but there was no guarantee of success. The gods were bound by no laws and no morality. The best behavior and the greatest devotion to the cult of the gods were no defense against the divine and cosmic caprice.

In the earliest civilizations, human relations were guided by laws, often set down in written codes. The basic question about law concerned its legitimacy: Why, apart from the lawgiver's power to coerce obedience, should anyone obey the law? For Old Kingdom Egyptians, the answer was simple: The king was bound to act in accordance with *maat*, and so his laws were righteous. For the Mesopotamians, the answer was almost the same: The king was a representative of the gods, so the laws he set forth were authoritative.

The Hebrews introduced some important new ideas. Their unique God was capable of great anger and destruction, but he was open to persuasion and subject to morality. He was therefore more predictable and comforting, for all the terror of his wrath. The biblical version of the flood story, for instance, reveals the great difference between the Hebrew God and the Babylonian deities. The Hebrew God was powerful and wrathful, but he was not arbitrary. He chose to destroy his creatures for their moral failures.

Such a world offers the possibility of order in the universe and on this earth. There is also the possibility of justice among human beings, for the Hebrew God had provided his people with law. Through his prophet Moses, he had provided humans with regulations that would enable them to live in peace and justice. If they would abide by the law and live upright lives, they and their descendants could expect happy and prosperous lives. This idea was different from the uncertainty of the Babylonian view, but like it and its Egyptian partner, it left no doubt of the certainty of the divine. Cosmic order, human survival, and justice all depended on God.

TOWARD THE GREEKS AND WESTERN THOUGHT

WHY WAS Greek rationalism such an important break with earlier intellectual traditions?

Greek thought offered different approaches and answers to many of the concerns we have been discussing. Calling attention to some of those differences will help convey the distinctive outlook of the Greeks and the later cultures within Western civilization that have drawn heavily on Greek influence.

Greek ideas had much in common with the ideas of earlier peoples. The Greek gods had most of the characteristics of the Mesopotamian deities. Magic and incantations played a part in the lives of most Greeks, and Greek law, like that of earlier peoples, was usually connected with divinity. Many, if not most, Greeks in the ancient world must have lived their lives with notions similar to those other peoples held. The surprising thing is that some Greeks developed ideas that were strikingly different and, in so doing, set part of humankind on an entirely new path.

As early as the sixth century B.C.E., some Greeks living in the Ionian cities of Asia Minor raised questions and suggested answers about the nature of the world that produced an intellectual revolution. In their speculations, they made guesses that were completely naturalistic and made no reference to supernatural powers. By putting the question of the world's origin in a naturalistic form, the Greeks may have begun the unreservedly rational investigation of the universe and, in so doing, initiated both philosophy and science.

This rationalistic, skeptical way of thinking carried over into practical matters. The school of medicine led by Hippocrates of Cos (about 400 B.C.E.) attempted to understand, diagnose, and cure disease without any attention to supernatural forces. By the fifth century B.C.E., the historian Thucydides could analyze and explain human behavior completely in terms of human nature and chance, leaving no place for the gods or supernatural forces. The same absence of divine or supernatural forces characterized Greek views of law and justice. Most Greeks, of course, liked to think that, in a vague way, law came ultimately from the gods. In practice, however, and especially in the democratic states, they knew that laws were made by humans and should be obeyed because they represented the expressed consent of the citizens.

SUMMARY

HOW DID life in the Neolithic Age differ from the Paleolithic?

Early Humans and Their Culture During the Paleolithic period, humans lived by hunting, fishing, and gathering food. They used tools, fire, and language; they believed in the supernatural. Around 10,000 B.C.E., humans started domesticating animals and plants for food. This Neolithic Revolution, which took place at different times in different parts of the world, was based on different crops in different environments. Civilization emerged, first in Mesopotamia, approximately during the Bronze Age, 3100 to 1200 B.C.E. *page 4*

WHY DID the first cities develop?

Early Civilizations to about 1000 B.C.E. Around 3000 B.C.E., civilizations along the Tigris and Euphrates Rivers in Mesopotamia, and the Nile River in Egypt, started to produce written records. Civilization in southern Mesopotamia was founded by Sumerians. Semitic Akkadians from northern Babylonia established the first empire in history; Sumerians returned to power in the Third Dynasty of Ur. Egypt's pharaohs united lands along the Nile. Hieroglyphs and tombs have left us an extensive record of life in ancient Egypt. *page 6*

WHAT WERE the great empires of the ancient Middle East?

Ancient Near Eastern Empires Between about 1400 B.C.E. and 500 B.C.E., new peoples and empires emerged in the Middle East. The Kassites and Mitannians were warrior peoples who ruled over the inhabitants of Babylonia and northern Syria/Mesopotamia, respectively. The Hittites based an empire in what is now Turkey. The Assyrian military supported a large Middle Eastern empire that lasted for almost half a millennium. Nebuchadnezzar overthrew the Assyrians and established a short-lived Neo-Babylonian dynasty. *page 20*

WHAT WERE the Persian rulers' attitudes toward the cultures they ruled?

The Persian Empire In the late sixth and early fifth centuries B.C.E., the Persian Empire reached the height of its power and geographical expansion under Cyrus the Great and Darius the Great. By assimilating cultures and peoples, the empire successfully combined a measure of autonomy among its twenty-nine satrapies (provinces) with a centralized authority based on the king's rule as a semidivine autocrat. Tolerance of other religions, use of the common language of Aramaic and existing writing systems, and an efficient communications system contributed to the Persians' imperial power. The Persian Empire was also built on the use of non-Persian soldiers and the art, architecture, and raw materials of its conquered lands. *page 23*

HOW WAS Hebrew monotheism different from Mesopotamian and Egyptian polytheism?

Palestine Judaism, Christianity, and Islam all owe many of their beliefs and practices to the Israelites who settled in Palestine before 1200 B.C.E. Israelites under Moses conquered Canaan in the thirteenth century B.C.E., and their kingdom reached its peak in the tenth century B.C.E. in the reigns of David and Solomon before splintering. Polytheistic Canaanites had lived in Syria-Palestine and through the coastal Phoenicians gave the Greeks the predecessor of the alphabet we use today. *page 26*

WHAT SOCIAL and political contrasts existed between ancient Middle Eastern and Greek civilizations?

General Outlook of Mideastern Cultures Most people of the ancient Mideast believed humans were inseparable from nature, and the gods were powerful and capricious. The Hebrew God reflected a different perspective on humanity's relationship with nature and with divine power. All the ancient Middle Eastern attitudes toward religion, philosophy, science, and society in general differ markedly from what we will learn about the Greeks. *page 28*

WHY WAS Greek rationalism such an important break with earlier intellectual traditions?

Toward the Greeks and Western Thought By the sixth century B.C.E., some Greeks started thinking about the world in ways that became the hallmark of Western civilization: They began to seek naturalistic, rational explanations for material phenomena and human behavior. Philosophy and science, as we understand them, could only develop once the Greeks had discarded supernatural explanations and reliance on divine intervention as ways of understanding the world. By the fifth century B.C.E., Greek thinkers had inaugurated the study of medicine and history, and by the fourth century B.C.E., Greek law and democracy had begun to evolve into forms recognizable to us. *page 29*

Review Questions

1. How was life during the Paleolithic Age different from life during the Neolithic Age? What advances account for the difference? Were these advances so significant that they warrant referring to the Neolithic as a revolutionary era?
2. What differences do you see in the political and intellectual outlooks of the Egyptian and Mesopotamian civilizations? How do their religious views compare? What influence did geography have on their religious outlooks?
3. What was significant about Cyrus the Great and Darius the Great? During their reigns, how did the Persians treat the cultures and peoples of subject lands?
4. What role did religious faith play in the political history of the Jews? Why did Middle Eastern civilizations regard the concept of Hebrew monotheism as a radical idea?
5. How did Greek thinkers diverge from the intellectual traditions of the Middle East? What new kinds of questions did Greeks ask?

Key Terms

Ahura Mazda (p. 25)
Aramaic (p. 26)
Bronze Age (p. 6)
civilization (p. 6)
culture (p. 4)
cuneiform (p. 10)
hieroglyphics (p. 18)
Homo sapiens (p. 4)
Lower Egypt (p. 15)
monotheism (p. 27)
Neolithic Age (p. 5)
nomes (p. 17)
Paleolithic (p. 4)
pharaoh (p. 16)
Phoenicians (p. 26)
ten lost tribes (p. 27)
Upper Egypt (p. 15)

For additional learning resources related to this chapter, please go to **www.myhistorylab.com**

PEARSON myhistorylab

2

The Rise of Greek Civilization

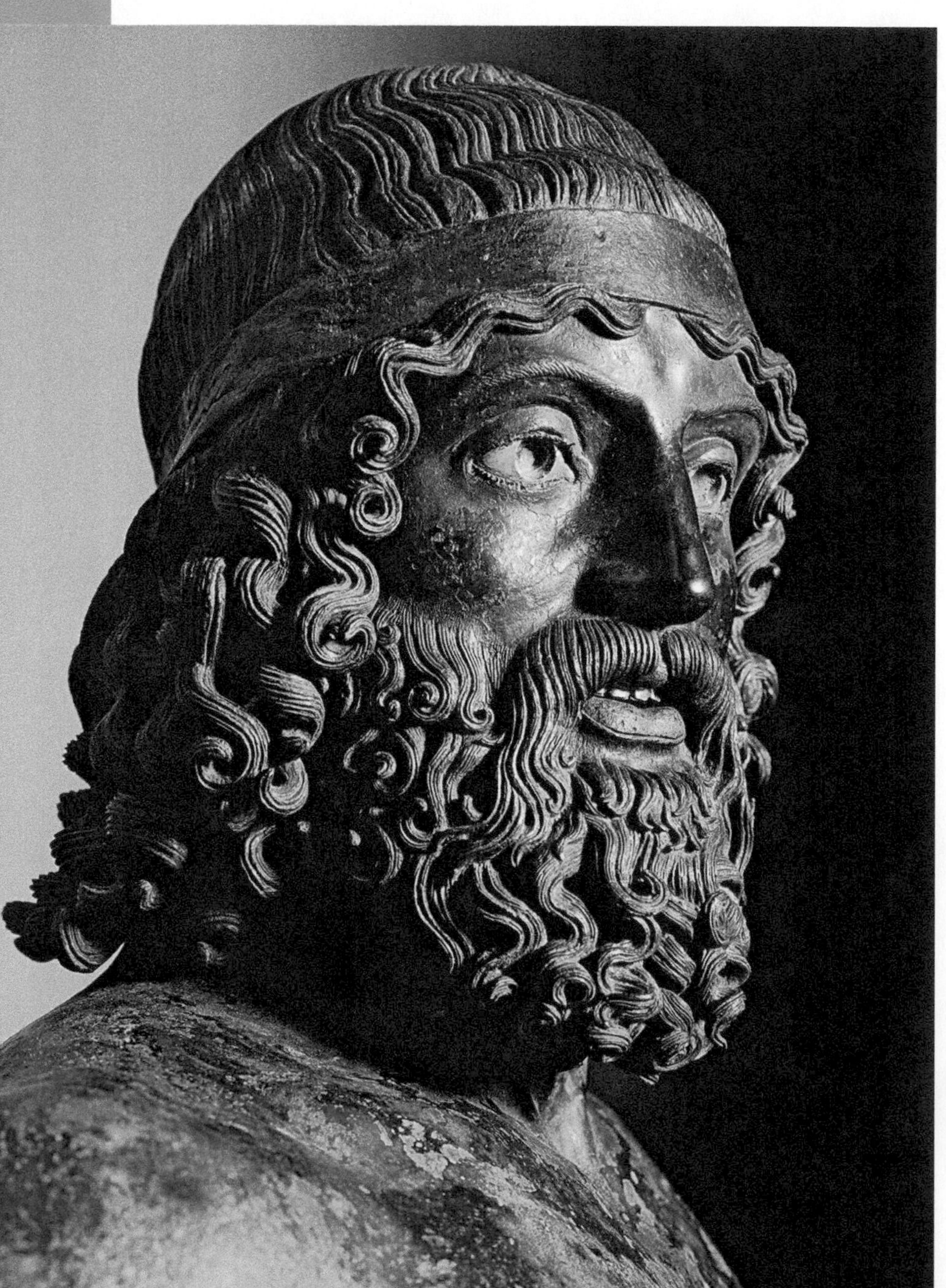

In 1972, this striking bronze statue was found off the coast of Riace, southern Italy. Possibly a votive statue from the sanctuary of Delphi in Greece, it may have been the work of the sculptor Phidias (ca. 490–430 B.C.E.).

Erich Lessing/Art Resource, N.Y.

In what ways does this statue reflect the confident worldview of the Ancient Greeks?

THE BRONZE AGE ON CRETE AND ON THE MAINLAND TO ABOUT 1150 B.C.E. *page 34*

IN WHAT ways were the Minoan and Mycenaean civilizations different?

THE GREEK "MIDDLE AGES" TO ABOUT 750 B.C.E. *page 37*

WHAT WERE the Greek Dark Ages?

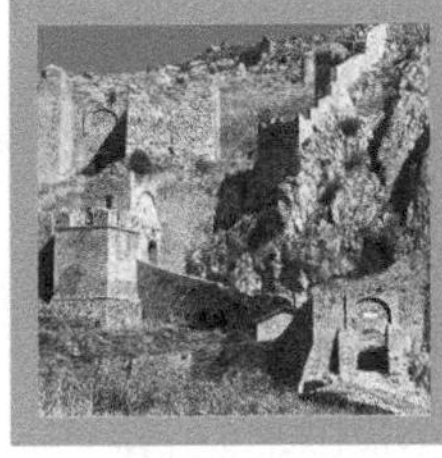

THE *POLIS* *page 39*

DESCRIBE THE *polis* and how it affected society and government.

EXPANSION OF THE GREEK WORLD *page 40*

HOW AND why did the Greeks colonize large parts of the Mediterranean?

THE MAJOR STATES *page 43*

HOW WERE the government and politics of Athens different from those of Sparta?

LIFE IN ARCHAIC GREECE *page 46*

WHAT ROLE did religion play in the lives of ordinary Greeks?

THE PERSIAN WARS *page 50*

WHAT WAS the significance of the wars between the Greeks and the Persians?

Minoan Civilization of Crete (2100–1150 B.C.E.), and the Aegean's first civilization, named for a legendary king on the island.

Mycenaean Civilization occupying mainland Greece during the Late Helladic era (1580–1150 B.C.E.).

About 2000 B.C.E., Greek-speaking peoples settled the lands surrounding the Aegean Sea and established communities that made major contributions to the Western heritage. The Greeks' location at the eastern end of the Mediterranean put them in touch, early in their history, with Mesopotamia, Egypt, Asia Minor, and Syria-Palestine. The Greeks acknowledged debts to the cultures of these regions but were conscious (and proud) of the ways in which their way of life was unique. ■

THE BRONZE AGE ON CRETE AND ON THE MAINLAND TO ABOUT 1150 B.C.E.

IN WHAT ways were the Minoan and Mycenaean civilizations different?

The Bronze Age civilizations in the region the Greeks would rule arose on the island of Crete, on the islands of the Aegean, and on the mainland of Greece. Crete was the site of the earliest Bronze Age settlements, and modern scholars have called the civilization that arose there **Minoan**, after Minos, the legendary king of Crete. A later Bronze Age civilization was centered at the mainland site of Mycenae and is called **Mycenaean**.

THE MINOANS

With Greece to the north, Egypt to the south, and Asia to the east, Crete was a cultural bridge between the older civilizations and the new one of the Greeks. The Bronze Age came to Crete not long after 3000 B.C.E., and the Minoan civilization, which powerfully influenced the islands of the Aegean and the mainland of Greece, arose in the third and second millennia B.C.E.

The Minoans produced a civilization that was new and unique in its character and beauty. Its most striking creations are the palaces uncovered at such sites as Phaestus, Haghia Triada, and, most important, Cnossus. Each of these palaces was built around a central court surrounded by a labyrinth of rooms. Some sections of the palace at Cnossus were four stories high. The palace design and the paintings show the influence of Syria, Asia Minor, and Egypt, but the style and quality are unique to Crete.

In contrast to the Mycenaean cities on the mainland of Greece, Minoan palaces and settlements lacked strong defensive walls. This evidence that the Minoans built without defense in mind has raised questions and encouraged speculation. Some scholars, pointing also to evidence that Minoan religion was more matriarchal than the patriarchal religion of the Mycenaeans and their Greek descendants, have argued that the civilizations of Crete, perhaps reflecting the importance of women, were inherently more tranquil and pacific than others. An earlier and different explanation for the absence of fortifications was that the protection provided by the sea made them unnecessary. The evidence is not strong enough to support either explanation, and the mystery remains.

Along with palaces, paintings, pottery, jewelry, and other valuable objects, excavations have revealed clay writing tablets like those found in Mesopotamia. The tablets, preserved accidentally when a great fire that destroyed the royal palace at Cnossus hardened them, have three distinct kinds of writing on them: a kind of picture writing called *hieroglyphic*, and two different linear scripts called Linear A and Linear B. The languages of the two other scripts remain unknown, but Linear B proved to be an early form of Greek. The contents of the tablets, primarily inventories, reveal an organization centered on the palace and ruled by a king who was supported by an extensive bureaucracy that kept remarkably detailed records.

This statuette of a female with a snake in each of her hands is thought to represent either the Minoan snake goddess herself or one of her priestesses performing a religious ritual. It was found on Crete and dates from around 1600 B.C.E.

Max Alexander/Dorling Kindersley © Archaeological Receipts Fund (TAP)

What might goddess worship tell us about gender roles in ancient Crete?

This sort of organization is typical of early civilizations in the Near East, but as we shall see, is nothing like that of the Greeks after the Bronze Age. Yet the inventories were written in a form of Greek. If they controlled Crete throughout the Bronze Age, why should Minoans, who were not Greek, have written in a language not their own? This question raises the larger one of what the relationship was between Crete and the Greek mainland in the Bronze Age and leads us to an examination of mainland culture.

THE MYCENAEANS

In the third millennium B.C.E.—the Early Helladic Period—most of the Greek mainland, including many of the sites of later Greek cities, was settled by people who used metal, built some impressive houses, and traded with Crete and the islands of the Aegean. The names they gave to places, names that were sometimes preserved by later invaders, make it clear they were not Greeks and they spoke a language that was not Indo-European (the language family to which Greek belongs). Not long after the year 2000 B.C.E., many of these Early Helladic sites were destroyed by fire, some were abandoned, and still others appear to have yielded peacefully to an invading people. These signs of invasion probably signal the arrival of the Greeks and the advent of a civilization historians have named Mycenaean for Mycenae, one of its cities. The presence of the Greek Linear B tablets at Cnossus suggests that Greek invaders also established themselves in Crete, and there is good reason to believe that at the height of Mycenaean power (1400–1200 B.C.E.), Crete was part of the Mycenaean world.

Mycenaean Culture The Mycenaean people were warriors, as their art, architecture, and weapons reveal. The success of their campaigns and the defense of their territory required strong central authority, and all available evidence shows that the kings provided it. Their palaces, in which the royal family and its retainers lived, were located within the walls; most of the population lived outside the walls. As on Crete, paintings usually covered the palace walls, but instead of peaceful landscapes and games, the Mycenaean murals depicted scenes of war and boar hunting.

About 1500 B.C.E., Mycenaean kings were constructing *tholos* tombs. These large, beehivelike chambers were built of enormous well-cut and fitted stones and were approached by an unroofed passage (*dromos*) cut horizontally into the side of the hill. Only a strong king whose wealth was great, whose power was unquestioned, and who commanded the labor of many people could undertake such a project. His wealth probably came from plundering raids, piracy, and trade.

The citadel of Mycenae, a major center of the Greek civilization of the Bronze Age, was built of enormously heavy stones. The lion gate at its entrance was built in the thirteenth century B.C.E.

Joe Cornish/Dorling Kindersley © Archaeological Receipts Fund (TAP)

Why did the Mycenaeans devote so much time and energy to the construction of heavily fortified outposts?

The Rise and Fall of Mycenaean Power At the height of their power (1400–1200 B.C.E.), the Mycenaeans were prosperous and active. They enlarged their cities, expanded their trade, and even established commercial colonies in the East. Sometime about 1250 B.C.E., they probably sacked Troy, on the coast of northwestern Asia Minor, giving rise to the epic poems of Homer—the *Iliad* and the *Odyssey*. (See Map 2–1.) Around 1200 B.C.E., however, the Mycenaean world showed signs of trouble, and by 1100 B.C.E., it was gone. Its palaces were destroyed, many of its cities were abandoned, and its art, way of life, and system of writing were buried and forgotten.

MAP 2–1 **The Aegean Area in the Bronze Age** The Bronze Age in the Aegean area lasted from about 1900 to about 1100 B.C.E. Its culture on Crete is called Minoan and was at its height about 1900–1400 B.C.E. Bronze Age Helladic culture on the mainland flourished from about 1600–1200 B.C.E.

What societal differences between the Mycenaean civilization on mainland Greece and the Minoan civilization of Crete might be a direct result of the geographic differences between the two civilizations?

What happened? Some recent scholars, noting evidence that the Aegean island of Thera (modern Santorini) suffered a massive volcanic explosion in the middle to late second millennium B.C.E., have suggested that this natural disaster was responsible. However, the Mycenaean towns were not destroyed all at once; many fell around 1200 B.C.E., but some flourished for another century, and the Athens of the period was never destroyed or abandoned. No theory of natural disaster can account for this pattern, leaving us to seek less dramatic explanations for the end of Mycenaean civilization.

CHRONOLOGY OF THE RISE OF GREECE

ca. 2900–1150 B.C.E.	Minoan period
ca. 1900 B.C.E.	Arrival of the Greeks on the mainland
ca. 1600–1150 B.C.E.	Mycenaean period
ca. 1250 B.C.E.	Sack of Troy
ca. 1200–1150 B.C.E.	Fall of the Mycenaean kingdoms
ca. 1150–750 B.C.E.	The Greek Dark Ages
ca. 750–500 B.C.E.	Greek colonial expansion
ca. 725 B.C.E.	Homer flourished
ca. 700 B.C.E.	Hesiod flourished
ca. 650 B.C.E.	Spartan constitution militarizes the state
546–510 B.C.E.	Athenian tyranny of Pisistratus and Hippias
508 B.C.E.	Clisthenes inaugurates Athenian democracy
499 B.C.E.	Miletus rebels against Persia
490 B.C.E.	Persian Wars: Darius
480–479 B.C.E.	Persian Wars: Xerxes

The Dorian Invasion Some scholars have suggested that piratical sea raiders, known as Dorians, destroyed Pylos and, perhaps, other sites on the mainland. Archaeology has not provided material evidence of whether there was a single Dorian invasion or a series of them, and it is impossible as yet to say with any certainty what happened at the end of the Bronze Age in the Aegean. The chances are good, however, that Mycenaean civilization ended gradually over the century between 1200 B.C.E. and 1100 B.C.E. Its end may have been the result of internal conflicts among the Mycenaean kings combined with continuous pressure from outsiders, who raided, infiltrated, and eventually dominated Greece and its neighboring islands. There is reason to believe that Mycenaean society suffered internal weaknesses due to its organization around the centralized control of military force and agricultural production. This rigid organization may have deprived it of flexibility and vitality, leaving it vulnerable to outside challengers.

THE GREEK "MIDDLE AGES" TO ABOUT 750 B.C.E.

WHAT WERE the Greek Dark Ages?

The immediate effects of the Dorian invasion were disastrous for the inhabitants of the Mycenaean world. The palaces and the kings and bureaucrats who managed them were destroyed. The wealth and organization that had supported the artists and merchants were likewise swept away by a barbarous people who did not have the knowledge or social organization to maintain them. The chaos resulting from the collapse of the rigidly controlled palace culture produced severe depopulation and widespread poverty that lasted for a long time.

GREEK MIGRATIONS

Another result of the invasion was the spread of the Greek people eastward from the mainland to the Aegean islands and the coast of Asia Minor. The Dorians themselves, after occupying most of the Peloponnesus, occupied the southern Aegean islands and the southern part of the Anatolian coast.

These migrations made the Aegean a Greek lake. The fall of the advanced Minoan and Mycenaean civilizations, however, virtually ended trade with the old civilizations of the Near East, nor was there much internal trade among the different parts of Greece. The Greeks were forced to turn inward, and each community was left largely to its own devices.

The Age of Homer

For a picture of society in these "Dark Ages," the best source is Homer. His epic poems, the ***Iliad*** and the ***Odyssey***, emerged from a tradition of oral poetry whose roots extend into the Mycenaean Age. Although the poems tell of the deeds of Mycenaean Age heroes, the world they describe clearly differs from the Mycenaean world. Homer's heroes are not buried in *tholos* tombs but are cremated; they worship gods in temples, whereas the Mycenaeans had no temples; they have chariots but do not know their proper use in warfare. Certain aspects of the society described in the poems appear instead to resemble the world of the tenth and ninth centuries B.C.E., and other aspects appear to belong to the poet's own time, when population was growing at a swift pace and prosperity was returning, thanks to changes in Greek agriculture, society, and government.

Iliad Homer's poem narrates a dispute between Agamemnon the king and his warrior Achilles, whose honor is wounded and then avenged.

Odyssey Homer's epic poem tells of the wanderings of the hero Odysseus.

Government and Society In the Homeric poems, the power of the kings is much less than that of the Mycenaean rulers. Homeric kings had to consult a council of nobles before they made important decisions. The nobles felt free to discuss matters in vigorous language and in opposition to the king's wishes. The king could ignore the council's advice, but it was risky for him to do so.

QUICK REVIEW

Homeric Kings

- Homeric kings had less power than their Mycenaean predecessors
- Homeric kings made decisions in consultation with nobles
- Right to speak at royal councils limited to noblemen, but common soldiers were not ignored

Only noblemen had the right to speak in council, but the common people could not be entirely ignored. If a king planned a war or a major change of policy during a campaign, he would not fail to call the common soldiers to an assembly; they could listen and express their feelings by acclamation, though they could not take part in the debate.

Homeric society, nevertheless, was sharply divided into classes, the most important division being the one between nobles and everyone else. Birth determined noble status, and wealth usually accompanied it. Below the nobles were three other classes: *thetes*, landless laborers, and slaves. We do not know whether the *thetes* owned the land they worked outright (and so were free to sell it) or worked a hereditary plot that belonged to their clan (and was, therefore, not theirs to dispose of as they chose). The worst condition was that of the free, but landless, hired agricultural laborer. The slave, at least, was attached to a family household and so was protected and fed. In a world where membership in a settled group gave the only security, the free laborers were desperately vulnerable. Slaves were few in number and were mostly women, who served as maids and concubines.

arete The highest virtue in Homeric society: the manliness, courage, and excellence that equipped a hero to acquire and defend honor.

Homeric Values The Homeric poems reflect an aristocratic code of values that powerfully influenced all future Greek thought. Those values were physical prowess; courage; fierce protection of one's family, friends, property; and, above all, personal honor and reputation. Achilles, the great hero of the *Iliad*, refuses to fight in battle, allowing his fellow Greeks to be slain and almost defeated, because Agamemnon has wounded his honor by taking away his battle prize. He returns not out of a sense of duty to the army, but to avenge the death of his dear friend Patroclus.

The highest virtue in Homeric society was ***arete***—manliness, courage in the most general sense, and the excellence proper to a hero. This quality was best revealed in a contest, or *agon*. Homeric battles are not primarily group combats, but a series of individual contests between great champions. One of the prime forms of entertainment is the athletic contest, and such a contest celebrates the funeral of Patroclus.

Black-Figure Hydria Five women filling hydriae in a fountain house.

"Hydria (water jug)". Greek, Archaic period, ca. 520 B.C. Athens, Attica, Greece the Priam Painter. Ceramic, black-figure, H: 0.53 cm Diam (with handles): 0.37 cm. William Francis Warden Fund.

What place did women have in the Ancient Greek household?

The central ethical idea in Homer can be found in the instructions that Achilles' father gives him when he sends him off to fight at Troy: "Always be the best and distinguished above others." Here in a nutshell we have the chief values of the aristocrats of Homer's world: to vie for individual supremacy in *arete* and to defend and increase the honor of the family.

Women in Homeric Society In the world described by Homer, the role of women was chiefly to bear and raise children, but the wives of the heroes also had a respected position, presiding over the household, overseeing the servants, and safeguarding the family property. They were prized for their beauty, constancy, and skill at weaving. Unlike Greek women in later centuries, the women of the higher class depicted in Homer are seen moving freely about their communities in town and country. They have a place alongside their husbands at the banquets in the great halls and take part in the conversation.

QUICK REVIEW

Women in a Warrior Society

- Women relegated to domestic roles
- Chief functions were to bear children and manage their husbands' estates
- Upper-class women had more freedom than later Greek women

THE *POLIS*

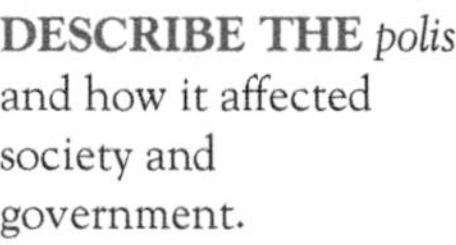

DESCRIBE THE *polis* and how it affected society and government.

The characteristic Greek institution was the *polis* (plural *poleis*). The common translation of that word as "city-state" is misleading, for it says both too much and too little. All Greek *poleis* began as little more than agricultural villages or towns, and many stayed that way, so the word "city" is inappropriate. All of them were states, in the sense of being independent political units, but they were much more than that. The *polis* was thought of as a community of relatives; all its citizens, who were theoretically descended from a common ancestor, belonged to subgroups, such as fighting brotherhoods or *phratries*, clans, and tribes, and worshipped the gods in common ceremonies.

Aristotle argued that the *polis* was a natural growth and the human being was by nature "an animal who lives in a *polis*." Humans alone have the power of speech and from it derive the ability to distinguish good from bad and right from wrong, "and the sharing of these things is what makes a household and a *polis*." Without law and justice, human beings are the worst and most dangerous of the animals. With them, humans can be the best, and justice exists only in the *polis*. These high claims were made in the fourth century B.C.E., hundreds of years after the *polis* came into existence, but they accurately reflect an attitude that was present from the first.

Entrance to Acrocorinth with its three gateways.

Joe Cornish © Dorling Kindersley

DEVELOPMENT OF THE *POLIS*

Originally the word *polis* referred only to a citadel—an elevated, defensible rock to which the farmers of the neighboring area could retreat in case of attack. The **Acropolis** in Athens and the hill called Acrocorinth in Corinth are examples. For some time, such high places and the adjacent farms made up the *polis*. The towns grew gradually and without planning, as their narrow, winding, and disorderly streets show. For centuries they had no walls. Unlike the city-states of the Near East, they were not placed for commercial convenience on rivers or the sea. Nor did they grow up around a temple to serve the needs of priests and to benefit from the needs of worshippers. The availability of farmland and of a natural fortress determined their location. They were placed either well inland or far enough away from the sea to avoid piratical raids. Only later and gradually did the ***agora***—a marketplace and civic center—appear within the *polis*. The *agora* was to become the heart of the Greeks' remarkable social life, distinguished by conversation and argument carried on in the open air.

Acropolis At the center of the city of Athens, the most famous example of a citadel.

agora Place for markets and political assemblies.

Some *poleis* probably came into existence early in the eighth century B.C.E. The institution was certainly common by the middle of the century, for all the colonies that were established by the Greeks in the years after 750 B.C.E. took the form of the *polis*. Once the new institution had been fully established, true monarchy disappeared. The original form of the *polis* was an aristocratic republic dominated by the nobility through its council of nobles and its monopoly of the magistracies. About 750 B.C.E., coincident with the development of the *polis*, the Greeks borrowed a writing system from one of the Semitic scripts and added vowels to create the first true alphabet. This new Greek alphabet was easier to learn than any earlier writing system, leading to a much wider literacy.

THE *HOPLITE* PHALANX

hoplite A true infantry soldier that began to dominate the battlefield in the late eighth century B.C.E.

phalanx Tight military formation of men eight or more ranks deep.

A new military technique was crucial to the development of the *polis*. In earlier times, small troops of cavalry and individual "champions" who first threw their spears and then came to close quarters with swords may have borne the brunt of fighting. Toward the end of the eighth century B.C.E., however, the ***hoplite* phalanx** came into being and remained the basis of Greek warfare thereafter.

The *hoplite* was a heavily armed infantryman who fought with a spear and a large shield. Most scholars believe that these soldiers were formed into a phalanx in close order, usually at least eight ranks deep, although some argue for a looser formation. As long as the *hoplites* fought bravely and held their ground, there would be few casualties and no defeat, but if they gave way, the result was usually a rout. All depended on the discipline, strength, and courage of the individual soldier. At its best, the phalanx could withstand cavalry charges and defeat infantries not as well protected or disciplined. Until defeated by the Roman legion, it was the dominant military force in the eastern Mediterranean.

In every way, the phalanx was a communal effort that relied not on the extraordinary actions of the individual, but on the courage of a considerable portion of the citizenry. This style of fighting produced a single, decisive battle that reduced the time lost in fighting other kinds of warfare; it spared the houses, livestock, and other capital of the farmer-soldiers who made up the phalanx, and it also reduced the number of casualties. It perfectly suited the farmer-soldier-citizen, who was the backbone of the *polis*, and, by keeping wars short and limiting their destructiveness and expense, it helped the *polis* prosper.

The phalanx and the *polis* arose together, and both heralded the decline of the kings. The phalanx, however, was not made up only of aristocrats. Most of the *hoplites* were farmers working small holdings. The immediate beneficiaries of the royal decline were the aristocrats, but because the existence of the *polis* depended on small farmers, their wishes could not long be wholly ignored. The rise of the *hoplite* phalanx created a bond between the aristocrats and the yeomen family farmers who fought in it. This bond helps explain why class conflicts were muted for some time. It also guaranteed, however, that the aristocrats, who dominated at first, would not always be unchallenged.

EXPANSION OF THE GREEK WORLD

HOW AND why did the Greeks colonize large parts of the Mediterranean?

From the middle of the eighth century B.C.E. until well into the sixth century B.C.E., the Greeks vastly expanded their territory, their wealth, and their contacts with other peoples. A burst of colonizing activity placed *poleis* from Spain to the Black Sea. (See Map 2–2.)

THE GREEK COLONY

The Greeks did not lightly leave home to join a colony. The voyage by sea was dangerous and uncomfortable, and at the end of it were uncertainty and danger. Only powerful pressures like overpopulation and hunger for land drove thousands from their homes to establish new *poleis*.

MAP EXPLORATION

Interactive map: To explore this map further, go to www.myhistorylab.com

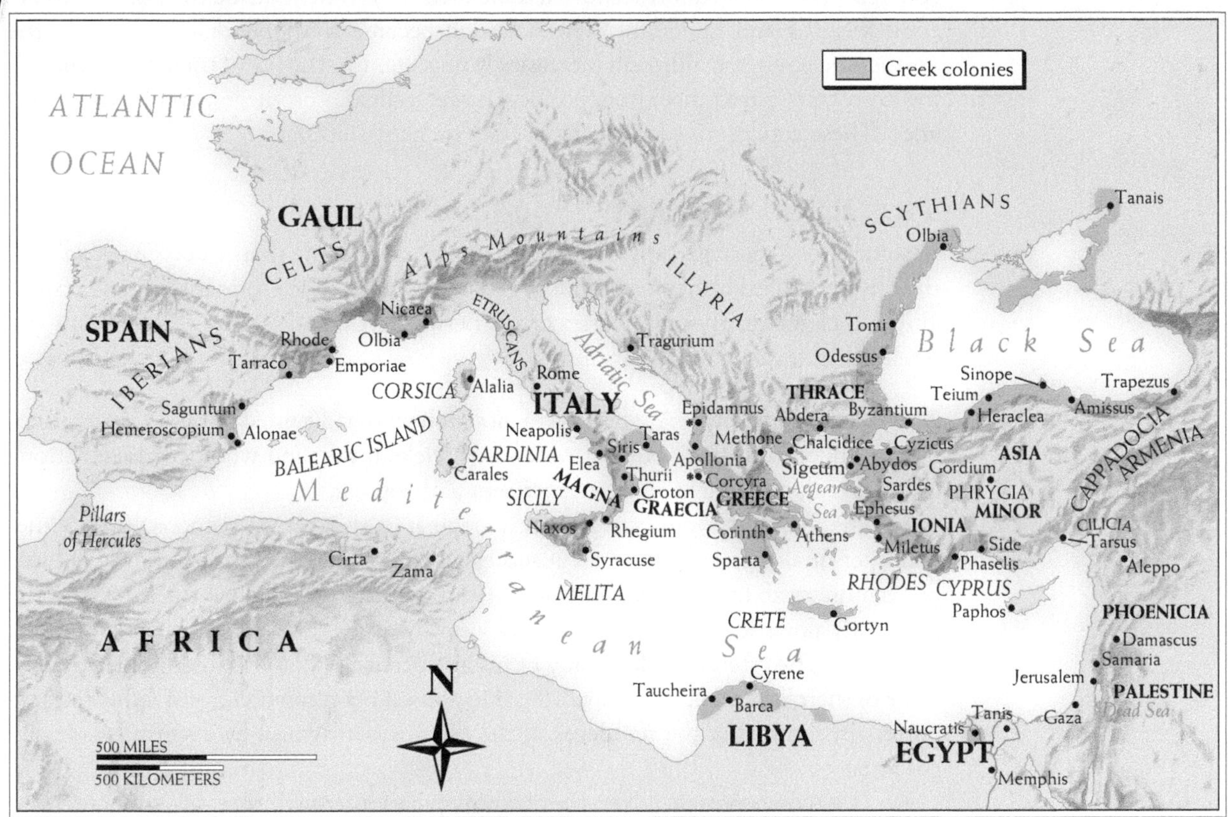

MAP 2–2 **Greek Colonization** The height of Greek colonization was between about 750 and 550 B.C.E. Greek colonies stretched from the Mediterranean coasts of Spain and Gaul (modern France) in the west to the Black Sea and Asia Minor in the east.

Note the area of penetration in the various colonized areas on this map. How is this indicative of a colonization achieved mainly by means of the sea?

The colony, although sponsored by the mother city, was established for the good of the colonists rather than for the benefit of those they left behind. The colonists tended to divide the land they settled into equal shares, reflecting an egalitarian tendency inherent in the ethical system of the yeoman farmers in the mother cities. Most colonies, though independent, were friendly with their mother cities. Each might ask the other for aid in time of trouble and expect to receive a friendly hearing, although neither was obligated to help the other.

Colonization had a powerful influence on Greek life. By relieving the pressure of a growing population, it provided a safety valve that allowed the *poleis* to escape civil wars. By confronting the Greeks with the differences between themselves and the new peoples they met, colonization gave them a sense of cultural identity and fostered a **Panhellenic** ("all-Greek") spirit that led to the establishment of common religious festivals. The most important ones were at Olympia, Delphi, Corinth, and Nemea.

Panhellenic ("all Greek") Sense of cultural identity that all Greeks felt in common with one another.

Colonization also encouraged trade and industry. The influx of new wealth from abroad and the increased demand for goods from the homeland stimulated a more intensive use of the land and an emphasis on crops for export, chiefly the olive and the wine grape. The manufacture of pottery, tools, weapons, and fine artistic metalwork, as well as perfumed oil, the soap of the ancient Mediterranean world, was likewise encouraged. New opportunities allowed some men, sometimes outside the nobility, to become wealthy and important. The new rich became a troublesome element in the aristocratic *poleis*, for, although increasingly important in the life of their states, the ruling aristocrats barred them from political power, religious privileges, and social acceptance. These conditions soon created a crisis in many states.

The Tyrants (about 700–500 B.C.E.)

In some cities—perhaps only a small percentage of the more than 1,000 Greek *poleis*—the crisis produced by new economic and social conditions led to or intensified factional divisions within the ruling aristocracy. Between 700 and 500 B.C.E., the result was often the establishment of a tyranny.

The Rise of Tyranny A tyrant was a monarch who had gained power in an unorthodox or unconstitutional, but not necessarily wicked, way and who exercised a strong one-man rule that might well be beneficent and popular.

The founding tyrant was usually a member of the ruling aristocracy who either had a personal grievance or led an unsuccessful faction. He often rose to power because of his military ability and support from the *hoplites*. He generally had the support of the politically powerless group of the newly wealthy and of the poor farmers. When he took power, he often expelled many of his aristocratic opponents and divided at least some of their land among his supporters. He pleased his commercial and industrial supporters by destroying the privileges of the old aristocracy and by fostering trade and colonization.

The tyrants presided over a period of population growth that saw an increase especially in the number of city dwellers. They responded with a program of public works that included the improvement of drainage systems, care for the water supply, the construction and organization of marketplaces, the building and strengthening of city walls, and the erection of temples. They introduced new local festivals and elaborated the old ones. They patronized the arts, supporting poets and artisans with gratifying results. All this activity contributed to the tyrant's popularity, to the prosperity of his city, and to his self-esteem.

The End of the Tyrants By the end of the sixth century B.C.E., tyranny had disappeared from the Greek states and did not return in the same form or for the same reasons. The last tyrants were universally hated for their cruelty and repression. They left bitter memories in their own states and became objects of fear and hatred everywhere.

Besides the outrages individual tyrants committed, the very concept of tyranny was inimical to the idea of the *polis*. The notion of the *polis* as a community to which every member must be responsible, the connection of justice with that community, and the natural aristocratic hatred of monarchy all made tyranny seem alien and offensive. The rule of a tyrant, however beneficent, was arbitrary and unpredictable. Tyranny came into being in defiance of tradition and law, and the tyrant governed without either. He was not answerable in any way to his fellow citizens.

From a longer perspective, however, the tyrants made important contributions to the development of Greek civilization. They encouraged economic changes that helped secure the future prosperity of Greece. They increased communication with the rest of the Mediterranean world and cultivated crafts and technology, as well as arts and literature. Most important of all, they broke the grip of the aristocracy and put the productive powers of the most active and talented of its citizens fully at the service of the *polis*.

QUICK REVIEW

Greek Tyranny

- Tyrants were men who took power through illegal means
- Rule was not always oppressive
- Tyrannies faded away around the sixth century B.C.E.

THE MAJOR STATES

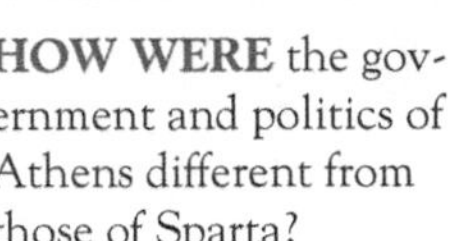

HOW WERE the government and politics of Athens different from those of Sparta?

Generalization about the *polis* becomes difficult not long after its appearance, for although the states had much in common, some of them developed in unique ways. Sparta and Athens, which became the two most powerful Greek states, had especially unusual histories.

SPARTA

Peloponnesus Southern half of the Greek peninsula.

Helots Slaves to the Spartans who revolted and nearly destroyed Sparta in 650 B.C.E.

At first Sparta—located on the **Peloponnesus**, the southern peninsula of Greece—seems not to have been strikingly different from other *poleis*. About 725 B.C.E., however, the pressure of population and land hunger led the Spartans to launch a war of conquest against their western neighbor, Messenia. The First Messenian War gave the Spartans as much land as they would ever need. The reduction of the Messenians to the status of serfs, or **Helots**, meant the Spartans did not even need to work the land that supported them.

The turning point in Spartan history came about 650 B.C.E., when, in the Second Messenian War, the Helots rebelled with the help of Argos and other Peloponnesian cities. After they had suppressed the revolt, the Spartans were forced to reconsider their way of life. They could not expect to keep down the Helots, who outnumbered them perhaps ten to one, and still maintain the old free and easy habits typical of most Greeks. Faced with the choice of making drastic changes and sacrifices or abandoning their control of Messenia, the Spartans chose to turn their city forever after into a military academy and camp.

A large Spartan plate from the second quarter of the sixth century B.C.E.

Hirmer Fotoarchiv

How did Spartan society differ from that of other Greek city-states?

Spartan Society The new system that emerged late in the sixth century B.C.E. exerted control over each Spartan from birth, when officials of the state decided which infants were physically fit to survive. At the age of seven, the Spartan boy was taken from his mother and turned over to young instructors. He was trained in athletics and the military arts and taught to endure privation, to bear physical pain, and to live off the country, by theft if necessary. At twenty, the Spartan youth was enrolled in the army, where he lived in barracks with his companions until the age of thirty. Marriage was permitted, but a strange sort of marriage it was, for the Spartan male could visit his wife only infrequently and by stealth. At thirty he became a full citizen, an "equal." Military service was required until the age of sixty; only then could the Spartan retire to his home and family.

This educational program extended to women, too, although they were not given military training. Like males, female infants were examined for fitness to survive. Girls were given gymnastic training, were permitted greater freedom of movement than among other Greeks, and were equally indoctrinated with the idea of service to Sparta.

The entire system was designed to change the natural feelings of devotion to family and children into a more powerful commitment to the *polis*. Privacy, luxury, and even comfort were sacrificed to the purpose of producing soldiers whose physical powers, training, and discipline made them the best in the world. Nothing that might turn the mind away from duty was permitted.

Spartan Government The Spartan constitution was mixed, containing elements of monarchy, oligarchy, and democracy. There were two kings, whose power was limited by law and also by the rivalry that usually existed between the two royal houses. Their functions were chiefly religious and military. A Spartan army rarely left home without a king in command.

A spartan warrior.

Nick Nicholls © The British Museum

A council of elders, consisting of twenty-eight men over the age of sixty, elected for life, and the kings, represented the oligarchic element. These elders had important judicial functions, sitting as a court in cases involving the kings. They also were consulted before any proposal was put before the assembly of Spartan citizens.

The Spartan assembly consisted of all males over thirty. This was thought to be the democratic element in the constitution, but its membership included only a small percentage of the entire population. Theoretically, they were the final authority, but in practice, only magistrates, elders, and kings participated in debate, and voting was usually by acclamation. Therefore, the assembly's real function was to ratify decisions already made or to decide between positions favored by the leading figures.

The Peloponnesian League By about 550 B.C.E., the Spartan system was well established, and its limitations were plain. Suppression of the Helots required all the effort and energy that Sparta had. The Spartans could expand no further, but they could not allow unruly independent neighbors to cause unrest that might inflame the Helots.

When the Spartans defeated Tegea, their northern neighbor, they imposed an unusual peace. Instead of taking away land and subjugating the defeated state, Sparta left the Tegeans their land and their freedom. In exchange, they required the Tegeans to follow the Spartan lead in foreign affairs and to supply a fixed number of soldiers to Sparta on demand. This became the model for Spartan relations with the other states in the Peloponnesus. Soon Sparta was the leader of an alliance that included every Peloponnesian state but Argos; modern scholars have named this alliance the Peloponnesian League. It provided Sparta with security and made it the most powerful *polis* in Hellenic history.

Athens

Attica Region (about 1,000 square miles) that Athens dominated.

Athens—located in **Attica**—was slow to come into prominence and to join in the new activities that were changing the more advanced states. The reasons were several: Athens was not situated on the most favored trade routes of the eighth and seventh centuries B.C.E.; its large area (about 1,000 square miles) allowed population growth without great pressure; and the many villages and districts within this territory were not fully united into a single *polis* until the seventh century B.C.E.

Aristocratic Rule In the seventh century B.C.E., Athens was a typical aristocratic *polis*. Its people were divided into four tribes and into several clans and brotherhoods (*phratries*). The aristocrats held the most land and the best land, and dominated religious and political life. The **Areopagus**, a council of nobles deriving its name from the hill where it held its sessions, governed the state. Annually the council elected nine magistrates, called *archons*, who joined the Areopagus after their year in office. Because the *archons* served for only a year, were checked by their colleagues, and looked forward to a lifetime as members of the Areopagus, the aristocratic Areopagus, not the *archons*, was the true master of the state.

Areopagus Council heading Athens's government comprised of a group of nobles that annually chose the city's nine *archons*, the magistrates who administered the *polis*.

Pressure for Change In the seventh century B.C.E., the peaceful life of Athens was disturbed, in part by quarrels within the nobility and in part by the beginnings of an agrarian crisis. In 621 B.C.E., a man named Draco was given special authority to codify and publish laws for the first time. Draco's work was probably limited to laws concerning homicide and was aimed at ending blood feuds between clans, but it set an important precedent: The publication of laws strengthened the hand of the state against the local power of the nobles.

The root of Athens's troubles was agricultural. Many Athenians worked family farms, from which they obtained most of their living. It appears that they planted wheat, the staple crop, year after year without rotating fields or using enough fertilizer. Shifting to more intensive agricultural techniques and to the planting of fruit and olive trees and grapevines required capital, leading the less successful farmers to acquire excessive debt. Inevitably, many Athenians defaulted and were enslaved. Revolutionary pressures grew among the poor, who began to demand the abolition of debt and a redistribution of the land.

Bust of Solon.

Bust of Solon. Rudolf Lesch Fine Arts Inc., New York, New York.

Reforms of Solon In the year 594 B.C.E., as tradition has it, the Athenians elected Solon as the only *archon*, with extraordinary powers to legislate and revise the constitution. Immediately, he attacked the agrarian problem by canceling current debts and forbidding future loans secured by the person of the borrower. He helped bring back many Athenians enslaved abroad and freed those in Athens enslaved for debt.

In the short run, therefore, Solon did resolve the economic crisis, but his other economic actions had profound success in the long run. He forbade the export of wheat and encouraged that of olive oil. This policy had the initial effect of making wheat more available in Attica and encouraging the cultivation of olive oil and wine as cash crops. By the fifth century B.C.E., the cultivation of cash crops had become so profitable that much Athenian land was diverted from grain production, and Athens became dependent on imported wheat. Solon also changed the Athenian standards of weights and measures to conform with those of Corinth and Euboea and the cities of the east. This change also encouraged commerce and turned Athens in the direction that would lead it to great prosperity in the fifth century B.C.E. Solon also encouraged industry by offering citizenship to foreign artisans.

Solon also changed the constitution. Citizenship had previously been the privilege of all male adults whose fathers were citizens; to their number he added those immigrants who were tradesmen and merchants. All these Athenian citizens were divided into four classes on the basis of wealth, measured by annual agricultural production. The two highest classes alone could hold the *archonship*, the chief magistracy in Athens, and sit on the Areopagus.

Men of the third class were allowed to serve as *hoplites*. They could be elected to a council of 400 chosen by all the citizens, 100 from each tribe. The *thetes* made up the last class. They voted in the assembly for the *archons* and the council members and on any other business brought before them by the *archons* and the council. They also sat on a new popular court established by Solon. This new court was recognized as a court of appeal, and by the fifth century B.C.E., almost all cases came before it. In Solon's Athens, as everywhere in the world before the twentieth century, women took no part in the political or judicial process.

Pisistratus the Tyrant Solon's efforts to avoid factional strife failed. Within a few years contention reached such a degree that no *archons* could be chosen. Out of this turmoil emerged the first Athenian tyranny. Pisistratus, a nobleman, leader of a faction, and military hero, briefly seized power in 560 B.C.E. and again in 556 B.C.E., but each time his support was inadequate, and he was driven out. At last, in 546 B.C.E., he came back at the head of a mercenary army from abroad and established a successful tyranny.

Pisistratus sought to increase the power of the central government at the expense of the nobles, but he made no formal change in the Solonian constitution. The assembly, councils, and courts met; the magistrates and councils were elected. Pisistratus merely saw to it that his supporters dominated these bodies. The intended effect was to blunt the sharp edge of tyranny with the appearance of a constitutional government. The unintended effect was to give the Athenians more experience in the procedures of self-government and a growing taste for it.

Spartan Intervention Pisistratus was succeeded by his oldest son, Hippias, who followed his father's ways at first. In 514 B.C.E., however, his brother Hipparchus was murdered as a result of a private quarrel. Hippias became nervous, suspicious, and harsh. Led by their ambitious king, Cleomenes I, the Spartans marched into Athenian territory in 510 B.C.E. and deposed Hippias, who went into exile to the Persian court. The tyranny was over.

The Spartans must have hoped to leave Athens in friendly hands, and indeed Cleomenes' friend Isagoras held the leading position in Athens after the withdrawal of the Spartan army. Isagoras, however, faced competitors, chief among them Clisthenes. Clisthenes lost out in the initial political struggle among the noble factions. Clisthenes then took an unprecedented action—he turned to the people for political support and won it with a program of great popular appeal. In response, Isagoras called in the Spartans again who drove Clisthenes out. But the people refused to tolerate an aristocratic restoration and drove out the Spartans and Isagoras with them. Clisthenes and his allies returned, ready to put their program into effect.

Clisthenes, the Founder of Democracy A central aim of Clisthenes' reforms was to diminish the influence of traditional localities and regions in Athenian life, for these were an important source of power for the nobility and of factions in the state. In 508 B.C.E., he made the *deme*, the equivalent of a small town in the country or a ward in the city, the basic unit of civic life. The *deme* was a purely political unit that elected its own officers. The distribution of *demes* in each tribe guaranteed that no region would dominate any of them.

A new council of 500 replaced the Solonian council of 400. The council's main responsibility was to prepare legislation for the assembly to discuss, but it also had important financial duties and received foreign emissaries. Final authority in all things rested with the assembly of all adult male Athenian citizens. Debate in the assembly was free and open; any Athenian could submit legislation, offer amendments, or argue the merits of any question.

As a result of the work of Solon, Pisistratus, and Clisthenes, Athens entered the fifth century B.C.E. well on the way to prosperity and democracy. It was much more centralized and united than it had been, and it was ready to take its place among the major states that would lead the defense of Greece against the dangers that lay ahead.

QUICK REVIEW

Clisthenes' Democracy

- Clisthenes sought to weaken his opponents by dividing Attica into *demes*
- Increased Solon's council from four to five hundred
- All adult male Athenians were members of the popular assembly

LIFE IN ARCHAIC GREECE

WHAT ROLE did religion play in the lives of ordinary Greeks?

SOCIETY

As the "Dark Ages" ended, the features that would distinguish Greek society thereafter took shape. The artisan and the merchant grew more important as contact with the non-Hellenic world became easier. Most people, however, continued to make their living from the land.

Farmers Ordinary country people rarely leave a written record of their thoughts or activities, and we have no such record from ancient Greece. The poet Hesiod (ca. 700 B.C.E.), however, was certainly no aristocrat. He presented himself as a small farmer, and his *Works and Days* gives some idea of the life of such a farmer. The crops included grain—chiefly barley, but also wheat; grapes for making wine; olives for food and oil; green vegetables, especially the bean; and some fruit. Sheep and goats provided milk and cheese. He and small farmers like him tasted meat chiefly from sacrificial animals at festivals.

These farmers worked hard to make a living. The hardest work came in October, at the start of the rainy season, the time for the first plowing. Autumn and winter were the time for cutting wood, building wagons, and making tools. Late winter was the time to tend to the vines, May was the time to harvest the grain, July to winnow and store it. Only at the height of summer's heat did Hesiod allow for rest, but when September came, it was time to harvest the grapes. As soon as that task was done the cycle started again.

An amphora decorated with a symposium scene.

Ashmolean Museum, University of Oxford, UK/The Bridgeman Art Library

Aristocrats Most aristocrats were rich enough to employ many hired laborers, sometimes sharecroppers, and sometimes even slaves, to work their extensive lands. They could therefore enjoy leisure for other activities. The center of aristocratic social life was the drinking party, or ***symposium***. The sessions began with prayers and libations to the gods. Usually there were games, such as dice or *kottabos*, in which wine was flicked from the cups at different targets. Sometimes dancing girls or flute girls offered entertainment. Frequently the aristocratic participants provided their own amusements with songs, poetry, or even philosophical disputes. Characteristically, these took the form of contests, with some kind of prize for the winner, for aristocratic values continued to emphasize competition and the need to excel, whatever the arena.

symposium A men's drinking party at the center of aristocratic social life in archaic Greece.

This aspect of aristocratic life appears in the athletic contests that became widespread early in the sixth century. The games included running events; the long jump; the discus and javelin throws; the pentathlon, which included all of these; boxing; wrestling; and the chariot race. Only the rich could afford to raise, train, and race horses, so the chariot race was a special preserve of aristocracy. The nobility also especially favored wrestling, and the *palaestra*, or fields, where they practiced became an important social center for the aristocracy. The contrast between the hard, drab life of the farmers and the leisured and lively one of the aristocrats could hardly have been greater. (See "Encountering the Past: Greek Athletics," page 48.)

Religion

Like most ancient peoples, the Greeks were **polytheists**, and religion played an important part in their lives. Much of Greek art and literature was closely connected with religion, as was the life of the *polis* in general.

polytheists Worshippers of many gods

Olympian Gods The Greek pantheon consisted of the twelve gods who lived on Mount Olympus, led by Zeus, the father of the Gods. These gods were seen as behaving much like mortals, with all the foibles of humans, except they were superhuman in these as well as in their strength and immortality. In contrast, Zeus, at least, was seen as a source of human justice, and even the Olympians were understood to be subordinate to the Fates. Each *polis* had one of the Olympians as its guardian deity and worshipped that god in its own special way, but all the gods were Panhellenic.

Immortality and Morality Besides the Olympians, the Greeks also worshipped countless lesser deities connected with local shrines. They even worshipped human heroes, real or legendary, who had accomplished great deeds and had earned immortality and divine status. The worship of these deities was not a very emotional experience. It was a matter of offering prayer, libations, and gifts in return for protection and favors from the god during the lifetime of the worshipper. The average human had no hope of immortality, and these devotions involved little moral teaching.

ENCOUNTERING THE PAST

Greek Athletics

Athletic contests were an integral part of Greek civilization throughout its entire history. They were much more than entertainments. They were religious festivals in which the Greeks celebrated the virtues and attitudes that they considered central to their way of life. International or Panhellenic ("all-Greek") contests were scheduled in alternating annual cycles. The most prestigious of these were the games that began to be celebrated in honor of Zeus at the southern mainland city of Olympia in 776 B.C.E.

The Greeks' primary interest was not team sports, but contests in which individuals could prove their superiority. Races of various lengths were the heart of Olympic competition, but there were also field events such as discus and javelin throws and combat sports such as wrestling and boxing. Only male athletes were admitted to the games, and by the fifth century B.C.E., all contestants (except those in a race in full armor) competed nude. The official prizes were simple wreaths, but *poleis* lavishly rewarded the native sons who brought home these tokens of victory.

WHY DID the Greeks prefer individual contests to team sports? What motivated them to train and compete?

A foot race, probably a sprint, at the Panathenaic Games in Athens, ca. 530 B.C.E.

National Archives and Records Administration

Why was public athletic competition so important to Ancient Greek men? What values were highlighted by such competitions?

Most Greeks seem to have held to the commonsense notion that justice lay in paying one's debts. They thought that civic virtue consisted of worshipping the state deities in the traditional way, performing required public services, and fighting in defense of the state. To them, private morality meant to do good to one's friends and harm to one's enemies.

The Cult of Delphian Apollo In the sixth century B.C.E., the influence of the cult of Apollo at Delphi and of his oracle there became great. The oracle was the most important of several that helped satisfy the human craving for a clue to the future. The priests of Apollo preached moderation; the two famous sayings identified with Apollo—"Know thyself" and "Nothing in excess"—exemplified their advice. Humans needed self-control (*sophrosynē*). Its opposite was arrogance (***hubris***), brought on by excessive wealth or good fortune. *Hubris* led to moral blindness and, finally, to divine vengeance. This theme of moderation and the dire consequences of its absence was central to Greek popular morality and appears frequently in Greek literature.

hubris Arrogance produced by excessive wealth or good fortune.

The Cult of Dionysus and the Orphic Cult The somewhat cold religion of the Olympian gods and of the cult of Apollo did little to assuage human fears or satisfy human hopes and passions. For these needs, the Greeks turned to other deities and rites. Of these deities, the most popular was Dionysus, a god of nature and fertility, of the grapevine, drunkenness, and sexual abandon. The Orphic cult, named after its supposed founder, the mythical poet Orpheus, provided its followers with more hope than did the worship of the twelve Olympians. Cult followers are thought to have refused to kill animals or eat their flesh and to have believed in the transmigration of souls, which offered the prospect of some form of life after death.

Poetry

The poetry of the sixth century B.C.E. also reflected the great changes sweeping through the Greek world. The lyric style—poetry meant to be sung, either by a chorus or by one person—predominated. Sappho of Lesbos, Anacreon of Teos, and Simonides of Cos composed personal poetry, often relating the pleasure and agony of love. Alcaeus of Mytilene, an aristocrat driven from his city by a tyrant, wrote bitter invective.

This Attic cup from the fifth century B.C.E. shows the two great poets from the island of Lesbos, Sappho (center) and Alcaeus (far left).

Hirmer Fotoarchiv

What role did poetry play in Ancient Greek culture?

Perhaps the most interesting poet of the century from a political point of view was Theognis of Megara. Theognis was the spokesperson for the old, defeated aristocracy of birth. He divided everyone into two classes, the noble and the base; the former were the good, the latter, bad. Those nobly born must associate only with others like themselves if they were to preserve their virtue; if they mingled with the base, they became base. Those born base, however, could never become noble. Only nobles could aspire to virtue and possessed the critical moral and intellectual qualities—respect or honor and judgment. These qualities could not be taught; they were innate. Even so, they had to be carefully guarded against corruption by wealth or by mingling with the base.

Intermarriage between the noble and the base was especially condemned. Such ideas remained alive in aristocratic hearts throughout the next century and greatly influenced later thinkers, Plato among them.

THE PERSIAN WARS

WHAT WAS the significance of the wars between the Greeks and the Persians?

The Greeks' period of fortunate isolation and freedom ended in the sixth century B.C.E. They had established colonies along most of the coast of Asia Minor from as early as the eleventh century B.C.E. The colonies maintained friendly relations with the mainland but developed a flourishing economic and cultural life independent of their mother cities and of their eastern neighbors. In the middle of the sixth century B.C.E., however, these Greek cities of Asia Minor came under the control of Lydia and its king, Croesus (ca. 560–546 B.C.E.).

THE IONIAN REBELLION

The Ionian Greeks (those living on the central part of the west coast of Asia Minor and nearby islands) had been moving toward democracy and were not pleased to find themselves under the monarchical rule of Persia. That rule, however, was not overly burdensome at first. The Persians ruled the Greek cities through local individuals, who governed their cities as "tyrants." Most of the tyrants, however, were not harsh, the Persian tribute was not excessive, and the Greeks enjoyed general prosperity. Neither the death of the Persian king Cyrus the Great fighting on a distant frontier in 530 B.C.E., nor the suicide of his successor Cambyses, nor the civil war that followed it in 522–521 B.C.E. produced any disturbance in the Greek cities. When Darius emerged as Great King in 521 B.C.E., he found **Ionia** perfectly obedient.

Ionia Western coast of Asia Minor.

The private troubles of the ambitious tyrant of Miletus, Aristagoras, ended this calm. He had urged a Persian expedition against the island of Naxos; when it failed, he feared the consequences and organized the Ionian rebellion of 499 B.C.E. To gain support, he overthrew the tyrannies and proclaimed democratic constitutions. Then he turned to the mainland states for help, petitioning first Sparta, the most powerful Greek state. The Spartans, however, would have none of Aristagoras's promises of easy victory and great wealth.

Aristagoras next sought help from the Athenians, who were related to the Ionians and had close ties of religion and tradition with them. Besides, Hippias, the deposed tyrant of Athens, was an honored guest at the court of Darius, who had already made it plain that he favored the tyrant's restoration. The Persians, moreover, controlled both sides of the Hellespont, the route to the grain fields beyond the Black Sea that were increasingly vital to Athens. Perhaps some Athenians already feared that a Persian attempt to conquer the Greek mainland was only a matter of time. The Athenian assembly agreed to send a fleet of twenty ships to help the rebels. The Athenian expedition was strengthened by five ships from Eretria in Euboea, which participated out of gratitude for past favors.

In 498 B.C.E., the Athenians and their allies made a surprise attack on Sardis, the old capital of Lydia and now the seat of the *satrap*, and burned it. This action caused the revolt to spread throughout the Greek cities of Asia Minor outside Ionia, but the Ionians could not follow it up. The Athenians withdrew and took no further part. Gradually the Persians reimposed their will. In 495 B.C.E., they defeated the Ionian fleet at Lade, and in the next year they wiped out Miletus. The Ionian rebellion was over.

MAP 2–3 The Persian Invasion of Greece This map traces the route taken by the Persian king Xerxes in his invasion of Greece in 480 B.C.E. The gray arrows show movements of Xerxes' army, the purple arrows show movements of his navy, and the green arrows show movements of the Greek army and navy.

Although Xerxes' army had superior numbers, how did Greece's geography favor the Greek cities over the Persians?

Overview The Greek Wars Against Persia

560–546 B.C.E.	Greek cities of Asia Minor conquered by Croesus of Lydia
546 B.C.E.	Cyrus of Persia conquers Lydia and gains control of Greek cities
499–494 B.C.E.	Greek cities rebel (Ionian rebellion)
490 B.C.E.	Battle of Marathon
480–479 B.C.E.	Xerxes' invasion of Greece
480 B.C.E.	Battles of Thermopylae, Artemisium, and Salamis
479 B.C.E.	Battles of Plataea and Mycale

THE WAR IN GREECE

In 490 B.C.E., the Persians launched an expedition directly across the Aegean to punish Eretria and Athens, to restore Hippias, and to gain control of the Aegean Sea. (See Map 2–3 on page 51.) They landed their infantry and cavalry forces first at Naxos, destroying it for its successful resistance in 499 B.C.E. Then they destroyed Eretria and deported its people deep into the interior of Persia.

Marathon Rather than submit and accept the restoration of the hated tyranny of Hippias, the Athenians chose to resist the Persian forces bearing down on them and risk the same fate that had just befallen Eretria. Miltiades, an Athenian who had fled from Persian service, led the city's army to confront the Persians at Marathon.

A Persian victory at Marathon would have destroyed Athenian freedom and led to the conquest of all the mainland Greeks. The greatest achievements of Greek culture, most of which lay in the future, would never have occurred. But the Athenians won a decisive victory, instilling them with a sense of confidence and pride in their *polis*, their unique form of government, and themselves.

The Great Invasion Internal troubles prevented the Persians from taking swift revenge for their loss at Marathon. Almost ten years elapsed before Darius's successor, Xerxes, in 481 B.C.E., gathered an army of at least 150,000 men and a navy of more than 600 ships to conquer Greece. In Athens, Themistocles, who favored making Athens into a naval power, had become the leading politician. During his *archonship* in 493 B.C.E., Athens had already built a fortified port at Piraeus. A decade later the Athenians came upon a rich vein of silver in the state mines, and Themistocles persuaded them to use the profits to increase their fleet. By 480 B.C.E., Athens had over 200 ships, the backbone of a navy that was to defeat the Persians.

Of the hundreds of Greek states, only thirty-one—led by Sparta, Athens, Corinth, and Aegina—were willing to fight as the Persian army gathered south of the Hellespont. In the spring of 480 B.C.E., Xerxes launched his invasion. The Persian strategy was to march into Greece, destroy Athens, defeat the Greek army, and add the Greeks to the number of Persian subjects. The huge Persian army needed to keep in touch with the fleet for supplies. If the Greeks could defeat the Persian navy, the army could not remain in Greece long. Themistocles knew that the Aegean was subject to sudden devastating storms. His strategy was to delay the Persian army and then to bring on the kind of naval battle he might hope to win. (See "Compare & Connect: Greek Strategy in the Persian War," on pages 54–55.)

The Greek League, founded specifically to resist this Persian invasion, met at Corinth as the Persians were ready to cross the Hellespont. They chose Sparta as leader and first confronted the Persians at Thermopylae, the "hot gates," on land and off Artemisium at sea. The opening between the mountains and the sea at Thermopylae was so narrow that a small army could hold it against a much larger one. The Spartans sent their king, Leonidas, with 300 of their own citizens and enough allies to make a total of about 9,000.

Severe storms wrecked many Persian ships while the Greek fleet waited safely in a protected harbor. Then Xerxes attacked Thermopylae, and for two days the Greeks butchered his best troops without serious loss to themselves. On the third day, however, a traitor showed the Persians a mountain trail that permitted them to come on the Greeks from behind. Many allies escaped, but Leonidas and his 300 Spartans all died fighting. At about the same time, the Greek and Persian fleets fought an indecisive battle at Artemisium. The fall of Thermopylae, however, forced the Greek navy to withdraw. The Persian army moved into Attica and burned Athens.

Defeating the Persians A sea battle in the narrow waters to the east of the island of Salamis, to which the Greek fleet withdrew after the battle at Artemisium, decided the fate of Greece. Because the Greek ships were fewer, slower, and less maneuverable than those of the Persians, the Greeks put soldiers on their ships and relied chiefly on hand-to-hand combat. In the ensuing battle the Persians lost more than half their ships and retreated to Asia with a good part of their army, but the danger was not over yet.

The Persian general Mardonius spent the winter in central Greece, and in the spring he unsuccessfully tried to win the Athenians away from the Greek League. The Spartan regent, Pausanias, then led the largest Greek army up to that time to confront Mardonius in Boeotia. At Plataea, in the summer of 479 B.C.E., the Persians suffered a decisive defeat.

Meanwhile the Ionian Greeks urged King Leotychidas, the Spartan commander of the fleet, to fight the Persian fleet. At Mycale, on the coast of Samos, Leotychidas destroyed the Persian camp and its fleet. The Persians fled the Aegean and Ionia. For the moment, at least, the Persian threat was gone.

COMPARE & CONNECT

GREEK STRATEGY IN THE PERSIAN WAR

In the summer of 480 B.C.E., Xerxes, Great King of Persia, took an enormous invading army into Greece. During the previous year those Greeks who meant to resist met to plan a defense. After abandoning an attempt to make a stand at Tempe in Thessaly, they fell back to central Greece, at Thermopylae on land and Artemisium at sea. Herodotus is our main source and his account of the Greek strategy is not clear. How did the Greeks hope to check the Persians? Did they hope to stop them for good at Thermopylae, or was the idea to force a sea battle at Artemisium? Were both the army and the fleet intended only to fight holding actions until the Athenians fled to Salamis and the Peloponnesus? Scholars have long argued these questions, which have been sharpened by the discovery of the "Themistocles Decree," an inscription from the third century B.C.E. which purports to be an Athenian decree passed in 480 before the Battle of Artemisium. The authenticity of the decree is still in question, but if it reflects a reliable tradition it must influence our view in important ways.

QUESTIONS

1. In Herodotus's account what is the state of the Athenian preparation?
2. What light does it reflect on the original Greek strategy for the war?
3. Was the Themistocles Decree passed before or after the battle at Thermopylae? What light does this decree shed on Greek strategy?
4. How do the two documents compare?
5. Are they incompatible?

I. THE ACCOUNT OF HERODOTUS

In this passage Herodotus describes Athens after the Greek defeat at Thermopylae.

Meanwhile, the Grecian fleet, which had left Artemisium, proceeded to Salamis, at the request of the Athenians, and there cast anchor. The Athenians had begged them to take up this position, in order that they might convey their women and children out of Attica, and further might deliberate upon the course which it now behooved them to follow. Disappointed in the hopes which they had previously entertained, they were about to hold a council concerning the present posture of their affairs. For they had looked to see the Peloponnesians drawn up in full force to resist the enemy in Boeotia, but found nothing of what they had expected; nay, they learnt that the Greeks of those parts, only concerning themselves about their own safety, were building a wall across the Isthmus, and intended to guard the Peloponnese, and let the rest of Greece take its chance. These tidings caused them to make the request whereof I spoke, that the combined fleet should anchor at Salamis.

So while the rest of the fleet lay to off this island, the Athenians cast anchor along their own coast. Immediately upon their arrival, proclamation was made, that every Athenian should save his children and household as he best could; whereupon some sent their families to Aegina, some to Salamis, but the greater number to Troezen. This removal was made with all possible haste, partly from a desire to obey the advice of the oracle, but still more for another reason. The Athenians say they have in their acropolis a huge serpent which lives in the temple, and is the guardian of the whole place. Nor do they only say this, but, as if the serpent really dwelt there, every month they lay out its food, which consists of a honey-cake. Up to this time the honey-cake had always been consumed; but now it lay untouched. So the priestess told the people what had happened; whereupon they left Athens the more readily, since they believed that the goddess had abandoned the citadel.

Source: Herodotus, *Histories*, trans. by George Rawlinson, 8.40.41.

A Greek *hoplite* attacking a Persian soldier. The contrast between the Greek's metal body armor, large shield, and long spear and the Persian's cloth and leather garments indicates one reason the Greeks won. This Attic vase was found on Rhodes and dates from ca. 475 B.C.E.

Greek. Vase, Red-figured. Attic. ca. 480–470 B.C. Neck amphora, Nolan type. Side 1: "Greek warrior attacking a Persian." Said to be from Rhodes. Terracotta. H. 13-11/16 in. The Metropolitan Museum of Art, Rogers Fund, 1906. (06.1021.117) Photograph © 1986 The Metropolitan Museum of Art

How did conflict with Persia shape the image Greeks had of themselves and their society?

II. THE THEMISTOCLES DECREE

The Gods

Resolved by the Council and the People
Themistocles, son of Neokles, of Phrearroi, made the motion:

To entrust the city to Athena the Mistress of Athens and to all the other Gods to guard and defend from the Barbarian for the sake of the land. The Athenians themselves and the foreigners who live in Athens are to send their children and women to safety in Troizen, their protector being Pittheus, the founding hero of the land. They are to send the old men and their movable possessions to safety on Salamis. The treasurers and priestesses are to remain on the acropolis guarding the property of the gods.

All the other Athenians and foreigners of military age are to embark on the 200 ships that are ready and defend against the Barbarian for the sake of their own freedom and that of the rest of the Greeks along with the Lakedaimonians, the Korinthians. the Aiginetans, and all others who wish to share the danger.

The generals are to appoint, starting tomorrow, 200 trierarchs [captains], one to a ship, from among those who have land and house in Athens and legitimate children and who are not older than fifty; to these men the ships are to be assigned by lot. They are to enlist marines, 10 to each ship, from men between the ages of twenty and thirty, and four archers. They are to distribute the servicemen [the marines and archers] by lot at the same time as they assign the trierarchs to the ships by lot. The generals are to write up the rest ship by ship on white boards, (taking) the Athenians from the lexiarchic registers, the foreigners from those registered with the polemarch. They are to write them up assigning them by divisions, 200 of about one hundred (men) each, and to write above each division the name of the trireme and of the trierarch and the servicemen, so that they may know on which trireme each division is to embark. When all the divisions have been composed and allotted to the triremes, the Council and the generals are to man all the 200 ships, after sacrificing a placatory offering to Zeus the Almighty and Athena and Nike and Poseidon the Securer.

When the ships have been manned, with 100 of them they are to meet the enemy at Artemision in Euboia, and with the other 100 they are to lie off Salamis and the coast of Attica and keep guard over the land. In order that all Athenians may be united in their defense against the Barbarian those who have been sent into exile for ten years are to go to Salamis and to stay there until the People come to some decision about them, while those who have been deprived of citizen rights are to have their rights restored . . .

Source: "Waiting for the Barbarian, Greece and Rome," second series, 8 trans. by Michael H. Jameson (Oxford, 1961), pp. 5–18. By permission of the Oxford University Press.

SUMMARY

IN WHAT ways were the Minoan and Mycenaean civilizations different?

The Bronze Age on Crete and on the Mainland to about 1150 B.C.E. During the Bronze Age, the Minoan and Mycenaean civilizations ruled over the Greek mainland and Aegean islands. The Minoan civilization on Crete is renowned for its beautiful palaces. They were the organizational center of Minoan society, and Minoan kings employed a large bureaucracy. The lack of defensive walls is a notable feature of Minoan settlements. On the Greek mainland, starting around 1600 B.C.E., the Mycenaean culture was warlike and ruled by strong kings. Mycenaeans traded widely. Historians and archaeologists have suggested various explanations for the fact that, by 1100 B.C.E., the Mycenaean culture had disappeared. *page 34*

WHAT WERE the Greek Dark Ages?

The Greek "Middle Ages" to about 750 B.C.E. The Dorian invasion destroyed the Mycenaean palace culture. The Greek peoples spread around the Aegean. Trade diminished; writing and other arts disappeared. Oral poetry flourished, and Homer's *Iliad* and *Odyssey* provide both great stories and insights into life in the Greek "Dark Ages." The aristocratic values of the tenth and ninth centuries B.C.E. idealized the individual hero. *page 37*

DESCRIBE THE *polis* and how it affected society and government.

The *Polis* Greek social and political values are exemplified in the Greeks' characteristic form of community, the *polis*. Early *poleis* developed around 800 B.C.E. in locations that featured fertile farmland and, nearby, natural defensive positions. Later *poleis* always included an *agora*, a marketplace and civic center. *Polis* society was made possible by a new military technology, the *hoplite* phalanx. The power of the kings and, later, the aristocrats was undermined by the emergence of the farmer-soldier-citizen in the *polis*. *page 39*

HOW AND why did the Greeks colonize large parts of the Mediterranean?

Expansion of the Greek World For about two centuries starting around 750 B.C.E., the Greeks colonized widely throughout the Mediterranean world. Trade became an increasingly important part of the Greek economy. Exposure to other peoples and cultures fostered consciousness of Greek cultural identity and led to Panhellenic feelings. In some *poleis*, new social and economic conditions led to rule by tyrants. But by late in the sixth century B.C.E., tyrants had lost favor with the populace, and by the end of the century, they were gone. *page 40*

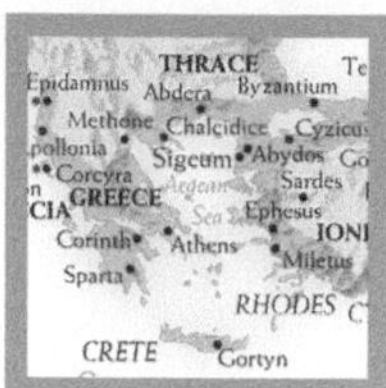

HOW WERE the government and politics of Athens different from those of Sparta?

The Major States The two most powerful Greek *poleis*, Sparta and Athens, developed differently. Starting around 725 B.C.E., Sparta gained land and power over the Messenians through warfare. Late in the sixth century B.C.E., Spartan society was reorganized along military lines to ensure that Sparta could continue its hold over Messenia. By 500 B.C.E., Sparta headed a Peloponnesian League, a mighty military alliance. In Athens, meanwhile, political and economic innovations included the publication of laws; by the fifth century B.C.E., prosperity and democracy had taken root in Athens. *page 43*

WHAT ROLE did religion play in the lives of ordinary Greeks?

Life in Archaic Greece Social class shaped everyday life for the ancient Greeks. Greeks were polytheistic, worshipping the Olympian gods and other deities through sacrifices and athletic contests. Lyric poetry treated topics ranging from love to politics. *page 46*

WHAT WAS the significance of the wars between the Greeks and the Persians?

The Persian Wars Cyrus the Great came to power in Persia in 559 B.C.E. and set about unifying and expanding his territory. For almost a century, starting around 550 B.C.E. and continuing into the mid–fifth century B.C.E., Greece faced intermittent military challenges from the Persian Empire. After Lydia came under Persian rule in 546 B.C.E., the Ionian Greeks sought military assistance from first the Spartans (who refused to get involved) and then the Athenians, who in 498 B.C.E. helped them in a short-lived revolt. Eventually the Persians withdrew from the Aegean Sea and Ionia. *page 50*

Review Questions

1. How were the Minoan and the Mycenaean civilizations similar? How were they different?

2. What was a *polis?* What role did geography play in its development? What contribution did it make to the development of Hellenic civilization?

3. How did the political, social, and economic institutions of Athens and Sparta compare around 500 B.C.E.? What explains Sparta's uniqueness? How did Athens make the transition from aristocracy to democracy?

4. Why did the Greeks and Persians go to war in 490 and 480 B.C.E.? Why were the Greeks victorious over the Persians?

KEY TERMS

Acropolis (p. 39)
agora (p. 39)
Areopagus (p. 44)
arete (p. 38)
Attica (p. 44)
Helots (p. 43)
hoplite (p. 40)
hubris (p. 48)
Iliad (p. 38)
Ionia (p. 49)
Minoan (p. 34)
Mycenaean (p. 34)
Odyssey (p. 38)
Panhellenic ("all Greek") (p. 41)
Peloponnesus (p. 43)
phalanx (p. 40)
polytheists (p. 47)
symposium (p. 47)

For additional learning resources related to this chapter, please go to **www.myhistorylab.com**

myhistorylab

3

Classical and Hellenistic Greece

The Winged Victory of Samothrace. This is one of the great masterpieces of Hellenistic sculpture. It appears to be the work of the Rhodian sculptor Pythokritos, about 200 B.C.E. The statue stood in the Sanctuary of the Great Gods on the Aegean island of Samothrace on a base made in the shape of a ship's prow. The goddess is seen as landing on the ship to crown its victorious commander and crew.

The Nike of Samothrace, goddess of victory. Marble figure (190 B.C.E.) from Rhodos, Greece. Height 328 cm, MA 2369, Louvre, Dpt. des Antiquités Grecques/Romaines, Paris, France. Photograph © Erich Lessing/Art Resource, NY

How were Greek cultural values reflected in *The Winged Victory of Samothrace?*

The Greeks' remarkable victory over the Persians (480–479 B.C.E.) marked the start of an era of great achievement. Fear of another Persian incursion into the Aegean led the Greeks to contemplate some kind of arrangement for their joint defense. The Spartans refused to make commitments that would take them away from their homeland, but the Athenians were eager for leadership opportunities. They negotiated a military alliance called the Delian League. It laid the foundation for an Athenian Empire, and fear of Athenian expansion led other states to ally with Sparta. The Greek world was polarized and finally erupted in a self-destructive civil war. In 338 B.C.E., Philip of Macedon intervened, took control, and ended the era of the independent polis.

AFTERMATH OF VICTORY

WHAT LED to the foundation of the Delian League?

The unity of the Greeks had shown strain even in the life-and-death struggle against the Persians. Within two years of the Persian retreat, it gave way almost completely and yielded to a division of the Greek world into two spheres of influence dominated by Sparta and Athens. The need of the Ionian Greeks to obtain and defend their freedom from Persia and the desire of many Greeks to gain revenge and financial reparation for the Persian attack brought on the split. (See Map 3–1.)

MAP 3–1 Classical Greece Greece in the Classical period (ca. 480–338 B.C.E.) centered on the Aegean Sea. Although there were important Greek settlements in Italy, Sicily, and all around the Black Sea, the area shown in this general reference map embraced the vast majority of Greek states.

Why was Athens not able to control its vast empire? What are some of the factors that led to its decline?

THE DELIAN LEAGUE AND THE RISE OF CIMON

Sparta had led the Greeks to victory, and it was natural to look to the Spartans to continue the campaign against Persia. But Sparta was ill-suited to the task, which required both a long-term commitment far from the Peloponnesus and continuous naval action.

Athens had become the leading naval power in Greece, and the same motives that had led the Athenians to support the Ionian revolt prompted them to try to drive the Persians from the Aegean and the Hellespont. The Ionians were at least as eager for the Athenians to take the helm as the Athenians were to accept the responsibility and opportunity.

In the winter of 478–477 B.C.E., the islanders and the Greeks from the coast of Asia Minor and other Greek cities on the Aegean met with the Athenians on the sacred island of Delos and swore oaths of alliance. The aims of this new **Delian League** were to free those Greeks who were under Persian rule, to protect all against a Persian return, and to obtain compensation from the Persians by attacking their lands and taking booty. An assembly in which each state, including Athens, had one vote was supposed to determine league policy. Athens, however, was clearly designated the leader.

Delian League Pact joined in 478 B.C.E. by Athenians and other Greeks to continue the war with Persia.

From the first, the league was remarkably successful. The Persians were driven from Europe and the Hellespont, and the Aegean was cleared of pirates. In 467 B.C.E., a great victory at the Eurymedon River in Asia Minor routed the Persians and added several cities to the league.

Cimon, son of Miltiades, the hero of Marathon, became the leading Athenian soldier and statesman soon after the war with Persia. Cimon, who was to dominate Athenian politics for almost two decades, pursued a policy of aggressive attacks on Persia and friendly relations with Sparta. Cimon led the Athenians and the Delian League to victory after victory, and his own popularity grew with his successes.

THE FIRST PELOPONNESIAN WAR: ATHENS AGAINST SPARTA

WHAT WAS the cause of the Peloponnesian War, and what was the end result?

In 465 B.C.E., the island of Thasos rebelled from the Delian League, and Cimon put the rebellion down after a siege of more than two years. When Cimon returned to Athens from Thasos, he was charged with taking bribes for having refrained from conquering Macedonia, although conquering Macedonia had not been part of his assignment. He was acquitted; the trial was only a device by which his political opponents tried to reduce his influence. Their program at home was to undo the gains made by the Areopagus and bring about further democratic changes. In foreign policy, Cimon's enemies wanted to break with Sparta and contest its claim to leadership over the Greeks. The head of this faction was Ephialtes.

THE BREACH WITH SPARTA

When the Thasians began their rebellion, they asked Sparta to invade Athens the next spring, and the *ephors*, the annual magistrates responsible for Sparta's foreign policy, agreed. An earthquake, however, accompanied by a rebellion of the Helots that threatened the survival of Sparta, prevented the invasion. The Spartans asked their allies, the Athenians among them, for help, and Cimon persuaded the Athenians to send it. While Cimon was in the Peloponnesus helping the Spartans, Ephialtes stripped the Areopagus of almost all its power. In 462 B.C.E., Ephialtes was assassinated, and Pericles replaced him as leader of the democratic faction. In the spring of 461 B.C.E., Cimon was ostracized, and Athens made an alliance with Argos, Sparta's traditional enemy. Almost overnight, Cimon's domestic and foreign policies had been overturned.

THE DIVISION OF GREECE

The new regime at Athens, led by Pericles and the democratic faction, was confident and ambitious. When Megara, getting the worst of a border dispute with Corinth, withdrew from the Peloponnesian League, the Athenians accepted the Megarians as

Peloponnesian Wars Series of wars between Athens and Sparta beginning in 460 B.C.E.

allies. Sparta, however, resented the defection of Megara to Athens, leading to the outbreak of the first of the **Peloponnesian Wars**, the first phase in a protracted struggle between Athens and Sparta. The Athenians conquered Aegina and gained control of Boeotia. At this moment Athens was supreme and apparently invulnerable, controlling the states on its borders and dominating the sea. (See Map 3–2.)

About 455 B.C.E., however, the tide turned. A disastrous defeat met an Athenian fleet that had gone to aid an Egyptian rebellion against Persia. The great loss of men, ships, and prestige caused rebellions in the empire, forcing Athens to make a truce in Greece to subdue its allies in the Aegean. In 449 B.C.E., the Athenians ended the war against Persia.

In 446 B.C.E., the war on the Greek mainland broke out again. Rebellions in Boeotia and Megara removed Athens's land defenses and brought a Spartan invasion. Rather than fight, Pericles, the commander of the Athenian army, agreed to a peace of thirty years by the terms of which he abandoned all Athenian possessions on the Greek mainland outside of Attica. In return, the Spartans gave formal recognition to the Athenian Empire. From then on, Greece was divided into two power blocs: Sparta with its alliance on the mainland, and Athens ruling its empire in the Aegean.

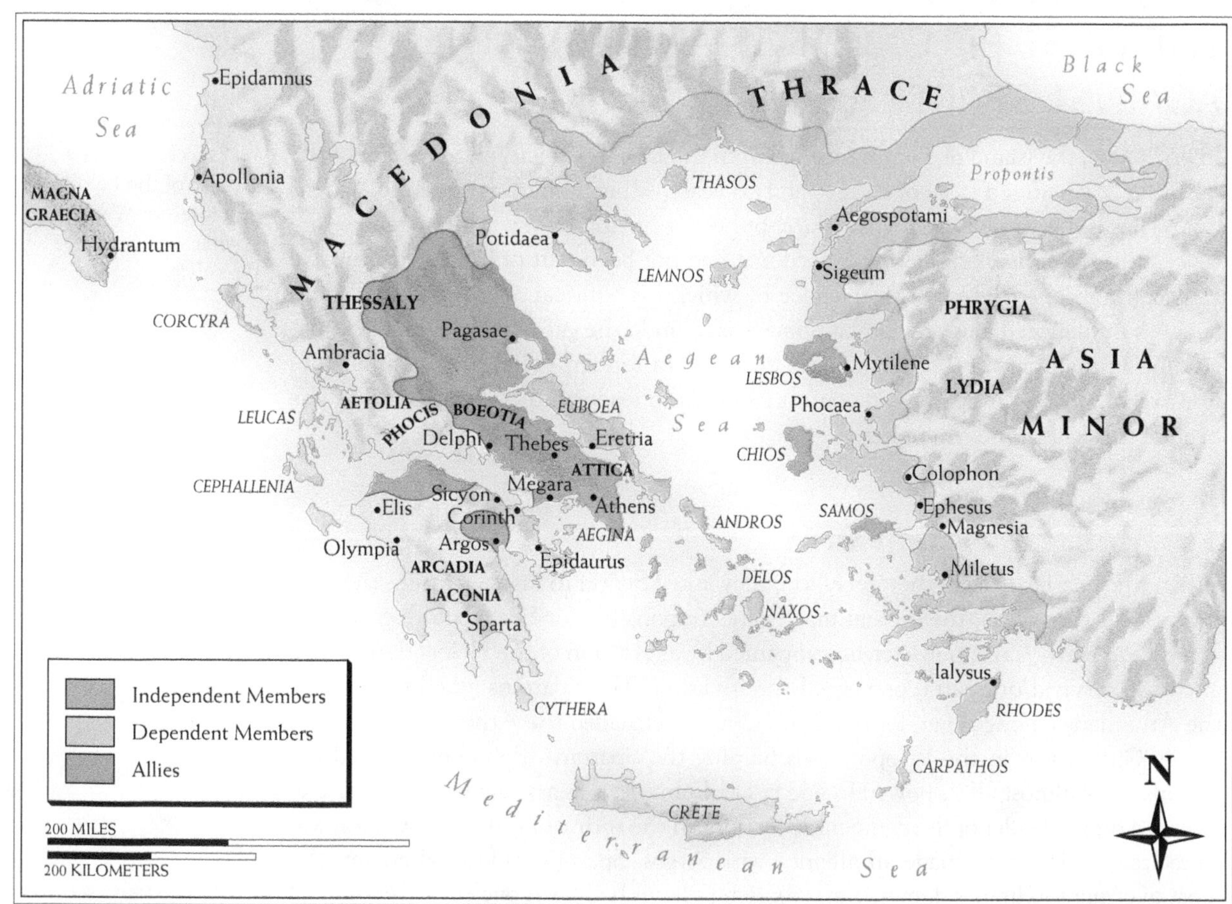

MAP 3–2 **The Athenian Empire about 450 B.C.E.** The Athenian Empire at its fullest extent. We see Athens and the independent states that provided manned ships for the imperial fleet but paid no tribute; dependent states that paid tribute; and states allied to, but not actually in, the empire.

Why would some of the weakest and most dependent Greek states be located in Asia Minor and Thrace?

CLASSICAL GREECE

HOW DID democracy work in fifth-century B.C.E. Athens?

The Athenian Empire

Because of the peace with Persia, the Athenians were compelled to find a new justification for their empire. They called for a Panhellenic congress to meet at Athens to discuss rebuilding the temples the Persians had destroyed and to consider how to maintain freedom of the seas. When Sparta's reluctance to participate prevented the congress, Athens felt free to continue to collect funds from the allies, both to maintain its navy and to rebuild the Athenian temples. Athenian propaganda suggested that henceforth the allies would be treated as colonies and Athens as their mother city, the whole to be held together by good feeling and common religious observances.

There is little reason, however, to believe the allies were taken in or were truly content with their lot. Nothing could cloak the fact that Athens was becoming the master and its allies mere subjects. The change from alliance to empire came about because of the pressure of war and rebellion and largely because the allies were unwilling to see to their own defense. Although the empire had many friends among the lower classes and the democratic politicians in the subject cities, it was seen more and more as a tyranny. Athenian prosperity and security, however, had come to depend on the empire, and the Athenians were determined to defend it.

Athenian Democracy

Even as the Athenians were tightening their control over their empire, they were expanding democracy at home. Under the leadership of Pericles, they evolved the freest government the world had yet seen.

Democratic Legislation Legislation was passed making the *hoplite* class eligible for the *archonship*, and, in practice, no one was thereafter prevented from serving in this office on the basis of his property class. Pericles himself proposed a law introducing pay for jury members, opening that important duty to the poor. Circuit judges were reintroduced, a policy making swift impartial justice available even to the poorest residents in the countryside.

Finally, Pericles himself introduced a bill limiting citizenship to those who had two citizen parents. Democracy was defined as the privilege of those who held citizenship, making citizenship a valuable commodity. Limiting it increased its value. Women, resident aliens, and slaves were also denied participation in government in all the Greek states.

(a)

(b)

An Athenian silver four-drachma coin (tetradrachm) from the fifth century B.C.E. (440–430 B.C.E.). On the front (a) is the profile of Athena and on the back (b) is her symbol of wisdom, the owl. The silver from which the coins were struck came chiefly from the state mines at Sunium in southern Attica.

Hirmer Fotoarchiv

How did the Athenians use economic exploitation to transform the Delian League into the Athenian Empire?

How Did the Democracy Work? Within the citizen body, the extent of Athenian democracy was remarkable. The popular assembly—a collection of the people, not their representatives—had to approve every decision of the state. Every judicial decision was subject to appeal to a popular court chosen from an annual panel of jurors widely representative of the Athenian population. (See "Encountering the Past, Going to Court in Athens.") Most officials were selected by lot without regard to class. All public officials were subject to scrutiny before taking office and could be called to account or be removed from office during their tenure. They were held to compulsory

ENCOUNTERING THE PAST

Going to Court in Athens

The Athenians placed the administration of justice directly into the hands of their fellow citizens, including the poorest ones. Each year 6,000 Athenian males, between a quarter and a fifth of the citizen body, signed on to a panel. (Because women were not considered citizens, they were not allowed to sit on juries or sue in the courts.) From this panel on any given day, jurors were assigned to specific courts and cases. The usual size of a jury was 501, although there were juries of from 51 to as many as 1,501 members.

Unlike in a modern American court, there was no public prosecutor, no lawyers at all, and no judge. The jury was everything. Private citizens registered complaints and argued their own cases. In deciding fundamental matters of justice and fairness, the Athenian democrat put little faith in experts.

In the courtroom the plaintiff and defendant would each present his case for himself, rebut his opponent, cite the relevant laws and precedents, produce witnesses, and sum up. No trial lasted more than a day. The jury did not deliberate but just voted by secret ballot. A simple majority decided the verdict. If a penalty was called for and not prescribed by law (as few were), the plaintiff proposed one penalty, and the defendant a different one. The jury voted to choose one of these but could not propose any other. Normally, this process led both sides to suggest moderate penalties, for an unreasonable suggestion would alienate the jury. To further deter frivolous lawsuits, the plaintiff had to pay a large fine if he did not win a stated percentage of the jurors' votes.

The Athenian system of justice had obvious flaws. Decisions could be quirky and unpredictable because they were unchecked by precedent. Juries could be prejudiced, and the jurors had no defense except their own intelligence and knowledge against speakers who cited laws incorrectly and distorted history. Speeches—unhampered by rules of evidence and relevance, and without the discipline judges impose—could be fanciful, false, and deceptive.

For all its flaws, however, the Athenian system was simple, speedy, open, and easily understood by the citizens. It counted, as always, on the common sense of the ordinary Athenian, and contained provisions aimed at producing moderate penalties and deterring unreasonable lawsuits. No legal technicalities or experts came between the citizens and their laws.

Water Clock and Jury Ballots. Participants in an Athenian trial could speak for only a limited time. A water clock (*clepsydra*) like this kept the time. In front of it are two ballots used by the jurors to vote in favor of the plaintiff or the defendant.

Picture Desk/The Art Archive/Agora Museum Athens/Dagli Orti

What characteristics of Athenian democracy were revealed by the conduct of Athenian justice?

WHAT WERE the advantages and disadvantages of the Athenian justice system? Do you think it would lead to fair and just results?

examination and accounting at the end of their term. There was no standing army, no police force, open or secret, and no way to coerce the people.

Pericles was elected to the generalship fifteen years in a row and thirty times in all, not because he was a dictator but because he was a persuasive speaker, a skillful politician, a respected military leader, an acknowledged patriot, and patently incorruptible. When he lost the people's confidence, they did not hesitate to depose him from office. In 443 B.C.E., however, he stood at the height of his power. The defeat of the Athenian fleet in the Egyptian campaign and the failure of Athens's continental campaigns had persuaded him to favor a conservative policy, seeking to retain the empire in the Aegean and live at peace with the Spartans. It was in this direction that he led Athens's imperial democracy in the years after the First Peloponnesian War. (See "Compare & Connect: Athenian Democracy—Pro and Con," on pages 66–67.)

The Women of Athens: Legal Status and Everyday Life

Men dominated Greek society, like most societies all over the world throughout history. This was true of the democratic city of Athens in the great days of Pericles, in the fifth century B.C.E., no less than of any other Greek city. The actual position of women in classical Athens, however, has been the subject of much controversy.

The bulk of the evidence, coming from the law, from philosophical and moral writings, and from information about the conditions of daily life and the organization of society, shows that women were excluded from most aspects of public life. They could not vote, could not take part in the political assemblies, could not hold public office, and could not take any direct part in politics.

In the private aspects of life women were always under the control of a male guardian—a father, a husband, or some other male relative.

The main function and responsibility of a respectable Athenian woman of a citizen family was to produce male heirs for the *oikos*, or household, of her husband. Because the pure and legitimate lineage of the offspring was important, women were carefully segregated from men outside the family and were confined to the women's quarters in the house. The only public function of women—an important one—was in the various rituals and festivals of the state religion. Apart from these activities, Athenian women were expected to remain at home out of sight, quiet, and unnoticed. Pericles told the widows and mothers of the Athenian men who died in the first year of the Peloponnesian War only this: "Your great glory is not to fall short of your natural character, and the greatest glory of women is to be least talked about by men, whether for good or bad."

The picture of the legal status of women derived from these sources is largely accurate. It does not fit well, however, with other evidence from mythology, from pictorial art, and from the tragedies and comedies by the great Athenian dramatists. These often show women as central characters and powerful figures in both the public and the private spheres, suggesting that Athenian women may have played a more complex role than their legal status suggests.

An Exceptional Woman: Aspasia Pericles' life did not conform to his own prescription. After divorcing his first wife, he entered a liaison that was unique in his time, to a woman who was, in her own way, as remarkable as the great Athenian leader. His companion was Aspasia, a young woman who had left her native Miletus

COMPARE & CONNECT

ATHENIAN DEMOCRACY—PRO AND CON

The first democracy in the world's history appeared in Athens at the end of the sixth century B.C.E. By the middle of the fifth century the Athenian constitution had broadened to give all adult males participation in all aspects of government.

Although most Greek states remained oligarchic, some adopted the Athenian model and became democratic, but democracy was harshly criticized by members of the upper classes, traditionalists, and philosophers. In the following documents Pericles, the most famous Athenian political leader, and an anonymous pamphleteer present contrasting evaluations of the Athenian democracy.

QUESTIONS

1. What virtues does Pericles find in the Athenian constitution?
2. Against what criticisms is he defending it?
3. What are the author's objections to democracy?
4. How would a defender of the Athenian constitution and way of life meet his complaints?
5. To what extent do these descriptions agree?
6. How do they disagree?

I. PERICLES' FUNERAL ORATION

In 431 B.C.E., the first year of the Peloponnesian War, Pericles delivered a speech to honor and commemorate the Athenian soldiers who died in the fighting. A key part of it was the praise of the Athenian democratic constitution, which, he argued, justified the sacrifice they had made.

Our constitution does not copy the laws of neighbouring states; we are rather a pattern to others than imitators ourselves. Its administration favours the many instead of the few; this is why it is called a democracy. If we look to the laws, they afford equal justice to all in their private differences; if to social standing, advancement in public life falls to reputation for capacity, class considerations not being allowed to interfere with merit; nor again does poverty bar the way, if a man is able to serve the state, he is not hindered by the obscurity of his condition. The freedom which we enjoy in our government extends also to our ordinary life. There, far from exercising a jealous surveillance over each other, we do not feel called upon to be angry with our neighbour for doing what he likes, or even to indulge in those injurious looks which cannot fail to be offensive, although they inflict no positive penalty. But all this ease in our private relations does not make us lawless as citizens. Against this fear is our chief safeguard, teaching us to obey the magistrates and the laws, particularly such as regard the protection of the injured, whether they are actually on the statute book, or belong to that code which, although unwritten, yet cannot be broken without acknowledged disgrace.

Source: Thucydides, *The Peloponnesian War* 2.37, trans. by Richard Crawley.

II. ATHENIAN DEMOCRACY: AN UNFRIENDLY VIEW

The following selection comes from an anonymous pamphlet thought to have been written in the midst of the Peloponnesian War. Because it has come down to us among the works of Xenophon, but cannot be his work, it is sometimes called "The Constitution of the Athenians" by Pseudo-Xenophon. It is also common to refer to the unknown author as "The Old Oligarch"—although neither his age nor his purpose is known—because of the obviously anti-democratic tone of the work. Such opinions were common among members of the upper classes in Athens late in the fifth century B.C.E. *and thereafter.*

Now, in discussing the Athenian constitution, I cannot commend their present method of running the state, because in choosing it they preferred that the masses should do better than the respectable citizens; this, then, is my reason for not commending it. Since, however, they have made this choice, I will demonstrate how well they preserve their constitution and handle the other affairs for which the rest of the Greeks criticize them.

Again, some people are surprised at the fact that in all fields they give more power to the masses, the poor, and the common people than they do to the respectable elements of society, but it will become clear that they preserve the democracy by doing precisely this. When the poor, the ordinary people, and the lower classes flourish and increase in numbers, then the power of the democracy will be increased; if, however, the rich and the respectable flourish, the democrats increase the strength of their opponents. Throughout the world the aristocracy are opposed to democracy, for they are naturally least liable to loss of self-control and injustice and most meticulous in their regard for what is respectable, whereas the masses display extreme ignorance, indiscipline, and wickedness, for poverty gives them a tendency towards the ignoble, and in some cases the lack of money leads to their being uneducated and ignorant.

It may be objected that they ought not to grant each and every man the right of speaking in the Ekklesia and serving on the Boule, but only the ablest and best of them; however, in this also they are acting in their own best interests by allowing the mob also a voice. If none but the respectable spoke in the Ekklesia and the Boule, the result would benefit that class and harm the masses; as it is, anyone who wishes rises and speaks, and as a member of the mob he discovers what is to his own advantage and that of those like him.

But someone may say: "How could such a man find out what was advantageous to himself and the common people?" The Athenians realize that this man, despite his ignorance and badness, brings them more advantage because he is well-disposed to them than the ill-disposed, respectable man would, despite his virtue and wisdom. Such practices do not produce the best city, but they are the best way of preserving democracy. For the common people do not wish to be deprived of their rights in an admirably governed city, but to be free and to rule the city; they are not disturbed by inferior laws, for the common people get their strength and freedom from what you define as inferior laws.

Pericles (ca. 495–429 B.C.E.) was the leading statesman of Athens for much of the fifth century. This is a Roman copy in marble of the Greek bronze bust that was probably cast in the last decade of Pericles' life.

Library of Congress

What does the sustained power of Pericles tell us about Athenian democracy?

Source: *Aristotle and Xenophon on Democracy and Oligarchy*, trans. with introductions and commentary by J. M. Moore (Berkeley and Los Angeles: University of California Press, 1975), pp. 37–38.

The Acropolis was both the religious and civic center of Athens. In its final form it is the work of Pericles and his successors in the late fifth century B.C.E. This photograph shows the Parthenon and to its left, the Erechtheum.

Meredith Pillon, Greek National Tourism Organization

Why did Pericles devote so much energy and so many resources to the construction of public buildings and monuments?

and come to live in Athens. The ancient writers refer to her as a *hetaira*, a kind of high-class courtesan who provided men with both erotic and other kinds of entertainment.

Aspasia represented something completely different from Athenian women. She was not a child, not a sheltered and repressed creature confined to the narrow world of slave women, children, and female relatives, but a beautiful, independent, brilliantly witty young woman capable of holding her own in conversation with the best minds in Greece and of discussing and illuminating any question with her husband. There can be no doubt that Pericles loved her passionately. He took her into his house, and whether or not they were formally and legally married, he treated her as his one and only beloved wife.

QUICK REVIEW

Aspasia

- Pericles' female companion
- Highly intelligent and well educated
- Pericles discussed politics with her and respected her ideas

SLAVERY

The Greeks had some form of slavery from the earliest times, but true chattel slavery was initially rare. The most common forms of bondage were different kinds of serfdom in relatively backward areas such as Crete, Thessaly, and Sparta. Another early form of bondage involving a severe, but rarely permanent, loss of freedom resulted from default in debt.

True chattel slavery began to increase about 500 B.C.E. and remained important to Greek society thereafter. The main sources of slaves were war captives and the captives of pirates. Like the Chinese, Egyptians, and many other peoples, the Greeks regarded foreigners as inferior, and most slaves working for the Greeks were foreigners.

The chief occupation of the Greeks, as of most of the world before our century, was agriculture. Most Greek farmers worked small holdings too poor to support even one slave, but some had one or two slaves to work alongside them. The upper classes had larger farms that were let out to free tenant farmers or were worked by slaves, generally under an overseer who was himself a slave.

Larger numbers of slaves labored in industry, especially in mining. Most manufacturing was on a small scale, with shops using one, two, or a handful of slaves. Slaves worked as craftsmen in almost every trade, and, like agricultural slaves on small farms, they worked alongside their masters. Many slaves were domestic servants or shepherds. Publicly held slaves served as policemen, prison attendants, clerks, and secretaries.

The number of slaves in ancient Greece and their importance to Greek society are the subjects of controversy. We have no useful figures of the absolute number of slaves or their percentage of the free population in the classical period (fifth and fourth centuries B.C.E.), and estimates range from 20,000 to 100,000. Accepting the mean between the extremes, 60,000, and estimating the free population at its height at about 40,000 households, would yield a figure of fewer than two slaves per family. Estimates suggest that only a quarter to a third of free Athenians owned any slaves at all.

QUICK REVIEW

Chattel Slavery

- Proliferated about 500 B.C.E.
- Most slaves were prisoners of war or abducted by pirates
- Slaves worked in every craft and many professions

RELIGION IN PUBLIC LIFE

In Athens, as in the other Greek states, religion was more a civic than a private matter. Participation in the rituals of the state religion was not a matter of faith, but of patriotism and good citizenship. In its most basic form, it had little to do with morality. Greek religion emphasized not moral conduct to orthodox belief, but the faithful practice of rituals meant to win the favor of the gods. To fail to carry out these duties or to attack the gods in any way was seen as a blow against the state and was severely punished.

Famous examples of such blasphemies and their punishment occurred late in the fifth and early in the fourth centuries B.C.E. The best known is the case of the philosopher Socrates. In 399 B.C.E., Socrates was convicted of not honoring the state's gods and of introducing new divinities, and he was put to death. This was connected with the further charge of corrupting the youths, both acts believed to do harm to the well-being of Athens. In ancient Greece there was no thought of separating religion from civic and political life.

THE GREAT PELOPONNESIAN WAR

HOW DID the Peloponnesian War affect the faith in the *polis*?

During the first decade after the Thirty Years' Peace of 445 B.C.E., the willingness of each side to respect the new arrangements was tested and not found wanting. About 435 B.C.E., however, a dispute in a remote and unimportant part of the Greek world ignited a long and disastrous war that shook the foundations of Greek civilization.

CAUSES

The spark that ignited the conflict was a civil war at Epidamnus, a Corcyraean colony on the Adriatic. This civil war caused a quarrel between Corcyra (modern Corfu) and its mother city and traditional enemy, Corinth, an ally of Sparta. The Corcyraean fleet was second in size only to that of Athens, and the Athenians feared that its capture by Corinth would threaten Athenian security. As a result, they made an alliance with the previously neutral Corcyra, angering Corinth and leading to a series of crises in 433–432 B.C.E. that threatened to bring the Athenian Empire into conflict with the Peloponnesian League.

In the summer of 432 B.C.E., the Spartans met to consider the grievances of their allies. Persuaded, chiefly by the Corinthians, that Athens was an insatiably aggressive power seeking to enslave all the Greeks, they voted for war. In the spring of 431 B.C.E., its army marched into Attica, the Athenian homeland.

STRATEGIC STALEMATE

The Spartan strategy was traditional: to invade the enemy's country and threaten the crops, forcing the enemy to defend them in a *hoplite* battle. Such a battle the Spartans were sure to win because they had the better army and they outnumbered the Athenians at least two to one. Any ordinary *polis* would have yielded or fought and lost.

This storage jar *(amphora)*, made about 540 B.C.E., is attributed to the anonymous Athenian master artist called the Amasis painter. It shows Dionysus, the god of wine, revelry, and fertility, with two of his ecstatic female worshippers called maenads.

Cliché Bibliothèque Nationale de France—Paris

What role did the gods play in the daily life of Classical Athens?

Athens, however, had an enormous navy, an annual income from the empire, a vast reserve fund, and long walls that connected the fortified city with the fortified port of Piraeus.

The Athenians' strategy was to allow devastation of their own land to prove that Spartan invasions could not hurt Athens. At the same time, the Athenians launched seaborne raids on the Peloponnesian coast to hurt Sparta's allies. Pericles expected that within a year or two—three at most—the Peloponnesians would become discouraged and make peace, having learned their lesson.

The plan required restraint and the leadership only a Pericles could provide. In 429 B.C.E., however, after a devastating plague and a political crisis that had challenged his authority, Pericles died. After his death, no dominant leader emerged to hold the Athenians to a consistent policy. Two factions vied for influence: One, led by Nicias, wanted to continue the defensive policy, and the other, led by Cleon, preferred a more aggressive strategy. In 425 B.C.E., the aggressive faction was able to win a victory that changed the course of the war. Four hundred Spartans surrendered. Sparta offered peace at once to get them back. The great victory and the prestige it brought Athens made it safe to raise the imperial tribute, without which Athens could not continue to fight. The Athenians indeed wanted to continue, for the Spartan peace offer gave no adequate guarantee of Athenian security.

In 424 B.C.E., the Athenians undertook a more aggressive policy. They sought to make Athens safe by conquering Megara and Boeotia. Both attempts failed, and defeat helped discredit the aggressive policy, leading to a truce in 423 B.C.E. Meanwhile, Sparta's ablest general, Brasidas, took a small army to Thrace and Macedonia. He captured Amphipolis, the most important Athenian colony in the region. In 422 B.C.E., Cleon led an expedition to undo the work of Brasidas. At Amphipolis, both he and Brasidas died in battle. The removal of these two leaders of the aggressive factions in their respective cities paved the way for the Peace of Nicias, named for its chief negotiator, which was ratified in the spring of 421 B.C.E.

The Fall of Athens

The peace, officially supposed to last fifty years and, with a few exceptions, guarantee the status quo, was in fact fragile. Neither side carried out all its commitments, and several of Sparta's allies refused ratification. In 415 B.C.E., Alcibiades persuaded the Athenians to attack Sicily to bring it under Athenian control. This ambitious and unnecessary undertaking ended in disaster in 413 B.C.E., when the entire expedition was destroyed. It shook Athens's prestige, reduced its power, provoked rebellions, and brought the wealth and power of Persia into the war on Sparta's side.

It is remarkable that the Athenians could continue fighting despite the disaster. Their allies rebelled, however, and Persia paid for fleets to sustain them. When its fleet was caught napping and was destroyed at Aegospotami in 405 B.C.E., Athens could not build another. The Spartans, under Lysander, a clever and ambitious general who was responsible for obtaining Persian support, cut off the food supply through the Hellespont, and the Athenians were starved into submission. In 404 B.C.E., they surrendered unconditionally; the city walls were dismantled, Athens was permitted no fleet, and the empire was gone. The Great Peloponnesian War was over.

COMPETITION FOR LEADERSHIP IN THE FOURTH CENTURY B.C.E.

HOW DID Athens and Sparta compete for leadership in the Greek world?

Athens's defeat did not bring domination to the Spartans. Instead, the period from 404 B.C.E. until the Macedonian conquest of Greece in 338 B.C.E. was a time of intense rivalry among the Greek cities, each seeking to achieve leadership and control over the others.

The Hegemony of Sparta

The collapse of the Athenian Empire created a vacuum of power in the Aegean and opened the way for Spartan leadership or hegemony. Under the leadership of Lysander, the Spartans made a mockery of their promise to free the Greeks by stepping into the imperial role of Athens in the cities along the European coast and the islands of the Aegean. In most of the cities, Lysander installed a board of ten local oligarchs loyal to him and supported them with a Spartan garrison. Tribute brought in an annual revenue almost as great as that the Athenians had collected.

The increasing arrogance of Sparta's policies alienated some of its allies, especially Thebes and Corinth. In 404 B.C.E., Lysander installed an oligarchic government in Athens. Democratic exiles took refuge in Thebes and Corinth and raised an army to challenge the oligarchy. Sparta's conservative king, Pausanias, replaced Lysander, arranging a peaceful settlement and, ultimately, the restoration of democracy. Thereafter, Athenian foreign policy remained under Spartan control, but otherwise Athens was free.

In 405 B.C.E., Darius II of Persia died and was succeeded by Artaxerxes II. His younger brother, Cyrus, received Spartan help in recruiting a Greek mercenary army to help him contest the throne. The Greeks marched inland as far as Mesopotamia, where they defeated the Persians at Cunaxa in 401 B.C.E., but Cyrus was killed in the battle. The Greeks were able to march back to the Black Sea and safety; their success revealed the potential weakness of the Persian Empire.

The Greeks of Asia Minor had supported Cyrus and were now afraid of Artaxerxes' revenge. The Spartans accepted their request for aid and sent an army into Asia, attracted by the prospect of prestige, power, and money. In 396 B.C.E., the command of Sparta's army was given to a new king, Agesilaus, who dominated Sparta until his death in 360 B.C.E.

Agesilaus collected much booty and frightened the Persians. They sent a messenger with money and promises of further support to friendly factions in all of the Greek states likely to help them against Sparta. By 395 B.C.E., Thebes was able to organize an alliance that included Argos, Corinth, and a resurgent Athens. The result was the Corinthian War (395–387 B.C.E.), which put an end to Sparta's Asian adventure. In 394 B.C.E., the Persian fleet destroyed Sparta's maritime empire. Meanwhile, the Athenians rebuilt their walls, enlarged their navy, and even recovered some of their lost empire in the Aegean. The war ended when the exhausted Greek states accepted a peace dictated by the Great King of Persia.

The Persians, frightened now by the recovery of Athens, turned the management of Greece over to Sparta. Agesilaus broke up all alliances except the Peloponnesian League. He used or threatened to use the Spartan army to interfere in other *poleis* and put friends of Sparta in power within them. Sparta reached a new level of lawless arrogance in 382 B.C.E., when it seized Thebes during peacetime without warning or pretext. In 379 B.C.E., a Spartan army made a similar attempt on Athens. That action persuaded the Athenians to join with Thebes, which had rebelled from Sparta a few months earlier, to wage war on the Spartans. In 371 B.C.E., the Thebans, led by their great generals Pelopidas and Epaminondas, defeated the Spartans at Leuctra. The Theban victory brought the end of Sparta as a power of the first rank.

THE HEGEMONY OF THEBES: THE SECOND ATHENIAN EMPIRE

Thebes's power after its victory at Leuctra lay in its democratic constitution, its control over Boeotia, and its two outstanding and popular generals. One of these generals, Pelopidas, died in a successful attempt to gain control of Thessaly. The other, Epaminondas, made Thebes dominant over all of Greece north of Athens and the Corinthian Gulf and challenged the reborn Athenian Empire in the Aegean. All this activity provoked resistance, and by 362 B.C.E., Thebes faced a Peloponnesian coalition as well as Athens. Epaminondas, once again leading a Boeotian army into the Peloponnesus, confronted this coalition at the Battle of Mantinea. His army was victorious, but Epaminondas himself was killed, and Theban dominance died with him.

The Second Athenian Confederation, which Athens had organized in 378 B.C.E., was aimed at resisting Spartan aggression in the Aegean. Its constitution avoided the abuses of the Delian League, but the Athenians soon began to repeat them anyway. This time, however, they did not have the power to put down resistance. When the collapse of Sparta and Thebes and the restraint of Persia removed any reason for voluntary membership, Athens's allies revolted. By 355 B.C.E., Athens had to abandon most of the empire. After two centuries of almost continuous warfare, the Greeks returned to the chaotic disorganization that characterized the time before the founding of the Peloponnesian League.

THE COMPETITION FOR LEADERSHIP OF GREECE

479 B.C.E.	Battles of Plataea and Mycale
478–477 B.C.E.	Formation of the Delian League
465–463 B.C.E.	Thasos attempts to leave the league
462 B.C.E.	Pericles begins to lead Athens
460–445 B.C.E.	First Peloponnesian War
454 B.C.E.	Athens is defeated in Egypt
449 B.C.E.	Athens makes peace with Persia
435 B.C.E.	Corinth attacks Corcyra
432–404 B.C.E.	Great Peloponnesian War
421 B.C.E.	Peace of Nicias
415–413 B.C.E.	Athens's Sicilian campaign
404 B.C.E.	Sparta defeats Athens
404–403 B.C.E.	Thirty Tyrants govern Athens
382 B.C.E.	Sparta seizes Thebes
378 B.C.E.	Second Athenian Confederation
371 B.C.E.	Thebes defeats Sparta at Leuctra
362 B.C.E.	End of Theban hegemony
338 B.C.E.	Philip of Macedon dominates Greece
336–323 B.C.E.	Reign of Alexander the Great

THE CULTURE OF CLASSICAL GREECE

WHAT ARE the achievements of Classical Greece?

The repulse of the Persian invasion released a flood of creative activity in Greece that was rarely, if ever, matched anywhere at any time. The century and a half between the Persian retreat and the conquest of Greece by Philip of Macedon (479–338 B.C.E.) produced achievements of such quality as to justify the designation of that era as the Classical Period. Ironically, we often use the term *classical* to suggest calm and serenity, but the word that best describes Greek life, thought, art, and literature in this period is *tension.*

THE FIFTH CENTURY B.C.E.

Two sources of tension contributed to the artistic outpouring of fifth-century B.C.E. Greece. One arose from the conflict between the Greeks' pride in their accomplishments and their concern that overreaching would bring retribution. The second source of tension was the conflict between the soaring hopes and achievements of individuals and the claims and limits their fellow citizens in the *polis* put on them. These tensions were felt throughout Greece. They had the most spectacular consequences, however, in Athens in its Golden Age, the time between the Persian and the Peloponnesian wars.

Attic Tragedy Nothing reflects Athens's concerns better than Attic tragedy, which emerged as a major form of Greek poetry in the fifth century B.C.E. The tragedies were presented in a contest as part of the public religious observations in honor of the god Dionysus. The festivals in which they were shown were civic occasions.

Attic tragedy served as a forum in which the poets raised vital issues of the day, enabling the Athenian audience to think about them in a serious, yet exciting, context. On rare occasions, the subject of a play might be a contemporary or historic event, but almost always it was chosen from mythology. Until late in the century, the tragedies always dealt solemnly with difficult questions of religion, politics, ethics, morality, or some combination of these. The plays of the dramatists Aeschylus and Sophocles, for example, follow this pattern. The plays of Euripides, written toward the end of the century, are less solemn and more concerned with individual psychology.

QUICK REVIEW

Athenian Drama

- Plays were staged at festivals honoring the gods
- Plays were presented in the temple of Dionysus
- Playwrights used the theater to encourage citizens to think about the issues of the day

Old Comedy Comedy was introduced into the Dionysian festival early in the fifth century B.C.E. Cratinus, Eupolis, and the great master of the genre called Old Comedy, Aristophanes (ca. 450–385 B.C.E.), the only one from whom we have complete plays, wrote political comedies. They were filled with scathing invective and satire against such contemporary figures as Pericles, Cleon, Socrates, and Euripides.

Architecture and Sculpture The great architectural achievements of Periclean Athens, as much as Athenian tragedy, illustrate the magnificent results of the union and tension between religious and civic responsibilities, on the one hand, and the transcendent genius of the individual artist, on the other. Beginning in 448 B.C.E. and continuing to the outbreak of the Great Peloponnesian War, Pericles undertook a great building program on the Acropolis. The income from the empire paid for it. Pericles' main purpose seems to have been to represent visually the greatness and power of Athens, by emphasizing intellectual and artistic achievement—civilization rather than military and naval power. It was as though these buildings were tangible proof of Pericles' claim that Athens was "the school of Hellas"—that is, the intellectual center of all Greece.

Philosophy The tragic dramas, architecture, and sculpture of the fifth century B.C.E. all indicate an extraordinary concern with human beings—their capacities, their limits, their nature, and their place in the universe. The same concern is clear in the development of philosophy.

To be sure, some philosophers continued the speculation about the nature of the cosmos (as opposed to human nature) that began with Thales in the sixth century B.C.E. Parmenides of Elea and his pupil Zeno, in opposition to the earlier philosopher Heraclitus, argued that change was only an illusion of the senses. Reason and reflection showed that reality was fixed and unchanging, because it seemed evident that nothing could be created out of nothingness. Empedocles of Acragas further advanced such fundamental speculations by identifying four basic elements: fire, water, earth, and air. Like Parmenides, he thought that reality was permanent, but he thought it was not immobile; two primary forces, he contended, love and strife—or, as we might say, attraction and repulsion—moved the four elements.

The three orders of Greek architecture, Doric, Ionic, and Corinthian, have had an enduring impact on Western architecture.

What role did public spaces play in Athenian life?

Empedocles' theory is clearly a step on the road to the atomist theory of Leucippus of Miletus and Democritus of Abdera. According to this theory, the world consists of innumerable tiny, solid, indivisible, and unchangeable particles—or "atoms"—that move about in the void. The size of the atoms and the arrangements they form when joined produce the secondary qualities that our senses perceive, such as color and shape. These secondary qualities are merely conventional—the result of human interpretation and agreement—unlike the atoms themselves, which are natural.

Previous to the atomists, Anaxagoras of Clazomenae, an older contemporary and a friend of Pericles, had spoken of tiny fundamental particles called *seeds*, which were put together on a rational basis by a force called *nous*, or "mind." Anaxagoras was thus suggesting a distinction between matter and mind. The atomists, however, regarded "soul," or mind, as material and believed purely physical laws guided everything. In these conflicting positions, we have the beginning of the enduring philosophical debate between materialism and idealism.

These speculations were of interest to few people, and in fact, most Greeks were suspicious of them. A group of professional teachers who emerged in the mid-fifth century began a far more influential debate. Called *Sophists*, they traveled about and received pay for teaching such practical techniques of persuasion as rhetoric, dialectic, and argumentation. Reflecting the human focus characteristic of fifth-century thought, they refrained from speculations about the physical universe, instead applying reasoned analysis to human beliefs and institutions. In doing so, they identified a central problem of human social life and the life of the *polis*: the conflict between nature and custom, or law. The more traditional among them argued that law itself was in accord with nature and was of divine origin, a view that fortified the traditional beliefs of the *polis*.

Others argued, however, that laws were merely the result of convention—an agreement among people—and not in accord with nature. The laws could not pretend to be a positive moral force but merely had the negative function of preventing people from harming each other. The most extreme Sophists argued that law was contrary to nature, a trick whereby the weak control the strong.

History The first prose literature in the form of history was Herodotus's account of the Persian War. "The father of history," as he has been deservedly called, was born shortly before the outbreak of the war. His account goes far beyond all previous chronicles, genealogies, and geographical studies and attempts to explain human actions and to draw instruction from them.

Although his work was completed about 425 B.C.E. and shows a few traces of Sophist influence, its spirit is that of an earlier time. Herodotus accepted the evidence of legends and oracles, although not uncritically, and often explained human events in terms of divine intervention. Yet the *History* is typical of its time in celebrating the crucial role of human intelligence. Nor was Herodotus unaware of the importance of institutions. His pride in the superiority of the Greek *polis*, in the discipline it inspired in its citizen soldiers, and in the superiority of the Greeks' voluntary obedience to law over the Persians' fear of punishment is unmistakable.

Thucydides, the historian of the Peloponnesian War, was born about 460 B.C.E. and died a few years after the end of the Great Peloponnesian War. He was very much a product of the late fifth century B.C.E. His work, which was influenced by the secular, human-centered, skeptical rationalism of the Sophists, also reflects the scientific attitude of the school of medicine named for his contemporary, Hippocrates of Cos.

The Hippocratic school, known for its pioneering work in medicine and scientific theory, emphasized an approach to the understanding, diagnosis, and treatment of disease that combined careful observation with reason. In the same way, Thucydides took pains to achieve factual accuracy and tried to use his evidence to discover meaningful patterns of human behavior. His work has proved to be, as he hoped, "a possession forever." Its description of the terrible civil war between the two basic kinds of *poleis* is a final and fitting example of the tension that was the source of both the greatness and the decline of Classical Greece.

QUICK REVIEW

Heredotus

- "Father of history"
- Assigned human intelligence a crucial role in determining the course of events
- Credited Greece's victory over Persia to citizens' love of liberty

THE FOURTH CENTURY B.C.E.

Historians often speak of the Peloponnesian War as the crisis of the *polis* and of the fourth century B.C.E. as the period of its decline. The Greeks of the fourth century B.C.E. did not know, however, that their traditional way of life was on the verge of destruction. Still, thinkers recognized that they lived in a time of troubles, and they responded in various ways. Some looked to the past and tried to shore up the weakened structure of the *polis*; others tended toward despair and looked for new solutions; and still others averted their gaze from the public arena altogether. All these responses are apparent in the literature, philosophy, and art of the period.

Drama The tendency of some to turn away from the life of the *polis* and inward to everyday life, the family, and their own individuality is apparent in the poetry of the fourth century B.C.E. A new genre, called Middle Comedy, replaced the political subjects and personal invective of the Old Comedy with a comic-realistic depiction of daily life, plots of intrigue, and a mild satire of domestic situations. Significantly, the role of the chorus, which in some way represented the *polis*, was diminished quite a bit. These trends all continued and were carried even further in the New Comedy. Its leading playwright, Menander (342–291 B.C.E.), completely abandoned mythological subjects in favor of domestic tragicomedy.

Tragedy faded as a robust and original form. It became common to revive the great plays of the previous century. No tragedies written in the fourth century B.C.E. have been preserved. The plays of Euripides, which rarely won first prize when first

The theater at Epidaurus was built in the fourth century B.C.E. The city contained the Sanctuary of Asclepius, a god of healing, and drew many visitors who packed the theater at religious festivals.

Hirmer Fotoarchiv

What was the relationship between religion and theater in Classical Athens?

The striding god from Artemisium is a bronze statue dating from about 460 B.C.E. It was found in the sea near Artemisium, the northern tip of the large Greek island of Euboea, and is now on display in the Athens archaeological museum. Exactly whom he represents is not known. Some have thought him to be Poseidon holding a trident; others believe he is Zeus hurling a thunderbolt. In either case, he is a splendid representative of the early Classical Period of Greek sculpture.

National Archaeological Museum, Athens

What does the striding god tell us about Classical Greek attitudes toward the male human body?

produced for Dionysian festival competitions, became increasingly popular in the fourth century and after. Euripides was less interested in cosmic confrontations of conflicting principles than in the psychology and behavior of individual human beings.

Sculpture The same movement away from the grand, the ideal, and the general, and toward the ordinary, the real, and the individual is apparent in the development of Greek sculpture. To see these developments, one has only to compare the statue of the striding god from Artemisium (ca. 460 B.C.E.), thought to be either Zeus on the point of releasing a thunderbolt or Poseidon about to throw his trident, or the Doryphoros of Polycleitus (ca. 450–440 B.C.E.) with the Hermes of Praxiteles (ca. 340–330 B.C.E.) or the Apoxyomenos attributed to Lysippus (ca. 330 B.C.E.).

Philosophy and the Crisis of the *Polis*

Socrates Probably the most complicated response to the crisis of the *polis* may be found in the life and teachings of Socrates (469–399 B.C.E.). Because he wrote nothing, our knowledge of him comes chiefly from his disciples Plato and Xenophon and from later tradition. Socrates was committed to the search for truth and for the knowledge about human affairs that he believed reason could discover. His method was to question and cross-examine men, particularly those reputed to know something, such as craftsmen, poets, and politicians.

The result was always the same. Those Socrates questioned might have technical information and skills but seldom had any knowledge of the fundamental principles of human behavior. It is understandable that Athenians so exposed should be angry with their examiner, and it is not surprising they thought Socrates was undermining the beliefs and values of the *polis*. Socrates' unconcealed contempt for democracy, which seemingly relied on ignorant amateurs to make important political decisions without any certain knowledge, created further hostility. Moreover, his insistence on the primacy of his own individualism and his determination to pursue philosophy even against the wishes of his fellow citizens reinforced this hostility and the prejudice that went with it.

In 399 B.C.E., an Athenian jury condemned him to death on the charges of bringing new gods into the city and of corrupting the youth. His dialectical inquiries had angered many important people. He was given a chance to escape but, as Plato's *Crito* tells us, he refused to do so because of his veneration of the laws. Socrates' career set the stage for later responses to the travail of the *polis*. He recognized its difficulties and criticized its shortcomings, and he turned away from an active political life, but he did not abandon the idea of the *polis*. He fought as a soldier in its defense, obeyed its laws, and sought to put its values on a sound foundation by reason.

Plato Plato (429–347 B.C.E.) was by far the most important of Socrates' associates and is a perfect example of the pupil who becomes greater than his master. He was the first systematic philosopher and therefore the first to place political ideas in their full philosophical context. Plato came from a noble Athenian family, and he looked forward to an active political career until the excesses of the Thirty Tyrants and the execution of Socrates discouraged him from that pursuit.

Academy School founded by Plato in Athens to train statesmen and citizens.

In 386 B.C.E., he founded the **Academy**, a center of philosophical investigation and a school for training statesmen and citizens. It had a powerful impact on Greek thought and lasted until the emperor Justinian closed it in the sixth century C.E.

Like Socrates, Plato firmly believed in the *polis* and its values. Its virtues were order, harmony, and justice, and one of its main objects was to produce good people. Like his master, Plato thought the *polis* was in accord with nature. He accepted Socrates' doctrine of the identity of virtue and knowledge. He made it plain what that knowledge was: *episteme*—science—a body of true and unchanging wisdom open to only a few philosophers, whose training, character, and intellect allowed them to see reality. Only such people were qualified to rule; they would prefer the life of pure contemplation but would accept their responsibility and take their turn as philosopher kings. The training of such an individual required a specialization of function and a subordination of that individual to the community even greater than that at Sparta. This specialization would lead to Plato's definition of justice: Each person should do only that one thing to which his or her nature is best suited.

Plato understood that the *polis* of his day suffered from terrible internal stress, class struggle, and factional divisions. His solution, however, was not that of some Greeks—that is, conquest and resulting economic prosperity. For Plato, the answer was in moral and political reform. The way to harmony was to destroy the causes of strife: private property, the family—anything, in short, that stood between the individual citizen and devotion to the *polis*.

Concern for the redemption of the *polis* was at the heart of Plato's system of philosophy. He began by asking the traditional questions: What is a good man, and how is he made? The goodness of a human being belonged to moral philosophy, and when goodness became a function of the state, it became political philosophy. Because goodness depended on knowledge of the good, it required a theory of knowledge and an investigation of what kind of knowledge goodness required. The answer must be

Overview The Three Great Greek Intellectuals

SOCRATES (469–399 B.C.E.)	One of the first Greek intellectuals to recognize the shortcomings of the *polis*. He believed in the existence of truth and the power of reason to discover it. He made no attempt to conceal his contempt for Athenian democracy—a political system that he said empowered the ignorant to make decisions about things they did not understand. Socrates was eventually tried and executed for undercutting the Athenian way of life.
PLATO (429–347 B.C.E.)	The most important of Socrates' followers, he was the first to formulate a consistent worldview and a method for exploring all of life's fundamental questions. Like Socrates, Plato believed in the *polis* and saw it as consistent with humanity's social nature. He established the Academy in 386 B.C.E., a school for training statesmen and citizens. Plato believed power should be entrusted to philosophers only and that the *polis* could only be redeemed by improving its ability to produce good citizens.
ARISTOTLE (384–322 B.C.E.)	The most prominent of Plato's students, he founded the Lyceum (the school of the Peripatetics). Unlike Plato's students at the Academy, Aristotle's students gathered, ordered, and analyzed data from all fields of knowledge. He wrote on logic, physics, astronomy, biology, ethics, rhetoric, literary criticism, and politics. Aristotle believed human beings are social creatures and that the *polis* was necessary to realize their potential. He also stated that a moderate constitution was necessary to create a state dominated by the middle class, not by the rich or the poor.

metaphysical and so required a full examination of metaphysics. Even when the philosopher knew the good, however, the question remained how the state could bring its citizens to the necessary comprehension of that knowledge. The answer required a theory of education. Even purely logical and metaphysical questions, therefore, were subordinate to the overriding political questions. In this way, Plato's need to find a satisfactory foundation for the beleaguered *polis* contributed to the birth of systematic philosophy.

Aristotle Aristotle (384–322 B.C.E.) was a pupil of Plato's and owed much to the thought of his master, but his different experience and cast of mind led him in new directions. He was born at Stagirus, the son of the court doctor of neighboring Macedon. As a young man, he went to Athens to study at the Academy, where he stayed until Plato's death. Then he joined a Platonic colony at Assos in Asia Minor, and from there he moved to Mytilene. In both places he did research in marine biology, and biological interests played a large part in all his thoughts. In 342 B.C.E., Philip, the king of Macedon, appointed him tutor to his son, the young Alexander. (See "The Hellenistic World," page 79.)

Lyceum School founded by Aristotle in Athens that focused on the gathering and analysis of data from all fields of knowledge.

In 336 B.C.E., Aristotle returned to Athens, where he founded his own school, the **Lyceum**. Unlike the Academy, the members of the Lyceum took little interest in mathematics and were concerned with gathering, ordering, and analyzing all human knowledge. Almost all of what we possess of their work is in the form of philosophical and scientific studies, whose loose organization and style suggest they were lecture notes. The range of subjects treated is astonishing, including logic, physics, astronomy, biology, ethics, rhetoric, literary criticism, and politics.

In each field, the method is the same. Aristotle began with observation of the empirical evidence, which in some cases was physical and in others was common opinion. To this body of information, he applied reason and discovered inconsistencies or difficulties. To deal with these, he introduced metaphysical principles to explain the problems or to reconcile the inconsistencies.

His view on all subjects, like Plato's, was teleological; that is, both Plato and Aristotle recognized purposes apart from and greater than the will of the individual human being. Plato's purposes, however, were contained in ideas, or forms, that were transcendental concepts outside the experience of most people. For Aristotle, the purposes of most things were easily inferred by observation of their behavior in the world. Aristotle's most striking characteristics are his moderation and his common sense. His epistemology finds room for both reason and experience; his metaphysics gives meaning and reality to both mind and body; his ethics aims at the good life, which is the contemplative life, but recognizes the necessity for moderate wealth, comfort, and pleasure.

All these qualities are evident in Aristotle's political thought. Like Plato, he opposed the Sophists' assertion that the *polis* was contrary to nature and the result of mere convention. His response was to apply to politics the teleology he saw in all nature. In his view, matter existed to achieve an end, and it developed until it achieved its form, which was its end. There was constant development from matter to form, from potential to actual. Therefore, human primitive instincts could be seen as the matter out of which the human's potential as a political being could be realized. The *polis* made individuals self-sufficient and allowed the full realization of their potentiality. It was therefore natural.

It was also the highest point in the evolution of the social institutions that serve the human need to continue the species—marriage, household, village, and, finally, *polis*. For Aristotle, the purpose of the *polis* was neither economic nor military, but moral. According to Aristotle, "The end of the state is the good life" (*Politics* 1280b), the life lived "for the sake of noble actions" (1281a), a life of virtue and morality.

Characteristically, Aristotle was less interested in the best state—the utopia that required philosophers to rule it—than in the best state that was practically possible, one that

would combine justice with stability. The constitution for that state he called *politeia*, not the best constitution, but the next best, the one most suited to, and most possible for most states. Its quality was moderation, and it naturally gave power to neither the rich nor the poor, but to the middle class, which must also be the most numerous. The middle class possessed many virtues; because of its moderate wealth, it was free of the arrogance of the rich and the malice of the poor. For this reason, it was the most stable class.

The stability of the constitution also came from its being a mixed constitution, blending in some way the laws of democracy and of oligarchy. Aristotle's scheme was unique because of its realism and the breadth of its vision. Aristotle combined the practical analysis of political and economic realities with the moral and political purposes of the traditional defenders of the *polis*. The result was a passionate confidence in the virtues of moderation and of the middle class, and the proposal of a constitution that would give it power. It is ironic that the ablest defense of the *polis* came soon before its demise.

THE HELLENISTIC WORLD

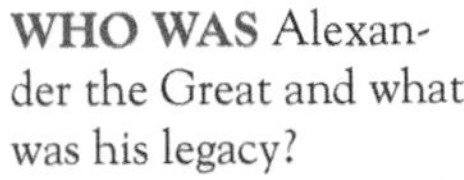

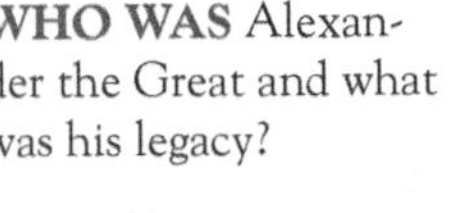

WHO WAS Alexander the Great and what was his legacy?

Hellenistic Term that describes the cosmopolitan civilization, established under the Macedonians, that combined aspects of Greek and Middle Eastern cultures.

The term ***Hellenistic*** was coined in the nineteenth century to describe the period of three centuries during which Greek culture spread far from its homeland to Egypt and deep into Asia. The new civilization formed in this expansion was a mixture of Greek and Near Eastern elements, although the degree of mixture varied from time to time and place to place. The Hellenistic world was larger than the world of Classical Greece, and its major political units were much larger than the city-states, though these persisted in different forms. The new political and cultural order had its roots in the rise to power of a Macedonian dynasty that conquered Greece and the Persian Empire in two generations.

THE MACEDONIAN CONQUEST

The quarrels among the Greeks brought on defeat and conquest by a new power that suddenly rose to eminence in the fourth century B.C.E.: the kingdom of Macedon (see Map 3–1, page 60). By Greek standards, Macedon was a backward, semibarbaric land. It had no *poleis* and was ruled loosely by a king. A council of nobles checked the royal power and could reject a weak or incompetent king. Hampered by constant wars with the barbarians, internal strife, loose organization, and lack of money, Macedon played no great part in Greek affairs up to the fourth century B.C.E.

The Macedonians were of the same stock as the Greeks and spoke a Greek dialect, and the nobles, at least, thought of themselves as Greeks. The kings claimed descent from Heracles and the royal house of Argos. They tried to bring Greek culture into their court and won acceptance at the Olympic games. If a king could be found to unify this nation, it was bound to play a greater part in Greek affairs.

Hermes and Dionysus

Praxiteles (c. 400–300 B.C.E.), *Hermes and Dionysus* c. 350–330 B.C.E. National Archeological Museum, Olympia. Scala/ Art Resource, NY

In what ways does the sculpture represent a departure from earlier Classical works?

Philip of Macedon That king was Philip II (r. 359–336 B.C.E.), who, although still under thirty, took advantage of his appointment as regent to overthrow his infant nephew and make himself king. His talents for war and diplomacy and his boundless ambition made him the ablest king in Macedonian history. Using both diplomatic and military means, he pacified the tribes on his frontiers and strengthened his own hold on the throne. Then he began to undermine Athenian control of the northern Aegean. He took Amphipolis, which gave him control of gold and silver mines. The income allowed him to found new cities, to bribe politicians in foreign towns, and to reorganize his army into the finest fighting force in the world.

The Macedonian Army Philip created a versatile and powerful army that was at once national and professional, unlike the amateur armies of citizen-soldiers who fought for the individual *poleis*. The infantry was drawn from among Macedonian farmers and the frequently rebellious Macedonian hill people. In time, these two elements were integrated to form a loyal and effective national force. Infantrymen were armed with thirteen-foot pikes instead of the more common nine-foot pikes and stood in a more open phalanx formation than the *hoplite* phalanx of the *poleis*. The effectiveness of this formation depended more on the skillful use of the pike than the weight of the charge. In Macedonian tactics, the role of the phalanx was not to be the decisive force, but to hold the enemy until a massed cavalry charge could strike a winning blow on the flank or into a gap. The cavalry was made up of Macedonian nobles and clan leaders, called Companions, who lived closely with the king and developed a special loyalty to him.

Philip also employed mercenaries who knew the latest tactics used by mobile light-armed Greek troops and were familiar with the most sophisticated siege machinery known to the Greeks. With these mercenaries, and with draft forces from among his allies, he could expand on his native Macedonian army of as many as 40,000 men.

The Invasion of Greece So armed, Philip turned south toward central Greece. Since 355 B.C.E., the Phocians had been fighting against Thebes and Thessaly. Philip gladly accepted the request of the Thessalians to be their general, defeated Phocis, and treacherously took control of Thessaly. Swiftly he turned northward again to Thrace and gained domination over the northern Aegean coast and the European side of the straits to the Black Sea. This conquest threatened the vital interests of Athens, which still had a formidable fleet of three hundred ships.

The Athens of 350 B.C.E. was not the Athens of Pericles. It had neither imperial revenue nor allies to share the burden of war, and its own population was smaller than in the fifth century. The Athenians, therefore, were reluctant to go on expeditions themselves or even to send out mercenary armies under Athenian generals, for they had to be paid out of taxes or contributions from Athenian citizens.

The leading spokesman against these tendencies and the cautious foreign policy that went with them was Demosthenes (384–322 B.C.E.), one of the greatest orators in Greek history. He was convinced that Philip was a dangerous enemy to Athens and the other Greeks. He spent most of his career urging the Athenians to resist Philip's encroachments. He was right, for beginning in 349 B.C.E., Philip attacked several cities in northern and central Greece and firmly planted Macedonian power in those regions.

The years between 346 B.C.E. and 340 B.C.E. were spent in diplomatic maneuvering, each side trying to win useful allies. At last, Philip attacked Perinthus and Byzantium, the lifeline of Athenian commerce; in 340 B.C.E., he besieged both cities and declared war. The Athenian fleet saved both, and so in the following year, Philip marched into Greece. Demosthenes performed wonders in rallying the Athenians and winning Thebes over to the Athenian side. In 338 B.C.E., however, Philip defeated the allied forces at Chaeronea in Boeotia. The decisive blow in this great battle was a cavalry charge led by Alexander, the eighteen-year-old son of Philip.

The Macedonian Government of Greece The Macedonian settlement of Greek affairs was not as harsh as many had feared, although in some cities the friends of Macedon came to power and killed or exiled their enemies. Athens was spared from attack on the condition that it give up what was left of its empire and follow the lead of Macedon. The rest of Greece was arranged so as to remove all dangers to Philip's rule. To guarantee his security, Philip placed garrisons at Thebes, Chalcis, and Corinth.

In 338 B.C.E., Philip called a meeting of the Greek states to form the federal League of Corinth. The constitution of the league provided for autonomy, freedom from tribute and garrisons, and suppression of piracy and civil war. The league delegates would make foreign policy in theory without consulting their home governments or Philip. All this was a facade; not only was Philip of Macedon president of the league, but he was also its ruler. The defeat at Chaeronea ended Greek freedom and autonomy. Although it maintained its form and way of life for some time, the *polis* had lost control of its own affairs and the special conditions that had made it unique.

Philip did not choose Corinth as the seat of his new confederacy simply from convenience or by accident. It was at Corinth that the Greeks had gathered to resist a Persian invasion almost 150 years earlier. And it was there in 337 B.C.E. that Philip announced his intention to invade Persia in a war of liberation and revenge, as leader of the new league. In the spring of 336 B.C.E., however, as he prepared to begin the campaign, Philip was assassinated.

ALEXANDER THE GREAT

Philip's first son, Alexander III (356–323 B.C.E.), later called Alexander the Great, succeeded his father at the age of twenty. The young king also inherited his father's daring plans to conquer Persia.

The Conquest of the Persian Empire The Persian Empire was vast and its resources enormous. The usurper Cyrus and his Greek mercenaries, however, had shown it to be vulnerable when they penetrated deep into its interior in the fourth century B.C.E. Its size and disparate nature made it hard to control and exploit. Its rulers faced constant troubles on its far-flung frontiers and intrigues within the royal palace. Throughout the fourth century, they had used Greek mercenaries to suppress uprisings. At the time of Philip II's death in 336 B.C.E., a new and inexperienced king, Darius III, was ruling Persia. Yet with a navy that dominated the sea, a huge army, and vast wealth, it remained a formidable opponent.

In 334 B.C.E., Alexander crossed the Hellespont into Asia. His army consisted of about 30,000 infantry and 5,000 cavalry; he had no navy and little money. These facts determined his early strategy—he must seek quick and decisive battles to gain money and supplies from the conquered territory, and he must move along the coast to neutralize the Persian navy by depriving it of ports.

Alexander met the Persian forces of Asia Minor at the Granicus River, where he won a smashing victory in characteristic style. (See Map 3–3, page 82.) He led a cavalry charge across the river into the teeth of the enemy on the opposite bank. He almost lost his life in the process, but he won the devotion of his soldiers. That victory left the coast of Asia Minor open. Alexander captured the coastal cities, thus denying them to the Persian fleet.

In 333 B.C.E., Alexander marched inland to Syria, where he met the main Persian army under King Darius at Issus. Alexander himself led the cavalry charge that broke the Persian line and sent Darius fleeing into central Asia Minor. He continued along the coast and captured previously impregnable Tyre after a long and ingenious siege, putting an end to the threat of the Persian navy. He took Egypt with little trouble and was greeted as liberator, pharaoh, and son of Re (an Egyptian god whose Greek equivalent was Zeus). At Tyre, Darius sent Alexander a peace offer, yielding his entire empire west of the Euphrates River and his daughter in exchange for an alliance and an end to the invasion. But Alexander aimed at conquering the whole empire and probably whatever lay beyond.

In the spring of 331 B.C.E., Alexander marched into Mesopotamia. At Gaugamela, near the ancient Assyrian city of Nineveh, he met Darius, ready for a last stand. Once again, Alexander's tactical genius and personal leadership carried the day. The Persians were broken, and Darius fled once more. Alexander entered Babylon, again hailed as liberator and king.

MAP EXPLORATION

Interactive map: To explore this map further, go to www.myhistorylab.com

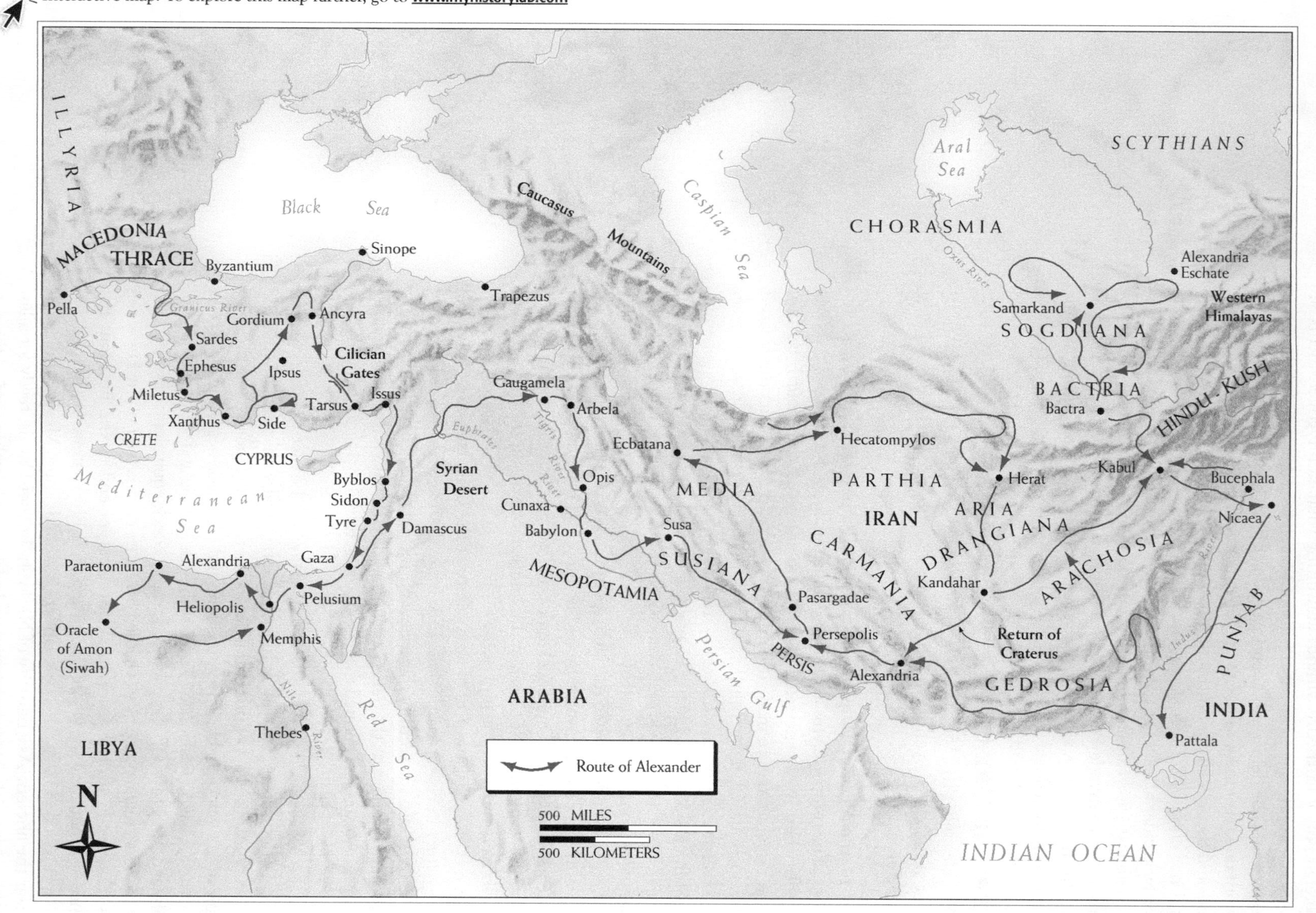

MAP 3–3 Alexander's Campaigns The route taken by Alexander the Great in his conquest of the Persian Empire, 334 to 323 B.C.E. Starting from the Macedonian capital at Pella, he reached the Indus Valley before being turned back by his own restive troops. He died of fever in Mesopotamia.

Before crossing into Mesopotamia, what considerations determined Alexander's route? Was his aim merely to defeat the Persians?

In January 330 B.C.E., he came to Persepolis, the Persian capital, which held splendid palaces and the royal treasury. This bonanza ended his financial troubles and put a vast sum of money into circulation, with economic consequences that lasted for centuries. After a stay of several months, Alexander burned Persepolis to dramatize the destruction of the native Persian dynasty and the completion of Hellenic revenge for the earlier Persian invasion of Greece.

The new regime could not be secure while Darius lived, so Alexander pursued him eastward. Just south of the Caspian Sea, he came on the corpse of Darius, killed by his relative Bessus. The Persian nobles around Darius had lost faith in him and had joined in the plot. The murder removed Darius from Alexander's path, but now he had to catch Bessus, who proclaimed himself successor to Darius. The pursuit of Bessus (who was soon caught), combined with his own great curiosity and longing to go to the most distant places, took Alexander to the frontier of India.

In 327 B.C.E., Alexander took his army through the Khyber Pass in an attempt to conquer the lands around the Indus River (modern Pakistan). He reduced the king of these lands, Porus, to vassalage but pushed on in the hope of reaching the river called Ocean that the Greeks believed encircled the world. Finally, his weary men refused to go on. By the spring of 324 B.C.E., the army was back at the Persian Gulf and celebrated in the Macedonian style, with a wild spree of drinking.

The Death of Alexander Alexander was filled with plans for the future: for the consolidation and organization of his empire; for geographical exploration; for building new cities, roads, and harbors; and perhaps for further conquests in the west. There is even some evidence that he asked to be deified and worshipped as a god, although we cannot be sure if he really did so or why. In June 323 B.C.E., however, he was overcome by a fever and died in Babylon at the age of thirty-three. His memory has never faded, and he soon became the subject of myth, legend, and romance. From the beginning, estimates of him have varied. Some have seen in him a man of grand and noble vision who transcended the narrow limits of Greek and Macedonian ethnocentrism and sought to realize the solidarity of humankind in a great world state. Others have seen him as a calculating despot, given to drunken brawls, brutality, and murder.

The truth is probably somewhere in between. Alexander was one of the greatest generals the world has seen; he never lost a battle or failed in a siege, and with a modest army he conquered a vast empire. He had rare organizational talents, and his plan for creating a multinational empire was the only intelligent way to consolidate his conquests. He established many new cities—seventy, according to tradition—mostly along trade routes. These cities encouraged commerce and prosperity and introduced Hellenic civilization into new areas. It is hard to know if even Alexander could have held together the vast new empire he had created, but his death proved that only he would have had a chance to succeed.

The Successors

Nobody was prepared for Alexander's sudden death, and a weak succession further complicated affairs. His able and loyal Macedonian generals at first hoped to preserve the empire for the Macedonian royal house, and to this end they appointed themselves governors of the various provinces of the empire. The conflicting ambitions of these strong-willed men, however, led to prolonged warfare among them. In these conflicts three of the original number were killed, and all of the direct members of the Macedonian royal house were either executed or murdered. In 306 and 305 B.C.E., the surviving governors proclaimed themselves kings of their various holdings.

Three of these Macedonian generals founded dynasties of significance in the spread of Hellenistic culture:

- Ptolemy I, 367–283 B.C.E.; founder of Dynasty 31 in Egypt, the Ptolemies, of whom Cleopatra, who died in 30 B.C.E., was the last
- Seleucus I, 358–280 B.C.E.; founder of the Seleucid Dynasty in Mesopotamia
- Antigonus I, 382–301 B.C.E.; founder of the Antigonid Dynasty in Asia Minor and Macedon

For the first 75 years or so after the death of Alexander, the world ruled by his successors enjoyed considerable prosperity. The vast sums of money that he and they put into circulation greatly increased the level of economic activity. The opportunities for service and profit in the East attracted many Greeks and relieved their native cities of some of the pressure of the poor. The opening of vast new territories to Greek trade, the increased demand for Greek products, and the new availability of desired goods, as well as the conscious policies of the Hellenistic kings, all helped the growth of commerce.

The new prosperity, however, was not evenly distributed. The urban Greeks, the Macedonians, and the Hellenized natives who made up the upper and middle classes lived in comfort and even luxury, but the rural native peasants did not. Unlike the independent men who owned and worked the relatively small and equal lots of the *polis* in earlier times, Hellenistic farmers were reduced to subordinate, dependent peasant status, working on large plantations of decreasing efficiency. During prosperous times these distinctions were bearable, although even then there was tension between the two groups. After a while, however, the costs of continuing wars, inflation, and a gradual lessening of the positive effects of the introduction of Persian wealth all led to economic crisis. The kings bore down heavily on the middle classes, who were skilled at avoiding their responsibilities, however. The pressure on the peasants and the city laborers became great too, and they responded by slowing down their work and even by striking. In Greece, economic pressures brought clashes between rich and poor, demands for the abolition of debt and the redistribution of land, and even, on occasion, civil war.

These internal divisions, along with international wars, weakened the capacity of the Hellenistic kingdoms to resist outside attack. By the middle of the second century B.C.E., they had all, except for Egypt, succumbed to an expanding Italian power, Rome. The two centuries between Alexander and the Roman conquest, however, were of great and lasting importance. They saw the entire eastern Mediterranean coast, Greece, Egypt, Mesopotamia, and the old Persian Empire formed into a single political, economic, and cultural unit.

HELLENISTIC CULTURE

HOW DID Hellenistic culture differ from the culture of Classical Greece?

The career of Alexander the Great marked a significant turning point in Greek thought as it was represented in literature, philosophy, religion, and art. His conquests and the establishment of the successor kingdoms put an end to the central role of the *polis* in Greek life and thought. Deprived of control of their foreign affairs, and with a foreign monarch determining their important internal arrangements, the post-Classical cities lost the political freedom that was basic to the old outlook. They were cities, perhaps—in a sense, even city-states—but not *poleis*. As time passed, they changed from sovereign states to municipal towns merged into military empires. Never again in antiquity would there be either a serious attack on or defense of the *polis*, for its importance was gone. For the most part, the Greeks after Alexander turned away from political solutions for their problems. Instead, they sought personal responses to their hopes and fears, particularly in religion, philosophy, and magic. The confident, sometimes arrogant, humanism of the fifth century B.C.E. gave way to a kind of resignation to fate, a recognition of helplessness before forces too great for humans to manage.

PHILOSOPHY

These developments are noticeable in the changes that overtook the established schools of philosophy as well as in the emergence of two new and influential groups of philosophers: the Epicureans and the Stoics. Athens's position as the center of philosophical studies was reinforced, for the Academy and the Lyceum continued in operation, and the new schools were also located in Athens. The Lyceum turned gradually away from the universal investigations of its founder, Aristotle, even from his scientific interests, to become a center chiefly of literary and especially historical studies.

The Academy turned even further away from its tradition. It adopted the systematic Skepticism of Pyrrho of Elis. Under the leadership of Arcesilaus and Carneades, the Skeptics of the Academy became skilled at pointing out fallacies and weaknesses in the philosophies of the rival schools. They thought that nothing could be known and so consoled themselves and their followers by suggesting that nothing mattered. It was easy for them, therefore, to accept conventional morality and the world as it was.

One of the masterpieces of Hellenistic sculpture, the *Laocoön*. This is a Roman copy. According to legend, Laocoön was a priest who warned the Trojans not to take the Greeks' wooden horse within their city. This sculpture depicts his punishment. Great serpents sent by the goddess Athena, who was on the side of the Greeks, devoured Laocoön and his sons before the horrified people of Troy.

Direzione Generale Musei Vaticani

How does the sculpture reflect the attitudes and anxieties of Hellenistic Greeks?

The Epicureans Epicurus of Athens (342–271 B.C.E.) formulated a new teaching, embodied in the school he founded in his native city in 306 B.C.E. His philosophy conformed to the mood of the times in that its goal was not knowledge, but human happiness, which he believed a style of life based on reason could achieve. He took sense perception to be the basis of all human knowledge. The reality and reliability of sense perception rested on the acceptance of the physical universe described by the atomists, Democritus and Leucippus. The **Epicureans** proclaimed atoms were continually falling through the void and giving off images that were in direct contact with the senses. These falling atoms could swerve in an arbitrary, unpredictable way to produce the combinations seen in the world.

Epicurus thereby removed an element of determinism that existed in the Democritean system. When a person died, the atoms that composed the body dispersed so the person had no further existence or perception and therefore nothing to fear after death. Epicurus believed the gods existed, but that they took no interest in human affairs. This belief amounted to a practical atheism, and Epicureans were often thought to be atheists.

Epicureans People who believed the proper pursuit of humankind is undisturbed withdrawal from the world.

The purpose of Epicurean physics was to liberate people from their fear of death, of the gods, and of all nonmaterial or supernatural powers. Epicurean ethics were hedonistic, that is, based on the acceptance of pleasure as true happiness. But pleasure for Epicurus was chiefly negative: the absence of pain and trouble. The goal of the Epicureans was *ataraxia*, the condition of being undisturbed, without trouble, pain, or responsibility. Ideally, a man should have enough means to allow him to withdraw from the world and avoid business and public life. Epicurus even advised against marriage and children. He preached a life of genteel, restrained selfishness that might appeal to intellectual men of means but was not calculated to be widely attractive.

The Stoics Soon after Epicurus began teaching in his garden in Athens, Zeno of Citium in Cyprus (335–263 B.C.E.) established the Stoic school. Like the Epicureans, the **Stoics**

Stoics People who sought freedom from passion and harmony with nature.

sought the happiness of the individual. Quite unlike them, the Stoics proposed a philosophy almost indistinguishable from religion. They believed humans must live in harmony within themselves and with nature; for the Stoics, God and nature were the same. The guiding principle in nature was divine reason (*Logos*), or fire. Every human had a spark of this divinity, and after death it returned to the eternal divine spirit. From time to time the world was destroyed by fire, from which a new world arose.

The aim of humans, and the definition of human happiness, was the virtuous life: a life lived in accordance with natural law. To live such a life required the knowledge only the wise possessed. They knew what was good, what was evil, and what was neither, but "indifferent." According to the Stoics, good and evil were dispositions of the mind or soul: prudence, justice, courage, temperance, and so on, were good, whereas folly, injustice, cowardice, and the like, were evil. Life, health, pleasure, beauty, strength, wealth, and so on, were neutral—morally indifferent—for they did not contribute either to happiness or to misery. Human misery came from an irrational mental contraction—from passion, which was a disease of the soul. The wise sought *apatheia*, or freedom from passion, because passion arose from things that were morally indifferent.

Politically, the Stoics fit well into the new world. They thought of it as a single *polis* in which all people were children of the same God. Although they did not forbid political activity, and many Stoics took part in political life, withdrawal was obviously preferable because the usual subjects of political argument were indifferent. Because the Stoics strove for inner harmony of the individual, their aim was a life lived in accordance with the divine will, their attitude fatalistic, and their goal a form of apathy. They fit in well with the reality of post–Alexandrian life. In fact, Stoicism facilitated the task of creating a new political system that relied not on the active participation of the governed, but merely on their docile submission.

Literature

Hellenistic literature reflects the new intellectual currents, the new conditions of literary life, and the new institutions created in that period. The center of literary production in the third and second centuries B.C.E. was the new city of Alexandria in Egypt. There the Ptolemies, the monarchs of Egypt during that time, founded the museum—a great research institute where royal funds supported scientists and scholars—and the library, which contained almost half a million papyrus scrolls.

The library contained much of the great body of past Greek literature, most of which has since been lost. The Alexandrian scholars made copies of what they judged to be the best works. They edited and criticized these works from the point of view of language, form, and content, and wrote biographies of the authors. Their work is responsible for the preservation of most of what remains to us of ancient literature.

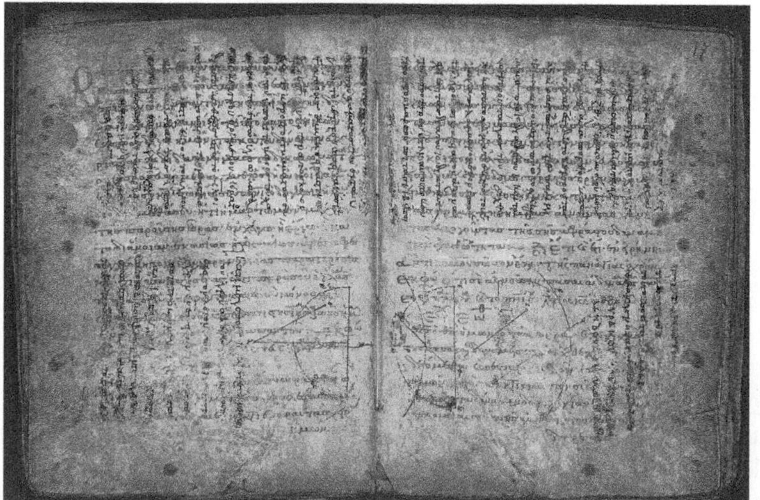

The Archimedes Palimpsest A page from *On Floating Bodies.*

What contributions did Hellenistic thinkers make to mathematics and science?

Architecture and Sculpture

The advent of the Hellenistic monarchies greatly increased the opportunities open to architects and sculptors. Money was plentiful, rulers sought outlets for conspicuous display, new cities needed to be built and beautified, and the well-to-do wanted objects of art.

The new cities were usually laid out on the grid plan introduced in the fifth century B.C.E. by Hippodamus of Miletus. Temples were built on the classical model, and the covered portico, or *stoa*, became a popular addition to the *agoras* of the Hellenistic towns.

Reflecting the cosmopolitan nature of the Hellenistic world, leading sculptors accepted commissions wherever they were attractive. The result was a certain uniformity of style, although Alexandria, Rhodes, and the kingdom of Pergamum in Asia Minor developed their own distinctive characteristics. For the most part, Hellenistic sculpture moved away from the balanced tension and idealism of the fifth century B.C.E. toward the sentimental, emotional, and realistic mode of the fourth century B.C.E. These qualities are readily apparent in the marble statue called the *Laocoön*, carved at Rhodes in the second century B.C.E. and afterward taken to Rome.

Mathematics and Science

Among the most spectacular and remarkable intellectual developments of the Hellenistic Age were those that came in mathematics and science. The burst of activity in these subjects drew their inspiration from several sources. The stimulation and organization provided by the work of Plato and Aristotle should not be ignored. Alexander's interest in science, evidenced by the scientists he took with him on his expedition and the aid he gave them in collecting data, provided further impetus.

The expansion of Greek horizons geographically and the consequent contacts with Egyptian and Babylonian knowledge were also helpful. Finally, the patronage of the Ptolemies and the opportunity for many scientists to work with one another at the museum at Alexandria provided a unique opportunity for scientific work. The work the Alexandrians did formed the greater part of the scientific knowledge available to the Western world until the scientific revolution of the sixteenth and seventeenth centuries C.E.

Euclid's *Elements* (written early in the third century B.C.E.) remained the textbook of plane and solid geometry until recent times. Archimedes of Syracuse (ca. 287–212 B.C.E.) made further progress in geometry, established the theory of the lever in mechanics, and invented hydrostatics.

These advances in mathematics, once they were applied to the Babylonian astronomical tables available to the Hellenistic world, spurred great progress in astronomy. As early as the fourth century B.C.E., Heraclides of Pontus (ca. 390–310 B.C.E.) had argued that Mercury and Venus circulate around the sun and not Earth. He appears to have made other suggestions leading to a heliocentric theory of the universe. Most scholars, however, give credit for that theory to Aristarchus of Samos (ca. 310–230 B.C.E.), who asserted that the sun, along with the other fixed stars, did not move and that Earth revolved around the sun in a circular orbit and rotated on its axis while doing so. The heliocentric theory ran contrary not only to the traditional view codified by Aristotle, but also to what seemed to be common sense.

Hellenistic scientists mapped the earth as well as the sky. Eratosthenes of Cyrene (ca. 275–195 B.C.E.) calculated the circumference of Earth to within about 200 miles. He wrote a treatise on geography based on mathematical and physical reasoning and the reports of travelers. Despite the new data that were available to later geographers, Eratosthenes' map was in many ways more accurate than the one Ptolemy of Alexandria constructed, which became standard in the Middle Ages.

The Hellenistic Age contributed little to the life sciences, such as biology, zoology, and medicine. Even the sciences that had such impressive achievements to show in the third century B.C.E. made little progress thereafter. In fact, to some extent, there was a retreat from science. Astrology and magic became subjects of great interest as scientific advance lagged.

SUMMARY

WHAT LED to the foundation of the Delian League?

Aftermath of Victory The tenuous unity the Greeks had shown while fighting against the Persians disintegrated. Sparta and Athens emerged as leaders of two spheres of influence. Sparta was uninterested in continued aggression against Persia. The Athenians and the Ionians shared an interest in driving the Persians out of the Aegean region; with others, they formed the Delian League under Athenian leadership. *page 60*

WHAT WAS the cause of the Peloponnesian War, and what was the end result?

The First Peloponnesian War: Athens Against Sparta Pericles led a democratic, but aggressive, Athens. The Peloponnesian Wars were the manifestation of the conflict between Sparta and Athens. After an initial victory, Athens seemed almost invincible, but soon military defeat abroad and rebellion at home weakened Athens so much that Sparta invaded. Pericles agreed to a thirty peace, abandoning all Athenian possessions on the Greek mainland outside of Attica, but gaining Spartan recognition of the Athenian Empire. *page 61*

HOW DID democracy work in fifth-century B.C.E. Athens?

Classical Greece Athenian government had become more democratic than any previous political system. All male citizens gained important rights, regardless of their property class. The official status of women was severely circumscribed, both in public and in private. Greek art, drama, and mythology suggest that women may have had more freedom and power than a strict reading of the documentary evidence would allow. Before around 500 B.C.E. there was little chattel slavery in Greece—although serfdom and bond slavery were more or less common in various times and places—but later war captives and other foreigners were held as chattel slaves. Slaves worked in agriculture, industry, and households and served as shepherds, policemen, and secretaries. Most Athenians did not own any slaves, and those who did generally owned only a few. *page 63*

HOW DID the Peloponnesian War affect the faith in the *polis*?

The Great Peloponnesian War The Thirty Years' Peace of 445 B.C.E. lasted just over ten years, until a conflict between Corcyra and Corinth drew in their allies, Athens and Sparta, respectively. Sparta violated a clause of the peace that required arbitration of all disagreements between Athens and Sparta, and instead, in 431 B.C.E., invaded Attica. The outnumbered Athenians followed a daring strategy and won an important victory in 425 B.C.E. After a mix of victories and defeats, both sides signed the Peace of Nicias in 421 B.C.E. This peace, too, was short-lived; this time the Athenians were the aggressors, against Sicily, in a disastrous 415 B.C.E. expedition that brought the Persians into the war on Sparta's side. The Athenians fought on, however, until 404 B.C.E., when they surrendered unconditionally. *page 69*

HOW DID Athens and Sparta compete for leadership in the Greek world?

Competition for Leadership in the Fourth Century B.C.E. After defeating Athens, Sparta had a golden opportunity to claim leadership, but Spartan arrogance—among other problems—caused their allies the Persians to turn against them. Theban victory at Leuctra in 371 B.C.E. brought an end to Spartan hegemony. But Theban dominance was short-lived, ending in 362 B.C.E. in a defeat at the hands of the Athenians. Athens, however, repeated many of the same mistakes that had cost it allies in the Delian League, and by 355 B.C.E., Athens again had to abandon most of its empire. Greece descended into chaos. *page 71*

WHAT ARE the achievements of Classical Greece?

The Culture of Classical Greece Classical Greece produced dramas, architecture and sculpture, and philosophical and historical works. The Golden Age of Athens, between the Persian and Peloponnesian Wars, is epitomized by Attic tragedy, including the works of Aeschylus, Sophocles, and Euripedes. The buildings of the Acropolis are the product of Athenian religious and civic sensibility and individual artistry and achievement. Philosophy continued to explore questions about the natural world. Herodotus and Thucydides wrote histories that are models of the genre. Sociopolitical changes brought about by the Peloponnesian War were reflected in drama and sculpture, especially in the philosophical traditions of Socrates, Plato, and Aristotle. *page 72*

WHO WAS Alexander the Great and what was his legacy?

The Hellenistic World Greek culture mixed with Middle Eastern elements and spread throughout the eastern

Mediterranean, Egypt, and far into Asia. This Hellenistic world was largely the result of military conquests by a short-lived, father-and-son Macedonian dynasty. Philip of Macedon introduced tactical innovations into the Macedonian army, and he coupled military force with diplomacy to conquer Greece. In 336 B.C.E., Philip was assassinated and succeeded by his son Alexander. Alexander led his troops to victory in Persia, Egypt, Mesopotamia, and as far as what is now Pakistan. After his death, three of Alexander's generals founded significant dynasties that helped spread Hellenism in Egypt, Mesopotamia, and Asia Minor. Within Greece, class conflict and other internal divisions were exacerbated by the new wealth Alexander's conquests had brought to the region. *page 79*

HOW DID Hellenistic culture differ from the culture of Classical Greece?

Hellenistic Culture The true *polis* was destroyed by the Macedonian invasion. Greeks turned from the political to the personal. In Athenian philosophy, the Epicureans (whose goal was hedonistic human happiness) and Stoics (who sought happiness through harmony and freedom from passion) gained prominence. Hellenistic Alexandria fostered literature and humanistic scholarship. Hellenistic styles in architecture and sculpture diffused over a wide area. Mathematics and science—especially astronomy—blossomed. *page 84*

REVIEW QUESTIONS

1. What caused the Great Peloponnesian War? What strategies did Athens and Sparta hope would bring them victory? Why did Sparta win?
2. What were the tensions that characterized Greek life in the Classical Period, and how were they reflected in its art, literature, and philosophy? How does Hellenistic art differ from art of the Classical Period?
3. How and why did Philip II conquer Greece? Why was Athens unable to stop him? Was his success due to Macedon's strength or to the weaknesses of the Greek city-states?
4. What were the consequences of Alexander the Great's early death? What were his lasting achievements? Did he consciously promote Greek civilization, or was he only an egomaniac devoted to endless conquest?
5. What were the most significant elements that made up Hellenistic civilization and culture?

KEY TERMS

Academy (p. 76)
Delian League (p. 61)
Epicureans (p. 85)
Hellenistic (p. 79)
Lyceum (p. 78)
Peloponnesian Wars (p. 62)
Stoics (p. 85)

For additional learning resources related to this chapter, please go to **www.myhistorylab.com**

4

Rome: From Republic to Empire

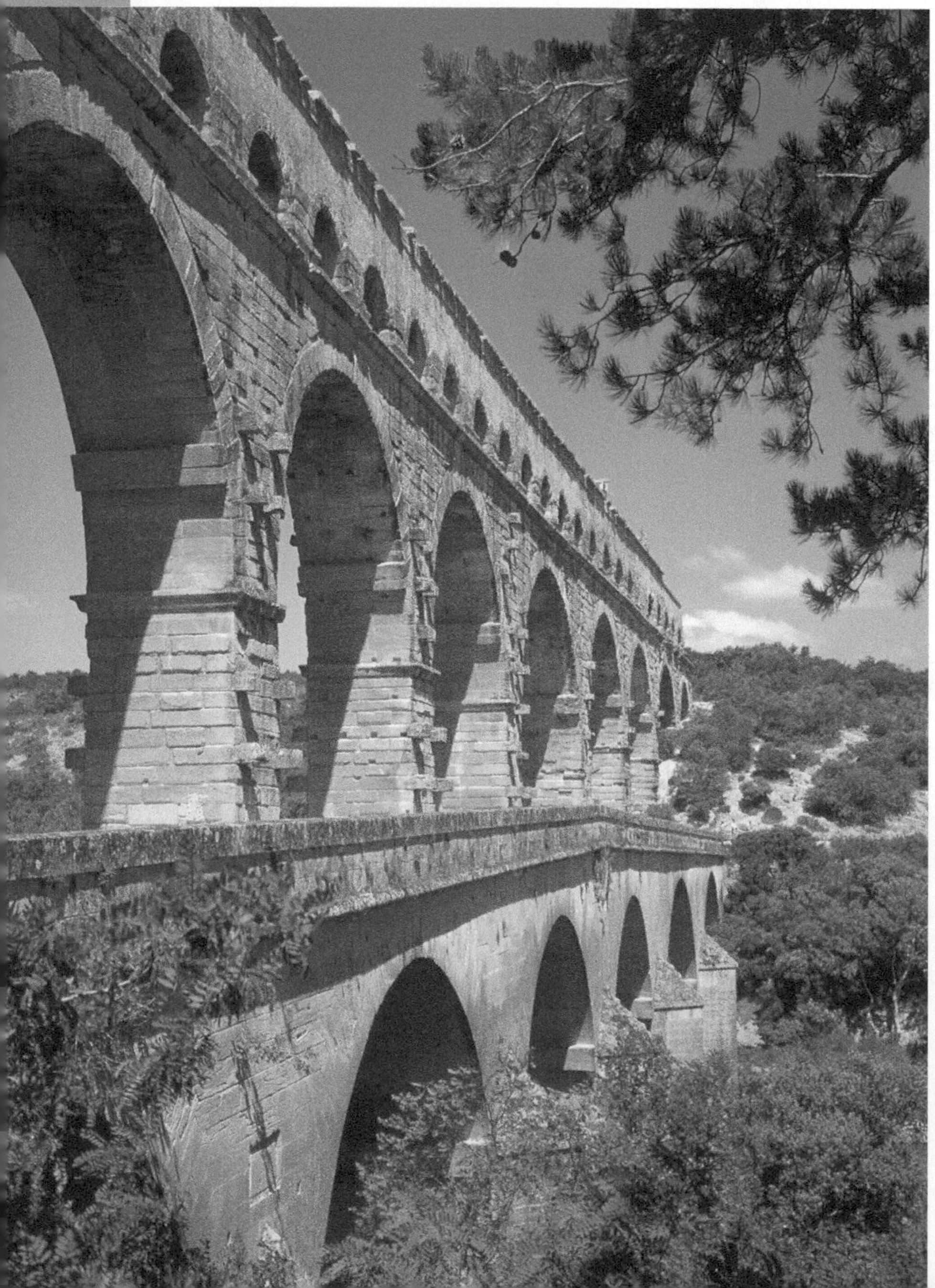

The Pont du Gard, an aqueduct and bridge, was built in the first century B.C.E. in southern France in Rome's first province beyond the Alps.

Walter S. Clark/Photo Researchers, Inc.

How did the Romans use their engineering prowess to help bind together their growing empire?

THE ETRUSCANS *page 92*

WHO WERE the Etruscans and how did they influence Rome?

ROYAL ROME *page 93*

HOW DID ideas about the family influence society and government in early Rome?

THE REPUBLIC *page 95*

WHAT ROLE did consuls, the Senate, and the Assembly play in Republican government?

CIVILIZATION IN THE EARLY ROMAN REPUBLIC *page 103*

HOW DID contact with the Hellenistic world affect Rome?

ROMAN IMPERIALISM: THE LATE REPUBLIC *page 105*

HOW DID the expansion of Rome change the Republic?

THE FALL OF THE REPUBLIC *page 109*

WHAT EVENTS led to the fall of the Republic?

he Romans started with a small village in central Italy and went on to unite the peoples of the Western world and sustain the longest period of peace in Western history. By adopting Hellenistic culture and spreading it through their empire, they laid a universal Graeco-Roman foundation for Western civilization. The effects of their achievement are still being felt.

PREHISTORIC ITALY

The culture of Italy developed late. Paleolithic settlements gave way to the Neolithic mode of life only around 2500 B.C.E. The Bronze Age came around 1500 B.C.E. About 1000 B.C.E., bands of new arrivals—warlike peoples speaking a set of closely related languages we call *Italic*—began to infiltrate Italy from across the Adriatic Sea and around its northern end. By 800 B.C.E., they occupied the highland pastures of the Apennines, and within a short time, they began to challenge the earlier settlers for control of the tempting western plains. It would be the descendants of these tough mountain people—Umbrians, Sabines, Samnites, and Latins—together with others soon to arrive—Etruscans, Greeks, and Celts—who would shape the future of Italy.

THE ETRUSCANS

WHO WERE the Etruscans and how did they influence Rome?

The Etruscans exerted the most powerful external influence on the Romans. Their civilization arose in Etruria (now Tuscany), west of the Apennines between the Arno and Tiber Rivers, about 800 B.C.E. (See Map 4–1.)

GOVERNMENT

The Etruscans brought civilization with them. Their settlements were self-governing, fortified city-states, of which twelve formed a loose religious confederation. At first, kings ruled these cities, but they were replaced by an agrarian aristocracy, which ruled through a council and elected annual magistrates. The Etruscans were a military ruling

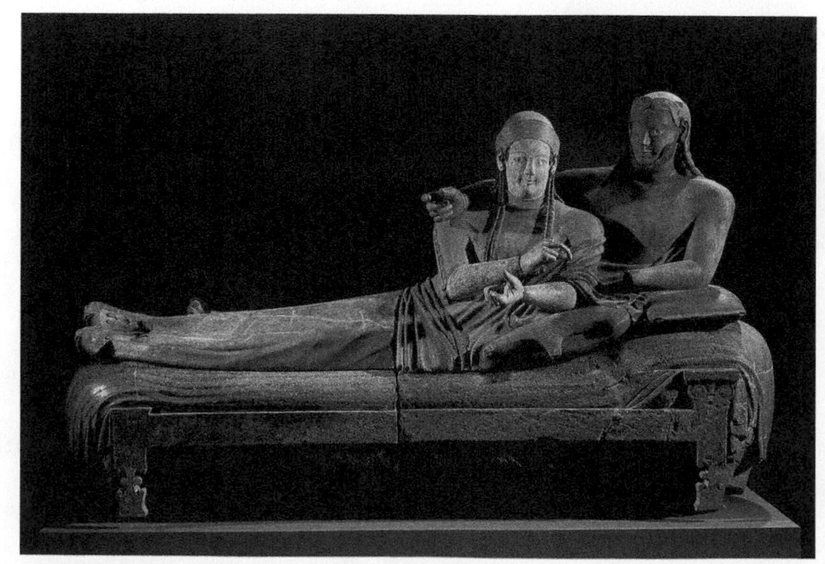

Much of what we know of the Etruscans comes from their funery art. This sculpture of an Etruscan couple is part of a sarcophagus.

Sarcophagus of a Couple. Etruscan, 6th B.C.E. Terracotta. H: 114 cm. Louvre, Paris, France. Copyright Erich Lessing/Art Resource, NY

What contributions did the Etruscans make to Roman culture?

MAP 4–1 Ancient Italy This map of ancient Italy and its neighbors before the expansion of Rome shows major cities and towns as well as several geographical regions and the locations of some of the Italic and non-Italic peoples.

Why, geographically, was Rome ideal to become the center for Italy's inland communication and trade?

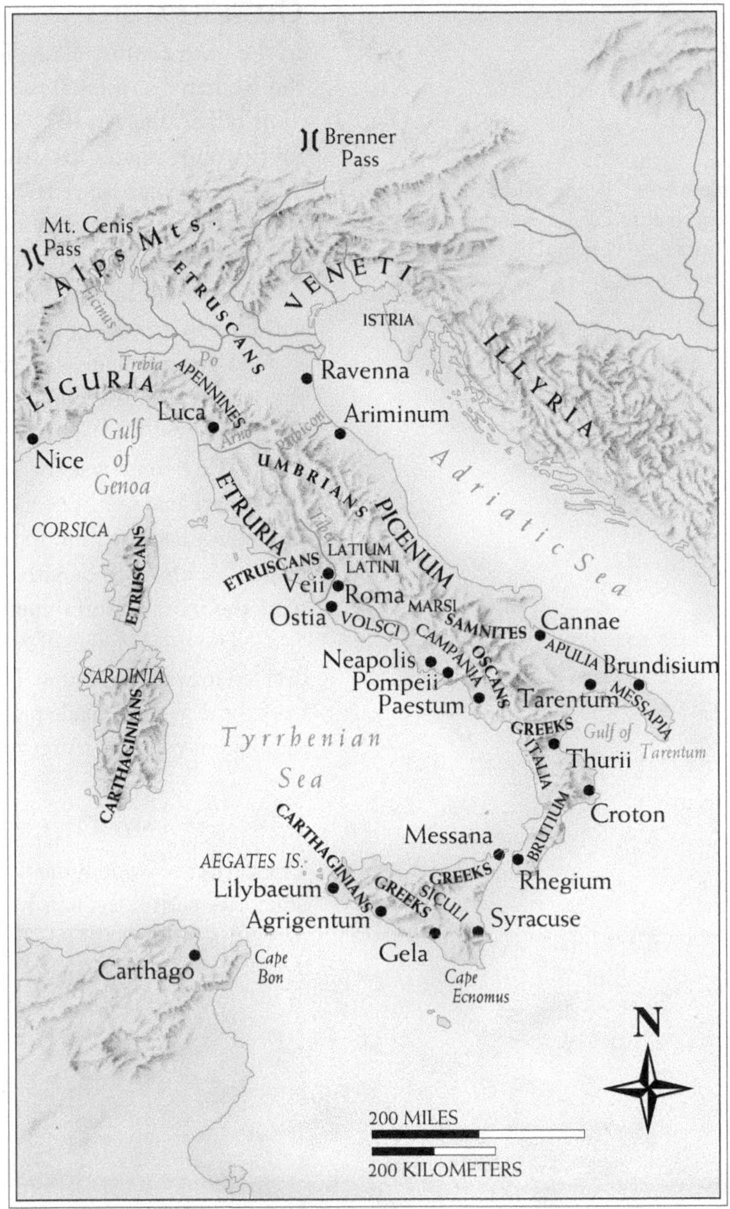

class that exploited the native Italians (the predecessors of the later Italic speakers), who worked the Etruscans' land and mines and served as infantry in Etruscan armies. This aristocracy accumulated wealth through agriculture, industry, piracy, and commerce with the Carthaginians and the Greeks.

Religion

The Etruscans' influence on the Romans was greatest in religion. They imagined a world filled with gods and spirits, many of them evil. To deal with such demons, the Etruscans developed complicated rituals and powerful priesthoods. Divination by sacrifice and omens in nature helped discover the divine will, and careful attention to precise rituals directed by priests helped please the gods. After a while the Etruscans, influenced by the Greeks, worshipped gods in the shape of humans and built temples for them.

Dominion

In the seventh and sixth centuries B.C.E., the Etruscan aristocracy expanded their power in Italy and across the sea to Corsica and Elba. They conquered **Latium** (a region that included the small town of Rome) and Campania, where they became neighbors of the Greeks of Naples. In the north, they got as far as the Po Valley. Etruscan power reached its height some time before 500 B.C.E. and then rapidly declined. About 400 B.C.E., Celtic peoples from the area the Romans called **Gaul** (modern France) broke into the Po Valley and drove out the Etruscans. Eventually, even the Etruscan heartland in Etruria lost its independence and was incorporated into Roman Italy.

Latium Region located in present-day Italy that included the small town of Rome.

Gaul Area that is now modern France.

ROYAL ROME

HOW DID ideas about the family influence society and government in early Rome?

Rome was an unimportant town in Latium until the Etruscans conquered it, but its location—fifteen miles from the mouth of the Tiber River at the point at which hills made further navigation impossible—gave it advantages over its Latin neighbors. The island in the Tiber southwest of the Capitoline Hill made the river fordable, so Rome was naturally a center for communication and trade, both east-west and north-south.

GOVERNMENT

In the sixth century B.C.E., Rome came under Etruscan control. Led by Etruscan kings, the Roman army, equipped and organized like the Greek phalanx, gained control of most of Latium. An effective political and social order that gave extraordinary power to the ruling figures in both public and private life made this success possible. To their kings the Romans gave the awesome power of ***imperium***—the right to issue commands and to enforce them by fines, arrests, and corporal, or even capital, punishment. Although it tended apparently to remain in the same family, kingship was elective. The Roman Senate had to approve the candidate for the office, and a vote of the people gathered in an assembly formally granted the *imperium*. A basic characteristic of later Roman government—the granting of great power to executive officers contingent on the approval of the Senate and, ultimately, the people—was already apparent in this structure.

imperium Right held by a Roman king to enforce commands by fines, arrests, and corporal and capital punishment.

The Senate was the second branch of the early Roman government. Ostensibly, the Senate had neither executive nor legislative power; it met only when the king summoned it to advise him. In reality its authority was great, for the senators, like the king, served for life. The Senate, therefore, had continuity and experience, and its members were the most powerful men in the state.

The third branch of government, the curiate assembly, was made up of all citizens, as divided into thirty groups. The assembly met only when the king summoned it; he determined the agenda, made proposals, and recognized other speakers, if any. Usually, the assembly was called to listen and approve.

FAMILY AND GENDER IN EARLY ROME

The center of Roman life was the family. At its head stood the father, whose power and authority within the family resembled those of the king within the state. Over his children, the father held broad powers analogous to *imperium* in the state. The father was also the chief priest of the family.

Thus, early Roman society was hierarchical and dominated by males. Throughout her life, a woman was under the control of some adult male. Before her marriage it was her father, afterward her husband or, when neither was available, a guardian chosen from one of her male relatives. Nonetheless, women of the upper classes had a position of influence and respect greater than the classical Greeks. Just as the husband was *paterfamilias*, the wife was *materfamilias*. She was mistress within the home, controlling access to the storerooms, keeping the accounts, and supervising the slaves and the raising of the children. She also was part of the family council and a respected adviser on all questions concerning the family.

Busts of a Roman couple, from the period of the Republic. Although some have identified the individuals as Cato the Younger and his daughter Porcia, no solid evidence confirms this claim.

Bust of Cato and Porcia. Roman sculpture. Vatican Museums, Vatican State. Photograph © Scala/Art Resource, NY

How did the Romans view the relationship between husband and wife?

CLIENTAGE

Clientage was one of Rome's most important institutions. The patron provided his client with protection, both physical and legal. He gave him economic assistance in the form of a land grant, the opportunity to work as a tenant farmer or a laborer on the patron's land, or simply hand-

Overview The Rise of the Plebeians to Equality in Rome

509 B.C.E.	Kings expelled; republic founded
450–449 B.C.E.	Laws of the Twelve Tables published
445 B.C.E.	Plebeians gain right of marriage with patricians
367 B.C.E.	Licinian-Sextian Laws open consulship to plebeians
300 B.C.E.	Plebeians attain chief priesthoods
287 B.C.E.	Laws passed by plebeian assembly made binding on all Romans

outs. In return, the client would fight for his patron, work his land, and support him politically. Public opinion and tradition reinforced these mutual obligations.

In the early history of Rome, patrons were rich and powerful, whereas clients were poor and weak, but as time passed, rich and powerful members of the upper classes became clients of even more powerful men, chiefly for political purposes. Because the client-patron relationship was hereditary and sanctioned by religion and custom, it played an important part in the life of the Roman Republic.

Patricians and Plebeians

In the royal period, a class distinction based on birth divided Roman society in two. The wealthy **patrician** upper class held a monopoly of power and influence. Its members alone could conduct state religious ceremonies, sit in the Senate, or hold office. They formed a closed caste by forbidding marriage outside their own group.

patricians Upper class of Roman families that originally monopolized all political authority. Only they could serve as priests, senators, and magistrates.

The **plebeian** lower class must have consisted originally of poor, dependent small farmers, laborers, and artisans, the clients of the nobility. As Rome and its population grew, families that were rich, but outside the charmed circle of patricians, grew wealthy. From early times, therefore, there were rich plebeians, and incompetence and bad luck must have produced some poor patricians. The line between the classes and the monopoly of privileges remained firm, nevertheless, and the struggle of the plebeians to gain equality occupied more than two centuries of republican history.

plebeians Commoner class of Roman families, usually families of small farmers, laborers, and artisans who were early clients of the patricians.

THE REPUBLIC

WHAT ROLE did consuls, the Senate, and the Assembly play in Republican government?

Roman tradition tells us that the outrageous behavior of the last kings led the noble families to revolt in 509 B.C.E., bringing the monarchy to a sudden close and leading to the creation of the Roman Republic.

Constitution

The Consuls The Roman constitution was an unwritten accumulation of laws and customs. The Romans were a conservative people and were never willing to deprive their chief magistrates of the great powers the monarchs had exercised. They elected two patricians to the office of consul and endowed them with *imperium*. Two financial officials called *quaestors*, whose number ultimately reached eight, assisted them. Like the

consuls Elected magistrates from patrician families chosen annually to lead the army, oversee the state religion, and sit as judges.

kings, the **consuls** led the army, had religious duties, and served as judges. The power of the consuls, however, was limited legally and institutionally as well as by custom.

The power of the consulship was granted not for life, but only for a year. Each consul could prevent any action by his colleague simply by saying no to his proposal, and the consuls shared their religious powers with others. Even the *imperium* was limited. Although the consuls had full powers of life and death while leading an army, within the sacred boundary of the city of Rome, the citizens had the right to appeal all cases involving capital punishment to the popular assembly.

The many checks on consular action tended to prevent initiative, swift action, and change, but this was just what a conservative, traditional, aristocratic republic wanted. Only in the military sphere did divided counsel and a short term of office create important problems. The Romans tried to get around the difficulties by sending only one consul into the field or, when this was impossible, allowing each consul sole command on alternate days. In serious crises, the consuls, with the advice of the Senate, could appoint a *dictator* to the command and could retire in his favor. The *dictator*'s term of office was limited to six months, but his own *imperium* was valid both inside and outside the city without appeal.

proconsulships Extension of terms for consuls who had important work to finish.

censors Men of unimpeachable reputation, chosen to carry the responsibility for enrolling, keeping track of, and determining the status and tax liability of each citizen.

These devices worked well enough in the early years of the republic, when Rome's battles were near home. Longer wars and more sophisticated opponents, however, revealed the system's weaknesses and required significant changes. Long campaigns prompted the invention of the **proconsulship** in 325 B.C.E., whereby the term of a consul serving in the field was extended. This innovation contained the seeds of many troubles for the constitution.

Lictors were attendants of the Roman magistrates who held the power of *imperium*, the right to command. In republican times these magistrates were the consuls, praetors, and proconsuls. The lictors were men from the lower classes—some were even former slaves. They constantly attended the magistrates when the latter appeared in public. The lictors cleared a magistrate's way in crowds and summoned, arrested, and punished offenders for him. They also served as their magistrate's house guard.

Alinari/Art Resource, NY

How did the lictors serve to reinforce the power and status of Roman magistrates?

The creation of the office of *praetor* also helped provide commanders for Rome's many campaigns. The basic function of the *praetors* was judicial, but they also had *imperium* and served as generals. *Praetors*' terms were also for one year.

At first, the consuls identified citizens and classified them according to age and property. After the middle of the fifth century B.C.E., this job was delegated to a new office, that of *censor*. The Senate elected two ***censors*** every five years. They conducted a census and drew up the citizen rolls. Their task was not just clerical; the classification of the citizens fixed taxation and status, so the censors had to be men of fine reputation, former consuls. They soon acquired additional powers. By the fourth century B.C.E., they compiled the roll of senators and could strike senators from that roll not only for financial, but also for moral, reasons. As the prestige of the office grew, it became the ultimate prize of a Roman political career.

The Senate and the Assembly With the end of the monarchy, the Senate became the single continuous, deliberative body in the Roman state, greatly increasing its influence and power. Its members were prominent patricians, often leaders of clans and patrons of many clients. The Senate soon gained control of the state's finances and of foreign policy. Neither magistrates nor popular assemblies could lightly ignore its formal advice.

The most important assembly in the early republic was the *centuriate assembly*, which was, in a sense, the Roman army acting in a political capacity. The assembly elected the consuls and several other magistrates, voted on bills put before it, made decisions of war and peace, and also served as the court of appeal against decisions of the magistrates affecting the life or property of a citizen. In theory, the assembly had final authority, but the Senate exercised great, if informal, influence.

The Struggle of the Orders The laws and constitution of the early republic gave to the patricians almost a monopoly of power and privilege. The plebeians undertook a campaign to achieve political, legal, and social equality, and this attempt, which succeeded after two centuries of intermittent effort, is called the *Struggle of the Orders*.

The most important source of plebeian success was the need for their military service. According to tradition, the plebeians, angered by patrician resistance to their demands, withdrew from the city and camped on the Sacred Mount. There they formed a plebeian tribal assembly and elected plebeian **tribunes** to protect them from the arbitrary power of the magistrates. They declared the tribune inviolate and sacrosanct. By extension of his right to protect the plebeians, the tribune gained the power to veto any action of a magistrate or any bill in a Roman assembly or the Senate.

tribunes Officials elected by the plebeian tribal assembly given the power to protect plebeians from abuse by patrician magistrates.

Next, the plebeians obtained access to the laws, when early Roman custom in all its harshness and simplicity was codified in the Twelve Tables around 450 B.C.E. In 445 B.C.E., plebeians gained the right to marry patricians. The main prize, the consulship, the patricians did not yield easily. Not until 367 B.C.E. did legislation—the Licinian-Sextian Laws—provide that at least one consul could be a plebeian. Before long, plebeians held other offices—even the dictatorship and the censorship. In 300 B.C.E., they were admitted to the most important priesthoods, the last religious barrier to equality. In 287 B.C.E., the plebeians completed their triumph. They once again withdrew from the city and secured the passage of a law whereby decisions of the plebeian assembly bound all Romans and did not require the approval of the Senate.

It might seem that the Roman aristocracy had given way under the pressure of the lower class. Yet the victory of the plebeians did not bring democracy. An aristocracy based strictly on birth had given way to an aristocracy more subtle, but no less restricted, based on a combination of wealth and birth. A relatively small group of rich and powerful families, both patrician and plebeian, known as *nobiles*, attained the highest offices in the state. The significant distinction was no longer between patrician and plebeian but between the *nobiles* and everyone else.

QUICK REVIEW

The Struggle of the Orders

- Fueled by tensions between plebeians and patricians
- Plebeians used power of the army to gain concessions
- Plebeians made slow and incremental progress toward greater rights

The Conquest of Italy

Not long after the fall of the monarchy in 509 B.C.E., a coalition of Romans, Latins, and Italian Greeks drove the Etruscans out of Latium for good. Throughout the fifth century B.C.E., the powerful Etruscan city of Veii, only twelve miles north of the Tiber River, raided Roman territory. After a hard struggle and a long siege, the Romans took Veii in 392 B.C.E., more than doubling the size of Rome.

Roman policy toward defeated enemies used both the carrot and the stick. When the Romans made friendly alliances with some, they gained new soldiers for their army. When they treated others more harshly by annexing their land, they achieved a similar end. Service in the Roman army was based on property, and the distribution to poor Romans of conquered land made soldiers of previously useless men. It also gave the poor a stake in Rome and reduced the pressure against its aristocratic regime.

QUICK REVIEW

Roman Italy

- 392 B.C.E.: Rome destroys Veii and seizes its territory
- Rome tried to build constructive relationships with conquered Italian cities
- Colonies of veteran soldiers established on annexed land

Gallic Invasion and Roman Reaction At the beginning of the fourth century B.C.E., a disaster struck. In 387 B.C.E., the Gauls, barbaric Celtic tribes from across the Alps, defeated the Roman army and burned Rome. The Gauls sought plunder, not conquest, so they extorted a ransom from the Romans and returned to the north. Rome's power appeared to be wiped out.

By about 350 B.C.E., however, the Romans were more dominant than ever. Their success in turning back new Gallic raids added to their power and prestige. As the Romans tightened their grip on Latium, the Latins became resentful. In 340 B.C.E., they demanded independence from Rome or full equality and launched a war of independence that lasted until 338 B.C.E. The victorious Romans dissolved the Latin League, and their treatment of the defeated opponents provided a model for the settlement of Italy.

Roman Policy toward the Conquered The Romans did not destroy any of the Latin cities or their people, nor did they treat them all alike. Some near Rome received full Roman citizenship. Others farther away gained municipal status, which gave them the private rights of intermarriage and commerce with Romans, but not the public rights of voting and holding office in Rome. They retained the rights of local self-government and could obtain full Roman citizenship if they moved to Rome. They followed Rome in foreign policy and provided soldiers to serve in the Roman legions.

Still other states became allies of Rome on the basis of treaties, which differed from city to city.

On some of the conquered land, the Romans placed colonies, permanent settlements of veteran soldiers in the territory of recently defeated enemies. The colonists retained their Roman citizenship and enjoyed home rule; in return for the land they had been given, they were a kind of permanent garrison to deter or suppress rebellion. These colonies were usually connected to Rome by a network of military roads. The roads guaranteed that a Roman army could swiftly reinforce an embattled colony or put down an uprising in any weather.

The Roman settlement of Latium reveals even more clearly than before the principles by which Rome was able to conquer and dominate Italy. The excellent army and the diplomatic skill that allowed Rome to separate its enemies help explain its conquests. The reputation for harsh punishment of rebels, and the sure promise that such punishment would be delivered, was made unmistakably clear. But the positive side, represented by Rome's organization of the defeated states, is at least as important. The Romans did not regard the status given each newly conquered city as permanent. They held out to loyal allies the prospect of improving their status—even of achieving the ultimate prize, full Roman citizenship. In so doing, the Romans gave their allies a stake in Rome's future success and a sense of being colleagues, though subordinate ones, rather than subjects. The result, in general, was that most of Rome's allies remained loyal even when put to the severest test.

Defeated Samnites The next great challenge to Roman arms came in a series of wars with a tough mountain people of the southern Apennines, the Samnites. Some of Rome's allies rebelled, and soon the Etruscans and Gauls joined in the war against Rome. But most of the allies remained loyal. In 295 B.C.E., at Sentinum, the Romans defeated an Italian coalition, and by 280 B.C.E., they were masters of central Italy. Their power extended from the Po Valley south to Apulia and Lucania.

Now the Romans were in direct contact with the Greek cities of southern Italy. Roman intervention in a quarrel between Greek cities brought them face to face with Pyrrhus, king of Epirus. He defeated the Romans twice but suffered many casualties. When one of his officers rejoiced at the victory, Pyrrhus told him, "If we win one more battle against the Romans, we shall be completely ruined." This "Pyrrhic victory" led him to withdraw to Sicily in 275 B.C.E. The Greek cities that had hired him were forced to join the Roman confederation. By 265 B.C.E., Rome ruled all Italy as far north as the Po River, an area of 47,200 square miles.

Rome and Carthage

The conquest of southern Italy brought the Romans face to face with the great naval power of the western Mediterranean, Carthage. (See Map 4–2.) Late in the ninth century B.C.E., the Phoenician city of Tyre had planted a colony on the coast of northern Africa near modern Tunis, calling it the New City, or Carthage. The city was located on a defensible site and commanded an excellent harbor that encouraged commerce.

Beginning in the sixth century B.C.E., the Carthaginians expanded their domain to include the coast of northern Africa west beyond the Straits of Gibraltar and eastward into Libya. Overseas, they came to control the southern part of Spain, Sardinia, Corsica, Malta, the Balearic Islands, and western Sicily. Carthage profited greatly from the mines of Spain and from an absolute monopoly of trade imposed on the western Mediterranean.

Rome became a naval power late in its history to defeat Carthage in the First Punic War (264–241 B.C.E.). This sculpture in low relief shows a Roman ship, propelled by oars, with both ram and soldiers, ready either to ram or board an enemy.

A Roman Warship. Direzione Generale Musei Vaticani

How did competition for seaborne trade contribute to the outbreak of hostilities between Rome and Carthage?

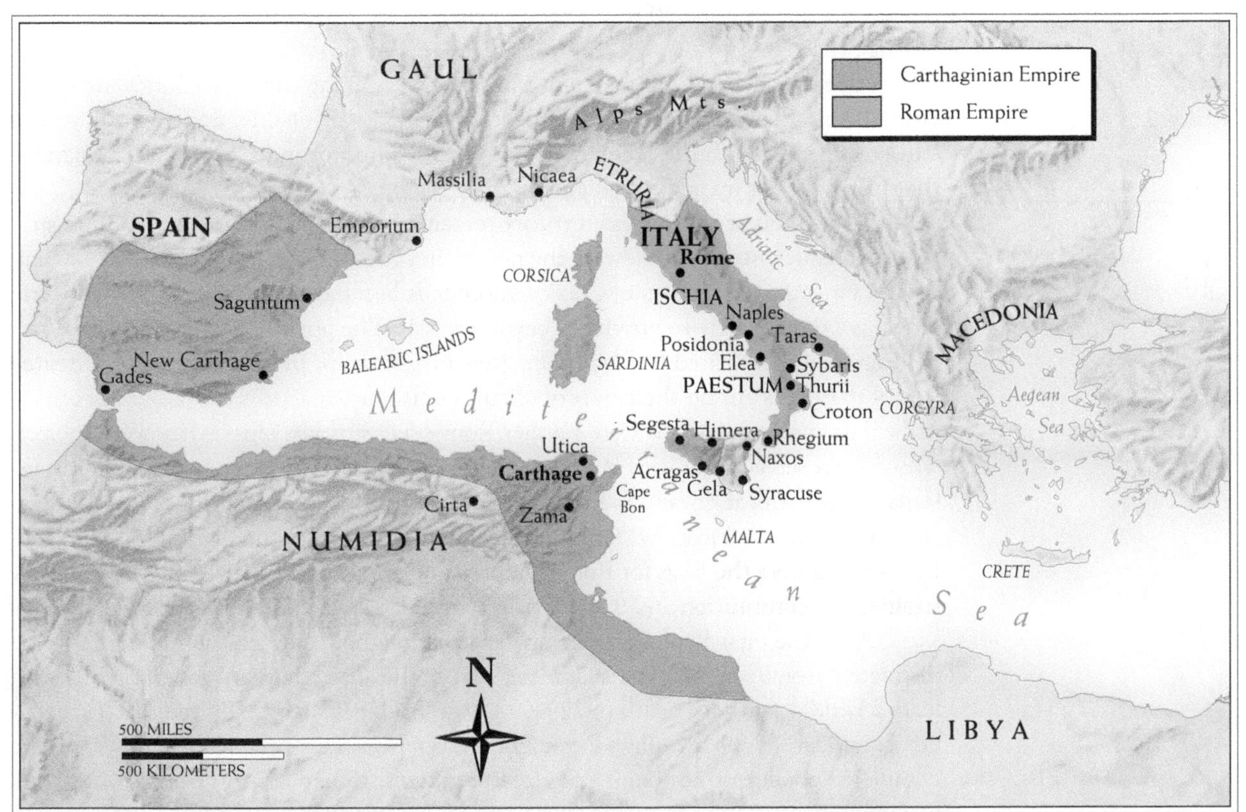

MAP 4–2 **The Western Mediterranean Area During the Rise of Rome** This map illustrates the theater of conflict between the growing Roman dominions and those of Carthage in the third century B.C.E. The Carthaginian Empire stretched westward from the city (in modern Tunisia) along the North African coast and into southern Spain.

What economic and political effects did the Punic Wars have on Rome?

An attack by Hiero, tyrant of Syracuse, on the Sicilian city of Messana just across from Italy, first caused trouble between Rome and Carthage. Messana had been seized by a group of Italian mercenary soldiers who called themselves *Mamertines*, the sons of the war god Mars. When Hiero defeated the Mamertines, some of them called on the Carthaginians to help save their city. Carthage agreed and sent a garrison, for the Carthaginians wanted to prevent Syracuse from dominating the straits. One Mamertine faction, however, fearing that Carthage might take undue advantage of the opportunity, asked Rome for help.

QUICK REVIEW

Path to War

- Carthage's power expanded throughout western Mediterranean in sixth century B.C.E.
- Carthage claimed exclusive rights to trade in the Mediterranean
- Conflict over Sicilian city of Messana sparked war

In 264 B.C.E., the request came to the Senate. Because a Punic garrison (the Romans called the Carthaginians *Phoenicians*; in Latin the word is *Poeni* or *Puni*—hence the adjective *Punic*) was in place at Messana, any intervention would be not against Syracuse, but against the mighty empire of Carthage. Unless Rome intervened, however, Carthage would gain control of all Sicily and the straits. The assembly voted to send an army to Messana and expelled the Punic garrison. The First Punic War was on.

The First Punic War (264–241 B.C.E.) The war in Sicily soon settled into a stalemate until the Romans built a fleet to cut off supplies to the besieged Carthaginian cities at the western end of Sicily. When Carthage sent its own fleet to raise the siege, the Romans destroyed it. In 241 B.C.E., Carthage signed a treaty giving up Sicily and the islands between Italy and Sicily; it also agreed to pay a war indemnity in ten annual installments. Neither side was to attack the allies of the other. The peace was realistic and not unduly harsh. If it had been carried out in good faith, it might have brought lasting peace.

A rebellion, however, broke out in Carthage among the mercenaries, newly recruited from Sicily, who now demanded their pay. In 238 B.C.E., while Carthage was still preoccupied with the rebellion, Rome seized Sardinia and Corsica and demanded that Carthage pay an additional indemnity.

The conquest of overseas territory presented the Romans with new administrative problems. Instead of following the policy they had pursued in Italy, they made Sicily a province and Sardinia and Corsica another. It became common to extend the term of the governors of these provinces beyond a year. The governors were unchecked by colleagues and exercised full *imperium*. New magistracies, in effect, were thus created free of the limits put on the power of officials in Rome.

The new populations were neither Roman citizens nor allies; they were subjects who did not serve in the army but paid tribute instead. The old practice of extending citizenship and, with it, loyalty to Rome thus stopped at the borders of Italy. Rome collected taxes on these subjects by "farming" them out at auction to the highest bidder. These innovations were the basis for Rome's imperial organization in the future. In time, they strained the constitution and traditions and threatened the existence of the republic.

After the First Punic War, campaigns against the Gauls and across the Adriatic distracted Rome. Meanwhile Hamilcar Barca, the Carthaginian governor of Spain from 237 B.C.E. until his death in 229 B.C.E., was leading Carthage on the road to recovery. Hamilcar sought to build a Punic Empire in Spain. He improved the ports and the commerce conducted in them, exploited the mines, gained control of the hinterland, won over many of the conquered tribes, and built a strong and disciplined army. Hamilcar's successor, his son-in-law Hasdrubal, pursued the same policies.

The Second Punic War (218–202 B.C.E.) On Hasdrubal's assassination in 221 B.C.E., the army chose as his successor Hannibal, son of Hamilcar Barca. Hannibal was at that time twenty-five years old. He quickly consolidated and extended the Punic Empire in Spain. A few years before his accession, Rome had received an offer of alliance from the people of Saguntum, a Spanish town about one hundred miles south of the Ebro River. The Romans accepted the friendship and the responsibilities it entailed. At first, Hannibal avoided any action against Saguntum, but the Saguntines, confident of Rome's protection, began to interfere with some of the Spanish tribes allied with Hannibal. When the Romans sent an embassy to Hannibal warning him to let Saguntum alone, he ignored the warning and captured the town. The Romans sent an ultimatum to Carthage demanding the surrender of Hannibal. Carthage refused, and Rome declared war in 218 B.C.E.

Between the close of the First Punic War and the outbreak of the Second, Rome had repeatedly provoked Carthage, taking Sardinia in 238 B.C.E. and interfering in Spain, but had not prevented Carthage from building a powerful and dangerous empire in Spain. Hannibal saw to it that the Romans paid the price for these blunders. By September 218 B.C.E., he was across the Alps, in Italy and among the friendly Gauls.

Hannibal defeated the Romans at the Ticinus River and crushed the joint consular armies at the Trebia River. In 217 B.C.E., he outmaneuvered and trapped another army at Lake Trasimene. The key to success, however, would be defection by Rome's allies. Hannibal released Italian prisoners without harm or ransom and moved his army south of Rome to encourage rebellion. But the allies remained firm.

In 216 B.C.E., Hannibal marched to Cannae in Apulia to tempt the Romans into another open fight. They sent off an army of some 80,000 men to meet him. Almost the entire Roman army was wiped out. It was the worst defeat in Roman history. Rome's prestige was shattered, and most of its allies in southern Italy, as well as Syracuse in Sicily, went over to Hannibal. For more than a decade, no Roman army would dare face Hannibal in the field.

Hannibal, however, had neither the numbers nor the supplies to besiege walled cities, nor did he have the equipment to take them by assault. The Romans appointed Publius Cornelius Scipio (237–183 B.C.E.), later called Africanus, to the command in Spain with proconsular *imperium*. Scipio was not yet twenty-five and had held no high office, but he was a general almost as talented as Hannibal. Within a few years, young Scipio had conquered all of Spain and had deprived Hannibal of any hope of help from that region.

In 204 B.C.E., Scipio landed in Africa and forced the Carthaginians to accept a peace, the main clause of which was the withdrawal of Hannibal and his army from Italy. Hannibal had won every battle but lost the war, for he had not counted on the determination of Rome and the loyalty of its allies. Hannibal's return inspired Carthage to break the peace and to risk all in battle. In 202 B.C.E., Scipio and Hannibal faced each other at the Battle of Zama. The generalship of Scipio and the desertion of Hannibal's mercenaries gave the victory to Rome. The new peace terms reduced Carthage to the status of a dependent ally of Rome. Rome now ruled the seas and the entire Mediterranean coast from Italy westward.

QUICK REVIEW

Hannibal on the Offensive

- 218 B.C.E.: crossed Alps and dealt Rome a series of defeats
- 216 B.C.E.: defeated Romans in Battle of Cannae, worst defeat in Roman history
- Victory at Cannae convinced some Roman allies to change sides

The Republic's Conquest of the Hellenistic World

The East By the middle of the third century B.C.E., the eastern Mediterranean had reached a condition of stability based on a balance of power among the three great Hellenistic kingdoms that allowed an established place even for lesser states. Two aggressive monarchs, Philip V of Macedon (221–179 B.C.E.) and Antiochus III of the Seleucid kingdom (223–187 B.C.E.), threatened this equilibrium, however. Philip and Antiochus moved swiftly, the latter against Syria and Palestine, the former against cities in the Aegean, in the Hellespontine region, and on the coast of Asia Minor.

SIGNIFICANT DATES IN ROME'S RISE TO EMPIRE

509 B.C.E.	Republic founded
387 B.C.E.	Gauls sack Rome
338 B.C.E.	Rome defeats the Latin League
295 B.C.E.	Rome defeats the Samnites
287 B.C.E.	"Struggle of the Orders" ends
275 B.C.E.	Pyrrhus abandons Italy to Rome
264–241 B.C.E.	First Punic War
218–202 B.C.E.	Second Punic War
215–205 B.C.E.	First Macedonian War
200–197 B.C.E.	Second Macedonian War
189 B.C.E.	Rome defeats Antiochus
172–168 B.C.E.	Third Macedonian War
149–146 B.C.E.	Third Punic War
154–133 B.C.E.	Roman Wars in Spain

The threat that a more powerful Macedon might pose to Rome's friends and, perhaps, even to Italy persuaded the Romans to intervene. Philip had already attempted to meddle in Roman affairs when he formed an alliance with Carthage during the Second Punic War, provoking a conflict known as the First Macedonian War (215–205 B.C.E.). In 200 B.C.E., in an action that began the Second Macedonian War, the Romans sent an ultimatum to Philip ordering him not to attack any Greek city and to pay reparations to Pergamum. These orders were meant to provoke, not avoid, war, and Philip refused to obey. Two years later the Romans sent out a talented young general, Flamininus, who demanded that Philip withdraw from Greece entirely. In 197 B.C.E., with Greek support, Flamininus defeated Philip at Cynoscephalae, ending the war. The Greek cities freed from Philip were made autonomous, and in 196 B.C.E., Flamininus proclaimed the freedom of the Greeks.

Soon after the Romans withdrew from Greece, they came into conflict with Antiochus, who was expanding his power in Asia and on the European side of the Hellespont. On the pretext of freeing the Greeks from Roman domination, he landed an army on the Greek mainland. The Romans routed Antiochus at Thermopylae and quickly drove him from Greece. In 189 B.C.E., they crushed his army at Magnesia in Asia Minor. Once again, the Romans took no territory for themselves and left several Greek cities in Asia free. They regarded Greece, and now Asia Minor, as a kind of protectorate in which they could intervene or not as they chose.

This relatively mild policy was destined to end as the stern and businesslike policies of the conservative censor Cato gained favor in Rome. A new harshness was to be applied to allies and bystanders, as well as to defeated opponents.

In 179 B.C.E., Perseus succeeded Philip V as king of Macedon. He tried to gain popularity in Greece by favoring the democratic and revolutionary forces in the cities. The Romans, troubled by his threat to stability, launched the Third Macedonian War (172–168 B.C.E.), and in 168 B.C.E. Aemilius Paulus defeated Perseus at Pydna. The peace that followed this war, reflecting the changed attitude at Rome, was harsh.

The West Harsh as the Romans had become toward the Greeks, they treated the people of the Iberian Peninsula (Spain and Portugal), whom they considered barbarians, even worse. They committed dreadful atrocities, lied, cheated, and broke treaties to exploit and pacify the natives, who fought back fiercely in guerrilla style. From 154 to 133 B.C.E., the fighting waxed, and it became hard to recruit Roman soldiers to participate in the increasingly ugly war. At last, in 134 B.C.E., Scipio Aemilianus took the key city of Numantia by siege and burned it to the ground. This put an end to the war in Spain.

Roman treatment of Carthage was no better. Although Carthage lived up to its treaty with Rome faithfully and posed no threat, some Romans refused to abandon their hatred of the traditional enemy. At last the Romans took advantage of a technical breach of the peace to destroy Carthage. In 146 B.C.E., Scipio Aemilianus took the city, plowed up its land, and put salt in the furrows as a symbol of the permanent abandonment of the site. The Romans incorporated it as the province of Africa, one of six Roman provinces, including Sicily, Sardinia-Corsica, Macedonia, Hither Spain, and Further Spain.

CIVILIZATION IN THE EARLY ROMAN REPUBLIC

HOW DID contact with the Hellenistic world affect Rome?

Close and continued association with the Greeks of the Hellenistic world wrought important changes in the Roman style of life and thought. The Roman attitude toward the Greeks ranged from admiration for their culture and history to contempt for their constant squabbling, their commercial practices, and their weakness.

RELIGION

The Greeks influenced Roman religion almost from the beginning. The Romans identified their own gods with Greek equivalents and incorporated Greek mythology into their own. Mostly, however, Roman religious practice remained simple and Italian, until the third century B.C.E. brought important new influences from the East.

Traditional Religion and Character In early Rome the family stood at the center of religious observance, and gods of the household and farm were most important. In the early days, before they were influenced by the Etruscans and Greeks, Roman religion knew little of mythology: Their gods were impersonal forces, *numina*, rather than deities in human or superhuman form. Their image of an afterlife was vague and insubstantial. Morality played little role in Roman religion but, since failure to perform the necessary rites correctly could bring harm on the entire state, everyone had to participate in religious observance as a civic duty and evidence of patriotism.

ENCOUNTERING THE PAST

ROMAN COMEDY

In Rome, as in Greece, religious festivals were public entertainments involving gladiatorial contests, chariot races, and dramas. Initially, Roman audiences sat on hillsides and watched performances staged on temporary wooden platforms. Toward the end of the republican period, however, wealthy Romans began to donate permanent amphitheaters to their communities, and theaters spread to all the lands Rome ruled.

Tragedies modeled on Greek examples were staged in Rome, but the works of the republic's best playwrights—Plautus (ca. 254–184 B.C.E.) and Terence (ca. 195–159 B.C.E.)—belong to the genre of Hellenistic New Comedy. The standard set for such plays was a city street where stock characters (clever slaves, dim-witted masters, young lovers, and shrewish women) enacted plots involving a tangle of mistaken identities, love affairs, and domestic disputes. The result was very similar to the situation comedies that are staples of modern television.

IS THERE any significance in the fact that the great plays that survive from the era of the Roman Republic are comedies, not tragedies?

This mosaic shows a scene from Roman comedy in which musicians played a significant role.

Who made up the audience for Roman comedy?

In 205 B.C.E., the Senate approved the public worship of Cybele, the Great Mother goddess from Phrygia in Asia Minor. Hers was a fertility cult accompanied by ecstatic, frenzied, and sensual rites that so outraged conservative Romans that they soon banned the cult. Similarly, the Senate banned the worship of Dionysus, or Bacchus, in 186 B.C.E. In the second century B.C.E., interest in Babylonian astrology also grew, and the Senate's attempt in 139 B.C.E. to expel the "Chaldaeans," as the astrologers were called, did not prevent the continued influence of their superstition.

Education

Education in the early republic was entirely the responsibility of the family, the father teaching his own son at home. It is not clear whether in these early times girls received any education, though they certainly did later on. The boys learned to read, write, calculate, and how to farm. They memorized the laws of the Twelve Tables, learned how to perform religious rites, heard stories of the great deeds of early Roman history and particularly those of their ancestors, and engaged in the physical training appropriate for potential soldiers.

Hellenized Education In the third century B.C.E., the Romans came into contact with the Greeks of southern Italy, and this contact changed Roman education. Greek teachers introduced the study of language, literature, and philosophy, as well as the idea of a liberal education, or what the Romans called ***humanitas***, the root of our concept of the humanities. The aim of education changed from the mastery of practical, vocational skills to an emphasis on broad intellectual training, critical thinking, an interest in ideas, and the development of a well-rounded person. The new emphasis required students to learn Greek, for Rome did not yet have a literature of its own. Hereafter, educated Romans were expected to be bilingual.

humanitas Wide-ranging intellectual curiosity and habits of critical thinking that are the goals of liberal education.

In the late republic, Roman education, though still entirely private, became more formal and organized. From the ages of seven to twelve, boys went to elementary school. At school the boys learned to read and write, using a wax tablet and a stylus, and to do simple arithmetic with an abacus and pebbles (*calculi*). Discipline was harsh and corporal punishment frequent. From twelve to sixteen, boys went to a higher school, where instructors provided a liberal education, using Greek and Latin literature as their subject matter.

At sixteen, some boys went on to advanced study in rhetoric. The instructors were usually Greek. They trained their charges by studying models of fine speech of the past and by having them write, memorize, and declaim speeches suitable for different occasions.

This style of education broadened the Romans' understanding through the careful study of a foreign language and culture. It made them a part of the older and wider culture of the Hellenistic world, a world they had come to dominate and needed to understand.

Education for Women Though the evidence is limited, we can be sure that girls of the upper classes received an education equivalent at least to the early stages of a boy's

This carved relief from the second century C.E. shows a schoolmaster and his pupils. The pupil at the right is arriving late.

Rheinisches Landesmuseum, Trier, Germany. Alinari/Art Resource, NY

Why was education so important to the future success of elite Roman boys?

education. They were probably taught by tutors at home rather than going to school, as was increasingly the fashion among boys in the late republic. Young women did not study with philosophers and rhetoricians, for they were usually married by the age at which the men were pursuing their higher education. Still, some women continued their education and became prose writers or poets.

Slavery

Like most other ancient peoples, the Romans had slaves from early in their history, but slavery became a basic element in the Roman economy and society only during the second century B.C.E., after the Romans had conquered most of the lands bordering the Mediterranean. In the time between the beginning of Rome's first war against Carthage (264 B.C.E.) and the conquest of Spain (133 B.C.E.), the Romans enslaved some 250,000 prisoners of war, greatly increasing the availability of slave labor and reducing its price. Many slaves worked as domestic servants, feeding the growing appetite for luxury of the Roman upper class; at the other end of the spectrum, many worked in the mines of Spain and Sardinia. Some worked as artisans in small factories and shops or as public clerks. Slaves were permitted to marry, and they produced sizable families. As in Greece, domestic slaves and those used in crafts and commerce could earn money, keep it, and, in some cases, use it to purchase their own freedom. *Manumission* (the freeing of slaves) was common among the Romans.

The unique development in the Roman world was the emergence of an agricultural system that employed and depended on a vast number of slaves. By the time of Jesus, there were between 2 and 3 million slaves in Italy, and about 35 to 40 percent of the total population, most of them part of great slave gangs that worked the vast plantations the Romans called ***latifundia***. *Latifundia* owners sought maximum profits and treated their slaves simply as means to that end. The slaves often worked in chains, were oppressed by brutal foremen, and lived in underground prisons.

latifundia Great estates that produced capital-intensive cash crops for the international market.

Such harsh treatment led to serious slave rebellions of a kind we do not hear of in other ancient societies. A rebellion in Sicily in 134 B.C.E. kept the island in turmoil for more than two years, and the rebellion of the gladiators led by Spartacus in 73 B.C.E. produced an army of 70,000 slaves that repeatedly defeated the Roman legions and overran southern Italy before it was brutally crushed.

Slavery retained its economic and social importance in the first century of the imperial period, but its centrality began to decline in the second. The reasons for this decline are rather obscure. A rise in the cost of slaves and a consequent reduction in their economic value seem to have been factors. More important, it appears, was a general economic decline that permitted increasing pressure on the free lower classes. More and more they were employed as ***coloni***—tenant farmers. Over centuries, these increasingly serflike *coloni* replaced most agricultural slave labor.

coloni Tenant farmers who were bound to the lands they worked.

ROMAN IMPERIALISM: THE LATE REPUBLIC

HOW DID the expansion of Rome change the Republic?

Rome's expansion in Italy and overseas was accomplished without a grand general plan. Whether intended or not, Rome's expansion brought the Romans an empire and, with it, power, wealth, and responsibilities. The need to govern an empire beyond the seas would severely test the republican constitution, Roman society, and the Roman character.

The Aftermath of Conquest

War and expansion changed the economic, social, and political life of Italy. Before the Punic Wars, most Italians owned their own farms, which provided the greater part of

This wall painting from the first century B.C.E. comes from the villa of Publius Fannius Synistor at Pompeii and shows a woman playing a cithera.

Roman. Paintings. Pompeian, Boscoreale. 1st Century B.C. *Lady Playing the Cithara.* Wall painting from the east wall of large room in the villa of Publius Fannius Synistor. Fresco on lime plaster. H. 6 ft. 1 1/2 in. W. 6 ft. 1 1/2 in. (18 × 187 cm.) The Metropolitan Museum of Art, Rogers Fund, 1903. (03.14.5) Photograph © 1986 The Metropolitan Museum of Art

What social and political functions were played by the Roman villa?

the family's needs. Fourteen years of fighting in the Second Punic War did terrible damage to Italian farmland. Many veterans returning from the wars found it impossible or unprofitable to go back to their farms. Some moved to Rome, where they could find work as laborers, but most stayed in the country as tenant farmers or hired hands. Often, the wealthy converted the abandoned land into *latifundia* for growing cash crops—grain, olives, and grapes for wine—or into cattle ranches.

The upper classes had plenty of capital to operate these estates because of profits from the war and from exploiting the provinces. Land was cheap, and so was slave labor. By fair means and foul, large landholders obtained great quantities of public land and forced small farmers from it. These changes separated the people of Rome and Italy more sharply into rich and poor, landed and landless, privileged and deprived. The result was political, social, and, ultimately, constitutional conflict that threatened the existence of the republic.

The Gracchi

By the middle of the second century B.C.E., the problems caused by Rome's rapid expansion troubled perceptive Roman nobles. The fall in status of peasant farmers made it harder to recruit soldiers and came to present a political threat as well. The patron's traditional control over his clients was weakened when they fled from their land. Even those former landowners who worked on the land of their patrons as tenants or hired hands were less reliable. The introduction of the secret ballot in the 130s B.C.E. made them even more independent.

Tiberius Gracchus In 133 B.C.E., Tiberius Gracchus tried to solve these problems. He became tribune for 133 B.C.E. on a program of land reform; some of the most powerful members of the Roman aristocracy helped him draft the bill. They meant it to be a moderate attempt at solving Rome's problems. The bill's target was public land that had been acquired and held illegally, some of it for many years. The bill allowed holders of this land to retain as many as five hundred iugera (approximately 320 acres), but the state would reclaim anything over that and redistribute it in small lots to the poor, who would pay a small rent to the state and could not sell what they had received.

The bill aroused great hostility. Its passage would hurt many senators who held vast estates. Others thought it would be a bad precedent to allow any interference with property rights, even if they involved illegally held public land. Still others feared the political gains that Tiberius and his associates would make if the beneficiaries of their law were properly grateful to its drafters.

When Tiberius put the bill before the tribal assembly, one of the tribunes, M. Octavius, interposed his veto. Tiberius went to the Senate to discuss his proposal, but the senators continued their opposition. Unwilling to give up, he put his bill before the tribal assembly again. Again Octavius vetoed. So Tiberius, strongly supported by the people, had Octavius removed from office, violating the constitution. The assembly's removal of a magistrate implied a fundamental shift of power from the Senate to the people. If the assembly could pass laws the Senate opposed and a tribune vetoed, and if they could remove magistrates, then Rome would become a democracy like Athens instead of a traditional oligarchy.

Tiberius proposed a second bill, harsher than the first and more appealing to the people, for he had given up hope of conciliating the Senate. This bill, which passed the assembly, provided for a commission to carry it out. When King Attalus of Pergamum died and left his kingdom to Rome, Tiberius proposed using the Pergamene revenue to finance the commission. This proposal challenged the Senate's control both of finances and of foreign affairs. Hereafter there could be no compromise: Either Tiberius or the Roman constitution must go under.

Tiberius understood the danger he would face if he stepped down from the tribunate, so he announced his candidacy for a second successive term, striking another blow at tradition. His opponents feared he might go on to hold office indefinitely, to dominate Rome in what appeared to them a demagogic tyranny. At the elections a riot broke out, and a mob of senators and their clients killed Tiberius and some three hundred of his followers and threw their bodies into the Tiber River. The Senate had put down the threat to its rule, but at the price of the first internal bloodshed in Roman political history.

The tribunate of Tiberius Gracchus changed Roman politics. Heretofore Roman political struggles had generally been struggles for honor and reputation between great families or coalitions of such families. Fundamental issues were rarely at stake. The revolutionary proposals of Tiberius, however, and the senatorial resort to bloodshed created a new situation. From then on, Romans could pursue a political career that was not based solely on influence within the aristocracy; pressure from the people might be an effective substitute. In the last century of the republic, politicians who sought such backing were called ***populares***, whereas those who supported the traditional role of the Senate were called ***optimates***, or "the best men."

populares Politicians who followed Tiberius's example of politics and governing.

optimates ("the best men") Opponents of Tiberius and defenders of the traditional prerogatives of the Senate.

equestrians Men rich enough to qualify for cavalry service.

Gaius Gracchus The tribunate of Gaius Gracchus (brother of Tiberius) was much more dangerous than that of Tiberius. All the tribunes of 123 B.C.E. were his supporters, so there could be no veto, and a recent law permitted the reelection of tribunes. Gaius's program appealed to a variety of groups. First, he revived the agrarian commission, which had been allowed to lapse. Because there was not enough good public land left to meet the demand, he proposed to establish new colonies: two in Italy and one on the old site of Carthage. Among other popular acts, he put through a law stabilizing the price of grain in Rome, which involved building granaries to guarantee an adequate supply. Finally, Gaius undercut his opponents by passing legislation to the advantage of the **equestrians** (men rich enough to qualify for cavalry service), effectively pitting the republic's two wealthiest classes, the senators and the equestrians, against each other.

Gaius easily won reelection as tribune for 122 B.C.E. He aimed at giving citizenship to the Italians, both to resolve their dissatisfaction and to add them to his political coalition. But the common people did not want to share the advantages of Roman citizenship. The Senate seized on this proposal to drive a wedge between Gaius and his supporters.

The Romans did not reelect Gaius for 121 B.C.E., leaving him vulnerable to his enemies. A hostile consul provoked an incident that led to violence. The Senate invented an extreme decree ordering the consuls to see to it that no harm came to the republic; in effect, this decree established martial law. Gaius was hunted down and killed, and a senatorial court condemned and put to death some 3,000 of his followers without any trial.

This statue of an unknown member of the Roman nobility from late in the first century illustrates a fundamental custom. He carries the images of two of his ancestors, probably his father and grandfather.

Marble. Musei Capitolini, Rome, Italy. Photograph ©Scala/Art Resource, NY

What role did illustrious ancestors play in the lives of elite Roman men?

MARIUS AND SULLA

For the moment, the senatorial oligarchy had fought off the challenge to its traditional position. Before long, it faced more serious dangers arising from troubles abroad. The first grew out of a dispute over the succession to the throne of Numidia, a client kingdom of Rome's near Carthage.

Marius and the Jugurthine War The victory of Jugurtha, who became king of Numidia, and his massacre of Roman and Italian businessmen in the province, gained Roman attention. Although the Senate was reluctant to become involved, pressure from the equestrians and the people forced the declaration of what became known as the Jugurthine War in 111 B.C.E.

As the war dragged on, the people, sometimes with good reason, suspected the Senate of taking bribes from Jugurtha. They elected C. Marius (157–86 B.C.E.) to the consulship for 107 B.C.E. The assembly, usurping the role of the Senate, assigned him to Numidia.

Marius quickly defeated Jugurtha, but Jugurtha escaped, and guerrilla warfare continued. Finally, Marius's subordinate, L. Cornelius Sulla (138–78 B.C.E.), trapped Jugurtha and brought the war to an end. Marius celebrated the victory, but Sulla, an ambitious though impoverished descendant of an old Roman family, resented being cheated of the credit he thought he deserved. Rumors credited Sulla with the victory and diminished Marius's role. Thus were the seeds planted for a mutual hostility that would last until Marius's death.

While the Romans were fighting Jugurtha, a far greater danger threatened Rome from the north. In 105 B.C.E., two barbaric tribes, the Cimbri and the Teutones, had come down the Rhone Valley and crushed a Roman army at Arausio (Orange) in southern France. When these tribes threatened again, the Romans elected Marius to his second consulship to meet the danger. He served five consecutive terms until 100 B.C.E., when the crisis was over.

While the barbarians were occupied elsewhere, Marius used the time to make important changes in the army. He began using volunteers for the army, mostly the dispossessed farmers and rural proletarians whose problems the Gracchi had not solved. Volunteers were most likely to enlist with a man who was a capable soldier and influential enough to obtain what he needed for them. They looked to him rather than to the state for their rewards. He, however, had to obtain these favors from the Senate if he was to maintain his power and reputation. Marius's innovation created both the opportunity and the necessity for military leaders to gain enough power to challenge civilian authority. The promise of rewards won these leaders the personal loyalty of their troops, and that loyalty allowed them to frighten the Senate into granting their demands.

The Wars against the Italians (90–88 B.C.E.) For a decade Rome avoided serious troubles, but in that time the Senate took no action to deal with Italian discontent. Frustrated, the Italians revolted in 90 B.C.E. and established a separate confederation with its own capital and coinage.

Employing the traditional device of divide and conquer, the Romans immediately offered citizenship to those cities that remained loyal and soon made the same offer to the rebels if they laid down their arms. Even then, hard fighting was needed to put down the uprising, but by 88 B.C.E., the war against the allies was over. All the Italians became Roman citizens with the protections that citizenship offered.

Sulla's Dictatorship During the war against the allies, Sulla had performed well. He was elected consul for 88 B.C.E. and was given command of the war against Mithridates, who was leading a major rebellion in Asia. At this point, the seventy-year-old Marius emerged from obscurity and sought the command for himself. With popular and equestrian support, he got the assembly to transfer the command to him. Sulla, defending the rights of the Senate and his own interests, marched his army against Rome. This was the first time a Roman general had used his army against fellow citizens. Marius and his friends fled, and Sulla regained the command. No sooner had he left again for

Asia, than Marius joined with the consul Cinna and seized Rome. He outlawed Sulla and massacred the senatorial opposition. Marius died soon after his election to a seventh consulship, for 86 B.C.E.

Cinna now was the chief man at Rome. Supported by Marius's men, he held the consulship from 87 to 84 B.C.E. His future depended on Sulla's fortunes in the East.

By 85 B.C.E., Sulla had driven Mithridates from Greece and had crossed over to Asia Minor. Eager to regain control of Rome, he negotiated a compromise peace. In 83 B.C.E., he returned to Italy and fought a civil war that lasted for more than a year. Sulla won and drove the followers of Marius from Italy. He had himself appointed dictator, not in the traditional sense, but to remake the state.

Sulla's first step was to wipe out the opposition. The names of those proscribed were posted in public. As they were outlaws, anyone could kill them and receive a reward. Sulla proscribed not only political opponents, but also his personal enemies and men whose only crime was their wealth. With the proceeds from the confiscations, Sulla rewarded his veterans, perhaps as many as 100,000 men, and thereby built a solid base of support.

Sulla had enough power to make himself the permanent ruler of Rome. He was traditional enough to want to restore senatorial government but reformed so as to prevent the misfortunes of the past. To deal with the decimation of the Senate caused by the proscriptions and the civil war, he enrolled three hundred new members, many of them from the equestrian order and the upper classes of the Italian cities. The office of tribune, which the Gracchi had used to attack senatorial rule, was made into a political dead end.

Sulla's most valuable reforms improved the quality of the courts and the entire legal system. He created new courts to deal with specified crimes, bringing the number of courts to eight. Because both judge and jurors were senators, the courts, too, enhanced senatorial power. These actions were the most permanent of Sulla's reforms, laying the foundation for Roman criminal law.

Sulla retired to a life of ease and luxury in 79 B.C.E. He could not, however, undo the effect of his own example—that of a general using the loyalty of his own troops to take power and to massacre his opponents, as well as innocent men. These actions proved to be more significant than his constitutional arrangements.

THE FALL OF THE REPUBLIC

WHAT EVENTS led to the fall of the Republic?

Within a year of Sulla's death, his constitution came under assault. To deal with an armed threat to its powers, the Senate violated the very procedures meant to defend them.

POMPEY, CRASSUS, CAESAR, AND CICERO

The Senate gave the command of the army to Pompey (106–48 B.C.E.), who was only twenty-eight and had never been elected to a magistracy. Then, when Sertorius, a Marian general, resisted senatorial control, the Senate appointed Pompey proconsul in Spain in 77 B.C.E. In 71 B.C.E., Pompey returned to Rome with new glory, having put down the rebellion of Sertorius. In 73 B.C.E., the Senate made another extraordinary appointment to put down a great slave rebellion led by the gladiator Spartacus. Marcus Licinius Crassus, a rich and ambitious senator, received powers that gave him command of almost all of Italy. Together with the newly returned Pompey, he crushed the rebellion in 71 B.C.E. Extraordinary commands of this sort proved to be the ruin of the republic.

Crassus and Pompey were ambitious men whom the Senate feared. Both demanded special honors and election to the consulship for the year 70 B.C.E. They joined forces, though they disliked and were jealous of each other. They both won election and repealed most of Sulla's constitution. This opened the way for further attacks on senatorial control and for collaboration between ambitious generals and demagogic tribunes.

In 67 B.C.E., a special law gave Pompey *imperium* for three years over the entire Mediterranean and fifty miles in from the coast. It also gave him the power to raise troops and money to rid the area of pirates. The assembly passed the law over senatorial opposition, and in three months Pompey cleared the seas of piracy. Meanwhile, a new war had broken out with Mithridates. In 66 B.C.E., the assembly transferred the command to Pompey, giving him unprecedented powers. He held *imperium* over all Asia, with the right to make war and peace at will. His *imperium* was superior to that of any proconsul in the field.

Once again, Pompey justified his appointment. He defeated Mithridates and drove him to suicide. By 62 B.C.E., he had extended Rome's frontier to the Euphrates River and had organized the territories of Asia so well that his arrangements remained the basis of Roman rule well into the imperial period. When Pompey returned to Rome in 62 B.C.E., he had more power, prestige, and popular support than any other Roman in history.

Rome had not been quiet in Pompey's absence. Crassus was the foremost among those who had reason to fear Pompey's return. Although rich and influential, Crassus did not have the confidence of the Senate, a firm political base of his own, or the kind of military glory needed to rival Pompey. During the 60s B.C.E., therefore, he allied himself with various popular leaders.

The ablest of these men was Gaius Julius Caesar (100–44 B.C.E.). Caesar was an ambitious young politician whose daring and rhetorical skill made him a valuable ally in winning the discontented of every class to the cause of the *populares*. Though Crassus was the senior partner, each needed the other to achieve what both wanted: significant military commands with which to build a reputation, a political following, and a military force to compete with Pompey's.

The chief opposition to Crassus's candidates for the consulship for 63 B.C.E. came from Cicero (106–43 B.C.E.). Cicero, though he came from outside the senatorial aristocracy, was no *popularis*. His program was to preserve the republic against demagogues and ambitious generals by making the government more liberal. He wanted to unite the stable elements of the state—the Senate and the equestrians—in a harmony of the orders. This program did not appeal to the senatorial oligarchy, but the Senate preferred Cicero to Catiline, a dangerous and popular politician thought to be linked with Crassus. Cicero and Antonius were elected consuls for 63 B.C.E., with Catiline running third.

Cicero soon learned of a plot hatched by Catiline. Catiline had run in the previous election on a platform of cancellation of debts; this appealed to discontented elements in general, but especially to the heavily indebted nobles and their many clients. Made desperate by defeat, Catiline planned to stir up rebellions around Italy, to cause confusion in the city, and to take it by force. Quick action by Cicero defeated Catiline.

The First Triumvirate

Toward the end of 62 B.C.E., Pompey landed at Brundisium. Surprisingly, he disbanded his army, celebrated a great triumph, and returned to private life. He had delayed his return in the hope of finding Italy in such a state as to justify his keeping the army and dominating the scene. Cicero's quick suppression of Catiline prevented his plan. Pompey, therefore, had either to act illegally or to lay down his arms.

Pompey had achieved amazing things for Rome and simply wanted the Senate to approve his excellent arrangements in the East and to make land allotments to his vet-

erans. But the Senate was jealous and fearful of overmighty individuals and refused his requests. Pompey was driven to an alliance with his natural enemies, Crassus and Caesar. They formed the First Triumvirate, a private political arrangement that enabled them, by working together, to dominate the republic.

A Bust of Julius Caesar.

Bust of Julius Caesar (100–44 B.C.E.). Roman statesman. Museo Archeologico Nazionale, Naples, Italy. Photograph © Scala/Art Resource, NY

What circumstances allowed for the rise of men like Caesar and Pompey to positions of unprecedented power?

Julius Caesar and His Government of Rome

Caesar was elected to the consulship for 59 B.C.E. The triumvirs' program was quickly enacted. Caesar got the extraordinary command that would give him a chance to earn the glory and power with which to rival Pompey: the governorship of Illyricum and Gaul for five years. A land bill settled Pompey's veterans comfortably, and his eastern settlement was ratified. Crassus, much of whose influence came from his position as champion of the equestrians, won for them a great windfall by having the government renegotiate a tax contract in their favor. To guarantee themselves against any reversal of these actions, the triumvirs continued their informal but effective collaboration, arranging for the election of friendly consuls and the departure of potential opponents.

Caesar was now free to seek the military success he craved. His province included Cisalpine Gaul in the Po Valley (by now occupied by many Italian settlers as well as Gauls) and Narbonese Gaul beyond the Alps (modern Provence).

Relying first on the excellent quality of his army and the experience of his officers and then on his own growing military ability, Caesar made great progress. By 56 B.C.E., he had conquered most of Gaul, but he had not yet consolidated his victories firmly. He therefore sought an extension of his command, but quarrels between Crassus and Pompey so weakened the Triumvirate that the Senate was prepared to order Caesar's recall.

To prevent the dissolution of his base of power, Caesar persuaded Crassus and Pompey to meet with him at Luca in northern Italy to renew the coalition. They agreed that Caesar would get another five-year command in Gaul, and Crassus and Pompey would be consuls again in 55 B.C.E. After that, they would each receive an army and a five-year command. Caesar was free to return to Gaul and finish the job. The capture of Alesia in 51 B.C.E. marked the end of the serious Gallic resistance and of Gallic liberty. For Caesar, it brought the wealth, fame, and military power he wanted. He commanded thirteen loyal legions, a match for his enemies as well as for his allies.

By the time Caesar was ready to return to Rome, the Triumvirate had dissolved and a crisis was at hand. At Carrhae, in 53 B.C.E., Crassus died trying to conquer the Parthians, successors to the Persian Empire. His death broke one link between Pompey and Caesar. The death of Caesar's daughter Julia, who had been Pompey's wife, dissolved another.

As Caesar's star rose, Pompey became jealous and fearful. In the late 50s B.C.E., political rioting at Rome caused the Senate to appoint Pompey sole consul. This grant of unprecedented power and responsibility brought Pompey closer to the senatorial aristocracy in mutual fear of, and hostility to, Caesar. The Senate wanted to bring Caesar back to Rome as a private citizen after his proconsular command expired. He would then be open to attack for past illegalities. Caesar tried to avoid the trap by asking permission to stand for the consulship in absentia.

Early in January 49 B.C.E., the more extreme faction in the Senate had its way. It ordered Pompey to defend the state and Caesar to lay down his command by a specified day. For Caesar, this meant exile or death, so he ordered his legions to cross the Rubicon River, the boundary of his province. (See Map 4–3, page 112.) This action started a civil war. In 45 B.C.E., Caesar defeated the last forces of his enemies under Pompey's sons at Munda in Spain.

Caesar made few changes in the government of Rome. The Senate continued to play its role, in theory. But its increased size, its packing with supporters of Caesar, and his own monopoly of military power made the whole thing a sham. He treated the

MAP EXPLORATION

Interactive map: To explore this map further, go to www.myhistorylab.com

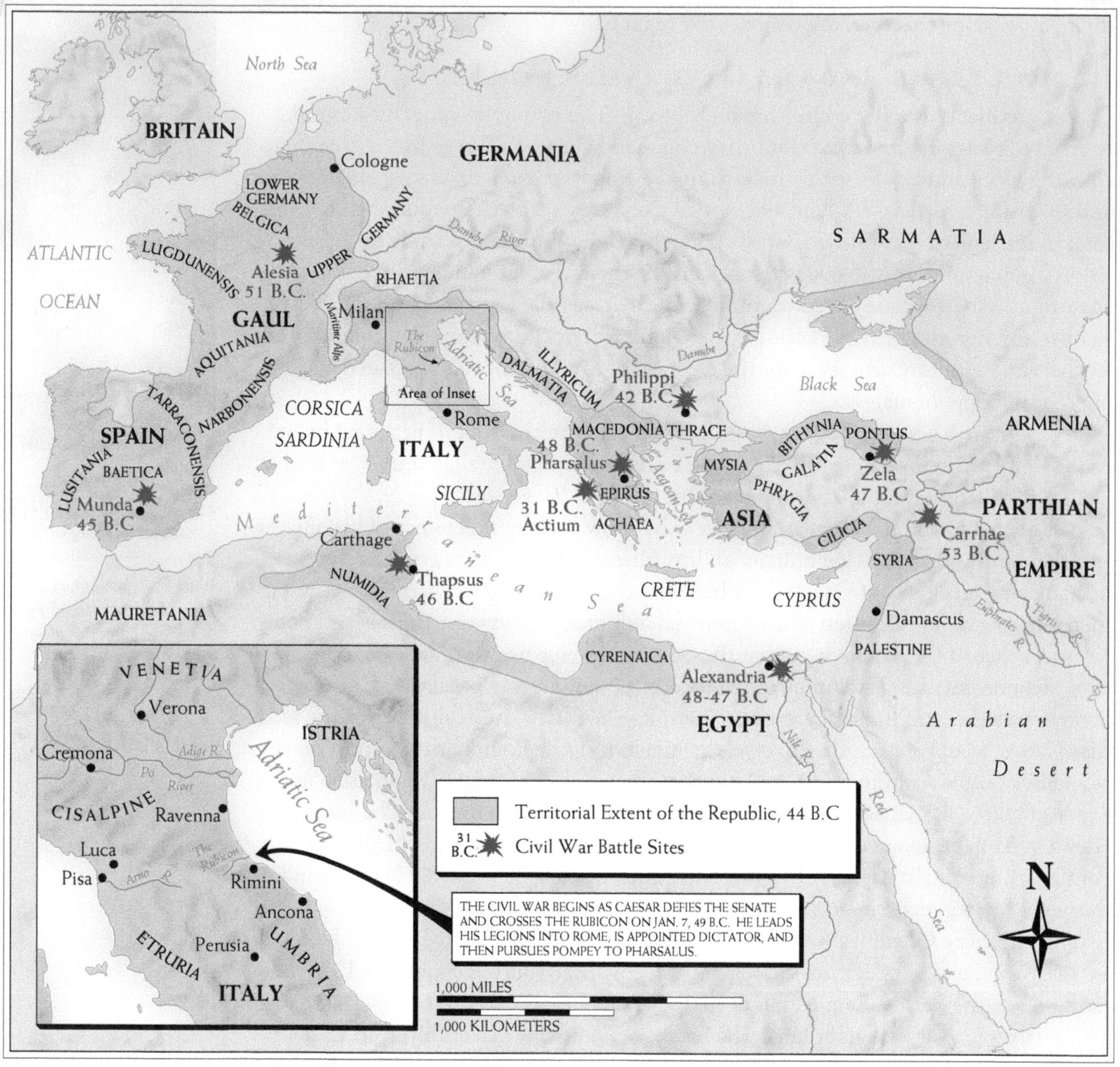

MAP 4–3 The Civil Wars of the Late Roman Republic This map shows the extent of the territory controlled by Rome at the time of Caesar's death and the sites of the major battles of the civil wars of the late republic.

What was the principal goal of Roman foreign policy during the period of the Roman Republic? How did this goal contribute to Roman expansion?

Senate as his creature, sometimes with disdain. The enemies of Caesar were quick to accuse him of aiming at monarchy. (See "Compare & Connect: Did Caesar Want to Be King?," on pages 114–115.) A conspiracy under the leadership of Gaius Cassius Longinus and Marcus Junius Brutus included some sixty senators. On 15 March 44 B.C.E., Caesar entered the Senate, characteristically without a bodyguard, and was stabbed to death. The assassins regarded themselves as heroic tyrannicides but did not have a clear plan of action to follow the tyrant's death. No doubt they simply expected the republic to be restored in the old way, but things had gone too far for that. There followed instead thirteen more years of civil war, at the end of which the republic received its final burial.

The Second Triumvirate and the Triumph of Octavian

Caesar had had legions of followers, and he had a capable successor in Mark Antony. But the dictator had named his eighteen-year-old grandnephew, Gaius Octavius (63 B.C.E.–14 C.E.), as his heir and had left him three-quarters of his vast wealth. Octavius gathered an army, won the support of many of Caesar's veterans, and became a figure of importance—the future Augustus.

At first, the Senate tried to use Octavius against Antony, but when the conservatives rejected his request for the consulship, Octavius broke with them. Following Sulla's grim precedent, he took his army and marched on Rome. There he finally assumed his adopted name, C. Julius Caesar Octavianus. Modern historians refer to him at this stage in his career as Octavian, although he insisted on being called Caesar. In August 43 B.C.E., he became consul and declared the assassins of Caesar outlaws. Brutus and Cassius had an army of their own, so Octavian made a pact with Mark Antony and M. Aemilius Lepidus, a Caesarean governor of the western provinces. They took control of Rome and had themselves appointed "triumvirs to put the republic in order," with great powers. This was the Second Triumvirate, and unlike the first, it was legally empowered to rule almost dictatorially.

In 42 B.C.E., the triumviral army defeated Brutus and Cassius at Philippi in Macedonia, and the last hope of republican restoration died with the tyrannicides. Each of the triumvirs received a command. The junior partner, Lepidus, was given Africa, Antony took the rich and inviting East, and Octavian got the West and the many troubles that went with it. Octavian had to fight a war against Sextus, the son of Pompey, who held Sicily. He also had to settle 100,000 veterans in Italy, confiscating much property and making many enemies. Helped by his friend Agrippa, he defeated Sextus Pompey in 36 B.C.E.

Meanwhile Antony was in the East, chiefly at Alexandria with Cleopatra, the queen of Egypt. In 36 B.C.E., he attacked Parthia, with disastrous results. Octavian had promised to send troops to support Antony's Parthian campaign but never sent them. Antony was forced to depend on the East for support, and this meant reliance on Cleopatra. Octavian understood the advantage of representing himself as the champion of the West, Italy, and Rome. Meanwhile he represented Antony as the man of the East and the dupe of Cleopatra, her tool in establishing Alexandria as the center of an empire and herself as its ruler.

By 32 B.C.E., all pretense of cooperation ended. Octavian and Antony each tried to put the best face on what was essentially a struggle for power. Lepidus had been put aside some years earlier. Antony sought senatorial support and promised to restore the republican constitution. Octavian seized and published what was alleged to be the will of Antony, revealing his gifts of provinces to the children of Cleopatra. This caused the conflict to take the form of East against West, Rome against Alexandria.

In 31 B.C.E., the matter was settled at Actium in western Greece. Agrippa, Octavian's best general, cut off the enemy by land and sea, forcing and winning a naval battle. Octavian pursued Antony and Cleopatra to Alexandria, where both committed suicide. The civil wars were over, and at the age of thirty-two, Octavian was absolute master of the Mediterranean world. His power was enormous, but he had to restore peace, prosperity, and confidence. All of these required establishing a constitution that would reflect the new realities without offending unduly the traditional republican prejudices that still had so firm a grip on Rome and Italy.

COMPARE & CONNECT

DID CAESAR WANT TO BE KING?

After the retirement and death of Sulla, his constitution was quickly destroyed, his attempt to restore the rule of the Senate proven a failure. The remaining years of the Roman Republic were occupied with a struggle among dynasts and senatorial factions to achieve dominance. From 49 to 46 B.C.E. Caesar and Pompey fought a great civil war that ended in total defeat for Pompey and the senatorial forces. Caesar was unchallenged master of the Roman world. His problem was to invent a system of government that would avoid the pitfalls of divided rule and yet rest upon widespread popular support. From antiquity to the present time, men have argued that his solution was nothing less than monarchy pure and simple. Others have denied that this was his goal. The question cannot be settled, for Caesar was assassinated before he could put his plans into practice, yet it is important to consider the problem both because of its intrinsic interest and because it represents a significant stage in the transition from republic to empire.

QUESTIONS

1. What does Cassius Dio think Caesar wanted?
2. What is the opinion of Nicolaus of Damascus?
3. What is the significance of the debate?

I. CASSIUS DIO

Cassius Dio was a Greek of the third century C.E. *who became a senator under the Roman Empire. He wrote an eighty-book history of Rome from the beginning to 229* C.E. *Here he tells the story of the growing suspicion among his enemies and the plots arising among them.*

When he had reached this point, the conduct of the men plotting against him became no longer doubtful, and in order to embitter even his best friends against him they did their best to traduce the man and finally called him "king,"—a name which was often heard in their consultations. When he refused the title and rebuked in a way those that so saluted him, yet did nothing by which he could be thought to be really displeased at it, they secretly adorned his statue, which stood on the rostra, with a diadem. And when Gaius Epidius Marullus and Lucius Casetius Flavus, tribunes, took it down, he became thoroughly angry, although they uttered no insulting word and furthermore spoke well of him before the people as not desiring anything of the sort. At this time, though vexed, he remained quiet; subsequently, however, when he was riding in from Albanum, some men again called him king, and he said that his name was not king but Caesar: then when those tribunes brought suit against the first man that termed him king, he no longer restrained his wrath but showed evident irritation, as if these officials were actually aiming at the stability of his government. . . .

Something else that happened not long after these events proved still more clearly that while pretendedly he shunned the title, in reality he desired to assume it. When he had entered the Forum at the festival of the Lupercalia . . . Antony with his fellow priests saluted him as king and surrounding his brows with a diadem said: "The people gives this to you through my hands." He answered that Jupiter alone was king of the Romans and sent the diadem to him to the Capitol, yet he was not angry and caused it to he inscribed in the records that the royalty presented to him by the people through the consul he had refused to receive. It was accordingly suspected that this had been done by some prearranged plan and that he was anxious for the name but wished to be somehow compelled to take it, and the consequent hatred against him was intense.

Source: CassiusDio, 44.8–11, trans. by H.B. Foster, pp. 414–417.

A profile of Brutus, one of Caesar's assassins, appeared on this silver coin. The reverse shows a cap of liberty between two daggers and reads "Ides of March."

Getty Images, Inc–Liaison

What were the political goals of Caesar's assassins?

II. NICOLAUS OF DAMASCUS

Nicolaus was born to a distinguished Greek family in the first century B.C.E. *He served as adviser and court historian to Herod the Great of Judea. In addition to the biography of the young Augustus, from which the following selection is taken, he wrote dramas, philosophical works, and a multivolume history of the world.*

Such was the people's talk at that time. Later, in the course of the winter, a festival was held in Rome, called Lupercalia, in which old and young men together take part in a procession, naked except for a girdle, and anointed, railing at those whom they meet and striking them with pieces of goat's hide. When this festival came on Marcus Antonius was chosen director. He proceeded through the Forum, as was the custom, and the rest of the throng followed him. Caesar was sitting in a golden chair on the Rostra, wearing a purple toga. At first Licinius advanced toward him carrying a laurel wreath, though inside it a diadem was plainly visible. He mounted up, pushed up by his colleagues (for the place from which Caesar was accustomed to address the assembly was high), and set the diadem down before Caesar's feet. Amid the cheers of the crowd he placed it on Caesar's head. Thereupon Caesar called Lepidus, the master of horse, to ward him off, but Lepidus hesitated. In the meanwhile Cassius Longinus, one of the conspirators, pretending to be really well disposed toward Caesar so that he might the more readily escape suspicion, hurriedly removed the diadem and placed it in Caesar's lap. Publius Casca was also with him. While Caesar kept rejecting it, and among the shouts of the people, Antonius suddenly rushed up, naked and anointed, just as he was in the procession, and placed it on his head. But Caesar snatched it off, and threw it into the crowd. Those who were standing at some distance applauded this action, but those who were near at hand clamored that he should accept it and not repel the people's favor. Various individuals held different views of the matter. Some were angry, thinking it an indication of power out of place in a democracy; others, thinking to court favor, approved; still others spread the report that Antonius had acted as he did not without Caesar's connivance. There were many who were quite willing that Caesar be made king openly. All sorts of talk began to go through the crowd. When Antonius crowned Caesar a second time, the people shouted in chorus, 'Hail, King,' but Caesar still refusing the crown, ordered it to be taken to the temple of Capitolme Jupiter, saying that it was more appropriate there. Again the same people applauded as before. There is told another story, that Antonius acted thus wishing to ingratiate himself with Caesar, and at the same time was cherishing the hope of being adopted as his son. Finally, he embraced Caesar and gave the crown to some of the men standing near to place it on the head of the statue of Caesar which was near by. This they did. Of all the occurrences of that time this was not the least influential in hastening the action of the conspirators, for it proved to their very eyes the truth of the suspicions they entertained.

Source: Nicolaus of Damascus, *Life of Augustus*, 19–22, trans. by Clayton M. Hall (Menascha, WI: George Banta, 1923), p. 41. Reprinted by permission of Clayton M. Hall.

Summary

Prehistoric Italy The Neolithic era came late to Italy, around 2500 B.C.E., followed by the Bronze Age starting around 1500 B.C.E. Bands of warring peoples speaking Italic languages invaded from across the Adriatic and along the northeastern coast starting around 1000 B.C.E.; within two centuries they had occupied the Appenines and were challenging the earlier settlers on the western plains. These peoples shaped Italy's history. *page 92*

WHO WERE the Etruscans and how did they influence Rome?

The Etruscans Etruscan civilization emerged in Etruria around 800 B.C.E. The Etruscans formed a military ruling class that held power over the native Italians. Etruscan religion exerted a strong influence throughout the region. Etruscans expanded their domains and controlled large holdings in Italy, Corsica, and Elba. Etruscan power had peaked by 500 B.C.E., then declined rapidly under attack by the Gauls around 400 B.C.E. *page 92*

HOW DID ideas about the family influence society and government in early Rome?

Royal Rome Rome's location on the Tiber River made it an important center for communication and trade. In the sixth century B.C.E., under the leadership of Etruscan kings, Rome developed political institutions that would endure through the Roman Republic, imperial Rome, and beyond. The kings of Rome held the power of *imperium*, but they were checked by the Senate and the curiate assembly. The family was the center of Roman life. Women and children had some protections. Upper-class women had positions of influence and respect greater than those available to Greek women. *Clientage* entailed mutual obligations between client and patron; the relationship was hereditary and sanctioned by religion. The two classes in royal Rome were *patricians*, a closed upper class that monopolized power, and the *plebeians*, who were originally poor but eventually came to include wealthy families unable to join the patrician class. *page 93*

WHAT ROLE did consuls, the Senate, and the Assembly play in Republican government?

The Republic In 509 B.C.E., the noble families revolted successfully against the monarchy and created the Roman Republic. A limited form of the *imperium* was exercised by the consuls. Over the following centuries, the powers of the Senate increased substantially. Plebeians chafed against the limits on their political participation and other rights, leading to the Struggle of the Orders. By the middle of the third century B.C.E., Rome controlled the Italian peninsula. Conflict between Rome and Carthage in Sicily erupted in the First Punic War, through which Rome won control of Sicily. By mismanaging the peace, however, the Romans set the stage for the Second Punic War, in which Rome faced Hannibal. After winning every battle, Hannibal lost the war when the Roman general Scipio defeated the Carthaginians. Meanwhile, Rome had started meddling in Macedonian affairs, participating in the three Macedonian Wars. Rome's victory at the conclusion of the Third Macedonian War in 168 B.C.E. resulted in an uncharacteristically harsh peace. *page 95*

HOW DID contact with the Hellenistic world affect Rome?

Civilization in the Early Roman Republic Educated Romans were bilingual, in Latin and Greek; Greek mythology was incorporated into Roman religion; education became Hellenized, and Greeks took on significant roles in the formal educational system. Girls did not attend school, but among the upper classes they were tutored at home. Slavery increased dramatically as the Romans enslaved prisoners of war. Manumission was common, and former slaves enjoyed social and economic mobility. The development of the *latifundia* system of agriculture—basically, cash-crop plantations that depended on slave labor—fueled the growth of a harsher and more oppressive form of slavery, with the result that significant slave rebellions occurred. Slavery declined gradually; in agriculture, tenant farmers called *coloni* slowly filled the economic niche of slavery. *page 103*

HOW DID the expansion of Rome change the Republic?

Roman Imperialism: The Late Republic War, expansion, and the administration of an empire fundamentally altered Roman culture. The availability of cheap land and labor sharpened class differences throughout Italy. Tiberius Gracchus's unconstitutional tactics in attempting to pass land reform legislation in 133 B.C.E. led eventually to a riot in which Tiberius and three hundred of his supporters were killed. Roman politics was changed forever. Fundamental issues were now clearly at stake. Tiberius's brother Gaius Gracchus assumed the tribunate in 123 B.C.E. and passed some populist reforms, but he too was assassinated. Soon senatorial privilege was challenged from abroad, through the Jugurthine War that began in 111 B.C.E. Two ambitious generals, Marius and Sulla, gained power through their victories. Later, fighting barbarian tribes to the north, Marius introduced innovations into the army that made soldiers more loyal to their general than to the state. All Italians gained citizenship after a revolt. Between 88 and 83 B.C.E., Marius and Sulla dragged the Romans into civil war in their competition for power; Sulla won, assassinated his opponents, and attempted to reform the constitution and government institutions. *page 105*

WHAT EVENTS led to the fall of the Republic?

The Fall of the Republic Soon after Sulla's death, Crassus and Pompey intimidated the Senate into granting them extraordinary powers. By 60 B.C.E., when Crassus, Pompey, and Caesar all found their ambitions thwarted by the Senate, they formed the First Triumvirate, an informal political alliance to further their own private goals. Caesar was elected consul in 59 B.C.E. and enacted the triumvirs' program. Through impressive military conquest and intense diplomacy, Caesar held on to power until his assassination fifteen years later. Mark Antony and Gaius Octavius vied to succeed Caesar, although they joined with M. Aemilius Lepidus to form the Second Triumvirate to fight against Caesar's assassins in a civil war. After the triumvirate won, Octavian patronized the Roman arts and fostered the impression that Antony was a stooge of Cleopatra. When the power struggle between Octavian and Antony degenerated into battle, at Actium in 31 B.C.E., Octavian's forces won. *page 109*

REVIEW QUESTIONS

1. How did the institutions of family and clientage and the establishment of patrician and plebeian classes contribute to the stability of the early Roman Republic? What was "the Struggle of the Orders"? What methods did plebeians use to get what they wanted?
2. Until 265 B.C.E., how and why did Rome expand its territory? How was Rome able to conquer and to control Italy? Why did Romans and Carthaginians clash in the First and Second Punic Wars? Could the wars have been avoided? What problems did the victory create for Rome?
3. What social, economic, and political problems faced Italy in the second century B.C.E.? How did Tiberius and Gaius Gracchus propose to solve them? What were the political implications of the Gracchan reform program? Why did reform fail?
4. What were the problems that plagued the Roman Republic in the last century B.C.E.? What caused these problems, and how did the Romans try to solve them? To what extent were ambitious, power-hungry generals responsible for the destruction of the republic?

KEY TERMS

censors (p. 96)
coloni (p. 105)
consuls (p. 96)
equestrians (p. 107)
Gaul (p. 93)
humanitas (p. 104)
imperium (p. 94)
latifundia (p. 105)
Latium (p. 93)
optimates (p. 107)
patricians (p. 95)
plebeians (p. 95)
populares (p. 107)
proconsulships (p. 96)
tribunes (p. 97)

For additional learning resources related to this chapter, please go to **www.myhistorylab.com**

myhistorylab

5

The Roman Empire

This statue of Emperor Augustus (r. 27 B.C.E.–14 C.E.), now in the Vatican, stood in the villa of Augustus's wife, Livia. The figures on the elaborate breastplate are all of symbolic significance. At the top, for example, Dawn in her chariot brings in a new day under the protective mantle of the sky god; in the center, Tiberius, Augustus's future successor, accepts the return of captured Roman army standards from a barbarian prince; and at the bottom, Mother Earth offers a horn of plenty.

Vatican Museums & Galleries, Vatican City/Superstock

What does this statue tell us about the Romans' vision of themselves and their empire?

THE AUGUSTAN PRINCIPATE *page 120*

HOW DID Augustus transform Roman politics and government?

CIVILIZATION OF THE CICERONIAN AND AUGUSTAN AGES *page 122*

HOW DID political developments shape the culture of the Ciceronian and Augustan ages?

IMPERIAL ROME, 14 TO 180 C.E. *page 124*

HOW WAS imperial Rome governed and what was life like for its people?

THE RISE OF CHRISTIANITY *page 130*

WHO WAS Jesus of Nazareth?

THE CRISIS OF THE THIRD CENTURY *page 136*

HOW DID economic developments lead to the political and military crisis of the third century?

THE LATE EMPIRE *page 138*

WHAT FACTORS contributed to the decline and eventual fall of Rome?

ARTS AND LETTERS IN THE LATE EMPIRE *page 144*

HOW DID arts and letters in Late Rome reflect the developing relationship between pagan and Christian ideas?

THE PROBLEM OF THE DECLINE AND FALL OF THE EMPIRE IN THE WEST *page 145*

WHY WERE new conquests so important to the vitality of the Roman Empire?

Octavian's victory over Mark Antony in 31 B.C.E. *ended a century of civil strife that had begun with the murder of Tiberius Gracchus. Octavian (subsequently known as Augustus) stabilized Rome by establishing a monarchy hidden behind a republican facade. The unification of the Mediterranean world promoted peace and economic expansion. The spread of Latin and Greek as the empire's official languages promoted growth of a common Classical tradition that had a great influence on the development of a new religion that appeared in the first century* C.E.*: Christianity.*

In the third century C.E.*, Rome's institutions began to fail, and its emperors resorted to drastic measures to try to maintain order. The result was growing centralization and militarization of an increasingly authoritarian government. A wave of invasions in the second half of the fifth century finally initiated the empire's collapse.*

THE AUGUSTAN PRINCIPATE

HOW DID Augustus transform Roman politics and government?

If the problems facing Octavian after the Battle of Actium in 31 B.C.E. were great, so were his resources for addressing them. He was the master of a vast military force, the only one in the Roman world, and he had loyal and capable assistants. Of enormous importance was the rich treasury of Egypt, which Octavian treated as his personal property. The people of Italy were eager for an end to civil war and a return to peace, order, and prosperity. The memory of Julius Caesar's fate, however, was still fresh in Octavian's mind. Its lesson was that it was dangerous to flaunt unprecedented powers and to disregard all republican traditions.

During the civil war Octavian's powers came from his triumviral status, whose dubious legality and unrepublican character were an embarrassment. From 31 B.C.E. on, he held the consulship each year, but this circumstance was neither strictly legal nor satisfactory. On 13 January 27 B.C.E., Octavian put forward a new plan in dramatic style, coming before the Senate to give up all his powers and provinces. In what was surely a rehearsed response, the Senate begged him to reconsider. At last he agreed to accept the provinces of Spain, Gaul, and Syria with proconsular power for military command and to retain the consulship in Rome. The other provinces would be governed by the Senate as before. Because the provinces he retained were border provinces that contained twenty of Rome's twenty-six legions, his true power was undiminished. The Senate, however, responded with almost hysterical gratitude, voting him many honors. Among them was the semireligious title **Augustus**, which implied veneration, majesty, and holiness. From this time on, historians speak of Rome's first emperor as Augustus and of his regime as the *Principate* (from *princeps*, or "first citizen"). This would have pleased him, for it helps conceal the novel, unrepublican nature of the regime and the naked power on which it rested.

Augustus ("revered") Name by which the Senate hailed Octavian for his restoration of the republic.

ADMINISTRATION

Augustus made important changes in the government of Rome, Italy, and the provinces. Most of his reforms reduced inefficiency and corruption, ended the danger to peace and order from ambitious individuals, and lessened the distinction between Romans and Italians, senators and equestrians. The assemblies lost their significance as a working part of the constitution, and the Senate took on most of the functions of the assemblies. Augustus purged the old Senate of undesirable members and fixed its number at six hundred. He recruited its members from wealthy men of good character, who entered after serving as lesser magistrates. Augustus controlled the elections and en-

This scene from Augustus's *Ara Pacis*, the Altar of Peace, in Rome shows the general Marcus Agrippa (63–12 B.C.E.) in procession with the imperial family. Agrippa was a powerful deputy, close friend, and son-in-law of Augustus. He was chiefly responsible for the victory over Marc Antony at the Battle of Actium in 31 B.C.E.

Museum of the Ara Pacis, Rome, Italy

How did ties of family and clientage shape Roman politics?

sured that promising young men, whatever their origin, served the state as administrators and provincial governors. In this way, many equestrians and Italians who had no connection with the Roman aristocracy entered the Senate. For all his power, Augustus was always careful to treat the Senate with respect and honor.

Augustus divided Rome into regions and wards with elected local officials. He gave the city its first public fire department and police force. He carefully controlled grain distribution to the poor and created organizations to provide an adequate water supply. The Augustan period was one of great prosperity, based on the wealth brought in by the conquest of Egypt, on the great increase in commerce and industry made possible by general peace, on a vast program of public works, and on the revival of small farming by Augustus's resettled veterans.

The union of political and military power in the hands of the *princeps* enabled him to install rational, efficient, and stable government in the provinces for the first time. The emperor, in effect, chose the governors, removed the incompetent or rapacious, and allowed the effective ones to keep their provinces for longer periods. Also, he allowed much greater local autonomy, giving considerable responsibility to the upper classes in the provincial cities and towns and to the tribal leaders in less civilized areas.

The Army and Defense

The main external problem facing Augustus—and one that haunted all his successors—was the northern frontier. Rome needed to pacify the regions to the north and the northeast of Italy and to find defensible frontiers against the recurring waves of barbarians. Augustus's plan was to push forward into central Europe to create the shortest possible defensive line. The eastern part of the plan succeeded, and the campaign in the West started well. In 9 C.E., however, the German tribal leader Herrmann, or Arminius, as the Romans called him, ambushed and destroyed three Roman legions, and the aged Augustus abandoned the campaign, leaving a problem of border defense that bedeviled his successors.

Under Augustus, the armed forces achieved professional status. Together with the auxiliaries from the provinces, these forces formed a frontier army of about 300,000 men. The army permanently based in the provinces brought Roman culture to the natives. As time passed, the provincials on the frontiers became Roman citizens who helped strengthen Rome's defenses against the barbarians outside.

Religion and Morality

A century of political strife and civil war had undermined many of the foundations of traditional Roman society. To repair the damage, Augustus sought to preserve and restore the traditional values of the family and religion in Rome and Italy. He introduced laws curbing adultery and divorce and encouraging early marriage and the procreation of legitimate children. Augustus also worked at restoring the dignity of formal Roman religion, building many temples, reviving old cults, invigorating the priestly colleges, and banning the worship of newly introduced foreign gods.

CIVILIZATION OF THE CICERONIAN AND AUGUSTAN AGES

HOW DID political developments shape the culture of the Ciceronian and Augustan ages?

The high point of Roman culture came in the last century of the republic and during the Principate of Augustus. Both periods reflected the dominant influence of Greek culture, especially its Hellenistic mode. Yet in spirit and sometimes in form, the art and writing of both periods show uniquely Roman qualities.

The Late Republic

Cicero The towering literary figure of the late republic was Cicero (106–43 B.C.E.). Cicero believed in a world governed by divine and natural law that human reason could perceive and human institutions reflect. He looked to law, custom, and tradition to produce both stability and liberty. His literary style, as well as his values and ideas, were an important legacy for the Middle Ages and, reinterpreted, for the Renaissance.

History The last century of the republic produced some historical writing, much of which is lost to us. Sallust (86–35 B.C.E.) wrote a history of the years 78 to 67 B.C.E., but only a few fragments remain to remind us of his reputation as the greatest of republican historians. Julius Caesar wrote important treatises on the Gallic and civil wars. They are not fully rounded historical accounts, but chiefly military narratives written from Caesar's point of view and to enhance his repuation.

Law The period from the Gracchi to the fall of the republic was important in the development of Roman law. Before that time, Roman law was essentially national and had developed chiefly by juridical decisions, case by case. Contact with foreign peoples and the influence of Greek ideas, however, forced a change. Quite early, the edicts of the magistrates who dealt with foreigners developed the idea of the ***jus gentium***, or "law of peoples," as opposed to that arising strictly from the experience of the Romans. In the first century B.C.E., the influence of Greek thought made the idea of *jus gentium* identical with that of the ***jus naturae***, or "natural law," taught by the Stoics.

jus gentium Law of all peoples as opposed to the law that reflected only Roman practice.

jus naturae Law of nature that enshrined the principles of divine reason that Cicero and the Stoics believed governed the universe.

Overview The Great Augustan Poets

VERGIL (70–19 B.C.E.)	The most important of the Augustan poets, Vergil wrote somewhat artificial pastoral idylls. Vergil transformed the early Greek poet's praise of simple labor into a hymn to the human enterprise—the civilizing of the world of nature. His most important poem, the *Aeneid*, celebrated Italy's traditional religious cults and institutions.
HORACE (65–8 B.C.E.)	The son of a freedman, Horace was a highly skillful lyric poet. He produced a collection of genial, sometimes humorous, poems called *satires* and a number of *odes*, songs that glorify the Augustan order. He skillfully adapted Latin to the forms of Greek verse.
PROPERTIUS (50–16 B.C.E.)	Propertius joined Vergil and Horace as a member of the poetic circle favored by Augustus's wealthy friend Maecenas. He wrote elegies that were renowned for their grace and wit.
OVID (43 B.C.E.–18 C.E.)	Ovid was the only one of the great poets to run spectacularly afoul of Augustus. His poetic celebrations of the loose sexual mores of sophisticated Roman aristocrats did not serve the *princeps's* purpose. When Ovid published a poetic textbook on the art of seduction, *Ars Amatoria*, Augustus exiled him to a remote region of the empire.

Poetry The time of Cicero was also the period of two of Rome's greatest poets, Lucretius and Catullus, each representing a different aspect of Rome's poetic tradition. The Hellenistic poets and literary theorists saw two functions for the poet: entertainer and teacher. They thought the best poet combined both roles, and the Romans adopted the same view. Lucretius (ca. 99–55 B.C.E.) pursued a similar path in his epic poem *De Rerum Natura* (*On the Nature of the World*). In it, he set forth the scientific and philosophical ideas of Epicurus and Democritus with the zeal of a missionary trying to save society from fear and superstition.

Catullus (ca. 84–54 B.C.E.) was a thoroughly different kind of poet. He wrote poems that were personal—even autobiographical. He offered no moral lessons and was not interested in Rome's glorious history and in contemporary politics. In a sense, he is an example of the proud, independent, pleasure-seeking nobleman who characterized part of the aristocracy at the end of the republic.

The Age of Augustus

The spirit of the Augustan Age, the Golden Age of Roman literature, was different, reflecting the new conditions of society. Under Augustus, all patronage flowed from the *princeps*, usually through his chief cultural adviser, Maecenas.

The major poets of this time, Vergil and Horace, had lost their property during the civil wars. The patronage of the *princeps* allowed them the leisure and the security to write poetry, but it also made them dependent on him and limited their freedom of expression. These poets were not mere propagandists, however. It seems clear that mostly they believed in the virtues of Augustus and his reign and sang its praises with some degree of sincerity.

Vergil Vergil (70–19 B.C.E.) was the most important of the Augustan poets. Vergil's greatest work is the *Aeneid*, a long national epic that placed the history of Rome in the great tradition of the Greeks and the Trojan War. Its hero, the Trojan warrior Aeneas,

This mosaic found in Tunisia shows the poet Vergil reading from his *Aeneid* to the Muses of Epic and Tragedy.

Roger Wood/CORBIS/Bettmann

What does the mosaic imply about the relationship between Greek and Roman literature?

personifies the ideal Roman qualities of duty, responsibility, serious purpose, and patriotism. As the Romans' equivalent of Homer, Vergil glorified not the personal honor and excellence of the Greek epic heroes, but the civic greatness, peace, and prosperity that Augustus and the Julian family had given to imperial Rome.

Horace Horace (65–8 B.C.E.) was the son of a freedman. His *Odes*, which are ingenious in their adaptation of Greek meters to the requirements of Latin verse, best reveal his great skills as a lyric poet. Two of the odes are directly in praise of Augustus, and many of them glorify the new Augustan order, the imperial family, and the empire.

Propertius Sextus Propertius lived in Rome in the second half of the first century B.C.E., a contemporary of Vergil and Horace. Like them, he was part of the poetic circle around Augustus's friend Maecenas. He wrote witty and graceful elegies.

Ovid The career of Ovid (43 B.C.E.–18 C.E.) reveals the darker side of Augustan influence on the arts. He wrote light and entertaining love elegies that reveal the sophistication and the loose sexual code of a notorious sector of the Roman aristocracy whose values and amusements were contrary to the seriousness and family-centered life Augustus was trying to foster. Ovid's *Ars Amatoria*, a poetic textbook on the art of seduction, angered Augustus and was partly responsible for the poet's exile in 8 C.E. His most popular work is the *Metamorphoses*, a kind of mythological epic that turns Greek myths into charming stories in a graceful and lively style.

History The achievements of Augustus, his emphasis on tradition, and the continuity of his regime with the glorious history of Rome encouraged both historical and antiquarian prose works. Livy's (59 B.C.E.–17 C.E.) *History of Rome* treated the period from the legendary origins of Rome until 9 B.C.E. Its purpose was moral, and he set up historical models as examples of good and bad behavior and, above all, patriotism. He glorified Rome's greatness and connected it with Rome's past, as Augustus tried to do.

Architecture and Sculpture Augustus was as great a patron of the visual arts as he was of literature. His building program beautified Rome, glorified his reign, and contributed to the general prosperity and his own popularity. The Greek classical style, which aimed at serenity and the ideal type, influenced most of the building. The same features were visible in the portrait sculpture of Augustus and his family. The greatest monument of the age is the *Ara Pacis*, or "Altar of Peace," dedicated in 9 B.C.E. Part of it shows a procession in which Augustus and his family appear to move forward, followed in order by the magistrates, the Senate, and the people of Rome. There is no better symbol of the new order.

IMPERIAL ROME, 14 TO 180 C.E.

HOW WAS imperial Rome governed and what was life like for its people?

THE EMPERORS

Because Augustus was ostensibly only the "first citizen" of a restored republic and the Senate and the people theoretically voted him his powers, he could not legally name his successor. In fact, however, he plainly designated his heirs by lavishing favors on

them and by giving them a share in the imperial power and responsibility. Tiberius (r. 14–37 C.E.), his immediate successor, was at first embarrassed by the ambiguity of his new role, but soon the monarchical and hereditary nature of the regime became clear. Gaius (Caligula, r. 37–41 C.E.), Claudius (r. 41–54 C.E.), and Nero (r. 54–68 C.E.) were all descended from either Augustus or his wife, Livia, and all were elevated because of that fact.

Gaius Caesar Germanicus succeeded Tiberius in 37 at the age of twenty-five. He restored the use of trials for treason that had darkened the reign of Tiberius and was vicious and cruel. He claimed to be divine even while alive and was thought to aim at a despotic monarchy like that of the Ptolemies in Egypt. Caligula spent the large amount of money in the state treasury and tried to get more by seizing the property of wealthy Romans. He was widely thought to be insane.

In 41 C.E., the naked military basis of imperial rule was revealed when the Praetorian Guard, having assassinated Caligula, dragged the lame, stammering, and frightened Claudius from behind a curtain and made him emperor. Claudius left the throne to his stepson Nero. Nero's incompetence and unpopularity, and especially his inability to control his armies, led to a serious rebellion in Gaul in 68 C.E. The year 69 saw four different emperors assume power in quick succession as different Roman armies took turns placing their commanders on the throne.

Marcus Aurelius, emperor of Rome from 161 to 180 C.E., was one of the five "good emperors" who brought a period of relative peace and prosperity to the empire. This is the only Roman bronze equestrian statue that has survived.

Capitoline Museums, Rome, Italy/Canali PhotoBank, Milan/Superstock

From the Roman point of view, what made Marcus Aurelius a "good emperor"?

Vespasian (r. 69–79 C.E.) emerged victorious from the chaos, and his sons, Titus (r. 79–81 C.E.) and Domitian (r. 81–96 C.E.), carried forward his line, the Flavian dynasty. Vespasian, a tough soldier from the Italian middle class, was the first emperor who did not come from the old Roman nobility.

The assassination of Domitian put an end to the Flavian dynasty. Because Domitian had no close relative who had been designated as successor, the Senate put Nerva (r. 96–98 C.E.) on the throne to avoid chaos. He was the first of the five "good emperors," who included Trajan (r. 98–117 C.E.), Hadrian (r. 117–138 C.E.), Antoninus Pius (r. 138–161 C.E.), and Marcus Aurelius (r. 161–180 C.E.).

The Administration of the Empire

The provinces flourished economically and generally accepted Roman rule easily. (See Map 5–1, page 126.) Imperial policy usually combined an attempt to unify the empire and its various peoples with a respect for local customs and differences. Roman citizenship was spread ever more widely, and by 212 C.E., almost every free inhabitant of the empire was a citizen. Latin became the language of the western provinces. Although the East remained essentially Greek in language and culture, even it adopted many aspects of Roman life.

Local Municipalities From an administrative and cultural standpoint, the empire was a collection of cities and towns and had little to do with the countryside. Roman policy during the Principate was to raise urban centers to the status of Roman municipalities, with the rights and privileges attached to them. Therefore, the Romans enlisted the upper classes of the provinces in their own government, spread Roman law and culture, and won the loyalty of the influential people.

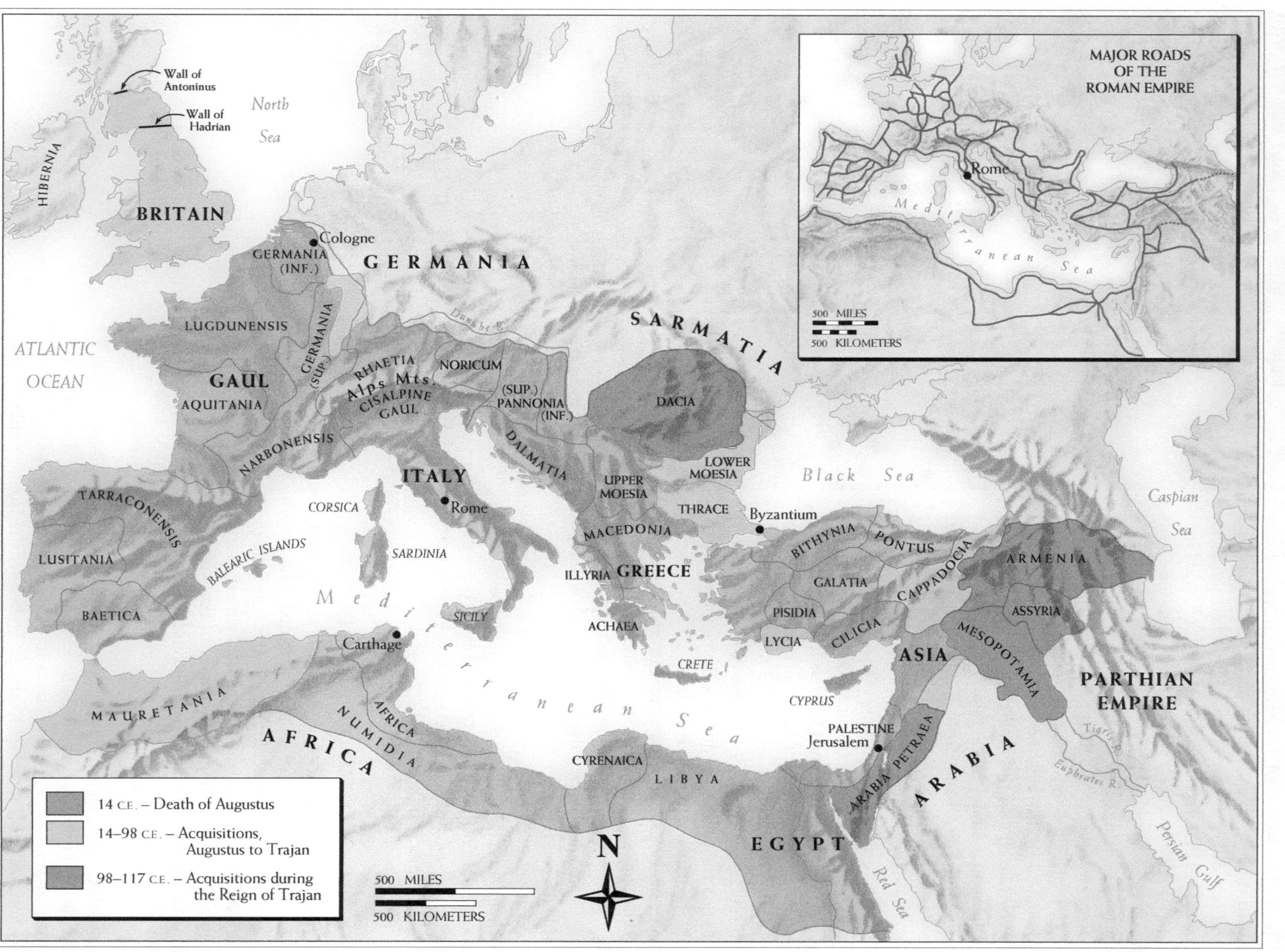

MAP 5–1 Provinces of the Roman Empire to 117 C.E. The growth of the empire to its greatest extent is here shown in three stages—at the death of Augustus in 14 C.E., at the death of Nerva in 98, and at the death of Trajan in 117. The division into provinces is also shown. The insert shows the main roads that tied the far-flung empire together.

What boundaries, both manmade and natural, did the Roman Empire have at each stage of its expansion?

There were exceptions to this picture of success. The Jews found their religion incompatible with Roman demands and were savagely repressed when they rebelled in 66–70, 115–117, and 132–135 C.E. In Egypt, the Romans exploited the peasants with exceptional ruthlessness and did not pursue a policy of urbanization.

As the efficiency of the bureaucracy grew, so did the number and scope of its functions and therefore its size. The emperors came to take a broader view of their responsibilities for the welfare of their subjects than before. More and more the emperors intervened when municipalities got into difficulties, usually financial, sending imperial troubleshooters to deal with problems. The importance and autonomy of the municipalities shrank as the central administration took a greater part in local affairs. The price paid for the increased efficiency that centralized control offered was the loss of the vitality of the cities throughout the empire.

The success of Roman civilization also came at great cost to the farmers who lived outside of Italy. Taxes, rents, mandatory gifts, and military service drew capital away from the countryside to the cities on a scale not previously seen in the Graeco-Roman world. More and more the rich life of the urban elite came at the expense of millions of previously stable farmers.

SIGNIFICANT DATES FROM THE IMPERIAL PERIOD

THE JULIO-CLAUDIAN DYNASTY

27 B.C.E.–14 C.E.	Augustus
ca. 4 B.C.E.–30 C.E.	Jesus of Nazareth
14–37 C.E.	Tiberius
37–41 C.E.	Gaius "Caligula"
41–54 C.E.	Claudius
54–68 C.E.	Nero
69 C.E.	"Year of the Four Emperors"

THE FLAVIAN DYNASTY

69–79 C.E.	Vespasian
79–81 C.E.	Titus
81–96 C.E.	Domitian
ca. 70–100 C.E.	Composition of the Gospels

THE "GOOD EMPERORS"

96–98 C.E.	Nerva
98–117 C.E.	Trajan
117–138 C.E.	Hadrian
138–161 C.E.	Antoninus Pius
161–180 C.E.	Marcus Aurelius

Foreign Policy Augustus's successors, for the most part, accepted his conservative and defensive foreign policy. Trajan was the first emperor to take the offensive in a sustained way. Between 101 and 106 C.E., he crossed the Danube and, after hard fighting, established the new province of Dacia between the Danube and the Carpathian Mountains. His intent was probably to defend the empire more aggressively by driving wedges into the territory of threatening barbarians. The same strategy dictated the invasion of the Parthian Empire in the East (113–117 C.E.). Trajan's early success was astonishing, and he established three new provinces in Armenia, Assyria, and Mesopotamia. But his lines were overextended. Rebellions sprang up, and the campaign crumbled. Trajan was forced to retreat, and he died before getting back to Rome.

Hadrian's reign marked an important shift in Rome's frontier policy. Heretofore, Rome had been on the offensive against the barbarians. Hadrian hardened the Roman defenses, building a stone wall in the south of Scotland and a wooden one across the Rhine-Danube triangle. The Roman defense became rigid, and initiative passed to the barbarians.

Agriculture: The Decline of Slavery and the Rise of the *Coloni* The defense of its frontiers put enormous pressure on the human and financial resources of the empire, but the effect of these pressures was not immediately felt. Internal peace and efficient

Spoils from the temple in Jerusalem were carried in triumphal procession by Roman troops. This relief from Titus's arch of victory in the Roman Forum celebrates his capture of Jerusalem after a two-year siege. The Jews found it difficult to reconcile their religion with Roman rule and frequently rebelled.

Scala/Art Resource, NY

Why was the relationship between the Romans and the Jews so contentious?

Imperial Roman Cameo of Livia and Tiberius.

©Burstein Collection/CORBIS

What role did elite Roman women play in Roman politics?

administration benefited agriculture as well as trade and industry. Farming and trade developed together as political conditions made it easier to sell farm products at a distance.

Small farms continued to exist, but the large estate, managed by an absentee owner and growing cash crops, dominated agriculture. At first, as in the republican period, slaves mostly worked these estates, but in the first century, this began to change. Economic pressures forced many of the free lower classes to become tenant farmers, or *coloni*, and eventually the *coloni* replaced slaves as the mainstay of agricultural labor. Eventually, they were tied to the land they worked, much as were the manorial serfs of the Middle Ages. Whatever its social costs, the system was economically efficient, however, and contributed to the general prosperity.

Women of the Upper Classes

By the late years of the Roman republic, women of the upper classes had achieved a considerable independence and influence. Some of them had become wealthy through inheritance and were well educated. Women conducted literary salons and took part in literary groups. Marriage without the husband's right of *manus* became common, and some women conducted their sexual lives as freely as men. Such women were reluctant to have children and increasingly employed contraception and abortion to avoid childbirth.

Augustus tried to restore Rome to an earlier ideal of decency and family integrity that reduced the power and sexual freedom of women. He also introduced legislation to encourage the procreation of children, but the new laws seem to have had little effect. In the first imperial century, several powerful women played an important, if unofficial, political role. In later centuries, women were permitted to make wills and inherit from children. At the turn of the first century, the Emperor Domitian freed women from the need for guardianship.

QUICK REVIEW

Elite Women

- Upper-class women were rich, educated, and influential
- Divorce was common and women used contraception
- Augustus's efforts to restore a more traditional model of the family failed

Life in Imperial Rome: The Apartment House

The civilization of the Roman Empire depended on the vitality of its cities. The typical city had about 20,000 inhabitants, and perhaps only three or four had a population of more than 75,000. The population of Rome, however, was certainly greater than

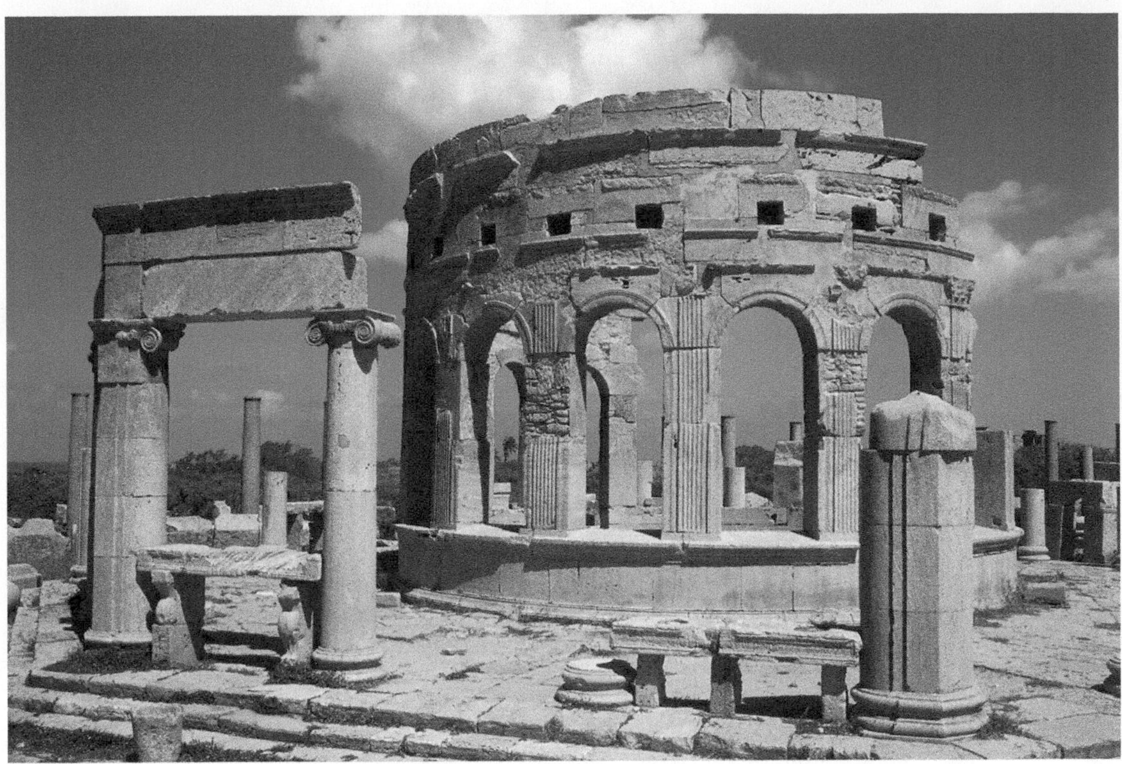

The largest city of the ancient region of Tripolitania, Leptis Magna was located sixty-two miles southeast of Tripoli on the Mediterranean coast of Libya in North Africa. In its heyday, it was one of the richest cities in the Roman Empire, and it contains some of the finest remains of Roman architecture. The city was lavishly rebuilt by the Emperor Septimius Severus (r. 193–211 C.E.), who was born at Leptis in146 C.E.

Peter Wilson/Rough Guides DK

How did the Romans use buildings and monuments to establish their presence in conquered territories?

500,000, perhaps more than a million. The rich lived in elegant homes called *domūs*. Though only a small portion of Rome's population lived in them, *domūs* took up as much as a third of the city's space. Public space for temples, markets, baths, gymnasiums, theaters, forums, and governmental buildings took up another quarter of Rome's territory.

This left less than half of Rome's area to house the mass of its inhabitants, who were squeezed into multiple dwellings that grew increasingly tall. Most Romans during the imperial period lived in apartment buildings called *insulae*, or "islands," that rose to a height of five or six stories and sometimes even more.

These buildings were divided into separate apartments (*cenicula*). The apartments were cramped and uncomfortable. They had neither central heating nor open fireplaces; heat and fire for cooking came from small portable stoves. The apartments were hot in summer, cold in winter, and stuffy and smoky when the stoves were lit. There was no plumbing, so tenants needed to go into the streets to wells or fountains for water and to public baths and latrines, or to less regulated places.

Despite these difficulties, the attractions of the city and the shortage of space caused rents to rise, making life in the *insulae* buildings expensive, uncomfortable, and dangerous. The houses were lightly built of concrete and brick and were far too high for the limited area of their foundations, and so they often collapsed. Laws limiting the height of buildings were not always obeyed and did not, in any case, always prevent disaster.

Even more serious was the threat of fire. Wooden beams supported the floors, and torches, candles, and oil lamps lit the rooms and braziers heated them. Fires broke out easily and, without running water, they usually led to disaster.

The Culture of the Early Empire

The years from 14 to 180 C.E. were a time of general prosperity and a flourishing material and artistic culture, but one not as brilliant and original as in the Age of Augustus.

Literature In Latin literature, the period between the death of Augustus and the time of Marcus Aurelius is known as the Silver Age. In contrast to the hopeful, positive optimists of the Augustans, the writers of the Silver Age were gloomy, negative, and pessimistic. In the works of the former period, praise of the emperor, his achievements, and the world abounds; in the latter, criticism and satire lurk everywhere.

The writers of the second century C.E. appear to have turned away from contemporary affairs and even recent history. Historical writing was about remote periods so there would be less danger of irritating imperial sensibilities. In the third century C.E., romances written in Greek became popular and offer further evidence of the tendency of writers of the time to seek and offer escape from contemporary realities.

Architecture The main contribution of the Romans lay in two new kinds of buildings—the great public bath and a new freestanding kind of amphitheater—and in the advances in engineering that made these large structures possible. While keeping the basic post-and-lintel construction used by the Greeks, the Romans added to it the principle of the semicircular arch, borrowed from the Etruscans. The arch, combined with the post and lintel, produced the great Colosseum built by the Flavian emperors. When used internally in the form of vaults and domes, the arch permitted great buildings like the baths, of which the most famous and best preserved are those of the later emperors Caracalla (r. 211–217) and Diocletian (r. 284–305).

Society One of the dark sides of Roman society, at least since the third century B.C.E., had been its increasing addiction to the brutal contests involving gladiators. By the end of the first century C.E., emperors regularly appealed to this barbaric entertainment as a way of winning the acclaim of their people. On broader fronts in Roman society, by the second century C.E., troubles were brewing that foreshadowed the difficult times ahead.

In the first century C.E., members of the upper classes vied with one another for election to municipal office and for the honor of doing service to their communities. By the second century C.E., the emperors had to intervene to correct abuses in local affairs and even to force unwilling members of the ruling classes to accept public office.

These difficulties reflected more basic problems. The prosperity that the end of civil war and the influx of wealth from the East brought could not sustain itself beyond the first half of the second century C.E. Population also appears to have declined for reasons that remain mysterious. The cost of government kept rising. The ever-increasing need for money compelled the emperors to raise taxes, to press hard on their subjects, and to bring on inflation by debasing the coinage. These elements brought about the desperate crises that ultimately destroyed the empire.

THE RISE OF CHRISTIANITY

WHO WAS Jesus of Nazareth?

Christianity emerged, spread, survived, and ultimately conquered the Roman Empire despite its origin among poor people from an unimportant and remote province of the empire. Christianity faced the hostility of the established religious institutions of its native Judea. It also had to compete against the official cults of Rome and the highly sophisticated philosophies of the educated classes and against such other "mystery" religions as the cults of Mithra, Isis, and Osiris. The Christians also faced the opposition of the imperial government and formal persecution. Yet Christianity achieved toleration and finally exclusive command as the official religion of the empire.

ENCOUNTERING THE PAST

CHARIOT RACING

Romans invested heavily in facilities for staging public entertainments, and among the earliest and most popular of these were race tracks. Romans were building race courses by the seventh and sixth centuries B.C.E. They called their tracks "circuses" ("circular") because of their curved layout. Rome's Circus Maximus ("Greatest Circus") was one of the earliest as well as the largest and most famous. It was used for a variety of events (riding exhibitions, wild animal hunts, etc.), but nothing rivaled the popularity of chariot racing.

The races staged in the Circus Maximus involved seven laps around the track, a distance of about 2.7 miles. As many as twelve chariots might compete at one time. Various numbers of horses could be used to pull a chariot, but the most common arrangement was the *quadriga*, the four-horse team. Short straightaways, sharp turns, and a crowded field made for a dangerous and, therefore, crowd-pleasing race. Raw speed was often less important than strength, courage, and endurance. Racing companies called *factiones* were formed to sponsor stables and professional riders. They were known by their colors. The two first were the reds and the whites. They were eventually joined by the blues, greens, purples, and golds. Betting on the races was heavy, and factions went to extremes to win victories. Horses were drugged and drivers bribed—or murdered when they proved uncooperative.

Romans bet heavily on the kind of chariot races shown on this low relief and were fanatically attached to their favorite riders and stables.

© Araldo de Luca/CORBIS

WHY DID Roman politicians and emperors find it worth their while to spend lavishly on amusements like chariot races?

JESUS OF NAZARETH

An attempt to understand this amazing outcome must begin with the story of Jesus of Nazareth. Jesus was born in the province of Judea in the time of Augustus. He was a most effective teacher in the tradition of the prophets. This tradition promised the coming of a Messiah (in Greek, *christos*—so Jesus Christ means "Jesus the Messiah"), the redeemer who would make Israel triumph over its enemies and establish the kingdom of God on earth. In fact, Jesus seems to have insisted the Messiah would not establish an earthly kingdom but would bring an end to the world as human beings knew it at the Day of Judgment. Until then (a day his followers believed would come soon), Jesus taught the faithful to abandon sin and worldly concerns; to follow him and his way; to follow the moral code described in the Sermon on the Mount, which preached love, charity, and humility; and to believe in him and his divine mission.

Jesus won a considerable following, especially among the poor, which caused great suspicion among the upper classes. His novel message and his criticism of the religious practices connected with the temple at Jerusalem and its priests provoked the hostility of the religious establishment. A misunderstanding of the movement made it easy to convince the Roman governor, Pontius Pilate, that Jesus and his followers might be dangerous revolutionaries. He was put to death in Jerusalem by the cruel and degrading device of crucifixion, probably in 30 C.E. His followers believed he was resurrected on the third day after his death, and that belief became a critical element in the religion they propagated throughout the Roman Empire and beyond.

This second-century statue in the Lateran Museum in Rome shows Jesus as the biblical Good Shepherd.

The Good Shepherd, marble, Height: as restored cm 99, as perserved cm 55, head cm 15.5. Late 3rd century A.D. Vatican Museums, Lateran Museums, Pio-Christian Museum, Inv. 28590. Courtesy of the Vatican Museums

How did the image of Jesus evolve in the two centuries following his death?

agape Common meal, or "love feast," that was the central ritual of the church in early Christianity.

Eucharist ("thanksgiving") Celebration of the Lord's Supper in which bread and wine were blessed and consumed.

The new belief spread quickly to the Jewish communities of Syria and Asia Minor. It might, however, have had only a short life as a despised Jewish heresy were it not for the conversion and career of Paul.

Paul of Tarsus

Paul was born Saul, a citizen of the Cilician city of Tarsus in Asia Minor. He had been trained in Hellenistic culture and was a Roman citizen. But he was also a zealous member of the Jewish sect known as the Pharisees, the group that was most strict in its adherence to Jewish law. He took part in the persecution of the early Christians until his own conversion outside Damascus about 35 C.E., after which he changed his name from Saul to Paul.

The great problem facing the early Christians was to resolve their relationship to Judaism. If the new faith was a version of Judaism, then it must adhere to the Jewish law and seek converts only among Jews. James, called the brother of Jesus, was a conservative who held to that view, whereas the Hellenist Jews tended to see Christianity as a new and universal religion. Paul supported the position of the Hellenists and soon won many converts among the Gentiles. After some conflict within the sect, Paul won out.

Paul believed that the followers of Jesus should be *evangelists* (messengers) to spread the gospel, or "good news," of God's gracious gift. He taught that Jesus would soon return for the Day of Judgment, and that all who would, should believe in him and accept his way. Faith in Jesus as the Christ was necessary, but not sufficient, for salvation, nor could good deeds alone achieve it. That final blessing of salvation was a gift of God's grace that would be granted to all who asked for it.

Organization

Paul and the other apostles did their work well. The new religion spread throughout the Roman Empire and even beyond its borders. It had its greatest success in the cities and among the poor and uneducated. The rites of the early communities appear to have been simple and few. Baptism by water removed original sin and permitted participation in the community and its activities. The central ritual was a common meal called the ***agape***, or "love feast," followed by the ceremony of the **Eucharist**, or "thanksgiving," a celebration of the Lord's Supper in which unleavened bread was eaten and unfermented wine was drunk. There were also prayers, hymns, or readings from the Gospels.

Not all the early Christians were poor, and the rich provided for the poor at the common meals. The sense of common love fostered in these ways focused the community's attention on the needs of the weak, the sick, the unfortunate, and the unprotected. This concern gave the early Christian communities a warmth and a human appeal that stood in marked contrast to the coldness and impersonality of the pagan cults. No less attractive were the promise of salvation, the importance to God of each human soul, and the spiritual equality of all in the new faith.

The future of Christianity depended on its communities finding an organization that would preserve unity within the group and help protect it against enemies outside. At first, the churches had little formal organization. By the second century C.E., as their numbers grew, the Christians of each city tended to accept the authority and leadership of bishops (*episkopoi*, or "overseers"). The congregations elected bishops to lead them in worship and to supervise funds. As time passed, the bishops extended their authority over the Christian communities in outlying towns and the countryside.

The bishops kept in touch with one another, maintained communications between different Christian communities, and prevented doctrinal and sectarian splintering, which would have destroyed Christian unity. They maintained internal disci-

pline and dealt with the civil authorities. After a time they began the practice of coming together in councils to settle difficult questions, to establish orthodox opinion, and even to expel as heretics those who would not accept it. It is unlikely that Christianity could have survived the travails of its early years without such strong internal organization and government.

THE PERSECUTION OF CHRISTIANS

The new faith soon incurred the distrust of the pagan world and of the imperial government. At first, Christians were thought of as a Jewish sect and were therefore protected by Roman law. It soon became clear, however, that they were different, both mysterious and dangerous. They denied the existence of the pagan gods and so were accused of atheism. Their refusal to worship the emperor was judged treasonous. Because they kept mostly to themselves, took no part in civic affairs, engaged in secret rites, and had an organized network of local associations, they were misunderstood and suspected. By the end of the first century, "the name alone"—that is, simple membership in the Christian community—was a crime.

But, for the most part, the Roman government did not take the initiative in attacking Christians in the first two centuries. (See "Compare & Connect: Christianity in the Roman Empire—Why Did the Romans Persecute the Christians?," on pages 134–135.) Mobs, not the government, started most persecutions in this period. Though they lived quiet, inoffensive lives, some Christians must have seemed unbearably smug and self-righteous. Unlike the tolerant, easygoing pagans, who were generally willing to accept the new gods of foreign people and add them to the pantheon, the Christians denied the reality of the pagan gods. They proclaimed the unique rightness of their own way and looked forward to their own salvation and the damnation of nonbelievers. It is not surprising, therefore, that pagans disliked these strange and unsocial people, tended to blame misfortunes on them, and, in extreme cases, turned to violence.

QUICK REVIEW

Reasons for Persecution

- Christians were ardent missionaries
- Christians had a network of communities throughout the empire
- Christians were secretive about their beliefs and practices

THE EMERGENCE OF CATHOLICISM

Division within the Christian Church may have been an even greater threat to its existence than persecution from outside. Most Christians never accepted complex, intellectualized opinions but held to what even then were traditional, simple, conservative beliefs. This body of majority opinion, considered to be universal, or **catholic**, was enshrined by the church that came to be called Catholic. The Catholic Church's doctrines were deemed **orthodox**, that is, "holding the right opinions," whereas those holding contrary opinions were **heretics**.

catholic ("universal") As in "universal" majority of Christians.

orthodox ("correct") As in "correct" faith in Christianity.

heretics "Takers" of contrary positions, namely in Christianity.

The need to combat heretics, however, compelled the orthodox to formulate their own views more clearly and firmly. By the end of the second century C.E., an orthodox canon included the Old Testament, the Gospels, and the Epistles of Paul, among other writings. The orthodox declared the Catholic Church itself to be the depository of Christian teaching and the bishops to be its receivers. They also drew up a creed or brief statements of faith to which true Christians should adhere.

In the first century, all that was required of one to be a Christian was to be baptized, to partake of the Eucharist, and to call Jesus the Lord. By the end of the second century, an orthodox Christian—that is, a member of the Catholic Church—was required to accept its creed, its canon of holy writings, and the authority of the bishops. The loose structure of the apostolic church had given way to an organized body with recognized leaders able to define its faith and to exclude those who did not accept it.

COMPARE & CONNECT

CHRISTIANITY IN THE ROMAN EMPIRE — Why Did the Romans Persecute the Christians?

The rise of Christianity and its spread throughout the Mediterranean presented a serious problem to the magistrates of the Roman Empire. Like most pagans, the Romans were tolerant of most religious beliefs. Persecution on religious grounds was unusual among the Romans. The Christians, however, were very different from votaries of Isis, Mithra, Magna Mater, even from the Jews. The Romans did, in fact, persecute the Christians with varying degrees of severity. The following passages shed light on the character of and reasons for these persecutions.

QUESTIONS

1. Why did Nero blame the Christians?
2. On what grounds did Pliny punish the Christians?
3. What was the reaction of Trajan?
4. How did the approach of the two emperors compare?

I. THE PERSECUTION BY NERO

In 64 C.E., a terrible fire broke out in Rome that destroyed a good part of the city. Here the historian Tacitus tells us how the Emperor Nero dealt with its aftermath.

The next thing was to seek means of propitiating the gods, and recourse was had to the Sibylline books, by the direction of which prayers were offered to Vulcanus, Ceres, and Proserpina. Juno, too, was entreated by the matrons, first, in the Capitol, then on the nearest part of the coast, whence water was procured to sprinkle the fane and image of the goddess. And there were sacred banquets and nightly vigils celebrated by married women. But all human efforts, all the lavish gifts of the emperor, and the propitiations of the gods, did not banish the sinister belief that the conflagration was the result of an order. Consequently, to get rid of the report, Nero fastened the guilt and inflicted the most exquisite tortures on a class hated for their abominations, called Christians by the populace. Christus, from whom the name had its origin, suffered the extreme penalty during the reign of Tiberius at the hands of one of our procurators, Pontius Pilatus, and a most mischievous superstition, thus checked for the moment, again broke out not only in Judaea, the first source of the evil, but even in Rome, where all things hideous and shameful from every part of the world find their centre and become popular. Accordingly, an arrest was first made of all who pleaded guilty; then, upon their information, an immense multitude was convicted, not so much of the crime of firing the city, as of hatred against mankind. Mockery of every sort was added to

Thrown to the lions in 275 C.E. by the Romans for refusing to recant his Christian beliefs, St. Mamai is an important martyr in the iconography of Georgia, a Caucasian kingdom that embraced Christianity early in the fourth century.

Courtesy of the Library of Congress

How did persecution by the Romans shape Christians' image of themselves?

their deaths. Covered with the skins of beasts, they were torn by dogs and perished, or were nailed to crosses, or were doomed to the flames and burnt, to serve as a nightly illumination, when daylight had expired.

Nero offered his gardens for the spectacle, and was exhibiting a show in the circus, while he mingled with the people in the dress of a charioteer or stood aloft on a car. Hence, even for criminals who deserved extreme and exemplary punishment, there arose a feeling of compassion; for it was not, as it seemed, for the public good, but to glut one man's cruelty, that they were being destroyed.

Source: Tacitus, *Annals* 15.44, trans. by A. J. Church and W. J. Brodribb.

II. THE EMPEROR TRAJAN AND THE CHRISTIANS

Pliny the Younger was governor of the Roman province of Bithynia in Asia Minor about 112 B.C.E. Confronted by problems caused by Christians, he wrote to the Emperor Trajan to report his policies and to ask for advice. The following exchange between governor and emperor provides evidence of the challenge Christianity posed to Rome and the Roman response.

TO THE EMPEROR TRAJAN

Having never been present at any trials of the Christians, I am unacquainted with the method and limits to be observed either in examining or punishing them.

In the meanwhile, the method I have observed towards those who have been denounced to me as Christians is this: I interrogated them whether they were Christians; if they confessed it, I repeated the question twice again, adding the threat of capital punishment; if they still persevered, I ordered them to be executed. For whatever the nature of their creed might be, I could at least feel no doubt that contumacy and inflexible obstinacy deserved chastisement. There were others also possessed with the same infatuation, but being citizens of Rome, I directed them to be carried thither. . . .

TRAJAN TO PLINY

The method you have pursued, my dear Pliny, in sifting the cases of those denounced to you as Christians is extremely proper. It is not possible to lay down any general rule which can be applied as the fixed standard in all cases of this nature. No search should be made for these people, when they are denounced and found guilty they must be punished; with the restriction, however, that when the party denies himself to be a Christian, and shall give proof that he is not (that is, by adoring our Gods he shall be pardoned on the ground of repentance even though he may have formerly incurred suspicion). Informations without the accuser's name subscribed must not be admitted in evidence against anyone, as it is introducing a very dangerous precedent, and by no means agreeable to the spirit of the age.

Source: From Pliny the Younger, *Letters*, trans. by W. Melmoth, rev. by W. M. Hutchinson (London: William Heinemann, Ltd; Cambridge, MA: Harvard University Press, 1925).

Rome as a Center of the Early Church

During this same period, the church in Rome came to have special prominence. As the center of communications and the capital of the empire, Rome had natural advantages. After the Roman destruction of Jerusalem in 135 C.E., no other city had any convincing claim to primacy in the church. Besides having the largest single congregation of Christians, Rome also benefited from the tradition that Jesus' apostles Peter and Paul were martyred there.

Peter, moreover, was thought to be the first bishop of Rome. The Gospel of Matthew (16:18) reported Jesus' statement to Peter: "Thou art Peter [in Greek, *Petros*] and upon this rock [in Greek, *petra*] I will build my church." Because of the city's early influence and because of the Petrine doctrine derived from the Gospel of Matthew, later bishops of Rome claimed supremacy in the Catholic Church.

THE CRISIS OF THE THIRD CENTURY

HOW DID economic developments lead to the political and military crisis of the third century?

Dio Cassius, a historian of the third century C.E., described the Roman Empire after the death of Marcus Aurelius as declining from "a kingdom of gold into one of iron and rust." Although we have seen that the gold contained more than a little impurity, there is no reason to quarrel with Dio's assessment of his own time.

Barbarian Invasions

The pressure on Rome's frontiers reached massive proportions in the third century. In the East, a new power threatened the frontiers. In 224 C.E. a new Iranian dynasty, the Sassanians, seized control from the Parthians and brought new vitality to Persia. They soon recovered Mesopotamia and in 260 C.E. they humiliated the Romans by taking the emperor Valerian (r. 253–260) prisoner; he died in captivity.

On the western and northern frontiers, the pressure came not from a well-organized rival empire, but from an ever-increasing number of German tribes. Though the Germans had been in contact with the Romans at least since the second century B.C.E., civilization had not much affected them. Always eager for plunder, these tough barbarians were attracted by the civilized delights they knew existed beyond the frontier of the Rhine and Danube Rivers.

The most aggressive of the Germans in the third century C.E. were the Goths. Centuries earlier they had wandered from their ancestral home near the Baltic Sea into southern Russia. In the 220s and 230s C.E., they began to put pressure on the Danube frontier. By about 250 C.E., they were able to penetrate the empire and overrun the Balkans. The need to meet this threat and the one the Persian Sassanids posed in the East made the Romans weaken their western frontiers, and other Germanic peoples—the Franks and the Alemanni—broke through in those regions. There was danger that Rome would be unable to meet this challenge.

QUICK REVIEW

Germanic Tribes

- Germans had been in contact with Romans since second century B.C.E.
- Most aggressive of the Germans in the third century C.E. were the Goths
- Weakness of the Roman army heightened the danger posed by Germanic tribes

The unprecedentedly numerous and simultaneous attacks, no doubt, caused Rome's perils but its internal weakness encouraged these attacks. The Roman army was not what it had been in its best days. By the second century C.E., it was made up mostly of romanized provincials. The training and discipline with which the Romans had conquered the Mediterranean world had declined.

Economic Difficulties

These changes were a response to the great financial needs the barbarian attacks caused. To raise money, the emperors invented new taxes, debased the coinage, and even sold the palace furniture. But it was still hard to recruit troops.

The same forces that caused problems for the army damaged society at large. The shortage of workers for the large farms, which had all but wiped out the independent family farm, reduced agricultural production. Distracted by external threats, the emperors were less able to preserve domestic peace. Piracy, brigandage, and the neglect of roads and harbors hampered trade. So, too, did the debasement of the coinage and the inflation in general. Imperial taxation and confiscations of the property of the rich removed badly needed capital from productive use.

More and more, the government had to demand services that had been given gladly in the past. Because the empire lived hand to mouth, with no significant reserve fund and no system of credit financing, the emperors had to compel the people to provide food, supplies, money, and labor. The upper classes in the cities were made to serve as administrators without pay and to meet deficits in revenue out of their own pockets. All these difficulties weakened Rome's economic strength when it was most needed.

The Social Order

The new conditions caused important changes in the social order. Hostile emperors and economic losses decimated the Senate and the traditional ruling class. Men coming up through the army took their places. The whole state began to take on an increasingly military appearance. Titles were assigned to ranks in society as to ranks in the army. The most important distinction was between the *honestiores* (senators, equestrians, the municipal aristocracy, and the soldiers) and the lower classes, or *humiliores*. *Honestiores* were given a privileged position before the law. They were given lighter punishments, could not be tortured, and alone had the right of appeal to the emperor.

As time passed, it became more difficult to move from the lower order to the higher, another example of the growing rigidity of the late Roman Empire. Peasants were tied to their lands, artisans to their crafts, soldiers to the army, merchants and shipowners to the needs of the state, and citizens of the municipal upper class to the collection and payment of increasingly burdensome taxes. Freedom and private initiative gave way before the needs of the state and its ever-expanding control of its citizens.

Civil Disorder

Marcus Aurelius' son and heir, Commodus, was killed on the last day of 192 C.E. The succeeding year was similar to the year 69. Three emperors ruled in swift succession, with Septimius Severus emerging to establish firm rule and a dynasty. The murder of Alexander Severus, the last of the dynasty, in 235 C.E., brought on a half century of internal anarchy and foreign invasion.

The empire seemed on the point of collapse. But the two conspirators who overthrew and succeeded the emperor Gallienus (r. 253–268) proved to be able soldiers. Claudius II Gothicus (268–270 C.E.) and Aurelian (270–275 C.E.) drove back the barbarians and stamped out internal disorder. The soldiers who followed Aurelian on the throne were good fighters who made significant changes in Rome's system of defense. Around Rome, Athens, and other cities, they built heavy walls that could resist barbarian attack. They drew back their best troops from the frontiers, relying chiefly on a newly organized heavy cavalry and a mobile army near the emperor's own residence.

Hereafter, mercenaries, who came from among the least civilized provincials and even from among the Germans, largely made up the army. The officers gave personal loyalty to the emperor rather than to the empire. These officers became a foreign,

This porphyry sculpture on the corner of the church of San Marco in Venice shows Emperor Diocletian (r. 284–305 C.E.) and his three imperial colleagues. Dressed for battle, they clasp one another to express their mutual solidarity.

John Heseltine © Dorling Kindersley

Why did Diocletian find it necessary to divide the Roman Empire?

hereditary caste of aristocrats that increasingly supplied high administrators and even emperors. In effect, the Roman people hired an army of mercenaries, who were only technically Roman, to protect them.

THE LATE EMPIRE

WHAT FACTORS contributed to the decline and eventual fall of Rome?

During the fourth and fifth centuries, the Romans strove to meet the many challenges, internal and external, that threatened the survival of their empire. Growing pressure from barbarian tribes pushing against its frontier intensified the empire's tendency to smother individuality, freedom, and initiative, in favor of an intrusive and autocratic centralized monarchy. Economic and military weakness increased, and it became even harder to keep the vast empire together. Hard and dangerous times may well have helped the rise of Christianity, encouraging people to turn away from the troubles of this world to be concerned about the next.

THE FOURTH CENTURY AND IMPERIAL REORGANIZATION

The period from Diocletian (r. 284–305 C.E.) to Constantine (r. 306–337 C.E.) was one of reconstruction and reorganization after a time of civil war and turmoil. Diocletian was from Illyria (the former Yugoslavia of the twentieth century). A man of undistinguished birth, he rose to the throne through the ranks of the army. He knew that the job of defending and governing the entire empire was too great for one individual.

tetrarchy Coalition of four men, each of whom was responsible for a different part of the empire, established by Diocletian.

Diocletian therefore decreed the introduction of the **tetrarchy**, the rule of the empire by four men with power divided territorially. (See Map 5–2.) He allotted the provinces of Thrace, Asia, and Egypt to himself. His co-emperor, Maximian, shared with him the title of Augustus and governed Italy, Africa, and Spain. In addition, two

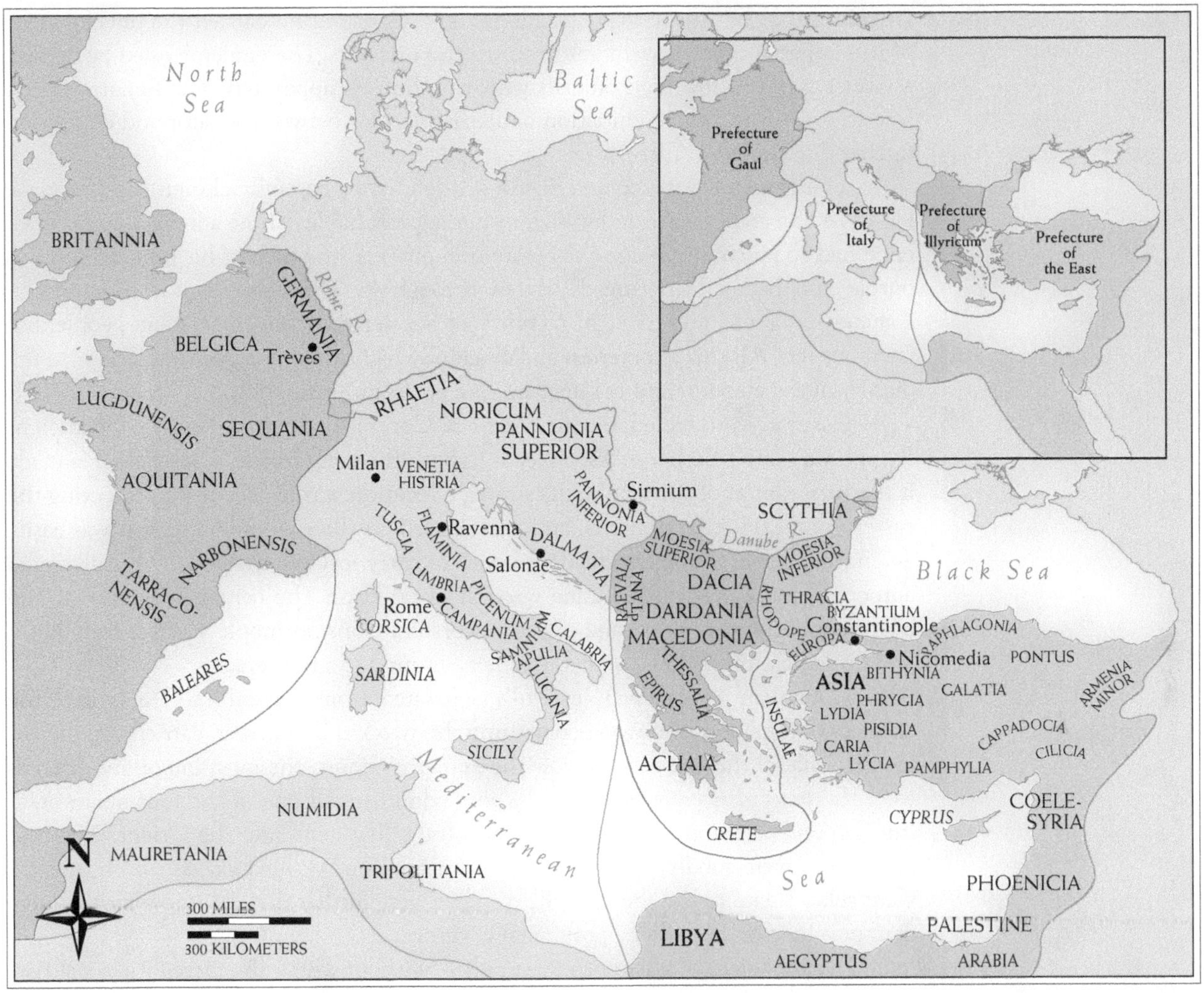

MAP 5–2 Divisions of the Roman Empire Under Diocletian Diocletian divided the sprawling empire into four prefectures for more effective government and defense. The inset map shows their boundaries, and the larger map gives some details of regions and provinces. The major division between the East and the West was along the line running south between Pannonia and Moesia.

Did Diocletian's tetrarchy likely postpone or expedite the eventual fall of the Roman Empire?

men were given the subordinate title of Caesar: Galerius, who was in charge of the Danube frontier and the Balkans, and Constantius, who governed Britain and Gaul.

This arrangement not only afforded a good solution to the military problem but also provided for a peaceful succession. Diocletian was the senior Augustus, but each tetrarch was supreme in his own sphere. The Caesars were recognized as successors to each half of the empire, and marriages to daughters of the Augusti enhanced their loyalty.

In 305 C.E., Diocletian retired and compelled his co-emperor to do the same. But his plan for a smooth succession failed. In 310, there were five Augusti and no Caesars. Out of this chaos, Constantine, son of Constantius, produced order. In 324, he defeated his last opponent and made himself sole emperor, uniting the empire once again; he reigned until 337. Mostly, Constantine carried forward the policies of Diocletian. He supported Christianity, however, which Diocletian had tried to suppress.

Development of Autocracy Diocletian and Constantine carried the development of the imperial office toward autocracy to the extreme. The emperor ruled by decree, consulting only a few high officials whom he himself appointed. The Senate had no role whatever, and the elimination of all distinctions between senator and equestrian further diminished its dignity.

The emperor was a remote figure surrounded by carefully chosen high officials. He lived in a great palace and was almost unapproachable. Those admitted to his presence had to prostrate themselves before him and kiss the hem of his robe, which was purple and had golden threads woven through it. The emperor was addressed as *dominus*, or "lord," and his right to rule was not derived from the Roman people, but from heaven. All this remoteness and ceremony had a double purpose: to enhance the dignity of the emperor and to safeguard him against assassination.

Constantine erected the new city of Constantinople on the site of ancient Byzantium on the Bosporus, which leads to both the Aegean and Black Seas. He made it the new capital of the empire. Its strategic location was excellent for protecting the eastern and Danubian frontiers, and, surrounded on three sides by water, it was easily defended. This location also made it easier to carry forward the policies that fostered autocracy and Christianity. Rome was full of tradition, the center of senatorial and even republican memories, and of pagan worship. Constantinople was free from both, and its dedication in 330 C.E. marked the beginning of a new era.

A civilian bureaucracy, carefully separated from the military to reduce the chances of rebellion by anyone combining the two kinds of power, carried out the autocratic rule of the emperors. Below the emperor's court, the most important officials were the *praetorian* prefects, each of whom administered one of the four major areas into which the empire was divided: Gaul, Italy, Illyricum, and the Orient. The four prefectures were subdivided into twelve territorial units called *dioceses*, each under a vicar subordinate to the prefect. The dioceses were further divided into almost a hundred provinces, each under a provincial governor.

A vast system of spies and secret police, without whom the increasingly rigid organization could not be trusted to perform, supervised the entire system. Despite these efforts, the system was corrupt and inefficient.

The cost of maintaining a 400,000-man army, as well as the vast civilian bureaucracy, the expensive imperial court, and the imperial taste for splendid buildings, strained an already weak economy. Diocletian's attempts to establish a reliable currency failed, leading instead to increased inflation. To deal with it, he resorted to price control with his Edict of Maximum Prices in 301 C.E. For each product and each kind of labor, a maximum price was set, and violations were punishable by death. The edict still failed.

QUICK REVIEW

Constantinople

- Dedicated by Constantine in 330 C.E.
- Situated on the Bosporus midway between eastern and Danube frontiers
- Marked the start of a new empire

Peasants unable to pay their taxes and officials unable to collect them tried to escape. Diocletian resorted to stern regimentation to keep all in their places and at the service of the government. The terror of the third century forced many peasants to seek protection in the *villa*, or "country estate," of a large and powerful landowner and to become tenant farmers. As social boundaries hardened, these *coloni* and their descendants became increasingly tied to their estates.

Division of the Empire The peace and unity Constantine established did not last long. Constantius II (r. 337–361) won the struggle for succession after his death. Constantius's death, in turn, left the empire to his young cousin Julian (r. 361–363 C.E.), whom Christians called the Apostate because of his attempt to stamp out Christianity and restore paganism. Julian undertook a campaign against Persia to put a Roman on the throne of the Sassanids and end the Persian menace once and for all. He penetrated deep into Persia but was killed in battle. His death ended the expedition and the pagan revival.

The Germans in the West took advantage of the eastern campaign to attack along the Rhine and upper Danube Rivers. In addition, even greater trouble was brewing along the middle and upper Danube. The eastern Goths, known as the Ostrogoths, occupied that territory. They were being pushed hard by their western cousins, the Visigoths, who in turn had been driven from their home in the Ukraine by the fierce Huns, a nomadic people from central Asia.

The emperor Valentinian I (r. 364–375 C.E.) saw he could not defend the empire alone and appointed his brother Valens (r. 364–378 C.E.) as co-ruler. Valentinian made his own headquarters at Milan and spent the rest of his life fighting and defeating the Franks and the Alemanni in the West. Valens was given control of the East. The empire was once again divided in two. The two emperors maintained their own courts, and the halves of the empire became increasingly separate and different. Latin was the language of the West and Greek of the East.

In 376, the Visigoths, pursued by the Huns, won rights of settlement and material assistance within the empire from the eastern emperor Valens (r. 364–378) in exchange for defending the eastern frontier as *foederati*, or special allies of the empire. The Visigoths, however, did not keep their bargain with the Romans and plundered the Balkan provinces. Nor did the Romans comply. They treated the Visigoths cruelly, even forcing them to trade their children for dogs to eat. Valens attacked the Goths and died, along with most of his army, at Adrianople in Thrace in 378. Theodosius I (r. 379–395 C.E.), an able and experienced general, was named co-ruler in the East. Theodosius tried to unify the empire again, but his death in 395 left it divided and weak.

The Rural West The two parts of the empire went their different ways. The West became increasingly rural as barbarian invasions intensified. The *villa*, a fortified country estate, became the basic unit of life. There, *coloni* gave their services to the local magnate in return for economic assistance and protection from both barbarians and imperial officials. Many cities shrank to no more than tiny walled fortresses ruled by military commanders and bishops. The upper classes moved to the country and asserted an ever-greater independence from imperial authority. The new world emerging in the West by the fifth century and afterwards was increasingly made up of isolated units of rural aristocrats and their dependent laborers. The only institution providing a high degree of unity was the Christian Church. The pattern for the early Middle Ages in the West was already formed.

The Byzantine East In the East the situation was different. Constantinople became the center of a vital and flourishing culture we call *Byzantine* that lasted until the fifteenth century. Because of its defensible location, the skill of its emperors, and the firmness and strength of its base in Asia Minor, it could deflect and repulse barbarian attacks. A strong navy allowed commerce to flourish in the eastern Mediterranean and, in good times, far beyond. Cities continued to prosper, and the emperors made their will good over the nobles in the countryside. The civilization of the Byzantine Empire was a unique combination of classical culture, the Christian religion, Roman law, and Eastern artistic influences. (See Chapter 6). Thus, when we contemplate the decline and fall of the Roman Empire in the fourth and fifth centuries, we are speaking only of the West. A form of classical culture persisted in the Byzantine East for a thousand years more.

The Triumph of Christianity

The rise of Christianity to dominance in the empire was closely connected with the political and cultural experience of the third and fourth centuries. Political chaos and decentralization had religious and cultural consequences.

Religious Currents in the Empire In some provinces, native languages replaced Latin and Greek, sometimes even for official purposes. The classical tradition that had been the basis of imperial life became the exclusive possession of a small, educated aristocracy. In religion, the public cults had grown up in an urban environment and were largely political in character. As the importance of the cities diminished, so did the significance of their gods. People might still take comfort in the worship of the friendly, intimate deities of family, field, hearth, storehouse, and craft, but these gods were too petty to serve their needs in a confused and frightening world. The only universal worship was of the emperor, but he was far off, and obeisance to his cult was more a political than a religious act.

In the troubled fourth and fifth centuries, people sought powerful, personal deities who would bring them safety and prosperity in this world and immortality in the next. Paganism was open and tolerant. Many people worshipped new deities alongside the old and even intertwined elements of several to form a new amalgam by the device called syncretism.

Manichaeism was an especially potent rival of Christianity. Named for its founder, Mani, a Persian who lived in the third century C.E., this movement contained aspects of various religious traditions, including Zoroastrianism from Persia and both Judaism and Christianity. The Manichaeans pictured a world in which light and darkness, good and evil, were constantly at war. Good was spiritual and evil was material. The movement reached its greatest strength in the fourth and fifth centuries, and some of its central ideas persisted into the Middle Ages.

Christianity had something in common with these cults and answered many of the same needs their devotees felt. None of them, however, attained Christianity's universality, and none appears to have given the early Christians as much competition as the ancient philosophies or the state religion.

Imperial Persecution By the third century, Christianity had taken firm hold in the eastern provinces and in Italy. It had not made much headway in the West, however. (See Map 5–3.) As times became bad and the Christians became more numerous and visible, popular opinion came to blame disasters, natural and military, on the Christians.

About 250, the emperor Decius (r. 249–251 C.E.) invoked the aid of the gods in his war against the Goths and required all citizens to worship the state gods publicly. True Christians could not obey, and Decius started a major persecution. Many Christians—even some bishops—yielded to threats and torture, but others held out and were killed. Valerian (r. 253–260 C.E.) resumed the persecutions, partly to confiscate the wealth of rich Christians. His successors, however, found other matters more pressing, and the persecution lapsed until the end of the century.

By the time of Diocletian, the increasing number of Christians included high officials. But hostility to the Christians had also grown on every level. Diocletian's effort to bolster imperial power with the aura of divinity boded ill for the church, and in 303 he launched the most serious persecution inflicted on the Christians in the Roman Empire. He confiscated church property and destroyed churches and their sacred books. He deprived upper-class Christians of public office and judicial rights, imprisoned clergy, and enslaved Christians of the lower classes. He fined anyone refusing to sacrifice to the public gods. A final decree required public sacrifices and libations. The persecution horrified many pagans, and the plight and the demeanor of the martyrs aroused pity and sympathy.

Ancient states could not carry out a program of terror with the thoroughness of modern totalitarian governments, so the Christians and their church survived to enjoy what they must have considered a miraculous change of fortune. In 311, Galerius, who had been one of the most vigorous persecutors, was influenced, perhaps by his Christian wife, to issue the Edict of Toleration, permitting Christian worship.

The victory of Constantine and his emergence as sole ruler of the empire changed the condition of Christianity from a precariously tolerated sect to the religion the emperor favored. This put it on the path to becoming the official and only legal religion in the empire.

Emergence of Christianity as the State Religion The sons of Constantine continued to favor the new religion, but the succession of Julian the Apostate in 360 posed a new threat. Though he refrained from persecution, he tried to undo the work of Constantine by withdrawing the privileges of the church, removing Christians from high offices, and introducing a new form of pagan worship. His reign, however, was short, and his work did not last. In 394, Theodosius forbade the celebration of pagan cults and abolished the pagan religious calendar. At his death, Christianity was the official religion of the Roman Empire.

The establishment of Christianity as the state religion did not put an end to the troubles of the Christians and their church; instead, it created new ones and complicated some old ones. The favored position of the church attracted converts for the wrong reasons and diluted the moral excellence and spiritual fervor of its adherents. The problem of the relationship between church and state arose, presenting the possibility that religion would become subordinate to the state, as it had been in the classical world and in earlier civilizations. In the East, that largely happened.

In the West, the weakness of the emperors permitted church leaders to exercise remarkable independence. In 390, Ambrose, bishop of Milan, excommunicated Theodosius I for a massacre he had carried out, and the emperor did penance. This act provided an important precedent for future assertions of the church's autonomy and authority, but it did not end secular interference and influence in the church.

MAP EXPLORATION

Interactive map: To explore this map further, go to www.myhistorylab.com

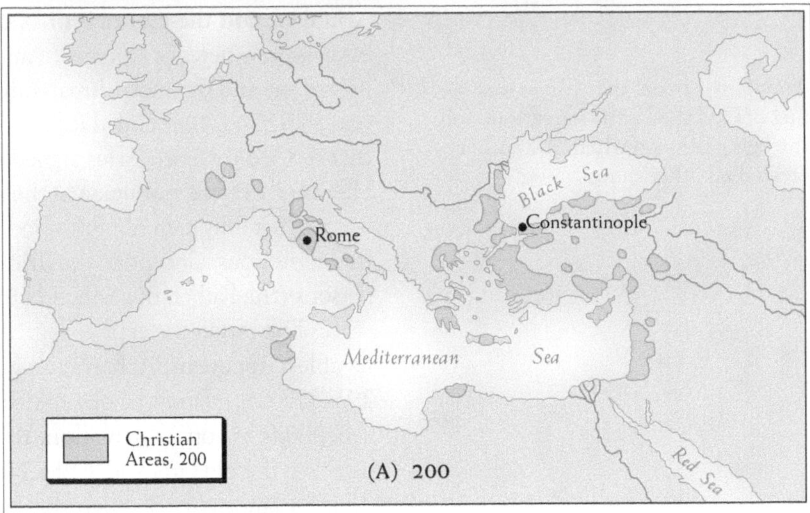

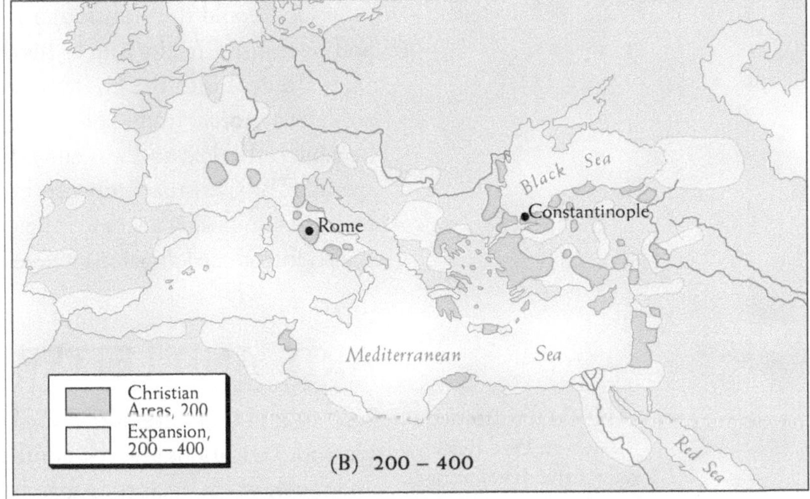

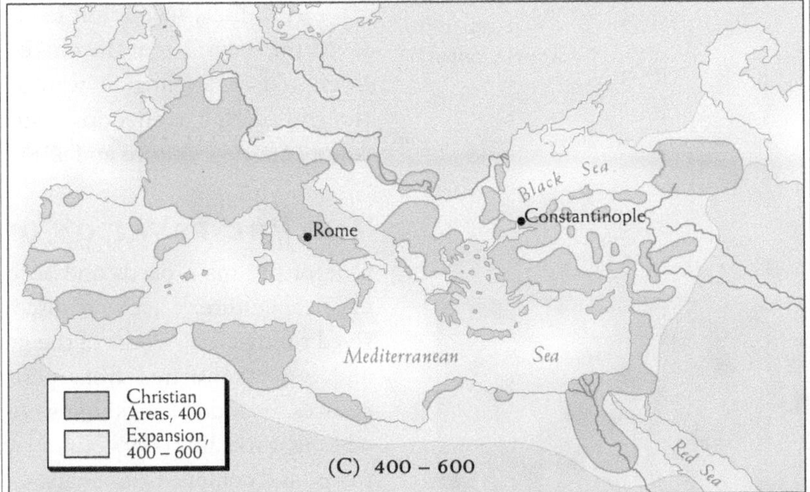

MAP 5–3 **The Spread of Christianity** Christianity grew swiftly in the third, fourth, fifth, and sixth centuries—especially after the conversion of the emperors in the fourth century. By 600, on the eve of the birth of the new religion of Islam, Christianity was dominant throughout the Mediterranean world and most of Western Europe.

How important was state acceptance of Christianity to the religion's growth in the Roman Empire?

Arianism Belief that Christ was the first of God the Father's creations and the being through whom the Father created all other things.

Arianism and the Council of Nicea Internal divisions proved to be even more troubling as new heresies emerged. Among the many controversial views that arose, the most important and the most threatening was **Arianism.** A priest named Arius of Alexandria (ca. 280–336 C.E.) founded it. The issue creating difficulty was the relation of God the Father to God the Son. Arius argued that Jesus was a created being, unlike God the Father. He was, therefore, not made of the substance of God and was not eternal. For Arius, Jesus was neither fully man nor fully God, but something in between. Arius's view did away with the mysterious concept of the Trinity, the difficult doctrine that holds that God is three persons (the Father, the Son, and the Holy Spirit) and also one in substance and essence.

The Arian concept appeared simple, rational, and philosophically acceptable. To its ablest opponent, Athanasius, however, it had serious shortcomings. Athanasius (ca. 293–373 C.E.), later bishop of Alexandria, saw the Arian view as an impediment to any acceptable theory of salvation, to him the most important religious question. He adhered to the old Greek idea of salvation as involving the change of sinful mortality into divine immortality through the gift of "life." Only if Jesus were both fully human and fully God could the transformation of humanity to divinity have taken place in him and be transmitted by him to his disciples.

To deal with the controversy, Constantine called a council of Christian bishops at Nicaea, not far from Constantinople, in 325. At Nicaea, Athanasius's view won out, became orthodox, and was embodied in the Nicene Creed. But Arianism persisted and spread. The Christian emperors hoped to bring unity to their increasingly decentralized realms by imposing a single religion. Over time it did prove to be a unifying force, but it also introduced divisions where none had existed before.

ARTS AND LETTERS IN THE LATE EMPIRE

HOW DID arts and letters in Late Rome reflect the developing relationship between pagan and Christian ideas?

The art and literature of the late empire reflect the confluence of pagan and Christian ideas and traditions and the conflict between them. Much of the literature is polemical and much of the art is propaganda.

A military revolution led by provincials whose origins were in the lower classes saved the empire from the chaos of the third century. Yet the new ruling class was not interested in leveling; it wanted instead to establish itself as a new aristocracy. It thought of itself as effecting a great restoration rather than a revolution and sought to restore classical culture and absorb it.

The Preservation of Classical Culture

One of the main needs and accomplishments of this period was the preservation of classical culture. Ways were discovered to make it available and useful to the newly arrived ruling class. Works of the great classical authors were reproduced in many copies and were transferred from perishable and inconvenient papyrus rolls to sturdier codices, bound volumes that were as easy to use as modern books. Scholars also digested long works like Livy's *History of Rome* into shorter versions, wrote learned commentaries, and compiled grammars. Original works by pagan writers of the late empire were neither numerous nor especially distinguished.

Carving of the Crucifixion.

c. 420 C.E. (ivory). British Museum, London, UK/Bridgeman Art Library

What place did Christianity have in the Roman world at the time of the fall of the Western Roman Empire?

Christian Writers

The late empire, however, did see a great outpouring of Christian writings, including many examples of Christian apologetics, in poetry and prose, and sermons, hymns, and biblical commentaries. Christianity could also boast important scholars. Jerome (348–420 C.E.), thoroughly trained in classical Latin literature and rhetoric, produced a revised version of the Bible in Latin. Commonly called the **Vulgate**, it became the Bible the Catholic Church used. Probably the most important eastern scholar was Eusebius of Caesarea (ca. 260–340 C.E.). His most important work, his *Ecclesiastical History*, was an attempt to set forth the Christian view of history.

Vulgate Latin translation of the Bible that became the standard text for the Catholic Church.

The closeness and also the complexity of the relationship between classical pagan culture and that of the Christianity of the late empire are nowhere better displayed than in the career and writings of Augustine (354–430 C.E.), bishop of Hippo in North Africa. He was born at Carthage and was trained as a teacher of rhetoric. His training and skill in pagan rhetoric and philosophy made him peerless among his contemporaries as a defender of Christianity and as a theologian.

His greatest works are his *Confessions*, an autobiography describing the road to his conversion, and *The City of God*. The latter was a response to the pagan charge that the abandonment of the old gods and the advent of Christianity caused the Visigoths' sack of Rome in 410. The optimistic view some Christians held that God's will worked its way in history and was easily comprehensible needed further support in the face of this calamity. Augustine sought to separate the fate of Christianity from that of the Roman Empire. He contrasted the secular world, the City of Man, with the spiritual, the City of God. The former was selfish, the latter unselfish; the former evil, the latter good. All states, even a Christian Rome, were part of the City of Man and were therefore corrupt and mortal. Only the City of God was immortal, and it, consisting of all the saints on earth and in heaven, was untouched by earthly calamities.

Though the *Confessions* and *The City of God* are Augustine's most famous works, they emphasize only a part of his thought. His treatises *On the Trinity* and *On Christian Education* reveal the great skill with which he supported Christian belief with the learning, logic, and philosophy of the pagan classics. Augustine believed faith is essential and primary (a thoroughly Christian view), but it is not a substitute for reason (the foundation of classical thought). Instead, faith is the starting point for, and liberator of, human reason, which continues to be the means by which people can understand what faith reveals.

THE PROBLEM OF THE DECLINE AND FALL OF THE EMPIRE IN THE WEST

WHY WERE new conquests so important to the vitality of the Roman Empire?

The massive barbarian invasions of the fifth century put an end to effective imperial government in the West. For centuries people have speculated about the causes of the collapse of the ancient world. Some blame the slavery and a resulting failure to make advances in science and technology. Others blame excessive government interference in the economic life of the empire and still others the destruction of the urban middle class, the carrier of classical culture.

A simpler and more obvious explanation might begin with the observation that the growth of so mighty an empire as Rome's was by no means inevitable. Rome's greatness had come from conquests that provided the Romans with the means to expand still further, until there were not enough Romans to conquer and govern any more peoples and territory. When pressure from outsiders grew, the Romans lacked the resources to advance and defeat the enemy as in the past. The tenacity and success of their resistance for so long were remarkable. Without new conquests to provide the immense wealth needed to defend and maintain internal prosperity, the Romans finally yielded to unprecedented onslaughts by fierce and numerous attackers. Perhaps we would do well to think of the problem as did Edward Gibbon, the author of the great eighteenth-century study of Rome's collapse and transformation. Instead of asking why Rome fell, "we should rather be surprised that it had subsisted so long."

Summary

HOW DID Augustus transform Roman politics and government?

The Augustan Principate After defeating Mark Antony at Actium in 31 B.C.E., Octavian started transforming his rule into the functional equivalent of a monarchy. In 26 B.C.E., he made a show of giving up his powers, no doubt expecting the Senate to beg him to keep them, as it in fact did. From then on he was referred to as Augustus. He introduced administrative reforms, widened the talent pool from which senators were selected, and generally improved his subjects' standard of living. He professionalized the military and attempted to secure the northern frontier. He modeled austere morality and supported traditional Roman religion. *page 120*

HOW DID political developments shape the culture of the Ciceronian and Augustan ages?

Civilization of the Ciceronian and Augustan Ages Roman culture flourished in the late republican period and in the Principate of Augustus. Hellenistic influences permeated the arts and literature, but the great works are clearly Roman in character. History, poetry, and law all found able practitioners in the late republic. Augustus simplified patronage for the arts. Augustan literature features some of the most recognizable names of the period: Vergil, Horace, Ovid, among others. Augustus also supported the visual arts; some of Rome's loveliest monuments were built under his reign. *page 122*

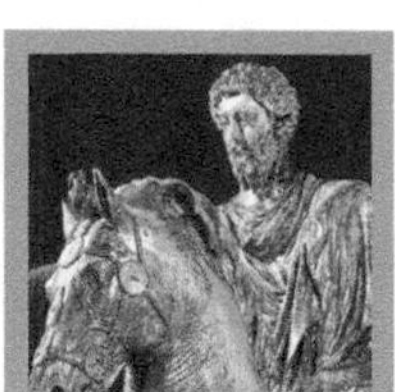

HOW WAS imperial Rome governed and what was life like for its people?

Imperial Rome, 14– to 180 C.E. The monarchical, hereditary rule of Augustus's successors was based on undisguised military power. In 69 C.E., Vespasian, the first emperor who was not a descendant of Roman nobility, assumed the throne. His Flavian dynasty was followed by the five "good emperors." The provinces were generally peaceful during this period. Latin was spoken throughout the West; in the East, Greek was still the predominant language. Culturally, "Romanitas" spread throughout the cities and towns of the empire. The situation for Jews and for peasant farmers was not attractive. Border defenses, particularly in the north, were a recurring problem for the empire. Women's status improved. Many people lived in *insulae*, multistory apartment buildings that were cramped and uncomfortable. Latin literature experienced a Silver Age between 14 and 180 C.E., offering a more critical worldview than the works of the Augustan period. Architecture flourished. By the second century C.E., problems such as a decline in the vitality of local government, a stagnating economy, the expense of defense, and probably a mysterious decline in population were foreshadowing crises to come. *page 124*

WHO WAS Jesus of Nazareth?

The Rise of Christianity Jesus of Nazareth was born in Judaea under the reign of Augustus. He gained a large following, particularly among the poor, with a message of a coming Day of Judgment and criticism of existing religious practices. Feared and misunderstood by the authorities, Jesus was crucified in Jerusalem, probably in 30 C.E. Written decades after his death, the Gospels present Jesus as the Son of God, a redeemer who was resurrected after death. The writings of Paul of Tarsus are especially important, since he makes the case that Christianity is a new and universal religion. The *agape* ("love feast") created a sense of solidarity across classes among early Christians, and it helped the religion spread throughout the Roman Empire and beyond. By the end of the second century C.E., the Catholic Church had been institutionalized as the definer of Christian orthodoxy. *page 130*

HOW DID economic developments lead to the political and military crisis of the third century?

The Crisis of the Third Century External military threats and internal social weakness interacted in a vicious circle. Commodus came to power in 180 C.E. When he was assassinated in 192 C.E., civil war again erupted and military strongman Septimius Severus emerged victorious. In the third century C.E., others invaded the outskirts of the empire. Repelling these challenges required more resources than the society could spare; labor shortages, inflation, and neglect of infrastructure such as roads weakened Rome's economy. Social stratification increased. Invasions and anarchy characterized the middle of the third century C.E. *page 136*

WHAT FACTORS contributed to the decline and eventual fall of Rome?

The Late Empire During the fourth and fifth centuries, the empire was reorganized and divided, and Christianity gained followers and power. Diocletian introduced the tetrarchy, but it did not lead to a smooth succession when he and his co-emperor retired in 305 C.E. Diocletian and Constantine both ruled autocratically from Eastern cities. Diocletian tried to suppress

Christianity, whereas Constantine supported it. Constantine's death was followed by yet another struggle for power. By the end of the fourth century, the empire had been divided permanently. Christianity's continued viability depended on its ability to cope with political interference and doctrinal disputes. *page 138*

HOW DID arts and letters in Late Rome reflect the developing relationship between pagan and Christian ideas?

Arts and Letters in the Late Empire Much of the art and literature of the late empire reflects the relationship between Christianity and pagan religions. The empire's new rulers came from the lower classes of the provinces; in their efforts to restore classical culture, they inevitably reshaped it. Christian writings were numerous, the most significant among them the works of Augustine in which he combined Christian faith and pagan (Classical) reason. *page 144*

WHY WERE new conquests so important to the vitality of the Roman Empire?

The Problem of the Decline and Fall of the Empire in the West Imperial government fell in the West in the fifth century in the face of barbarian invasions. Ever since, historians and commentators have offered explanations, many of which seem specious. Like the early-twentieth-century historian Edward Gibbon, the authors believe the question should be more properly framed as, "How did the Roman Empire last as long as it did?" rather than, "Why did the Roman Empire decline and fall?" The Roman Empire could not expand forever; without the infusion of new people and new wealth that territorial conquest provided, the Roman Empire could not survive. *page 145*

REVIEW QUESTIONS

1. How did Augustus alter Rome's constitution and government? How did his innovations solve the problems that had plagued the republic? Why were the Romans willing to accept him?
2. How did the literature of the Golden Age differ from that of the Silver Age? What did poets contribute to the success of Augustus's reforms?
3. Why were Christians persecuted by the Roman authorities? What enabled them to acquire such an enormous following by the fourth century C.E.?
4. What were the political, social, and economic problems that beset Rome in the third and fourth centuries C.E.? How did Diocletian and Constantine deal with them? Were these men able to halt Rome's decline? Were there problems they could not solve?

KEY TERMS

agape(p. 132)
Arianism (p. 144)
Augustus (p. 120)
catholic (p. 133)
Eucharist (p. 132)
heretics (p. 133
jus gentium (p. 122)
jus naturale (p. 122)
orthodox (p. 133)
tetrarchy (p. 138)
Vulgate (p. 145)

6

Late Antiquity and the Early Middle Ages:

Creating a New European Society and Culture (476–1000)

This illustration from a fourteenth-century "Life of the Prophet" shows Muhammad's family—his daughter Fatima, her husband Ali, and Muhammad's father-in-law Abu Bakr—traveling together. Muhammad himself is not shown because like God he cannot be portrayed in Islamic art. Hence, whenever Muslims travel, Muhammad is in their midst but cannot be seen with the naked eye.

The New York Public Library/Art Resource, NY

How do Muslims see the relationship between Muhammad, Jesus, and Moses?

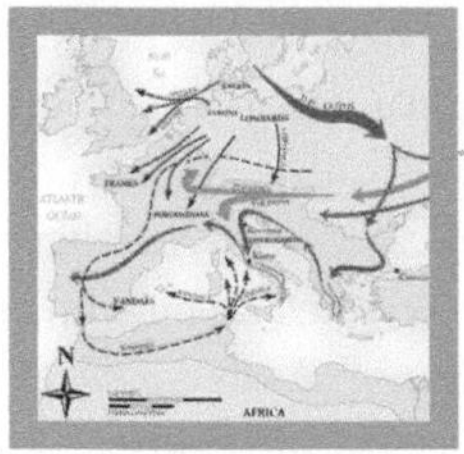

HOW DID Germanic migrations contribute to the fall of the Roman Empire?

HOW DID the Byzantine Empire continue the legacy of Rome?

HOW DID Islamic culture influence the West?

HOW DID the developing Christian church influence Western society during the early Middle Ages?

HOW DID the reign of Clovis differ from that of Charlemagne?

WHAT WERE the characteristics of a feudal society?

Scholars increasingly view the period between 250 C.E. and 800 C.E.—called Late Antiquity—as a single world, both cohesive and moving apart, bounded by the Roman and Sassanian (Persian) Empires. The Western and Eastern (Byzantine) empires of Rome never succumbed culturally to barbarian and Muslim invaders. In the East, the Sassanians created a powerful empire and deeply penetrated Rome's provinces. By the mid-eighth century, Arab conquests extended Muslim influence from the Middle East to North Africa and Spain. In Western Europe, Germanic heritage, Judeo-Christian religion, Roman language and law, and Greco-Byzantine administration and culture gradually combined to create a uniquely European way of life.

ON THE EVE OF THE FRANKISH ASCENDANCY

HOW DID Germanic migrations contribute to the fall of the Roman Empire?

As we have already seen, by the late third century, the Roman Empire had become too large for a single emperor to govern and was beginning to fail. (See Chapter 5.) The emperor Diocletian (r. 284–305) tried to strengthen the empire by dividing it between himself and a co-emperor. The result was a dual empire with an eastern and a western half, each with its own emperor and, eventually, imperial bureaucracy and army. A critical shift of the empire's resources and orientation to the eastern half accompanied these changes. As imperial rule weakened in the West and strengthened in the East, it also became increasingly autocratic.

Diocletian's reign was followed by factional strife. His eventual successor, Constantine the Great (r. 306–337), briefly reunited the empire by conquest (his three sons and their successors would divide it again) and ruled as sole emperor of the eastern and western halves after 324. In that year, he moved the capital of the empire from Rome to Byzantium, an ancient Greek city that stood at the crossroads of the major sea and land routes between Europe and Asia Minor. Here, Constantine built the new city of Constantinople, which he dedicated in 330. As the imperial residence and the new administrative center of the empire, Constantinople gradually became a "new Rome." When the barbarian invasions of non-Roman Germanic and eastern peoples began in the late fourth century, the West was in political and economic disarray, and imperial power and prestige had shifted decisively to Constantinople and the East.

GERMANIC MIGRATIONS

The German tribes did not burst in on the West all of a sudden. Before the massive migrations from the north and the east, Roman and Germanic cultures had commingled peacefully for centuries. Beginning in 376 with a great influx of Visigoths, or "west Goths," into the empire, this peaceful coexistence ended. The Visigoths, accomplished horsemen and fierce warriors, were themselves pushed into the empire by the emergence of a notoriously violent people, the Huns, from what is now Mongolia. The Visigoths ultimately reached southern Gaul and Spain. Soon to be Christianized, they won rights of settlement and material assistance within the empire from the Eastern emperor Valens (r. 364–378) in exchange for defending the eastern frontier as *foederati*, or the emperor's "special" allies. Instead of the promised assistance, however, the Visigoths received harsh treatment from their new allies. After repeated conflicts, the Visigoths rebelled and overwhelmed Valens at the Battle of Adrianople in 378. (See Chapter 5.)

Thereafter, the Romans passively permitted the settlement of barbarians within the heart of the Western empire. The Vandals crossed the Rhine in 406 and within three decades gained control of northwest Africa and much of the Mediterranean. The Burgundians, who came on the heels of the Vandals, settled in Gaul. Most important for subsequent Western history were the Franks, who settled northern and central

Gaul, some along the seacoast (the Salian Franks) and others along the Rhine, Seine, and Loire Rivers (the Ripuarian Franks).

Why was there so little Roman resistance to these Germanic tribes? The invaders were successful because they came in rapid succession upon a badly overextended Western empire divided politically by ambitious military commanders and weakened by decades of famine, pestilence, and over-taxation. The Eastern empire retained enough wealth and vitality to field new armies or to buy off the invaders. The Western empire, in contrast, succumbed not only because of moral decay and materialism, but also because of a combination of military rivalry, political mismanagement, disease, and sheer poverty.

New Western Masters

In the early fifth century, Italy and the "eternal city" of Rome suffered devastating blows. In 410 the Visigoths, under Alaric (ca. 370–410), sacked Rome. In 452 the Huns, led by Attila—the "scourge of God"—invaded Italy. Rome was sacked still again, in 455—this time by the Vandals.

By the mid–fifth century, power in Western Europe had passed decisively from the hands of the Roman emperors to those of barbarian chieftains. In 476, the traditional date historians give for the fall of the Roman Empire, the barbarian Odovacer (ca. 434–493) deposed the last Western emperor Romulus Augustulus. The Eastern emperor Zeno (r. 474–491) recognized Odovacer's authority in the West, and Odovacer acknowledged Zeno as sole emperor, contenting himself to serve as Zeno's Western viceroy. In a later coup in 493, Theodoric (ca. 454–526), king of the Ostrogoths, or "east Goths," replaced Odovacer. Theodoric then governed with the full acceptance of the Roman people, the emperor in Constantinople, and the Christian church. By the end of the fifth century, the barbarians from west and east had saturated the Western empire. (See Map 6–1.)

MAP EXPLORATION

Interactive map: To explore this map further, go to www.myhistorylab.com

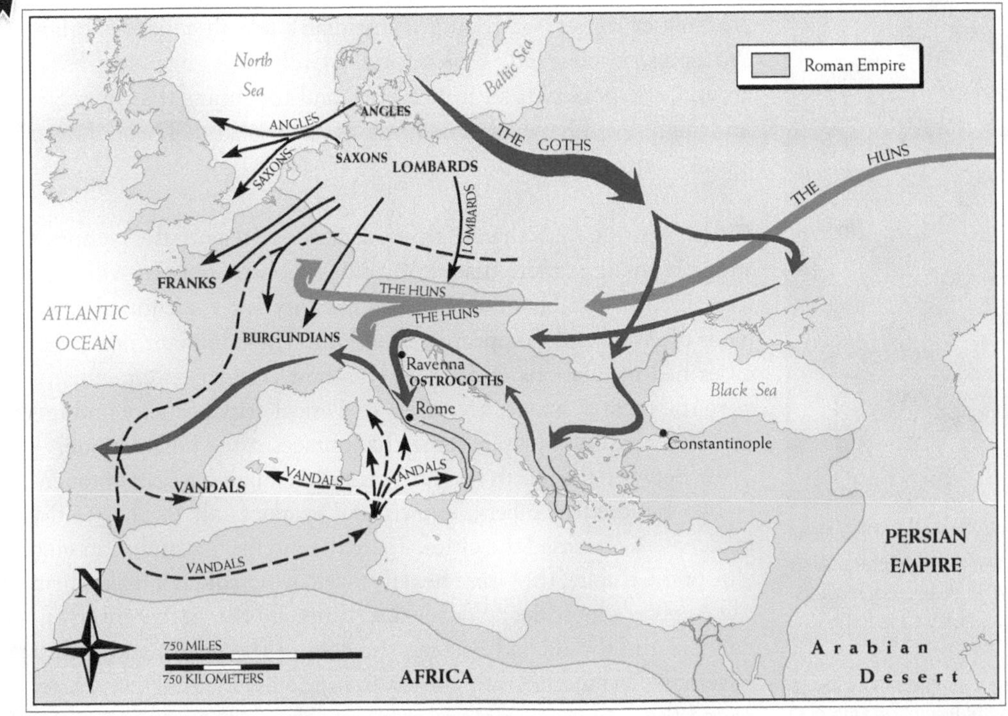

MAP 6–1 **Barbarian Migrations into the West in the Fourth and Fifth Centuries** The forceful intrusion of Germanic and non-Germanic barbarians into the Roman Empire from the last quarter of the fourth century through the fifth century made for a constantly changing pattern of movement and relations. The map shows the major routes taken by the usually unwelcome newcomers and the areas most deeply affected by the main groups.

Which part of the empire was least affected by barbarian migrations?

These barbarian military victories did not, however, obliterate Roman culture; Western Europe's new masters were willing to learn from the people they had conquered. They admired Roman culture and had no desire to destroy it. Except in Britain and northern Gaul, Roman law, Roman government, and Latin, the Roman language, coexisted with the new Germanic institutions.

All things considered, a gradual interpenetration of two strong cultures—a creative tension—marked the period of the Germanic migrations. The stronger culture was the Roman, and it became dominant in a later fusion. Despite Western military defeat, the Goths and the Franks became far more romanized than the Romans were germanized. Latin language, Nicene Catholic Christianity, and eventually Roman law and government were to triumph in the West during the Middle Ages.

THE BYZANTINE EMPIRE

HOW DID the Byzantine Empire continue the legacy of Rome?

As the Roman Empire in the West succumbed to Germanic and other barbarian invasions, imperial power shifted to the eastern part of the Roman Empire, whose center was the city of Constantinople or Byzantium (modern-day Istanbul). It remained the sole imperial capital until the eighth century, when Charlemagne revived the Western empire and reclaimed its imperial title. In historical usage, the term *Byzantine* indicates the Hellenistic Greek, Roman, and Judaic monotheistic elements that distinguish the culture of the East from the Latin West.

Built during the reign of Justinian, Hagia Sophia (Church of the Holy Wisdom) is a masterpiece of Byzantine and world architecture. After the Turkish conquest of Constantinople in 1453, Hagia Sophia was transformed into a mosque with four minarets, still visible today.

Turkish Tourism and Information Office

What does Justinian's construction of the Hagia Sophia tell us about the relationship between church and state in the Byzantine Empire?

THE REIGN OF JUSTINIAN

The Byzantine Empire reached its pinnacle during the reign of Emperor Justinian (r. 527–565) and his like-minded wife, Empress Theodora (d. 548). A strongman ruler who expected all his subjects, clergy and laity, high and low, to submit absolutely to his hierarchical control, Justinian spent, built, and destroyed on a grand scale. Theodora, the daughter of a circus bear trainer, had been an entertainer in her youth and, if Justinian's tell-all court historian, Procopius, is believed, a prostitute as well. Whatever her background, she possessed an intelligence and toughness that matched and might even have exceeded that of her husband. Theodora was a true co-ruler.

Cities During Justinian's thirty-eight-year reign, the empire's strength lay in its more than 1,500 cities. Constantinople, with perhaps 350,000 inhabitants, was the largest city and the cultural crossroads of Asian and European civilizations. The dominant provincial cities had populations of 50,000. The most popular entertainments were the theater, where, according to clerical critics, nudity and immorality were on display, and the chariot races at the Hippodrome.

Between the fourth and fifth centuries, urban councils of roughly two hundred members, known as *Decurions*, all local, wealthy landowners, governed the cities. Being the intellectual and economic elite of the empire, they were heavily taxed, which did not make them the emperor's most docile or loyal servants. By the sixth century, fidelity to the throne had become the coin of the realm, and special governors, lay and clerical, chosen from the landholding classes, replaced the *decurion* councils as more reliable instruments of the emperor's sovereign will. As the sixth and seventh centuries saw the beginning of new barbarian invasions of the empire from the north and the east, such political tightening was imperative.

Law The imperial goal—as reflected in Justinian's policy of "one God, one empire, one religion"—was to centralize government by imposing legal and doctrinal conformity throughout. To this end, the emperor ordered a collation and revision of Roman law. What Justinian wanted was loyal and docile subjects guided by clear and enforceable laws. The result was the *Corpus Juris Civilis*, or "body of civil law." This work laid the foundation for most subsequent European law. Because bringing subjects under the authority of a single sovereign was the fundamental feature of Roman law, rulers seeking to centralize their states especially benefited from Justinian's legal legacy.

Empress Theodora and Her Attendants. The union of political and spiritual authority in the person of the empress is shown by the depiction on Theodora's mantle of three magi carrying gifts to the Virgin and Jesus.

The Court of Empress Theodora. Byzantine early Christian mosaic. San Vitale, Ravenna, Italy Photograph © Scala/Art Resource, NY

What role did the Empress Theodora play in Byzantine politics?

Reconquest in the West Justinian sought to reconquer the imperial provinces lost to the barbarians in the West. Beginning in 533, his armies overran the Vandal kingdom in North Africa and Sicily, the Ostrogothic kingdom in Italy, and part of Spain. But the price paid in blood and treasure was enormous, particularly in Italy, where prolonged resistance by the Ostrogoths did not end until 554. By Justinian's death, his empire was financially exhausted, and plague had ravaged the population of Constantinople and much of the East. Although Byzantine rule survived in Sicily and parts of southern Italy until the eleventh century, most of Justinian's Western and North African conquests were soon lost to Lombard invaders from north of the Alps and to the Muslim Arabs. (See Map 6–2, page 154.)

QUICK REVIEW

Theodora (d. 548)

- Justinian's wife and his chief counselor
- Daughter of a circus performer who began her career as a prostitute
- A true co-ruler

The Spread of Byzantine Christianity

In the late sixth and seventh centuries, nomadic, pagan tribes of Avars, Slavs, and Bulgars invaded and occupied the Balkan provinces of the eastern empire, threatening a "dark age" there. More than once, these fierce raiders menaced Constantinople itself. Yet after almost two centuries of intermittent warfare, the Slavs and Bulgars eventually converted to Eastern Orthodoxy or Byzantine Christianity. Hoping to build a cultural-linguistic firewall against menacing Franks from the West who had conquered the Avars and were attempting to convert his people to Roman Catholicism in Latin, a language they did not understand, the Slav Duke Rastislav of Moravia turned in the ninth century to Constantinople for help. In response, the emperor sent two learned missionaries to convert the Moravians: the brothers, priests, and future saints Constantine, later known as Cyril, and Methodius. In Moravia, the two created a new, Greek-based alphabet, which permitted the Slavs to create their own written language. That language gave the Christian gospels and Byzantine theology a lasting Slavic home. Later, after the Bulgars conquered and absorbed many of the Slavs, that alphabet was elevated to a broader script known as Cyrillic after St. Cyril. Known today as Old Church Slavonic, it has ever since been the international Slavic language through which Byzantine Christianity penetrated eastern Europe.

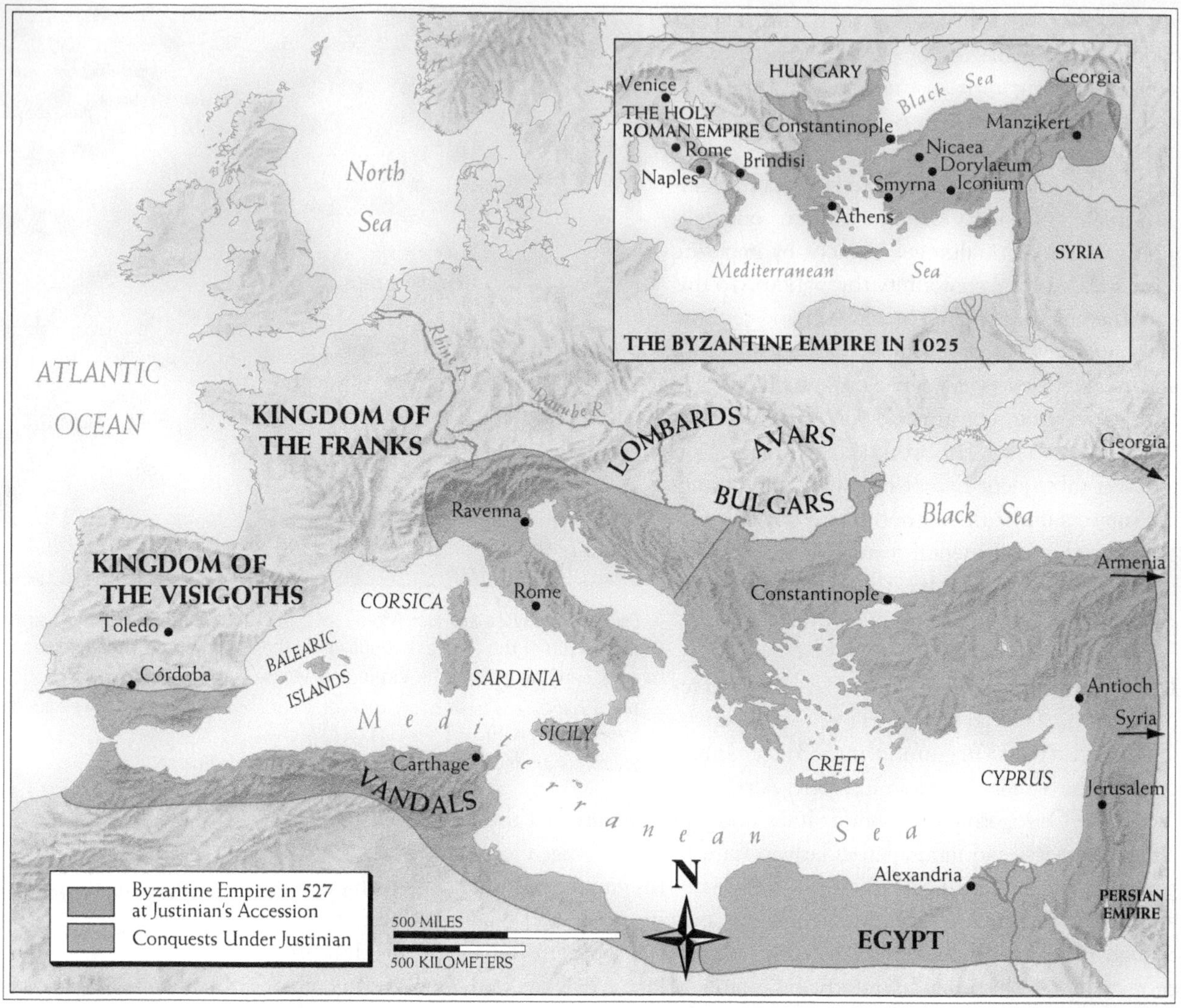

MAP 6–2 **The Byzantine Empire at the Time of Justinian's Death** Justinian reconquered lands in the West that once belonged to the Roman Empire. From 500 to 1100, the Byzantine Empire was the center of Christian civilization. The inset shows the empire in 1025, before its losses to the Seljuk Turks.

In the second half of the first millennium C.E., how did the power and influence of Rome and Constantinople compare?

Persians and Muslims

During the reign of Emperor Heraclius (r. 610–641), the Byzantine Empire took a decidedly Eastern, as opposed to a Western Roman, direction. Heraclius spent his entire reign resisting Persian and Islamic invasions, the former successfully, the latter in vain. In 628 he defeated the Persian Sassanid king Chosroes and took back one of Western Christendom's great lost relics: a piece of Christ's Cross that Chosroes had carried off when he captured Jerusalem in 614. After 632, however, Islamic armies overran much of the empire, directly attacking Constantinople for the first time in the mid-670s. Not until Leo III of the Isaurian dynasty (r. 717–740) did the Byzantines succeed in repelling Arab armies and regaining most of Asia Minor, having lost forever Syria, Egypt, and North Africa. The setback was traumatic and forced a major restructuring of the diminished empire, creating a new system of provincial government under the direct authority of imperial generals. In the tenth century, a reinvigorated Byzantium went on the offensive, pushing back the Muslims in Armenia and northern Syria and conquering the Bulgar kingdom in the Balkans.

But like Justinian's conquests in the sixth century, these may have overtaxed the empire's strength; and in the eleventh century, Byzantine fortunes rapidly reversed. After inflicting a devastating defeat on the Byzantine army at Manzikert in Armenia in 1071, Muslim Seljuk Turks overran most of Asia Minor, from which the Byzantines had drawn most of their tax revenue and troops. The empire never fully recovered, yet its end—which came when the Seljuks' cousins, the Ottoman Turks, captured Constantinople in 1453—was still almost four centuries away. In 1092, after two decades of steady Turkish advance, the Eastern emperor Alexius I Comnenus (r. 1081–1118) called for Western aid, which helped spark the First Crusade. It also heightened tensions between Latin West and Greek East and exposed the riches of Constantinople to predatory Western eyes. A century later (1204), the Fourth Crusade was diverted from Jerusalem to Constantinople, not, however, to rescue the city, but rather to inflict more damage on it and on the Byzantine Empire than all previous non-Christian invaders had done before. (See Chapter 7.)When the Byzantines eventually recovered the city in 1261, Byzantine power was a shadow of its former self, the empire was impoverished, and the Turks had become a constant threat.

ISLAM AND THE ISLAMIC WORLD

HOW DID Islamic culture influence the West?

A new drama began to unfold in the sixth century with the awakening of a rival far more dangerous to the West than the German tribes: the new faith of **Islam**. By the time of Muhammad's death (632), Islamic armies were beginning to absorb the attention and the resources of the emperors in Constantinople and the rulers in the West.

Islam New religion appearing in Arabia in the sixth century in response to the work of the Prophet Muhammad.

MUHAMMAD'S RELIGION

Muhammad (570–632), an orphan, was raised by a family of modest means. As a youth, he worked as a merchant's assistant, traveling the major trade routes. When he was twenty-five, he married a wealthy widow from the city of Mecca, the religious and commercial center of Arabia. Thereafter, himself a wealthy man, he became a kind of social activist, criticizing Meccan materialism, paganism, and unjust treatment of the poor and needy. At about age forty, a deep religious experience heightened his commitment to reform and it transformed his life. He began to receive revelations from the angel Gabriel, who recited God's word to him at irregular intervals. These revelations were collected after his death into the Islamic holy book, the **Qur'an** (literally, a "reciting"), which his followers compiled between 650 and 651. The basic message Muhammad received was a summons to all Arabs to submit to God's will. Followers of Muhammad's religion came to be called *Muslim* ("submissive" or "surrendering"); *Islam*, itself, means "submission."

Qur'an Sacred book comprised of a collection of the revealed texts that God had chosen Muhammad to convey.

The message was not a new one. A long line of Jewish prophets going back to Noah had reiterated it. According to Muslims, however, this line ended with Muhammad, who, as the last of God's chosen prophets, became "the Prophet." The Qur'an also recognized Jesus Christ as a prophet but denied that he was God's co-eternal and co-equal son. Like Judaism, Islam was a monotheistic and theocentric religion, not a trinitarian one like Christianity.

Mecca was a major pagan pilgrimage site (the **Ka'ba**, which became Islam's holiest shrine, housed a sacred black meteorite that was originally a pagan object of worship). Muhammad's condemnation of idolatry and immorality threatened the trade that flowed from the pilgrims, enraging the merchants of the city. Persecuted for their attacks on traditional religion, Muhammad and his followers fled Mecca in 622 for

Ka'ba One of Arabia's holiest shrines located in Mecca, the birthplace of Muhammad.

Hegira Forced flight of Muhammad and his followers to Medina, 240 miles north of Mecca. This event marks the beginning of the Islamic calendar.

Medina, 240 miles to the north. This event came to be known as the ***Hegira*** ("flight") and marks the beginning of the Islamic calendar.

In Medina, Muhammad organized his forces and drew throngs of devoted followers. He raided caravans going back and forth to Mecca. He also had his first conflicts with Medina's Jews, who were involved in trade with Mecca. By 624, he was able to conquer Mecca and make it the center of the new religion.

During these years the basic rules of Islamic practice evolved. True Muslims were expected (1) to be honest and modest in all their dealings and behavior; (2) to be unquestionably loyal to the Islamic community; (3) to abstain from pork and alcohol at all times; (4) to wash and pray facing Mecca five times a day; (5) to contribute to the support of the poor and needy; (6) to fast during daylight hours for one month each year; and (7) to make a pilgrimage to Mecca and visit the Ka'ba at least once in a lifetime. The last requirement reflects the degree to which Islam was an assimilationist religion: it "Islamicized" a major pagan religious practice.

Islam also permitted Muslim men to have up to four wives—provided they treated them all justly and gave each equal attention—and as many concubines as they wished. A husband could divorce a wife with a simple declaration, whereas, to divorce her husband, a wife had to show good cause before a religious judge. A wife was expected to be totally loyal and devoted to her husband and was allowed to show her face to no man but him. (See "Compare & Connect: The Battle of the Sexes in Christianity and Islam," pages 158–159.)

ulema ("Persons with correct knowledge") Scholarly elite leading Islam.

In contrast to Christianity, Islam drew no rigid distinction between the clergy and the laity. A lay scholarly elite developed, however, and held moral authority within Islamic society in domestic and religious matters. This elite, known as the ***ulema***, or "persons with correct knowledge," served a social function similar to that of a professional priesthood or rabbinate. Its members were men of great piety and obvious learning whose opinions came to have the force of law in Muslim society. They also saw that Muslim rulers adhered to the letter of the Qur'an.

Islamic Diversity

The success of Islam lay in its ability to unify and inspire tribal Arabs and other non-Jewish and non-Christian people. Islam also appealed to Arab pride, for it deemed Muhammad to be history's major religious figure and his followers to be God's chosen people.

caliphate Office of the leader of the Muslim community.

As early as the seventh century, however, disputes arose among Muslims over the nature of Islamic society and authority within it that left permanent divisions. Disagreement over the true line of succession to Muhammad—the **caliphate**—was one source of discord. Another disagreement related to this was over doctrinal issues involving the extent to which Islam was an inclusive religion, open to sinners as well as to the virtuous. Several groups emerged from these disputes. The most radical was the Kharijites, whose leaders seceded from the camp of the caliph Ali (656–661) because Ali compromised with his enemies on a matter of principle. Righteous and judgmental, the Kharijites wanted all but the most rigorously virtuous Muslims excluded from the community of the faithful. In 661, a Kharijite assassinated Ali.

Shi'a The "party" of Ali. They believed Ali and his descendants were Muhammad's only rightful successors.

Another, more influential group was the **Shi'a**, or "partisans of Ali" (*Shi'at Ali*). The Shi'a looked on Ali and his descendants as the rightful successors of Muhammad not only by virtue of kinship, but also by the expressed will of the Prophet himself. To the Shi'a, Ali's assassination revealed the most basic truth of a devout Muslim life: A true *imam*, or "ruler," must expect to suffer unjustly even unto death in the world, and so, too, must his followers. A distinctive theology of martyrdom has ever since been a mark of Shi'a teaching. And the Shi'a, until modern times, have been an embattled minority within mainstream Islamic society.

A third group, which has been dominant for most of Islamic history, was the majority centrist **Sunnis** (followers of ***sunna***, or "tradition"). Sunnis have always put loyalty to the community of Islam above all else and have spurned the exclusivism and purism of the Kharijites and the Shi'a.

Sunnis Followers of the *sunna*, "tradition." They emphasize loyalty to the fundamental principles of Islam.

ISLAMIC EMPIRES

Under Muhammad's first three successors—the caliphs Abu Bakr (r. 632–634), Umar (r. 634–644), and Uthman (r. 644–655)—Islam expanded by conquest throughout the southern and eastern Mediterranean, into territories mostly still held today by Islamic states. In the eighth century, Muslim armies occupied parts of Spain in the West and of India in the East, producing a truly vast empire. (See Map 6–3.) The capital of this empire moved, first, from Mecca to Damascus in Syria, and then, in 750, to Baghdad in Iraq after the Abbasid dynasty replaced the Umayyads in a struggle for the caliphate. Thereafter, the huge Muslim Empire gradually broke up into separate states, some with their own line of caliphs claiming to be the true successors of Muhammad.

The early Muslim conquests would not have been so rapid and thorough had the contemporary Byzantine and Persian empires not been exhausted by decades of war. The Muslims struck at both empires in the 630s, completely overrunning the Persian Empire by 651. Most of the inhabitants in Byzantine Syria and Palestine, although Christian, were Semites like the Arabs. Any religious unity they felt with the Byzantine Greeks may have been offset by hatred of the Byzantine army of occupation and by resentment at Constantinople's efforts to impose Greek "orthodox" beliefs on the Monophysite churches

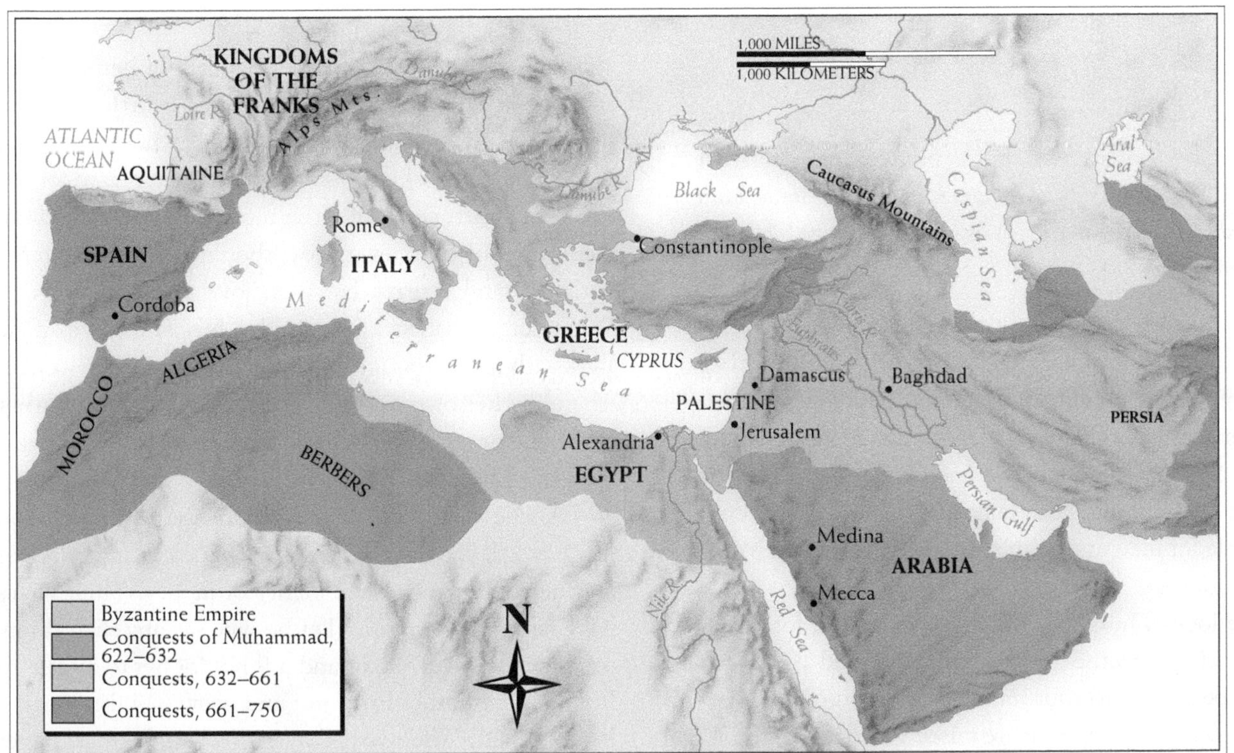

MAP 6–3 **Muslim Conquests and Domination of the Mediterranean to about 750 C.E.** Within 125 years of Muhammad's rise, Muslims came to dominate Spain and all areas south and east of the Mediterranean.

How were Muslims able to dominate much of the area east and south of the Mediterranean within 125 years of Muhammad's rise?

COMPARE & CONNECT

THE BATTLE OF THE SEXES IN CHRISTIANITY AND ISLAM

In early Christianity man and woman were viewed as one and the same offspring, Eve born of Adam, for which reason they were forever after drawn irresistibly to one another. What one did to the other, one also did to oneself, so tightly were they bound. And that bond between husband and wife made their relationship all the more caring and charitable.

Muhammad's role as a husband was by all accounts exemplary: a spouse who dealt shrewdly and fairly with his wives, a splendid model for his followers. In the teaching of the Qur'an, all conflict between husband and wife was to be resolved by talking and, that failing, by the husband's departure from the marital bed. Heeding the example of the Prophet and the teaching of the Qur'an, devout Muslim men viewed a husband's hitting a wife as a last resort in his disciplining of her. Yet, when a wife flagrantly disobeyed (*nashiz*) her husband, or, much worse, was unfaithful to him, hitting often became the husband's and society's first response.

QUESTIONS

1. How does the marriage bond differ in the Christian and Muslim faiths? What does it mean to Christians to say that husband and wife are one flesh? Is that also the way spouses are perceived in Islam?

2. How successful is male discipline of self and of wife in Islam? Is Christian marriage too egalitarian and, hence, more vulnerable to failure?

3. If marriage is a mirror of a religion, what does it reveal Christianity and Islam to be?

I. CHRISTIAN MARRIAGE

St. John Chrysostom (347–407) elaborated the relationship between Christian spouses in his Homily on Christian Spouses: *"Wives, be subject to your husbands, as to the Lord . . . Husbands, love your wives as Christ loved the Church." (Ephesians 5:22–25)*

There is no relationship between human beings so close as that of husband and wife, if they are united as they ought to be . . . God did not fashion woman independently from man . . . nor did He enable woman to bear children without man . . . He made the one man Adam to be the origin of all mankind, both male and female, and made it impossible for men and women to be self-sufficient [without one another] . . .

The love of husband and wife is [thus] the force that wields society together . . . Why else would [God] say, "Wives, be subject to your husbands?" Because when harmony prevails, the children are raised well, the household is kept in order . . . and great benefits, both for families and for states result . . .

Having seen the amount of obedience necessary, hear now about the amount of love that is needed. [If] you want your wife to be obedient to you . . . then be responsible for the same providential care of her as Christ has for the Church. Even if you see her belittling you, or despising and mocking you . . . subject her to yourself through affection, kindness, and your great regard for her . . . One's partner for life, the mother of one's children, the source of one's every joy, should never be fettered with fear and threats, but with love and patience . . . What sort of satisfaction could a husband have, if he lives with his wife as if she were a slave and not a woman [there] by her own free will. [So] suffer anything for her sake, but never disgrace her, for Christ never did this with the Church . . .

A wife should never nag her husband [saying] "You lazy coward, you have no ambition! Look at our relatives and neighbors; they have plenty of money. Their wives have far more than I do." Let no wife say any such thing; she is her husband's body, and it is not for her to dictate to her head, but rather to submit and obey . . . Likewise, if a husband has a wife who behaves this way, he must never exercise his authority by insulting and abusing her.

Source: Don S. Browning et al., *Sex, Marriage, and Family in World Religions* (New York: Columbia University Press), pp. 106–108.

Muslims are enjoined to live by the divine law, or Shari'a, and have a right to have disputes settled by an arbiter of the Shari'a. Here we see a husband complaining about his wife before the state-appointed judge, or *qadi*. The wife, backed up by two other women, points an accusing finger at the husband. In such cases, the first duty of the *qadi*, who should be a learned person of faith, is to try to effect a reconciliation before the husband divorces his wife, or the wife herself seeks a divorce.

Bibliothèque Nationale de France, Paris

What role did clerics play in Islamic society?

II. MUSLIM MARRIAGE

Chroniclers Abu Hamid Al-Ghazali (1058–1111), Ihya'Ulum, 2:34–35 (11th c. C.E.) elaborate the teaching of Qur'an 4:34: "Men are the protectors and maintainers of women because God has given [men] more strength . . . and because they support [women] from their means."

Treating women well and bearing their ill treatment [is] required for marriage . . . God said, "keep them good company." [Among] the last things the Messenger [Muhammad] recommended was to take care of your slaves. Do not burden them with things beyond their capacity, and observe God's exhortations relating to your wives, for they are like slaves in your hands. You took them in trust from God and made them your wives by His words . . .

One should know that treating one's wife well does not only mean not harming her; it also means to endure ill treatment and be patient when she gets angry and loses her temper, a [method] the Messenger used to forgive his wives who argued with him and turned away from him for the whole day . . .

'A'ishah [a wife of the Prophet] once got angry and said to the Prophet . . . "You, who claims to be the Prophet of God!" The Messenger of God smiled and tolerated her in the spirit of forgiveness and generosity . . . It is believed that the first love story in Islam was that of Prophet Muhammad and 'A'ishah. The Prophet used to say to his other wives: "Do not upset me by saying bad things about 'A'ishah, for she is the only woman in whose company I have received the revelation [of God]! Anas [Ibn Malik, a ninth-century. chronicler] reported that the Prophet was the most compassionate person in matters concerning women and children . . .

Respond to [as he did to women's] harshness by teasing, joking, and kidding them, for it is certain this softens women's hearts. The Prophet said, "The people with the most perfect faith are those with the best ethics and those who are the kindest toward their families." Umar [a companion of the Prophet and the second caliph of Islam] once said: "One should always be like a child with his family, but when they need him they should find [in him] a man."

Source: Don S. Browning et al., *Sex, Marriage, and Family*, pp. 190–91, 194–95.

A Muslim and a Christian play the *ud*, or lute, together, from a thirteenth-century *Book of Chants* in the Escorial Monastery of Madrid. Medieval Europe was deeply influenced by Arab–Islamic culture, transmitted particularly through Spain. Some of the many works in Arabic on musical theory were translated into Latin and Hebrew, but the main influence on music came from the arts of singing and playing spread by minstrels.

A Moor and a Christian playing the lute, miniature in a book of music from the "Cantigas" of Alphonso X "the Wise" (1221–1284). Thirteenth century (manuscript). Monastero de El Excorial, El Escorial, Spain/Index/Bridgeman Art Library

How would you characterize Muslim-Christian relations in medieval Spain?

of Egypt and Syria. As a result, many Egyptian and Syrian Christians, hoping for deliverance from Byzantine oppression, appear to have welcomed the Islamic conquerors.

Although Islam gained converts from among the Christians in the Near East, North Africa, and Spain, its efforts to invade northern Europe were rebuffed. The ruler of the Franks, Charles Martel, defeated a raiding party of Arabs on the western frontier of Europe at Poitiers (today in central France) in 732. This victory and the failure to capture Constantinople ended any Arab effort to expand into Western or Central Europe.

THE WESTERN DEBT TO ISLAM

Arab invasions and their presence in the Mediterranean area during the early Middle Ages contributed both directly and indirectly to the formation of Western Europe. They did so indirectly by driving Western Europeans back onto their native tribal and inherited Judeo-Christian, Greco-Roman, and Byzantine resources, from which they created a Western culture of their own. Also, by diverting the attention and energies of the Byzantine Empire during the formative centuries, the Arabs have prevented it from expanding into and reconquering Western Europe. That allowed two Germanic peoples to gain ascendancy: first, the Franks and then the Lombards, who invaded Italy in the sixth century and settled in the Po valley around the city of Milan.

Despite the hostility of the Christian West to the Islamic world, there was nonetheless much creative interchange between these two different cultures, and the West profited greatly and directly from it. At this time, Arab civilizations were the more advanced, enjoying their golden age, and they had much to teach a toddling West. Between the eighth and tenth centuries, Cordoba, the capital of Muslim Spain, was a model multicultural city embracing Arabs, Berbers from North Africa, Christian converts to Islam, and Jews. Cordoba was a conduit for the finest Arabian tableware, leather, silks, dyes, aromatic ointments, and perfumes into the West. The Arabs taught Western farmers how to irrigate fields and Western artisans how to tan leather and refine silk. The West also gained from its contacts with Arabic scholars. Thanks to the skills of Islamic scholars, ancient Greek works on astronomy, mathematics, and medicine became available in Latin translation to Westerners. Down to the sixteenth century, the basic gynecological and child-care manuals guiding the work of Western midwives and physicians were compilations made by the Baghdad physician Al-Razi (Rhazes), the philosopher and physician Ibn-Sina (Avicenna) (980–1037), and Ibn Rushd (known in the West as Averröes, 1126–1198), who was also Islam's greatest authority on Aristotle. Jewish scholars also thrived amid the intellectual culture Islamic scholars created. The greatest of them all, Moses Maimonides (1135–1204), wrote in both Arabic and Hebrew.

WESTERN SOCIETY AND THE DEVELOPING CHRISTIAN CHURCH

HOW DID the developing Christian church influence Western society during the early Middle Ages?

Facing barbarian invasions from the north and east and a strong Islamic presence in the Mediterranean, the West found itself in decline during the fifth and sixth centuries. As trade waned, cities rapidly fell on hard times, depriving the West of centers for the exchange of goods and ideas that might enable it to look and live beyond itself.

While these social changes were occurring, one institution remained firmly entrenched and increasingly powerful within the declining cities of the waning Roman Empire: the Christian church. As the Western empire crumbled, Roman governors withdrew and populations emigrated to the countryside, where the resulting vacuum of authority was filled by local bishops and cathedral chapters. The local cathedral became the center of urban life and the local bishop the highest authority for those who remained in the cities. In Rome, on a larger and more fateful scale, the pope took control of the city as the Western emperors gradually departed and died out. Left to its own devices, Western Europe soon discovered that the Christian church was its best repository of Roman administrative skills and classical culture. Alone in the West, the church retained an effective hierarchical administration, scattered throughout the old empire, staffed by the best educated minds in Europe and centered in emperor-less Rome.

Monastic Culture

Throughout late antiquity the Christian church gained the services of growing numbers of monks, who were not only loyal to its mission, but also objects of great popular respect. Monastic culture proved again and again to be the peculiar strength of the church during the Middle Ages.

The popularity of monasticism began to grow as Roman persecution of Christians waned and Christianity became the favored religion of the empire during the fourth century. Christians came to view monastic life—embracing, as it did, the biblical "counsels of perfection" (chastity, poverty, and obedience)—as the purest form of religious practice, going beyond the baptism and creed that identified ordinary believers. This view evolved during the Middle Ages into a belief in the general superiority of the clergy and in the church's mission over the laity and the state. That belief served the papacy in later confrontations with secular rulers.

The first monks were hermits who had withdrawn from society to pursue a more perfect way of life. Anthony of Egypt (ca. 251–356), the father of hermit monasticism, went into the desert to pray and work, setting an example followed by hundreds in Egypt, Syria, and Palestine in the fourth and fifth centuries.

Hermit monasticism was soon joined by the development of communal monasticism. In the first quarter of the fourth century, Pachomius (ca. 286–346) organized monks in southern Egypt into a highly regimented community in which monks shared a life of labor, order, and discipline enforced by a strict penal code. Basil the Great (329–379) popularized communal monasticism throughout the East, providing a less severe rule than Pachomius, one that directed monks into such worldly services as caring for orphans, widows, and the infirm in surrounding communities.

Athanasius (ca. 293–373) and Martin of Tours (ca. 315–399) introduced monasticism to the West. The teachings of John Cassian (ca. 360–435) and Jerome (ca. 340–420) then helped shape the basic values and practices of Western monasticism. The great organizer of Western monasticism, however, was Benedict of Nursia (ca. 480–547). Benedict founded a monastery at Monte Cassino near Naples, Italy, in 529 and wrote *Rule for Monasteries*, a sophisticated and comprehensive plan for every activity of the monks, even detailing the manner in which they were to sleep. Periods of devotion (about four hours each day) were set aside for the "work of God." That is, regular prayers, liturgical activities, and study alternated with manual labor (farming). This program permitted not a moment's idleness and carefully nurtured the religious, intellectual, and physical well-being of the cloistered monks. The monastery was directed by an abbot, whose command the monks had to obey unquestioningly. During the early Middle Ages, Benedictine missionaries Christianized both England and Germany. Their disciplined organization and devotion to hard work made the Benedictines an economic and political power as well as a spiritual force wherever they settled.

The Doctrine of Papal Primacy

Constantine and his successors, especially the Eastern emperors, ruled religious life with an iron hand and consistently looked on the church as little more than a department of the state. At first, state control of religion was also the rule in the West. Most of the early popes were mediocre and not very influential. To increase their influence, in the fifth and sixth centuries, they took advantage of imperial weakness and distraction to develop a new defense: the powerful weaponry of papal primacy. This doctrine raised the Roman pope, or pontiff, to unassailable supremacy within the church when it came to defining church doctrine. It also put him in a position to make important secular claims, paving the way to repeated conflicts between church and state, pope and emperor, throughout the Middle Ages.

Papal primacy was first asserted as a response to the decline of imperial Rome. It was also a response to the claims of the patriarchs of the Eastern church, who, after imperial power was transferred to Constantinople, looked on the bishop of Rome as an equal, but no superior. Roman pontiffs, understandably jealous of such claims and resentful of the political interference of Eastern emperors, launched a counteroffensive. Pope Damasus I (r. 366–384) took the first of several major steps in the rise of the Roman church when he declared a Roman "apostolic" primacy. Pointing to Jesus' words to Peter in the Gospel of Matthew (16:18) ("Thou art Peter, and upon this rock I will build my church"), he claimed himself and all other popes to be Peter's direct successors as the unique "rock" on which the Christian church was built. Pope Leo I (r. 440–461) took still another fateful step by assuming the title *pontifex maximus*, or "supreme priest." He further proclaimed himself to be endowed with a "plentitude of power," thereby establishing the supremacy of the bishop of Rome over all other bishops. During Leo's reign, an imperial decree recognized his exclusive jurisdiction over the Western church. At the end of the fifth century, Pope Gelasius I (r. 492–496) proclaimed the authority of the clergy to be "more weighty" than the power of kings, because priests had charge of divine affairs and the means of salvation.

Events as well as ideology favored the papacy. As barbarian and Islamic invasions isolated the West by diverting the attention of the Byzantine empire, they also prevented both emperors and the Eastern patriarchs from interfering in the affairs of the Western church. At the same time, the Franks became a new political ally of the church. The power of the exarch of Ravenna—the Byzantine emperor's viceroy in the West—was eclipsed in the late sixth century by invading Lombards who conquered most of Italy. Thanks to Frankish prodding, the Lombards became Nicene Christians loyal to Rome and a new counterweight to Eastern power and influence in the West. In an unprecedented act, Pope Gregory I, "the Great" (r. 590–604), instead of looking to the emperor in Constantinople for protection, negotiated an independent peace treaty with the Lombards.

QUICK REVIEW

Papal Primacy

- First asserted as a response to the decline of imperial Rome
- Pope Leo I (440–461) took the title *pontifex maximus*
- Constantinople lost influence over papacy as Byzantine control of Italy decreased

The Religious Division of Christendom

In both East and West, religious belief alternately served and undermined imperial political unity. Since the fifth century, the patriarch of Constantinople had blessed Byzantine emperors in that city (the "second Rome"), attesting the close ties between rulers and the Eastern Church. While Orthodox Christianity was the religion that mattered most, it was not the only religion in the empire with a significant following. Nor did Byzantine rulers view religion as merely a political tool. From time to time, Christian heresies also received imperial support. Moreover, with imperial encouragement, Christianity absorbed pagan religious practices and beliefs that were too deeply rooted in rural and urban cultures to be eradicated, thus turning local gods and their shrines into Christian saints and holy places.

Over time, the differences between Eastern and Western Christianity grew. One issue even divided Justinian and his wife Theodora. Whereas Justinian remained strictly orthodox in his Christian beliefs, Theodora supported a divisive Eastern teaching that the Council of Chalcedon in 451 had condemned as a heresy, namely, that Christ had a single, immortal nature and was not both eternal God and mortal man in one and the same person. In reaction to the **Monophysite** controversy, orthodox Christianity became even more determined to protect the sovereignty of God.

Monophysites Believers in a single, immortal nature of Christ; not both eternal God and mortal man in one and the same person.

A similar dispute appeared in Eastern debates over the relationship among the members of the Trinity, specifically whether the Holy Spirit proceeded only from the Father, as the Nicene-Constantinopolitan Creed taught, or from the Father and the Son (*filioque* in Latin), an idea that became increasingly popular in the West and was eventually adopted by the Western church and inserted into its creed. These disputes, which appear trivial and are almost unintelligible to many people today, seemed vitally important to many Christians at the time.

Another major rift between the Christian East and West was over the veneration of images in worship. In 726, Emperor Leo III (r. 717–741) forbade the use of images and icons that portrayed Christ, the Virgin Mary, and the saints throughout Christendom. As their veneration had been commonplace for centuries, the decree came as a shock, especially to the West where it was rejected as heresy. **Iconoclasm**, as the change in policy was called, drove the popes into the camp of the Franks, where they found in Charlemagne an effective protector against the Byzantine world. (See page 000.)

Iconoclasm Opposition to the use of images in Christian worship.

A third difference between East and West was the Eastern emperors' pretension to absolute sovereignty, both secular and religious. Expressing their sense of sacred mission, the emperors presented themselves in the trappings of holiness and directly interfered in matters of church and religion, what is called **Caesaropapism**, or the emperor acting as if he were pope as well as caesar. To a degree unknown in the West, Eastern emperors appointed and manipulated the clergy, convening church councils and enforcing church decrees. By comparison, the West nurtured a distinction between church and state that became visible in the eleventh century.

Caesaropapism Emperor acting as if he were pope as well as caesar.

The Eastern church also rejected several disputed requirements of Roman Christianity. It denied the existence of Purgatory, permitted lay divorce and remarriage, allowed priests, but not bishops, to marry, and conducted religious services in the languages that people in a given locality actually spoke (the so-called "vernacular" languages) instead of Greek and Latin.

Having piled up over the centuries, these various differences ultimately resulted in a schism between the two churches in 1054. In that year a Western envoy of the pope, Cardinal Humbertus, visited the Patriarch of Constantinople, Michael Cerularius, in the hope of overcoming the differences that divided Christendom. The patriarch was not, however, welcoming. Relations between the two men quickly deteriorated, and cardinal and patriarch engaged in mutual recriminations and insults. Before leaving the city, Humbertus left a bull of excommunication on the altar of Hagia Sophia. In response, the patriarch proclaimed all Western popes to have been heretics since the sixth century! Nine hundred and eleven years would pass before this breach was repaired. In a belated ecumenical gesture in 1965, a Roman pope met with the patriarch of Constantinople to revoke the mutual condemnations of 1054.

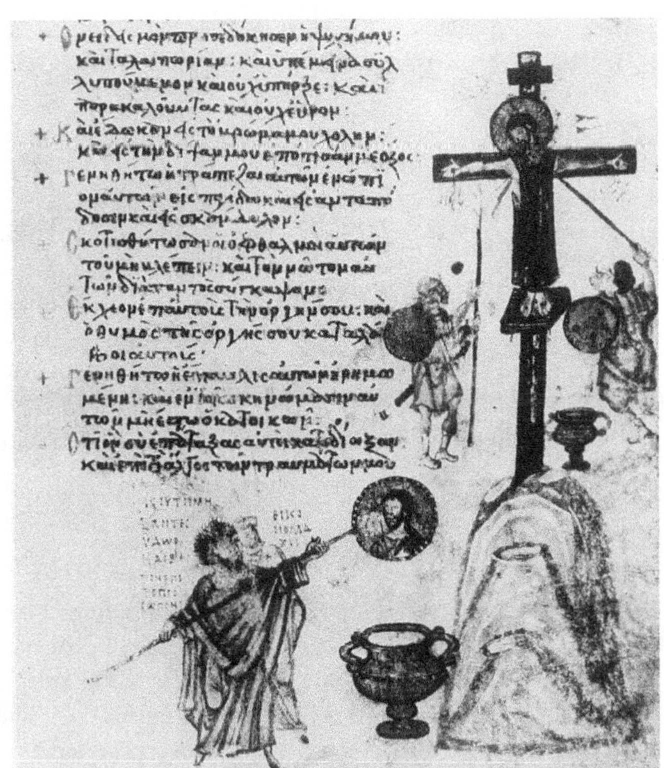

A ninth-century Byzantine manuscript shows an iconoclast whiting out an image of Christ. The Iconoclastic Controversy was an important factor in the division of Christendom into separate Latin and Greek branches.

State Historical Museum, Moscow

Why were religious and political disputes so often intertwined in the Byzantine Empire?

Overview Major Political and Religious Developments of the Early Middle Ages

313	Emperor Constantine issues the Edict of Milan
325	Council of Nicaea defines Christian doctrine
410	Rome invaded by Visigoths under Alaric
413–426	Saint Augustine writes *City of God*
451	Council of Chalcedon further defines Christian doctrine
451–453	Europe invaded by the Huns under Attila
476	Barbarian Odovacer deposes Western emperor and rules as king of the Romans
489–493	Theodoric establishes kingdom of Ostrogoths in Italy
529	Saint Benedict founds monastery at Monte Cassino
533	Justinian codifies Roman law
622	Muhammad's flight from Mecca (*Hegira*)
711	Muslim invasion of Spain
732	Charles Martel defeats Muslims between Poitiers and Tours
754	Pope Stephen II and Pepin III ally

THE KINGDOM OF THE FRANKS: FROM CLOVIS TO CHARLEMAGNE

HOW DID the reign of Clovis differ from that of Charlemagne?

A warrior chieftain, Clovis (ca. 466–511), who converted to Catholic Christianity around 496, founded the first Frankish dynasty, the Merovingians, named for Merovich, an early leader of one branch of the Franks. Clovis and his successors united the Salian and Ripuarian Franks, subdued the Arian Burgundians and Visigoths, and established the kingdom of the Franks within ancient Gaul, making the Franks and the Merovingian kings a significant force in Western Europe. The Franks themselves occupied a broad belt of territory that extended throughout modern France, Belgium, the Netherlands, and western Germany, and their loyalties remained strictly tribal and local.

Governing the Franks

In attempting to govern this sprawling kingdom, the Merovingians encountered what proved to be the most persistent problem of medieval political history—the competing claims of the "one" and the "many." On the one hand, the king struggled for a centralized government and transregional loyalty, and on the other, powerful local magnates strove to preserve their regional autonomy and traditions.

The Merovingian kings addressed this problem by making pacts with the landed nobility and by creating the royal office of counts. The counts were men without possessions to whom the king gave great lands in the expectation that they would be, as the landed aristocrats often were not, loyal officers of the kingdom. Like local aristocrats, however, the Merovingian counts also let their immediate self-interest gain the upper hand. Once established in office for a period of time, they, too, became territorial rulers in their own right, so the Frankish kingdom progressively fragmented into independent regions and tiny principalities. The Frankish custom of dividing the kingdom equally among the king's legitimate male heirs furthered this tendency.

By the seventh century, the Frankish king was king in title only and had no effective executive power. Real power came to be concentrated in the office of the "mayor of the palace," spokesperson at the king's court for the great landowners of the three regions into which the Frankish kingdom was divided: Neustria, Austrasia, and Burgundy. Through this office, the Carolingian dynasty rose to power.

The Carolingians controlled the office of the mayor of the palace from the ascent to that post of Pepin I of Austrasia (d. 639) until 751, when, with the enterprising connivance of the pope, they simply seized the Frankish crown. Pepin II (d. 714) ruled in fact, if not in title, over the Frankish kingdom. His illegitimate son, Charles Martel ("the Hammer," d. 741), created a great cavalry by bestowing lands known as benefices, or **fiefs**, on powerful noblemen. In return, they agreed to be ready to serve as the king's army.

fiefs ("Lands") Granted to cavalry men to fund their equipment and service.

The fiefs so generously bestowed by Charles Martel to create his army came in large part from landed property he usurped from the church. The Carolingians created counts almost entirely from among the same landed nobility from which the Carolingians themselves had risen. The Merovingians, in contrast, had tried to compete directly with these great aristocrats by raising landless men to power. By playing to strength rather than challenging it, the Carolingians strengthened themselves, at least for the short term. The church, by this time dependent on the protection of the Franks against the Eastern emperor and the Lombards, could only suffer the loss of its lands in silence. Later, although they never returned them, the Franks partially compensated the church for these lands.

The Frankish Church The church came to play a large and enterprising role in the Frankish government. By Carolingian times, monasteries were a dominant force. Their intellectual achievements made them respected centers of culture. Their religious teaching and example imposed order on surrounding populations. Their relics and rituals made them magical shrines to which pilgrims came in great numbers. Also, thanks to their many gifts and internal discipline and industry, many had become profitable farms and landed estates, their abbots rich and powerful magnates. Already in Merovingian times, the higher clergy were employed along with counts as royal agents.

It was the policy of the Carolingians, perfected by Charles Martel and his successor, Pepin III ("the Short," d. 768), to use the church to pacify conquered neighboring tribes—Frisians, Thüringians, Bavarians, and especially the Franks' archenemies, the Saxons. Conversion to Nicene Christianity became an integral part of the successful annexation of conquered lands and people. Christian bishops in missionary districts and elsewhere became lords, appointed by and subject to the king. In this ominous integration of secular and religious policy lay the seeds of the later investiture controversy of the eleventh and twelfth centuries. (See Chapter 7.)

The church served more than Carolingian territorial expansion. Pope Zacharias (r. 741–752) also sanctioned Pepin the Short's termination of the Merovingian dynasty and supported the Carolingian accession to outright kingship of the Franks. With the pope's public blessing, Pepin was proclaimed king by the nobility in council in 751. Zacharias's successor, Pope Stephen II (r. 752–757), did not let Pepin forget the favor of his predecessor. In 753, when the Lombards besieged Rome, Pope Stephen crossed the Alps and appealed directly to Pepin to cast out the invaders and to guarantee papal claims to central Italy, largely dominated at this time by the Eastern emperor. In 755, the Franks defeated the Lombards and gave the pope the lands surrounding Rome, creating what came to be known as the **Papal States**.

Papal States Central part of Italy where Pope Stephen II became the secular ruler when confirmed by the Franks in 755.

QUICK REVIEW
Church and State

- Church played a large role in Frankish government
- Christian bishops became lords in service of the king
- Franks confirm pope as ruler of the Papal States in 755

The papacy had looked to the Franks for an ally strong enough to protect it from the Eastern emperors. It is an irony of history that the church found in the Carolingian dynasty a Western imperial government that drew almost as slight a boundary between state and church and between secular and religious policy as did Eastern emperors. Although Carolingian patronage was eminently preferable to Eastern domination for the popes, it proved in its own way to be no less constraining.

The Reign of Charlemagne (768–814)

Charlemagne, the son of Pepin the Short, continued the role of his father as papal protector in Italy and his policy of territorial conquest in the north. By the time of his death on January 28, 814, Charlemagne's kingdom embraced modern France, Belgium, Holland, Switzerland, almost the whole of western Germany, much of Italy, a portion of Spain, and the island of Corsica. (See Map 6–4.)

The New Empire Encouraged by his ambitious advisers, Charlemagne came to harbor imperial designs. He desired to be not only king of all the Franks but a universal emperor as well. Although he permitted the church its independence, he looked after it with a paternalism almost as great as that of any Eastern emperor. He used the church, above all, to promote social stability and hierarchical order throughout the kingdom—as an aid in the creation of a great Frankish Christian Empire. Charlemagne fulfilled his imperial pretensions on Christmas Day 800, when Pope Leo III (r. 795–816) crowned him emperor in Rome. This event began what would come to be known as the **Holy Roman Empire**, a revival of the old Roman Empire in the West, based in Germany after 870.

Holy Roman Empire The domain of the German monarchs who revived the use of the Roman imperial title during the Middle Ages.

In 799, Pope Leo III had been imprisoned by the Roman aristocracy but escaped to the protection of Charlemagne, who restored him as pope. The fateful coronation of Charlemagne was thus, in part, an effort by the pope to enhance the church's stature and to gain some leverage over this powerful king. It was, however, no papal coup d'état; Charlemagne's control over the church remained as strong after the event as before. If the coronation benefited the church, as it certainly did, it also served Charlemagne's purposes.

The New Emperor Charlemagne stood a majestic six feet three and a half inches tall. He was restless, ever ready for a hunt. Informal and gregarious, he insisted on the presence of friends even when he bathed. He was widely known for his practical jokes, lusty good humor, and warm hospitality. His capital, Aachen, was a festive palace city to which people and gifts came from all over the world. In 802, Charlemagne even received from the caliph of Baghdad, Harun-al-Rashid, a white elephant, whose transport across the Alps was as great a wonder as the creature itself.

Problems of Government Charlemagne governed his kingdom through counts, of whom there were perhaps as many as 250, strategically located within the administrative districts into which the kingdom was divided. Carolingian counts tended to be local magnates who possessed the armed might and the self-interest to enforce the will of a generous king. Counts had three main duties: to maintain a local army loyal to the king, to collect tribute and dues, and to administer justice throughout their districts.

This last responsibility a count undertook through a district law court known as the *mallus*. The *mallus* received testimony from witnesses familiar with the parties involved in a dispute or criminal case, much as a modern court does. On occasion, in difficult cases where the testimony was insufficient to determine guilt or innocence, recourse would be taken to judicial duels or to a variety of "divine" tests or ordeals. Among these was the length of time it took a defendant's hand to heal after immersion in boiling water. In another, a defendant was thrown with his hands and feet bound into a river or pond that a priest had blessed. If he floated, he was pronounced guilty, because the pure water had obviously rejected him; if, however, the water received him and he sank, he was deemed innocent and quickly retrieved.

As in Merovingian times, many counts used their official position and new judicial powers to their own advantage and became little despots within their districts. As the strong became stronger, they also became more independent. They began to look on the land grants with which they were paid as hereditary possessions rather than generous royal donations—a development that began to fragment Charlemagne's kingdom. Charlemagne tried to oversee his overseers and improve local justice by creating special royal envoys. Known as *missi dominici*, these were lay and clerical agents (counts, archbishops, and bishops) who made annual visits to districts other than their own. Yet their impact was marginal. Permanent provincial governors, bearing the title of prefect, duke, or margrave, were created in what was still another attempt to supervise the counts and organize the outlying regions of the kingdom. Yet as these governors became established in their areas, they proved no less corruptible than the others.

Charlemagne never solved the problem of creating a loyal bureaucracy. Ecclesiastical agents proved no better than secular ones in this regard. Landowning bishops had not only the same responsibilities, but also the same secular lifestyles and aspirations as the royal counts. *Capitularies*, or royal decrees, discouraged the more outrageous behav-

MAP 6–4 **The Empire of Charlemagne to 814** Building on the successes of his predecessors, Charlemagne greatly increased the Frankish domains. Such traditional enemies as the Saxons and the Lombards fell under his sway.

What reasons might Charlemagne have had for expanding the Frankish domains into the regions in which he did?

QUICK REVIEW

Carolingian Administration

- 250 counts administred empire
- Counts tended to become despots in their own regions
- Charlemagne often appointed churchmen to government offices

ior of the clergy. However, Charlemagne also sensed, and rightly so as the Gregorian reform of the eleventh century would prove, that the emergence of a distinctive, reform-minded class of ecclesiastical landowners would be a danger to royal government. He purposefully treated his bishops as he treated his counts, that is, as vassals who served at the king's pleasure.

Alcuin and the Carolingian Renaissance Charlemagne accumulated great wealth in the form of loot and land from conquered tribes. He used part of this booty to attract Europe's best scholars to Aachen, where they developed court culture and education. By making scholarship materially as well as intellectually rewarding, Charlemagne attracted such scholars as Theodulf of Orleans, Angilbert, his own biographer Einhard, and the renowned Anglo-Saxon master Alcuin of York (735–804). In 782, at almost fifty years of age, Alcuin became director of the king's palace school. He brought classical and Christian learning to Aachen in schools run by the monasteries. Alcuin was handsomely rewarded for his efforts with several monastic estates, including that of Saint Martin of Tours, the wealthiest in the kingdom.

Although Charlemagne also appreciated learning for its own sake, his grand palace school was not created simply for the love of classical scholarship. Charlemagne wanted to upgrade the administrative skills of the clerics and officials who staffed the royal bureaucracy. By preparing the sons of the nobility to run the religious and secular offices of the realm, court scholarship served kingdom building. The school provided basic instruction in the seven liberal arts, with special concentration on grammar, logic, rhetoric, and the basic mathematical arts. It therefore provided training in reading, writing, speaking, sound reasoning, and counting—the basic tools of bureaucracy.

Interior of the palace chapel of Charlemagne, Aachen.

French Government Tourist Office

What were the most important achievements of the Carolingian Renaissance?

Among the results of this intellectual activity was the appearance of a more accurate Latin in official documents and the development of a clear style of handwriting known as *Carolingian minuscule*. By making reading both easier and more pleasurable, Carolingian minuscule helped lay the foundations of subsequent Latin scholarship. It also increased lay literacy.

A modest renaissance of antiquity occurred in the palace school as scholars collected and preserved ancient manuscripts for a more curious posterity. These scholarly activities aimed at concrete reforms and helped bring uniformity to church law and liturgy, educate the clergy, and improve monastic morals. Through personal correspondence and visitations, Alcuin created a genuine, if limited, community of scholars and clerics at court. He did much to infuse the highest administrative levels with a sense of comradeship and common purpose.

Breakup of the Carolingian Kingdom

In his last years, an ailing Charlemagne knew his empire was ungovernable. The seeds of dissolution lay in regionalism, that is, the determination of each region, no matter how small, to look first—and often only—to its own self-interest. Despite his skill and resolve, Charlemagne's realm became too fragmented among powerful regional magnates. Charlemagne had been forced to recognize and even to enhance the power of regional magnates to gain needed financial and military support. But as in the Merovingian kingdom, the tail came increasingly also to wag the dog in the Carolingian.

MAJOR DEVELOPMENTS OF THE EARLY MIDDLE AGES

313	Emperor Constantine legalizes Christianity
ca. 251–356	Anthony of Egypt inspires the monastic movement
410	Visigoths sack the city of Rome
476	Deposition of Romulus Augustulus, last Western Roman emperor
ca. 466–511	Clovis founds the Franks' Merovingian dynasty
527–565	Reign of Byzantine emperor Justinian
622	Muhammad's *Hegira*, the foundation of Islam
732	Charles Martel stops the Muslim advance at Tours
751	Pepin III founds the Carolingian dynasty
768–814	Reign of Charlemagne
ca. 875–950	Invasions, feudal fragmentation, and the Dark Ages

Louis the Pious The Carolingian kings did not give up easily, however. Charlemagne's only surviving son and successor was Louis the Pious (r. 814–840). After Charlemagne's death, Louis no longer referred to himself as king of the Franks. He bore instead the single title of emperor. The assumption of this title reflected not only the Carolingian pretense to be an imperial dynasty, but also Louis's determination to unify his kingdom and raise its people above mere regional and tribal loyalties.

Unfortunately, Louis's own fertility joined with Salic, or Frankish, law and custom to prevent the attainment of this high goal. Louis had three sons by his first wife. According to Salic law, a ruler partitioned his kingdom equally among his surviving sons (Salic law forbade women to inherit the throne). Louis, who saw himself as an emperor and no mere king, recognized that a tripartite kingdom would hardly be an empire and acted early in his reign, in 817, to break this legal tradition. This he did by making his eldest son, Lothar (d. 855), co-regent and sole imperial heir by royal decree. To Lothar's brothers he gave important, but much lesser, *appanages*, or assigned hereditary lands; Pepin (d. 838) became king of Aquitaine, and Louis "the German" (d. 876) became king of Bavaria, over the eastern Franks.

In 823, Louis's second wife, Judith of Bavaria, bore him a fourth son, Charles, later called "the Bald" (d. 877). Mindful of Frankish law and custom and determined her son should receive more than just a nominal inheritance, the queen incited the brothers Pepin and Louis against Lothar, who fled for refuge to the pope. More important, Judith was instrumental in persuading Louis to adhere to tradition and divide the kingdom equally among his four living sons. As their stepmother and the young Charles rose in their father's favor, the three brothers, fearing still further reversals, decided to act against their father. Supported by the pope, they joined forces and defeated their father in a battle near Colmar in 833.

As the bestower of crowns on emperors, the pope had an important stake in the preservation of the revived Western empire and the imperial title. Louis's belated agreement to an equal partition of his kingdom threatened to weaken the pope as well as the royal family. Therefore, the pope condemned Louis and restored Lothar to his original inheritance. But Lothar's regained imperial dignity only stirred anew the resentments of his brothers, including his stepbrother, Charles, who joined in renewed warfare against him.

The Treaty of Verdun and Its Aftermath In 843, with the Treaty of Verdun, peace finally came to the surviving heirs of Louis the Pious. (Pepin had died in 838.) The great Carolingian Empire was divided into three equal parts. Lothar received a middle section, known as Lotharingia, which embraced roughly modern Holland, Belgium, Switzerland, Alsace-Lorraine, and Italy. Charles the Bald acquired the western part of the kingdom, or roughly modern France. And Louis the German took the eastern part, or roughly modern Germany.

The Treaty of Verdun proved to be only the beginning of Carolingian fragmentation. When Lothar died in 855, his middle kingdom was divided equally among his three surviving sons, the eldest of whom, Louis II, retained Italy and the imperial title. This partition of the partition sealed the dissolution of the great empire of Charlemagne.

This seventy-five-foot-long Viking burial ship from the early ninth century is decorated with beastly figures. It bore a dead queen, her servant, and assorted sacrificed animals to the afterlife. The bodies of the passengers were confined within a burial cabin at midship surrounded with a treasure trove of jewels and tapestries.

Dorling Kindersley Media Library. Universitets Oldsaksamling © Dorling Kindersley

How did the Viking invasions disrupt European life in the early Middle Ages?

In Italy the demise of the Carolingian emperors enhanced for the moment the power of the popes, who had become adept at filling vacuums. The popes were now strong enough to excommunicate weak emperors and override their wishes. In a major church crackdown on the polygyny of the Germans, Pope Nicholas I (r. 858–867) excommunicated Lothar II for divorcing his wife. After the death of the childless emperor Louis II in 875, Pope John VIII (r. 872–882) installed Charles the Bald as emperor against the express last wishes of Louis II.

When Charles the Bald died in 877, both the papal and the imperial thrones suffered defeat. They became pawns in the hands of powerful Italian and German magnates, respectively. The last Carolingian emperor died in 911. This internal political breakdown of the empire and the papacy coincided with new barbarian attacks.

Vikings, Magyars, and Muslims The late ninth and tenth centuries saw successive waves of Normans (North-men), better known as Vikings, from Scandinavia, Magyars, or Hungarians, the great horsemen from the eastern plains, and Muslims from the south. The political breakdown of the Carolingian Empire coincided with these new external threats, both probably set off by overpopulation and famine in northern and eastern Europe.

Taking to the sea in rugged longboats of doubled-hulled construction, the Vikings terrified their neighbors to the south, invading and occupying English and European coastal and river towns. In the 880s, the Vikings even penetrated to Aachen and besieged Paris. In the ninth century, the Vikings turned York in northern England into a major trading post for their woolens, jewelry, and ornamental wares. Erik the Red made it to Greenland, and his son, Leif Erikson wintered in Newfoundland and may even have reached New England five hundred years before Columbus. In the eleventh century, Christian conversions and the English defeat of the Danes and Norwegians effectively restricted the Vikings to their Scandinavian homelands.

Magyars, the ancestors of the modern Hungarians, swept into Western Europe from the eastern plains, while Muslims made incursions across the Mediterranean from North Africa. The Franks built fortified towns and castles in strategic locations, and when they could, they bought off the invaders with grants of land and payments of silver. In the resulting turmoil, local populations became more dependent than ever on local strongmen for life, limb, and livelihood—the essential precondition for the maturation of feudal society.

FEUDAL SOCIETY

WHAT WERE the characteristics of a feudal society?

The Middle Ages were characterized by a chronic absence of effective central government and the constant threat of famine, disease, and foreign invasion. In this state of affairs, the weaker sought the protection of the stronger, and the true lords and masters became those who could guarantee immediate security from violence and starvation. The term *feudal society* refers to the social, political, military, and economic system that emerged from these conditions.

ORIGINS

The origins of feudal government can be found in the divisions and conflicts of Merovingian society. In the sixth and seventh centuries, it became customary for individual freemen who did not already belong to families or groups that could protect them to place themselves under the protection of more powerful freemen. In this way the latter built up armies and became local magnates, and the former solved the problem of simple survival. Freemen who so entrusted themselves to others came to be described as **vassals**, *vassi* or

vassal A person granted an estate or cash payments in return for rendering services to a lord.

"those who serve," from which evolved the term *vassalage*, meaning the placement of oneself in the personal service of another who promises protection in return.

Landed nobles, like kings, tried to acquire as many such vassals as they could, because military strength in the early Middle Ages lay in numbers. Because it proved impossible to maintain these growing armies within the lord's own household (as was the original custom) or to support them by special monetary payments, the practice evolved of simply granting them land as a "tenement." Vassals were expected to dwell on these *benefices*, or fiefs, and maintain horses, armor, and weapons in good order. Originally, vassals therefore were little more than gangs-in-waiting.

Vassalage and the Fief

Vassalage involved "fealty" to the lord. To swear fealty was to promise to refrain from any action that might in any way threaten the lord's well-being and to perform personal services for him on his request. Chief among the expected services was military duty as a mounted knight. This could involve a variety of activities: a short or long military expedition, escort duty, standing castle guard, or placing his own fortress at the lord's disposal, if the vassal had one. Limitations were placed on the number of days a lord could require services from a vassal. In France in the eleventh century, about forty days of service a year were considered sufficient. It also became possible for vassals to buy their way out of military service by a monetary payment, known as scutage. The lord, in turn, could use this payment to hire mercenaries, who often proved more efficient than contract-conscious vassals.

Beginning with the reign of Louis the Pious (r. 814–840), bishops and abbots swore fealty to the king and received their offices from him as a *benefice*. The king formally "invested" these clerics in their offices during a special ceremony in which he presented them with a ring and a staff, the symbols of high spiritual office. Long a sore point with the church, lay investiture of the clergy provoked a serious confrontation of church and state in the late tenth and eleventh centuries. At that time, reform-minded clergy rebelled against what they then believed to be a kind of involuntary clerical vassalage. Even reform-minded clerics, however, welcomed the king's grants of land and power to the clergy.

The lord's obligations to his vassals were specific. First, he was obligated to protect the vassal from physical harm and to stand as his advocate in public court. After fealty was sworn and homage paid, the lord provided for the vassal's physical maintenance by the bestowal of a *benefice*, or fief. The fief was simply the physical or material wherewithal to meet the vassal's military and other obligations. It could take the form of liquid wealth, as well as the more common grant of real property.

Daily Life and Religion

The Humble Carolingian Manor The agrarian economy of the early Middle Ages was organized and controlled through village farms known as manors. On these, peasants labored as tenants for a lord, that is, a more powerful landowner who allotted them land and tenements in exchange for their services and a portion of their crops. The part of the land tended for the lord was the *demesne*, on average about one-quarter to one-third of the arable land. All crops grown there were harvested for the lord. The manor also included common meadows for grazing animals and forests reserved exclusively for the lord to hunt in.

Peasants were treated according to their personal status and the size of their tenements. A freeman, that is, a peasant with his own modest *allodial*, or hereditary property (property free from the claims of an overlord), became a **serf** by surrendering his property to a greater landowner—a lord—in exchange for protection and assistance. The freeman received his land back from the lord with a clear definition of his economic and legal rights. Although the land was no longer his property, he had full

serf Peasant bound to the land he worked.

possession and use of it, and the number of services and amount of goods he was to supply to the lord were carefully spelled out.

Peasants who entered the service of a lord with little real property (perhaps only a few farm implements and animals) ended up as unfree serfs. Such serfs were far more vulnerable to the lord's demands, often spending up to three days a week working the lord's fields. Peasants who had nothing to offer a lord except their hands had the lowest status and were the least protected from excessive demands on their labor.

By the time of Charlemagne, the moldboard plow and the three-field system of land cultivation were coming into use. The moldboard plow cut deep into the soil, turning it to form a ridge, which provided a natural drainage system and permitted the deep planting of seeds. This made cultivation possible in the regions north of the Mediterranean, where soils were dense and waterlogged from heavy precipitation. The **three-field system** alternated fallow with planted fields each year, and this increased the amount of cultivated land by leaving only one-third fallow in a given year. It also better adjusted crops to seasons. In fall, one field was planted with winter crops of wheat or rye, to be harvested in early summer. In late spring, a second field was planted with summer crops of oats, barley, and beans. The third field was left fallow, to be planted in its turn with winter and summer crops. The new summer crops, especially beans, restored nitrogen to the soil and helped increase yields. (See "Encountering the Past: Medieval Cooking.")

three-field system Developed by medieval farmers, a system in which three fields were utilized during different growing seasons to limit the amount of nonproductive plowing and to restore soil fertility through crop rotation.

These developments made possible what has been called the "expansion of Europe within Europe." They permitted the old lands formerly occupied by barbarians to be cultivated and filled with farms and towns. This, in turn, led to major population growth in the north and ultimately a shift of political power from the Mediterranean to northern Europe.

The Cure of Carolingian Souls The lower clergy lived among, and were drawn from, peasant ranks. They fared hardly better than peasants in Carolingian times. As owners of the churches on their lands, the lords had the right to raise chosen serfs to the post of parish priest, placing them in charge of the churches on the lords' estates. Church law directed a lord to set a serf free before he entered the clergy. Lords, however, preferred a "serf priest," one who not only said the Mass on Sundays and holidays, but who also continued to serve his lord during the week.

The ordinary people looked to religion for comfort and consolation. They especially associated religion with the major Christian holidays and festivals, such as Christmas and Easter. They baptized their children, attended mass, tried to learn the Lord's Prayer and the Apostles' Creed, and received the last rites from the priest as death approached. Because local priests on the manors were no better educated than their congregations, religious instruction in the meaning of Christian doctrine and practice remained at a bare minimum.

Fragmentation and Divided Loyalty

In addition to the fragmentation brought about by the multiplication of vassalage, effective occupation of land led gradually to claims of hereditary possession. Hereditary possession became a legally recognized principle in the ninth century and laid the basis for claims to real ownership. Fiefs given as royal donations became hereditary possessions and, over time, sometimes even the real property of the possessor.

Further, vassal obligations increased in still another way as enterprising freemen sought to accumulate as much land as possible. One man could become a vassal to several different lords. This development led in the ninth century to the "liege lord"—the one master the vassal must obey even against his other masters, should a direct conflict arise among them.

The problem of loyalty was reflected both in the literature of the period, with its praise of the virtues of honor and fidelity, and in the ceremonial development of the very

ENCOUNTERING THE PAST

Medieval Cooking

Medieval cooks served things that modern diners would recognize: roasts, pastas, meat pies, and custards. But where modern chefs are preoccupied primarily with the taste of their fare, medieval cooks worried about the effect of their dishes on diners' health. Medieval physicians traced illness to imbalances among the so-called four humors: blood, black bile, yellow bile, and phlegm. Because the humors were generated by food, recipes had to be planned like medicines. Health depended on maintaining a balance between the poles of the opposites that the humors nurtured: wet–dry, cold–warm. If not moderated by cool, wet seasonings, a spicy dish might produce an excess of hot, dry humors that made one ill.

Medieval people correctly intuited a link between diet and health, but from the modern point of view this did them little good. A fixation on meat as a prestige food meant vegetables were little appreciated. Most Europeans survived on a diet of mush or a porridge made by boiling bread in milk.

Medieval cooks were expected to be artists as well as scientists. Formal dining called for elaborately constructed dishes, such as castles executed in pastry or cooked birds stuffed back into their feathered skins. Dishes were sometimes tinted strange colors, modeled into odd shapes, or rendered otherwise amusing to the eye.

[Top] The Lord of the Manor Dining [Bottom] Kitchen Scene, Chopping Meat

From *The Luttrell Psalter,* by permission of The British Library (1000102.021)

What was the relationship between the lord of the manor and the serfs and others who inhabited the manor?

DID THE medieval understanding of the link between diet and health differ from the modern understanding—or was only the explanation different?

act of commendation by which a freeman became a vassal. In the mid–eighth century, an oath of fealty highlighted the ceremony. A vassal reinforced his promise of fidelity to the lord by swearing a special oath with his hand on a sacred relic or the Bible. In the tenth and eleventh centuries, paying homage to the lord involved not only swearing such an oath, but also placing the vassal's hands between the lord's and sealing the ceremony with a kiss.

As the centuries passed, personal loyalty and service became secondary to the acquisition of property. In developments that signaled the waning of feudal society in the tenth century, the fief came to overshadow fealty, the *benefice* became more important than vassalage, and freemen would swear allegiance to the highest bidder.

Feudal arrangements nonetheless provided stability throughout the early Middle Ages and aided the difficult process of political centralization during the High Middle Ages (c. 1000–1300). The genius of feudal government lay in its adaptability. Contracts of different kinds could be made with almost anybody, as circumstances required. The process embraced a wide spectrum of people, from the king at the top to the lowliest vassal in the remotest part of the kingdom. The foundations of the modern nation-state would emerge in France and England from the fine-tuning of essentially feudal arrangements as kings sought to adapt their goal of centralized government to the reality of local power and control.

SUMMARY

HOW DID Germanic migrations contribute to the fall of the Roman Empire?

On the Eve of the Frankish Ascendancy In the late fourth century, the Western empire was weakening, and the Visigoths were being forced out of their own home territories by invading Huns. The Visigoths defeated the Romans in the ensuing conflict. Soon other barbarians had established territories within the Western empire. By the mid–fifth century, Rome had been sacked repeatedly, and by the end of the century the Western empire was history. Roman culture endured, although it was transformed through its contact with the Germanic peoples. Christianity, too, endured and changed through cultural contact. *page 150*

HOW DID the Byzantine Empire continue the legacy of Rome?

The Byzantine Empire The eastern portion of the Roman Empire endured as the Byzantine Empire. Although the empire lasted until Constantinople (the capital) fell to the Turks in 1453, it peaked under Justinian, in the mid–sixth century. Although Justinian and his wife, the empress Theodora, were both Christians, she was a believer in Monophysitism, a heresy that influenced the later course of the empire's history. Justinian codified Roman law, which was to prove influential in the West for centuries. Justinian supported Orthodox Christianity, although some of his successors supported other forms of Christianity. Constantinople and smaller urban centers formed the economic, administrative, and cultural backbone of the empire. The empire's eastern orientation increased under Heraclius in the early seventh century. In the early eighth century, Leo's Caesaropapism led him to attempt to ban the use of images in churches. *page 152*

HOW DID Islamic culture influence the West?

Islam and the Islamic World In the seventh century, Muhammad founded a new religion on the Arabian peninsula. In 624, Muhammad's Medina-based army conquered Mecca, and in the following years the basic rules of Islamic life were articulated. Islam expanded substantially, until by 750 the Islamic Empire stretched from Spain through North Africa, the southern and eastern Mediterranean, and eastward into India. But this was the peak of Muslim territorial expansion, and Islam did not spread farther than Spain into the remnants of the Western Roman Empire. The West profited from its contact with Islam, since much of the Arab world's technology and scholarship was superior to Europe's in the early Middle Ages. *page 155*

HOW DID the developing Christian church influence Western society during the early Middle Ages?

Western Society and the Developing Christian Church As trade declined throughout the West, people migrated from cities to farmlands. New types of relationships between landowners and peasants emerged, including serfdom, the manorial system, and the feudal system. The Christian church provided a strong element of continuity with the educational and administrative achievements of the Roman Empire. Monastic culture took shape. Christianity was a potent unifying and civilizing force within the West, although it was also the source of a fundamental rift with the Eastern Empire. By the middle of the eighth century, the papacy in Rome faced military threats from the north and doctrinal threats from the East; Pope Stephen boldly initiated an alliance with the Franks that influenced history for the next millennium or more. *page 160*

HOW DID the reign of Clovis differ from that of Charlemagne?

The Kingdom of the Franks: From Clovis to Charlemagne Clovis founded the first Frankish dynasty, the Merovingians. Then the Carolingian dynasty made strategic alliances with the landed nobility and with the church. The most illustrious Carolingian ruler, Charlemagne, conquered additional lands and, on Christmas Day in 800 had himself crowned Holy Roman Emperor by Pope Leo III. His capital, Aachen, was a center of scholarship and intelligent administration. The social organization of the manor and innovations such as new plows improved agricultural productivity. Soon after Charlemagne's death in 814, his empire disintegrated as it was divided up, messily, among his grandsons. The late ninth and early tenth centuries were truly "dark ages" in Europe: Both secular and church-based organizations were weak, and at the same time invaders such as the Vikings were attacking. Peasants sought security at almost any price, so the institution of feudalism spread and matured. *page 164*

WHAT WERE the characteristics of a feudal society?

Feudal Society The feudal system was built around the exchange of land, labor, and military protection. Vassals would swear fealty to a more powerful individual, in return for the promise of protection. Kings and nobles built their military strength by acquiring increasing numbers of vassals; as the system developed, benefices replaced residence in the lord's household, scutage replaced direct military service, and other innovations formalized and institutionalized the relationships of feudal society. All participants in the feudal system constantly negotiated and competed for advantage. Loyalties could become divided as vassals swore fealty to multiple lords to gain multiple landholdings. Eventually, vassals could claim hereditary possession of the lands they worked, reducing their sense of obligation to lords. Nonetheless, feudalism provided a first glimpse of many of the political and legal institutions that developed into the modern nation-state. *page 170*

REVIEW QUESTIONS

1. What changes took place in the Frankish kingdom between its foundation and the end of Charlemagne's reign? What were the characteristics of Charlemagne's government? Why did Charlemagne encourage learning at his court? Why did his empire break apart?
2. How and why was the history of the eastern half of the former Roman Empire so different from that of its western half? Did Justinian strengthen or weaken the Byzantine Empire? How does his reign compare to Charlemagne's?
3. What were the tenets of Islam? How were the Muslims able to build an empire so quickly? What contributions did the Muslims make to the development of Western Europe?
4. How and why did feudal society begin? What were the essential features of feudalism? Do you think modern society could slip back into a feudal pattern?

KEY TERMS

Caesaropapism (p. 163)
caliphate (p. 156)
fiefs (p. 165)
Hegira (p. 156)
Holy Roman Empire (p. 166)
iconoclasm (p. 163)
Islam (p. 155)
Ka'ba (p. 155)
Monophysites (p. 163)
Papal States (p. 165)
Qur'an (p. 155)
serf (p. 171)
Shi'a (p. 156)
Sunnis (p. 157)
three-field system (p. 172)
ulema (p. 156)
vassal (p. 170)

For additional learning resources related to this chapter, please go to **www.myhistorylab.com**

PEARSON myhistorylab

7

The High Middle Ages: The Rise of European Empires and States (1000–1300)

In medieval Europe, the traditional geocentric or earth-centered universe was usually depicted by concentric circles. In this popular German work on natural history, medicine, and science, Konrad von Megenberg (1309–1374) depicted the universe in a most unusual but effective manner. The seven known planets are contained within straight horizontal bands that separate the earth, below, from heaven, populated by the saints, above.

Konrad von Megenberg. *Buch der Natur* (Book of Nature). Augsburg: Johannes Bämler, 1481. Rosenwald Collection. Courtesy of the Library of Congress. Rare Book and Special Collections Division.

How were medieval ideas of social and political hierarchy reflected in medieval models of the universe?

OTTO I AND THE REVIVAL OF THE EMPIRE *page 178*

HOW WAS Otto able to secure the power of his Saxon dynasty?

THE REVIVING CATHOLIC CHURCH *page 179*

WHAT EXPLAINS the popularity of the Cluniac reform movement?

ENGLAND AND FRANCE: HASTINGS (1066) TO BOUVINES (1214) *page 188*

HOW DID England and France develop strong monarchies?

FRANCE IN THE THIRTEENTH CENTURY: THE REIGN OF LOUIS IX *page 193*

IN WHAT ways was Louis IX of France the "ideal" medieval monarch?

THE HOHENSTAUFEN EMPIRE (1152–1272) *page 194*

HOW DID the policies of the Hohenstaufens lead to the fragmentation of Germany?

Europe in the High Middle Ages (1000–1300) was characterized by political expansion and consolidation and by intellectual flowering and synthesis. This may indeed have been a more creative era than the Italian Renaissance or the German Reformation.

The borders of western Europe were secured against invaders, and Europeans, who had long been the prey of foreign powers, mounted a military and economic offensive against the East. By adapting feudal traditions, the rulers of England and France established nuclei for centrally governed nation-states. The parliaments and popular assemblies that emerged in some places enabled the propertied classes to exert some political influence. Germany and Italy, however, resisted the general trend toward political consolidation and remained fragmented until the nineteenth century.

The distinctive Western belief in the separation of church and state was established during the High Middle Ages. The popes acquired monarchical authority over the church and prevented it from being absorbed into Europe's emerging nation-states. Their methods, however, led to accusations that the papacy was diverting the church from its spiritual mission into the murky world of politics.

OTTO I AND THE REVIVAL OF THE EMPIRE

HOW WAS Otto able to secure the power of his Saxon dynasty?

The fortunes of both the old empire and the papacy began to revive after the dark period of the late ninth century and the early tenth century. In 918, the Saxon Henry I ("the Fowler," d. 936), the strongest of the German dukes, became the first non-Frankish king of Germany.

UNIFYING GERMANY

Henry rebuilt royal power by forcibly combining the duchies of Swabia, Bavaria, Saxony, Franconia, and Lotharingia. He secured imperial borders by checking the invasions of the Hungarians and the Danes. Although much smaller than Charlemagne's empire, the German kingdom Henry created placed his son and successor Otto I (r. 936–973) in a strong territorial position.

The able Otto maneuvered his own kin into positions of power in Bavaria, Swabia, and Franconia. He refused to recognize each duchy as an independent hereditary entity, as the nobility increasingly expected, treating each instead as a subordinate member of a unified kingdom. In a truly imperial gesture in 951, he invaded Italy and proclaimed himself its king. In 955, he won his most magnificent victory by defeating the Hungarians at Lechfeld. That victory secured German borders against new barbarian attacks, further unified the German duchies, and earned Otto the well-deserved title "the Great."

EMBRACING THE CHURCH

As part of a careful rebuilding program, Otto, following the example of his predecessors, enlisted the church. Bishops and abbots—men who possessed a sense of universal empire, yet because they did not marry, could not found competitive dynasties—were made princes and agents of the king.

In 961, Otto, who had long aspired to the imperial crown, responded to a call for help from Pope John XII (r. 955–964), who was then being bullied by an Italian enemy of the German king, Berengar of Friuli. In recompense for this rescue, Pope John crowned Otto emperor on February 2, 962. Otto, for his part, recognized the existence of the Papal States and proclaimed himself their special protector. Over time, such

close cooperation between emperor and pope put the church more than ever under royal control.

Pope John belatedly recognized the royal web in which the church was becoming entangled and joined the Italian opposition to the new emperor. This turnabout brought Otto's swift revenge. An ecclesiastical synod over which Otto presided deposed Pope John and proclaimed that henceforth no pope could take office without first swearing an oath of allegiance to the emperor. Under Otto I, popes ruled at the emperor's pleasure.

Otto's successors—Otto II (r. 973–983) and Otto III (r. 983–1002)—became so preoccupied with running the affairs of Italy that their German base began to disintegrate, sacrificed to imperial dreams. The Ottonians reached far beyond their grasp when they tried to subdue Italy. As the briefly revived empire began to crumble in the first quarter of the eleventh century, the church, long unhappy with Carolingian and Ottonian domination, prepared to declare its independence and exact its own vengeance.

THE REVIVING CATHOLIC CHURCH

WHAT EXPLAINS the popularity of the Cluniac reform movement?

During the late ninth and early tenth centuries, the clergy had become tools of kings and magnates, and the papacy a toy of Italian nobles. The church was about to gain renewed respect and authority, however, thanks not only to the failing fortunes of the overextended Ottonian empire, but also to a new, determined force for reform within the church itself.

THE CLUNY REFORM MOVEMENT

The great monastery in Cluny in east-central France gave birth to a profoundly important monastic reform movement. The reformers of Cluny were aided by widespread popular respect for the church that found expression in lay religious fervor and generous baronial patronage of religious houses. Since the fall of the Roman Empire, popular support for the church had been especially inspired by the example set by monks. Monks remained the least secularized and most spiritual of the church's clergy. Their cultural achievements were widely admired, their relics and rituals were considered magical, and their high religious ideals and sacrifices were imitated by the laity.

William the Pious, duke of Aquitaine, founded Cluny in 910. Although the reformers who emerged at Cluny were loosely organized and their demands not always consistent, they shared a determination to maintain a spiritual church. They absolutely rejected the subservience of the clergy, especially that of the German bishops, to royal authority. They taught that the pope in Rome was sole ruler over all the clergy.

No local secular rulers, the Cluniacs asserted, could have any control over their monasteries. And they further denounced the sins of the flesh of the "secular" parish clergy, who maintained concubines in a relationship akin to marriage. The Cluny reformers thus resolved to free the clergy from both kings and "wives"—to create an independent and chaste clergy. Thus, the distinctive Western separation of church and state, and the celibacy of the Catholic clergy, both of which continue today, had their definitive origins in the Cluny reform movement.

Cluny rapidly became a center from which reformers were dispatched to other monasteries throughout France and Italy. Under its aggressive abbots, especially Saint Odo (r. 926–946), it grew to embrace almost fifteen hundred dependent cloisters, each devoted to monastic and church reform. In the latter half of the eleventh century, the Cluny reformers reached the summit of their influence when the papacy itself embraced their reform program.

The monastery at Cluny.

Kenneth J. Conant/French Embassy

In the late ninth and early tenth centuries the proclamation of a series of church decrees, called the Peace of God, reflected the influence of the Cluny movement. These decrees tried to lessen the endemic warfare of medieval society by threatening excommunication for all who, at any time, harmed members of such vulnerable groups as women, peasants, merchants, and the clergy. The Peace of God was subsequently reinforced by the Truce of God, a church order proclaiming that all men must abstain from violence and warfare during a certain part of each week (eventually from Wednesday night to Monday morning) and in all holy seasons.

Popes devoted to reforms like those urged by Cluny came to power during the reign of Emperor Henry III (r. 1039–1056). Pope Leo IX (r. 1049–1054) promoted regional synods to oppose *simony* (the selling of spiritual things, especially church offices) and clerical marriage (celibacy was not strictly enforced among the secular clergy until after the eleventh century). He also placed Cluniacs in key administrative posts in Rome.

During the turbulent minority of Henry III's successor, Henry IV (r. 1056–1106), reform popes began to assert themselves more openly. Pope Stephen IX (1057–1058) reigned without imperial ratification, contrary to the earlier declaration of Otto I. Pope Nicholas II (1059–1061) decreed in 1059 that a body of high church officials and advisers, known as the College of Cardinals, would henceforth choose the pope, establishing the procedures for papal succession that the Catholic Church still follows. With this action, the papacy declared its full independence from both local Italian and distant royal interference. Rulers continued nevertheless to have considerable indirect influence on the election of popes.

The Investiture Struggle: Gregory VII and Henry IV

Alexander's successor was Pope Gregory VII (r. 1073–1085), a fierce advocate of Cluny's reforms who had entered the papal bureaucracy a quarter of a century earlier during the pontificate of Leo IX. It was he who put the church's declaration of independence to the test. Cardinal Humbert, a prominent reformer, argued that lay investiture of the clergy—that is, the appointment of bishops and other church officials by secular officials and rulers—was the worst form of simony. In 1075, Pope Gregory embraced these arguments and condemned, under penalty of excommunication, lay investiture of clergy at any level.

Gregory's prohibition came as a jolt to royal authority. Since the days of Charlemagne, emperors had routinely passed out bishoprics to favored clergy. Bishops, who received royal estates, were the emperors' appointees and servants of the state. Henry IV's Carolingian and Ottonian predecessors had carefully nurtured the theocratic character of the empire in both concept and administrative bureaucracy. The church and religion had become integral parts of government.

Now the emperor, Henry IV, suddenly found himself ordered to secularize the empire by drawing a distinct line between the spheres of temporal and spiritual—royal and ecclesiastical—authority and jurisdiction. Henry considered Gregory's action a direct challenge to his authority. The territorial princes, however, eager to see the emperor weakened, were quick to see the advantages of Gregory's ruling. If a weak emperor could not gain a bishop's ear, then a strong prince might, thus bringing the offices of the church into his orbit of power. In the hope of gaining an advantage over both the emperor and the clergy in their territory, the princes fully supported Gregory's edict.

The lines of battle were quickly drawn. Henry assembled his loyal German bishops at Worms in January 1076 and had them proclaim their independence from Gregory. Gregory promptly responded with the church's heavy artillery: He excommunicated Henry and absolved all Henry's subjects from loyalty to him. This turn of events delighted the German princes, and Henry found himself facing a general revolt led by the duchy of Saxony. He had no recourse but to come to terms with Gregory. In a famous scene, Henry prostrated himself outside Gregory's castle retreat at Canossa on January 25, 1077. There he reportedly stood barefoot in the snow off and on for three days before the pope agreed to absolve him.

Papal power had at this moment reached a pinnacle. But Gregory's power, as he must have known when he restored Henry to power, was soon to be challenged.

Henry regrouped his forces, regained much of his power within the empire, and soon acted as if the humiliation at Canossa had never occurred. In March 1080, Gregory excommunicated Henry once again, but this time the action was ineffectual. In 1084, Henry, absolutely dominant, installed his own antipope, Clement III, and forced Gregory into exile, where he died the following year. It appeared as if the old practice of kings controlling popes had been restored—with a vengeance. Clement, however, was never recognized within the church, and Gregory's followers, who retained wide popular support, later regained power.

The settlement of the investiture controversy came in 1122 with the Concordat of Worms. Emperor Henry V (r. 1106–1125) formally renounced his power to invest bishops with ring and staff. In exchange, Pope Calixtus II (r. 1119–1124) recognized the emperor's right to be present and to invest bishops with fiefs before and after their investment with ring and staff by the church. The old church-state back-scratching in this way continued, but now on different terms. The clergy received their offices and attendant religious powers solely from ecclesiastical authority and no longer from kings and emperors. Rulers continued to bestow lands and worldly goods on high clergy in the hope of influencing them. The Concordat of Worms thus made the clergy more independent, but not necessarily less worldly.

QUICK REVIEW

Investiture Struggle

- Investiture struggle centered on authority to appoint and control clergy
- Pope Gregory excommunicated Henry IV when he proclaimed his independence from papacy
- Crisis settled in 1122 with Concordat of Worms

The Crusades

If an index of popular piety and support for the pope in the High Middle Ages is needed, the **Crusades** amply provide it. What the Cluny reform was to the clergy, the Crusades to the Holy Land were to the laity: an outlet for the heightened religious zeal, much of it fanatical, of the late eleventh and twelfth centuries.

Crusades Campaigns authorized by the church to combat heresies and rival faiths.

Late in the eleventh century, the Byzantine Empire was under severe pressure from the Seljuk Turks, and the Eastern emperor, Alexius I Comnenus (r. 1081–1118), appealed for Western aid. At the Council of Clermont in 1095, Pope Urban II (r. 1088–1099) responded positively to that appeal, setting the First Crusade in motion. (See "Compare & Connect: Christian *Jihad*, Muslim *Jihad*," pages 184–185.) This event has puzzled some historians, because the First Crusade was a risky venture. Yet the pope, the nobility, and Western society at large had much to gain by removing large numbers of nobility temporarily from Europe. Too many idle, restless noble youths spent too great a part of their lives feuding with each other and raiding other people's lands. The nobility, in turn, saw that fortunes could be made in foreign wars. Pope Urban may well have believed that the Crusade would reconcile and reunite Western and Eastern Christianity.

The early Crusades were inspired by genuine religious piety and carefully orchestrated by a revived papacy. Popes promised the first Crusaders a plenary indulgence should they die in battle. That was a complete remission of the temporal punishment due them for unrepented mortal sins, and hence a release from suffering for them in purgatory. In addition to this spiritual reward, the prospect of a Holy War against the Muslim infidel also propelled the Crusaders.

En route the Crusaders also began a general cleansing of Christendom that would intensify during the thirteenth-century papacy of Pope Innocent III. Accompanied by the new mendicant orders of Dominicans and Franciscans, Christian knights attempted to rid Europe of Jews as well as Muslims. Along the Crusaders' routes, especially in the Rhineland, Jewish communities were subjected to pogroms.

The First Victory The Crusaders had not assembled merely to defend Europe's outermost borders against Muslim aggression. Their goal was to rescue the holy city of Jerusalem, which had been in the hands of the Muslims since the seventh century. To this end, three great armies—tens of thousands of Crusaders—gathered in France, Germany, and Italy and, taking different routes, reassembled in Constantinople in 1097. (See Map 7–1.) From there, they soundly defeated one Muslim army after another in a

MAP EXPLORATION

Interactive map: To explore this map further, go to www.myhistorylab.com

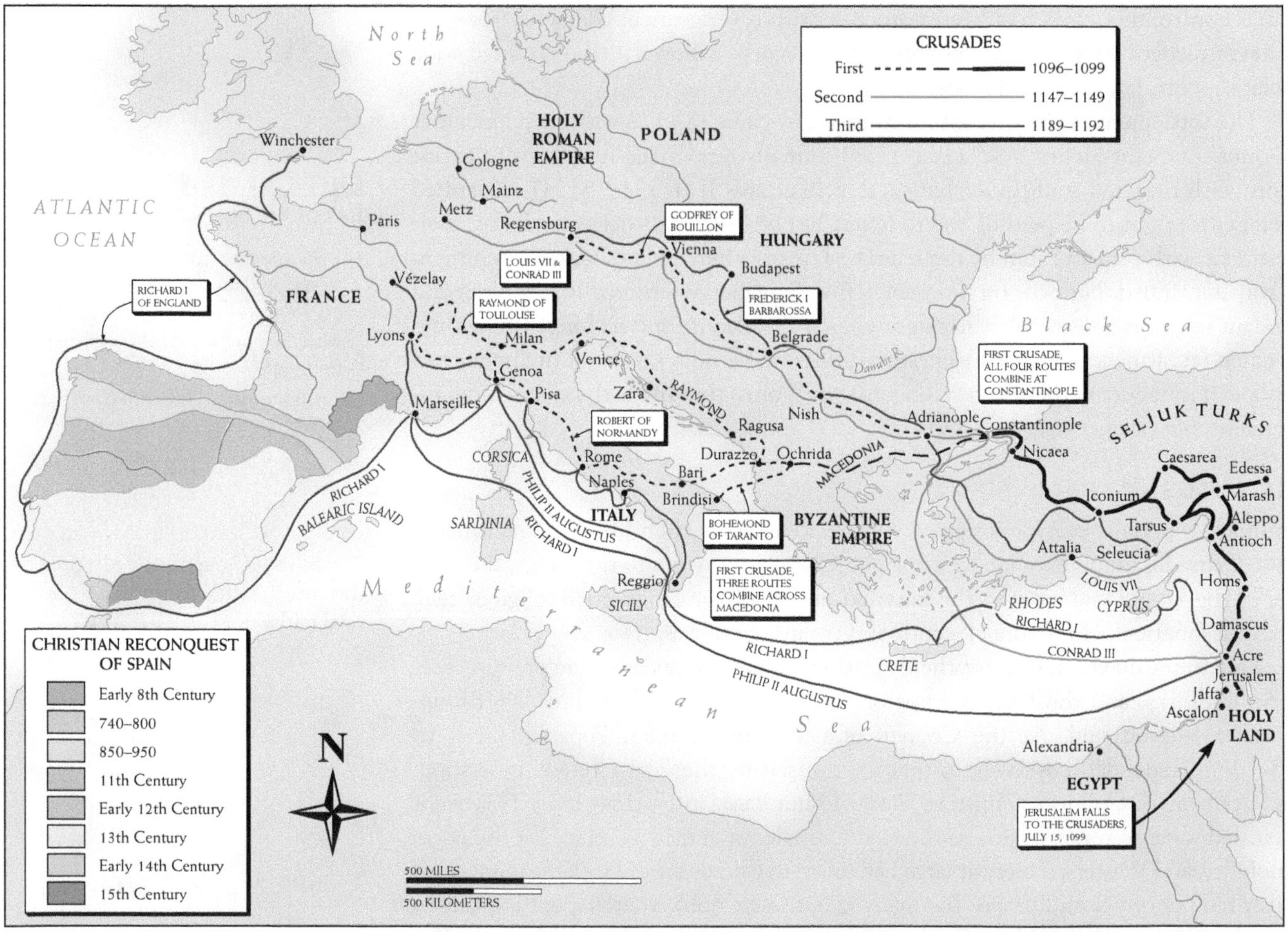

MAP 7–1 **The Early Crusades** Routes and several leaders of the Crusades during the first century of the movement are shown. The names on this map do not exhaust the list of great nobles who went on the First Crusade. The even showier array of monarchs of the Second and Third Crusades still left the Crusades, on balance, ineffective in achieving their goals.

Compare and contrast the scope and result of each of the first three Crusades. Overall, how successful were these Crusades?

steady advance toward Jerusalem, which they captured on July 15, 1099. The Crusaders owed their victory to superior military discipline and weaponry and were also helped by the deep political divisions within the Islamic world that prevented a unified Muslim resistance.

The victorious Crusaders divided conquered territories into the feudal states of Jerusalem, Edessa, and Antioch, which were apportioned to them as fiefs from the pope. The Crusaders, however, remained small islands within a great sea of Muslims, who looked on the Western invaders as savages to be slain or driven out. Once settled in the Holy Land, the Crusaders found themselves increasingly on the defensive. Now an occupying rather than a conquering army, they became obsessed with fortification, building castles and forts throughout the Holy Land, the ruins of which can still be seen today.

Once secure within their new enclaves, the Crusaders ceased to live off the land, as they had done since departing Europe, and increasingly relied on imports from home. As they developed the economic resources of their new possessions, the once fierce warriors were transformed into international traders and businessmen.

The Second and Third Crusades Native resistance broke the Crusaders' resolve around mid-century, and the forty-year-plus Latin presence in the East began to crumble. Edessa fell to Islamic armies in 1144. A Second Crusade, preached by Christendom's most eminent religious leader, the Cistercian monk Bernard of Clairvaux (1091–1153), attempted a rescue but met with dismal failure. In October 1187, Saladin (1138–1193), king of Egypt and Syria, reconquered Jerusalem. Save for a brief interlude in the thirteenth century, the holiest of cities remained thereafter in Islamic hands until the twentieth century.

Thirteenth-century statue of St. Maurice, patron saint of Magdeburg, Germany. An Egyptian Christian who commanded a Roman legion, St. Maurice was executed in 286 C.E. after refusing to worship the Roman gods. Portrayed as a white man for centuries, during the era of the Crusades, Maurice became a perfect talisman for Europeans venturing eastward.

Constantin Beyer

What made St. Maurice so appealing to the Crusaders?

A Third Crusade in the twelfth century (1189–1192) attempted yet another rescue, led by the most powerful Western rulers: Hohenstaufen emperor Frederick Barbarossa, Richard the Lion-Hearted, the king of England, and Philip Augustus, the king of France. It became instead a tragicomic commentary on the passing of the original crusading spirit. Frederick Barbarossa drowned while fording a small stream, the Saleph River, near the end of his journey across Asia Minor. Richard the Lion-Hearted and Philip Augustus reached Palestine, only to shatter the Crusaders' unity and chances of victory by their intense personal rivalry.

The long-term results of the first three Crusades had little to do with their original purpose. Politically and religiously they were a failure. The Holy Land reverted as firmly as ever to Muslim hands. The Crusades had, however, been a safety valve for violence-prone Europeans. More importantly, they stimulated Western trade with the East, as Venetian, Pisan, and Genoan merchants followed the Crusaders across Byzantium to lucrative new markets. The need to resupply the Christian settlements in the Near East also created new trade routes and reopened old ones long closed by Islamic supremacy over the Mediterranean.

The Fourth Crusade It is a commentary on both the degeneration of the original crusading ideal and the Crusaders' true historical importance that a Fourth Crusade transformed itself into a piratical, commercial venture controlled by the Venetians. In 1202, 30,000 Crusaders arrived in Venice to set sail for Egypt. When they could not pay the price of transport, the Venetians negotiated an alternative venture: the conquest of Zara, a rival Christian port on the Adriatic. Zara, however, proved to be only their first digression; in 1204, they beseiged, captured, and sacked Constantinople itself.

This stunning event brought Venice new lands and maritime rights that assured its domination of the eastern Mediterranean. Constantinople was now the center for Western

COMPARE & CONNECT

CHRISTIAN *JIHAD*, MUSLIM *JIHAD*

On November 26, 1095, Pope Urban II summoned the First Crusade to the Holy Land, its mission to take back Jerusalem from the Muslims. In a seeming propaganda and smear campaign, Urban depicted Muslims as savages. Roughly four years later, July 15, 1099, Western Crusaders captured the holy city with overwhelming force and untold carnage.

Eighty-eight years later, October 2, 1187, the fabled Sultan of Egypt and Syria, Saladin, returned Jerusalem to the Muslim fold by defeating the Third Crusade. During his march to Jerusalem, he massacred captured members of the Christian military religious orders of the Knights Templars and the Hospitallers, who were escorts and protectors of Christians journeying back and forth to the Holy Land.

QUESTIONS

1. Were the Christian Crusades, as the pope argued, a legitimate reclamation of the Christian Holy Land, or a preemptive Christian *jihad*?
2. Did Saladin's counteroffensive have stronger legal and moral grounds?
3. What role did religion play in the behavior of both sides?

I. POPE URBAN II (R. 1088–1099) PREACHES THE FIRST CRUSADE

When Pope Urban II summoned the First Crusade in a sermon at the Council of Clermont on November 26, 1095, he painted at savage picture of the Muslims who controlled Jerusalem. Urban also promised the Crusaders, who responded by the tens of thousands, remission of their unrepented sins and assurance of heaven. Robert the Monk is one of four witnesses who has left us a summary of the sermon.

From the confines of Jerusalem and the city of Constantinople a horrible tale has gone forth and very frequently has been brought to our ears, namely, that a race from the kingdom of the Persians [that is, the Seljuk Turks], an accursed race, a race utterly alienated from God, a generation forsooth which has not directed its heart and has not entrusted its spirit to God, has invaded the lands of those Christians and has depopulated them by the sword, pillage and fire; it has led away a part of the captives into its own country, and a part it has destroyed by cruel tortures; it has either entirely destroyed the churches of God or appropriated them for the rites of its own religion. They destroy the altars, after having defiled them with their uncleanness. They circumcise the Christians, and the blood of the circumcision they either spread upon the altars or pour into the vases of the baptismal font. When they wish to torture people by a base death, they perforate their navels, and dragging forth the extremity of the intestines, bind it to a stake; then with flogging they lead the victim around until the viscera having gushed forth, the victim falls prostrate upon the ground. Others they bind to a post and pierce with arrows. Others they compel to extend their necks and then, attacking them with naked swords, attempt to cut through the neck with a single blow. What shall I say of the abom-

Krak des Chavaliers served as the headquarters of the Knights of St. John (Hospitallers) during the Crusades. This fortress is among the most notable surviving examples of medieval military architecture.

Dorling Kindersley Media Library/Alistair Duncan © Dorling Kindersley

What does the merger of military and religious values tell us about the Crusaders and their motives?

inable rape of the women? The kingdom of the Greeks is now dismembered by them and deprived of territory so vast in extent that it can not be traversed in a march of two months. On whom therefore is the labor of avenging these wrongs and of recovering this territory incumbent, if not upon you? . . .

Jerusalem is the navel of the world; the land is fruitful above others, like another paradise of delights. This the Redeemer of the human race has made illustrious by His advent, has beautified by residence, has consecrated by suffering, has redeemed by death, has glorified by burial. This royal city, therefore, situated at the centre of the world, is now held captive by His enemies, and is in subjection to those who do not know God, to the worship of the heathens. She seeks therefore and desires to be liberated, and does not cease to implore you to come to her aid. From you especially she asks succor, because, as we have already said, God has conferred upon you above all nations great glory in arms.

Accordingly undertake this journey for the remission of your sins, with the assurance of the imperishable glory of the kingdom of heaven.

Source: Translations and reprints from *Original Sources of European History*, Vol. 1 (Philadelphia: Department of History, University of Pennsylvania, 1910), pp. 5–7.

II. SALADIN (R. 1174–1193) DEFEATS THE THIRD CRUSADE: THE REPORT OF AN EYEWITNESS

[En route to liberating Jerusalem] Saladin sought out the Templars and Hospitallers . . . saying: 'I shall purify the land of these two impure races.' He ordered them to be beheaded, choosing to have them dead rather than in prison. With him [were] scholars and sufis [mystics] . . . devout men and ascetics, each begging to kill one of them . . . Saladin, his face joyful, sat on his dais [while] the unbelievers [Christians] showed black despair . . . There were some who slashed and cut [the Christians] cleanly, and were thanked for it. Some refused and failed to act . . . I [the eye-witness] saw the man who laughed scornfully as he slaughtered [the Christians] . . . How much praise he won! [How great] the eternal rewards he secured by the blood he had shed . . . ! How many ills did he cure by the ills he brought upon a Templar . . . ! I saw how he killed unbelief to give life to Islam, and destroyed polytheism [i.e. Trinitarian Christianity] to build monotheism . . .

[Later, during the conquest of Jerusalem] the Franks [i.e. Crusaders] saw how violently the Muslims attacked [and] decided to ask for safe-conduct out of the city [agreeing to] hand Jerusalem over to Saladin . . . A deputation . . . asked for terms, but . . . Saladin refused to grant [them]. 'We shall deal with you,' he said, 'just as you dealt with the population of Jerusalem when you took it [from us] in 1099, with murder and enslavement and other such savageries . . . ! Despairing of this approach, [one of the city's Christian leaders] said: 'Know, O Sultan, that there are many of us in this city . . . At the moment we are fighting [against you] half-hearted in the hope to be spared by you as you have spared others—this because of our horror of death and our love of life. However, if we see that death is inevitable . . . we shall kill our children and our wives, burn our possessions, so as not to leave you with . . . a single man or woman to enslave [and we will also raze the city]. Saladin took counsel with his advisers [and] agreed to give the Franks assurances of safety on the understanding that each man, rich and poor alike [would pay] the appropriate ransom.

Source: From chronicles of Imad Ad-Din and Ibn Al-Athir, in Francesco Gabrieli, ed. and trans., *Arab Historians of the Crusades* (London: Routledge & Kegan Paul, 1957), pp. 138–140 and Carole Hillenbrand, *The Crusades: Islamic Perspectives* (Chicago: Fitzroy Dearborn Publishers, 1999), p. 554.

SIGNIFICANT DATES FROM THE PERIOD OF THE HIGH MIDDLE AGES

910	Cluniac reform begins
955	Otto I defeats Magyars
1059	College of Cardinals empowered to elect popes
1066	Norman conquest of England
1075–1122	Investiture Controversy
1095–1099	First Crusade
1144	Edessa falls; Second Crusade
1152	Hohenstaufen dynasty founded
1154	Plantagenet dynasty founded
1187	Jerusalem falls to Saladin
1189–1192	Third Crusade
1202	Fourth Crusade sacks Constantinople
1209	Albigensian Crusade
1210	Franciscan Order founded
1215	Fourth Lateran Council; Magna Carta
1250	Death of Frederick II

trade throughout the Near East. Western control of Constantinople continued until 1261, when eastern emperor Michael Paleologus (r. 1261–1282) finally recaptured the city. This fifty-seven-year occupation of Contstantinople did nothing to heal the political and religious divisions between East and West.

The Pontificate of Innocent III (r. 1198–1216)

Pope Innocent III was a papal monarch in the Gregorian tradition of papal independence from secular domination. He proclaimed and practiced as none before him the doctrine of the plenitude of papal power. Although this pretentious theory greatly exceeded Innocent's ability to practice it, he and his successors did not hesitate to act on the ambitions it reflected. When Philip II, the king of France, tried unlawfully to annul his marriage, Innocent placed France under interdict, suspending all church services save baptism and the last rites. The same punishment befell England with even greater force when King John refused to accept Innocent's nominee for archbishop of Canterbury. Later in the chapter it will be shown how Innocent also intervened frequently and forcefully in the political affairs of the Holy Roman Empire.

The New Papal Monarchy Innocent made the papacy a great secular power, with financial resources and a bureaucracy equal to those of contemporary monarchs. During his reign the papacy transformed itself, in effect, into an efficient ecclesio-commercial complex, which reformers would attack throughout the later Middle Ages. Innocent consolidated and expanded ecclesiastical taxes on the laity, the chief of which was "Peter's pence." Innocent also imposed an income tax of 2.5 percent on the clergy.

Crusades in France and the East Innocent's predilection for power politics also expressed itself in his use of the Crusade, the traditional weapon of the church against Islam, to suppress internal dissent and heresy. Heresy had grown under the influence of native religious reform movements that tried, often naïvely, to disassociate the church from the growing materialism of the age and to keep it pure of political scheming. Heresy also stemmed from anticlericalism fed by real clerical abuses that the laity could see for themselves, such as immorality, greed, and poor pastoral service.

The idealism of these movements was too extreme for the papacy. In 1209, Innocent launched a Crusade against the **Albigensians**, also known as Cathars, or "pure ones." These advocates of an ascetic, dualist religion were concentrated in the area of Albi in Languedoc in southern France, but they also had adherents among the laity in Italy and Spain. The Albigensians generally sought a pure and simple religious life, claiming to follow the model of the apostles of Jesus in the New Testament. Yet they denied the Old Testament and its God of wrath, as well as God's incarnation in Jesus Christ; despite certain Christian influenced ideas, they were non-Christians. Their idea of a church was an invisible spiritual force, not a real-world institution.

Albigensians Heretical sect that advocated a simple, pious way of life following the example set by Jesus and the Apostles, but rejecting key Christian doctrines.

The Crusades against the Albigensians were carried out by powerful noblemen from northern France and ended with a special Crusade led by King Louis VIII of France from 1225 to 1226, which destroyed the Albigensians as a political entity. Pope Gregory IX (r. 1227–1241) introduced the **Inquisition** into the region to complete the work of the Crusaders. This institution, a formal tribunal to detect and punish heresy, had been in use by the church since the mid–twelfth century as a way for bishops to maintain diocesan discipline. During Innocent's pontificate it became centralized in the papacy. Papal legates were dispatched to chosen regions to conduct interrogations, trials, and executions.

QUICK REVIEW

Suppression of the Albigensians

- 1209: Pope Innocent III launches Crusade against Albigensians
- 1226: Louis VIII's armies devastate Albigensian region
- Pope Gregory IX follows up by sending the Inquisition to the region

The Fourth Lateran Council Under Innocent's direction, the Fourth Lateran Council met in 1215 to formalize church discipline throughout the hierarchy, from pope to parish priest. The council enacted many important landmarks in ecclesiastical legislation. It gave full dogmatic sanction to the controversial doctrine of **transubstantiation**, according to which the bread and wine of the Lord's Supper become the true body and blood of Christ when consecrated by a priest in the sacrament of the Eucharist. It also enhanced the power and authority of the clergy, because it specified that only they could perform the miracle of the Eucharist.

Inquisition Formal ecclesiastical court dedicated to discovering and punishing heresy.

transubstantiation Christian doctrine which holds that, at the moment of priestly consecration, the bread and wine of the Lord's Supper become the body and blood of Christ.

In addition, the council made annual confession and Easter communion mandatory for every adult Christian. This legislation formalized the sacrament of penance as the church's key instrument of religious education and discipline in the later Middle Ages.

Franciscans and Dominicans During his reign, Pope Innocent gave official sanction to two new monastic orders: the Franciscans and the Dominicans. No other action of the pope had more of an effect on spiritual life. Unlike other regular clergy, the members of these mendicant orders, known as *friars*, did not confine themselves to the cloister. They went out into the world to preach the church's mission and to combat heresy, begging or working to support themselves (hence the term *mendicant*).

Lay interest in spiritual devotion, especially among urban women, was particularly intense at the turn of the twelfth century. In addition to the heretical Albigensians, there were movements of Waldensians, Beguines, and Beghards, each of which stressed biblical simplicity in religion and a life of poverty in imitation of Christ. Such movements were especially active in Italy and France. Their heterodox teachings—teachings that, although not necessarily heretical, nonetheless challenged church

Dominicans (left) **and Franciscans** (right). Unlike the other religious orders, the Dominicans and Franciscans did not live in cloisters but wandered about preaching and combating heresy. They depended for support on their own labor and the kindness of the laity.

Cliché Bibliothèque Nationale de France, Paris

What was the relationship between the rise of the Dominicans and Franciscans and medieval urbanization?

orthodoxy—and the critical frame of mind they promoted caused the pope deep concern. Innocent feared they would inspire lay piety to turn militantly against the church. The Franciscan and Dominican orders, however, emerged from the same background of intense religiosity. By sanctioning them and thus keeping their followers within the confines of church organization, the pope provided a response to heterodox piety as well as an answer to lay criticism of the worldliness of the papal monarchy.

The Franciscan order was founded by Saint Francis of Assisi (1182–1226), the son of a rich Italian cloth merchant, who became disaffected with wealth and urged his followers to live a life of extreme poverty. Pope Innocent recognized the order in 1210, and its official rule was approved in 1223. The Dominican order, the Order of Preachers, was founded by Saint Dominic (1170–1221), a well-educated Spanish cleric, and was sanctioned in 1216. Both orders received special privileges from the pope and were solely under his jurisdiction.

Pope Gregory IX (r. 1227–1241) canonized Saint Francis only two years after Francis's death. Two years after the canonization, however, Gregory canceled Saint Francis's own *Testament* as an authoritative rule for the Franciscan order. He did so because he found it to be an impractical guide for the order and because the unconventional nomadic life of strict poverty it advocated conflicted with papal plans to enlist the order as an arm of church policy. Most Franciscans themselves, under the leadership of moderates like Saint Bonaventure, general of the order between 1257 and 1274, also came to doubt the wisdom of extreme asceticism. In the fourteenth century, the pope condemned a radical branch, the Spiritual Franciscans, extreme followers of Saint Francis who considered him almost a new Messiah. In his condemnation, the pope declared absolute poverty a fictitious ideal that not even Christ endorsed.

Beguines Sisterhoods of pious, self-supporting single women.

The Dominicans, a less factious order, combated doctrinal error through visitations and preaching. They conformed new convents of **Beguines** (lay religious sisterhoods of single lay women in the Netherlands and Belgium; see Chapter 8) to the church's teaching, led the church's campaign against heretics in southern France, and staffed the offices of the Inquisition after Pope Gregory centralized it in 1223. The great Dominican theologian Thomas Aquinas (d. 1274) was canonized in 1322 for his efforts to synthesize faith and reason in an enduring definitive statement of Catholic belief. (See Chapter 8.)

The Dominicans and the Franciscans strengthened the church among the laity. Through the institution of so-called Third Orders, they provided ordinary men and women the opportunity to affiliate with the monastic life and pursue the high religious ideals of poverty, obedience, and chastity while remaining laypeople. Such organizations helped keep lay piety orthodox and within the church during a period of heightened religiosity.

ENGLAND AND FRANCE: HASTINGS (1066) TO BOUVINES (1214)

HOW DID England and France develop strong monarchies?

In 1066, the death of the childless Anglo-Saxon ruler Edward the Confessor occasioned the most important change in English political life. Edward's mother was a Norman, giving the duke of Normandy a competitive, if not the best, hereditary claim to the English throne. Before his death, Edward, who was not a strong ruler, acknowledged that claim and even directed that his throne be given to William, the reigning duke of Normandy (d. 1087). Yet the Anglo-Saxon assembly, which customarily bestowed the royal power, had a mind of its own and vetoed Edward's last wishes, choosing instead Harold Godwinsson. This action triggered the swift conquest of

The *Battle of Hastings* Detail of the *Bayeux Tapestry*. c. 1073–1083. Wool embroidery on linen, height 200 (50.7 cm).

Centre Guillaume Le Conquerant. Detail of the *Bayeux Tapestry*—XIth century. By special permission of the City of Bayeux

How did the Battle of Hastings alter the political landscape of England?

England by the powerful Normans. William's forces defeated Harold's army at Hastings on October 14, 1066. Within weeks of the invasion William was crowned king of England in Westminster Abbey, both by right of heredity and by right of conquest.

William the Conqueror

Thereafter, William embarked on a twenty-year conquest that eventually made all of England his domain. Every landholder, whether large or small, was henceforth his vassal, holding land legally as a fief from the king. William organized his new English nation shrewdly. He established a strong monarchy whose power was not fragmented by independent territorial princes. He kept the Anglo-Saxon tax system and the practice of court writs (legal warnings) as a flexible form of central control over localities. And he took care not to destroy the Anglo-Saxon quasi-democratic tradition of frequent "parleying"—that is, the holding of conferences between the king and lesser powers who had vested interests in royal decisions. The result was a unique blending of the "one" and the "many," a balance between monarchical and parliamentary elements that has ever since been a feature of English government—although the English Parliament as we know it today did not formally develop as an institution until the late thirteenth century.

For administration and taxation purposes William commissioned a county-by-county survey of his new realm, a detailed accounting known as the *Domesday Book* (1080–1086). The title of the book may reflect the thoroughness and finality of the survey. As none would escape the doomsday judgment of God, so no property was overlooked by William's assessors.

QUICK REVIEW

William the Conqueror (d. 1087)

- October 14, 1066: Normans defeated Anglo-Saxons at the Battle of Hastings
- William's rule in England combined elements of continental feudalism and Anglo-Saxon tradition
- *Domesday Book* contained county-by-county survey of William's kingdom

Henry II

William's son, Henry I (r. 1100–1135), died without a male heir, throwing England into virtual anarchy until the accession of Henry II (r. 1154–1189). Henry tried to recapture the efficiency and stability of his grandfather's regime, but in the process he steered the English monarchy rapidly toward an oppressive rule. Thanks to his inheritance from his father (the count of Anjou) and his marriage to Eleanor of Aquitaine (ca. 1122–1204), Henry brought to the throne virtually the entire west coast of France.

The union with Eleanor created the Angevin, or English-French, Empire. Eleanor married Henry while he was still the count of Anjou and not yet king of England. The marriage occurred eight weeks after the annulment of Eleanor's fifteen-year marriage to the ascetic French king Louis VII in March 1152. Although the annulment was granted on grounds of consanguinity (blood relationship), the true reason for the

Overview A Comparison of Leaders in the High Middle Ages

	ENGLAND	FRANCE	GERMANY
LEADER	Henry II	Louis IX	Frederick II
REIGN	(1154–1189)	(1226–1270)	(1212–1250)
ACCOMPLISHMENTS	Henry brought to the throne greatly expanded French holdings. The union with Eleanor created the Angevin (English–French) Empire. Henry conquered a part of Ireland and made the king of Scotland his vassal.	Louis IX embodied the medieval view of the perfect ruler. His greatest achievements lay at home. The French bureaucracy became an instrument of order and fair play in government under Louis. He abolished private wars and serfdom within his domain. Respected by the kings of Europe, Louis became an arbiter among the world's powers.	Within a year and a half of Frederick's crowning, the treacherous reign of Otto IV came to an end on the battlefields of Bouvines.
FAILURES	As Henry acquired new lands abroad, he became more autocratic at home. He tried to recapture the efficiency and stability of his grandfather's regime but in the process steered the English monarchy toward an oppressive rule.	Had Louis ruthlessly confiscated English territories on the French coast, he might have lessened, if not averted altogether, the conflict underlying the Hundred Years' War.	During his reign, Frederick effectively turned dreams of a unified Germany into a nightmare of disunity. Living mostly outside of Germany during his rule, he did little to secure the rights of the emperor in Germany. Frederick's relations with the pope were equally disastrous, leading to his excommunication on four different occasions.

dissolution of the marriage was Louis's suspicion of her infidelity. According to rumor, Eleanor had been intimate with a cousin.

In addition to gaining control of most of the coast of France, Henry also conquered part of Ireland and made the king of Scotland his vassal. Louis VII saw a mortal threat to France in this English expansion. He responded by adopting what came to be a permanent French policy of containment and expulsion of the English from their continental holdings in France.

Eleanor of Aquitaine and Court Culture

Eleanor of Aquitaine was a powerful influence on both politics and culture in twelfth-century France and England. She accompanied her first husband, King Louis VII, on the Second Crusade, becoming an example for women of lesser stature, who were also then venturing in increasing numbers into war and business and other areas previously considered the province of men. After marrying Henry, she settled in Angers, the chief town of Anjou, where she sponsored troubadours and poets at her lively court. Eleanor spent the years 1154 to 1170 as Henry's queen in England. She separated from Henry in 1170, partly because of his public philandering and cruel treatment of her, and took revenge on him by joining ex-husband Louis VII in provoking Henry's three surviving sons, who were unhappy with their inheritance, into an unsuccessful rebellion against their father in 1173. From 1179 until his death in 1189, Henry kept Eleanor under mild house arrest to prevent any further such mischief from her.

After her separation from Henry in 1170 and until her confinement in England, Eleanor lived in Poitiers with her daughter Marie, the countess of Champagne, and the two made the court of Poitiers a famous center for the literature of courtly love. The most famous courtly literature was that of Chrétien de Troyes, whose stories of King Arthur and the Knights of the Round Table recounted the tragic story of Sir Lancelot's secret and illicit love for Arthur's wife, Guinevere.

Popular Rebellion and Magna Carta

As Henry II acquired new lands abroad, he became more autocratic at home. He forced his will on the clergy in the Constitutions of Clarendon (1164). These measures limited judicial appeals to Rome, subjected the clergy to the civil courts, and gave the king control over the election of bishops. The result was strong political resistance from both the nobility and the clergy. The archbishop of Canterbury, Thomas à Becket (1118?–1170), once Henry's compliant chancellor, broke openly with the king and fled to Louis VII. Becket's subsequent assassination in 1170 and his canonization by Pope Alexander III in 1172 helped focus popular resentment against the king's heavy-handed tactics.

Under Henry's successors, the brothers Richard I, the Lion-Hearted (r. 1189–1199), and John (r. 1199–1216), new burdensome taxation in support of unnecessary foreign Crusades and a failing war with France turned resistance into outright rebellion. The last straw for the English was the defeat of the king's forces by the French at Bouvines in 1214. With the full support of the clergy and the townspeople, English barons revolted against John. The popular rebellion ended with the king's grudging recognition of **Magna Carta**, or "Great Charter," in 1215.

Magna Carta ("Great Charter") Document spelling out limitations on royal authority agreed to by John in 1215. It created the foundation for modern English law.

The Magna Carta put limits on autocratic behavior of the kind exhibited by the Norman kings and Plantagenet kings. It also secured the rights of the privileged against the monarchy. In Magna Carta the privileged preserved their right to be represented at the highest levels of government in important matters like taxation. The monarchy, however, was also preserved and kept strong. This balancing act, which gave power to both sides, had always been the ideal of feudal government.

Although King John continued to resist the Magna Carta in every way, and succeeding kings ignored it, Magna Carta nonetheless became a cornerstone of modern English law.

Philip II Augustus

The English struggle in the High Middle Ages had been to secure the rights of the privileged many, not the authority of the king. The French, by contrast, faced the opposite problem. In 987, noblemen chose Hugh Capet to succeed the last Carolingian ruler, replacing the Carolingian dynasty with the Capetian, a third Frankish dynasty that ruled France for twelve generations, until 1328. For two centuries thereafter, until the reign of Philip II Augustus (r. 1180–1223), powerful feudal princes contested Capetian rule, burying the principle of election.

During this period, after a rash attempt to challenge the more powerful French nobility before they had enough strength to do so, the Capetian kings concentrated their limited resources on securing the royal domain, their uncontested territory around Paris and the Île-de-France to the northeast. Aggressively exercising their feudal rights, French kings, especially after 1100, gained near absolute obedience from the noblemen in this area and established a solid base of power. By the reign of Philip II Augustus, Paris had become the center of French government and culture, and the Capetian dynasty a secure hereditary monarchy. Thereafter, the kings of France could impose their will on the French nobles, who were always in law, if not in political fact, the king's sworn vassals.

In an indirect way the Norman conquest of England helped stir France to unity and made it possible for the Capetian kings to establish a truly national monarchy. The duke of Normandy, who after 1066 was master of the whole of England, was also among the vassals of the French king in Paris. Capetian kings understandably watched with alarm as the power of their Norman vassal grew. Other powerful vassals of the king also watched with alarm. King Louis VI, the Fat (r. 1108–1137), entered an alliance with Flanders, traditionally a Norman enemy. King Louis VII (r. 1137–1180), assisted by a

ENCOUNTERING THE PAST

PILGRIMAGE

Thomas à Becket's tomb at Canterbury quickly became one of the most frequented pilgrimage shrines in Europe. The perennially popular Canterbury Tales *of Geoffrey Chaucer (ca. 1345–1400) provides a fictional account of one such trip. As Chaucer describes it, a medieval pilgrimage was both a spiritual and a social event. Because travel to distant shrines involved self-sacrifice (danger and expense), clergy often imposed pilgrimages as penances for sins. Pilgrims also set out on their own in the hope that contact with a saint's relics or the waters of a sacred well or spring would provide a miraculous cure for a bodily affliction. Parents even brought the corpses of dead infants to shrines to beg the saints to bring them back to life.*

The most prestigious pilgrimages were those to the Holy Lands and to the graves of St. Peter in Rome and St. James at Compostela in northern Spain. Pilgrim traffic was so great that businesses sprang up along these routes to assist travelers. Transportation, shelter, emergency services, and even guidebooks were available. Pilgrims, particularly to distant locales, often traveled in groups, and an opportunity to share stories and adventures with others made for diverting entertainment. Travel then, as now, was highly educational.

A thirteenth-century stained glass window depicts pilgrims traveling to Canterbury Cathedral.

How did pilgrimages stimulate the economic development of medieval Europe?

WHY WERE pilgrimages so popular with medieval people?

brilliant minister, Suger, abbot of St. Denis and famous for his patronage of Gothic architecture, found allies in the great northern French cities and used their wealth to build a royal army.

When he succeeded Louis VII as king, Philip II Augustus inherited financial resources and a skilled bureaucracy that put him in a strong position. He was able to resist the competition of the French nobility and the clergy and to focus on the contest with the English king. Confronted at the same time with an internal and an international struggle, he proved successful in both. His armies occupied all the English king's territories on the French coast except for Aquitaine. As a showdown with the English neared on the continent, however, Holy Roman Emperor Otto IV (r. 1198–1215) entered the fray on the side of the English, and the French found themselves assailed from both east and west. But when the international armies finally clashed at Bouvines in Flanders on July 27, 1214, in what history records as the first great European battle, the French won handily over the opposing Anglo-Flemish-German army. This victory unified France politically around the monarchy and thereby laid the foundation for French ascendancy in the later Middle Ages.

FRANCE IN THE THIRTEENTH CENTURY: THE REIGN OF LOUIS IX

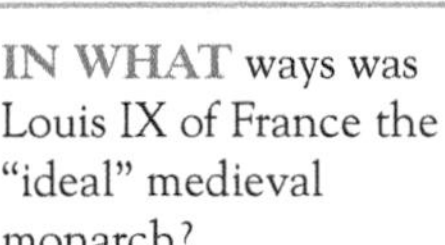
IN WHAT ways was Louis IX of France the "ideal" medieval monarch?

Coming to power after the French victory at Bouvines (1214), Louis IX (r. 1226–1270) inherited a unified and secure kingdom. Not beset by the problems of sheer survival, and a reformer at heart, Louis found himself free to concentrate on what medieval people believed to be the business of civilization.

GENEROSITY ABROAD

Magnanimity in politics is not always a sign of strength, and Louis could be very magnanimous. Although in a strong position during negotiations for the Treaty of Paris (1259), which momentarily settled the dispute between France and England, he refused to take advantage of it to drive the English from their French possessions. Had he done so and ruthlessly confiscated English territories on the French coast, he might have lessened, if not averted altogether, the conflict underlying the Hundred Years' War, which began in the fourteenth century. Instead he surrendered disputed territory on the borders of Gascony to the English king, Henry III, and confirmed Henry's possession of the duchy of Aquitaine.

Although he occasionally chastised popes for their crude political ambitions, Louis remained neutral during the long struggle between the German Hohenstaufen emperor Frederick II and the papacy and his neutrality worked to the pope's advantage. Louis also remained neutral when his brother, Charles of Anjou, intervened in Italy and Sicily against the Hohenstaufens, again to the pope's advantage. Urged on by the pope and his noble supporters, Charles was crowned king of Sicily in Rome, and his subsequent defeat of the son and grandson of Frederick II ended the Hohenstaufen dynasty. For such service to the church, both by action and by inaction, the Capetian kings of the thirteenth century received many papal favors.

ORDER AND EXCELLENCE AT HOME

Louis's greatest achievements lay at home. The efficient French bureaucracy, which his predecessors had used to exploit their subjects, became under Louis an instrument of order and fair play in local government. He sent forth royal commissioners (*enquêteurs*) whose mission was to monitor the royal officials responsible for local governmental administration and to ensure that justice would truly be meted out to all. These royal ambassadors were received as genuine tribunes of the people. Louis further abolished private wars and serfdom within his royal domain. He gave his subjects the judicial right of appeal from local to higher courts and made the tax system, by medieval standards, more equitable. The French people came to associate their king with justice; consequently, national feeling, the glue of nationhood, grew strong during his reign.

Respected by the kings of Europe and possessed of far greater moral authority than the pope, Louis became an arbiter among the world's powers. During his reign French society and culture became an example to all of Europe, a pattern that would continue into the modern period. Northern France became the showcase of monastic reform, chivalry, and Gothic art and architecture. Louis's reign also coincided with the golden age of Scholasticism, which saw the convergence of Europe's greatest thinkers on Paris.

Louis's perfection remained, however, that of a medieval king. He sponsored the French Inquisition. He led two French Crusades against the Muslims, which, although inspired by the purest religious motives, proved to be personal disasters. During the first (1248–1254), Louis was captured and had to be ransomed out of Egypt. He died of a fever during the second in 1270. It was especially for this selfless, but also useless, service on behalf of the church that Louis later received the rare honor of sainthood.

THE HOHENSTAUFEN EMPIRE (1152–1272)

HOW DID the policies of the Hohenstaufens lead to the fragmentation of Germany?

During the twelfth and thirteenth centuries, stable governments developed in both England and France. The story within the Holy Roman Empire, which embraced Germany, Burgundy, and northern Italy by the mid-thirteenth century, was different. (See Map 7–2.) There, primarily because of the efforts of the Hohenstaufen dynasty to extend imperial power into southern Italy, disunity and blood feuding remained the order of the day for two centuries. It left as a legacy the fragmentation of Germany until the nineteenth century.

FREDERICK I BARBAROSSA

The investiture struggle had earlier weakened imperial authority. After the Concordat of Worms, the German princes were the supreme lay powers within the rich ecclesiastical territories and held a dominant influence over the appointment of the church's bishops.

The power of the emperor promised to return, however, with the accession to the throne of Frederick I Barbarossa (r. 1152–1190) of the Hohenstaufen dynasty, the strongest line of emperors yet to succeed the Ottonians. This new dynasty not only reestablished imperial authority but also started a new, deadlier phase in the contest between popes and emperors.

Frederick I confronted powerful feudal princes in Germany and Lombardy and a pope in Rome who still looked on the emperor as his creature. However, the incessant strife among the princes and the turmoil caused by the papacy's pretensions to great political power alienated many people. Such popular sentiment presented Frederick with an opportunity to recover imperial authority and he was shrewd enough to take advantage of it. Frederick especially took advantage of the contemporary revival of Roman law, which served him on two fronts. On one hand, it praised centralized authority, that of king or emperor, against the nobility; on the other, it stressed the secular origins of imperial power against the tradition of Roman election of the emperor and papal coronation of him, thus reducing papal involvement to a minimum.

QUICK REVIEW

Frederick I Barbarossa (r. 1152–1190)

- Founder of the Hohenstaufen dynasty
- From base in Switzerland waged war to control the German nobility
- Efforts to conquer Italy ended in defeat at Legnano in 1176

From his base in Switzerland, Frederick attempted to hold his empire together by invoking feudal bonds. He was relatively successful in Germany, thanks largely to the fall from power and exile in 1180 of his strongest German rival, Henry the Lion (d. 1195), the duke of Saxony. Although he could not defeat the many German duchies, Frederick never missed an opportunity to remind each German ruler of his prescribed duties as one who held his land legally as a fief of the emperor.

Italian popes proved to be the greatest obstacle to Frederick's plans to revive his empire. In 1155, he restored Pope Adrian IV (r. 1154–1159) to power in Rome after a religious revolutionary had taken control of the city. For his efforts, Frederick won a coveted papal coronation—and strictly on his terms, not on those of the pope. Despite fierce resistance to him in Italy, led by Milan, the door to Italy had opened, and an imperial assembly sanctioned his claims to Italian lands.

As this challenge to royal authority was occurring, Cardinal Roland, a skilled lawyer, became Pope Alexander III (r. 1159–1181). In a clever effort to strengthen the papacy against growing imperial influence, the new pope had, while still a cardinal, negotiated an alliance between the papacy and the Norman kingdom of Sicily. Thus, Frederick now found himself at war with the pope, Milan, and Sicily.

By 1167, the combined forces of the north Italian communes had driven Frederick back into Germany, and a decade later, in 1176, Italian forces soundly defeated his armies at Legnano. In the Peace of Constance in 1183, which ended the hostilities, Frederick recognized the claims of the Lombard cities to full rights of self-rule, a great blow to his imperial plans.

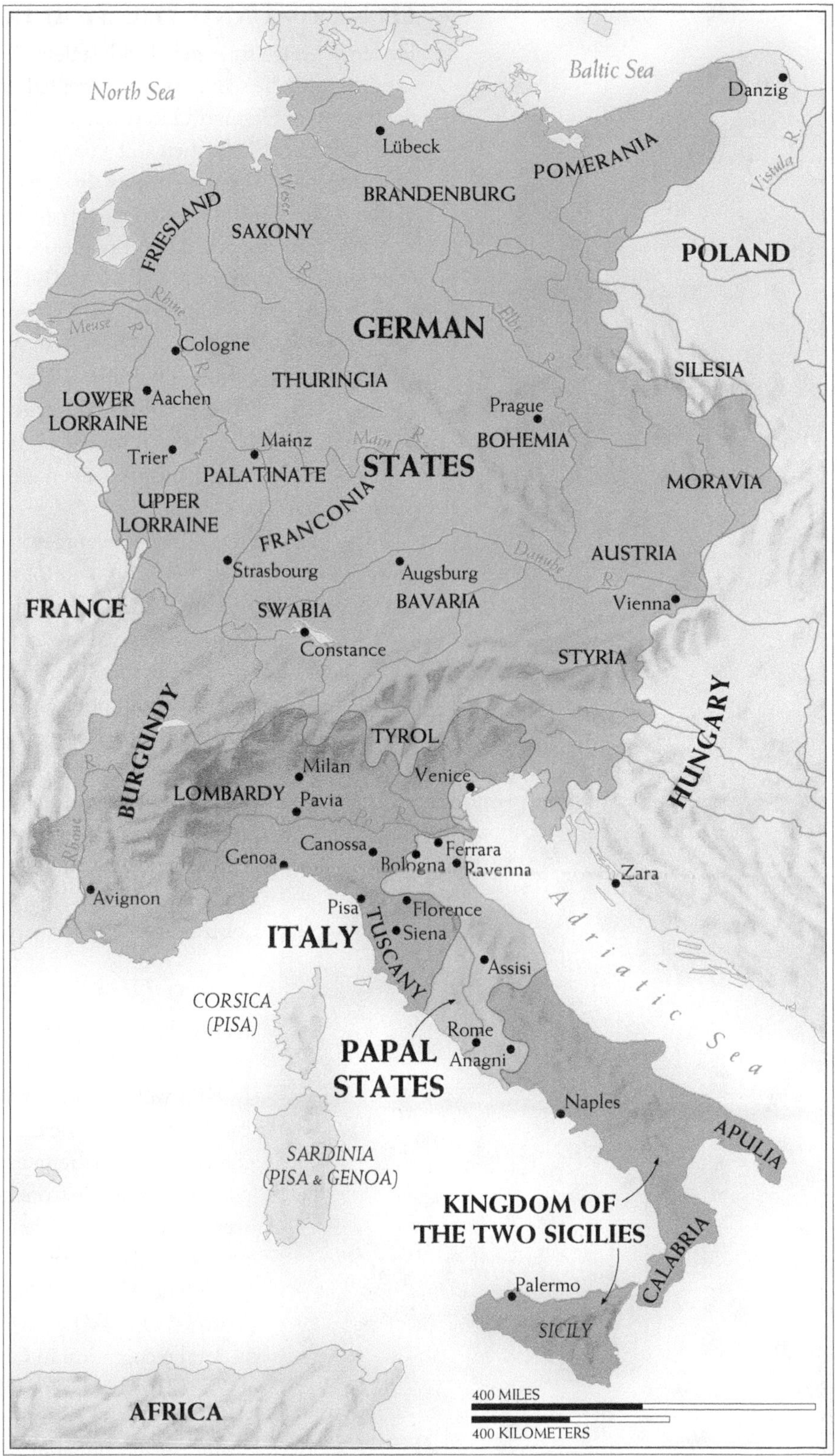

MAP 7–2 Germany and Italy in the Middle Ages Medieval Germany and Italy were divided lands. The Holy Roman Empire (Germany) embraced hundreds of independent territories that the emperor ruled only in name. The papacy controlled the Rome area and tried to enforce its will on Romagna. Under the Hohenstaufens (mid–twelfth to mid–thirteenth centuries), internal German divisions and papal conflict reached new heights; German rulers sought to extend their power to southern Italy and Sicily.

How did Roman emperors, German rulers, and the papacy all vie for power in Germany and Italy in the Middle Ages?

Henry VI and the Sicilian Connection

Frederick's reign thus ended with stalemate in Germany and defeat in Italy. After the Peace of Constance, he seems to have accepted the reality of the empire's division among the feudal princes of Germany. However, in the last years of his reign he seized an opportunity to gain control of Sicily, then still a papal ally, and form a new territorial base of power for future emperors. The opportunity arose when the Norman ruler of the kingdom of Sicily, William II (r. 1166–1189), sought an alliance with Frederick that would free him to pursue a scheme to conquer Constantinople. In 1186, a fateful marriage occurred between Frederick's son, the future Henry VI (r. 1190–1197), and Constance, the eventual heiress to the kingdom of Sicily, which promised to change the balance of imperial-papal power.

It proved, however, to be but another well-laid plan that went astray. The Sicilian kingdom became a fatal distraction for succeeding Hohenstaufen kings, tempting them to sacrifice their traditional territorial base in northern Europe to dreams of imperialism. Equally disastrous for the Hohenstaufens, the union of the empire with Sicily left Rome encircled, ensuring even greater emmity from a papacy already thoroughly distrustful of the emperor.

When Henry VI became emperor in 1190, he thus faced a hostile papacy, German princes more defiant than ever of the emperor, and an England whose adventurous king, Richard the Lion-Hearted, plotted against Henry VI with the old Hohenstaufen enemy, the exiled duke of Saxony, Henry the Lion.

It was into these circumstances that the future Emperor Frederick II was born in 1194. Heretofore the German princes had not recognized birth alone as qualifying one for the imperial throne, although the offspring of the emperor did have the inside track. To ensure baby Frederick's succession and stabilize his monarchy, Henry campaigned vigorously for recognition of the principle of hereditary succession. He won many German princes to his side by granting them what he asked for himself and his son: full hereditary rights to their own fiefs. Not surprisingly, the encircled papacy strongly opposed hereditary succession and joined dissident German princes against Henry.

Ekkehard and Uta, ca. 1240–1250 This famous noble pair founded Naumburg Cathedral in Germany in the middle of the thirteenth century and are exemplary studies of medieval nobility.

How was the importance of noble patronage reflected in the decoration and organization of medieval churches and cathedrals?

Otto IV and the Welf Interregnum

Henry died in September 1197, leaving his son Frederick a ward of the pope. Henry's brother succeeded him as German king, but the Welf family, who were German rivals of the Hohenstaufens, put forth their own candidate, whom the English supported. The French, beginning a series of interventions in German affairs, stuck with the Hohenstaufens. The papacy supported first one side and then the other, depending on which seemed most to threaten it. The struggle for power threw Germany into anarchy and civil war.

The Welf candidate, Otto of Brunswick, outlasted his rival and was crowned Otto IV by his followers in Aachen in 1198, thereafter winning general recognition in Germany. In October 1209, Pope Innocent III (r. 1198–1216) boldly meddled in German politics by crowning Otto emperor in Rome. After his papal coronation, Otto proceeded to attack Sicily, an old imperial policy threatening to Rome. Four months after crowning Otto emperor, Pope Innocent excommunicated him.

Frederick II

Casting about for a counterweight to the treacherous Otto, the pope joined with the French, who had remained loyal to the Hohenstaufens. In December 1212, with papal, French, and German support,

Innocent's ward, Frederick of Sicily, son of the late Hohenstaufen emperor Henry VI, was crowned king of the Romans in the German city of Mainz. Within a year and a half, Philip Augustus ended the reign of Otto IV on the battlefield of Bouvines, and three years later (1215), Frederick II was crowned emperor again, this time in the sacred imperial city of Aachen.

During his reign, Frederick effectively turned dreams of a unified Germany into a nightmare of disunity, assuring German fragmentation into modern times. Frederick seemed to desire only the imperial title for himself and his sons and was willing to give the German princes whatever they wanted to secure it. It was this eager compliance with their demands that laid the foundation for six centuries of German division. In 1220, he recognized the jurisdictional claims of the ecclesiastical princes of Germany, and twelve years later (1232) he extended the same recognition to the secular princes. Frederick's concessions amounted to an abdication of imperial power in Germany.

Frederick's relations with the pope were equally disastrous, leading to his excommunication on four different occasions. He was also determined to control Lombardy and Sicily, a policy that was anathema to the pope. The papacy came to view Frederick as the Antichrist, the biblical beast of the Apocalypse, whose persecution of the faithful signaled the end of the world.

The papacy won the long struggle that ensued, although its victory was arguably a Pyrrhic one. During this bitter contest, Pope Innocent IV (r. 1243–1254) launched the church into European politics on a massive scale, a policy that left the church vulnerable to criticism from both religious reformers and royal apologists. Pope Innocent organized the German princes against Frederick, who—thanks to Frederick's grand concessions—were a superior force and able to gain full control of Germany by the 1240s.

When Frederick died in 1250, the German monarchy died with him. The princes established their own informal electoral college in 1257, which thereafter controlled the succession. The princes elected directly, and his offspring had no hereditary right to succeed him. The last male Hohenstaufen was executed in 1268.

Romanesque and Gothic Architecture

The High Middle Ages witnessed the peak of Romanesque art and the transition to the Gothic. Romanesque literally means "like Rome," and the art and architecture of the High Middle Ages embraced the classical style of ancient Rome. Romanesque churches are fortress-like. Rounded arches, thick stone walls, and heavy columns support their vaults or ceilings. In the early Middle Ages this architecture expressed the church's role as a refuge for the faithful and a new world power. Developed under the Carolingians and Ottonians, the Romanesque attained its perfection and predominated between 1050 and 1200.

Appearing first in mid-twelfth-century France, Gothic art and architecture evolved directly from the Romanesque. Gothic architecture's distinctive feature is a ribbed, crisscrossed ceiling, with pointed arches in place of rounded ones, a clever construction technique that allows Gothic churches to soar far above their Romanesque predecessors. The greater weight on the walls was off-loaded by exterior "flying" buttresses built directly into them. With the walls thus shored up, they could be filled with wide expanses of stained glass windows that flooded the churches with colored light.

Transept, Cathedral of St. James, Santiago de Compostela.

Achim Bednorz/© Achim Bednorz, Koln

How did Gothic architecture embody the religious values of the High Middle Ages?

SUMMARY

HOW WAS Otto able to secure the power of his Saxon dynasty?

Otto I and the Revival of the Empire In 918, Henry I became the first Saxon king of Germany; eighteen years later his son Otto I took power, continuing his program of unification and expansion. He invaded Italy in 951 and proclaimed himself king. By the end of his reign, Otto the Great had even established authority over the Papal States and the pope himself. The Ottonian dynasty faltered in the early eleventh century, however, because Otto I's successors did not pay enough attention to events in Germany, and the church established an independent base of power for itself. By contrast, during this same period the Capetian kings in France focused on their home turf and built the basis for enduring royal power. *page 178*

WHAT EXPLAINS the popularity of the Cluniac reform movement?

The Reviving Catholic Church The Catholic Church shed the secular control of the ninth and tenth centuries to emerge as a powerful independent institution. The reform movement based at the French monastery in Cluny spread throughout Europe and was endorsed by the pope. In 1075, Pope Gregory VII outlawed lay investiture of the clergy; this led to a battle of wills between popes and emperors, until the 1122 Concordat of Worms formalized a new relationship between church and state. Meanwhile, the Crusades provided an outlet for popular religious zeal. Repeated Christian expeditions to the Holy Lands did not do much to encourage Muslim respect for Europeans, but the Crusades did stimulate trade and expose the West to the civilizations of the East. Around 1200, Pope Innocent III asserted increased papal power, suppressed internal dissent, clarified church doctrine, and sanctioned two new monastic orders: the Franciscans and the Dominicans. *page 179*

HOW DID England and France develop strong monarchies?

England and France: Hastings (1066) to Bouvines (1214) William, the duke of Normandy, won the Battle of Hastings in 1066 and soon was crowned king of England. Building on Anglo-Saxon traditions, he created a strong monarchy that used parleying to channel communications between the king and other leaders. William's grandson Henry married Eleanor of Aquitaine, creating the Angevin Empire. Later kings of England became more oppressive, raised taxes, and caused other problems, until English barons revolted and forced King John to recognize the Magna Carta in 1215. In roughly this same period in France, the Capetian kings first concentrated on securing their territory, then on exercising authority over the nobility. By 1214, in the battle at Bouvines against a combined English and German force, the French were able to defeat their opponents. *page 188*

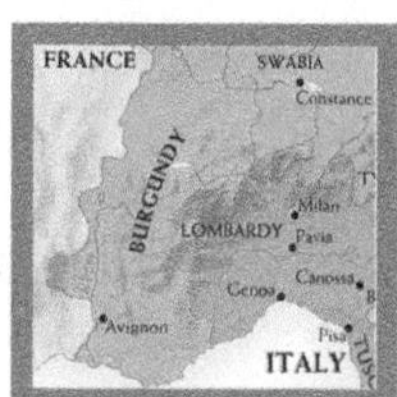

IN WHAT ways was Louis IX of France the "ideal" medieval monarch?

France in the Thirteenth Century: The Reign of Louis IX In the middle of the thirteenth century, Louis IX enjoyed almost fifty years as the ruler of a unified and secure France. He was able to focus his energies on domestic reform and the cultivation of culture and religion. He improved the justice system and presided over the emergence of Paris as the intellectual capital of Europe. He was fiercely religious, sponsoring the French Inquisition and leading two Crusades. In his dealings with foreigners, especially the English, he might be accused of naïveté; he failed to press his advantage at the Treaty of Paris in 1259 and allowed the English to maintain their claims on various French lands, thereby setting the stage for the Hundred Years' War in the next century. *page 193*

HOW DID the policies of the Hohenstaufens lead to the fragmentation of Germany?

The Hohenstaufen Empire (1152–1272) While stable governments that balanced central authority with the local needs of the populace were developing in England and France, the leaders of the Holy Roman Empire were squandering their opportunities to develop a sustainable political structure, a failure that would have negative repercussions through centuries of German history. Throughout the Hohenstaufen dynasty, conflicts with the popes and imperial schemes to control Italian lands distracted Frederick I Barbarossa and his successors from the task of maintaining the allegiance of the nobility and keeping their territory unified. By the late thirteenth century, the Hohenstaufen dynasty had lost all meaningful power and Germany was fragmented. *page 194*

Review Questions

1. How did the Saxon king Otto I rebuild the German Empire and use the church to achieve his political goals? How did his program fit with the aspirations of the Cluny reform movement? What was at stake for each of the disputants in the investiture controversy? Who won?

2. What developments in western and eastern Europe led to the start of the crusading movement? How did the Crusades to the Holy Lands affect Europe and the Muslim world?

3. Why were France and England able to coalesce into reasonably strong states, but not Germany?

KEY TERMS

Albigensians (p. 186)
Beguines (p. 188)
Crusades (p. 181)
Inquisition (p. 187)
Magna Carta (p. 191)
transubstantiation (p. 187)

For additional learning resources related to this chapter, please go to **www.myhistorylab.com**

PEARSON myhistorylab

8

Medieval Society:

Hierarchies, Towns, Universities, and Families (1000–1300)

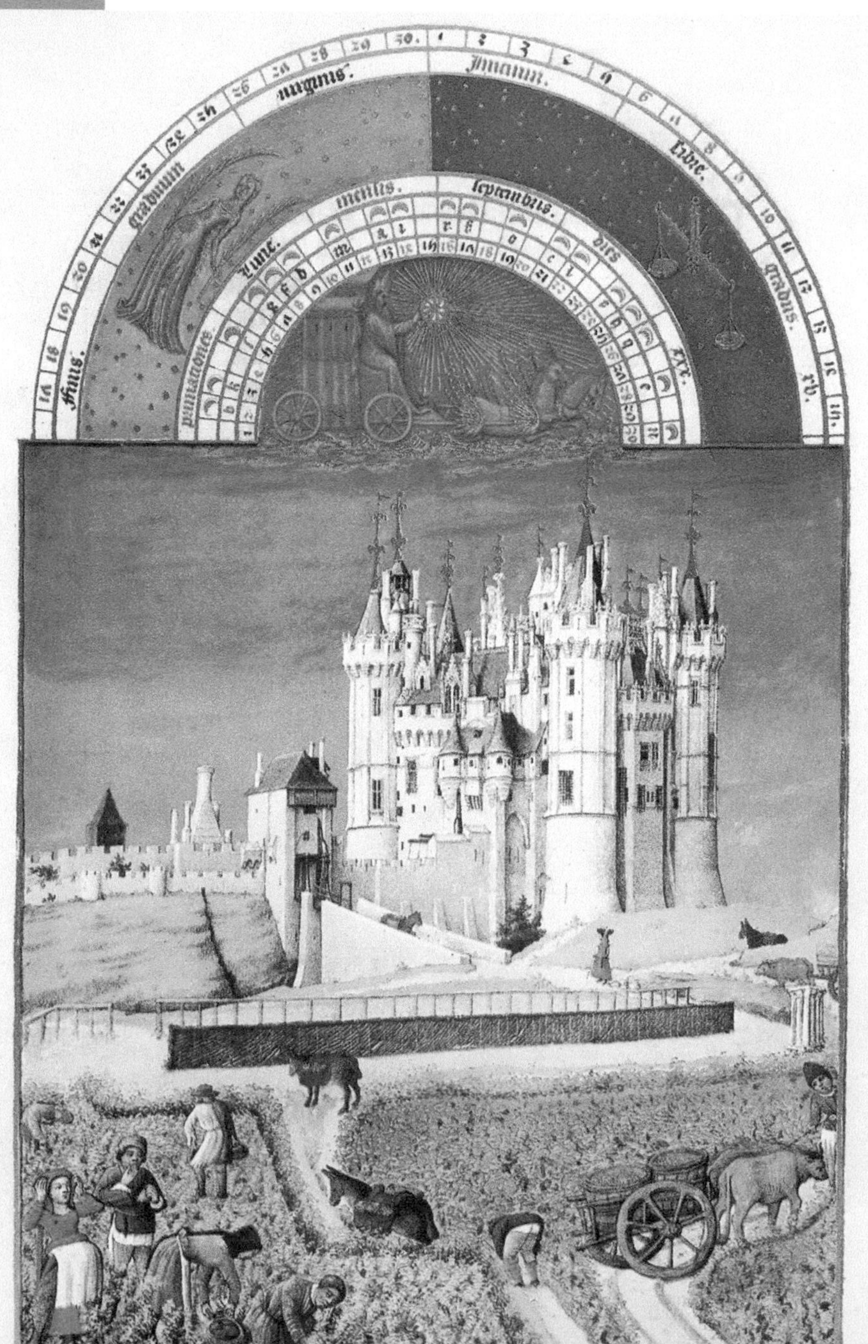

The livelihood of towns and castles depended on the labor of peasants in surrounding villages. Here a peasant family collects the September grape harvest from a vineyard outside a fortified castle in France in preparation for making wine.

The Granger Collection

How did the labor of peasants make the lifestyle of medieval elites possible?

THE TRADITIONAL ORDER OF LIFE *page 202*

WHAT WAS the relationship between the three basic groups in medieval society?

TOWNS AND TOWNSPEOPLE *page 208*

WHAT PROCESSES led to the rise of towns and a merchant class?

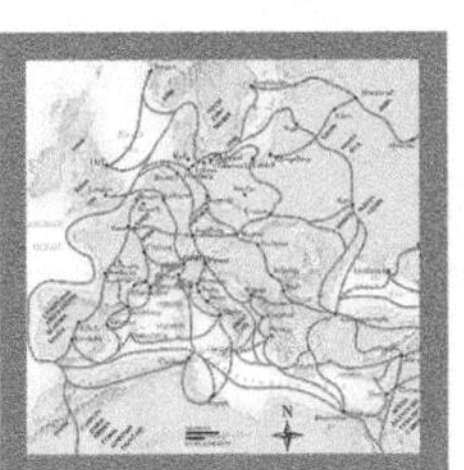

SCHOOLS AND UNIVERSITIES *page 212*

WHAT INTELLECTUAL trends accompanied the rise of universities?

WOMEN IN MEDIEVAL SOCIETY *page 215*

WHAT WAS life like for women during the Middle Ages?

THE LIVES OF CHILDREN *page 218*

WHAT WERE the characteristics of childhood in the Middle Ages?

From the tenth to the twelfth centuries, increasing political stability helped Europe advance on multiple fronts. Agricultural production increased, population exploded, and trade and urban life revived. Crusades multiplied contacts with foreign lands that stimulated both economic and cultural development. A new merchant class, the ancestors of modern capitalists, appeared to serve the West's growing markets, and an urban proletariat developed.

Muslim intellectuals guided Europe's scholars in the rediscovery of Classical literature, and an explosion of information led to the rise of the university. Literacy increased among the laity and a renaissance in art and thought blossomed in the twelfth century. The creative vigor that surged through Europe in the High Middle Ages became tangible in the awesome Gothic churches that were the supreme products of medieval art and science.

THE TRADITIONAL ORDER OF LIFE

WHAT WAS the relationship between the three basic groups in medieval society?

In the art and literature of the Middle Ages, three basic social groups were represented: those who fought as mounted knights (the landed nobility), those who prayed (the clergy), and those who labored in fields and shops (the peasantry and village artisans). After the revival of towns in the eleventh century, a fourth social group emerged: long-distance traders and merchants.

The Joys and Pains of the Medieval Joust This scene from a manuscript from c. 1300–1349 idealizes medieval noblewomen and the medieval joust. Revived in the late Middle Ages, jousts were frequently held in peacetime. They kept the warring skills of noblemen sharp and became popular entertainment. Only the nobility were legally allowed to joust, but over time, uncommon wealth enabled a persistent commoner to qualify.

Universitatsbibliothek Heidelberg.

What medieval values are reflected in this manuscript illustration? What significance do you attach to the fact that the spectators are women?

NOBLES

As a distinctive social group, not all nobles were originally great men with large hereditary lands. Many rose from the ranks of feudal vassals or warrior knights. The successful vassal attained a special social and legal status based on his landed wealth (accumulated fiefs), his exercise of authority over others, and his distinctive social customs—all of which set him apart from others in medieval society. By the late Middle Ages, a distinguishable higher and lower nobility living in both town and country had evolved. The higher were the great landowners and territorial magnates, who had long been the dominant powers in their regions, while the lower were comprised of petty landlords, descendants of minor knights, newly rich merchants able to buy country estates, and wealthy farmers patiently risen from ancestral serfdom.

Warriors Arms were the nobleman's profession; to wage war was his sole occupation and reason for living. In the eighth century, the adoption of stirrups made mounted warriors, or cavalry, indispensable to a successful army (stirrups permitted the rider to strike a blow without falling off the horse). Good horses and the accompanying armor and weaponry of horse warfare were expensive. Thus only those with means could pursue the life of a cavalryman. The nobleman's fief gave him the means to acquire the expensive military equipment that his rank required. He maintained that enviable position as he had gained it, by fighting for his chief.

The nobility accordingly celebrated the physical strength, courage, and constant activity of warfare. Warring gave them both new riches and an opportunity to gain honor and glory. Knights were paid a share in the plunder of victory, and in war everything became fair game. They looked down on the peasantry as cowards who ran and hid during war. They held urban merchants, who amassed wealth by business methods strange to feudal society, in equal contempt. The nobility possessed as strong a sense of superiority over these "unwarlike" people as the clergy did over the general run of the laity.

Knighthood The nobleman nurtured his sense of distinctiveness within medieval society by the chivalric ritual of dubbing to knighthood. This ceremonial entrance into the noble class became almost a religious sacrament. A bath of purification, confession, communion, and a prayer vigil preceded the ceremony. Thereafter, the priest blessed the knight's standard, lance, and sword. As prayers were chanted, the priest girded the knight with his sword and presented him his shield, enlisting him as much in the defense of the church as in the service of his lord. Dubbing raised the nobleman to a state as sacred in his sphere as clerical ordination made the priest in his.

In the twelfth century, knighthood was legally restricted to men of high birth. This circumscription of noble ranks came in reaction to the growing wealth, political power, and successful social climbing of newly rich townspeople (mostly merchants), who formed a new urban patriciate that was increasingly competitive with the lower nobility. Kings remained free, however, to raise up knights at will and did not shrink from increasing royal revenues by selling noble titles to wealthy merchants. But the law was building fences—fortunately, with gates—between town and countryside in the High Middle Ages.

Sportsmen In peacetime, the nobility had two favorite amusements: hunting and tournaments. Where they could, noblemen progressively monopolized the rights to game, forbidding commoners from hunting in their "lord's" forests. This practice built resentment among common people to the level of revolt. Free game, fishing, and access to wood were basic demands in the petitions of grievance and the revolts of the peasantry throughout the High and later Middle Ages.

Tournaments also sowed seeds of social disruption, but more within the ranks of the nobility itself. As regions competed fiercely with one another for victory and glory, even mock battles with blunted weapons proved to be deadly. Often, tournaments got out of hand, ending with bloodshed and animosity among the combatants. The church came to oppose tournaments as occasions of pagan revelry and senseless violence. Kings and princes also turned against them as sources of division within their realms. (See "Encountering the Past: Warrior Games," page 204.)

Courtly Love From the repeated assemblies in the courts of barons and kings, set codes of social conduct, or "courtesy," developed in noble circles. With the French leading the way, mannered behavior and court etiquette became almost as important as expertise on the battlefield. Knights became literate gentlemen, and lyric poets sang and moralized at court. The cultivation of a code of behavior and a special literature to eulogize it was not unrelated to problems within the social life of the nobility. Noblemen were notorious philanderers; their illegitimate children mingled openly with their legitimate offspring in their houses. The advent of courtesy was, in part, an effort to reform this situation.

Although the poetry of courtly love was sprinkled with frank eroticism and the beloved in these epics were married women pursued by those to whom they were not married, the poet usually recommended love at a distance, unconsummated by sexual intercourse. Court poets depicted those who succumbed to illicit carnal love as reaping at least as much suffering as joy.

Lovers playing chess on an ivory mirror back, ca. 1300.

The Bridgeman Art Library International

What role did romantic love play in the relationships between elite men and women?

Social Divisions No medieval social group was absolutely uniform—not the nobility, the clergy, the townspeople, or even the peasantry. Noblemen formed a broad spectrum—from minor vassals without subordinate vassals to mighty barons, the principal vassals of a king or prince, who had many vassals of their own. Dignity and status within the nobility were directly related to the exercise of authority over others; a chief with many vassals obviously far excelled the small country nobleman who served another and was lord over none but himself.

ENCOUNTERING THE PAST

Warrior Games

The cultural environment surrounding the medieval nobility—poetry, songs, arts, and entertainments—glorified war. This was consistent with the interests of a warrior class whose men spent their lives fighting and training for battle. A young nobleman might receive his first horse and dagger at the age of two. By the time he turned fourteen, he was ready to handle adult weapons.

Tournaments (mock combats) provided him with both practical training and diversion. They proved so popular with all members of society that they survived as pastimes even after changes in warfare diminished the need for a knight's traditional skills.

The military preoccupations of the knights influenced the behavior of other members of medieval society. Aristocratic women hunted but were limited to the role of spectators at entertainments such as tournaments. Some clergy were famous sportsmen and warriors, but, like women, their taste for violence was usually satisfied vicariously by rooting for champions at tournaments and by playing chess, backgammon, and competitive games such as Tick, Tack, Toe. Commoners attended tournaments and developed similar warlike games and sports of their own. The equivalent of a tournament for men and boys of the lower classes was a rough ball game—an early version of rugby, soccer, or football. Medieval people were ingenious at inventing diversions for their idle hours, as Pieter Breughel's painting *Children's Games* (1560) documents. It depicts boys and girls engaged in seventy-eight different activities.

Breughel, *Children's Games.*

Pieter the Elder Breughel (1525–1569), *Children's Games*, 1560. Oil on oakwood, 118 × 161 cm. Kunsthistoriches Museum, Vienna, Austria. Photo copyright Erich Lessing/Art Resource, NY

What similarities and differences do you note between contemporary children's games and those depicted by Breughel?

WHY DID the medieval nobility play warlike games? How did these influence the behavior of other members of society?

In the late Middle Ages, the landed nobility suffered a steep economic and political decline. Climatic changes and agricultural failures created large famines, and the great plague (see Chapter 9) brought unprecedented population loss. Changing military tactics occasioned by the use of infantry and heavy artillery during the Hundred Years' War made the noble cavalry nearly obsolete. Also, the alliance of wealthy towns with kings challenged the nobility within their own domains. A waning of the landed nobility occurred after the fourteenth century when the effective possession of land and wealth counted more than lineage for membership in the highest social class. Still a shrinking nobility continued to dominate society down to the nineteenth century, and they have been with us ever since.

Clergy

Unlike the nobility and the peasantry, the clergy was an open estate. Although the clerical hierarchy reflected the social classes from which the clergy came, one was still a cleric by religious training and ordination, not by the circumstances of birth or military prowess.

Regular and Secular Clerics There were two basic types of clerical vocation: the regular clergy and the secular clergy. The **regular clergy** was made up of the orders of monks who lived according to a special ascetic rule (*regula*) in cloisters separated from the world. They were the spiritual elite among the clergy, and monks' personal sacrifices and high religious ideals made them much respected in high medieval society.

regular clergy Monks and nuns who lived under the *regula* ("rule") of a cloister.

Many monks (and also nuns, who increasingly embraced the vows of poverty, obedience, and chastity without a clerical rank) secluded themselves altogether. The regular clergy, however, were never completely cut off from the secular world. They maintained frequent contact with the laity through such charitable activities as feeding the destitute and tending the sick, through liberal arts instruction in monastic schools, through special pastoral commissions from the pope, and as supplemental preachers and confessors in parish churches during Lent and other peak religious seasons. It became the mark of the Dominican and Franciscan friars to live a common life according to a special rule and still to be active in a worldly ministry. Some monks, because of their learning and rhetorical skills, even rose to prominence as secretaries and private confessors to kings and queens.

The **secular clergy**, those who lived and worked directly among the laity in the world (*saeculum*), formed a vast hierarchy. At the top were the high prelates—the wealthy cardinals, archbishops, and bishops, who were drawn almost exclusively from the nobility—and below them the urban priests, the cathedral canons, and the court clerks. Finally, there was the great mass of poor parish priests, who were neither financially nor intellectually far above the common people they served. Until the Gregorian reform in the eleventh century, parish priests lived with women in a relationship akin to marriage, and the communities they served accepted their concubines and children. Because of their relative poverty, priests often took second jobs as teachers, artisans, or farmers. Their parishioners also accepted and even admired this practice.

secular clergy Clergy, such as bishops and priests, who lived and worked among the laity in the *saeculum* ("world").

QUICK REVIEW

Clergy

- Secular clergy worked and lived among the laity
- Regular clergy were monks and nuns who lived under the rule of a cloister
- Regular clergy maintained contact with the secular world

New Orders One of the results of the Gregorian reform was the creation of new religious orders aspiring to a life of poverty and self-sacrifice in imitation of Christ and the first apostles. The more important were the Canons Regular (founded 1050–1100), the Carthusians (founded 1084), the Cistercians (founded 1098), and the Praemonstratensians (founded 1121). Carthusians, Cistercians, and Praemonstratensians practiced extreme austerity in their quest to recapture the pure religious life of the early church.

Strictest of them all were the Carthusians. Members lived in isolation and fasted three days a week. They also devoted themselves to long periods of silence and even self-flagellation in their quest for perfect self-denial and conformity to Christ.

The Cistercians (from Citeaux in Burgundy) were a reform wing of the Benedictine order. They hoped to avoid the materialistic influences of urban society and maintain uncorrupted the original *Rule* of Saint Benedict, which their leaders believed Cluny was compromising. The Cistercians accordingly stressed anew the inner life and spiritual goals of monasticism. They located their houses in remote areas and denied themselves worldly comforts and distractions.

The Canons Regular were independent groups of secular clergy (and also earnest laity) who, in addition to serving laity in the world, adopted the *Rule* of Saint Augustine (a monastic guide dating from around the year 500) and practiced the ascetic virtues of regular clerics. By merging the life of the cloister with traditional clerical duties, the Canons Regular foreshadowed the mendicant friars of the thirteenth century—the Dominicans and the Franciscans, who combined the ascetic ideals of the cloister with an active ministry in the world.

The monasteries and nunneries of the established orders recruited candidates from among wealthy social groups. Crowding in these convents and the absence of patronage gave rise in the thirteenth century to lay satellite convents known as Beguine houses. These convents housed religiously earnest single women from the upper and middle social strata. In the German city of Cologne, one hundred such houses were established between 1250 and 1350, each with eight to twelve "sisters."

Prominence of the Clergy The clergy constituted a far greater proportion of medieval society than modern society. Estimates suggest that 1.5 percent of fourteenth-century Europe was in clerical garb. The clergy were concentrated in urban areas, especially in towns with universities and cathedrals, where, in addition to studying, they found work in a wide variety of religious services. In large university towns, the clergy might exceed 10 percent of the population.

Despite the moonlighting of poorer parish priests, the clergy as a whole, like the nobility, lived on the labor of others. Their income came from the regular collection of tithes and church taxes according to an elaborate system that evolved in the High and later Middle Ages. The church was, of course, a major landowner and regularly collected rents and fees. Monastic communities and high prelates amassed great fortunes. The immense secular power attached to high clerical posts can be seen in the intensity of the investiture struggle. (See Chapter 7.)

For most of the Middle Ages, the clergy were the "first estate," and theology was the queen of the sciences. Theologians elaborated the distinction between the clergy and the laity to the clergy's benefit. Secular rulers were not supposed to tax the clergy, who were holy persons, without special permission from the ecclesiastical authorities. Clerical crimes were under the jurisdiction of special ecclesiastical courts, not the secular courts. Because churches and monasteries were deemed holy places, they, too, were free from secular taxation and legal jurisdiction. By the late Middle Ages, townspeople increasingly resented the special immunities of the clergy. They complained that the clergy had greater privileges, yet fewer responsibilities, than all others who lived within the town walls.

PEASANTS

manor A self-sufficient rural community that was a fundamental institution of medieval life.

The largest and lowest social group in medieval society was the one on whose labor the welfare of all the others depended: the agrarian peasantry. Many peasants lived on and worked the **manors** of the nobility. All were to one degree or another dependent on their lords and were considered to be their property. The manor in Frankish times was a plot of land within a village, ranging from twelve to seventy-five acres in size, assigned to a certain member by a settled tribe or clan. This member and his family became lords of the land, and those who came to dwell there formed a smaller, self-sufficient community within a larger village. In the early Middle Ages, such manors consisted of the dwellings of the lord and his family, the huts of the peasants, agricultural sheds, and fields.

QUICK REVIEW

Peasant Life

- Peasants were the largest and lowest social group
- Many peasants worked on manors
- The lord was the supreme authority on his manor

The Duties of Tenancy The landowner or lord of the manor required a certain amount of produce (grain, eggs, and the like) and a certain number of services from the peasant families that came to dwell on and farm his land. The tenants were free to divide the labor as they wished and could keep what goods remained after the lord's levies were met. A powerful lord might own many such manors.

There were both servile and free manors. The tenants of the latter had originally been freemen known as *coloni*. (See Chapter 5.) Original inhabitants of the territory and petty landowners, they swapped their small possessions for a guarantee of security from a more powerful lord, who came in this way to possess their land. Unlike the pure serfdom of the servile manors, whose tenants had no original claim to a part of the land, the tenancy obligations on free manors tended to be limited, and the tenants' rights more carefully defined. It was a milder serfdom. Tenants of servile manors were, by comparison, far more vulnerable to the whims of their landlords. These two types of manors tended, however, to merge. The most common situation was the manor on which tenants of greater and lesser degrees of servitude dwelt together, their services to the lord defined by their personal status and local custom. In many regions free, self-governing peasant communities existed without any overlords and tenancy obligations.

The lord held both judicial and police powers. The lord also had the right to subject his tenants to exactions known as **banalities**. He could, for example, force them to breed their cows with his bull and to pay for the privilege, to grind their bread grains in his mill, to bake their bread in his oven, to make their wine in his wine press, to buy their beer from his brewery, and even to surrender to him the tongues or other choice parts of all animals slaughtered on his lands. The lord also collected a serf's best animal as an inheritance tax. Without the lord's permission, serfs could neither travel nor marry outside the manor in which they served.

In this eleventh-century manuscript, peasants harvest grain, trim vines, and plow fields behind yoked oxen.

The Labors of the 12 Months. Pietro de Crescenzi, Le Rustican. Ms.340/603. France, c. 1460. Location: Musée Condé, Chantilly, France. Giraudon/Art Resource, NY

How did the changing seasons shape the activities of medieval serfs?

The Life of a Serf Exploited as the serfs may appear to have been from a modern point of view, their status was far from chattel slavery. It was to the lord's advantage to keep his serfs healthy and happy; his welfare, like theirs, depended on a successful harvest. Serfs had their own dwellings and modest strips of land and lived by the produce of their own labor and organization. They could market for their own profit what surpluses might remain after the harvest. They were free to choose their spouses within the local village, although they needed the lord's permission to marry a wife or husband from another village. Serfs could pass their property (their dwellings and field strips) and worldly goods on to their children.

banalities Monopolies maintained by landowners giving them the right to demand that tenants pay to grind all their grain in the landowner's mill and bake all their bread in his oven.

Despite the social distinctions between free and servile serfs—and, within these groups, between those who owned plows and oxen and those who possessed only hoes—the common dependence on the soil forced close cooperation. The ratio of seed to grain yield was consistently poor. There was rarely an abundance of bread and ale, the staple peasant foods. Two important American crops, potatoes and corn (maize), were unknown in Europe until the sixteenth century. Pork was the major source of protein, and every peasant household had its pigs. At slaughter time a family might also receive a little tough beef. Basically, however, everyone depended on the grain crops. When they failed or fell short, peasants went hungry unless their lord had surplus stores he was willing to share.

Changes in the Manor Two basic changes occurred in the evolution of the manor from the early to the later Middle Ages. The first was its fragmentation and the rise to dominance of the single-family holding. Such technological advances as the collar harness (ca. 800), the horseshoe (ca. 900), and the three-field system of crop rotation facilitated this development by making it easier for small family units to support themselves. As the lords parceled out their land to new tenants, their own plots became progressively smaller. This increase in tenants and decrease in the lord's fields brought about a corresponding reduction in the labor services exacted from the tenants. Also, the bringing of new fields into production increased individual holdings and modified labor services. In France, by the reign of Louis IX (r. 1226–1270), only a few days of labor a year were required, whereas in the time of Charlemagne (r. 768–814) peasants had worked the lords' fields several days a week.

As the single-family unit replaced the clan as the basic nuclear group, assessments of goods and services fell on individual fields and households, no longer on manors as a whole. Family farms replaced manorial units. The peasants' carefully nurtured communal life made possible a family's retention of its land and dwelling after the death of the head of the household. In this way, land and property remained in the possession of a single family from generation to generation.

The second change in the evolution of the manor was the conversion of the serf's dues into money payments, a change brought about by the revival of trade and the rise of the towns. This development, completed by the thirteenth century, permitted serfs to hold their land as rent-paying tenants and to overcome their servile status. Although tenants thereby gained more freedom, they were not necessarily better off materially. Whereas servile workers could have counted on the benevolent assistance of their landlords in hard times, rent-paying workers were left, by and large, to their own devices. Their independence caused some landlords to treat them with indifference and even resentment.

By the mid-fourteenth century, a declining nobility in England and France, faced with the ravages of the great plague and the Hundred Years' War, tried to turn back the historical clock by increasing taxes on the peasantry and restricting their migration into the cities. The peasantry responded with armed revolts. They stand out at the end of the Middle Ages as violent testimony to the breakup of medieval society. As growing national sentiment would break its political unity and heretical movements would end its nominal religious unity, peasant revolts revealed the absence of medieval social unity.

TOWNS AND TOWNSPEOPLE

WHAT PROCESSES led to the rise of towns and a merchant class?

In the eleventh and twelfth centuries, towns held only about 5 percent of Western Europe's population. Nonetheless, in the Middle Ages cities and towns were where the action was. There one might find the whole of medieval society, including its most creative segments.

The Chartering of Towns

Feudal lords, both lay and clerical, originally dominated towns. The lords created the towns by granting charters to those who would agree to live and work within them. The charters guaranteed their safety and gave inhabitants a degree of independence unknown on the land. The purpose was originally to concentrate skilled laborers who could manufacture the finished goods lords and bishops wanted. By the eleventh century, skilled serfs began to pay their manorial dues in manufactured goods, rather than in field labor, eggs, chickens, and beans, as they had done earlier. In return for a fixed rent and proper subservience, serfs were also encouraged to move to the towns. There they gained special rights and privileges from the charters.

As towns grew and beckoned, serfs fled the countryside with their skills going directly to the new urban centers. There they found the freedom and profits that might lift an industrious craftsperson into higher social ranks. As this migration of serfs to the towns accelerated, the lords in the countryside offered them more favorable terms of tenure to keep them on the land. But serfs could not easily be kept down on the farms after they had discovered the opportunities of town life. In this way, the growth of towns improved the lot of serfs generally.

THE RISE OF MERCHANTS

Not only did rural society give the towns their craftspeople and day laborers, the first merchants themselves may also have been enterprising serfs. Not a few long-distance traders were men who had nothing to lose and everything to gain by the enormous risks of foreign trade. They traveled together in armed caravans and convoys, buying goods and products as cheaply as possible at the source, and selling them for all they could get in Western ports. (See Map 8–1.) At first, traditional social groups—nobility, clergy, and peasantry—considered the merchants an oddity. Over time the powerful grew to respect the merchants, and the weak to imitate them, because wherever the merchants went, they left a trail of wealth behind.

MAP EXPLORATION

Interactive map: To explore this map further, go to www.myhistorylab.com

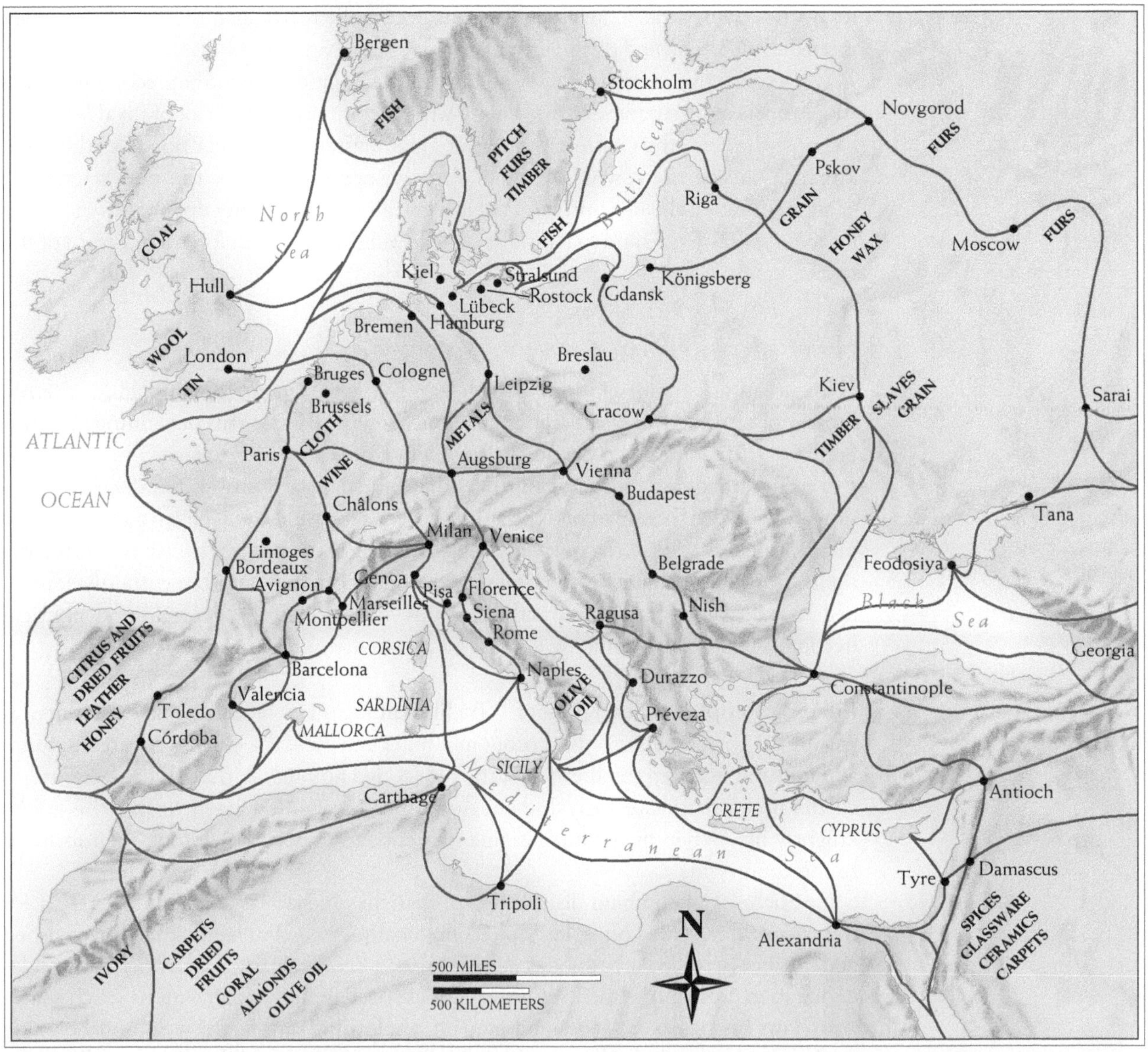

MAP 8–1 **Some Medieval Trade Routes and Regional Products** The map shows some of the channels that came to be used in interregional commerce and what was traded in a particular region.

Given the kinds of items traded, was international trade essential or peripheral to the lives of medieval people?

Challenging the Old Lords

As they grew in wealth and numbers, merchants formed their own protective associations and were soon challenging traditional seigneurial authority. They especially wanted to end the tolls and tariffs regional authorities imposed on the surrounding countryside. Such regulations hampered the flow of commerce on which both merchant and craftsperson in the growing urban export industries depended. Merchant guilds or protective associations also sprang up in the eleventh century and were followed in the twelfth century by those of craftspeople. Both quickly found themselves in conflict with the norms of a comparatively static agricultural society.

Merchants and craftspeople needed simple and uniform laws and a fluid government sympathetic to their new forms of business activity—not the fortress mentality of the lords of the countryside. The result was a struggle with the old nobility within and outside the towns. This conflict led towns in the High and later Middle Ages to form their own independent communes and to ally themselves with kings against the nobility in the countryside, a development that eventually rearranged the centers of power in medieval Europe and dissolved classic feudal government.

Because the merchants were so clearly the engine of the urban economy, small shopkeepers and artisans identified more with them than with the aloof royal lords and bishops who were the chartered town's original masters. The lesser nobility (the small knights) outside the towns also embraced the opportunities of the new mercantile economy. During the eleventh and twelfth centuries, the burgher upper class increased its economic strength and successfully challenged the old urban lords for control of the towns.

New Models of Government

With urban autonomy came new models of self-government. Around 1100, the old urban nobility and the new burgher upper class merged. From this new ruling class was born the aristocratic town council, which henceforth governed towns.

guild An association of merchants or craftsmen that offered protection to its members and set rules for their work and products.

Enriching and complicating the situation, small artisans and craftspeople also slowly developed their own protective associations, or **guilds**, and began to gain a voice in government. Within town walls, people thought of themselves as citizens with basic rights, not subjects liable to their masters' whim. Economic hardship certainly continued to exist among the lower urban groups, despite their basic legal and political freedoms, but social mobility was at least a possibility in the towns.

Keeping People in Their Places Traditional measures of success had great appeal within the towns. Despite their economic independence, the wealthiest urban groups admired and imitated the lifestyle of the old landed nobility. Although the latter treated the urban patriciate with disdain, successful merchants longed to live the noble, knightly life. When merchants became rich enough to do so, they took their fortunes to the countryside.

Such social climbing disturbed city councils, and when merchants departed for the countryside, towns often lost out economically. A need to be socially distinguished and distinct pervaded urban society. Towns tried to control this need by defining grades of luxury in dress and residence for the various social groups and vocations. Such sumptuary laws restricted the types and amount of clothing one might wear and how one might decorate one's dwelling architecturally. In this way, people were forced to dress and live according to their station in life. The intention of such laws was positive: to maintain social order and dampen social conflict by keeping everyone clearly and peacefully in their place.

Social Conflict and Protective Associations (Guilds) Despite unified resistance to external domination, medieval towns were not internally harmonious social units. Conflict between haves and have-nots was inevitable, especially because medieval towns had little concept of social and economic equality. Only families of long standing in the town who owned property had full rights of citizenship and a direct say in the town's government at the highest levels. Government, in other words, was inbred and aristocratic.

Conflict also existed between the poorest workers in the export trades (usually the weavers and wool combers) and the economically better off and socially ascending independent workers and small shopkeepers. The better-off workers also had their differences with the merchants, whose export trade often brought competitive foreign goods into the city. So independent workers and small shopkeepers organized to restrict foreign trade to a minimum and corner the local market in certain items.

Over time, the formation of artisan guilds gave workers in the trades a direct voice in government. Ironically, the long-term effect of this gain limited the social mobility of the poorest artisans. The guilds gained representation on city councils, where, to discourage imports, they used their power to enforce quality standards and fair prices on local businesses. These actions tightly restricted guild membership, squeezing out poorer artisans and tradesmen. Unrepresented artisans and craftspeople constituted a true urban proletariat prevented by law from forming their own guilds or entering existing ones. The efforts by guild-dominated governments to protect local craftspeople and industries tended to narrow trade and depress the economy for all.

QUICK REVIEW

Town Society

- Townspeople were very conscious of class distinctions
- Laws were enacted to limit competition among social classes
- Urban self-government tended to become progressively inbred and aristocratic

Towns and Kings

By providing kings with the resources they needed to curb factious noblemen, towns became a major force in the transition from feudal societies to national governments. In many places kings and towns formally allied against the traditional lords of the land. Towns attracted kings and emperors for obvious reasons. They were a ready source of educated bureaucrats and lawyers who knew Roman law, the ultimate tool for running kingdoms and empires. Kings could also find money in the towns in great quantity, enabling them to hire their own armies instead of relying on the nobility. Towns had the human, financial, and technological resources to empower kings. By such alliances, towns won royal political recognition and guarantees for their constitutions.

It was also in the towns' interest to have a strong monarch as their protector against despotic local lords and princes, who were always eager to integrate or engulf the towns within their expanding territories. Unlike a local magnate, a king tended to remain at a distance, allowing towns to exercise their precious autonomy. A king was thus the more desirable overlord. It was also an advantage for a town to conduct its long-distance trade in the name of a powerful monarch.

QUICK REVIEW

Basis of the Alliance

- Towns were a source of human, financial, and technological resources for kings
- Effective royal government created the best environment for commerce
- In many places, towns and kings allied against traditional lords

Jews in Christian Society

The major urban centers, particularly in France and Germany, attracted many Jews during the late twelfth and thirteenth centuries. Jews gathered there both by choice and for safety in the increasingly hostile Christian world. Mutually wary of one another, Christians and Jews limited direct contact with one another to exchanges between their merchants and scholars. The church expressly forbade Jews from hiring Christians in their businesses and from holding any public authority over them. Jews freely conducted their own small businesses, catering to private clients, both Christian and Jewish. The wealthier Jews became bankers to kings and popes. Jewish intellectual and religious culture, always elaborate and sophisticated, both dazzled and threatened

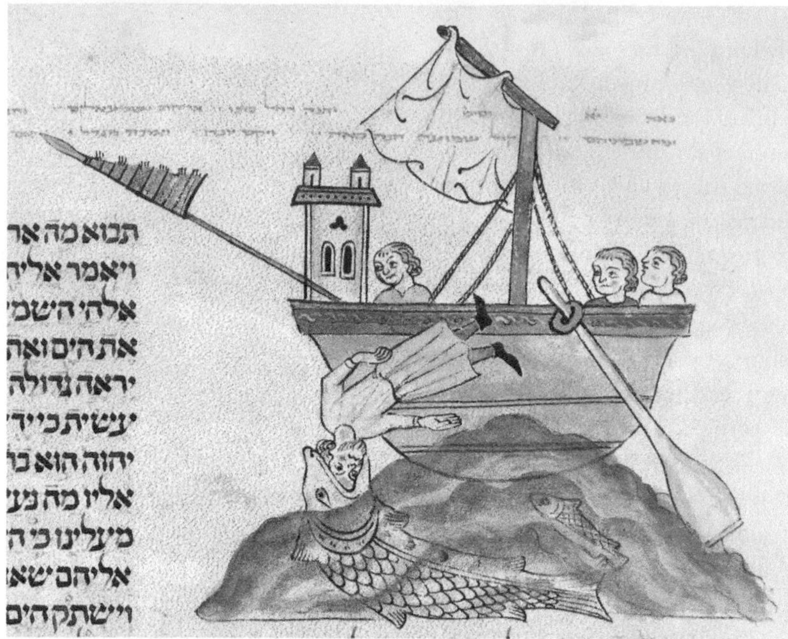

Jonah is swallowed by a great fish in a scene from a thirteenth-century Hebrew Torah from Portugal, an example of the rich Jewish heritage of medieval Iberia.

Instituto da Biblioteca Nacional, Lisbon, Portugal/Bridgeman Art Library

What conditions in Spain allowed for the development of a wealthy and influential Jewish community?

Christians who viewed it from outside. These various factors—the separateness of Jews, their exceptional economic power, and their rich cultural strength—contributed to envy, suspicion, and distrust among many Christians, whose religious teaching held Jews responsible for the death of Christ.

Between the late twelfth and fourteenth centuries, Jews were exiled from France and persecuted elsewhere. Two factors lay behind this unprecedented surge in anti-Jewish sentiment. The first was a desire by kings to confiscate Jewish wealth and property, and to eliminate the Jews as economic competitors with the monarchy. The church's increasing political vulnerability to the new dynastic monarchies also contributed to the surge in anti-Jewish sentiment. Faced with the loss of its political power, the church became more determined than ever to maintain its spiritual hegemony. Beginning with the Crusades and the creation of new mendicant orders, the church reasserted its claims to spiritual sovereignty over Europe, instigating campaigns against dissenters, heretics, witches, Jews, and infidels at home and abroad.

SCHOOLS AND UNIVERSITIES

WHAT INTELLECTUAL trends accompanied the rise of universities?

In the twelfth century, Byzantine and Spanish Islamic scholars made it possible for the works of Aristotle on logic, the mathematical and astronomical writings of Euclid and Ptolemy, the basic works of Greek physicians and Arab mathematicians, and the larger texts of Roman law to circulate among Western scholars. Islamic scholars preserved these works and wrote extensive, thought-provoking commentaries on them, which were translated into Latin and made available to Western scholars and students. This renaissance of ancient knowledge produced an intellectual ferment that gave rise to Western universities.

University of Bologna

The first important Western university, established by Emperor Frederick I Barbarossa in 1158, was in Bologna. Originally, the term *university* meant simply a corporation of individuals (students and masters) who joined for their mutual protection from overarching episcopal authority (the local bishop oversaw the university) and from the local townspeople. Because townspeople then looked on students as foreigners without civil rights, such protective unions were necessary. They followed the model of an urban trade guild.

Bolognese students also "unionized" to guarantee fair rents and prices from their often reluctant hosts. And students demanded regular, high-quality teaching from their masters. In Italy, students actually hired their own teachers, set pay scales, and drew up desired lecture topics. Masters who did not keep their promises or live up to student expectations were boycotted. Price gouging by townspeople was met with the threat to move the university to another town.

Masters also formed their own protective associations and established procedures and standards for certification to teach within their ranks. The first academic degree was a certificate that licensed one to teach, a *licentia docendi*. It granted graduates in the liberal arts program—the program basic to all higher learning—as well as those in the higher professional sciences of medicine, theology, and law, "the right to teach anywhere" (*ius ibique docendi*).

Bologna was famous for the revival of Roman law. During the Frankish era and later, from the seventh to the eleventh centuries, only the most rudimentary manuals of Roman law had survived. With the growth of trade and towns in the late eleventh century, Western scholars had come into contact with the larger and more important parts of the *Corpus juris civilis* of Justinian, which had been lost during the intervening centuries. (See Chapter 6.) The study and dissemination of this recovered material was now undertaken in Bologna.

As Bologna was the model for southern European universities (those of Spain, Italy, and southern France) and the study of law, so Paris became the model for northern European universities and the study of theology. Oxford and Cambridge in England and (much later) Heidelberg in Germany were among its imitators. All these universities required a foundation in the liberal arts for advanced study in the higher sciences of medicine, theology, and law. The **liberal arts** program consisted of the *trivium* (grammar, rhetoric, and logic) and the *quadrivium* (arithmetic, geometry, astronomy, and music), the language arts and the mathematical arts.

In this medieval school scene, a teacher and his wife, with switches, teach children their music lessons.

German Information Center

Why did elites send their sons to school? What skills did they hope they would acquire?

Cathedral Schools

liberal arts The medieval university program that consisted of the *trivium* (TRI-vee-um): grammar, rhetoric, and logic, and the *quadrivium* (qua-DRI-vee-um): arithmetic, geometry, astronomy, and music.

Before the emergence of universities, the liberal arts were taught in cathedral and monastery schools to train the clergy. By the late eleventh and twelfth centuries, cathedral schools also began to provide lectures for nonclerical students, broadening their curricula to include training for purely secular vocations.

After 1200, increasing numbers of future notaries and merchants who had no particular interest in becoming priests, but who needed Latin and related intellectual disciplines to fill their secular positions, studied side by side with aspiring priests in cathedral and monastery schools. By the thirteenth century, the demand for secretaries and notaries in growing urban and territorial governments and for literate personnel in the expanding merchant firms gave rise to schools for secular vocational preparation. With the appearance of these schools, the church began to lose its monopoly on higher education.

University of Paris

The University of Paris grew institutionally out of the cathedral school of Notre Dame, among others. King Philip Augustus and Pope Innocent III gave the new university its charter in 1200. At Paris the college, or house system, originated. In Paris, the most famous college was the Sorbonne, founded for theology students around 1257 by Robert de Sorbon, chaplain to the king. In Oxford and Cambridge, the colleges became the basic unit of student life and were indistinguishable from the university proper.

As a group, Parisian students had power and prestige. They enjoyed royal protections and privileges that were denied to ordinary citizens. Many Parisian students were well-to-do, many of whom were spoiled and petulant. They did not endear themselves to the townspeople, whom they considered inferior. Townspeople's resentments sometimes led to violence against students.

Overview Two Schools of the High Middle Ages

UNIVERSITY OF BOLOGNA	• Chartered in 1158 • First of the great medieval schools to acquire recognition as a university • Students hired professors, set pay scales, and assigned lecture topics • Europe's premier center for advanced studies in law
UNIVERSITY OF PARIS	• Chartered in 1200 • Provided the model for the schools of northern Europe • Students given protections and privileges exceeding those of other citizens • Teachers were required to be examined thoroughly before being licensed • Twenty or more years were needed to earn a doctorate in theology

THE CURRICULUM

Scholasticism Method of study associated with the medieval university.

Before the "renaissance" of the twelfth century, when many Greek and Arabic texts became available to Western scholars and students in Latin translations, the education available within cathedral and monastery schools had been limited. Students learned grammar, rhetoric, and elementary geometry and astronomy. They had the classical Latin grammars of Donatus and Priscian, Saint Augustine's treatise *On Christian Doctrine* and Cassiodorus's treatise On *Divine and Secular Learning.* The writings of Boethius provided instruction in arithmetic and music and preserved the small body of Aristotle's works on logic then known in the West. After the textual finds of the early twelfth century, Western scholars possessed the whole of Aristotle's logic, the astronomy of Ptolemy, the writings of Euclid, and many Latin classics. By the mid–thirteenth century, almost all of Aristotle's works circulated in the West.

In the High Middle Ages, the learning process was basic. The assumption was that truth already existed; one did not have to go out and find it. Such conviction made logic and dialectic the focus of education. Students wrote commentaries on authoritative texts, especially those of Aristotle and the Church Fathers. This method of study, based on logic and dialectic, was known as **Scholasticism.** It reigned supreme in all the faculties—in law and medicine as well as in philosophy and theology. Students read the traditional authorities in their field, formed short summaries of their teaching, disputed them with their peers, and then drew conclusions.

In this engraving, a teacher at the University of Paris leads fellow scholars in a discussion. As shown here, all of the students wore the scholar's cap and gown.

CORBIS/Bettmann

How was the medieval understanding of knowledge reflected in medieval approaches to classroom instruction?

Few books existed for students and those available were expensive hand-copied works. Students had to master a subject through lecture, discussion, and debate. This required memorization and the ability to think on one's feet. Rhetoric, or persuasive argument, was the ultimate goal, an ability to eloquently defend the knowledge one had gained by logic and dialectic.

PHILOSOPHY AND THEOLOGY

Scholastics quarreled over the proper relationship between philosophy, by which they meant almost exclusively the writings of Aristotle, and theology, which they believed to be a "science" based on divine revelation. The problem between philosophy and theology arose because, in Christian eyes, Aristotle's writings contained heresy. Aristotle, for example, taught the eternality of the world, which called into question the Judeo-Christian teaching that God created the world in time, as the book of Genesis said. Church authorities wanted the works of Aristotle and other ancient authorities to be submissive handmaidens to Christian truth.

Abelard When philosophers and theologians applied the logic and metaphysics of Aristotle to the interpretation of Christian revelation, many believed it posed a mortal threat to biblical truth and church authority. Few philosophers and theologians gained greater notoriety for such wrongful interpretation of the Scriptures than Peter Abelard (1079–1142). No one promoted the new Aristotelian learning more boldly than he, nor did any other pay more dearly for it. His bold subjection of church teaching to Aristotelian logic and dialectic made him many powerful enemies at a time when there was no tenure to protect genius and free speech in schools and universities. Accused of multiple transgressions of church doctrine, he recounted in an autobiography the "calamities" that had befallen him over a lifetime because of his boldness.

His critics especially condemned him for his subjective interpretations of Scripture. Rather than a God-begotten cosmic ransom of humankind from the Devil, Christ's crucifixion, he argued, redeemed Christians by virtue of its impact on their hearts and minds when they heard the story. Abelard's ethical teaching stressed intent over deed: The motives of the doer made an act good or evil, not the act itself. Inner feelings were thus more important for receiving divine forgiveness than the church's sacrament of penance administered by a priest.

Abelard's native genius and youthful disrespect for seniority and tradition gained him powerful enemies in high places. He gave those enemies the opportunity to strike him down when, in Paris, where he became Master of Students at Notre Dame, he seduced a bright, seventeen-year-old niece of a powerful canon, who hired him to be her tutor in his home. Her name was Héloïse and their passionate affair ended in public scandal, with Héloïse pregnant. Intent on punishing Abelard and ending his career, the enraged uncle exposed their secret marriage and hired men to castrate Abelard.

In the aftermath of those terrible events, the lovers entered cloisters nearby Paris: Héloïse at Argentueil, Abelard at St. Denis. She continued to love Abelard and relive their passion in her mind, while Abelard became a self-condemning recluse, assuring Héloïse in his letters to her that his "love" had only been wretched desire. In 1121, a church synod ordered all his writings to be burned. Another synod in 1140 condemned nineteen propositions from his philosophical and theological works as heresy. Retracting his teaching, Abelard lived out the remaining two years of his life in an obscure priory near Chalons. As for Héloïse, she lived another twenty years and gained renown for her positive efforts to reform the rules for the cloistered life of women, under which she had suffered.

WOMEN IN MEDIEVAL SOCIETY

WHAT WAS life like for women during the Middle Ages?

The image and the reality of medieval women are two different things. Male Christian clergy, whose ideal was a celibate life of chastity, poverty, and obedience, strongly influenced the image. Drawing on the Bible and classical medical, philosophical, and legal traditions predating Christianity, Christian thinkers depicted women as physically, mentally, and morally weaker than men.

Image and Status

Both within and outside Christianity, this image of women was contradicted. In chivalric romances and courtly love literature of the twelfth and thirteenth centuries, as in the contemporaneous cult of the Virgin Mary, women were put on pedestals and treated as

COMPARE & CONNECT

FAITH AND LOVE IN THE HIGH MIDDLE AGES

Separate and apart in their respective cloisters, Abelard and Héloïse performed a lengthy post-mortem on their tragic love affair in letters to one another. Therein, they showed their open wounds and shared completely different assessments of where their love had led them. Unhappy in the cloister, Héloïse had only regret for what they had lost, while Abelard, having found his true self in the cloister, looked back on their relationship only with shame.

QUESTIONS

1. Did the expectations of contemporary religion and culture contribute to the tragedy of their love?
2. Did they have only themselves to blame?
3. Which of the two understood the situation better? Who, in the end, was the stronger?

I. HÉLOÏSE TO ABELARD

Why, after our conversion [and entrance into the cloisters], which you alone decreed, am I fallen into such neglect and oblivion that I am neither refreshed by your presence, nor comforted by a letter in your absence . . . When I was enjoying carnal pleasures with you, many were uncertain whether I did so from love or from desire. Now the end [result] shows the spirit [in which I acted]. I have forbidden myself all pleasures so that I might obey your will. I have reserved nothing for myself, save this one thing: to be entirely yours . . .

When we enjoyed the delights of love . . . we were spared divine wrath. But when we corrected the unlawful with the lawful [by marriage] and covered the filth of fornication with the honesty of marriage, the wrath of the Lord vehemently fell upon us . . . For men taken in the most flagrant adultery what you suffered [castration] would have been a proper punishment. But what others might merit by adultery, you incurred by a [proper] marriage. What an adulteress brings to her lover, your own wife brought to you! And this did not happen when we were still indulging our old pleasures, but when we were separated and living chaste lives apart . . .

So sweet to me were those delights of lovers that they can neither displease me nor pass from my memory. Whatever I am doing, they always come to mind. Not even when I am asleep do they spare me . . . [At] Mass, when prayer ought to be pure, the memory of those delights thoroughly captivate my wretched soul rather than heed my prayers. And although I ought to lament what I have done, I sigh rather for what I now have to forego. Not only the things that we did, but the places and the times in which we did them are so fixed with you in my mind that I reenact them all . . . At times the thoughts of my mind

superior to men in purity. If the church harbored misogynist sentiments, it also condemned them, as in the case of the late-thirteenth-century *Romance of the Rose* and other popular bawdy literature.

The learned churchman Peter Lombard (1100–1169), whose *Four Books of the Sentences* every theological student annotated, asked why Eve had been created from Adam's rib rather than from his head or his feet? The answer: God took Eve from Adam's side because she was meant neither to rule over man, nor to be man's slave, but rather to stand squarely at his side, as his companion and partner in mutual aid and trust. By such insis-

are betrayed by the very motions of my body . . . 'O wretched person that I am, who shall deliver me from this body of death?' Would that I might truthfully add what follows: 'I thank God through Jesus Christ our Lord.'

II. ABELARD TO HÉLOÏSE

Heloise, my lust sacrificed our bodies to such great infamy that no reverence for honor, nor for God, or for the days of our Lord's passion, or for any solemn thing whatsoever could I be stopped from wallowing in that filth . . . [and although you resisted] I made you consent. Wherefore most justly . . . of that part of my body have I been diminished wherein was the seat of my lust . . . God truly loved you [Heloise], not I. My love . . . was lust, not love. I satisfied my wretched desires in you . . . So weep for your Savior, not for your seducer, for your Redeemer, not for your defiler, for the Lord who died for you, not for me, his servant, who is now truly free for the first time . . .

O how detestable a loss [it would have been] if, given over to carnal pleasure, you were to bring forth a few children . . . for the world, when you are now delivered of a numerous progeny [i.e. the young nuns who are Heloise's wards in the cloister]. Nor would you then be more than a woman, you who now transcend even men, and have turned the curse of Eve into the blessing of Mary [by your chastity in the cloister]. O how indecent it would be for those holy hands of yours, which now turn the pages of sacred books, to serve the obscenities of womanly cares.

Source: *Letters of Abelard and Héloïse*, trans. by Charles Moncrieff (New York: Alfred A. Knopf, 1942), pp. 59–61, 78, 81, 97–98, 100, 103.

Adam and Eve were not cast out of the Garden of Eden because of their sexual lust for one another but rather for their disobedience to God in eating the forbidden fruit from the Tree of Knowledge of Good and Evil. St. Augustine who, like Abelard, was known to exhibit a certain weakness for the charms of the opposite sex, taught that before their Fall, Adam and Eve had complete control over their libidos as opposed to their libidos having complete control over them. Their minds and hearts filled only with thoughts of God when, without any shame or self-indulgence, they engaged in sexual intercourse. Abelard and Héloïse's sexual lust and shame serve as a commentary on fallen humankind, tracing back to Adam and Eve.

Courtesy of the Library of Congress, Rare book and Special Collections Division

How would you explain the fact that so many medieval books were highly ornate and richly decorated?

tence on the spiritual equality of men and women and their shared responsibility in marriage, the church to this extent also helped protect the dignity of women.

Germanic law treated women better than Roman law had done, recognizing basic rights that forbade their treatment as chattel. All major Germanic law codes recognized the economic freedom of women: their right to inherit, administer, dispose of, and confer property and wealth on their children. They could also press charges in court against men for bodily injury and rape, whose punishment, depending on the circumstances, ranged from fines, flogging, and banishment to blinding, castration, and death.

(a)

(b)

(c)

A fourteenth-century English manuscript shows women at their daily tasks: carrying jugs of milk from the sheep pen, feeding the chickens, carding and spinning wool.

By permission of The British Library

What role did ordinary women play in the economic life of medieval Europe?

Life Choices

The nunnery was an option for single women from the higher social classes. Entrance required a dowry and could be almost as expensive as a wedding, although usually cheaper. Within the nunnery, a woman could rise to a position of leadership as an abbess or a mother superior, exercising authority denied her in much of secular life. The nunneries of the established religious orders remained under male supervision, however, so that even abbesses had to answer to higher male authority.

In the ninth century, under the influence of Christianity, the Carolingians made monogamous marriage official policy. Heretofore they had practiced polygamy and concubinage and permitted divorce. The result was both a boon and a burden to women. On one hand, wives gained greater dignity and legal security. On the other hand, a wife's labor as household manager and bearer of children greatly increased.

Working Women

Most medieval women were neither housewives nor nuns, but workers like their husbands. Between the ages of ten and fifteen, girls were apprenticed and gained trade skills much as did boys. If they married, they often continued their trade, operating their bake or dress shops next to their husbands' businesses, or becoming assistants and partners in the shops of their husbands. Women appeared in virtually every "blue-collar" trade, from butcher to goldsmith, but mostly worked in the food and clothing industries. Women belonged to guilds, just like men, and they became craft masters. By the fifteenth century, townswomen increasingly had the opportunity to go to school and gain at least vernacular literacy.

Women's gender, however, excluded them from the learned professions of scholarship, medicine, and law. Women's freedom of movement within a profession was more often regulated than a man's and their wages for the same work were not as great. Still, women remained as prominent and as creative a part of workaday medieval society as men. Rare was the medieval woman who considered herself merely a wife.

THE LIVES OF CHILDREN

WHAT WERE the characteristics of childhood in the Middle Ages?

The image of medieval children and the reality of their lives were also two different things. Until recently, historians were inclined to believe that parents were emotionally distant from their children during the Middle Ages. Evidence of low esteem for children comes from a variety of sources.

Children as "Little Adults"

Some historians maintain that medieval art and sculpture rarely portray children as being different from adults. If, pictorially, children and adults look alike, does that mean that people in the Middle Ages were unaware that childhood was a separate period of life requiring special care and treatment? High infant and child mortality also existed, which, one theorizes, could only have discouraged parents from making a deep emotional investment in their children.

During the Middle Ages, children also assumed adult responsibilities early in life. The children of peasants labored in the fields alongside their parents as soon as they could physically manage the work. Urban artisans and burghers sent their children out of their homes into apprenticeships in various crafts and trades between the ages of eight and twelve. Could loving parents remove a child from the home at so tender an age?

The practice of infanticide is another striking suggestion of low esteem for children in ancient and early medieval times. According to the Roman historian Tacitus (ca. 55–120), the Romans exposed unwanted children, especially girls, at birth to regulate family size. Infanticide, particularly of girls, continued to be practiced in the early Middle Ages, if its condemnation in penance books and by church synods is any measure.

Childhood as a Special Stage

Despite such evidence of parental distance and neglect, there is another side to the story. Since the early Middle Ages, physicians and theologians had understood childhood to be a distinct and special stage of life. Isidore (560–636), bishop of Seville and a leading intellectual authority throughout the Middle Ages, distinguished six ages of life, the first four of which were infancy, childhood, adolescence, and youth.

According to the medical authorities, infancy proper extended from birth to anywhere between six months and two years and covered the period of speechlessness and suckling. The period thereafter, until age seven, was considered a higher level of infancy, marked by the beginning of a child's ability to speak and his or her weaning. At seven, when a child could think, act decisively, and speak clearly, childhood proper began. At this point a child could be reasoned with, profit from regular discipline, and begin to learn vocational skills. At seven a child was ready for schooling, private tutoring, or apprenticeship in a chosen craft or trade. Until physical growth was complete, which could extend to twenty-one years of age, the child or youth remained legally under the guardianship of parents or a surrogate authority.

There is evidence that high infant and child mortality, rather than distancing parents from their children, actually made them all the more precious to them. Both in learned and in popular medicine, sensible as well as fanciful cures existed for the leading killers of children (diarrhea, worms, pneumonia, and fever). When infants and children died, medieval parents can be found grieving as pitiably as modern parents do. In the art and literature of the Middle Ages, we find mothers baptizing dead infants and children, even carrying them to pilgrim shrines in the hope of miraculous revival.

Clear evidence of special attention being paid to children may be seen in children's toys and aids (walkers and potty chairs). Medieval authorities on child rearing widely condemned child abuse and urged moderation in disciplining and punishing children. In church art and drama, parents were urged to love their children as Mary loved Jesus. Early apprenticeships may also be seen as an expression of parental love and concern. In the Middle Ages, no parental responsibility was greater than that of equipping a child for useful and gainful work. Certainly, by the High Middle Ages if not earlier, children were widely viewed as special creatures with their own needs and rights.

SUMMARY

WHAT WAS the relationship between the three basic groups in medieval society?

The Traditional Order of Life The nobility were warriors who lived off the labor of others and resided in mansions or castles in the countryside. The clergy constituted a noticeable portion of the medieval population. The "regular" clergy, who lived separately from the world, and the "secular" clergy, who lived among the laity, had their own hierarchies and responsibilities. The agrarian peasantry were the largest and most significant group. During the Middle Ages, families were the basic socioeconomic unit. *page 202*

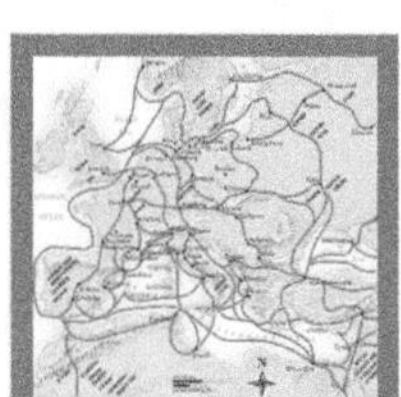

WHAT PROCESSES led to the rise of towns and a merchant class?

Towns and Townspeople Towns grew in size and significance. The nobility and upper clergy's newfound taste for fancy manufactured goods was an early impetus for the growth of towns. Ironically, as towns grew and artisans and traders gained status, it was generally the nobility that suffered. Throughout Europe, it was common for townspeople and kings to form alliances that impinged on the traditional powers of the nobility. Cities, especially in France and Germany, also attracted large numbers of Jews. *page 208*

WHAT INTELLECTUAL trends accompanied the rise of universities?

Schools and Universities Starting in Bologna in 1158, Western universities taught the *trivium* (language arts) and the *quadrivium* (math). Scholasticism, the favored method of study, relied on logic, memorization, argumentation, and recitation. Most of the content of the instruction came from Latin translations of Greek and Arabic texts. Scholastics quarreled over the proper relationship of philosophy and theology. The life of Peter Abelard illustrates the danger of overly independent thinking in the Middle Ages. *page 212*

WHAT WAS life like for women during the Middle Ages?

Women in Medieval Society The male Christian clergy portrayed women in the Middle Ages as having two options: subjugated housewife or confined nun. The vast majority of them, in fact, worked in a range of trades, although they were concentrated in the food and clothing industries. Nuns avoided the problems associated with pregnancy and could attain some power. Aristocratic women could manage large households. *page 215*

WHAT WERE the characteristics of childhood in the Middle Ages?

The Lives of Children Most historians have probably misunderstood the lives of children in the Middle Ages. Children had a 30 to 50 percent chance of dying before they turned five, so some historians have suggested that parents would not risk making a big emotional investment in young children. Children worked as soon as they were able and are depicted in medieval art as "little adults," so some historians have wondered whether people in the Middle Ages had an understanding of childhood as a distinct phase of life, with its own needs. But medieval medical and clerical authorities did, in fact, write about childhood as a special stage in life, and evidence indicates that parents and society at large cherished their babies and children. *page 218*

Review Questions

1. How did the responsibilities of the nobility differ from those of the clergy and peasantry during the High Middle Ages? What led to the revival of trade and the growth of towns in the twelfth century? How did towns change medieval society?
2. What were the strengths and weaknesses of the educations provided by medieval universities? How would you evaluate the standard curriculum?
3. How would you define Scholasticism? What was the Scholastic program and method of study? Who were the main critics of Scholasticism, and what were their complaints?
4. Do Germanic law and Roman law reflect different understandings of the position of women in society? How did options and responsibilities differ for women in each of the social classes? What are the theories concerning the concept of childhood in the Middle Ages?

KEY TERMS

banalities (p. 207)
guild (p. 210)
liberal arts (p. 213)
manor (p. 206)
regular clergy (p. 205)
Scholasticism (p. 214)
secular clergy (p. 205)

For additional learning resources related to this chapter, please go to **www.myhistorylab.com**

PEARSON myhistorylab

9

The Late Middle Ages:

Social and Political Breakdown (1300–1453)

A procession of flagellants at Tournai in Flanders in 1349, marching with the crucified Christ and scourging themselves in imitation of his suffering.

What was the psychological impact of the Black Death on medieval Europe?

THE BLACK DEATH *page 224*

WHAT WERE the social and economic consequences of the "Black Death"?

THE HUNDRED YEARS' WAR AND THE RISE OF NATIONAL SENTIMENT *page 228*

HOW DID the Hundred Years' War contribute to a growing sense of national identity in France and England?

ECCLESIASTICAL BREAKDOWN AND REVIVAL: THE LATE MEDIEVAL CHURCH *page 232*

HOW DID secular rulers challenge papal authority in the fourteenth and fifteenth centuries?

MEDIEVAL RUSSIA *page 239*

HOW DID Mongol rule shape Russia's development?

The West endured so many calamities as the Middle Ages drew to a close that European civilization seemed in imminent danger of collapse. From 1337 to 1453, France and England were locked in a bloody conflict called the Hundred Years' War. Between 1347 and 1350, a devastating plague swept through Europe and carried off a third of its population. In 1378, a quarrel between competing candidates for the papacy began a schism that kept the church divided for thirty-nine years. In 1453, the Turks overran Constantinople and charged up the Danube valley toward the heart of Europe.

These crises were accompanied by intellectual developments that undercut many of the assumptions about faith, life, and the social order that had comforted earlier generations. Some philosophers concluded that human reason is much more limited in scope than the Scholastics had realized. Feudal institutions, which had been assumed to be divinely ordained, were assaulted by kings who aspired to absolute monarchy. Competing claims to authority were made by kings and popes, and both of these leaders were challenged by political theorists who argued that subjects had the right to hold rulers accountable for how they used their power. ■

THE BLACK DEATH

WHAT WERE the social and economic consequences of the "Black Death"?

The virulent plague known as the Black Death struck fourteenth-century Europe when it was already suffering from overpopulation and malnutrition.

Preconditions and Causes of the Plague

In the fourteenth century, nine-tenths of the population worked the land. The three-field system of crop production increased the amount of arable land and with it the food supply. As that supply grew, however, so did the population. It is estimated that Europe's population doubled between the years 1000 and 1300 and began thereafter to outstrip food production.

Between 1315 and 1317, crop failures produced the greatest famine of the Middle Ages. Densely populated urban areas such as the industrial towns of the Netherlands suffered greatly. Decades of overpopulation, economic depression, famine, and bad health progressively weakened Europe's population and made it highly vulnerable to a virulent bubonic plague that struck with full force in 1348.

Black Death Virulent plague that struck in Sicily in 1347 and spread through Europe. It discolored the bodies of its victims. By the early fifteenth century, the plague may have reduced the population of western Europe by two-fifths.

The **Black Death** followed the trade routes from Asia into Europe. Rats, or more precisely, the fleas the rats bore, on ships from the Black Sea area most likely brought it to Western Europe. Appearing in Constantinople in 1346 and Sicily in late 1347, it entered Europe through the ports of Venice, Genoa, and Pisa in 1348. From there it swept rapidly through Spain and southern France and into northern Europe. Areas that lay outside the major trade routes, like Bohemia, appear to have remained virtually unaffected. Bubonic plague made numerous reappearances in succeeding decades. (See Map 9–1.)

Popular Remedies

Contemporaries could neither explain the plague nor defend themselves against it. To them, the Black Death was a catastrophe with no apparent explanation and against which there was no known defense. (See "Encountering the Past: Medieval Medicine," page 227.) Throughout much of Western Europe, it inspired an obsession with death and dying and a deep pessimism that endured long after the plague years.

Popular wisdom held that a corruption in the atmosphere caused the disease. Some blamed poisonous fumes released by earthquakes. Many wore aromatic amulets

MAP EXPLORATION

Interactive map: To explore this map further, go to www.myhistorylab.com

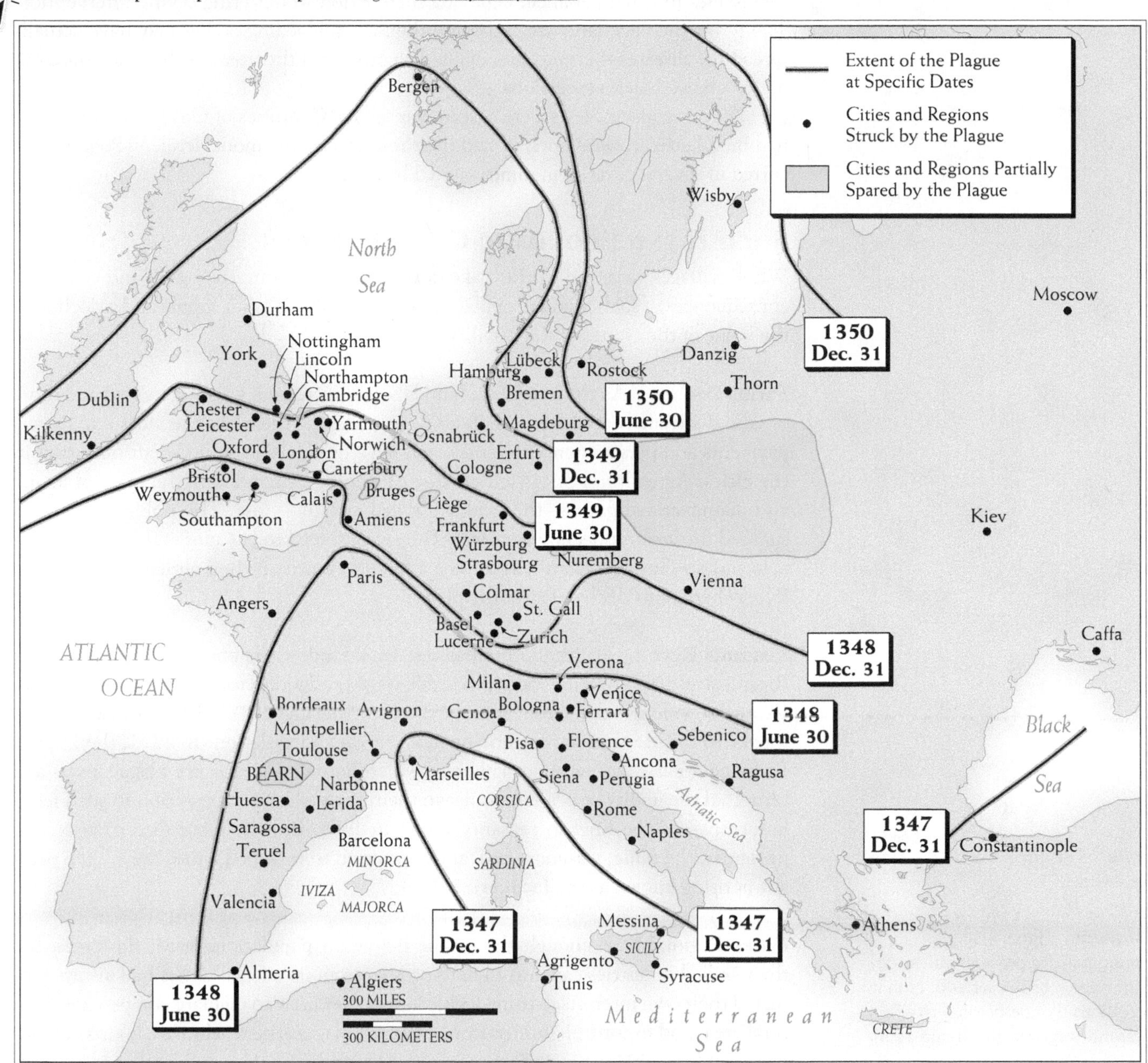

MAP 9–1 **Spread of the Black Death** Apparently introduced by seaborne rats from Black Sea areas where plague-infested rodents had long been known, the Black Death brought huge human, social, and economic consequences. One of the lower estimates of Europeans dying is 25 million. The map charts the plague's spread in the mid–fourteenth century. Generally following trade routes, the plague reached Scandinavia by 1350, and some believe it then went on to Iceland and even Greenland. Areas off the main trade routes were largely spared.

What does the spread of the plague indicate about the networks of trade routes and economic development in Europe in the mid-fourteenth century?

as a remedy. There was a wide range of psychological and emotional responses to the crisis. One extreme reaction was processions of flagellants, religious fanatics who beat themselves in ritual penance, believing such action would bring divine intervention. The terror the flagellants created—and their dirty, bleeding bodies may have actually spread the disease—became so socially disruptive and threatening that the church finally outlawed such processions.

In some places, Jews were cast as scapegoats. Centuries of Christian propaganda had bred hatred toward Jews, as had their role as society's moneylenders. Pogroms occurred in several cities, sometimes incited by the flagellants.

Social and Economic Consequences

Whole villages vanished in the wake of the plague. Among the social and economic consequences of such high depopulation were a shrunken labor supply and a decline in the value of the estates of the nobility.

Farms Decline As the number of farm laborers decreased, wages increased and those of skilled artisans soared. Many serfs chose to commute their labor services into money payments and pursue more interesting and rewarding jobs in skilled craft industries in the cities. Agricultural prices fell because of waning demand, and the price of luxury and manufactured goods—the work of skilled artisans—rose. The noble landholders suffered the greatest decline in power. They were forced to pay more for finished products and for farm labor, while receiving a smaller return on their agricultural produce. Everywhere rents declined after the plague.

Peasants Revolt To recoup their losses, some landowners converted arable land to sheep pasture, substituting more profitable wool production for labor-intensive grains. Others abandoned the farms, leasing them to the highest bidder. Landowners also sought to reverse their misfortune by new repressive legislation. In 1351, the English Parliament passed a Statute of Laborers, which limited wages to pre-plague levels and restricted the ability of peasants to leave their masters' land. Opposition to such legislation sparked the English peasants' revolt in 1381. In France the direct tax on the peasantry, the ***taille***, was increased, and opposition to it helped ignite the French peasant uprising known as the **Jacquerie**.

taille The direct tax on the French peasantry.

Jacquerie (From "Jacques Bonhomme," a peasant caricature) Name given to the series of bloody rebellions that desperate French peasants waged beginning in 1358.

Cities Rebound Although the plague hit urban populations hard, the cities and their skilled industries came in time to prosper from its effects. Cities had always protected their own interests, passing legislation as they grew to regulate competition from rural areas and to control immigration. After the plague, the reach of such laws extended beyond the cities to include the surrounding lands of nobles and landlords, many of whom now peacefully integrated into urban life.

Expensive clothes and jewelry, furs from the north, and silks from the south were in great demand in the decades after the plague. The prices of manufactured and luxury items rose to new heights, which, in turn, encouraged workers to migrate from the countryside to the city and learn the skills of artisans. Townspeople profited coming and going. As wealth poured into the cities and per capita income rose, the prices of agricultural products from the countryside, now less in demand, declined.

The church also gained and lost. It suffered as a landholder and was politically weakened, yet it also received new revenues from the vastly increased demand for religious services for the dead and the dying, along with new gifts and bequests.

ENCOUNTERING THE PAST

Medieval Medicine

Medieval medicine was a mix of practices ranging from diet, exercise regimens, and medicines to prayer, magical amulets, and incantations. Celestial forces (the stars and planets) were assumed to influence human physical and mental states, and physicians turned to astrology for help in explaining illnesses and devising treatments. In a world where lives tended to be short and suffering difficult to ease, people were desperate for cures and willing to take advice from any source. The wealthy sought help from university-trained physicians. These men were the most prestigious, if not inevitably the most effective, healers. They relied on diet and medication to treat internal illnesses. Apothecaries supplied their patients with medicinal herbs, and surgeons performed any physical operations they prescribed. Some surgeons had university educations, but many were humble barbers who learned their trade as apprentices.

Bloodletting was prescribed as a treatment for illness and a preservative of health, for medical theory held that illness was a result of an imbalance of humors (fluids) in the body. Greek science maintained there were four elements (earth, air, fire, and water), each associated with a quality (hot, cold, moist, and dry). The mix of these in the body determined its condition, and treatment called for draining off excesses or shifting humors to different locations in the body. Physicians commonly diagnosed problems by examining urine and blood and checking pulses. The urine flask was the medieval equivalent of the stethoscope—the badge of the physician.

A Caricature of Physicians (Early Sixteenth Century). A physician carries a uroscope (for collecting and examining urine); discolored urine signaled an immediate need for bleeding. The physician/surgeon wears surgical shoes and his assistant carries a flail—a comment on the risks of medical services.

Hacker Art Books Inc.

How did medieval doctors respond to the challenges the plague presented?

WHAT KIND of medical help was available to medieval people?

New Conflicts and Opportunities

The economic and political power of local artisans and trade guilds grew steadily in the late Middle Ages, along with the demand for their goods and services. The merchant and patrician classes found it increasingly difficult to maintain their traditional dominance and grudgingly gave guild masters a voice in city government. As the guilds won political power, they encouraged restrictive legislation to protect local industries. The restrictions, in turn, caused conflict between master artisans, who wanted to keep their numbers low and expand their industries at a snail's pace, and the many journeymen, who were eager to rise to the rank of master. To the long-existing conflict between the guilds and the ruling urban patriciate was now added one within the guilds themselves.

Also, after 1350, the results of the plague put two traditional "containers" of monarchy—the landed nobility and the church—on the defensive. Kings now exploited growing national sentiment in an effort to centralize their governments and

Overview Effects of the Black Death

SOCIAL	Rumors abounded that unpopular minorities were spreading the disease. Serfs began to abandon farming for more lucrative jobs in towns.
ECONOMIC	Agricultural profits diminished because consumers were fewer. Prices rose for luxury and manufactured goods as artisans became scarce.
CULTURAL	Churches saw increased demand for masses for the dead. Deep pessimism, superstition, and obsession with death were inspired.
POLITICAL	Nobles used their monopoly of political power to reverse declining fortunes. Laws passed freezing low wages and ordering peasants to stay on the land.

economies. At the same time, the battles of the Hundred Years' War demonstrated the military superiority of paid professional armies over the traditional noble cavalry, thus bringing the latter's future role into question. The plague also killed many members of the clergy—perhaps one-third of the German clergy fell victim as they dutifully ministered to the sick and dying. This reduction in clerical ranks occurred in the same century that saw the pope move from Rome to Avignon in southeast France (1309–1377) and the Great Schism (1378–1417) divide the Church into warring factions.

THE HUNDRED YEARS' WAR AND THE RISE OF NATIONAL SENTIMENT

HOW DID the Hundred Years' War contribute to a growing sense of national identity in France and England?

To field the armies and collect the revenues that made their existence possible, late medieval rulers depended on carefully negotiated alliances among a wide range of lesser powers. To maintain the order they required, the Norman kings of England and the Capetian kings of France fine-tuned traditional feudal relationships by stressing the duties of lesser to higher powers and the unquestioning loyalty noble vassals owed to the king. The result was a degree of centralized royal power unseen before in these lands and a growing national consciousness that together equipped both France and England for international warfare.

The Causes of the War

The conflict that came to be known as the Hundred Years' War began in May 1337 and lasted until October 1453. The English king Edward III (r. 1327–1377), the grandson of Philip the Fair of France (r. 1285–1314), may have started the war by asserting a claim to the French throne after the French king Charles IV (r. 1322–1328), the last of Philip the Fair's surviving sons, died without a male heir. The French barons had no intention of placing the then fifteen-year-old Edward on the French throne. They chose instead the first cousin of Charles IV, Philip VI of Valois (r. 1328–1350), the first of a new French dynasty that would rule into the sixteenth century.

But there was, of course, more to the war than just an English king's assertion of a claim to the French throne. England and France were then emergent territorial powers in too close proximity to one another. Edward was actually a vassal of Philip VI, holding several sizable French territories as fiefs from the king of France. English possession of any French land was repugnant to the French because it threatened the royal policy of centralization. England and France also quarreled over control of Flanders, which, although a French fief, was subject to political influence from England because its principal industry, the manufacture of cloth, depended on supplies of imported English wool. Compounding these frictions was a long history of prejudice and animosity between the French and English people, who constantly confronted one another on the high seas and in ports. Taken together, these various factors made the Hundred Years' War a struggle for national identity as well as for control of territory.

Edward III pays homage to his feudal lord Philip VI of France. Legally, Edward was a vassal of the king of France.

Archives Snark International/Art Resource, NY

What tensions were there between ties of vassalage and national identity?

French Weakness For most of the conflict, until after 1415, the major battles ended in often stunning English victories. (See Map 9–2, page 230.) The primary reason for these French failures was internal disunity caused by endemic social conflicts. Unlike England, fourteenth-century France was still struggling to make the transition from a splintered feudal society to a centralized "modern" state.

Desperate to raise money for the war, French kings resorted to such financial policies as depreciating the currency and borrowing heavily from Italian bankers, which aggravated internal conflicts. In 1355, in a bid to secure funds, the king turned to the **Estates General**, a representative council of townspeople, clergy, and nobles. Although it levied taxes at the king's request, its independent members also exploited the king's plight to broaden their own regional sovereignty, thereby deepening territorial divisions.

Estates General Assembly of representatives from France's propertied classes.

France's defeats also reflected English military superiority. The English infantry was more disciplined than the French, and English archers carried a formidable weapon, the longbow, capable of firing six arrows a minute with enough force to pierce an inch of wood or the armor of a knight at two hundred yards.

Finally, French weakness during the Hundred Years' War was due, in no small degree, to the comparative mediocrity of its royal leadership. English kings were far shrewder.

Progress of the War

The war had three major stages of development, each ending with a seemingly decisive victory by one or the other side.

The Conflict During the Reign of Edward III In the first stage of the war, Edward embargoed English wool to Flanders, sparking urban rebellions by merchants and the trade guilds. The Flemish cities revolted against the French and in 1340 signed an alliance with England acknowledging Edward as king of France. On June 23 of that same year, in the first great battle of the war, Edward defeated the French fleet in the Bay of Sluys, but his subsequent effort to invade France by way of Flanders failed.

In 1346, Edward attacked Normandy and, after a series of easy victories that culminated at the Battle of Crécy, seized the port of Calais. Exhaustion of both sides and the onset of the Black Death forced a truce in late 1347, as the war entered a brief lull. In 1356, near Poitiers, the English won their greatest victory, routing France's noble cavalry and taking the French king, John II the Good (r. 1350–1364), captive back to England. A complete breakdown of political order in France followed.

MAP EXPLORATION

Interactive map: To explore this map further, go to www.myhistorylab.com

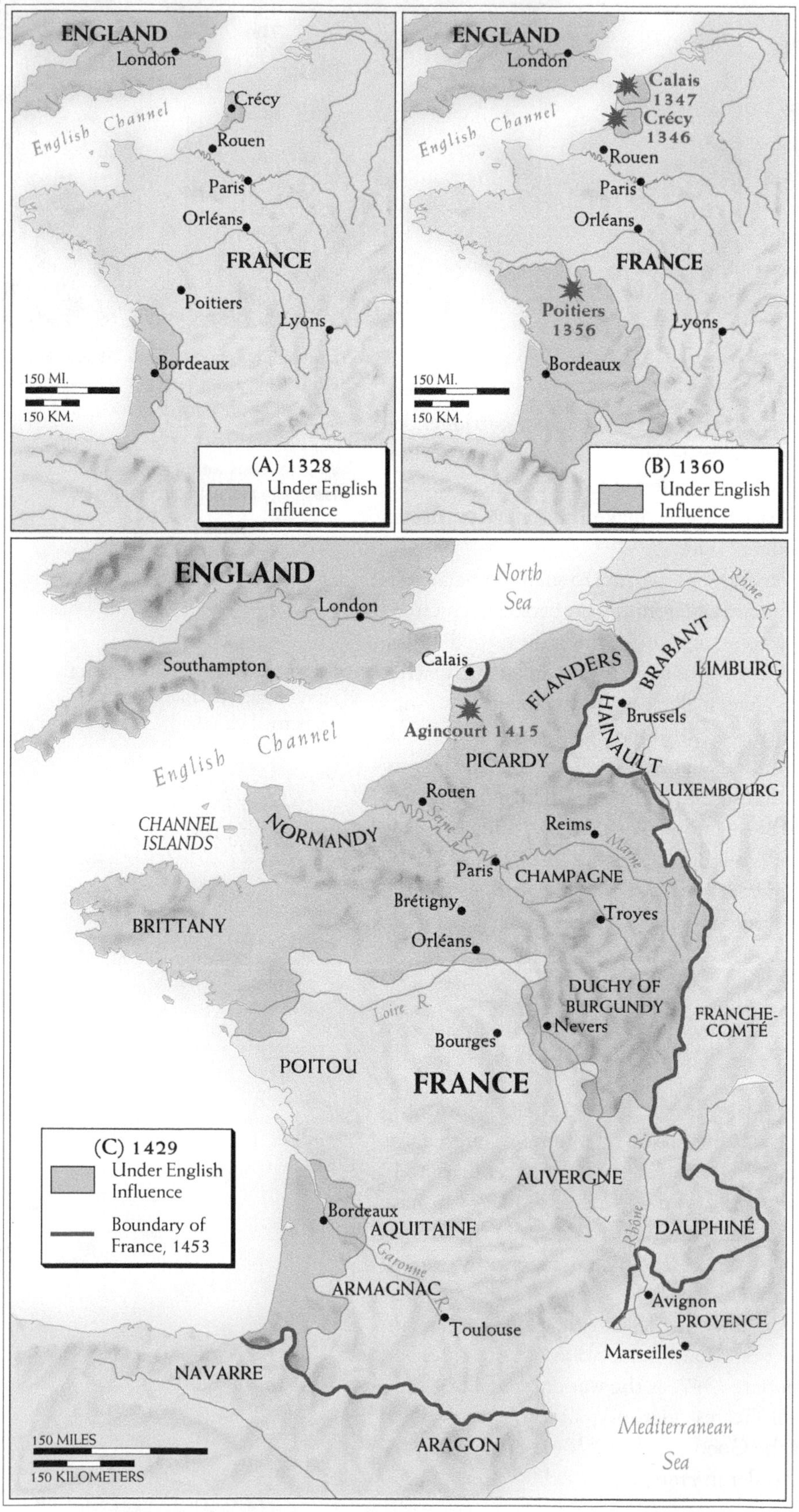

Power in France now lay with the Estates General. Led by the powerful merchants of Paris, that body took advantage of royal weakness, demanding and receiving rights similar to those the Magna Carta had granted to the English privileged classes. Yet, unlike the English Parliament, which represented the interests of a comparatively unified English nobility, the French Estates General was too divided to be an instrument for effective government.

To secure their rights, the French privileged classes forced the peasantry to pay ever-increasing taxes and to repair their war-damaged properties without compensation. This bullying became more than the peasants could bear, and they rose up in several regions in a series of bloody rebellions known as the Jacquerie in 1358. The nobility quickly put down the revolt, matching the rebels atrocity for atrocity.

On May 9, 1360, another milestone of the war was reached when England forced the Peace of Brétigny-Calais on the French. This agreement declared an end to Edward's vassalage to the king of France and affirmed his sovereignty over English territories in France (including Gascony, Guyenne, Poitou, and Calais). France also agreed to pay a ransom of 3 million gold crowns to win King John the Good's release. In return, Edward simply renounced his claim to the French throne.

Such a partition was unrealistic, and sober observers on both sides knew it could not last. France struck back in the late 1360s and, by the time of Edward's death in 1377, had beaten the English back to coastal enclaves and the territory around Bordeaux.

MAP 9–2 **The Hundred Years' War** The Hundred Years' War went on intermittently from the late 1330s until 1453. These maps show the remarkable English territorial gains up to the sudden and decisive turning of the tide of battle in favor of the French by the forces of Joan of Arc in 1429.

Using the map as a reference, what were the major English victories or French weaknesses that led to England's significant influence in France by 1429?

French Defeat and the Treaty of Troyes After Edward's death the English war effort lessened, partly because of domestic problems within England. During the reign of Richard II (r. 1377–1399), England had its own version of the Jacquerie. In June 1381, long-oppressed peasants and artisans joined in a great revolt of the underprivileged classes under the leadership of John Ball, a secular priest, and Wat Tyler, a journeyman. As in France, the revolt was brutally crushed within the year, but it left the country divided for decades.

England recommenced the war under Henry V (r. 1413–1422), who took advantage of internal French turmoil created by the rise to power of the duchy of Burgundy. With France deeply divided, Henry V struck hard in Normandy, routing the French at Agincourt on October 25, 1415. In the years thereafter, belatedly recognizing that the defeat of France would leave them easy prey for the English, the Burgundians closed ranks with French royal forces. The renewed French unity was shattered in September 1419 when the duke of Burgundy was assassinated. The duke's son and heir, determined to avenge his father's death, joined forces with the English.

France now became Henry V's for the taking—at least in the short run. The Treaty of Troyes in 1420 disinherited the legitimate heir to the French throne and proclaimed Henry V the successor to the French king, Charles VI. When Henry and Charles died within months of one another in 1422, the infant Henry VI of England was proclaimed in Paris to be king of both France and England.

The son of Charles VI went into retreat in Bourges, where, on the death of his father, he became Charles VII to most of the French people, who ignored the Treaty of Troyes. Displaying unprecedented national feeling inspired by the remarkable Joan of Arc, they soon rallied to his cause and united in an ultimately victorious coalition.

A contemporary portrait of Joan of Arc (1412–1431) in the National Archives in Paris.

Anonymous, 15th century. Joan of Arc. Franco-Flemish miniature. Archives Nationales, Paris, France. Photograph copyright Bridgeman-Giraudon/Art Resource, NY

Who felt threatened by Joan of Arc? Why?

Joan of Arc and the War's Conclusion Joan of Arc (1412–1431), a peasant from Domrémy in Lorraine in eastern France, presented herself to Charles VII in March 1429, declaring that the King of Heaven had called her to deliver besieged Orléans from the English. Charles's desperation overcame his skepticism, and he gave Joan his leave. Circumstances worked perfectly to her advantage. The English force, already exhausted by a six-month siege, was at the point of withdrawal when Joan arrived with fresh French troops. After repulsing the English from Orléans, the French enjoyed a succession of victories they popularly attributed to Joan. She rather had given the French something military experts could not: an enraged sense of national identity and destiny.

Within a few months of the liberation of Orléans, Charles VII received his crown in Rheims, ending the nine-year "disinheritance" prescribed by the Treaty of Troyes. The king now forgot his liberator as quickly as he had embraced her. When the Burgundians captured Joan in May 1430, he might have secured her release, but did little to help her. She was turned over to the Inquisition in English-held Rouen. She was executed as a relapsed heretic on May 30, 1431.

In 1435, the duke of Burgundy made peace with Charles, allowing France to force the English back. By 1453, when the war ended, the English held only their coastal enclave of Calais.

SIGNIFICANT DATES FROM THE PERIOD OF THE LATE MIDDLE AGES

1309–1377	Avignon Papacy
1340	Sluys, first major battle of Hundred Years' War
1346	Battle of Crécy and seizure of Calais
1347	Black Death strikes
1356	Battle of Poitiers
1358	Jacquerie disrupts France
1360	Peace of Brétigny-Calais
1378–1417	Great Schism
1381	English Peasants' Revolt
1414–1417	Council of Constance
1415	Battle of Agincourt
1420	Treaty of Troyes
1431	Joan of Arc executed as a heretic
1431–1449	Council of Basel
1453	End of Hundred Years' War

QUICK REVIEW

Joan of Arc (1412–1431)

- March 1429: Joan appears at Charles's court-in-exile
- Joan inspires French to a string of victories starting with Orléans
- Captured by the Burgundians in May 1430 and executed by the English as a heretic in May 1431

The Hundred Years' War devastated France, but it also awakened French nationalism and hastened the transition there from a feudal monarchy to a centralized state. It saw Burgundy become a major European political power. It also encouraged the English, in response to the seesawing allegiance of the Netherlands throughout the conflict, to develop their own clothing industry and foreign markets. In both France and England, the burden of the on-again, off-again war fell most heavily on the peasantry, who were forced to support it with taxes and services.

ECCLESIASTICAL BREAKDOWN AND REVIVAL: THE LATE MEDIEVAL CHURCH

HOW DID secular rulers challenge papal authority in the fourteenth and fifteenth centuries?

The Thirteenth-Century Papacy

The late Middle Ages was a time of turmoil for the Catholic Church. As early as the reign of Pope Innocent III (r. 1198– 1216), when papal power reached its height, there were ominous developments. Innocent's transformation of the papacy into a great secular power weakened the church spiritually even as it strengthened it politically. Thereafter, the church as a papal monarchy increasingly parted company with the church as the "body of the faithful." It was against this perceived "papal church" and in the name of the "true Christian church" that both reformers and heretics protested until the Protestant Reformation.

What Innocent began, his successors perfected. Under Urban IV (r. 1261–1264), the papacy established its own law court, the *Rota Romana*, which tightened and centralized the church's legal proceedings. The latter half of the thirteenth century saw an elaboration of the system of clerical taxation. In the same period, papal power to determine appointments to many major and minor church offices was greatly broadened. The thirteenth-century papacy became a powerful political institution governed by its own law and courts, serviced by an efficient international bureaucracy, and preoccupied with secular goals.

Papal centralization of the church undermined both diocesan authority and popular support. Rome's interests, not local needs, came to control church appointments, policies, and discipline. To its critics, the church in Rome was hardly more than a legalized, "fiscalized," bureaucratic institution.

Political Fragmentation More than internal religious disunity was undermining the thirteenth-century church. The demise of imperial power meant the papacy in Rome was no longer the leader of anti-imperial sentiment in Italy. Instead of being the center of Italian resistance to the emperor, popes now found themselves on the defensive against their old allies.

Rulers with a stake in Italian politics now directed the intrigue formerly aimed at the emperor toward the College of Cardinals. Such efforts to control the decisions of the college led Pope Gregory X (r. 1271–1276) to establish the practice of sequestering the cardinals immediately upon the death of the pope. The purpose of this so-called conclave of cardinals was to minimize political influence on the election of new popes, but the college became so politicized that it proved to be of little avail.

In 1294, such a conclave, in frustration after a deadlock of more than two years, chose a saintly, but inept, hermit as Pope Celestine V. Celestine abdicated under suspicious circumstances after only a few weeks in office. Celestine's tragicomic reign shocked the Cardinals into electing his opposite, Pope Boniface VIII (r. 1294–1303), a nobleman and a skilled politician. His pontificate, however, would mark the beginning of the end of papal pretensions to great-power status.

Boniface VIII and Philip the Fair

Boniface came to rule when England and France were maturing as nation-states. Boniface had the further misfortune of bringing to the papal throne memories of the way earlier popes had brought kings and emperors to their knees. Painfully he was to discover that the papal monarchy of the early thirteenth century was no match for the new political powers of the late thirteenth century.

The Royal Challenge to Papal Authority France and England were on the brink of all-out war when Boniface became pope in 1294. As both countries mobilized for war, they used the pretext of preparing for a Crusade to tax the clergy heavily. Viewing English and French taxation of the clergy as an assault on traditional clerical rights, Boniface took a strong stand against it. On February 5, 1296, he issued a bull, *Clericis laicos*, which forbade lay taxation of the clergy without papal approval and revoked all previous papal dispensations in this regard.

In England, Edward I retaliated by denying the clergy the right to be heard in royal court, in effect removing from them the protection of the king. But France's Philip IV "the fair" (r. 1285–1314) struck back with a vengeance: In August 1296, he forbade the exportation of money from France to Rome, thereby denying the papacy the revenues it needed to operate. Boniface had no choice but to come to terms quickly with Philip. He conceded Philip the right to tax the French clergy "during an emergency."

Boniface's fortunes appeared to revive in 1300, a "Jubilee year." During such a year, all Catholics who visited Rome and fulfilled certain conditions had the penalties for their unrepented sins remitted. Tens of thousands of pilgrims flocked to Rome, and Boniface, heady with this display of popular religiosity, reinserted himself into international politics. He championed Scottish resistance to England, for which he received a firm rebuke from an outraged Edward I and from Parliament.

Pope Boniface VIII (r. 1294–1303), depicted here, opposed the taxation of the clergy by the kings of France and England and issued one of the strongest declarations of papal authority over rulers, the bull *Unam Sanctam*. This statue is in the Museo Civico, Bologna, Italy.

Statue of Pope Boniface VIII. Museo Civico, Bologna. Scala/Art Resource, NY

What tools did the papacy have to ensure the implementation of its policies?

But once again a confrontation with the king of France proved the more costly. Philip seemed to be eager for another fight with the pope. He arrested Boniface's Parisian legate, Bernard Saisset. Accused of heresy and treason, Saisset was tried and convicted in the king's court. Thereafter, Philip demanded that Boniface recognize the process against Saisset, something Boniface could do only if he was prepared to surrender his jurisdiction over the French episcopate. Boniface could not sidestep this challenge, and he acted swiftly to champion Saisset as a defender of clerical political independence within France. A bull, *Ausculta fili*, or "Listen, My Son," was sent to Philip in December 1301, pointedly informing him that "God has set popes over kings and kingdoms."

Unam Sanctam (1302) Philip unleashed a ruthless antipapal campaign. Increasingly placed on the defensive, Boniface made a last-ditch stand against state control of national churches. On November 18, 1302, he issued the bull *Unam Sanctam*. This famous statement of papal power declared that temporal authority was "subject" to the spiritual power of the church. On its face a bold assertion, *Unam Sanctam* was, in truth, the desperate act of a besieged papacy. (See "Compare & Connect: Who Runs the World: Priests or Princes?" pages 234–235.)

After *Unam Sanctam*, the French and their Italian allies moved against Boniface with force. Philip's chief minister, Guillaume de Nogaret, denounced Boniface to the French clergy as a heretic and common criminal. In mid-August 1303, his army surprised the pope at his retreat in Anagni, beat him up, and almost executed him before an aroused populace returned him safely to Rome. The ordeal, however, proved to be too much, and Boniface died in October 1303.

Boniface's immediate successor, Benedict XI (r. 1303–1304), excommunicated Nogaret for his deed, but there was to be no lasting papal retaliation. Benedict's successor, Clement V (r. 1305–1314), was forced into French subservience.

COMPARE & CONNECT

WHO RUNS THE WORLD: PRIESTS OR PRINCES?

In one of the boldest papal bulls in the history of Christianity, Pope Boniface VIII declared the temporal authority of rulers to be subject to papal authority. Behind that ideology lay a long, bitter dispute between the papacy and the kings of France and England. Despite the strained scholastic arguments from each side's apologists, the issue was paramount and kingdoms were at stake. The debaters were Giles of Rome and John of Paris, the former a philosopher and papal adviser, the latter a French Dominican and Aristotle expert. Quoting ecclesiastical authorities, Giles defended a papal theocracy, while John made the royal case for secular authority.

QUESTIONS

1. Are the arguments pro and con logical and transparent?
2. How is history invoked to support their positions?
3. Which of the two seems to have the better authorities behind his arguments?

I. GILES OF ROME, *ON ECCLESIASTICAL POWER* (1301)

Hugh of St. Victor . . . declares that the spiritual power has to institute the earthly power and to judge it if it has not been good . . . We can clearly prove from the order of the universe that the church is set above nations and kingdoms [Jeremias 1:10] . . . It is the law of divinity that the lowest are led to the highest through intermediaries . . . At Romans 13 . . . the Apostle, having said that there is no power except from God, immediately added: "And those that are, are ordained of God." If then there are two swords [governments], one spiritual, the other temporal, as can be gathered from the words of the Gospel, "Behold, here are two swords" (Luke 22:38), [to which] the Lord at once added, "It is enough" because these two swords suffice for the church, [then] it follows that these two swords, these two powers and authorities, are [both] from God, since there is no power except from God. But, therefore they must be rightly ordered since, what is from God must be ordered. [And] they would not be so

Papal ring: gold with an engraving on each side and set with a square stone.

Dorling Kindersley Media Library. Geoff Dann © The British Museum

What were the most important sources of the papacy's wealth and power?

In 1309, Clement moved the papal court to Avignon, an imperial city on the southeastern border of France. Situated on land that belonged to the pope, the city maintained its independence from the French king. In 1311, Clement made it his permanent residence. There the papacy would remain until 1377.

ordered unless one sword was led by the other and one was under the other since, as Dionysius said, the law of divinity which God gave to all created things requires this . . . Therefore the temporal sword, as being inferior, is led by the spiritual sword, as being superior, and the one is set below the other as an inferior below a superior.

It may be said that kings and princes ought to be subject spiritually but not temporally . . . But those who speak thus have not grasped the force of the argument. For if kings and princes were only spiritually subject to the church, one sword would not be below the other, nor temporalities below spiritualities; there would be no order in the powers, the lowest would not be led to the highest through intermediaries. If they are ordered, the temporal sword must be below the spiritual, and [royal] kingdoms below the vicar of Christ, and that by law . . . [then] the vicar of Christ must hold dominion over temporal affairs.

II. JOHN OF PARIS, *TREATISE ON ROYAL AND PAPAL POWER* (1302–1303)

It is easy to see which is first in dignity, the kingship or the priesthood . . . A kingdom is ordered to this end, that an assembled multitude may live virtuously . . . and it is further ordered to a higher end which is the enjoyment of God; and responsibility for this end belongs to Christ, whose ministers and vicars are the priests. Therefore, the priestly power is of greater dignity than the secular and this is commonly conceded . . .

But if the priest is greater in himself than the prince and is greater in dignity, it does not follow that he is greater in all respects. For the lesser secular power is not related to the greater spiritual power as having its origin from it or being derived from it as the power of a proconsul is related to that of the emperor, which is greater in all respects since the power of the former is derived from the latter. The relationship is rather like that of a head of a household to a general of armies, since one is not derived from the other but both from a superior power. And so the secular power is greater than the spiritual in some things, namely in temporal affairs, and in such affairs it is not subject to the spiritual power in any way because it does not have its origin from it, but rather both have their origin immediately from the one supreme power, namely, the divine. Accordingly the inferior power is not subject to the superior in all things, but only in those where the supreme power has subordinated it to the greater. [For example] a teacher of literature or an instructor in morals directs the members of a household to a very noble end: the knowledge of truth. [That] end is more noble than [that] of a doctor who is concerned with a lower end, namely, the health of bodies. But who would say therefore that the doctor should be subjected to the teacher in preparing his medicines . . . ? Therefore, the priest is greater than the prince in spiritual affairs and, on the other hand, the prince is greater in temporal affairs.

Source: Brian Tierney, *The Crisis of Church and State 1050–1300* (Toronto: Toronto University Press, 1996), pp. 198–199, 209–209.

After Boniface's humiliation, popes never again seriously threatened kings and emperors, despite continuing papal excommunications and political intrigue. The relationship between church and state now tilted in favor of the state, and the control of religion fell into the hands of powerful monarchies. Ecclesiastical authority would become subordinate to larger secular political policies.

QUICK REVIEW

The Hundred Years' War and the Papacy

- Both Edward I and Philip the Fair taxed their clergy to raise funds for coming war
- Boniface's efforts to stop taxation of clergy were met with retaliation by both monarchs
- Boniface was forced to back down

Avignon papacy Period from 1309 to 1377 when the papal court was situated in Avignon, France, and gained a reputation for greed and worldly corruption.

THE AVIGNON PAPACY (1309–1377)

The **Avignon papacy** was in appearance, although not always in fact, under strong French influence. Under Clement V, the French dominated the College of Cardinals, testing the papacy's agility both politically and economically.

Pope John XXII Pope John XXII (r. 1316–1334), the most powerful Avignon pope, tried to restore papal independence and to return to Italy. This goal led him into war with the Visconti, the powerful ruling family of Milan, and a costly contest with Emperor Louis IV (r. 1314–1347). John had challenged Louis's election as emperor in 1314 in favor of the rival Habsburg candidate. When John obstinately and without legal justification refused to recognize Louis's election, the emperor declared him deposed and put in his place an antipope. Two outstanding pamphleteers wrote lasting tracts for the royal cause: William of Ockham, whom John excommunicated in 1328, and Marsilius of Padua (ca. 1290–1342), whose teaching John declared heretical in 1327.

In his *Defender of Peace* (1324), Marsilius of Padua stressed the independent origins and autonomy of secular government. Clergy were subjected to the strictest apostolic ideals and confined to purely spiritual functions, and all power of coercive judgment was denied the pope. Marsilius argued that spiritual crimes must await an eternal punishment. This assertion directly challenged the power of the pope to excommunicate rulers and place countries under interdict. The *Defender of Peace* depicted the pope as a subordinate member of a society over which the emperor ruled supreme and in which temporal peace was the highest good.

John XXII made the papacy a sophisticated international agency and adroitly adjusted it to the growing European money economy. The more the Curia, or papal court, mastered the latter, however, the more vulnerable it became to criticism. Under John's successor, Benedict XII (r. 1334–1342), the papacy became entrenched in Avignon. His high-living French successor, Clement VI (r. 1342–1352), placed papal policy in lockstep with the French. In this period the cardinals became barely more than lobbyists for policies their secular patrons favored.

National Opposition to the Avignon Papacy As Avignon's fiscal tentacles probed new areas, monarchies took strong action to protect their interests. The latter half of the fourteenth century saw legislation restricting papal jurisdiction and taxation in France, England, and Germany. In England, where the Avignon papacy was identified with the French enemy after the outbreak of the Hundred Years' War, Parliament passed statutes that restricted payments and appeals to Rome and the pope's power to make high ecclesiastical appointments several times between 1351 and 1393.

In France, the so-called Gallican, or French, liberties regulated ecclesiastical appointments and taxation. These national rights over religion had long been exercised in fact, and the church legally acknowledged them in the *Pragmatic Sanction of Bourges* in 1438. In German and Swiss cities in the fourteenth and fifteenth centuries, local governments also limited and even overturned traditional clerical privileges and immunities.

JOHN WYCLIFFE AND JOHN HUSS

The popular lay religious movements that most successfully assailed the late medieval church were the Lollards in England and the Hussites in Bohemia. The Lollards looked to the writings of John Wycliffe (d. 1384) to justify their demands, while moderate and extreme Hussites turned to those of John Huss (d. 1415), although both Wycliffe and Huss would have disclaimed the extremists who revolted in their names.

Wycliffe was an Oxford theologian and a philosopher of high standing. His work initially served the anticlerical policies of the English government. After 1350, English kings greatly reduced the power of the Avignon papacy to make ecclesiastical appointments and to collect taxes within England, a position that Wycliffe strongly supported. His views on clerical poverty followed original Franciscan ideals and, more by accident than by design, gave justification to government restriction and even confiscation of church properties within England.

Wycliffe also maintained that personal merit, not rank and office, was the true basis of religious authority. This was a dangerous teaching, because it raised allegedly pious laypeople above allegedly corrupt ecclesiastics, regardless of the latter's official stature. It thus threatened secular as well as ecclesiastical dominion and jurisdiction. At his posthumous condemnation by the pope, Wycliffe was accused of the ancient heresy of Donatism—the teaching that the efficacy of the church's sacraments did not only lie in their true performance, but also depended on the moral character of the clergy who administered them. Wycliffe also anticipated certain Protestant criticisms of the medieval church by challenging papal infallibility, the sale of indulgences (pardons for unrepented sins), the authority of Scripture, and the dogma of transubstantiation.

A portrayal of John Huss as he was led to the stake at Constance. After his execution, his bones and ashes were scattered in the Rhine River to prevent his followers from claiming them as relics. This pen-and-ink drawing is from Ulrich von Richenthal's *Chronicle of the Council of Constance* (ca. 1450).

CORBIS/Bettmann

How did Czech nationalism and a desire for religious reform combine in the movement centered on John Huss?

The Lollards, English advocates of Wycliffe's teaching, preached in the vernacular, disseminated translations of Holy Scripture, and championed clerical poverty. After the English peasants' revolt in 1381, an uprising filled with egalitarian notions that could find support in Wycliffe's teaching, Lollardy was officially viewed as subversive. Opposed by an alliance of church and crown, it became a capital offense in England by 1401.

Heresy was less easily brought to heel in Bohemia, where it coalesced with a strong national movement. The University of Prague, founded in 1348, became the center for both Czech nationalism and a religious reform movement. The latter began within the bounds of orthodoxy. It was led by local intellectuals and preachers, the most famous of whom was John Huss, the rector of the university after 1403. The Czech reformers supported vernacular translations of the Bible and were critical of traditional ceremonies and allegedly superstitious practices, particularly those relating to the sacrament of the Eucharist.

Wycliffe's teaching appears early to have influenced the movement. Regular traffic between England and Bohemia had existed since the marriage in 1381 of Anne of Bohemia to King Richard II. Czech students studied at Oxford and returned with Wycliffe's writings.

Huss became the leader of the pro-Wycliffe faction at the University of Prague. In 1410, his activities brought about his excommunication, and Prague was placed under papal interdict. In 1414, Huss won an audience with the newly assembled Council of Constance. Within weeks of his arrival in early November 1414, he was accused of heresy and imprisoned. He died at the stake on July 6, 1415, and was followed there less than a year later by his colleague Jerome of Prague.

The reaction in Bohemia to the execution of these national heroes was fierce revolt. Militant Hussites, the Taborites, set out to transform Bohemia by force into a religious and social paradise under the military leadership of John Ziska. After a decade of belligerent protest, the Hussites won significant religious reforms and control over the Bohemian church from the Council of Basel.

QUICK REVIEW

John Huss

- 1403: Huss becomes rector of the University of Prague and begins religious reform movement
- Reformers used vernacular translations of the Bible and rejected practices they saw as superstitious
- Huss was burned at the stake as a heretic in 1415

The Great Schism (1378–1417) and the Conciliar Movement to 1449

Pope Gregory XI (r. 1370–1378) reestablished the papacy in Rome in January 1377, ending what had come to be known as the "Babylonian Captivity" of the church in Avignon, a reference to the biblical bondage of the Israelites. The return to Rome proved to be short-lived, however.

Urban VI and Clement VII On Gregory's death, the cardinals, in Rome, elected an Italian archbishop as Pope Urban VI (r. 1378–1389), who immediately announced his intention to reform the Curia. The cardinals, most of whom were French, responded by calling for the return of the papacy to Avignon. The French king, Charles V (r. 1364–1380), wanting to keep the papacy within the sphere of French influence, lent his support to what came to be known as the Great Schism.

On September 20, 1378, five months after Urban's election, thirteen cardinals, all but one of whom was French, formed their own conclave and elected Pope Clement VII (r. 1378–1397), a cousin of the French king. Allegiance to the two papal courts divided along political lines. England and its allies (the Holy Roman Empire, Hungary, Bohemia, and Poland) acknowledged Urban VI, whereas France and those in its orbit (Naples, Scotland, Castile, and Aragon) supported Clement VII.

Two approaches were initially taken to end the schism. One tried to win the mutual cession of both popes, thereby clearing the way for the election of a new pope. The other sought to secure the resignation of the one in favor of the other. Both approaches proved fruitless. Each pope considered himself fully legitimate, and too much was at stake for either to make a magnanimous concession. One way remained: the deposition of both popes by a special council of the church.

Conciliar Theory of Church Government The correctness of a conciliar deposition of a pope was debated a full thirty years before any direct action was taken. Advocates of conciliar theory sought to fashion a church in which a representative council could effectively regulate the actions of the pope. The conciliarists defined the church as the whole body of the faithful, of which the elected head, the pope, was only one part. The conciliarists further argued that a council of the church acted with greater authority than the pope alone.

Justice in the late Middle Ages. Depicted are the most common forms of corporal and capital punishment in Europe in the late Middle Ages and the Renaissance. At top: burning, hanging, drowning. At center: blinding, quartering, the wheel, cutting of hair (a mark of great shame for a freeman). At bottom: thrashing, decapitation, amputation of hand (for thieves).

Herzog August Bibliothek Wolfenbuttel

Why were medieval punishments so often carried out in public?

The Council of Pisa (1409–1410) On the basis of the arguments of the conciliarists, cardinals representing both popes convened a council on their own authority in Pisa in 1409, deposed both the Roman and the Avignon popes, and elected a new pope, Alexander V. To the council's consternation, neither pope accepted its action, and Christendom suddenly faced the spectacle of three contending popes. Although most of Latin Christendom accepted Alexander and his Pisan successor John XXIII (r. 1410–1415), the popes of Rome and Avignon refused to step down.

The Council of Constance (1414–1417) The intolerable situation ended when Emperor Sigismund prevailed on John XXIII to summon a new council in Constance in 1414, which the Roman pope Gregory XII also recognized. In a famous declaration entitled *Sacrosancta*, the council asserted its supremacy and elected a new pope, Martin V (r. 1417–1431), after the three contending popes had either resigned or been deposed.

The Council of Basel (r. 1431–1449) Conciliar government of the church peaked at the Council of Basel, when the council directly negotiated church doctrine with heretics. In 1432, the Hussites of Bohemia entered into negotiations with the council and, in November 1433, an agreement among the emperor, the council, and the Hussites gave the Bohemians jurisdiction over their church similar to what the French and the English held.

The end of the Hussite wars and the new reform legislation curtailing the pope's powers of appointment and taxation were the high points of the Council of Basel and ominous signs of what lay ahead for the church. The exercise of such power by a council did not please the pope, and in 1438, he upstaged the Council of Basel by negotiating a reunion with the Eastern church. Although the agreement, signed in Florence in 1439, was short-lived, it restored papal prestige and signaled the demise of the conciliar movement. Having overreached itself, the

Council of Basel collapsed in 1449. A decade later, Pope Pius II (r. 1458–1464) issued the papal bull *Execrabilis* (1460) condemning appeals to councils as "erroneous and abominable" and "completely null and void."

Consequences A major consequence of the conciliar movement was the devolving of greater religious responsibility onto the laity and secular governments. Without effective papal authority and leadership, secular control of national or territorial churches increased. Kings asserted their power over the church in England and France. In German, Swiss, and Italian cities, magistrates and city councils reformed and regulated religious life.

QUICK REVIEW

Church Councils

- Council of Pisa (1409–1410): Attempt to resolve schism ended in creating a third pope
- Council of Constance (1414–1417): Three popes resigned or were deposed and Martin V was chosen as new pope
- Council of Basel (1431–1449): Entered into negotiations with the Hussites

MEDIEVAL RUSSIA

HOW DID Mongol rule shape Russia's development?

In the late tenth century, Prince Vladimir of Kiev (r. 980–1015), then Russia's dominant city, received delegations of Muslims, Roman Catholics, Jews, and Greek Orthodox Christians, each of which hoped to persuade the Russians to embrace their religion. Vladimir chose Greek Orthodoxy, which became the religion of Russia, adding strong cultural bonds to the close commercial ties that had long linked Russia to the Byzantine Empire.

Politics and Society

Vladimir's successor, Yaroslav the Wise (r. 1016–1054), developed Kiev into a magnificent political and cultural center, with architecture rivaling that of Constantinople. He also pursued contacts with the West in an unsuccessful effort to counter the political influence of the Byzantine emperors. After his death, rivalry among their princes slowly divided Russians into three cultural groups: the Great Russians, the White Russians, and the Little Russians (Ukrainians). Autonomous principalities also challenged Kiev's dominance, and it became just one of several national centers. Government in the principalities combined monarchy (the prince), aristocracy (the prince's council of noblemen), and democracy (a popular assembly of all free adult males). The broadest social division was between freemen and slaves. Freemen included the clergy, army officers, **boyars** (wealthy landowners), townspeople, and peasants.

boyars Wealthy landowners among the freemen in late medieval Russia.

Mongol Rule (1243–1480)

In the thirteenth century, Mongol, or Tatar, armies swept through China, much of the Islamic world, and Russia. Ghengis Khan (1155–1227) invaded Russia in 1223, and Kiev fell to his grandson Batu Khan in 1240. Russian cities became dependent, tribute-paying principalities of the segment of the Mongol Empire known as the *Golden Horde*. The conquerors stationed their own officials in all the principal Russian towns to oversee taxation and the conscription of Russians into Tatar armies.

The Mongols, however, left Russian political and religious institutions largely intact and, thanks to their far-flung trade, brought most Russians greater prosperity. Princes of Moscow collected tribute for their overlords and grew wealthy under Mongol rule. As that rule weakened, the Moscow princes took control of the territory surrounding the city. Gradually the principality of Moscow expanded through land purchases, colonization, and conquest. In 1380, Grand Duke Dimitri of Moscow (r. 1350–1389) defeated Tatar forces at Kulikov Meadow, a victory that marked the beginning of the decline of the Mongol hegemony. Another century would pass, however, before Ivan III, the Great (d. 1505), would bring all of northern Russia under Moscow's control and end Mongol rule (1480). Moscow replaced Kiev as the political and religious center of Russia. After Constantinople fell to the Turks in 1453, the city became, in Russian eyes, the "third Rome."

Genghis Khan Holding an Audience. This Persian miniature shows the great conqueror and founder of the Mongol empire with members of his army and entourage as well as an apparent supplicant (lower right).

The Art Archive/Picture Desk, Inc./Kobal Collection

What threat did the Mongols pose to medieval Europe?

Summary

WHAT WERE the social and economic consequences of the "Black Death"?

The Black Death Between 1347 and the early fifteenth century, close to 40 percent of the population of western Europe was killed by the Black Death. People had no idea what the bubonic plague was, how it was transmitted, or how to treat the sick. The fear inspired by the disease itself, and by the responses to it, influenced European attitudes and religious beliefs for centuries. The sharp reduction in population changed fundamental social, economic, and political patterns. Increased demand and reduced supply of luxury goods brought more power and wealth to cities and to skilled artisans; the landed nobility suffered economically as demand for food diminished. *page 224*

HOW DID the Hundred Years' War contribute to a growing sense of national identity in France and England?

The Hundred Years' War and the Rise of National Sentiment The so-called Hundred Years' War between England and France actually lasted for more than a century, from 1337 to 1453, although there were long intervals of peace during this period. The direct cause of the war was controversy over the succession to the French throne. Despite a smaller population, less wealth, and fighting on enemy soil, England got the better of France in most of the significant early battles. England began the conflict as a more cohesive state than France. Eventually, however, the French began to see past regional rivalries, and Joan of Arc inspired an emergent national pride. *page 228*

HOW DID secular rulers challenge papal authority in the fourteenth and fifteenth centuries?

Ecclesiastical Breakdown and Revival: The Late Medieval Church Through the thirteenth century, popes had worked to centralize church power. As nation-states gained cohesiveness, kings started to challenge papal authority. Throughout most of the fourteenth century, the papacy was based in Avignon, France, rather than Rome. The conciliar theory proposed that the pope just oversee a church that should rightfully be dominated by the faithful as a group. The Council of Basel in the fifteenth century provided a model of lay rights and responsibilities for other church and national organizations. *page 232*

HOW DID Mongol rule shape Russia's development?

Medieval Russia Kiev was the most important city in Russia around the turn of the millennium, so Prince Vladimir of Kiev's selection of Greek Orthodoxy as the state religion had ramifications that endure to the present. Starting in the eleventh century, Kiev lost its preeminence, and Russians split into three geographic and cultural groupings: the Great Russians, the White Russians, and the Little Russians or Ukrainians. In 1223, Ghengis Khan sent a Mongol (or Tatar) army into Russia. The Golden Horde brought much of Russia into the Mongol Empire. Mongol rule ended in 1480, by which time Moscow was the dominant city within Russia. *page 239*

Review Questions

1. What were the causes of the Black Death? Why did it spread so quickly? What were its effects on European society? How important do you think disease is in changing the course of history?
2. What were the causes of the Hundred Years' War? What advantages did each side have? Why were the French ultimately victorious?
3. What changes took place in the church and in its relationship to secular society between 1200 and 1450? How did it respond to political threats from increasingly powerful monarchs? How great an influence did the church have on secular events?
4. What is meant by the term "Avignon papacy"? What caused the Great Schism? How was it resolved? Why did kings in the late thirteenth and early fourteenth centuries have more power over the church than it had over them? What did kings hope to achieve through their struggles with the church?
5. How did the Kievan and medieval Russian states develop in terms of religion, politics, and social structure? What effect did Mongol rule have on Russian lands?

Key Terms

Avignon papacy (p. 236)
Black Death (p. 224)
boyars (p. 239)
Estates General (p. 229)
Jacquerie (p. 226)
taille (p. 226)

For additional learning resources related to this chapter, please go to **www.myhistorylab.com**

PEARSON myhistorylab

10

Renaissance and Discovery

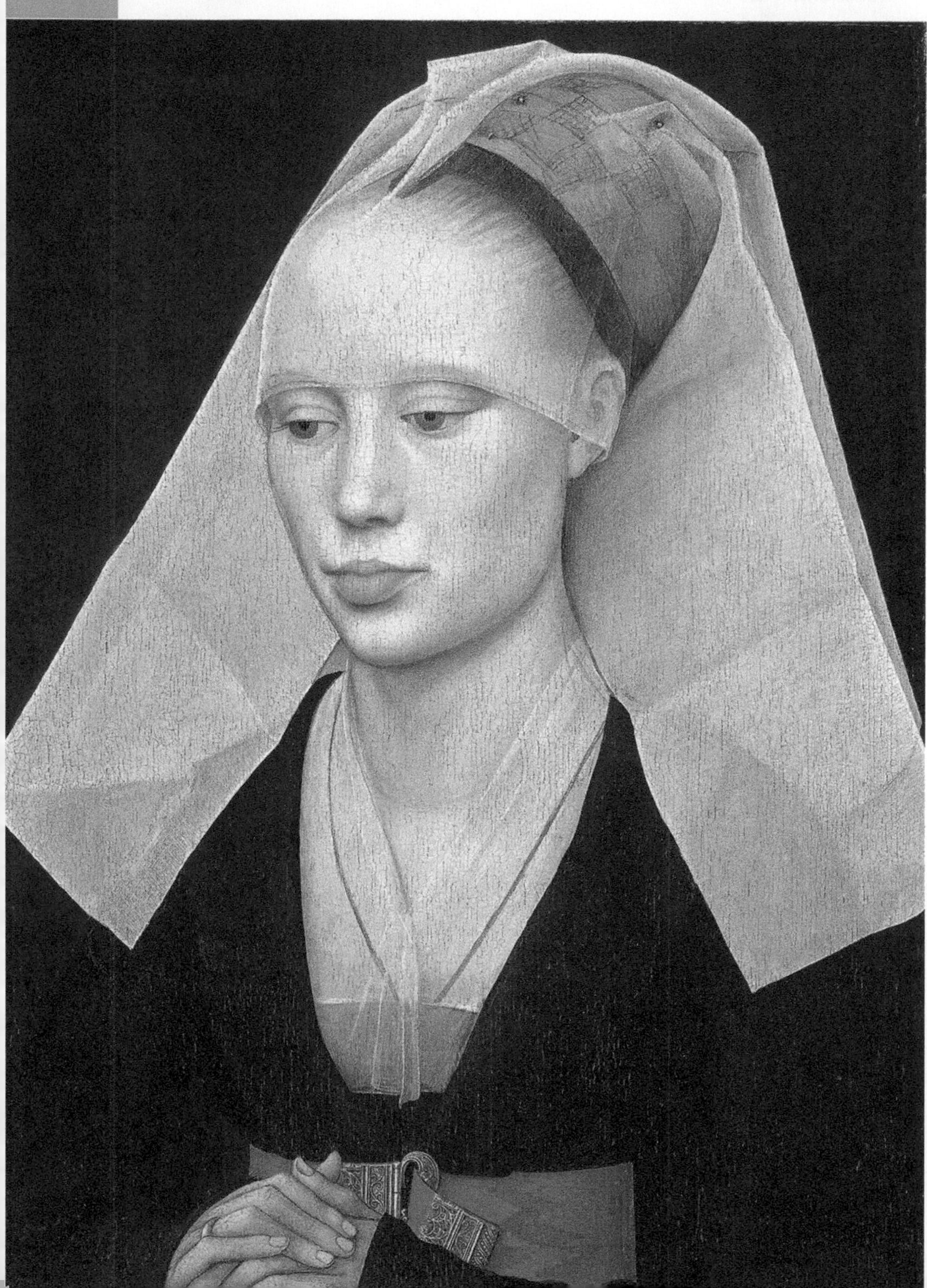

The Renaissance celebrated human beauty and dignity. Here the Flemish painter Rogier van der Weyden (1400–1464) portrays an ordinary woman more perfectly on canvas than she could ever have appeared in life.

Rogier van der Weyden (Netherlandish, 1399.1400–1464), *Portrait of a Lady.* 1460. .370 × .270 (14 1/16 X 10 5/8) framed: .609 × .533 × .114 (24 X 21 X 4 1/2). Photo: Bob Grove. Andrew W. Mellon Collection. Photograph © Board of Trustees, National Gallery of Art, Washington, DC

What personal qualities might the painter have wanted viewers to see in his subject?

THE RENAISSANCE IN ITALY (1375–1527) *page 244*

HOW DID humanism affect culture and the arts in fourteenth- and fifteenth-century Italy?

ITALY'S POLITICAL DECLINE: THE FRENCH INVASIONS (1494–1527) *page 253*

WHAT WERE the causes of Italy's political decline?

REVIVAL OF MONARCHY IN NORTHERN EUROPE *page 256*

HOW WERE the powerful monarchies of northern Europe different from their predecessors?

THE NORTHERN RENAISSANCE *page 259*

HOW DID the northern Renaissance affect culture in Germany, England, France, and Spain?

VOYAGES OF DISCOVERY AND THE NEW EMPIRES IN THE WEST AND EAST *page 262*

WHAT WERE the motives for European voyages of discovery, and what were the consequences?

The late medieval period was an era of creative disruption. The social order that had persisted in Europe for a thousand years failed, but Europe did not decline. It merely changed direction. By the late fifteenth century, its population had nearly recovered from the losses inflicted by the plagues, famines, and wars of the fourteenth century. Able rulers were establishing stable, centralized governments, and Italy's city-states were doing especially well. Italy's strategic location enabled it to dominate world trade, which still centered on the Mediterranean. Italy's commercial wealth gave its leaders means to provide patronage for education and the arts and fund the famous Italian Renaissance.

Renaissance scholars, the humanists, revived the study of classical Greek and Latin languages and literature. They reformed education and, thanks to the invention of the printing press, became the first scholars able to reach out to the general public. In their eagerness to educate ordinary men and women, they championed the use of vernacular languages as vehicles for art and serious thought.

During the late fifteenth and the sixteenth centuries, powerful nations arose in Western Europe and sponsored voyages of exploration that spread Europe's influence around the globe. The colonies they planted and empires they built yielded a flood of gold, information, and new materials that transformed the Western way of life.

THE RENAISSANCE IN ITALY (1375–1527)

HOW DID humanism affect culture and the arts in fourteenth- and fifteenth-century Italy?

The Renaissance (which means "rebirth" in French) was a time of transition from medieval to modern times. Medieval Europe, especially before the twelfth century, had been a fragmented feudal society with an agricultural economy, and the church largely dominated its thought and culture. Renaissance Europe, especially after the fourteenth century, was characterized by growing national consciousness and political centralization, an urban economy based on organized commerce and capitalism, and growing lay and secular control of thought and culture, including religion. Italy between 1375 and 1527, a century and a half of cultural creativity, most strikingly reveals the distinctive features of the Renaissance.

Florentine women doing needlework, spinning, and weaving. These activities took up much of a woman's time and contributed to the elegance of dress for which Florentine men and women were famed.

Palazzo Schifanoia, Ferrara. Alinari/Art Resource, NY

How important was the textile industry to the cultural development of Renaissance Florence?

The Italian City-State

Renaissance society first took shape within the merchant cities of late medieval Italy. Italy had always had a cultural advantage over the rest of Europe because its geography made it the natural gateway between East and West. Venice, Genoa, and Pisa had traded uninterruptedly with the Near East throughout the Middle Ages, maintaining vibrant urban societies by virtue of such trade. When commerce revived on a large scale in the eleventh century, Italian merchants had quickly mastered the business skills of organization, bookkeeping, scouting new markets, and securing monopolies. During the thirteenth and fourteenth centuries, trade-rich cities became powerful city-states, dominating the political and economic life of the surrounding countryside. By the fifteenth century, the great Italian cities were the bankers for much of Europe.

Growth of City-States The endemic warfare between pope and emperor and the Guelf (propapal) and Ghibelline (proimperial) factions this warfare spawned assisted the growth of Italian cities and urban culture. Either of these factions might successfully have subdued the cities had they permitted each other to concentrate on doing so. Instead, they chose to weaken one another, which strengthened the merchant oligarchies of the cities.

Unlike the great cities of northern Europe, which kings and territorial princes dominated, the great Italian cities remained free to expand on their own. Becoming independent states, they absorbed the surrounding countryside, assimilating the local nobility in a unique urban meld of old and new rich. Five such major, competitive states evolved: the duchy of Milan, the republics of Florence and Venice, the Papal States, and the kingdom of Naples. (See Map 10–1.)

Social Class and Conflict Social strife and competition for political power became so intense within the cities that most evolved into despotisms just to survive. Florence was the most striking example of social division and anarchy. Four distinguishable social groups existed within the city. There was the old rich, or *grandi*, the nobles and merchants who traditionally ruled the city. The emergent newly rich merchant class, capitalists and bankers known as the *popolo grosso*, or "fat people," formed a second group. In the late thirteenth and early fourteenth centuries, they began to challenge the old rich for political powers. Then there were the middle-burgher ranks of guild masters, shop owners, and professionals, the smaller businesspeople who, in Florence, as elsewhere, tended to side with the new rich against the conservative policies of the old rich. Finally, there was the *popolo minuto*, or the "little people," the lower economic classes. In 1457, one-third of the population of Florence, about 30,000 people, was officially listed as paupers, that is, as having no wealth at all.

These social divisions produced conflict at every level of society, to which was added the ever-present fear of foreign intrigue. In 1378, a great uprising of the poor, known as the Ciompi Revolt, occurred. It resulted from a combination of three factors that made life unbearable for those at the bottom of society: the feuding between the old rich and the new rich; the social anarchy created when the Black Death cut the city's population almost in half; and the collapse of the great banking houses of Bardi and Peruzzi, which left the poor more vulnerable than ever. The Ciompi Revolt established a chaotic four-year reign of power by the lower Florentine classes. True stability did not return to Florence until the ascent to power of the Florentine banker and statesman, Cosimo de' Medici (1389–1464) in 1434.

Despotism and Diplomacy Cosimo de' Medici was the wealthiest Florentine and a natural statesman. He controlled the city internally from behind the scenes, manipulating the constitution and influencing elections. His grandson, Lorenzo the Magnificent (1449–1492; r. 1478–1492), ruled Florence in almost totalitarian fashion during the last, chaotic quarter of the fifteenth century. The assassination of his brother in

MAP EXPLORATION

Interactive map: To explore this map further, go to www.myhistorylab.com

MAP 10–1 **Renaissance Italy** The city-states of Renaissance Italy were self-contained principalities whose internal strife was monitored by their despots and whose external aggression was long successfully controlled by treaty.

How did city-states help shape the political climate of Renaissance Italy?

1478 by a rival family, the Pazzi, who had long plotted with the pope against the Medicis, made Lorenzo a cautious and determined ruler.

Despotism elsewhere was even less subtle. To prevent internal social conflict and foreign intrigue from paralyzing their cities, the dominant groups cooperated to install hired strongmen, or despots. Known as a *podestà,* the despot's sole purpose was to maintain law and order. He held executive, military, and judicial authority, and his mandate was direct and simple: to permit, by whatever means required, the normal flow of business activity without which neither the old rich and new rich, nor the poor of a city, could long survive, much less prosper. Because despots could not count on the loyalty of the divided populace, they operated through mercenary armies obtained through military brokers known as ***condottieri***.

condottieri Military brokers from whom one could hire a mercenary army.

Mercifully, the political turbulence and warfare of the times also gave birth to the art of diplomacy. Through their diplomats, the various city-states stayed abreast of foreign military developments and, when shrewd enough, gained power and advantage over their enemies without actually going to war. Most city-states established resident embassies in the fifteenth century for that very purpose. Their ambassadors not only represented them in ceremonies and at negotiations, but they also became their watchful eyes and ears at rival courts.

The Italian city proved a congenial climate for an unprecedented flowering of thought and culture. Italian Renaissance culture was promoted vigorously in all the major city-states. Such widespread support occurred because the main requirement for patronage of the arts and letters was the one thing that Italian cities of the High Renaissance had in abundance: great wealth.

HUMANISM

The most important Renaissance intellectual movement, humanism, was the scholarly study of the Latin and Greek classics and of the ancient Church Fathers, both for its own sake and in the hope of reviving respected ancient norms and values. Humanists advocated the ***studia humanitatis***, a liberal arts program of study embracing grammar, rhetoric, poetry, history, politics, and moral philosophy. Not only were these subjects considered a joy in themselves, but they also celebrated the dignity of humankind and prepared people for a life of virtuous action.

***studia humanitatis* (humanism)** Scholarship of the Renaissance that championed the study of Latin and Greek classics and Christian church fathers as an end in itself and as a guide to reforming society. Some claim it is an un-Christian philosophy emphasizing human dignity, individualism, and secular values.

The first humanists were orators and poets. They wrote original literature in both classical and vernacular languages, inspired by and modeled on the newly discovered works of the ancients. They also taught rhetoric within the universities. When humanists were not employed as teachers of rhetoric, princely and papal courts sought their talents as secretaries, speechwriters, and diplomats.

The study of classical and Christian antiquity had existed before the Italian Renaissance. There were memorable recoveries of ancient civilization during the Carolingian renaissance of the ninth century, within the cathedral school of Chartres in the twelfth century, during the great Aristotelian revival in Paris in the thirteenth century, and among the Augustinians in the early fourteenth century. These precedents, however, only partially compare with the achievements of the Italian Renaissance of the fourteenth and fifteenth centuries. The latter was far more secular and lay-dominated, had much broader interests, was blessed with many more recovered manuscripts, and its scholars possessed far superior technical skills than those who had delivered the earlier "rebirths" of antiquity.

Unlike their Scholastic rivals, humanists were less bound to recent tradition; nor did they focus all their attention on summarizing and comparing the views of recognized authorities. Their most respected sources were classical and biblical, not medieval philoso-

ENCOUNTERING THE PAST

THE GARDEN

Gardens were sources of both necessities and pleasures for the people of the Middle Ages and the Renaissance, and every household from the grandest to the humblest had one. In addition to their practical functions, gardens had religious and social associations. They were enclosed behind walls, fences, or hedges to protect their contents, and they served as private retreats in a world that offered little shelter for privacy. They called to mind the Garden of Eden and the more sensuous pleasures of the garden described in the Bible's Song of Songs (4:12). They were symbols of paradise and reminders of the temptations that led to Adam's fall.

Wealthy people had gardens (adorned with grottoes and fountains) that were designed primarily for pleasure. They provided ideal settings for the romantic trysts of courtly lovers. Even great houses, however, like the cottages of the poor, also had gardens devoted to much more utilitarian purposes. A medieval/Renaissance household depended on its garden for much of its food and medicine. The fruit it produced was mainly used to concoct sweet drinks, and it was the source of the limited range of vegetables medieval people consumed: cabbage, lentils, peas, beans, onions, leeks, beets, and parsnips. The herbs and flowers from gardens were highly prized as flavorings for a diet heavy on bland, starchy foods. They were also the era's most effective medicines.

A wealthy man oversees apple picking at harvest time in a fifteenth-century French orchard. In the town below, individual house gardens can be seen. Protective fences, made of woven sticks, keep out predatory animals.

By permission of the British Library

WHAT WERE some of the purposes that gardens served during the Middle Ages and early Renaissance?

Teresa McClean, *Medieval English Gardens* (New York: Viking Press, 1980), pp. 64, 133; Marilyn Stokstad and Jerry Stannard, *Gardens of the Middle Ages* (Lawrence, KS: Spencer Museum, 1983), pp. 19–21, 61.

phers and theologians. Avidly searching out manuscript collections, Italian humanists made the full riches of Greek and Latin antiquity available to contemporary scholars.

Petrarch, Dante, and Boccaccio Francesco Petrarch (1304–1374) was the "father of humanism." Petrarch celebrated ancient Rome in his *Letters to the Ancient Dead*, fancied personal letters to Cicero, Livy, Vergil, and Horace. He also wrote a Latin epic poem (*Africa*, a poetic historical tribute to the Roman general Scipio Africanus) and biographies of famous Roman men (*Lives of Illustrious Men*). His most famous contemporary work was a collection of highly introspective love sonnets to a certain Laura, a married woman he admired romantically from a safe distance. His critical textual studies, elitism, and contempt for the learning of the Scholastics were features many later humanists also shared. As with many later humanists, Classical and Christian values coexist uneasily in his work.

Petrarch was, however, far more secular in orientation than his famous near-contemporary Dante Alighieri (1265–1321), whose *Vita Nuova* and *Divine Comedy* form, with Petrarch's sonnets, the cornerstones of Italian vernacular literature. Petrarch's student and friend Giovanni Boccaccio (1313–1375) was also a pioneer of humanist studies. His *Decameron*—one hundred often bawdy tales told by three men and seven women in a safe country retreat away from the plague that ravaged Florence in 1348 (see Chapter 9)—is both a stinging social commentary (it exposes sexual and economic misconduct) and a sympathetic look at human behavior.

Educational Reforms and Goals Humanists delighted in taking their mastery of ancient languages directly to the past, refusing to be slaves to later tradition. Such an attitude not only made them innovative educators, but also kept them constantly in search of new sources of information. In the search, they assembled magnificent manuscript collections, treating them as potent medicines for the ills of contemporary society, and capable of enlightening the minds of any who would immerse themselves in them.

The goal of humanist studies was wisdom eloquently spoken, both knowledge of the good and the ability to move others to desire it. Learning was not meant to remain abstract and unpracticed. "It is better to will the good than to know the truth," Petrarch taught, and it became a motto of many later humanists, who, like Petrarch, believed learning ennobled people.

Christine de Pisan, who has the modern reputation of being the first European feminist, presents her internationally famous book *The Treasure of the City of Ladies,* also known as *The Book of Three Virtues,* to Isabella of Bavaria amid her ladies in waiting.

Historical Picture Archive/CORBIS/Bettmann

How does Pisan's widowhood help explain her intellectual career?

The ideal of a useful education and well-rounded people inspired far-reaching reforms in traditional education. Vittorino da Feltre (d. 1446) exemplified the ideals of humanist teaching. Not only did he have his students read the difficult works of Pliny, Ptolemy, Terence, Plautus, Livy, and Plutarch, but he also subjected them to vigorous physical exercise and games.

Despite the grinding scholarly process of acquiring ancient knowledge, humanistic studies were not confined to the classroom. As Baldassare Castiglione's (1478–1529) *Book of the Courtier* illustrates, the rediscovered knowledge of the past was both a model and a challenge to the present. Written as a practical guide for the nobility at the court of Urbino, a small duchy in central Italy, it embodies the highest ideals of Italian humanism. The successful courtier is said to be one who knows how to integrate knowledge of ancient languages and history with athletic, military, and musical skills, while at the same time practicing good manners and exhibiting a high moral character.

Privileged, educated noblewomen also promoted the new education and culture at royal courts. Among them was Christine de Pisan (1363?–1434), the Italian-born daughter of the physician and astrologer of French king Charles V. She became an expert in classical, French, and Italian languages and literature. Married at fifteen and the widowed mother of three at twenty-seven, she wrote lyric poetry to support herself and was much read throughout the courts of Europe. Her most famous work, *The Treasure of the City of Ladies,* is a chronicle of the accomplishments of the great women of history.

QUICK REVIEW

Humanist Education

- Humanists sought reform of education to serve humanist values
- *Book of the Courtier*: Provided practical advice for conduct at court
- Women profited from education reform and helped guide it

The Florentine "Academy" and the Revival of Platonism Of all the important recoveries of the past made during the Italian Renaissance, none stands out more than the revival of Greek studies in fifteenth-century Florence. Renaissance thinkers were especially attracted to the Platonic tradition and to those Church Fathers who tried to synthesize Platonic philosophy with Christian teaching. The Florentine Platonic Academy evolved under the patronage of Cosimo de' Medici and the supervision of Marsilio Ficino (1433–1499) and Pico della Mirandola (1463–1494). The Academy was actually not a formal school, but an informal gathering of influential Florentine humanists devoted to the revival of the works of Plato and the Neoplatonists: Plotinus, Proclus, Porphyry, and Dionysius the Areopagite. To this end, Ficino edited and published the complete works of Plato.

The appeal of Platonism lay in its flattering view of human nature. It distinguished between an eternal sphere of being and the perishable world in which humans actually lived. Human reason was believed to belong to the former—to have preexisted in this pristine world and still to commune with it, to which human knowledge of eternal mathematical and moral truth bore direct witness.

Strong Platonic influence is evident in Pico's *Oration on the Dignity of Man*, perhaps the most famous Renaissance statement on the nature of humankind. (See "Compare & Connect: Is the 'Renaissance Man' a Myth?" pages 250–251.) The *Oration* drew on Platonic teaching to depict humans as the only creatures in the world who possessed the freedom to be whatever they chose, able at will to rise to the height of angels or just as quickly to wallow with pigs.

QUICK REVIEW

Humanists and Plato

- Humanists led revival of Greek studies
- Humanists were particularly attracted to Platonic tradition
- Plato's appeal lay in his view of human nature

Critical Work of the Humanists: Lorenzo Valla Because they were guided by scholarly ideals of philological accuracy and historical truth, the humanists could become critics of tradition even when that was not their intention. Dispassionate critical scholarship shook long-standing foundations, not the least of which were those of the medieval church.

The work of Lorenzo Valla (1406–1457), author of the standard Renaissance text on Latin philology, *Elegances of the Latin Language* (1444), reveals the explosive character of the new learning. Although a good Catholic, Valla became a hero to later Protestant reformers. His popularity among them stemmed from his exposé of the *Donation of Constantine* and his defense of predestination against the advocates of free will.

The fraudulent *Donation*, written in the eighth century, purported to be a grant of vast territories that the Roman emperor Constantine (r. 307–337) donated to the pope. Using textual analysis and historical logic, Valla demonstrated that the document was filled with anachronistic terms, such as *fief*, and contained information that could not have existed in a fourth-century document. In the same dispassionate way, he also pointed out errors in the Latin Vulgate, still the authorized version of the Bible for the Western church.

Such discoveries did not make Valla any less loyal to the church, nor did they prevent his faithful fulfillment of the office of apostolic secretary in Rome under Pope Nicholas V (r. 1447–1455). Nonetheless, historical humanistic criticism of this type also served those less loyal to the medieval church. Young humanists formed the first identifiable group of Martin Luther's supporters.

Civic Humanism Education, humanists believed, should promote individual virtue and public service, hence the designation, civic humanism. The most striking examples of this were found in Florence, where three humanists served as chancellors of the city: Coluccio Salutati (1331–1406), Leonardo Bruni (ca. 1370–1444), and Poggio Bracciolini (1380–1459). Each used his rhetorical skills to rally the Florentines against the aggression of Naples and Milan. Bruni and Poggio wrote adulatory histories of the city. Another accomplished humanist scholar, Leon Battista Alberti (1402–1472), was a noted Florentine architect and builder. However, many modern scholars doubt that humanistic scholarship really accounted for such civic activity and rather view the three famous humanist chancellors of Florence as men who simply wanted to exercise power.

Toward the end of the Renaissance, many humanists became cliquish and snobbish, an intellectual elite more concerned with narrow scholarly interests and writing

COMPARE & CONNECT

IS THE "RENAISSANCE MAN" A MYTH?

As several illustrations in this chapter attest, the great artists of the Renaissance (Raphael, Leonardo da Vinci, Albrecht Dürer) romanticized their human subjects and made them larger than life. Not only was the iconic "Renaissance man" perfectly proportioned physically, but he was also effective in what he undertook, endowed with the divine freedom and power to be and to do whatever he chose.

QUESTIONS

1. Who or what are Pico's and Dürer's glorified humans? Is the vaunted "Renaissance Man" real or fictional?
2. What is one to make of an era fixated on the perfect body and mind?
3. Is Martin Luther's rejoinder (the bondage of the will) a breath of fresh air or religious misanthropy?

I. PICO DELLA MIRANDOLA, *ORATION ON THE DIGNITY OF MAN* (CA. 1486)

One of the most eloquent descriptions of the Renaissance image of human beings comes from the Italian humanist Pico della Mirandola (1463–1494). In his famed Oration on the Dignity of Man *(ca. 1486), Pico describes humans as free to become whatever they choose.*

Pico's "Renaissance Man" stands in stark contrast to the devout Christian pilgrim of the Middle Ages. The latter found himself always at the crossroads of heaven and hell, in constant fear of sin, death, and the devil, regularly confessing his sins and receiving forgiveness in an unending penitential cycle. Had the Middle Ages misjudged human nature? Was there a great transformation in human nature between the Middle Ages and the Renaissance?

The best of artisans [God] ordained that that creature (man) to whom He had been able to give nothing proper to himself should have joint possession of whatever had been peculiar to each of the different kinds of being. He therefore took man as a creature of indeterminate nature and, assigning him a place in the middle of the world, addressed him thus: "Neither a fixed abode nor a form that is thine alone nor any function peculiar to thyself have we given thee, Adam, to the end that according to thy longing and according to thy judgment thou mayest have and possess what abode, what form, and what functions thou thyself shalt desire. The nature of all other beings is limited and constrained within the bounds of laws prescribed by Us. Thou, constrained by no limits, in accordance with thine own free will, in whose hand We have placed thee, shall ordain for thyself the limits of thy nature. We have set thee at the world's center that thou mayest from thence more easily observe whatever is in the world. We have made thee neither of heaven nor of earth, neither mortal nor immortal, so that with freedom of choice and with honor, as though the maker and molder of thyself, thou mayest fashion thyself in whatever shape thou shalt prefer. Thou shalt have the power to degenerate into the lower forms of life, which are brutish. Thou shalt have the power, out of thy soul's judgment, to be reborn into the higher forms, which are divine." O supreme generosity of God the Father, O highest and most marvelous felicity of man! To him it is granted to have whatever he chooses, to be whatever he wills.

Source: Giovanni Pico della Mirandola, *Oration on the Dignity of Man*, in *The Renaissance Philosophy of Man*, ed. by E. Cassirer et al. (Chicago: Phoenix Books, 1961), pp. 224–225.

Albrecht Dürer (1471–1528), *Self-portrait at Age 28 with Fur Coat*.

1500. Oil on wood, 67 × 49 cm. Alte Pinakothek, Munich, Germany. Photograph © Scala/Art Resource, NY

What might Dürer be saying about himself in this self-portrait?

II. ALBRECHT DÜRER

In 1500, Albrecht Dürer, then twenty-eight, painted the most famous self-portrait of the European Renaissance and Reformation, one that celebrated his own beauty and genius by imposing his face on a portrayal of Christ, a work of art that has been called "the birth of the modern artist."

Fourteen years later (1514), on the occasion of his mother's death, Dürer engraved another famous image of himself, only now as a man in deep depression, or melancholy, his mind darkened and his creativity throttled.

In this self-portrait he is neither effective nor handsome, much less heroic and divine, not a self-portrait of a Renaissance man.

Albrecht Dürer, *Melencolia I* (1514).

Engraving. 23.8 X 18.9 cm. Courtesy of the Library of Congress.

What symbols did Dürer employ to suggest the effects of melancholy?

III. MARTIN LUTHER, *ON THE BONDAGE OF THE WILL* (1525)

The greater challenge to the Renaissance man came from Martin Luther, who met his "Pico" in the northern humanist Desiderius Erasmus. Like Pico, Erasmus, flying in the face of Reformation theology, conceived free will to be "a power of the human will by which a man may apply himself to those things that lead to eternal salvation, or turn away from the same." Of such thinking, Luther made short-shift.

It is in the highest degree wholesome and necessary for a Christian to know whether or not his will has anything to do in matters pertaining to salvation . . . We need to have in mind a clear-cut distinction between God's power and ours and God's work and ours, if we would live a godly life . . . The will, be it God's or man's, does what it does, good or bad, under no compulsion, but just as it wants or pleases, as if totally free . . . Wise men know what experience of life proves, that no man's purposes ever go forward as planned, but events overtake all men contrary to their expectation. . . . Who among us always lives and behaves as he should? But duty and doctrine are not therefore condemned, rather they condemn us.

God has promised His grace to the humbled, that is, to those who mourn over and despair of themselves. But a man cannot be thoroughly humbled till he realizes that his salvation is utterly beyond his own powers, counsels, efforts, will and works, and depends absolutely on the will, counsel, pleasure, and work of Another: GOD ALONE. As long as he is persuaded that he can make even the smallest contribution to his salvation, he . . . does not utterly despair of himself, and so is not humbled before God, but plans for himself a position, an occasion, a work, which shall bring him final salvation. But he who [no longer] doubts that his destiny depends entirely only on the will of God . . . waits for God to work in him, and such a man is very near to grace for his salvation. So if we want to drop this term ("free will") altogether, which would be the safest and most Christian thing to do, we may, still in good faith, teach people to use it to credit man with 'free will' in respect not of what is above him, but of what is below him . . . However, with regard to God and in all that bears on salvation or damnation, he has no 'free will' but is a captive, prisoner and bond-slave, either to the will of God, or to the will of Satan.

Source: Martin Luther, *On the Bondage of the Will*, ed. by J. I Packer & O. R. Johnston (Westwood, NJ: Fleming H. Fevell Co., 1957), pp. 79, 81, 83, 87, 100, 104, 107, 137.

pure, classical Latin than with revitalizing civic and social life. In reaction to this elitist trend, the humanist historians Niccolò Machiavelli (1469–1527) and Francesco Guicciardini (1483–1540) wrote in Italian and made contemporary history their primary source and subject matter. Here, arguably, we can see the two sides of humanism: deep scholarship and practical politics.

Renaissance Art

In Renaissance Italy, as in Reformation Europe, the values and interests of the laity were no longer subordinated to those of the clergy. In education, culture, and religion, the laity assumed a leading role and established models for the clergy to emulate. This development was due in part to the church's loss of international power during the great crises of the late Middle Ages. The rise of national sentiment and the emergence of national bureaucracies staffed by laymen, not clerics, and the rapid growth of lay education over the fourteenth and fifteenth centuries also encouraged it. Medieval Christian values were adjusted to a more this-worldly spirit.

This new perspective on life is prominent in the painting and sculpture of the High Renaissance (1450–1527), when art and sculpture reached their full maturity. Whereas medieval art tended to be abstract and formulaic, Renaissance art emphatically embraced the natural world and human emotions. Renaissance artists gave their works a rational, even mathematical, order—perfect symmetry and proportionality reflecting a belief in the harmony of the universe.

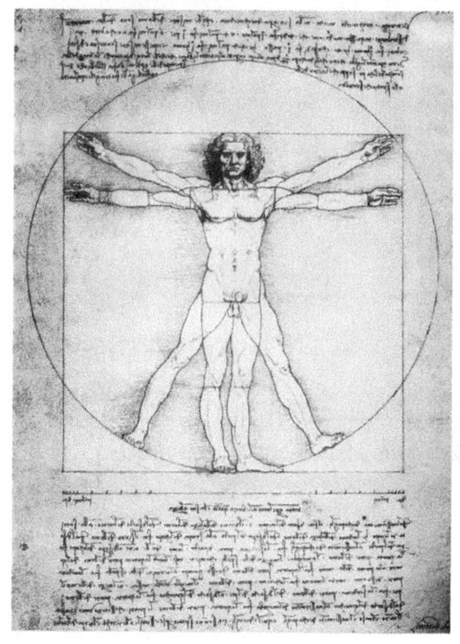

The Vitruvian Man, by Leonardo da Vinci, c. 1490. Like most other Renaissance artists, Leonardo sought to portray human beauty and perfection. This sketch is named after the first-century C.E. Roman architect Marcus Pollio Vitruvius, who used squares and circles to demonstrate the human body's symmetry and proportionality.

Corbis/Bettmann

Why did da Vinci use geometry to demonstrate man's perfection?

mannerism Reaction against the simplicity, symmetry, and idealism of High Renaissance art. It made room for the strange, even the abnormal, and gave free reign to the subjectivity of the artist. The name reflects a tendency by artists to employ "mannered" ("affected") techniques—distortions that expressed individual perceptions and feelings.

Renaissance artists were helped by the development of new technical skills during the fifteenth century. In addition to the availability of oil paints, two special techniques gave them an edge: the use of shading to enhance naturalness (*chiaroscuro*) and the adjustment of the size of figures to give the viewer a feeling of continuity with the painting (*linear perspective*). These techniques enabled the artist to portray space realistically and to paint a more natural world. The result, compared to their flat Byzantine and Gothic counterparts, was a three-dimensional canvas filled with energy and life.

Giotto (1266–1336), the father of Renaissance painting, signaled the new direction. An admirer of Saint Francis of Assisi, whose love of nature he shared, Giotto painted a more natural world. Though still filled with religious seriousness, his work was no longer an abstract and unnatural depiction of the world. The painter Masaccio (1401–1428) and the sculptor Donatello (1386–1466) also portrayed the world around them literally and naturally. The great masters of the High Renaissance—Leonardo da Vinci (1452–1519), Raphael (1483–1520), and Michelangelo Buonarroti (1475–1564)—reached the heights of such painting.

Leonardo da Vinci A true master of many skills, Leonardo exhibited the Renaissance ideal of the universal person. One of the greatest painters of all time, he also advised Italian princes and the French king Francis I (r. 1515–1547) on military engineering. He advocated scientific experimentation, dissected corpses to learn anatomy, and was a self-taught botanist. His inventive mind foresaw such modern machines as airplanes and submarines. His great skill in conveying inner moods through complex facial expression is apparent not only in his most famous painting, the *Mona Lisa,* but in his self-portrait as well.

Raphael A man of great kindness and a painter of great sensitivity, his contemporaries loved Raphael as much for his person as for his work. He is most famous for his tender madonnas and the great fresco in the Vatican, *The School of Athens,* a virtually perfect example of Renaissance technique. It depicts Plato and Aristotle surrounded by other great philosophers and scientists of antiquity who bear the features of Raphael's famous contemporaries.

Michelangelo The melancholy genius Michelangelo also excelled in a variety of arts and crafts. His eighteen-foot sculpture of David, which long stood majestically in the great square of Florence, is a perfect example of Renaissance devotion to harmony, symmetry, and proportion, all serving the glorification of the human form. Four different popes commissioned works by Michelangelo. The frescoes in the Vatican's Sistine Chapel are the most famous, painted during the pontificate of Pope Julius II (r. 1503–1513), who also set Michelangelo to work on his own magnificent tomb.

His later works mark, artistically and philosophically, the passing of High Renaissance painting and the advent of a new style known as **mannerism**, which reached its peak in the late sixteenth and early seventeenth centuries. A reaction to the simplicity and symmetry of High Renaissance art, which also had a parallel in contemporary music and literature, mannerism made room for the strange and the abnormal, giving freer reign to the individual perceptions and feelings of the artist, who now felt free to paint, compose, or write in a "mannered," or "affected," way. Tintoretto (d. 1594) and El Greco (d. 1614) are mannerism's supreme representatives.

Combining the painterly qualities of all the other Renaissance masters, Raphael created scenes of tender beauty and subjects sublime in both flesh and spirit.

Musée du Louvre, Paris/Giraudon, Paris/SuperStock

How did Raphael use the depiction of human emotion to comment on the nature of divine truth?

Slavery in the Renaissance

Throughout Renaissance Italy, slavery flourished as extravagantly as art and culture. A thriving Western slave market existed as early as the twelfth century, when the Spanish sold Muslim slaves captured in raids and war to wealthy Italians and other buyers. In addition to widespread household or domestic slavery, collective plantation slavery, following East Asian models, also developed in the eastern Mediterranean during the High Middle Ages. In the savannas of Sudan and the Venetian estates on the islands of Cyprus and Crete, gangs of slaves cut sugarcane, setting the model for later slave plantations in the Mediterranean and the New World.

After the Black Death (1348–1350) reduced the supply of laborers everywhere in Western Europe, the demand for slaves soared. Slaves were imported from Africa, the Balkans, Constantinople, Cyprus, Crete, and the lands surrounding the Black Sea.

Tatars and Africans appear to have been the worst treated, but as in ancient Greece and Rome, slaves at this time were generally accepted as family members and integrated into households. Not a few women slaves became mothers of their masters' children. Fathers often adopted children of such unions and raised them as their legitimate heirs. It was also in the interest of their owners to keep slaves healthy and happy; otherwise they would be of little use and even become a threat. Slaves nonetheless remained a foreign and suspected presence in Italian society; they were, as all knew, uprooted and resentful people.

SIGNIFICANT DATES FROM THE ITALIAN RENAISSANCE (1375–1527)

1434	Medici rule established in Florence
1454–1455	Treaty of Lodi
1494	Charles VIII of France invades Italy
1495	League of Venice
1499	Louis XII invades Italy
1500	The Borgias conquer Romagna
1512–1513	The Holy League defeats the French
1515	Francis I invades Italy
1527	Sack of Rome by imperial soldiers

ITALY'S POLITICAL DECLINE: THE FRENCH INVASIONS (1494–1527)

WHAT WERE the causes of Italy's political decline?

As a land of autonomous city-states, Italy had always relied on internal cooperation for its peace and safety from foreign invasion—especially by the Turks. Such cooperation was maintained during the second half of the fifteenth century, thanks to a political alliance known as the Treaty of Lodi (1454–1455). Its terms brought Milan and Naples, long traditional enemies, into the alliance with Florence. These three stood together for decades against Venice, which frequently joined the Papal States to maintain an internal balance of power. However, when a foreign enemy threatened Italy, the five states could also present a united front.

Around 1490, after the rise to power of the Milanese despot Ludovico il Moro, hostilities between Milan and Naples resumed. The peace that the Treaty of Lodi made possible ended in 1494 when Naples, supported by Florence and the Borgia Pope Alexander VI (r. 1492–1503), threatened Milan. Ludovico made a fatal response to these new political alignments: He appealed to the French for aid. French kings had ruled Naples from 1266 to 1442 before being driven out by Duke Alfonso of Sicily. Breaking a wise Italian rule, Ludovico invited the French to reenter Italy and revive their dynastic claim to Naples. In his haste to check rival Naples, Ludovico did not recognize sufficiently that France also had dynastic claims to Milan. Nor did he foresee how insatiable the French appetite for new territory would become once French armies had crossed the Alps and encamped in Italy.

Charles VIII's March Through Italy

The French king Louis XI had resisted the temptation to invade Italy while nonetheless keeping French dynastic claims in Italy alive. His successor, Charles VIII (r. 1483–1498), an eager youth in his twenties, responded to Ludovico's call with lightning speed. Within five months, he had crossed the Alps (August 1494) and raced as conqueror through Florence and the Papal States into Naples. As Charles approached Florence, its Florentine ruler, Piero de' Medici, who was allied with Naples against Milan, tried to placate the French king by handing over Pisa and other Florentine possessions. Such appeasement only brought about Piero's exile by a citizenry that was being revolutionized by a radical Dominican preacher named Girolamo Savonarola (1452–1498). Savonarola convinced the fearful Florentines that the French king's arrival was a long-delayed and fully justified divine vengeance on their immorality.

That allowed Charles to enter Florence without resistance. Between Savonarola's fatal flattery and the payment of a large ransom, the city escaped destruction. After Charles's departure, Savonarola exercised virtual rule over Florence for four years, but the Florentines eventually tired of his puritanical tyranny and executed him (May 1498).

Charles's lightning march through Italy also struck terror in non-Italian hearts. Ferdinand of Aragon (r. 1479–1516), who had hoped to expand his own possessions in Italy from his base in Sicily, now found himself vulnerable to a French-Italian axis. In response he created a new counteralliance—the League of Venice. Formed in March 1495, the League brought Venice, the Papal States, and Emperor Maximilian I (r. 1493–1519) together with Ferdinand against the French. When Milan, which had come to regret inviting the French into Italy, joined the League, Charles was forced to retreat.

Pope Alexander VI and the Borgia Family

The French returned to Italy under Charles's successor, Louis XII (r. 1498–1515). This time a new Italian ally, the Borgia pope, Alexander VI, assisted them. He placed papal policy in tandem with the efforts of his powerful family to secure a political base in Romagna in north central Italy.

In Romagna, several principalities had fallen away from the church during the Avignon papacy. Venice, the pope's ally within the League of Venice, continued to contest the Papal States for their loyalty. Seeing that a French alliance would allow him to reestablish control over the region, Alexander worked hard to secure French favor and to make it possible for both the French king and the pope to realize their am-

bitions within Italy. Louis invaded Milan in August 1499. In 1500, Louis and Ferdinand of Aragon divided Naples between them, and the pope and his illegitimate son, Cesare Borgia, conquered the cities of Romagna without opposition. Alexander's victorious son was given the title "duke of Romagna."

Pope Julius II

Cardinal Giuliano della Rovere, a strong opponent of the Borgia family, succeeded Alexander VI as Pope Julius II (r. 1503–1513). He suppressed the Borgias and placed their newly conquered lands in Romagna under papal jurisdiction. Julius raised the Renaissance papacy to its peak of military prowess and diplomatic intrigue, gaining him the title of "warrior pope."

Assisted by his powerful allies, Pope Julius drove the Venetians out of Romagna in 1509 and fully secured the Papal States. Having realized this long-sought papal goal, Julius turned to the second major undertaking of his pontificate: ridding Italy of his former ally, the French invader. Julius, Ferdinand of Aragon, and Venice formed a second Holy League in October 1511 and were joined by Emperor Maximilian I and the Swiss. In 1512, the league had the French in full retreat, and the Swiss defeated them in 1513 at Novara.

The French were nothing if not persistent. They invaded Italy a third time under Louis's successor, Francis I (r. 1515–1547). French victory won the Concordat of Bologna from the pope in August 1516, an agreement that gave the French king control over the French clergy in exchange for French recognition of the pope's superiority over church councils and his right to collect annates in France. This concordat helped keep France Catholic after the outbreak of the Protestant Reformation, but the new French entry into Italy set the stage for the first of four major wars with Spain in the first half of the sixteenth century: the Habsburg-Valois wars, none of which France won.

QUICK REVIEW

The Warrior Pope

- Julius II's (r. 1503–1513) reign marked the pinnacle of the papacy's military prowess
- After securing Romagna and the Papal States, he set about pushing the French out of Italy
- Julius formed a Holy League with Ferdinand of Aragon and Venice in 1511 for this purpose

Niccolò Machiavelli

The foreign invasions made a shambles of Italy. One who watched as French, Spanish, and German armies wreaked havoc on Italy was Niccolò Machiavelli (1469–1527). The more he saw, the more convinced he became that Italian political unity and independence were ends that justified any means.

A humanist and a careful student of ancient Rome, Machiavelli was impressed by the way Roman rulers and citizens had then defended their homeland. They possessed *virtù*, the ability to act decisively and heroically for the good of their country. Stories of ancient Roman patriotism and self-sacrifice were Machiavelli's favorites, and he lamented the absence of such traits among his compatriots.

Machiavelli also held republican ideals, which he did not want to see vanish from Italy. He believed a strong and determined people could struggle successfully with fortune. He scolded the Italian people for the self-destruction their own internal feuding was causing. He wanted an end to that behavior above all, so a reunited Italy could drive all foreign armies out.

His fellow citizens were not up to such a challenge. The juxtaposition of what Machiavelli believed the ancient Romans had been, with the failure of his contemporaries to attain such high ideals, made him the famous cynic whose name—in the epithet "Machiavellian"—has become synonymous with ruthless political expediency. Only a strongman, he concluded, could impose order on so divided and selfish a people; the salvation of Italy required, for the present, cunning dictators.

It has been argued that Machiavelli wrote *The Prince* in 1513 as a cynical satire on the way rulers actually do behave and not as a serious recommendation of unprincipled despotic rule. But Machiavelli seems to have been in earnest when he advised rulers to discover the advantages of fraud and brutality, at least as a temporary means to

Santi di Tito's portrait of Machiavelli, perhaps the most famous Italian political theorist, who advised Renaissance princes to practice artful deception and inspire fear in their subjects if they wished to be successful.

Scala/Art Resource, NY

Should we consider Machiavelli a humanist? Why or why not?

the higher end of a unified Italy. He apparently hoped to see a strong ruler emerge from the Medici family, which had captured the papacy in 1513 with the pontificate of Leo X (r. 1513–1521). At the same time, the Medici family retained control over the powerful territorial state of Florence. *The Prince* was pointedly dedicated to Lorenzo de' Medici, duke of Urbino and grandson of Lorenzo the Magnificent.

Whatever Machiavelli's hopes may have been, the Medicis were not destined to be Italy's deliverers. The second Medici pope, Clement VII (r. 1523–1534), watched helplessly as the army of Emperor Charles V sacked Rome in 1527, also the year of Machiavelli's death.

REVIVAL OF MONARCHY IN NORTHERN EUROPE

HOW WERE the powerful monarchies of northern Europe different from their predecessors?

After 1450, the emergence of truly sovereign rulers set in motion a shift from divided feudal monarchy to unified national monarchies. Dynastic and chivalric ideals of feudal monarchy did not, however, vanish. Territorial princes remained on the scene and representative bodies persisted and even grew in influence. Still, in the late fifteenth and early sixteenth centuries, the old problem of the one and the many was now progressively decided in favor of national monarchs.

The feudal monarchy of the High Middle Ages was characterized by the division of the basic powers of government between the king and his semiautonomous vassals. The nobility and the towns then acted with varying degrees of unity and success through evolving representative assemblies, such as the English Parliament, the French Estates General, and the Spanish *Cortés*, to thwart the centralization of royal power into a united nation. But after the Hundred Years' War and the Great Schism in the church, the nobility and the clergy were in decline and less able to block growing national monarchies.

The increasingly important towns now began to ally with the king. Loyal, business-wise townspeople, not the nobility and the clergy, increasingly staffed royal offices and became the king's lawyers, bookkeepers, military tacticians, and foreign diplomats. This new alliance between king and town broke the bonds of feudal society and made possible the rise of sovereign states.

In a sovereign state, the powers of taxation, war making, and law enforcement no longer belong to semiautonomous vassals, but are concentrated in the monarch and exercised by his or her chosen agents. Taxes, wars, and laws become national, rather than merely regional, matters. Only as monarchs became able to act independently of the nobility and representative assemblies could they overcome the decentralization that impeded nation building.

The many were, of course, never totally subjugated to the one. But in the last half of the fifteenth century, rulers demonstrated that the law was their creature. They appointed civil servants whose vision was no longer merely local or regional. These royal ministers and agents could become closely attached to the localities they administered in the ruler's name, and regions were able to secure congenial royal appointments. Nonetheless, these new executives remained royal executives, bureaucrats whose outlook was now "national" and whose loyalty was to the "state."

Monarchies also began to create standing national armies in the fifteenth century. The noble cavalry receded as the infantry and the artillery became the backbone of royal armies. Mercenary soldiers were recruited from Switzerland and Germany to form the major part of the "king's army." Professional soldiers who fought for pay and booty proved far more efficient than feudal vassals who fought simply for honor's sake. Monarchs who failed to meet their payrolls, however, now faced a new danger of mutiny and banditry by foreign troops.

The growing cost of warfare in the fifteenth and sixteenth centuries increased the monarch's need for new national sources of income. The great obstacle was the stubborn belief of the highest social classes that they were immune from government taxation. The nobility guarded their properties and traditional rights and despised taxation as an insult and a humiliation. Royal revenues accordingly had to grow at the expense of those least able to resist and least able to pay.

The monarchs had several options when it came to raising money. As feudal lords, they could collect rents from their royal domains. They could also levy national taxes on basic food and clothing. The rulers could also levy direct taxes on the peasantry, which they did through agreeable representative assemblies of the privileged classes in which the peasantry did not sit. Innovative fund-raising devices in the fifteenth century included the sale of public offices and the issuance of high-interest government bonds. Rulers still did not levy taxes on the powerful nobility, but instead, they borrowed from rich nobles and the great bankers of Italy and Germany. In money matters, the privileged classes remained as much the kings' creditors and competitors as their subjects.

FRANCE

Charles VII (r. 1422–1461) was a king made great by those who served him. His ministers and advisors created a permanent professional army and helped develop a strong economy, diplomatic corps, and national administration during Charles's reign. These sturdy tools in turn enabled Charles's son and successor, the ruthless Louis XI (r. 1461–1483), to make France a great power.

French nation building had two political cornerstones in the fifteenth century. The first was the collapse of the English Empire in France following the Hundred Years' War. The second was the defeat of Charles the Bold (r. 1467–1477) and his duchy of Burgundy. Louis XI and Habsburg emperor Maximilian I divided the conquered Burgundian lands between them, with the treaty-wise Habsburgs getting the better part. The dissolution of Burgundy ended its constant intrigue against the French king and left Louis XI free to secure the monarchy. Between the newly acquired Burgundian lands and his own inheritance, the king was able to end his reign with a kingdom almost twice the size of that he had inherited.

A strong nation is a two-edged sword. Because Louis's successors inherited a secure and efficient government, they felt free to pursue what proved ultimately to be a bad foreign policy. Conquests in Italy in the 1490s and a long series of losing wars with the Habsburgs in the first half of the sixteenth century left France, by the mid-sixteenth century, once again a defeated nation almost as divided as it had been during the Hundred Years' War.

SPAIN

Both Castile and Aragon had been poorly ruled and divided kingdoms in the mid–fifteenth century, but the union of Isabella of Castile (r. 1474–1504) and Ferdinand of Aragon (r. 1479–1516) in 1469 changed that situation. Although the marriage of Ferdinand and Isabella dynastically united the two kingdoms, they remained constitutionally separated. Each retained its respective government agencies—separate laws, armies, coinage, and taxation—and cultural traditions.

Ferdinand and Isabella could do together what neither was able to accomplish alone: subdue their realms, secure their borders, venture abroad militarily, and Christianize the whole of Spain. Between 1482 and 1492 they conquered the Moors in Granada. Naples became a Spanish possession in 1504. By 1512, Ferdinand had secured his northern borders by conquering the kingdom of Navarre. Internally, the Spanish king and queen won the allegiance of the *Hermandad*, a powerful league of cities and towns that served them against stubborn noble landowners. The crown also extended its authority over the wealthy chivalric orders, further limiting the power of the nobility.

Spain had long been remarkable among European lands as a place where three religions—Islam, Judaism, and Christianity—coexisted with a certain degree of toleration. That toleration was to end dramatically under Ferdinand and Isabella, who made Spain the prime exemplar of state-controlled religion.

Ferdinand and Isabella exercised almost total control over the Spanish church as they placed religion in the service of national unity. They appointed the higher clergy and the officers of the Inquisition. The latter, run by Tomás de Torquemada (d. 1498), Isabella's confessor, was a key national agency established in 1479 to monitor the activity of converted Jews (*conversos*) and Muslims (*Moriscos*) in Spain. In 1492, the Jews were exiled and their properties confiscated. In 1502, nonconverting Moors in Granada were driven into exile by Cardinal Francisco Jiménez de Cisneros (1437–1517).

Despite a certain internal narrowness, Ferdinand and Isabella were rulers with wide horizons. They contracted anti-French marriage alliances that came to determine a large part of European history in the sixteenth century. In 1496, their eldest daughter, Joanna, later known as "the Mad," married Archduke Philip, the son of Emperor Maximilian I. The fruit of this union, Charles I, was the first to rule over a united Spain; by his inheritance and election as emperor in 1519, his empire almost equaled in size that of Charlemagne. A second daughter, Catherine of Aragon, wed Arthur, the son of the English king Henry VII. After Arthur's premature death, she was betrothed to his brother, the future King Henry VIII (r. 1509–1547), whom she married eight years later, in 1509. The failure of this marriage became the key factor in the emergence of the Anglican church and the English Reformation.

QUICK REVIEW

Unification of Spain

- Aragon and Castile unified by marriage of Ferdinand and Isabella
- 1492: The last Muslim state in the Iberian peninsula, Granada, falls
- Ferdinand and Isabella sought to create religious uniformity in their lands by force

The new power of Spain was also revealed in Ferdinand and Isabella's promotion of overseas exploration. They sponsored the Genoese adventurer Christopher Columbus (1451–1506), who arrived at the islands of the Caribbean while sailing west in search of a shorter route to the spice markets of the Far East. This patronage led to the creation of the Spanish Empire in Mexico and Peru, whose gold and silver mines helped make Spain Europe's dominant power in the sixteenth century.

England

The latter half of the fifteenth century was a period of especially difficult political trial for the English. Following the Hundred Years' War, civil warfare broke out between two rival branches of the royal family: the House of York and the House of Lancaster. The roots of the war lay in succession irregularities after the forced deposition of the erratic king Richard II (r. 1377–1399). This conflict, known to us today as the Wars of the Roses (because York's symbol, according to legend, was a white rose and Lancaster's a red rose), kept England in turmoil from 1455 to 1485.

The duke of York and his supporters in the prosperous southern towns challenged the Lancastrian monarchy of Henry VI (r. 1422–1461). In 1461, Edward IV (r. 1461–1483), son of the duke of York, seized power and instituted a strong-arm rule that lasted more than twenty years; it was only briefly interrupted, in 1470–1471, by Henry VI's short-lived restoration. Assisted by able ministers, Edward effectively increased the power and finances of the monarchy. His brother, Richard III (r. 1483–1485), usurped the throne from Edward's son. Richard's reign saw the growth of support for the exiled Lancastrian Henry Tudor, who returned to England to defeat Richard on Bosworth Field in August 1485.

Early British pound coin, 1545, showing Henry VII on throne.

Dorling Kindersley Media Library/Chas Howson © The British Museum

Henry Tudor ruled as Henry VII (r. 1485–1509), the first of the new Tudor dynasty that would dominate England throughout the sixteenth century. He succeeded in disciplining the English nobility through a special instrument of the royal will known as the

Court of Star Chamber. Created with the sanction of Parliament in 1487, the court was intended to end the perversion of English justice by "over-mighty subjects," that is, powerful nobles who used intimidation and bribery to win favorable verdicts in court cases.

Henry shrewdly used English law to further the ends of the monarchy. He managed to confiscate lands and fortunes of nobles with such success that he was able to govern without dependence on Parliament for royal funds, always a cornerstone of a strong monarchy. In these ways, Henry began to shape a monarchy that would develop into one of early modern Europe's most exemplary governments during the reign of his granddaughter, Elizabeth I (r. 1558–1603).

THE HOLY ROMAN EMPIRE

Germany and Italy were the striking exceptions to the steady development of politically centralized lands in the last half of the fifteenth century. In Germany, territorial rulers and cities resisted every effort at national consolidation and unity. By the late fifteenth century, Germany was hopelessly divided into some three hundred autonomous political entities.

The princes and the cities did work together to create the machinery of law and order, if not of union, within the divided empire. Emperor Charles IV (r. 1346–1378) and the major German territorial rulers reached an agreement in 1356 known as the **Golden Bull**. It established a seven-member electoral college consisting of the archbishops of Mainz, Trier, and Cologne; the duke of Saxony; the margrave of Brandenburg; the count Palatine; and the king of Bohemia. This group also functioned as an administrative body. They elected the emperor and, in cooperation with him, provided what transregional unity and administration existed.

Golden Bull Arrangements agreed to by the Holy Roman Emperor and the major German territorial rulers in 1356 that helped stabilize Germany.

In the fifteenth century, an effort was made to control incessant feuding by the creation of an imperial diet known as the *Reichstag*. This was a national assembly of the seven electors, the nonelectoral princes, and representatives from the sixty-five imperial free cities. The cities were the weakest of the three bodies represented in the diet. During such an assembly in Worms in 1495, the members won from Emperor Maximilian I an imperial ban on private warfare, the creation of a Supreme Court of Justice to enforce internal peace, and an imperial Council of Regency to coordinate imperial and internal German policy. The emperor only grudgingly conceded the latter because it gave the princes a share in executive power.

These reforms were still a poor substitute for true national unity. In the sixteenth and seventeenth centuries, the territorial princes became virtually sovereign rulers in their various domains. Such disunity aided religious dissent and conflict. It was in the cities and territories of still feudal, fractionalized, backward Germany that the Protestant Reformation broke out in the sixteenth century.

THE NORTHERN RENAISSANCE

HOW DID the northern Renaissance affect culture in Germany, England, France, and Spain?

The scholarly works of northern humanists created a climate favorable to religious and educational reforms on the eve of the Reformation. Northern humanism was initially stimulated by the importation of Italian learning through such varied intermediaries as students who had studied in Italy, merchants who traded there, and the Brothers of the Common Life. This last was an influential lay religious movement that began in the Netherlands and permitted men and women to live a shared religious life without making formal vows of poverty, chastity, and obedience.

The northern humanists, however, developed their own distinctive culture. They tended to come from more diverse social backgrounds and to be more devoted to religious reforms than their Italian counterparts. They were also more willing to write for lay audiences as well as for a narrow intelligentsia. Thanks to the invention of printing with movable type, it became possible for humanists to convey their educational ideals to laypeople and clerics alike. Printing gave new power and influence to elites in both church and state, who now could popularize their viewpoints freely and widely.

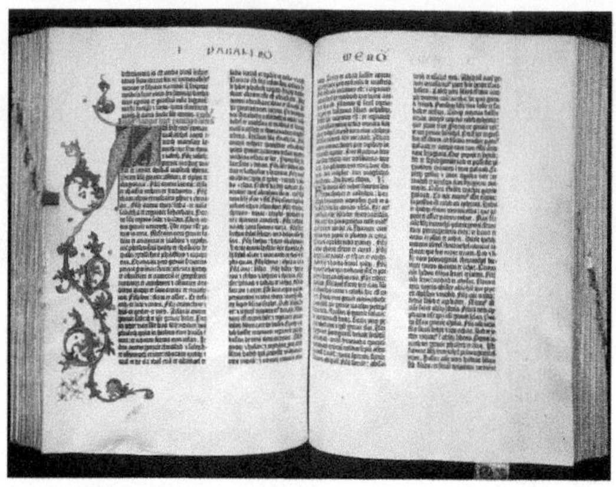

The printing press made possible the diffusion of Renaissance learning. No book stimulated more at this time than did the Bible. With Gutenberg's publication of a printed Bible in 1454, scholars gained access to a dependable, standardized text, so Scripture could be discussed and debated as never before.

How did the advent of printing change the nature of the Renaissance?

The Printing Press

A variety of forces converged in the fourteenth and fifteenth centuries to give rise to the invention of the printing press. Since the days of Charlemagne, kings and princes had encouraged schools and literacy to help provide educated bureaucrats to staff the offices of their kingdoms. By the fifteenth century, a new literate lay public had been created, thanks to the enormous expansion of schools and universities during the late Middle Ages. The invention of a cheap way to manufacture paper also helped make books economical and broaden their content.

In response to the demand for books that the expansion of lay education and literacy created, Johann Gutenberg (d. 1468) invented printing with movable type in the mid–fifteenth century in the German city of Mainz, the center of printing for the whole of Western Europe. Thereafter, books were rapidly and handsomely produced on topics both profound and practical and were intended for ordinary lay readers, scholars, and clerics alike.

Literacy deeply affected people everywhere, nurturing self-esteem and a critical frame of mind. By standardizing texts, the print revolution made anyone who could read an instant authority. Rulers in church and state now had to deal with a less credulous and less docile laity. Print was also a powerful tool for political and religious propaganda. Kings could now indoctrinate people as never before, and clergymen found themselves able to mass-produce both indulgences and pamphlets.

Erasmus

The far-reaching influence of Desiderius Erasmus (1466?–1536), the most famous northern humanist, illustrates the impact of the printing press. Through his printed works, Erasmus gained fame both as an educational and as a religious reformer. A lifelong Catholic, his life and work make clear that many loyal Catholics wanted major reforms in the church long before the Reformation made them a reality.

Erasmus aspired to unite classical ideals of humanity and civic virtue with the Christian ideals of love and piety. He believed disciplined study of the classics and the Bible, if begun early enough, was the best way to reform individuals and society. He summarized his own beliefs with the phrase *philosophia Christi*, a simple, ethical piety in imitation of Christ. He set this ideal in stark contrast to what he believed to be the dogmatic, ceremonial, and bullying religious practices of the later Middle Ages.

Erasmus was a true idealist, who expected more from people than the age's theologians believed them capable of doing. To promote what he deemed to be the essence of Christianity, he made ancient Christian sources available in their original versions, believing that if people would only imbibe the pure sources of the faith, they would recover the moral and religious health the New Testament promises. To this end, Erasmus edited the works of the Church Fathers and produced a Greek edition of the New Testament (1516), later adding a new Latin translation of the latter (1519). Martin Luther used both of those works when he translated the New Testament into German in 1522.

These various enterprises did not please the church authorities. They remained unhappy with Erasmus's "improvements" on the Vulgate, Christendom's Bible for over a thousand years, and his popular anticlerical writings. At one point in the mid–sixteenth century, all of Erasmus's works were on the church's *Index of Forbidden Books*. Luther also condemned Erasmus for his views on the freedom of human will. Still, Erasmus's works put sturdy tools of reform in the hands of both Protestant and Catholic reformers.

Albrecht Dürer (1471–1528), *Portrait of the Moorish Woman Katharina*, drawing.

Uffizi Florence, Italy. Albrecht Dürer (1471–1528), *Portrait of the Moorish Woman Katharina*. Drawing. Uffizi Florence, Italy. Photograph © Foto Marburg/Art Resource, NY

What might explain the interest of early modern artists in ordinary people as subjects?

Humanism and Reform

In Germany, England, France, and Spain, humanism stirred both educational and religious reform.

Germany Rudolf Agricola (1443–1485), the "father of German humanism," spent ten years in Italy and introduced Italian learning to Germany when he returned. Conrad Celtis (d. 1508), the first German poet laureate, and Ulrich von Hutten (1488–1523), a fiery knight, gave German humanism a nationalist coloring hostile to non-German cultures, particularly Roman culture.

The controversy that brought von Hutten onto the historical stage and unified reform-minded German humanists was the Reuchlin affair. Johann Reuchlin (1455–1522) was Europe's foremost Christian authority on Hebrew and Jewish learning. Around 1506, supported by the Dominican order in Cologne, a Christian who had converted from Judaism began a movement to suppress Jewish writings. When this man, whose name was Pfefferkorn, attacked Reuchlin, many German humanists, in the name of academic freedom and good scholarship—not for any pro-Jewish sentiment—rushed to Reuchlin's defense. When Martin Luther came under attack in 1517 for his famous ninety-five theses against indulgences, many German humanists saw a repetition of the Scholastic attack on Reuchlin and rushed to his side.

England Thomas More (1478–1535), a close friend of Erasmus, is the best known English humanist. His *Utopia* (1516), a conservative criticism of contemporary society, rivals the plays of Shakespeare as the most read sixteenth-century English work. *Utopia* depicted an imaginary society based on reason and tolerance that overcame social and political injustice by holding all property and goods in common and requiring everyone to earn their bread by their own work.

More became one of Henry VIII's most trusted diplomats. His repudiation of the Act of Supremacy (1534), which made the king of England head of the English church in place of the pope (see Chapter 11), and his refusal to recognize the king's marriage to Anne Boleyn, however, led to his execution in July 1535. Although More remained Catholic, humanism in England, as also in Germany, helped prepare the way for the English Reformation.

France The French invasions of Italy made it possible for Italian learning to penetrate France, stirring both educational and religious reform. Guillaume Budé (1468–1540), an accomplished Greek scholar, and Jacques Lefèvre d'Etaples (1454–1536), a biblical authority, were the leaders of French humanism. Lefèvre's scholarly works exemplified the new critical scholarship and influenced Martin Luther. Guillaume Briçonnet (1470–1533), the bishop of Meaux, and Marguerite d'Angoulême (1492–1549), sister of King Francis I, the future queen of Navarre, and a successful spiritual writer in her own right, cultivated a generation of young reform-minded humanists. The future Protestant reformer John Calvin was a product of this native reform circle.

Spain Whereas in England, France, and Germany, humanism prepared the way for Protestant reforms, in Spain it entered the service of the Catholic Church. Here the key figure was Francisco Jiménez de Cisneros (1437–1517), a confessor to Queen Isabella and, after 1508, the "Grand Inquisitor"—a position that allowed him to enforce

Overview Humanism and Reform

GERMANY	• Rudolf Agricola, the father of German humanism, brought Italian learning to Germany. • German humanism was given a nationalist coloring hostile to non-German cultures. • The Reuchlin affair caused the unification of reform-minded German humanists. • When Martin Luther came under attack in 1517, many German humanists rushed to his side.
ENGLAND	• Thomas More is the best known English humanist. • More's *Utopia* depicted a tolerant, just society that held property and goods in common. • Humanism in England played a key role in preparing the way for the English Reformation.
FRANCE	• Guillaume Budé and Jacques Lefèvre d'Etaples were the leaders of French humanism. • Lefèvre's works exemplified the new critical scholarship and influenced Martin Luther. • A new generation was cultivated by Marguerite d'Angoulême. • The future Protestant reformer John Calvin was a product of this native reform circle.
SPAIN	• Unlike the other countries, in Spain humanism entered the service of the Catholic Church. • Francisco Jiménez de Cisneros was the key figure in Spanish humanism. • In Jiménez's *Complutensian Polygot Bible*, Hebrew, Greek, and Latin appeared together. • This with church reform helped keep Spain strictly Catholic in the Age of Reformation.

the strictest religious orthodoxy. His great achievement, taking fifteen years to complete, was the *Complutensian Polyglot Bible*, a six-volume work that placed the Hebrew, Greek, and Latin versions of the Bible in parallel columns. Such scholarly projects and internal church reforms joined with the repressive measures of Ferdinand and Isabella to keep Spain strictly Catholic throughout the Age of Reformation.

VOYAGES OF DISCOVERY AND THE NEW EMPIRES IN THE WEST AND EAST

WHAT WERE the motives for European voyages of discovery, and what were the consequences?

The discovery of the Americas dramatically expanded the horizons of Europeans, both geographically and intellectually. Knowledge of the New World's inhabitants and the exploitation of its mineral and human wealth set new cultural and economic forces in motion throughout Western Europe.

Beginning with the voyages of the Portuguese and Spanish in the fifteenth century, commercial supremacy progressively shifted from the Mediterranean and Baltic seas to the Atlantic seaboard, setting the stage for global expansion. (See Map 10–2.)

THE PORTUGUESE CHART THE COURSE

Seventy-seven years before Columbus, who sailed under the flag of Spain, set foot in the Americas, Prince Henry "the Navigator" (1394–1460), brother of the king of Portugal, captured the North African Muslim city of Ceuta. His motives were mercenary and religious, both a quest for gold and spices and the pious work of saving the souls of Muslims and pagans who had no knowledge of Christ. Thus began the Portuguese exploration of the African coast, first in search of gold and slaves, and then by century's end, of a sea route around Africa to Asia's spice markets.

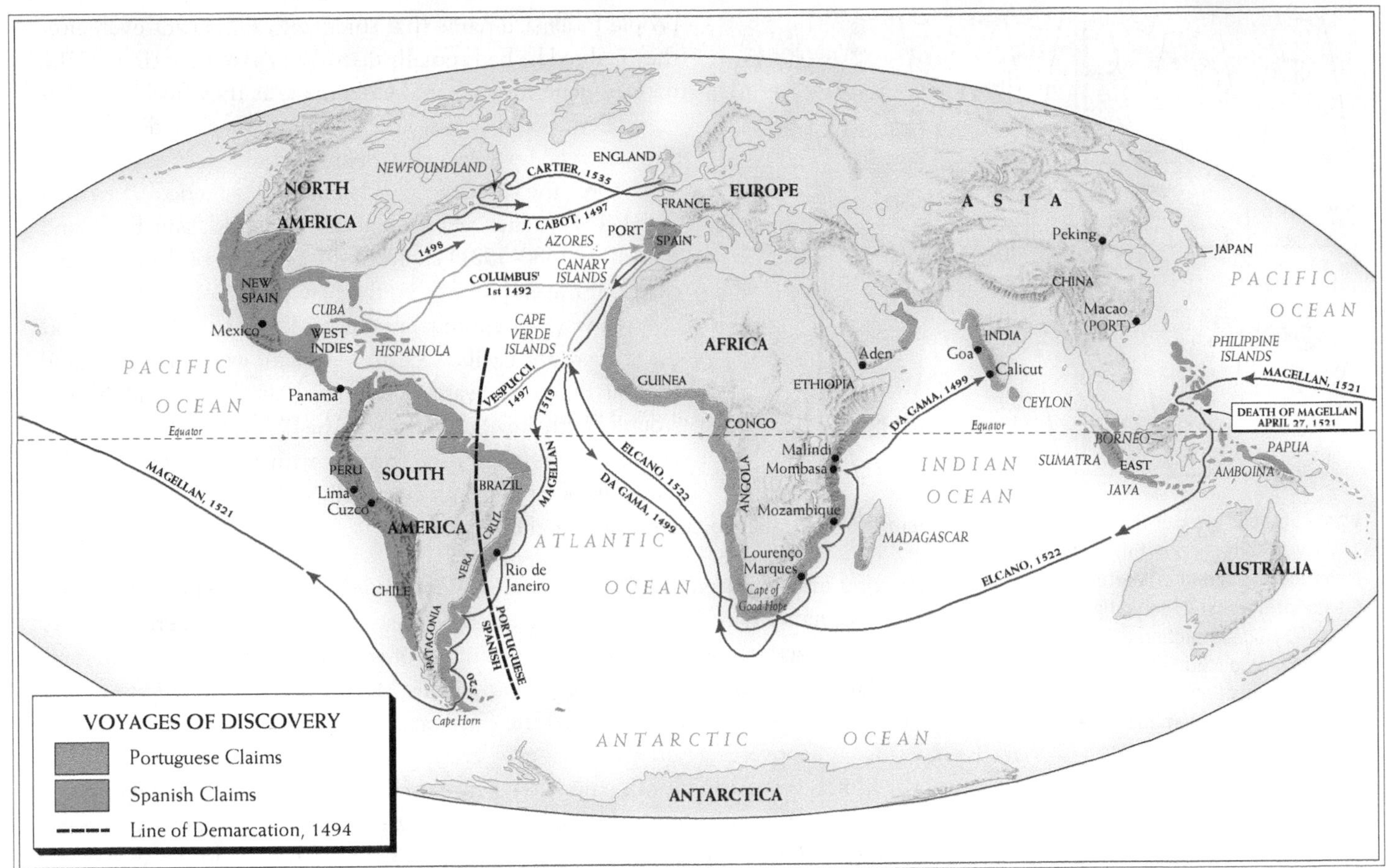

MAP 10–2 European Voyages of Discovery and the Colonial Claims of Spain and Portugal in the Fifteenth and Sixteenth Centuries

The map depicts Europe's global expansion in the fifteenth and sixteenth centuries.

What reasons did European explorers have for their many voyages of discovery?

Before there was a sea route to the East, Europeans could only get spices through the Venetians, who bought or bartered them from Muslim merchants in Egypt and the Ottoman Empire. The Portuguese resolved to beat this powerful Venetian-Muslim monopoly by sailing directly to the source.

Bartholomew Dias (ca. 1450–1500) pioneered the eastern Portuguese Empire after safely rounding the Cape of Good Hope at the tip of Africa in 1487. A decade later, in 1498, Vasco da Gama (1469–1525) stood on the shores of India. When he returned to Portugal, he carried a cargo of spices worth sixty times the cost of the voyage. Later, the Portuguese established colonies in Goa and Calcutta on the coast of India, whence they challenged the Arabs and the Venetians for control of the spice trade.

The Portuguese had concentrated their explorations on the Indian Ocean. The Spanish turned west, believing they could find a shorter route to the East Indies by sailing across the Atlantic. Instead, Christopher Columbus (1451–1506) discovered the Americas.

The Spanish Voyages of Columbus

Thirty-three days after departing the Canary Islands, on October 12, 1492, Columbus landed in San Salvador (Watlings Island) in the eastern Bahamas. Thinking he was in the East Indies, he mistook his first landfall as an outer island of Japan. Not until his third voyage to the Caribbean in 1498 did Columbus realize that Cuba was not Japan and South America was not China.

Naked, friendly natives met Columbus and his crew on the beaches of the New World. They were Taino Indians, who spoke a variant of a language known as Arawak. Believing the island on which he landed to be the East Indies, Columbus called these

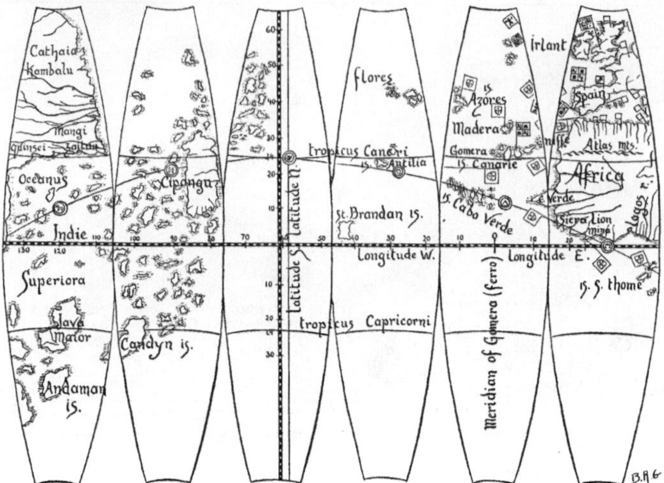

What Columbus knew of the world in 1492 was contained in this map by the Nuremberg geographer Martin Behaim, creator of the first spherical globe of the earth. The ocean section of Behaim's globe is reproduced here. Departing the Canary Islands (in the second section from the right), Columbus expected his first major landfall to be Japan (Cipangu, in the second section from the left). When he landed at San Salvador, he thought he was on the outer island of Japan. Thus, when he arrived in Cuba, he thought he was in Japan.

What errors in his understanding of geography led Columbus to conclude he could reach Japan by sailing west?

people Indians, a name that stuck with Europeans even after they realized he had actually discovered a new continent. The natives' generosity amazed Columbus, as they freely gave his men all the corn, yams, and sexual favors they desired. He also observed how easily the Spanish could enslave them.

On the heels of Columbus, Amerigo Vespucci (1451–1512), after whom America is named, and Ferdinand Magellan (1480–1521) explored the coastline of South America. Their travels proved that the new lands Columbus had discovered were an entirely unknown continent that opened on the still greater Pacific Ocean. Magellan, who was continuing the search for a westward route to the Indies, made it all the way around South America and across the Pacific to the Philippines, where he was killed in a skirmish with the inhabitants. The remnants of his squadron eventually sailed on to Spain, making them the first sailors to circumnavigate the globe.

Intended and Unintended Consequences Columbus's first voyage marked the beginning of more than three centuries of a vast Spanish empire in the Americas. What began as voyages of discovery became expeditions of conquest, not unlike the warfare Christian Aragon and Castile waged against Islamic Moors. Those wars had just ended in 1492, and their conclusion imbued the early Spanish explorers with a zeal for conquering and converting non-Christian peoples.

Much to the benefit of Spain, the voyages of discovery created Europe's largest and longest surviving trading bloc and spurred other European countries to undertake their own colonial ventures. The wealth extracted from its American possessions financed Spain's commanding role in the religious and political wars of the sixteenth and seventeenth centuries, while fueling a Europe-wide economic expansion.

European expansion also had a profound biological impact. Europeans introduced numerous new species of fruits, vegetables, and animals into the Americas and brought American species back to Europe. European expansion also spread European diseases. Vast numbers of Native Americans died from measles and smallpox epidemics, while Europeans died from a virulent form of syphilis that may have originated in the Americas.

For the Native Americans, the voyages of discovery were the beginning of a long history of conquest, disease, and slave labor they could neither evade nor survive. In both South and North America, Spanish rule left a lasting imprint of Roman Catholicism, economic dependency, and hierarchical social structure, all still visible today. (See Chapter 18.)

The Spanish Empire in the New World

When the first Spanish explorers arrived, the Aztec Empire dominated Mesoamerica, which stretches from Central Mexico to Guatemala, and the Inca Empire dominated Andean South America. Both were rich, and their conquest promised the Spanish the possibility of acquiring large quantities of gold.

The Aztecs in Mexico The forebears of the Aztecs had arrived in the Valley of Mexico early in the twelfth century, where they lived as a subservient people. In 1428, however, they began a period of imperial expansion. By the time of Spanish conquest, the Aztecs ruled almost all of central Mexico from their capital Tenochtitlán (modern-day Mexico City). The Aztecs' brutal rule bred resentment and fear among their subject peoples.

In 1519, Hernán Cortés (1485–1547) landed in Mexico with about five hundred men and a few horses. He opened communication with Moctezuma II (1466–1520), the Aztec emperor. Moctezuma may initially have believed Cortés to be the god Quetzalcoatl, who, according to legend, had been driven away centuries earlier but had promised to return. Whatever the reason, Moctezuma hesitated to confront Cortés, attempting at first to appease him with gold, which only whetted Spanish appetites. Cortés forged alliances with the Aztecs' subject peoples, most importantly, with Tlaxcala, an independent state and traditional enemy of the Aztecs. His forces then marched on Tenochtitlán, where Moctezuma welcomed him. Cortés soon seized Moctezuma, who died in unexplained circumstances. The Aztecs' wary acceptance of the Spaniards turned to open hostility. The Spaniards were driven from Tenochtitlán and were nearly wiped out, but they returned and laid siege to the city. The Aztecs, under their last ruler, Cuauhtemoc (ca. 1495–1525), resisted fiercely, but were finally defeated in 1521.

Armored Spanish soldiers, under the command of Pedro de Alvarado (d. 1541) and bearing crossbows, engage unprotected and crudely armed Aztecs, who are nonetheless portrayed as larger than life by Spanish artist Diego Duran (sixteenth century).

Codex Duran: Pedro de Alvarado (c. 1485–1541), companion-at-arms of Hernando Cortés (1485–1547) besieged by Aztec warriors (vellum) by Diego Duran (16th century), Codex Duran, Historia De Las Indias (16th century). Biblioteca Nacional, Madrid, Spain. The Bridgeman Art Library International Ltd.

How accurate are the depictions of Spanish *conquistadors* and Aztec warriors in this image?

The Incas in Peru The second great Native American civilization the Spanish conquered was that of the Incas in the highlands of Peru. Like the Aztecs, the Incas also began to expand rapidly in the fifteenth century and, by the time of the Spanish conquest, controlled an enormous empire.

In 1532, largely inspired by Cortés's example in Mexico, Francisco Pizarro (c. 1478–1541) landed on the western coast of South America with about two hundred men to take on the Inca Empire. Pizarro lured Atahualpa (ca. 1500–1533), the Inca ruler, into a conference and then seized him, killing hundreds of Atahualpa's followers in the process. The imprisoned Atahualpa tried to ransom himself with a hoard of gold, but instead of releasing him, Pizarro executed him in 1533. The Spaniards then captured Cuzco, the Inca capital, but Inca resistance did not end until the 1570s.

The conquests of Mexico and Peru are among the most dramatic and brutal events in modern history. Small military forces armed with advanced weapons subdued, in a remarkably brief time, two powerful peoples. The spread of European diseases, especially smallpox, among the Native Americans, also aided the conquest. But beyond the drama and bloodshed, these conquests, as well as those of other Native American peoples, marked a fundamental turning point. Native American cultures endured, accommodating themselves to European dominance, but the Spanish conquests of the early sixteenth century marked the beginning of the transformation of South America into Latin America.

The Church in Spanish America

Roman Catholic priests had accompanied the earliest explorers and the conquerors of the Native Americans. They were filled with zeal not only to convert the inhabitants to Christianity, but also to bring to them European learning and civilization.

Tension, however, existed between the early Spanish conquerors and the mendicant friars who sought to minister to the Native Americans. Without conquest, the church could not convert the Native Americans, but the priests often deplored the harsh conditions imposed on the native peoples. By far the most effective and outspoken clerical critic of the Spanish conquerors was Bartolomé de Las Casas (1474–1566), a Dominican. He contended that conquest was not necessary for conversion.

Despite such protests, by the end of the sixteenth century, the Church in Spanish America had become largely an institution upholding the colonial status quo. Although individual priests defended the communal rights of Indian peoples, the colonial Church prospered as the Spanish elite prospered by exploiting the resources and peoples of the New World. The Church became a great landowner through crown grants and bequests from Catholics who died in the New World. The monasteries took on an economic as well as a spiritual life of their own. Whatever its concern for the spiritual welfare of the Native Americans, the Church remained one of the indications that Spanish America was a conquered world. By the end of the colonial era in the late eighteenth century, the Roman Catholic Church had become one of the most conservative forces in Latin America.

THE ECONOMY OF EXPLOITATION

From the beginning, both the Native Americans and their lands were drawn into the Atlantic economy and the world of competitive European commercialism. For the Indians of Latin America and, somewhat later, the black peoples of Africa, that drive for gain meant forced labor.

The colonial economy of Latin America had three major components: mining, agriculture, and shipping. Each involved labor, servitude, and the intertwining of the New World economy with that of Spain.

conquistadores "Conquerors."

Mining The early ***conquistadores***, or "conquerors," were primarily interested in gold, but by the mid–sixteenth century, silver mining provided the chief source of metallic wealth. The great mining centers were Potosí in Peru and somewhat smaller sites in northern Mexico. Exploring for silver continued throughout the colonial era. Its production by forced labor for the benefit of Spaniards and the Spanish crown epitomized the wholly extractive economy that stood at the foundation of colonial life.

hacienda Large landed estate that characterized most Spanish colonies.

Agriculture The major rural and agricultural institution of the Spanish colonies was the ***hacienda***, a large landed estate owned by persons originally born in Spain (*peninsulares*) or persons of Spanish descent born in America (*creoles*). Laborers on the *hacienda* were usually subject in some legal way to the owner and were rarely free to move from working for one landowner to another.

The *hacienda* economy produced two major products: foodstuffs for mining areas and urban centers and leather goods used in mining machinery. Both farming and ranching were subordinate to the mining economy.

In the West Indies, the basic agricultural unit was the plantation. In Cuba, Hispaniola, Puerto Rico, and other islands, the labor of black slaves from Africa produced sugar to supply an almost insatiable demand for the product in Europe.

A final major area of economic activity in the Spanish colonies was urban service occupations, including government offices, the legal profession, and shipping. Those who worked in these occupations were either *peninsulares* or *creoles*, with the former dominating more often than not.

Labor Servitude All this extractive and exploitive economic activity required labor, and the Spanish in the New World decided early that the native population would supply it. A series of social devices was used to draw them into the new economic life the Spanish imposed.

encomienda Legal grant of the right to the labor of a specific number of Indians for a particular period of time. This was used as a Spanish strategy for exploiting the labor of the natives.

The first of these was the ***encomienda***, a formal grant of the right to the labor of a specific number of Indians, usually a few hundred, but sometimes thousands, for a particular period of time. The *encomienda* was in decline by the mid–sixteenth century because the Spanish monarchs feared its holders might become too powerful. There were also humanitarian objections to this particular kind of exploitation of the Indians.

The passing of the *encomienda* led to a new arrangement of labor servitude: the *repartimiento*. This device required adult male Indians to devote a certain number of days of labor annually to Spanish economic enterprises. *Repartimiento* service was often harsh, and some Indians did not survive their stint. The limitation on labor time led some Spanish managers to abuse their workers on the assumption that fresh workers would soon replace them.

The eventual shortage of workers and the crown's pressure against extreme versions of forced labor led to the use of free labor. The freedom, however, was more in appearance than reality. Free Indian laborers were required to purchase goods from the landowner or mine owner, to whom they became forever indebted. This form of exploitation, known as *debt peonage*, continued in Latin America long after the nineteenth-century wars of liberation.

Black slavery was the final mode of forced or subservient labor in the New World. Both the Spanish and the Portuguese had earlier used African slaves in Europe. The sugar plantations of the West Indies and Brazil now became the major center of black slavery.

The conquest, the forced labor of the economy of exploitation, and the introduction of European diseases had devastating demographic consequences for the Native Americans. Within a generation, the native population of New Spain (Mexico) was reduced to an estimated 8 percent of its numbers, from 25 million to 2 million.

The Impact on Europe

Among contemporary European intellectuals, Columbus's discovery increased skepticism about the wisdom of the ancients. If traditional knowledge about the world had been so wrong geographically, how trustworthy was it on other matters? For many, Columbus's discovery demonstrated the folly of relying on any fixed body of presumed authoritative knowledge. Both in Europe and in the New World, there were those who condemned the explorers' treatment of American natives, as more was learned about their cruelty. Three centuries later, however, on the third centenary of Columbus's discovery (1792), the great thinkers of the age lionized Columbus for having opened up new possibilities for civilization and morality.

On the material side, the influx of spices and precious metals into Europe from the new Portuguese and Spanish Empires was a mixed blessing. It contributed to a steady rise in prices during the sixteenth century that created an inflation rate estimated at 2 percent a year. The new supply of bullion from the Americas joined with enlarged European production to increase greatly the amount of coinage in circulation, and this increase, in turn, fed inflation. Prices doubled in Spain by 1550, quadrupled by 1600. In Luther's Wittenberg in Germany, the cost of basic food and clothing increased almost 100 percent between 1519 and 1540.

The new wealth enabled governments and private entrepreneurs to sponsor basic research and expansion in the printing, shipping, mining, textile, and weapons industries. There is also evidence of large-scale government planning in such ventures as the French silk industry and the Habsburg-Fugger development of mines in Austria and Hungary.

In the thirteenth and fourteenth centuries, capitalist institutions and practices had already begun to develop in the rich Italian cities. Those who owned the means of production, either privately or corporately, were clearly distinguished from the workers who operated them. Wherever possible, entrepreneurs created monopolies in basic goods. High interest was charged on loans—actual, if not legal, usury. The "capitalist" virtues of thrift, industry, and orderly planning were everywhere in evidence—all intended to permit the free and efficient accumulation of wealth.

The late fifteenth and the sixteenth centuries saw the maturation of this type of capitalism together with its attendant social problems. The new wealth and industrial expansion raised the expectations of the poor and the ambitious and heightened the reactionary tendencies of the wealthy. This effect, in turn, aggravated the traditional social divisions between the clergy and the laity, the urban patriciate and the guilds, and the landed nobility and the agrarian peasantry.

These divisions indirectly prepared the way for the Reformation as well, by making many people critical of traditional institutions and open to new ideas—especially those that seemed to promise greater freedom and a chance at a better life.

SUMMARY

HOW DID humanism affect culture and the arts in fourteenth- and fifteenth-century Italy?

The Renaissance in Italy (1375–1527) The Renaissance first appeared in Italy and thrived from 1375 to 1527. This period, a transition between the medieval and modern worlds, was a time of unprecedented cultural creativity. Italian city-states, with their extensive trade networks and their competition with one another, were great incubators for artistic expression, political innovation, and humanistic studies. The significance of "humanism" is debated by scholars today, but for Renaissance Italians humanism implied studies of Classical languages and arts that offered moral preparation for a life of virtuous action. Authors and artists, including Petrarch, Dante, Boccaccio, Leonardo da Vinci, Raphael, and Michelangelo, exemplify the values of Renaissance humanism. *page 244*

WHAT WERE the causes of Italy's political decline?

Italy's Political Decline: The French Invasions (1494–1527) In the late fifteenth century, the balance of power among Italian city-states that had been enforced by the Treaty of Lodi started to unravel. In 1495, at the invitation of the Milanese leader Ludovico il Moro, French king Charles VIII invaded Italy and conquered Florence. This invasion triggered several rounds of diplomacy, alliance making, and strategic marriages involving families of popes, the leaders of Italian city-states, French kings, and the rulers of Aragon and Brittany, among others. A quarter century of military conflicts led to political fragmentation and military weakness in Italy. In 1513, Niccolò Machiavelli wrote *The Prince*, in which he argued that only a strong and cunning dictator could unify Italy. *page 253*

HOW WERE the powerful monarchies of northern Europe different from their predecessors?

Revival of Monarchy in Northern Europe Sovereign monarchies, in which kings and their appointed agents—usually townspeople, not nobility—control national policies on taxation, warfare, and law enforcement, emerged in France, Spain, and England in the late fifteenth century. In France, Charles VII and, later, Louis XI were able to capitalize on the French victories over England and Burgundy, to expand French territory, build trade and industry, and suspend the Estates General. In Spain, Isabella of Castile and Ferdinand of Aragon married in 1469, and they proceeded to impose state control on religion, arrange marriages for their children that would shape future European history, and sponsor global exploration. In England, Henry VII founded the Tudor dynasty and found ways to govern without consulting Parliament. The Holy Roman Empire (Germany) was northern Europe's chief example of a country that failed to develop a strong centralized monarchy. *page 256*

HOW DID the northern Renaissance affect culture in Germany, England, France, and Spain?

The Northern Renaissance The Renaissance spread from Italy to northern Europe through traders and merchants, students, religious practitioners, and others. Northern humanists, however, were more interested in religious reforms and in spreading humanism to a broad audience than Italian humanists had been. Gutenberg's invention of the moveable-type printing press facilitated the wide dissemination of texts. Erasmus exemplified northern humanists' interest in reform of the Catholic Church. In Germany, England, and France, humanism laid the groundwork for the Reformation, but in Spain, the humanist movement, like most other aspects of culture, was controlled by Ferdinand and Isabella and therefore did not challenge the church. *page 259*

WHAT WERE the motives for European voyages of discovery, and what were the consequences?

Voyages of Discovery and the New Empire in the West and East In the fifteenth century, Europeans began the process of expansion that eventually led to European control over huge regions of the globe. Searching for gold, spices, and later, slaves, the Portuguese, Spanish, and others established maritime trade routes to the coasts of Africa, India, and the Americas. Spain established an empire in what became Latin America, introducing Catholicism, new forms of social, political, and economic organization—including servitude—and diseases to which the indigenous peoples had no resistance. Mexico lost approximately 92 percent of its population within a generation after the Spanish conquest. Spain's empire brought new ideas and products to Europe and led to inflation. *page 262*

Review Questions

1. How would you define Renaissance humanism? In what ways was the Renaissance a break with the Middle Ages? Who were the leading literary and artistic figures of the Italian Renaissance? What defined them as people of the Renaissance?
2. What was the purpose and outcome of the French invasion of Italy in 1494? Given the cultural productivity of Renaissance Italy, is it a valid assumption that creative work thrives best in periods of calm and peace?
3. How did the northern Renaissance differ from the Italian Renaissance? In what ways was Erasmus the embodiment of the northern Renaissance?
4. What prompted the voyages of discovery? How did the Spanish establish their empire in the Americas? What did native peoples experience during and after the conquest?

KEY TERMS

condottieri (p. 246)
conquistadores (p. 266)
encomienda (p. 266)
Golden Bull (p. 259)
hacienda (p. 266)
mannerism (p. 252)
***studia humanitas* (humanism)** (p. 246)

For additional learning resources related to this chapter, please go to **www.myhistorylab.com**

PEARSON myhistorylab

11

The Age of Reformation

Painted on the eve of the Reformation, Matthias Grunewald's (ca. 1480–1528) *Crucifixion* shows a Christ who takes all the sins of the world into his own body, as his mother, Mary Magdalene, and John the Baptist share the pain of his afflictions.

Musée Unterlinden, Colmar, France/SuperStock

How did images such as this one convey the teachings of Christianity to worshippers?

WHAT WAS the social and religious background of the Reformation?

WHY DID Martin Luther challenge the church?

WHERE DID other reform movements develop and how were they different from Luther's?

WHAT WERE the political ramifications of the Reformation?

HOW DID royal dynastic concerns shape the Reformation in England?

WHAT WAS the Counter-Reformation and how successful was it?

WHAT WAS the social significance of the Reformation and how did it affect family life?

WHAT WAS family life like in early modern Europe?

HOW WAS the transition from medieval to modern reflected in the works of the great literary figures of the era?

In the second decade of the sixteenth century, a powerful religious movement began in northern Germany. Reformers, attacking what they believed to be superstitions and abuses of authority, rebelled against the medieval church. The Protestant Reformation that resulted from their efforts opposed aspects of the Renaissance—especially the optimistic view of human nature that humanist scholars derived from classical literature. The reformers did, however, embrace some Renaissance ideas, particularly educational reforms and training in ancient languages that equipped scholars to go to the original sources of important texts. Protestant challenges to Catholic practices were based on appeals to the Hebrew and Greek Scriptures. ■

SOCIETY AND RELIGION

WHAT WAS the social and religious background of the Reformation?

The Protestant Reformation occurred at a time of sharp conflict between the emerging nation-states of Europe bent on conformity and centralization within their realms, and the self-governing towns and villages long accustomed to running their own affairs. Many townspeople and village folk perceived in the religious revolt an ally in their struggle to remain politically free and independent.

Social and Political Conflict

The Reformation broke out first in the free imperial cities of Germany and Switzerland, and the basic tenets of Lutheran and Zwinglian Protestantism remained visible in subsequent Protestant movements. There were about sixty-five free imperial cities, each a small kingdom unto itself. Most had Protestant movements, but with mixed success and duration. Some quickly turned Protestant and remained so. Some were Protestant only for a short time. Still others developed mixed confessions.

A seeming life-and-death struggle with higher princely or royal authority was not the only conflict late medieval cities were experiencing. They also coped with deep social and political divisions. Certain groups favored the Reformation more than others. In many places, guilds whose members were economically prospering and socially rising were in the forefront of the Reformation. Evidence also suggests that people who felt pushed around and bullied by either local or distant authority—a guild by an autocratic local government, or a city or region by a powerful prince or king—often perceived an ally in the Protestant movement.

Social and political experience naturally influenced religious change in town and countryside. A Protestant sermon or pamphlet praising religious freedom seemed directly relevant, for example, to the townspeople of German and Swiss cities who faced incorporation into the territory of a powerful local prince, who looked on them as his subjects rather than as free citizens. Like city dwellers, the peasants on the land also heard in the Protestant message a promise of political liberation, even a degree of social betterment. More than the townspeople, the peasants found their traditional liberties—from fishing and hunting rights to representation at local diets—progressively being chipped away by the secular and ecclesiastical landlords of the age.

Popular Religious Movements and Criticism of the Church

The Protestant Reformation could also not have occurred without the monumental challenges to the medieval church during its "exile" in Avignon, the Great Schism, the Conciliar period, and the Renaissance papacy. For sizable numbers of people in future Protestant lands, the medieval church had ceased to provide a viable foundation for religious piety. Many intellectuals and laypeople felt a sense of spiritual crisis. Between the secular pretensions of the papacy and the dry teaching of Scholastic theologians, laity and clerics alike began to seek a more heartfelt, idealistic, and—often, in the eyes of the pope—heretical religious piety. The late Middle Ages were marked by independent lay and clerical efforts to reform local religious practice and by widespread experimentation with new religious forms.

A variety of factors contributed to the growing lay criticism of the church. Urban laypeople were increasingly knowledgeable about the world around them and about the rulers who controlled their lives. They traveled widely—as soldiers, pilgrims, explorers, and traders. New postal systems and the printing press increased the information at their disposal. A new age of books and libraries raised literacy and heightened curiosity. Laypeople were able to shape the cultural life of their communities.

For many participants in lay religious movements, a simple religion of love and self-sacrifice like that of Jesus and the first disciples seemed to be the ideal. To that end, the laity sought a more egalitarian church—one that gave the members as well as the head of the church a voice—and also a more spiritual church—one that lived manifestly according to its New Testament model.

Martin Schongauer (c. 1430–1491), a German engraver, portrays the devil's temptation of St. Anthony in the wilderness as a robust physical attack by demons rather than the traditional melancholic introspection.

National Gallery of Art, Washington DC

How did sixteenth-century people imagine the devil and his place in everyday life?

The Modern Devotion One of the more constructive lay religious movements in northern Europe on the eve of the Reformation was that of the Brothers of the Common Life, also known as the Modern Devotion, a kind of boarding school for reform-minded laity. The brothers fostered religious life outside formal church offices and apart from formal religious vows—a lay religious life of prayer and study without surrendering the world. Centered at Zwolle and Deventer in the Netherlands, the brother and (less numerous) sister houses of the Modern Devotion spread rapidly throughout northern Europe and influenced parts of southern Europe as well. In these houses clerics and laity shared a common life, stressing individual piety and practical religion. Lay members were not expected to take special religious vows or to wear a special religious dress, nor did they abandon their ordinary secular vocations.

The brothers were also educators. They worked as copyists, sponsored many religious and some classical publications, ran hospices for poor students, and conducted schools for the young—especially boys preparing for the priesthood or a monastic vocation. Thomas à Kempis (d. 1471) summarized the philosophy of the brothers in what became the most popular religious book of the period, the *Imitation of Christ*. This semi-mystical guide to the inner life was intended primarily for monks and nuns but was also widely read by laity who wanted to pursue the ascetic life.

Lay Control over Religious Life On the eve of the Reformation, Rome's international network of church offices, which had unified Europe religiously during the Middle Ages, was falling apart in many areas. This collapse was hurried along by a growing sense of regional identity, an increasingly competent local secular administration, and a newly emerging nationalism. The long-entrenched *benefice* system of the medieval church had permitted important ecclesiastical posts to be sold to the highest bidders and had often failed to enforce the requirement that priests and bishops had to live in their parishes and dioceses. Such a system threatened a vibrant, lay spiritual life. Rare was the late medieval German town that did not have complaints about the maladministration, concubinage, or financial greed of its clergy—especially the higher clergy (bishops, abbots, and prelates).

The sale of indulgences, in particular, had been repeatedly attacked before Luther came on the scene. On the eve of the Reformation, this practice had expanded to permit people to buy release from time in purgatory for both themselves and their deceased loved ones. Rulers and magistrates had little objection to their sale and might even encourage it, as long as a generous portion of the income the sales generated remained in the local coffers. Yet when an indulgence was offered primarily for the benefit of distant interests, as with the sale of indulgences to raise money for a new Saint Peter's basilica in Rome that Luther protested, resistance arose also for strictly financial reasons: Their sale drained away local revenues.

City governments also undertook to improve local religious life on the eve of the Reformation by endowing preacherships. These positions, supported by *benefices*, made possible the hiring of well-trained pastors who provided regular preaching and pastoral care beyond the performance of the Mass. These preacherships often became platforms for Protestants.

Magistrates also carefully restricted the growth of ecclesiastical properties and clerical privileges. During the Middle Ages, canon and civil law had recognized special clerical rights in both property and person. Churches and monasteries were exempted from the taxes and laws that affected others. Law also deemed it inappropriate for holy persons (clergy) to burden themselves with such "dirty jobs" as military service, compulsory labor, standing watch at city gates, and other ordinary civic obligations. Moreover, the clergy came to enjoy an immunity from the jurisdiction of civil courts.

QUICK REVIEW
Anticlericalism

- Corruption and incompetence marred church administration
- City governments took steps to improve the situation by endowing preacherships
- Fifteenth century witnessed a growing sense that clerical privileges were undeserved

Already on the eve of the Reformation, measures were passed to restrict these clerical privileges and to end their abuses. Governments grew tired of church interference in what to them were strictly secular political spheres of competence and authority. Secular authorities accordingly began to scrutinize the church's acquisition of new properties, finding ways to get around its right of asylum when it interrupted the administration of justice, and generally bringing the clergy under local tax codes.

MARTIN LUTHER AND THE GERMAN REFORMATION TO 1525

WHY DID Martin Luther challenge the church?

Unlike England and France, late medieval Germany lacked the political unity to enforce "national" religious reforms during the late Middle Ages. As popular resentment of clerical immunities and ecclesiastical abuses spread among German cities and towns, an unorganized "national" opposition to Rome formed. German humanists had long given voice to such criticism, and by 1517 it was pervasive enough to provide a solid foundation for Martin Luther's protest of indulgences and the theology that legitimated them.

The son of a successful Thüringian miner, Luther (1483–1546) was educated in Mansfeld, Magdeburg (where the Brothers of the Common Life had been his teachers), and Eisenach. Between 1501 and 1505, he attended the University of Erfurt, where the nominalist teachings of William of Ockham and Gabriel Biel (d. 1495) prevailed. (See Chapter 8.) After receiving his master-of-arts degree in 1505, Luther registered with the law faculty in accordance with his parents' wishes. But he never began the study of law. To the disappointment of his family, he instead entered the Order of the Hermits of Saint Augustine in Erfurt on July 17, 1505.

Ordained in 1507, Luther pursued a traditional course of study. In 1510, he journeyed to Rome on the business of his order, finding there justification for the many criticisms of the church he had heard in Germany. In 1511, he moved to the Augustinian monastery in Wittenberg, where he earned his doctorate in theology in 1512, thereafter to become a leader within the monastery, the new university, and the spiritual life of the city.

Justification by Faith Alone

Luther was especially plagued by the disproportion between his own sense of sinfulness and the perfect righteousness God required for salvation, according to traditional church teaching. His insight into the meaning of "justification by faith alone" (*sola fide*) was a gradual process between 1513 and 1518. The righteousness that God demands, he concluded, did not result from charitable acts and religious ceremonies but was given in full measure to any and all who believe in and trust Jesus Christ as their perfect righteousness satisfying to God.

The medieval church had always taught that salvation was a joint venture, a combination of divine mercy and human good works, what God alone could do and what man was expected to do in return. Luther also believed that faith without charitable service to one's neighbor was dead. The issue was not whether good works should be done, but how those works should be regarded. It was unbiblical, Luther argued, to treat works as contributing to one's eternal salvation, something only an almighty God could bestow.

Good works were expected over a lifetime, Luther taught, but not because they earned salvation. The believer who is bound to Christ by faith already possesses God's perfect righteousness. It is this knowledge of faith that sets narcissistic souls free to serve their neighbors selflessly. Such service is ethical, not soteriological—a good work, not a saving work. God is pleased when those who believe in him do good works, and he expects his people always to do them, but he does not take those works into account when he is merciful and bestows eternal life, which would make God a puppet of man.

The Attack on Indulgences

Luther's doctrine of justification by faith was incompatible with the church's practice of issuing indulgences, for an **indulgence** was a remission of the obligation to perform a "work of satisfaction" for a sin. The medieval church taught that after priests absolved penitents of guilt, penitents still had to pay penalties for their sins. They could discharge their penalties in this life by prayers, fasting, almsgiving, retreats, and pilgrimages. If their works of satisfaction were insufficient at the time of their deaths, they would continue to suffer for them in purgatory.

indulgence Remission of the obligation to perform a "work of satisfaction" for a sin.

Indulgences were originally given to Crusaders who could not complete their penances because they had fallen in battle. By the late Middle Ages, indulgences had become an aid to laypeople made genuinely anxious by their fear of a future suffering in purgatory for neglected penances or unrepented sins. In 1343, Pope Clement VI (r. 1342–1352) proclaimed the existence of a "treasury of merit," an infinite reservoir of good works in the church's possession that could be dispensed at the pope's discretion. In 1476, Pope Sixtus IV (r. 1471–1484) extended indulgences to the unrepented sins of all Christians in purgatory.

By Luther's time, indulgences were regularly dispensed for small cash payments, modest sums that were regarded as a good work of almsgiving. Indulgence preachers presented them to the laity as remitting not only their own future punishments, but also those of dead relatives presumed still to be suffering in purgatory.

In 1517, Pope Leo X (r. 1513–1521) revived a plenary Jubilee Indulgence that had first been issued by Pope Julius II (r. 1503–1513), the proceeds of which were to rebuild St. Peter's Basilica in Rome. Such an indulgence promised forgiveness of all outstanding unrepented sins upon the completion of certain acts. That indulgence was subsequently preached on the borders of Saxony in the territories of the future Archbishop Albrecht of Mainz. The famous indulgence preacher John Tetzel (d. 1519) was enlisted to preach the indulgence in Albrecht's territories.

A contemporary caricature depicts John Tetzel, the famous indulgence preacher. The last lines of the jingle read: "As soon as gold in the basin rings, right then the soul to Heaven springs." It was Tetzel's preaching that spurred Luther to publish his ninety-five theses.

Courtesy Stiftung Luthergedenkstaten in Sachsen-Anhalt/Lutherhalle, Wittenberg

Why did Luther find the practice of indulgences particularly offensive?

When Luther posted his ninety-five theses against indulgences on the door of Castle Church in Wittenberg (October 31, 1517), he protested especially the impression Tetzel created that indulgences remitted sins and released unrepentant sinners from punishment in purgatory. Luther believed these claims went far beyond the traditional practice and seemed to make salvation something that could be bought and sold.

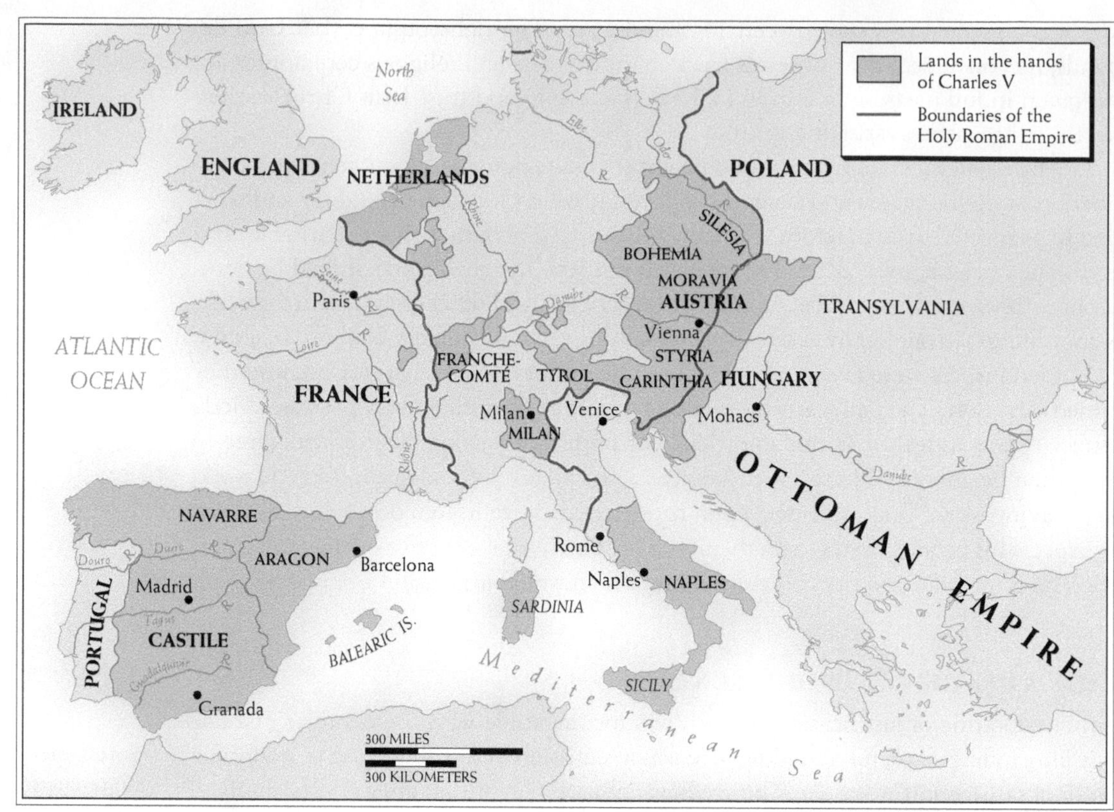

MAP 11–1 The Empire of Charles V Dynastic marriages and simple chance concentrated into Charles's hands rule over the lands shown here, plus Spain's overseas possessions. Crowns and titles rained down on him; his election in 1519 as emperor gave him new distractions and responsibilities.

Were the acquisitions of large portions of Europe more of a burden than a privilege for Charles V?

ELECTION OF CHARLES V

The ninety-five theses were embraced by Nuremberg humanists, who translated and widely circulated them. This made Luther a central figure in an already organized national German cultural movement against foreign influence and competition, particularly on the part of the Italians. In October, he was summoned before the general of the Dominican order in Augsburg to answer for his criticism of the church. Yet as sanctions were being prepared against him, Emperor Maximilian I died (January 12, 1519)—a fortunate event for the budding Reformation, because it turned attention away from heresy in Saxony to the contest for a new emperor.

In that contest, the pope backed the French king, Francis I. However, Charles I of Spain, a youth of nineteen, successfully succeeded his grandfather as Emperor Charles V. (See Map 11–1.) Charles was blessed by both the long tradition of the Habsburg imperial rule and a massive campaign chest that secured the votes of the seven imperial electors. The most prominent among the seven was Frederick the Wise, Luther's lord and protector. Frederick took great pride in his new University of Wittenberg, and he was not about to let any harm come to his famous court preacher.

LUTHER'S EXCOMMUNICATION AND THE DIET OF WORMS

QUICK REVIEW

The Condemnation of Luther

- June 15, 1520: Papal bull condemns Luther as a heretic
- April 1521: Luther refuses to recant before the imperial diet in Worms
- May 26, 1521: Luther placed under imperial ban, making his heresy a crime punishable by the state

In the same month in which Charles was elected emperor, Luther debated the Ingolstadt professor John Eck in Leipzig (June 27, 1519). During this contest, Luther challenged the infallibility of the pope and the inerrancy of church councils, appealing, for the first time, to the sovereign authority of Scripture alone. He burned all his bridges to the old church when he further defended certain teachings of John Huss, who had been condemned to death for heresy at the Council of Constance.

In 1520, Luther signaled his new direction with three famous pamphlets. The *Address to the Christian Nobility of the German Nation* urged the German princes to force reforms on the Roman church, especially to curtail its political and economic power in Germany. The *Babylonian Captivity of the Church* attacked the traditional seven sacraments, arguing that only two, baptism and the Eucharist, were unquestionably biblical, and it exalted the authority of Scripture, church councils, and secular princes over that of the pope. The eloquent *Freedom of a Christian* summarized the new teaching of salvation by faith alone.

On June 15, 1520, Leo's papal bull *Exsurge Domine* ("Arise, O Lord") condemned Luther for heresy and gave him sixty days to retract. The final bull of excommunication was issued on January 3, 1521.

In April 1521, Luther presented his views before the Diet of Worms, over which the newly elected Emperor Charles V presided. Ordered to recant, Luther declared that to do so would be to act against Scripture, reason, and his conscience. On May 26, 1521, he was placed under the imperial ban, which made him an "outlaw" to secular as well as religious authority. For his own protection, friends disguised and hid him in Wartburg Castle at the instruction of Elector Frederick. There, he spent almost a year, from April 1521 to March 1522. During his stay, he translated the New Testament into German using Erasmus's new Greek text and Latin translation, while overseeing by correspondence the first steps of the Reformation in Wittenberg.

In 1520, Luther's first portrait, shown here, depicted him as a tough, steely eyed monk. Afraid that this portrayal might convey defiance rather than reform to Emperor Charles V, Elector Frederick the Wise of Saxony, Luther's protector, ordered court painter Lucas Cranach to soften the image. The result was a Luther placed within a traditional monk's niche reading an open Bible, a reformer, unlike the one depicted here, who was prepared to listen as well as to instruct.

Martin Luther as a monk 1521. © Foto Marburg/Art Resource, NY

Why was Luther so concerned about his public image?

Imperial Distractions: War with France and the Turks

The Reformation was greatly helped in these early years by the emperor's war with France and the advance of the Ottoman Turks into eastern Europe. Against both adversaries Charles V, who remained a Spanish king with dynastic responsibilities in Spain and Austria, needed loyal German troops, to which end he sought friendly relations with the German princes. Between 1521 and 1559, Spain (the Habsburg dynasty) and France (the Valois dynasty) fought four major wars over disputed territories within Italy and along their respective borders.

Thus preoccupied, the emperor agreed through his representatives at the German Diet of Speyer (1526) that each German territory was free to enforce the Edict of Worms (1521) against Luther "so as to be able to answer in good conscience to God and the emperor." That concession in effect gave the German princes, who five years earlier had refused to publish the emperor's condemnation of Luther, territorial sovereignty in religious matters. It also bought the Reformation time to put down deep roots in Germany and Switzerland.

How the Reformation Spread

In the late 1520s and 1530s, the Reformation passed from the free hands of the theologians and pamphleteers into the firmer ones of the magistrates and princes. In many cities, the latter quickly mandated new religious reforms. The elector of Saxony and the prince of Hesse, the two most powerful German Protestant rulers, led the politicization of religious reform within their territories. Like the urban magistrates, the German princes recognized the political and economic opportunities offered them by the demise of the Roman Catholic Church in their lands. In the 1530s, German Protestant lands formed a powerful defensive alliance, the Schmaldkaldic League, and prepared for war with the Catholic emperor.

A handwritten manuscript depicts the execution of Jaklein Rohrbach. The sixteenth-century German radical burns at a stake inside a ring of fire.

Courtesy of the Library of Congress

Why were heretics seen as such a threat to established authority and order?

The Peasants' Revolt

In its first decade, the Reformation suffered more from internal division than from imperial interference. By 1525, Luther had become almost as much an object of protest within Germany as was the pope. Original allies, sympathizers, and fellow travelers increasingly declared their independence from Wittenberg.

COMPARE & CONNECT

A RAW DEAL FOR THE COMMON MAN, OR HIS JUST DESSERTS?

Beginning in the late fifteenth century, German feudal lords, both secular and ecclesiastical, increased labor and crop quotas on their peasant tenants, while restricting their freedoms and overriding their customary laws as well. In 1525, massive revolts occurred in southern Germany, in what became the largest social uprising before the French Revolution. Among those responding directly to the revolt were two highly respected authorities: Wittenberg theologian Martin Luther and Nuremberg artist Albrecht Dürer.

QUESTIONS

1. What is there in Luther's religious teaching that might have led the peasants to think he would support their revolt? What personal interest might he have had in turning them his way? What does he advise them to do to address their grievances properly?

2. Does Dürer's 1527 sketch *Memorial to the Peasants' Revolt*, depicting a peasant sitting atop a chicken coop with a sword thrust through his back, suggest a greater sympathy for the peasants on his part? Or is it possible that both Luther and Dürer agreed that the peasants received their just desserts for rebelling against lawful authority?

I. MARTIN LUTHER, *AN ADMONITION TO PEACE* (1525)

ON STOPPING THE WAR

We have no one on earth to thank for this mischievous rebellion, except you lords and princes, especially you blind bishops and mad priests and monks . . . In your government you do nothing but flay and rob your subjects in order that you may lead a life of splendor and pride, until the poor common folk can bear it no longer . . .

[As for] the peasants, they must take the name and title of a people who fight because they will not and ought not endure wrong or evil, according to the teaching of nature. You should have *that* name, and let the name of Christ alone . . . [As for your so-called 'Christian' demands for] freedom of game, birds, fish, wood, forests, labor services, tithes, imposts, excises, and release from the death tax, these I leave to the lawyers, for they are things that do not concern a Christian who is a martyr on this earth . . . Let the name of Christian alone and act in some other name, as men and women who want human and natural rights.

Source: Cited by Steven Ozment, *The Age of Reform* (New Haven, CT: Yale University Press, 1980), pp. 280–282.

II. MARTIN LUTHER, *AGAINST THE ROBBING AND MURDERING PEASANTS* (1525)

FINAL WORDS

[The princes] should have no mercy on obstinate, hardened, blinded peasants who refuse to listen to reason. Let everyone, as he is able, strike, hew, stab, and slay, as though among mad dogs, so that by doing so he may show mercy to those [non-rebelling peasants] who have been ruined, put to flight, and led astray by these rebelling peasants [so that] peace and safety may return . . .

Source: Ozment, *The Age of Reform,* p. 284.

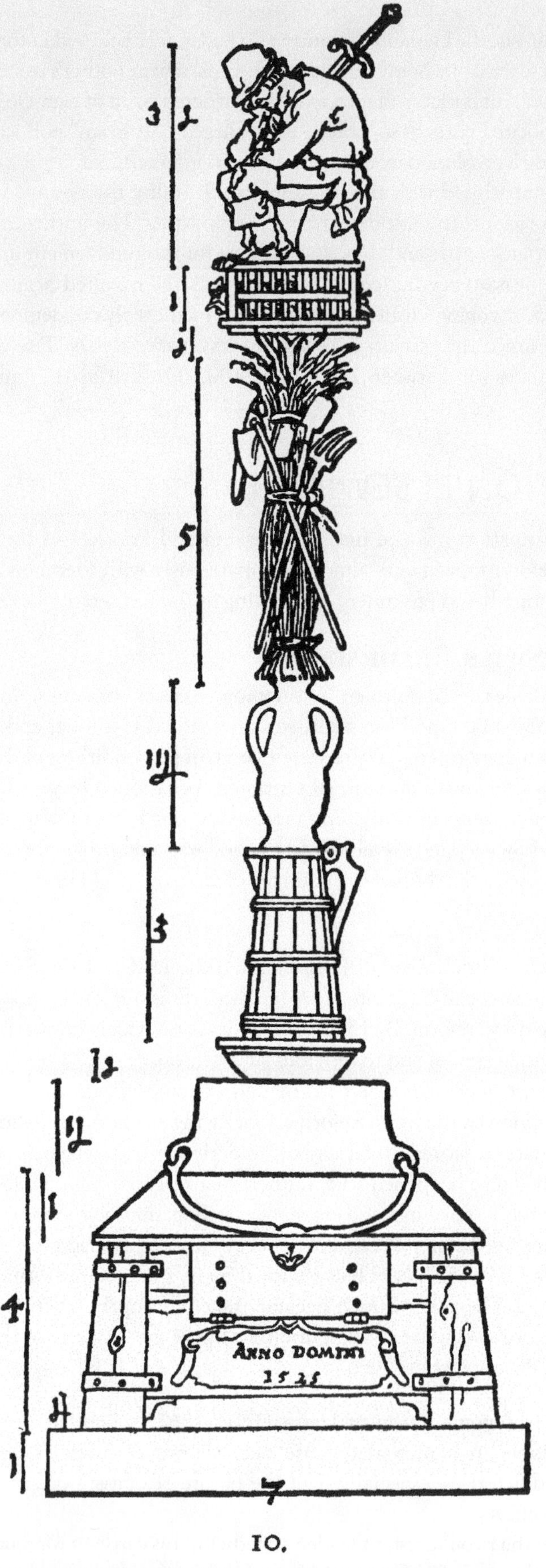

III. *AN OPEN LETTER CONCERNING THE HARD BOOK AGAINST THE PEASANTS* (1525)

FINAL WORDS

From the start I had two fears. If the peasants became lords, the devil would become abbot; if these tyrants became lords, the devil's dam would become abbess. Therefore I wanted to do two things: quiet the peasants and instruct the lords. The peasants were unwilling, and now they have their reward. The lords will not hear, and they shall have their reward also.

Source: Ozment, *The Age of Reform*, p. 287.

IV. ALBRECHT DÜRER, *MEMORIAL TO THE PEASANTS' REVOLT* (1527)

Dürer's "Memorial to the Peasants," drawn in 1527, the year before his death, appeared in a book devoted to "phrase perspectives in art." Fearing that Protestant iconoclasm (destruction of icons) and the coming of religious wars would remove decorative art from the churches, his book was to be a primer for artists who in the aftermath of such destruction would have to learn the art of painting all over again. The sketch shows a peasant sitting atop a chicken coop with a sword thrust through his back, the classic iconography of betrayal.

At this time Dürer's peers, friends, and associates condemned the Peasants' Revolt as strongly as Luther. During the war Dürer painted portraits of the Fuggers, the great merchant family the peasants despised, and also Margrave Casimir of Brandenburg-Ansbach, a brutal slayer of peasants and Anabaptists. Within this context might Dürer's slain rebellious peasant, like Luther's, have gotten his just due?

Source: Joseph Leo Koerner, *The Moment of Self-Portraiture in Renaissance Art* (Chicago: Chicago University Press, 1993), p. 235.

The caption reads: "He who wants to commemorate his victory over the rebellious peasants might use to that end a structure such as I portray here."

Illustration from Jane Campbell Hutchinson, *Albrecht Dürer: A Biography* (Princeton, NJ: Princeton University Press, 1990)

What was this monument meant to say about the Peasants' War?

Like the German humanists, the German peasantry also had at first believed Luther to be an ally. Peasant leaders, several of whom had been Lutherans, saw in Luther's teaching about Christian freedom and his criticism of monastic landowners a point of view close to their own. They openly solicited Luther's support of their alleged "Christian" political and economic rights, including a revolutionary demand of release from serfdom.

Luther had initially sympathized with the peasants, condemning the tyranny of the princes and urging them to meet the just demands of the peasants. The Lutherans, however, were not social revolutionaries and they saw no hope for their movement if it became intertwined with a peasant revolution. When the peasants revolted against their landlords in 1524–1525, invoking Luther's name, Luther predictably condemned them as "un-Christian" and urged the princes to crush the revolt mercilessly. Tens of thousands of peasants (estimates run between 70,000 and 100,000) died by the time the revolt was suppressed.

THE REFORMATION ELSEWHERE

WHERE DID other reform movements develop and how were they different from Luther's?

Although the German Reformation was the first, Switzerland and France had their own independent church reform movements almost simultaneously with Germany's. From them developed new churches as prominent and lasting as the Lutheran.

Zwingli and the Swiss Reformation

Switzerland was a loose confederacy of thirteen autonomous *cantons*, or states, and their allied areas. Some cantons became Protestant, some remained Catholic, and a few others managed to effect a compromise. There were two main preconditions of the Swiss Reformation. First was the growth of national sentiment occasioned by popular opposition to foreign mercenary service. (Providing mercenaries for Europe's warring nations was a major source of Switzerland's livelihood.) Second was a desire for church reform that had persisted in Switzerland since the councils of Constance (1414–1417) and Basel (1431–1449).

The Reformation in Zurich Ulrich Zwingli (1484–1531), the leader of the Swiss Reformation, had been humanistically educated. He credited Erasmus over Luther with having set him on the path to reform. By 1518, Zwingli was also widely known for his opposition to the sale of indulgences and to religious superstition.

In 1519, he won the post of people's priest in the main church of Zurich. From his new position, Zwingli engineered the Swiss Reformation. Zwingli's reform guideline was simple and effective: Whatever lacked literal support in Scripture was to be neither believed nor practiced. As had also happened with Luther, that test soon raised questions about such honored traditional teachings and practices as fasting, transubstantiation, the worship of saints, pilgrimages, purgatory, clerical celibacy, and certain sacraments. A disputation held on January 29, 1523, concluded with the city government's sanction of Zwingli's Scripture test. Thereafter Zurich became the center of the Swiss Reformation. The new regime imposed a harsh discipline that made the city one of the first examples of puritanical Protestantism.

The Marburg Colloquy Landgrave Philip of Hesse (1504–1567) sought to unite Swiss and German Protestants in a mutual defense pact. However, Luther's and Zwingli's bitter theological differences, especially over the nature of Christ's presence in the Eucharist, spoiled his efforts.

Philip of Hesse brought the two Protestant leaders together in his castle in Marburg in early October 1529, to work out their differences. However, the effort proved to be in vain. Although cooperation between the two Protestant sides did not cease altogether, the disagreement splintered the Protestant movement theologically and politically.

Swiss Civil Wars As the Swiss cantons divided themselves between Protestantism and Catholicism, civil wars erupted. There were two major battles, both at Kappel, one in June 1529 and a second in October 1531. The first ended in a Protestant victory, which forced the Catholic cantons to break their foreign alliances and to recognize the rights of Swiss Protestants. After the second battle, Zwingli lay wounded on the battlefield, and when discovered, he was unceremoniously executed. The subsequent treaty confirmed the right of each canton to determine its own religion.

Anabaptists and Radical Protestants

The moderate pace and seemingly low ethical results of the Lutheran and Zwinglian reformations discontented many people, among them some of the original followers of Luther and Zwingli. These were devout fundamentalist Protestants who desired a more rapid and thorough implementation of Apostolic Christianity. They accused the reform movements that went before them of having gone only halfway. The most important of these radical groups were the **Anabaptists**, the sixteenth-century ancestors of the modern Mennonites and Amish. The Anabaptists were especially distinguished by their rejection of infant baptism and their insistence on only adult baptism, as was the case with Jesus, who was baptized as an adult. Only a thoughtful consenting adult, able to understand the Scriptures and what the biblical way of life required, could enter the covenant of faith.

Anabaptists ("rebaptizers") The most important of several groups of Protestants forming more radical organizations that sought a more rapid and thorough restoration of the "primitive Christianity" described in the New Testament.

Conrad Grebel and the Swiss Brethren Conrad Grebel (1498–1526), with whom Anabaptism originated, performed the first adult rebaptism in Zurich in January 1525. Initially a co-worker of Zwingli's and an even greater biblical literalist, Grebel broke openly with him. In a religious disputation in October 1523, Zwingli supported the city government's plea for a peaceful, gradual removal of resented traditional religious practices—not the rush to perfection the Anabaptists demand.

The alternative of the Swiss Brethren, as Grebel's group came to be called, was embodied in the *Schleitheim Confession* of 1527. This document distinguished Anabaptists not only by their practice of adult baptism, but also by their pacifism, refusal to swear oaths, and nonparticipation in the offices of secular government. By both choice and coercion, Anabaptists physically separated from established society to form a more perfect communion modeled on the first Christians. Because of the close connection between religious and civic life in the sixteenth century, the political authorities also viewed such separatism as a threat to basic social bonds, even as a form of sedition.

The Anabaptist Reign in Münster Brutal measures were universally applied against nonconformists after Anabaptist extremists came to power in the German city of Münster in 1534–1535. Led by two Dutch emigrants, a baker, Jan Matthys of Haarlem, and a tailor, Jan Beukelsz of Leiden, the Anabaptists in Münster forced Lutherans and Catholics in the city either to convert or to emigrate. After their departure, the city was blockaded by besieging armies. Under such pressures, Münster was transformed into an Old Testament theocracy, replete with charismatic leaders and the practice of polygamy.

These developments shocked the outside world, and Protestant and Catholic armies united to crush the radicals. After this episode, moderate, pacifistic Anabaptism became the norm among most nonconformists. Menno Simons (1496–1561), the founder of the Mennonites, set an example of nonprovocative separatist Anabaptism, which became the historical form in which Anabaptist sects survived down to the present.

Spiritualists and Antrinitarians Another diverse and highly individualistic group of Protestant dissenters was the Spiritualists. These were mostly isolated individuals distinguished by their disdain for external, institutional religion. They believed the only religious authority was the Spirit of God, which spoke not in some past revelation, but here and now in the heart and mind of every listening individual.

A final group of persecuted radical Protestants also destined for prominence in the modern world was the Antitrinitarians. These were exponents of a commonsense, rational, and ethical religion. These thinkers were the strongest opponents of Calvinism, especially its belief in original sin and predestination, and have a deserved reputation as defenders of religious toleration.

Portrait of John Calvin.
Library of Congress

John Calvin and the Genevan Reformation

In the second half of the sixteenth century, Calvinism replaced Lutheranism as the dominant Protestant force in Europe. Calvinists believed strongly in both divine predestination and the individual's responsibility to reorder society according to God's plan. They were determined to transform society so men and women lived their lives externally as they professed to believe internally, and were presumably destined to live eternally.

The namesake of Calvinism and its perfect embodiment, John Calvin (1509–1564), was born into a well-to-do French family, the son of the secretary to the bishop of Noyon. It was probably in the spring of 1534 that Calvin experienced that conversion to Protestantism by which he said his "long stubborn heart" was "made teachable" by God. His own hard experience became a personal model of reform by which he would measure the recalcitrant citizenry of Geneva. His mature theology stressed the sovereignty of God's will over all creation and the necessity of humankind's conformity to it.

Political Revolt and Religious Reform in Geneva Whereas in Saxony religious reform paved the way for a political revolution against the emperor, in Geneva a political revolution against the local prince-bishop laid the foundation for the religious change. Genevans revolted against their resident prince-bishop in the late 1520s, and the city council assumed his legal and political powers in 1527.

In late 1533, the Protestant city of Bern dispatched two reformers to Geneva: Guillaume Farel (1489–1565) and Antoine Froment (1508–1581). In the summer of 1535, after much internal turmoil, the Protestants triumphed, and the traditional Mass and other religious practices were removed. On May 21, 1536, Geneva voted officially to adopt the Reformation.

Calvin, an exile from France, arrived in Geneva after these events, in July 1536, and was persuaded by Ferel to stay and assist the Reformation. He agreed and drew up articles for the governance of the new church, as well as a catechism to guide and discipline the people. Both were presented for approval to the city councils in early 1537. Opponents feared Calvin and Farel were going too far too fast. Geneva's powerful Protestant ally, Bern, which had adopted a more moderate Protestant reform, pressured Geneva's magistrates to restore traditional religious ceremonies and holidays that Calvin and Farel had abolished. When the reformers opposed these actions, they were exiled from the city.

Calvin went to Strasbourg, a model Protestant city, where he became pastor to French exiles and wrote biblical commentaries. He also produced a second edition of his masterful *Institutes of the Christian Religion*, which many consider the definitive theological statement of the Protestant faith. Most importantly, he learned from the Strasbourg reformer Martin Bucer how to achieve his goals.

Calvin's Geneva In 1540, Geneva elected officials both favorable to Calvin and determined to establish full Genevan political and religious independence from Bern.

They knew Calvin would be a valuable ally in that undertaking and invited him to return. This he did in September 1540, never to leave the city again. Within months of his return, the city implemented new ecclesiastical ordinances that provided for cooperation between the magistrates and the clergy in matters of internal discipline.

The controversial doctrine of predestination was at the center of Calvin's theology as justification by faith was at Luther's. Calvin did not discuss predestination until the end of his great theological work *Institutes of the Christian Religion*. Explaining why he delayed its discussion, he described predestination as a doctrine only for mature Christians. For true believers, predestination recognized that the world and all who dwell in it are in God's hands from eternity to eternity, regardless of all else. By believing that, and living as the Bible instructed them to do, Calvinists found consoling, presumptive evidence that they were among God's elect.

Possessed of such assurance, Calvinists turned their energies to transforming society spiritually and morally. The consistory, or Geneva's regulatory court, became his instrument of power. Composed of the elders and the pastors and presided over by one of the city's chief magistrates, that body implemented the strictest moral discipline.

After 1555, Geneva became home to thousands of exiled Protestants who had been driven out of France, England, and Scotland. Refugees numbering more than 5,000, most of them utterly loyal to Calvin, made up more than one-third of Geneva's population. All of Geneva's magistrates were now devout Calvinists, greatly strengthening Calvin's position in the city.

QUICK REVIEW

Theocracy in Geneva

- Magistrates and clergy cooperated to enforce Calvin's vision
- Consistory handed out punishments for moral and religious transgressions
- Calvin and his followers showed little mercy to their opponents

POLITICAL CONSOLIDATION OF THE LUTHERAN REFORMATION

WHAT WERE the political ramifications of the Reformation?

By 1530, the Reformation was in Europe to stay. It would, however, take several decades and major attempts to eradicate it, before all would recognize this fact. With the political triumph of Lutheranism in the empire by the 1550s, Protestant movements elsewhere gained a new lease on life.

THE DIET OF AUGSBURG

Charles V devoted most of his first decade as emperor to the pursuit of politics and military campaigns outside the empire, particularly in Spain and Italy. In 1530, he returned to the empire to direct the Diet of Augsburg. This assembly of Protestant and Catholic representatives had been called to address the growing religious division within the empire in the wake of the Reformation's success. With its terms dictated by the Catholic emperor, the diet adjourned with a blunt and unrealistic order to all Lutherans to revert to Catholicism.

The Reformation was by this time too firmly established for that to occur. In February 1531, the Lutherans responded with the formation of their own defensive alliance, the Schmalkaldic League. The league took as its banner the **Augsburg Confession**, a moderate statement of Protestant beliefs that had been spurned by the emperor at the Diet of Augsburg. Under the leadership of Landgrave Philip of Hesse and Elector John Frederick of Saxony, the league achieved a stalemate with the emperor, who was again distracted by renewed war with France and the ever-resilient Turks.

Augsburg Confession Moderate Protestant creed endorsed by the Schmalkaldic League (a defensive alliance of Lutherans).

THE EXPANSION OF THE REFORMATION

In the 1530s, German Lutherans formed regional consistories, judicial bodies composed of theologians and lawyers, which oversaw and administered the new Protestant churches and replaced the old Catholic episcopates. Educational reforms provided for compulsory primary education, schools for girls, a humanist revision of the traditional curriculum, and instruction of the laity in the new religion.

The Reformation also entrenched itself elsewhere. Introduced into Denmark by King Christian II (r. 1513–1523), Lutheranism thrived there under Frederick I (r. 1523–1533), who joined the Schmalkaldic League. Under Christian III (r. 1536–1559), Lutheranism became the official state religion.

In Sweden, King Gustavus Vasa (r. 1523–1560), supported by a Swedish nobility greedy for church lands, embraced Lutheranism, confiscated church property, and subjected the clergy to royal authority at the Diet of Vesteras (1527).

In politically splintered Poland, Lutherans, Anabaptists, Calvinists, and even Antitrinitarians found room to practice their beliefs. Primarily because of the absence of a central political authority, Poland became a model of religious pluralism and toleration in the second half of the sixteenth century.

Reaction Against Protestants

Charles V made abortive efforts in 1540–1541 to enforce a compromise between Protestants and Catholics. As these and other conciliar efforts failed, he turned to a military solution. In 1547, imperial armies crushed the Protestant Schmalkaldic League, defeating and capturing John Frederick of Saxony and Philip of Hesse. The emperor established puppet rulers in Saxony and Hesse and issued an imperial law mandating that Protestants everywhere readopt old Catholic beliefs and practices.

The Peace of Augsburg

The Reformation was too entrenched by 1547 to be ended even by brute force. Confronted by fierce resistance and weary from three decades of war, the emperor was forced to relent. After a defeat by Protestant armies in 1552, Charles reinstated the Protestant leaders and guaranteed Lutherans religious freedoms in the Peace of Passau (August 1552). With this declaration, he effectively surrendered his lifelong quest for European religious unity.

The Peace of Augsburg in September 1555 made the division of Christendom permanent. This agreement recognized in law what had already been well established in practice: *Cuius regio, eius religio,* meaning the ruler of a land would determine its religion. People discontented with the religion of their region were permitted to migrate to another.

The Peace of Augsburg did not extend official recognition to Calvinism and Anabaptism as legal forms of Christian belief and practice. Anabaptists had long adjusted to such exclusion by forming their own separatist communities. Calvinists, however, were not separatists. They remained determined to secure the right to worship publicly as they pleased, and to shape society according to their own religious convictions. While Anabaptists retreated and Lutherans enjoyed the security of an established religion, Calvinists organized to lead national revolutions throughout northern Europe in the second half of the sixteenth century.

THE ENGLISH REFORMATION TO 1553

HOW DID royal dynastic concerns shape the Reformation in England?

Lollardy, humanism, and widespread anticlerical sentiments prepared the way for Protestant ideas, which entered England in the early sixteenth century.

The Preconditions of Reform

In the early 1520s, future English reformers met in Cambridge to discuss Lutheran writings smuggled into England by merchants and scholars. One of these future reformers was William Tyndale (ca. 1492–1536), who translated the New Testament into English

in 1524–1525 while in Germany. Printed in Cologne and Worms, Tyndale's New Testament began to circulate in England in 1526.

Cardinal Thomas Wolsey (ca. 1475–1530), the chief minister of King Henry VIII (r. 1509–1547), and Sir Thomas More (1478–1535), Wolsey's successor, guided royal opposition to incipient English Protestantism. The king himself defended the seven sacraments against Luther, receiving as a reward the title "Defender of the Faith" from Pope Leo X.

The King's Affair

Lollardy and humanism may have provided some native seeds for religious reform, but it was Henry's unhappy marriage to Catherine of Aragon (d. 1536) and obsession to get a male heir that broke the soil and allowed the seeds to take root. In 1509, Henry had married Catherine, the daughter of Ferdinand and Isabella of Spain and the aunt of Emperor Charles V. By 1527, the union had produced only one surviving child, a daughter, Mary. Although women could inherit the throne, Henry fretted over the political consequences of leaving only a female heir.

Hans Holbein the Younger (1497–1543) was the most famous portrait painter of the Reformation. Here he portrays a seemingly almighty Henry VIII.

What qualities did Holbein intend the viewer to see in Henry VIII?

Henry came even to believe that God had cursed his union with Catherine, who had many miscarriages and stillbirths. The reason lay in Catherine's previous marriage to Henry's brother Arthur. After Arthur's premature death, Henry's father, Henry VII, betrothed her to Henry to keep the English alliance with Spain intact. The two were wed in 1509, a few days before Henry VIII received his crown. Because marriage to the wife of one's brother was prohibited by both canon and biblical law (see Leviticus 18:16, 20:21), the marriage had required a special dispensation from Pope Julius II.

By 1527, Henry was also thoroughly enamored of Anne Boleyn, one of Catherine's ladies-in-waiting. He determined to put Catherine aside and take Anne as his wife. This he could not do in Catholic England, however, without a papal annulment of the marriage to Catherine. Therein lay a special problem. Pope Clement VII was then a prisoner of Emperor Charles V, who also happened to be Catherine's nephew, and he was not about to encourage the pope to annul the royal marriage. Even if such coercion had not existed, it would have been virtually impossible for the pope to grant an annulment of a marriage that not only had survived for eighteen years but had also been made possible in the first place by a special papal dispensation.

Cardinal Wolsey, who aspired to become pope, was placed in charge of securing the royal annulment. When he failed to secure the annulment through no fault of his own, he was dismissed in disgrace in 1529. Thomas Cranmer (1489–1556) and Thomas Cromwell (1485–1540), both of whom harbored Lutheran sympathies, thereafter became the king's closest advisers. Finding the way to a papal annulment closed, Henry's new advisers struck a different course: Why not simply declare the king supreme in English spiritual affairs as he was in English temporal affairs? Then the king could settle the king's affair himself.

The "Reformation Parliament"

In 1529, Parliament convened for what would be a seven-year session that earned it the title of the "Reformation Parliament." During this period, it passed a flood of legislation that harassed, and finally placed royal reins on, the clergy. In so doing, it established a precedent that would remain a feature of English government: Whenever fundamental changes are made in religion, the monarch must consult with and work through Parliament. In January 1531, the Convocation (a legislative assembly representing the English clergy) publicly recognized Henry as head of the church in England "as far as the law of Christ allows." In 1532, Parliament published official grievances against the church, ranging from alleged indifference to the needs of the laity to an

Act of Supremacy Act of 1534 proclaiming Henry VIII "the only supreme head on earth of the Church of England."

QUICK REVIEW

Legal Break with Rome

- 1531: Convocation recognizes Henry VIII as head of the church in England
- 1532: Parliament gives the king jurisdiction over the clergy and canon law
- 1534: Parliament ends all payments to Rome and gives king jurisdiction over ecclesiastical appointments

excessive number of religious holidays. In the same year, Parliament passed the Submission of the Clergy, which effectively placed canon law under royal control and thereby the clergy under royal jurisdiction.

In January 1533, Henry wed the pregnant Anne Boleyn, with Thomas Cranmer officiating. In February 1533, Parliament made the king the highest court of appeal for all English subjects. In March 1533, Cranmer became archbishop of Canterbury and led the Convocation in invalidating the king's marriage to Catherine. In 1534, Parliament ended all payments by the English clergy and laity to Rome and gave Henry sole jurisdiction over high ecclesiastical appointments. The Act of Succession in the same year made Anne Boleyn's children legitimate heirs to the throne, and the **Act of Supremacy** declared Henry "the only supreme head in earth of the Church of England."

When Thomas More and John Fisher, bishop of Rochester, refused to recognize the Act of Succession and the Act of Supremacy, Henry had them executed, making clear his determination to have his way regardless of the cost. In 1536 and 1538, Parliament dissolved England's monasteries and nunneries.

Wives of Henry VIII

Henry's domestic life lacked the consistency of his political life. In 1536, Anne Boleyn was executed for alleged treason and adultery, and her daughter Elizabeth, like Elizabeth's half-sister Mary before her, was declared illegitimate by her father. His third wife, Jane Seymour, died in 1537 shortly after giving birth to the future Edward VI. Henry wed Anne of Cleves sight unseen on the advice of Cromwell, the purpose being to create by the marriage an alliance with the Protestant princes of Germany. Neither the alliance nor the marriage proved worth the trouble; the marriage was annulled by Parliament, and Cromwell was dismissed and executed. Catherine Howard, Henry's fifth wife, was beheaded for adultery in 1542. His last wife, Catherine Parr, a patron of humanists and reformers, for whom Henry was the third husband, survived him to marry still a fourth time—obviously she was a match for the English king.

The King's Religious Conservatism

Henry's boldness in politics and domestic affairs did not extend to religion. Despite the break with Rome, Henry remained decidedly conservative in his religious beliefs. With the Ten Articles of 1536, he made only mild concessions to Protestant tenets. Otherwise Catholic doctrine was maintained in a country filled with Protestant sentiment.

Angered by the growing popularity of Protestant views, even among his chief advisers, Henry struck directly at them in the Six Articles of 1539. These reaffirmed transubstantiation, denied the Eucharistic cup to the laity, declared celibate vows inviolable, provided for private Masses, and ordered the continuation of oral confession. England had to await Henry's death before it could become a genuinely Protestant country.

The Protestant Reformation under Edward VI

When Henry died in 1547, his son and successor, Edward VI (d. 1553), was only ten years old. Edward reigned under the successive regencies of Edward Seymour, who became the duke of Somerset (1547–1550), and the earl of Warwick, who became known as the duke of Northumberland (1550–1553). During this time, England enacted the Protestant Reformation. The new king and Somerset corresponded directly with John Calvin.

In 1547, the chantries, places where endowed Masses had traditionally been said for the dead, were dissolved. In 1549, the Act of Uniformity imposed Thomas Cranmer's *Book of Common Prayer* on all English churches. Images and altars were removed from the churches in 1550. The Second Act of Uniformity, passed in 1552, imposed a revised *Book of Common Prayer* on all English churches. A forty-two-article confession of faith, also written by Thomas Cranmer, set forth a moderate Protestant doctrine. It taught justification by faith and the supremacy of Holy Scripture, denied transubstantiation (although not the real presence), and recognized only two sacraments.

All these changes were short-lived, however. In 1553, Catherine of Aragon's daughter succeeded Edward (who had died in his teens) to the throne as Mary I (d. 1558) and restored Catholic doctrine and practice with a single-mindedness rivaling that of her father. It was not until the reign of Anne Boleyn's daughter, Elizabeth I (r. 1558–1603), that England worked out a lasting religious settlement.

CATHOLIC REFORM AND COUNTER-REFORMATION

WHAT WAS the Counter-Reformation and how successful was it?

The Protestant Reformation did not take the medieval church completely by surprise. There were many internal criticisms and efforts at reform before there was a Counter-Reformation in reaction to Protestant successes.

Sources of Catholic Reform

Before the Reformation began, ambitious proposals had been made for church reform. But sixteenth-century popes, ever mindful of how the councils of Constance and Basel had stripped the pope of his traditional powers, squelched such efforts to change the laws and institutions of the church.

Despite such papal foot-dragging, the old church was not without its reformers. Many new religious orders also sprang up in the sixteenth century to lead a broad revival of piety within the church. The first of these orders was the Theatines, founded in 1524, to groom devout and reform-minded leaders at the higher levels of the church hierarchy. Another new order, whose mission pointed in the opposite direction, was the Capuchins. Recognized by the pope in 1528, they sought to return to the original ideals of Saint Francis and became popular among the ordinary people to whom they directed their ministry. The Somaschi, who became active in the mid-1520s, and the Barnabites, founded in 1530, worked to repair the moral, spiritual, and physical damage done to people in war-torn Italy. For women, there was the influential new order of Ursulines. Founded in 1535, it established convents in Italy and France for the religious education of girls from all social classes.

Ignatius of Loyola and the Jesuits

Of the various reform groups, none was more instrumental in the success of the Counter-Reformation than the Society of Jesus, the new order of Jesuits. Organized by Ignatius of Loyola in the 1530s, the church recognized it in 1540. The society grew within a century from its original 10 members to more than 15,000 members scattered throughout the world, with thriving missions in India, Japan, and the Americas.

The founder of the Jesuits, Ignatius of Loyola (1491–1556), developed a program of religious and moral self-discipline that came to be embodied in the *Spiritual Exercises*. This psychologically perceptive devotional guide contained mental and emotional exercises designed to teach one absolute spiritual self-mastery over one's feelings. It taught that a person could shape his or her own behavior—even create a new religious self—through disciplined study and regular practice.

The exercises of Ignatius were intended to teach good Catholics to deny themselves and submit without question to higher church authority and spiritual direction. Perfect discipline and self-control were the essential conditions of such obedience. To these were added the enthusiasm of traditional spirituality and mysticism and uncompromising loyalty to the church's cause. This potent combination helped counter the

MAP EXPLORATION

Interactive map: To explore this map further, go to www.myhistorylab.com

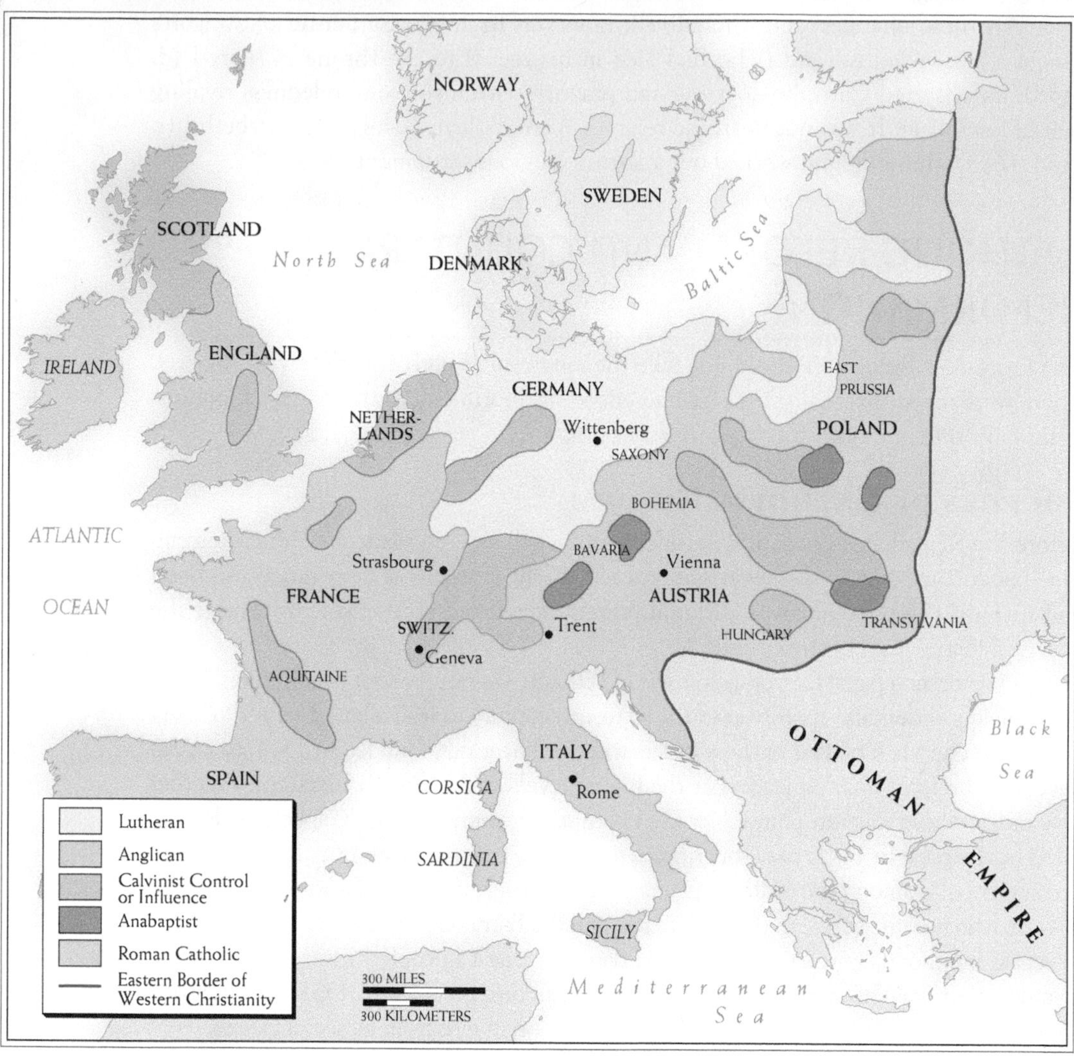

MAP 11–2 **The Religious Situation about 1560** By 1560, Luther, Zwingli, and Loyola were dead, Calvin was near the end of his life, the English break from Rome was complete, and the last session of the Council of Trent was about to assemble. This map shows the "religious geography" of western Europe at the time.

How would you characterize Christianity in western Europe at this time? Which reform movements seem to have had the most success?

Reformation and win many Protestants back to the Catholic fold, especially in Austria and parts of Germany. (See Map 11–2.)

The Council of Trent (1545–1563)

The broad success of the Reformation and the insistence of the Emperor Charles V forced Pope Paul III (r. 1534–1549) to call a general council of the church to reassert church doctrine. The council met in 1545 in the imperial city of Trent in northern Italy. There were three sessions, spread over eighteen years, with long interruptions due to war, plague, and imperial and papal politics. The council met from 1545 to 1547, from 1551 to 1552, and from 1562 to 1563, a period that spanned the reigns of four different popes.

The council's most important reforms concerned internal church discipline. Steps were taken to curtail the selling of church offices and other religious goods. Many bishops who resided in Rome were forced to move to their dioceses. Trent strengthened the authority of local bishops so they could effectively discipline popular religious practices. The bishops were also subjected to new rules that required them to be highly visible by preaching regularly and conducting annual visitations of their diocesan parishes. Parish priests were required to be neatly dressed, better educated, strictly celibate, and active among their parishioners. To train priests, Trent also called for a seminary in every diocese.

Not a single doctrinal concession was made to the Protestants, however. Instead, the Council of Trent reaffirmed the traditional Scholastic education of the clergy; the role of good works in salvation; the authority of tradition; the seven sacraments; transubstantiation; the withholding of the Eucharistic cup from the laity; clerical celibacy; purgatory; the veneration of saints, relics, and sacred images; and indulgences. The council resolved medieval Scholastic quarrels in favor of the theology of Saint Thomas Aquinas, further enhancing his authority within the church. Thereafter, the church offered its strongest resistance to groups like the Jansenists, who endorsed the medieval Augustinian tradition, a source of alternative Catholic, as well as many Protestant, doctrines.

Rulers initially resisted Trent's reform decrees, fearing a revival of papal political power and new confessional conflicts within their lands. Over time, however, and with the pope's assurances that religious reforms were his sole intent, the new legislation took hold, and parish life revived under a devout and better trained clergy.

THE SOCIAL SIGNIFICANCE OF THE REFORMATION IN WESTERN EUROPE

WHAT WAS the social significance of the Reformation and how did it affect family life?

The Lutheran, Zwinglian, and Calvinist reformers all sought to work within the framework of reigning political power. Luther, Zwingli, and Calvin saw themselves and their followers as subject to definite civic responsibilities and obligations. They wanted reform to take shape within reigning laws and institutions. They thus remained highly sensitive to what was politically and socially possible in their age.

The Revolution in Religious Practices and Institutions

The Reformation may have been politically conservative, but by the end of the sixteenth century, it had brought about radical changes in traditional religious practices and institutions in those lands where it succeeded.

Religion in Fifteenth-Century Life In the fifteenth century, on the streets of the great cities of Europe that later turned Protestant, the clergy and the religious were everywhere. They made up 6 to 8 percent of the urban population, and they exercised considerable political as well as spiritual power. They legislated and taxed, they tried cases in special church courts, and they enforced their laws with threats of excommunication. The church calendar regulated daily life. About one-third of the year was given over to some kind of religious observance or celebration.

Monasteries, and especially nunneries, were prominent and influential institutions. The children of society's most powerful citizens resided there. Local aristocrats identified with particular churches and chapels, whose walls recorded their lineage and proclaimed their generosity. On the streets, friars begged alms from passersby. In the churches, the Mass and liturgy were read entirely in Latin. Images of saints were regularly displayed, and on certain holidays their relics were paraded about and venerated.

SIGNIFICANT DATES FROM THE PERIOD OF THE PROTESTANT REFORMATION

1517	Luther posts ninety-five theses against indulgences
1519	Charles V becomes Holy Roman Emperor
1521	Diet of Worms condemns Luther
1524–1525	Peasants' Revolt in Germany
1527	The Schleitheim Confession of the Anabaptists
1529	Marburg Colloquy between Luther and Zwingli
1529	England's Reformation Parliament convenes
1531	Formation of Protestant Schmalkaldic League
1533	Henry VIII weds Anne Boleyn
1534	England's Act of Supremacy
1534–1535	Anabaptists take over Münster
1536	Calvin arrives in Geneva
1540	Jesuits, founded by Ignatius of Loyola, recognized as order by pope
1546	Luther dies
1547	Armies of Charles V crush Schmalkaldic League
1547–1553	Edward VI, king of England
1555	Peace of Augsburg
1553–1558	Mary Tudor, queen of England
1545–1563	Council of Trent
1558–1603	Elizabeth I, queen of England; the Anglican settlement

Local religious shrines enjoyed a booming business. Pilgrims gathered there by the hundreds—even thousands—many sick and dying, all in search of a cure or a miracle, but also for diversion and entertainment. Several times during the year, special preachers arrived in the city to sell letters of indulgence.

People everywhere complained about the clergy's exemption from taxation and also often from the civil criminal code. People also grumbled about having to support church offices whose occupants actually lived and worked elsewhere, turning the cure of souls over to poorly trained and paid substitutes. Townspeople expressed concern that the church had too much influence over education and culture.

Religion in Sixteenth-Century Life In these same cities, after the Reformation had firmly established itself, few changes in politics and society were evident. The same aristocratic families governed as before, and the rich generally got richer and the poor poorer. Overall numbers of clergy fell by two-thirds, and religious holidays shrank by one-third. Cloisters were nearly gone, and many that remained were transformed into hospices for the sick and poor or into educational institutions, their endowments turned over to these new purposes.

The churches were reduced in number by at least one-third, and worship was conducted almost completely in the vernacular. Indulgence preachers no longer appeared. Local shrines were closed down, and anyone found openly venerating saints, relics, and images was subject to fine and punishment.

Copies of Luther's translation of the New Testament (1522) or, more often, excerpts from it could be found in private homes, and the new clergy encouraged meditation on the Bible. The clergy could marry, and most did. They paid taxes and were punished for their crimes in civil courts. Committees composed of roughly equal numbers of laity and clergy, over whose decisions secular magistrates had the last word, regulated domestic moral life.

Not all Protestant clergy remained enthusiastic about this new lay authority in religion. And the laity was also ambivalent about certain aspects of the Reformation. Over half of the original converts returned to the Catholic fold before the end of the sixteenth century.

The Reformation and Education

Another major cultural achievement of the Reformation was its implementation of many of the educational reforms of humanism in new Protestant schools and universities. Many Protestant reformers in Germany, France, and England were humanists. And even when their views on church doctrine and human nature separated them from the humanist movement, the Protestant reformers continued to share a common opposition to Scholasticism and a belief in the unity of wisdom, eloquence, and action. The humanist program of studies, providing the language skills to deal authoritatively with original sources, proved to be a more appropriate tool for the elaboration of Protestant doctrine than it did for Scholastic dialectic, which remained ascendant in the Counter-Reformation.

When, in August 1518, Philip Melanchthon (1497–1560), "the praeceptor of Germany," a young humanist and professor of Greek, arrived at the University of Wittenberg, his first act was to reform the curriculum on the humanist model. Together, Luther and Melanchthon restructured the University of Wittenberg's curriculum. Commentaries on Lombard's *Sentences* were dropped, as was canon law. Straightforward historical study replaced old Scholastic lectures on Aristotle. Students read primary sources directly, rather than by way of accepted Scholastic commentators. Candidates for theological degrees defended the new doctrine on the basis of their own study of the Bible. New chairs of Greek and Hebrew were created.

In Geneva, John Calvin and his successor, Theodore Beza, founded the Genevan Academy, which later evolved into the University of Geneva. That institution, created primarily to train Calvinist ministers, pursued ideals similar to those set forth by

Luther and Melanchthon. Calvinist refugees who studied there later carried Protestant educational reforms to France, Scotland, England, and the New World.

Some famous contemporaries decried what they saw as a narrowing of the original humanist program as Protestants took it over. Humanist culture and learning nonetheless remained indebted to the Reformation. The Protestant endorsement of the humanist program of studies remained as significant for the humanist movement as the latter had been for the Reformation. Protestant schools and universities consolidated and preserved for the modern world many of the basic pedagogical achievements of humanism. There, the *studia humanitatis,* although often as little more than a handmaiden to theological doctrine, found a permanent home, one that remained hospitable even in the heyday of conservative Protestantism.

The Reformation and the Changing Role of Women

The Protestant reformers favored clerical marriage and opposed monasticism and the celibate life. From this position, they challenged the medieval tendency alternately to degrade women as temptresses (following the model of Eve) and to exalt them as virgins (following the model of Mary). Protestants opposed the popular antiwoman and antimarriage literature of the Middle Ages. They praised woman in her own right, but especially in her biblical vocation as mother and housewife. Although wives remained subject to their husbands, new laws gave them greater security and protection.

Protestants placed a high value on marriage and family life. In opposition to the celibate ideal of the Middle Ages, Protestants stressed, as no religious movement before them had ever done, the sacredness of home and family. The ideal of the companionate marriage—that is, of husband and wife as co-workers in a special God-ordained community of the family, sharing authority equally within the household—led to an expansion of the grounds for divorce in Protestant lands as early as the 1520s. Women gained an equal right with men to divorce and remarry in good conscience—unlike the situation in Catholicism, where only a separation from bed and table, not divorce and remarriage, was permitted a couple in a failed marriage. The reformers were more willing to permit divorce and remarriage on grounds of adultery and abandonment than were secular magistrates, who feared liberal divorce laws would lead to social upheaval.

Typical of reforms and revolutions in their early stages, Protestant doctrines emboldened women as well as men. Renegade nuns wrote exposés of the nunnery in the name of Christian freedom and justification by faith, declaring the nunnery was no special woman's place at all and that supervisory male clergy made their lives as unpleasant and burdensome as any abusive husband. Women in the higher classes, who enjoyed new social and political freedoms during the Renaissance, found in Protestant theology a religious complement to their greater independence in other walks of life. Some cloistered noblewomen, however, protested the closing of nunneries, arguing that the cloister provided them a more interesting and independent way of life than they would have known in the secular world.

Because Protestants wanted women to become pious housewives, they encouraged the education of girls to literacy in the vernacular, with the expectation that they would thereafter model their lives on the Bible. However, women also found biblical passages that made clear their equality to men in the presence of God. Education also gave some women roles as independent authors on behalf of the Reformation. Although small advances from a modern perspective, these were also steps toward the emancipation of women.

FAMILY LIFE IN EARLY MODERN EUROPE

WHAT WAS family life like in early modern Europe?

Changes in the timing and duration of marriage, family size, and infant and child care suggest that family life was under a variety of social and economic pressures in the sixteenth and seventeenth centuries.

ENCOUNTERING THE PAST

Table Manners

Humanists believed that education ought to mix pleasure with discipline. The family meal was, therefore, a suitable occasion for instructing the young in the lessons of life. Learning required neatness, order, respect, and attentiveness—traits that Hans Sachs, a sixteenth-century father, wanted his children to learn at his table.

Listen you children who are going to table.
Wash your hands and cut your nails.
Do not sit at the head of the table;
This is reserved for the father of the house.
Do not commence eating until a blessing has been said.
. . .permit the eldest to begin first.
Proceed in a disciplined manner.
Do not snort or smack like a pig.
Do not reach violently for bread. . . .
Do not stir food around on your plate or linger over it. . . .
Rushing through your meal is bad manners.
Do not reach for more food while your mouth is still full,
Nor talk with your mouth full. . . .
Chew your food with your mouth closed.
Do not lick the corners of your mouth like a dog. . . .
Do not belch or cry out. . . .
Do not stare at a person as if you were watching him eat.
Do not elbow the person sitting next to you. . . .
Do not rock back and forth on the bench, lest you let loose a stink. . . .
If sexual play occurs at table, pretend you do not see it. . . .
Do not pick your nose. . . .
Let no one wipe his mouth on the table cloth. . . .
Silently praise and thank God for the food he has graciously provided.

Source: From Steven Ozment, *When Fathers Ruled: Family Life in Reformation Europe,* trans. by Steven Ozment (Cambridge, MA: Harvard University Press, 1983), pp. 142–143.

A Family Meal

In Max Geisberg, *The German Single-Leaf Woodcuts,* ill: *1500–1550,* rev. and ed. by W. L. Strauss (New York: Hacker Art Books, 1974). Used by permission of Hacker Art Books

What role did the family play in early modern religious life?

HOW DO table manners prepare a child for life?

Later Marriages

Between 1500 and 1800, men and women in Western Europe married at later ages than they had in previous centuries: men in their mid- to late-twenties, and women in their early- to mid-twenties. Late marriage in the West reflected the difficulty couples had supporting themselves independently. It simply took the average couple a longer time than before to prepare themselves materially for marriage. In the sixteenth century, one in five women never married, and these, combined with the estimated 15 percent who were unmarried widows, constituted a large unmarried female population. A later marriage was also a shorter marriage; in an age when few people lived into their sixties couples who married in their thirties spent less time together than couples who married in their twenties. Also, because women who bore children for the first time at advanced ages had higher mortality rates, late marriage meant more frequent remarriage for men. As the rapid growth of orphanages and foundling homes between 1600 and 1800 makes clear, delayed marriage increased premarital sex and the number of illegitimate children.

Arranged Marriages

Marriage tended to be "arranged" in the sense that the parents met and discussed the terms of the marriage before the prospective bride and bridegroom became direct parties to the preparations. The wealth and social standing of the bride and the bridegroom, however, were not the only things considered when youth married. By the fifteenth century, it was usual for the future bride and bridegroom to have known each other and to have had some prior relationship. Parents did not force total strangers to live together, and children had a legal right to resist a coerced marriage, which was by definition invalid. The best marriage was one desired by both the bride and groom and their families.

Family Size and Birth Control

The West European family was conjugal, or nuclear, consisting of a father and a mother and two to four children who survived into adulthood. This nuclear family lived within a larger household, including in-laws, servants, laborers, and boarders. The average husband and wife had six to seven children, a new birth about every two years. Of these, an estimated one-third died by age five, and one-half by their teens. Rare was the family, at any social level, that did not experience child death.

Artificial birth control (sponges, acidic ointments) has existed since antiquity. The church's condemnation of *coitus interruptus* (male withdrawal before ejaculation) during the thirteenth and fourteenth centuries suggests the existence of a contraceptive mentality, that is, a conscious, regular effort at birth control. Early birth control measures, when applied, were not very effective, and for both historical and moral reasons, the church opposed them.

Wet Nursing

The church allied with the physicians of early modern Europe on another intimate family matter. Both condemned women who hired wet nurses to suckle their newborn children. The practice was popular among upper-class women and reflected their social standing. It appears to have increased the risk of infant mortality by exposing infants to a strange and shared milk supply from women who were often not as healthy as the infants' own mothers and lived under less sanitary conditions. Nursing was distasteful to some upper-class women, whose husbands also preferred that they not do it. Because the church forbade lactating women from indulging in sexual intercourse, a nursing wife

Overview The Reformation and the Changing Role of Women

EDUCATION	• Encouraged female literacy in the vernacular • Women found biblical passages that suggested they were equal to men • Women became independent authors
LATER MARRIAGES	• Men and women tended to wait until their mid- to late twenties to marry • Later marriages meant marriages of shorter duration • Remarriage was now more common for men who lost wives in childbearing
ARRANGED MARRIAGES	• Bride and groom often knew each other in advance of marriage • Emotional feeling for one another was increasingly respected by parents • Forced marriages were, by definition, invalid and often failed
FAMILY SIZE	• Large households consisted of in-laws, servants, laborers, and boarders • The average husband and wife had seven or eight children but most families experienced infant mortality and child death
WET NURSING	• Church and physicians condemned the use of wet nurses • Upper-class women viewed the use of wet nurses as a symbol of high rank • The practice increased the rate of infant mortality

could become a reluctant lover. Nursing also had a contraceptive effect. Some women prolonged nursing their children to delay a new pregnancy, and some husbands cooperated in this form of family planning. For other husbands, however, especially noblemen and royalty who desired an abundance of male heirs, nursing seemed to rob them of offspring and jeopardize their patrimony—hence their support of hired wet nurses.

Loving Families?

The traditional Western European family had features that seem cold and distant. Children between the ages of eight and thirteen were routinely sent from their homes into apprenticeships, school, or employment in the homes and businesses of relatives, friends, and occasionally strangers. The emotional ties between spouses also seem to have been as tenuous as those between parents and children. Widowers and widows often married again within a few months of their spouses' deaths, and marriages with extreme difference in age between partners suggest limited affection.

In response to modern-day criticism, an early modern parent might well have asked, "What greater love can parents have for their children than to equip them well for a worldly vocation?" A well-apprenticed child was a self-supporting child, and hence a child with a future. In light of the comparatively primitive living conditions, contemporaries also appreciated the purely utilitarian and humane side of marriage and understood when widowers and widows quickly remarried. Marriages with extreme disparity in age, however, were no more the norm in early modern Europe than the practice of wet nursing, and they received just as much criticism and ridicule.

LITERARY IMAGINATION IN TRANSITION

HOW WAS the transition from medieval to modern reflected in the works of the great literary figures of the era?

As Europe approached the seventeenth century, it was no longer medieval but neither was it yet modern. The great literary figures of the era produced transitional works that combined traditional values and fresh perspectives on human life.

Miguel de Cervantes Saavedra: Rejection of Idealism

Spanish literature of the sixteenth and seventeenth centuries reflects the peculiar religious and political history of Spain in this period. Traditional Catholic teaching was a major influence on Spanish life. Since the joint reign of Ferdinand and Isabella (1479–1504), the church had received the unqualified support of the reigning political power.

A second influence on Spanish literature was the aggressive piety of Spanish rulers. Their intertwining of Catholic piety and political power underlay a third influence: preoccupation with medieval chivalric virtues, in particular, questions of honor and loyalty. The novels and plays of the period almost invariably focus on a special test of character, bordering on the heroic, that threatens honor and reputation. In this regard, Spanish literature remained more Catholic and medieval than that of England and France, where major Protestant movements had occurred. The writer generally acknowledged to be Spain's greatest, Cervantes, was preoccupied in his work with the strengths and weaknesses of traditional religious idealism.

Cervantes (1547–1616) had only a smattering of formal education. He educated himself by wide reading in popular literature and immersion in the "school of life." As a young man, he worked in Rome for a Spanish cardinal. As a soldier, he was decorated for gallantry in the Battle of Lepanto against the Turks (1571). He also spent five years as a slave in Algiers after his ship was pirated in 1575. Later, while working as a tax collector, he was imprisoned several times for padding his accounts, and it was in prison that he began, in 1603, to write his most famous work, *Don Quixote*.

The first part of *Don Quixote* appeared in 1605. The intent of this work seems to have been to satirize the chivalric romances then popular in Spain. But Cervantes could not conceal his deep affection for the character he created as an object of ridicule. Cervantes presented Don Quixote as a none-too stable middle-aged man. Driven mad by reading too many chivalric romances, he had come to believe he was an aspiring knight who had to prove his worthiness by brave deeds. To this end, he donned a rusty suit of armor and chose for his inspiration an unworthy peasant girl (Dulcinea), whom he fancied to be a noble lady to whom he could, with honor, dedicate his life.

Don Quixote's foil—Sancho Panza, a clever, worldly wise peasant who serves as Quixote's squire—watches with bemused skepticism as his lord repeatedly makes a fool of himself as he gallops across the countryside. The story ends tragically with Don Quixote's humiliating defeat at the hand of a well-meaning friend who, disguised as a knight, bested Quixote in combat and forced him to renounce his quest for knighthood. Don Quixote did not, however, come to his senses but rather returned to his village to die a brokenhearted old man.

Throughout the novel, Cervantes juxtaposes the down-to-earth realism of Sancho Panza with the old-fashioned religious idealism of Don Quixote. The reader perceives that Cervantes admired the one as much as the other and meant to portray both as representing attitudes necessary for a happy life.

William Shakespeare: Dramatist of the Age

William Shakespeare.

Library of Congress

There is much less factual knowledge about Shakespeare (1564–1616) than we would expect of the greatest playwright in the English language. He apparently worked as a schoolteacher for a time and in this capacity gained his broad knowledge of Renaissance literature. His own reading and enthusiasm for the learning of his day are manifest in the many literary allusions that appear in his plays.

Shakespeare lived the life of a country gentleman. There is none of the Puritan distress over worldliness in his work. He took the new commercialism and the bawdy pleasures of the Elizabethan Age in stride and with amusement. He was a radical neither in politics nor religion. The few allusions in his works to the Puritans seem more critical than complimentary.

That Shakespeare was interested in politics is apparent from his historical plays and the references to contemporary political events that fill all his plays. He viewed government through the character of the individual ruler, whether Richard III or Elizabeth Tudor, rather than in terms of ideal systems or social goals. By modern standards, he was a political conservative, accepting the social rankings and the power structure of his day and demonstrating unquestioned patriotism.

Elizabethan drama was already a distinctive form when Shakespeare began writing. Unlike French drama of the seventeenth century, which was dominated by classical models, English drama developed in the sixteenth and seventeenth centuries as a blending of many forms: classical comedies and tragedies, medieval morality plays, and contemporary Italian short stories.

Shakespeare wrote histories, comedies, and tragedies. *Richard III* (1593), an early play, stands out among the histories, although some scholars view the picture it presents of Richard as an unprincipled villain as "Tudor propaganda." Shakespeare's comedies, although not attaining the heights of his tragedies, surpass his history plays in originality.

Shakespeare's tragedies are considered his unique achievement. Four of these were written within a three-year period: *Hamlet* (1603), *Othello* (1604), *King Lear* (1605), and *Macbeth* (1606). The most original of the tragedies, *Romeo and Juliet* (1597), transformed an old popular story into a moving drama of "star-cross'd lovers."

Shakespeare's works struck universal human themes, many of which were deeply rooted in contemporary religious traditions. His plays were immensely popular with both the playgoers and the play readers of Elizabethan England. Still today, the works of no other dramatist from his age are performed in theaters or on film more regularly than his.

SUMMARY

WHAT WAS the social and religious background of the Reformation?

Society and Religion The Protestant Reformation had roots in political, social, and economic concerns. The emergence of centralizing national governments was challenging local custom and authority through much of Europe; in Germany and Switzerland, the free imperial cities were important early hotbeds of Protestantism. Often, groups (such as guilds) or regions in which people felt controlled by authority figures were particularly receptive to Protestantism. Laypeople were gaining power to criticize, and attempt to reform, the church, both because they were gaining cultural authority in general and because the church's crises had cost it so much credibility. *page 272*

WHY DID Martin Luther challenge the church?

Martin Luther and the German Reformation to 1525 Martin Luther, like many other Germans, was concerned about the church's sale of indulgences and other financial and political arrangements. An ordained priest with a doctorate in theology, he developed the doctrine of justification by faith alone, which offers salvation to believers in Christ. In 1517, Luther posted ninety-five theses against indulgence on the door of a church in Wittenberg. This sparked the Reformation. In the following years, Luther developed and publicized his theology; he was excommunicated in 1521. German humanists, peasants, and others supported Luther and his ideas, although Luther urged princes to suppress the peasants' revolt of 1524–1525. *page 274*

WHERE DID other reform movements develop and how were they different from Luther's?

The Reformation Elsewhere In Switzerland, France, and elsewhere in Europe, variations of Protestantism developed. In the 1520s, Ulrich Zwingli orchestrated the Swiss Reformation, from his post as the people's priest in the main church of Zurich. Zwingli believed a literal reading of Scripture should guide Christian beliefs and practices. More radical groups emerged, including Anabaptists, who believed baptism should only be performed on adults, who were capable of choosing their religion. John Calvin and his followers wanted to transform society morally, starting in Geneva in 1540. In the second half of the sixteenth century, Calvinism displaced Lutheranism as Europe's dominant form of Protestantism. *page 280*

WHAT WERE the political ramifications of the Reformation?

Political Consolidation of the Lutheran Reformation Between 1530 and 1552, the emperor Charles V made repeated attempts to persuade or force Protestants to revert to Catholicism. The 1555 Peace of Augsburg formalized Lutheranism's official status in the empire. Lutheranism also became the official state religion in Denmark and Sweden. Calvinists and Anabaptists, among others, were still excluded from official recognition throughout Europe. *page 283*

HOW DID royal dynastic concerns shape the Reformation in England?

The English Reformation to 1553 King Henry VIII's marital history had dramatic consequences for England's religion: Because Henry wanted to marry Anne Boleyn, and because Pope Clement VII would not annul Henry's marriage to Catherine of Aragon, Parliament decreed that the king, not the pope, was the "supreme head on earth of the Church of England." But, by the 1530s, many of Henry's subjects were far more sympathetic to Protestantism than the king himself was; Henry's Church of England differed little from the Catholic Church. Only under the reign of his son, Edward VI, was Protestantism really instituted in England. *page 284*

WHAT WAS the Counter-Reformation and how successful was it?

Catholic Reform and Counter-Reformation Protestants were not the only critics of the Catholic Church. Although the popes resisted reform, many new reform-oriented orders were established in the sixteenth century. Ignatius of Loyola founded what became one of the most significant of these orders, the Jesuits, who stressed a powerful combination of discipline and traditional spirituality. Between 1545 and 1563, a council of the church met at Trent to reassert Catholic doctrine. As a result of the Council of Trent, internal church discipline was reformed, but doctrine became even more strongly traditional and scholastic in orientation. Improvements in the education and behavior of local clergy helped revive parish life. *page 287*

WHAT WAS the social significance of the Reformation and how did it affect family life?

The Social Significance of the Reformation in Western Europe Although the Reformation was politically conservative, it revolutionized religious practice and institutions in part of Europe. In cities that became Protestant, many aspects of life were transformed. The numbers of clergy in these cities declined by two-thirds, one-third of all churches were closed, there were one-third fewer religious holidays, and most cloisters were closed. Some changes did not endure: More than half the original converts to Protestantism returned to the Catholic Church by the end of the sixteenth century. Protestant reformers helped disseminate humanist learning and culture. The ideal of the companionate marriage and other Protestant views helped improve the status of women. *page 289*

WHAT WAS family life like in early modern Europe?

Family Life in Early Modern Europe Marriage occurred at a later age in the sixteenth through eighteenth centuries than it had previously in Europe and England. One reason for this shift was that, in a time of population growth, it took couples longer to accumulate the capital needed to raise a family. Parents were involved in arranging their children's marriages, although the couple's own wishes also carried significant weight. Generally, two to four children survived to adulthood in the European nuclear family. Birth control was not very effective; wet nursing was controversial. Although they sometimes exhibited it in ways that may seem strange to us, early modern parents almost certainly loved their children, and probably also each other. *page 291*

HOW WAS the transition from medieval to modern reflected in the works of the great literary figures of the era?

Literary Imagination in Transition Miguel de Cervantes Saavedra and William Shakespeare are among the most renowned authors of this period. Cervantes lived and worked in Catholic Spain; Shakespeare was a product of Protestant England. Their writings reflect their very different situations and interests. Cervantes's most famous work, *Don Quixote*, pays homage to the tradition of chivalric romance. Shakespeare's dramas cover a wide range of topics, including history; his universal themes and brilliant technique explain his enduring popularity. *page 294*

REVIEW QUESTIONS

1. What were the main problems of the church that contributed to the Protestant Reformation? On what did Luther and Zwingli agree? On what did they disagree? What about Luther and Calvin?
2. What was the Catholic Reformation? What were the major reforms instituted by the Council of Trent? Did the Protestant Reformation have a healthy effect on the Catholic Church?
3. Why did Henry VIII break with the Catholic Church? Did he establish a truly Protestant religion in England? What problems did his successors face as a result of his religious policies?
4. What impact did the Reformation have on women in the sixteenth and seventeenth centuries? What new factors and pressures affected relations between men and women, family size, and child care during this period?

KEY TERMS

Act of Supremacy (p. 286)
Anabaptists (p. 281)
Augsburg Confession (p. 283)
indulgence (p. 275)

12

The Age of Religious Wars

The massacre of worshipping Protestants at Vassy, France (March 1, 1562), which began the French wars of religion. An engraving by an unidentified seventeenth-century artist.

The Granger Collection

How did politics and religion combine to produce civil war in sixteenth-century France?

RENEWED RELIGIOUS STRUGGLE *page 300*

HOW DID religious conflict in Europe evolve over the course of the second half of the sixteenth century?

THE FRENCH WARS OF RELIGION (1562–1598) *page 301*

WHAT CAUSED the civil war between the Huguenots and the Catholics in France and what was the outcome?

IMPERIAL SPAIN AND PHILIP II (R. 1556–1598) *page 305*

HOW WAS Philip II able to dominate international politics for much of the latter half of the sixteenth century?

ENGLAND AND SPAIN (1553–1603) *page 308*

WHAT ROLE did Catholic and Protestant extremism play in the struggle for supremacy between England and Spain?

THE THIRTY YEARS' WAR (1618–1648) *page 313*

WHAT TOLL did the Thirty Years' War take on Germany?

*olitical rivalries and religious conflicts combined to make the late sixteenth and the early seventeenth centuries an "age of religious wars." The era was plagued by civil conflicts within nations and by battles among nations. Catholic and Protestant factions contended within France, the Netherlands, and England. The Catholic monarchies of France and Spain attacked the Protestant regimes in England and the Netherlands. Ultimately, every major nation in Europe was drawn into a conflict that devastated Germany: the Thirty Years' War (1618–1648).* ■

RENEWED RELIGIOUS STRUGGLE

HOW DID religious conflict in Europe evolve over the course of the second half of the sixteenth century?

During the first half of the sixteenth century, religious conflict had been confined to central Europe and was primarily a struggle by Lutherans and Zwinglians to secure rights and freedoms for themselves. In the second half of the century, the focus shifted to Western Europe—to France, the Netherlands, England, and Scotland—and became a struggle by Calvinists for recognition. After the Peace of Augsburg (1555) and acceptance of the principle that a region's ruler determined its religion (*cuius regio, eius religio*), Lutheranism became a legal religion in the Holy Roman Empire. The Peace of Augsburg did not, however, extend recognition to non-Lutheran Protestants. Anabaptists and other sectarians continued to be scorned as heretics and anarchists, and Calvinists were not strong enough to gain legal standing.

Outside the empire, the struggle for religious freedom had intensified in most countries. After the Council of Trent adjourned in 1563, Catholics began a Jesuit-led international counteroffensive against Protestants. At the time of John Calvin's death in 1564, Geneva had become both a refuge for Europe's persecuted Protestants and an international school for Protestant resistance, producing leaders equal to the new Catholic challenge.

Counter-Reformation A reorganization of the Catholic Church that equipped it to meet the challenges posed by the Protestant Reformation.

Genevan Calvinism and Catholicism as revived by the Council of Trent were two equally dogmatic, aggressive, and irreconcilable church systems. Calvinism adopted an organization that magnified regional and local religious authority. Boards of presbyters, or elders, represented the individual congregations of Calvinists, directly shaping policy. By contrast, the **Counter-Reformation** sponsored a centralized episcopal church system hierarchically arranged from pope to parish priest and stressing unquestioning obedience to the person at the top. Calvinism proved attractive to proponents of political decentralization who opposed such hierarchical rule, in principle, whereas the Roman Catholic Church, an institution also devoted to one head and one law, found absolute monarchy congenial.

Contrast between an eighteenth-century Catholic baroque church in Ottobeuren, Bavaria, and a seventeenth-century Calvinist plain church in the Palatinate. The ornamental Catholic church (left) inspires worshippers to self-transcendence, while the undecorated Protestant church (right) focuses attention on God's word.

(Left) Vanni/Art Resource, NY (Right) German National Museum, Nuremberg, Germany

How did the baroque style reflect early modern Catholicism?

Why did Protestant churches such as this one avoid ornament and decoration?

Overview Main Events of French Wars of Religion

1559	Treaty of Cateau-Cambrésis ends Habsburg-Valois wars
1559	Francis II succeeds to French throne under regency of his mother, Catherine de Médicis
1562	Protestant worshippers massacred at Vassy in Champagne by the duke of Guise
1572	The Saint Bartholomew's Day Massacre leaves thousands of Protestants dead
1589	Assassination of Henry III brings the Huguenot Henry of Navarre to throne as Henry IV
1593	Henry IV embraces Catholicism
1598	Henry IV grants Huguenots religious and civil freedoms in the Edict of Nantes
1610	Henry IV assassinated

As religious wars engulfed Europe, the intellectuals perceived the wisdom of religious pluralism and toleration more quickly than did the politicians. A new skepticism, relativism, and individualism in religion became respectable in the sixteenth and seventeenth centuries. (See Chapter 14.) The French essayist Michel de Montaigne (1533–1592) asked in scorn of the dogmatic mind, "What do I know?" The Lutheran Valentin Weigel (1533–1588), surveying a half century of religious strife in Germany, advised people to look within themselves for religious truth and no longer to churches and creeds.

Such skeptical views gained currency in larger political circles only at the cost of painful experience. Religious strife and civil war were best held in check where rulers tended to subordinate theological doctrine to political unity, urging tolerance, moderation, and compromise—even indifference—in religious matters. Rulers of this kind came to be known as ***politiques***, and the most successful among them was Elizabeth I of England. By contrast, Mary I of England, Philip II of Spain, and Oliver Cromwell, all of whom took their religion with the utmost seriousness and refused any compromise, did not, in the end, achieve their political goals.

politiques Rulers who tended to subordinate theological doctrine to political unity.

Huguenots French Protestants.

THE FRENCH WARS OF RELIGION (1562–1598)

WHAT CAUSED the civil war between the Huguenots and the Catholics in France and what was the outcome?

French Protestants, known as **Huguenots**, were already under surveillance in France in the early 1520s when Lutheran writings and doctrines began to circulate in Paris. The capture of the French king Francis I by the forces of Emperor Charles V at the Battle of Pavia in 1525 provided a motive for the first wave of Protestant persecution in France. The French government hoped thereby to pacify the Habsburg victor, a fierce opponent of German Protestants, and to win their king's swift release.

A second major crackdown came a decade later. When Protestants plastered Paris and other cities with anti-Catholic placards on October 18, 1534, mass arrests of suspected Protestants followed. The government retaliation drove John Calvin and other members of the French reform party into exile. Save for a few brief interludes, the French monarchy remained a staunch foe of the Protestants until the ascension to the throne of Henry IV of Navarre in 1589.

The Habsburg-Valois wars (see Chapter 11) had ended with the Treaty of Cateau-Cambrésis in 1559, after which Europe experienced a moment of peace. The same year, however, marked the beginning of internal French conflict and a shift of the European balance of power away from France to Spain. The premature death of the

French king, Henry II, brought to the throne his sickly fifteen-year-old son, Francis II, who died after reigning only a year (1559–1560). With the monarchy weakened, three powerful families saw their chance to control France and began to compete for the young king's ear: the Bourbons, whose power lay in the south and west; the Montmorency-Chatillons, who controlled the center of France; and the strongest among them, the Guises, who were dominant in eastern France.

The Guises had little trouble establishing firm control over the young king. Throughout the latter half of the sixteenth century, the name "Guise" remained interchangeable with militant, reactionary Catholicism. The Bourbon and Montmorency-Chatillon families, in contrast, developed strong Huguenot sympathies, largely for political reasons. The Bourbon Louis I, prince of Condé (d. 1569), and the Montmorency-Chatillon admiral Gaspard de Coligny (1519–1572) became the political leaders of the French Protestant resistance.

Appeal of Calvinism

Often for different reasons, ambitious aristocrats and discontented townspeople joined Calvinist churches in opposing the Guise-dominated French monarchy. Although they made up only about one-fifteenth of the population, Huguenots held important geographic areas and were heavily represented among the more powerful segments of French society. A good two-fifths of the French aristocracy became Huguenots. Many apparently hoped to establish within France a principle of territorial sovereignty akin to what the Peace of Augsburg had secured within the Holy Roman Empire. Calvinism thus served the forces of political decentralization.

John Calvin and Theodore Beza sought to advance their cause by currying favor with powerful aristocrats. Beza converted Jeanne d'Albert, the mother of the future Henry IV. The prince of Condé was apparently converted in 1558 under the influence of his Calvinist wife. For many aristocrats—Condé probably among them—Calvinist religious convictions proved useful to their political goals.

The military organization of Condé and Coligny progressively merged with the religious organization of the French Huguenot churches, creating a potent combination that benefited both political and religious dissidents. Calvinism justified and inspired political resistance, while the resistance made Calvinism a viable religion in Catholic France. Each side had much to gain from the other.

Catherine de Médicis (1519–1589) exercised power in France during the reigns of her three sons Francis II (r. 1559–1560), Charles IX (r. 1560–1574), and Henry III (r. 1574–1589).

Getty Images, Inc.—Liaison

What role did Catherine de Médicis play in France's wars of religion?

Catherine de Médicis and the Guises

Following Francis II's death in 1560, the queen mother, Catherine de Médicis (1519–1589) became regent for her minor son, Charles IX (r. 1560–1574). At a meeting in Poissy, she tried unsuccessfully to reconcile the Protestant and Catholic factions. Fearing the power and guile of the Guises, Catherine, whose first concern was always to preserve the monarchy, sought allies among the Protestants. In 1562, after conversations with Beza and Coligny, she issued the January Edict, which granted Protestants freedom to worship publicly outside towns—although only privately within them—and to hold synods. In March 1562, this royal toleration came to an abrupt end when the duke of Guise surprised a Protestant congregation at Vassy in Champagne and massacred many worshippers. That event marked the beginning of the French wars of religion.

Had Condé and the Huguenot armies rushed immediately to the queen's side after this attack, Protestants might well have secured an alliance with the crown. The queen mother's fear of Guise power was great. Condé's hesitation, however, placed the young king and the queen mother, against their deepest wishes, under firm Guise control. Cooperation with the Guises became the only alternative to capitulation to the Protestants.

The Peace of Saint-Germain-en-Laye During the first French war of religion, fought between April 1562 and March 1563, the duke of Guise was assassinated. A brief resumption of hostilities in 1567–1568 was followed by the bloodiest of all the conflicts, between September 1568 and August 1570. In this period, Condé was killed, and Huguenot leadership passed to Coligny. In the peace of Saint-Germain-en-Laye (1570), which ended the third war, the crown, acknowledging the power of the Protestant nobility, granted the Huguenots religious freedoms within their territories and the right to fortify their cities.

Perpetually caught between fanatical Huguenot and Guise extremes, Queen Catherine had always sought to balance one side against the other. After the Peace of Saint-Germain-en-Laye, the crown tilted manifestly toward the Bourbon faction and the Huguenots, and Coligny became Charles IX's most trusted adviser. Unknown to the king, Catherine began to plot with the Guises against the ascendant Protestants. As she had earlier sought Protestant support when Guise power threatened to subdue the monarchy, she now sought Guise support as Protestant influence grew.

There was reason for Catherine to fear Coligny's hold on the king. Louis of Nassau, the leader of Protestant resistance to Philip II in the Netherlands, had gained Coligny's ear. Coligny used his influence to win the king of France over to a planned French invasion of the Netherlands to support the Dutch Protestants. This would have placed France squarely on a collision course with mighty Spain. Catherine recognized far better than her son that France stood little chance in such a contest.

The Saint Bartholomew's Day Massacre When Catherine lent her support to the infamous Saint Bartholomew's Day Massacre of Protestants, she did so out of a far less reasoned judgment. Her decision appears to have been made in near panic. On August 22, 1572, Coligny was struck down, although not killed, by an assassin's bullet. Catherine had apparently been party to this Guise plot to eliminate Coligny. After its failure, she feared both the king's reaction to her complicity with the Guises and the Coligny's response. Catherine convinced Charles that a Huguenot coup was afoot, inspired by Coligny, and that only the swift execution of Protestant leaders could save the crown from a Protestant attack on Paris.

On Saint Bartholomew's Day, August 24, 1572, Coligny and 3,000 fellow Huguenots were butchered in Paris. Within three days coordinated attacks across France killed an estimated 20,000 Huguenots. It is a date that has ever since lived in infamy for Protestants.

The event changed the nature of the struggle between Protestants and Catholics both within and beyond the borders of France. It was thereafter no longer an internal contest between Guise and Bourbon factions for French political influence, nor was it simply a Huguenot campaign to win basic religious freedoms. Henceforth, in Protestant eyes, it became an international struggle for sheer survival against an adversary whose cruelty justified any means of resistance.

QUICK REVIEW

Saint Bartholomew's Day Massacre

- August 24, 1572: 3,000 Huguenots ambushed in Paris and killed
- Within three days, some 20,000 Huguenots were killed throughout France
- Massacre changed the nature of the conflict between Protestants and Catholics throughout Europe

Protestant Resistance Theory Only as Protestants faced suppression and sure defeat did they begin to sanction active political resistance. At first, they tried to practice the biblical precept of obedient subjection to worldly authority (Romans 13:1).

The exiled Scots reformer John Knox (1513–1572), who had seen Mary of Guise, the Regent of Scotland, and Mary I of England crush his cause, laid the groundwork for later Calvinist resistance. In his famous *First Blast of the Trumpet against the Terrible Regiment of Women* (1558), he declared that the removal of a heathen tyrant was not only permissible, but also a Christian duty. He had the Catholic queen of England in mind.

After the great massacre of French Protestants on Saint Bartholomew's Day 1572, Calvinists everywhere came to appreciate the need for an active defense of their religious rights. Classical Huguenot theories of resistance appeared in three major works of the 1570s. The first was the *Franco-Gallia* of François Hotman (1573), a humanist argument that the representative Estates General of France historically held higher authority than the French king. The second was Theodore Beza's *On the Right of Magistrates over Their Subjects* (1574), which justified the correction and even the overthrow of tyrannical rulers by lower authorities. Finally, Philippe du Plessis Mornay's *Defense of Liberty against Tyrants* (1579) admonished princes, nobles, and magistrates beneath the king, as guardians of the rights of the body politic, to take up arms against tyranny in other lands.

The Rise to Power of Henry of Navarre

Henry III (r. 1574–1589) was the last of Henry II's sons to wear the French crown. He found the monarchy wedged between a radical Catholic League, formed in 1576 by Henry of Guise, and vengeful Huguenots. Like the queen mother, Henry sought to steer a middle course. In this effort, he received support from a growing body of neutral Catholics and Huguenots, who put the political survival of France above its religious unity. Such *politiques* were prepared to compromise religious creeds to save the nation.

The Peace of Beaulieu in May 1576 granted the Huguenots almost complete religious and civil freedom. France, however, was not ready then for such sweeping toleration. Within seven months of the Peace, the Catholic League forced Henry to return to the illusory quest for absolute religious unity in France. In October 1577, the king truncated the Peace of Beaulieu and once again limited areas of permitted Huguenot worship. Thereafter, Huguenot and Catholic factions returned to their accustomed anarchical military solutions. The Protestants were led by Henry of Navarre, a legal heir to the French throne by virtue of his descent in a direct male line from St. Louis IX (d. 1270).

In the mid-1580s, the Catholic League, with Spanish support, became dominant in Paris. In what came to be known as the Day of the Barricades, Henry III attempted to rout the league with a surprise attack in 1588. The effort failed, and the king had to flee Paris. Forced by his weakened position into unkingly guerrilla tactics, and also emboldened by news of the English victory over the Spanish Armada in 1588, Henry had both the duke and the cardinal of Guise assassinated. Led by still another Guise brother, the Catholic League reacted with a fury that matched the earlier Huguenot response to the Massacre of Saint Bartholomew's Day. The king was now forced to strike an alliance with the Protestant Henry of Navarre in April 1589.

As the two Henrys prepared to attack the Guise stronghold of Paris, however, an enraged Dominican friar killed Henry III. Thereupon, the Bourbon Huguenot Henry of Navarre succeeded the childless Valois king to the French throne as Henry IV (r. 1589–1610). Pope Sixtus V and Philip II were aghast at the sudden prospect of a Protestant France. They had always wanted France to be religiously Catholic and politically weak, and they now acted to achieve that end. Spain rushed troops to support the besieged Catholic League.

Henry IV of France (r. 1589–1610) on horseback, painted in 1594.

Réunion des Musées Nationaux/Art Resource, NY

What did Henry IV hope to accomplish with the Edict of Nantes?

Henry came to the throne as a *politique*, long weary with religious strife and fully prepared to place political peace above absolute religious unity. He believed a royal policy of tolerant Catholicism would be the best way to achieve such peace. On July 25, 1593, he publicly abandoned the Protestant faith and embraced the traditional and majority religion of his country. "Paris is worth a Mass," he is reported to have said. Most of the French church and people, having known internal strife too long, rallied to his side. By 1596, the Catholic League was dispersed, its ties with Spain were broken, and the wars of religion in France, to all intents, had ground to a close.

The Edict of Nantes

On April 13, 1598, Henry IV's famous Edict of Nantes proclaimed a formal religious settlement. The following month, on May 2, 1598, the Treaty of Vervins ended hostilities between France and Spain.

In 1591, Henry IV had already assured the Huguenots of at least qualified religious freedoms. The Edict of Nantes made good that promise. It recognized minority religious rights within what was to remain an officially Catholic country. This religious truce—and it was never more than that—granted the Huguenots, who by this time numbered well over a million, freedom of public worship, the right of assembly, admission to public offices and universities, and permission to maintain fortified towns. They were to exercise most of the new freedoms, however, within their own towns and territories. Concession of the right to fortify their towns revealed the continuing distrust between French Protestants and Catholics. As significant as it was, the edict only transformed a long hot war between irreconcilable enemies into a long cold war.

A Catholic fanatic assassinated Henry IV in May 1610. Although he is best remembered for the Edict of Nantes, Henry IV's political and economic policies were equally important. They laid the foundations for the transformation of France into the absolute state it would become under Cardinal Richelieu and Louis XIV. (See Chapter 13.)

IMPERIAL SPAIN AND PHILIP II (R. 1556–1598)

Pillars of Spanish Power

HOW WAS Philip II able to dominate international politics for much of the latter half of the sixteenth century?

Until the English defeated the mighty Spanish Armada in 1588, no one person stood larger in the second half of the sixteenth century than Philip II of Spain. Philip was heir to the intensely Catholic and militarily supreme western Habsburg kingdom.

New World Riches and Population Growth Populous and wealthy Castile gave Philip a solid home base. The regular arrival in Seville of bullion from the Spanish colonies in the New World provided additional wealth. He nonetheless never managed to erase the debts his father left or to finance his own foreign adventures fully.

The new American wealth brought dramatic social change to the peoples of Europe during the second half of the sixteenth century. As Europe became richer, it was also becoming more populous. In the economically and politically active towns of France, England, and the Netherlands, populations had tripled and quadrupled by the early seventeenth century. Europe's population exceeded 70 million by 1600.

The combination of increased wealth and population triggered inflation. A steady 2 percent a year rise in prices in much of Europe had serious cumulative effects by the mid–sixteenth century. There were more people and more coinage in circulation than before, but less food and fewer jobs; wages stagnated while prices doubled and tripled in much of Europe.

This was especially the case in Spain. Because the new wealth was concentrated in the hands of a few, the traditional gap between the haves—the propertied, privileged, and educated classes—and the have-nots widened. Nowhere did the unprivileged suffer more than in Spain, where the Castilian peasantry, the backbone of Philip II's great empire, became the most heavily taxed people of Europe.

Efficient Bureaucracy and Military Philip II shrewdly organized the lesser nobility into a loyal and efficient national bureaucracy. A reclusive man, he managed his kingdom by pen and paper rather than by personal presence. He was also a learned and pious Catholic, although some popes suspected he used religion as much for political as for devotional purposes. That he was a generous patron of the arts and culture can be seen in his unique retreat outside Madrid, the Escorial, a combination palace, church, tomb, and monastery.

Supremacy in the Mediterranean During the first half of Philip's reign, attention focused almost exclusively on the Mediterranean and the Turkish threat. By history, geography, and choice, Spain had traditionally been Catholic Europe's champion against Islam. During the 1560s, the Turks advanced deep into Austria, and their fleets dominated the Mediterranean. Between 1568 and 1570, armies under Philip's half brother, Don John of Austria (1547–1578), the illegitimate son of Charles V, suppressed and dispersed the Moors in Granada.

In May 1571, a Holy League of Spain, Venice, Genoa, and the pope, again under Don John's command, formed to check Turkish belligerence in the Mediterranean. In the largest naval battle of the sixteenth century, Don John's fleet engaged the Ottoman navy under Ali Pasha off Lepanto in the Gulf of Corinth on October 7, 1571. Before the engagement ended, over a third of the Turkish fleet had been sunk or captured, and 30,000 Turks had died. The resilient Ottomans would rebuild and regroup, but, for the moment, the Mediterranean belonged to Spain, and the Europeans were left to fight each other. Philip's armies also suppressed resistance in neighboring Portugal, when Philip inherited the throne of that kingdom in 1580. The union with Portugal not only enhanced Spanish sea power, but it also brought Portugal's overseas empire in Africa, India, and Brazil into the Spanish orbit.

The Revolt in the Netherlands

The spectacular Spanish military success in southern Europe was not repeated in northern Europe. When Philip attempted to impose his will within the Netherlands and on England and France, he learned the lessons of defeat.

Cardinal Granvelle The Netherlands was the richest area not only of Philip's Habsburg kingdom, but of Europe as well. In 1559, Philip departed the Netherlands for Spain, never again to return. His half sister, Margaret of Parma, assisted by a special council of state, became regent in his place. The council was headed by the extremely able Antoine Perrenot (1517–1586), known after 1561 as Cardinal Granvelle, who hoped to break down the traditional local autonomy of the seventeen Netherlands provinces by stages and establish in its place a centralized royal government directed from Madrid.

The merchant towns of the Netherlands were, however, Europe's most independent; many, like magnificent Antwerp, were also Calvinist strongholds. Two members of the council of state led a stubborn opposition to the Spanish overlords, who now attempted to reimpose their traditional rule with a vengeance. They were the Count of Egmont (1522–1568) and William of Nassau, the Prince of Orange (1533–1584), known as "the Silent" because of his small circle of confidants.

In 1561, Cardinal Granvelle proceeded with his plans for the ecclesiastical reorganization of the Netherlands. It was intended to tighten the control of the Catholic hierarchy over the country and to accelerate its consolidation as a Spanish ward. Organizing the Dutch nobility in opposition, Orange and Egmont succeeded in gaining Granvelle's removal from office in 1564. Aristocratic control of the country after Granvelle's departure, however, proved woefully inefficient. Popular unrest grew, especially among urban artisans, who joined the congregations of radical Calvinist preachers in large numbers.

The Compromise The year 1564 also saw the first fusion of political and religious opposition to Regent Margaret's government. This opposition resulted from Philip II's unwise insistence on trying to enforce the decrees of the Council of Trent throughout the Netherlands. William of Orange's younger brother, Louis of Nassau, who had been raised a Lutheran, led the opposition with support from the Calvinist-inclined lesser nobility and townspeople. A national covenant called the *Compromise* was drawn up, a solemn pledge to resist the decrees of Trent and the Inquisition. When Regent Margaret's government spurned the protesters as "beggars" in 1566, Calvinists rioted throughout the country. Louis called for aid from French Huguenots and German Lutherans, and a full-scale rebellion against the Spanish regency appeared imminent.

The Duke of Alba The rebellion failed to materialize, however, because the higher nobility of the Netherlands would not support it. Their shock at Calvinist iconoclasm and anarchy was as great as their resentment of Granvelle's more subtle repression. Philip, determined to make an example of the Protestant rebels, dispatched the duke of Alba to suppress the revolt. His army of 10,000 journeyed northward from Milan in 1567 in a show of combined Spanish and papal might. Before Alba's reign of terror ended, the counts of Egmont and Horn and several thousand suspected heretics were publicly executed.

Resistance and Unification William of Orange was an exile in Germany during these turbulent years. He now emerged as the leader of a broad movement for the independence of the Netherlands from Spain. The northern, Calvinist-inclined provinces of Holland, Zeeland, and Utrecht, of which Orange was the *Stadholder*, or governor, became his base. As in France, political resistance in the Netherlands gained both organization and inspiration by merging with Calvinism.

The early victories of the resistance attest to the popular character of the revolt. A case in point is the capture of the port city of Brill by the "Sea Beggars," an international group of anti-Spanish exiles and criminals, among them many Englishmen. In 1572, the Beggars captured Brill and other seaports in Zeeland and Holland. Mixing with the native population, they quickly sparked rebellions against Alba in town after town and spread the resistance southward. In 1574, the people of Leiden heroically resisted a long Spanish siege. The Dutch opened the dikes and flooded their country to repulse the hated Spanish. The faltering Alba had by that time ceded power to Don Luis de Requesens, who replaced him as commander of the Spanish forces in the Netherlands in November 1573.

QUICK REVIEW

Resistance to the Spanish

- William of Orange emerged as leader of the movement for the Netherlands' independence
- Political resistance gained organization and inspiration by merging with Calvinism
- Early victories demonstrate the popular character of the revolt

The Pacification of Ghent The greatest atrocity of the war came after Requesens's death in 1576. Spanish mercenaries, leaderless and unpaid, ran amok in Antwerp on November 4, 1576, leaving 7,000 people dead in the streets. The event came to be known as the Spanish Fury.

These atrocities accomplished in just four days what neither religion nor patriotism had previously been able to do. The ten largely Catholic southern provinces (what is roughly modern Belgium) now came together with the seven largely Protestant northern provinces (what is roughly the modern Netherlands) in unified opposition to Spain. This union, known as the Pacification of Ghent, was accomplished on November 8, 1576. It declared internal regional sovereignty in matters of religion, a key clause that permitted political cooperation among the signatories, who were not agreed over religion. Four provinces initially held out, but they soon made the resistance unanimous by joining the all-embracing Union of Brussels in January 1577. For the next two years, the Spanish faced a unified and determined Netherlands.

Confronted by unified Netherlands' resistance, Spain signed the humiliating Perpetual Edict in February 1577, which provided for the removal of all Spanish troops from the Netherlands within twenty days. The withdrawal gave the country to William of Orange and effectively ended, for the time being, whatever plans Philip may have had for using the Netherlands as a staging area for an invasion of England.

The Union of Arras and the Union of Utrecht The Spanish, however, were nothing if not persistent. Don John and Alexander Farnese of Parma, the Regent Margaret's son, revived Spanish power in the southern provinces, where fear of Calvinist extremism had moved the leaders to break the Union of Brussels. In January 1579, the southern provinces formed the Union of Arras and soon made peace with Spain. The northern provinces responded by forming the Union of Utrecht.

The Milch Cow, a sixteenth-century satirical painting depicting the Netherlands as a cow in whom all the great powers of Europe have an interest. Elizabeth of England is feeding her (England had long-standing commercial ties with Flanders); Philip II of Spain is attempting to ride her (Spain was trying to reassert its control over the entire area); William of Orange is trying to milk her (he was the leader of the anti-Spanish rebellion); and the king of France holds her tail (France hoped to profit from the rebellion at Spain's expense).

The *Milch Cow.* Rijksmuseum, Amsterdam

What made the Netherlands a focal point for international conflict in the sixteenth century?

Netherlands Independence Seizing what now appeared to be a last opportunity to break the back of Netherlands' resistance, Philip II declared William of Orange an outlaw and placed a bounty of 25,000 crowns on his head. The act predictably stiffened the resistance of the northern provinces.

Spanish efforts to reconquer the Netherlands continued into the 1580s. William of Orange, assassinated in July 1584, was succeeded by his seventeen-year-old son, Maurice (1567–1625), who, with the assistance of England and France, continued the Dutch resistance. Fortunately for the Netherlands, Philip II began now to meddle directly in French and English affairs. He signed a secret treaty with the Guises (the Treaty of Joinville in December 1584) and sent armies under Alexander Farnese into France in 1590. Hostilities with the English, who openly aided the Dutch rebels, also increased. Gradually, they built to a climax in 1588, when Philip's great Armada was defeated in the English Channel.

These new fronts overextended Spain's resources, thus strengthening the Netherlands. Spanish preoccupation with France and England now permitted the northern provinces to drive out all Spanish soldiers by 1593. In 1596, France and England formally recognized their independence. Peace was not, however, concluded with Spain until 1609, when the Twelve Years' Truce gave the northern provinces virtual independence. Full recognition came with the Peace of Westphalia in 1648.

ENGLAND AND SPAIN (1553–1603)

WHAT ROLE did Catholic and Protestant extremism play in the struggle for supremacy between England and Spain?

Before Edward VI died in 1553, he agreed to a device to make the Protestant Lady Jane Grey his successor in place of the Catholic Mary Tudor (r. 1553–1558). Yet popular support for the principle of hereditary monarchy was too strong to deprive Mary of her rightful rule. Uprisings in London and elsewhere led to Jane Grey's removal from the throne within days of her crowning, and she was eventually beheaded.

Portrait of Mary I (r. 1553–1558), Queen of England.

Queen Mary I, 1554 (oil on panel) by Sir Anthonis Mor (Antonio Moro) (1517/20–76/7). Prado, Madrid, Spain/Bridgeman Art Library

Why did Mary I's policies toward Spain spark so much resentment among her subjects?

MARY I (R. 1553–1558)

Once enthroned, Mary proceeded to act even beyond the worst fears of the Protestants. In 1554, she entered a highly unpopular political marriage with Philip (later Philip II) of Spain, a symbol of militant Catholicism to English Protestants. Mary's domestic measures were equally shocking to the English people and even more divisive. During her reign, Parliament repealed the Protestant statutes of Edward and reverted to the Catholic religious practice of her father, Henry VIII. The great Protestant leaders of the Edwardian Age—John Hooper, Hugh Latimer, and Thomas Cranmer—were executed for heresy. Hundreds of Protestants either joined them in martyrdom or fled to the Continent.

ELIZABETH I (R. 1558–1603)

Mary's successor was her half sister, Elizabeth I, the daughter of Henry VIII and Anne Boleyn. Elizabeth had remarkable and enduring successes in both domestic and foreign policy. Between 1559 and 1603, she guided a religious settlement through Parliament that prevented religious differences from tearing England apart in the sixteenth century. A ruler who subordinated religious to political unity, Elizabeth merged a centralized episcopal system that she firmly controlled with broadly defined Protestant doctrine and traditional Catholic ritual.

In 1559, an Act of Supremacy passed Parliament, repealing all the anti-Protestant legislation of Mary Tudor and asserting Elizabeth's right as "supreme governor" over both spiritual and temporal affairs. In the same year, the Act of Uniformity mandated for every English parish a revised version of the second *Book of Common Prayer* (1552). In 1563, the issuance of the Thirty-Nine Articles, a revision of Thomas Cranmer's original forty-two, made a moderate Protestantism the official religion within the Church of England.

Catholic and Protestant Extremists Elizabeth hoped to avoid both Catholic and Protestant extremism by pursuing a middle way. Elizabeth could not prevent the emergence of subversive Catholic and Protestant zealots, however. When she ascended the throne, Catholics were in the majority in England. The extremists among them, encouraged by the Jesuits and aided by the Spanish, plotted against her.

Catholic extremists hoped eventually to replace Elizabeth with Mary Stuart, Queen of Scots. Elizabeth acted swiftly against Catholic assassination plots, rarely letting her emotions override her political instincts. Despite proven cases of Catholic treason and even attempted regicide, she executed fewer Catholics during her forty-five years on the throne than Mary Tudor had executed Protestants during her brief five-year reign.

Elizabeth showed little mercy, however, to any who threatened the unity of her rule. She dealt cautiously with the Puritans, who were Protestants working within the national church to "purify" it of every vestige of "popery" and to make its Protestant doctrine more precise. Sixteenth-century Puritans were not true separatists. They enjoyed popular support and were led by widely respected men like Thomas Cartwright (d. 1603). They worked through Parliament to create an alternative national church of semiautonomous congregations governed by representative presbyteries (hence, **Presbyterians**), following the model of Calvin and Geneva. Elizabeth dealt firmly, but subtly, with them, conceding nothing that lessened the hierarchical unity of the Church of England and her control over it.

Presbyterians Puritans who favored a national church of semiautonomous congregations governed by representative presbyteries.

The more extreme Puritans wanted every congregation to be autonomous, a law unto itself, with neither higher episcopal nor presbyterian control. They came to be known as **Congregationalists**. Elizabeth and her second archbishop of Canterbury, John Whitgift (d. 1604), refused to tolerate this group, whose views on independence they found patently subversive. The Conventicle Act of 1593 gave such separatists the option either to conform to the practices of the Church of England or face exile or death.

Congregationalists The more extreme Puritans who believed every congregation ought to be autonomous, a law unto itself controlled by neither bishops nor presbyterian assemblies.

Deterioration of Relations with Spain A series of events led inexorably to war between England and Spain, despite the sincere desires of both Philip II and Elizabeth to avoid a confrontation. In 1567, the Spanish duke of Alba marched his mighty army into the Netherlands, which was, from the English point of view, simply a convenient staging area for a Spanish invasion of England. Pope Pius V (r. 1566–1572), who favored a military conquest of Protestant England, "excommunicated" Elizabeth for heresy in 1570. This mischievous act encouraged both internal resistance and international intrigue against the queen. Two years later, as noted earlier, the piratical sea beggars, many of whom were Englishmen, occupied the port of Brill in the Netherlands and aroused the surrounding countryside against the Spanish.

In 1571, England signed a mutual defense pact with France. Also in the 1570s, Elizabeth's famous seamen John Hawkins (1532–1595) and Sir Francis Drake (1545?–1596) began to prey regularly on Spanish shipping in the Americas.

After the Saint Bartholomew's Day Massacre, Elizabeth was the only protector of Protestants in France and the Netherlands. In 1585, she signed the Treaty of Nonsuch, which provided English soldiers and cavalry to the Netherlands. Funds that had previously been funneled covertly to support Henry of Navarre's army in France now flowed openly.

An idealized likeness of Elizabeth Tudor when she was a princess, attributed to Flemish court painter L. B. Teerling, ca. 1551. The painting shows her blazing red hair and alludes to her learning by the addition of books.

What qualities did Teerling intend the viewer to see in the young Elizabeth?

Mary, Queen of Scots These events made a tinderbox of English–Spanish relations. The spark that finally touched it off was Elizabeth's execution of Mary, Queen of Scots (1542–1587).

COMPARE & CONNECT

A GREAT DEBATE OVER RELIGIOUS TOLERANCE

On October 27, 1553, the Spanish physician and amateur theologian Michael Servetus died at the stake in Geneva for alleged "blasphemies against the Holy Trinity." A bold and confident man, he had also incurred the wrath of Rome before badgering John Calvin in Geneva on theological issues. In the wake of Servetus's execution, Calvin was much criticized for fighting heresy with capital punishment. In 1544, he came to his own defense in a tract entitled *Defense of the Orthodox Faith in the Holy Trinity Against the Monstrous Errors of Michael Servetus of Spain*. Thereafter, Sebastian Castellio, an accomplished humanist and former rector of the college in Geneva, whom Calvin had driven out of the city years earlier, began a series of writings against Calvin. One of his titles, *Whether Heretics Should Be Punished By the Sword of the Magistrates*, was an anonymous anthology on religious toleration that included a supporting excerpt from John Calvin himself! Writing over the years under several pseudonyms for safety's sake, Castellio excerpted statements from Calvin's works and put them in a sustained "debate" with his own more liberal point of view.

QUESTIONS

1. Why does Calvin believe that heresy deserves capital punishment?
2. What are Castellio's best rebuttal arguments?
3. Why does Castellio write under pseudonyms?

I. *WHETHER HERETICS SHOULD BE PUNISHED BY THE SWORD OF THE MAGISTRATES*

CALVIN: Kings are duty bound to defend the doctrine of piety.

CASTELLIO: [Yes, but] to kill a man is not to defend doctrine, but rather to kill a man . . .

CALVIN: What of today? The majority of people have lost all sense of shame and openly mock God. They burst as boldly into God's awesome mysteries as pigs poke their snouts into costly storehouses.

CASTELLIO: Calvin appears to be criticizing himself. For truly the awesome mysteries of God are the Trinity, predestination, and election. But this man [Calvin] speaks so assuredly about these matters that one would think he was in Paradise. So thorny is his own teaching about the Trinity . . . that by his own curiosity he weakens and makes doubtful the consciences of the simple. He has taught so crudely about predestination that innumerable men have been seduced into a security as great as that which existed before the Flood . . .

Tell me, in brief, what you think about predestination.

CALVIN: I have been taught the following about predestination: All men are not created in an equal state. Rather in eternity, God, by inevitable decree, determined in advance those whom he would save and those whom he would damn to destruction. Those whom he has deemed worthy of salvation have been chosen by his mercy without consideration of their worthiness. And those given damnation, he shuts off from life by a just and irreprehensible, albeit incomprehensible, judgment.

CASTELLIO: So you maintain that certain men are created by God already marked for damnation so that they cannot be saved?

CALVIN: Precisely.

CASTELLIO: But what if they *should* obey God? Would they not then be saved?

CALVIN: They would then be saved. However, they are not able to obey God, because God excludes them from the knowledge of his name and the spirit of his justification so that they can and will do only evil and are inclined only to every kind of sin.

CASTELLIO: Hence, they have that inclination [to sin] from God's creation and predestination?

CALVIN: They have it so, just as surely as God has created the wolf with the inclination to eat sheep!

CASTELLIO: Therefore they have been damned and rejected by God even before they existed?

CALVIN: Exactly.

CASTELLIO: But are they not damned for their sins?

CALVIN: Indeed so. Those who were destined to that [damned] lot are completely worthy of it.

CASTELLIO: When were they worthy of it?

CALVIN: When they were destined to it?

CASTELLIO: Then they have 'been' before they 'are'. Do you see what you are saying?!

CALVIN: I don't understand.

CASTELLIO: If they were worthy, then they 'were.' For to be worthy is to be. And if you concede that they have been damned before they are, then they have 'been' before they were.

CALVIN: God elects the foolish things of the world to confound the wise.

CASTELLIO: Calvin and his kind reject the foolish things of the world so that they may exalt the wise [themselves]. Hence, they admit hardly anyone into . . . their circle who is not accomplished in sciences and languages . . . If Christ himself came to them, he would certainly be turned away if he spoke no Latin . . .

[But] Christ wishes to be judged by common sense and refers the matters of the gospel to human judgment . . . He would never have employed such analogies had he wished to deprive us of our common sense. And who would have believed him had he taught things repugnant to nature and contradictory to human experience . . .? What kind of master would he have been, had he said to the woman who cried out to him and washed his feet with her hair: "O woman, whatever your sin, it was done by God's decree!

Source: Steven Ozment, *Mysticism and Dissent: Religious Ideology and Social Protest in the Sixteenth Century* (New Haven, CT: Yale University Press, 1973), pp. 171–179.

Despite her Protestant sympathies, Queen Elizabeth I of England (r. 1558–1603) steered clear of both Catholic and Protestant extremism. Despite proven cases of Catholic treason and even attempted regicide, she executed fewer Catholics during her forty-five years on the throne than Mary Tudor had executed Protestants during her brief five-year reign.

Courtesy of the Library of Congress, Rare Book and Special Collections Division

How did Elizabeth I want to be seen by her people?

ENCOUNTERING THE PAST

Going to the Theater

The Elizabethan era was a Golden Age for English theater. During the late Middle Ages, troupes of players had toured the countryside performing morality plays. The church often sponsored these companies, for plays offered religious education and moral instruction as well as entertainment. The rural theater was nothing more than a circular field ringed with mounds of earth on which spectators sat. Four tents were pitched at the points of the compass to give actors opportunities to enter and exit the action as the plot required.

During the fifteenth century, players began to stage their productions in the courtyards of urban inns. Inns were renovated to provide permanent stages and more complex sets. The enclosed space also made it possible to limit the audience to paying customers and to turn theater into a profitable business enterprise. The urban setting altered the content as well as the staging of plays. The allegorical moralizing of the medieval country theater was replaced by a more ribald, worldly entertainment, and the inn setting provided the workmen and young women who comprised much of the audience with rooms to which to retreat for performances of their own.

London's theater world matured in the late sixteenth and early seventeenth centuries in the work of Shakespeare and his contemporaries. Special theaters (notably the Rose and the Globe, for which Shakespeare wrote) were built in the 1590s on the south bank of the river Thames. Plays were hugely popular with Londoners. Women were excluded from the stage, so all parts were acted by men and boys. Audiences (particularly in "the pit," the ground floor) were rowdy. They responded to the witty repartee and bawdy action on stage and overindulged in the food and drink sold during the performance.

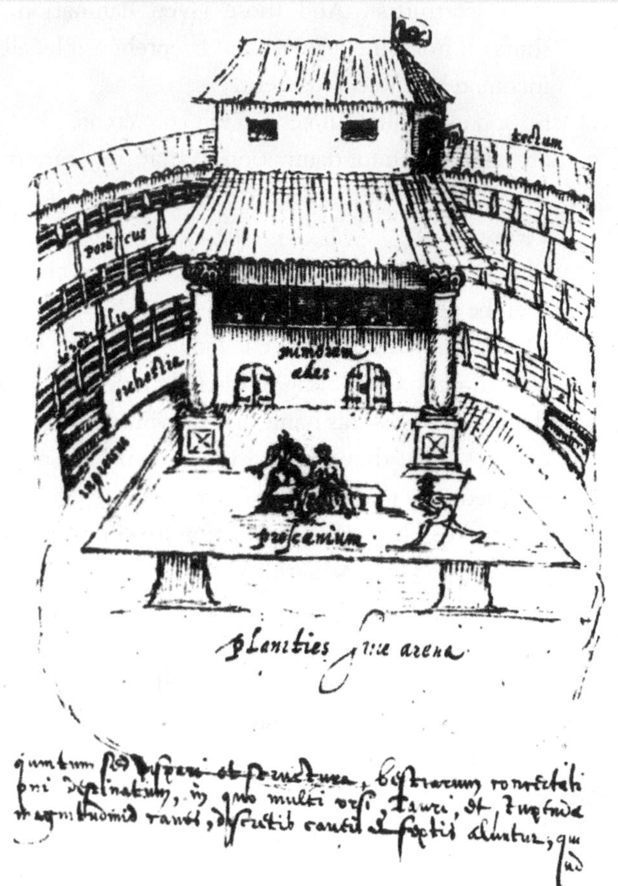

A seventeenth-century sketch of the Swan Theatre, which stood near Shakespeare's Globe Theatre on the south bank of the Thames.

The Bridgeman Art Library

Who went to the theater in the seventeenth century? What kinds of plays did they see?

HOW DID medieval theater differ from the theater of Elizabeth's era?

Mary Stuart was the daughter of King James V of Scotland and Mary of Guise and had resided in France from the time she was six years old. This thoroughly French and Catholic queen had returned to Scotland after the death of her husband, the French king Francis II, in 1561. There she found a successful, fervent Protestant Reformation legally sanctioned the year before by the Treaty of Edinburgh (1560).

In 1568, a public scandal forced Mary's abdication and flight to her cousin Elizabeth in England. Mary's reputed lover, the earl of Bothwell, was, with cause, suspected of having killed her legal husband, Lord Darnley. When a packed court acquitted Bothwell, he subsequently married Mary. The outraged reaction from Protestant nobles forced Mary to surrender the throne to her one-year-old son, the future James VI of Scotland and, later, Elizabeth's successor as King James I of England. Because of Mary's clear claim to the Eng-

lish throne, she was an international symbol of a possible Catholic England and consumed by the desire to be England's queen. For this reason, her presence in England, where she resided under house arrest for nineteen years, was a constant discomfort to Elizabeth.

In 1583, Elizabeth's vigilant secretary, Sir Francis Walsingham, uncovered a plot against Elizabeth involving the Spanish ambassador Bernardino de Mendoza. After Mendoza's deportation in January 1584, popular antipathy toward Spain and support for Protestant resistance in France and the Netherlands became massive throughout England.

In 1586, Walsingham uncovered still another plot against Elizabeth, the so-called Babington plot, after Anthony Babington, who was caught seeking Spanish support for an attempt on the queen's life. This time he had uncontestable proof of Mary's complicity. Mary was executed on February 18, 1587. This event dashed all Catholic hopes for a bloodless reconversion of Protestant England. Philip II ordered his Armada to make ready for the invasion of England.

The Armada On May 30, 1588, 130 ships bearing 25,000 sailors and soldiers under the command of the duke of Medina-Sidonia set sail for England. In the end, however, the English won a stunning victory. The invasion barges that were to transport Spanish soldiers from the galleons onto English shores were prevented from leaving Calais and Dunkirk. The swifter English and Netherlands' ships, helped by what came to be known as an "English wind," dispersed the waiting Spanish fleet, over one-third of which never returned to Spain.

The news of the Armada's defeat gave heart to Protestant resistance everywhere. Although Spain continued to win impressive victories in the 1590s, it never fully recovered. By the time of Philip's death on September 13, 1598, his forces had been rebuffed on all fronts. His seventeenth-century successors were all inferior leaders who never knew responsibilities equal to his, nor did Spain ever again know such imperial grandeur. The French soon dominated the Continent, and in the New World the Dutch and the English whittled away at Spain's overseas empire.

Elizabeth died on March 23, 1603, leaving behind her a strong nation poised to expand into a global empire.

QUICK REVIEW

The Spanish Armada

- Assembled for invasion of Protestant England
- Comprised of 130 ships bearing 25,000 sailors and soldiers
- Failure of Armada in May 1588 dealt a severe blow to Spain's military power

THE THIRTY YEARS' WAR (1618–1648)

WHAT TOLL did the Thirty Years' War take on Germany?

The Thirty Years' War in the Holy Roman Empire was the last and most destructive of the wars of religion. What made the Thirty Years' War so devastating was the entrenched hatred of the various sides and their seeming determination to sacrifice all for their religious beliefs. When the hostilities ended in 1648, the peace terms shaped the map of northern Europe much as we know it today.

PRECONDITIONS FOR WAR

Fragmented Germany In the second half of the sixteenth century, Germany was an almost ungovernable land of about 360 autonomous political entities. The Peace of Augsburg (1555) had given each of them significant sovereignty within its own borders. Many of these little lands also had great-power pretensions.

Because of its central location, Germany had always been Europe's highway for merchants and traders going north, south, east, and west. Europe's rulers pressed in on Germany both because of trade and because some held lands or legal privileges within certain German principalities. German princes, in their turn, looked to import and export markets beyond German borders and opposed efforts to consolidate the Holy Roman Empire, lest their territorial rights, confirmed by the Peace of Augsburg, be overturned. German princes were not loath to turn to Catholic France or to the kings of Denmark and Sweden for allies against the Habsburg emperor.

After the Council of Trent, Protestants in the empire suspected the existence of an imperial and papal conspiracy to re-create the Catholic Europe of pre-Reformation times. The imperial diet, which the German princes controlled, demanded strict observance of the constitutional rights of Germans, as set forth in agreements with the emperor since the mid–fourteenth century. In the late sixteenth century, the emperor ruled only to the degree to which he was prepared to use force of arms against his subjects.

Religious Division Religious conflict accentuated the international and internal political divisions. (See Map 12–1.) During this period, the population within the Holy Roman Empire was about equally divided between Catholics and Protestants, the latter having perhaps a slight numerical edge by 1600. The terms of the Peace of Augsburg had attempted to freeze the territorial holdings of the Lutherans and the Catholics (the so-called *ecclesiastical reservation*). In the intervening years, however, the Lutherans had gained and kept political control in some Catholic areas, as had the Catholics in a few previously Lutheran areas. Such territorial reversals, or the threat of them, only increased the suspicion and antipathy between the two sides.

The Lutherans had been far more successful in securing their rights to worship in Catholic lands than the Catholics had been in securing such rights in Lutheran lands. The Catholic rulers, who were in a weakened position after the Reformation, had made, but resented, concessions to Protestant communities within their territories. With the passage of time, they demanded that all ecclesiastical princes, electors, archbishops, bishops, and abbots who had deserted the Catholic for the Protestant side be immediately deprived of their religious offices and that their ecclesiastical holdings be promptly returned to Catholic control in accordance with the ecclesiastical reservation. However, the Lutherans and, even more so, the Calvinists in the Palatinate ignored this stipulation at every opportunity.

Calvinism and the Palatinate As elsewhere in Europe, Calvinism was the political and religious leaven within the Holy Roman Empire on the eve of the Thirty Years' War. Unrecognized as a legal religion by the Peace of Augsburg, it gained a strong foothold within the empire when Frederick III (r. 1559–1576), a devout convert to Calvinism, became Elector Palatine (ruler within the Palatinate; see Map 12–1) and made it the official religion of his domain. By 1609, Palatine Calvinists headed a Protestant defensive alliance that received support from Spain's sixteenth-century enemies: England, France, and the Netherlands.

The Lutherans came to fear the Calvinists almost as much as they did the Catholics. By their bold missionary forays into the empire, Palatine Calvinists seemed to the Lutherans to threaten the Peace of Augsburg—and hence the legal foundation of the Lutheran states. Also, outspoken Calvinist criticism of the doctrine of Christ's real presence in the Eucharist shocked the more religiously conservative Lutherans.

QUICK REVIEW

Religious Divisions in the Holy Roman Empire

- By 1600 slightly more Protestants than Catholics in Holy Roman Empire
- Peace of Augsburg (1555) did not succeed in freezing religion of territories
- Divisions within Protestant camp complicated situation

Maximilian of Bavaria and the Catholic League If the Calvinists were active within the Holy Roman Empire, so also were their Catholic counterparts, the Jesuits. From staunchly Catholic Bavaria, the Jesuits launched successful missions throughout the empire, winning such major cities as Strasbourg and Osnabrück back to the Catholic fold by 1600. In 1609, Maximilian I, duke of Bavaria (r. 1597–1651), organized a Catholic league to counter a new Protestant alliance that had been formed in the same year under the leadership of Calvinist Elector Palatine, Frederick IV (r. 1583–1610). When the league fielded a great army under the command of Count Johann von Tilly, the stage was set, both internally and internationally, for the worst of the religious wars, the Thirty Years' War.

Four Periods of War

The war went through four distinguishable periods. During its course, it drew in every major Western European nation—at least diplomatically and financially, if not by direct

MAP EXPLORATION

Interactive map: To explore this map further, go to www.myhistorylab.com

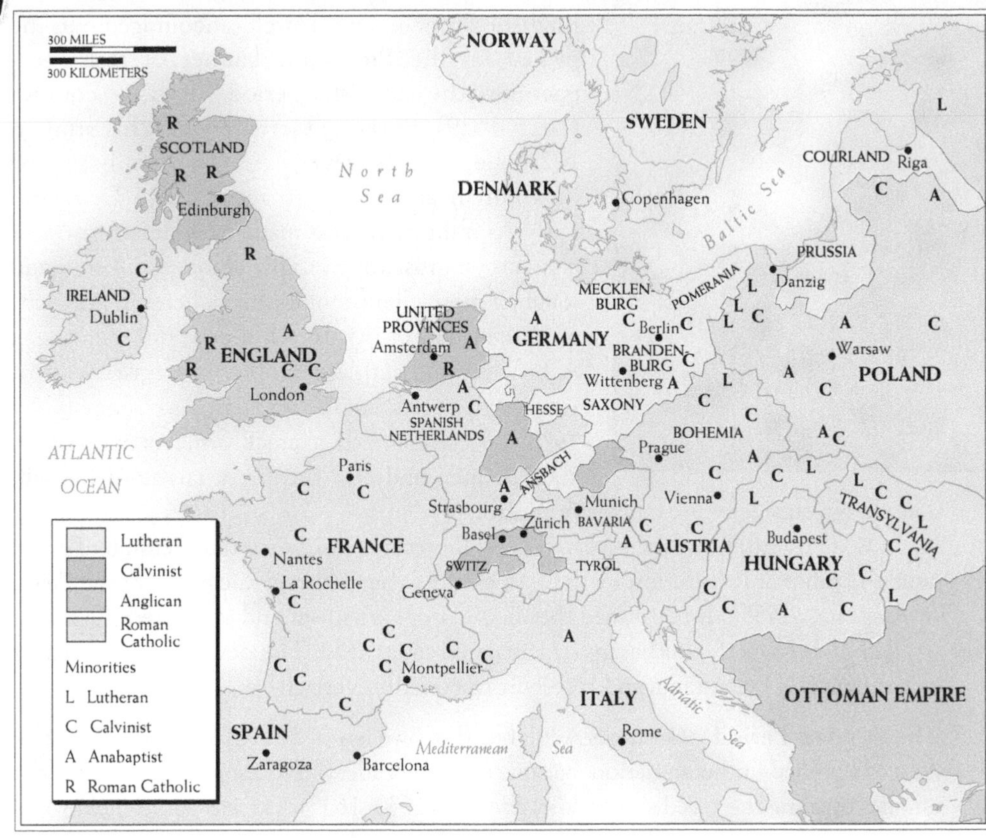

MAP 12–1 **Religious Divisions about 1600** By 1600, few could seriously expect Christians to return to a uniform religious allegiance. In Spain and southern Italy, Catholicism remained relatively unchallenged, but note the existence elsewhere of large religious minorities, both Catholic and Protestant.

How would you explain the division between Catholic and Protestant regions in Europe?

military intervention. The four periods were the Bohemian (1618–1625); the Danish (1625–1629); the Swedish (1630–1635); and the Swedish-French (1635–1648).

The Bohemian Period The war broke out in Bohemia after the ascent to the Bohemian throne in 1618 Habsburg Ferdinand, archduke of Styria, who was also heir to the imperial throne and a fervent Catholic. No sooner had Ferdinand become king of Bohemia than he revoked the religious freedoms of Bohemian Protestants. The Protestant nobility in Prague responded to Ferdinand's act in May 1618 by throwing his regents out the window of the royal palace. The event has ever since been known as the "defenestration of Prague." In the following year Ferdinand became Holy Roman Emperor as Ferdinand II (r. 1619–1637), by the unanimous vote of the seven electors. The Bohemians, however, defiantly deposed him in Prague and declared the Calvinist elector Palatine, Frederick V (r. 1616–1623), their king.

What had begun as a revolt of the Protestant nobility against an unpopular king of Bohemia escalated into an international war. Spain sent troops to Ferdinand, who found more motivated allies in Maximilian of Bavaria and the Lutheran elector John George I of Saxony (r. 1611–1656).

Ferdinand's army routed Frederick V's troops at the Battle of White Mountain in 1620. By 1622, Ferdinand had not only subdued and re-Catholicized Bohemia, but conquered the Palatinate as well. Meanwhile, Maximilian of Bavaria pressed the conflict into northwestern Germany, laying claim to land as he went.

The Danish Period These events raised new fears that a reconquest and re-Catholicization of the empire now loomed, which was precisely Ferdinand II's design. The Lutheran king Christian IV (r. 1588–1648) of Denmark, who already

Bohemian protesters throw three of Emperor Ferdinand II's agents out of windows at Hradschin Castle in Prague to protest his revocation of Protestant freedoms.

Bildarchiv Preussischer Kulturbesitz/Art Resource, NY

How did this event lead to the outbreak of the Thirty Years' War?

held territory within the empire as the duke of Holstein, was eager to extend Danish influence over the coastal towns of the North Sea. With English, French, and Dutch encouragement, he picked up the Protestant banner of resistance, opening the Danish period of the conflict (1625–1629). Entering Germany with his army in 1626, he was, however, quickly humiliated by Maximilian and forced to retreat into Denmark.

As military success made Maximilian stronger and an untrustworthy ally, Emperor Ferdinand sought a more pliant tool for his policies in Albrecht of Wallenstein (1583–1634), a powerful mercenary. A brilliant and ruthless military strategist, Wallenstein carried Ferdinand's campaign into Denmark. By 1628, he commanded a crack army of more than 100,000 men and also became a law unto himself, completely outside of the emperor's control.

Wallenstein, however, had so broken Protestant resistance that Ferdinand could issue the Edict of Restitution in 1629, reasserting the Catholic safeguards of the Peace of Augsburg (1555). It reaffirmed the illegality of Calvinism and it ordered the return of all church lands the Lutherans had acquired since 1552. The new edict struck panic in the hearts of Protestants and Habsburg opponents everywhere.

The Swedish Period Gustavus Adolphus II of Sweden (r. 1611–1632), a deeply pious king of a unified Lutheran nation, became the new leader of Protestant forces within the empire, opening the Swedish period of the war (1630–1635). He was controlled by two interested bystanders: (1) the French minister Cardinal Richelieu (1585–1642), whose foreign policy was to protect French interests by keeping the Habsburg armies tied down in Germany, and (2) the Dutch, who had not forgotten Spanish Habsburg rule in the sixteenth century. In alliance with the electors of Brandenburg and Saxony and led by their great general Gustavus Adolphus, the Swedes won a smashing victory at Breitenfeld in 1630—one that reversed the course of the war so dramatically that it has been regarded as the most decisive engagement of the long conflict.

Gustavus Adolphus died at the hands of Wallenstein's forces during the Battle of Lützen (November 1632)—a costly engagement for both sides that created a brief standstill. Ferdinand had long resented Wallenstein's independence, although he was the major factor in imperial success. In 1634, Ferdinand had Wallenstein assassinated. The episode is a telling commentary on this war without honor. Despite the deep religious motivations, greed and political gain were the real forces at work in the Thirty Years' War.

In the Peace of Prague in 1635, the German Protestant states, led by Saxony, reached a compromise with Ferdinand. France and the Netherlands, however, continued to support Sweden. Desiring to maximize their investment in the war, they refused to join the agreement. Their resistance to settlement plunged the war into its fourth and most devastating phase.

The Swedish-French Period The French openly entered the war in 1635, sending men and munitions as well as financial subsidies. Thereafter, the war dragged on for thirteen years, with French, Swedish, and Spanish soldiers looting the length and breadth of Germany. By the time peace talks began at Münster and Osnabrück in Westphalia in 1644, the war had killed an estimated one-third of the German population. It has been called the worst European catastrophe since the Black Death of the fourteenth century.

The Treaty of Westphalia

The Treaty of Westphalia in 1648 ended all hostilities within the Holy Roman Empire. It was the first general peace in Europe after a war unprecedented for its number of warring parties. (See Map 12–2.) The treaty rescinded Ferdinand's Edict of Restitution and reasserted the major feature of the religious settlement of the Peace of Augsburg ninety-three years earlier: The ruler of a land determines the official religion of that land. The treaty also gave the Calvinists their long-sought legal recognition. The independence of the Swiss Confederacy and the United Provinces of the Netherlands, long recognized in fact, was now proclaimed in law. Bavaria became an elector state, Brandenburg-Prussia emerged as the most powerful northern German state, and the other German princes became supreme over their principalities.

By confirming the territorial sovereignty of Germany's many political entities, the Treaty of Westphalia perpetuated German division and political weakness into the modern period. The petty regionalism within the empire also reflected on a small scale the drift of larger European politics. In the seventeenth century, distinctive nation-states, each with their own political, cultural, and religious identity, reached maturity and firmly established the competitive nationalism of the modern world.

MAP EXPLORATION

Interactive map: To explore this map further, go to www.myhistorylab.com

MAP 12–2 **Europe in 1648** At the end of the Thirty Years' War, Spain still had extensive possessions. Austria and Brandenburg-Prussia were rising powers, the independence of the United Provinces and Switzerland was recognized, and Sweden had footholds in northern Germany.

What does this map indicate about the German lands and the Holy Roman Empire in 1648?

SUMMARY

HOW DID religious conflict in Europe evolve over the course of the second half of the sixteenth century?

Renewed Religious Struggle The Peace of Augsburg recognized Lutheranism as a legal religion in the Holy Roman Empire in 1555. For the remainder of the sixteenth century, religious strife centered on the conflict between Calvinism and Catholicism. Calvinism and Catholicism both were dogmatic, aggressive, and irreconcilable. Slowly some intellectuals—and a very few political leaders—came to adopt a more skeptical, tolerant view of religion, but in the meantime the Thirty Years' War between 1618 and 1648 drew every nation of Europe into some degree of religious conflict. *page 300*

WHAT CAUSED the civil war between the Huguenots and the Catholics in France and what was the outcome?

The French Wars of Religion (1562–1598) The rulers of France repeatedly cracked down on France's Protestant Huguenots. After the death of King Henry II, the French monarchy was weak. Although Calvinists made up only a small part of the population, France's Calvinists included much of the aristocracy. Catherine de Médicis attempted with some success to play Catholics and Huguenots off against each other. In 1593, a few years after the Bourbon Huguenot Henry of Navarre took the French throne, Henry renounced his Protestantism in favor of Catholicism; his 1598 Edict of Nantes sanctioned minority religious rights within Catholic France. *page 301*

HOW WAS Philip II able to dominate international politics for much of the latter half of the sixteenth century?

Imperial Spain and the Reign of Philip II (r. 1556–1598) Philip II, who ruled Spain through most of the second half of the sixteenth century, controlled vast territories, many people, and much wealth. For the first twenty-five years or so of Philip's reign, his attention was focused on the demographic and economic changes within his kingdom, defense against the Turks in the Mediterranean, and the annexation of Portugal (which led to control over Portugal's wealthy colonies). The second half of his reign was overshadowed by unrest and, eventually, defeat in the Netherlands. *page 305*

WHAT ROLE did Catholic and Protestant extremism play in the struggle for supremacy between England and Spain?

England and Spain (1553–1603) Catholic Mary I ruled England for five bloody years. Many Protestants were martyred or exiled during her reign. She married Spain's Prince Philip. Her half sister, Elizabeth I, succeeded her and ruled for most of the second half of the sixteenth century (r. 1558–1603). Elizabeth was probably the most successful European leader of her time. She steered a middle course between extremes in all areas, most notably religion, where she created the moderate Anglican church. She took firm measures against extremist Puritans (with the Conventicle Act), against would-be assassins (she executed Mary Queen of Scots for plotting against her), and Spain (the English navy defeated Spain's Armada in 1588). *page 308*

WHAT TOLL did the Thirty Years' War take on Germany?

The Thirty Years' War (1618–1648) Germany's political fragmentation, and conflict throughout Europe among Lutherans, Catholics, and Calvinists, set the stage for the Thirty Years' War. This devastating conflict drew in all the major lands of Europe before it was over; it has shaped the map of Europe up to the present. There were four distinct phases to the war, named after the region that was most actively involved in fighting at that time: the Bohemian period (1618–1625), the Danish period (1625–1629), the Swedish period (1630–1635), and the Swedish-French period (1635–1648). Finally, the 1648 Treaty of Westphalia put an end to hostilities and, among other provisions, reasserted the right of each ruler to determine the religion in his or her land. *page 313*

Review Questions

1. What part did politics play in the religious positions adopted by France's leaders? How did the French monarchy decide which side to favor? What led to the infamous Saint Bartholomew's Day Massacre? What resulted from it?
2. How did Spain acquire the dominant position in Europe in the sixteenth century? What were its strengths and weaknesses as a nation? What were Philip II's goals? Which did he fail to achieve? Why?
3. What changes occurred in the religious policies of England's government in the process of establishing the Anglican church? What were Mary I's political objectives? What was Elizabeth I's "settlement"? How was it imposed on England? Who were her opponents? What were their criticisms of her?
4. Why was the Thirty Years' War fought? Could matters have been resolved without war? To what extent did politics determine the outcome of the war? What were the terms and objectives of the Treaty of Westphalia?

Key Terms

Congregationalists (p. 309)
Counter-Reformation (p. 300)
Huguenots (p. 301)
politiques (p. 301)
Presbyterians (p. 309)

For additional learning resources related to this chapter, please go to **www.myhistorylab.com**

PEARSON myhistorylab

13

European State Consolidation in the Seventeenth and Eighteenth Centuries

Peter the Great (r. 1682–1725), seeking to make Russia a military power, reorganized the country's political and economic structures. His reign saw Russia enter fully into European power politics.

The Apotheosis of Tsar Peter the Great 1672–1725 by unknown artist, 1710. Historical Museum, Moscow, Russia/E.T. Archive

How would you reconcile this image of Peter the Great with his reputation as a modernizer and reformer?

WHAT WAS the Dutch Golden Age and what led to its decline?

WHAT FACTORS led to the different political paths taken by England and France in the seventeenth century?

HOW DID conflicts over taxation and religion lead to civil war in Stuart England?

WHY WERE efforts to establish absolute monarchy successful in France but unsuccessful in England?

WHAT WERE the main characteristics that defined the Polish, Austrian, and Prussian states in the seventeenth and eighteenth centuries?

HOW DID Peter the Great transform Russia into a powerful, centralized nation?

WHAT WAS the attitude of the Ottoman rulers toward religion in their empire and how was this reflected in their policies?

Between the early seventeenth and mid–twentieth centuries, no region so dominated other parts of the world politically, militarily, and economically as Europe. Such had not been the case before this period, nor would it be so after World War II. This era of European dominance coincided with a shift of power with Europe itself from the Mediterranean—in particular, Spain and Portugal—to the states of northern Europe.

By the mid–1700s, five states—Great Britain, France, Austria, Prussia, and Russia—organized themselves politically and came to dominate Europe, and later, large areas of the world through military might and economic strength. These states arose at the expense of Spain, Portugal, the United Provinces of the Netherlands, Poland, Sweden, the Ottoman Empire, and the Holy Roman Empire. ■

THE NETHERLANDS: GOLDEN AGE TO DECLINE

WHAT WAS the Dutch Golden Age and what led to its decline?

The seven provinces that became the United Provinces of the Netherlands emerged as a nation after revolting against Spain in 1572. During the seventeenth century, the Dutch engaged in a series of naval wars with England. Then, in 1672, the armies of Louis XIV invaded the Netherlands. Prince William III of Orange (1650–1702), the grandson of William the Silent (1533–1584) and the hereditary chief executive, or *stadtholder*, of Holland, the most important of the provinces, rallied the Dutch and eventually led the entire European coalition against France. As a part of that strategy, he answered the invitation of Protestant English aristocrats in 1688 to assume, along with his wife Mary, the English throne.

During both the seventeenth and eighteenth centuries, the political and economic life of the Netherlands differed from that of the rest of Europe. The other major nations pursued paths toward strong central government. By contrast, the Netherlands was formally a republic. Each of the provinces retained considerable authority. The Dutch deeply distrusted monarchy and the ambitions of the House of Orange. Nonetheless, when confronted with major military challenges, the Dutch would permit the House of Orange and, most notably, William III to assume dominant leadership. When William died in 1702 and the wars with France ended in 1714, the Dutch reverted to their republican structures.

The technologically advanced fleet of the Dutch East India Company, shown here at anchor in Amsterdam, linked the Netherlands' economy with that of Southeast Asia.

Andries van Eertvelt (1590–1652), *The Return to Amsterdam of the Fleet of the Dutch East India Company in 1599.* Oil on copper. Johnny van Haeften Gallery, London, UK. The Bridgeman Art Library

What role did naval power play in producing the Golden Age of the Netherlands?

Although the provinces making up the Netherlands were traditionally identified with the Protestant cause in Europe, toleration marked Dutch religious life. While governments in other European states attempted to impose a single religion on their people or tore themselves apart in religious conflict, in the Netherlands peoples of differing religious faiths lived together peacefully.

Urban Prosperity

Beyond the climate of religious toleration, what most amazed seventeenth-century contemporaries about the Dutch Republic was its economic prosperity. Its remarkable economic achievement was built on the foundations of high urban consolidation, transformed agriculture, extensive trade and finance, and an overseas commercial empire.

In the Netherlands, more people lived in cities than in any other area of Europe. Key transformations in Dutch farming that served as the model for the rest of Europe made this urban transformation possible. During the seventeenth century, the Dutch drained and reclaimed land from the sea, which they used for highly profitable farming.

Dutch fishermen dominated the market for herring and supplied much of the continent's dried fish. The Dutch also supplied textiles to many parts of Europe. The overseas trades also supported a vast shipbuilding and ship supply industry. The most advanced financial system of the day supported all of this trade, commerce, and manufacturing.

The final foundation of Dutch prosperity was a seaborne empire. Dutch traders established a major presence in East Asia, particularly in spice-producing areas of Java, the Moluccas, and Sri Lanka. The vehicle for this penetration was the Dutch East Indies Company (chartered in 1602). The company eventually displaced Portuguese dominance in the spice trade of East Asia and for many years prevented English traders from establishing a major presence there.

Economic Decline

The decline in political influence of the United Provinces of the Netherlands occurred in the eighteenth century. After the death of William III of Britain in 1702, unified political leadership vanished. Naval supremacy slowly but steadily passed to the British. The fishing industry declined, and the Dutch lost their technological superiority in shipbuilding. Similar stagnation overtook the Dutch domestic industries.

What saved the United Provinces from becoming completely insignificant in European affairs was its continued financial dominance. Well past the middle of the eighteenth century, Dutch banks continued to finance European trade, and the Amsterdam stock exchange remained an important financial institution.

TWO MODELS OF EUROPEAN POLITICAL DEVELOPMENT

WHAT FACTORS led to the different political paths taken by England and France in the seventeenth century?

The United Netherlands, like Venice and the Swiss cantons, was a republic governed without a monarch. Elsewhere in Europe, monarchy of two fundamentally different patterns predominated in response to the military challenges of international conflict.

The two models became known as ***parliamentary monarchy*** and ***political absolutism***. England embodied the first, and France, the second. The political forces that led to the creation of these two models had arisen from military concerns. During the second half of the sixteenth century, changes in military organization, weapons, and tactics sharply increased the cost of warfare. Because their traditional sources of income could not finance these growing expenses, in addition to the other costs of government, monarchs sought new revenues. Only monarchies that succeeded in building a secure financial base that was not deeply dependent on the support of noble estates, diets, or assemblies achieved absolute rule. The French monarchy succeeded in this effort, whereas the English monarchy failed. That success and failure led to the two models of government—*absolutism* in France and *parliamentary monarchy* in England—that shaped subsequent political development in Europe.

political absolutism Government by a ruler with absolute authority.

parliamentary monarchy Rule by a monarch with some parliamentary guidance or input.

CONSTITUTIONAL CRISIS AND SETTLEMENT IN STUART ENGLAND

HOW DID conflicts over taxation and religion lead to civil war in Stuart England?

James I

In 1603 James VI, the son of Mary Stuart, Queen of Scots, who had been King of Scotland since 1567 succeeded without opposition or incident the childless Elizabeth I as James I of England. He also inherited a large royal debt and a fiercely divided church. A strong believer in the divine right of kings, he expected to rule with a minimum of consultation beyond his own royal court.

Parliament met only when the monarch summoned it, which James hoped to do rarely. In place of parliamentarily approved revenues, James developed other sources of income, largely by levying new custom duties known as *impositions*. Members of Parliament regarded this as an affront to their authority over the royal purse, but they did not seek a serious confrontation. Rather, throughout James's reign they wrangled and negotiated.

Puritans English Protestants who advocated the "further reformation" of the Anglican Church.

The religious problem also festered under James. Since the days of Elizabeth, **Puritans** within the Church of England had sought to eliminate elaborate religious ceremonies and replace the hierarchical episcopal system of church governance under bishops appointed by the king with a more representative Presbyterian form like that of the Calvinist churches in Scotland and on the Continent. At the Hampton Court Conference of January 1604, James rebuffed the Puritans and firmly declared his intention to maintain and even enhance the Anglican episcopacy.

Religious dissenters began to leave England. In 1620, Puritan separatists founded Plymouth Colony on Cape Cod Bay in North America, preferring flight from England to Anglican conformity. Later in the 1620s, a larger, better financed group of Puritans left England to found the Massachusetts Bay Colony.

James's court became a center of scandal and corruption. He governed by favorites, of whom the most influential was the duke of Buckingham, whom rumor made the king's homosexual lover. Buckingham controlled royal patronage and openly sold peerages and titles to the highest bidders—a practice that angered the nobility because it cheapened their rank.

James's foreign policy roused further opposition and doubt about his Protestant loyalty. In 1604, he concluded a much needed peace with Spain, England's longtime adversary. The war had been ruinously expensive, but his subjects considered the peace a sign of pro-Catholic sentiment. James's unsuccessful attempt to relax penal laws against Catholics further increased suspicions, as did his wise hesitancy in 1618 to rush English troops to the aid of German Protestants at the outbreak of the Thirty Years' War. In 1624, shortly before James's death, England again went to war against Spain, largely in response to parliamentary pressures.

Overview Two Models of Government

	FRANCE'S ABSOLUTISM	ENGLAND'S PARLIAMENTARY MONARCHY
RELIGIOUS FACTORS	Louis XIV, with the support of Catholics, crushed Protestantism for religious uniformity.	A strong Protestant religious movement known as Puritanism limited the monarchy.
INSTITUTIONAL DIFFERENCES	Opposition to the monarchy lacked a tradition of liberties, representation, or bargaining tools.	Parliament was to be consulted, and it appealed to concepts of liberty when conflicts arose.
ECONOMIC POLICIES	Louis XIV made French nobility dependent on his good will by supporting their status.	Political groups invoked traditional liberties to resist the monarchy's economic intrusions.
ROLE OF PERSONALITIES	Louis XIV had guidance from Cardinals Mazarin and Richelieu, training him to be hardworking.	The four Stuart monarchs, acting on whims, had trouble simply making people trust them.

ENCOUNTERING THE PAST

EARLY CONTROVERSY OVER TOBACCO AND SMOKING

King James defended sports from the Puritan charge that all amusements were sinful when enjoyed on the Sabbath, but the king did not favor all popular pleasures. He was ardently opposed to tobacco, one of the novelties that Europeans discovered in the Americas. Tobacco smoking excited opposition almost from the start. Spanish missionaries associated it with pagan religious practices. Sir Francis Bacon (1561–1626) noted it was addictive, and it was condemned by both Christian and Muslim clerics. None of this, however, impeded the spreading use of the pipe.

In 1604, James published a work that left smokers in no doubt as to his opinion of them and their practice. In *A Counterblast to Tobacco* he wrote, "Have you not reason then to be ashamed, and to forbear this filthy novelty . . . ? In your abuse thereof sinning against God, harming yourselves in person . . . [with a] custom loathsome to the eye, hateful to the nose, harmful to the brain, dangerous to the lungs, and the black stinking fume thereof, nearest resembling the horrible Stygian smoke of the pit that is bottomless." [*A Counterblast to Tobacco* (1604), reprinted by the Rodale Press, London, 1954, p. 36.] James tried to stem the use of tobacco by heavily taxing it. When this had the result of encouraging smugglers, James lowered the tax. That, however, produced a stream of revenue that became increasingly important to his government. In 1614, he made the importation of tobacco a royal monopoly, and by 1619, Virginia was shipping 40,000 pounds of tobacco to England annually. James's government, like modern ones, put itself in the odd position of depending on taxes imposed to stop the practice that produced those taxes.

Practically from the moment of its introduction into Europe tobacco smoking was controversial. Here a court jester is portrayed as exhaling rabbits from a pipe as three pipe-smoking gentlemen look on.

What activities did early modern writers associate with tobacco smoking?

CHARLES I

Parliament had favored the war with Spain but would not adequately finance it because its members distrusted the monarchy. Unable to gain adequate funds from Parliament, Charles I (r. 1625–1649), like his father, resorted to extra-parliamentary measures. These included levying new tariffs and duties, attempting to collect discontinued taxes, and subjecting English property owners to a so-called forced loan (a tax theoretically to be repaid) and then imprisoning those who refused to pay.

When Parliament met in 1628, its members would grant new funds only if Charles recognized the Petition of Right. This document required that henceforth there should be no forced loans or taxation without the consent of Parliament, that no freeman should be imprisoned without due cause, and that troops should not be billeted in private homes. Charles agreed to the petition, but whether he would keep his word was doubtful. The next year after further disputes, Charles dissolved Parliament and did not recall it until 1640.

Years of Personal Rule Charles might have ruled indefinitely without Parliament had not his religious policies provoked war with Scotland. James I had allowed a wide variety of religious observances in England, Scotland, and Ireland; by contrast, Charles hoped to impose religious conformity at least within England and Scotland. In 1637, Charles and his

QUICK REVIEW

Charles I (r. 1625–1649)

- 1629: Charles dissolves Parliament in face of criticism of his policies
- Unable to wage foreign wars without funds granted by Parliament
- 1640: Efforts to enforce religious conformity within England and Scotland force Charles to reconvene Parliament

One of the key moments in the conflict between Charles I and Parliament occurred in January 1642 when Charles personally arrived at the House of Commons intent on arresting five members who had been responsible for opposing him. They had already escaped. Thereafter Charles departed London to raise his army. The event was subsequently often portrayed in English art. The present illustration is from an eighteenth-century engraving.

The Granger Collection, New York

How did Charles I see the relationship between himself and Parliament?

Oliver Cromwell's New Model Army defeated the royalists in the English Civil War. After the execution of Charles I in 1649, Cromwell dominated the short-lived English republic, conquered Ireland and Scotland, and ruled as Lord Protector from 1653 until his death in 1658.

Dorling Kindersley Media Library

What kind of government did Cromwell think was best for England?

high-church Archbishop William Laud (1573–1645), against the opposition of both the English Puritans and the Presbyterian Scots, tried to impose on Scotland the English episcopal system and a prayer book almost identical to the Anglican Book of Common Prayer.

The Scots rebelled, and Charles, with insufficient resources for war, was forced in 1640 to call Parliament. It refused even to consider funds for war until the king agreed to redress a long list of political and religious grievances. The king, in response, immediately dissolved that Parliament—hence its name, the Short Parliament (April–May 1640). When the Scots defeated an English army at the Battle of Newburn in the summer of 1640, Charles reconvened Parliament—this time on its terms—for a long and fateful duration.

The Long Parliament and Civil War

The landowners and the merchant classes represented in Parliament had long resented the king's financial measures and paternalistic rule. The Puritans in Parliament resented his religious policies and distrusted the influence of his Roman Catholic wife. What became known as the Long Parliament (1640–1660) thus acted with widespread support and general unanimity when it convened in November 1640.

Parliament abolished the courts that had enforced royal policy and prohibited the levying of new taxes without its consent. In addition, Parliament resolved that no more than three years should elapse between its meetings and that the king could not dissolve it without its own consent.

In January 1642, Charles invaded Parliament, intending to arrest certain of his opponents, but they escaped. The king then left London and began to raise an army. Shocked, a majority of the House of Commons passed the Militia Ordinance, which gave Parliament authority to raise an army of its own. The die was now cast. For the next four years (1642–1646), civil war engulfed England with the king's supporters known as Cavaliers and the parliamentary opposition as Roundheads.

Oliver Cromwell and the Puritan Republic

Two factors led finally to Parliament's victory. The first was an alliance with Scotland in 1643 that committed Parliament to a Presbyterian system of church government. The second was the reorganization of the parliamentary army under Oliver Cromwell (1599–1658), a country squire of iron discipline and strong, independent religious sentiment.

Defeated militarily by June 1645, Charles for the next several years tried to take advantage of divisions within Parliament, but Cromwell and his army foiled him. Members who might have been sympathetic to the monarch were expelled from Parliament in December 1648. After a trial by a special court, Charles was executed on January 30, 1649, as a public criminal. Parliament then abolished the monarchy, the House of Lords, and the Anglican Church.

From 1649 to 1660, England became officially a Puritan republic, although Cromwell dominated it. When in 1653, the House of Commons wanted to disband his expensive army of 50,000 men, Cromwell instead disbanded Parliament. He ruled thereafter as Lord Protector.

Cromwell's military dictatorship, however, proved no more effective than Charles's rule and became just as harsh and hated. People deeply resented his Puritan prohibitions of drunkenness, theatergoing, and dancing. Political liberty vanished in the name of religious conformity. When Cromwell died in 1658, the English were ready by 1660 to restore both the Anglican Church and the monarchy.

Charles II and the Restoration of the Monarchy

After negotiations with the army, Charles II (r. 1660–1685) returned to England amid great rejoicing. England returned to the status quo of 1642, with a hereditary monarch,

a Parliament of Lords and Commons that met only when the king summoned it, and the Anglican Church, with its bishops and prayer book, supreme in religion.

The king, however, had secret Catholic sympathies and favored religious toleration. He wanted to allow loyal Catholics and Puritans to worship freely. Yet ultraroyalists in Parliament between 1661 and 1665, through a series of laws known as the Clarendon Code, excluded Roman Catholics, Presbyterians, and Independents from the official religious and political life of the nation.

In 1670 by the Treaty of Dover, England and France formally allied against the Dutch, their chief commercial competitor. In a secret portion of this treaty, Charles pledged to announce his conversion to Catholicism as soon as conditions in England permitted this to happen. In return for this announcement (which Charles never made), Louis XIV promised to pay Charles a substantial subsidy. In an attempt to unite the English people behind the war with Holland, and as a sign of good faith to Louis XIV, Charles issued a Declaration of Indulgence in 1672, suspending all laws against Roman Catholics and non-Anglican Protestants. Parliament refused to fund the war, however, until Charles rescinded the measure. After he did so, Parliament passed the Test Act requiring all civil and military officials of the crown to swear an oath against the doctrine of transubstantiation—which no loyal Roman Catholic could honestly do. Parliament had aimed the Test Act largely at the king's brother, James, duke of York, heir to the throne and a recent, devout convert to Catholicism.

In 1678, a notorious liar named Titus Oates swore before a magistrate that Charles's Catholic wife, through her physician, was plotting with Jesuits and Irishmen to kill the king so James could assume the throne. Parliament believed Oates. In the ensuing hysteria, known as the Popish Plot, several innocent people were tried and executed.

More suspicious than ever of Parliament, Charles II turned again to increased customs duties and the assistance of Louis XIV for extra income. By these means, he was able to rule from 1681 to 1685 without recalling Parliament.

QUICK REVIEW

The Long Parliament (1640–1660)

- Acted with widespread support and general unanimity
- Demanded codification and expansion of Parliament's powers
- Raised an army in response to Charles I's invasion of Parliament in January 1642

THE "GLORIOUS REVOLUTION"

When James II (r. 1685–1688) became king, he immediately demanded the repeal of the Test Act. When Parliament balked, he dissolved it and proceeded to appoint Catholics to high positions in both his court and the army. In 1687, he issued another Declaration of Indulgence suspending all religious tests and permitting free worship. In June 1688, James imprisoned seven Anglican bishops who had refused to publicize his suspension of laws against the Catholics. Each of these actions represented a direct royal attack on the local authority of nobles, landowners, the church, and other corporate bodies whose members believed they possessed particular legal privileges.

The English had hoped that James would be succeeded by Mary (r. 1689–1694), his Protestant eldest daughter. She was the wife of William III of Orange, the leader of European opposition to Louis XIV. But on June 20, James II's Catholic second wife gave birth to a son. There was now a Catholic male heir to the throne. The Parliamentary opposition invited William to invade England to preserve its "traditional liberties," that is, the Anglican Church and parliamentary government.

William of Orange arrived with his army in November 1688 and was received with considerable popular support. James fled to France, and Parliament, in 1689, proclaimed William III and Mary II the new monarchs, thus completing the **"Glorious Revolution."** William and Mary, in turn, recognized a Bill of Rights that limited the powers of the monarchy and guaranteed the civil liberties of the English privileged classes. The Bill of Rights also prohibited Roman Catholics from occupying the English throne. The Toleration Act of 1689 permitted worship by all Protestants and outlawed only Roman Catholics and those who denied the Christian doctrine of the Trinity.

Glorious Revolution Parliament's 1688 declaration of a vacant throne and proclamation that William and Mary were its heirs.

QUICK REVIEW

James II (r. 1685–1688)

- Policy of toleration of Catholicism alienated Parliament
- June 20, 1688: Birth of son alarms opponents
- James forced to leave England and William and Mary of Orange invited to become new monarchs

The parliamentary measure closing this century of strife was the Act of Settlement (1701), which provided for the English crown to go to the Protestant House of Hanover in Germany if Queen Anne (r. 1702–1714), the second daughter of James II and the heir to the childless William III, died without issue. Thus, at Anne's death in 1714, the Elector of Hanover became King George I of Great Britain (r. 1714–1727) since England and Scotland had been combined in an Act of Union in 1707.

The Age of Walpole

George I almost immediately confronted a challenge to his title. James Edward Stuart (1688–1766), the Catholic son of James II, landed in Scotland in December 1715 but met defeat less than two months later.

Despite the victory over the Stuart pretender, the political situation after 1715 remained in flux until Sir Robert Walpole (1676–1745) took over the helm of government. Walpole maintained peace abroad and promoted the status quo at home. Britain's foreign trade spread from New England to India. Because the central government refrained from interfering with the local political influence of nobles and other landowners, they were willing to serve as local government administrators, judges, and military commanders, and to collect and pay the taxes to support a powerful military force, particularly a strong navy. As a result, Great Britain became not only a European power of the first order but eventually a world power as well.

The power of the British monarchs and their ministers had real limits. Parliament could not wholly ignore popular pressure. Newspapers and public debate flourished. Free speech could be exercised, as could freedom of association. There was no large standing army. There existed significant religious toleration. Walpole's enemies could and did openly oppose his policies, which would not have been possible on the Continent. Consequently, the English state combined considerable military power with both religious and political liberty. British political life became the model for all progressive Europeans who questioned the absolutist political developments of the Continent.

RISE OF ABSOLUTE MONARCHY IN FRANCE: THE WORLD OF LOUIS XIV

WHY WERE efforts to establish absolute monarchy successful in France but unsuccessful in England?

Fronde Widespread rebellions in France between 1649 and 1652 (named after a slingshot used by street ruffians) aimed at reversing the drift toward absolute monarchy and preserving local autonomy.

The French monarchy, which had faced numerous challenges from strong, well-armed nobles and discontented Protestants during the first half of the seventeenth century, only gradually achieved the firm authority for which it became renowned later in the century. The groundwork for Louis XIV's (r. 1643–1715) absolutism had been laid by two powerful chief ministers, Cardinal Richelieu (1585–1642) under Louis XIII (r. 1610–1643), and then by Cardinal Mazarin (1602–1661). Both Richelieu and Mazarin attempted to impose direct royal administration on France. The centralizing policies of Richelieu and then of Mazarin, however, finally provoked a series of widespread rebellions among French nobles between 1649 and 1652 known as the ***Fronde*** (after the slingshots used by street boys).

Though unsuccessful, these rebellions convinced Louis XIV and his advisors that heavy-handed policies could endanger the throne. Thereafter Louis would concentrate unprecedented authority in the monarchy, but he would be more subtle than his predecessors. His genius was to make the monarchy the most important and powerful political institution in France while also assuring the nobles and other wealthy groups of their social standing and influence on the local level.

YEARS OF PERSONAL RULE

On the death of Mazarin in 1661, Louis XIV assumed personal control of the government at the age of twenty-three. Louis devoted enormous personal energy to his political tasks. He ruled through councils that controlled foreign affairs, the army, domestic administration, and economic regulations. Each day he spent hours with the ministers of these councils, whom he chose from families long in royal service or from among people just beginning to rise in the social structure. Unlike the more ancient noble families, the latter had no real or potential power bases in the provinces and depended solely on the king for their standing in both government and society.

Louis made sure, however, that the nobility and other major social groups would benefit from the growth of his own authority. Although he controlled foreign affairs and limited the influence of noble institutions on the monarchy, he never tried to abolish those institutions or limit their local authority. The crown, for example, usually conferred informally with regional judicial bodies, called *parlements*, before making rulings that would affect them. Likewise, the crown would rarely enact economic regulations without consulting local opinion.

Gold Fleur-de-Lis with Gold Crown.

Neil Lukas © Dorling Kindersley, Courtesy of l'Etablissement Public du Musée et du Domaine National de Versailles

Why was it so important to Louis XIV to look like a king at all times?

VERSAILLES

Louis and his advisors became masters of propaganda and political image creation. Louis never missed an opportunity to impress the grandeur of his crown on the French people, but most especially on the French nobility. The central element of the image of the monarchy was the palace of Versailles, which, when completed, was the largest secular structure in Europe. More than any other monarch of the day, Louis XIV used the physical setting of his court to exert political control. Versailles was a temple to royalty, designed and decorated to proclaim the glory of the Sun King, as Louis was known. A spectacular estate with magnificent fountains and gardens, it housed thousands of the more important nobles, royal officials, and servants. Some nobles paid for their own residence at the palace, thus depleting their resources; others required royal patronage to remain in residence. In either case they became dependent on the monarch. Although it consumed over half Louis's annual revenues, Versailles paid significant political dividends.

Palace of Versailles, garden facade. The terrace later became part of the Hall of Mirrors.

Chateau de Versailles, France/The Bridgeman Art Library

What political motives were behind the transformation of Versailles into the seat of the French monarchy?

Because Louis ruled personally, he was himself the chief source of favors and patronage in France. To emphasize his prominence, he organized life at court around every aspect of his own daily routine. Elaborate etiquette governed every detail of life at Versailles. Moments near the king were important to most court nobles because they were effectively excluded from the real business of government. The king's rising and dressing were times of rare intimacy, when nobles could whisper their special requests in his ear. Fortunate nobles held his night candle when he went to his bed.

KING BY DIVINE RIGHT

An important source for Louis's concept of royal authority was his devout tutor, the political theorist Bishop Jacques-Bénigne Bossuet (1627–1704). Bossuet defended what he called the "**divine right of kings**" and cited examples of Old Testament rulers divinely appointed by and answerable only to God. Although kings might be duty bound to reflect God's will in their rule, yet as God's regents on earth they could not be bound to the dictates of mere nobles and parliaments. Such assumptions lay behind Louis XIV's alleged declaration: "*L'état, c'est moi*" ("I am the state"). (See "Compare & Connect: The Debate over the Origin and Character of Political Authority," pages 330–331.)

divine right of kings The belief that God appoints kings and that kings are accountable only to God for how they use their power.

COMPARE & CONNECT

THE DEBATE OVER THE ORIGIN AND CHARACTER OF POLITICAL AUTHORITY

During the second half of the seventeenth century a profound dispute occurred among European political philosophers over the origin and character of political authority. Some political philosophers, here illustrated by the French bishop Jacques-Bénigne Bossuet, contended that monarchs governed absolutely by virtue of authority derived from God. Other philosophers, here illustrated by the English writer John Locke, contended that political authority originated in the consent of the governed and that such authority was inherently limited in its scope.

QUESTIONS

1. Why might Bossuet have wished to make such extravagant claims for absolute royal power? How might these claims be transferred to any form of government?
2. How does Bossuet's argument for absolute royal authority lead also to the need for a single uniform religion in France?
3. Why does Locke find an absolute monarch in conflict with his subjects and they with him?
4. How do Locke's views serve to provide a foundation for parliamentary government?
5. How might subjects governed according to Bossuet's and Locke's principles relate differently to their monarchs and to the officials of monarchs administering their local communities?

I. BISHOP BOSSUET DEFENDS THE DIVINE RIGHT OF KINGS

The revolutions of the seventeenth century caused many to fear anarchy far more than tyranny, among them the influential French bishop Jacques-Bénigne Bossuet (1627–1704), the leader of French Catholicism in the second half of the seventeenth century. Louis XIV made him court preacher and tutor to his son, for whom Bossuet wrote a celebrated universal history. In the following excerpt, Bossuet defends the divine right and absolute power of kings. He depicts kings as embracing in their person the whole body of the state and the will of the people they govern and, as such, as being immune from judgment by any mere mortal.

The royal power is absolute. . . . The prince need render account of his acts to no one. "I counsel thee to keep the king's commandment, and that in regard of the oath of God. Be not hasty to go out of his sight; stand not on an evil thing for he doeth whatsoever pleaseth him. Where the word of a king is, there is power; and who may say unto him, What doest thou? Whoso keepeth the commandment shall feel no evil thing" [Eccles. 8:2–5]. Without this absolute authority the king could neither do good nor repress evil. It is necessary that his power be such that no one can hope to escape him, and finally, the only protection of individuals against the public authority should be their innocence. This confirms the teaching of St. Paul: "Wilt thou then not be afraid of the power? Do that which is good" [Rom. 13:3].

God is infinite, God is all. The prince, as prince, is not regarded as a private person: he is a public personage, all the state is in him; the will of all the people is included in his. As all perfection and all strength are united in God, so all the power of individuals is united in the person of the prince. What grandeur that a single man should embody so much! . . .

Behold an immense people united in a single person; behold this holy power, paternal and absolute; behold the secret cause which governs the whole body of the state, contained in a single head: you see the image of God in the king, and you have the idea of royal majesty. God is holiness itself, goodness itself, and power itself. In these things lies the majesty of God. In the image of these things lies the majesty of the prince.

Source: From *Politics Drawn from the Very Words of Holy Scripture*, as quoted in James Harvey Robinson, ed., *Readings in European History*, vol. 2 (Boston: Athenaeum, 1906), pp. 275–276.

II. JOHN LOCKE DENOUNCES THE IDEA OF ABSOLUTE MONARCHY

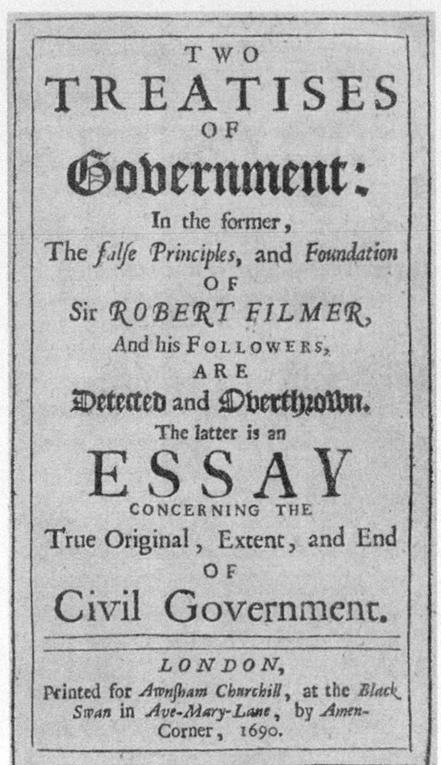

TWO
TREATISES
OF
Government:
In the former,
The false Principles, and Foundation
OF
Sir ROBERT FILMER,
And his FOLLOWERS,
ARE
Detected and Overthrown.
The latter is an
ESSAY
CONCERNING THE
True Original, Extent, and End
OF
Civil Government.

LONDON,
Printed for Awnsham Churchill, at the Black Swan in Ave-Mary-Lane, by Amen-Corner, 1690.

Title Page from *Two Treatises of Government* by John Locke, London, 1690.

Courtesy of the Library of Congress (Rosenwald Collection, Rare Book and Special Collections Division)

How did Locke challenge traditional notions of European monarchy?

John Locke (1632–1704) was the most important English philosopher of the late seventeenth century. As will be seen in Chapter 14, he wrote on a wide variety of subjects including both political philosophy and religious toleration. In 1690 he published his second Treatise of Civil Government. *In this work he defended limitations on government and rooted political authority in the consent of the governed. He drafted the treatise in the late 1670s in response to Tory assertions of absolute monarchy set forth by supporters of Charles II. The treatise was published in the wake of the Revolution of 1688 and was read at the time as a justification of that event. Locke's thought would almost a century later influence the American Declaration of Independence. In the passages below Locke explains that under absolute monarchy citizens must submit to an authority from which they can make no appeal. Consequently, there is a necessary conflict between citizens and the absolute monarchy. It was to escape such conflict and to secure property and liberty that human beings had left the state of nature to found civil society.*

Man being born . . . with a title to perfect freedom, and an uncontrolled enjoyment of all the rights and privileges of the law of nature, equally with any other man, or number of men in the world, hath by nature a power, not only to preserve his property, that is, his life, liberty and estate, against the injuries and attempts of other men; but to judge of, and punish the breaches of that law in others, as he is persuaded the offence deserve . . . [T]here and there only is political society, where every one of the members hath quitted this natural power, resigned it up into the hands of the community in all cases that excludes him not from appealing for protection to the law established by it. And thus all private judgment of every particular member being excluded, the community comes to be umpire, by settled standing rules, indifferent, and the same to all parties; and by men having authority from the community, for the execution of those rules, decides all the differences that may happen between any members of that society concerning any matter of right . . .

Whenever therefore any number of men are so united into one society, as to quit every one his executive power of the law of nature, and to resign it to the public, there and there only is a political, or civil society. . . .

Hence it is evident, that absolute monarchy, which by some men is counted the only government in the world, is indeed inconsistent with civil society, and so can be no form of civil government at all; for the end of civil society, being to avoid, and remedy those inconveniencies of the state of nature, which necessarily follow from every man's being judge in his own case, by setting up a known authority, to which every one of that society may appeal upon any injury received, or controversy that may arise, and which every one of the society ought to obey; whereever any persons are, who have not such an authority to appeal to, for the decision of any difference between them, there those persons are still in the state of nature; and so is every absolute prince, in respect of those who are under his dominion.

For he being supposed to have all, both legislative and executive power in himself alone, there is no judge to be found, no appeal lies open to any one, who may fairly, and indifferently, and with authority decide, and from whose decision relief and redress may be expected of any injury or inconveniency, that may be suffered from the prince, or by his order: so that such a man, however intitled, czar, or grand seignior, or how you please, is as much in the state of nature, with all under his dominion, as he is with the rest of mankind: for where-ever any two men are, who have no standing rule, and common judge to appeal to on earth, for the determination of controversies of right betwixt them, there they are still in the state of nature, and under all the inconveniencies of it. . .

Source: John Locke, *Of Civil Government*, paragraphs 87, 89, 90, 91 in *Two Treatises of Government*, a new ed. (London: C. and J. Rivington et al., 1824), pp. 179–183.

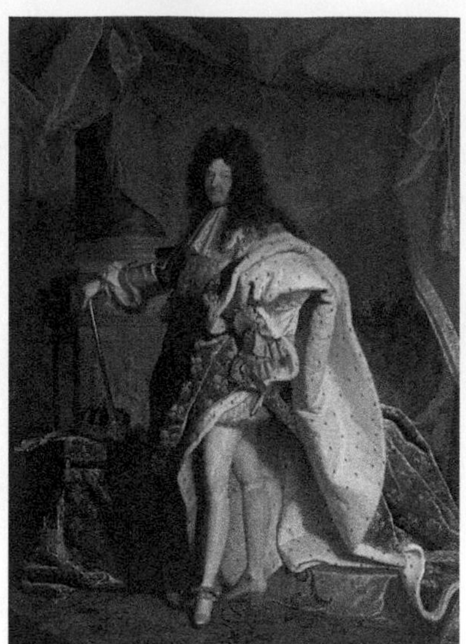

Louis XIV of France came to symbolize absolute monarchy though such government was not as absolute as the term implied. This state portrait was intended to convey the grandeur of the king and of his authority. The portrait was brought into royal council meetings when the king himself was absent.

Hyacinthe Rigaud (1659–1743), *Portrait of Louis XIV.* Louvre, Paris, France. Dorling Kindersley Media Library/Max Alexander. © Dorling Kindersley, courtesy of l'Etablissement public du musée et du domaine national de Versailles

What does this portrait tell us about Louis XIV's ideas about kingship?

Despite these claims, Louis's rule did not exert the oppressive control over the daily lives of his subjects that police states would do in the nineteenth and twentieth centuries. His absolutism functioned primarily in the classic areas of European state action—the making of war and peace, the regulation of religion, and the oversight of economic activity.

Louis's Early Wars

By the late 1660s, France was superior to any other European nation in population, administrative bureaucracy, army, and national unity. Because of the economic policies of Jean-Baptiste Colbert (1619–1683), his most brilliant minister, Louis could afford to raise and maintain a large and powerful army. Louis was particularly concerned to secure France's northern borders along the Spanish Netherlands, the Franche-Comté, Alsace, and Lorraine from which foreign armies had invaded France and could easily do so again. Louis was also determined to frustrate Habsburg ambitions that endangered France and, as part of that goal, sought to secure his southern borders toward Spain. Whether reacting to external events or pursuing his own ambitions, Louis's pursuit of French interests threatened and terrified neighboring states and led them to form coalitions against France.

The early wars of Louis XIV included conflicts with Spain and the United Netherlands. The first was the War of the Devolution in which Louis supported the alleged right of his first wife, Marie Thérèse, to inherit the Spanish Netherlands. In 1667, Louis's armies invaded Flanders and the Franche-Comté. He was repulsed by the Triple Alliance of England, Sweden, and the United Provinces. By the Treaty of Aix-la-Chapelle (1668), he gained control of certain towns bordering the Spanish Netherlands.

In 1670, with the secret Treaty of Dover, England and France became allies against the Dutch. Louis invaded the Netherlands again in 1672. The Prince of Orange, the future William III of England, forged an alliance with the Holy Roman Emperor, Spain, Lorraine, and Brandenburg against Louis, now regarded as a menace to the whole of Western Europe, Catholic and Protestant alike. The war ended inconclusively with the Peace of Nijmwegen, signed with different parties in successive years (1678, 1679). France gained more territory, including the Franche-Comté.

Louis's Repressive Religious Policies

Louis believed that political unity and stability required religious conformity. To that end he carried out repressive actions against both Roman Catholics and Protestants.

Gallican Liberties The French Roman Catholic Church's ecclesiastical independence of papal authority in Rome.

Jansenism Appearing in the 1630s, it followed the teachings of St. Augustine, who stressed the role divine grace played in human salvation.

Suppression of the Jansenists The French crown and the French Roman Catholic church had long jealously guarded their ecclesiastical independence or "**Gallican Liberties**" from papal authority in Rome. However, after the conversion to Roman Catholicism of Henry IV in 1593, the Jesuits, fiercely loyal to the authority of the pope, had monopolized the education of French upper-class men, and their devout students promoted the religious reforms and doctrines of the Council of Trent.

A Roman Catholic religious movement known as **Jansenism** arose in the 1630s in opposition to the theology and the political influence of the Jesuits. Jansenists adhered to the teachings of St. Augustine (354–430) that had also influenced many Protestant doctrines. Serious and uncompromising, they particularly opposed Jesuit teachings about free will. They believed with Augustine that original sin had so corrupted humankind that individuals could by their own effort do nothing good nor contribute anything to their own salvation.

On May 31, 1653, Pope Innocent X declared heretical five Jansenist theological propositions on grace and salvation. In 1660, Louis permitted the papal bull banning Jansenism to be enforced in France. Thereafter, Jansenists either retracted their views or went underground.

By persecuting the Jansenists, Louis XIV turned his back on the long tradition of protecting the Gallican Liberties of the French Church and fostered within the French Church a core of opposition to royal authority. This had long-term political significance. During the eighteenth century after the death of Louis XIV, the Parlement of Paris and other French judicial bodies would reassert their authority in opposition to the monarchy. These courts were sympathetic to the Jansenists because of their common resistance to royal authority. Jansenism, because of its austere morality, then also came to embody a set of religious and moral values that contrasted with what eighteenth-century public opinion saw as the corruption of the mid-eighteenth-century French royal court.

Portrait of Françoise d'Aubigne, Marquise de Maíntenon (1635–1719), Mistress and Second Wife of Louis XIV, by Pierre Mignard (1612–1695).

Portrait of Françoise d'Aubigne, Marquise de Maintenon (1635–1719), Mistress and Second Wife of Louis XIV, c. 1694. Oil on canvas, 128 ∞ 97 cm. Inv.: MV 3637. Chateaux de Versailles et de Trianon, Versailles. Bridgeman-Giraudon/Art Resource, NY

What role did elite women play in the court of Louis XIV?

Revocation of the Edict of Nantes After the Edict of Nantes in 1598, relations between the Catholic majority (nine-tenths of the French population) and the Protestant minority had remained hostile. After the Peace of Nijmwegen, Louis launched a methodical campaign against the Huguenots in an effort to unify France religiously. Louis hounded Huguenots out of public life, banning them from government office and excluding them from such professions as printing and medicine. He used financial incentives to encourage them to convert to Catholicism. In 1681, he bullied them by quartering troops in their towns. Finally, in October 1685, Louis revoked the Edict of Nantes, and extensive religious repression followed. Protestant churches and schools were closed, Protestant ministers exiled, nonconverting laity were condemned to be galley slaves, and Protestant children were baptized by Catholic priests.

The revocation was a major blunder. Henceforth, Protestants across Europe considered Louis a fanatic who must be resisted at all costs. More than a quarter million people, many of whom were highly skilled, left France. They formed new communities abroad and joined the resistance to Louis in England, Germany, Holland, and the New World. As a result of the revocation of the Edict of Nantes and the ongoing persecution of Jansenists, France became a symbol of religious repression in contrast to England's reputation for moderate, if not complete, religious toleration.

Louis's Later Wars

The League of Augsburg and the Nine Years' War After the Treaty of Nijmwegen in 1678–1679, Louis maintained his army at full strength and restlessly probed beyond his borders. In 1681 his forces occupied the free city of Strasbourg on the Rhine River, prompting new defensive coalitions to form against him. One of these, the League of Augsburg, grew to include England, Spain, Sweden, the United Provinces, and the major German states. Between 1689 and 1697, the League and France battled each other in the Nine Years' War, while England and France struggled to control North America. The Peace of Ryswick, signed in September 1697, which ended the war, secured Holland's borders and thwarted Louis's expansion into Germany.

War of the Spanish Succession On November 1, 1700, the last Habsburg king of Spain, Charles II (r. 1665–1700), died without direct heirs. He left his entire inheritance to Louis's grandson Philip of Anjou, who became Philip V of Spain (r. 1700–1746). Spain and the vast trade with its American empire appeared to have fallen to France. In September 1701, England, Holland, and the Holy Roman Empire formed the Grand Alliance to preserve the balance of power by once and for all securing Flanders as a neutral barrier between Holland and France and by gaining for the emperor, who was also a Habsburg, his fair share of the Spanish inheritance. Louis soon increased the political stakes by recognizing the Stuart claim to the English throne.

In 1701 the War of the Spanish Succession (1701–1714) began, and it soon enveloped Western Europe. John Churchill, the Duke of Marlborough (1650–1722) bested Louis's soldiers in every major engagement, although French arms triumphed in Spain. After 1709 the war became a bloody stalemate.

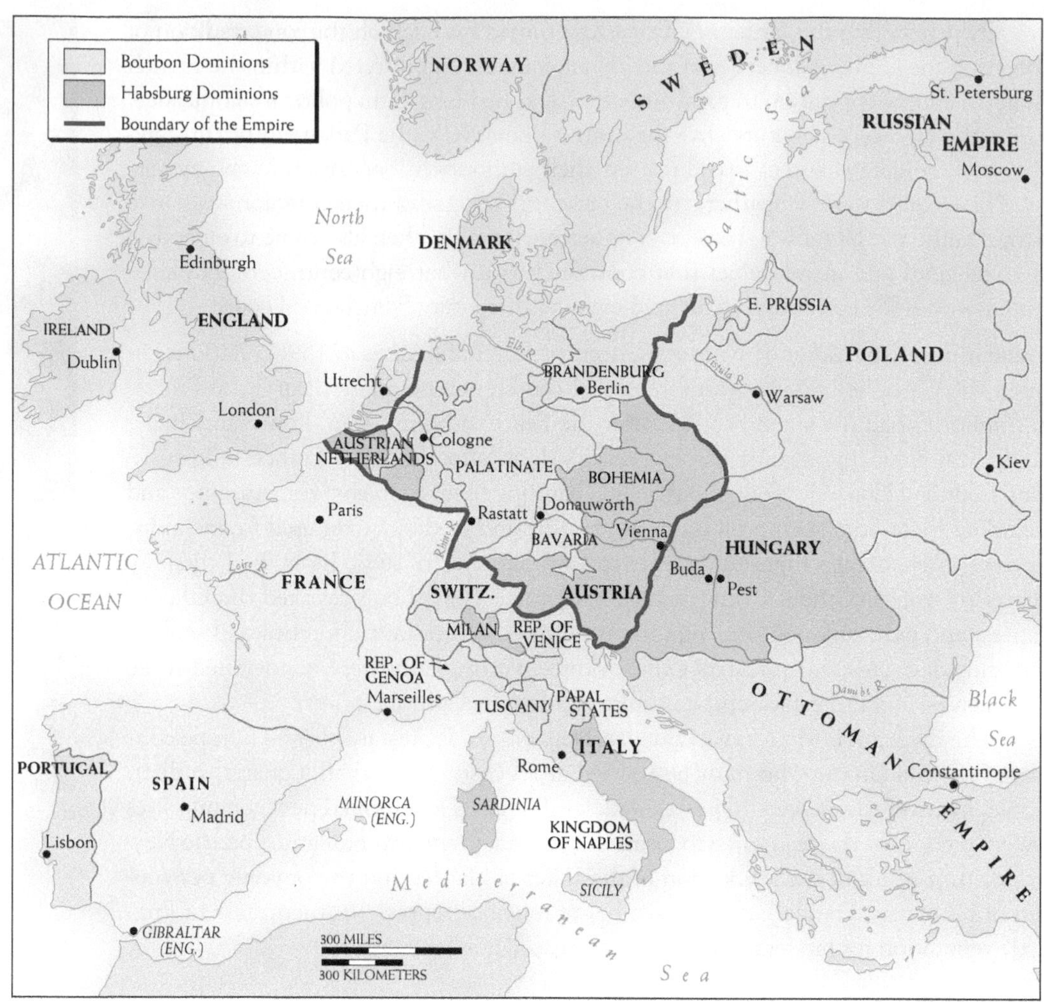

MAP 13–1 Europe in 1714 The War of the Spanish Succession ended a year before the death of Louis XIV. The Bourbons had secured the Spanish throne, but Spain had forfeited its possessions in Flanders and Italy.

How did the territorial makeup of Europe change during the long reign of Louis XIV?

France finally made peace with England at Utrecht in July 1713, and with Holland and the emperor at Rastatt in March 1714. Philip V remained king of Spain, but England got Gibraltar and the island of Minorca, making it a Mediterranean power. (See Map 13–1.) Louis also recognized the right of the House of Hanover to the English throne.

France after Louis XIV

Despite its military reverses in the War of the Spanish Succession, France remained a great power. It was less strong in 1715 than in 1680, but it still possessed the largest European population, an advanced, if troubled, economy, and the administrative structure bequeathed it by Louis XIV. Moreover, even if France and its resources had been drained by the last of Louis's wars, the other major states of Europe were similarly debilitated. Louis XIV was succeeded by his five-year-old great-grandson Louis XV (r. 1715–1774). The young boy's uncle, the duke of Orléans, became regent and remained so until his death in 1720. The regency, marked by financial and moral scandals, further undermined the faltering prestige of the monarchy.

John Law and the Mississippi Bubble The duke of Orléans was a gambler, and for a time he turned over the financial management of the kingdom to John Law (1671–1729), a Scottish mathematician and fellow gambler. Law believed an increase in the paper-money supply would stimulate France's economic recovery. With the permission of the regent, he established a bank in Paris that issued paper money. Law then

organized a monopoly, called the Mississippi Company, on trading privileges with the French colony of Louisiana in North America.

The Mississippi Company also took over the management of the French national debt. The company issued shares of its own stock in exchange for government bonds, which had fallen sharply in value. To redeem large quantities of bonds, Law encouraged speculation in the Mississippi Company stock. In 1719, the price of the stock rose handsomely. Smart investors, however, took their profits by selling their stock in exchange for paper money from Law's bank, which they then sought to exchange for gold. The bank, however, lacked enough gold to redeem all the paper money brought to it.

In February 1720, all gold payments were halted in France. Soon thereafter, Law himself fled the country. The Mississippi Bubble, as the affair was called, had burst. The fiasco brought disgrace on the government that had sponsored Law. The Mississippi Company was later reorganized and functioned profitably, but fear of paper money and speculation marked French economic life for decades.

Renewed Authority of the *Parlements* The duke of Orléans made a second decision that also lessened the power of the monarchy. He attempted to draw the French nobility once again into the decision-making processes of the government. He set up a system of councils on which nobles were to serve along with bureaucrats. The experiment failed. Nonetheless, the chief feature of eighteenth-century French political life was the attempt of the nobility to use its authority to limit the power of the monarchy. The most effective instrument in this process was the ***parlements***, or courts dominated by the nobility.

parlements French political institutions with customary rights of consultation and deliberation.

Throughout the eighteenth century, *parlements* succeeded in identifying their authority and resistance to the monarchy with wider public opinion. This situation meant that until the revolution in 1789, the *parlements* became natural centers not only for aristocratic, but also for popular resistance to royal authority. In a vast transformation from the days of Louis XIV, the *parlements* rather than the monarchy would come to be seen as more nearly representing the nation.

By 1726, the general political direction of the nation had come under the authority of Cardinal Fleury (1653–1743). He worked to maintain the authority of the monarchy, including ongoing repression of the Jansenists, while continuing to preserve the local interests of the French nobility. Like Walpole in Britain, he pursued economic prosperity at home and peace abroad. Again like Walpole, after 1740, Fleury could not prevent France from entering a worldwide colonial conflict. (See Chapter 17.)

CENTRAL AND EASTERN EUROPE

WHAT WERE the main characteristics that defined the Polish, Austrian, and Prussian states in the seventeenth and eighteenth centuries?

Central and eastern Europe were economically much less advanced than western Europe. Except for the Baltic ports, the economy was agrarian. There were fewer cities and many more large estates worked by serfs.

During the sixteenth and early seventeenth centuries, the political authorities in this region, which lay largely east of the Elbe River, were weak. During the last half of the seventeenth century, however, three strong dynasties, whose rulers aspired to the absolutism then being constructed in France, emerged in central and eastern Europe. They were Austria, Prussia, and Russia. By contrast, Poland during the eighteenth century became the single most conspicuous example in Europe of a land that failed to establish a viable centralized government.

POLAND: ABSENCE OF STRONG CENTRAL AUTHORITY

In no other part of Europe was the failure to maintain a competitive political position so complete as in Poland. The Polish monarchy was elective, but the deep distrust and divisions among the nobility usually prevented their electing a king from among

Sejm Central legislative body to which the Polish nobles belonged.

themselves. Most of the Polish monarchs were foreigners and the tools of foreign powers. The Polish nobles did have a central legislative body called the ***Sejm***, or diet. The diet, however, had a practice known as the *liberum veto*, whereby the staunch opposition of any single member, who might have been bribed by a foreign power, could require the body to disband. Such opposition, termed "exploding the diet," was most often the work of a group of dissatisfied nobles rather than of one person. Nonetheless, the requirement of unanimity was a major stumbling block to effective government. The price of this noble liberty would eventually be the disappearance of Poland from the map of Europe in the late eighteenth century.

The Habsburg Empire and the Pragmatic Sanction

The close of the Thirty Years' War marked a fundamental turning point in the history of the Austrian Habsburgs. Previously, in alliance with their Spanish cousins, they had hoped to bring all of Germany under their control and back to the Catholic fold. In this they had failed, and the decline of Spanish power meant that the Austrian Habsburgs were on their own. (See Map 13–2.)

After 1648, the Habsburg family retained a firm hold on the title of Holy Roman Emperor, but the power of the emperor depended less on the force of arms than on the cooperation he could elicit from the various political bodies in the empire. While establishing their new dominance among the German states, the Habsburgs also began to consolidate their power and influence within their hereditary possessions outside the Holy Roman Empire, which included the Crown of Saint Wenceslas, encompassing the kingdom of Bohemia (in the modern Czech Republic) and the duchies of Moravia and Silesia; and the Crown of Saint Stephen, which ruled Hungary, Croatia, and Transylvania.

In each of their many territories the Habsburgs ruled by virtue of a different title—king, archduke, duke—and they needed the cooperation of the local nobility, which was not always forthcoming. They repeatedly had to bargain with nobles in one part of Europe to maintain their position in another. Their domains were so geographically diverse and the people who lived in them of so many different languages and customs that almost no grounds existed on which to unify them politically.

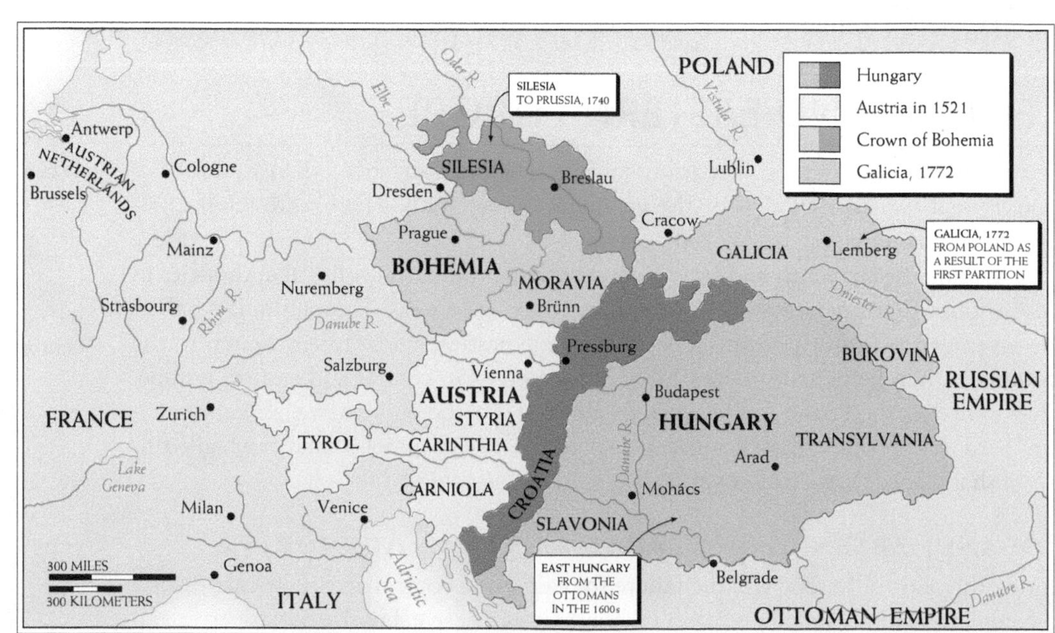

MAP 13–2 **The Austrian Habsburg Empire, 1521–1772** The empire had three main units—Austria, Bohemia, and Hungary. Expansion was mainly eastward: eastern Hungary from the Ottomans (seventeenth century) and Galicia from Poland (1772). Meantime, Silesia was lost after 1740, but the Habsburgs remained Holy Roman Emperors.

Why was expansion of the Austrian Habsburg Empire mostly eastward?

Despite these internal difficulties, Leopold I (r. 1658–1705) managed to resist the advances of the Ottoman Empire into central Europe, which included a siege of Vienna in 1683, and to thwart the aggression of Louis XIV. He achieved Ottoman recognition of his sovereignty over Hungary in 1699 and extended his territorial holdings over much of the Balkan peninsula and western Romania. These conquests allowed the Habsburgs to hope to develop Mediterranean trade through the port of Trieste on the northern coast of the Adriatic Sea and helped compensate for their loss of effective power over the Holy Roman Empire. Strength in the East gave them greater political leverage in Germany. Joseph I (r. 1705–1711) continued Leopold's policies.

When Charles VI (r. 1711–1740) succeeded Joseph, a new problem was added to the chronic one of territorial diversity. He had no male heir, and there was only the weakest of precedents for a female ruler of the Habsburg domains. Charles feared that on his death the Austrian Habsburg lands might fall prey to the surrounding powers, as had those of the Spanish Habsburgs in 1700. He was determined to prevent that disaster and to provide his domains with the semblance of legal unity. To those ends, he devoted most of his reign to seeking the approval of his family, the estates of his realms, and the major foreign powers for a document called the ***Pragmatic Sanction***.

Pragmatic Sanction Document recognizing Charles VI's daughter Maria Theresa as his heir.

This instrument provided the legal basis for a single line of inheritance within the Habsburg dynasty through Charles VI's daughter Maria Theresa (r. 1740–1780). When Charles VI died in October 1740, he believed that he had secured legal unity for the Habsburg Empire and a safe succession for his daughter. Despite the Pragmatic Sanction, however, his failure to provide his daughter with a strong army or a full treasury left her inheritance open to foreign aggression. In December 1740, Frederick II of Prussia invaded the Habsburg province of Silesia in eastern Germany. Maria Theresa had to fight for her inheritance.

Prussia and the Hohenzollerns

The rise of Prussia occurred within the German power vacuum created by the Peace of Westphalia. It is the story of the extraordinary Hohenzollern family, which had ruled Brandenburg since 1417. Through inheritance the family had acquired the duchy of Cleves, and the counties of Mark and Ravensburg in 1614, East Prussia in 1618, and Pomerania in 1648. Except for Pomerania, none of these lands shared a border with Brandenburg. Still, by the late seventeenth century, the geographically scattered Hohenzollern holdings represented a block of territory within the Holy Roman Empire, second in size only to that of the Habsburgs.

The person who began to forge these areas into a modern state was Frederick William (r. 1640–1688), who became known as the Great Elector. He established himself and his successors as the central uniting power by breaking the local noble estates, organizing a royal bureaucracy, and building a strong army.

Between 1655 and 1660, Sweden and Poland fought each other across the Great Elector's holdings in Pomerania and East Prussia. Frederick William had neither an adequate army nor the tax revenues to confront this threat. In 1655, the Brandenburg estates refused to grant him new taxes; however, he proceeded to collect them by military force. In 1659, a different grant of taxes, originally made in 1653, elapsed; Frederick William continued to collect them as well as those he had imposed by his own authority. He used the money to build an army, which allowed him to continue to enforce his will without the approval of the nobility. Similar coercion took place against the nobles in his other territories.

There was, however, a political and social trade-off between the Elector and his various nobles. In exchange for their obedience to the Hohenzollerns, the **Junkers**, or German noble landlords, received the right to demand obedience from their serfs. Frederick William also tended to choose as the local administrators of the tax structure

Junkers (Prussian nobles) They were allowed to demand absolute obedience from the serfs on their estates in exchange for their support of the Hohenzollerns.

men who would normally have been members of the noble branch of the old parliament. As the years passed, Junkers increasingly dominated the army officer corps, and this situation became even more pronounced during the eighteenth century. All officials and army officers took an oath of loyalty directly to the Elector. The army and the Elector thus came to embody the otherwise absent unity of the state.

The achievement of a royal title was one of the few state-building accomplishments of the Elector's heir, Frederick I (r. 1688–1713). In the War of the Spanish Succession, he put his army at the disposal of the Habsburg Holy Roman Emperor Leopold I. In exchange, the emperor permitted Frederick to assume the title of "King in Prussia" in 1701.

His successor, Frederick William I (r. 1713–1740), was both the most eccentric monarch to rule the Hohenzollern domains and one of the most effective. He organized the bureaucracy along military lines. The Prussian military grew from about 39,000 in 1713 to over 80,000 in 1740, making it the third or fourth largest army in Europe. Separate laws applied to the army and to civilians. Laws, customs, and royal attention made the officer corps the highest social class of the state. Military service thus attracted the sons of Junkers. In this fashion the army, the Junker nobility, and the monarchy became forged into a single political entity.

QUICK REVIEW

Frederick William's Army

- Grew from 39,000 in 1713 to over 80,000 in 1740
- Separate laws applied to the army and civilians
- The officer corps became the highest social class of the state

Although Frederick William I built the best army in Europe, he avoided conflict. His army was a symbol of Prussian power and unity, not an instrument for foreign adventures or aggression. At his death in 1740, he passed to his son Frederick II, later known as Frederick the Great (r. 1740–1786), this superb military machine but not the wisdom to refrain from using it. Almost immediately on coming to the throne, Frederick II upset the Pragmatic Sanction and invaded Silesia. He thus crystallized the Austrian-Prussian rivalry for the control of Germany that would dominate central European affairs for over a century.

RUSSIA ENTERS THE EUROPEAN POLITICAL ARENA

HOW DID Peter the Great transform Russia into a powerful, centralized nation?

The emergence of Russia in the late seventeenth century as an active European power was a wholly new factor in European politics.

THE ROMANOV DYNASTY

The reign of Ivan IV (r. 1533–1584), later known as Ivan the Terrible, had commenced well but ended badly. About midway in his reign he underwent a personality change that led him to move from a program of sensible reform of law, government, and the army toward violent personal tyranny. A period known as the "Time of Troubles" followed upon his death. In 1613, hoping to end the uncertainty, an assembly of nobles elected as tsar a seventeen-year-old boy named Michael Romanov (r. 1613–1645). Thus began the dynasty that ruled Russia until 1917.

Michael Romanov and his two successors, Aleksei (r. 1654–1676) and Theodore II (r. 1676–1682), brought stability and modest bureaucratic centralization to Russia. The country remained, however, weak and impoverished. After years of turmoil, the *boyars*, the old nobility, still largely controlled the bureaucracy. Furthermore, the government and the tsars faced the danger of mutiny from the *streltsy*, or guards of the Moscow garrison.

PETER THE GREAT

In 1682, Peter (r. 1682–1725)—ten years old at the time—ascended the fragile Russian throne as co-ruler with his half brother. He and the sickly Ivan V had come to power on the shoulders of the *streltsy*, who expected to be rewarded for their support. Violence and bloodshed had surrounded the disputed succession. Matters became even more confused when the boys' sister, Sophia, was named regent. Peter's followers overthrew her in 1689. From that date onward, Peter ruled personally, although in theory he shared the crown until Ivan died in 1696. The dangers and turmoil of his youth convinced Peter of two things: First, the power of the tsar must be made secure from the jealousy of the *boyars* and the greed of the *streltsy*; second, Russian military power must be increased.

Northwestern Europe, particularly the military resources of the maritime powers, fascinated Peter I, who eventually became known as Peter the Great. In 1697, he made a famous visit in transparent disguise to western Europe. An imitator of the first order, Peter returned to Moscow determined to copy what he had seen abroad, for he knew warfare would be necessary to make Russia a great power. Yet he understood his goal would require him to confront the long-standing power and traditions of the Russian nobles.

Taming the *Streltsy* and *Boyars* In 1698, while Peter was abroad, the *streltsy* had rebelled. On his return, Peter brutally suppressed the revolt. Approximately a thousand of the rebels were put to death, and their corpses remained on public display to discourage disloyalty. Peter then set about building a new military. He drafted an unprecedented 130,000 soldiers, and by the end of his reign he had a well-disciplined army of 300,000.

Peter also made a sustained attack on the *boyars* and their attachment to traditional Russian culture. After his European journey, he personally shaved the long beards of the court *boyars* and sheared off the customary long hand-covering sleeves of their shirts and coats, which had made them the butt of jokes among other European courts. Peter became highly skilled at balancing one group off against another while never completely excluding any as he set about to organize Russian government and military forces along the lines of the more powerful European states.

Developing a Navy In the mid-1690s, Peter oversaw the construction of ships to protect his interests in the Black Sea against the Ottoman Empire. In 1695, he began a war with the Ottomans and captured Azov on the Black Sea in 1696. Part of the reason for Peter's trip to western Europe in 1697 was to learn how to build still better warships, this time for combat on the Baltic. The construction of a Baltic fleet was essential in Peter's struggles with Sweden that over the years accounted for many of his major steps toward westernizing his realm.

Russian Expansion in the Baltic: The Great Northern War Following the end of the Thirty Years' War in 1648, Sweden had consolidated its control of the Baltic, thus preventing Russian possession of a port on that sea and permitting Polish and German access to the sea only on Swedish terms.

In 1697, Charles XII (r. 1697–1718) came to the Swedish throne. He was headstrong, to say the least, and perhaps insane. In 1700, Peter the Great began a drive to the west against Swedish territory to gain a foothold on the Baltic. The result was the Great Northern War (1700–1721). By 1709, Peter had decisively defeated the Swedes at the Battle of Poltava in Ukraine. Thereafter, the Swedes could maintain only a holding action against their enemies. When the Great Northern War came to a close in 1721, the Peace of Nystad confirmed the Russian conquest of Estonia, Livonia, and part of Finland. Henceforth, Russia possessed ice-free ports and a permanent influence on European affairs.

Founding St. Petersburg At one point, the domestic and foreign policies of Peter the Great intersected. This was at the site on the Gulf of Finland where he founded his new capital city of St. Petersburg in 1703. There he built government structures and compelled the *boyars* to construct town houses. He thus imitated those European monarchs who had copied Louis XIV by constructing smaller versions of Versailles. The

QUICK REVIEW

Peter I (r. 1682–1725)

- Resolved to increase power of the monarchy
- Imported products and people from the West in pursuit of this goal
- After 1697 tour of Europe, returned to Russia determined to westernize country

founding of St. Petersburg went beyond establishing a central imperial court, however; it symbolized a new Western orientation of Russia and Peter's determination to hold his position on the Baltic coast.

The Case of Peter's Son Aleksei Peter's son Aleksei had been born to his first wife whom he had divorced in 1698. By 1716, Peter was becoming convinced that his opponents looked to Aleksei as a focus for their possible sedition while Russia remained at war with Sweden. There was some truth to these concerns because the next year Aleksei went to Vienna where he attempted to enter into a vague conspiracy with the Habsburg emperor Charles VI.

Peter, who was investigating official corruption, realized his son might become a rallying point for those he accused. Early in 1718, when Aleksei reappeared in St. Petersburg, the tsar began to look into his son's relationships with Charles VI. During this six-month investigation, Peter personally interrogated Aleksei, who was eventually condemned to death and died under mysterious circumstances on June 26, 1718.

Table of Ranks Issued by Peter the Great to draw nobles into state service, it made rank in the bureaucracy or military, not lineage, the determinant of an individual's social status.

Reforms of Peter the Great's Final Years The interrogations surrounding Aleksei had revealed greater degrees of court opposition than Peter had suspected. Recognizing he could not eliminate his opponents the way he had attacked the *streltsy* in 1698, Peter undertook radical administrative reforms designed to bring the nobility and the Russian Orthodox Church more closely under the authority of persons loyal to the tsar.

EVENTS AND REIGNS

1533–1584	Ivan the Terrible
1584–1613	Time of Troubles
1613	Michael Romanov becomes tsar
1640–1688	Frederick William, the Great Elector
1643–1715	Louis XIV, the Sun King
1648	Independence of the Netherlands recognized
1682–1725	Peter the Great
1683	Turkish siege of Vienna
1688–1713	Frederick I of Prussia
1697	Peter the Great's European tour
1700–1721	The Great Northern War
1703	Saint Petersburg founded
1711–1740	The Great Northern War
1703	Saint Petersburg founded
1711–1740	Charles VI, the Pragmatic Sanction
1713	War of the Spanish Succession ends
1713–1740	Frederick William I of Prussia
1714	George I founds England's Hanoverian dynasty
1715	Louis XV becomes king of France
1720–1741	Robert Walpole dominates British politics
1726–1743	Cardinal Fleury
1727	George II
1740	Maria Theresa succeeds to the Habsburg throne
1740	Frederick II invades Silesia

Administrative Colleges In December 1717, Peter reorganized his domestic administration to sustain his own personal authority and to fight rampant corruption. To achieve this goal, Peter looked to Swedish institutions called *colleges*—bureaus of several persons operating according to written instructions rather than departments headed by a single minister. He created eight of these colleges to oversee matters such as the collection of taxes, foreign relations, war, and economic affairs. Each college was to receive advice from a foreigner. Peter divided the members of these colleges between nobles and persons he was certain would be personally loyal to himself.

Table of Ranks Peter made another major administrative reform with important consequences when in 1722 he published a **Table of Ranks**, which was intended to draw the nobility into state service. That table equated a person's social position and privileges with his rank in the bureaucracy or the military, rather than with his lineage among the traditional landed nobility. Peter thus made the social standing of individual *boyars* a function of their willingness to serve the central state.

Achieving Secular Control of the Church Peter also moved to suppress the independence of the Russian Orthodox Church. In 1721, Peter simply abolished the position of *patriarch*, the bishop who had been head of the church. In its place he established a government department called the *Holy Synod*, which

consisted of several bishops headed by a layman, called the *procurator general*. This body would govern the church in accordance with the tsar's secular requirements.

For all the numerous decisive actions Peter had taken since 1718, he still had not settled on a successor. Consequently, when he died in 1725, there was no clear line of succession to the throne. For more than thirty years, soldiers and nobles again determined who ruled Russia. Peter had laid the foundations of a modern Russia, but not the foundations of a stable state.

Ottoman Empire The authority Instanbul's Ottoman Turkish sultan exercised over the Balkans, the Middle East, and North Africa from the end of the Middle Ages to World War I.

THE OTTOMAN EMPIRE

WHAT WAS the attitude of the Ottoman rulers toward religion in their empire and how was this reflected in their policies?

Governing a remarkably diverse collection of peoples that ranged from Baghdad westward across the Arabian peninsula, Anatolia, the Balkan peninsula, and across North Africa from Egypt to Algiers, the **Ottoman Empire** was the largest and most stable political entity to arise in or near Europe following the collapse of the Roman Empire. (See Map 13–3.) It had achieved this power between the eleventh and early sixteenth centuries as Ottoman tribes migrated westward from the steppes of Asia.

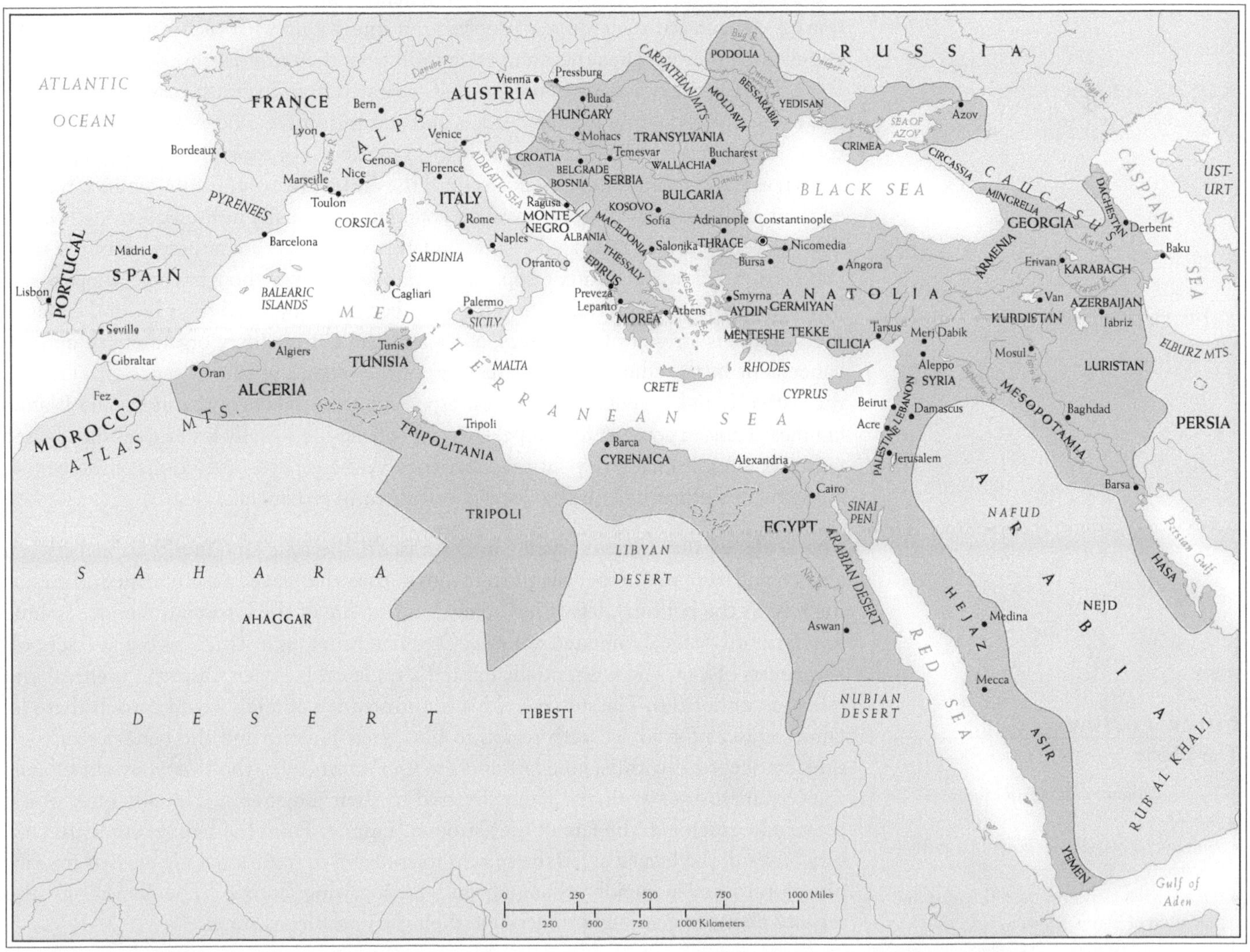

MAP 13–3 **The Ottoman Empire in the Late Seventeenth Century** By the 1680s, the Ottoman Empire had reached its maximum extent, but the Ottoman failure to capture Vienna in 1683 marked the beginning of a long and inexorable decline that ended with the empire's collapse after World War I.

From the late 1600s until 1918, which non-Turkish peoples would rise up against Turkish rule in the Ottoman Empire?

Religious Toleration and Ottoman Government

The Ottoman Empire was the dominant political power in the Muslim world after 1516, when it administered the holy cities of Mecca and Medina as well as Jerusalem, and arranged the safety of Muslim pilgrimages to Mecca. Yet its population was exceedingly diverse ethnically, linguistically, and religiously with significant numbers of Orthodox and Roman Catholic Christians and, after the late fifteenth century, thousands of Jews from Spain.

millets Communities of the officially recognized religions that governed portions of the Ottoman Empire.

The Ottomans extended far more religious toleration to their subjects than existed anywhere in Europe. The Ottoman sultans governed their empire through units, called **millets**, of officially recognized religious communities. Various laws and regulations applied to the persons who belonged to a particular millet rather than to a particular administrative territory. Non-Islamic persons in the empire, known as *dhimmis*, or followers of religions tolerated by law, could practice their religion and manage their internal community affairs through their own religious officials. They were, however, also second-class citizens generally unable to rise in the service of the empire, subject to certain restrictions, and required to pay special taxes. Nonetheless, they often attained economic success because they possessed the highest level of commercial skills in the empire. Because the Ottomans discouraged their various peoples from interacting with each other, the Islamic population rarely acquired these and other skills from their non-Islamic neighbors.

The Ottoman dynasty also kept itself separated from the most powerful families of the empire by recruiting military leaders and administrative officers from groups whom the sultans believed would be personally loyal to them. For example, through a practice known as the *devshirme*, the Ottomans, until the end of the seventeenth century, recruited their most elite troops from Christian communities usually in the Balkans. Christian boys so recruited were raised as Muslims and organized into elite military units, the most famous of which were infantry troops called *Janissaries*. It was thought these troops would be extremely loyal to the sultan and the state because they owed their life and status to the sultan. As a result of this policy, entry into the elite military organizations and advancement in the administrative structures of the empire remained generally closed to the native Islamic population and most especially to members of the most elite Islamic families. Thus, in contrast to Europe, few people from the socially leading families gained military, administrative, or political experience in the central institutions of the empire but remained primarily linked to local government in provincial cities.

The Role of the *Ulama* Again in contrast to the long-standing tension between church and state in Europe, Islamic religious authorities played a significant and enduring role in the political, legal, and administrative life of the Ottoman Empire. Islamic scholars, or *Ulama*, dominated not only Ottoman religious institutions but also schools and courts of law. There essentially existed a trade-off between Ottoman political and religious authorities. The sultan and his administrative officials would consult these Islamic scholars for advice with regard to how their policies and the behavior of their subjects accorded with Islamic law and the Qur'an. In turn, the *Ulama* would support the Ottoman state while the latter deferred to their judgments. This situation would prove a key factor in the fate of the Ottoman Empire. From the late seventeenth century onward, the *Ulama* urged the sultans to conform to traditional life even as the empire confronted a rapidly changing and modernizing Europe. The Janissaries also resisted changes that might undermine their own privileged status.

QUICK REVIEW

The *Ulama*

- *Ulama*: Dominant group of Muslim scholars
- Sultan and his advisors consulted with *Ulama*
- *Ulama* advised against modernization and adoption of European ideas

The End of Ottoman Expansion

From the fifteenth century onward, the Ottoman Empire had tried to push further westward into Europe. The Ottomans made their deepest military invasion into Europe in 1683, when they unsuccessfully besieged Vienna. Although that defeat proved to be

decisive, many observers at the time thought it the result only of an overreach of power by the Ottomans rather than as a symptom of a deeper decline, which was actually the case.

Gradually, from the seventeenth century onward, the authority of the grand vizier, the major political figure after the sultan, began to grow. This development meant that more and more authority lay with the administrative and military bureaucracy. Rivalries for power among army leaders and nobles, as well as their flagrant efforts to enrich themselves, weakened the effectiveness of the government. About the same time local elites in the various provincial cities of the empire began to assert their own influence.

External factors also accounted for both the blocking of Ottoman expansion in the late seventeenth century and then its slow decline thereafter. During the European Middle Ages, the Islamic world had far outdistanced Europe in learning, science, and military prowess. From the fifteenth century onward, however, Europeans had begun to make rapid advances in technology, wealth, and scientific knowledge. For example, they designed ships for the difficult waters of the Atlantic and thus eventually opened trade routes to the East around Africa and reached the Americas. As trade expanded, Europeans achieved new commercial skills, founded trading posts in South Asia, established the plantation economies and precious metal mines of the Americas, and became much wealthier. By the seventeenth century, Europeans, particularly the Dutch and Portuguese, imported directly from Asia or America commodities such as spices, sugar, and coffee that they had previously acquired through the Ottoman Empire. During the same decades, Europeans developed greater military and naval power and new weapons.

Devshirme. An Ottoman portrayal of the *Devshirme.* This miniature painting from about 1558 depicts the recruiting of young Christian children for the Sultan's elite Janissary corps.

British Library, London, UK/Bridgeman Art Library

What was the relationship between the Ottoman government and its Christian subjects?

During the 1690s, the Ottomans unsuccessfully fought a league of European states including Austria, Venice, Malta, Poland, and Tuscany, joined by Russia, which, as we have already seen, was emerging as a new aggressive power to the north. In early 1699, the defeated Ottomans negotiated the Treaty of Carlowitz, which required them to surrender significant territory lying not at the edges, but at the heart of their empire in Europe, including most of Hungary, to the Habsburgs. This treaty meant not only the loss of territory, but also of the revenue the Ottomans had long drawn from those regions. From this time onward, Russia and the Ottomans would duel for control of regions around the Black Sea with Russia achieving ever greater success by the close of the eighteenth century.

Despite these defeats, the Ottomans remained deeply inward looking, continuing to regard themselves as superior to the once underdeveloped European West. The Ottoman leaders, isolated from both their own leading Muslim subjects and from Europe, failed to understand what was occurring far beyond their immediate borders, especially European advances in military technology. When during the eighteenth century the Ottoman Empire began to recognize the new situation, it tended to borrow European technology and import foreign advisers, thus failing to develop its own infrastructure. Moreover, the powerful influence of the *Ulama* worked against imitation of Christian Europe. This influence by Muslim religious teachers occurred just as governments, such as that of Peter the Great, and secular intellectuals across Europe, through the influence of the Enlightenment (see Chapter 17), were increasingly diminishing the influence of the Christian churches in political and economic affairs. Consequently, European intellectuals began to view the once feared Ottoman Empire as a declining power and Islam as a backward-looking religion.

SUMMARY

WHAT WAS the Dutch Golden Age and what led to its decline?

The Netherlands: Golden Age to Decline By the mid–eighteenth century, Britain and France had emerged as the dominant powers in Western Europe and Spain had lost influence. The United Netherlands had enjoyed a Golden Age in the seventeenth century, and it was more urbanized than any other area of Europe. Dutch agriculture and financial systems were models for the rest of Europe, and the Dutch were the leading traders of Europe. After the death of William of Orange in 1702, the loose republican system that had given the Netherlands valuable flexibility turned into a handicap in the absence of leadership. *page 322*

WHAT FACTORS led to the different political paths taken by England and France in the seventeenth century?

Two Models of European Political Development In the seventeenth century, England and France developed two different forms of government that served as models for other European countries in the eighteenth century. In England, nobles and the wealthy were politically active and had a tradition of broad liberties, representation, and bargaining with the monarch through Parliament. The English nobility felt little admiration or affection for the Stuart monarchs. In France, members of the French nobility believed the strength of Louis XIV served their personal interests as well as those of the king. This led to the so-called absolutism of the French monarchy, which became the country's sole significant national institution. *page 323*

HOW DID conflicts over taxation and religion lead to civil war in Stuart England?

Constitutional Crisis and Settlement in Stuart England In the first half of the seventeenth century, many of the English suspected that their leaders were Catholic sympathizers. Oliver Cromwell led opposition in a civil war from 1642 to 1646, and then ruled until 1658. In 1660, the Stuart monarchy was restored under Charles II. His relationship with Parliament was testy. His brother and successor, the Catholic James II, was not as astute as Charles II. In 1688, members of Parliament invited William III of Orange to invade England and take the throne. After the success of the "Glorious Revolution," in 1689, William and Mary recognized a Bill of Rights, limiting the monarchy's powers, guaranteeing civil liberties to some, formalizing Parliament's role, and barring Catholics from the throne. The 1689 Toleration Act allowed Protestants freedom to worship but denied Catholics similar privileges. The monarchy in Great Britain passed to the house of Hanover, and George I sought support from the Whigs. Robert Walpole functioned as George's prime minister. Parliament checked royal influence and provided strong central political authority. Britain's economy was strong, and political life was remarkably free. *page 323*

WHY WERE efforts to establish absolute monarchy successful in France but unsuccessful in England?

Rise of Absolute Monarchy in France: The World of Louis XIV Louis XIV's monarchy gathered unprecedented power on the national level in the area of foreign and military affairs, domestic administration, and economic regulation. At the same time, Louis was careful to allow nobles to retain their local power and privileges. He ensured loyalty to the crown by employing nobles in his administration and crafted a political image as the "Sun King" based at Versailles. At this palace, Louis built a system of patronage that effectively excluded many nobles from government, even as it occupied them in ritual and ceremony all designed to promote Louis's personal rule and divine right monarchy. Louis's armies instilled fear in France's neighbors, prompting several alliances to be formed against France throughout his reign. He repressed the anti-Jesuit Jansenists and revoked the Edict of Nantes, which had ensured toleration of French Protestants. These policies reinforced Europe's image of Louis as a repressive fanatic and sowed the seeds of domestic opposition to the monarchy, not only among Jansenist sympathizers, but also in noble and judicial bodies. *page 328*

WHAT WERE the main characteristics that defined the Polish, Austrian, and Prussian states in the seventeenth and eighteenth centuries?

Central and Eastern Europe The economies and political structures of central and eastern Europe were weaker than those of the West. Late in the seventeenth century, Poland could not develop a strong central authority, while Austria, Prussia, and Russia emerged as political and military powers. The Habsburg Empire expanded so much that by the eighteenth and nineteenth centuries, Habsburg power and influence were based more on territories outside of Germany than within. Political unity was in short supply. The Hohenzollerns created a Prussian army that, according to an axiom, possessed the nation, rather than the other way around. *page 335*

HOW DID Peter the Great transform Russia into a powerful, centralized nation?

Russia Enters the European Political Arena In the seventeenth century, Russia became one of the nations of Europe, and the Romanov dynasty was founded. Russia's old nobility, the *boyars*, retained considerable authority until Peter (later Peter the Great) assumed personal rule in 1689. Peter was zealous in his efforts to westernize Russia, to curb the power of the *boyars* and Moscow garrison guards (the *streltsy*), and to increase the nation's military strength. He was remarkably successful in most of his efforts. His critical failure was that, when he died in 1725, he had not appointed a successor; for decades after his death, power reverted to nobles and soldiers. *page 338*

WHAT WAS the attitude of the Ottoman rulers toward religion in their empire and how was this reflected in their policies?

The Ottoman Empire The Ottoman Empire was diverse ethnically, linguistically, and religiously and offered more religious freedom than could be found anywhere in Europe. Social and political structures prevented leading families from interacting meaningfully with the ruling elite, which limited the infusion of new ideas and personalities into government. Military defeats in the late seventeenth century marked the beginning of the end for the Ottoman Empire. *page 341*

REVIEW QUESTIONS

1. Why did Britain and France remain leading powers while the United Netherlands declined? How did the structure of British government change under the political leadership of Walpole?
2. What similarities and differences do you see between the systems of government and religious policies in place in England and France at the end of the seventeenth century? What accounts for the path each nation took?
3. Why did the English king and Parliament come into conflict in the 1640s? What was the "Glorious Revolution"? How did England in 1700 differ from England in 1600?
4. How did Louis XIV consolidate his monarchy? How successful was his foreign policy? What were the domestic and international consequences of his religious policies?
5. How did Peter the Great's plan for building a greater Russia compare with the conduct of the Ottoman leaders who allowed their empire to decline?
6. How was the Hohenzollern family able to forge a conglomerate of diverse landholdings into the state of Prussia? How do the Hohenzollerns and the Habsburgs compare in the ways they dealt with the problems that confronted their domains?
7. What sorts of political and diplomatic problems did questions about successions to thrones create for various states between 1685 and 1740?

KEY TERMS

divine right of kings (p. 329)
Fronde (p. 328)
Gallican Liberties (p. 332)
Glorious Revolution (p. 327)
Jansenism (p. 332)
Junkers (p. 337)
millets (p. 342)
Ottoman Empire (p. 341)
parlements(p. 335)
parliamentary monarchy (p. 323)
political absolutism (p. 323)
Pragmatic Sanction (p. 337)
Puritans (p. 324)
Sejm (p. 336)
Table of Ranks (p. 340)

For additional learning resources related to this chapter, please go to **www.myhistorylab.com**

myhistorylab

14

New Directions in Thought and Culture in the Sixteenth and Seventeenth Centuries

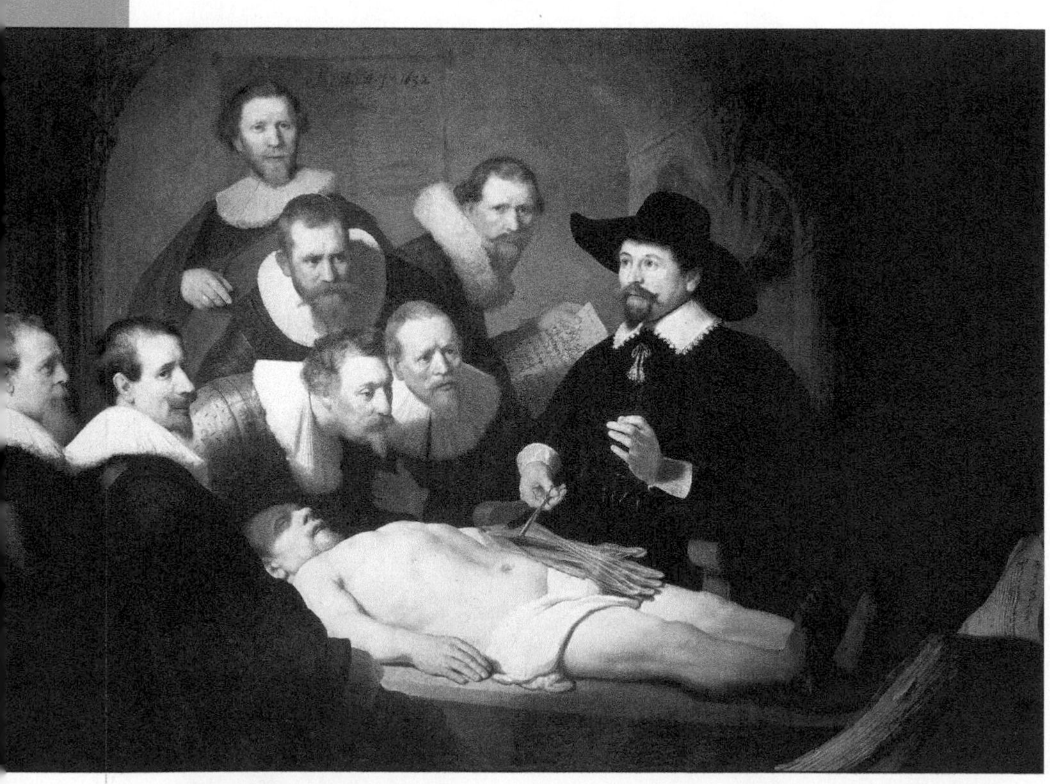

The great Dutch artist Rembrandt van Rijn (1606–1669) recorded the contemporary life of the United Provinces of the Netherlands during its Golden Age. The new sciences including medicine made much progress in the Netherlands, which was a center for publishing and instrument making and known for its religious toleration. *The Anatomy Lesson of Dr. Tulp* (1632) presents the dissection of a cadaver of an executed criminal by the noted Dutch physician Dr. Nicolass Tulp who stands on the right surrounded by other members of the Amsterdam Guild of Surgeons. Such dissections were a controversial part of new emerging medical education with only one a year permitted in Amsterdam. The dramatic use of light and darkness is characteristic of the painting of the baroque style.

Rembrandt van Rijn (1606–1669). *The Anatomy Lesson of Dr. Tulp*. Mauritshuis, The Hague, The Netherlands. SCALA/Art Resource, NY

What does this painting tell us about the development of medical education in the seventeenth century?

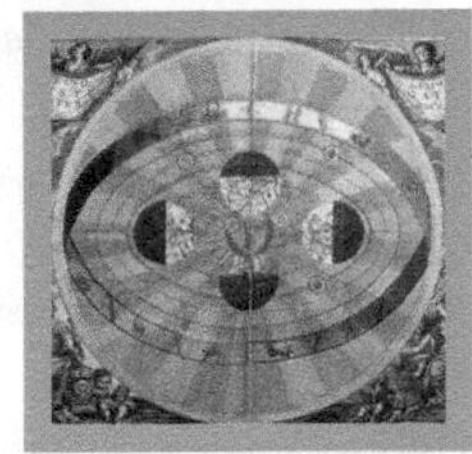

WHAT WAS the scientific revolution?

WHAT IMPACT did the new science have on philosophy?

WHAT WAS the social and political context for scientific inquiry in the seventeenth century?

WHAT ROLE did women play in the scientific revolution?

WHAT EFFORTS were made to reconcile the new science and religion?

WHAT EXPLAINS the witch hunts and panics of the sixteenth and seventeenth centuries?

HOW DID baroque art serve both religious and secular ends?

During the sixteenth and seventeenth centuries, science created a new view of the universe that challenged many previously held beliefs. Earth moved from the center of the universe and became only one of several planets orbiting a sun that was only one of countless stars. This new cosmology forced people to rethink humanity's place in the larger scheme of things. The new scientific ideas came into apparent conflict with traditional religion and raised doubts about the grounds for faith and morality. Europeans discovered the world was a much more complex place than their ancestors had imagined. The telescope opened the heavens to them while the microscope disclosed the existence of a realm of microorganisms. A spate of scientific discoveries added to the intellectual dislocation already created by the Reformation and contact with the New World. ■

THE SCIENTIFIC REVOLUTION

WHAT WAS the scientific revolution?

scientific revolution The emergence in the sixteenth century of rational and empirical methods of research that challenged traditional thought and promoted the rise of science and technology.

The process that established the new view of the universe is normally termed the ***scientific revolution***. The revolution-in-science metaphor must be used carefully, however. Not everything associated with the "new" science was necessarily new. Sixteenth- and seventeenth-century natural philosophers were often reexamining and rethinking theories and data from the ancient world and the late Middle Ages. Moreover, the word *revolution* normally denotes rapid, collective political change involving many people. The scientific revolution was not rapid. It was a complex movement with many false starts and brilliant people suggesting wrong as well as useful ideas. Nor did it involve more than a few hundred people who labored in widely separated studies and crude laboratories located in Poland, Italy, Denmark, Bohemia, France, and Great Britain. Furthermore, the achievements of the new science were not simply the function of isolated brilliant scientific minds. The leading figures of the scientific revolution often drew on the aid of artisans and craftspeople to help them construct new instruments for experimentation and to carry out those experiments. Finally, because the practice of science involves social activity as well as knowledge, the revolution also saw the establishment of new social institutions to support the emerging scientific enterprise.

Natural knowledge was only in the process of becoming science as we know it today during the era of the scientific revolution. In fact the word *scientist*, which was only coined in the 1830s, did not yet exist in the seventeenth century, nor did anything resembling the modern scientific career. Individuals devoted to natural philosophy might work in universities or in the court of a prince or even in their own homes and workshops. Only in the second half of the seventeenth century did formal societies and academies devoted to the pursuit of natural philosophy come into existence.

Although new knowledge emerged in many areas during the sixteenth and seventeenth centuries, including medicine, chemistry, and natural history, the scientific achievements that most captured the learned imagination and persuaded people of the cultural power of natural knowledge were those that occurred in astronomy.

NICOLAUS COPERNICUS REJECTS AN EARTH-CENTERED UNIVERSE

Nicolaus Copernicus (1473–1543) was a Polish priest and an astronomer. In 1543, the year of his death, Copernicus published *On the Revolutions of the Heavenly Spheres*. What Copernicus's work did was to provide an intellectual springboard for a complete criticism of the then-dominant view of the position of Earth in the universe. He had undertaken this task to help the papacy reform the calendar, so that it could correctly calculate the date for Easter based on a more accurate understanding of astronomy.

The Ptolemaic System In Copernicus's time, the standard explanation of the place of Earth in the heavens combined the mathematical astronomy of Ptolemy, contained in his work entitled the *Almagest* (150 C.E.), with the physical cosmology of Aristotle. Over the centuries, commentators on Ptolemy's work had developed several alternative **Ptolemaic systems**, on the basis of which they made mathematical calculations relating to astronomy. Most of these writers assumed Earth was the center of the universe, an outlook known as *geocentrism*. Drawing on Aristotle, these commentators assumed that above Earth lay a series of concentric spheres, one of which contained the moon, another the sun, and still others the planets and the stars. At the outer regions of these spheres lay the realm of God and the angels. Earth had to be the center because of its heaviness. The stars and the other heavenly bodies had to be enclosed in the spheres so they could move, since nothing could move unless something was actually moving it. The state of rest was presumed to be natural; motion required explanation.

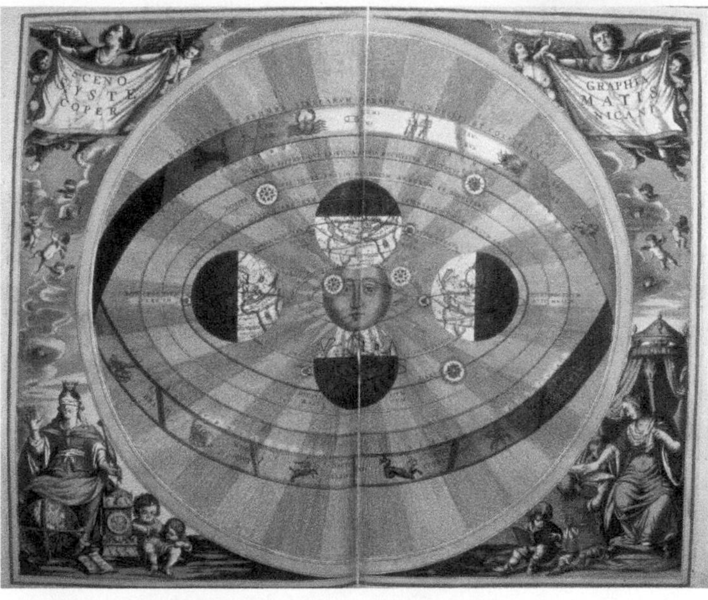

Scenographia: Systematis Copernicani Astrological Chart, ca. 1543.

British Library, London, UK/Bridgeman Art Library

What was the relationship between astronomy and astrology in the sixteenth century?

The Ptolemaic model gave rise to many problems, which had long been recognized. For example, at certain times the planets appeared to be going backwards. Complex mathematical models were developed to account for this phenomenon. Other intellectual, but nonobservational, difficulties related to the immense speed at which the spheres had to move around Earth. To say the least, the Ptolemaic systems were cluttered. They were effective, however, as long as one assumed Aristotelian physics to be correct.

Ptolemaic system Astronomical theory, named after Greek astronomer Ptolemy, that assumed Earth was the center point of a ball-shaped universe composed of concentric layers of rotating crystalline spheres to which the heavenly bodies were attached.

Copernicus's Universe Copernicus's *On the Revolutions of the Heavenly Spheres* challenged the Ptolemaic picture in the most conservative manner possible. He adopted many elements of the Ptolemaic model but transferred them to a *heliocentric* (sun-centered) model, which assumed Earth moved about the sun in a circle. The repositioning of the Earth had not been Copernicus's goal. Rather, he appears to have set out to achieve new intelligibility and mathematical elegance in astronomy by rejecting Aristotle's cosmology and by removing the earth from the center of the universe. His system was no more accurate than the existing ones for predicting the location of the planets. He had used no new evidence. The major impact of his work was to provide another way of confronting some of the difficulties inherent in Ptolemaic astronomy. The Copernican system did not immediately replace the old astronomy, but it allowed other people who were also discontented with the Ptolemaic view to think in new directions. Indeed, for at least a century, only a minority of natural philosophers and astronomers embraced the Copernican system.

QUICK REVIEW

On the Revolutions of the Heavenly Spheres

- Copernicus's work meant as a revision of Ptolemy's model
- If Earth was assumed to rotate around the sun, the model would be vastly simplified
- Model slow to attract adherents

Tycho Brahe and Johannes Kepler Make New Scientific Observations

The Danish astronomer Tycho Brahe (1546–1601) took the next major step toward the conception of a sun-centered system. He did not embrace Copernicus's view of the universe and actually spent most of his life advocating an Earth-centered system. Brahe's contribution was the construction of scientific instruments with which he made more extensive naked-eye observations of the planets than anyone else had ever done. His labors produced a vast body of astronomical data from which his successors could work.

When Brahe died, his assistant, Johannes Kepler (1571–1630), a German astronomer, took possession of these tables. Kepler was a convinced Copernican and a more consistently rigorous advocate of a heliocentric model than Copernicus himself had been. Like Copernicus, Kepler was deeply influenced by Renaissance Neoplatonism, which held the sun in special honor. In keeping with this outlook, Kepler was determined to find in Brahe's numbers mathematical harmonies that would support a sun-centered universe. Based on the mathematical relationships that emerged from his study of Brahe's observations, Kepler set forth the first astronomical model that actually portrayed motion—that is, the path of the planets—and those orbits were elliptical, not circular. Kepler published his findings in his 1609 book entitled *The New Astronomy*. He had used Copernicus's sun-centered universe and Brahe's empirical data to solve the problem of planetary motion.

Kepler had also defined a new problem. None of the available theories could explain why the planetary orbits were elliptical or, for that matter, why planetary motion was orbital at all rather than simply moving off along a tangent. That solution awaited the work of Sir Isaac Newton.

Galileo Galilei Argues for a Universe of Mathematical Laws

From Copernicus to Brahe to Kepler, there had been little new information about the heavens that might not have been known to Ptolemy. In 1609, however, the same year that Kepler published *The New Astronomy*, an Italian mathematician and natural philosopher named Galileo Galilei (1564–1642) first turned a telescope on the heavens. Using that recently invented Dutch instrument, he saw stars where none had been known to exist, mountains on the moon, spots moving across the sun, and moons orbiting Jupiter. The heavens were far more complex than anyone had suspected. In the *Starry Messenger* (1610) and *Letters on Sunspots* (1613), he used his considerable rhetorical skills to argue that his newly observed physical evidence, particularly the phases of Venus, required a Copernican interpretation of the heavens.

Galileo's career illustrates that the forging of the new science involved more than just presenting arguments and evidence. In 1610, he had left the University of Padua for Florence, where he became the philosopher and mathematician to the Grand Duke of Tuscany, who was a Medici. Galileo was now pursuing natural philosophy in a princely court and had become dependent on princely patronage. To win such support both for his continued work and for his theories, he named the moons of Jupiter after the Medicis. As a natural philosopher working with the new telescope, he had literally presented recently discovered heavenly bodies to his patron. By his political skills and his excellent prose, he had transformed himself into a high-profile advocate of Copernicanism. Galileo's problems with the Roman Catholic Church (see page 000) arose from both his ideas and his flair for self-advertisement.

Galileo not only popularized the Copernican system but also articulated the concept of a universe subject to mathematical laws. More than any other writer of the century, he argued that nature displayed mathematical regularity in its most minute details. For Galileo, the universe was rational; however, its rationality was not that of medieval scholastic logic, but of mathematics. Copernicus had thought that the heavens conformed to mathematical regularity; Galileo saw this regularity throughout physical nature.

A world of quantities was replacing one of qualities. The new natural philosophy portrayed nature as cold, rational, mathematical, and mechanistic. What was real and lasting was what was mathematically measurable. For many people, the power of the mathematical arguments that appeared irrefutable proved more persuasive than the new information from physical observation that produced so much controversy. Few intellectual shifts have wrought such momentous changes for Western civilization.

Sir Isaac Newton's experiments dealing with light passing through a prism became a model for writers praising the experimental method.

CORBIS/Bettmann

In what sense was Newton's work the culmination of the scientific revolution?

Isaac Newton Discovers the Laws of Gravitation

The question that continued to perplex seventeenth-century scientists who accepted the theories of Copernicus, Kepler, and Galileo was how the planets and other heavenly bodies moved in an orderly fashion. It was this issue of planetary motion that the Englishman Isaac Newton (1642–1727) addressed and, in so doing, established a basis for physics that endured for more than two centuries.

In 1687, Newton published *The Mathematical Principles of Natural Philosophy*, better known by its Latin title of *Principia Mathematica*. Galileo's mathematical bias permeated Newton's thought, as did his view that inertia applied to bodies both at rest and in motion. Newton reasoned that the planets and all other physical objects in the universe moved through mutual attraction, or gravity. Every object in the universe affected every other object through gravity. The attraction of gravity explained why the planets moved in an orderly, rather than a chaotic, manner. Newton demonstrated this relationship mathematically; he made no attempt to explain the nature of gravity itself.

Newton was a mathematical genius, but he also upheld the importance of empirical data and observation. Like Francis Bacon, he believed in empiricism—that one must observe phenomena before attempting to explain them. The final test of any theory or hypothesis for him was whether it described what was actually observed. Newton was a great opponent of the rationalism of the French philosopher René Descartes (see page 000), which he believed included insufficient guards against error. Consequently, as Newton's own theory of universal gravitation became increasingly accepted, so, too, was Baconian empiricism.

PHILOSOPHY RESPONDS TO CHANGING SCIENCE

WHAT IMPACT did the new science have on philosophy?

The revolution in scientific thought contributed directly to a major reexamination of Western philosophy. Several of the most important figures in the scientific revolution, such as Bacon and Descartes, were also philosophers discontented with the scholastic heritage. Newton's interests likewise extended to philosophy; he wrote broadly on many topics, including scientific method and theology.

Nature as Mechanism

If a single idea informed all of these philosophers, though in different ways, it was the idea of *mechanism*. The proponents of the new science sought to explain the world in terms of mechanical metaphors, or the language of machinery. Nature conceived as machinery removed much of the mystery of the world and the previous assumption of the presence of divine purpose in nature. The qualities that seemed to inhere in matter came to be understood as the result of mechanical arrangement. Some writers came to understand God as a kind of divine watchmaker or mechanic who had arranged the world as a machine that would thereafter function automatically. The drive to a mechanical understanding of

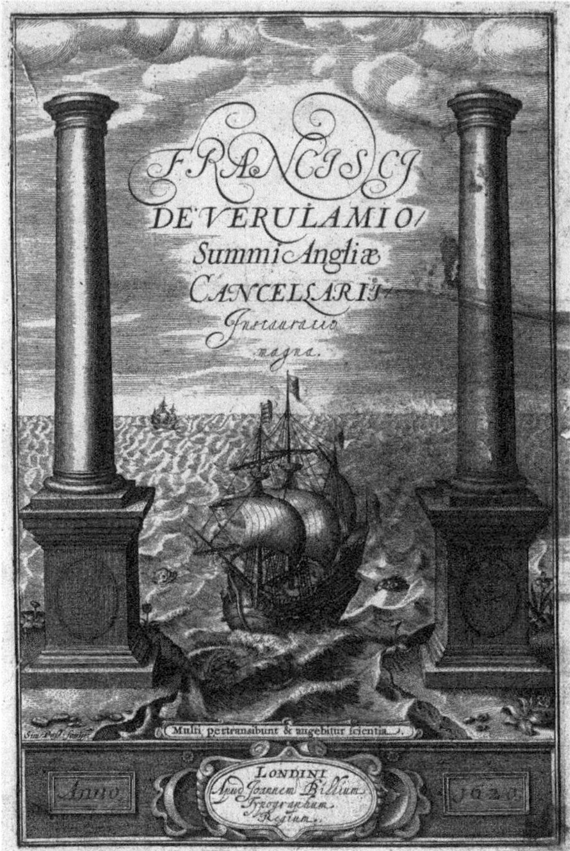

Published in 1620, *Novum Organum* ("new organ or instrument") by Francis Bacon is one of the most important works of the scientific revolution. In this and other works Bacon attacked the long-held belief that most truth had already been discovered. This allegorical image, from the frontispiece of *Novum Organum*, shows a ship striking out for unknown territories, seeking, as did Bacon, for a new understanding of the natural world. The ship is flanked by the mythical pillars of Hercules that stand at the point where the Mediterranean meets the Atlantic—the realm of the unknown and unexplored.

Courtesy of the Library of Congress

What sort of future did Bacon imagine for the human race?

nature also meant that the language of science and of natural philosophy would become largely that of mathematics.

This new mode of thinking transformed physical nature from a realm in which Europeans looked for symbolic or sacramental meaning related to the divine into a realm where they looked for utility or usefulness. Natural knowledge became the path toward the physical improvement of human beings through their ability to command and manipulate the processes of nature. Many people associated with the new science also believed such knowledge would strengthen the power of their monarchs.

Francis Bacon: The Empirical Method

Bacon (1561–1626) was an Englishman of almost universal accomplishment. He was a lawyer, a high royal official, and the author of histories, moral essays, and philosophical discourses. Traditionally, he has been regarded as the father of **empiricism** and of experimentation in science. Much of this reputation was actually unearned. Bacon was not a natural philosopher, except in the most amateur fashion. His real accomplishment was setting an intellectual tone and helping create a climate conducive to scientific work.

In books such as *The Advancement of Learning* (1605), the *Novum Organum* (1620), and *The New Atlantis* (1627), Bacon attacked the scholastic belief that most truth had already been discovered and only required explanation, as well as the scholastic reverence for authority in intellectual life. He urged contemporaries to strike out on their own in search of a new understanding of nature. Bacon was one of the first major European writers to champion innovation and change.

Bacon believed that human knowledge should produce useful results—deeds rather than words. In particular, knowledge of nature should be enlisted to improve the human condition. These goals required modifying or abandoning scholastic modes of learning and thinking. Scholastic philosophers could not escape from their syllogisms to examine the foundations of their thought and intellectual presuppositions. Bacon urged that philosophers and investigators of nature examine the evidence of their senses before constructing logical speculations. By directing natural philosophy toward an examination of empirical evidence, Bacon hoped it would achieve new knowledge and thus new capabilities for humankind.

Bacon boldly compared himself with Columbus, plotting a new route to intellectual discovery. The comparison is significant, because it displays the consciousness of a changing world that appears so often in writers of the late sixteenth and early seventeenth centuries. They were rejecting the past not from simple contempt or arrogance, but rather from a firm understanding that the world was much more complicated than their medieval forebearers had thought. Neither Europe nor European thought could remain self-contained. Like the new worlds on the globe, new worlds of the mind were also emerging.

Most of the people in Bacon's day, including the intellectuals influenced by humanism, thought that the best era of human history lay in antiquity. Bacon dissented vigorously from that view. He looked to a future of material improvement achieved through the empirical examination of nature. His own theory of induction from empirical evidence was unsystematic, but his insistence on appealing to experience influenced others whose methods were more productive. He and others of his outlook

empiricism The use of experiment and observation derived from sensory evidence to construct scientific theory or philosophy of knowledge.

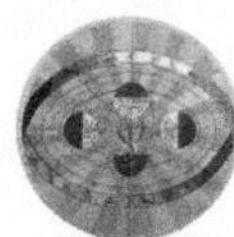

received almost daily support from the reports not only of European explorers, but also of ordinary seamen who now sailed all over the world and could describe wondrous cultures, as well as plants and animals, unknown to the European ancients.

Bacon believed that expanding natural knowledge had a practical purpose and its goal was human improvement. Some scientific investigation does have this character. Much pure research does not. Bacon, however, linked science and material progress in the public mind. This was a powerful idea that still influences Western civilization. It has made science and those who can appeal to the authority of science major forces for change and innovation. As a person actively associated with politics, Bacon also believed the pursuit of new knowledge would increase the power of governments and monarchies. Again, his thought in this area opened the way for the eventual strong links between governments and the scientific enterprise.

QUICK REVIEW

The Empirical Method

- Francis Bacon believed Scholasticism did nothing more than arrange old ideas
- Thinkers should reexamine the foundations of their thought
- Reliance on empirical evidence would yield the best results

René Descartes: The Method of Rational Deduction

Descartes (1596–1650) was a gifted mathematician who invented analytic geometry. His most important contribution, however, was to develop a scientific method that relied more on deduction—reasoning from general principle to arrive at specific facts—than empirical observation and induction.

In 1637, he published his *Discourse on Method*, in which he rejected scholastic philosophy and education and advocated thought founded on a mathematical model. (See "Compare & Connect: Descartes and Swift Debate the Scientific Enterprise," pages 354–355.) In the *Discourse*, he began by saying he would doubt everything except those propositions about which he could have clear and distinct ideas. This approach rejected all forms of intellectual authority, except the conviction of his own reason. Descartes concluded that he could not doubt his own act of thinking and his own existence. From this base, he proceeded to deduce the existence of God. The presence of God was important to Descartes because God guaranteed the correctness of clear and distinct ideas. Since God was not a deceiver, the ideas of God-given reason could not be false.

On the basis of such an analysis, Descartes concluded that human reason could fully comprehend the world. He divided existing things into two basic categories: thinking things and things occupying space—mind and body, respectively. Thinking was the defining quality of the mind, and extension (the property by which things occupy space) was the defining quality of material bodies. Human reason could grasp and understand the world of extension, which became the realm of the natural philosopher. That world had no place for spirits, divinity, or anything nonmaterial.

Descartes's emphasis on deduction, rational speculation, and internal reflection by the mind, all of which he explored more fully in his *Meditations* of 1641, has influenced philosophers from his time to the present. His deductive methodology, however, eventually lost favor to scientific induction, whereby scientists draw generalizations derived from and test hypotheses against empirical observations.

Queen Christina of Sweden (r. 1632–1654), shown here with the French philosopher and scientist René Descartes, was one of many women from the elite classes interested in the new science. In 1649 she invited Descartes to live at her court in Stockholm, but he died a few months after moving to Sweden.

Pierre-Louis the Younger Dumesnil (1698–1781), *Christina of Sweden (1626–89) and Her Court: Detail of the Queen and René Descartes (1596–1650) at the Table.* Oil on canvas. Chateau de Versailles, France/Bridgeman Art Library

What role did monarchs like Christina play in promoting scientific research?

COMPARE & CONNECT

DESCARTES AND SWIFT DEBATE THE SCIENTIFIC ENTERPRISE

Throughout the seventeenth and eighteenth century, various writers asserted that the growth of natural knowledge held the promise of improving the human situation. Others, who did not dispute the truth or correctness of the new natural knowledge, nonetheless questioned whether it could actually improve the human situation. In these two documents the French philosopher René Descartes upholds the former position while many decades later the English satirist Jonathan Swift questions the usefulness of the new natural knowledge pursued by the Royal Society of London and by implication by other European scientific academies.

QUESTIONS

1. How does Descartes compare the usefulness of science with previous speculative philosophy?
2. What, if any, limits does he place on the extension of scientific knowledge?
3. Why might Swift have so emphasized what he saw as the impracticality of science?
4. How might Swift's presentation be seen as manifesting jealousy of a literary figure toward the growing influence of science?
5. How does Swift's passage serve as an effort to refute the promise of science championed by Bacon and Descartes?

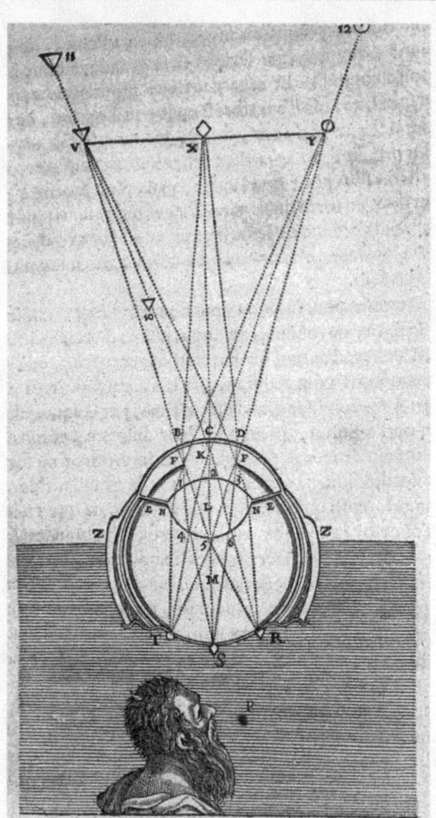

An Illustration from ***Discourse on Method,*** by René Descartes (1637).

Courtesy of the Library of Congress

What place did mathematics have in Descartes's vision of the universe?

I. DESCARTES EXPLORES THE PROMISE OF EXPANDING NATURAL KNOWLEDGE

In 1637, Descartes published his Discourse on Method. *He wrote against what he believed to be the useless speculations of scholastic philosophy. He championed the careful investigation of physical nature on the grounds that it would expand the scope of human knowledge beyond anything previously achieved and, in doing so, make human beings the masters of nature. This passage contains much of the broad intellectual and cultural argument that led to the ever-growing influence and authority of science from the seventeenth century onward.*

My speculations were indeed truly pleasing to me; but I recognize that other men have theirs, which perhaps please them even more. As soon, however, as I had acquired some general notions regarding physics, and on beginning to make trial of them in various special difficulties had observed how far they can carry us and how much they differ from the principles hitherto employed, I believed that I could not keep them hidden without grievously sinning against the law which lays us under obligation to promote, as far as in us lies, the general good of all mankind. For they led me to see that it is possible to obtain knowledge highly useful in life, and that in place of the speculative philosophy taught in the Schools we can have a practical philosophy, by means of which, knowing the force and the actions of fire, water, air, and of the stars, of the heavens, and of all the bodies that surround us—knowing them as distinctly as we know the various crafts of the artisans—we may in the same fashion employ them in all the uses for which they are suited, thus rendering ourselves the masters and possessors of nature. This is to be desired, not only with a view to the invention of an infinity of arts by which we would be enabled to enjoy without heavy labor the fruits of the earth and all its conveniences, but above all for the preservation of health, which is, without doubt, of all blessings in this life, the first of all goods and the foundation on which the others rest. For the mind is so dependent on the temper and disposition of the bodily organisms that if any means can ever be found to render men wiser and more capable than they have hitherto been, I believe that it is in the science of medicine that the means must be sought. . . . With no wish to depreciate it, I am yet sure there is no one, even of those engaged in the profession, who does not admit that all we know is almost nothing in comparison with what remains to be discovered; and that we could be freed from innumerable maladies, both of body and of mind, and even perhaps from the infirmities of age, if we had sufficient knowledge of their causes and of the remedies provided by nature.

Source: From René Descartes, *Discourse on Method*, in *Descartes's Philosophical Writings*, ed. by Norman Kemp Smith (New York: The Modern Library, 1958), pp. 130–131. Reprinted by permission of Macmillan Press Ltd.

II. JONATHAN SWIFT SATIRIZES SCIENTIFIC SOCIETIES

Swift, the greatest author of English satire in the eighteenth century, was a deeply pessimistic person who thought much of the promise held forth for scientific enterprise would never be realized. In the third voyage of Gulliver's Travels, *published in 1726, Swift portrays Gulliver as visiting the land of Lagardo where he encounters a learned academy filled with scholars pursuing outlandish projects. Swift lists the efforts of a whole series of Projectors, each of which is more impractical than the next. This passage in which Swift pillories the various people who hoped to receive patronage for projects from persons associated with the Royal Society of London remains one of the most famous satires of science in the English language. That Swift wrote it is a testimony to the cultural authority that science had achieved by the early eighteenth century.*

Gulliver reports a conversation he encountered while visiting Lagardo:

"The Sum of his Discourse was to this Effect. That about Forty Years ago, certain Persons went up to *Laputa*, either upon Business or Diversion; and after five Months Continuance, came back with a very little Smattering in Mathematics, but full of Volatile Spirits acquired in that Airy Region. That these Persons upon their Return, began to dislike the Management of every Thing below; and fell into Schemes of putting all Arts, Sciences, Languages, and Mechanics upon a new Foot. To this End they procured a Royal Patent for erecting an Academy of *Projectors* in *Lagado*; And the Humour prevailed so strongly among the People, that there is not a Town of any Consequence in the Kingdom without such an Academy. In these Colleges, the Professors contrive new Rules and Methods of Agriculture and Building, and new Instruments and Tools for all Trades and Manufactures, whereby, as they undertake, one Man shall do the Work of Ten; a Palace may be built in a Week, of Materials so durable as to last for ever without repairing. All the Fruits of the Earth shall come to Maturity at whatever Season we think fit to chuse; and increase an Hundred Fold more than they do at present; with innumerable other happy Proposals. The only Inconvenience is, that none of these Projects are yet brought to Perfection; and in the mean time, the whole Country lies miserably waste, the Houses in Ruins, and the People without Food or Cloaths. By all which, instead of being discouraged they are Fifty Times more violently bent upon prosecuting their Schemes, driven equally on by Hope and Depair. . . ."

Gulliver then reports what he found occurring in the rooms of an academy in Lagardo:

"The first Man I saw . . . had been Eight Years upon a Project for extracting Sun-Beams out of Cucumbers, which were to be put into Vials hermetically sealed, and let out to warm the Air in raw inclement Summers. . . .

"I saw another at work to calcine ice into Gunpowder . . .

"There was another most ingenius Architect who had contrived a new Method for building Houses, by beginning at the Roof, and working downwards to the Foundation. . . .

In another Apartment I was highly pleased with a Projector, who had found a Device of plowing the Ground with Hogs, to save the Charges of Plows, Cattle, and Labour. The Method is this: In an Acre of Ground you bury at six Inches Distance, and eight deep, a quantity of Acorns, Dates, Chesnuts, and other Masts or Vegetables whereof these Animals are fondest; then you drive six Hundred or more of them into the Field, where in a few Days they will root up the whole Ground in search of their Food, and make it fit for sowing, at the same time manuring it with their Dung. It is true, upon Experiment they found the Charge and Trouble very great, and they had little or no Crop. However, it is not doubted that this Invention may be capable of great Improvement."

Source: Jonathan Swift, *Gulliver's Travels*, Part III, chaps. iv and v (New York: The Heritage Press, 1960), pp. 193–194, 197–199.

Thomas Hobbes: Apologist for Absolute Government

Nowhere did the impact of the methods of the new science so deeply affect political thought as in the thought of Thomas Hobbes (1588–1679), the most original political philosopher of the seventeenth century.

An urbane and much-traveled man, Hobbes enthusiastically supported the new scientific movement. During the 1630s, he visited Paris, where he came to know Descartes, and Italy, where he spent time with Galileo. He took special interest in the works of William Harvey (1578–1657), who was famous for his discovery of the circulation of blood through the body.

Hobbes had written works of political philosophy before the English Civil War, but the turmoil of that struggle led him in 1651 to publish his influential work *Leviathan*. His aim was to provide a rigorous philosophical justification for a strong central political authority. Hobbes portrayed human beings and society in a thoroughly materialistic and mechanical way. He traced all psychological processes to bare sensation and regarded all human motivations as egoistical, intended to increase pleasure and minimize pain.

According to Hobbes, human beings in their natural state are inclined to a "perpetual and restless desire" for power. Because all people want and, in their natural state, possess a natural right to everything, their equality breeds enmity, competition, diffidence, and perpetual quarreling—"a war of every man against every man." Hobbes, contrary to Aristotle and Christian thinkers like Thomas Aquinas (1225–1274), rejected the view that human beings are naturally sociable. Rather, they are self-centered creatures who lack a master. Thus, whereas earlier and later philosophers saw the original human state as a paradise from which humankind had fallen, Hobbes saw it as a state of natural, inevitable conflict in which neither safety, security, nor any final authority existed. Human beings in this state of nature were constantly haunted by fear of destruction and death.

Human beings escaped this terrible state of nature, according to Hobbes, only by entering into a particular kind of political contract according to which they agreed to live in a commonwealth tightly ruled by a recognized sovereign. This contract obliged every person, for the sake of peace and self-defense, to agree to set aside personal rights to all things and to be content with as much liberty against others as he or she would allow others against himself or herself.

The Famous Title Page Illustration for Hobbes's *Leviathan*. The ruler is pictured as absolute lord of his lands, but note that the ruler incorporates the mass of individuals whose self-interests are best served by their willing consent to accept him and cooperate with him.

Courtesy of the Library of Congress

How did Hobbes see the relationship between a monarch and his or her subjects?

Because, however, words and promises are insufficient to guarantee this agreement, the contract also established the coercive use of force by the sovereign to compel compliance. Believing the dangers of anarchy to be always greater than those of tyranny, Hobbes thought that rulers should be absolute and unlimited in their power, once established as authority. Hobbes's political philosophy has no room for protest in the name of individual conscience or for individual appeal to some other legitimate authority beyond the sovereign.

The specific structure of this absolute government was not of enormous concern to Hobbes. He believed absolute authority might be lodged in either a monarch or a legislative body, but once that person or body had been granted authority, there existed no argument for appeal. For all practical purposes, obedience to the Hobbesian sovereign was absolute.

Hobbes's argument for an absolute political authority that could assure order aroused sharp opposition. Monarchists objected to his willingness to assign sovereign authority to a legislature.

Republicans rejected his willingness to accept a monarchical authority. Many Christian writers, including those who supported the divine right of kings, furiously criticized his materialist arguments for an absolute political authority. Other Christian writers attacked his refusal to recognize the authority of either God or the church as standing beside or above his secular sovereign. The religious critique of Hobbes meant that his thought had little immediate practical impact, but his ideas influenced philosophical literature from the late seventeenth century onward.

John Locke: Defender of Moderate Liberty and Toleration

Locke (1632–1704) proved to be the most influential philosophical and political thinker of the seventeenth century. Although he was less original than Hobbes, his political writings became a major source of criticism of absolutism and provided a foundation for later liberal political philosophy in both Europe and America. His philosophical works dealing with human knowledge became the most important work of psychology for the eighteenth century.

Locke wrote two treatises on government that were eventually published in 1690. In the first of these, he rejected arguments for absolute government that based political authority on the patriarchal model of fathers ruling over a family. After the publication of this treatise, no major political philosopher again appealed to the patriarchal model. In that regard, though not widely read today, Locke's *First Treatise of Government* proved enormously important by clearing the philosophical decks, so to speak, of a long-standing traditional argument that could not stand up to rigorous analysis.

In his *Second Treatise of Government*, Locke presented an extended argument for a government that must necessarily be both responsible for and responsive to the concerns of the governed. Locke portrayed the natural human state as one of perfect freedom and equality in which everyone enjoyed, in an unregulated fashion, the natural rights of life, liberty, and property. Locke, contrary to Hobbes, regarded human beings in their natural state as creatures of reason and basic goodwill rather than of uncontrolled passion and selfishness. For Locke, human beings possess a strong capacity for dwelling more or less peacefully in society before they enter a political contract. What they experience in the state of nature is not a state of war, but a condition of competition and modest conflict that requires a political authority to sort out problems rather than to impose sovereign authority. They enter into the contract to form political society to secure and preserve the rights, liberty, and property that they already possess prior to the existence of political authority. In this respect, government exists to protect the best achievements and liberty of the state of nature, not to overcome them. Thus, by its very foundation, Locke's government is one of limited authority.

The conflict that Hobbes believed characterized the state of nature emerged for Locke only when rulers failed to preserve people's natural freedom and attempted to enslave them by absolute rule. The relationship between rulers and the governed is that of trust, and if the rulers betray that trust, the governed have the right to replace them.

In his *Letter Concerning Toleration* (1689), Locke used the premises of the as yet unpublished *Second Treatise* to defend extensive religious toleration among Christians, which he saw as an answer to the destructive religious conflict of the past two centuries. To make his case for toleration, Locke claimed that each individual was required to work out his or her own religious salvation and these efforts might lead various people to join different religious groups. For its part, government existed by its very nature to preserve property, not to make religious decisions for its citizens. Consequently, Locke urged a wide degree of religious toleration among differing voluntary Christian groups. He did not, however, extend toleration to Roman Catholics, whom he believed to have given allegiance to a foreign prince (i.e., the pope), to non-Christians, or to atheists, whom he believed could not be trusted to keep their word. Despite these limitations, Locke's *Letter Concerning Toleration* established a powerful foundation for the future extension of toleration, religious liberty, and the separation of church and state.

Finally, just as Newton had set forth laws of astronomy and gravitation, Locke hoped to elucidate the basic structures of human thought. He did so in the most immediately influential of his books, his *Essay Concerning Human Understanding* (1690), which became the major work of European psychology during the eighteenth century. There, Locke portrayed a person's mind at birth as a blank tablet whose content would be determined by sense experience. It was a reformer's psychology, which contended that the human condition could be improved by changing the environment.

Locke's view of psychology rejected the Christian understanding of original sin, yet he believed his psychology had preserved religious knowledge. He thought such knowledge came through divine revelation in Scripture and also from the conclusions that human reason could draw from observing nature. He hoped this interpretation of religious knowledge would prevent human beings from falling into what he regarded as fanaticism arising from the claims of alleged private revelations and irrationality arising from superstition. For Locke, reason and revelation were compatible and together could sustain a moderate religious faith that would avoid religious conflict.

THE NEW INSTITUTIONS OF EXPANDING NATURAL KNOWLEDGE

WHAT WAS the social and political context for scientific inquiry in the seventeenth century?

One of the most fundamental features of the expansion of science was the emerging idea that *genuinely new knowledge* about nature and humankind could be discovered. The proponents of the new natural knowledge and the new philosophy sought to pursue what Bacon called the advancement of learning. New knowledge would be continuously created. This outlook required new institutions.

Colbert was Louis XIV's most influential minister. He sought to expand the economic life of France and to associate the monarchy with the emerging new science from which he hoped might flow new inventions and productive technology. Here he is portrayed presenting members of the French Academy of Science to the monarch on the founding of the French Academy.

Henri Testelin (1616–1695) (after Le Brun). Minister of Finance Colbert presenting the members of the Royal Academy of Science (founded in 1667) to Louis XIV. Study for a tapestry. Photo: Gerard Blot. Chateaux de Versailles et de Triaanon, Versailles, France. Reunion des Musées Nationaux/Art Resource, NY

What role did Colbert believe science could play in the development of the French economy?

The expansion of natural knowledge had powerful social implications. Both the new science and the philosophical outlook associated with it opposed Scholasticism and Aristotelianism. These were not simply disembodied philosophical outlooks, but ways of approaching the world of knowledge most scholars in the universities of the day still believed in.

Not surprisingly, the advanced thinkers of the seventeenth century often criticized the universities. Some of the criticism of universities was exaggerated. Medical faculties, on the whole, welcomed the advancement of learning in their fields of study. Most of the natural philosophers had themselves received their education at universities. Moreover, however slowly new ideas might penetrate universities, the expanding world of natural knowledge would be taught to future generations. With that diffusion of science into the universities came new supporters of scientific knowledge beyond the small group of natural

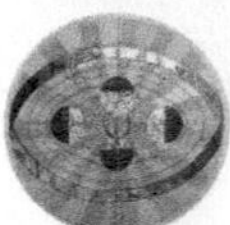

philosophers themselves. Universities also provided much of the physical and financial support for teaching and investigating natural philosophy and employed many scientists, the most important of whom was Newton himself.

Yet because of the reluctance of universities to rapidly assimilate the new science, its pioneers quickly understood that they required a framework for cooperating and sharing information that went beyond existing intellectual institutions. Consequently, they and their supporters established what have been termed "institutions of sharing" that allowed information and ideas associated with the new science to be gathered, exchanged, and debated. The most famous of these institutions was the Royal Society of London, founded in 1660, whose members consciously saw themselves as following the path Bacon had laid out almost a half century earlier. In addition to these major institutions, the new science was discussed and experiments were carried out in many local societies and academies.

These societies met regularly to hear papers and observe experiments. These groups also published information relating to natural philosophy and often organized libraries for their members. Perhaps most important, they attempted to separate the discussion and exploration of natural philosophy from the religious and political conflicts of the day. They intended science to exemplify an arena for the polite exchange of ideas and for civil disagreement and debate.

The activities of the societies also constituted a kind of crossroads between their own members always drawn from the literate classes, and people outside the elite classes, whose skills and practical knowledge might be important for advancing the new science. The latter included craftspeople who could manufacture scientific instruments, sailors whose travels had taken them to foreign parts and who might report on the plants and animals they had seen there, and workers who had practical knowledge of problems in the countryside.

The work, publications, and interaction of the scientific societies with both the government and private business established a distinct role and presence for scientific knowledge in European social life. By 1700, that presence was relatively modest, but it would grow steadily during the coming decades. The groups associated with the new science saw themselves as championing modern practical achievements of applied knowledge and urging religious toleration, mutual forbearance, and political liberty. Such people would form the social base for the eighteenth-century movement known as the **Enlightenment**.

Enlightenment The eighteenth-century movement led by the *philosophes* that held that change and reform were both desirable through the application of reason and science.

WOMEN IN THE WORLD OF THE SCIENTIFIC REVOLUTION

WHAT ROLE did women play in the scientific revolution?

The same factors that had long excluded women from participating in most intellectual life continued to exclude them from working in the emerging natural philosophy. Traditionally, the institutions of European intellectual life had all but excluded women. Women could and did exercise influence over princely courts where natural philosophers, such as Galileo, sought patronage, but they usually did not determine those patronage decisions or benefit from them. Queen Christina of Sweden (r. 1632–1654), who brought René Descartes to Stockholm to provide the regulations for a new science academy, was an exception. When various scientific societies were founded, women were not admitted to membership. In that regard, there were virtually no social spaces that might have permitted women to pursue science easily.

Margaret Cavendish, who wrote widely on scientific subjects, was the most accomplished woman associated with the new science in seventeenth-century England.

ImageWorks/Mary Evans Picture Library Ltd.

What role did women play in the scientific revolution?

Yet a few isolated women from two different social settings did manage to engage in the new scientific activity—noblewomen and women from the artisan class. In both cases, they could do so only through their husbands or male relatives.

The social standing of certain noblewomen allowed them to command the attention of ambitious natural philosophers who were part of their husband's social circle. Margaret Cavendish (1623–1673) actually made significant contributions to the scientific literature of the day. As a girl she had been privately tutored and become widely read. Her marriage to the duke of Newcastle introduced her into a circle of natural philosophers. She understood the new science, quarreled with the ideas of Descartes and Hobbes, and criticized the Royal Society for being more interested in novel scientific instruments than in solving practical problems. She was the only woman in the seventeenth century to be allowed to visit a meeting of the Royal Society of London.

Women associated with artisan crafts actually achieved greater freedom to pursue the new sciences than did noblewomen. Traditionally, women had worked in artisan workshops, often with their husbands, and might take over the business when their spouse died. In Germany, much study of astronomy occurred in these settings, with women assisting their fathers or husbands. One German female astronomer, Maria Cunitz, published a book on astronomy that many people thought her husband had written until he added a preface supporting her sole authorship. Elisabetha and Johannes Hevelius constituted a wife-and-husband astronomical team, as did Maria Winkelmann and her husband Gottfried Kirch. Winkelmann had worked jointly with her husband who was the official astronomer of the Berlin Academy of Sciences and was responsible for an official calendar the academy published. When her husband died in 1710, Winkelmann applied for permission to continue the work, basing her application for the post on the guild's tradition of allowing women to continue their husbands' work, in this case the completion of observations required to create an accurate calendar. After much debate, the academy formally rejected her application on the grounds of her gender, although its members knew of her ability and previous accomplishments. Years later, she returned to the Berlin Academy as an assistant to her son, who had been appointed astronomer. Again, the academy insisted that she leave, forcing her to abandon astronomy. She died in 1720.

Such policies of exclusion, however, did not altogether prevent women from acquiring knowledge about scientific endeavors. Margaret Cavendish had composed a *Description of a New World, Called the Blazing World* (1666) to introduce women to the new science. Other examples of scientific writings for a female audience were Bernard de Fontenelle's *Conversations on the Plurality of Worlds* and Francesco Algarotti's *Newtonianism for Ladies* (1737). During the 1730s, Emilie du Châtelet (1706–1749) aided Voltaire in his composition of an important French popularization of Newton's science. Her knowledge of mathematics was more extensive than his and crucial to his completing his book. She also translated Newton's *Principia* into French, an accomplishment made possible only by her exceptional understanding of advanced mathematics.

Still, with few exceptions, women were barred from science and medicine until the late nineteenth century, and not until the twentieth century did they enter these fields in significant numbers.

QUICK REVIEW

Women and Science

- Significant obstacles stood in the way of women doing scientific work
- A few elite women, notably Margaret Cavendish, were allowed to make contributions
- Women from the artisan classes had more opportunities than other women

THE NEW SCIENCE AND RELIGIOUS FAITH

WHAT EFFORTS were made to reconcile the new science and religion?

For many contemporaries, the new science posed a potential challenge to religion. Three major issues were at stake. First, certain theories and discoveries did not agree with biblical statements about the heavens. Second, who would decide conflicts between religion and science—church authorities or the natural philosophers? Finally, for many religious thinkers, the new science seemed to replace a universe of spiritual meaning and significance with a purely materialistic one.

THE CASE OF GALILEO

The condemnation of Galileo by Roman Catholic authorities in 1633 is the single most famous incident of conflict between modern science and religious institutions. The condemnation of Copernicanism and of Galileo occurred at a particularly difficult moment in the history of the Roman Catholic Church. In response to Protestant emphasis on private interpretation of Scripture, the Council of Trent (1545–1563) had stated that only the church itself possessed the authority to interpret the Bible. Furthermore, after the Council, the Roman Catholic Church had adopted a more literalist mode of reading the Bible in response to the Protestant emphasis on the authority of Scripture. Galileo's championing of Copernicanism took place in this particular climate of opinion and practice when the Roman Catholic Church, on the one hand, could not surrender the interpretation of the Bible to a layman and, on the other, had difficulty moving beyond a literal reading of the Bible, lest the Protestants accuse it of abandoning Scripture.

Galileo Galilei.

In a *Letter to the Grand Duchess Christina* (1615), Galileo, as a layman, had published his own views about how Scripture should be interpreted to accommodate the new science. To certain Roman Catholic authorities, his actions resembled those of a Protestant who looked to himself rather than the church to understand the Bible. In early 1616, the Roman Catholic Inquisition formally censured Copernicus's views, placing *On the Revolutions of the Heavenly Spheres* in the Index of Prohibited Books. The ground for the condemnation was Copernicus's disagreement with the literal word of the Bible and the biblical interpretations of the Church Fathers.

Galileo, who was not on trial in 1616, was formally informed of the condemnation of Copernicanism. Exactly what agreement he and the Roman Catholic authorities reached as to what he would be permitted to write about Copernicanism remains unclear. It appears that he agreed not to advocate that Copernican astronomy was actually physically true, but only to suggest that it could be true in theory.

In 1623, however, a Florentine acquaintance of Galileo's was elected as Pope Urban VIII. He gave Galileo permission to resume discussing the Copernican system, which he did in *Dialogue on the Two Chief World Systems* (1632). The book clearly was designed to defend the physical truthfulness of Copernicanism. Moreover, the voices in the dialogue favoring the older system appeared slow-witted—and those voices presented the views of Pope Urban. Feeling humiliated and betrayed, the pope ordered an investigation of Galileo's book. The actual issue in Galileo's trial of 1633 was whether he had disobeyed the mandate of 1616, and he was held to have done so even though the exact nature of that mandate was less than certain. Galileo was condemned, required to renounce his views, and placed under the equivalent of house arrest in his home near Florence for the last nine years of his life.

BLAISE PASCAL: REASON AND FAITH

Blaise Pascal (1623–1662), a French mathematician and a physical scientist who surrendered his wealth to pursue an austere, self-disciplined life, made one of the most influential efforts to reconcile faith and the new science. He aspired to write a work that would refute both dogmatism and skepticism. He never produced a definitive

Overview Major Works of the Scientific Revolution

YEAR	WORK	AUTHOR
1543	*On the Revolutions of the Heavenly Spheres*	Copernicus
1605	*The Advancement of Learning*	Bacon
1609	*The New Astronomy*	Kepler
1610	*The Starry Messenger*	Galileo
1620	*Novum Organum*	Bacon
1632	*Dialogue on the Two Chief World Systems*	Galileo
1637	*Discourse on Method*	Descartes
1651	*Leviathan*	Hobbes
1687	*Principia Mathematica*	Newton
1689	*Letter Concerning Toleration*	Locke
1690	*An Essay Concerning Human Understanding*	Locke
1690	*Treatises of Government*	Locke

refutation of the two sides. Rather, he formulated his views on these matters in piecemeal fashion in a provocative collection of reflections on humankind and religion published posthumously under the title *Pensées (Thoughts)*.

Pascal believed that in religious matters, only the reasons of the heart and a "leap of faith" could prevail. For him, religion was not the domain of reason and science. He saw two essential truths in the Christian religion: A loving God exists, and human beings, because they are corrupt by nature, are utterly unworthy of God. He believed the atheists and the deists of his age had overestimated reason. To Pascal, reason itself was too weak to resolve the problems of human nature and destiny. Ultimately, reason should drive those who truly heeded it to faith in God and reliance on divine grace.

Pascal made a famous wager with the skeptics. It is a better bet, he argued, to believe God exists and to stake everything on his promised mercy than not to do so. This is because, if God does exist, the believer will gain everything, whereas, should God prove not to exist, comparatively little will have been lost by having believed in him.

QUICK REVIEW

Blaise Pascal (1623–1662)

- French mathematician and physical scientist
- His *Pensées (Thoughts)* was meant to refute both dogmatism and skepticism
- Believed reason could lead humans to religion, but that religion operated beyond reason

Convinced that belief in God improved life psychologically and disciplined it morally (regardless of whether God proved in the end to exist), Pascal worked to strengthen traditional religious belief. He urged his contemporaries to seek self-understanding by "learned ignorance" and to discover humankind's greatness by recognizing its misery. He hoped thereby to counter what he believed to be the false optimism of the new rationalism and science.

The English Approach to Science and Religion

Francis Bacon established a key framework for reconciling science and religion that long influenced the English-speaking world. He argued there were two books of divine revelation: the Bible and nature. Because both books of revelation shared the same author, they must be compatible. Whatever discord might first appear between science and religion must eventually be reconciled.

Later in the seventeenth century, with the work of Newton, the natural universe became a realm of law and regularity. Most natural philosophers were devout people who saw in the new picture of physical nature a new picture of God. The Creator of

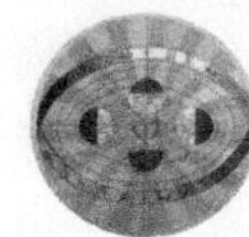

this rational, lawful nature must also be rational. To study nature was to come to a better understanding of that Creator. Science and religious faith were not only compatible, but also mutually supportive.

Finally, the new science and the technological and economic innovations associated with its culture came again, especially among English thinkers, to be interpreted as part of a divine plan. By the late seventeenth century, natural philosophy and its practical achievements had become associated in the public mind with consumption and the market economy. Scientific advance and economic enterprise came to be interpreted in the public mind as the fulfillment of God's plan: Human beings were meant to improve the world. This outlook provided a religious justification for the processes of economic improvement that would characterize much of eighteenth-century Western Europe.

CONTINUING SUPERSTITION

WHAT EXPLAINS the witch hunts and panics of the sixteenth and seventeenth centuries?

Despite the great optimism among certain European thinkers associated with the new ideas in science and philosophy, traditional beliefs and fears long retained their hold on Western culture.

Witch Hunts and Panic

Nowhere is the dark side of early modern thought and culture more strikingly visible than in the witch hunts and panics that erupted in almost every Western land. Between 1400 and 1700, courts sentenced an estimated 70,000 to 100,000 people to death for harmful magic (*maleficium*) and diabolical witchcraft.

Why did witch panics occur in the sixteenth and early seventeenth centuries? The disruptions created by religious division and warfare were major factors. (The peak years of the religious wars were also those of the witch hunts.) Some argue that the Reformation spurred the panics by taking away the traditional defenses against the devil and demons, thus compelling societies to protect themselves preemptively by searching out and executing witches. Political consolidation by secular governments and the papacy played an even greater role, as both aggressively conformed their respective realms in an attempt to eliminate competition for the loyalty of their subjects.

Village Origins

The roots of belief in witches are found in both popular and elite culture. In village societies, feared and respected "cunning folk" helped people cope with natural disasters and disabilities by magical means. Those who were most in need of security and influence, particularly old, impoverished single or widowed women, often made claims to such magical powers. In village society witch beliefs may also have been a way to defy urban Christian society's attempts to impose its orthodox beliefs, laws, and institutions on the countryside. Under church persecution local fertility cults, whose semipagan practices were intended to ensure good harvests, acquired the features of diabolical witchcraft.

Three witches charged with practicing harmful magic are burned alive in Baden in southwest Germany. On the left, two of them are feasting with demons at a sabbat

Bildarchiv Preussischer Kulturbesitz

Influence of the Clergy

Popular belief in magical power was the essential foundation of the witch hunts. Had ordinary people not believed that "gifted persons" could help or harm by magical means, and had they not been willing to accuse them, the hunts would never have occurred. However, the contribution of Christian theologians was equally great. In the late thirteenth century, the Church declared its magic to be the only true magic. Since such powers were not innate to humans, the theologians reasoned, they must come either from God or from the devil. Those from God were properly exercised within and by the church. Any who practiced magic outside and against the Church did so on behalf of the devil. From such reasoning grew allegations of "pacts" between nonpriestly magicians and Satan. Attacking accused witches became a way for the church to extend its spiritual hegemony.

Who Were the Witches?

Roughly 80 percent of the victims of witch hunts were women, most single and aged over forty. Three groups of women appear especially to have drawn the witch-hunter's attention. The first was widows, who, living alone in the world after the deaths of their husbands, were often dependent on help from others, unhappy, and known to strike out. A second group was midwives, whose work made them unpopular when mothers and newborns died during childbirth. (See "Encountering the Past: Midwives.") Finally, there were women healers and herbalists, who were targeted because their work gave them a moral and spiritual authority over people whom the church wished to reserve for its priests.

End of the Witch Hunts

Several factors helped end the witch hunts. One was the emergence of a more scientific point of view. In the seventeenth century, mind and matter came to be viewed as two independent realities, making it harder to believe that thoughts in the mind or words on the lips could alter physical things. With advances in medicine, the rise of insurance companies, and the availability of lawyers, people gained greater physical security against the physical afflictions and natural calamities that drove the witch panics. Finally, the witch hunts began to get out of hand. Tortured witches, when asked whom they saw at witches' sabbats, sometimes alleged having seen leading townspeople there, and even the judges themselves! At this point the trials ceased to serve the interests of those conducting them, becoming dysfunctional and threatening anarchy as well.

baroque Naturalistic style associated with seventeenth-century painting, sculpture, and architecture that emphasized the emotional connection between art and the observer.

BAROQUE ART

HOW DID baroque art serve both religious and secular ends?

Art historians use the term ***baroque*** to denote the style associated with seventeenth-century painting, sculpture, and architecture. Baroque painters depicted their subjects in a thoroughly naturalistic, rather than an idealized, manner. This faithfulness to nature paralleled the interest in natural knowledge associated with the rise of the new science and the deeper understanding of human anatomy that was achieved during this period. These painters, the most famous of whom was Michelangelo Caravaggio (1573–1610), also were devoted to picturing sharp contrasts between light and darkness, which created dramatic scenes in their painting. Consequently, both baroque painting and sculpture have been seen as theatrical and intending to draw the observer into an emotional involvement with the subject that is being portrayed.

The work of baroque artists served both religious and secular ends. Baroque painters, especially in Roman Catholic countries, often portrayed scenes from the Bible and from the lives of saints intended to instruct the observer in religious truths. Artists used the same style of painting, however, to present objects and scenes of everyday life in new realistic detail. Such was the case with Dutch painters of still lifes who portrayed all manner of elaborate foodstuffs as well as with artists such Louis LeNain (1593–1648) who painted scenes of French peasant life.

Bernini designed the elaborate Baldacchino that stands under the dome of St. Peter's Basilica. It is one of the major examples of baroque interior decoration.

Scala/Art Resource, NY

In what ways did baroque art reflect the values of seventeenth-century Catholicism?

Baroque art became associated, rightly or wrongly, with both Roman Catholicism and absolutist politics. The style first emerged in papal Rome, where Gian Lorenzo Bernini's great Tabernacle—situated under the dome of St. Peter's basilica, above the space where St. Peter is said to be buried—is the most famous example, along with the two vast colonnades outside the church. Bernini also created the dramatic sculpture of the Spanish mystic St. Teresa of Avila (1515–1582), depicting her in religious ecstasy.

The association of baroque art with Roman Catholicism had its counterpart in the secular world. Charles I (r. 1625–1649) of England employed the Roman Catholic

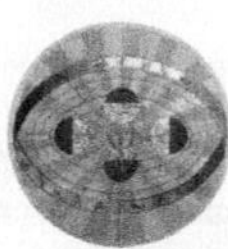

ENCOUNTERING THE PAST

MIDWIVES

Although women were excluded from formal medical training until well into the nineteenth century, the delivery of children was largely left to professional women called midwives. Midwifery was a trade often pursued by elderly or widowed women of the lower social classes. They underwent years of apprenticeship but were not permitted to organize themselves into guilds. They were licensed by civil and church authorities who were invariably men. Sometimes upper-class women were appointed to supervise them.

A reputation for respectability and discretion was essential for a midwife, for she witnessed some of life's most private moments and was privy to the intimate affairs of families. Her character was also assumed to have an effect on the outcome of a birth. A bad character was said to produce stillbirths and imperfectly formed infants. Carelessness or incompetence could, of course, void her license.

Midwives had religious and civic duties associated with births. In emergencies they could baptize failing infants. They registered births, and they were required to report to the authorities any suspicion of abortion or infanticide. A trusted midwife might also be called on to testify to a child's legitimacy.

Male physicians began to replace midwives in the eighteenth century, and civil authorities increasingly required persons who assisted at births to have a formal medical training that was not available to women. Midwives, however, never ceased to serve the poor and rural populations of Europe.

Until well into the eighteenth century, midwives oversaw the delivery of most children in Europe.

CORBIS

Why were midwives viewed with suspicion by many physicians?

WHY WAS midwifery long considered a female activity? Why did men eventually take charge of supervising the birthing process?

Flemish artist Peter Paul Rubens (1577–1640) to decorate the ceiling of the Banqueting Hall at his palace in London with paintings commemorating his father James I (r. 1603–1625). Charles's employment of him fed Puritan suspicions that the king harbored Roman Catholic sympathies. Consequently, it was not by coincidence that Charles I was led to his execution in 1649 through the Rubens-decorated Banqueting Hall to his death on the scaffold erected outside.

The most elaborate baroque monument to political absolutism was Louis XIV's palace at Versailles. (See Chapter 13.) Room after room was decorated with vast, dramatic paintings and murals presenting Louis as the Sun King. Monarchs across Europe, Protestant as well as Catholic, who hoped to imitate Louis's absolutism in their own domains, erected similar, if smaller, palaces filled with elaborate decoration.

SUMMARY

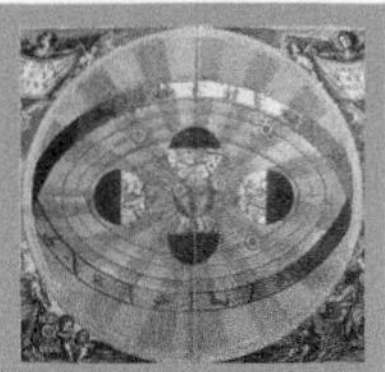

WHAT WAS the scientific revolution?

The Scientific Revolution What we now call "science" emerged as a field of inquiry in the seventeenth century as "natural philosophy." Copernicus, hoping to simplify Ptolemy's geocentric system, had tentatively proposed in the sixteenth century that the sun might be the center of circular planetary motion. Brahe disagreed and performed extensive observations attempting to support the geocentric model. Brahe's assistant Kepler used Brahe's data to propose, in a 1609 book, that the sun was at the center of elliptical planetary orbits. Also in 1609, Galileo was the first to study astronomy through a telescope. Galileo became a strong advocate for the heliocentric universe and popularized the idea that the universe is rational and subject to the laws of mathematics. Finally, Newton combined mathematical modeling and scientific observation to derive his famous laws of motion and theory of universal gravitation. *page 348*

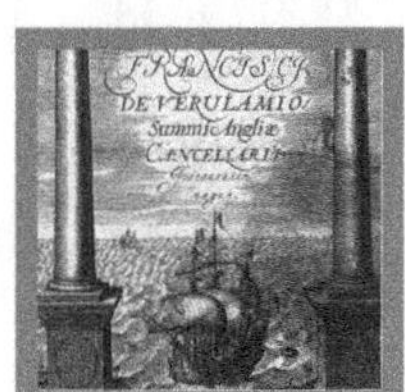

WHAT IMPACT did the new science have on philosophy?

Philosophy Responds to Changing Science Scientists of the seventeenth century were called natural philosophers, and there was some overlap between philosophers and natural philosophers. For this reason, and because of the challenges to traditional thinking posed by scientific work in this period, philosophers were profoundly influenced by the scientific revolution. Galileo's mathematical modeling of the physical world translated into a mechanistic worldview that was widespread among philosophers. Bacon, Descartes, Hobbes, and Locke all articulated philosophies that took aspects of the new science into account and also had implications for social and political organization. *page 351*

WHAT WAS the social and political context for scientific inquiry in the seventeenth century?

The New Institutions of Expanding Natural Knowledge Through the Reformation, most intellectuals had believed their task was to recover and elaborate on knowledge from the Classical/biblical period. The expansion of natural knowledge changed universities and existing centers of learning, and it led to the creation of new "institutions of sharing." Scientific societies encouraged new kinds of social mingling and the cross-fertilization of ideas. *page 358*

WHAT ROLE did women play in the scientific revolution?

Women in the World of the Scientific Revolution European universities had offered little room for scholarship by women; the institutions of science soon turned out to be even more exclusionary. Two categories of women were occasionally able to work around these constraints: noblewomen and female artisans. Women did write important scientific works and popularizations. *page 359*

WHAT EFFORTS were made to reconcile the new science and religion?

The New Science and Religious Faith The new science challenged religion in three ways: Some scientific observations contradicted biblical descriptions (e.g., of the heavens); it was unclear who should resolve any potential conflicts between science and religion, natural philosophers or church authorities; and the new philosophy's materialism seemed to some to preclude spirituality. Most natural philosophers worked hard to reconcile their work with religious views, and they were generally successful. Galileo's condemnation by the church, however, was a dramatic exception to the general rule of accommodation between science and religion. *page 361*

WHAT EXPLAINS the witch hunts and panics of the sixteenth and seventeenth centuries?

Continuing Superstition Through the seventeenth century, most Europeans believed in some form of magic and in the power of demons. "Magic," in the form of transubstantiation, was indeed at the heart of Christian ritual. Although such beliefs had been present for centuries, witch hunts and panics soared in the late sixteenth and early seventeenth centuries. Possible explanations for this phenomenon include the impact of wars and upheaval, spiritual insecurity in the aftermath of the Reformation, and villagers' sublimated hostility toward urban leaders. There is also a variety of possible explanations for why witch hunts died out in the seventeenth century. *page 363*

HOW DID baroque art serve both religious and secular ends?

Baroque Art In the seventeenth century, styles of painting, sculpture, and architecture collectively known as *baroque* came to prominence across Europe. Baroque depictions were naturalistic rather than idealized and sought to involve the observer on an emotional level through dramatic portrayals and contrasts of light and darkness. Catholic baroque art and architecture aimed to instruct and impress. Secular artists depicted everyday life but also created grandiose monuments to political absolutism, such as Louis XIV's palace at Versailles. *page 364*

REVIEW QUESTIONS

1. What contributions to the scientific revolution were made by Copernicus, Brahe, Kepler, Galileo, and Newton? Was the scientific revolution truly a revolution? Which has a greater impact on history, political or intellectual revolution?
2. How do the political philosophies of Hobbes and Locke compare? How did each view human nature? Would you rather live under a government designed by Hobbes or by Locke? Why?
3. What prevented women from playing a greater role in the development of the new science? How did family connections enable some women to contribute to the advance of natural philosophy?
4. What things account for the Church's condemnation of Galileo? How did Pascal try to reconcile faith and reason? How do you explain the fact that witchcraft and witch hunts flourished during an age of scientific enlightenment?
5. What purposes and goals did baroque painting, sculpture, and architecture serve in the religious and secular spheres?

KEY TERMS

baroque (p. 364)
empiricism (p. 352)
Enlightenment (p. 359)
Ptolemaic system (p. 349)
scientific revolution (p. 348)

For additional learning resources related to this chapter, please go to **www.myhistorylab.com**

myhistorylab

15

Society and Economy Under the Old Regime in the Eighteenth Century

During the eighteenth century farm women normally worked in the home and performed such tasks as churning butter as well as caring for children. As time passed, tasks such as making butter were mechanized and women were displaced from such work.

Francis Wheatley (RA) (1747–1801), *Morning*, signed and dated 1799, oil on canvas, 17½ × 21½ in. (44.5 × 54.5 cm), Yale Center for British Art, Paul Mellon Collection, USA/Bridgeman Art Library (B1977.14.120)

What role did women play in the family economy?

Old Regime Prerevolutionary era marked by absolutist monarchies, agrarian economies, tradition, hierarchy, and privilege.

*The French Revolution of 1789 was a turning point in European history. The era that led up to it—the ancien régime (**Old Regime**)—was characterized by absolutist monarchies and agrarian economies that suffered chronic scarcity of food. Tradition, hierarchy, corporateness, and privilege were dominant features of the era. Men and women saw themselves less as individuals than as members of groups. The social order seemed fixed and rigid, but there was some change. Population grew, and standards of living improved. As farming was slowly commercialized, food became more abundant, and as the Industrial Revolution took hold, consumer goods became more plentiful. The spirit of rationality that had fostered the scientific revolution of the seventeenth century thrived in the eighteenth, the "Age of Reason" or the "Enlightenment." In many ways, the Old Regime nourished the changes that terminated its way of life.* ■

MAJOR FEATURES OF LIFE IN THE OLD REGIME

HOW DID tradition, hierarchy, and privilege shape life in the Old Regime?

Socially, prerevolutionary Europe was based on (1) aristocratic elites possessing a wide variety of inherited legal privileges; (2) established churches intimately related to the state and the aristocracy; (3) an urban labor force usually organized into guilds; and (4) a rural peasantry subject to high taxes and feudal dues.

Maintenance of Tradition

During the eighteenth century, few persons outside the government bureaucracies, the expanding merchant groups, and the movement for reform called the Enlightenment (see Chapter 17) considered change or innovation desirable. This was especially true of social relationships. Both nobles and peasants, for different reasons, repeatedly called for the restoration of traditional, or customary, rights. The nobles asserted what they considered their ancient rights against the intrusion of the expanding monarchical bureaucracies. The peasants, through petitions and revolts, called for the revival or the maintenance of the customary manorial rights that allowed them access to particular lands, courts, or grievance procedures. Except for the early industrial development in Britain and the accompanying expansion of personal consumption, the eighteenth-century economy was also predominantly traditional.

Hierarchy and Privilege

Closely related to this traditional social and economic outlook was the hierarchical structure of the society. The medieval sense of rank and degree not only persisted but also became more rigid during the century.

Each state or society was considered a community composed of numerous smaller communities. The "community" might include the village, the municipality, the nobility, the church, the guild, a university, or the parish. In turn, each of these bodies enjoyed certain privileges, some great and some small. The privileges might involve exemption from taxation or from some especially humiliating punishment, the right to practice a trade or craft, the right of one's children to pursue a particular occupation, or, for the church, the right to collect the tithe.

THE ARISTOCRACY

WHAT WAS the foundation of the wealth and power for the eighteenth-century aristocracy?

The eighteenth century was the great age of the aristocracy. The nobility constituted approximately 1 to 5 percent of the population of any given country. Yet in every country, it was the single wealthiest sector of the population, had the widest degree of social, political, and economic power, and set the tone of polite society.

Varieties of Aristocratic Privilege

To be an aristocrat was a matter of birth and legal privilege. This much the aristocracy had in common across the Continent. In almost every other respect, they differed markedly from country to country.

The foundation of aristocratic life was the possession of land. English aristocrats and large landowners controlled local government as well as the English Parliament. This painting of Robert Andrews and his wife by Thomas Gainsborough (1728–1788) shows an aristocratic couple on their estate. The gun and the hunting dog in this portrait suggest the importance landowners assigned to the virtually exclusive hunting privileges they enjoyed on their land.

What key characteristics of the English aristocracy did the artist include in this portrait?

British Nobility The smallest, wealthiest, best defined, and most socially responsible aristocracy resided in Great Britain. It consisted of about four hundred families, and the eldest male members of each family sat in the House of Lords. Through the corruptions of the electoral system, these families also controlled many seats in the House of Commons. The nobles owned about one-fourth of all the arable land in the country. Increasingly, the British aristocracy invested its wealth in commerce, canals, urban real estate, mines, and even industrial ventures. They had few significant legal privileges, but their direct or indirect control of local government gave them immense political power and social influence.

French Nobility In France, the approximately 400,000 nobles were divided between nobles "of the sword," or those whose nobility was derived from military service, and those "of the robe," who had acquired their titles either by serving in the bureaucracy or by having purchased them.

The French nobles were also divided between those who held office or favor with the royal court at Versailles and those who did not. The court nobility reaped the immense wealth that could be gained from holding high office. The nobles' hold on such offices intensified during the century. Whereas these well-connected aristocrats were rich, the provincial nobility, called *hobereaux*, were often little better off than wealthy peasants.

Despite differences in rank, origin, and wealth, certain hereditary privileges set all French aristocrats apart from the rest of society. They were exempt from many taxes. The nobles were technically liable for payment of the *vingtième*, or the "twentieth," which resembled an income tax, but they rarely had to pay it in full. The nobles were not liable for the royal *corvées*, or forced labor on public works, which fell on the peasants. In addition to these exemptions, French nobles could collect feudal dues from their tenants and enjoyed exclusive hunting and fishing privileges.

Eastern European Nobilities East of the Elbe River, the character of the nobility became even more complicated and repressive. Throughout the area, the military traditions of the aristocracy remained important. In Poland, there were thousands of nobles, or *szlachta*, who were entirely exempt from taxes after 1741. Until 1768, these Polish aristocrats possessed the right of life and death over their serfs. Most of the Polish nobility were relatively poor. A few rich nobles who had immense estates exercised political power in the fragile Polish state.

In Austria and Hungary, the nobility continued to possess broad judicial powers over the peasantry through their manorial courts. They also enjoyed various degrees of exemption from taxation.

In Prussia, after the accession of Frederick the Great in 1740, the position of the Junker nobles became much stronger. Frederick drew his officers almost wholly from the Junker class. Nobles also increasingly made up the bureaucracy. As in other parts of eastern Europe, the Prussian nobles had extensive judicial authority over the serfs.

In Russia, Peter the Great's (r. 1682–1725) linking of state service and noble social status through the Table of Ranks (1722) established among Russian nobles a self-conscious class identity that had not previously existed. In 1785, in the Charter of the Nobility, Catherine the Great (r. 1762–1796) legally defined the rights and privileges of noble men and women in exchange for the assurance that the nobility would serve the state voluntarily. Noble privileges included the right of transmitting noble status to a nobleman's wife and children, the judicial protection of noble rights and property, considerable power over the serfs, and exemption from personal taxes.

Aristocratic Resurgence

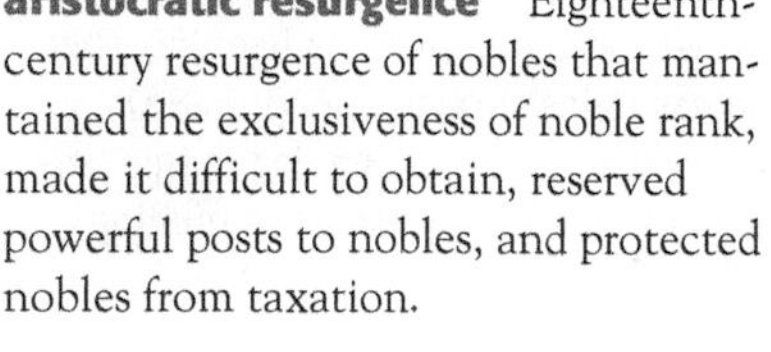

aristocratic resurgence Eighteenth-century resurgence of nobles that mantained the exclusiveness of noble rank, made it difficult to obtain, reserved powerful posts to nobles, and protected nobles from taxation.

The Russian Charter of the Nobility constituted one aspect of the broader European-wide development termed the ***aristocratic resurgence***. This was the nobility's reaction to the threat to their social position and privileges that they felt from the expanding power of the monarchies. This resurgence took several forms in the eighteenth century.

First, all nobilities tried to preserve their exclusiveness by making it more difficult to become a noble. Second, they pushed to reserve appointments to the officer corps of the armies, the senior posts in the bureaucracies and government ministries, and the upper ranks of the church exclusively for nobles. Third, the nobles attempted to use the authority of existing aristocratically controlled institutions against the power of the monarchies. These institutions included the British Parliament, the French courts, or *parlements*, and the local aristocratic estates and provincial diets in Germany and the Habsburg Empire. Finally, the nobility sought to improve its financial position by gaining further exemptions from taxation or by collecting higher rents or long-forgotten feudal dues from the peasantry. This aristocratic challenge to the monarchies was a fundamental political fact of the day and a potentially disruptive one.

THE LAND AND ITS TILLERS

HOW WERE peasants and serfs tied to the land in eighteenth-century Europe?

Land was the economic basis of eighteenth-century life. Well over three-fourths of all Europeans lived in the country. Except for the nobility and the wealthier nonaristocratic landowners, most people who dwelled on the land were poor, living in various states of economic and social dependency, exploitation, and vulnerability.

Peasants and Serfs

Rural social dependency related directly to the land. The nature of the dependency differed sharply for free peasants, such as English tenants and most French cultivators, and for the serfs of Germany, Austria, and Russia, who were legally bound to a particular plot of land and a particular lord. Yet everywhere, the class that owned most of the land also controlled the local government and the courts.

Obligations of Peasants The power of the landlord increased as one moved across Europe from west to east. Most French peasants owned some land, but there were a few serfs in eastern France. Nearly all French peasants were subject to certain feudal dues, called *banalités*. In Prussia and Austria, despite attempts by the monarchies late in the century to improve the lot of the serfs, the landlords continued to exercise almost complete control over them.

Serfs were worst off in Russia. Russian landlords, in effect, regarded serfs merely as economic commodities. They could demand as many as six days a week of labor, known as *barshchina*, from the serfs. Like Prussian and Austrian landlords, they enjoyed

the right to punish their serfs. Serfs had no legal recourse against the orders and whims of their lords. There was little difference between Russian serfdom and slavery.

In southeastern Europe, where the Ottoman Empire held sway, peasants were free, though landlords tried to exert authority in every way. During the seventeenth and eighteenth centuries, disorder originating in Constantinople (now Istanbul), the capital, spilled over into the Balkan peninsula. In this climate, landlords increased their authority by offering their peasants protection from bandits or rebels. These landlords also owned all the housing and tools the peasants needed to work the land and also furnished their seed grain. Consequently, despite legal independence, Balkan peasants under the Ottoman Empire became largely dependent on the landlords, though never to the extent of serfs in eastern Europe or Russia.

Emelyan Pugachev (1726–1775) led the largest peasant revolt in Russian history. In this contemporary propaganda picture he is shown in chains. An inscription in Russian and German was printed below the picture decrying the evils of revolution and insurrection.

Bildarchiv Preussischer Kulturbesitz

What factors contributed to peasant revolts in sixteenth-century Russia?

Peasant Rebellions Russia experienced vast peasant unrest, with well over fifty peasant revolts between 1762 and 1769. These culminated in Pugachev's Rebellion between 1773 and 1775, when Emelyan Pugachev (1726–1775) promised the serfs land of their own and freedom from their lords. All of southern Russia was in turmoil until the government brutally suppressed the rebellion.

Pugachev's was the largest peasant uprising of the eighteenth century, but smaller peasant revolts or disturbances took place in Bohemia in 1775, in Transylvania in 1784, in Moravia in 1786, and in Austria in 1789. There were almost no revolts in Western Europe, but England experienced many rural riots. The rebels usually sought to reassert traditional or customary rights against practices that they perceived as innovations. Peasant revolts were thus conservative in nature.

FAMILY STRUCTURES AND THE FAMILY ECONOMY

WHAT ROLE did the family play in the economy of preindustrial Europe?

HOUSEHOLDS

Northwestern Europe In northwestern Europe, the household almost invariably consisted of a married couple, their children through their early teenage years, and their servants. Except for the few wealthy people, households usually consisted of not more than five or six members. Furthermore, in these households, more than two generations of a family rarely lived under the same roof. The family structure of northwestern Europe was thus nuclear rather than extended.

Children lived with their parents only until their early teens. Then they normally left home, usually to enter the workforce of young servants who lived and worked in another household. A child of a skilled artisan might remain with his or her parents to learn a valuable skill, but only rarely would more than one child do so, because children earned more working outside the home.

Those young men and women who had left home would eventually marry and form their own independent households. Men were usually over twenty-six, and women over twenty-three when they married. The new couple usually had children as soon after marriage as possible. Frequently, the woman was already pregnant at marriage. Family and community pressure often compelled the man to marry her. In any case, premarital sexual relations were common. The new couple would soon employ a servant, who, together with their growing children, would undertake whatever form of livelihood the household used to support itself.

The word *servant* in this context does not refer to someone looking after the needs of wealthy people. Rather, in preindustrial Europe, a servant was a person—either male or female—who was hired, often under a clear contract, to work for the head of the household in exchange for room, board, and wages. The servant was usually young and by no means always socially inferior to his or her employer. Normally, the

QUICK REVIEW

Eastern European Peasants

- Power of landlords increased across Europe from west to east
- Peasants in southeastern Europe became more dependent on landlords over the course of the seventeenth and eighteenth centuries
- Russian serfs endured the worst conditions

servant was an integral part of the household and ate with the family. Being a servant for several years—often as many as eight or ten years—allowed young people to acquire the productive skills and the monetary savings necessary to begin their own household.

Eastern Europe As one moved eastward across the Continent, the structure of the household and the pattern of marriage changed. In eastern Europe, both men and women usually married before the age of twenty. Consequently, children were born to much younger parents. Often—especially among Russian serfs—wives were older than their husbands. Eastern European households were generally larger than those in the West. Frequently a rural Russian household consisted of more than nine, and possibly more than twenty, members, with three or perhaps even four generations of the same family living together. Early marriage made this situation more likely. In Russia, marrying involved not starting a new household, but remaining in and expanding one already established.

The landholding structure in eastern Europe accounts, at least in part, for these patterns of marriage and the family. The lords of the manor who owned land wanted to ensure that it would be cultivated, so they could receive their rents. Thus, in Poland, for example, landlords might forbid marriage between their own serfs and those from another estate and require widows and widowers to remarry quickly. Polish landlords also frowned on the hiring of free laborers—the equivalent of servants in the West—to help cultivate land. The landlords preferred to use other serfs. This practice inhibited the formation of independent households. In Russia, landlords ordered the families of young people in their villages to arrange marriages within a short set time. These lords discouraged single-generation family households because the death or serious illness of one person in such a household might mean the land assigned to it would go out of cultivation.

The Family Economy

During the seventeenth century the French Le Nain brothers painted scenes of French peasant life. Although the images softened many of the harsh realities of peasant existence, the clothing and the interiors were based on actual models and convey the character of the life of better-off French peasants whose lives would have continued very much the same into the eighteenth century.

Erich Lessing/Art Resource, NY

What explains the fascination of early modern artists with peasant life?

Throughout Europe, most people worked within the family economy. That is to say, the household was the basic unit of production and consumption. Depending on their ages and skills, everyone in the household worked. The need to survive poor harvests or economic slumps meant that no one could be idle. Within this family economy, all goods and income produced went to the benefit of the household rather than to the individual family member. On a farm, much of the effort went directly into raising food or producing other agricultural goods that could be exchanged for food. Few Western Europeans, however, had enough land to support their household from farming alone. Thus, one or more family members might work elsewhere and send wages home; for example, the father and older children might work as harvesters, fishermen, or engage in other labor either in the neighborhood or farther from home. If the father was such a migrant worker, his wife and their younger children would have to work the family farm. This was not an uncommon pattern.

The family economy also dominated the life of skilled urban artisans. The father was usually the chief artisan. He normally employed one or more servants but would expect his children to work in the enterprise also. He usually trained his eldest child in the trade. His wife often sold his wares or opened a small shop of her own. Wives of merchants also frequently ran their husbands' businesses, especially when the husband traveled to purchase new goods.

In Western Europe, the death of a father often brought disaster to the household. The continuing economic life of the family usually depended on his land or skills. The widow might take on the farm or the business, or his children might do so. The widow usually sought to remarry quickly to restore the labor and skills of a male to the household and to prevent herself from becoming dependent on relatives or charity.

In Eastern Europe, the family economy functioned in the context of serfdom and landlord domination. Peasants clearly thought in terms of their families and expanding the land available for cultivation. The village structure may have mitigated the pressures of the family economy, as did the multigenerational family. Dependence on the available land was the chief fact of life. There were many fewer artisan and merchant households, and there was far less geographical mobility than in Western Europe.

Women and the Family Economy

The family economy established many of the chief constraints on the lives and personal experiences of women in preindustrial society. Most of the historical research that has been undertaken on this subject relates to Western Europe. There, a woman's life experience was largely the function of her capacity to establish and maintain a household. For women, marriage was an economic necessity, as well as an institution that fulfilled sexual and psychological needs. Outside a household, a woman's life was vulnerable and precarious. Consequently, a woman devoted much of her life first to maintaining her parents' household and then to devising some means of getting her own household to live in as an adult. Bearing and rearing children were usually subordinate to these goals.

By the age of seven, a girl would have begun to help with the household work. The girl would remain in her parents' home as long as she made a real contribution to the family enterprise or as long as her labor elsewhere was not more remunerative to the family. An artisan's daughter might not leave home until marriage, because at home she could learn increasingly valuable skills associated with the trade. The situation was different for the much larger number of girls growing up on farms. Their parents and brothers could often do all the necessary farm work, and a girl's labor at home quickly became of little value to her family. She would then leave home, usually between the age of twelve and fourteen years. She might take up residence on another farm, but more likely she would migrate to a nearby town or city. She would then normally become a servant, once again living in a household, but this time in the household of an employer. Having left home, the young woman's chief goal was to accumulate enough capital for a dowry. Her savings would make her eligible for marriage, because they would allow her to make the necessary contribution to form a household with her husband. A young woman might well work for ten years or more to accumulate a dowry. This practice meant that marriage was usually postponed until her mid- to late twenties.

Within marriage, earning enough money or producing enough farm goods to ensure an adequate food supply dominated women's concerns. Domestic duties, childbearing, and child rearing were subordinate to economic pressures. Consequently, couples tried to limit the number of children they had, usually through the practice of *coitus interruptus*, the withdrawal of the male before ejaculation.

The work of married women differed markedly between city and country and was in many ways a function of their husbands' occupations. If the peasant household had enough land to support itself, the wife spent much of her time literally carrying things for her husband—water, food, seed, harvested grain, and the like. If the husband had to do work besides farming, such as fishing or migrant labor, the wife might actually be in charge of the farm and do the plowing, planting, and harvesting. In the city, the wife of an artisan or a merchant might be in charge of the household finances and help manage the business. When her husband died, she might take over the business and perhaps hire an artisan.

Despite all this economic activity, women found many occupations and professions closed to them because they were female. They labored with less education than men, because in such a society women at all levels of life consistently found fewer opportunities for education than did men. They often received lower wages than men for the same work.

QUICK REVIEW

Girlhood

- By age seven girls contributed to household work
- Most girls left home between the ages of twelve and fourteen
- A young woman's chief goal was to accumulate a dowry

CHILDREN AND THE WORLD OF THE FAMILY ECONOMY

For women of all social ranks, childbirth meant fear and vulnerability. Contagious diseases endangered both mother and child. Not all midwives were skillful practitioners. Furthermore, most mothers gave birth in conditions of immense poverty and wretched housing. Assuming both mother and child survived, the mother might nurse the infant, but often the child would be sent to a wet nurse. The wealthy may have done this for convenience, but economic necessity dictated it for the poor. The structures and customs of the family economy did not permit a woman to devote herself entirely to rearing a child.

The birth of a child was not always welcome. Through at least the end of the seventeenth century, unwanted or illegitimate births could lead to infanticide, especially among the poor. The late seventeenth and the early eighteenth centuries saw a new interest in preserving the lives of abandoned children. Although foundling hospitals established to care for abandoned children had existed before, their size and number expanded during these years. Such hospitals cared for thousands of children, and the demand for their services increased during the eighteenth century.

Sadness and tragedy surrounded abandoned children. Most of them were illegitimate infants from across the social spectrum. Many, however, were left with the foundling hospitals because their parents could not support them. Parents would sometimes leave personal tokens or saints' medals on the abandoned baby in the vain hope they might one day be able to reclaim the child. Few children were reclaimed. Leaving a child at a foundling hospital did not guarantee its survival. In Paris, only about 10 percent of all abandoned children lived to the age of ten.

Despite all these perils of early childhood, children did grow up and come of age across Europe. The world of the child may not have received the kind of attention it does today, but during the eighteenth century, the seeds of that modern sensibility were sown. Particularly among the upper classes, new interest arose in educating children. As economic skills became more demanding, literacy became more valuable, and literacy rates rose during the century. Yet most Europeans remained illiterate. Not until the late nineteenth century was the world of childhood inextricably linked to the process of education. Then children would be reared to become members of a national citizenry. In the Old Regime, they were reared to make their contribution to the economy of their parents' family and then to set up their own households.

THE REVOLUTION IN AGRICULTURE

WHAT LED to the agricultural revolution of the eighteenth century?

The main goal of traditional peasant society was a stability that would ensure the local food supply. Despite differences in rural customs across Europe, the tillers resisted changes that might endanger the sure supply of food, which they generally believed traditional methods of cultivation would provide. Failure of the harvest meant not only hardship, but also death from either outright starvation or malnutrition. Poor harvests also played havoc with prices. Even small increases in the cost of food could exert heavy pressure on peasant or artisan families.

Historians now believe that during the eighteenth century bread prices slowly but steadily rose, spurred largely by population growth. Prices rose faster than urban wages and brought no appreciable advantage to the small peasant producer. However, the rise in grain prices benefited landowners and those wealthier peasants who had surplus grain to sell. The rising grain prices gave landlords an opportunity to improve their incomes and lifestyle. To achieve those ends, landlords in Western Europe began a series of innovations in farm production that became known as the Agricultural Revolution. Landlords commercialized agriculture and thereby challenged the traditional peasant ways of

production. Peasant revolts and disturbances often resulted. The governments of Europe, hungry for new taxes and dependent on the goodwill of the nobility, used their armies and militias to smash peasants who defended traditional practices.

New Crops and New Methods

The drive to improve agricultural production began during the sixteenth and seventeenth centuries in the Low Countries, where the pressures of the growing population and the shortage of land required changes in cultivation. Dutch landlords and farmers devised better ways to build dikes and to drain land, so they could farm more land. They also experimented with new crops, such as clover and turnips, that would increase the supply of animal fodder and restore the soil.

English landlords provided the most striking examples of eighteenth-century agricultural improvement. They originated almost no genuinely new farming methods, but they popularized ideas developed in the previous century either in the Low Countries or in England. Some of these landlords and agricultural innovators became famous. For example, Jethro Tull (1674–1741) championed the use of iron plows to turn the earth more deeply and of planting wheat by a drill rather than by just casting seeds. His methods permitted land to be cultivated for longer periods without having to leave it fallow. Charles "Turnip" Townsend (1674–1738) instituted crop rotation, using wheat, turnips, barley, and clover. This new system of rotation replaced the fallow field with one sown with a crop that both restored nutrients to the soil and supplied animal fodder. The additional fodder meant that more livestock could be raised, increasing the quantity of manure available as fertilizer for the grain crops. Consequently, in the long run, both animals and human beings had more food. Finally, Robert Bakewell (1725–1795) pioneered new methods of animal breeding that produced more and better animals and more milk and meat.

This seed drill, devised by the English agricultural innovator Jethro Tull (1674–1741), increased wheat crops by planting seed deep in the soil rather than just casting it randomly on the surface.

Image Works/Mary Evans Picture Library Ltd.

How did technology contribute to the agricultural revolution?

Enclosure Replaces Open-Field Method Many of the agricultural innovations, which were adopted only slowly, were incompatible with the existing organization of land in England. Small cultivators who lived in village communities still farmed most of the soil. Each farmer tilled an assortment of unconnected strips. The two- or three-field systems of rotation left large portions of land fallow and unproductive each year. Animals grazed on the common land in the summer and on the stubble of the harvest in the winter. Until at least the mid-eighteenth century, the whole community decided what crops to plant. The entire system discouraged improvement and favored the poorer farmers, who needed the common land and stubble fields for their animals.

In 1700, approximately half the arable land in England was farmed by this open-field method. By the second half of the century, the rising price of wheat encouraged landlords to consolidate or enclose their lands to increase production. The **enclosures** were intended to use land more rationally and to achieve greater commercial profits. The process involved the fencing of common lands, the reclamation of previously untilled waste, and the transformation of strips into block fields. These procedures brought turmoil to the economic and social life of the countryside. Riots often ensued.

enclosures Process of land privatization and rationalization intended to produce greater commercial profits.

Because many English farmers either owned their strips or rented them in a manner that amounted to ownership, the larger landlords usually resorted to parliamentary acts to legalize the enclosure of the land, which they owned but rented to the farmers. Because the large landowners controlled Parliament, such measures passed easily. Between 1761 and 1792, almost 500,000 acres were enclosed through acts of Parliament, compared with 75,000 acres between 1727 and 1760. In 1801, a general enclosure act streamlined the process.

The enclosures permitted the extension of both farming and innovation, and thus increased food production on larger agricultural units. They also disrupted small traditional communities; they forced off the land independent farmers, who had needed the common pasturage, and poor cottage dwellers, who had lived on the reclaimed wasteland. The enclosures, however, did not depopulate the countryside. In some counties where the enclosures took place, the population increased. New soil had come into production, and services that supported farming also expanded.

QUICK REVIEW

Enclosure

- Traditional open-field method favored poorer farmers
- Landlords "enclosed" land over the course of the eighteenth century
- Enclosure led to the commercialization of British agriculture

The commercialization of agriculture, which spread from Britain slowly across the Continent during the next century, strained the paternal relationship between the governing and governed classes. Previously, landlords had often looked after the welfare of the lower orders through price controls or waivers of rent during hard times. As the landlords became increasingly concerned about profits, they began to leave the peasants to the mercy of the marketplace.

Limited Improvements in Eastern Europe Improving agriculture tended to characterize farm production west of the Elbe River. (See "Compare & Connect: Two Eighteenth-Century Writers Contemplate the Effects of Different Economic Structures," pages 380–381.) In Prussia, Austria, Poland, and Russia, agricultural improvement was limited. Nothing in the relationship of the serfs to their lords encouraged innovation. In eastern Europe, the chief method of increasing production was to bring previously untilled lands under the plow. By extending tillage, the great landlords sought to squeeze more labor from their serfs, rather than greater productivity from the soil. The only significant nutritional gain they achieved was the introduction of maize and the potato.

Expansion of the Population

The population explosion with which the entire world must contend today had its origins in the eighteenth century. Before that time, Europe's population had experienced dramatic increases, but plagues, wars, or famine had redressed the balance. Beginning in the second quarter of the eighteenth century, the population began to increase steadily. In 1700, Europe's population, excluding the European provinces of the Ottoman Empire, was probably between 100 million and 120 million people. By 1800, the figures had risen to almost 190 million and by 1850, to 260 million. Such extraordinary sustained growth put new demands on all resources and considerable pressure on the existing social organization.

The population expansion occurred across the Continent in both the country and the cities. Only a limited consensus exists among scholars about the causes of this growth. The death rate clearly declined. There were fewer wars and epidemics in the eighteenth century. Hygiene and sanitation also improved, but the most important factor may have been changes in the food supply.

Improved and expanding grain production made one contribution. Another and even more important change was the cultivation of the potato. This tuber was a product of the New World and came into widespread European production during the eighteenth century. On a single acre, a peasant family could grow enough potatoes to feed itself for an entire year.

The impact of the population explosion can hardly be overestimated. It created new demands for food, goods, jobs, and services. It provided a new pool of labor. Traditional modes of production and living had to be revised. More people lived in the countryside than could find employment there. Migration increased. There were also more people who might become socially and politically discontented. Because the population growth fed on itself, these pressures and demands continued to increase. The society and the social practices of the Old Regime literally outgrew their traditional bounds.

THE INDUSTRIAL REVOLUTION OF THE EIGHTEENTH CENTURY

WHY DID the Industrial Revolution begin in Britain?

The second half of the eighteenth century witnessed the beginning of the industrialization of the European economy. That achievement of sustained economic growth is known as the **Industrial Revolution**. At considerable social cost, industrialization made possible the production of more goods and services than ever before in human history. The new means of production demanded new kinds of skills, new discipline in work, and a large labor force. In the long run, industrialization raised the standard of living and overcame the poverty that most Europeans, who lived during the eighteenth century and earlier, had taken for granted. It gave human beings greater control over nature than they had ever known before, yet by the mid–nineteenth century, industrialism would also cause new and unanticipated problems with the environment.

Industrial Revolution Term coined by early-nineteenth-century observers to describe the changes that the spreading use of powered machinery made in society and economics.

A Revolution in Consumption

The inventions of the Industrial Revolution increased the supply of consumer goods as never before in history. The supply of goods was only one side of the economic equation, however. An unprecedented demand for the humble goods of everyday life created the supply. Those goods included clothing, buttons, toys, china, furniture, rugs, kitchen utensils, candlesticks, brassware, silverware, pewterware, glassware, watches, jewelry, soap, beer, wines, and foodstuffs. It was the ever-increasing demand for these goods that sparked the ingenuity of designers and inventors. Furthermore, consumer demand seemed unlimited.

Many social factors helped establish the markets for these consumer goods. During the seventeenth century, the Dutch had enjoyed enormous prosperity and had led the way in new forms of consumption. For reasons that are still not clear, during the eighteenth century, first the English and then the people on the Continent came to have more disposable income, allowing people to buy consumer goods that previous generations had inherited or did not possess. What is key to this change in consumption is that it depended primarily on expanding the various domestic markets in Europe.

This revolution, if that is not too strong a term, in consumption was not automatic. People became persuaded that they needed or wanted new consumer goods. Often, entrepreneurs caused it to happen by developing new methods of marketing. For example, the English porcelain manufacturer Josiah Wedgwood (1730–1795) first attempted to find customers among the royal family and the aristocracy. Once he had gained their business with luxury goods, then he produced a less expensive version of the chinaware for middle-class customers. He also used advertising, opened showrooms, and sent out salespeople with samples and catalogs of his wares. There seemed to be no limit to the markets for consumer goods that social emulation on the one hand and advertising on the other could stimulate. Manufacturers soon realized that by changing styles they could further increase demand, for the desire to have the latest in fashions and inventions prompted people to return to the market again and again.

This expansion of consumption quietly, but steadily, challenged the social assumptions of the day. Fashion publications made all levels of society aware of new styles. Clothing fashions could be copied. Servants could begin to dress well if not

Overview: Major Inventions in the Textile-Manufacturing Revolution

1733	James Kay's flying shuttle
1765	James Hargreaves's spinning jenny (patented 1770)
1769	James Watt's steam engine patent
1769	Richard Arkwright's water frame patent
1787	Edmund Cartwright's power loom

COMPARE & CONNECT

TWO EIGHTEENTH-CENTURY WRITERS CONTEMPLATE THE EFFECTS OF DIFFERENT ECONOMIC STRUCTURES

Among eighteenth-century public officials and commentators there existed a broad agreement that European economic life needed to be reorganized and stimulated to achieve greater productivity and wealth. These writers also understood that different modes of productive activity resulted in very different kinds of society. In these two documents a French writer bemoans problems of French agriculture and landholding while a Scottish writer praises the wealth and good society that flow from growing commerce and refinement of both mechanical and liberal arts.

QUESTIONS

1. Why does Turgot favor those farmers who can make investments in the land they rent from a proprietor?
2. What are the structures of the *métayer* system? Why did it lead to poor investments and lower harvests?
3. Why does Hume link industry and the arts?
4. How does he see a commercial, improving economy producing important intellectual outlooks and social skills?
5. What benefits to agriculture might Hume have assigned to prosperous cities, and what benefits might Turgot have seen agriculture contributing to urban life?

I. TURGOT DECRIES FRENCH LANDHOLDING

During the eighteenth century, many observers became keenly aware that different kinds of landholding led to different attitudes toward work and to different levels of production and wealth. Robert Jacques Turgot (1727–1781), who later became finance minister of France, analyzed these differences in an effort to reform French agriculture. He was especially concerned with arrangements that encouraged long-term investment. The métayer *system Turgot discusses was an arrangement whereby landowners had land farmed by peasants who received part of the harvest as payment for working the land, but the peasants had no long-term interest in improving the land. Virtually all observers regarded the system as inefficient.*

1. What really distinguishes the area of large-scale farming from the areas of small-scale production is that in the former areas the proprietors find farmers who provide them with a permanent revenue from the land and who buy from them the right to cultivate it for a certain number of years. These farmers undertake all the expenses of cultivation, the ploughing, the sowing and the stocking of the farm with cattle, animals and tools. They are really agricultural entrepreneurs, who possess, like the entrepreneurs in all other branches of commerce, considerable funds, which they employ in the cultivation of land. . . .

   They have not only the brawn but also the wealth to devote to agriculture. They have to work, but unlike workers, they do not have to earn their living by the sweat of their brow, but by the lucrative employment of their capital, just as the ship owners of Nantes and Bordeaux employ theirs in maritime commerce.
2. *Métayer* System The areas of small-scale farming, that is to say at least four-sevenths of the kingdom, are those where there are no agricultural entrepreneurs, where a proprietor who wishes to develop his land cannot find anyone to cultivate it except wretched peasants who have no resources other than their labor, where he is obliged to make, at his own expense, all the advances necessary for tillage, beasts, tools, sowing, even to the extent of advancing to his *métayer* the wherewithal to feed himself until the first harvest, where consequently a proprietor who did not have any property other than his estate would be obliged to allow it to lie fallow. After having deducted the costs of sowing and feudal dues with which the property is burdened, the proprietor shares with the *métayer* what remains of the profits, in accordance with the agreement they have concluded. The proprietor runs all the risks of harvest failure and any loss of cattle: he is the real entrepreneur. The *métayer* is

This is a detail of a 1739 map by Louis Bretez, a member of the Academy of Painting and Sculpture, showing an aerial view of the city of Paris. The primary function of the map was to reestablish Paris as the universal model of a capital city.

Library of Congress

What fueled the growth of Paris in the eighteenth century?

nothing more than a mere workman, a farm hand to whom the proprietor surrenders a share of his profits instead of paying wages. But in his work the proprietor enjoys none of the advantages of the farmer who, working on his own behalf, works carefully and diligently; the proprietor is obliged to entrust all his advances to a man who may be negligent or a scoundrel and is answerable for nothing.

This *métayer*, accustomed to the most miserable existence and without the hope and even the desire to obtain a better living for himself, cultivates badly and neglects to employ the land for valuable and profitable production; by preference he occupies himself in cultivating those things whose growth is less troublesome and which provide him with more foodstuffs, such as buckwheat and chestnuts which do not require any attention. He does not worry very much about his livelihood; he knows that if the harvest fails, his master will be obliged to feed him in order not to see his land neglected.

Source: From *Oeuvres, et documents les concernant*, by A. M. R. Turgot, ed. by F. Schelle, 5 vols. (Paris: F. Alcan, 1914), vol. II, pp. 448–450; *Documents of European Economic History*, as quoted and trans. by S. Pollard and C. Holmes, (London: Edward Arnold, 1968), pp. 38–39.

II. DAVID HUME PRAISES LUXURY AND THE REFINEMENT OF THE ARTS

David Hume (1711–1776) was a Scottish philosopher, historian, and economic commentator. He was deeply committed to the modernization of the Scottish and wider European economy through the growth of commerce and the fostering of improved means of mechanical production. In this essay published in 1752 he outlined the beneficial social consequence he saw resulting from commercial wealth and new mechanical inventions. He believed such economic activity not only increased riches but also produced a population capable of providing a national defense. He was quite concerned to demonstrate that luxury and the economy that fostered it would not lead to moral decay.

In times when industry and the arts flourish, men are kept in perpetual occupation, and enjoy, as their reward, the occupation itself, as well as those pleasures which are the fruit of their labour. The mind acquires new vigour; enlarges its powers and faculties; and by an assiduity in honest industry, both satisfies its natural appetites, and prevents the growth of unnatural ones, which commonly spring up, when nourished by ease and idleness. . . .

Another advantage of industry and of refinements in the mechanical arts, is, that they commonly produce some refinements in the liberal; nor can one be carried to perfection, without being accompanied, in some degree, with the other. . . .

The more these refined arts advance, the more sociable men become . . . They flock into cities; love to receive and communicate knowledge; to show their wit or their breeding; their taste in conversation or living, in clothes or furniture. Curiosity allures the wise; vanity the foolish, and pleasure both. Particular clubs and societies are everywhere formed: Both sexes meet in an easy and sociable manner: and the tempers of men, as well as their behaviour, refine apace. So that, beside the improvements which they receive from knowledge and the liberal arts, it is impossible but they must feel an encrease of humanity, from the very habit of conversing together, and contributing to each other's pleasure and entertainment. Thus *industry, knowledge*, and *humanity*, are linked together by an indissoluble chain, and are found, from experience as well as reason, to be peculiar to the more polished, and, what are commonly denominated, the more luxurious ages. . . .

But industry, knowledge, and humanity are not advantageous in private life alone: They diffuse their beneficial influence on the *public*, and render the government as great and flourishing as they make individuals happy and prosperous. The encrease and consumption of all the commodities . . . are advantageous to society; because . . . they are a kind of *storehouse* of labour, which, in the exigencies of state, may be turned to the public service. In a nation, where there is no demand for such superfluities, men sink into indolence, lose all enjoyment of life, and are useless to the public, which cannot maintain or support its fleets and armies, from the industry of such slothful members.

Source: David Hume, "Of Refinement in the Arts (1752)," in *Essays: Moral, Political and Literary* (Indianapolis, IN: Liberty Classics, 1985), pp. 270–272.

luxuriously. Changes in the consumption of food and drink demanded new kinds of dishware for the home. Tea and coffee became staples. The brewing industry became fully commercialized. Those developments entailed the need for new kinds of cups and mugs and many more of them.

There would always be critics of this consumer economy. Yet, the ever-increasing consumption and production of the goods of everyday life became a hallmark of modern Western society from the eighteenth century to our own day. It would be difficult to overestimate the importance of the desire for consumer goods and the higher standard of living that they made possible in Western history after the eighteenth century. The presence and accessibility of such goods became the hallmark of a nation's prosperity. It was the absence of such consumer goods, as well as of civil liberties, that during the 1980s led to such deep discontent with the communist regimes in Eastern Europe and the former Soviet Union.

QUICK REVIEW

Josiah Wedgwood (1730–1795)

- Started as producer of luxury goods
- Once established, produced less expensive items for middle-class customers
- Took advantage of middle-class desire to emulate social superiors

Industrial Leadership of Great Britain

Great Britain was the home of the Industrial Revolution and, until the middle of the nineteenth century, remained the industrial leader of Europe. Several factors contributed to the early start in Britain.

Great Britain took the lead in the consumer revolution that expanded the demand for goods that could be efficiently supplied. It seems to have been in Britain that a world of fashion first developed that led people to want to accumulate goods. In addition to the domestic consumer demand, the British economy benefited from demand from the colonies in North America.

Britain was also the single largest free-trade area in Europe. The British had good roads and waterways without internal tolls or other trade barriers. The country had rich deposits of coal and iron ore. Its political structure was stable, and property was absolutely secure. The sound systems of banking and public credit established a stable climate for investment. Taxation in Britain was heavy, but it was efficiently and fairly collected, largely from indirect taxes. Furthermore, British taxes received legal approval through Parliament, with all social classes and all regions of the nation paying the same taxes.

Finally, British society was mobile by the standards of the time. Persons who had money or could earn it could rise socially. The British aristocracy would receive into its ranks people who had amassed large fortunes. Even persons of wealth who did not join the aristocracy could enjoy their riches, receive social recognition, and exert political influence.

New Methods of Textile Production

The industry that pioneered the Industrial Revolution and met the growing consumer demand was the production of textiles for clothing. Textile production developed not in cities, but in the countryside. Although the eighteenth-century economy was primarily agricultural, manufacturing also permeated rural areas. The peasant family living in a one- or two-room cottage, rather than the factory, was the basic unit of production. The same peasants who tilled the land in spring and summer often spun thread or wove textiles in the winter.

Under what is termed the ***domestic***, or putting-out, ***system of textile production***, agents of urban textile merchants took wool or other unfinished fibers to the homes of peasants, who spun it into thread. The agent then transported the thread to other peasants, who wove it into the finished product. The merchant sold the wares.

domestic system of textile production Means by which urban merchants obtained their wares. They bought wool or other unfinished fiber for distribution to peasant workers who took it home, spun it into thread, wove it into cloth, and returned the finished product to the merchants for sale.

By the mid–eighteenth century, however, production bottlenecks had developed within the domestic system. The demand for cotton textiles was growing more rapidly than production, especially in Britain, which had a large domestic and North American market for these goods. Inventors devised some of the most famous machines of the early Industrial Revolution to meet consumer demand for cotton textiles.

The Spinning Jenny Thanks to the invention of the flying shuttle in the 1730s, weavers had the technical capacity to produce enough cotton fabric to meet market demand. It was not until 1765, however, when James Hargreaves (d. 1778) invented the **spinning jenny**, that spinners began to be able to provide weavers with adequate supplies of thread. Hargreaves's machine spun 16 spindles of thread simultaneously. By the close of the century, capacity had increased to 120 spindles.

spinning jenny Invented by James Hargreaves in 1765, this machine spun sixteen spindles of thread simultaneously.

The Water Frame The spinning jenny broke the bottleneck between the productive capacity of the spinners and the weavers, but it was still a piece of machinery used in the cottage. The invention that took cotton textile manufacture out of the home and put it into the factory was Richard Arkwright's (1732–1792) **water frame**, patented in 1769. This was a water-powered device designed to permit the production of cotton fabric. From the 1780s onward, the cotton industry could meet an ever-expanding demand. Cotton output increased by 800 percent between 1780 and 1800. By 1815, cotton composed 40 percent of the value of British domestic exports and by 1830, just over 50 percent.

water frame Invented in 1769 by Richard Arkwright, this water-powered device produced a cotton fabric and was suitable for use in factories.

The Industrial Revolution had commenced in earnest by the 1780s, but the full economic and social ramifications of this unleashing of human productive capacity were not really felt until the early nineteenth century. The expansion of industry and the incorporation of new inventions often occurred slowly. Nor did all the social ramifications of industrialism appear immediately. The first cotton mills used water power, were located in the country, and rarely employed more than two dozen workers. Not until the late-century application of the steam engine, perfected by James Watt (1736–1819) in 1769, to run textile machinery could factories easily be located in or near urban centers. The steam engine not only vastly increased and regularized the available energy but also made possible the combination of urbanization and industrialization.

The Steam Engine

More than any other invention, the steam engine permitted industrialization to grow on itself and to expand into one area of production after another. This machine provided for the first time in human history a steady and essentially unlimited source of inanimate power.

Thomas Newcomen had invented the first engine using steam power early in the eighteenth century. It was driven by injecting steam into a cylinder to push up a piston that fell back when the steam condensed. The machine was heavy and energy inefficient, but it was widely used in Britain to pump water out of coal and tin mines. During the 1760s, James Watt, a Scottish engineer, experimented with the Newcomen machine and achieved much greater efficiency by separating the condenser from the piston and the cylinder. His design, however, required precisely tooled metalwork, a technical liability that Matthew Boulton, a successful toy and button maker, and John Wilkinson, a cannon manufacturer, helped him overcome. In 1776, a Watt steam engine found its first commercial application: pumping water from mines in Cornwall.

By the early nineteenth century, the steam engine had become the prime mover for all industry. With its application to ships and then to wagons on iron rails, the steam engine also revolutionized transportation.

Iron Production

The manufacture of high-quality iron has been basic to modern industrial development. Iron is the chief element of all heavy industry and of land or sea transport. During the early eighteenth century, British ironmakers produced somewhat less than 25,000 tons of iron annually. Three factors held back the production. First, charcoal rather than coke was used to smelt the ore. Charcoal, derived from wood, was becoming scarce as forests in Britain diminished, and it does not burn at as high a temperature as coke, derived from coal. Second, until the perfection of the steam engine, furnaces could not achieve high enough blasts. Finally, the demand for iron was limited. The elimination of the first two problems also eliminated the third.

Eventually, British ironmakers began to use coke, and the steam engine provided new power for the blast furnaces. Coke was an abundant fuel because of Britain's large coal deposits. The steam engine both improved iron production and increased the demand for iron.

In 1784, Henry Cort (1740–1800) introduced a new puddling process, that is, a new method for melting and stirring molten ore. Cort's process allowed the removal of more slag (the impurities that bubbled to the top of the molten metal) and thus the production of purer iron. Cort also developed a rolling mill that continuously shaped the still-molten metal into bars, rails, or other forms. Previously, the metal had to be pounded into these forms. All these innovations achieved a better, more versatile, cheaper product. The demand for iron consequently grew. By the early nineteenth century, the British produced over a million tons annually. The lower cost of iron, in turn, lowered the cost of steam engines and allowed them to be used more widely.

The Impact of the Agricultural and Industrial Revolutions on Working Women

The transformation of agriculture and industry led to a series of seemingly modest changes that, taken collectively, diminished the importance and the role of those women already in the workforce.

Women had been an important part of traditional European agriculture. They worked in and often were permitted to glean the grain left over after the general harvest. Women also managed industries like milking and cheese production. However, primarily in Western Europe, increasing commercialization and mechanization eroded these traditional roles. Machinery operated by men displaced the work of women in the field and their skills in dairying and home industry, particularly in Britain. Even nonmechanized labor came to favor men. For example, during the late eighteenth century, heavy scythes wielded by men replaced the lighter sickles that women had used to harvest grain. Moreover, the drive to maximize profits led landlords to enclose lands and curtail customary rights like gleaning. This transformation of farming constricted women's ability to earn their living from the land.

A similar process took place in textile manufacturing, where mechanization deprived many women of one of their most traditional means of earning income. Before mechanization thousands of women worked at spinning wheels to produce thread that hand-loom weavers, who were often their husbands, then wove. The earlier, small spinning jennies did not immediately disrupt this situation because women could use them in the loft of a home, but the larger ones required a factory setting where men often ran the machinery. As a result, most women spinners were put out of work, and those women who did move into the factory labor force performed less skilled work than men.

Consumption of all forms of consumer goods increased greatly in the eighteenth century. This engraving illustrates a shop, probably in Paris. Here women, working apparently for a woman manager, are making dresses and hats to meet the demands of the fashion trade.

Bildarchiv Preussischer Kulturbesitz

Many working women, displaced from spinning thread or from farming, slowly turned to cottage industries, such as knitting, button making, straw plaiting, bonnet making, or glove stitching, that invariably earned them less than their former occupations had. The work and skills these occupations involved were considered inferior; and because it paid so poorly, women who did this work might become prostitutes or engage in other criminal activity. Consequently, the reputations and social standing of many working women suffered.

Among women who did not work in the cottage industries, thousands became domestic servants in the homes of landed or commercial families. During the nineteenth century, such domestic service became the largest area of female employment.

By the end of the eighteenth century, the work and workplaces of men and women were becoming increasingly separate and distinct. This shift in female employment pro-

duced several long-term results. First, women's work, whether in cottage industries or domestic service, became associated with the home rather than with places where men worked. Second, the laboring life of most women was removed from the new technologies in farming, transportation, and manufacturing. Woman's work thus appeared traditional, and people assumed women could do only such work. Third, during the nineteenth and early twentieth centuries, Europeans also assumed most women worked only to supplement a husband's income. Finally, because the work women did was considered marginal and only as supplementing a male income, men were paid much more than women. Most people associate the Industrial Revolution with factories, but for many working women, these revolutions led to a life located more in homes than ever before.

THE GROWTH OF CITIES

WHAT PROBLEMS arose as a result of the growth of cities?

Remarkable changes occurred in the pattern of city growth between 1500 and 1800. In 1500, within Europe (excluding Hungary and Russia) 156 cities had a population greater than 10,000. Only four of those cities—Paris, Milan, Venice, and Naples—had populations larger than 100,000. By 1800, 363 cities had 10,000 or more inhabitants, and 17 of them had populations larger than 100,000. The percentage of the European population living in urban areas had risen from just over 5 percent to just over 9 percent. A major shift in urban concentration from southern, Mediterranean Europe to the north had also occurred.

Patterns of Preindustrial Urbanization

The eighteenth century witnessed a considerable growth of towns. London grew from about 700,000 inhabitants in 1700 to almost 1 million in 1800. By the time of the French Revolution, Paris had more than 500,000 inhabitants. Berlin's population tripled during the century, reaching 170,000 in 1800. Warsaw had 30,000 inhabitants in 1730, but almost 120,000 in 1794. St. Petersburg, founded in 1703, numbered more than 250,000 inhabitants a century later. The number of smaller cities with 20,000 to 50,000 people also increased considerably. This urban growth must, however, be kept in perspective. Even in France and Great Britain, probably somewhat less than 20 percent of the population lived in cities. And the town of 10,000 inhabitants was much more common than the giant urban center.

Growth of Capitals and Ports Between 1600 and 1750, the cities that grew most vigorously were capitals and ports. This situation reflects the success of monarchical state building during those years and the consequent burgeoning of bureaucracies, armies, courts, and other groups who lived in the capitals. The growth of port cities, in turn, reflects the expansion of European overseas trade—especially that of the Atlantic routes. Except for Manchester in England and Lyons in France, the new urban conglomerates were nonindustrial cities.

Furthermore, between 1600 and 1750, cities with populations of fewer than 40,000 inhabitants declined. These included older landlocked trading centers, medieval industrial cities, and ecclesiastical centers. They contributed less to the new political regimes, and the expansion of the putting-out system transferred production from medieval cities to the countryside because rural labor was cheaper than urban labor.

The Emergence of New Cities and the Growth of Small Towns In the mid-eighteenth century, a new pattern emerged. The rate of growth of existing large cities declined, new cities emerged, and existing smaller cities grew. Several factors were at work in the process. First was the general overall population increase. Second, the early stages of the Industrial Revolution, particularly in Britain, occurred in the countryside and fostered the growth of smaller towns and cities located near factories. Factory organization itself led to new concentrations of population.

Cities also grew as a result of the new prosperity of European agriculture, even where there was little industrialization. Improved agricultural production promoted the growth of nearby market towns and other urban centers that served agriculture or allowed more prosperous farmers to have access to consumer goods and recreation. This new pattern of urban growth—new cities and the expansion of smaller existing ones—would continue into the nineteenth century.

Urban Classes

Social divisions were as marked in eighteenth-century cities as they were in nineteenth-century industrial centers. The urban rich were often visibly segregated from the urban poor. Aristocrats and the upper middle class lived in fashionable town houses, often constructed around newly laid-out green squares. The poorest town dwellers usually congregated along the rivers. Small merchants and artisans lived above their shops. Whole families might live in a single room. Modern sanitary facilities were unknown. Pure water was rare. Cattle, pigs, goats, and other animals roamed the streets. All reports on the cities of Europe during this period emphasize both the striking grace and beauty of the dwellings of the wealthy and the dirt, filth, and stench that filled the streets. (See "Encountering the Past: Water, Washing, and Bathing.")

Poverty was not just an urban problem; it was usually worse in the countryside. In the city, however, poverty was more visible in the form of crime, prostitution, vagrancy, begging, and alcoholism. It did not require the Industrial Revolution and the urban factories to make the cities into hellholes for the poor and the dispossessed.

The Upper Classes At the top of the urban social structure stood a generally small group of nobles, large merchants, bankers, financiers, clergy, and government officials. These upper-class men controlled the political and economic affairs of the town. Normally, they constituted a self-appointed and self-electing oligarchy that governed the city through its corporation or city council. In a few cities on the Continent, artisan guilds controlled the corporations, but generally, the local nobility and the wealthiest commercial people dominated the councils.

The Middle Class Another group in the city was the prosperous, but not always immensely wealthy, merchants, trades people, bankers, and professional people. They were the most dynamic element of the urban population and made up the middle class, or bourgeoisie. The middle class itself was and would remain diverse and divided, with persons employed in the professions often resentful of those who drew their incomes from commerce. Less wealthy members of the middle class of whatever occupation resented wealthier members who might be connected to the nobility through social or business relationships.

The middle class had less wealth than most nobles, but more than urban artisans. Middle-class people lived in the cities and towns, and their sources of income had little or nothing to do with the land. In one way or another, they all benefited from expanding trade and commerce, whether as merchants, lawyers, or small-factory owners. They saw themselves as willing to put their capital and energy to work, whereas they portrayed the nobility as idle. The members of the middle class tended to be economically aggressive and socially ambitious. The middle class normally supported reform, change, and economic growth. They also wanted more rational regulations for trade and commerce, as did some progressive aristocrats.

The middle class was made up of people whose lives fostered the revolution in consumption. On one hand, as owners of factories and of wholesale and retail businesses, they produced and sold goods for the expanding consumer market; on the other hand, members of the middle class were among the chief consumers. They were also the people whose social values most fully embraced the commercial spirit. They might not enjoy the titles or privileges of the nobility, but they could enjoy material comfort

ENCOUNTERING THE PAST

Water, Washing, and Bathing

Clear water was scarce in Europe until the end of the nineteenth century. Households that did not have wells drew their water from streams, rivers, and public wells or fountains. Governments did nothing to assure the purity of a resource whose importance was less appreciated than it is today. Where the average American now uses about 210 liters of water per day, an individual in the eighteenth century may have needed only about 7.5 liters.

Public bathhouses were common during the Middle Ages. Bodily cleanliness was associated with spiritual purity, and aristocrats and townspeople bathed frequently. In the late medieval period, however, physicians began to argue that bathing was unhealthy. They reasoned that it opened the pores of the skin and allowed *miasma* (bad air) to infect the body with disease. Until the end of the eighteenth century, medical texts advised people to wash only the parts of the body that are publicly visible (hands, face, neck, and feet). Clean clothing was, however, considered indispensable. A switch from wool to linen garments, which began in the sixteenth century, made laundering easier, and social mores of the Renaissance-Reformation era placed a great deal of emphasis on the quality and appearance of one's clothing. Consequently, garments were washed much more frequently than bodies.

Attitudes began to change again toward the middle of the eighteenth century. Bathing was once more seen as healthful (particularly as the germ theory of disease received acceptance). Public baths reappeared in the nineteenth century, and great engineering projects were undertaken to provide urban dwellers with sewage disposal and clean water (see Chapter 23).

In the eighteenth century, washing linen clothing by hand was a major task of women servants.

J. B. S. Chardin, *The Washerwoman.* Nationalmuseum med Prins Eugens Waldemarsudde. Photo: The National Museum of Fine Arts

Why was washing such a time-consuming task in the eighteenth century?

WHAT CAUSED bathing customs to fluctuate from age to age?

and prosperity. It was this style of life that less well-off people could emulate as they sought to acquire consumer goods for themselves.

During the eighteenth century, the relationship between the middle class and the aristocracy was complicated. On one hand, the nobles, especially in England and France, increasingly embraced the commercial spirit associated with the middle class by improving their estates and investing in cities. On the other hand, wealthy members of the middle class often tried to imitate the lifestyle of the nobility by purchasing landed estates. The aspirations of the middle class for social mobility, however, conflicted with the determination of the nobles to maintain and reassert their own privileges and to protect their own wealth.

The bourgeoisie was not rising to challenge the nobility; rather, both were seeking to increase their existing political power and social prestige. The tensions that arose between the nobles and the middle class during the eighteenth century normally involved issues of power sharing or access to political influence, rather than clashes over values or goals associated with class.

The middle class in the cities also feared the lower urban classes as much as they envied the nobility. The lower orders were a potentially violent element in society, a threat to property, and, in their poverty, a drain on national resources. The lower classes, however, were much more varied than either the city aristocracy or the middle class cared to admit.

Artisans Shopkeepers, artisans, and wage earners were the single largest group in any city. They were grocers, butchers, fishmongers, carpenters, cabinetmakers, smiths, printers, hand-loom weavers, and tailors, to give a few examples. They had their own culture, values, and institutions. Like the peasants, economic vulnerability made them, in many respects, conservative. These urban classes also contributed to the revolution in consumption, however. They could buy more goods than ever before, and, to the extent their incomes permitted, many of them sought to copy the domestic consumption of the middle class.

The lives of these artisans and shopkeepers centered on their work and their neighborhoods. They usually lived near or at their place of employment. Most of them worked in shops with fewer than a half dozen other artisans. Their primary institution had historically been the guild, but by the eighteenth century, the guilds rarely exercised the influence their predecessors had in medieval or early modern Europe.

Nevertheless, the guilds were not to be ignored. They played a conservative role. Rather than seeking economic growth or innovation, they tried to preserve the jobs and skills of their members. To lessen competition, they attempted to prevent too many people from learning a particular skill.

The guilds also provided a framework for social and economic advancement. At an early age, a boy might become an apprentice to learn a craft or trade. After several years, he would be made a journeyman. Still later, if successful and competent, he might become a master. The artisan could also receive social benefits from the guilds, including aid for his family during sickness or the promise of admission for his son. The guilds were the chief protection for artisans against the workings of the commercial market. They were particularly strong in central Europe.

The Urban Riot

The artisan class, with its generally conservative outlook, maintained a rather fine sense of social and economic justice based largely on traditional practices. The most sensitive area was the price of bread, the staple food of the poor. If a baker or a grain merchant announced a price that was considered unjustly high, a riot might well ensue. Artisan leaders would confiscate the bread or grain and sell it for what the urban crowd considered a "just price." They would then give the money paid for the grain or bread to the baker or merchant. Thus, bread and food riots, which occurred throughout Europe, were not irrational acts of screaming, hungry people, but highly ritualized social phenomena of the Old Regime and its economy of scarcity.

Other kinds of riots also characterized eighteenth-century society and politics. The riot was a way in which people who were excluded in every other way from the political processes could make their will known. Sometimes religious bigotry led to urban riots. For example, in 1753, London Protestant mobs compelled the government to withdraw an act to legalize Jewish naturalization.

In these riots and in food riots, violence was normally directed against property rather than people. The rioters themselves were not disreputable people, but usually small shopkeepers, freeholders, artisans, and wage earners. They usually wanted only to restore a traditional right or practice that seemed endangered. Nevertheless, their actions could cause considerable turmoil and destruction.

During the last half of the century, urban riots increasingly involved political ends. Though often simultaneous with economic disturbances, the political riot always had nonartisan leadership or instigators. In fact, an eighteenth-century "crowd" was

often the tool of the upper classes. Such outbursts indicate that the crowd or mob had entered the European political and social arena well before the revolution in France.

THE JEWISH POPULATION: THE AGE OF THE GHETTO

HOW DID the suppression of Jews in European cities lead to the formation of ghettos?

Although the small Jewish communities of Amsterdam and other Western European cities became famous for their intellectual life and financial institutions, the Jewish population of Europe was concentrated in Poland, Lithuania, and Ukraine, where no fewer than 3 million Jews dwelled. Perhaps 150,000 Jews lived in the Habsburg lands, primarily Bohemia, around 1760. Fewer than 100,000 Jews lived in Germany. France had approximately 40,000 Jews. England and Holland each had a Jewish population of fewer than 10,000. There were even smaller groups of Jews elsewhere.

Jews dwelled in most nations without enjoying the rights and privileges that other subjects had unless monarchs specifically granted them to Jews. Jews were regarded as a kind of resident alien whose residence might well be temporary or changed at the whim of rulers.

No matter where they dwelled, Old Regime Jews lived apart in separate communities from non-Jewish Europeans. These communities might be distinct districts of cities, known as **ghettos**, or in primarily Jewish villages in the countryside. Jews were also treated as a distinct people religiously and legally. In Poland for much of the century, they were virtually self-governing. In other areas, they lived under the burden of discriminatory legislation. Except in England, Jews could not and did not mix in the mainstream of the societies in which they dwelled. This period, which may be said to have begun with the expulsion of the Jews from Spain at the end of the fifteenth century, is known as the age of the ghetto, or separate community.

ghettos Separate districts in cities and entire villages in the countryside where Jews lived apart from Christians in eighteenth-century Europe.

During the seventeenth century, a few Jews had helped finance the wars of major rulers. These financiers often became close to the rulers and were known as "court Jews." The court Jews and their financial abilities became famous. They tended to marry among themselves.

Most European Jews, however, lived in poverty. They occupied the most undesirable sections of cities or poor villages. Some were small-time moneylenders, but most worked at the lowest occupations. Their religious beliefs, rituals, and community set them apart. Virtually all laws and social institutions kept them socially inferior to and apart from their Christian neighbors.

Under the Old Regime, it is important to emphasize that this discrimination was based on religious separateness. Jews who converted to Christianity were welcomed, even if not always warmly, into the major political and social institutions of gentile European society. Until the last two decades of the eighteenth century, in every part of Europe, however, those Jews who remained loyal to their faith were subject to various religious, civil, and social disabilities. They could not pursue the professions freely, they often could not change residence without official permission, and they were excluded from the political structures of the nations in which they lived. Jews could be expelled from their homes, and their property could be confiscated. They could be required to listen to sermons that insulted their religion. Their children could be taken away from them and given Christian instruction. They knew their non-Jewish neighbors might suddenly turn against them and kill them.

In subsequent chapters, it will be shown how the end of the Old Regime brought major changes in the lives of European Jews and in their relationship to the larger culture.

During the Old Regime, European Jews were separated from non-Jews, typically in districts known as ghettos. Relegated to the least desirable section of a city or to rural villages, most lived in poverty. This watercolor painting depicts a street in Kazimlesz, the Jewish quarter of Cracow, Poland.

What was life like for the majority of Europe's Jews during the Old Regime?

SUMMARY

HOW DID tradition, hierarchy, and privilege shape life in the Old Regime?

Major Features of Life in the Old Regime Many aspects of life in the eighteenth century still followed traditional patterns. European economies were dominated by agriculture; nothing mattered more to most individuals—or their governments—than the grain harvest. Society was more oriented toward the past than the future. Rights accrued not to individuals, but to groups. *page 370*

WHAT WAS the foundation of the wealth and power for the eighteenth-century aristocracy?

The Aristocracy The aristocratic resurgence that took place across Europe was a noteworthy feature of eighteenth-century European social history. The nobility made up between 1 percent and 5 percent of the population in most European countries. They were wealthy and powerful; their income came largely from land ownership. In England especially, they also invested in various ventures, including industries. Other aristocratic characteristics varied from country to country, but nobles throughout Europe all tried to preserve noble exclusivity, to resist the growing power of the monarchies, and to improve their financial status. *page 370*

HOW WERE peasants and serfs tied to the land in eighteenth-century Europe?

The Land and Its Tillers Land was the basis of noble wealth, and its cultivation was the task of the huge class of peasants and serfs. Landowners controlled local government and the courts; continental Europe's tax burden fell on those who tilled the soil. Landowners' power increased the farther east one went in Europe. In Prussia, Austria, and Russia, a serf's life was nothing but a commodity to an aristocrat. Peasants revolted violently and repeatedly. *page 372*

WHAT ROLE did the family play in the economy of preindustrial Europe?

Family Structures and the Family Economy The "family economy" was the norm throughout Europe before the Industrial Revolution. In northwestern Europe, the "household" was generally a nuclear family and its servants. Premarital sex was common, and people married in their twenties, usually after spending several years earning wages. Eastern European "households" were larger, with more than nine members of three generations living together. Landowners in eastern Europe discouraged families from separating into multiple households. Everyone worked, who could, with the goal of supporting the family unit. The death of the father could easily spell disaster for the family. Women's economic contributions to the household were more important than their reproductive capacities. Women and babies experienced high mortality rates, and many infants were abandoned for economic reasons. *page 373*

WHAT LED to the agricultural revolution of the eighteenth century?

The Revolution in Agriculture Europe's population in 1750 was between 100 and 120 million people; by 1800, there were almost 190 million, and by 1850, there were 260 million. Historians have proposed many explanations for this population growth. One factor was the introduction of the potato from America. Increasing population led to increasing demand and prices for wheat and bread. This hurt peasants but helped larger landowners. Landlords began to treat crop cultivation as a commercial operation and introduced new techniques that increased crop yields. The economic and social organization of farming also changed: The enclosure movement in England rationalized the use of land and saw higher productivity. Governments sided with landowners, and serf revolts were suppressed. In eastern Europe, land ownership and social structures were less encouraging of agricultural innovation. *page 376*

WHY DID the Industrial Revolution begin in Britain?

The Industrial Revolution of the Eighteenth Century Europe's economy of scarcity was replaced by a demand-driven cycle of growth. Advertising and social emulation fueled consumer demand. In Great Britain political and economic factors were also favorable for innovation. The domestic system of textile production was the first area of industry to be transformed, through the invention of the spinning jenny in 1765, the water frame in 1769, and the power loom in the late 1780s. The 1769 steam engine was applied to industries ranging from mining to textiles to transportation. Iron became the backbone of industrial machinery. As work was reorganized to accommodate the new machines, labor was increasingly segregated by gender, and women's work was systematically devalued. *page 379*

WHAT PROBLEMS arose as a result of the growth of cities?

The Growth of Cities Many cities grew substantially between 1500 and 1800. Between 1600 and 1750, capital cities and ports grew most vigorously; most smaller cities actually lost population. After 1750, smaller cities began to grow more rapidly than larger ones, and entirely new cities emerged. City dwellers led radically different lives, depending on their social class. The upper classes lived quite comfortably and often controlled city government. The middle class had aspirations and fears that led them to support reform, change, and economic growth. Artisans, the largest group, were generally conservative. Bread riots were sparked by artisans who believed merchants were not charging "just" prices; other forms of riots could be fueled by religious prejudice or political agendas. *page 385*

HOW DID the suppression of Jews in European cities lead to the formation of ghettos?

The Jewish Population: The Age of the Ghetto Jews were segregated and discriminated against on religious grounds throughout Europe. The vast majority of Jews lived in eastern Europe, particularly Poland, Lithuania, and the Ukraine. In most countries Jews were treated as resident aliens, without political or civil rights and socially inferior; only in England was it possible for Jews to mingle with mainstream society. This was the age of the ghetto, or separate community, which were either distinct districts within cities or separate Jewish villages in rural areas. Most Jews were poor; one exceptional category was the so-called court Jews, who helped finance royal projects (usually wars). Jews, especially children, were sometimes forcibly converted to Christianity, and they were sometimes killed for their religious beliefs. *page 389*

REVIEW QUESTIONS

1. How did the situation of the English aristocracy differ from that of the French? What kind of privileges distinguished European aristocrats from other social groups?
2. What was the family economy? How did households in northwestern Europe differ from those in eastern Europe? In what ways were the lives of women constrained by the family economy?
3. What caused the Agricultural Revolution? To what extent did the English aristocracy contribute to it? What explains the growth of Europe's population in the eighteenth century? How did population growth change consumption?
4. What caused the Industrial Revolution of the eighteenth century? Why did Great Britain take the lead in the Industrial Revolution? What was city life like during the eighteenth century? How did the lifestyle of the upper class differ from that of the middle and lower classes? What were some of the causes of urban riots?

KEY TERMS

aristocratic resurgence (p. 372)
domestic system of textile production (p. 382)
enclosures (p. 377)
ghettos (p. 389)
Industrial Revolution (p. 379)
Old Regime (p. 370)
spinning jenny (p. 383)
water frame (p. 383)

16

The Transatlantic Economy, Trade Wars, and Colonial Rebellion

General James Wolfe was mortally wounded during his victory over the French at Quebec in 1759. This painting by the American artist Benjamin West (1738–1820) became famous for portraying the dying Wolfe and the officers around him in poses modeled after classical statues.

Getty Images Inc.–Hulton Archive Photos

What does the presence of Native Americans at Wolfe's death suggest about their role in colonial conflicts?

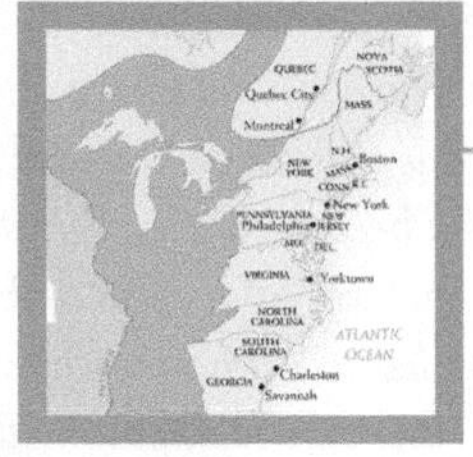

PERIODS OF EUROPEAN OVERSEAS EMPIRES *page 394*

HOW DID European contact with the rest of the world evolve in the centuries since the Renaissance?

MERCANTILE EMPIRES *page 395*

WHAT WERE the characteristics of European mercantile empires?

THE SPANISH COLONIAL SYSTEM *page 396*

HOW DID Spanish colonial organization reflect its imperial goals?

BLACK AFRICAN SLAVERY, THE PLANTATION SYSTEM, AND THE ATLANTIC ECONOMY *page 397*

WHAT WERE the origins of slavery in the Americas?

MID-EIGHTEENTH-CENTURY WARS *page 404*

WHY DID mid-eighteenth-century European wars often involve both continental and global conflicts?

THE AMERICAN REVOLUTION AND EUROPE *page 408*

WHAT WERE the causes of the American Revolution?

During the eighteenth century, Europeans began to make wars on a global scale. Austria and Prussia struggled in central Europe, and Great Britain and France competed for colonies abroad. The result was a new balance of power on the Continent and on the high seas. Prussia became one of Europe's leading nations and Great Britain won a world empire. Wars forced European states to subordinate financial planning to military policy and led to economic decisions that had far-reaching political consequences. These included the American Revolution, the development of enlightened absolutist monarchies, a financial crisis for the French monarchy, and reform of Spain's American empire.

PERIODS OF EUROPEAN OVERSEAS EMPIRES

HOW DID European contact with the rest of the world evolve in the centuries since the Renaissance?

Since the Renaissance, European contacts with the rest of the world have gone through four distinct stages. The first was that of the European discovery, exploration, initial conquest, and settlement of the New World. The second era—that of the mercantile empires, which are largely the concern of this chapter—was one of colonial trade rivalry among Spain, France, and Great Britain. The achievement of commercial goals, however, often sparked intense rivalry and conflict in key imperial trouble spots. As a result, the various imperial ventures led to the creation of large navies and a series of major naval wars at the midcentury—wars that in turn became linked to warfare on the European continent.

A fundamental element in these first two periods of European imperial ventures in the Americas was the presence of slavery. By the eighteenth century, the slave population of the New World consisted almost entirely of a black population that had either recently been forcibly imported from Africa or born to slaves whose forebearers had been forcibly imported from Africa. The Atlantic economy and the societies that arose in the Americas were, consequently, the creation of both Europeans and Africans while, as a result of the Spanish conquest, Native Americans were pressed toward the margins of those societies.

Finally, during the second period, both the British colonies of the North American seaboard and the Spanish colonies of Mexico and Central and South America emancipated themselves from European control. This same revolutionary era witnessed the beginning of the antislavery movement that extended through the third quarter of the nineteenth century.

The third stage of European contact with the non-European world occurred in the nineteenth century. During that period, European governments largely turned from their involvement in the Americas and carved out new formal empires involving the direct European administration of indigenous peoples in Africa and Asia.

The last period of the European empire occurred during the mid- and late twentieth century, with the decolonization of peoples who had previously lived under European colonial rule. (See Chapter 29.)

During the four-and-one-half centuries before decolonization, Europeans exerted political, military, and economic dominance over much of the rest of the world that was far disproportional to the geographical size or population of Europe. What allowed the Europeans initially to exert such influence and domination for so long over so much of the world was not any innate cultural superiority, but a technological supremacy related to naval power and gunpowder. Ships and guns allowed the Europeans to exercise their will almost wherever they chose.

MERCANTILE EMPIRES

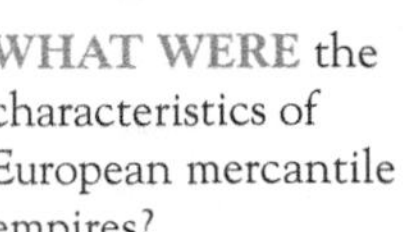

WHAT WERE the characteristics of European mercantile empires?

Navies and merchant shipping were the keystones of the mercantile empires that were meant to bring profit to a nation rather than to provide areas for settlement. The Treaty of Utrecht (1713) established the boundaries of empire during the first half of the eighteenth century.

Except for Brazil, which Portugal governed, and Dutch Guiana, Spain controlled all of mainland South America. In North America, it ruled Florida, Mexico, California, and the Southwest. The Spanish also governed Central America and the islands of Cuba, Puerto Rico, Trinidad, and the eastern part of Hispaniola that is today the Dominican Republic. The British Empire consisted of the colonies along the North Atlantic seaboard, Nova Scotia, Newfoundland, Bermuda, Jamaica, and Barbados. Britain also possessed a few trading stations on the Indian subcontinent. The French domains covered the Saint Lawrence River valley and the Ohio and Mississippi River valleys. They included the West Indian islands of Saint Domingue (modern Haiti on the western part of Hispaniola), Guadeloupe, and Martinique, and also stations in India and on the West Coast of Africa. The Dutch controlled Surinam, or Dutch Guiana, in South America, Cape Colony in what is today South Africa, and trading stations in West Africa, Sri Lanka, and Bengal in India. Most importantly, they also controlled the trade with Java in what is now Indonesia.

mercantilism Economic theory in which governments heavily regulated economic activity and promoted empires in order to produce a positive balance of trade.

MERCANTILIST GOALS

Critics have coined the term ***mercantilism*** to describe the economic theories that drove Europe's quest for empires. Mercantilists believed bullion was the measure of a country's wealth, and they advocated courses of action that encouraged its accumulation. The goal was to maintain an excess of exports over imports, for a favorable trade balance siphoned gold and silver away from trading partners. Mercantilists assumed the world's resources were limited and one nation's economy could grow only at the expense of others.

The economic well-being of the home country was the primary goal of the mercantilist system. It was taken for granted that a colony was the inferior partner in its relationship with its European sponsor. Colonies were established to provide markets and natural resources to support industries in the home country. The home country furnished its colonies with military security and political administration. Colonies were expected to remain subordinate and trade only with their homelands. Each country maintained monopolistic control of its colonies' commerce by means of navigation laws, tariffs, and regulations that prohibited trade with other colonies and European states.

Mercantilism worked better in theory than practice, for it was at odds with economic realities and human nature. Colonial and home markets failed to mesh. Spain could not produce sufficient goods for all of South America, and manufacturing in Britain's North American colonies competed with factories in England. It was also impossible to prevent trade among colonies belonging to different countries. English colonists, for instance, could buy sugar more cheaply from the French West Indies than from English suppliers, and efforts to prevent them simply encouraged smuggling and ultimately goaded them to rebel.

During the seventeenth and eighteenth centuries, European maritime nations established overseas empires and set up trading monopolies within them in an effort to magnify their economic strength. As this painting of the Old Custom House Quay in London suggests, trade from these empires and the tariffs imposed on it were expected to generate revenue for the home country. But behind many of the goods carried in the great sailing ships in the harbor and landed on these docks lay the labor of African slaves working on the plantations of North and South America.

Samuel Scott, *Old Custom House Quay* Collection. V & A Images, The Victoria and Albert Museum, London

How did eighteenth-century Europeans envision the relationship between European countries and their overseas colonies?

FRENCH–BRITISH RIVALRY

Major flash points existed between France and Britain in North America. Their colonists quarreled endlessly with each other over the coveted regions of the lower Saint Lawrence River valley, upper New England, and, later, the Ohio River valley. Other rivalries arose over fishing rights, the fur trade, and alliances with Native Americans. The heart of the eighteenth-century colonial rivalry in the Americas, however, lay in the West Indies. The West Indies plantations raised tobacco, cotton, indigo, coffee, and, above all, sugar, for which there existed huge markets in Europe. Only slave labor allowed the profitable cultivation of these products during the seventeenth and eighteenth centuries. (See "Encountering the Past: Sugar Enters the Western Diet," page 400.)

India was another area of French–British rivalry. In India, both France and Britain traded through privileged chartered companies that enjoyed a legal monopoly. The East India Company was the English institution; the French equivalent was the *Compagnie des Indes*. The original European footholds in India were trading posts called *factories*. They existed through privileges granted by various Indian governments that in theory were themselves subject to the decaying Mughal Empire, which exercised little effective authority.

QUICK REVIEW
Sites of Rivalry

- North America: Colonists quarrel over land and trade rights
- Indian subcontinent: French and British companies compete for trade rights
- French and European companies took control of local governments in India

Two circumstances in the mid–eighteenth century changed this situation in India. First, the administration and government of several Indian states had decayed. Second, to maintain their own security and to expand their privileges, each of the two companies began in effect to take over the government of some of the regions. Each group of Europeans hoped to checkmate the other.

The Dutch maintained their extensive commercial empire further to the east in what today is Indonesia. By the eighteenth century, the other European powers more or less acknowledged Dutch predominance in that region.

THE SPANISH COLONIAL SYSTEM

HOW DID Spanish colonial organization reflect its imperial goals?

Until the mid–eighteenth century, the primary purpose of the Spanish Empire was to supply Spain with the precious metals mined in the New World.

Colonial Government and the Regulation of Trade

Because Queen Isabella of Castile (r. 1474–1504) had commissioned Columbus, the technical legal link between the New World and Spain was the crown of Castile. The Castilian monarch assigned the government of America to the Council of the Indies, which, with the monarch, nominated the viceroys of New Spain (Mexico) and Peru. These viceroys served as the chief executives in the New World and carried out the laws issued by the Council of the Indies. Virtually all power flowed from the top of this political structure downward; in effect, local initiative or self-government scarcely existed.

The colonial political structures functioned largely to support Spanish commercial self-interests. The *Casa de Contratación* (House of Trade) in Seville regulated all trade with the New World. A complicated system of trade and bullion fleets administered from Seville maintained Spain's trade monopoly. Each year, a fleet of commercial vessels (the *flota*), controlled by Seville merchants and escorted by warships, carried merchandise from Spain to a few specified ports in America. After selling their wares, the ships were loaded with silver and gold bullion and then sailed back to Spain. The *flota* system always worked imperfectly, but trade outside it was illegal.

Colonial Reform under the Spanish Bourbon Monarchs

A crucial change occurred in the Spanish colonial system in the early eighteenth century. The War of the Spanish Succession (1701–1714) and the Treaty of Utrecht (1713) replaced the Spanish Habsburgs with the Bourbons of France on the Spanish throne. Philip V (r. 1700–1746) and his successors tried to use French administrative skills to reassert the imperial trade monopoly, which had decayed under the last Spanish Habsburgs, and thus to improve the domestic economy and revive Spanish power in Europe.

Under Philip V, Spanish coastal patrol vessels tried to suppress smuggling in American waters. An incident arising from this policy led to war with England in 1739, the year in which Philip established the viceroyalty of New Granada in the area that today includes Venezuela, Colombia, and Ecuador. The goal was to strengthen the royal government there.

The great midcentury wars exposed the vulnerability of the Spanish empire to naval attack and economic penetration. As an ally of France, Spain emerged as one of the defeated powers in 1763. Government circles then became convinced that the colonial system had to be reformed.

The Silver Mines of Potosi. Worked by conscripted Indian laborers under extremely harsh conditions, these mines provided Spain with a vast treasure in silver.

Hispanic Society of America

How did American silver shape the development of early modern Spain?

Charles III (r. 1759–1788) attempted to reassert Spain's control of the empire. Like his Bourbon predecessors, Charles emphasized royal ministers rather than councils. Thus, the role of both the Council of the Indies and the *Casa de Contratación* diminished. After 1765, Charles abolished the monopolies of Seville and Cádiz and permitted other Spanish cities to trade with America. He also opened more South American and Caribbean ports to trade and authorized commerce between Spanish ports in America. In 1776, he organized a fourth viceroyalty in the region of Río de la Plata, which included much of present-day Argentina, Uruguay, Paraguay, and Bolivia. (See Map 16–1, page 398.)

To increase the efficiency of tax collection and end bureaucratic corruption, Charles III introduced the institution of the *intendant* into the Spanish Empire. These loyal, royal bureaucrats were patterned on the domestic French *intendants* made so famous and effective as agents of French royal administration under the absolutism of Louis XIV.

The late-eighteenth-century Bourbon reforms did stimulate the imperial Spanish economy. Trade expanded and became more varied. These reforms, however, also brought the empire more fully under direct Spanish control. Many *peninsulares* (persons born in Spain) entered the New World to fill new posts, which were often the most profitable jobs in the region. As a result of these policies, the *creoles* (persons of European descent born in the Spanish colonies) came to feel they were second-class subjects. In time, their resentment would provide a major source of the discontent leading to the wars of independence in the early nineteenth century.

BLACK AFRICAN SLAVERY, THE PLANTATION SYSTEM, AND THE ATLANTIC ECONOMY

WHAT WERE the origins of slavery in the Americas?

Within various parts of Europe itself, slavery had existed since ancient times. Black slaves from Africa were not uncommon in various parts of the Mediterranean, and a few found their way into northern Europe. In the fifteenth century, they were typically used as personal servants or displayed because of the novelty of their color in royal courts or in wealthy homes.

Yet, from the sixteenth century onward, first within the West Indies and the Spanish and Portuguese settlements in South America and then in the British colonies on the South Atlantic seaboard of North America, slave labor became a fundamental social and economic factor. The development of those plantation economies based on slave labor led to unprecedented interaction between the peoples of Europe and Africa and between the European settlers in the Americas and Africa.

MAP EXPLORATION

Interactive map: To explore this map further, go to www.myhistorylab.com

MAP 16–1 **Viceroyalties in Latin America in 1780** The late-eighteenth-century viceroyalites in Latin America display the effort of the Spanish Bourbon monarchy to establish more direct control of the colonies. They sought this control through the introduction of more royal officials and by establishing more governmental districts.

Given the size of the Spanish viceroyalties, how effective do you think Spain was in controlling its Latin American territories and trade?

From that point onward, Africa and Africans were drawn into the Western experience as never before in history.

The African Presence in the Americas

Once they had encountered and begun to settle the New World, the Spanish and Portuguese faced a severe shortage of labor. At first, they used Native Americans as laborers, but during the sixteenth century as well as afterward, disease killed hundreds of thousands of the native population. The Spanish and Portuguese then turned to the labor of imported African slaves. Settlers in the English colonies of North America during the seventeenth century turned more slowly to slavery, with the largest number coming to the Chesapeake Bay region of Virginia and Maryland and then later into the low country of the Carolinas.

The major sources for slaves were slave markets on the West African Coast from Senegambia to Angola. Slavery and an extensive slave trade had existed in West Africa for centuries. Just as particular social and economic conditions in Europe had led to the voyages of exploration and settlement, political and military conditions in Africa and warfare among various African nations similarly created a supply of slaves that certain African societies were willing to sell to Europeans.

The West Indies, Brazil, and Sugar Although citizens of the United States mark the beginning of slavery in 1619 with the arrival of African slaves on a Dutch ship in Jamestown, Virginia, over a century of slave trading in the West Indies and South America had preceded that event. Indeed, by the late sixteenth century, Africans had become a major social presence in the West Indies and in the major cities of both Spanish and Portuguese South America. In these places, African slaves equaled or more generally surpassed the numbers of white European settlers in what soon constituted multiracial societies.

Within much of Spanish South America, the numbers of slaves declined during the late seventeenth century, and slavery became somewhat less fundamental there than elsewhere. Slavery continued to expand its influence, however, in Brazil and in the Caribbean through the spreading cultivation of sugar to meet the demand of the European market. By the close of the seventeenth century, the Caribbean islands were the world center for the production of sugar and the chief supplier for the ever-growing demand for it. The opening of new areas of cultivation and other economic enterprises required additional slaves during the eighteenth century, a period of major slave importation. A vast increase in the number of Africans brought as slaves to the Americas occurred during the eighteenth century, with most arriving in the Caribbean or Brazil.

Newly imported African slaves were needed because the fertility rate of the earlier slave population was low and the death rate high from disease, overwork, and malnutrition. Restocking through the slave trade meant the slave population of the West Indies and Brazil consisted of African-born persons rather than of persons of African descent. Consequently, one of the key factors in the social life of many of the areas of American slavery during the eighteenth century was the presence of persons newly arrived from Africa, carrying with them African languages, religion, culture, and local African ethnic identities that they would infuse into the already existing slave communities.

Slavery and the Transatlantic Economy

Different nations dominated the slave trade in different periods. During the sixteenth century, the Portuguese and the Spanish were most involved. The Dutch supplanted them during most of the seventeenth century. Thereafter, during the late seventeenth and eighteenth centuries, the English were the chief slave traders. French traders also participated in the trade.

ENCOUNTERING THE PAST

Sugar Enters the Western Diet

Sugarcane requires tropical temperatures and abundant rainfall. It could not be cultivated in Europe, and, prior to the discovery of the Americas, European consumers had to import it from Arab lands at great expense. It was a luxury item that few could afford.

Columbus quickly recognized the Caribbean's potential as a sugar-producing region, and he carried cane to the New World in 1493. Within a decade slaves were being used to grow it on Santo Domingo. Demand for sugar grew steadily until, by the eighteenth century, the small Caribbean islands that produced it (with slave labor) had become the most valuable real estate on earth. North American colonies imported large amounts of sugar to make rum, and it became Britain's largest colonial import. The market for it accelerated as Europeans acquired a taste for other tropical products—coffee, tea, and chocolate. Enormous quantities of these stimulants (all sweetened with sugar) were consumed in the seventeenth and eighteenth centuries.

As production increased, prices fell, but demand never slackened. The greater availability of a former luxury item persuaded people they were improving their living standards by consuming more and more of it. During the nineteenth century, the custom developed in Western countries to end meals with desserts—foods sweetened with sugar.

WHY DID demand for sugar steadily accelerate in Western societies from the sixteenth century to the present?

Sugar was both raised and processed on plantations such as this one in Brazil.

Library of Congress

Why were sugar production and African slavery so closely intertwined?

Slavery touched most of the economy of the transatlantic world. Colonial trade followed roughly a geographic triangle. European goods—often guns—were carried to Africa to be exchanged for slaves, who were then taken to the West Indies, where they were traded for sugar and other tropical products, which were then shipped to Europe. Another major trade pattern existed between New England and the West Indies with New England fish, rum, or lumber being traded for sugar. All the shippers who handled cotton, tobacco, and sugar depended on slavery, though they might not have had direct contact with the institution, as did all the manufacturers and merchants who produced finished products for the consumer market.

As had been the case during previous centuries, eighteenth-century political turmoil in Africa, such as the civil wars in the Kingdom of Kongo (modern Angola and Republic of Congo), increased the supply of slaves during that period. Similar political unrest and turmoil in the Gold Coast area (modern Ghana) during the eighteenth century increased the supply of African captives to be sold into American slavery. Consequently, warfare in West Africa, often far into the interior, and the economic development of the American Atlantic seaboard were closely related.

This eighteenth-century print shows bound African captives being forced to a slaving port. It was largely African middlemen who captured slaves in the interior and marched them to the coast.

North Wind Picture Archives

Under what circumstances were most Africans enslaved?

THE EXPERIENCE OF SLAVERY

The Portuguese, Spanish, Dutch, French, and English slave traders forcibly transported several million (perhaps more than 9 million; the exact numbers are disputed) Africans to the New World—the largest forced intercontinental migration in human history. The conditions of slaves' passage across the Atlantic were wretched. Many Africans died during the crossing. (See "Compare & Connect: The Atlantic Passage," pages 402–403.)

The newly arrived Africans were subjected to a process known as *seasoning*, during which they were prepared for the laborious discipline of slavery and made to understand that they were no longer free. The process might involve receiving new names, acquiring new work skills, and learning, to some extent, the local European language. Generally, North American plantation owners were only willing to purchase such recently arrived Africans seasoned in the West Indies.

Language and Culture Within the sharply restricted confines of slavery, the recently arrived Africans were able, at least for a time, to sustain elements of their own culture and social structures. From the West Indies southward throughout the eighteenth century, there were more people whose first language was African rather than European. It would take more than two generations for the colonial language to dominate, and even then the result was often a dialect combining an African and a European language.

Through these languages, Africans on plantation estates could organize themselves into nations with similar, though not necessarily identical, ethnic ties to regions of West Africa. These nations that the plantation experience organized and sustained also became the basis for a wide variety of religious communities among African slaves who had roots in their African experience. In this manner, some Africans maintained a loyalty to the Islamic faith of their homeland. Many of the African nations on plantations, such as those of Brazil, organized lay religious brotherhoods that carried out various kinds of charitable work within the slave communities.

The shared language of a particular African nation in the Americas enabled the slaves to communicate among themselves during revolts such as those in South Carolina in 1739, in Jamaica in the early 1760s, and, most successfully, during the Haitian Revolution of the 1790s.

Daily Life The life conditions of plantation slaves differed from colony to colony. Black slaves living in Portuguese areas had the fewest legal protections. In the Spanish colonies, the church attempted to provide some protection for black slaves but devoted more effort toward the welfare of Native Americans. Slave codes were developed in the British and the French colonies during the seventeenth century, but they provided only the most limited protection to slaves while assuring dominance to their owners.

COMPARE & CONNECT

THE ATLANTIC PASSAGE

Slavery lay at the core of the eighteenth-century transatlantic economy. At the heart of slavery lay the forced transportation in slave ships across the Atlantic of millions of Africans to the Americas. The frightening and horrific character of the Atlantic Passage became widely known through the memoirs of sailors and slave trade captains. Later the groups that after the mid-eighteenth century sought the abolition of slavery made known the inhumanity of the passage through published attacks on the slave trade and by providing illustrations of slave ships such as that of the *Brooks*.

QUESTIONS

1. Who are the various people described in this document who in one way or another were involved in or profited from the slave trade?
2. What dangers did the Africans face on the voyage?
3. What contemporary attitudes could have led this captain to treat and think of his human cargo simply as goods to be transported?
4. How might the publication of the interior compartments of a slave ship have served the cause of antislavery? How and why might this illustration of a slave ship have proved more persuasive in rousing antislavery sentiment than a prose description?
5. How would this illustration and the description of the Atlantic Passage have contrasted with contemporary illustrations and memoirs of victorious naval battles on the high seas?

I. A SLAVE TRADER DESCRIBES THE ATLANTIC PASSAGE

During 1693 and 1694, Captain Thomas Phillips carried slaves from Africa to Barbados on the ship Hannibal. *The financial backer of the voyage was the Royal African Company of London, which held an English crown monopoly on slave trading. Phillips sailed to the west coast of Africa, where he purchased the Africans who were sold into slavery by an African king. Then he set sail westward.*

Having bought my complement of 700 slaves, 480 men and 220 women, and finish'd all my business at Whidaw [on the Gold Coast of Africa], I took my leave of the old king and his *cappasheirs* [attendants], and parted, with many affectionate expressions on both sides, being forced to promise him that I would return again the next year, with several things he desired me to bring from England. . . . I set sail the 27th of July in the morning, accompany'd with the East-India Merchant, who had bought 650 slaves, for the Island of St. Thomas . . . from which we took our departure on August 25th and set sail for Barbadoes.

We spent in our passage from St. Thomas to Barbadoes two months eleven days, from the 25th of August to the 4th of November following: in which time there happened such sickness and mortality among my poor men and Negroes. Of the first we buried 14, and of the last 320, which was a great detriment to our voyage, the Royal African Company losing ten pounds by every slave that died, and the owners of the ship ten pounds ten shillings, being the freight agreed on to be paid by the charter-party for every Negro delivered alive ashore to the African Company's agents at Barbadoes. . . . The loss in all amounted to near 6500 pounds sterling.

The distemper which my men as well as the blacks mostly died of was the white flux, which was so violent and inveterate that no medicine would in the least check it, so that when any of our men were seized with it, we esteemed him a dead man, as he generally proved. . . .

The Negroes are so incident to [subject to] the small-pox that few ships that carry them escape without it, and sometimes it makes vast havoc and destruction among them. But tho' we had 100 at a time sick of it, and that it went thro' the ship, yet we lost not above a dozen by it. All the assistance we gave the diseased was only as much water as they desir'd to drink, and some palm-oil to annoint their sores, and they would generally recover without any other helps but what kind nature gave them. . . .

But what the smallpox spar'd, the flux swept off, to our great regret, after all our pains and care to give them their messes in due order and season, keeping their lodgings as clean and sweet as possible, and enduring so much misery and stench so long among a parcel of creatures nastier than swine, and after all our expectations to be defeated by their mortality. . . .

No gold-finders can endure so much noisome slavery as they do who carry Negroes; for those have some respite and satisfaction, but we endure twice the misery; and yet by their mortality our voyages are ruin'd, and we pine and fret ourselves to death, and take so much pains to so little purpose.

Source: From Thomas Phillips, "Journal," *A Collection of Voyages and Travels*, Vol. 6, ed. by Awnsham and John Churchill (London: Henry Linot, 1746), as quoted in Thomas Howard, ed., *Black Voyage: Eyewitness Accounts of the Atlantic Slave Trade* (Boston: Little, Brown and Company, 1971), pp. 85–87.

II. THE SLAVE SHIP *BROOKES*

This print records the main decks of the 320-ton slave ship *Brookes*.

The average space for each African destined for slavery in the Americas was 78 inches by 16 inches. The Africans were normally shackled to assure discipline and to prevent their injuring the crew. Iron shackles also prevented Africans from committing suicide on the voyage.

The ship measured 25 feet wide and 100 feet long.

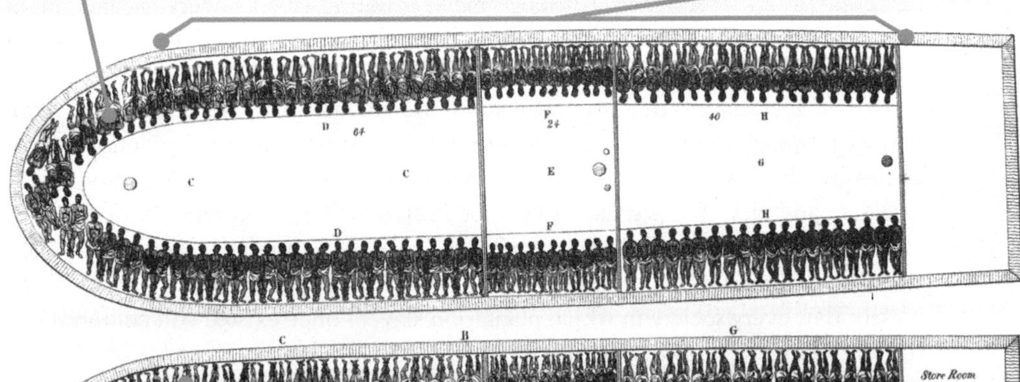

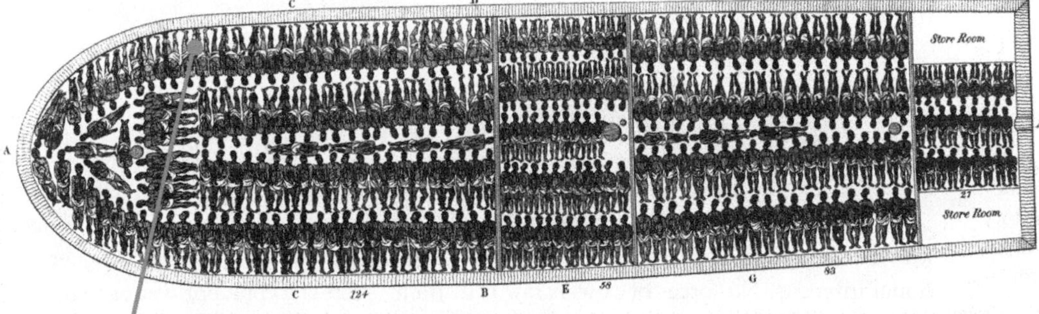

Through the most inhumane use of space efficiency, 609 slaves could be crammed onboard for the nightmarish passage to America. A Parliamentary inquiry in 1788 found that the ship had been designed to carry no more than approximately 450 persons.

Library of Congress

What does this image reveal about conditions aboard slave ships?

Source: (See "*A Slave Trader Describes the Atlantic Passage.*")

Slaves on the plantations of the American South were the chattel property of their masters and their lives were grim. Some artists sought to disguise this harsh reality by depicting the lighter moments of slave society, as in this scene of slaves dancing.

Getty Images Inc.–Hulton Archive Photos

What elements of African culture are depicted in this painting?

Slave owners always feared a revolt, and legislation and other regulations were intended to prevent one. Slave masters were permitted to whip slaves and inflict other harsh corporal punishment. Furthermore, slaves were often forbidden to gather in large groups lest they plan a revolt. In most of these slave societies, the law did not recognize slave marriages. Legally, the children of slaves were slaves, and the owner of their parents owned them too. Owners could separate slave families, or their members could be sold separately after owners died. The slaves' welfare and their lives were sacrificed to the continuing expansion of the sugar, rice, and tobacco plantations that made their owners wealthy and that produced goods for European consumers.

Conversion to Christianity Most African slaves transported to the Americas were, like the Native Americans, eventually converted to Christianity. Some African religious practices survived in muted forms, gradually separated from African religious belief. Although slaves did manage to mix Christianity with their previous African religions, their conversion to Christianity was nonetheless another example, like that of the Native Americans, of the crushing of a set of non-European cultural values in the context of the New World economies and social structures.

European Racial Attitudes Many Europeans considered Africans to be savages or less than civilized. Still others looked down on them simply because they were slaves. In virtually all these plantation societies, race was an important element in keeping black slaves in subservience. Although racial thinking about slavery became important primarily in the nineteenth century, that slaves were black and masters were white was as fundamental to the system as that slaves were chattel property.

The plantations that stretched from the middle Atlantic colonies of North America through the West Indies and into Brazil constituted a vast corridor of slave societies in which social and economic subordination was based on both involuntary servitude and race. These societies had not existed before the European discovery and exploitation of the Americas. In its complete dependence on slave labor and racial differences, this kind of society was unique in both European and world history. To the present day, every society in which plantation slavery once existed still contends with the long-term effects of that institution.

QUICK REVIEW

Slaves' Lives

- Conditions on plantations varied from colony to colony
- Slave masters had all but unlimited power over slaves
- Race-based slavery in the Americas created a kind of society that was unique in world history

MID-EIGHTEENTH-CENTURY WARS

WHY DID mid-eighteenth-century European wars often involve both continental and global conflicts?

From the standpoint of international relations, the state system of the mid–eighteenth century was quite unstable and tended to lead the major states of Europe into prolonged warfare. The statesmen of the period generally assumed that warfare could further national interests. No forces or powers saw it in their interest to prevent war or maintain peace. Consequently, nations often viewed periods of peace at the conclusion of a war simply as opportunities to recoup their strength, so that they could start fighting again to seize another nation's territory or disrupt another empire's trading monopoly.

The two fundamental areas of great power rivalry were the overseas empires and central and eastern Europe. Conflict in one of these regions repeatedly overlapped with conflict in the other, and this interaction influenced strategy and the pattern of alliances among the great powers.

The War of Jenkins's Ear

By the mid–eighteenth century, the West Indies had become a hotbed of trade rivalry and illegal smuggling. Much to British chagrin, the Spanish government took its own alleged trading monopoly seriously and maintained coastal patrols, which boarded and searched English vessels to look for contraband.

In 1731, during one such boarding operation, there was a fight, and the Spaniards cut off the ear of an English captain named Robert Jenkins. Thereafter he carried about his severed ear preserved in a jar of brandy. This incident was of little importance until 1738, when Jenkins appeared before the British Parliament, reportedly brandishing his ear as an example of Spanish atrocities to British merchants in the West Indies. The British merchant and West Indian planters lobbied Parliament to relieve Spanish intervention in their trade. Sir Robert Walpole (1676–1745), the British prime minister, could not resist these pressures. In late 1739, Britain went to war with Spain. This war might have been a relatively minor event, but because of developments in continental European politics, it became the opening encounter to a series of European wars fought across the world until 1815.

The War of the Austrian Succession (1740–1748)

In December 1740, after being king of Prussia for less than seven months, Frederick II (r. 1740–1786) seized the Austrian province of Silesia in eastern Germany. The invasion shattered the provisions of the Pragmatic Sanction (see Chapter 13) and upset the continental balance of power.

Maria Theresa Preserves the Habsburg Empire The Prussian seizure of Silesia could have marked the opening of a general hunting season on Habsburg holdings and the beginning of revolts by Habsburg subjects. Instead, it led to new political allegiances. Maria Theresa's (r. 1740–1780) great achievement was not the reconquest of Silesia, which eluded her, but the preservation of the Habsburg Empire as a major political power. She won loyalty and support from her various subjects not merely through her heroism, but by granting new privileges to the nobility. Most significantly, the empress recognized Hungary as the most important of her crowns and promised the Magyar nobility local autonomy. She thus preserved the Habsburg state, but at considerable cost to the power of the central monarchy.

France Draws Great Britain into the War The war over the Austrian succession and the British–Spanish commercial conflict could have remained separate disputes. What united them was the role of France. Aggressive court aristocrats compelled the elderly Cardinal Fleury (1653–1743), first minister of Louis XV (r. 1715–1774), to abandon his planned naval attack on British trade and instead to support the Prussian aggression against Austria, the traditional enemy of France. This was among the more fateful decisions in French history.

In the first place, aid to Prussia consolidated a new and powerful state in Germany. That new power could, and indeed later did, endanger France. Second, the French move against Austria brought Great Britain into the continental war, as Britain sought to make sure the Low Countries remained in the friendly hands of Austria, not France. In 1744, the British–French conflict expanded beyond the Continent when France supported Spain against Britain in the New World. As a result, French military and economic resources were badly divided. The war ended in a stalemate in 1748 with the Treaty of Aix-la-Chapelle. Prussia retained Silesia, and Spain renewed Britain's privilege from the Treaty of Utrecht (1713) to import slaves into the Spanish colonies.

Overview Eighteenth-Century Conflicts

DATE	WAR	PARTICIPANTS	FACTORS
1739	The War of Jenkins's Ear	Great Britain vs. Spain	Sparked by British captain Robert Jenkins's account of atrocities inflicted on British merchants by Spaniards
1740–1748	The War of the Austrian Succession	Prussia and France vs. Austria and Great Britain	France and Great Britain were dragged into this war after Prussia seized an Austrian province
1756–1763	The Seven Years' War	France and Austria vs. Prussia	Prussia was aided financially by Great Britain in this war that continued in America between France and Britain
1776–1783	The American Revolution	Great Britain vs. Colonial America	Fought for American independence from Great Britain; France and Spain joined the colonists before war's end

The "Diplomatic Revolution" of 1756

Although the Treaty of Aix-la-Chapelle had brought peace in Europe, France and Great Britain continued to struggle unofficially in the Ohio River valley and in upper New England. These clashes were the prelude to what is known in American history as the French and Indian War, which formally erupted in the summer of 1755.

Before war commenced again in Europe, however, a dramatic shift of alliances took place, in part, as a result of the events in North America. The British king, George II (r. 1727–1760), who was also the Elector of Hanover in Germany, thought the French might attack Hanover in response to the conflict in America. In January 1756, Britain and Prussia signed the Convention of Westminster, a defensive alliance aimed at preventing the entry of foreign troops into the German states. Whereas George II feared a French attack on Hanover, Frederick II feared an alliance of Russia and Austria. The convention meant that Great Britain, the ally of Austria since the wars of Louis XIV, had now joined forces with Austria's major eighteenth-century enemy.

Maria Theresa was despondent over this development. It delighted her foreign minister, Prince Wenzel Anton Kaunitz (1711–1794), however. He had long hoped for an alliance with France to help dismember Prussia and, in May 1756, France and Austria signed a defensive alliance. France would now fight to restore Austrian supremacy in central Europe.

The Seven Years' War (1756–1763)

Once again, however, Frederick II precipitated a European war that extended into a colonial theater.

Frederick the Great Opens Hostilities In August 1756, Frederick II opened what would become the Seven Years' War by invading Saxony. Frederick considered this to be a preemptive strike against a conspiracy by Saxony, Austria, and France to destroy Prussian power. The invasion itself, however, created the very destructive alliance that Frederick feared. In the spring of 1757, France and Austria made a new alliance dedicated to the destruction of Prussia. Sweden, Russia, and many of the smaller German states joined them.

Two factors saved Prussia. First, Britain furnished considerable financial aid. Second, in 1762, Empress Elizabeth of Russia (r. 1741–1762) died. Her successor, Tsar Peter III, immediately made peace with Prussia, thus relieving Frederick of one enemy and allowing him to hold off Austria and France. The Treaty of Hubertusburg of 1763 ended the continental conflict with no significant changes in prewar borders.

This scene, painted by artist Edward Penny, shows Robert Clive receiving a sum of money from Siraj-ud-daulah, the Mughal Nawab of Bengal, for injured officers and soldiers at Plassey. Clive's victory in 1757 at the Battle of Plassey brought English domination of the Indian subcontinent for almost two centuries. Clive had won the battle largely through bribing many of the Nawab's troops and potential allies.

Erich Lessing © The Trustees of the British Museum/Art Resource, NY

What role did private companies play in the British domination of India?

William Pitt's Strategy for Winning North America The survival of Prussia was less impressive to the rest of Europe than were the victories of Great Britain in every theater of conflict. The architect of these victories was William Pitt the Elder (1708–1778).

North America was the center of Pitt's real concern. Put simply, he wanted all of North America east of the Mississippi for Great Britain, and that was what he won. He sent more than 40,000 regular English and colonial troops against the French in Canada and achieved unprecedented cooperation with the American colonies, whose leaders realized they might finally defeat their French neighbors. The French government was unwilling and unable to direct similar resources against the English in America. In September 1759, on the Plains of Abraham, overlooking the valley of the Saint Lawrence River at Quebec City, the British army under James Wolfe defeated the French under Louis Joseph de Montcalm. The French Empire in Canada was ending.

Moreover, the major islands of the French West Indies fell to British fleets. Between 1755 and 1760, the value of the French colonial trade fell by more than 80 percent. In India, British victories opened the way for the eventual conquest of Bengal in northeast India and later of all of India by the British East India Company. (See Chapter 25.) Never had Great Britain or any other European power experienced such a complete worldwide military victory.

The Treaty of Paris of 1763 The Treaty of Paris of 1763 reflected somewhat less of a victory than Britain had won on the battlefield. Britain received all of Canada, the Ohio River valley, and the eastern half of the Mississippi River valley. Britain returned Pondicherry and Chandernagore in India and the West Indian sugar islands of Guadeloupe and Martinique to the French.

The Seven Years' War had been a vast worldwide conflict. At great internal sacrifice, Prussia had permanently wrested Silesia from Austria and had turned the Holy Roman Empire into an empty shell. France, though still having sources of colonial income, was no longer a great colonial power. The Spanish Empire remained largely intact, but the British were still determined to penetrate its markets. In India, the British East India Company continued to impose its own authority on the decaying indigenous governments. In North America, the British government faced the task of organizing its new territories. From this time until World War II, Great Britain was a world power, not just a European one.

The quarter century of warfare also caused a long series of domestic crises among the European powers. The financial burdens of the wars had astounded all contemporaries. Every power had to increase its revenues to pay its war debt and finance its preparation for the next combat. Nowhere did this search for revenue lead to more far-ranging consequences than in the British colonies in North America.

QUICK REVIEW

Treaty of Paris (1763)

- Ended the Seven Years' War
- Britain gave France generous terms
- War launched Britain as a global power

THE AMERICAN REVOLUTION AND EUROPE

WHAT WERE the causes of the American Revolution?

The revolt of the British colonies in North America marked the beginning of the end of European colonial domination of the American continents. The War of the American Revolution also continued the conflict between France and Great Britain. The French support of the Americans deepened the existing financial and administrative difficulties of the French monarchy.

MAP EXPLORATION

Interactive map: To explore this map further, go to www.myhistorylab.com

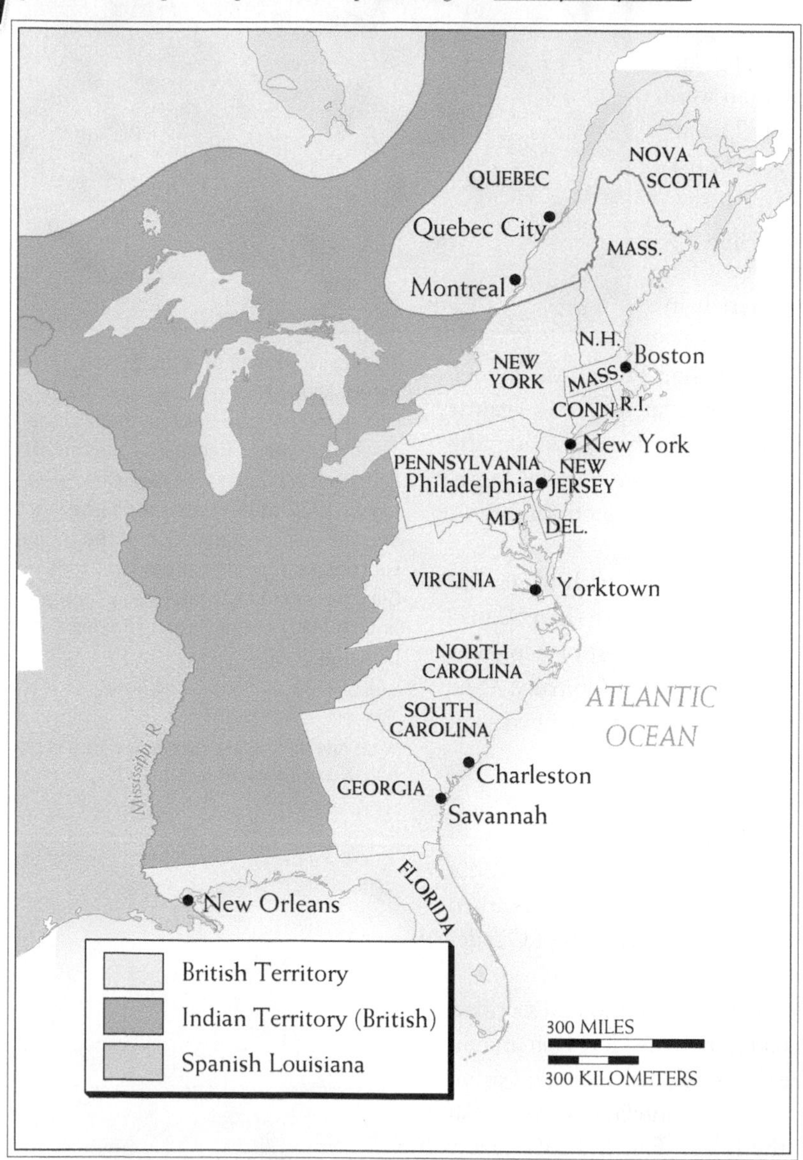

MAP 16–2 **North America in 1763** In the year of the victory over France, the English colonies lay along the Atlantic seaboard. The difficulties of organizing authority over the previous French territory in Canada and west of the Appalachian Mountains would contribute to the coming of the American Revolution.

How costly would it seem to conquer and control the territory encompassing the British colonies, former French Canada, and land east of the Mississippi River?

Resistance to the Imperial Search for Revenue

After the Treaty of Paris of 1763, the British government faced two imperial problems. The first was the sheer cost of maintaining their empire, which the British felt they could no longer carry alone. Since the American colonies had been the chief beneficiaries of the conflict, the British felt it was rational for the colonies henceforth to bear part of the cost of their protection and administration. The second problem was the vast expanse of new territory in North America that the British had to organize. This included all the land from the mouth of the Saint Lawrence River to the Mississippi River, with its French settlers and, more importantly, its Native Americans. (See Map 16–2.)

The British drive for revenue began in 1764 with the passage of the Sugar Act. The measure attempted to produce more revenue from imports into the colonies by the rigorous collection of what was actually a lower tax. The next year, Parliament passed the Stamp Act, which put a tax on legal documents and other items such as newspapers.

The Americans responded that they alone, through their colonial assemblies, had the right to tax themselves and that they were not represented in Parliament. Furthermore, they feared that if their colonial government was financed from outside, they would lose control over it. In October 1765, the Stamp Act Congress met in America and drew up a protest to the crown. The colonists agreed to refuse to import British goods. In 1766, Parliament repealed the Stamp Act, but through the Declaratory Act said it had the power to legislate for the colonies.

The Stamp Act crisis set the pattern for the next ten years. Parliament, under the leadership of a royal minister, would approve revenue or administrative legislation. The Americans would then resist by reasoned argument, economic pressure, and violence. Then the British would repeal the legislation, and the process would begin again. Each time, tempers on both sides became more frayed and positions more irreconcilable. With each clash, the Americans more fully developed their own thinking about political liberty.

The Crisis and Independence

Many Americans fiercely objected to the British Parliament's attempts to tax the colonies. This print of a British tax collector being tarred and feathered warned officials of what could happen to them if they tried to collect these taxes.

Philip Dawe (c. 1750–c. 1785), *The Bostonians Paying the Excise-Man or Tarring & Feathering.* London, 1774. Colored Engraving. The Gilder Lehman Collection on deposit at the Pierpont Morgan Library. GL 4961.01. Photography: Joseph Zehavi. The Pierpont Morgan Library/Art Resource, NY

How did Americans evade, intimidate, and harass British officials?

In 1767, Charles Townshend (1725–1767), as Chancellor of the Exchequer, the British finance minister, led Parliament to pass a series of revenue acts relating to colonial imports. The colonists again resisted. The ministry sent over its own customs agents to administer the laws. To protect these new officers, the British sent troops to Boston in 1768. The obvious tensions resulted. In March 1770, the Boston Massacre, in which British troops killed five citizens, took place. That same year, Parliament repealed all of the Townshend duties except the one on tea.

In May 1773, Parliament passed a new law relating to the sale of tea by the East India Company. The measure permitted the direct importation of tea into the American colonies. It actually lowered the price of tea while retaining the tax imposed without the colonists' consent. In some cities, the colonists refused to permit the unloading of the tea; in Boston, a shipload of tea was thrown into the harbor.

The British ministry of Lord North (1732–1792) was determined to assert the authority of Parliament over the colonies. During 1774, Parliament passed a series of laws known in American history as the **Intolerable Acts**. These measures closed the port of Boston, reorganized the government of Massachusetts, allowed troops to be quartered in private homes, and removed the trials of royal customs officials to England. The same year, the Quebec Act extended the boundaries of Quebec to include the Ohio River valley. The Americans regarded the Quebec Act as an attempt to prevent their mode of self-government from spreading beyond the Appalachian Mountains.

During these years, citizens critical of British policy had established committees of correspondence throughout the colonies. In September 1774, these committees organized the First Continental Congress in Philadelphia. This body hoped to persuade Parliament to restore self-government in the colonies and abandon its direct supervision of colonial affairs. Conciliation, however, was not forthcoming. By April 1775, the Battles of Lexington and Concord had been fought.

The Second Continental Congress gathered in May 1775. It still sought conciliation with Britain, but the pressure of events led it to begin to conduct the government of the colonies. By August 1775, George III had declared the colonies in rebellion. On July 4, 1776, the Continental Congress adopted the Declaration of Independence. Thereafter, the War of the American Revolution continued until 1781, when the forces of George Washington defeated those of Lord Cornwallis at Yorktown. Early in 1778, however, the war had widened into a European conflict when Benjamin Franklin (1706–1790) persuaded the French government to support the rebellion. In 1779, the Spanish also joined the war against Britain. The 1783 Treaty of Paris concluded the conflict, and the thirteen American colonies finally established their independence.

Intolerable Acts Series of laws passed by Parliament in 1774 that closed the port of Boston, reorganized the government of Massachusetts, quartered soldiers in private homes, and transferred trials of customs officials accused of crimes to England.

American Political Ideas

The American colonists looked to the English Revolution of 1688 as having established many of their own fundamental political liberties, as well as those of the English. Consequently, the colonists employed a theory that had developed to justify an aristocratic rebellion to support their own popular revolution. These Whig political ideas, largely derived from the writings of John Locke, were, however, only a part of the English ideological heritage that affected the Americans. Throughout the eighteenth century, they had become familiar with a series of British political writers called the Commonwealthmen, who held republican political ideas that had their intellectual roots in the most radical thought of the Puritan revolution. During the early eighteenth century, these writers argued that the government of Sir Robert Walpole and his successors was corrupt and that it undermined liberty. They regarded much parliamentary taxation as simply a means of financing political corruption. They also considered standing armies instruments of tyranny. In Great Britain, this republican political tradition had only a marginal impact. Three thousand miles away, however, the policy of Great Britain toward America following the Treaty of Paris of 1763 and certain political events in Britain had made many colonists believe the worst fears of the Commonwealthmen were coming true. All these events coincided with the accession of George III to the throne.

Events in Great Britain

George III believed that a few powerful Whig families and the ministries they controlled had bullied and dominated his two immediate royal predecessors. George III also believed he should have ministers of his own choice and Parliament should function under royal, rather than aristocratic, management. Between 1761 and 1770, George tried one minister after another, but each, in turn, failed to gain enough support from the various factions in the House of Commons. Finally, in 1770, he turned to Lord North, who remained the king's first minister until 1782. The Whig families and other political spokespersons claimed that George III was attempting to impose a tyranny. What they meant was that the king was attempting to curb the power of a particular group of the aristocracy.

The Challenge of John Wilkes In 1763, the various factions that opposed the king coalesced around John Wilkes (1725–1797), a London political radical, member of Parliament, and publisher of a newspaper called *The North Briton*. Wilkes used his paper to attack Lord Bute, the king's first minister, for his handling of peace negotiations with France. Bute had him arrested, but Wilkes's privileges as a member of Parliament won his release. The courts ruled that the vague warrant by which he had been arrested was illegal. The House of Commons, however, convicted him of libel and expelled him. Wilkes fled the country and was outlawed, but many saw him as a victim of political persecution.

In 1768, Wilkes returned to England and was reelected to Parliament. The House of Commons, however, bowed to the wishes of the king and refused to seat him. Although he won three subsequent elections, the House ignored the verdict of the electorate and seated a rival government-supported candidate. Shopkeepers, artisans, and small property owners took to the streets to support Wilkes, and aristocrats who wanted to humiliate the king also backed him. Wilkes maintained that his was the cause of English liberty, and his supporters adopted the slogan, "Wilkes and Liberty." Wilkes became lord mayor of London and was finally seated by Parliament in 1774.

The American colonists followed these developments closely, for they seemed to confirm the colonists' suspicion that the king and Parliament were conspiring against English liberty. The Wilkes affair highlighted the arbitrary power of the monarch, the corruption of the House of Commons, and the contempt of both for the electorate. These aspects of tyranny seemed, to the colonists, to be at the heart of their struggles with England.

Movement for Parliamentary Reform The political influences between America and Britain operated both ways. The colonial demand for no taxation without repre-

SIGNIFICANT DATES FROM THE EIGHTEENTH CENTURY

1713	Treaty of Utrecht
1739	War of Jenkins's Ear
1740–1748	War of the Austrian Succession
1756–1763	Seven Years' War
1763	John Wilkes challenges the British monarchy
1764	Sugar Act
1765	Stamp Act
1770	Boston Massacre
1773	Boston Tea Party
1774	First Continental Congress
1776–1783	War of the American Revolution

sentation and the criticism of the adequacy of the British system of representation struck at the core of the eighteenth-century British political structure. British subjects at home who were no more directly represented in the House of Commons than were the Americans could adopt the colonial arguments. The colonial questioning of the tax-levying authority of the House of Commons was related to the protest of John Wilkes. Both were protesting the power of a largely self-selected aristocratic political body. Moreover, both the colonial leaders and Wilkes appealed over the head of legally constituted political authorities to popular opinion and popular demonstrations.

The American colonists also demonstrated to Europe how a politically restive people in the Old Regime could fight tyranny and protect political liberty. They established revolutionary, but orderly, political bodies that could function outside the existing political framework. The legitimacy of these bodies lay not in existing law, but in the alleged consent of the governed.

The Yorkshire Association Movement By the close of the 1770s, many in Britain resented the mismanagement of the American war, the high taxes, and Lord North's ministry. In northern England in 1778, Christopher Wyvil (1740–1822), a landowner and retired clergyman, organized the Yorkshire Association Movement. Its members intended that the association examine, and suggest reforms for, the entire government. The Association Movement was thus a popular attempt to establish an extra-legal institution to reform the government. The movement collapsed during the early 1780s because its supporters, unlike Wilkes and the American rebels, were not willing to appeal for broad popular support. Nonetheless, the agitation of the Association Movement provided many people with experience in political protest.

Parliament was, however, influenced by the Association Movement. In April 1780, the Commons advocated a reduction in the power of the crown. In 1782, Parliament implemented an "economical" reform, which abolished some sources of royal patronage, and in 1783, Parliament forced Lord North to form a ministry with Charles James Fox (1749–1806), a longtime critic of the king. In the same year, the king turned to William Pitt the Younger (1759–1806) for help in creating a more pliable House of Commons. During the election of 1784, Pitt used immense amounts of royal patronage to fill the House of Commons with men friendly to the king. Efforts to reform Parliament faded, and by the mid-1780s, the king's political dominance had been restored. Its resurgence was, however, short-lived. George III succumbed to mental illness, and the regency that had to be established to govern for him could not aggressively exercise royal authority.

QUICK REVIEW

The Yorkshire Association Movement

- Started in 1778 by Christopher Wyvil
- Demanded moderate change in corrupt system of parliamentary elections
- Movement faded in the early 1780s

Broader Impact of the American Revolution

The Americans—through their state constitutions, the Articles of Confederation, and the federal Constitution adopted in 1788—had demonstrated to Europe the possibility of government without kings and hereditary nobilities. They had established the example of a nation in which written documents based on popular consent and popular sovereignty—rather than on divine law, natural law, tradition, or the will of kings—were the highest political and legal authority. The political novelty of these assertions should not be ignored.

Americans embraced democratic ideals, but they did not create a thoroughly democratic society. The equality of white male citizens—both before the law and in society—was endorsed. All white males were promised a chance to improve their social standing and economic lot by hard work and individual enterprise, and they alone were enfranchised. Slaves were not freed. Nor were the issues of women's rights and those of Native Americans addressed. Still, the American colonists of the eighteenth century produced a freer society than any the world had yet seen. Their revolution was a genuinely radical movement, whose influence would spread and inspire Europeans to question their traditional modes of government.

SUMMARY

HOW DID European contact with the rest of the world evolve in the centuries since the Renaissance?

Periods of European Overseas Empires There have been four stages in Europe's interactions with the rest of the world: (1) by the end of the seventeenth century, discovery and settlement of the New World, introduction of the transatlantic plantation economy, and market penetration of Southeast Asia; (2) by the 1820s, mercantile empires, with resulting competition among European powers, and independence in most of the Americas; (3) in the nineteenth century, formal empires ruled directly by Europe; and (4) by the late twentieth century, decolonization. Prior to colonial independence, Europeans generally treated indigenous peoples as inferior. Ships and guns gave Europeans insurmountable advantages. This chapter covers the mercantile period. *page 394*

WHAT WERE the characteristics of European mercantile empires?

Mercantile Empires Mercantilism, an economic theory based on the economy of scarcity, assumed the growth of one nation came at the expense of another. The goal of the mercantile system was for each European power to monopolize trade with its colonies, with the profits—in the form of gold and silver bullion—enriching each ruling country. Colonial rivalries could grow into conflicts between European nations. French–British rivalry was intense in the West Indies and in India. Dutch power in what is now Indonesia was acknowledged by other Europeans. *page 395*

HOW DID Spanish colonial organization reflect its imperial goals?

The Spanish Colonial System Spain attempted to impose control on trade with the colonies by restricting the American ports to which Spanish ships could sail. Smugglers, however, always found ways to carry out their work. The political system under which the Spanish colonies were administered concentrated power in the crown; local officials were appointed through royal patronage. In 1700, when the French Bourbon king Philip V took the Spanish throne, he tried to introduce effective French administrative techniques to Spain's empire. Spain was defeated in Europe's mid-eighteenth-century wars, and Charles III tried to use imperial reform and colonial trade liberalization to bolster Spain's economy. He was successful initially, but he stoked resentments that would erupt into colonial rebellion. *page 396*

WHAT WERE the origins of slavery in the Americas?

Black African Slavery, the Plantation System, and the Atlantic Economy The transatlantic plantation economy created social, political, and production systems unlike any others in world history. Although slavery was practiced in many other times and places, the extent to which the plantation economy depended on slave labor made it unique. The racist element in the justification for the trade in black African human beings left a cultural legacy that is still with us. The sheer volume and economic impact of the slave trade itself, and the goods produced by slave labor, make slavery one of the most important elements in the history of the Americas, and an important factor in the histories of Europe and of Africa as well. *page 397*

WHY DID mid-eighteenth-century European wars often involve both continental and global conflicts?

Mid-Eighteenth-Century Wars The mid-eighteenth-century European state system encouraged warfare. Monarchs thought they could use war to further their own ends without risking the lives of their subjects or the stability of their societies. Overseas empires and central and eastern Europe saw repeated international rivalries. The 1739 British–Spanish conflict, the War of Jenkins's Ear, began a period of European warfare that lasted until 1815. Prussia, Austria, France, and other European nations fought wars that spilled over into colonial conflicts. Maria Theresa preserved the Habsburg Empire, at the cost of power sharing with the nobility and with the Hungarian Magyars. Frederick II saved Prussia, becoming "Frederick the Great." Britain's William Pitt the Elder set his country on the path to a global dominance it would enjoy for the next century and a half by deploying troops into colonial battlefields. *page 404*

WHAT WERE the causes of the American Revolution?

The American Revolution and Europe The Treaty of Paris of 1763 left Britain with the problems of financing its empire and administering vast new North

American territories. Starting in 1764, Britain passed a series of taxes on the American colonies that it intended to collect more aggressively. In each case, American resistance led Britain to rescind most of the legislation. Tensions increased. In 1776, the colonists' Continental Congress declared independence from Britain. France and Spain entered the war as American allies, and the Americans' victory was ratified by the 1783 Treaty of Paris. Through this period, Britain's King George III alienated Whigs and convinced radical political theorists that he wanted to impose tyranny. The writings and examples offered by John Wilkes in Britain, and the revolutionaries in America, provided a new vocabulary for advocates of liberty and new models for free sovereign government. *page 408*

Review Questions

1. What were the main points of conflict between Britain and France in North America, the West Indies, and India? How was the Spanish colonial empire in the Americas organized and managed?
2. What was the nature of slavery in the Americas? How was it integrated into the economies of the Americas, Europe, and Africa? What was the plantation system?
3. What were the results of the Seven Years' War? Which countries emerged in a stronger position? Why?
4. To what extent were the colonists who began the American Revolution influenced by European ideas and political developments? What influence did their actions and arguments have on Europe?

KEY TERMS

Intolerable Acts (p. 409)

mercantilism (p. 395)

For additional learning resources related to this chapter, please go to **www.myhistorylab.com**

myhistorylab

17

The Age of Enlightenment:

Eighteenth-Century Thought

The salon of Madame Marie-Thérèse Geoffrin (1699–1777) was one of the most important Parisian gathering spots for Enlightenment writers during the middle of the eighteenth century. Well-connected women such as Madame Geoffrin were instrumental in helping the *philosophes* they patronized to bring their ideas to the attention of influential people in French society and politics.

Chateaux de Malmaison et Bois-Preau, Rueil-Malmaison. Bridgeman-Giraudon/Art Resource, NY

What does the importance of salons tell us about Enlightenment culture?

FORMATIVE INFLUENCES ON THE ENLIGHTENMENT *page 416*

WHAT WAS the intellectual and social background of the Enlightenment?

THE *PHILOSOPHES* *page 419*

WHO WERE the *philosophes?*

THE ENLIGHTENMENT AND RELIGION *page 420*

HOW DID the *philosophes* challenge traditional religious ideas and institutions?

THE ENLIGHTENMENT AND SOCIETY *page 422*

HOW DID the *philosophes* apply Enlightenment ideas to social and economic problems?

POLITICAL THOUGHT OF THE *PHILOSOPHES* *page 424*

HOW DID the *philosophes* apply Enlightenment ideas to political issues?

WOMEN IN THE THOUGHT AND PRACTICE OF THE ENLIGHTENMENT *page 427*

WHAT ROLE did women play in the Enlightenment?

ROCOCO AND NEOCLASSICAL STYLES IN EIGHTEENTH-CENTURY ART *page 428*

HOW DID rococo and neoclassicism styles reflect and contribute to the prevailing trends of the age?

ENLIGHTENED ABSOLUTISM *page 430*

WHAT WAS enlightened absolutism?

The modern world's faith in the possibility and desirability of change is a key intellectual inheritance from the eighteenth century's self-proclaimed Enlightenment. The leaders of the movement were convinced that human reason could comprehend the processes of nature and manipulate them to create a better world. They believed the rational order that the scientific revolution had discovered in the physical universe should also exist in human societies. They insisted that all traditional beliefs and institutions be exposed to rational critique, which would inevitably inspire innovation and improvement. Some of the era's monarchs caught the spirit of the age and used the power of "enlightened absolutism" to implement rational plans for reordering their subjects' lives.

FORMATIVE INFLUENCES ON THE ENLIGHTENMENT

WHAT WAS the intellectual and social background of the Enlightenment?

The Newtonian worldview, the political stability and commercial prosperity of Great Britain after 1688, the need for administrative and economic reform in France after the wars of Louis XIV, and the consolidation of what is known as a *print culture* were the chief factors that fostered the ideas of the Enlightenment and the call for reform throughout Europe.

IDEAS OF NEWTON AND LOCKE

Isaac Newton (1642–1727) and John Locke (1632–1704) were the major intellectual forerunners of the Enlightenment. Newton's formulation of the law of universal gravitation exemplified the newly perceived power of the human mind. Newtonian physics had portrayed a pattern of mechanical and mathematical rationality in the physical world. During the eighteenth century, thinkers from a variety of backgrounds began to apply this insight to society. If nature was rational, they reasoned, society, too, should be organized rationally. Furthermore, Newton had encouraged natural philosophers to approach the study of nature directly and to avoid metaphysics and supernaturalism. He had insisted on the use of empirical experience to check rational speculation. This emphasis on concrete experience became a key feature of Enlightenment thought.

As explained in Chapter 14, Newton's success in physics had inspired his fellow countryman John Locke to explain human psychology in terms of experience. In *An Essay Concerning Human Understanding* (1690), Locke argued that all humans enter the world a **tabula rasa**, or blank page. Personality is the product of the sensations that impinge on an individual from the external world throughout his or her life. This essentially behaviorist theory implied that human nature is changeable and can be molded by modifying the surrounding physical and social environment. Locke's was thus a reformer's psychology that suggested the possibility of improving the human condition. Locke's psychology also, in effect, rejected the Christian doctrine that sin permanently flawed human beings.

tabula rasa (a blank page) John Locke's *An Essay Concerning Human Understanding* (1690) theorized that at birth the human mind is a tabula rasa.

THE EXAMPLE OF BRITISH TOLERATION AND POLITICAL STABILITY

The domestic stability of Great Britain after the Revolution of 1688 furnished a living example of a society in which, to many contemporaries, enlightened reforms appeared to benefit everyone. England permitted religious toleration to all except Unitarians and Roman Catholics, and even they were not actively persecuted. Relative freedom of the press and free speech prevailed. The authority of the monarchy was limited, and political sovereignty resided in Parliament. The courts protected citizens from arbitrary government action. The army was small. Furthermore, the domestic economic life of Great Britain displayed far less regulation than that of France or other continental nations, and English commerce flourished. Many writers of the continental Enlightenment contrasted what they regarded as the wise, progressive features of English life with the absence of religious toleration, the extensive literary censorship, the possibility of arbitrary arrest, the overregulation of the economy, and the influence of aristocratic military values in their own nations and most particularly in France.

The Emergence of a Print Culture

The Enlightenment flourished in a *print culture*, that is, a culture in which books, journals, newspapers, and pamphlets had achieved a status of their own. During the eighteenth century, the volume of printed material—books, journals, magazines, and daily newspapers—increased sharply throughout Europe, notably in Britain. One of the driving forces behind this expansion of printed materials was the increase in literacy that occurred across Europe.

A growing concern with everyday life and material concerns—with secular as opposed to religious issues—accompanied this expansion of printed forms. Toward the end of the seventeenth century, half the books published in Paris were religious; by the 1780s, only about 10 percent were. Prose came to be valued as highly as poetry, and the novel emerged as a distinct literary genre. Novels often came to provide the moral and social instruction that books of piety once furnished.

Books were not inexpensive in the eighteenth century, but they, and the ideas they conveyed, circulated in a variety of ways to reach a broad public. Private and public libraries grew in number, allowing single copies to reach many readers. Authors might also publish the same material in book form, in journals, and in newspapers.

Within both aristocratic and middle-class society, people were increasingly expected to be familiar with books and secular ideas. Popular publications fostered the value of polite conversation and the reading of books. Coffeehouses became centers for discussing writing and ideas. (See "Encountering the Past: Coffeehouses and Enlightenment," page 418.)

The expanding market for printed matter allowed writers to earn a living from their work for the first time, making authorship an occupation. Parisian ladies who hosted fashionable salons sought out popular writers. Some writers, notably Alexander Pope (1688–1744) in England and Voltaire in France, grew wealthy, providing an example for their young colleagues. In a challenge to older aristocratic values, status for authors in this new print culture was based on merit and commercial competition, not heredity and patronage.

Printing shops were the productive centers for the books and newspapers that spread the ideas of the Enlightenment.

The Granger Collection

How did printing help make the wide dissemination of Enlightenment ideas possible?

ENCOUNTERING THE PAST

Coffeehouses and Enlightenment

Europe's first coffee imports came from the Ottoman Empire, where coffee drinking was encouraged by the Islamic prohibition of alcohol. Venice, which had close commercial ties with the Ottomans, opened the first European coffeehouse in the 1640s. By the middle of the eighteenth century, thousands of similar facilities were scattered across Europe.

Because no alcohol was served, behavior in a coffeehouse tended to be better than in a tavern, and coffeehouses provided social contexts for discussions of current events and serious issues. Proprietors of coffeehouses attracted customers by furnishing copies of newspapers and journals. Some even sponsored lectures on such topics as Newtonian physics or the relationship between science and religion. Respectable women did not frequent coffeehouses, but men of many different professional backgrounds and varying interests did. The coffeehouse provided a common meeting ground for persons interested in debating ideas and hearing the latest news and rumors from courts and governments. Although the discussion in such places often centered on issues of political liberty and freedom of thought, the great quantities of coffee and sugar their customers consumed were produced by the slaves who labored on Caribbean and Brazilian plantations.

Business, science, religion, and politics were discussed in London coffeehouses such as this.

Who went to coffeehouses? Why were they such popular meeting places?

HOW DID the coffeehouse work with the print culture to create an informed public?

A division, however, soon emerged between high and low literary culture. Successful authors of the Enlightenment addressed themselves to monarchs, nobles, the upper middle classes, and professional groups, and they were read and accepted in these upper levels of society. Other aspiring authors lived marginally, writing professionally for whatever newspaper or journal that would pay for their work. Many of these lesser writers grew resentful, blaming a corrupt society for their lack of success. From their anger, they often espoused radical ideas or took moderate Enlightenment ideas to radical extremes, transmitting them in this embittered form to their often lower-class audience.

An expanding literate public and the growing influence of secular printed materials created a new and increasingly influential social force called *public opinion*. This force—the collective effect on political and social life of views circulated in print and discussed in the home, the workplace, and centers of leisure—seems not to have existed before the middle of the eighteenth century. The emergence of public opinion changed the cultural and political climate in Europe. Governments could no longer operate wholly in secret or with disregard to the larger public sphere. They, as well as their critics, had to explain and discuss their views and policies openly. Government efforts to limit the freedom of the press underscored the challenge public opinion posed to traditional intellectual, social, and political authorities.

THE *PHILOSOPHES*

WHO WERE the *philosophes?*

The writers and critics who flourished in the expanding print culture and who took the lead in forging the new attitudes favorable to change, championed reform, and advocated toleration were known as the *philosophes*.

A few of these *philosophes*, particularly those in Germany, were university professors. Most, however, were free agents who might be found in London coffeehouses, Edinburgh drinking spots, the salons of fashionable Parisian ladies, the country houses of reform-minded nobles, or the courts of the most powerful monarchs on the Continent. In eastern Europe, they were often royal bureaucrats. They were not an organized group; they disagreed on many issues and did not necessarily like or respect each other.

The *philosophes* drew the bulk of their readership from the prosperous commercial and professional urban classes. These people as well as forward-looking aristocrats discussed the reformers' writings and ideas in local philosophical societies, Freemason lodges, and clubs. Although the writers of the Enlightenment did not consciously champion the goals or causes of the middle class, they did provide an intellectual ferment and a major source of ideas that could be used to undermine existing social practices and political structures based on aristocratic privilege. Moreover, the *philosophes* generally supported the expansion of trade, the improvement of agriculture and transport, and the invention of new manufacturing machinery, events that were transforming the society and the economy of the eighteenth century and enlarging the business and commercial classes.

The chief bond among the *philosophes* was their common desire to reform religion, political thought, society, government, and the economy for the sake of human liberty. Though challenged over the last three centuries, no other single set of ideas has done so much to shape and define the modern Western world.

VOLTAIRE—FIRST AMONG THE *PHILOSOPHES*

By far the most influential of the philosophes was François-Marie Arouet, known to posterity by his pen name Voltaire (1694–1778). In 1726, to escape the wrath of a powerful aristocrat whom he had offended, Voltaire went into exile in England. In 1728, Voltaire returned to France and, in 1733, published *Letters on the English*, which appeared in French the next year. The book praised the virtues of the English, especially their religious liberty, and implicitly criticized the abuses of French society. Voltaire then moved to Cirey from which, if necessary, he could easily escape France into what was then the nearby independent duchy of Lorraine. In 1738, with the considerable help of Countess Emilie de Chatelet (1706–1749), he published *Elements of the Philosophy of Newton*, which more than any other single book popularized the thought of Isaac Newton across the continent.

Voltaire's most popular work is probably *Candide* (1759), an attack on war, religious persecution, and unwarranted (as he saw it) optimism about the human condition. Like most *philosophes*, Voltaire believed society could and should be improved, but he was not confident that reforms could be sustained. The Enlightenment is associated with optimistic attitudes, but its sunny outlook radiated more hopefulness than certainty.

Statue of Voltaire by Jean-Antoine Houdon (Theatre Français, Paris).

Musée Lambinet, Versailles/Giraudon/Art Resource, NY

Why is Voltaire thought by many to be the most important *philosophe*?

THE ENLIGHTENMENT AND RELIGION

HOW DID the *philosophes* challenge traditional religious ideas and institutions?

For many, but not all, *philosophes* of the eighteenth century, ecclesiastical institutions, especially in their frequently privileged position as official parts of the state, were the chief impediment to human improvement and happiness.

The critical *philosophes* complained that both established and nonestablished Christian churches hindered the pursuit of a rational life and the scientific study of humanity and nature. According to the doctrine of original sin—either Protestant or Catholic—meaningful improvement in human nature on earth was impossible. Religion thus turned attention away from this world to the world to come. Mired in conflicts over obscure doctrines, the churches promoted intolerance and bigotry, inciting torture, war, and other forms of human suffering. With this attack, the *philosophes* were challenging not only a set of ideas, but also some of Europe's most powerful institutions, as the churches were deeply enmeshed in the power structure of the Old Regime.

DEISM

The *philosophes*, although critical of many religious institutions and frequently anticlerical, did not oppose all religion. What the *philosophes* sought, however, was religion without fanaticism and intolerance, a religious life that would largely substitute human reason for the authority of churches. The Newtonian worldview had convinced many writers that nature was rational. Therefore, the God who had created nature must also be rational, and the religion through which that God was worshipped should be rational. Most of them believed the life of religion and of reason could be combined, giving rise to a a broad set of ideas known as **deism**.

deism The *philosophes*' theology. A rational religion, a faith without fanaticism and intolerance that acknowledged the sovereign authority of reason.

The deists' informal creed had two major points. The first was a belief in the existence of God, which they thought the contemplation of nature could empirically justify, and in this respect many Protestant and Roman Catholic writers fully agreed with them. Because nature provided evidence of a rational God, that deity must also favor rational morality. So the second point in the deists' creed was a belief in life after death, when rewards and punishments would be meted out according to the virtue of the lives people led on this earth.

Deism, Enlightenment writers urged, was empirical, tolerant, reasonable, and capable of encouraging virtuous living. Deists hoped that wide acceptance of their faith would end rivalry among the various Christian sects and with it religious fanaticism, conflict, and persecution. They also felt deism would remove the need for priests and ministers, who, in their view, were often responsible for fomenting religious differences and denominational hatred. Deistic thought led some contemporaries to believe God had revealed himself in different ways and that many religions might embody divine truth. There was never a formal or extensive deist movement, but deist ideas spread informally throughout the culture and provided for some people a framework for a nondogmatic religious outlook.

TOLERATION

The *philosophes* presented religious toleration as a primary social condition for the virtuous life. Again Voltaire took the polemical lead in championing this cause. In 1762, the Roman Catholic political authorities in the city of Toulouse tortured and then executed a Huguenot named Jean Calas, who had been accused of murdering his son to prevent him from converting to Roman Catholicism. Voltaire made the dead man's cause his own, winning a reversal of the judicial decision against the unfortunate man in 1765. For Voltaire, the case illustrated the fruits of religious fanaticism and the need

for rational reform of judicial processes. In 1779, the German playwright and critic Gotthold Lessing (1729–1781) wrote *Nathan the Wise*, a plea for toleration not only of different Christian groups, but also of religious faiths other than Christianity.

Radical Enlightenment Criticism of Christianity

Some *philosophes* went beyond the formulation of a rational religious alternative to Christianity and the advocacy of toleration to attack the churches and the clergy with vehemence. The Scottish philosopher David Hume (1711–1776) argued in "Of Miracles," a chapter in his *Inquiry into Human Nature* (1748), that no empirical evidence supported the belief in divine miracles central to much of Christianity. Voltaire repeatedly questioned the truthfulness of priests and the morality of the Bible. In *The Decline and Fall of the Roman Empire* (1776), Edward Gibbon (1737–1794), the English historian, explained the rise of Christianity in terms of natural causes rather than the influence of miracles and piety. A few, but actually very few, *philosophes* went further than criticism. Most of the *philosophes*, however, sought not the abolition of religion, but its transformation into a humane force that would encourage virtuous living.

QUICK REVIEW

***Philosophes'* Critique of Religion**

- Europe's churches seen as the chief impediment to progress
- Piety and religious authoritarianism believed to hinder science
- Religion focused attention on afterlife and away from the here and now

Jewish Thinkers in the Age of Enlightenment

Despite their emphasis on toleration, the *philosophes*' criticisms of traditional religion often reflected an implicit contempt not only for Christianity but also, and sometimes more vehemently, for Judaism and, as we see later, for Islam as well. The Enlightenment view of religion thus served in some ways to further stigmatize Jews and Judaism in the eyes of non-Jewish Europeans.

Enlightenment values also, however, allowed certain Jewish intellectuals to rethink the relationship of their communities to the wider European culture from which they had largely lived apart. Baruch Spinoza (1632–1677) set the example for a secularized version of Judaism, and Moses Mendelsohn (1729–1786) established the main outlines of an assimilationist position.

The new science of the mid–seventeenth century deeply influenced Spinoza, the son of a Jewish merchant of Amsterdam. Like his contemporaries, Hobbes and Descartes, he looked to the power of human reason to reconceptualize traditional thought. In that regard his thinking reflected the age of scientific revolution and looked toward the later Enlightenment. In his *Ethics*, the most famous of his works, Spinoza closely identified God and nature, or the spiritual and material worlds. In his *Theologico-Political Treatise* (1670), Spinoza directly anticipated much of the religious criticism of the Enlightenment and its attacks on the power of superstition in human life. Spinoza described the origins of religion in thoroughly naturalistic terms. Spinoza's extensive rational and historical criticism of the biblical narratives disturbed Christian and Jewish contemporaries who saw him as a writer seeking to lead people away from all religion. During his lifetime the controversial character of his writings led both Jews and Protestants to criticize him as an atheist.

Dutch Jewish philosopher Baruch Spinoza.
Library of Congress
Why did Spinoza face attack from both Christians and Jews?

Moses Mendelsohn, the leading Jewish philosopher of the eighteenth century, was known as the "Jewish Socrates." Writing almost a century after Spinoza, he also advocated the entry of Jews into modern European life. In contrast to Spinoza, however, Mendelsohn argued that a Jew could combine loyalty to Judaism with adherence to rational, Enlightenment values. Mendelsohn's most influential work was *Jerusalem, or, On Ecclesiastical Power and Judaism* (1783) in which he argued both for extensive religious toleration and for maintaining the religious distinction of Jewish communities. Unlike Spinoza, Mendelsohn wished to advocate religious toleration while genuinely sustaining the traditional religious practices and faith of Judaism. Nevertheless, Mendelsohn believed Jewish communities should not have the right to excommunicate their members over differences in theological opinions or even if their members embraced modern secular ideas. He thus sought both toleration of Jews within European society and toleration by Jews of a wider spectrum of opinion within their own communities. His hope was that the rationalism of the Enlightenment would provide the foundation for both types of toleration.

QUICK REVIEW

Baruch Spinoza (1632–1677)

- Dutch Jewish thinker who was influenced by the scientific revolution
- Closely identified God and nature
- Recognized no reality beyond the natural order

Topkapi Palace, Istanbul Inside the imperial harem, a sanctuary from the outside world, this elegant room was used to entertain the sultan, who watched the proceedings from his large throne.

Tony Souter © Dorling Kindersley

What role did images of the East play in the Enlightenment critique of European society and government?

Islam in Enlightenment Thought

Islam continued to be seen as a rival to Christianity. European writers repeated what other Christian critics had said for centuries. They portrayed Islam as a false religion, Muhammad as an impostor and a false prophet, and attacked Islam as an exceptionally carnal or sexually promiscuous religion. European universities did endow professorships to study Arabic during the seventeenth century, but these university scholars generally agreed with theological critics that Islam too often embodied religious fanaticism.

Enlightenment *philosophes* spoke with two voices regarding Islam. Voltaire indicated his opinion along with that of many of his contemporaries in the title of his 1742 tragedy, *Fanaticism, or Mohammed the Prophet*. For Voltaire, Muhammad and Islam in general represented simply one more example of the religious fanaticism he had so often criticized among Christians. Some Enlightenment writers, however, spoke well of the Islamic faith. The deist John Toland, who opposed prejudice against both Jews and Muslims, contended that Islam derived from early Christian writings and was thus a form of Christianity. Other commentators approved of Islam's tolerance and the charitable work of Muslims.

One of the most positive commentators on eighteenth-century Islam was a woman. Between 1716 and 1718, Lady Mary Wortley Montagu (1689–1762) lived in Istanbul with her husband, the British ambassador to Turkey. She wrote a series of letters about her experiences there that was published the year after her death. In these *Turkish Embassy Letters*, she praised much about Ottoman society and urged the English to copy the Turkish practice of vaccination against smallpox. Nevertheless, the European voices demanding fairness and expressing empathy for Islam were rare throughout the eighteenth century.

QUICK REVIEW

Islam and the Enlightenment

- Eighteenth-century writers continued long-standing European hostility toward Islam
- *Philosophes* both damned and praised Islam
- Muslims showed little interest in Western Europe

Muslims were not curious about the Christian West. Only a handful of Muslims from the Ottoman Empire visited Western Europe in the eighteenth century, and no Islamic writers showed much interest in contemporary European authors. The *Ulema*, the Islamic religious establishment, reinforced these attitudes. They taught that God's revelations to Muhammad meant Islam had replaced Christianity as a religion and therefore there was little for Muslims to learn from Christian culture.

THE ENLIGHTENMENT AND SOCIETY

HOW DID the *philosophes* apply Enlightenment ideas to social and economic problems?

The *Encyclopedia*: Freedom and Economic Improvement

The midcentury witnessed the publication of the *Encyclopedia*, one of the greatest monuments of the Enlightenment and its most monumental undertaking in the realm of print culture. Under the heroic leadership of Denis Diderot (1713–1784) and Jean

Le Rond d'Alembert (1717–1783), seventeen volumes appeared between 1751 and 1772. No other work of the Enlightenment so illustrated the movement's determination to probe life on earth rather than in the religious realm.

The *Encyclopedia* was the product of the collective effort of more than a hundred authors, and its editors had at one time or another solicited articles from all the major French *philosophes*. It included the most advanced critical ideas of the time on religion, government, and philosophy. The *Encyclopedia* also included numerous important articles and illustrations on manufacturing, canal building, ship construction, and improved agriculture, making it an important source of knowledge about eighteenth-century social and economic life.

The project had been designed to secularize learning and to undermine intellectual assumptions that lingered from the Middle Ages and the Reformation. The articles on politics, ethics, and society ignored divine law and concentrated on humanity and its immediate well-being. For the authors, the good life lay here and now and was to be achieved through the application of reason to human relationships. The publication of the *Encyclopedia* spread Enlightenment thought more fully over the Continent, penetrating German and Russian intellectual and political circles.

Denis Diderot was the heroic editor of the *Encylopedia*, published in seventeen volumes of text and eleven volumes of prints between 1751 and 1772. Through its pages many of the chief ideas of the Enlightenment reached a broad audience of readers.

Jean-Simon Berthelemy (1743-1811), "Denis Diderot" (1713–1784). Writer and Encyelopaedist. Oil on canvas, 55 x 46 cm. Inv.: P 2082. Photo: Bulloz. Musée de la Ville de Paris, Musée Carnavalet, Paris, France/Art Resource, NY

What topics were covered in the *Encyclopedia*? What were the editors' goals?

Beccaria and Reform of Criminal Law

Although the term did not appear until later, the idea of *social science* originated with the Enlightenment. *Philosophes* hoped to end human cruelty by discovering social laws and making people aware of them. These concerns are most evident in the *philosophes'* work on law and prisons.

In 1764, Marquis Cesare Beccaria (1738–1794), an Italian aristocrat and *philosophe*, published *On Crimes and Punishments*, in which he applied critical analysis to the problem of making punishments both effective and just. He thought the criminal justice system should ensure a speedy trial and certain punishment and the intent of punishment should be to deter further crime. The purpose of laws was not to impose the will of God or some other ideal of perfection, but to secure the greatest good or happiness for the greatest number of human beings. This utilitarian philosophy based on happiness in this life permeated most Enlightenment writing on practical reforms.

The Physiocrats and Economic Freedom

Economic policy was another area in which the *philosophes* saw existing legislation and administration preventing the operation of natural social laws. They believed mercantilist legislation (designed to protect a country's trade from external competition) and the regulation of labor by governments and guilds actually hampered the expansion of trade, manufacture, and agriculture. In France, these economic reformers were called the physiocrats. The physiocrats believed the primary role of government was to protect property and to permit its owners to use it freely.

Adam Smith on Economic Growth and Social Progress

The most important economic work of the Enlightenment was Adam Smith's (1723–1790) *Inquiry into the Nature and Causes of the Wealth of Nations* (1776). Smith believed economic liberty was the foundation of a natural economic system. As a result, he urged that the mercantile system of England—including the navigation acts governing colonial trade, the bounties the government gave to favored merchants and industries, most tariffs, trading monopolies, and the domestic regulation of labor and manufacture—be abolished. The best way to encourage economic growth, he maintained, was to unleash individuals to pursue their own selfish economic interests.

Mercantilism assumed that the earth's resources were limited and scarce, so one nation could acquire wealth only at the expense of others. Smith's book challenged this assumption. He saw the resources of nature—water, air, soil, and minerals—as boundless. To him, they demanded exploitation for the enrichment and comfort of humankind. In effect, Smith was saying the nations and peoples of Europe need not be poor. Smith is usually regarded as the founder of **laissez-faire** economic thought and policy, which favors a limited role for the government in economic life. He was not opposed, however, to all government intervention in economic activity. The state, he believed, should provide schools, armies, navies, and roads, and it should fund commercial ventures that were desirable, but beyond the means of private enterprise.

laissez-faire Policy of noninterference, especially the policy of government noninterference in economic affairs or business.

Within *The Wealth of Nations*, Smith, like other Scottish thinkers of the day, embraced an important theory of human social and economic development, known as the *four-stage theory*. According to this theory, human societies move through four stages of development: the hunting and gathering stage, the pastoral or herding stage, the agricultural stage, and, finally, the commercial stage. Smith and other Scottish writers described the passage of human society through these stages as a movement from barbarism to civilization.

To Europeans, this outlook helped justify their economic and imperial domination of the world during the following century. They repeatedly portrayed themselves as bringing a higher level of civilization to people elsewhere who, according to the four-stage theory, lived in lower stages of human social and economic development. Europeans thus imbued with the spirit of the Enlightenment presented themselves as carrying out a civilizing mission to the rest of the world.

POLITICAL THOUGHT OF THE *PHILOSOPHES*

HOW DID the *philosophes* apply Enlightenment ideas to political issues?

Nowhere was the *philosophes*' reformist agenda, as well as tensions among themselves, so apparent as in their political thought. The most important political thought of the Enlightenment occurred in France. The French *philosophes*, however, were divided over how to solve their country's problems. Their proposed solutions spanned a wide political spectrum, from aristocratic reform to democracy to absolute monarchy.

MONTESQUIEU AND *SPIRIT OF THE LAWS*

Charles Louis de Secondat, baron de Montesquieu (1689–1755), was a lawyer, a noble of the robe, and a member of a provincial *parlement*. He also belonged to the Bordeaux Academy of Science, before which he presented papers on scientific topics. Although living comfortably within the bosom of French society, he saw the need for reform.

In his most enduring work, *Spirit of the Laws* (1748), Montesquieu pursued an empirical method, taking illustrative examples from the political experience of both ancient and modern nations. From these, he concluded that no single set of political laws could apply to all peoples at all times and in all places. Whether the best form of government for a country was a monarchy or a republic, for example, depended on that country's size, population, social and religious customs, economic structure, traditions, and climate. Only a careful examination and evaluation of these elements could reveal what mode of government would most benefit a particular people.

For France, Montesquieu favored a monarchical government tempered and limited by various intermediary institutions, including the aristocracy, the towns, and the other corporate bodies that enjoyed liberties the monarch had to respect. In France, he regarded the aristocratic courts, or *parlements*, as a major example of an intermediary association. Their role was to limit the power of the monarchy and thus to preserve the liberty of its subjects. In championing these aristocratic bodies and the general oppositional role of the aristocracy, Montesquieu was a political conservative. He adopted this conservatism in the hope of achieving reform, however, for he believed the oppressive and inefficient absolutism of the monarchy accounted for the degradation of French life.

One of Montesquieu's most influential ideas was that of the division of power in government. Executive, legislative, and judicial power should reside in separate branches of the government. He thought any two branches could check and balance the power of the other. Montesquieu's analysis illustrated his strong belief that monarchs should be subject to constitutional limits on their power and that a separate legislature, not the monarch, should formulate laws. For this reason, although he set out to defend the political privileges of the French aristocracy, Montesquieu's ideas have had a profound effect on the constitutional form of liberal democracies for more than two centuries.

Rousseau: A Radical Critique of Modern Society

Jean-Jacques Rousseau (1712–1778) held a different view of the exercise and reform of political power from Montesquieu's. Rousseau hated the world and the society in which he lived. It seemed to him impossible for human beings living according to the commercial values of his time to achieve moral, virtuous, or sincere lives. He contended that human beings in a primeval state of nature had been good, but that as they eventually formed social relations and then social institutions, they had lost that goodness. Society itself was the source of human evil for Rousseau, and one manifestation of that unnatural evil was unequal distribution of property.

Rousseau questioned the concepts of material and intellectual progress and the morality of a society in which commerce, industry, and the preservation of property rights were regarded as among the most important human activities. The other *philosophes* generally believed life would improve if people could enjoy more of the fruits of the earth or could produce more goods. Rousseau raised the more fundamental questions of what constitutes the good life and how can human society be reshaped to achieve that life.

Jean-Jacques Rousseau.
Library of Congress

Rousseau carried these same concerns into his political thought. His most extensive discussion of politics appeared in *The Social Contract* (1762). Rousseau suggested that society is more important than its individual members, because they are what they are only by virtue of their relationship to the larger community. Independent human beings living alone can achieve little. Through their relationship to the larger political community, they become moral creatures capable of significant action. The question then becomes: What kind of community allows people to behave morally?

Rousseau envisioned a society in which each person could maintain personal freedom while behaving as a loyal member of the larger community. Drawing on the traditions of Plato and Calvin, he defined freedom as obedience to law. In his case, the law to be obeyed was that created by the general will. In a society with virtuous customs and morals in which citizens have adequate information on important issues, the concept of the general will is normally equivalent to the will of a majority of voting citizens. Democratic participation in decision making would bind the individual citizen

Overview Major Works of the Enlightenment and Their Publication Dates

DATE	WORK	AUTHOR
1670	*Theologico-Political Treatise*	Spinoza
1677	*Ethics*	Spinoza
1687	*Principia Mathematica*	Newton
1690	*An Essay Concerning Human Understanding*	Locke
1696	*Christianity Not Mysterious*	Toland
1721	*Persian Letters*	Montesquieu
1733	*Letters on the English*	Voltaire
1738	*Elements of the Philosophy of Newton*	Voltaire
1748	*Spirit of the Laws*	Montesquieu
1748	*Inquiry into Human Nature*	Hume
1750	*Discourse on the Moral Effects of the Arts and Sciences*	Rousseau
1751	*Encyclopedia* (Vol. 1)	Edited by Diderot
1755	*Discourse on the Origin of Inequality*	Rousseau
1759	*Candide*	Voltaire
1762	*The Social Contract* and *Émile*	Rousseau
1763	*Treatise on Tolerance*	Voltaire
1764	*Philosophical Dictionary*	Voltaire
1764	*On Crimes and Punishments*	Beccaria
1776	*The Decline and Fall of the Roman Empire*	Gibbon
1776	*The Wealth of Nations*	Smith
1779	*Nathan the Wise*	Lessing
1783	*Jerusalem, or, On Ecclesiastical Power and Judaism*	Mendelsohn
1792	*Vindication of the Rights of Woman*	Wollstonecraft
1793	*Religion Within the Limits of Reason Alone*	Kant

to the community. Rousseau believed the general will, thus understood, must always be right and that to obey the general will is to be free. This argument led him to the notorious conclusion that under certain circumstances some people must be forced to be free. Rousseau's politics thus constituted a justification for radical direct democracy and for collective action against individual citizens.

Rousseau had only a marginal impact on his own time. He proved, however, to be a figure to whom later generations returned. Leading figures in the French Revolution were familiar with his writing, and he influenced writers in the nineteenth and twentieth centuries who were critical of the general tenor and direction of Western culture.

Enlightened Critics of European Empires

Most European thinkers associated with the Enlightenment favored the extension of European empires across the world. A few Enlightenment voices, however, did criticize the European empires on moral grounds, especially the European conquest of the Americas, the treatment of Native Americans, and the enslavement of Africans on the two American continents. The most important of these critics were Denis Diderot and two German philosophers, Immanuel Kant and Johann Gottlieb Herder (1744–1803).

Three ideas in particular provided the grounds for this criticism. First, the Enlightenment critics of their empires argued for a form of shared humanity that the sixteenth-century European conquerors and their successors in the Americas and in other areas of imperial conquest had ignored. Kant, Diderot, and Herder rejected this dismissive outlook and the harsh policies that had flowed from it. A second of these critical ideas was the conviction that the people whom Europeans had encountered in the Americas had possessed cultures that should have been respected and understood rather than destroyed. For Herder, human beings living in different societies possessed the capacity as human beings to develop in culturally different fashions. He thus embraced an outlook later known as cultural relativism. A third idea, closely related to the second, was that human beings may develop distinct cultures possessing intrinsic values that cannot be compared, one to the detriment of another, because each culture possesses deep inner social and linguistic complexities that make any simple comparison impossible. Indeed, Diderot, Kant, and Herder argued that being a human includes the ability to develop a variety of distinctly different cultures.

WOMEN IN THE THOUGHT AND PRACTICE OF THE ENLIGHTENMENT

WHAT ROLE did women play in the Enlightenment?

Women, especially in France, helped significantly to promote the careers of the *philosophes*. In Paris, the salons of women such as Marie-Thérèse Geoffrin (1699–1777), Julie de Lespinasse (1733–1776), and Claudine de Tencin (1689–1749) gave the *philosophes* access to useful social and political contacts and a receptive environment in which to circulate their ideas. Moreover, the women who organized the salons were well connected to political figures who could help protect the *philosophes* and secure royal pensions for them.

Despite this help and support from the learned women of Paris, the *philosophes* were on the whole not strong feminists. Many urged better and broader education for women. They criticized the education women did receive as overly religious, and they tended to reject ascetic views of sexual relations. In general, however, they displayed traditional views toward women and advocated no radical changes in their social condition.

Montesquieu, for example, maintained, in general, that the status of women in a society was the result of climate, the political regime, culture, and women's physiology. He believed women were not naturally inferior to men and should have a wider role in society. Yet Montesquieu's willingness to consider social change for women in European life had limits. Although in the *Spirit of the Laws* he indicated a belief in the equality of the sexes, he still retained a traditional view of marriage and family and expected men to dominate those institutions. Furthermore, although he supported the right of women to divorce and opposed laws that oppressed them, he upheld the ideal of female chastity.

The views about women expressed in the *Encyclopedia* were less generous than those of Montesquieu. The *Encyclopedia* suggested ways to improve women's lives, but in general, it did not emphasize that the condition of women needed reform. Almost all the contributors were men, and the editors, Diderot and d'Alembert, evidently saw no need to include many articles by women. The Encyclopedists discussed women primarily within a family context—as daughters, wives, and mothers—and presented motherhood as a woman's most important occupation. On sexual behavior, the Encyclopedists upheld an unquestioned double standard.

Mary Wollstonecraft in *A Vindication of the Rights of Woman* defended equality of women with men on the grounds of men and women sharing the capacity of human reason.

CORBIS/Bettmann

How sympathetic were the *philosophes* as a group to the ideas of Mary Wollstonecraft?

One of the most surprising and influential analyses of the position of women came from Jean-Jacques Rousseau. This most radical of all Enlightenment political theorists urged a traditional and conservative role for women. In his novel *Émile* (1762) (discussed again in Chapter 19), he set forth a radical version of the view that men and women occupy separate spheres. Only men were to populate the world of citizenship, political action, and civic virtue. Women were relegated to the domestic sphere. Many of these attitudes were not new—some have roots as ancient as Roman law—but Rousseau's powerful presentation and the influence of his other writings gave them new life in the late eighteenth century. Rousseau deeply influenced many leaders of the French Revolution, who, as shall be seen in the next chapter, often incorporated his view on gender roles in their policies.

Paradoxically, Rousseau achieved a vast following among women in the eighteenth century. One explanation for this influence is that his writings, although they did not advocate liberating women or expanding their social or economic roles, did stress the importance of their emotions. He portrayed the domestic life and the role of wife and mother as a noble and fulfilling vocation, giving middle- and upper-class women a sense that their daily occupations had a purpose. He assigned them a degree of influence in the domestic sphere that they could not have competing with men outside it.

In 1792, in *A Vindication of the Rights of Woman*, Mary Wollstonecraft (1759–1797) brought Rousseau before the judgment of the rational Enlightenment ideal of progressive knowledge. The immediate incentive for this essay was her opposition to certain policies of the French Revolution, unfavorable to women, that Rousseau had inspired. Wollstonecraft accused Rousseau and others after him who upheld traditional roles for women of attempting to narrow women's vision and limit their experience. She argued that to confine women to the separate domestic sphere because of supposed limitations of their physiology was to make them the sensual slaves of men. Confined in this separate sphere, they were the victims of male tyranny, their obedience was blind, and they could never achieve their own moral or intellectual identity. Denying good education to women would impede the progress of all humanity. With these arguments, Wollstonecraft was demanding for women the kind of liberty that male writers of the Enlightenment had been championing for men for more than a century. In doing so, she placed herself among the *philosophes* and broadened the agenda of the Enlightenment to include the rights of women as well as those of men.

ROCOCO AND NEOCLASSICAL STYLES IN EIGHTEENTH-CENTURY ART

HOW DID rococo and neoclassicism reflect and contribute to the prevailing trends of the age?

rococo Style that embraced lavish, often lighthearted decoration with an emphasis on pastel colors and the play of light.

Two contrasting styles dominated eighteenth-century European art and architecture. The **rococo** style embraced lavish, often lighthearted decoration with an emphasis on pastel colors and the play of light. **Neoclassicism** embodied a return to figurative and architectural models drawn from the Renaissance and the ancient world.

Rococo architecture and decoration originated in early-eighteenth-century France. After Louis XIV's death in 1715, the Regent Philippe d'Orleans (1674–1723) and the French aristocracy spent less time at Versailles and began to enjoy the diversions of Paris. There, wealthy French aristocrats built houses known as *hôtels*. Their designers compensated for the relatively small scale and nondescript exteriors of these

The color, the light, and the elaborate decorative details associated with rococo style are splendidly exemplified in the Imperial Hall (*Kaisarsaal*) built in Würzburg, Bavaria, according to the design of Balthasar Neumann (1687–1753).

Art Resource, N.Y.

What values are reflected in rococo architecture?

neoclassicism Style that embodied a return to figurative and architectural models drawn from the Renaissance and the ancient world.

mansions with interiors that were elaborately decorated and painted in light colors to make the rooms seem brighter and more spacious. Beyond such domestic and personally intimate settings in France, the rococo style spread across Europe and was adapted to many public buildings and churches.

The paintings associated with rococo art often portrayed the aristocracy, and particularly the French aristocracy, at play. The paintings showed not reality, but an idealized landscape with carefree men and women pursuing a life of leisure, romance, and seduction.

As the eighteenth century wore on, the way of life illustrated in rococo paintings and of more popular prints produced from them convinced many people in France that the monarchy, the court, and the aristocracy were frivolous and decadent. In reality, as seen in Chapter 15, many French and European aristocrats were hardworking and disciplined. Nonetheless, the lighthearted carelessness of rococo art increased hostility toward the political and social elites of the Old Regime.

Contemporaries, moreover, did not have to wait for the tumult of the French Revolution to view art that directly criticized the society rococo art portrayed. The mid–eighteenth century witnessed a new admiration for the art of the ancient world. Neoclassicism constituted a return to themes, topics, and styles drawn from antiquity itself and from the Renaissance appeal to antiquity.

Figures in neoclassical paintings rarely suggest movement and often seem to stand still in a kind of tableau illustrating a moral theme. These paintings were didactic rather than emotional or playful. Their subject matter was usually concerned with public life or public morals, rather than depicting intimate family life, daily routine, or the leisure activity favored by rococo painters.

Many neoclassical painters used scenes of heroism and self-sacrifice from ancient history to draw contemporary moral and political lessons. Such scenes provided a sharp moral contrast to rococo works in which lovers seek only pleasure and escape from care. Some neoclassical artists intended their paintings to be a form of direct political

The Panthéon in Paris (construction commencing 1758) embodied the neoclassical style used for a Jesuit church. After the French Revolution it became a national momument where famous figures of the Enlightenment and Revolution were buried. The bodies of both Voltaire and Rousseau were transferred there during the 1790s.

Jacques Germain Soufflot (1713–1780), Facade of the Panthéon (formerly Church of Ste. Genevieve), 1757. Panthéon, Paris, France. © Bridgeman-Giraudon/Art Resource, NY

Why were so many eighteenth-century Europeans drawn to the neoclassical style?

criticism. Jacques-Louis David (1748–1825), the foremost French neoclassical painter, used ancient republican themes in the 1780s to emphasize the corruption of French monarchical government.

The *philosophes* themselves became the subjects of neoclassical artists. The French sculptor Jean-Antoine Houdon (1741–1828) produced numerous portraits in stone of leading *philosophes* including Voltaire and Rousseau as well as American admirers of the Enlightenment such as Benjamin Franklin (1706–1790) and Thomas Jefferson (1743–1826). Even religious structures built in the neoclassical style were, by the end of the century, transformed to monuments to the Enlightenment and Revolution. Modeled on its ancient pagan namesake in Rome, the Panthéon in Paris was begun in 1758 as a Jesuit church. During the French Revolution, the new government transformed it into a national monument where the remains of French heroes could be interred.

ENLIGHTENED ABSOLUTISM

WHAT WAS enlightened absolutism?

Most of the *philosophes* favored neither Montesquieu's reformed and revived aristocracy nor Rousseau's democracy as a solution to contemporary political problems. Like other thoughtful people of the day in other stations and occupations, they looked to the existing monarchies. Voltaire and other *philosophes*, such as Diderot, who visited Catherine II of Russia, and the physiocrats, some of whom were ministers to Louis XV and Louis XVI, did not wish to limit the power of monarchs. Rather, they sought to use that power to rationalize economic and political structures and liberate intellectual life.

During the last third of the century, some observers believed that several European rulers had embraced many of the reforms the *philosophes* advocated. Historians use the term *enlightened absolutism* for this form of monarchical government in which the central absolutist administration was strengthened and rationalized at the cost of other, lesser centers of political power, such as the aristocracy, the church, and the parliaments or diets that had survived from the Middle Ages. The monarchs most closely associated with it are Frederick II (r. 1740–1786) of Prussia, Joseph II of Austria (r. 1765–1790), and Catherine II (r. 1762–1796) of Russia.

The humanitarian and liberating zeal of the Enlightenment writers was, however, only part of what motivated the policies of these rulers. Frederick II, Joseph II, and Catherine II were also determined to play major diplomatic and military roles in Europe. In no small measure, they adopted Enlightenment policies favoring the rational economic and social integration of their realms because these policies also increased their military strength and political power.

Frederick the Great of Prussia

More than any other ruler of the age, Frederick the Great of Prussia embodied enlightened absolutism. Drawing upon the accomplishments of his Hohenzollern forebearers, he forged a state that commanded the loyalty of the military, the Junker nobility, the Lutheran clergy, a growing bureaucracy recruited from an educated middle class, and university professors. Because the authority of the Prussian monarchy and the military were so strong and because the nobles, bureaucracy, clergy, and professors were so loyal, Frederick had the confidence to permit a more open discussion of Enlightenment ideas and to put into effect more Enlightenment values, such as extensive religious toleration, than any other continental ruler. Consequently, in marked contrast to France, Prussians sympathetic to the Enlightenment tended to support the state rather than criticize it.

Frederick the Great of Prussia.
Library of Congress

Promotion Through Merit Reflecting an important change in the European view of the ruler, Frederick frequently described himself as "the first servant of the State" contending that his own personal and dynastic interests should always be subordinate to the good of his subjects. Like earlier Hohenzollern rulers, he protected the local social and political interests of the Prussian nobility as well as their role in the army, but he also required nobles who sought positions in his well-paid bureaucracy to qualify for those jobs by merit. By 1770, a Prussian Civil Service Commission oversaw the education and examinations required for all major government appointments. Frederick thus made it clear that merit rather than privilege of birth would determine who served the Prussian state.

During his reign Frederick created few new nobles, and those persons whom he did ennoble earned their titles by merit, for having served the king and the state well. Because the Prussian state required academic training for appointment to positions of authority, nobles attended the universities. There they studied with middle-class Prussians who were training to serve the state either as Protestant clergy or bureaucrats. Consequently, nobles, clergy, and bureaucrats in Prussia shared a similar educational background that combined a moderate exposure to Enlightenment ideas with broadly shared religious values and loyalty to the state.

Religious Toleration No single policy so associated Frederick with the Enlightenment as that of full religious toleration. Continuing the Hohenzollern policy of toleration for foreign workers who brought important skills into Prussia, Frederick allowed Catholics and Jews to settle in his predominantly Lutheran country, and he protected the Catholics living in Silesia after he conquered that province from the Habsburgs in the 1740s. (See Chapter 13.) He even stated that he would be willing to build mosques for Turks should they move into his country. His religious toleration won the strong support of philosophers, such as Immanuel Kant and Moses Mendelsohn. Frederick nonetheless tended to appoint Protestants to most key positions in the bureaucracy and army.

Administrative and Economic Reforms Frederick also ordered a new codification of Prussian law, which was completed after his death. His objective was to rationalize the existing legal system and make it more efficient, eliminating regional peculiarities, reducing aristocratic influence, abolishing torture, and limiting the number of capital crimes.

The midcentury wars had inflicted considerable economic damage on Prussia. Thereafter, Frederick used the power of the state to foster economic growth. He sought to develop Prussian agriculture. Under state supervision, swamps were drained, new crops introduced, and peasants encouraged and sometimes compelled to migrate where they were needed. Frederick also established a land-mortgage credit association to help landowners raise money for agricultural improvements. Despite these efforts, however, most Prussians did not prosper under Frederick's reign, and the burden of taxation, reflecting his protection of the interests of the nobles, fell disproportionately on peasants and townspeople.

Joseph II of Austria

No eighteenth-century ruler so embodied rational, impersonal force as did the emperor Joseph II of Austria. He was the son of Maria Theresa and co-ruler with her from 1765 to 1780. Thereafter, he ruled alone until his death in 1790. Joseph II sincerely wished to improve the lot of his people. He was much less a political opportunist and cynic than either Frederick the Great of Prussia or Catherine the Great of Russia. Nonetheless, the ultimate result of his well-intentioned efforts was a series of aristocratic and peasant rebellions extending from Hungary to the Austrian Netherlands.

Centralization of Authority As explained in Chapter 13, of all the rising states of the eighteenth century, Austria was the most diverse in its people and problems. The Habsburgs never succeeded in creating either a unified administrative structure or a strong aristocratic loyalty to the dynasty. To preserve the monarchy during the War of the Austrian Succession (1740–1748), Maria Theresa had guaranteed the aristocracy considerable independence, especially in Hungary.

Maria Theresa strengthened the power of the crown outside of Hungary by increasing the size of the empire's administrative bureaucracy. Her efficient tax agents collected from the clergy as well as the nobles in Austria and Bohemia. She appointed councils to handle various kinds of problems, and she brought education under state control to ensure her government a sufficient supply of trained officials. Her concern for schools extended to increasing opportunities for primary education at the local level. She also tried to protect peasants and serfs by using the royal bureaucracy to enforce limits on the amount of labor noble landowners could demand from their tenants. Her concern was not solely humanitarian. She wanted to preserve the pool of manpower from which she drew her soldiers.

Joseph II was more determined than his mother, and his projected reforms were more wide ranging. He sought to overcome the pluralism of the Habsburg holdings by imposing central authority on areas of political and social life in which Maria Theresa had wisely chosen not to interfere.

In particular, Joseph sought to reduce Hungarian autonomy. To avoid having to guarantee Hungary's existing privileges or extend new ones at the time of his coronation, he refused to have himself crowned king of Hungary and even had the Crown of Saint Stephen, symbol of the Hungarian state, sent to the Imperial Treasury in Vienna. He reorganized local government in Hungary to increase the authority of his own officials. He also required the use of German in all governmental matters.

Ecclesiastical Policies Another target of Joseph's royal absolutism was the church. Maria Theresa was devout, but she had not allowed the church to limit her authority. Although she had attempted to discourage certain of the more extreme modes of Roman Catholic popular religious piety, such as public flagellation, she was adamantly opposed to religious toleration. (See "Compare & Conneect: Maria Theresa and Joseph II of Austria Debate Toleration," pages 434–435.)

Joseph II was also a practicing Catholic, but based on both Enlightenment values and pragmatic politics, he favored a policy of toleration. In October 1781, Joseph extended freedom of worship to Lutherans, Calvinists, and the Greek Orthodox. Joseph also granted the right of private worship to Jews and relaxed the financial and social burdens imposed on them, though he did not give Jews full equality with other Habsburg subjects.

Above all, Joseph sought to bring the Roman Catholic Church directly under royal control. He forbade the bishops of his realms to communicate directly with the pope. Since he considered religious orders that did not run schools or hospitals to be unproductive, he dissolved more than six hundred monasteries, confiscated their lands, and used some of their revenue to found new parishes in areas where there was a shortage of priests. He also reorganized the training of priests. In effect, Joseph's policies made Roman Catholic priests the employees of the state, ending the influence of the Roman Catholic Church as an independent institution in Habsburg lands.

Economic and Agrarian Reform Like Frederick of Prussia, Joseph sought to improve the economic life of his domains. He abolished many internal tariffs, encouraged road building, and improved river transport. He personally inspected farms and manufacturing districts. Joseph also reconstructed the judicial system to make laws more uniform and rational and to lessen the influence of local landlords. All these improvements were expected to bring new unity to the state and more taxes into the imperial coffers in Vienna.

Joseph's policies toward serfdom and the land were a far-reaching extension of those Maria Theresa had initiated. During his reign, he introduced reforms that touched the very heart of the rural social structure. He did not abolish the authority of landlords over their peasants, but he did seek to make that authority more moderate and subject to the oversight of royal officials. He abolished serfdom as a legally sanctioned state of servitude. He granted peasants a wide array of personal freedoms, including the right to marry, to engage in skilled work, and to have their children learn a skill without having to secure the landlord's permission. Joseph reformed the procedures of the manorial courts and opened avenues of appeal to royal officials. He also encouraged landlords to change land leases, so that peasants could more easily inherit land or transfer it to other peasants. His goal in all these efforts to reduce traditional burdens on peasants was to make them more productive and industrious farmers.

Near the end of his reign, Joseph proposed a new and daring system of land taxation. He decreed in 1789 that all proprietors of the land were to be taxed regardless of social status. No longer were the peasants alone to bear the burden of taxation. He commuted *robot* (forced peasant labor) into a monetary tax, only part of which was to go to the landlord, the rest reverting to the state. Angry nobles blocked the implementation of this decree, and it died with Joseph in 1790. This and others of Joseph's earlier measures, however, brought turmoil throughout the Habsburg realms. Peasants revolted over disagreements with landlords about their newly granted rights. The nobles of the various Habsburg realms protested the taxation scheme. The Magyars resisted Joseph's centralization measures in Hungary and forced him to rescind them. Joseph was succeeded by his brother Leopold II (r. 1790–1792). Although sympathetic to Joseph's goals, Leopold was forced to repeal many of the most controversial decrees, such as that on taxation.

QUICK REVIEW

Joseph II of Austria (r. 1765–1790)

- Attempted widespread reforms based on Enlightenment principles
- Resistance forced Joseph to rescind most of his centralizing efforts
- Abolished serfdom and gave peasants more personal freedom

Catherine the Great of Russia

Joseph II never grasped the practical necessity of forging political constituencies to support his policies. Catherine II, who had been born a German princess, but who became empress of Russia, understood only too well the fragility of the Romanov dynasty's base of power.

After the death of Peter the Great in 1725, the court nobles and the army repeatedly determined the Russian succession. Such had been the case for almost forty years when, in 1762, Peter III came to the throne. He was a weak ruler whom many contemporaries considered mad. He immediately exempted the nobles from compulsory military service and then rapidly made peace with Frederick the Great, for whom he held unbounded admiration. That decision probably saved Prussia from military defeat in the Seven Years' War. The one positive feature of this unbalanced creature's life was his marriage in 1745 to a young German princess born in the small duchy of Anhalt Zerbst. This was the future Catherine the Great.

COMPARE & CONNECT

MARIA THERESA AND JOSEPH II OF AUSTRIA DEBATE TOLERATION

The issue of religious toleration was widely debated throughout the age of Enlightenment. Many rulers feared that their domains would be overcome by religious turmoil and potential political unrest if their subjects could pursue religious freedom. The issue divided the Empress Maria Theresa and her son Joseph II who since 1765 had been co-rulers of the Austrian Empire. In 1777 they exchanged important letters setting forth their sharply differing views of the subject.

Joseph believed some religious toleration should be introduced into the Habsburg realms. Maria Theresa refused to consider toleration. The toleration of Protestants that is in dispute related only to Lutherans and Calvinists. Maria Theresa died in 1780; the next year Joseph issued an edict of toleration.

QUESTIONS

1. How does Joseph define toleration, and why does Maria Theresa believe it is the same as religious indifference?
2. Why does Maria Theresa fear that toleration will bring about political as well as religious turmoil?
3. Why does Maria Theresa think that Joseph's belief in toleration has come from Joseph's acquaintance with wicked books?

I. JOSEPH TO MARIA THERESA, JULY 20, 1777

It is only the word "toleration" which has caused the misunderstanding. You have taken it in quite a different meaning [from mine expressed in an earlier letter]. God preserve me from thinking it a matter of indifference whether the citizens turn Protestant or remain Catholic, still less, whether they cleave to, or at least observe, the cult which they have inherited from their fathers! I would give all I possess if all the Protestants of your states would go over to Catholicism.

The word "toleration," as I understand it, means only that I would employ any person, without distinction of religion, in purely temporal matters, allow them to own property, practice trades, be citizens, if they were qualified and if this would be of advantage to the State and its industry. Those who, unfortunately, adhere to a false faith, are far further from being converted if they remain in their own country than if they migrate into another, in which they can hear and see the convincing truths of the Catholic faith. Similarly, the undisturbed practice of their religion makes them far better subjects and causes them to avoid irreligion, which is a far greater danger to our Catholics than if one lets them see others practice their religion unimpeded.

II. MARIA THERESA TO JOSEPH, LATE JULY 1777

Without a dominant religion? Toleration, indifference are precisely the true means of undermining everything, taking away every foundation; we others will then be the greatest losers. . . . He is no friend of humanity, as the popular phrase is, who allows everyone his own thoughts. I am speaking only in the political sense, not as a Christian, nothing is so necessary and salutary as religion. Will you allow everyone to fashion his own religion as he pleases? No fixed cult, no subordination to the Church—what will then become of us? The result will not be quiet and content-

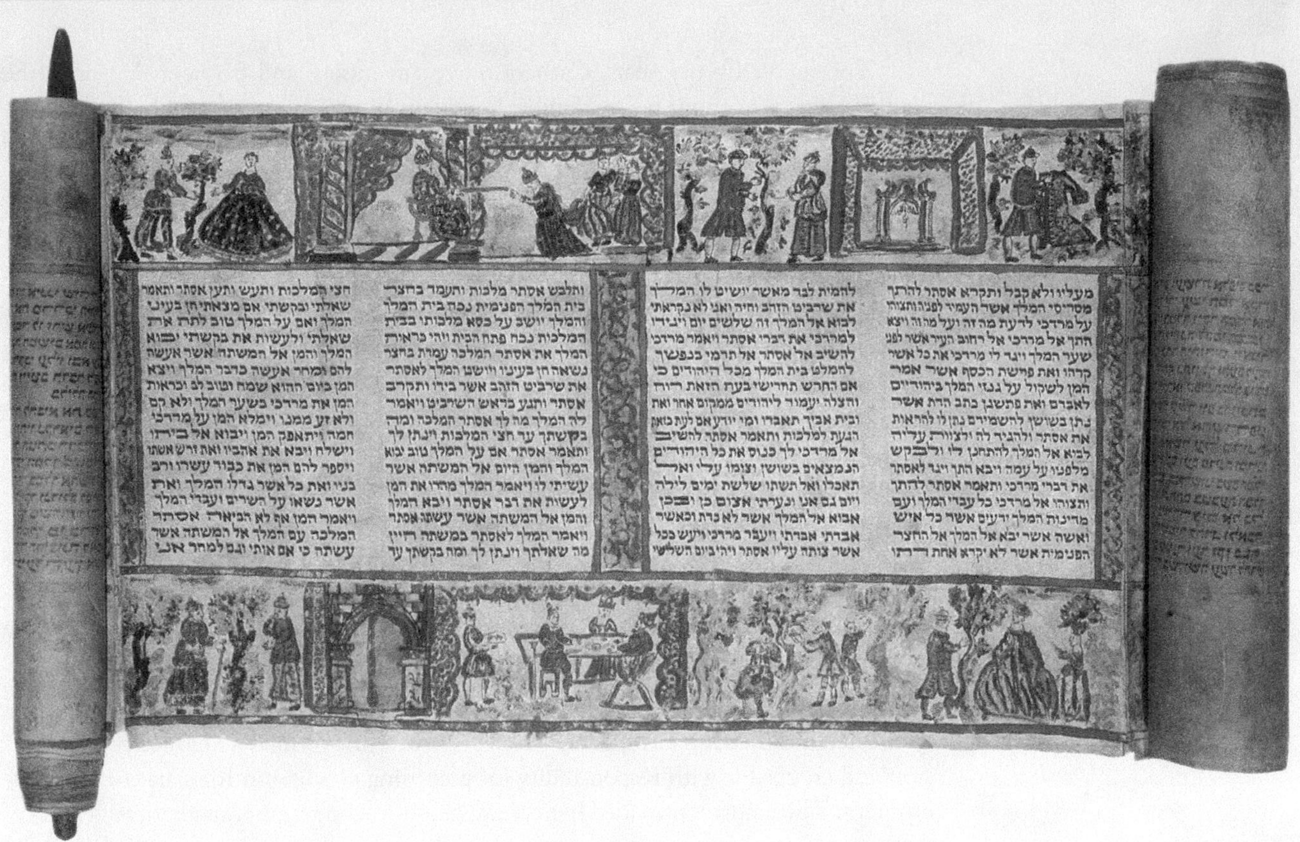

An eighteenth-century scroll of the biblical Book of Esther. According to the story, Queen Esther, who was married to King Ahasuerus of Persia, was responsible for thwarting a plan to annihilate all Jews in the Persian Empire.

Courtesy of the Library of Congress

What challenges did European Jews face in the eighteenth century?

ment; its outcome will be the rule of the stronger and more unhappy times like those which we have already seen. A manifesto by you to this effect can produce the utmost distress and make you responsible for many thousands of souls. And what are my own sufferings, when I see you entangled in opinions so erroneous? What is at stake is not only the welfare of the State but your own salvation. . . . Turning your eyes and ears everywhere, mingling your spirit of contradiction with the simultaneous desire to create something, you are ruining yourself and dragging the Monarchy down with you into the abyss. . . . I only wish to live so long as I can hope to descend to my ancestors with the consolation that my son will be as great, as religious as his forebearer, that he will return from his erroneous views, from those wicked books whose authors parade their cleverness at the expense of all that is most holy and most worthy of respect in the world, who want to introduce an imaginary freedom which can never exist and which degenerates into license and into complete revolution.

Source: As quoted in *The Habsburg and Hohenzollern Dynasties in the Seventeenth and Eighteenth Centuries* ed. by C. A. Macartney (New York: Walker, 1970), pp. 151–153. Reprinted by permission of Walker and Co.

For almost twenty years, Catherine lived in misery and frequent danger at the court. During that time, she befriended important nobles and read widely the books of the *philosophes*. A few months after his accession as tsar, Peter was deposed and murdered with Catherine's approval, if not her aid, and she was immediately proclaimed empress.

Catherine's familiarity with the Enlightenment and the general culture of Western Europe convinced her Russia was backward and that it needed major reforms to remain a great power. She understood that any significant reform must have a wide base of political and social support, especially since she had assumed the throne through a palace coup. In 1767, she summoned a legislative commission to advise her on revising the law and government of Russia. There were more than five hundred delegates, drawn from all sectors of Russian life.

Russian law, however, was not revised for more than half a century. In 1768, Catherine dismissed the commission before several of its key committees had reported. Yet the meeting had not been useless, for it had gathered a vast amount of information about the conditions of local administration and economic life throughout Russia. The inconclusive debates and the absence of programs from the delegates themselves suggested that most Russians saw no alternative to an autocratic monarchy, and Catherine had no intention of departing from absolutism.

Limited Administrative Reform In 1767, Catherine formed a Legislative Commission and charged it with responsibility for proposing changes in Russian law and government. The empress provided her commissioners, who represented various sectors of Russian society, with a set of *Instructions* drawn from the political works of the *philosophes*. A year later, Catherine dismissed the commission before several of its key committees reported, but its members had not wasted their time. The commission had gathered vast amounts of information about local administration and economic life, and the upshot of discussions among the commissioners was that few Russians saw any alternative to autocratic monarchy. Their consensus provided support for Catherine's exercise of enlightened absolutism.

Economic Growth Part of Catherine's program was to continue the economic development begun under Peter the Great. She attempted to suppress internal barriers to trade. Exports of grain, flax, furs, and naval stores grew dramatically. She also favored the expansion of the small Russian urban middle class that was so vital to trade.

Territorial Expansion Catherine's limited administrative reforms and her policy of economic growth had a counterpart in the diplomatic sphere. The Russian drive for warm-water ports continued. (See Map 17–1.) This goal required warfare with the Turks. In 1769, as a result of a minor Russian incursion, the Ottoman Empire declared war on Russia. The Russians responded with a series of strikingly successful military moves, occupying the Ottoman provinces on the Danube River. The conflict dragged on until 1774, when the Treaty of Kuchuk-Kainardji gave Russia a direct outlet on the Black Sea, free navigation rights in its waters, and free access through the Bosporus. Crimea became an independent state, which Catherine painlessly annexed in 1783.

The Partition of Poland

The Russian military successes increased Catherine's domestic political support, but they made the other states of eastern Europe uneasy. These anxieties were overcome by an extraordinary division of Polish territory known as the First Partition of Poland.

The Russian victories along the Danube River were most unwelcome to Austria, which also harbored ambitions of territorial expansion in that direction. At the same time, the Ottoman Empire was pressing Prussia for aid against Russia. Frederick the Great made a proposal to Russia and Austria that would give each something it wanted, prevent conflict among the powers, and save appearances. After long, complicated secret negotiations, Russia agreed to abandon the conquered Danubian provinces. In compensation, it received a large portion of Polish territory with almost 2 million inhabitants. As a reward for remaining neutral, Prussia annexed most of the territory between East Prussia and Prussia proper. This land allowed Frederick to unite two previously separate sections of his realm. Finally, Austria took Galicia in southern Poland, with its important salt mines, and other Polish territory with more than 2.5 million inhabitants.

MAP EXPLORATION

To explore this interactive map, go to www.myhistorylab.com

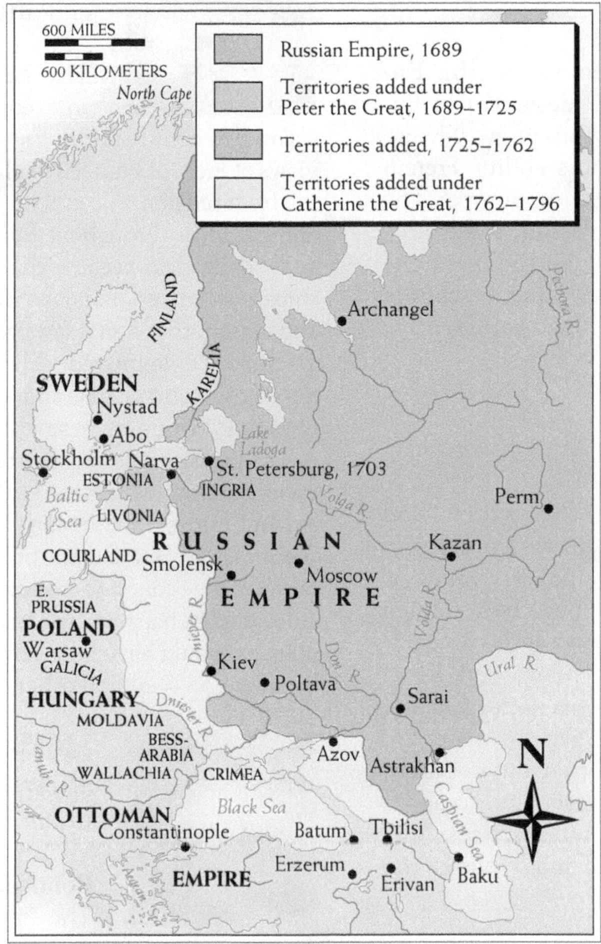

MAP 17–1 **Expansion of Russia, 1689–1796** The overriding territorial aim of the two most powerful Russian monarchs of the eighteenth century, Peter the Great (in the first quarter of the century) and Catherine the Great (in the last half of the century), was to secure navigable outlets to the sea in both the north and the south for Russia's vast empire, hence Peter's push to the Baltic Sea and Catherine's to the Black Sea. Russia also expanded into Central Asia and Siberia during this time period.

Which empire came into direct conflict with Russian expansion?

The partition of Poland clearly demonstrated that any nation without a strong monarchy, bureaucracy, and army could no longer compete within the European state system. It also demonstrated that the major powers in eastern Europe were prepared to settle their own rivalries at the expense of such a weak state. If Polish territory had not been available to ease tensions, international rivalries might have led to warfare among Russia, Austria, and Prussia.

The End of the Eighteenth Century in Central and Eastern Europe

During the last two decades of the eighteenth century, all three regimes based on enlightened absolutism became more conservative and politically repressive. In Prussia and Austria, the innovations of the rulers stirred resistance among the nobility. In Russia, fear of peasant unrest was the chief factor.

By the close of the century, fear of, and hostility to, change permeated the ruling classes of central and eastern Europe. This reaction had begun before 1789, but the events in France bolstered and sustained it for almost half a century. Paradoxically, nowhere did the humanity and liberalism of the Enlightenment encounter greater rejection than in those states that had been governed by "enlightened" rulers.

SUMMARY

WHAT WAS the intellectual and social background of the Enlightenment?

Formative Influences on the Enlightenment The ideas of the Enlightenment were based on the Newtonian worldview, Locke's psychology, Britain's wealth and stability, French reform, and the emerging print culture in Europe. The print culture facilitated increasing secularism, made writing an economically viable profession, and allowed the emergence of collective public opinion. Literary culture was generally divided between high and low. *page 416*

WHO WERE the *philosophes?*

The *Philosophes* The writers and critics of the eighteenth century who believed religion, politics, society, and the economy could be reformed to better support human liberty—the *philosophes*—included Montesquieu, Diderot, Rousseau, Hume, and Kant. Voltaire was the most influential, and his satire *Candide* reflects the *philosophes'* concerns and general attitudes. They were not an organized group, and they did not agree on all issues, but they all sought to use reason and common sense to improve institutions and social practices. The commercial and professional classes read and discussed the *philosophes'* works. *page 419*

HOW DID the *philosophes* challenge traditional religious ideas and institutions?

The Enlightenment and Religion Many eighteenth-century *philosophes* were hostile to the church and religious institutions in general. They did not, however, in general oppose religion itself. Deism was a movement that understood religion as something natural and rational, with God as the "divine watchmaker" who had created the universe, set it in motion according to certain laws, and then left it alone. Deists believed the existence of God could be proved empirically, and they believed in life after death, when virtue would be rewarded and sin punished. *Philosophes* valued religious toleration, although they did not always practice it. Jewish thinkers—particularly Spinoza and Mendelsohn—both contributed to, and responded to, the ideas of the Enlightenment. Enlightenment thinkers had less direct contact with Islam, and most sources of information about Islam available in the West were hostile. *page 420*

HOW DID the *philosophes* apply Enlightenment ideas to social and economic problems?

The Enlightenment and Society In an effort to secularize learning, *philosophes* compiled the *Encyclopedia*, a compendium of the views of most of France's leading *philosophes* on subjects ranging from religion to canal building. It helped spread Enlightenment ideas throughout Europe. The *philosophes* wanted to apply their ideas because they believed that human relationships obeyed rational laws through empirical examination and reason, that social laws could be learned, and that society could be improved. They criticized mercantilism and hoped to reform prisons and legal punishments. Many French economic reformers were physiocrats, who believed government's primary role was to provide only the protections necessary to allow owners to use their property to best advantage. Adam Smith's 1776 *Inquiry into the Nature and Causes of the Wealth of Nations* is described as the founding document for laissez-faire economic policy. One unsophisticated concept embedded in his work, the "four-stage theory" of social development, would have long-term consequences in relationships between the West and other cultures. *page 422*

HOW DID the *philosophes* apply Enlightenment ideas to political issues?

Political Thought of the *Philosophes* The French *philosophes* were the most discontented of a discontented lot. France's problems gave the *philosophes* more to criticize there than elsewhere in Europe at the time. The French *philosophes* proposed a wide array of reforms. Montesquieu and Rousseau both had a substantial influence on future political developments, and they represent two very different perspectives. Montesquieu believed that only empirical study could determine the best government for a given country. He advocated the division of political power. Rousseau was a radical, who raised the fundamental question of what constitutes the good life. He believed society was more important than the individual, because only within a properly functioning society could an individual live a moral life. A few thinkers criticized European treatment of and attitudes toward native peoples living in European empires, especially in the Americas, but such views would not gain significant public resonance until the end of the nineteenth century. *page 424*

WHAT ROLE did women play in the Enlightenment?

Women in the Thought and Practice of the Enlightenment The salons of French women were instrumental in spreading the ideas of the *philosophes*, but most of the *philosophes* were at best weak advocates of reforms that would help women. Some *philosophes* advocated improvements in education for women. But many *philosophes*—even the otherwise radical Rousseau!—had very traditional ideas about gender roles, and endorsed the double standard that frowned on female sexual expression. The beliefs that women were physiologically inferior to men and women's activities and aspirations should be limited to the domestic sphere were widely endorsed by *philosophes*. Late in the eighteenth century, Mary Wollstonecraft's *A Vindication of the Rights of Woman* placed women's rights within the Enlightenment agenda. *page 427*

HOW DID rococo and neoclassicism styles reflect and contribute to the prevailing trends of the age?

Rococo and neoclassical Styles in Eighteenth-Century Art In the early eighteenth century, the rococo style of art and architecture flourished in the private estates of monarchs and aristocrats and also in public buildings, both secular and religious. Rococo expressed frivolity, sensuality, and ornamentation that, by representing political and social elites of the Old Regime, eventually helped to increase popular hostility toward the decadence and corruption among the privileged strata of society. In the second half of the century, rococo gave way to neoclassicism, which embodied a didactic and disciplined attitude that hearkened back to the Renaissance and antiquity. Neoclassical works were concerned with public life and moral questions about civic virtue and self-sacrifice. Its works of art and architecture became identified with Enlightenment thought and criticism of the Old Regime and eventually with the French Revolution. *page 428*

WHAT WAS enlightened absolutism?

Enlightened Absolutism Many *philosophes* were fundamentally monarchists, although they believed monarchies should be reformed. In the last third of the eighteenth century, enlightened absolutism emerged under Frederick II of Prussia, Joseph II of Austria, and Catherine II of Russia. Frederick the Great tried to improve Prussian agriculture and the economy, with limited success. He widened religious toleration, codified Prussian law, and described himself as "the first servant of the State." Joseph II of Austria was unsuccessful in many of his reform efforts, and his successor repealed many of them. Catherine the Great empowered the local nobility and had some success in growing Russia's economy. She expanded Russian territory through various means including the partition of Poland. Late in the eighteenth century, all three of these regimes became increasingly conservative and politically repressive. After the French Revolution, central and eastern Europe's ruling classes began to resist change and oppose Enlightenment values. *page 430*

REVIEW QUESTIONS

1. What were the major formative influences on the *philosophes*? Why did the *philosophes* consider organized religion their greatest enemy? What were the basic tenets of deism? What were the attitudes of the *philosophes* toward women?
2. How did the arguments of the mercantilists differ from the theories developed by Adam Smith in *The Wealth of Nations*? How did each side in this debate view the earth's resources?
3. What political views were held by Montesquieu and Rousseau? Was Rousseau a child of the Enlightenment, or was he its opponent? Which did Rousseau value more, the individual or society?
4. What were the main Enlightenment attitudes about women? What was the significance of Mary Wollstonecraft?
5. How did the eighteenth-century styles of rococo and neoclassicism reflect and contribute to the prevailing political and social trends of the age?
6. Were the enlightened monarchs true believers in the ideals of the *philosophes* or was their "enlightenment" merely a pose or veneer? Was their power really absolute?

KEY TERMS

deism (p. 420)
laissez-faire (p. 424)
neoclassicism (p. 429)
rococo (p. 428)
tabula rasa (p. 416)

For additional learning resources related to this chapter, please go to **www.myhistorylab.com**

PEARSON myhistorylab

18

The French Revolution

On July 14, 1789, crowds stormed the Bastille, a prison in Paris. This event, whose only practical effect was to free a few prisoners, marked the first time the populace of Paris redirected the course of the revolution.

Anonymous, France, eighteenth century, *Siege of the Bastille, 14 July, 1789*. Musée de la Ville de Paris, Musée Carnavalet, Paris, France. Bridgeman–Giraudon/Art Resource, NY

What made the Bastille a target of popular anger and resentment?

THE CRISIS OF THE FRENCH MONARCHY *page 442*

HOW DID the financial weakness of the French monarchy lay the foundations of revolution in 1789?

THE REVOLUTION OF 1789 *page 444*

HOW DID the calling of the Estates General lead to revolution?

THE RECONSTRUCTION OF FRANCE *page 448*

HOW DID the National Constituent Assembly reorganize France?

THE END OF THE MONARCHY: A SECOND REVOLUTION *page 455*

WHAT LED to the radicalization of the French Revolution?

EUROPE AT WAR WITH THE REVOLUTION *page 457*

HOW DID Europe respond to the French Revolution?

THE REIGN OF TERROR *page 458*

HOW DID war and ideology combine to create the Reign of Terror?

THE THERMIDORIAN REACTION *page 461*

WHAT COURSE did the French Revolution take after 1794?

n 1789, the long-festering conflict between the French monarchy and aristocracy turned into a revolution that overturned the political and social order of France. Amidst the turmoil, small-town lawyers, artisans, and others of low birth exercised more control over events than kings and nobles. Neither France nor Europe would ever be the same. ■

THE CRISIS OF THE FRENCH MONARCHY

HOW DID the financial weakness of the French monarchy lay the foundations of revolution in 1789?

Although the French Revolution would shatter many of the political, social, and ecclesiastical structures of Europe, its origins lay in a much more mundane problem. By the late 1780s, the French royal government could not command sufficient taxes to finance itself.

The Monarchy Seeks New Taxes

The French monarchy emerged from the Seven Years' War (1756–1763) defeated, deeply in debt, and unable thereafter to put its finances on a sound basis. French support of the American revolt against Great Britain further deepened the financial difficulties of the government. Given the economic vitality of France, the debt was neither overly large nor disproportionate to the debts of other European powers. The problem lay with the inability of the royal government to tap the nation's wealth through taxes to service and repay the debt.

The debt was symptomatic of the failure of the late-eighteenth-century French monarchy to come to terms with the political power of aristocratic institutions and, in particular, the *parlements*.

For twenty-five years after the Seven Years' War, a standoff occurred between the monarchy and the aristocracy, as one royal minister after another attempted to devise new tax schemes that would tap the wealth of the nobility, only to be confronted by opposition from both the *Parlement* of Paris and provincial *parlements*.

Well meaning, but weak and vacillating, Louis XVI (r. 1774–1792) stumbled from concession to concession until he finally lost all power to save his throne.

Joseph Siffred Duplessis (1725–1802), *Louis XVI*. Versailles, France. Photograph copyright Bridgeman—Giraudon/Art Resource, NY

In what sense was Louis XVI a weak king? Could a stronger one have prevented the revolution?

In 1770, Louis XV (r. 1715–1774) appointed René Maupeou (1714–1792) as chancellor. The new minister was determined to break the *parlements* and increase taxes on the nobility. He abolished the *parlements* and exiled their members to different parts of the country. He then began an ambitious program to make the administration more efficient. What ultimately doomed Maupeou's policy was less the resistance of the nobility than the unexpected death from smallpox of Louis XV in 1774. His successor, Louis XVI (r. 1774–1792), in an attempt to regain what he conceived to be popular support, dismissed Maupeou, restored all the *parlements*, and confirmed their old powers.

Although the *parlements* spoke for aristocratic interests, they appear to have enjoyed public support. By the second half of the eighteenth century, many French nobles shared with the wealthy professional and commercial classes similar economic interests and similar goals for administrative reforms that would support economic growth. Moreover, throughout these initial and later disputes with the monarchy, the *parlements*, though completely dominated by the aristocracy, used the language of liberty and reform to defend their cause.

The monarchy was unable to rally public opinion to its side because it had lost much of its moral authority. The sexually scandalous life of Louis XV was known throughout France, and the memory of his behavior lingered long after his death. Marie Antoinette (1755–1793), the wife of Louis XVI, also rightly or wrongly, gained a reputation for sexual misconduct and personal extravagance. Furthermore, Louis XVI and his family continued to live at Versailles, rarely leaving its grounds to mix with his subjects and with the aristocracy, who now, unlike in the days of Louis XIV, often dwelled in Paris or on their estates. Hence, the French monarch stood at a distinct popular disadvantage in his clashes first with the *parlements* and later with other groupings of the aristocracy.

This late-eighteenth-century cartoon satirizes the French social structure. It shows a poor man in chains, who represents the vast majority of the population, supporting an aristocrat, a bishop, and a noble of the robe. The aristocrat is claiming feudal rights, the bishop holds papers associating the church with religious persecution and clerical privileges, and the noble of the robe holds a document listing the rights of the noble-dominated *parlements*.

CORBIS/Bettmann

What does this cartoon suggest about the relationship between the crown, the clergy, and the aristocracy in eighteenth-century France?

Necker's Report

France's successful intervention on behalf of the American colonists against the British only worsened the financial problems of Louis XVI's government. Nonetheless, the new royal director-general of finances, Jacques Necker (1732–1804), a Swiss banker, produced a public report in 1781 that suggested the situation was not as bad as had been feared. Necker's report also revealed that a large portion of royal expenditures went to pensions for aristocrats and other royal court favorites. This revelation angered court aristocratic circles, and Necker soon left office. His financial sleight of hand, nonetheless, made it more difficult for government officials to claim a real need to raise new taxes.

Calonne's Reform Plan and the Assembly of Notables

The monarchy hobbled along until 1786. By this time, Charles Alexandre de Calonne (1734–1802) was the minister of finance. Calonne proposed to encourage internal trade, to lower some taxes, such as the *gabelle* on salt, and to transform the *corvée*, peasants' labor services on public works, into money payments. He also sought to remove internal barriers to trade and reduce government regulation of the grain trade. More importantly, Calonne wanted to introduce a new land tax that all landowners would have to pay regardless of their social status. Calonne also intended to establish new local assemblies made up of landowners to approve land taxes; in these assemblies the voting power would have depended on the amount of land a person owned rather than on his social status. All these proposals would have undermined both the political and the social power of the French aristocracy.

Calonne needed public support for such bold new undertakings. In February 1787, he met with an Assembly of Notables, nominated by the royal ministry from the upper ranks of the aristocracy and the church, to seek support for his plan. The Assembly adamantly refused to give it and called for the reappointment of Necker, who they believed had left the country in sound fiscal condition. In addition, they claimed that only the Estates General of France, a medieval institution that had not met since 1614, could consent to new taxes. The notables believed that calling the Estates General, which had been traditionally organized to allow aristocratic and church dominance, would actually allow the nobility to have a direct role in governing the country alongside the monarchy.

QUICK REVIEW

Calonne's Reform Plan

- Charles Alexandre de Calonne (1734–1802): minister of finance under Louis XVI
- Wanted to encourage internal trade, lower some taxes, and transform peasants' services to money payments
- Most significant proposal was a new tax on landowners

Deadlock and the Calling of the Estates General

Again, Louis XVI backed off. He replaced Calonne with Étienne Charles Loménie de Brienne (1727–1794), archbishop of Toulouse and the chief opponent of Calonne at the Assembly of Notables. Once in office, Brienne found, to his astonishment, that the financial situation was as bad as his predecessor had asserted. Brienne himself now sought to reform the land tax but received no more cooperation from the aristocracy than had his predecessors.

At the same time, local aristocratic *parlements* and estates in the provinces were making their own demands. They wanted to restore the privileges they had enjoyed during the early seventeenth century, before Richelieu and Louis XIV had crushed their independence. Furthermore, bringing the financial crisis to a new point of urgency, bankers refused in the summer of 1788 to extend necessary short-term credit to the government. Consequently, in July 1788, the king, through Brienne, agreed to convoke the Estates General the next year. Brienne resigned, and Necker replaced him.

THE REVOLUTION OF 1789

HOW DID the calling of the Estates General lead to revolution?

The Estates General Becomes the National Assembly

The Estates General had been called because of the political deadlock between the French monarchy and the vested interests of aristocratic institutions and the church. Almost immediately after it was summoned, however, the three groups, or estates, represented within it clashed with each other. The First Estate was the clergy, the Second Estate the nobility, and the **Third Estate** was, theoretically, everyone else in the kingdom, although its representatives were drawn primarily from wealthy members of the commercial and professional middle classes. All the representatives in the Estates General were men. During the widespread public discussions preceding the meeting of the Estates General, representatives of the Third Estate made it clear they would not permit the monarchy and the aristocracy to decide the future of the nation.

Third Estate Members of the commercial and professional middle classes, or everyone but the clergy (the First Estate) and the nobility (the Second Estate).

Debate over Organization and Voting Before the Estates General gathered, a public debate over its proper organization drew the lines of basic disagreement. The aristocracy made two important attempts to limit the influence of the Third Estate. First, a reconvened Assembly of Notables demanded that each estate have an equal number of representatives. Second, in September 1788, the *Parlement* of Paris ruled that voting in the Estates General should be conducted by order rather than by head—that is, each estate, or order, in the Estates General, rather than each individual member, should have one vote. This procedure would in all likelihood have ensured the aristocratically dominated First and Second Estates could always outvote the Third by a vote of two estates to one estate.

In many respects the interests of the aristocracy and the most prosperous and well-educated members of the Third Estates had converged during the eighteenth century. Yet a fundamental social distance separated the members of the two orders. Many aristocrats were much richer than members of the Third Estate, and noblemen had all but monopolized the high command in the army and navy. The Third Estate had also experienced various forms of political and social discrimination from the nobility. The resistance of the nobility to voting by head confirmed the suspicions and resentments of the members of the Third Estate.

Doubling the Third In the face of widespread public uproar over the aristocratic effort to dominate composition and procedures of the Estates General, the royal council eventually decided that strengthening the Third Estate would best serve the interests of the monarchy and the cause of fiscal reform. In December 1788, the council announced the Third Estate would elect twice as many representatives as either the nobles or the clergy. This so-called doubling of the Third Estate meant it could easily dominate the Estates General if voting proceeded by head rather than by order. The method of voting had not yet been decided when the Estates General gathered at Versailles in May 1789.

The *Cahiers de Doléances* When the representatives came to the royal palace, they brought with them *cahiers de doléances*, or lists of grievances, registered by the local electors, to be presented to the king. The overwhelming demand of the *cahiers* was for equality of rights among the king's subjects. Yet it is also clear that the *cahiers* that originated among the nobility were not radically different from those of the Third Estate. There was broad agreement that the French government needed major reform, that greater equality in taxation and other matters was desirable, and that many aristocratic privileges must be abandoned. But that conflict among the estates, rather than cooperation, was to be the case became clear almost from the moment the Estates General opened.

The National Assembly and the Tennis Court Oath The complaints, demands, and hopes for reform expressed in the *cahiers* could not, however, be discussed until the questions of the organization and voting in the Estates General had been decided. For several weeks there was a standoff. Then, on June 1, the Third Estate invited the clergy and the nobles to join them in organizing a new legislative body. A few priests did so. On June 17, that body declared itself the National Assembly, and on June 19 by a narrow margin, the Second Estate voted to join the Assembly.

At this point, Louis XVI hoped to reassert a role in the proceedings. He intended to call a "Royal Session" of the Estates General for June 23 and closed the room where the National Assembly had been gathering. On June 20, finding themselves thus unexpectedly locked out of their usual meeting place, the National Assembly moved to a nearby indoor tennis court. There, its members took an oath to continue to sit until they had given France a constitution. Louis XVI ordered the National Assembly to desist, but many clergy and nobles joined the Assembly in defiance of the royal command.

Overview The Estates General Becomes the National Assembly

DEBATE OVER ORGANIZATION AND VOTING	• Public debate over proper organization • Spokespeople denounced the claims of the aristocracy • Resistance of nobility confirmed suspicions of Third Estate members
DOUBLING THE THIRD	• Council announces Third Estate would elect more representatives • Doubling meant Third Estate could dominate the Estates General • Liberal nobles and clergy supported the Third Estate
THE *CAHIERS DE DOLÉANCES*	• Lists of grievances brought to the royal palace by representatives • Documents recorded government waste, indirect taxes, and corruption • Demand was for equality of rights among the king's subjects
THE THIRD ESTATE CREATES THE NATIONAL ASSEMBLY	• Third Estate refused to sit as a separate order as the king desired • For several weeks there was a standoff • Clergy and nobles joined Third Estate, becoming National Assembly
THE TENNIS COURT OATH	• National Assembly took oath to sit until they gave France a constitution • The king eventually stipulated and requested the Estates to join them • Henceforth, monarchy could govern only in cooperation with Assembly

On June 27, the king, now having completely lost control of the events around him, capitulated and formally requested the First and Second Estates to meet with the National Assembly, where voting would occur by head rather than by order. The National Assembly, which renamed itself the National Constituent Assembly because of its intention to write a new constitution, was composed of a majority of members drawn from all three orders, who shared liberal goals for the administrative, constitutional, and economic reform of the country. The revolution in France against government by privileged hereditary orders, however, rapidly extended beyond events occurring at Versailles.

QUICK REVIEW
National Assembly

- June 17, 1789: Third Estate declares itself National Assembly
- Tennis Court Oath: pledge to sit until France had a constitution
- June 27, 1789: king capitulates to National Assembly

Fall of the Bastille

Two new forces soon intruded on the scene. First, Louis XVI again attempted to regain the political initiative by mustering royal troops near Versailles and Paris. On the advice of Queen Marie Antoinette, his brothers, and the most conservative aristocrats at court, he seemed to be contemplating the use of force against the National Constituent Assembly. On July 11, without consulting Assembly leaders, Louis abruptly dismissed Necker, his minister of finance. Louis's gathering troops and dismissal of Necker marked the beginning of a steady, but consistently poorly executed, royal attempt to undermine the Assembly and halt the revolution.

The second new factor to impose itself on the events at Versailles was the populace of Paris, which numbered more than 600,000 people. Those Parisians who had elected representatives to the Third Estate had continued to meet after the elections. By June they were organizing a citizen militia and collecting arms to protect the Assembly and the revolution it had begun.

On July 14, large crowds of Parisians, most of them small shopkeepers, tradespeople, artisans, and wage earners, marched to the Bastille to get weapons for the militia. Through miscalculations and ineptitude by the governor of the fortress, the troops in the Bastille fired into the crowd, killing ninety-eight people and wounding many others. Thereafter, the crowd stormed the fortress.

On July 15, the militia of Paris, by then called the National Guard, offered its command to a young liberal aristocrat, the Marquis de Lafayette (1757–1834). This hero of the American Revolution gave the guard a new insignia: the red and blue stripes from the colors of the coat of arms of Paris, separated by the white stripe of the royal flag. The emblem became the revolutionary *cockade* (badge) and eventually the tricolor flag of revolutionary France.

QUICK REVIEW
July 14, 1789

- June 1789: fear of attack by king spread throughout Paris
- July 14: 800 mostly working-class people march on the Bastille to demand weapons for the city's militia
- Bastille was stormed after soldiers fired on crowd

The attack on the Bastille marked the first of many crucial *journées*, days on which the populace of Paris redirected the course of the revolution. The fall of the fortress signaled that the National Constituent Assembly alone would not decide the political future of the nation. As the news of the taking of the Bastille spread, similar disturbances took place in provincial cities. A few days later, Louis XVI again bowed to the force of events and personally visited Paris, where he wore the revolutionary *cockade* and recognized the organized electors as the legitimate government of the city and the legitimacy of the National Guard.

The "Great Fear" and the Night of August 4

Simultaneous with the popular urban disturbances, a movement known as the "Great Fear" swept across much of the French countryside. Rumors that royal troops would be sent into the rural districts intensified the peasant disturbances that had begun during the spring. On the night of August 4, 1789, aristocrats in the National Constituent Assembly attempted to halt the spreading disorder in the countryside. By prearrangement, several liberal nobles and clerics rose in the Assembly and renounced their feudal rights, dues, and tithes. After the night of August 4, all French citizens were subject to the same and equal laws. This dramatic session of the Assembly effectively abolished the major social institutions of the Old Regime and created an unforeseen situation that required a vast legal and social reconstruction of the nation.

Both the attack on the Bastille and the Great Fear displayed characteristics of the urban and rural riots that had occurred often in eighteenth-century France. A deep economic downturn had struck France in 1787 and continued into 1788. The harvests for both years had been poor, and the food prices in 1789 were higher than at any time since 1703. Wages had not kept up with the rise in prices. Throughout the winter of 1788–1789, an unusually cold one, many people suffered from hunger. Wage and food riots had erupted in several cities. These economic problems fanned the fires of revolution.

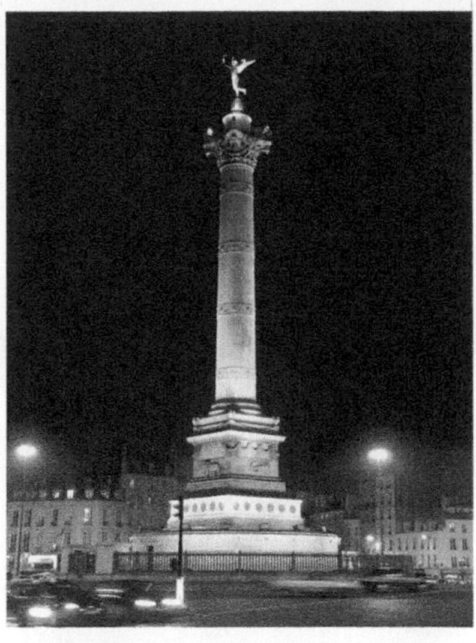

The July Column, which stands in the former location of the Bastille. The "Spirit of Liberty" is on top of the column.

James McConnachie © Rough Guides

The Declaration of the Rights of Man and Citizen

On August 27, 1789, the Assembly issued the Declaration of the Rights of Man and Citizen. This declaration drew on the political language of the Enlightenment and the Declaration of Rights that the state of Virginia had adopted in June 1776.

The French declaration proclaimed that all men were "born and remain free and equal in rights." Governments existed to protect those rights. All political sovereignty resided in the nation and its representatives. All citizens were to be equal before the law and were to be "equally admissible to all public dignities, offices, and employments, according to their capacity, and with no other distinction than that of their virtues and talents." There were to be due process of law and presumption of innocence until proof of guilt. Freedom of religion was affirmed. Taxation was to be apportioned equally according to the capacity to pay. Property constituted "an inviolable and sacred right."

It was not accidental that the Declaration of the Rights of Man and Citizen specifically applied to men and not to women. As discussed in Chapter 17, much of the political language of the Enlightenment, and especially that associated with Rousseau, separated men and women into distinct gender spheres. According to this view, which influenced legislation during the revolution, men were suited for citizenship, women for motherhood and the domestic life. Nonetheless, in the charged atmosphere of the summer of 1789, many politically active and informed Frenchwomen hoped the guarantees of the declaration would be extended to them. Those hopes would be disappointed during the years of the revolution and for many decades thereafter.

Nonetheless, over the succeeding two centuries the universalist language of the Declaration of the Rights of Man and Citizen would provide an intellectual framework for bringing into the realm of active civic life many groups that were excluded in the late eighteenth century. (See "Compare & Connect: The Declaration of the Rights of Man and Citizen Opens the Door for Disadvantaged Groups to Demand Equal Civic Rights," pages 450–451.)

The Parisian Women's March on Versailles

Louis XVI stalled before ratifying both the Declaration of the Rights of Man and Citizen and the aristocratic renunciation of feudalism. His hesitations fueled suspicions that he might again try to resort to force. Moreover, bread remained scarce and expensive. On October 5, some 7,000 Parisian women armed with pikes, guns, swords, and knives marched to Versailles demanding more bread. Deeply suspicious of the monarch and believing that he must be kept under the watchful eye of the people, the Parisians

The women of Paris marched to Versailles on October 5, 1789. The following day the royal family was forced to return to Paris with them. Henceforth, the French government would function under the constant threat of mob violence.

Anonymous, eighteenth century, *To Versailles, to Versailles.* The women of Paris going to Versailles, 7 October, 1789. French. Musée de la Ville de Paris, Musée Carnavalet, Paris, France. Photograph copyright Bridgeman—Giraudon/Art Resource, NY

What role did women play in Parisian politics during the revolution?

demanded that Louis and his family return to Paris with them. The monarch had no real choice. On October 6, 1789, his carriage followed the crowd into the city, where he and his family settled in the old palace of the Tuileries in the heart of Paris.

The National Constituent Assembly also soon moved to Paris. Thereafter, both Paris and France remained relatively stable and peaceful until the summer of 1792. A decline in the price of bread in late 1789 helped to calm the atmosphere.

THE RECONSTRUCTION OF FRANCE

HOW DID the National Constituent Assembly reorganize France?

In Paris, the National Constituent Assembly set about reorganizing France. In government, it pursued a policy of constitutional monarchy; in administration, rationalism; in economics, unregulated freedom; and in religion, anticlericalism. Throughout its proceedings and following the principles of the Declaration of the Rights of Man and Citizen, the Assembly was determined to protect property in all its forms.

QUICK REVIEW

National Constituent Assembly Policies

- Determined to protect private property
- Forbid formation of workers' organizations
- Confiscated and sold church lands

Political Reorganization

In the Constitution of 1791, the National Constituent Assembly established a constitutional monarchy. The major political authority of the nation would be a unicameral Legislative Assembly, in which all laws would originate. The monarch was allowed a suspensive veto that could delay, but not halt, legislation. The Assembly also had the power to make war and peace.

Active and Passive Citizens The constitution provided for an elaborate system of indirect elections to thwart direct popular pressure on the government. The citizens of France were divided into active and passive categories. Only active citizens—that is, men paying annual taxes equal to three days of local labor wages—could vote. They chose electors, who then, in turn, voted for the members of the legislature. Further property qualifications were required to serve as an elector or member of the legislature. Only about 50,000 citizens of a population of about 25 million could qualify as electors or members of the Legislative Assembly. Women could neither vote nor hold office. These constitutional arrangements effectively transferred political power from aristocratic wealth to all forms of propertied wealth in the nation.

Olympe de Gouges's Declaration of the Rights of Woman The laws that excluded women from voting and holding office did not pass unnoticed. In 1791, Olympe de Gouges (d. 1793), a butcher's daughter from Montauban in northwest France who became a major revolutionary radical in Paris, composed a Declaration of the Rights of Woman, which she ironically addressed to Queen Marie Antoinette. Much of the document reprinted the Declaration of the Rights of Man and Citizen, adding the word *woman* to the various original clauses. That strategy demanded that women be regarded as citizens and not merely as daughters, sisters, wives, and mothers of citizens. Olympe de Gouges further outlined rights that would permit women to own property and require men to recognize the paternity of their children. She called for equality of the sexes in marriage and improved education for women. Her declaration illustrated how the simple listing of rights in the Declaration of the Rights of Man and Citizen created a structure of universal civic expectations even for those it did not cover. (See "Compare & Connect: The Declaration of the Rights of Man and Citizen Opens the Door for Disadvantaged Groups to Demand Equal Civic Rights," pages 450–451.)

Departments Replace Provinces In reconstructing the local and judicial administration, the National Constituent Assembly applied the rational spirit of the Enlightenment. It abolished the ancient French provinces, such as Burgundy and Brittany, and established in their place eighty-three administrative units called departments, or *départements*, of generally equal size named after rivers, mountains, and other geographical features. (See Map 18–1, page 452.)

All the ancient judicial courts, including the seigneurial courts and the *parlements*, were also abolished and replaced by uniform courts with elected judges and prosecutors. Procedures were simplified, and the most degrading punishments, such as branding, torture, and public flogging, were removed from the books.

Economic Policy

In economic matters, the National Constituent Assembly suppressed the guilds and liberated the grain trade. The Assembly established the metric system to provide the nation with uniform weights and measures. (See "Encountering the Past: The Metric System," page 453.)

Workers' Organizations Forbidden The new policies of economic freedom and uniformity disappointed both peasants and urban workers. In 1789, the Assembly placed the burden of proof on the peasants to rid themselves of the residual feudal dues for which compensation was to be paid. On June 14, 1791, the Assembly crushed the attempts of urban workers to protect their wages by enacting the Chapelier Law, which forbade workers' associations. Peasants and workers were henceforth to be left to the freedom and mercy of the marketplace.

Confiscation of Church Lands While these various reforms were being put into effect, the financial crisis that had occasioned the calling of the Estates General persisted. The continuing financial problem led the Assembly to take what may well have been, for the future of French life and society, its most decisive action. The Assembly decided to finance the debt by confiscating and then selling the land and property of the Roman Catholic Church in France. The results were further inflation, religious schism, and civil war. In effect, the National Constituent Assembly had opened a new chapter in the relations of church and state in Europe.

COMPARE & CONNECT

THE DECLARATION OF THE RIGHTS OF MAN AND CITIZEN OPENS THE DOOR FOR DISADVANTAGED GROUPS TO DEMAND EQUAL CIVIC RIGHTS

The National Assembly passed the Declaration of the Rights of Man and Citizen on August 26, 1789. The principles of the declaration were very broad and in theory could be extended beyond the domestic male French citizens to whom it applied. Within months various civically disadvantaged groups stepped forward to demand inclusion within the newly proclaimed realm of civic rights. These included free persons of color from French Caribbean colony of St. Domingue and French women. It should be noted that during the same period French Jews also asked to have the principles of religious toleration proclaimed in the Declaration of the Rights of Man and Citizen extended to themselves.

QUESTIONS

1. How does Raymond portray himself as free but still clearly victimized by the Assembly in St. Domingue, composed only of white members?
2. How does Raymond invoke the principles of the Declaration of the Rights of Man and Citizen to apply pressure on the French National Assembly?
3. What are the specific parallels that de Gouges drew between the rights of man and the rights of woman?
4. How does her declaration suggest civic responsibilities for women as well as rights?
5. On what grounds might the same people who championed the Declaration of the Rights of Man and Citizen in 1789 deny the extension of those rights to the various groups that soon demanded inclusion under the ideals of the declaration?

I. A FREE PERSON OF COLOR FROM ST. DOMINGUE DEMANDS RECOGNITION OF HIS STATUS

In the spring of 1791, Julian Raymond, a free person of color from the French Caribbean colony of St. Domingue (Haiti), petitioned the French National Assembly to recognize persons such as himself as free citizens. The National Assembly did so in May 1791 but later rescinded the decree. Only in March, 1792 did the Assembly firmly recognize the civic equality of such persons. The background for the request and for the confusion of the French National Assembly over the matter was the eruption of the slave revolution in Haiti, which is discussed in Chapter 20.

Remaining to this day under the oppression of the white colonists, we dare hope that we do not ask the National Assembly in vain for the rights, which it has declared, belong to every man.

In our just protests, if the troubles, the calumnies that you have witnessed until today under the legislation of white colonists, and finally, if the truths which we had the honor of presenting yesterday to the bar of the Assembly do not overcome the unjust pretensions of the while colonial legislators who want to [proceed] without our participation, we beg the Assembly not to jeopardize the little remaining liberty we have, that of being able to abandon the ground soaked with the blood of our brothers and of permitting us to flee the sharp knife of the laws they will prepare against us.

If the Assembly has decided to pass a law which lets our fate depend on twenty-nine whites [in the colonial Assembly], our decided enemies, we demand to add an amendment to the decree which would be rendered in this situation, that free men of color can emigrate with their fortunes so that they can be neither disturbed nor hindered by the whites.

Mr. President, this is the last recourse which remains for us to escape the vengeance of the white colonists who menace us for not having given up our claims to the rights which the National Assembly has declared belong to every man.

Source: As quoted in Laura Mason and Tracey Rizzo, *The French Revolution: A Document Collection* (Boston: Houghton Mifflin Company, 1999), p. 109.

II. OLYMPE DE GOUGES ISSUES A DECLARATION OF THE RIGHTS OF WOMAN

In September 1791, Olympe de Gouges published a Declaration of the Rights of Woman that paralleled in many respects the Declaration of the Rights of Man and Citizen proclaimed two years earlier. A self-educated woman and butcher's daughter, she had written widely on a number of reform topics. Radical as she was, she remained loyal to the monarchy and was eventually executed by the revolutionary government in 1793.

Mothers, daughters, sisters [and] representatives of the nation demand to be constituted into a national assembly. . . . Consequently, the sex that is as superior in beauty as it is in courage during the sufferings of maternity recognizes and declares in the presence and under the auspices of the Supreme Being, the following Rights of Woman and of Female Citizens.

ARTICLE I

Woman is born free and lives equal to man in her rights. Social distinctions can be based only on the common utility.

ARTICLE II

The purpose of any political association is the conservation of the natural and imprescriptible rights of woman and man; these rights are liberty property, security, and especially resistance to oppression. . . .

ARTICLE IV

Liberty and justice consist of restoring all that belongs to others; thus, the only limits on the exercise of the natural rights of woman are perpetual male tyranny; these limits are to be reformed by the laws of nature and reason. . . .

ARTICLE VI

The law must be the expression of the general will; all female and male citizens must contribute either personally or through their representatives to its formation; it must be the same for all: male and female citizens, being equal in the eyes of the law, must be equally admitted to all honors, positions, and public employment according to their capacity and without other distinctions besides those of their virtues and talents. . . .

This is an example of the French Revolution–era clothing worn by the *sans-culottes* or members of the poorer classes and their leaders.

Dorling Kindersley Media Library/Mark Hamilton © Dorling Kindersley

What political and social values are revealed by the clothes of the *sans-culottes*?

ARTICLE X

No one is to be disquieted for his very basic opinions; woman has the right to mount the scaffold; she must equally have the right to mount the rostrum, provided that her demonstrations do not disturb the legally established public order. . . .

ARTICLE XIII

For the support of the public force and the expenses of administration, the contributions of woman and man are equal; she shares all the duties and all the painful tasks; therefore, she must have the same share in the distribution of positions, employment, offices, honors, and jobs. . . .

ARTICLE XVII

Property belongs to both sexes whether united or separate; for each it is an inviolable and sacred right; no one can be deprived of it, since it is the true patrimony of nature, unless the legally determined public need obviously dictates it, and then only with a just and prior indemnity.

POSTSCRIPT

Woman, wake up; the tocsin of reason is being heard throughout the whole universe; discover your rights.

Source: As quoted in Darline Gay Levy, Harriet Branson Applewhite, and Mary Durham Johnson, eds., *Women in Revolutionary Paris, 1789–1795* (Urbana: University of Illinois Press, 1980), pp. 87–96.

MAP EXPLORATION

Interactive map: To explore this map further, go to www.myhistorylab.com

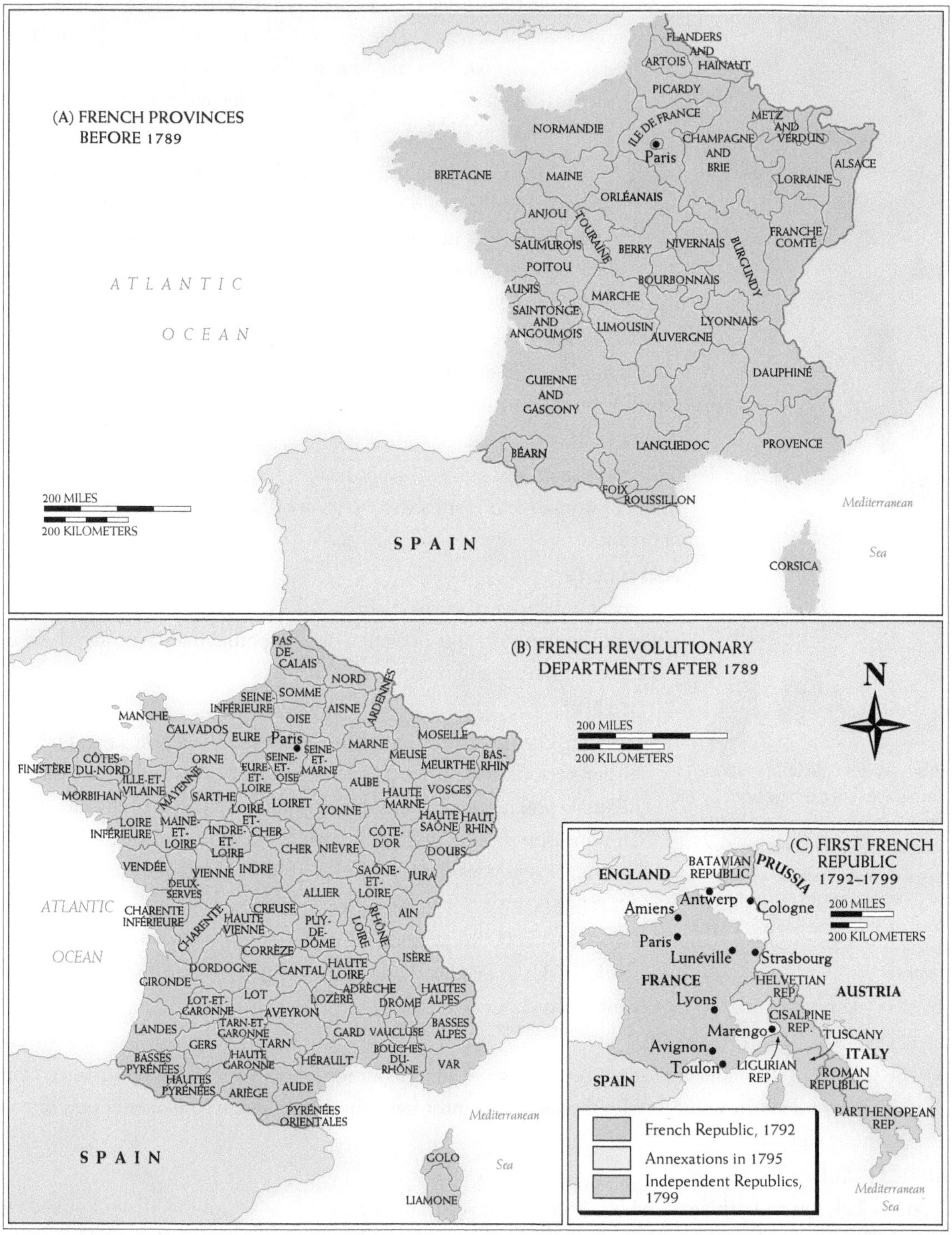

MAP 18–1 French Provinces and the Republic In 1789, the National Constituent Assembly redrew the map of France. The ancient provinces (A) were replaced with a large number of new, smaller departments (B). This redrawing of the map was part of the Assembly's effort to impose greater administrative rationality in France. The borders of the republic (C) changed as the French army conquered new territory.

What do the revolutionary departments suggest about prevailing attitudes toward administrative governance after 1789?

ENCOUNTERING THE PAST

The Metric System

France's revolutionaries hoped to realize the Enlightenment dream of dispelling superstition and obscurity by establishing the reign of science in all things. One of the revolution's lasting achievements was to simplify commercial transactions by eliminating the numerous local systems of weights and measures that had sprung up during the Middle Ages. There were political as well as economic motives for promoting the use of a common standard of measurement throughout the country. It symbolized France's existence as a single "indivisible" republic.

The metric (from *meter*) system, which the Assembly adopted (and is widely used today), was based on the work of astronomers. The revolutionaries wanted nature to establish the basic unit of measurement, and they chose the height of the arch of meridians (the highest point reached by the sun around the earth) in the latitude of Paris as their reference point. The meter was defined as one ten-millionth of one-quarter of that meridian. All other measurements of length were defined as decimal fractions or multiples of the meter. The gram, the standard for measuring weights, was decreed to be the weight of a cube of pure water measuring 0.01 meter on each side. Each measurement of weight was a decimal fraction or multiple of the gram.

Scientists quickly took to the new system, but the public resisted and clung to familiar weights and measures. Not until 1840 did political pressure, rationality, and convenience succeed in establishing use of the metric system throughout France. By the end of the nineteenth century, most of continental Europe had adopted it and it had been introduced to Latin America. It spread throughout Asia and Africa in the twentieth century. Today, English-speaking countries constitute the primary exceptions to its use. Scientists, engineers, and physicians employ it, but many people in the United States and Great Britain, despite encouragement, have declined to follow suit.

Jean-Baptiste Delambre (1749–1822) was one of the French astronomers whose measurements of the arch of meridians formed the basis for establishing the length of the meter.

Image Works/Mary Evans Picture Library Ltd.

How did Enlightenment ideas shape the French government's response to the fiscal crisis of the late eighteenth century?

HOW WAS the metric system consistent with the principles of the Enlightenment? Why has its use spread so widely?

The *Assignats* Having chosen to plunder the church, the Assembly authorized the issuance of *assignats*, or government bonds, in December 1789. Their value was guaranteed by the revenue to be generated from the sale of church property. Initially, a limit was set on the quantity of *assignats* to be issued. The bonds, however, proved so acceptable to the public that they began to circulate as currency. The Assembly decided to issue an ever-larger number of them to liquidate the national debt and to create a large body of new property owners with a direct stake in the revolution. Within a few months, however, the value of the *assignats* began to fall and inflation increased, putting new stress on the urban poor.

The *assignats* were government bonds that were backed by confiscated church lands. They circulated as money. When the government printed too many of them, inflation resulted and their value fell.

Bildarchiv Preussischer Kulturbesitz

How did fiscal problems undermine the Republican government in the early years of the revolution?

The Civil Constitution of the Clergy

The confiscation of church lands required an ecclesiastical reconstruction. In July 1790, the National Constituent Assembly issued the Civil Constitution of the Clergy, which transformed the Roman Catholic Church in France into a branch of the secular state. The Assembly, which also dissolved all religious orders in France except those that cared for the sick or ran schools, consulted neither Pope Pius VI (r. 1775–1799) nor the French clergy about these sweeping changes.

The Civil Constitution of the Clergy was the major blunder of the National Constituent Assembly. The measure immediately created immense opposition within the French church, even from bishops who had long championed Gallican liberties over papal domination. In the face of this resistance, the Assembly unwisely ruled that all clergy must take an oath to support the Civil Constitution. Only seven bishops and a little less than half the lower clergy did so. In reprisal, the Assembly designated those clergy who had not taken the oath as "refractory" and removed them from their clerical functions.

Angry reactions were swift. Refractory priests celebrated Mass in defiance of the Assembly. In February 1791, Pope Pius condemned not only the Civil Constitution of the Clergy, but also the Declaration of the Rights of Man and Citizen. Within France itself, the pope's action created a crisis of conscience and political loyalty for all sincere Catholics. Religious devotion and revolutionary loyalty became incompatible for many people.

Counterrevolutionary Activity

The revolution had other enemies besides the pope and devout Catholics. As it became clear that the old political and social order was undergoing fundamental and probably permanent change, many aristocrats, eventually over 16,000, left France. Known as the **émigrés**, they settled in countries near the French border, where they sought to foment counterrevolution. Among the most important of their number was the king's younger brother, the count of Artois (1757–1836). In the summer of 1791, his agents and the queen persuaded Louis XVI to attempt to flee the country.

émigrés French aristocrats and enemies of the revolution who fled to countries on France's borders and set up bases for counterrevolutionary activities.

Flight to Varennes On the night of June 20, 1791, Louis and his immediate family, disguised as servants, left Paris. They traveled as far as Varennes on their way to Metz in eastern France where a royalist military force was waiting for them. At Varennes the king was recognized, and his flight was halted. On June 24, a company of soldiers escorted the royal family back to Paris. It now seemed to many that the king was the chief counterrevolutionary in France and that the constitutional monarchy might not last long. Profound distrust dominated the political scene.

Declaration of Pillnitz Two months later, on August 27, 1791, under pressure from the *émigrés*, Emperor Leopold II (r. 1790–1792) of Austria, who was the brother of Marie Antoinette, and King Frederick William II (r. 1786–1797) of Prussia issued the Declaration of Pillnitz. The two monarchs promised to intervene in France to protect the royal family and to preserve the monarchy if the other major European powers agreed. This provision rendered the declaration meaningless because, at the time, Great Britain would not have given its consent. The declaration was, however, taken seriously in France, where the revolutionaries saw the nation surrounded by aristocratic and monarchical foes seeking to undo all that had been accomplished since 1789.

THE END OF THE MONARCHY: A SECOND REVOLUTION

WHAT LED to the radicalization of the French Revolution?

The National Constituent Assembly drew to a close in September 1791, having completed its task of reconstructing the government and the administration of France. The Assembly had passed a measure that forbade any of its own members to sit in the Legislative Assembly the new constitution established. That new Assembly filled with entirely new members met on October 1 and immediately had to confront the challenges flowing from the resistance to the Civil Constitution of the Clergy, the king's flight, and the Declaration of Pillnitz.

Emergence of the Jacobins

Ever since the original gathering of the Estates General, deputies from the Third Estate had organized themselves into clubs composed of politically like-minded persons. The most famous and best organized of these clubs were the **Jacobins**. They had been the most advanced political group in the National Constituent Assembly and had pressed for a republic rather than a constitutional monarchy. They drew their political language from the most radical thought of the Enlightenment, most particularly Rousseau's emphasis on equality, popular sovereignty, and civic virtue.

Jacobins The best organized of the political clubs, they embraced the most radical of the Enlightenment's political theories, and they wanted a republic, not a constitutional monarchy.

Factionalism plagued the Legislative Assembly throughout its short life (1791–1792). A group of Jacobins known as the *Girondists* assumed leadership of the Assembly. On April 20, 1792, the Girondists led the Legislative Assembly to declare war on Austria, by this time governed by Francis II (r. 1792–1835) and allied to Prussia. The Girondists believed the war would preserve the revolution from domestic enemies and bring the most advanced revolutionaries to power. Paradoxically, Louis XVI and other monarchists also favored the war. They thought the conflict would strengthen the executive power (the monarchy). The king also hoped that foreign armies might defeat French forces and restore the Old Regime. Both sides were playing a dangerously deluded political game. The war radicalized French politics and within months led to what is usually called the second revolution, which overthrew the constitutional monarchy and established a republic.

Initially, the war effort went poorly. In July 1792, the duke of Brunswick, commander of the Prussian forces, issued a manifesto threatening to destroy Paris if the French royal family were harmed. This statement stiffened support for the war and increased distrust of the king.

Late in July, under radical working-class pressure, the government of Paris passed from the elected council to a committee, or *commune*, of representatives from the sections (municipal wards) of the city. Thereafter the Paris commune became an independent political force casting itself in the role of the protector of the gains of the revolution against both internal and external enemies.

On August 10, 1792, a large crowd invaded the Tuileries palace and forced Louis XVI and Marie Antoinette to take refuge in the Legislative Assembly. The crowd fought with the royal Swiss guards. When Louis was finally able to call off the troops, several hundred of them and many Parisian citizens lay dead in the most extensive violence since the fall of the Bastille. Thereafter the royal family was imprisoned in comfortable quarters, but the king was allowed to perform none of his political functions.

The Convention and the Role of the *Sans-Culottes*

The September Massacres Early in September, the Parisian crowd again made its will felt. During the first week of the month, in what are known as the **September Massacres**, the Paris Commune summarily executed or murdered about 1,200 people who

September Massacres The execution ordered by the Paris Commune of approximately 1,200 aristocrats, priests, and common criminals who, because they were being held in city jails, were assumed to be counterrevolutionaries.

were in the city jails. Some of these people were aristocrats or priests, but most were simply common criminals. News of this event along with the massacre of the Swiss guards as well as the imprisonment of the royal family spread rapidly across Europe, rousing new hostility toward the revolutionary government.

The Paris Commune then compelled the Legislative Assembly to call for the election by universal male suffrage of still another new assembly to write a democratic constitution. That body, called the **Convention** after the American Constitutional Convention of 1787, met on September 21, 1792. The previous day, the French army filled with patriotic recruits willing to die for the revolution had halted the Prussian advance at the Battle of Valmy in eastern France. Victory on the battlefield had confirmed the victory of democratic forces at home. As its first act, the Convention declared France a republic—that is, a nation governed by an elected assembly without a monarch.

Convention The newly elected French body that met on September 21, 1792, whose first act was to declare France a republic—a nation governed by an elected assembly without a king.

Goals of the *Sans-culottes* The second revolution had been the work of Jacobins more radical than the Girondists and of the people of Paris known as the ***sans-culottes***. The *sans-culottes* were shopkeepers, artisans, wage earners, and, in a few cases, factory workers. The politics of the Old Regime had ignored them, and the policies of the National Constituent Assembly had left them victims of unregulated economic liberty. The government, however, required their labor and their lives if the war was to succeed. From the summer of 1792 until the summer of 1794, their attitudes, desires, and ideals were the primary factors in the internal development of the revolution.

sans-culottes Parisians (shopkeepers, artisans, wage earners, and factory workers who had been ignored by the Old Regime) who, along with radical Jacobins, began the second revolution in France.

The *sans-culottes* generally knew what they wanted. The Parisian tradespeople and artisans sought immediate relief from food shortages and rising prices through price controls. They believed all people have a right to subsistence, and they resented most forms of social inequality. This attitude made them intensely hostile to the aristocracy and the original leaders of the revolution of 1789 from the Third Estate, who, they believed, simply wanted to share political power, social prestige, and economic security with the aristocracy.

In politics they were antimonarchical, strongly republican, and suspicious even of representative government. They believed the people should make the decisions of government to an extent as great as possible. The Paris Commune organized the previous summer was their chief political vehicle and crowd action their chief instrument of action.

The Policies of the Jacobins The goals of the *sans-culottes* were not wholly compatible with those of the Jacobins, republicans who sought representative government. Jacobin hatred of the aristocracy and hereditary privilege did not extend to a general suspicion of wealth. From the time of Louis XVI's flight to Varennes onward, however, the more extreme Jacobins began to cooperate with leaders of the Parisian *sans-culottes* and the Paris Commune to overthrow the monarchy. Once the Convention began to deliberate, these Jacobins, known as the *Mountain*, worked with the *sans-culottes* to carry the revolution forward and to win the war. This willingness to cooperate with the forces of the popular revolution separated the Mountain from the Girondists, who were also members of the Jacobin Club.

Execution of Louis XVI On January 21, 1793, the Convention executed Louis XVI.

18th century CE. "Execution of Louis XVI." Aquatint. French. Musée de la Ville de Paris, Musée Carnavalet, Paris, France. Copyright Bridgeman-Giraudon/Art Resource, NY

What events led to the radicalization of the revolution and the execution of Louis XVI?

Execution of Louis XVI By the spring of 1793, several issues had brought the Mountain and its *sans-culottes* allies to dominate the Convention and the revolution. In December 1792, Louis XVI was put on trial as mere "Citizen Capet," the original medieval name of the royal family. An overwhelming majority convicted Louis of conspiring against the liberty of the people and the security of the state. Condemned to death by a smaller majority, he was beheaded on January 21, 1793.

The next month, the Convention declared war on Great Britain and Holland, and a month later on Spain. Soon thereafter, the Prussians renewed their offensive and drove the French out of Belgium. To make matters worse, General Dumouriez (1739–1823), the Girondist victor of Valmy, deserted to the enemy. Finally, in March 1793, a royalist revolt led by aristocratic officers and priests erupted in the Vendée in western France and roused much popular support. Thus, the revolution found itself at war with most of Europe and much of the French nation. The Girondists had led the country into the war but had been unable either to win it or to suppress the enemies of the revolution at home. The Mountain stood ready to take up the task.

EUROPE AT WAR WITH THE REVOLUTION

HOW DID Europe respond to the French Revolution?

Initially, the rest of Europe had been ambivalent toward the revolutionary events in France. Those people who favored political reform regarded the revolution as wisely and rationally reorganizing a corrupt and inefficient government. The major foreign governments thought that the revolution meant France would cease to be an important factor in European affairs for years.

EDMUND BURKE ATTACKS THE REVOLUTION

In 1790, however, the Irish-born writer and British statesman Edmund Burke (1729–1799) argued a different position in *Reflections on the Revolution in France*. Burke condemned the reconstruction of the French administration as the application of a blind rationalism that ignored the historical realities of political development and the concrete complexities of social relations. He also forecast further turmoil as people without political experience tried to govern France, predicted the possible deaths of Louis XVI and Marie Antoinette at the hands of the revolutionaries, and forecast that the revolution would end in military despotism. As the revolutionaries proceeded to attack the church, the monarchy, and finally the rest of Europe, Burke's ideas came to have many admirers. By the outbreak of the war with Austria in April 1792, the other European monarchies recognized, along with Burke, the danger of both the ideas and the aggression of revolutionary France. In response, one government after another turned to repressive domestic policies.

SUPPRESSION OF REFORM IN BRITAIN

In Great Britain, William Pitt the Younger (1759–1806), the prime minister, who had unsuccessfully supported moderate reform of Parliament during the 1780s, turned against both reform and popular movements. The government suppressed the London Corresponding Society, founded in 1792 as a working-class reform group. In Birmingham, the government sponsored mob action to drive Joseph Priestley (1733–1804), a famous chemist and a radical political thinker, out of the country. In early 1793, Pitt secured parliamentary approval for acts suspending *habeas corpus* and making the writing of certain ideas treasonable. With less success, Pitt also attempted to curb freedom of the press. All political groups who dared oppose the government faced being associated with sedition.

THE SECOND AND THIRD PARTITIONS OF POLAND, 1793, 1795

The final two partitions of Poland occurred as a direct result of fears by the eastern powers that the principles of the French Revolution were establishing themselves in Poland. After the first partition in 1772, Polish leaders had commenced reforms to provide for a stronger state. In 1791, a group of nobles known as the Polish Patriots actually issued a new constitution. Frederick William II of Prussia (r. 1786–1797) promised to defend the new Polish constitutional order because he believed that a stronger Poland was in Prussia's interest against the growing Russian power. Catherine the Great of Russia also understood that a reformed Polish state would diminish Russian influence in Poland and eastern Europe.

In April 1792, conservative Polish nobles who opposed the reforms invited Russia to restore the old order. In response to the Russian invasion, Frederick William II moved his troops from the west where they were confronting the French revolutionary army to his eastern frontier with Poland. However, rather than protecting Poland as he had promised, Frederick William reached an agreement with Catherine early in 1793 to carry out a second partition of Poland. The reformed constitution was abolished, and the new Polish government remained under the influence of Russia.

In the spring of 1794, Polish officers mutinied against efforts to unite their forces with the Russian army. As the rebellion expanded, the language and symbols of the French Revolution appeared in Polish cities. Before long, Prussia, Austria, and Russia sent troops into Poland. On November 4 in the single bloodiest day of combat in the decade, Russian troops killed well over 10,000 Poles outside Warsaw. Polish officers and troops who escaped Poland after the last partition later fought with the armies of the French Revolution and Napoleon against the forces of the partitioning powers.

THE REIGN OF TERROR

HOW DID war and ideology combine to create the Reign of Terror?

WAR WITH EUROPE

France's invasion and reorganization of the Austrian Netherlands roused the other European powers to hostile action, and heads of state were further alarmed, in November 1792, when the Convention announced it would aid all peoples everywhere who wanted to cast off the burdens of aristocracy and monarchy. The British, whose commerce was directly threatened, were on the point of declaring war on France when the Convention beat them to it (February 1793). By the time the Jacobins took charge of France's government in April 1793, France was at war with Austria, Prussia, Great Britain, Spain, Sardinia, and Holland.

This widening of the war in the winter and spring of 1792–1793 brought new, radical political actions within France as the revolutionary government mobilized itself and the nation for the conflict. Throughout France, there was the sense that a new kind of war had erupted. In this war the major issue was not protection of national borders as such, but rather the defense of the bold new republican political and social order that had emerged since 1789. The immediate need to protect the revolution from enemies, real or imagined, from across the spectrum of French political and social life was considered more important than the security of property or even of life. These actions to protect the revolution and silence dissent came to be known as the **Reign of Terror**.

Reign of Terror Extreme measures employed by the French government in an effort to protect the revolution.

THE REPUBLIC DEFENDED

To mobilize for war, the revolutionary government organized a collective executive in the form of powerful committees. These, in turn, sought to organize all French national life on a wartime footing. The result was an immense military effort dedicated both to protecting and promoting revolutionary ideals.

The Committee of Public Safety In April 1793, the Convention established a Committee of General Security and a Committee of Public Safety to carry out the executive duties of the government. The Committee of Public Safety eventually enjoyed almost dictatorial power. Its members saw their task as saving the revolution from mortal enemies at home and abroad.

The *Levée en Masse* The major problem for the Convention was to wage the war and at the same time to secure domestic support for the war effort. In early June 1793, the Parisian *sans-culottes* invaded the Convention and successfully demanded the expulsion of the Girondist members. That action further radicalized the Convention and gave the Mountain complete control. On August 23, Lazare Carnot (1753–1823), the member of the Committee of Public Safety in charge of the military, began a mobilization for victory by issuing a ***levée en masse***, a military requisition on the entire population, conscripting males into the army and directing economic production to military purposes.

levée en masse Order for total military mobilization of both men and property.

Following the *levée en masse*, the Convention on September 29, 1793, established a ceiling on prices in accord with *sans-culotte* demands. During these same months, the armies of the revolution also successfully crushed many of the counterrevolutionary disturbances in the provinces. Never before had Europe seen a nation organized in this way, nor one defended by a citizen army, which, by late 1794, with over a million men, had become larger than any ever organized in European history.

Other events within France astounded Europeans even more. The Reign of Terror had begun. Those months of quasi-judicial executions and murders stretching from the autumn of 1793 to the midsummer of 1794 are probably the most famous or infamous period of the revolution. They can be understood only in the context of the war on one hand and the revolutionary expectations of the Convention and the *sans-culottes* on the other.

The "Republic of Virtue" and Robespierre's Justification of Terror

The presence of armies closing in on the nation made it easy to dispense with legal due process. The people who sat in the Convention and those sitting on the Committee of Public Safety, however, did not see their actions simply in terms of expediency made necessary by war. They also believed they had created something new in world history, a "republic of virtue." In this republic, civic virtue largely understood in terms of Rousseau's *Social Contract*, the sacrifice of one's self and one's interest for the good of the republic, would replace selfish aristocratic and monarchical corruption. It was in the name of the public good that the Committee of Public Safety carried out the policies of the terror.

The person who embodied this republic of virtue defended by terror was Maximilien de Robespierre (1758–1794), who, by late 1793, had emerged as the dominant figure on the Committee of Public Safety. A shrewd and sensitive politician, Robespierre had opposed the war in 1792 because he feared it might aid the monarchy. He depended largely on the support of the *sans-culottes* of Paris, but he continued to dress as he had before the revolution in powdered wig and knee breeches. For him, the republic of virtue meant whole-hearted support of the republican government, the renunciation of selfish gains from political life, and the assault on foreign and domestic enemies of the revolution.

Maximilien Robespierre (1758–1794) emerged as the most powerful revolutionary figure in 1793 and 1794, dominating the Committee of Public Safety. He considered the Terror essential for the success of the revolution.

Musée des Beaux-Arts, Lille. Bridgeman—Giraudon/Art Resource, NY

What future did Robespierre imagine for France?

Repression of the Society of Revolutionary Republican Women

Revolutionary women established their own distinct institutions during these months. In May 1793, Pauline Léon and Claire Lacombe founded the Society of Revolutionary Republican Women. Its purpose was to fight the internal enemies of the revolution. Members of the society and other women filled the galleries of the Convention to hear the debates and cheer their favorite speakers. The society became increasingly radical, however. Its members sought stricter controls on the price of food and other commodities, worked to ferret out food hoarders, and brawled with working market women whom they thought to be insufficiently revolutionary. The women of the society also demanded the right to wear the revolutionary *cockade* that male citizens usually wore in their hats. By October 1793, the Jacobins in the Convention had begun to fear the turmoil the society was causing and banned all women's clubs and societies. The debates over these decrees show that the Jacobins believed the society opposed many of their economic policies, but the deputies used Rousseau's language of separate spheres for men and women to justify their exclusion of women from active political life.

There were other examples of repression of women in 1793. Olympe de Gouges, author of the Declaration of the Rights of Woman, opposed the Terror and accused Jacobins of corruption. She was guillotined in November 1793. The same year, women were formally excluded from serving in the French army and from the galleries of the Convention. The exclusion of women from public political life was part of the establishment of the Jacobin republic of virtue, because in such a republic men would be active citizens in the military and political sphere and women would be active only in the domestic sphere.

De-Christianization

The most dramatic step taken by the republic of virtue, and one that illustrates its imposition of political values to justify the Terror, was an the Convention's attempt to de-Christianize France. In November 1793, the Convention proclaimed a new calendar dating from the first day of the French Republic. There were twelve months of thirty days each, with names associated with the seasons and climate. Every tenth day, rather than every seventh, was a holiday. In November 1793, the Convention decreed the Cathedral of Notre Dame in Paris to be a "Temple of Reason."

The legislature then sent trusted members, known as deputies on mission, into the provinces to enforce de-Christianization by closing churches, persecuting clergy and believers (both Roman Catholic and Protestant), occasionally forcing priests to marry, and sometime simply by killing priests and nuns. Churches were desecrated, torn down, or used as barns or warehouses. This radical religious policy attacking both clergy and religious property roused enormous popular opposition and alienated parts of the French provinces from the revolutionary government in Paris.

Revolutionary Tribunals

The Reign of Terror manifested itself in revolutionary tribunals that the Convention established during the summer of 1793. The mandate of these tribunals, the most prominent of which was in Paris, was to try the enemies of the republic, but the definition of who was an "enemy" shifted as the months passed. Those whom the tribunal condemned in Paris were beheaded on the guillotine, a recently invented instrument of efficient and supposedly humane execution. Other modes of execution, such as mass shootings and drowning, were used in the provinces.

The first victims of the Terror were Marie Antoinette, other members of the royal family, and aristocrats, who were executed in October 1793. Girondist politicians who had been prominent in the Legislative Assembly followed them. In early 1794, the Terror moved to the provinces, where the deputies on mission presided over the summary execution of thousands of people, most of whom were peasants, who had allegedly supported internal opposition to the revolution. One of the most infamous incidents occurred in Nantes on the west coast of France, where several hundred people, including many priests, were simply tied to rafts and drowned in the river Loire. The victims of the Terror were now coming from every social class, including the *sans-culottes*.

The Festival of the Supreme Being, which took place in June 1794, inaugurated Robespierre's new civic religion. Its climax occurred when a statue of Atheism was burned and another statue of Wisdom rose from the ashes.

Pierre-Antoine Demachy, *Festival of the Supreme Being at the Champ de Mars on June 8, 1794.* Musée de la Ville de Paris, Musée Carnavalet, Paris, France. Bridgeman—Giraudon/Art Resource, NY

Why did the French public fail to embrace the new revolutionary festivals and holidays?

THE END OF THE TERROR

Revolutionaries Turn Against Themselves In Paris during the late winter of 1794, Robespierre began to orchestrate the Terror against republican political figures of the left and right. On March 24, he secured the execution of certain extreme *sans-culottes* leaders known as the *enragés*. Robespierre then turned against other republicans in the Convention. Most prominent among them was Jacques Danton (1759–1794), who had provided heroic national leadership in the dark days of September 1792 and who had later served briefly on the Committee of Public Safety before Robespierre joined the group. Danton and others were accused of being insufficiently militant on the war, profiting monetarily from the revolution, and rejecting the link between politics and moral virtue. Danton was executed in April 1794. Robespierre thus exterminated the leadership of both groups that might have threatened his position.

Fall of Robespierre In May 1794, at the height of his power, Robespierre, considering the worship of "Reason" too abstract for most citizens, replaced it with the "Cult of the Supreme Being." This deistic cult reflected Rousseau's vision of a civic religion that would induce morality among citizens.

On July 26, Robespierre made an ill-tempered speech in the Convention, declaring that other leaders of the government were conspiring against him and the revolution. Similar accusations against unnamed persons had preceded his earlier attacks. No member of the Convention could now feel safe. On July 27—the Ninth of Thermidor on the revolutionary calendar—members of the Convention, by prearrangement, shouted him down when he rose to make another speech. That night Robespierre was arrested, and the next day he and approximately eighty of his supporters were executed.

THE THERMIDORIAN REACTION

WHAT COURSE did the French Revolution take after 1794?

The fall of Robespierre might simply have been one more shift in the turbulent politics of the revolution, but instead it proved to be a major turning point. The members of the Convention used the event to reassert their authority over the executive power of Committee of Public Safety. Within a short time, the Reign of Terror, which had claimed more than 25,000 victims, came to a close. It no longer seemed necessary since the war abroad was going well and the republican forces had crushed the provincial uprisings.

Thermidorian Reaction Tempering of revolutionary fervor that led to the establishment of a new constitutional regime.

This tempering of the revolution, called the **Thermidorian Reaction**, because of its association with the events of 9 Thermidore, consisted of the destruction of the machinery of terror and the establishment of a new constitutional regime. It resulted from a widespread feeling that the revolution had become too radical. The influence of generally wealthy middle-class and professional people soon replaced that of the *sans-culottes*.

In the weeks and months after Robespierre's execution, the Convention allowed the Girondists who had been in prison or hiding to return to their seats. A general amnesty freed political prisoners. Some, though by no means all, of the people responsible for the Terror were removed from public life. The Paris Commune was outlawed, and its leaders and deputies on mission were executed. The Paris Jacobin Club was closed, and Jacobin clubs in the provinces were forbidden to correspond with each other.

The executions of former terrorists marked the beginning of "the white terror." Throughout the country, people who had been involved in the Reign of Terror were attacked and often murdered. Jacobins were executed with little more due process than they had extended to their victims a few months earlier.

The Thermidorian Reaction also saw the repeal of legislation that had been passed in 1792 making divorce more equitable for women. As the passage of that measure suggests, the reaction did not extend women's rights or improve their education. The Thermidorians and their successors had seen enough attempts at political and social change. They sought to return family life to its status before the outbreak of the revolution. Political authorities and the church were determined to reestablish separate spheres for men and women and to reinforce traditional gender roles. As a result, Frenchwomen may have had less freedom after 1795 than before 1789.

THE FRENCH REVOLUTION

1789	
May 5	The Estates General opens at Versailles
June 17	The National Assembly is declared
June 20	The Tennis Court Oath
July 14	Fall of the Bastille
August 4	Surrender of feudal rights
August 27	Declaration of the Rights of Man and Citizen
October 5	Parisian women march on Versailles
1790	
July 14	Louis XVI accepts constitutional monarchy
1791	
June 20	The royal family attempts to flee
October 1	Formation of the Legislative Assembly
1792	
April 20	France declares war on Austria
September 2	The September Massacres
September 21	The Convention meets; monarchy is abolished
1793	
January 21	Louis XVI is executed
February 1	France declares war on Great Britain
April	Formation of the Committee of Public Safety
June 22	Adoption of the Constitution of 1793
August 23	Levée en masse proclaimed
October 16	Marie Antoinette is executed
November 10	The Cult of Reason and the revolutionary calendar
1794	
March 24	Execution of leaders of the *sans-culottes*
May 7	Cult of the Supreme Being proclaimed
June 10	The Law of 22 Prairial is adopted
July 27	Ninth of Thermidor; the fall of Robespierre
1795	
August 22	Constitution of the Year III and the Directory

ESTABLISHMENT OF THE DIRECTORY

The Thermidorian Reaction led to still another new constitution. The Convention issued the Constitution of the Year III, which reflected the Thermidorian determination to reject *both* constitutional monarchy and democracy. In recognition of the danger of a legislature with only one chamber and unlimited authority, this new document provided for a legislature of two houses. The executive body was to be a five-person Directory, chosen from a list supplied by the legislature. Property qualifications limited the franchise, except for soldiers, who were permitted to vote whether they had property or not.

Historically, the term *Thermidor* has come to be associated with political reaction. That association requires considerable qualification. By 1795, the political structure and society of the Old Regime in France based on rank and birth had given way permanently to a political system based on civic equality and social status based on property ownership. Representation was an established principle of politics. Henceforth, the question before France and eventually before all of Europe would be which new groups would be permitted representation. In the *levée en masse*, the French had demonstrated to Europe the power of the secular ideal of nationhood and of the willingness of citizen soldiers to embrace self-sacrifice.

The post-Thermidorian course of the French Revolution did not undo these stunning changes in the political and social contours of Europe. What triumphed in the Constitution of the Year III was the revolution of the holders of property. For this reason the French Revolution has often been considered a victory of the bourgeoisie, or middle class. The property that won the day, however, was not industrial wealth, but the wealth stemming from commerce, the professions, and land. The largest new propertied class to emerge from the revolutionary turmoil was the peasantry, who, as a result of the destruction of aristocratic privileges, now owned their own land.

Removal of the *Sans-culottes* from Political Life

The most decisively reactionary element in the Thermidorian Reaction and the new constitution was the removal of the *sans-culottes* from political life. With the war effort succeeding, the Convention severed its ties with the *sans-culottes*. True to their belief in an unregulated economy, the Thermidorians repealed the ceiling on prices. As a result, the winter of 1794–1795 brought the worst food shortages of the period. There were many food riots, which the Convention suppressed to prove that the era of the *sans-culottes journées* had come to a close. Royalist agents, who aimed to restore the monarchy, tried to take advantage of their discontent. On October 5, 1795—13 Vendémiaire—the sections of Paris led by the royalists rose up against the Convention. The government turned the artillery against the royalist rebels. A general named Napoleon Bonaparte (1769–1821) commanded the cannon, and with a "whiff of grapeshot," he dispersed the crowd.

By the Treaties of Basel in March and June 1795, the Convention concluded peace with Prussia and Spain. The legislators, however, feared a resurgence of both radical democrats and royalists in the upcoming elections. Consequently, the Convention ruled that at least two-thirds of the new legislature must have served in the Convention itself. The Two-Thirds Law, which sought to foster continuity but also clearly favored politicians already in office, quickly undermined public faith in the new constitutional order.

The suppression of the *sans-culottes*, the narrow franchise of the constitution, the Two-Thirds Law, and the Catholic royalist revival presented the Directory with challenges that it was never able to overcome. Because France remained at war with Austria and Great Britain, it needed a broader-based active loyalty than it was able to command. Instead, the Directory came to depend on the power of the army to govern France. All soldiers could vote. Moreover, within the army that the revolution had created and sustained were ambitious officers who were eager for power. As will be seen in the next chapter, the instability of the Directory, the growing role of the army, and the ambitions of its leaders held profound consequences not only for France but for the entire Western world.

SUMMARY

HOW DID the financial weakness of the French monarchy lay the foundations of revolution in 1789?

The Crisis of the French Monarchy The cost of the Seven Years' War had caused a financial crisis for all Europe's monarchies. France's financial situation was exacerbated by the expenses incurred in joining the colonists' side in the American Revolutionary War. The government needed to raise new taxes; new taxes had to be approved by the nobility. France's noble class had been trying to reassert power ever since the end of Louis XIV's reign. The monarch's need for cash presented a perfect opportunity for the aristocrats to gain concessions from the king. Through various negotiations and standoffs, the aristocracy forced Louis XVI to reconvene the Estates General, which had not met since 1614. *page 442*

HOW DID the calling of the Estates General lead to revolution?

The Revolution of 1789 The 1789 calling of the Estates General and the events that followed have shaped the meanings of nation, state, and citizenship ever since. The royal council doubled the Third Estate, potentially strengthening the hand of the bourgeoisie and the nobility. On June 20, 1789, as delegates to the Estates General were attempting to resolve procedural questions, the Third Estate launched the National Assembly. On July 14, 1789, a mob stormed the Bastille and injected a populist, urban element into the political drama. In the countryside, the "Great Fear" intensified ongoing peasant disturbances aimed at limiting aristocratic privilege; on August 4, 1789, nobles and liberals in the National Constituent Assembly renounced their privileges. From then on, all French men were subject to the same laws. On August 27, 1789, the Assembly issued the Declaration of the Rights of Man and Citizen. Again, women were not portrayed as holding political rights. On October 5, 1789, Parisian women marched on Versailles and forced Louis XVI to move to Paris. *page 444*

HOW DID the National Constituent Assembly reorganize France?

The Reconstruction of France The National Constituent Assembly reorganized France as a constitutional monarchy, with a rational administration, an unregulated economy, and a state-controlled church. Property, in all its forms, was protected, and wealth—rather than bloodlines and titles—determined power. The Assembly divided the citizenry into "active" (propertied males) and "passive" (everyone else) elements. Olympe de Gouges protested with her Declaration of the Rights of Woman. Local and judicial administration was reorganized, and workers' organizations were banned. Most significantly in the long term, the Assembly confiscated all land and property of the Roman Catholic Church in France, in order to pay the royal debt. Under the Civil Constitution of the Clergy, the Roman Catholic Church was brought under the direct control of the French state. These moves against the church created massive opposition. The royal family attempted to flee France. The National Constituent Assembly closed in September 1791, having transformed the nation. The newly reconstructed nation was not stable, however. *page 448*

WHAT LED to the radicalization of the French Revolution?

The End of the Monarchy: A Second Revolution The short-lived (1791–1792) Legislative Assembly was factionalized. Jacobins had lobbied for a republic during the National Constituent Assembly. A faction within the Jacobin faction, the Girondists, took the leadership of the Legislative Assembly. On April 20, 1792, the Legislative Assembly declared war on Austria. The Girondists hoped war would suppress the counterrevolution within France; Louis XVI also supported war with Austria, hoping war would strengthen the monarchy. Instead, the *sans-culottes* seized control. In August 1792, a Parisian mob forced the royal family to take refuge in the Legislative Assembly; from then on, Louis XVI was unable to function as a monarch. The Paris Commune executed 1,200 prisoners in the September Massacres, and on September 21, 1792, the Convention met to write a democratic constitution for a French republic. Radical Jacobins within the Convention who collaborated with the *sans-culottes* constituted the "Mountain." In February 1793, the Convention declared war on Great Britain, Holland, and Spain; in March, the Vendée in France erupted in a royalist revolt. *page 455*

HOW DID Europe respond to the French Revolution?

Europe at War with the Revolution British statesman Edmund Burke, in his 1790 *Reflections on the Revolution in France*, was the first observer to articulate theoretical criticisms of the French Revolution and to predict further turmoil as a result of the revolution. European governments adopted repressive policies in response to France's ideas and military actions. In response to Polish reforms inspired by the revolution, Austria, Prussia, and Russia partitioned Poland out of existence. William Pitt the Younger suppressed political freedoms in Great Britain. By April 1793, the governments of all the countries with which France was at war—Austria, Prussia, Great Britain, Spain, Sardinia, and Holland—formed the First Coalition, an alliance to protect their social structures, political systems, and economic interests from the aggression of the revolution. *page 457*

HOW DID war and ideology combine to create the Reign of Terror?

The Reign of Terror In 1793, mobilization for war touched almost every aspect of French life. The Committee of General Security and the Committee of Public Safety were formed in April 1793 to facilitate the war effort. In August, the entire nation was requisitioned into national service; France had Europe's first citizen army. At about the same time, the Reign of Terror began. Robespierre and others in the Convention believed they were creating a "republic of virtue." The Convention established revolutionary tribunals in the summer of 1793; the Terror's first victims were Marie Antoinette and other members of the royal family. The Society of Revolutionary Women was among the first groups to be suppressed; Olympe de Gouges was guillotined in November 1793. Also in November 1793, the Convention attempted to de-Christianize France. Robespierre opposed this move, fearing it would lead to a backlash. In May 1794, he established the "Cult of the Supreme Being," a deistic cult over which he presided. Executions increased in 1794, as Robespierre turned on his political enemies, and a new law permitted convictions even in the absence of substantial evidence. Finally, on July 27, 1794, Robespierre himself was arrested. He was executed the next day, and the Terror died out soon thereafter. *page 458*

WHAT COURSE did the French Revolution take after 1794?

The Thermidorian Reaction The Thermidorian Reaction represented a tempering of the revolution. Propertied middle-class and professional people replaced the *sans-culottes* as the most influential group. The "white terror" turned violence against some of those responsible for the Terror. Catholicism revived throughout the country. Some progressive social legislation was repealed; women had, if anything, fewer rights than they had in 1789. The Constitution of the Year III created a bicameral legislature, under a five-man executive Directory, all limited to property-holding men. Voting was also limited to property holders and—significantly—soldiers. As the power of the *sans-culottes* waned, they and royalists revolted in Paris in October 1795. Napoleon Bonaparte was the general in charge of putting down their insurrection. The wars with Prussia and Spain ended in 1795, but France remained at war with Austria and Great Britain. In the absence of broad public support, the Directory came to rely on the army for stability. *page 461*

REVIEW QUESTIONS

1. How did the financial weaknesses of the French monarchy pave the way for the revolution of 1789? What role did Louis XVI play in the French Revolution? Would a constitutional monarchy have succeeded, or did the revolution ultimately have little to do with the competence of the monarch?
2. How was the Estates General transformed into the National Assembly? Which social and political values associated with the Enlightenment are reflected in the Declaration of the Rights of Man and Citizen? Why has the Civil Constitution of the Clergy been called the greatest blunder of the National Assembly?
3. Why were some political factions dissatisfied with the constitutional settlement of 1791? Who were the *sans-culottes*? How did they acquire political influence? What drew the *sans-culottes* and the Jacobins together? What ended their cooperation?
4. Why did France go to war with Austria in 1792? What were the benefits and drawbacks for France of fighting an external war while in the midst of a domestic political revolution? What were the causes of the Terror? In what ways did the French Revolution both live up to and betray its motto: "liberty, equality and fraternity"?

KEY TERMS

Convention (p. 456)
émigrés (p. 454)
Jacobins (p. 455)
levée en masse (p. 459)
Reign of Terror (p. 458)
sans-culottes (p. 456)
September Massacres (p. 455)
Thermidorian Reaction (p. 462)
Third Estate (p. 444)

19

The Age of Napoleon and the Triumph of Romanticism

This portrait of Napoleon on his throne by Jean Ingres (1780–1867) shows him in the splendor of an imperial monarch who embodies the total power of the state.

Jean Auguste Dominique Ingres (1780-1867), *Napoleon on His Imperial Throne*, 1806. Oil on canvas, 259 162 cm. Musée des Beaux-Arts, Rennes. Photograph © Erich Lessing/Art Resource, NY

What does this painting tell us about the nature of Napoleon's rule?

HOW DID Napoleon come to power in France?

HOW DID the Consulate end the revolution in France?

HOW DID Napoleon build an empire?

WHY DID Napoleonic rule breed resentment in Europe?

WHAT WERE the consequences of the Congress of Vienna?

HOW DID Rousseau and Kant contribute to the development of romanticism?

HOW WERE the ideals of romanticism reflected in English and German literature and in Romantic art?

HOW DID Romantic religious thinkers view the religious experience?

WHAT WERE the Romantic views of history and national identity?

By the late 1790s, many French people—especially property owners, who now included the peasantry—were longing for more political stability than the Directory seemed able to provide. The army, an institution associated with the values and successes of the revolution, offered the best hope for securing the nation. The most political of its generals was Napoleon Bonaparte. Once in power, he consolidated many of the achievements of the revolution. Ultimately, however, he overthrew the republic, declared himself emperor, and embarked on a mission of conquest that continued for over a decade. France's military offensive overturned Europe's old political and social order and fostered fierce nationalism among the French and the countries that allied to defeat Napoleon.

The Napoleonic period saw the flowering of the Romantic Era in European cultural history. Some Romantic ideas (nationalism, for example) sprang from the French Revolution, but the revolutionaries had opposed others (respect for history and religion most specifically). ■

THE RISE OF NAPOLEON BONAPARTE

HOW DID Napoleon come to power in France?

The chief threat to the Directory came from royalists, who hoped to restore the Bourbon monarchy by legal means. Many of the *émigrés* had returned to France. Their plans for a restoration drew support from devout Catholics and from those citizens disgusted by the excesses of the revolution. The spring elections of 1797 replaced most incumbents with constitutional monarchists and their sympathizers, thus giving them a majority in the national legislature.

To preserve the republic and prevent a peaceful restoration of the Bourbons, the antimonarchist Directory staged a *coup d'état* on 18 Fructidor (September 4, 1797). They put their own supporters into the legislative seats their opponents had won. They then imposed censorship and exiled some of their enemies. At the request of the Directors, Napoleon Bonaparte, the general in charge of the French invasion of Italy, had sent a subordinate to Paris to guarantee the success of the coup. In 1797, as in 1795, the army and Bonaparte had saved the day for the government installed in the wake of the Thermidorian Reaction.

Napoleon Bonaparte was born in 1769 to a poor family of lesser nobles at Ajaccio, on the Mediterranean island of Corsica. He favored the revolution and was a fiery Jacobin. In 1793, he played a leading role in recovering the port of Toulon from the British. As a reward for his service, he was appointed a brigadier general. During the Thermidorian Reaction, his defense of the new regime on 13 Vendémiaire won him a command in Italy.

EARLY MILITARY VICTORIES

By 1795, French arms and diplomacy had shattered the enemy coalition, but France's annexation of Belgium guaranteed continued fighting with Britain and Austria. The invasion of Italy aimed to deprive Austria of its rich northern Italian province of Lombardy. In a series of lightning victories, Bonaparte crushed the Austrian and Sardinian armies. On his own initiative, and against the wishes of the government in Paris, he concluded the Treaty of Campo Formio in October 1797. The treaty took Austria out of the war and crowned Napoleon's campaign with success. Before long, France dominated all of Italy and Switzerland.

In November 1797, the triumphant Bonaparte returned to Paris as a hero and to confront France's only remaining enemy, Britain. He judged it impossible to cross the Channel and invade England at that time. Instead, he chose to attack British interests through the eastern Mediterranean by capturing Egypt from the Ottoman Empire. By this strategy, he hoped to drive the British fleet from the Mediterranean, cut off British communications with India, damage British trade, and threaten the British Empire.

Napoleon easily overran Egypt, but the invasion was a failure. Admiral Horatio Nelson (1758–1805) destroyed the French fleet at Abukir on August 1, 1798. The French army was cut off from France. To make matters worse, the situation in Europe was deteriorating. The invasion of Egypt had alarmed Russia, which had its own ambitions in the Near East. The Russians, the Austrians, and the Ottomans joined Britain to form the Second Coalition against France. In 1799, the Russian and Austrian armies defeated the French in Italy and Switzerland and threatened to invade France.

In this early-nineteenth-century cartoon, England, personified by a caricature of William Pitt, and France, personified by a caricature of Napoleon, are carving out their areas of interest around the globe.

Bildarchiv Preussischer Kulturbesitz

How accurate a picture of international politics in the Napoleonic era does this cartoon draw?

THE CONSTITUTION OF THE YEAR VIII

Economic troubles and the dangerous international situation eroded the Directory's fragile support. One of the Directors, the Abbé Siéyès (1748–1836), proposed a new constitution. The author of the pamphlet *What Is the Third Estate?* (1789) now wanted an executive body independent of the whims of electoral politics, a government based on the principle of "confidence from below, power from above." The change would require another *coup d'état* with military support. News of France's misfortunes had reached Napoleon in Egypt. Without orders and leaving his army behind, he returned to France in October 1799 to popular acclaim. Soon he joined Siéyès. On 19 Brumaire (November 10, 1799), his troops ensured the success of the coup.

Siéyès appears to have thought that Napoleon could be used and then dismissed, but he misjudged his man. Bonaparte quickly pushed Siéyès aside, and in December 1799, he issued the Constitution of the Year VIII. The new constitution established the rule of one man—the First Consul, Bonaparte.

THE CONSULATE IN FRANCE (1799–1804)

HOW DID the Consulate end the revolution in France?

The **Consulate** in effect ended the revolution in France. The leading elements of the Third Estate—that is, officials, landowners, doctors, lawyers, and financiers—had achieved most of their goals by 1799. The newly established dominant classes had little or no desire to share their new privileges with the lower social orders. Bonaparte seemed just the person to give them security. When he submitted his constitution to the voters in a plebiscite, they overwhelmingly approved it.

Consulate A republican facade for one-man government by Napoleon.

SUPPRESSING FOREIGN ENEMIES AND DOMESTIC OPPOSITION

Throughout much of the 1790s, the pressures of warfare, particularly conscription, had accounted for much French internal instability. Bonaparte justified the public's confidence in himself by making peace with France's enemies. Russia had already left the Second Coalition. The Treaty of Luneville early in 1801 took Austria out of the war. Britain was now alone and, in 1802, concluded the Treaty of Amiens, which brought peace to Europe.

Bonaparte also restored peace and order at home. He used generosity, flattery, and bribery to win over enemies. He issued a general amnesty and employed men from all political factions. He required only that they be loyal to him. Bonaparte, however, ruthlessly suppressed opposition. He established a highly centralized administration in which prefects responsible to the government in Paris managed all departments. He employed secret police. He stamped out the royalist rebellion in the west and made the rule of Paris effective in Brittany and the Vendée for the first time in years.

Napoleon also used and invented opportunities to destroy his enemies. A plot on his life in 1804 provided an excuse to attack the Jacobins, though it was the work of the royalists. Also in 1804, he violated the sovereignty of the German state of Baden to seize and execute the Bourbon duke of Enghien (1772–1804).

Concordat with the Roman Catholic Church

No single set of revolutionary policies had aroused so much domestic opposition as those regarding the French Catholic Church, nor were there any other policies to which fierce supporters of the revolution seemed so attached. In 1801, to the shock and dismay of his anticlerical supporters, Napoleon concluded a concordat with Pope Pius VII (r. 1800–1823). The concordat gave Napoleon what he most wanted. The agreement required both the refractory clergy and those who had accepted the revolution to resign. Their replacements received their spiritual investiture from the pope, but the state named the bishops and paid their salaries and the salary of one priest in each parish. In return, the church gave up its claims to its confiscated property.

The concordat declared, "Catholicism is the religion of the great majority of French citizens." This was merely a statement of fact and fell far short of what the pope had wanted: religious dominance for the Roman Catholic Church. The clergy had to swear an oath of loyalty to the state. The Organic Articles of 1802, which the government issued on its own authority without consulting the pope, established the supremacy of state over church. Similar laws were applied to the Protestant and Jewish communities, reducing still further the privileged position of the Catholic Church.

The Napoleonic Code

In 1802, a plebiscite ratified Napoleon as consul for life, and he soon produced another constitution that granted him what amounted to full power. He thereafter set about reforming and codifying French law. The result was the Civil Code of 1804, usually known as the Napoleonic Code.

The Napoleonic Code safeguarded all forms of property and tried to secure French society against internal challenges. All the privileges based on birth that the revolution had overthrown remained abolished. The conservative attitudes toward labor and women that had emerged during the revolution also received full support. Workers' organizations remained forbidden, and workers had fewer rights than their employers. Fathers were granted extensive control over their children and husbands over their wives.

The coronation of Napoleon, December 2, 1804, as painted by Jacques-Louis David. Having first crowned himself, the emperor is shown about to place the crown on the head of Josephine. Napoleon instructed David to paint Pope Pius VII with his hand raised in blessing.

Jacques-Louis David (1748–1825), *Consecration of the Emperor Napoleon I and Coronation of Empress Josephine,* 1806–1807. Louvre, Paris. Bridgeman–Giraudon/Art Resource, NY

What role did Pope Pius VII play in the coronation of Napoleon? Why was his participation important to Napoleon?

Establishing a Dynasty

In 1804, a failed assassination attempt provided Napoleon with a rationale for ending the republic and establishing an empire. He argued that as emperor he could found a dynasty, and the hereditary rights of his descendants would guarantee continuity of government and make assassination pointless. This necessitated yet another constitution, which received overwhelming ratification by a plebiscite. Napoleon invited the pope to the cathedral of Notre Dame to witness his coronation, but not to crown him. Emperor Napoleon I placed the crown on his own head.

NAPOLEON'S EMPIRE (1804–1814)

HOW DID Napoleon build an empire?

Between his coronation as emperor and his final defeat at Waterloo (1815), Napoleon conquered most of Europe. France's victories changed the map of the Continent. The wars put an end to the Old Regime and its feudal trappings throughout Western Europe and forced the eastern European states to reorganize themselves to resist Napoleon's armies.

CONQUERING AN EMPIRE

The Peace of Amiens (1802) between France and Great Britain was merely a truce. Napoleon's unlimited ambitions shattered any hope that it might last. He sent an army to restore the rebellious colony of Haiti to French rule. This move aroused British fears that he was planning a new French empire in America, because Spain had restored Louisiana to France in 1801. More serious were his interventions in the Dutch Republic, Italy, and Switzerland and his reorganization of Germany. The Treaty of Campo Formio had required a redistribution of territories along the Rhine River, and the petty princes of the region engaged in a scramble to enlarge their holdings. Among the results were the reduction of Austrian influence and the emergence of fewer, but larger, German states in the West, all dependent on Napoleon.

British Naval Supremacy Alarmed by these developments, the British issued an ultimatum. When Napoleon ignored it, Britain declared war in May 1803. By August 1805, the British prime minister, William Pitt the Younger, had persuaded Russia and Austria to form a Third Coalition against France. On October 21, 1805, the British admiral Lord Nelson destroyed the combined French and Spanish fleets at the Battle of Trafalgar off the Spanish coast. Trafalgar ended all French hope of invading Britain and guaranteed British control of the sea for the rest of the war. (See "Encountering the Past: Sailors and Canned Food," page 472.)

Napoleonic Victories in Central Europe On land the story was different. Even before Trafalgar, Napoleon had marched to the Danube River to attack his continental enemies. In mid-October he forced an Austrian army to surrender at Ulm and occupied Vienna. On December 2, 1805, in perhaps his greatest victory, Napoleon defeated the combined Austrian and Russian forces at Austerlitz. The Treaty of Pressburg that followed won major concessions from Austria. The Austrians withdrew from Italy and left Napoleon in control of everything north of Rome.

Overview Napoleon and the Continental System

1806	Napoleon establishes the Continental System, prohibiting all trade with England
1807	The peace conference at Tilsit results in Russia joining the Continental System and becoming an ally of Napoleon
1809 and 1810	Napoleon at the peak of his power
1810	Russia withdraws from the Continental System and resumes relations with Britain; Napoleon plans to crush Russia militarily
1812	Napoleon invades Russia; the Russians adopt a scorched earth policy and burn Moscow; the thwarted Napoleon deserts his dwindling army and rushes back to Paris

ENCOUNTERING THE PAST

Sailors and Canned Food

New technologies often emerge during wartime, and in 1803, Napoleon's navy carried out the first experiments with something that has become a staple of modern life: canned food. Earlier methods of food preservation (drying, salting, pickling, smoking, fermenting, or condensing) altered taste and destroyed nutrients. Navies were hampered by the fact that sailors who spent a long time at sea on a diet of bread and salted meat developed scurvy and other illnesses caused by malnutrition. If fleets were to undertake longer tours of duty at sea and armies campaign where they could not live off the land, some way had to be found to supply them with more healthy food.

In the 1790s, the French government offered a prize for anyone who could invent a superior method for preserving food. The challenge was met by Nicholas Appert, a Parisian chef, who invented canning. Appert did not know of the existence of the microbes that spoil food but he stumbled across a process that worked by destroying them. He sealed food in glass jars filled with water or sauce and cooked these jars in a hot water bath. The result was food that did not deteriorate and kept its taste and nutrients. Sailors on several of Napoleon's ships were the first (in 1803) to test Appert's new products.

In 1810, Appert published information about his process, and by 1813, an English company was canning food in tins (which were cheaper and more durable than glass jars). By the middle of the nineteenth century, canned goods had entered the diets of millions of people in western Europe and North America.

Nicholas Appert (1749–1841) invented canning as a way of preserving food nutritiously. Canned food could be transported over long distances without spoiling.

Private Collection/Bridgeman Art Library

Why was the French government so interested in discovering new ways of preserving food?

WHAT MOTIVATED the work that went into the discovery of the canning process?

Napoleon also made extensive political changes in Germany. In July 1806, he organized the Confederation of the Rhine, which included most of the western German princes. Their withdrawal from the Holy Roman Empire led Francis II to dissolve that ancient political body and henceforth to call himself Emperor Francis I of Austria.

At this point, Prussia, which had remained neutral, declared war on France, but Napoleon crushed the Prussians in famous encounters at Jena and Auerstädt (October 14, 1806). Two weeks later he entered Berlin. On June 13, 1807, he defeated the Russians at Friedland and moved on to Königsberg, the capital of East Prussia.

Treaty of Tilsit Unable to fight another battle and unwilling to retreat into Russia, Tsar Alexander I (r. 1801–1825) was ready to make peace. On July 7, 1807, he signed the Treaty of Tilsit, which confirmed France's gains. Prussia lost half its territory. Only the support of Alexander saved it from extinction. Prussia openly and Russia secretly became allies of Napoleon.

Napoleon organized conquered Europe much like the estate of a Corsican family. The great French Empire was ruled directly by the head of the clan, Napoleon. On its borders lay satellite states ruled by members of his family. This establishment of the Napoleonic family as the collective sovereigns of Europe provoked political opposition that needed only encouragement and assistance to flare up into serious resistance.

The Continental System

After the Treaty of Tilsit, such resistance could come only from Britain, and Napoleon knew he must defeat the British before he could feel safe. Unable to compete with the British navy, he planned to cut off all British trade with the European continent and thus to cripple British commercial and financial power. (See Map 19–1.)

Despite initial drops in exports and domestic unrest, the British economy survived. British control of the seas assured access to the growing markets of North and South America and of the eastern Mediterranean. At the same time, the Continental System badly hurt the European economies. Moreover, his tariff policies favored France, increased the resentment of foreign merchants, and made them less willing to enforce the system and more ready to engage in smuggling.

QUICK REVIEW

The Continental System

- Treaty of Tilsit left Britain as sole power opposing France
- Napoleon tried to cripple Britain's economy by closing continental ports to British commerce
- Policy created resentment in Europe

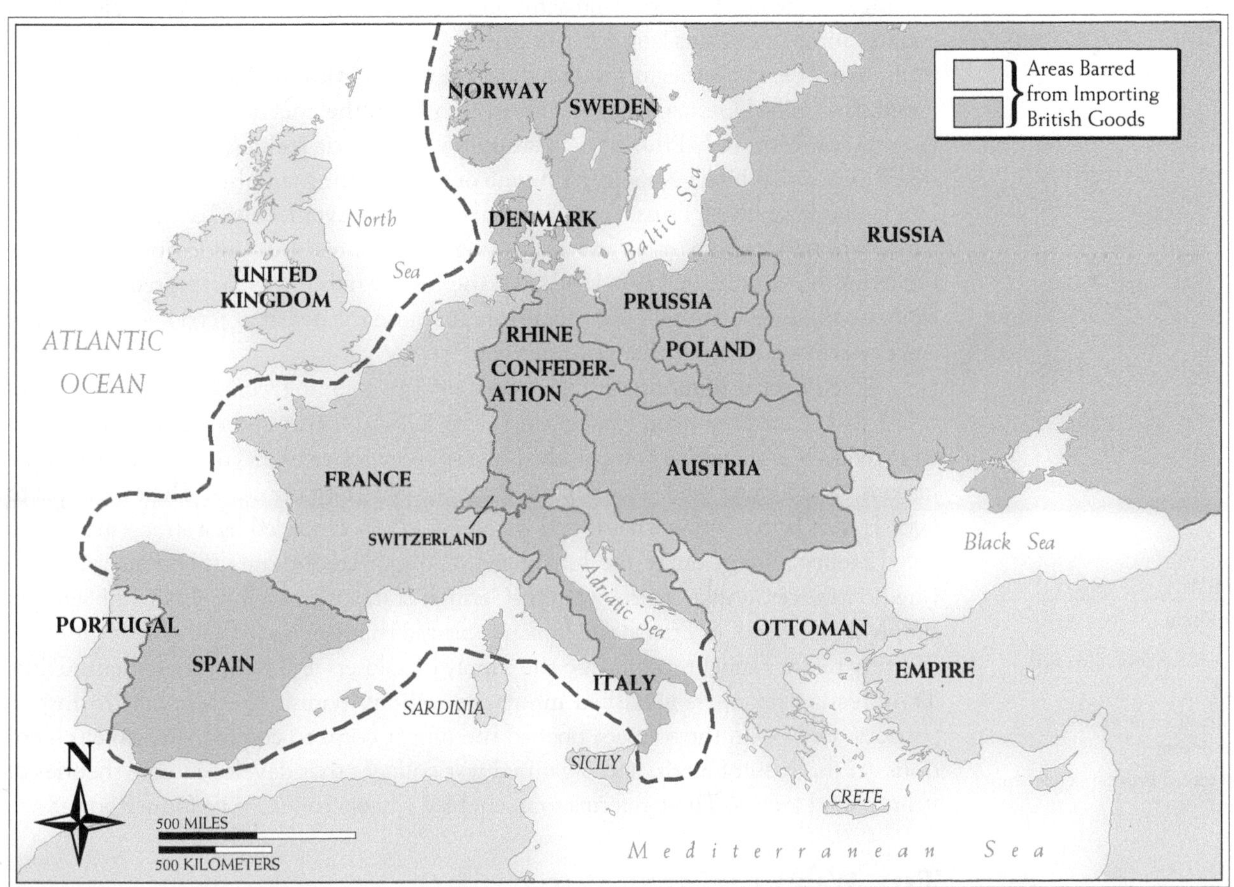

MAP 19–1 **The Continental System, 1806–1810** Napoleon hoped to cut off all British trade with the European continent and thereby drive the British from the war. The areas in peach indicate the French Empire. These lands, along with the Grand Empire and Napoleon's allies (in blue), made up the Continental System.

Did the Continental System deprive Britain of all its overseas trade? Did it guarantee free trade within continental Europe?

EUROPEAN RESPONSE TO THE EMPIRE

WHY DID Napoleonic rule breed resentment in Europe?

Wherever Napoleon ruled, he imposed the Napoleonic Code and abolished hereditary social distinctions. Feudal privileges disappeared, and the peasants were freed from serfdom and manorial dues. In the towns, the guilds and the local oligarchies that had been dominant for centuries were dissolved or deprived of their power. The established churches lost their traditional independence and were made subordinate to the state. Toleration replaced monopoly of religion by an established church. Despite these reforms, however, it was always clear that Napoleon's policies were intended first for his own glory and that of France. Consequently, before long, the conquered states and peoples grew restive.

German Nationalism and Prussian Reform

At the beginning of the nineteenth century, the Romantic Movement had begun to take hold. One of its basic features in Germany was the emergence of nationalism, which went through two distinct stages there. Initially, nationalistic writers emphasized the unique and admirable qualities of German culture, which, they argued, arose from the history of the German people. Such cultural nationalism prevailed until Napoleon's humiliation of Prussia at Jena in 1806. At that point many German intellectuals began to urge resistance to Napoleon on the basis of German nationalism. The French conquest endangered the independence and achievements of all German-speaking people. Only a people united through its language and culture could resist the French onslaught. Henceforth, many Germans sought to solve their internal political problems by attempting to establish a unified German state, reformed to harness the energies of the entire people.

After Tilsit, only Prussia could arouse such patriotic feelings. Elsewhere German rulers were either under Napoleon's thumb or collaborating with him. Defeated, humiliated, and diminished, Prussia continued to resist, however feebly. To Prussia fled German nationalists from other states, calling for reforms and unification that King Frederick William III (r. 1797–1840) and the Junker nobility in fact feared and hated. Reforms came about despite such opposition because the defeat at Jena had shown that the Prussian state had to change to survive.

The Prussian administrative and social reforms were the work of Baron vom Stein (1757–1831) and Prince von Hardenberg (1750–1822). Neither of these reformers intended to reduce the autocratic power of the Prussian monarch or to end the dominance of the Junkers, who formed the bulwark of the state and of the officer corps. Their plan was to fight France by becoming what it had become—a democracy led by a strong monarchy.

Stein's reforms broke the Junker monopoly of landholding. Serfdom was abolished. However, unlike in the western German states where all remnants of serfdom simply disappeared, in Prussia the Junkers ensured that vestiges of the system survived. Military reforms sought to increase the supply of soldiers and to improve their quality. The Prussian reformers abolished inhumane military punishments, sought to inspire patriotic feelings in the soldiers, opened the officer corps to commoners, gave promotions on the basis of merit, and organized war colleges that developed new theories of strategy and tactics. These reforms soon enabled Prussia to regain its former power.

QUICK REVIEW

German Nationalism

- After Tilsit, German nationalists fled to Prussia
- Nationalists called for German unification and reform
- Crisis situation forced Prussian leadership to accept reform

The Wars of Liberation

Spain France and Spain had been allies since 1796. In 1807, however, a French army came into the Iberian Peninsula to force Portugal to abandon its traditional alliance with Britain. The army stayed in Spain to protect lines of supply and communication. Napoleon used a revolt that broke out in Madrid in 1808 as a pretext to depose the Spanish Bourbons and to place his brother Joseph (1768–1844) on the Spanish throne.

Attacks on the privileges of the church increased public outrage. Many members of the upper classes were prepared to collaborate with Napoleon, but the peasants, urged on by the lower clergy and the monks, rebelled.

In Spain, Napoleon faced a new kind of warfare. Guerrilla bands cut lines of communication, killed stragglers, destroyed isolated units, and then disappeared into the mountains. The British landed an army under Sir Arthur Wellesley (1769–1852), later the duke of Wellington, to support the Spanish insurgents. Thus began the long peninsular campaign that would drain French strength from elsewhere in Europe and hasten Napoleon's eventual defeat. (See "Compare & Connect: The Experience of War in the Napoleonic Age," pages 476–477.)

Austria The French troubles in Spain encouraged the Austrians to renew the war in 1809. Since their defeat at Austerlitz, they had sought a war of revenge. The Austrians counted on Napoleon's distraction in Spain, French war weariness, and aid from other German princes. Napoleon was fully in command in France, however, and the German princes did not move. The French army marched swiftly into Austria and won the Battle of Wagram. The resulting Peace of Schönbrunn deprived Austria of much territory and 3.5 million subjects. Another spoil of victory was the Austrian archduchess Marie Louise (1791–1847), daughter of Emperor Francis I. Napoleon's wife, Josephine de Beauharnais (1763–1814), was forty-six and had borne him no children. His dynastic ambitions, as well as the desire for a royal marriage, led him to divorce Josephine and marry the eighteen-year-old Marie Louise.

The Invasion of Russia

The Franco-Russian alliance concluded at Tilsit was shaky. Russian nobles disliked the alliance because of the liberal politics of France and because the Continental System prohibited timber sales to Britain. The organization of the Polish Duchy of Warsaw as a Napoleonic satellite on the Russian doorstep and its enlargement with Austrian territory in 1809 after the Battle of Wagram angered Alexander. Napoleon's annexation of Holland in violation of the Treaty of Tilsit, his recognition of the French marshal Bernadotte (1763–1844) as the future King Charles XIV of Sweden, and his marriage to Marie Louise further disturbed the tsar. At the end of 1810, Russia withdrew from the Continental System and began to prepare for war. (See Map 19–2, page 478.)

Napoleon was determined to end the Russian military threat. He amassed an army of more than 600,000 men. He intended the usual short campaign crowned by a decisive battle, but the Russians retreated before his advance, destroying all food and supplies as they went. The so-called Grand Army of Napoleon could not live off the country, and the expanse of Russia made supply lines too long to maintain. Napoleon's advisers urged him to abandon the venture, but he feared an unsuccessful campaign would undermine his position in the empire and in France. He pinned his faith on the Russians' unwillingness to abandon Moscow without a fight.

In September 1812, Russian public opinion forced the army to give Napoleon the battle he wanted. At Borodino, not far west of Moscow, the bloodiest battle of the Napoleonic era cost the French 30,000 casualties and the Russians almost twice as many. Yet the Russian army was not destroyed. Napoleon won nothing substantial, and the battle was regarded as a defeat for him.

Fires set by the Russians soon engulfed Moscow and left Napoleon far from home with a badly diminished army lacking adequate supplies as winter came to a vast and unfriendly country. By October, what was left of the Grand Army was forced to retreat. By December, Napoleon realized the Russian fiasco would encourage plots against him at home. He returned to Paris, leaving the remnants of his army to struggle westward. Perhaps only 100,000 of the original 600,000 survived their ordeal.

COMPARE & CONNECT

THE EXPERIENCE OF WAR IN THE NAPOLEONIC AGE

The Napoleonic Wars spread violence across Europe. Different participants, writers, and artists portrayed the experience of war differently. William Napier reported his own heroism in a quite matter-of-fact manner. The German poet and historian Ernest Moritz Arndt recalled moments of intense nationalistic patriotism. The Spanish painter Goya portrayed a moment of enormous brutality suffered by the Spanish at the hands of French troops.

QUESTIONS

1. What were Napier's expectations of his men? Of his officers? Of himself?
2. Why does Arndt claim each of these various groups wanted war?
3. How does Arndt suggest the possibility of a united nation that did not yet actually exist?
4. How does Goya portray Spaniards as victims of harsh, unmerciful military violence?
5. How do Napier's memoir, Arndt's call to arms, and Goya's painting illustrate different points of view and ways of interpreting the violence of modern warfare?

I. A COMMANDER RECALLS AN INCIDENT IN SPAIN

William Napier, a British officer during the Napoleonic Wars and later a distinguished leader in the British army, describes his experiences in a battle that took place in Spain during 1811.

I arrived [with two companies] just in time to save Captain Dobbs, 52nd, and two men who were cut off from their regiment. The French were gathering fast about us, we could scarcely retreat, and Dobbs agreed with me that boldness would be our best chance; so we called upon the men to follow, and, jumping over a wall which had given us cover, charged the enemy with a shout which sent the nearest back. . . .

Only the two men of the 52nd followed us, and we four arrived unsupported at a second wall, close to a considerable body of French, who rallied and began to close upon us. Their fire was very violent, but the wall gave cover. I was, however, stung by the backwardness of my men, and told Dobbs I would save him or lose my life by bringing up the two companies; he entreated me not, saying I could not make two paces from the wall and live. Yet I did go back to the first wall, escaped the fire, and, reproaching the men gave them the word again, and returned to Dobbs, who was now upon the point of being taken; but again I returned alone! The soldiers had indeed crossed the wall in their front, but kept edging away to the right to avoid the heavy fire. Being now maddened by this second failure, I made another attempt, but I had not made ten paces when a shot struck my spine, and the enemy very ungenerously continued to fire at me when I was down. I escaped death by dragging myself by my hands—for my lower extremities were paralyzed—towards a small heap of stones which was in the midst of the field, and thus covering my head and shoulders. . . . However, Captain Lloyd and my company, and some of the 52nd, came up at that moment, and the French were driven away.

Source: Quoted in H. A. Bruce, *Life of Sir William Napier* (London: John Murray, 1864), 1:55–57.

II. A GERMAN WRITER DESCRIBES THE WAR OF LIBERATION

The German resistance to Napoleon as his army retreated from Moscow in 1813 was the first time in modern German history that people from virtually all German-speaking lands cooperated together. Ernest Moritz Arndt (1769–1860) described the excitement of that moment in a passage frequently reprinted in German history textbooks for more than a century.

Fired with enthusiasm, the people rose, "with God for King and Fatherland." Among the Prussians there was only one voice, one feeling, one anger and one love, to save the Fatherland and to free Germany. . . . War, war, sounded the cry from the Carpathians to the Baltic, from the Niemen to the Elbe. War! cried the nobleman and landed proprietor who had become impoverished. War! that peasant who was driving his last horse to death. . . . War! the citizen who was growing exhausted from quartering soldiers and paying taxes. War! the widow who was sending her only son to the front. War! the young girl who, with tears of pride and pain, was leaving her betrothed. . . . Even young women, under all sorts of disguises, rushed to arms; all wanted to drill, arm themselves and fight and die for the Fatherland. . . .

The most beautiful thing about all this holy zeal and happy confusion was . . . that the one great feeling for the Fatherland, its freedom and honor, swallowed all other feelings, caused all other considerations and relationships to be forgotten.

Source: *Documents of German History*, trans. by Louis L. Snyder.

III. FRANCISCO GOYA, *THE THIRD OF MAY, 1808* (PAINTED 1814–1815)

Napoleon had begun to send troops into Spain in 1807 after the king of Spain had agreed to aid France against Portugal, which was assisting Britain. By early 1808 Spain had essentially become an occupied nation. On May 2, riots took place in Madrid between French troops, many of whom were Islamic soldiers whom Napoleon had recruited in Egypt, and Spanish civilians. In response to that resistance the French general Murat ordered the execution of numerous citizens of Madrid, which occurred the night of May 2 and 3. The events of these two days marked the opening of the Spanish effort to rid their peninsula of French rule.

After the restoration of the Spanish monarchy, Francisco Goya (1745–1828) depicted the savagery of those executions in the most memorable war painting of the Napoleonic era, The Third of May, 1808. *There is one group of humble Spaniards who have already been shot, another in the process of execution, and a third group, some of whom are hiding their eyes, who will be the next victims.*

The painting illustrates two forces of Napoleonic warfare confronting each other: the professional solider and the guerilla *(a term coined during the Spanish resistance of this era). The* guerilla *must fight with what few resources he finds at his command and with few advanced weapons. By contrast, in this painting the soldiers, well disciplined and equipped with modern rifles, carry out the execution by the light of large technologically advanced lanterns fueled by either gas or oil with which Napoleon equipped his troops. Goya succeeds in making ordinary people and very poor clergy not only the victims, but also symbolic heroes of the national war of liberation.*

Goya y Lucientes, Francisco de Goya, recorded Napoleon's troops executing Spanish guerrilla fighters who had rebelled against the French occupation in *The Third of May, 1808*.

Francisco de Goya, *Los fusilamientos del 3 de Mayo, 1808*. 1814. Oil on canvas, 8'6" × 11'4". © Museo Nacional del Prado, Madrid

What factors contributed to the rise of resistance movements in occupied countries?

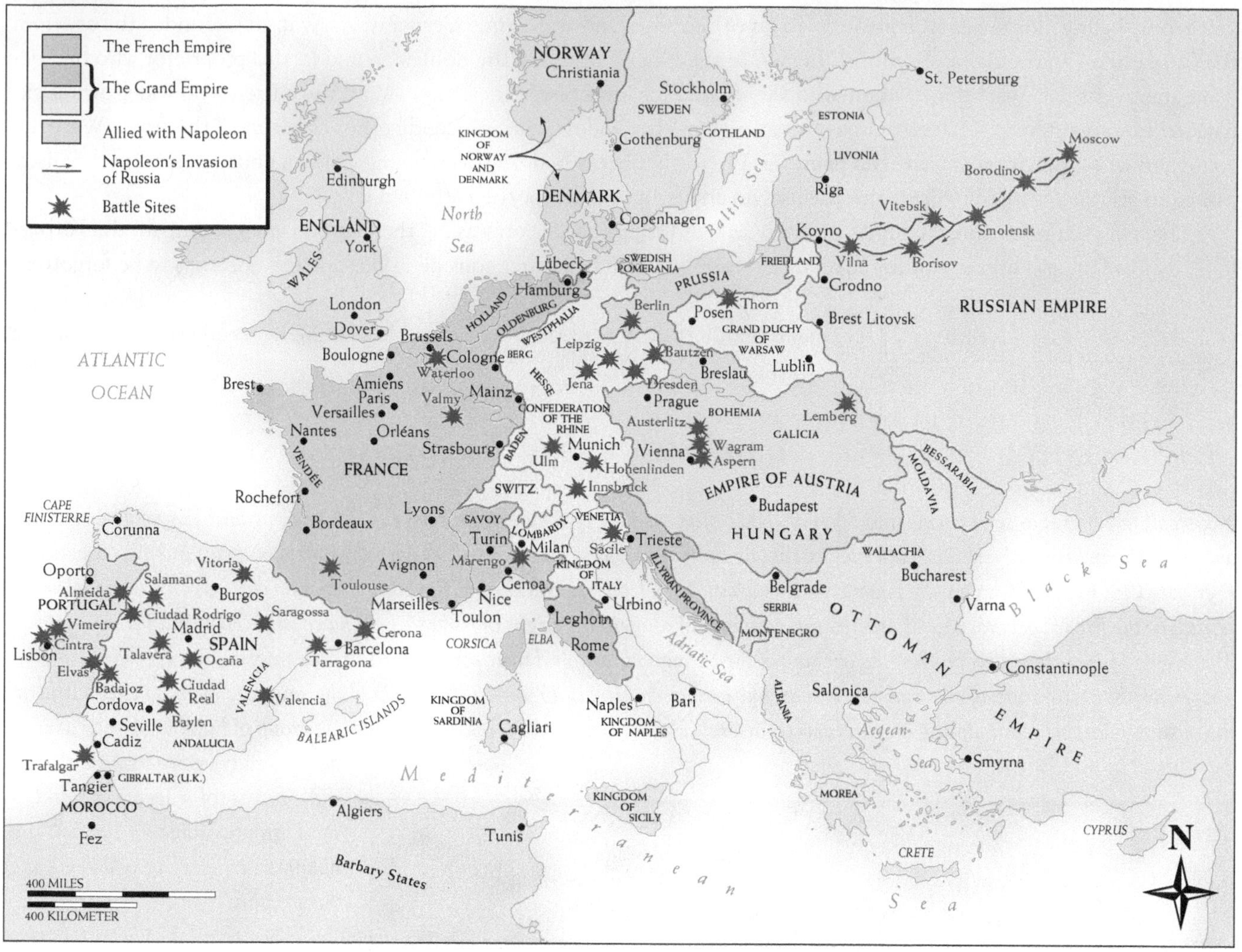

MAP 19–2 **Napoleonic Europe in Late 1812** By mid-1812 the areas shown in peach were incorporated into France, and most of the rest of Europe was directly controlled by or allied with Napoleon. But Russia had withdrawn from the failing Continental System, and the decline of Napoleon was about to begin.

Which areas in Europe were most problematic for Napoleon?

European Coalition

Even as the news of the disaster reached the West, the final defeat of Napoleon was far from certain. He was able to put down his opponents in Paris and raise another 350,000 men. Neither the Prussians nor the Austrians were eager to risk another contest with Napoleon, and even the Russians hesitated. The Austrian foreign minister, Prince Klemens von Metternich (1773–1859), would have been glad to make a negotiated peace that would leave Napoleon on the throne of a shrunken and chastened France rather than see Russia dominate Europe. Napoleon might have negotiated a reasonable settlement had he been willing to make concessions that would have split his jealous opponents. He would not consider that solution, however.

In 1813, patriotic pressure and national ambition brought together the last and most powerful coalition (Russia, Prussia, Austria, and Britain) against Napoleon. In October, the combined armies of the enemy decisively defeated him at Leipzig in what the Germans called the Battle of the Nations. In March 1814, the allied armies marched into Paris. A few days later, Napoleon abdicated and went into exile on the island of Elba, off the coast of central Italy.

QUICK REVIEW

Coalition of 1813

- Most powerful coalition created to oppose Napoleon
- Russia, Britain, Prussia, and Austria joined forces
- March 1814, allies defeat Napoleon at Leipzig

THE CONGRESS OF VIENNA AND THE EUROPEAN SETTLEMENT

WHAT WERE the consequences of the Congress of Vienna?

Fear of Napoleon and hostility to his ambitions had held the victorious coalition together. As soon as he was removed, the allies pursued their separate ambitions. The key person in achieving eventual agreement among them was Robert Stewart, Viscount Castlereagh (1769–1822), the British foreign secretary. Even before the victorious armies had entered Paris, he brought about the signing of the Treaty of Chaumont on March 9, 1814. It provided for the restoration of the Bourbons to the French throne and the contraction of France to its frontiers of 1792. Even more importantly, Britain, Austria, Russia, and Prussia agreed to form a Quadruple Alliance for twenty years to preserve whatever settlement they agreed on. Remaining problems—and there were many—and final details were left for a conference to be held at Vienna.

TERRITORIAL ADJUSTMENTS

The Congress of Vienna assembled in September 1814 but did not conclude its work until November 1815. The easiest problem the great powers faced was France. All the victors agreed that no single state should be allowed to dominate Europe, and all were determined to prevent France from doing so again. The restoration of the French Bourbon monarchy, which was temporarily popular, and a nonvindictive boundary settlement were designed to keep France calm and satisfied.

The powers also strengthened the states around France's borders to serve as barriers to renewed French expansion. They established the kingdom of the Netherlands in the north and added the important port of Genoa to strengthen Piedmont in the south. Prussia was given important new territories along the Rhine River to deter French aggression in the West. Austria gained full control of northern Italy to prevent a repetition of Napoleon's conquests there. As for the rest of Germany, most of Napoleon's territorial arrangements were left untouched and the Holy Roman Empire was not revived. In all these areas, the congress established the rule of legitimate monarchs and rejected any hint of the republican and democratic policies that had flowed from the French Revolution.

On these matters agreement was not difficult, but the settlement of eastern Europe sharply divided the victors. Alexander I of Russia wanted all of Poland under his rule. Prussia was willing to give it to him in return for all of Saxony, which had been allied with Napoleon. Austria, however, was unwilling to surrender its share of Poland or to see Prussian power grow or Russia penetrate deeper into central Europe. The Polish-Saxon question almost caused a new war among the victors, but defeated France provided a way out. The wily Talleyrand, now representing France at Vienna, suggested the weight of France added to that of Britain and Austria might bring Alexander to his senses. When news of a secret treaty among the three leaked out, the tsar agreed to become ruler of a smaller Poland, and Prussia settled for only part of Saxony. Thereafter, France was included as a fifth great power in all deliberations.

In this political cartoon of the Congress of Vienna, Talleyrand simply watches which way the wind is blowing, Castlereagh hesitates, while the monarchs of Russia, Prussia, and Austria form the dance of the Holy Alliance. The king of Saxony holds on to his crown and the republic of Geneva pays homage to the kingdom of Sardinia.

Bildarchiv Preussischer Kulturbesitz

Who were the winners and losers at the Congress of Vienna?

THE HUNDRED DAYS AND THE QUADRUPLE ALLIANCE

Napoleon's escape from Elba on March 1, 1815, further united the victors. Once back in power, Napoleon promised a liberal constitution and a peaceful foreign policy. The allies were not convinced. They declared Napoleon an outlaw (a new device under international law) and sent their armies to crush him. Wellington, with the crucial help of

SIGNIFICANT DATES FROM THE ERA OF NAPOLEONIC EUROPE

1797	The Treaty of Campo Formio
1798	Nelson defeats the French navy
1799	The Consulate is established in France
1801	Concordat between France and the papacy
1802	Treaty of Amiens
1803	War renewed between France and Britain
1804	Execution of the Duke of Enghien
	Napoleonic Civil Code issued
	Napoleon crowned emperor
1805	Nelson wins at Trafalgar (October 21)
	Battle of Austerlitz (December 2)
1806	Battle of Jena
	Continental System imposed (November 21)
1807	Treaty of Tilsit
1808	Spain revolts against Napoleon
1809	Battle of Wagram
	Napoleon marries Marie Louise of Austria
1810	Russia leaves the Continental System
1812	Invasion of Russia; battle at Borodino
1813	Leipzig ("Battle of the Nations")
1814	Treaty of Chaumont and the Quadruple Alliance
	Congress of Vienna convenes (September)
1815	Napoleon returns from Elba (March 1)
	Battle of Waterloo (June 18)
	Holy Alliance formed (September 26)
	Quadruple Alliance renewed (November 20)
1821	Napoleon dies on Saint Helena

the Prussians under Field Marshal von Blücher (1742–1819), defeated Napoleon at Waterloo in Belgium on June 18, 1815. Napoleon again abdicated and was exiled on Saint Helena, a tiny Atlantic island off the coast of Africa, where he died in 1821.

The Hundred Days, as the period of Napoleon's return is called, frightened the great powers and made the peace settlement harsher for France. Alexander proposed a Holy Alliance, whereby the monarchs promised to act together in accordance with Christian principles. Austria and Prussia signed, but Castlereagh thought it absurd, and England abstained. The Holy Alliance soon became a symbol of extreme political reaction.

England, Austria, Prussia, and Russia renewed the Quadruple Alliance on November 20, 1815. Henceforth, it was as much a coalition for maintaining peace as for pursuing victory over France. A coalition for such a purpose had never existed in European diplomacy before. It represented an important new departure in European affairs. The leaders of Europe had learned that a treaty should secure not victory, but peace. The diplomats aimed to establish a framework for stability, rather than to punish France. The great powers sought to ensure that each of them would respect the Vienna settlement and not use force to change it.

The congress has been criticized for failing to recognize and provide for the great forces that would stir the nineteenth century—nationalism and democracy. Such criticism is inappropriate. At the time nationalist pressures were relatively rare; the general desire was for peace. The settlement, like all other such agreements, aimed to solve past ills, and in that it succeeded. The measure of the success of the Vienna settlement is that it remained essentially intact for almost half a century and prevented general war for a hundred years. (See Map 19–3.)

THE ROMANTIC MOVEMENT

WHY DID the Romantics reject much of the Enlightenment?

romanticism Reaction against the rationalism and scientism of the Enlightenment, insisting on the importance of human feelings, intuition, and imagination as supplements for reason in the human quest to understand the world.

While the French Revolution and Napoleon's reign were unfolding, an important new intellectual movement called **romanticism** spread throughout Europe. It was a reaction against the rationalism and scientism of the Enlightenment. Romantics insisted on the importance of human feelings, intuition, and imagination as supplements for reason in the human quest to understand the world. Many encouraged a revival of Christianity and of the art, literature, and architecture of Europe's Christian Middle Ages. They were fascinated by folklore, folk songs, and fairy tales, and they took dreams, hallucinations, and sleepwalking seriously as phenomena that pointed to a world that lay beyond the reach of empirical observation, sensory data, and discursive reasoning.

MAP EXPLORATION

Interactive map: To explore this map further, go to www.myhistorylab.com

MAP 19–3 **Europe 1815, After the Congress of Vienna** The Congress of Vienna achieved the post-Napoleonic territorial adjustments shown on the map. The most notable arrangements dealt with areas along France's borders (the Netherlands, Prussia, Switzerland, and Piedmont) and in Poland and northern Italy.

In the European Settlement of 1815, did any single power dominate Europe?

Sturm and Drang ("Storm and Stress") Movement in German Romantic literature that emphasized feeling and emotion.

ROMANTIC QUESTIONING OF THE SUPREMACY OF REASON

HOW DID Rousseau and Kant contribute to the development of romanticism?

The romantic movement had roots in the individualism of the Renaissance, Protestant devotion and personal piety, sentimental novels of the eighteenth century, and dramatic German poetry of the ***Sturm and Drang*** (literally, "storm and stress") movement, which rejected the influence of French rationalism on German literature. However, two writers who were also closely related to the Enlightenment provided the immediate intellectual foundations for romanticism: Jean-Jacques Rousseau and Immanuel Kant.

Immanuel Kant.

Courtesy of the Library of Congress

Rousseau and Education

Rousseau's conviction that society and material prosperity had corrupted human nature profoundly influenced Romantic writers. Rousseau set forth his view on how the individual could develop to lead a good and happy life uncorrupted by society in his novel *Émile* (1762), a work that was for a long time far more influential than *The Social Contract*. In *Émile*, Rousseau stressed the difference between children and adults. He distinguished the stages of human maturation and urged that children be raised with maximum individual freedom. The parent or teacher would help most by providing the basic necessities of life and warding off what was manifestly harmful. Beyond that, the adult should stay completely out of the way. Rousseau thought that, because of their physical differences, men and women would naturally grow into social roles with different spheres of activity.

Rousseau also thought that adults should allow the child's sentiments, as well as its reason, to flourish. To Romantic writers, this concept of human development vindicated the rights of nature over those of artificial society. They thought such a form of open education would eventually lead to a natural society. Like Rousseau, the Romantics saw humankind, nature, and society as organically interrelated.

Kant and Reason

Immanuel Kant (1724–1804) wrote the two greatest philosophical works of the late eighteenth century: *The Critique of Pure Reason* (1781) and *The Critique of Practical Reason* (1788). He sought to accept the rationalism of the Enlightenment and to still preserve a belief in human freedom, immortality, and the existence of God. For Kant, the human mind does not simply reflect the world around it like a passive mirror; rather, the mind actively imposes on the world of sensory experience "forms of sensibility" and "categories of understanding." The mind itself generates these categories. This meant that human perceptions are as much the product of the mind's own activity as of sensory experience.

categorical imperative Kant's view that all human beings possess an innate sense of moral duty, an inner command to act in every situation as one would have other people act in that same situation.

Kant thought all human beings possess an innate sense of moral duty or an awareness of what he called a **categorical imperative**. This term refers to an inner command to act in every situation as one would have all other people always act in the same situation. Kant regarded the existence of this imperative of conscience as incontrovertible proof of humankind's natural freedom. On the basis of humankind's moral sense, Kant postulated the existence of God, eternal life, and future rewards and punishments.

To many Romantic writers, Kantian philosophy refuted the narrow rationality of the Enlightenment. Whether they called it "practical reason," "fancy," "imagination," "intuition," or simply "feeling," the Romantics believed that the human mind had the power to penetrate beyond the limits of largely passive human understanding as set forth by Hobbes, Locke, and Hume.

ROMANTIC LITERATURE

HOW WERE the ideals of romanticism reflected in English and German literature?

The term *Romantic* appeared in English and French literature as early as the seventeenth century. Neoclassical writers then used the word to describe literature they considered unreal, sentimental, or excessively fanciful. In both England and Germany, the term came to be applied to all literature that did not observe classical forms and rules and gave free play to the imagination. As an alternative to such dependence on the classical forms, August Wilhelm von Schlegel (1767–1845) praised the "Romantic" literature of Dante, Petrarch, Boccaccio, Shakespeare, the Arthurian legends, Cervantes, and Calderón. According to Schlegel, Romantic literature was to classical literature what the organic and living were to the merely mechanical.

The romantic movement had peaked in Germany and England before it became a major force in France under the leadership of Madame de Staël (1766–1817) and Victor Hugo (1802–1885). So influential was the classical tradition in France that not until 1816 did a French writer openly declare himself a Romantic. That was Henri Beyle (1783–1842), who wrote under the pseudonym Stendhal.

The English Romantic Writers

The English Romantics believed poetry was enhanced by freely following the creative impulses of the mind. In this belief, they directly opposed Lockean psychology, which regarded the mind as a passive receptor and poetry as a mechanical exercise of "wit" following prescribed rules.

Coleridge For Samuel Taylor Coleridge (1772–1834), the artist's imagination was God at work in the mind. As Coleridge expressed his views, the imagination was "a repetition in the finite mind of the eternal act of creation in the infinite I AM." Poetry thus could not be considered idle play. Rather, it was the highest of human acts, humankind's self-fulfillment in a transcendental world.

Samuel Taylor Coleridge.

British Information Services

Wordsworth William Wordsworth (1770–1850) was Coleridge's closest friend. Together they published *Lyrical Ballads* in 1798 as a manifesto of a new poetry that rejected the rules of eighteenth-century criticism. Among Wordsworth's most important later poems is his "Ode on Intimations of Immortality" (1803), written in part to console Coleridge, who was suffering a deep personal crisis. Its subject is the loss of poetic vision, something Wordsworth also felt then in himself. Nature, which he had worshipped, no longer spoke freely to him, and he feared it might never speak to him again. He had lost what he believed all human beings lose in the necessary process of maturation: their childlike vision and closeness to spiritual reality.

QUICK REVIEW

William Wordsworth (1770–1850)

- Rejected the rules of eighteenth-century literary criticism
- Believed that children existed in a more perfect spiritual state
- Believed that as people age they lose contact with natural and spiritual world

Lord Byron A true rebel among the Romantic poets was Lord Byron (1788–1824). In Britain, even most of the other Romantic writers distrusted and disliked him. Outside England, however, Byron was regarded as the embodiment of the new person the French Revolution had created. He rejected the old traditions (he was divorced and famous for his many love affairs) and championed the cause of personal liberty. Byron was outrageously skeptical and mocking, even of his own beliefs. In *Childe Harold's Pilgrimage* (1812), he created a brooding, melancholy Romantic hero. In *Don Juan* (1819), he wrote with ribald humor, acknowledged nature's cruelty as well as its beauty, and even expressed admiration for urban life.

The German Romantic Writers

Much Romantic poetry was also written on the Continent, but almost all major German Romantics wrote at least one novel. Romantic novels often were highly sentimental and borrowed material from medieval romances. The characters of Romantic novels were treated as symbols of the larger truth of life. Purely realistic description was avoided.

Schlegel Friedrich Schlegel (1767–1845) wrote a progressive early Romantic novel, *Lucinde* (1799), that attacked prejudices against women as capable of being little more than lovers and domestics. Schlegel's novel reveals the ability of the Romantics to become involved in the social issues of their day. He depicted Lucinde as the perfect friend and companion, as well as the unsurpassed lover, of the hero. Like other early Romantic novels, the work shocked contemporary morals by frankly discussing sexual activity and by describing Lucinde as equal to the male hero.

Goethe Towering above all of these German writers stood Johann Wolfgang von Goethe (1749–1832). Perhaps the greatest German writer of modern times, Goethe defies easy classification. Part of his literary production fits into the Romantic mold, and part of it was a condemnation of Romantic excesses. The book that made his early reputation was *The Sorrows of Young Werther*, published in 1774. This novel, like many others in the eighteenth century, is a series of letters. The hero falls in love with Lotte, who is married to another man. The letters explore their relationship with the sentimentalism that was characteristic of the age. This novel became popular throughout Europe. Romantic authors admired its emphasis on feeling and on living outside the bounds of polite society.

Goethe's masterpiece is *Faust*, a long dramatic poem. In Part I (1808), Faust, a world-weary scholar, promises his soul to the devil in exchange for knowledge. Faust seduces and abandons a young woman named Gretchen. When she dies, disgraced on earth but judged worthy of heaven, he struggles with grief and guilt. In Part II of the poem (completed in the year of Goethe's death, 1832), Faust has strange adventures with witches and mythological beings, but in the end he finds peace, understanding, and salvation by dedicating his life to the improvement of humankind.

ROMANTIC ART

HOW DID Romantic artists portray nature?

The art of the Romantic Era, like its poetry and philosophy, stood largely in reaction to that of the eighteenth century. Whereas the Rococo artists had looked to Renaissance models and neoclassical painters to the art of the ancient world, Romantic painters often portrayed scenes from medieval life. For them, the Middle Ages represented the social stability and religious reverence that was disappearing from their own era.

The Cult of the Middle Ages and Neo-Gothicism

Like many other early Romantic artists, the English landscape painter John Constable (1776–1837) was politically conservative. In *Salisbury Cathedral, from the Meadows*, he portrayed a stable world in which neither political turmoil nor industrial development challenged the traditional dominance of the church and the landed classes. Although the clouds and sky in the painting depict a severe storm, the works of both nature and humankind present a powerful sense of enduring order. The trees clearly have withstood this storm as they have withstood others for many years. The cathedral, built in the Middle Ages, has also stood majestically intact for centuries.

neo-Gothic Style of architecture in which Gothic motifs and forms are imitated.

Medieval structures not only appeared in Romantic painting. The **neo-Gothic** revival in architecture dotted the European landscape with modern imitations of them. Many medieval cathedrals were restored during this era, and new churches were designed to resemble their medieval forerunners. The British Houses of Parliament built in 1836–1837 were the most famous public buildings in the neo-Gothic style, but town halls, schools, and even railroad stations were designed to look like medieval buildings, while aristocratic country houses were rebuilt to resemble medieval castles.

Nature and the Sublime

Beyond their attraction to history, Romantic artists also sought to portray nature in all of its majestic power as no previous generation of European artists had ever done. Their works often sought to portray what they and others termed *the sublime*—that is, subjects from nature that aroused strong emotions, such as fear, dread, and awe, and raised questions about whether and how much we control our lives.

Caspar David Friedrich's *The Polar Sea* illustrated the power of nature to diminish the creations of humankind as seen in the wrecked ship on the right of the painting.

Kunsthalle, Hamburg, Germany/A.K.G., Berlin/SuperStock

What marks this as a Romantic painting?

Romantics saw nature as a set of infinite forces that overwhelmed the smallness of humankind. For example, in 1824, the German artist Caspar David Friedrich (1774–1840) in *The Polar Sea* painted the plight of a ship trapped and crushed by the force of a vast polar ice field. In direct contrast to eighteenth-century artists' portrayal of sunny Enlightenment, Friedrich also painted numerous scenes in which human beings stand shrouded in the mysterious darkness of night where moonlight and torches cast only fitful illumination.

An artist who similarly understood the power of nature but also depicted the forces of the new industrialism that was challenging them was Joseph Mallord William Turner (1775–1851) whose painting *Rain, Steam and Speed—The Great Western Railway* of 1844 illustrated the recently invented railway engine barreling through an enveloping storm. In this scene the new technology is both part of the natural world and strong enough to dominate it.

Friedrich's and Turner's paintings taken together symbolize the contradictory forces affecting Romantic artists—the sense of the power, awe, and mastery of nature coupled with the sense that the advance of industry represented a new kind of awesome human power that could challenge or even surpass the forces of nature itself.

RELIGION IN THE ROMANTIC PERIOD

HOW DID Romantic religious thinkers view the religious experience?

Romantic religious thinkers sought the foundations of religion in the inner emotions of humankind. Reacting to the anticlericalism of both the Enlightenment and the French Revolution, these thinkers also saw religious faith, experience, and institutions as central to human life. Their forerunners were the mystics of Western Christianity. One of the first great examples of a religion characterized by romantic impulses—Methodism—arose in mid–eighteenth-century England during the Enlightenment itself and became one of the most powerful forces in transatlantic religion during the nineteenth century.

METHODISM

Methodism Movement begun in England by John Wesley, an Oxford-educated Anglican priest, the first major religion to embody romanticism. It emphasized religion as a "method" for living more than a set of doctrines.

Methodism originated in the middle of the eighteenth century as a revolt against deism and rationalism in the Church of England. The leader of the Methodist movement was John Wesley (1703–1791). While at Oxford University studying to be an Anglican priest, Wesley organized a religious group known as the Holy Club. He soon left England for missionary work in the new colony of Georgia in America, where he arrived in 1735. While he was crossing the Atlantic, a group of German Moravians on the ship deeply impressed him with their unshakable faith and confidence during a storm. Wesley, who had despaired of his life, concluded they knew far better than he the meaning of justification by faith. When he returned to England in 1738, Wesley began to worship with Moravians in London. There, in 1739, he underwent a conversion experience.

Wesley discovered he could not preach his version of Christian conversion and practical piety in Anglican church pulpits. Therefore, late in 1739, he began to preach in the open fields near the cities and towns of western England. Thousands of humble people responded to his message of repentance and good works. Soon he and his brother Charles (1707–1788), who became famous for his hymns, began to organize Methodist societies. By the late eighteenth century, the Methodists had become a separate church. They ordained their own clergy and sent missionaries to America, where they eventually achieved their greatest success and influence.

Methodism stressed inward, heartfelt religion and the possibility of Christian perfection in this life. Many people, weary of the dry rationalism that derived from deism, found Wesley's ideal relevant to their own lives. The Methodist preachers emphasized the role of enthusiastic, emotional experience as part of Christian conversion. After Wesley, religious revivals became highly emotional in style and content.

John Wesley (1703–1791) was the founder of Methodism. He emphasized the role of emotional experience in Christian conversion.

CORBIS/Bettmann

How did Methodism differ from older, more mainstream forms of Christianity?

NEW DIRECTIONS IN CONTINENTAL RELIGION

Similar religious developments based on feeling appeared on the Continent. After the Thermidorian Reaction, a strong Roman Catholic revival took place in France. Its followers disapproved of both the religious policy of the revolution and the anticlericalism of the Enlightenment. The most important book to express these sentiments was *The Genius of Christianity* (1802) by Viscount François René de Chateaubriand (1768–1848). In this work, which became known as the "bible of Romanticism," Chateaubriand argued that the essence of religion is "passion." The foundation of faith in the church was the emotion that its teachings and sacraments inspired in the heart of the Christian.

No one stated the Romantic religious ideal more eloquently or with greater impact on the modern world than Friedrich Schleiermacher (1768–1834). In 1799, he published *Speeches on Religion to Its Cultured Despisers*. According to Schleiermacher, religion was neither dogma nor a system of ethics. It was an intuition or feeling of absolute dependence on an infinite reality. Religious institutions, doctrines, and moral activity expressed that primal religious feeling only in a secondary, or indirect, way.

ROMANTIC VIEWS OF NATIONALISM AND HISTORY

WHAT WERE the Romantic views of history and national identity?

A distinctive feature of romanticism, especially in Germany, was its glorification of both the individual person and individual cultures. Behind these views lay the philosophy of German idealism, which understood the world as the creation of subjective egos. The world is as it is because especially strong persons conceive of it in a particular way and impose their wills on the world and other people. This philosophy has ever since served to justify the glorification of great persons and their actions in overriding all opposition to their will and desires.

HERDER AND CULTURE

In addition to this philosophy, the influence of new historical studies lay behind the German glorification of individual cultures. German Romantic writers went in search of their own past in reaction to the copying of French manners in eighteenth-century Germany, the impact of the French Revolution, and the imperialism of Napoleon. An early leader in this effort was Johann Gottfried Herder (1744–1803). Herder saw human beings and societies as developing organically, like plants, over time. Human beings were different at different times and places.

Herder revived German folk culture by urging the collection and preservation of distinctive German songs and sayings. His most important followers in this work were the Grimm brothers, Jakob (1785–1863) and Wilhelm (1786–1859), famous for their collection of fairy tales. Herder's writings led to a broad revival of interest in history and philosophy. Although initially directed toward identifying German origins, such work soon expanded to embrace other world cultures. Eventually the ability of the Romantic imagination to be at home in any age or culture spurred the study of non-Western religion, comparative literature, and philology.

HEGEL AND HISTORY

The most important philosopher of history in the Romantic period was the German, Georg Wilhelm Friedrich Hegel (1770–1831). Hegel believed ideas develop in an evolutionary fashion that involves conflict. At any given time, a predominant set of ideas, which he termed the thesis, holds sway. Conflicting ideas, which Hegel termed the antithesis, challenge the thesis. As these patterns of thought clash, a synthesis emerges that eventually becomes the new thesis. Then the process begins all over again. Periods of world history receive their character from the patterns of thought that predominate during them.

Several important philosophical conclusions followed from this analysis. One of the most significant was the belief that all periods of history have been of almost equal value because each was, by definition, necessary to the achievements of those that came later. Also, all cultures are valuable because each contributes to the necessary clash of values and ideas that allows humankind to develop.

ISLAM, THE MIDDLE EAST, AND ROMANTICISM

The new religious, literary, and historical sensibilities of the Romantic period modified the European understanding of both Islam and the Arab world while at the same time preserving long-standing attitudes.

The energized Christianity associated with Methodist-like forms of Protestantism, on the one hand, and Chateaubriand's emotional Roman Catholicism, on the other, renewed the traditional sense of necessary conflict between Christianity and Islam. Indeed, the medieval Crusades against Islam fired the Romantic imagination. The general nineteenth-century association of nationalistic aspirations with romanticism also cast the Ottoman Empire and with it Islam in an unfavorable political light. Romantic poets and intellectuals championed the cause of the Greek Revolution (see Chapter 20) and revived older charges of Ottoman despotism.

When Napoleon invaded Egypt in 1799, he met stiff resistance. On July 25, however, the French won a decisive victory. This painting of that battle by Baron Antoine Gros (1771–1835) emphasizes French heroism and Muslim defeat. Such an outlook was typical of European views of Arabs and the Islamic world.

Antoine Jean Gros (1771–1835). Detail, *Battle of Aboukir, July 25, 1799*, c. 1806. Oil on canvas. Chateaux de Versailles et de Trianon, Versailles, France. Bridgeman—Giraudon/Art Resource, NY

What differences were there, if any, between Enlightenment and Romantic views of Islam and the Middle East?

By contrast, other Romantic sensibilities induced Europeans to see the Muslim world in a more positive fashion. The Romantic emphasis on the value of literature drawn from different cultures and ages allowed many nineteenth-century European readers to enjoy the stories from *The Thousand and One Nights*, which first appeared in English in 1778 from a French translation. As poets across Europe rejected classicism in literature in favor of folk stories and fairy tales, they saw the *Arabian Nights* as mysterious and exotic. In 1859, Edward FitzGerald (1809–1883) published his highly popular translation of the *Rubáiyát of Omar Khayyám* of Nishapur, a Persian poet of the twelfth century.

Herder's and Hegel's concepts of history gave both the Arab peoples and Islam distinct roles in history. For Herder, Arab culture was one of the numerous communities that composed the human race and manifested the human spirit. For Hegel, Islam represented an important stage of the development of the world spirit. However, Hegel believed Islam had fulfilled its role in history and no longer had any significant part to play.

The British historian and social commentator Thomas Carlyle (1795–1881) attributed new, positive qualities to Muhammad himself. In his book *On Heroes and Hero-Worship* (1841), Carlyle presented Muhammad as the embodiment of the hero as prophet. To Carlyle, Muhammad was straightforward and sincere. Carlyle's understanding of religion was similar to Schleiermacher's, and thus in his pages, Muhammad appeared as a person who had experienced God subjectively and had communicated a sense of the divine to others. Although friendly to Muhammad from a historical standpoint, Carlyle nonetheless saw him as one of many great religious figures and not, as Muslims believed, as the last of the prophets through whom God had spoken.

The person whose actions in the long run did perhaps the most to reshape the idea of both Islam and the Middle East in the European imagination was Napoleon himself. With his Egyptian expedition of 1798, the first European military invasion of the Near East since the Crusades, the study of the Arab world became an important activity within French intellectual life. For his invasion of Egypt to succeed, Napoleon believed he must make it clear he had no intention of destroying Islam but rather sought to liberate Egypt from the military clique that governed the country in the name of the Ottoman Empire. To that end, he took with him scholars of Arabic and Islamic culture whom he urged to converse with the most educated people they could meet. Napoleon personally met with the local Islamic leaders and had all of his speeches and proclamations translated into classical Arabic. Such cultural sensitivity and the serious efforts of the French scholars to learn Arabic and study the Qur'an impressed Egyptian scholars. It was on this expedition that the famous Rosetta Stone was discovered. Now housed in the British Museum, it eventually led to the decipherment of ancient Egypt's hieroglyphic writing. Two cultural effects in the West of Napoleon's invasion were an increase in the number of European visitors to the Middle East and a demand for architecture based on ancient Egyptian models. Perhaps the most famous example of this fad is the Washington Monument in Washington, D.C., which is modeled after ancient Egyptian obelisks.

SUMMARY

HOW DID Napoleon come to power in France?

The Rise of Napoleon Bonaparte In France in 1799, Napoleon Bonaparte made himself First Consul. He had taken advantage of the Directory's weaknesses, his own past military successes, and the naivete of politicians who thought Napoleon could be used as a figurehead, to grant himself powers comparable to those of Roman emperors. *page 468*

HOW DID the Consulate end the revolution in France?

The Consulate in France (1799–1804) The French Revolution ended with Napoleon's Consulate; the bourgeoisie and the peasants were satisfied. Napoleon seemed to offer stability, and the voters approved his constitution in a plebiscite. Napoleon signed treaties that brought peace to Europe and maneuvered to build coalitions and crush dissent at home. He concluded a concordat with the pope in 1801, which ratified the status quo but allowed Napoleon to replace clergy throughout France. Napoleon continued to increase his power and initiated codification of French law (the Napoleonic Code), which mostly endorsed changes that had been effected by the revolution while incrementally enhancing the state's power. By 1804, Napoleon was ready to crown himself emperor, making himself Napoleon I. *page 469*

HOW DID Napoleon build an empire?

Napoleon's Empire (1804–1814) Between 1804 and 1815, Napoleon conquered most of Europe, dismantling remnants of the Old Regime along the way. The revolution had mobilized France, and Napoleon took advantage of the fact that he could field more troops at once than any other military leader. Napoleon's greatest victory was probably his 1805 defeat of combined Austrian and Russian forces at Austerlitz. He occupied Vienna, reorganized Germany, caused the dissolution of the Holy Roman Empire, and reduced Prussia by half. Only Britain could compete with France. Napoleon's chief defeat had come in 1805 at the hands of Lord Nelson, at the Battle of Trafalgar. Napoleon attempted to weaken Britain through trade embargoes, but this turned out to hurt the Continental System more than it hurt Britain. *page 471*

WHY DID Napoleonic rule breed resentment in Europe?

European Response to the Empire Opposition to Napoleon fanned the flames of nationalism. Following his victory over the Prussians at Jena in 1806, nationalists called for Germany's unification. When he deposed the Bourbon monarchs of Spain in favor of his brother, the Spaniards rebelled. Austria's declaration of war on France gave him an opportunity to occupy Austrian territory, and in 1810, Russia's withdrawal from the Continental System prompted him to march on Moscow. The Russian winter forced him to retreat, and in October 1813, a powerful coalition defeated him. In the spring of 1814, he went into exile on the island of Elba. *page 474*

WHAT WERE the consequences of the Congress of Vienna?

The Congress of Vienna and the European Settlement In 1815 the Congress of Vienna broke new ground in international law by concluding treaties among states that prevented war in Europe for a century. France was reduced in size and its Bourbon dynasty restored. State boundaries were adjusted around France and in eastern Europe to enhance security. Napoleon attempted a comeback while the Congress was still debating these arrangements, but a British and Prussian force defeated him at Waterloo in June 1815, and he was exiled once again—this time to the island of Saint Helena. *page 479*

WHY DID the Romantics reject much of the Enlightenment?

The Romantic Movement Romanticism was an intellectual movement that emerged throughout Europe during the period of the French Revolution and Napoleonic rule. In a reaction against the Enlightenment, romanticism emphasized the value of intuition, spirituality, folklore, dreams, and other forms of human experience that lie beyond the realm of reason. *page 480*

HOW DID Rousseau and Kant contribute to the development of romanticism?

Romantic Questioning of the Supremacy of Reason Romanticism's intellectual foundations were laid largely by Jean-Jacques Rousseau and Immanuel Kant. Rousseau's belief that human nature is corrupted by society and by material prosperity, and his interest in childhood were reflected in the romantic movement's efforts to reform education and family life. Kant argued for the subjectivity of human knowledge. He theorized that because humans share an innate understanding of the categorical imperative, morality must be something independent of sensory experience. *page 481*

HOW WERE the ideals of romanticism reflected in English and German literature and in Romantic art at end of question?

Romantic Literature "Romantic literature" meant slightly different things in different countries and periods. In general, it meant literature that stressed the imaginative elements and was not bound by formal rules. Romantic literature peaked in England and Germany before France. English Romantics such as Coleridge and Wordsworth excelled in poetry that dealt with themes including morality, mortality, and creativity. German Romantics also wrote a great deal of poetry, but most of the major German Romantic authors wrote at least one novel. Goethe was the greatest German writer of the era, although he was a more complicated figure than the label "romantic" suggests. *Faust* was his seminal work. *page 481*

HOW DID Romantic artists portray nature?

Romantic Art The art of the romantic period, like its poetry and philosophy, reacted against the orderly, secular views of the Enlightenment that confidently sought to improve the world. Romantic artists looked to the Middle Ages for inspiration to capture the qualities of what they viewed as a more enduring order that emphasized social stability, religious reverence, the pastoral countryside, and nature in all its majestic and awesome force. The art of this era both feared and were impressed by the tremendous power of the industrializing world. *page 484*

HOW DID Romantic religious thinkers view the religious experience?

Religion in the Romantic Period Romanticism in religion stressed the individual's heartfelt response to the divine. Methodism developed in England in the eighteenth century as a reaction against deism and rationalism in the Church of England. Methodists believe in Christian perfectibility in this life; the enthusiastic emotional experience is part of Christian conversion. In France, Chateaubriand argued that passion is at the heart of religion. Schleiermacher described religion as a feeling of dependence on an infinite being. *page 485*

WHAT WERE the Romantic views of history and national identity?

Romantic Views of Nationalism and History Romanticism glorified both individuals and individual cultures. The German philosophy of idealism helped explain the relationship between the acts of strong individuals and the shaping of history. German Romantics also encouraged the study of folk culture. The German philosopher G. W. F. Hegel explained history in terms of the evolution of the prevailing ideas of a time and place. Europe's interest in the Arab world was revived by current events such as Napoleon's invasion of Egypt. The new European scholarship on Islam, however, perpetuated old Western stereotypes. *page 486*

REVIEW QUESTIONS

1. How did Napoleon rise to power? What were the stages by which he eventually made himself emperor? What were his major domestic achievements? Did his rule more nearly fulfill or betray the ideals of the French Revolution?
2. How did Napoleon acquire and rule his empire? Why did he invade Russia? Why did his campaign fail? Was he a military genius, or did his successes owe more to the ineptitude of his opponents?
3. Who were the principal personalities at the Congress of Vienna? What were the most significant problems they addressed? What was the long-term significance of the Congress?
4. How does the role Romantic writers assigned to feelings compare with the role Enlightenment writers claimed for reason? What questions did Rousseau and Kant raise about reason? How did the Romantic understanding of religion differ from Reformation Protestantism and Enlightenment deism? What was the importance of history to the Romantics? What inspired Romantic artists?

KEY TERMS

categorical imperative (p. 482)
Consulate (p. 469)
Methodism (p. 485)
neo-Gothic (p. 484)
romanticism (p. 480)
Sturm and Drang (p. 481)

For additional learning resources related to this chapter, please go to **www.myhistorylab.com**

myhistorylab

20

The Conservative Order and the Challenges of Reform (1815–1832)

In 1830, revolution again erupted in France as well as elsewhere on the Continent. Eugène Delacroix's *Liberty Leading the People* was the most famous image recalling that event. Note how Delacroix portrays persons from different social classes and occupations joining the revolution led by the figure of Liberty.

Eugène Delacroix (1798–1863), *Liberty Leading the People*, 1830. Oil on canvas, 260 × 325 cm–RF 129. Louvre/RMN Réunion des Musées Nationaux, France. Erich Lessing/Art Resource, NY

How did the French Revolution inspire movements for political change across Europe in the nineteenth century?

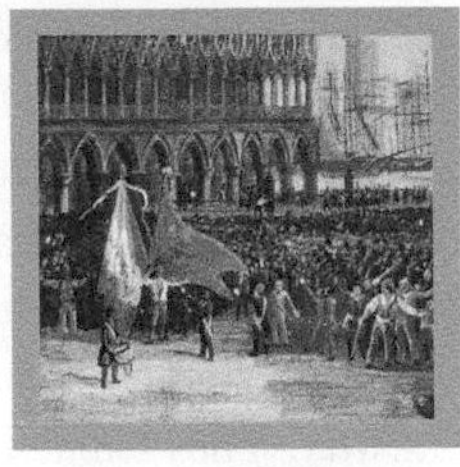

Reactionary movements that favored monarchy and aristocracy dominated European politics for the decade following the Congress of Vienna. However, nationalism and liberalism, two new ideologies, challenged the traditional understanding of the state as nothing more than a collection of properties belonging to a royal dynasty. Nationalists claimed that ethnicity was the true basis for statehood, and they wanted to redraw the map of Europe to reflect boundaries among ethnic groups. Liberals challenged the traditional order in a different way. They wanted governments to implement moderate political reforms and establish freer economic markets.

THE CHALLENGES OF NATIONALISM AND LIBERALISM

HOW DID early-nineteenth-century nationalists define the nation?

Throughout the nineteenth-century Western world, secular ideologies began to take hold of the learned and popular imaginations in opposition to the political and social status quo. These included nationalism, liberalism, republicanism, socialism, and communism.

THE EMERGENCE OF NATIONALISM

nationalism The belief that the people who share an ethnic identity (language, culture, and history) should also be recognized as having a right to a government and political identity of their own.

Nationalism proved to be the single most powerful European political ideology of the nineteenth and early twentieth centuries. As a political outlook, nationalism was and is based on the relatively modern concept that a nation is composed of people who are joined together by the bonds of a common language, as well as common customs, culture, and history, and who, because of these bonds, should be administered by the same government. The idea came into its own during the late eighteenth and the early nineteenth centuries.

Opposition to the Vienna Settlement Early-nineteenth-century nationalism directly opposed the principle upheld at the Congress of Vienna that legitimate monarchies or dynasties, rather than ethnicity, provide the basis for political unity. Nationalists naturally protested multinational states such as the Austrian and Russian Empires. They also objected to peoples of the same ethnic group, such as Germans and Italians, dwelling in a political unit smaller than that of the ethnic nation. Consequently, nationalists challenged both the domestic and the international order of the Vienna settlement.

Behind the concept of nationalism usually, though not always, lay the idea of popular sovereignty, since the qualities of peoples, rather than their rulers, determine a national character. This aspect of nationalism, however, frequently led to confusion or conflict over the status of minorities in regions ruled by a different ethnic majority.

Creating Nations In fact, it was nationalists who actually created nations in the nineteenth century. During the first half of the century, a particular, usually small, group of nationalistically minded writers or other intellectual elites, using the printed word, spread a nationalistic concept of the nation. In effect, they gave a people a sense of their past and a literature of their own. These small groups of early nationalists established the cultural beliefs and political expectations on which the later mass-supported nationalism of the second half of the century would grow.

Which language to use in the schools and in government offices was always a point of contention for nationalists. In France and Italy, official versions of the national language were imposed in the schools and they replaced local dialects. In parts of Scandinavia and eastern Europe, nationalists attempted to resurrect from earlier times what they regarded as purer versions of the national language. This process of establishing national languages led to far more linguistic uniformity in European nations than had existed before the nineteenth century.

Language could become such an effective cornerstone in the foundation of nationalism thanks largely to the emergence of the print culture discussed in Chapter 17. The uniform language found in printed works could overcome regional spoken dialects and establish itself as dominant. In most countries, spoken and written proficiency in the official, printed language became a path to social and political advancement. The growth of a uniform language helped persuade people who had not thought of themselves as constituting a nation that in fact they were one.

Meaning of Nationhood Nationalists used a variety of arguments and metaphors to express what they meant by *nationhood*. Some argued that gathering, for example, Italians into a unified Italy or Germans into a unified Germany, thus eliminating or at least federating the petty dynastic states that governed those regions, would promote economic and administrative efficiency. Adopting a tenet from political liberalism, certain nationalist writers suggested that nations determining their own destinies resembled individuals exploiting personal talents to determine their own careers. Some nationalists claimed that nations, like biological species in the natural world, were distinct creations of God. Other nationalists claimed a place for their nations in the divine order of things.

A significant difficulty for nationalism was, and is, determining which ethnic groups could be considered nations, with claims to territory and political autonomy. In theory, any of them could, but in reality, nationhood came to be associated with groups that were large enough to support a viable economy, that had a significant cultural history, that possessed a cultural elite that could nourish and spread the national language, and that had the military capacity to conquer other peoples or to establish and protect their own independence. (See "Compare & Connect: Mazzini and Lord Acton Debate the Political Principles of Nationalism," pages 494–495.)

Regions of Nationalistic Pressure During the nineteenth century, nationalists challenged the political status quo in six major areas of Europe. England had brought Ireland under direct rule in 1800. Irish nationalists, however, wanted independence or at least larger measures of self-government. German nationalists sought political unity for all German-speaking peoples, challenging the multinational structure of the Austrian Empire and pitting Prussia and Austria against each other. Italian nationalists sought to unify Italian-speaking peoples on the Italian peninsula and to drive out the Austrians. Polish nationalists, targeting primarily their Russian rulers, struggled to restore Poland as an independent nation. In eastern Europe, a host of national groups, including Hungarians, Czechs, Slovenes, and others, sought either independence or formal recognition within the Austrian Empire. Finally, in southeastern Europe on the Balkan peninsula and eastward, national groups, including Serbs, Greeks, Albanians, Romanians, and Bulgarians, sought independence from Ottoman and Russian control.

Early-Nineteenth-Century Political Liberalism

The word *liberal*, as applied to political activity, entered the European and American vocabulary during the nineteenth century. Its meaning has varied over time, and the values and beliefs of nineteenth-century liberals bear little resemblance to the values and beliefs identified with liberalism in America today.

COMPARE & CONNECT

MAZZINI AND LORD ACTON DEBATE THE POLITICAL PRINCIPLES OF NATIONALISM

No political force in the nineteenth and twentieth centuries was stronger than nationalism. It eventually replaced loyalty to a dynasty with loyalty based on ethnic considerations. It received new standing after World War I when the self-determination of nations became one of the cornerstones of the Paris Peace Treaties. Still later, former European colonies embraced this powerful idea. Yet from the earliest enunciation of the principles of nationalism the concept confronted major critics who understood its potential destructiveness. In these two documents Mazzini, the great Italian nationalist, sets forth his understanding of nationalism, and Lord Acton, the distinguished nineteenth-century English historian, points to the dangers lurking behind the ideas and realities of politics based on nationalism.

QUESTIONS

1. What qualities of a people does Mazzini associate with nationalism?
2. How and why does Mazzini relate nationalism to divine purposes?
3. Why does Acton see the principle of nationality as dangerous to liberty?
4. Why does Acton see nationalism as a threat to minority groups and to democracy?
5. How might the connection that Mazzini draws between nationalism and divine will serve to justify the repression of minority rights that Acton feared?

I. MAZZINI DEFINES NATIONALITY

In 1835 the Italian nationalist and patriot Giuseppe Mazzini (1805–1872) explained his understanding of nationalism. Note how he combines a generally democratic view of politics with a religious concept of the divine destiny of nations. Once in power, however, nationalist states in Europe and the rest of the world were often not democratic states.

The essential characteristics of a nationality are common ideas, common principles and a common purpose. A nation is an association of those who are brought together by language, by given geographical conditions or by the role assigned them by history, who acknowledge the same principles and who march together to the conquest of a single definite goal under the rule of a uniform body of law.

The life of a nation consists in harmonious activity (that is, the employment of all individual abilities and energies comprised within the association) towards this single goal. . . .

But nationality means even more than this. Nationality also consists in the share of mankind's labors which God assigns to a people. This mission is the task which a people must perform to the end that the Divine Idea shall be realized in this world; it is the work which gives a people its rights as a member of Mankind; it is the baptismal rite which endows a people with its own character and its rank in the brotherhood of nations. . . .

Nationality depends for its very existence upon its sacredness within and beyond its borders.

If nationality is to be inviolable for all, friends and foes alike, it must be regarded inside a country as holy, like a religion, and outside a country as a grave mission. It is necessary too that the ideas arising within a country grow steadily, as part of the general law of Humanity which is the source of all nationality. It is necessary that these ideas be shown to other lands in their beauty and purity, free from any alien mixture, from any slavish fears, from any skeptical hesitancy, strong and active, embracing in their evolution every aspect and manifestation of the life of the nation. These ideas, a necessary component in the order of universal destiny, must retain their originality even as they enter harmoniously into mankind's general progress.

The people must be the basis of nationality; its logically derived and vigorously applied principles its means; the strength of all its strength; the improvement of the life of all and the happiness of the greatest possible number its results; and the accomplishment of the task assigned to it by God its goal. This is what we mean by nationality.

Source: From Herbert H. Rowen, ed., *From Absolutism to Revolution, 1648–1848*, 2nd ed. © 1969. Reprinted by permission of Prentice Hall, Inc., Upper Saddle River, NJ, pp. 277–280.

II. LORD ACTON CONDEMNS NATIONALISM

As well as being an historian, Lord Acton (1834–1902) was an important nineteenth-century commentator on contemporary religious and political events. He was deeply concerned with the character and preservation of liberty. In his essay "Nationality" of 1862, Lord Acton's became one of the earliest voices to warn that nationalism, or what he here terms "the modern theory of nationality," could endanger liberty of both individuals and people who found themselves to be an ethnic minority within a state dominated by a different ethnic or nationalist majority. Acton's words would prove prophetic with regard to the fate of ethnic minorities within Europe for the next century. Acton also pointed out that the pursuit of nationalist goals might mean that a government would ignore the economic well-being of its peoples.

The greatest adversary of the rights of nationality is the modern theory of nationality. By making the State and the nation commensurate with each other in theory, it reduces practically to a subject condition all other nationalities that may be within the boundary. It cannot admit them to an equality with the ruling nation which constitutes the State, because the State would then cease to be national, which would be a contradiction of the principle of its existence. According, therefore, to the degree of humanity and civilization in that dominant body which claims all the rights of the community, the inferior races are exterminated, or reduced to servitude, or outlawed, or put in a condition of dependence.

If we take the establishment of liberty for the realization of moral duties to be the end of civil society, we must conclude that those states are substantially the most perfect which, like the British and Austrian Empires, include various distinct nationalities without oppressing them. Those in which no mixture of races has occurred are imperfect; and those in which its effects have disappeared are decrepit. A State which is incompetent to satisfy different races condemns itself; a State which labors to neutralize, to absorb, or to expel them, destroys its own vitality; a State which does not include them is destitute of the chief basis of self-government. The theory of nationality, therefore, is a retrograde step in history. . . .

[N]ationality does not aim either at liberty or prosperity, both of which it sacrifices to the imperative necessity of making the nation the mold and measure of the State. Its course will be marked with material as well as moral ruin, in order that a new invention may prevail over the works of God and the interests of mankind. There is no principle of change, no phrase of political speculation conceivable, more comprehensive, more subversive, or more arbitrary than this. It is a confutation of democracy, because it sets limits to the exercise of the popular will, and substitutes for it a higher principle.

Source: From John Emerich Edward Dalbert-Acton, First Baron Acton, *Essays in the History of Liberty*, ed. by J. Rufus Fears (Indianapolis, IN: Liberty Classics, 1985), pp. 431–433.

During the revolutionary months of 1848, Italian nationalists unfurled the tri-colored green,white and red Italian nationalist flag on St. Mark's Square in Venice to replace the flag of Austria, which then ruled the city. Austrian rule of Venice only ended in 1866.

Picture Desk Inc., Kobal Collection

What was the relationship between nationalism and militarism in the nineteenth century?

Political Goals Nineteenth-century liberals derived their political ideas from the writers of the Enlightenment, the example of English liberties, and the so-called principles of 1789 embodied in the French Declaration of the Rights of Man and Citizen. They sought to establish a political framework of legal equality, religious toleration, and freedom of the press. Their general goal was a political structure that would limit the arbitrary power of government against the persons and property of individual citizens. They generally believed the legitimacy of government emanated from the freely given consent of the governed. The popular basis of such government was to be expressed through elected representative, or parliamentary, bodies. Most importantly, free government required government ministers to be responsible to the representatives rather than to the monarch. Liberals sought to achieve these political arrangements through written constitutions. They wanted to see constitutionalism and constitutional governments installed across the Continent.

Those who espoused liberal political structures often were educated, relatively wealthy people, usually associated with the professions or commercial life, but who were excluded in one manner or another from the existing political processes. Although liberals wanted broader political participation, they did not advocate democracy. What they wanted was to extend representation to the propertied classes. Second only to their hostility to the privileged aristocracies was their contempt for the lower, unpropertied classes. Liberals transformed the eighteenth-century concept of aristocratic liberty into a new concept of privilege based on wealth and property rather than birth. By the middle of the century, this widely shared attitude meant that throughout Europe liberals had separated themselves from both the rural peasant and the urban working class, a division that was to have important consequences.

QUICK REVIEW

Liberal Political Program

- Derived from principles embodied in the Declaration of the Rights of Man and Citizen
- Favored equality before the law, religious toleration, and freedom of the press
- Wanted to see constitutional governments established throughout Europe

Economic Goals The economic goals of nineteenth-century liberals also divided them from working people. Following the Enlightenment ideas of Adam Smith, they sought to abolish the economic restraints associated with mercantilism or the regulated economies of enlightened absolutists. They wanted to manufacture and sell goods freely. To that end, they favored the removal of international tariffs and internal barriers to trade. Economic liberals opposed the old paternalistic legislation that established wages and labor practices by government regulation or by guild privileges. They saw labor as simply one more commodity to be bought and sold freely.

Because the social and political circumstances of various countries differed, the specific programs of liberals also differed from one country to another. Great Britain and France already had many structures liberals favored. The problem for liberals in both countries was to protect civil liberties, define the respective powers of the monarch and the elected legislature, and expand the electorate moderately while avoiding democracy.

The complex political situation in German-speaking Europe was different from that in France or Britain, and German liberalism differed accordingly from its French and British counterparts. In the German states and Austria, monarchs and aristocrats offered stiffer resistance to liberal ideas, leaving German liberals with less access to direct political influence. Little or no precedent existed for middle-class participation in the government or the military, and there was no strong tradition of civil or individual liberty. Most German liberals favored a united Germany and looked either to Austria or to Prussia as the instrument of unification. As a result, they were more tolerant of a strong state and monarchical power than other liberals were.

QUICK REVIEW

Liberal Economics

- Embraced the theories of Adam Smith
- Wanted free markets with limited governmental interference
- Saw labor as a commodity to be bought and sold

Relationship of Nationalism to Liberalism Nationalism could be, and often was, directly opposed to liberal political values. Some nationalists wanted their own particular ethnic group to dominate minority national or ethnic groups within a particular

region. Nationalists also often defined their own national group in opposition to other national groups whom they might regard as cultural inferiors or historical enemies. Furthermore, conservative nationalists might seek political autonomy for their own ethnic group but have no intention of establishing liberal political institutions thereafter. Nonetheless, although liberalism and nationalism were not identical, they were often compatible. By espousing representative government, civil liberties, and economic freedom, nationalist groups in one country could gain the support of liberals elsewhere in Europe who might not otherwise share their nationalist interests.

CONSERVATIVE GOVERNMENTS: THE DOMESTIC POLITICAL ORDER

WHAT EXPLAINS the strength of conservatism in the early nineteenth century?

Despite the challenges of liberalism and nationalism, the domestic political order that the restored conservative institutions of Europe established, particularly in Great Britain and eastern Europe, showed remarkable staying power. Not until World War I did their power and pervasive influence come to an end.

Conservative Outlooks

The major pillars of nineteenth-century **conservatism** were legitimate monarchies, landed aristocracies, and established churches. In the eighteenth century, these groups had often quarreled. Only the upheavals of the French Revolution and the Napoleonic era transformed them into natural, if sometimes reluctant, allies. In that sense, conservatism as an articulated outlook and set of cooperating institutions was as new a feature on the political landscape as nationalism and liberalism.

conservatism Form of political thought that, in mid-nineteenth-century Europe, promoted legitimate monarchies, landed aristocracies, and established churches.

The more theoretical political and religious ideas of the conservative classes were associated with thinkers such as Edmund Burke (see Chapter 18) and Friedrich Hegel (see Chapter 19). Conservatives shared other, less formal attitudes forged by the revolutionary experience. The execution of Louis XVI at the hands of radical democrats convinced most monarchs they could trust only aristocratic governments or governments of aristocrats in alliance with the wealthiest middle-class and professional people. The European aristocracies believed that no form of genuinely representative government would protect their property and influence. The churches equally distrusted popular movements, except their own revivals. They also feared and hated most of the ideas associated with the Enlightenment.

All the nations of Europe in the years immediately after 1815 confronted problems arising directly from their entering an era of peace after a quarter century of armed conflict. The wartime footing had allowed all the belligerent governments to exercise firm control over their populations. War had fueled economies and had furnished vast areas of employment in armies, navies, military industries, and agriculture. The onset of peace meant citizens could raise new political issues and that economies were no longer geared to supplying military needs. Thus, the conservative statesmen who led every major government in 1815 confronted new pressures that would cause various degrees of domestic unrest and would lead them to resort to differing degrees of repression.

Prince Klemens von Metternich (1773–1859) epitomized nineteenth-century conservatism.

Sir Thomas Lawrence (1769–1830), *Clemens Lothar Wenzel, Prince Metternich* (1773–1859), RCIN 404948, OM 905 WC 206. The Royal Collection © 2006, Her Majesty Queen Elizabeth II

Why was Metternich so hostile to liberalism and nationalism?

Liberalism and Nationalism Resisted in Austria and the Germanies

The early-nineteenth-century statesman who, more than any other epitomized conservatism, was the Austrian prince Metternich (1773–1859). It was Metternich who seemed to exercise chief control over the forces of European reaction.

Dynastic Integrity of the Habsburg Empire The Austrian government could make no serious compromises with the new political forces in Europe. To no other country were the programs of liberalism and nationalism potentially more dangerous. Germans and Hungarians, as well as Poles, Czechs, Slovaks, Slovenes, Italians, Croats, and other ethnic groups, peopled the Habsburg domains. Through client governments, Austria also dominated those parts of the Italian peninsula that it did not rule directly. For Metternich and other Austrian officials, the recognition of the political rights and aspirations of any of the various national groups would mean the probable dissolution of the empire. To safeguard dynastic integrity, Austria had to prevent the formation of a German national state that might absorb the German-speaking heart of the empire and exclude the other realms the Habsburgs governed.

QUICK REVIEW

Threats to Habsburg Empire

- Nationalism
- Liberal political reforms
- Ethnic divisions

Defeat of Prussian Reform An important victory for this holding policy came in Prussia in the years immediately after the Congress of Vienna. In 1815, Frederick William III (r. 1797–1840) had promised some form of constitutional government. After stalling, he formally reneged on his pledge in 1817. Instead, he created a new Council of State, which, although it improved administrative efficiency, was responsible to him alone. In 1819, the king moved further from reform. After a major disagreement over the organization of the army, he replaced his reform-minded ministers with hardened conservatives. On their advice, in 1823, Frederick William III established eight provincial estates, or diets. These bodies were dominated by the Junkers and exercised only an advisory function. The old bonds linking monarchy, army, and landholders in Prussia had been reestablished.

Student Nationalism and the Carlsbad Decrees Nonetheless, in the aftermath of the defeat of Napoleon, many young Germans continued to cherish nationalist and liberal expectations. University students who had grown up during the days of the reforms of Stein and Hardenberg and had read the writings of early German nationalists made up the most important of these groups. When they went to the universities, they continued to dream of a united Germany. They formed *Burschenschaften*, or student associations. Like student groups today, these clubs served numerous social functions, one of which was to replace old provincial attachments with loyalty to the concept of a united German state. It should also be noted that these clubs were often anti-Semitic. (See "Encountering the Past: Dueling in Germany.")

The activities of the *Burschenschaften* made the government uneasy. When, in early 1819, a student named Karl Sand, a *Burschenschaft* member, assassinated the conservative dramatist August von Kotzebue, Metternich used the incident to suppress institutions associated with liberalism. In July 1819, Metternich persuaded the major German states to issue the Carlsbad Decrees, which dissolved the *Burschenschaften*. The decrees also provided for university inspectors and press censors. The next year the German Confederation issued the Final Act, which limited the subjects that the constitutional chambers of Bavaria, Württemberg, and Baden could discuss. The measure also asserted the right of the monarchs to resist demands of constitutionalists. For many years thereafter, the secret police of the various German states harassed potential dissidents. In the opinion of the princes, these included almost anyone who sought even moderate social or political change.

In May 1820, Karl Sand, a German student and a member of a *Burschenschaft*, was executed for his murder of the conservative playwright August von Kotzebue the previous year. In the eyes of many young German nationalists, Sand was a political martyr.

Bildarchiv Preussischer Kulturbesitz

What role did universities play in the political upheavals of the first half of the nineteenth century?

Postwar Repression in Great Britain

The years 1819 and 1820 marked a high tide for conservative influence and repression in western as well as eastern Europe. After 1815, Great Britain experienced two years of poor harvests. At the same time, discharged sailors and soldiers and out-of-work industrial workers swelled the ranks of the unemployed.

ENCOUNTERING THE PAST

DUELING IN GERMANY

Dueling clubs were prestigious student organizations in the German universities of the nineteenth century. Europe's aristocracy had deep roots in the military, and dueling had long been the preferred method for resolving disputes among "gentlemen" (members of the upper class). The injury and loss of life this occasioned had prompted most western European governments to outlaw dueling by the mid-nineteenth century, but the conservative aristocratic-military class that dominated Germany kept it alive. Dueling was technically against the law, but it was socially acceptable and considered a test of manhood that elevated the status of those who practiced it.

Duels were a part of aristocratic life, and respect for the aristocracy was so great in Germany that any man who fought a duel elevated his social standing. The universities, whose students were drawn from the upper middle class and the aristocracy, congregated men for whom dueling was considered a form of character building. Duels elsewhere were usually fought with pistols, but students fenced with sabers. They seldom killed one another, but their weapons inflicted facial wounds—producing scars that served a man as a badge of honor for a lifetime. The fad for dueling persisted into the era of World War I, but it faded following the defeat of Germany's militaristic establishment in 1918.

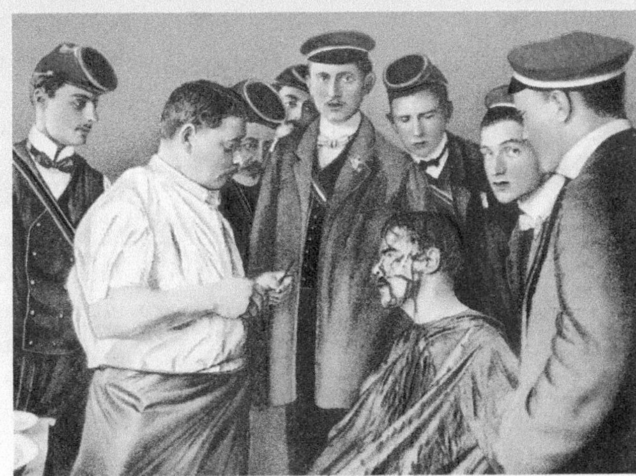

While fellow dueling-club members look on, a German student slashed in a duel is treated by a surgeon.

Image Works/Mary Evans Picture Library Ltd.

How would you explain the nineteenth-century German fad for dueling?

WHAT CAN you conclude about the politics of Germany in the nineteenth century from the fact that dueling became an avenue to social mobility?

Lord Liverpool's Ministry and Popular Unrest The Tory ministry of Lord Liverpool (1770–1828) was unprepared to deal with these problems of postwar dislocation. Instead, it sought to protect the interests of the landed and wealthy classes. In 1815, Parliament passed a Corn Law to maintain high prices for domestically produced grain (called "corn" in Britain) by levying import duties on foreign grain. The next year, Parliament replaced the income tax that only the wealthy paid with excise or sales taxes on consumer goods that both the wealthy and the poor paid. These laws continued a legislative trend that marked the abandonment by the British ruling class of its traditional role of paternalistic protector of the poor.

In light of these policies and the postwar economic downturn, it is hardly surprising that the lower social orders began to doubt the wisdom of their rulers and to demand political changes. Mass meetings called for the reform of Parliament. Reform clubs were organized. Radical newspapers demanded change. The government's answer to the discontent was repression.

"Peterloo" and the Six Acts This initial repression, in combination with improved harvests, calmed the political landscape for a time. By 1819, however, the people were restive again. In the industrial north, well-organized mass meetings demanded the reform of Parliament. The radical reform campaign culminated on August 16, 1819, with a meeting in the industrial city of Manchester at Saint Peter's Fields. Royal troops and the local militia were on hand to ensure order. As the speeches were about to begin, a local magistrate ordered the militia to move into the audience. The result was panic and death. At least eleven people in the crowd were killed; scores were injured. The event became known as the Peterloo Massacre, a phrase that drew a contemptuous comparison with Wellington's victory at Waterloo.

The Liverpool ministry decided to act once and for all to end these troubles. In December 1819, a few months after the German Carlsbad Decrees, Parliament passed a series of laws called the Six Acts, which (1) forbade large unauthorized, public meetings, (2) raised the fines for seditious libel, (3) speeded up the trials of political agitators, (4) increased newspaper taxes, (5) prohibited the training of armed groups, and (6) allowed local officials to search homes in certain disturbed counties. In effect, the Six Acts attempted to prevent radical leaders from agitating and to give the authorities new powers.

Bourbon Restoration in France

The abdication of Napoleon in 1814 opened the way for a restoration of Bourbon rule. The new king, Louis XVIII (r. 1814–1824), understood he could not turn back the clock to 1789. France had undergone too many irreversible changes. Consequently, Louis XVIII agreed to become a constitutional monarch, but under a constitution of his own making called the Charter.

QUICK REVIEW

Provisions of the Charter

- Combined hereditary monarchy and representative government
- Ratified most of the rights described in the Declaration of the Rights of Man and Citizen
- Did not challenge property rights of those who held land confiscated during the revolution

The Charter The Charter provided for a hereditary monarchy and a bicameral legislature. The monarch appointed the upper house, the Chamber of Peers, modeled on the British House of Lords; a narrow franchise with a high property qualification elected the lower house, the Chamber of Deputies. The Charter guaranteed most of the rights the Declaration of the Rights of Man and Citizen had enumerated. The Charter also promised not to challenge the property rights of the current owners of land that had been confiscated from aristocrats and the church. With this provision, Louis XVIII hoped to reconcile to his regime those who had benefited from the revolution.

Ultraroyalism This moderate spirit did not penetrate deeply into the ranks of royalist supporters whose families had suffered during the revolution. Rallying around Louis's brother and heir, the count of Artois (1757–1836), those people who were more royalist than the monarch now demanded their revenge. The ultraroyalist majority elected to the Chamber of Deputies in 1816 proved so dangerously reactionary that the king soon dissolved the chamber. The second election returned a more moderate majority. Several years of political give-and-take followed, with the king making mild accommodations to liberals.

In February 1820, however, the duke of Berri, son of Artois and heir to the throne after his father, was murdered by a lone assassin. The ultraroyalists persuaded Louis XVIII that the murder was the result of his ministers' cooperation with liberal politicians, and the king responded with repressive measures. By the early 1820s, the veneer of constitutionalism had worn away. Liberals were being driven out of politics and into a near illegal status.

THE CONSERVATIVE INTERNATIONAL ORDER

WHAT WERE the goals of the Concert of Europe?

At the Congress of Vienna, the major powers—Russia, Austria, Prussia, and Great Britain—had agreed to consult with each other from time to time on matters affecting Europe as a whole. The vehicle for this consultation was a series of postwar congresses, or conferences. Later, as differences arose among the powers, the consultations became more informal. This new arrangement for resolving mutual foreign policy issues was known as the *Concert of Europe*. It prevented one nation from taking a major action in international affairs without working in concert with and obtaining the assent of the others.

The Congress System

The first congress took place in 1818 at Aix-la-Chapelle in Germany near the border of Belgium. As a result of this gathering, the four major powers removed their troops from France, which had paid its war reparations, and readmitted France to good standing among the European nations. Despite unanimity on these decisions, the conference was not without friction. Tsar Alexander I (r. 1801–1825) suggested that the Quadruple Alliance (see Chapter 19) agree to uphold the borders and the existing governments of all European countries. Viscount Castlereagh (1769–1822), representing Britain, flatly rejected the proposal. He contended the Quadruple Alliance was intended only to prevent future French aggression. These disagreements appeared somewhat academic until revolutions broke out in southern Europe.

The Spanish Revolution of 1820

When the Bourbon Ferdinand VII of Spain (r. 1814–1833) was placed on his throne after Napoleon's downfall, he had promised to govern according to a written constitution. Once in power, however, he ignored his pledge, dissolved the *Cortés* (the parliament), and ruled alone. In 1820, army officers who were about to be sent to suppress revolution in Spain's Latin American colonies rebelled. In March, Ferdinand once again announced he would abide by the provisions of the constitution. Almost at the same time, in July 1820, revolution erupted in Naples, where the king of the Two Sicilies quickly accepted a constitution. There were other, lesser revolts in Italy, but none of them succeeded.

Metternich wanted to intervene, for he feared that disturbances in Italy might spread into the Habsburg lands. Britain, however, opposed joint intervention by the major powers in either Italy or Spain. When the Congress of Troppau met in late October 1820, Tsar Alexander persuaded the members of the Holy Alliance (Austria and Prussia) to endorse the Protocol of Troppau—a declaration of the right of stable governments to intervene to restore order in countries threatened by revolution. The decision to authorize Austrian intervention in Italy was, however, delayed until the Congress of Laibach met in January 1821. Austrian troops then marched into Naples and restored monarchy and nonconstitutional government to the Two Sicilies.

The final postwar congress took place in October 1822 at Verona. Its primary purpose was to resolve the situation in Spain. Once again, Britain balked at joint action. At Verona, Britain, in effect, withdrew from continental affairs. Austria, Prussia, and Russia agreed to support French intervention in Spain. In April 1823, a French army crossed the Pyrenees and within a few months suppressed the Spanish revolution. French troops remained in Spain to prop up King Ferdinand until 1827. France did not, however, use its intervention as an excuse to aggrandize its power or increase its territory. The same had been true of all the other interventions under the congress system. The great powers authorized these interventions to preserve or restore conservative regimes, not to conquer territory for themselves. Their goal was to maintain the international order established at Vienna.

The Congress of Verona and the Spanish intervention had a second diplomatic result. The new British foreign minister, George Canning (1770–1827), was much more interested in British commerce and trade than Castlereagh had been. Thus Canning sought to prevent the extension of European reaction to Spain's colonies in Latin America, which were then in revolt (see page 503). He intended to exploit these South American revolutions to break Spain's old trading monopoly with its colonies and gain access for Britain to Latin American trade. Britain soon recognized the Spanish colonies as independent states. Through the rest of the century, British commercial interests dominated Latin America.

An English poet appears as an Albanian. The famous English poet George Gordon, Lord Byron (1788–1824), was one of many European liberals who went to Greece to aid the cause of its independence. He died there of fever in 1824.

The Granger Collection, NY

Why were European liberals attracted to the cause of Greek independence?

Revolt Against Ottoman Rule in the Balkans

The Greek Revolution of 1821 While the powers were plotting conservative interventions in Italy and Spain, a third Mediterranean revolt erupted—in Greece. Ottoman weakness and instability troubled European diplomacy throughout the nineteenth century, raising what was known as "the Eastern Question": What should the European powers do about the Ottoman inability to assure political and administrative stability in its possessions in and around the eastern Mediterranean? Most of the major powers had a keen interest in those territories. Russia and Austria coveted land in the Balkans. France and Britain were concerned with the empire's commerce and with control of key naval positions in the eastern Mediterranean. Also at issue was the treatment of the Christian inhabitants of the empire and access to the Christian shrines in the Holy Land. The goals of the great powers often conflicted with the desire for independence of the many national groups in the Ottoman Empire. Yet, because the powers had little desire to strengthen the empire, they were often more sympathetic to nationalistic aspirations there than elsewhere in Europe.

These conflicting interests, as well as mutual distrust, prevented any direct intervention in Greek affairs for several years. Eventually, however, Britain, France, and Russia concluded that an independent Greece would benefit their strategic interests and would not threaten their domestic security. In 1827, they signed the Treaty of London, demanding Turkish recognition of Greek independence, and sent a joint fleet to support the Greek revolt. In 1828, Russia sent troops into the Ottoman holdings in what is today Romania, ultimately gaining control of that territory in 1829 with the Treaty of Adrianople. The treaty also stipulated the Turks would allow Britain, France, and Russia to decide the future of Greece. In 1830, a second Treaty of London declared Greece an independent kingdom.

Serbian Independence Since the late eighteenth century, Serbia had sought independence from the Ottoman Empire. During the Napoleonic wars, its fate had been linked to Russian policy and Russian relations with the Ottoman Empire. Between 1804 and 1813, a remarkable Serbian leader, Kara George (1762–1817), had led a guerrilla war against the Ottomans. This ultimately unsuccessful revolution helped build national self-identity and attracted the interest of the great powers.

In 1815 and 1816, a new leader, Milos Obrenovitch (1780–1860), succeeded in negotiating greater administrative autonomy for some Serbian territory, but most Serbs lived outside the borders of this new entity. In 1830, the Ottoman sultan formally granted independence to Serbia, and by the late 1830s, the major powers granted it diplomatic recognition.

Serbia's political structure, however, remained in doubt for many years. In 1833, Milos, now a hereditary prince, pressured the Ottoman authorities to extend the borders of Serbia, which they did. These new boundaries persisted until 1878. Serbian leaders continued to seek additional territory, however, creating tensions with Austria. The status of minorities, particularly Muslims, within Serbian territory, was also a problem. In the mid-1820s, Russia, which like Serbia was a Slav state and Eastern Orthodox in religion, became Serbia's formal protector. In 1856, Serbia came under the collective protection of the great powers, but the special relationship between Russia and Serbia would continue until the First World War and would play a decisive role in the outbreak of that conflict.

THE WARS OF INDEPENDENCE IN LATIN AMERICA

WHAT SPARKED the wars of independence in Latin America?

The wars of the French Revolution and, more particularly, those of Napoleon sparked movements for independence from European domination throughout Latin America. In less than two decades, between 1804 and 1824, France was driven from Haiti, Portugal lost control of Brazil, and Spain was forced to withdraw from all of its American empire except Cuba and Puerto Rico.

Revolution in Haiti

Between 1791 and 1804, the French colony of Haiti achieved independence. This event was of key importance for two reasons. First, it was sparked by policies of the French Revolution overflowing into its New World Empire. Second, the Haitian Revolution demonstrated that slaves of African origins could lead a revolt against white masters and mulatto freemen. The example of the Haitian Revolution for years thereafter terrified slaveholders throughout the Americas.

Once the French Revolution had broken out in France, the French National Assembly in 1791 decreed that free property-owning mulattos on Haiti should enjoy the same rights as white plantation owners. The Colonial Assembly in Haiti resisted the orders from France. In the same year, a full-fledged slave rebellion shook Haiti. It arose as a result of a secret conspiracy among the slaves. François-Dominique Toussaint L'Ouverture (1743–1803), himself a former slave, quickly emerged as its leader. Although the slave rebellion collapsed, mulattos and free black people on Haiti, who hoped to gain the rights the French National Assembly had promised, then took up arms against the white colonial masters. French officials sent by the revolutionary government in Paris soon backed them. Slaves now came to the aid of an invading French force, and in early 1793, the French abolished slavery in Haiti.

By this time both Spain and Great Britain were attempting to intervene in Haitian events to expand their own influence in the Caribbean. Both were opposed to the end of slavery and both coveted Haiti's rich sugar-producing lands. Toussaint L'Ouverture and his force of ex-slaves again supported the French against the Spanish and the British. By 1800, his army had achieved dominance throughout the island of Hispanola.

Toussaint L'Ouverture (1743–1803) began the revolt that led to Haitian independence in 1804.

Library of Congress

How did revolution in France contribute to revolution in Haiti?

The French government under Napoleon distrusted L'Ouverture and feared that his example would undermine French authority elsewhere in the Caribbean and North America. In 1802, Napoleon sent an army to Haiti and eventually captured L'Ouverture, who was sent back to France where he died in prison in 1803. Other Haitian military leaders of slave origin, the most important of whom was Jean-Jacques Dessalines (1758–1806), continued to resist. When Napoleon found himself again at war with Britain in 1803, he decided to abandon his American empire, selling Louisiana to the United States and withdrawing his forces from Haiti. Thus, the Haitian slave-led rebellion became the first successful assault on colonial government in Latin America. France formally recognized Haitian independence in 1804.

Wars of Independence on the South American Continent

Haiti's revolution, which involved the popular uprising of a repressed social group, proved to be the great exception in the Latin American drive for liberty from European masters. Generally speaking, on the South American continent, the **Creole** elite—merchants, landowners, and professional people of Spanish descent—led the movements against Spain and Portugal. The Creoles were determined that any drive for political independence from Spain and Portugal should not cause social disruption or the loss of their own privileges.

Creole Person of European, usually Spanish, descent born in the Americas.

Overview The Wars of Independence in Latin America

DATE	NATION	LEADER/S
1804	Haiti	Toussaint L'Ouverture and Jean-Jacques Dessalines
1820	Peru	José de San Martín
1821	New Spain	Miguel Hidalgo and José María Morelos
1821	Venezuela	Simón Bolívar

Creole Discontent Creole discontent with Spanish colonial government had many sources. (The Brazilian situation will be discussed separately. See page 505.) Latin American merchants wanted to trade more freely within the region and with North American and European markets. They wanted commercial regulations that would benefit them rather than Spain. They had also resented increases in taxation by the Spanish crown. Finally, Creoles resented Spanish policies that favored *peninsulares*—white people born in Spain—for political patronage, including appointments in the colonial government, church, and army.

Discontent was transformed into rebellion when, in 1807, Napoleon invaded Portugal and made his own brother king of Spain in 1808. The Portuguese royal family fled to Brazil and established its government there, but the Bourbon monarchy of Spain had, for the time being, been overthrown. That situation created an imperial political vacuum throughout Spanish Latin America and gave Creole leaders both the opportunity and the necessity to act.

The Creole elite feared a liberal Napoleonic monarchy in Spain would attempt to impose reforms in Latin America that would harm their economic and social interests. They also feared a French-controlled Spain would try to drain the region of the wealth and resources Napoleon needed for his wars. To protect their interests and to seize the opportunity to direct their own political destiny, between 1808 and 1810 Creole *juntas*, or political committees, claimed the right to govern different regions of Latin America. After the establishment of these local *juntas*, Spain never effectively reestablished its authority in South America. The establishment of the *juntas* also ended the privileges of the *peninsulares*, whose welfare had always depended on the favors of the Spanish crown. Creoles now took over positions in the government and army.

San Martín in Río de la Plata The vast size of Latin America, its geographical barriers, its distinct regional differences, and the absence of an even marginally integrated economy meant there would be several different paths to independence. The first region to assert itself was the Río de la Plata, or modern Argentina. In 1810, the *junta* in Buenos Aires not only thrust off Spanish authority, but also sent forces into Paraguay and Uruguay to liberate them from Spain. These armies were defeated, but Spain nevertheless lost control of both areas. Paraguay asserted its own independence. Brazil took over Uruguay.

These early defeats did not discourage the Buenos Aires government, which determined to liberate Peru, the stronghold of royalist power and loyalty on the continent. By 1817, José de San Martín (1778–1850), the leading general of the Río de la Plata forces, led an army in a daring march over the Andes Mountains and occupied Santiago in Chile, where the Chilean independence leader Bernardo O'Higgins (1778–1842) was established as the supreme dictator. From Santiago, San Martín organized a fleet that, in 1820, carried his army by sea to Peru. The next year, San Martín drove royalist forces from Lima and became Protector of Peru.

Simon Bolívar's Liberation of Venezuela While the army of San Martín had been liberating the southern portion of the continent, Simón Bolívar (1783–1830) had been pursuing a similar task in the north. Bolívar had been involved in the organization of a liberating *junta* in Caracas, Venezuela, in 1810. He was a firm advocate of both independence and a republic. Between 1811 and 1814, civil war broke out throughout Venezuela. Bolívar had to go into exile first in Colombia and then in Jamaica. In 1816, with help from Haiti, he returned to the continent. By the summer of 1821, Bolívar's forces captured Caracas, and he was named president.

Simón Bolívar was the liberator of much of Latin America. He inclined toward a policy of political liberalism.

© Christie's Images/CORBIS

Why did liberalism fail to take hold in the independent states of Latin America?

A year later, in July 1822, the armies of Bolívar and San Martín joined as they moved to liberate Quito, the capital of what is today Ecuador. At a famous meeting in Guayaquil, the two liberators sharply disagreed about the future political structure of Latin America. San Martín believed the peoples of the region required monarchies; Bolívar maintained his republicanism. Not long after the meeting, San Martín quietly retired from public life and went into exile in Europe. Meanwhile, Bolívar deliberately allowed the political situation in Peru to fall into confusion, and in 1823, he sent in troops to establish his control. On December 9, 1824, at the Battle of Ayacucho, the liberating army crushed the main Spanish royalist forces, ending Spain's effort to retain its South American empire.

Independence in New Spain

The drive for independence in New Spain, which included present-day Mexico as well as Texas, California, and the rest of the southwest United States, illustrates better than in any other region the socially conservative outcome of the Latin American colonial revolutions. As elsewhere, a local governing *junta* was organized in 1808. Before it had undertaken any significant measures, however, a Creole priest, Miguel Hidalgo y Costilla (1753–1811), in 1810, issued a call for rebellion to the Indians in his parish. Father Hidalgo set forth a program of social reform, including hints of changes in landholding. Soon he stood at the head of a loosely organized group of 80,000 followers, who captured several major cities and then marched on Mexico City. In July 1811, the revolutionary priest was captured and executed. Leadership of his movement then fell to José María Morelos y Pavón (1765–1815), a mestizo priest. Far more radical than Hidalgo, he called for an end to forced labor and for substantial land reforms. He was executed in 1815, ending five years of popular uprising.

The uprising and its demand for fundamental social reforms united all conservative political groups in Mexico, both Creole and Spanish. These groups opposed any kind of reform that might diminish their privileges. In 1820 the revolution in Spain had forced Ferdinand VII to accept a liberal constitution. Conservative Mexicans feared the new liberal monarchy would attempt to impose liberal reforms on Mexico. Therefore, for the most conservative of reasons, they rallied behind a former royalist general, Augustín de Iturbide (1783–1824), who declared Mexico independent of Spain in 1821. Shortly thereafter, Iturbide was declared emperor.

Brazilian Independence

Brazilian independence, in contrast to that of Spanish Latin America, came relatively simply and peacefully. As already noted, the Portuguese royal family, along with several thousand government officials and members of the court, fled to Brazil in 1807. The prince regent João addressed many of the local complaints, equivalent to those of the Spanish Creoles, by, for example, taking measures that expanded trade. In 1815, he made Brazil a kingdom, which meant it was no longer to be regarded merely as a colony of Portugal. Then, in 1820, a revolution occurred in Portugal, and its leaders demanded João's return to Lisbon. They also demanded the return of Brazil to colonial status. João, who had become King João VI in 1816 (r. 1816–1826), returned to Portugal but

MAP EXPLORATION

Interactive map: To explore this map further, go to www.myhistorylab.com

MAP 20–1 Latin America In 1830 By 1830 most of Latin America had been liberated from Europe. This map shows the initial borders of the states of the region with the dates of their independence. The United Provinces of La Plata formed the nucleus of what later became Argentina.

What caused the spread of independence throughout Latin America in the first quarter of the nineteenth century?

left his son Dom Pedro as regent in Brazil and encouraged him to be sympathetic to the political aspirations of the Brazilians. In September 1822, Dom Pedro embraced the cause of Brazilian independence against the recolonizing efforts of Portugal. By the end of the year, he had become emperor of an independent Brazil. Thus, in contrast to virtually all other nations of Latin America, Brazil achieved independence in a way that left no real dispute as to where the center of political authority lay.

Two other factors aided the peaceful transition to independence in Brazil. First, the political and social elite of Brazil wanted to avoid the destruction that the wars of

independence had unleashed in the Spanish American Empire. Second, these leaders had every intention of preserving slavery. The wars of independence elsewhere had generally led to the abolition of slavery or moved the new states closer to abolishing it. Warfare in Brazil might have caused social turmoil with similar consequences.

THE CONSERVATIVE ORDER SHAKEN IN EUROPE

HOW DID Russia, France, and Britain respond to challenges to the conservative order?

Beginning in the mid-1820s, the conservative governments of Russia, France, and Great Britain faced new political discontent. (See Map 20–2.) In Russia the result was suppression, in France revolution, and in Britain, accommodation. Belgium emerged as a newly independent state.

Russia: The Decembrist Revolt of 1825

Tsar Alexander I had come to the throne in 1801 after a palace coup against his father, Tsar Paul (r. 1796–1801). After flirting with Enlightenment ideas, Alexander turned permanently away from reform. Both at home and abroad, he took the lead in suppressing liberalism and nationalism. There would be no significant challenge to tsarist autocracy until his death.

Unrest in the Army As Russian forces drove Napoleon's army across Europe and then occupied defeated France, many Russian officers were exposed to the ideas of the French Revolution and the Enlightenment and some developed reformist sympathies. Unable to express themselves openly because of Alexander's repressive policies, they formed secret societies. Sometime during 1825, two such societies, the Southern Society and the Northern Society, apparently decided to carry out a *coup d'état* in 1826.

Dynastic Crisis In late November 1825, Tsar Alexander I died unexpectedly. His death created two crises. The first was dynastic. Alexander had no direct heir. Through a series of secret instructions made public only after his death, Alexander had named his younger brother, Nicholas (r. 1825–1855), as the new tsar. Once Alexander was dead, the legality of these instructions became uncertain. The tsar's brother Constantine acknowledged Nicholas as tsar, and Nicholas acknowledged Constantine. Then, in early December, the army command told Nicholas about a conspiracy among certain officers. Able to wait no longer, Nicholas had himself declared tsar.

The second crisis then unfolded. On December 26, 1825, the army was to take the oath of allegiance to Nicholas, who was less popular than Constantine and regarded as more conservative. Most regiments took the oath, but the Moscow regiment, whose chief officers, surprisingly, were not secret society members, marched into the Senate Square in Saint Petersburg and refused to swear allegiance. Late in the afternoon, Nicholas ordered the cavalry and the artillery to attack the insurgents. More than sixty people were killed. Early in 1826, Nicholas himself presided over the commission that investigated the Decembrist Revolt and the secret army societies. Five of the plotters were executed, and more than a hundred others were exiled to Siberia.

The Autocracy of Nicholas I Although Nicholas was neither an ignorant nor a bigoted reactionary, he came to symbolize the most

MAP EXPLORATION

Interactive map: To explore this map further, go to www.myhistorylab.com

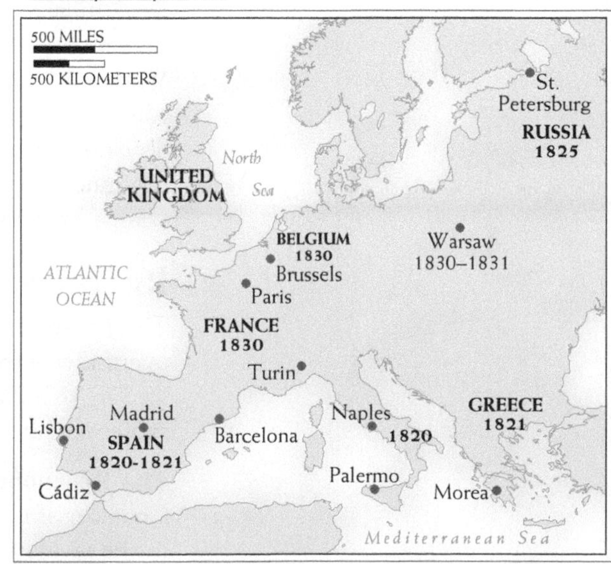

MAP 20–2 **Centers of Revolution, 1820–1831** The conservative order imposed by the great powers in post-Napoleonic Europe was challenged by various uprisings and revolutions, beginning in 1820–1821 in Spain, Naples, and Greece and spreading to Russia, Poland, France, and Belgium later in the decade.

Which countries were spared uprisings in this period?

When the Moscow regiment refused to swear allegiance to Nicholas, he ordered the cavalry and artillery to attack them. Although a total failure, the Decembrist Revolt came to symbolize the yearnings of all Russian liberals in the nineteenth century for a constitutional government.

The Insurrection of the Decembrists at Senate Square, St. Petersburg on 14th December, 1825 (w/c on paper) by Russian School (nineteenth century). Private Collection/Archives Charmet/Bridgeman Art Library

What pressures and tensions led to the Decembrist Revolt?

extreme form of nineteenth-century autocracy. He knew economic growth and social improvement in Russia required reform, but he was afraid of change. To remove serfdom would necessarily, in his view, have undermined the nobles' support of the tsar. So Nicholas turned his back on this and practically all other reforms. Literary and political censorship and a widespread system of surveillance by secret police flourished throughout his reign.

Official Nationality In place of reform, Nicholas and his closest advisers embraced a program called Official Nationality. Its slogan, published repeatedly in government documents, newspapers, journals, and schoolbooks, was "Orthodoxy, Autocracy, and Nationalism." The Russian Orthodox church was to provide the basis for morality, education, and intellectual life. The church, which, since the days of Peter the Great, had been an arm of the secular government, controlled the schools and universities. Autocracy meant the unrestrained power of the tsar as the only authority that could hold the vast expanse of Russia and its peoples together. Through the glorification of Russian nationality, Russians were urged to see their religion, language, and customs as a source of perennial wisdom that separated them from the moral corruption and political turmoil of the West. This program alienated serious Russian intellectuals from the tsarist government.

Revolt and Repression in Poland Nicholas I was also extremely conservative in foreign affairs, as became apparent in Poland in the 1830s. Most of Poland, which had been partitioned in the late eighteenth century and ceased to exist as an independent state, remained under Russian domination after the Congress of Vienna but was granted a constitutional government with a parliament, called the diet, that had limited powers. Under this arrangement, the tsar also reigned as king of Poland. Although both Alexander and Nicholas frequently infringed on the constitution and quarreled with the Polish diet, this arrangement held through the 1820s.

In late November 1830, after news of the French and Belgian revolutions of that summer had reached Poland, a small insurrection of soldiers and students broke out in Warsaw. Disturbances soon spread throughout the country. The tsar sent troops into the country and suppressed the revolt. In February 1832, Nicholas issued the Organic Statute, declaring Poland to be an integral part of the Russian Empire. The Polish uprising had confirmed the tsar's worst fears. Henceforth Russia and Nicholas became the gendarme of Europe, ever ready to provide troops to suppress liberal and nationalist movements.

Revolution in France (1830)

The Polish revolt was the most distant of several disturbances that flowed from the overthrow of the Bourbon dynasty in France during July 1830. When Louis XVIII had died in 1824, his brother, the count of Artois, the leader of the ultraroyalist faction, succeeded him as Charles X (r. 1824–1830).

The Reactionary Policies of Charles X Charles X's first action was to have the Chamber of Deputies in 1824 and 1825 indemnify aristocrats who had lost their lands in the revolution. He did this by lowering the interest rates on government bonds to create a fund to pay an annual sum to the survivors of the *émigrés* who had forfeited land. Middle-class bondholders, who lost income, resented this measure. Charles also restored the rule of primogeniture, whereby only the eldest son of an aristocrat inherited the family domains. To support the Roman Catholic Church, he enacted a law that punished sacrilege with imprisonment or death.

In the elections of 1827, the liberals gained enough seats in the Chamber of Deputies to compel the king to compromise. Liberals, however, wanted a genuinely

constitutional regime and remained unsatisfied. In 1829, the king replaced his moderate ministry with an ultraroyalist cabinet headed by the Prince de Polignac (1780–1847). The opposition, in desperation, opened negotiations with the liberal Orléans branch of the royal family.

This engraving captures one of the confrontations between workers and the king's forces in Paris on July 28, 1830.

Picture Desk, Inc./Kobal Collection

How does this depiction of the revolutionary events of 1830 in France differ from Delacroix's depiction of these same events in *Liberty Leading the People* on page 490?

The July Revolution In 1830, Charles X called for new elections, in which the liberals scored a stunning victory. Instead of accepting the new Chamber of Deputies, the king and his ministers decided to attempt a royalist seizure of power. In June and July 1830, Polignac sent a naval expedition against Algiers. News of the capture of Algiers and the founding of a French Empire in North Africa reached Paris on July 9. Taking advantage of the euphoria this victory created, Charles issued the Four Ordinances on July 25, 1830, staging what amounted to a royal *coup d'état*. These ordinances restricted freedom of the press, dissolved the recently elected Chamber of Deputies, limited the franchise to the wealthiest people in the country, and called for new elections.

The Four Ordinances provoked swift and decisive popular reaction. Liberal newspapers called on the nation to reject the monarch's actions. The workers of Paris, burdened since 1827 by an economic downturn, erected barricades in the streets. The king called out troops, and although more than 1,800 people died during the ensuing battles, the army was not able to gain control of Paris. On August 2, Charles X abdicated and went into exile in England. The Chamber of Deputies named a new ministry composed of constitutional monarchists. In an act that finally ended the rule of the Bourbon dynasty, it also proclaimed Louis Philippe (r. 1830–1848), the duke d'Orléans, the new king.

Had the liberals, who favored a constitutional monarchy, not acted quickly, the workers and shopkeepers of Paris might have attempted to form a republic. By seizing the moment, the middle class, the bureaucrats, and the moderate aristocratic liberals overthrew the restoration monarchy and still avoided a republic. These liberals feared a new popular revolution such as the one that had swept France in 1792. A fundamental political and social tension thus underlay the new monarchy. The revolution had succeeded thanks to a temporary alliance between hard-pressed laborers and the prosperous middle class, but these two groups soon realized that their basic goals were different.

Monarchy under Louis Philippe Politically, the July Monarchy, as the new regime was called, was more liberal than the restoration government. Socially, however, the Revolution of 1830 proved conservative. The hereditary peerage was abolished in 1831, but the everyday economic, political, and social influence of the landed oligarchy continued. Money was the path to power and influence in the government. There was much corruption.

Most importantly, the liberal monarchy displayed little or no sympathy for the lower and working classes. In 1830, the workers of Paris had called for the protection of jobs, better wages, and the preservation of the traditional crafts, rather than for the usual goals of political liberalism. The government of Louis Philippe ignored their demands and their plight. In late 1831, troops suppressed a workers' revolt in Lyons. In July 1832, an uprising occurred in Paris during the funeral of a popular Napoleonic general. Again the government called out troops, and more than eight hundred people were killed or wounded. In 1834, a large strike by silk workers in Lyons was crushed. Such discontent might be smothered for a time, but unless the government addressed the social and economic conditions that created it, new turmoil would eventually erupt.

The new French government of 1830 was only too happy to retain the control of the city of Algiers that Charles X had achieved less than a month before his overthrow. The occupation of Algeria gave French merchants in Marseilles new economic ties to North Africa. By the 1850s, the French had extended their rule, after constant warfare

Beginning in the 1820s Daniel O'Connell revolutionized the organization of Irish politics. He created a grass-roots organization and collected funds to finance Irish nationalist activities. He was also known as one of the great public speakers of his generation.

How did nineteenth-century Irish opposition to English occupation differ from earlier efforts to expel the English?

against Muslim tribesmen, as far as the northern Sahara desert. France now had a vast new empire, and French citizens and other Europeans also began to settle in Algeria in large numbers, especially in the cities. In the second half of the nineteenth century, the French government came to regard Algeria, despite its overwhelmingly Muslim population, as not a colony but an integral part of France itself.

Belgium Becomes Independent (1830)

The July Revolution in Paris sent sparks to other political tinder on the Continent. The revolutionary fires first flared in neighboring Belgium. The former Austrian Netherlands, Belgium had been merged with the kingdom of Holland in 1815. The two countries differed in language, religion, and economy, however, and the Belgian upper classes never reconciled themselves to Dutch rule.

On August 25, 1830, disturbances broke out in Brussels after the performance of an opera about a rebellion in Naples against Spanish rule. To end the rioting, the municipal authorities and people from the propertied classes formed a provisional national government. When compromise between the Belgians and the Dutch failed, King William I of Holland (r. 1815–1840) sent troops and ships against Belgium. By November 10, 1830, the Dutch had been defeated. A national congress then wrote a liberal Belgian constitution, which was issued in 1831.

Although the major powers saw the revolution in Belgium as upsetting the boundaries the Congress of Vienna had established, they were not inclined to intervene to reverse it. Russia, Prussia, and Austria were preoccupied with uprisings of their own and France under Louis Philippe hoped to dominate an independent Belgium. Britain could tolerate a liberal Belgium, as long as it was free of foreign domination.

In December 1830, Lord Palmerston (1784–1865), the British foreign minister, persuaded representatives of the powers in London to recognize Belgium as an independent and neutral state. In July 1831, Prince Leopold of Saxe-Coburg (r. 1831–1865), who had connections to the British royal family and was the husband of the daughter of Louis Philippe, became king of the Belgians.

The Great Reform Bill in Britain (1832)

In Great Britain, the revolutionary year of 1830 saw the election of a House of Commons that debated the first major bill to reform Parliament. The passage of the Great Reform Bill, which became law in 1832, was the result of a series of events different from those that occurred on the Continent. In Britain, the forces of conservatism and reform accommodated each other.

Political and Economic Reform Several factors contributed to this spirit of compromise. First, the commercial and industrial class was larger in Britain than in other countries. No government, could ignore their economic interests without damaging British prosperity. Second, Britain's liberal Whig aristocrats, who regarded themselves as the protectors of constitutional liberty, had a long tradition of favoring moderate reforms that would make revolutionary changes unnecessary. Finally, British law, tradition, and public opinion all showed a strong respect for civil liberties.

Catholic Emancipation Act English determination to maintain the union with Ireland brought about another key reform. In 1800, fearful that Irish nationalists might again rebel as they had in 1798 and perhaps turn Ireland into a base for a French invasion, William Pitt the Younger had persuaded Parliament to pass the Act of Union between Ireland and England. Ireland now sent a hundred members to the House of Commons. Only Protestant Irishmen, however, could be elected to represent their overwhelmingly Roman Catholic nation.

During the 1820s, under the leadership of Daniel O'Connell (1775–1847), Irish nationalists organized the Catholic Association to agitate for Catholic emancipation. In 1828, O'Connell secured his own election to Parliament, where he could not legally take his seat. The duke of Wellington, who was now prime minister, realized that henceforth Ireland might elect an overwhelmingly Catholic delegation. If they were not seated, civil war might erupt across the Irish Sea. Consequently, in 1829, Wellington and Robert Peel steered the Catholic Emancipation Act through Parliament. Roman Catholics could now become members of Parliament. This measure, together with the repeal in 1828 of restrictions against Protestant nonconformists, ended the Anglican monopoly on British political life.

Catholic emancipation was a liberal measure passed for a conservative purpose: the preservation of order in Ireland. It alienated many of Wellington's Anglican Tory supporters and split the Tory Party. When an election in 1830 seated a Parliament disposed to reform, Wellington's ministry fell, and King William IV asked Earl Grey (1764–1845), leader of the Whigs, to form the next government.

Legislating Change The Whig ministry presented the House of Commons with a major reform bill that had two broad goals. The first was to replace "rotten boroughs," or boroughs that had few voters, with representatives for the previously unrepresented manufacturing districts and cities. Second, the number of voters in England and Wales was to be increased by about 50 percent through a series of new franchises. In 1831, the House of Commons narrowly defeated the bill. Grey called for a new election and won a majority in favor of the bill. The House of Commons passed the reform bill, but the House of Lords rejected it. Mass meetings were held throughout the country. Riots broke out in several cities. Finally, William IV agreed to create enough new peers to give a third reform bill a majority in the House of Lords. Under this pressure, the measure became law in 1832.

The Great Reform Bill expanded the size of the English electorate, but it was not a democratic measure. It increased the number of voters by more than 200,000, or almost 50 percent, but it kept a property qualification for the franchise. Some members of the working class actually lost the right to vote because certain old franchise rights were abolished. New urban boroughs were created to allow the growing cities to have a voice in the House of Commons. Yet the passage of the reform act did not, as was once thought, constitute the triumph of middle-class interests in England: For every new urban electoral district, a new rural district was also drawn, and the aristocracy was expected to dominate rural elections. What the bill permitted was a wider variety of property to be represented in the House of Commons.

The success of the reform bill reconciled previously unrepresented property owners and economic interests to the political institutions of the country. The act laid the groundwork for further orderly reforms of the church, municipal government, and commercial policy. By admitting into the political forum people who sought change and giving them access to the legislative process, it made revolution in Britain unnecessary. Great Britain thus maintained its traditional institutions of government while allowing an increasingly diverse group of people to influence them.

SIGNIFICANT DATES FROM THE ERA OF POLITICAL REACTION AND REFORM

1814	Louis XVIII, Bourbon monarchy restored in France
1815	Holy Alliance (Russia, Austria, and Prussia); Quadruple Alliance (Russia, Austria, Prussia, and Britain)
1819	Carlsbad Decrees, Peterloo Massacre; The Six Acts passed in Great Britain
1820	Spanish revolution
1821	Greek revolution
1823	France intervenes to crush the Spanish revolution
1824	Charles X becomes king in France
1825	Decembrist Revolt in Russia
1829	Catholic Emancipation Act passed in Great Britain
1830	Charles X abdicates; Louis Philippe proclaimed king; Belgian revolution; Polish revolt
1832	Great Reform Bill passed in Great Britain

SUMMARY

HOW DID early-nineteenth-century nationalists define the nation?

The Challenges of Nationalism and Liberalism Secular ideologies including nationalism, liberalism, republicanism, socialism, and communism gained currency in nineteenth-century Europe. Nationalists opposed multinational states that were held together only by the legitimacy of their rulers, such as the Austrian and Russian Empires. The widespread existence of minority enclaves presented a practical problem for nineteenth-century nationalists. Nations were often created in the nineteenth century through the work of intellectual elites who used the print culture and schools to standardize a language and narrate a shared history. Nationalism was particularly fervent, and often politically disruptive, in nineteenth-century Ireland, Germany, Italy, Poland, eastern Europe, and the Balkans. Liberalism sought a political framework that institutionalized the "principles of 1789." Liberals were generally well educated and relatively wealthy; they did not trust the working class and did not want full democracy. They believed free trade would facilitate material progress. As a practical matter, nationalism and liberalism were often linked, although in some situations the goals of nationalists and liberals were directly contradictory. *page 492*

WHAT EXPLAINS the strength of conservatism in the early nineteenth century?

Conservative Governments: The Domestic Political Order Conservatism established itself as a coherent political program in Europe in response to nationalism and liberalism. Throughout Europe, the peace after 1815 presented problems. In Austria, Prince Metternich was the Continent's mastermind of conservatism. Austria found nationalism and liberalism particularly threatening. In Great Britain, popular unrest was suppressed. The Bourbon king Louis XVIII ascended the French throne. He was aware of the balancing act that his position required. Louis XVIII's moderation came to an end in 1820, however, when an heir to the throne was assassinated and ultraroyalists persuaded the king to break with liberal politicians. *page 497*

WHAT WERE the goals of the Concert of Europe?

The Conservative International Order The Concert of Europe was a device created at the Congress of Vienna whereby the major powers would meet from time to time to attempt to maintain international peace. It was unprecedented and surprisingly successful. The Spanish revolution of 1820 was consequential for Latin America, and, coupled with revolts in Italy, led Metternich to lobby the other powers for more active intervention in troubled regions. Greece and Serbia successfully revolted against the Ottoman Empire early in the nineteenth century. Independence movements throughout Latin America took various forms but had similar results. *page 500*

WHAT SPARKED the wars of independence in Latin America?

The Wars of Independence in Latin America The Napoleonic era marked the end of Europe's long domination of Latin America. A slave revolt, begun in 1794, won Haiti its independence. The Haitian slave revolt haunted the Creoles, who were growing discontented. Between 1808 and 1810, various Creole *juntas* governed different parts of Latin America, and Spain was never able to restore its authority over the continent. Different parts of Latin American took different paths toward independence. José de San Martín assembled an army and liberated Peru. In the north, Simón Bolívar began the fight that led to a republican Venezuela. Miguel Hidalgo y Costilla and José María Morelos y Pavón, both priests, were involved in early attempts for an independent New Spain but failed. Brazil's independence came relatively simply and peacefully. The prince regent, João, addressed local grievances and in 1815 declared Brazil a kingdom independent of Portugal. Latin America emerged from its wars for independence economically exhausted and politically unstable. *page 503*

HOW DID Russia, France, and Britain respond to challenges to the conservative order?

The Conservative Order Shaken in Europe Starting in the mid-1920s, political discontent led to suppression in Russia, revolution in France, independence in Belgium, and accommodation in Britain. The death of Tsar Alexander I in 1825 sparked a succession crisis, which led to the Decembrist Revolt of reform-minded army officers. Nicholas I feared reform at home and revolt abroad, so he ruled autocratically. In France, the Bourbon dynasty was overthrown in July 1830, after Charles X had attempted to concentrate political power in the monarchy. Louis Philippe's July Monarchy was politically liberal and socially conservative. Belgium revolted against the Dutch in 1830 and became a constitutional monarchy. In Britain, the Great Reform Bill widened the franchise and gave a broader section of Britain's population a stake in the existing political system. *page 507*

Review Questions

1. What is nationalism? What parts of Europe saw significant nationalist movements between 1815 and 1830? Which of these movements succeeded and which failed?
2. Which institutions and groups supported the conservative governments in Europe? What were the main threats to these governments?
3. What were the tenets of liberalism? What effects did liberalism have on political developments during the early nineteenth century? What relationship does liberalism have to nationalism?
4. What political changes took place in Latin America between 1804 and 1824? What were the main reasons for Creole discontent with Spanish rule? To what extent were Creole leaders influenced by Enlightenment political philosophy? Who were the major leaders in the fight for Latin American independence? Why did they succeed?
5. What kind of constitution was decreed for the restored monarchy in France? What were the causes of the Revolution of 1830? How do you explain the fact that although prior to 1820 Britain was moving down the same reactionary road as the other major European powers, events arrived at a different outcome in Britain?

KEY TERMS

conservatism (p. 497)
Creole (p. 503)
nationalism (p. 492)

For additional learning resources related to this chapter, please go to **www.myhistorylab.com**

myhistorylab

21

Economic Advance and Social Unrest (1830–1850)

In 1848 Ana Ipatescu helped to lead Transylvanian revolutionaries against Russian rule. Transylvania is part of present-day Romania. The revolutions of 1848 in eastern Europe were primarily uprisings of nationalist groups. Although generally repressed in the revolutions of that year, subject nationalities would prove a source of political upheaval and unrest in the region throughout the rest of the century, ultimately providing the spark for the outbreak of World War I.

The Art Archive/Picture Desk, Inc./Kobal Collection

Why was nationalism a particular problem in Eastern Europe?

TOWARD AN INDUSTRIAL SOCIETY *page 516*

HOW DID industrialization spread across Europe?

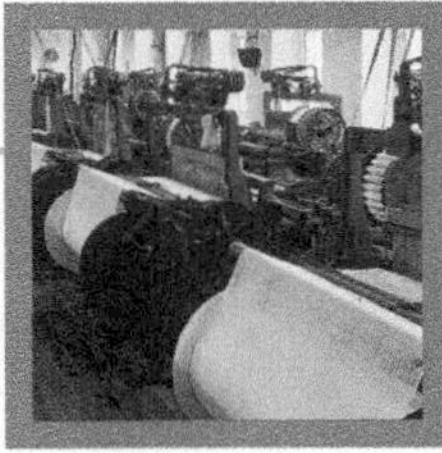

THE LABOR FORCE *page 519*

HOW DID industrialization change the European labor force?

FAMILY STRUCTURES AND THE INDUSTRIAL REVOLUTION *page 522*

HOW DID industrialization affect European families?

WOMEN IN THE EARLY INDUSTRIAL REVOLUTION *page 523*

WHAT ROLE did women play in the Industrial Revolution?

PROBLEMS OF CRIME AND ORDER *page 525*

HOW DID the establishment of police forces and the reform of prisons change society?

CLASSICAL ECONOMICS *page 526*

WHAT WERE the key assumptions of classical economic theory?

EARLY SOCIALISM *page 527*

HOW DID socialism challenge classical economics?

1848: YEAR OF REVOLUTIONS *page 531*

WHY DID a series of revolutions erupt across Europe in 1848?

By 1830, Great Britain had become an industrialized nation, and the rest of Europe was also soon to resound with the pounding of machinery and the grinding of railway engines. Between 1825 and 1850, while the groups that opposed industrialism made their final protests, intellectuals articulated major creeds that both supported and criticized the emerging society. These were years of uncertainty, a period of self-conscious transition leading to an unknown future. They culminated in 1848 with a continent-wide outbreak of revolution. ■

TOWARD AN INDUSTRIAL SOCIETY

HOW DID industrialization spread across Europe?

The Industrial Revolution had begun in eighteenth-century Great Britain with the advances in textile production described in Chapter 15. Natural resources, adequate capital, native technological skills, a growing food supply, a social structure that allowed considerable mobility, and strong foreign and domestic demand for goods had given Britain an edge in achieving a vast new capacity for production in manufacturing. Also, the French Revolution and the wars of Napoleon had finally destroyed the French Atlantic trade and thus disrupted continental economic life for two decades. The Latin American wars of independence opened the markets of South America to British goods. In North America, both the United States and Canada demanded British products. Through its control of India, Britain commanded the markets of southern Asia. British banks similarly dominated the international financial markets.

The wealth that Britain gained through textile production and its other industries of iron making, shipbuilding, china production, and the manufacture of other finished goods was invested all over the world, but especially in the United States and Latin America. This enormous activity provided the economic foundation for British dominance of the world scene throughout the nineteenth century.

Despite their economic lag, the continental nations were beginning to make material progress. By the 1830s, Belgium, France, and Germany had begun to imitate Britain. Industrial areas on the Continent were generally less concentrated than in Britain, nor did the Continent have large manufacturing districts, such as the British Midlands. Major pockets of production did exist in Western Europe, but most continental manufacturing still took place in the countryside. The slow pace of continental imitation of the British example meant that, at midcentury, peasants and urban artisans remained more important politically than industrial factory workers.

QUICK REVIEW

Britain's Advantages

- Natural resources, investment capital, technology, and an adequate food supply
- Relatively mobile society
- Strong foreign and domestic markets

POPULATION AND MIGRATION

While the process of industrialization spread, the population of Europe continued to grow on the base of the eighteenth-century population explosion. The number of people in France rose from 32.5 million in 1831 to 35.8 million in 1851. During approximately the same period, the population of Germany rose from 26.5 million to 33.5 million and that of Britain from 16.3 million to 20.8 million. More and more of the people of Europe lived in cities. By midcentury, one-half of the population of England and Wales and one-quarter of the population of France and Germany had become town dwellers. Eastern Europe, by contrast, remained overwhelmingly rural, with little industrial manufacturing.

The sheer numbers of human beings put considerable pressure on the physical resources of the cities. Existing housing, water, sewers, food supplies, and lighting were completely inadequate. Slums with indescribable filth grew, and disease, especially cholera, ravaged the population. Crime increased and became a way of life for those who could make a living in no other manner.

London's Crystal Palace during the International Exhibition of 1851.

Victoria & Albert Museum, London, Great Britain/Art Resource, NY

Who visited the International Exhibition? What was the exhibition meant to say about the future of British society?

The situation in the countryside was scarcely better. The enclosures of the late eighteenth century, the land redistribution of the French Revolution, and the emancipation of serfs in Prussia and later in Austria (1848) and Russia (1861) commercialized landholding. Liberal reformers had hoped the legal revolution in ownership would transform peasants into progressive, industrious farmers. Instead, most peasants became conservative landholders without enough land to make agricultural innovations or, oftentimes, even to support themselves. It is important to note the differing dates of rural emancipation across Europe. From Germany eastward, the pace of industrialization was much slower, in part because of the absence of a fluid market for free labor moving to the cities.

The specter of poor harvests still haunted Europe. The worst such experience of the century was the Irish famine of 1845 to 1848. (See "Encountering the Past: The Potato and the Great Hunger in Ireland.") By midcentury, the revolution in landholding led to greater agricultural production. It also resulted in a vast uprooting of people from the countryside into cities and from Europe into the rest of the world.

George Stephenson (1781–1848) invented the locomotive in 1814, but the "Rocket," his improved design shown here, did not win out over other competitors until 1829. In the following two decades the spread of railways transformed the economy of western Europe.

How did railways tie British communities together?

ENCOUNTERING THE PAST

THE POTATO AND THE GREAT HUNGER IN IRELAND

The potato was introduced to Europe from South America in the seventeenth century. It grew better than grain in parts of Europe that had cool, wet climates, and in these places it became the staple crop. On less than an acre of land, an Irish peasant could raise enough potatoes to feed eleven people for a year—and pay his rent (few owned their land). Reliance on a single food source is risky, however, for if that source fails, starvation threatens.

In 1845, a mysterious fungus blighted potato fields across Ireland, and half the crop was lost. In 1846, it reappeared and destroyed the entire harvest. The situation improved in 1847, but the blight struck again with devastating effects in 1848. The failure of the Irish potato crop was the worst natural disaster to strike Europe in the nineteenth century, and it created social catastrophe. Landlords drove peasants who could not pay their rent from the land, and the British government, which ruled Ireland, provided little aid.

Tens of thousands died, and many other thousands sought to escape "The Great Hunger" by emigrating to the United States and Britain. As a result, the population of Ireland began to fall. It stood at 8,197,000 in 1841. By 1901, it had declined to 4,459,000, and today Ireland is the only European country to have fewer inhabitants than it had in the nineteenth century.

Painter George Frederick Watts's 1850 depiction of a scene set during the Irish Potato Famine. So many people starved during the famine that workhouses could not shelter them all.

What did Watts want to convey about the victims of the famine with this painting?

WHY WAS the failure of a single crop such a disaster for Ireland? What long-range effect did it have on Ireland?

MAP EXPLORATION

Interactive map: To explore this map further, go to www.myhistorylab.com

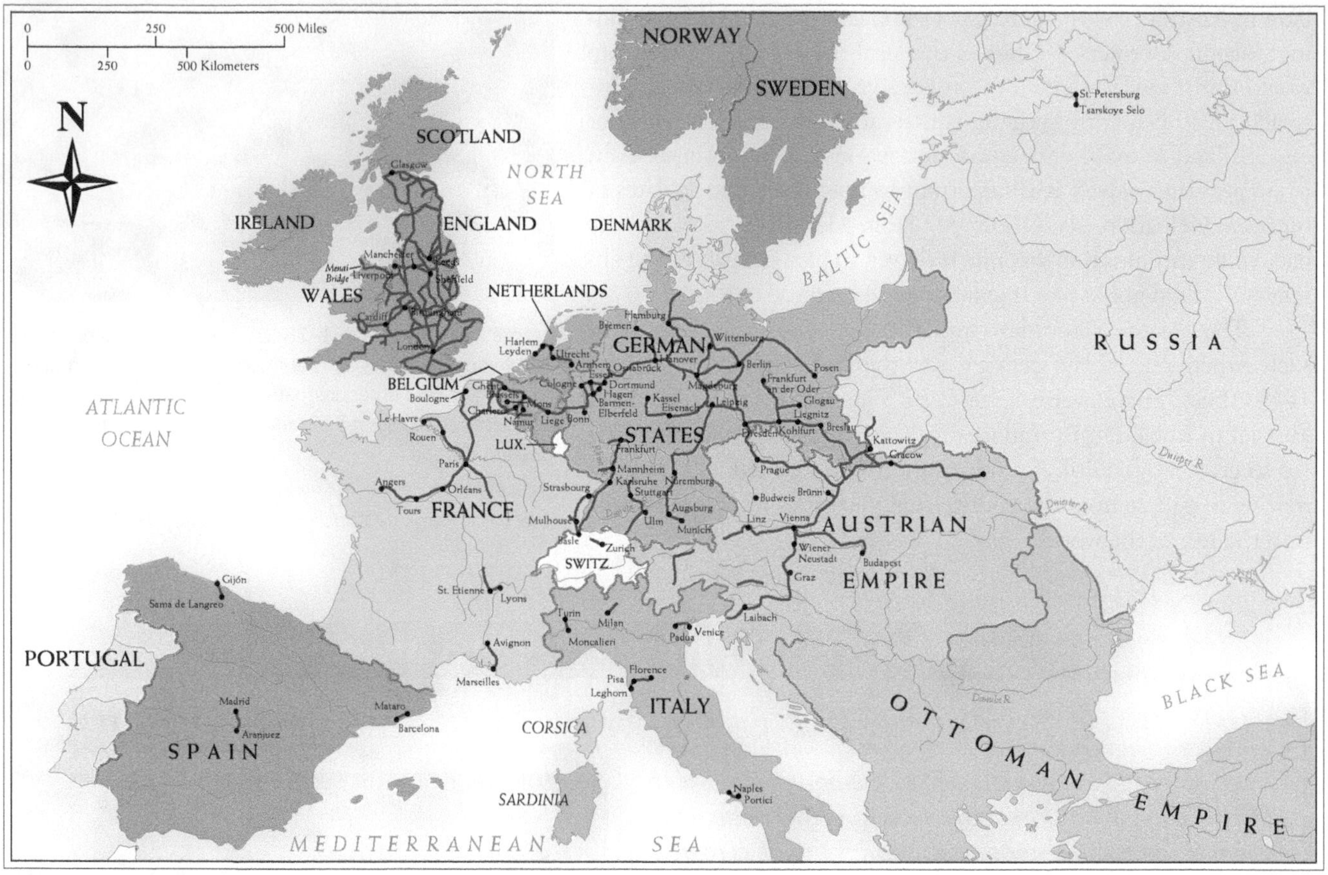

MAP 21–1 **European Railroads in 1850** At midcentury Britain had the most extensive rail network and the most industrialized economy in Europe, but rail lines were expanding rapidly in France, the German states, and Austria. Southern and eastern Europe had few railways and the Ottoman Empire had none.

What effect did railroads have on the European workforce?

Railways

Industrial advance itself had also contributed to this migration. The 1830s and 1840s opened the first great age of railway building. At midcentury, Britain had 9,797 kilometers of railway, France 2,915, and Germany 5,856. (See Map 21–1, page 518.) The railroads, plus canals and improved regular roads, meant people could leave the place of their birth more easily than ever before.

Railways epitomized the character of the industrial economy during the second quarter of the century. They represented investment in capital goods rather than in consumer goods. Consequently, there was a shortage of consumer goods at cheap prices. The railways in and of themselves also brought about still more industrialization. Embodying the most dramatic application of the steam engine, they sharply increased demand for iron and steel and then for a more skilled labor force. The new iron and steel capacity soon permitted the construction of ironclad ships and iron machinery rather than ships and machinery made of wood. These new capital industries led to the formation of vast industrial fortunes that would be invested in still newer enterprises. Industrialism had begun to grow on itself.

THE LABOR FORCE

HOW DID industrialization change the European labor force?

The composition and experience of the early-nineteenth-century labor force was varied. Some of the workforce was reasonably well off and enjoyed steady employment and decent wages. Other workers were the "laboring poor," who held jobs but earned little more than subsistence wages. Furthermore, the conditions of workers varied from decade to decade and from industry to industry within any particular decade.

Only the textile-manufacturing industry became thoroughly mechanized and moved into the factory setting during the first half of the century. Far more of the nonrural, nonagricultural workforce consisted of skilled artisans living in cities or small towns. They were attempting to maintain the value of their skills and control over their trades in the face of changing features of production.

THE EMERGENCE OF A WAGE-LABOR FORCE

During the nineteenth century, artisans as well as factory workers eventually came to participate in a wage-labor force in which their labor became a commodity of the labor marketplace. This process has often been termed *proletarianization*. In the process of becoming wage laborers, artisans gradually lost both significant ownership of the means of production, such as tools and equipment, and of control over the conduct of their own trades. The process occurred most rapidly wherever the factory system arose displacing previous skilled labor.

Factory workers also had to submit to various kinds of factory discipline that were virtually always unpopular and difficult to impose. Closing of factory gates to late workers, fines for such lateness, dismissal for drunkenness, and public scolding of faulty laborers were attempts to create human discipline that would match the mechanical regularity of the cables, wheels, and pistons. (See "Compare & Connect: Andrew Ure and John Ruskin Debate the Conditions of Factory Production," pages 520–521.)

Urban artisans in the nineteenth century entered the wage-labor force more slowly than factory workers, and machinery had little to do with the process. The emergence of factories in and of itself did not harm urban artisans. Where the urban artisans encountered difficulty and where they found their skills and livelihood threatened was in the organization of production.

In the eighteenth century, a European town or city workplace had usually consisted of a few artisans laboring for a master. They labored first as apprentices, then as journeymen, and eventually as masters in their own right, according to established guild regulations and practices. This guild system had allowed workers to exercise a considerable degree of control over labor recruitment and training, the pace of production, the quality of the product, and its price. In the nineteenth century, it became increasingly difficult for artisans to exercise corporate or guild direction and control over their trades. The legislation of the French Revolution had outlawed such organizations in France. Across Europe, political and economic liberals disapproved of labor and guild organizations and attempted to ban them.

Other destructive forces were also at work. The masters often found themselves under increased competitive pressure from larger, more heavily capitalized establishments or from the introduction of machine production into a previously craft-dominated industry. In many workshops masters began to follow a practice, known in France as *confection*, whereby goods, such as shoes, clothing, and furniture, were produced in standard sizes and styles rather than by special orders for individual customers.

This practice increased the division of labor in the workshop. Each artisan produced a smaller part of the more-or-less uniform final product. Thus, less skill was required of each artisan, and the particular skills a worker possessed became less valuable. To increase production and reduce costs, masters also tried to lower the wages

COMPARE & CONNECT

ANDREW URE AND JOHN RUSKIN DEBATE THE CONDITIONS OF FACTORY PRODUCTION

The factory was itself as much an invention of the Industrial Revolution as were the new machines the factory often housed. The factory required a new organization of labor. It also made possible the production of vast new quantities of manufactured goods. From its inception the factory system provoked both praise and criticism. Andrew Ure saw much positive good arising from factory production whereas John Ruskin became a vehement critic.

QUESTIONS

1. Why does Ure emphasize the willingness of workers to be employed in factories?
2. How does Ure portray the factory system as creating the possibility of new abundance?
3. How does Ruskin see the use of machinery reducing workers to a machine?
4. Is Ruskin's criticism of the division of labor a correct analysis or simply a well-crafted metaphorical criticism?
5. How might Andrew Ure have replied to Ruskin?

I. ANDREW URE PRAISES THE FACTORY SYSTEM

Andrew Ure (1778–1857) was a Scottisch physician and a great proponent of the benefits of the factory system. In 1835 he published The Philosophy of Manufactures, *which went through many editions from then until late in the century. He saw factories as not only increasing productivity but also providing a healthier environment than agricultural work or mining.*

Power looms used in the mass production of textiles during the Industrial Revolution.

Dorling Kindersley Medial Library/David Lyons © Dorling Kindersley. Courtesy of the Boott Cotton Mills Museum, Lowell, Massachusetts

How did the advent of factories change the relationship between work and home?

The term Factory, in technology, designates the combined operation of many orders of work—people, adult and young, in tending with assiduous skill a system of productive machines continuously impelled by a central power. This definition includes such organizations as cotton-mills, flax-mills, silk-mills, woolen-mills, and certain engineering works. . . . I conceive that this title, in its strictest sense, involves the idea of a vast automaton, composed of various mechanical and intellectual organs, acting in uninterrupted concert for the production of a common object, all of them being subordinated to a self-regulated moving force. . . .

In its precise acceptation, the Factory system is of recent origin, and may claim England for its birthplace. . . .

When the first water-frames for spinning cotton were erected at Cromford, in the romantic valley of the Derwent, about sixty years ago, mankind were little aware of the mighty revolution which the new system of labor was destined by Providence to achieve, not only in the structure of British society, but in the fortunes of the world at large.

Arkwright alone had the sagacity to discern, and the boldness to predict in glowing language, how vastly productive human industry would become, when no longer proportioned in its results to muscular effort, which is by its nature fitful and capricious, but when made to consist in the task of guiding the work of mechanical fingers and arms, regularly impelled with great velocity by some indefatigable physical power. . . .

In my recent tour, continued during several months, through the manufacturing districts, I have seen tens of thousands of old, young, and middle-aged of both sexes, many of them too feeble to get their daily bread by any of the former modes of industry, earning abundant food, raiment, and domestic accommodation, without perspiring at a single pore, screened meanwhile from the summer's sun and the winter's frost, in apartments more airy and salubrious than those of the metropolis, in which our legislative and fashionable aristocracies assemble. In those spacious halls the benignant power of steam summons around him his myriads of willing menials, and assigns to each the regulated task, substituting for painful muscular effort on their part, the energies of his own gigantic arm, and demanding in return only attention and dexterity to correct such little aberrations as casually occur in his workmanship. . . . Such is the factory system, replete with prodigies in mechanics and political economy, which promises, in its future growth, to become the great minister of civilization to the terraqueous globe, enabling this country, as its heart, to diffuse along with its commerce, the life-blood of science and religion to myriads of people still lying "in the region and shadow of death."

Source: Andrew Ure, *The Philosophy of Manufactures; or, An Exposition of the Scientific, Moral, and Commercial Economy of the Factory System* (London: Chas Knight, 1835), pp. 13 ff., as quoted in *Metternich's Europe*, ed. by Mack Walker (New York: Walker and Company, 1968), pp. 275–276, 278–279.

II. JOHN RUSKIN DECRIES THE IMPACT OF INDUSTRIAL PRODUCTION ON WORKERS

The Englishman John Ruskin (1819–1900) was the foremost mid-nineteenth-century critic of art and architecture. He commenced his career interested primarily in painting and then moved to architecture. In the course of that transition he became increasingly sensitive to the working conditions of the craftsmen who constructed the buildings he studied. Over time he became a major social critic of the new industrial order. His earliest statement of social criticism occurred in a chapter entitled "The Nature of Gothic" in his book of 1851 entitled The Stones of Venice. *Here Ruskin passionately attacked the mechanical routine of work associated with industrial machinery. He also attacked the concept of increasing work through the division of labor, which had been conceptualized by Adam Smith in* The Wealth of Nations *(1776). Smith had illustrated the division of labor by describing a pin factory. Ruskin here responds to Smith's analysis.*

You must either make a tool of the creature, or a man of him. You cannot make both. Men were not intended to work with the accuracy of tools, to be precise and perfect in all their actions. If you will have that precision out of them, and make their fingers measure degrees like cog-wheels, and their arms strike curves like compasses, you must unhumanize them. All the energy of their spirits must be given to make cogs and compasses of themselves. All their attention and strength must go to the accomplishment of the mean act . . . On the other hand, if you will make a man of the working creature, you cannot make a tool. Let him but begin to imagine, to think to try to do anything worth doing; and the engine-turned precision is lost at once. Out come all his roughness, all his dulness, all his incapability; shame upon shame, failure upon failure, pause after pause: but out comes the whole majesty of him also; . . .

It is verily this degradation of the operative into a machine, which, more than any other evil of the times, is leading the mass of the nations everywhere into vain, incoherent, destructive struggling for a freedom of which they cannot explain the nature to themselves. . . . It is not that men are ill read, but that they have no pleasure in the work by which they make their bread, and therefore look to wealth as the only means of pleasure. . . .

It is not, truly speaking, the labour that is divided; but the men:—Divided into mere segments of men—broken into small fragments and crumbs of life; so that all the little piece of intelligence that is left in a man is not enough to make a pin, or a nail, but exhausts itself in making the point of a pin or the head of a nail . . . . And all the evil to which that cry is urging our myriads can be met only in one way: not by teaching nor preaching, for to teach them is but to show them their misery, and to preach to them, if we do nothing more than preach, is to mock at it. It can be met only by a right understanding, on the part of all classes, of what kinds of labour are good for men, raising them, and making them happy; by a determined sacrifice of such convenience, or beauty, or cheapness as is to be got only by the degradation of the workman; and by equally determined demand for the products and results of healthy and ennobling labour.

Source: J. Ruskin, *Stones of Venice* (New York: Lovell, Coryell, and Co., n.d.), 2, pp. 162, 164, 165–166.

QUICK REVIEW
Factory Work

- Proletarianization: workers' loss of ownership of the means of production
- Factory work demanded submission to new kind of work discipline
- Artisans faced increasing pressure to become lifetime wage laborers

they paid for piecework. Those attempts often led to work stoppages or strikes. Migrants from the countryside or small towns into the cities created, in some cases, a surplus of relatively unskilled workers. They were willing to work for lower wages or under less favorable and protected conditions than traditional artisans. This situation made it much more difficult for urban journeymen ever to hope to become masters in charge of their own workshops. Increasingly, these artisans became lifetime wage laborers whose skills were simply bought and sold in the marketplace.

Working-Class Political Action: The Example of British Chartism

By midcentury, such artisans, proud of their skills and frustrated in their social and economic expectations, became the most radical political element in the European working class. From at least the 1830s onward, these artisans took the lead in one country after another in attempting to formulate new ways to protect their social and economic interests.

Chartism Political movement associated with the London Working Men's Association's 1838 proposal for political reform.

By the late 1830s, many British workers linked the solution of their economic plight to a program of political reform known as **Chartism**. In 1836, William Lovett (1800–1877) and other London radical artisans formed the London Working Men's Association. In 1838, the group issued the Charter, demanding six specific reforms. The Six Points of the Charter included universal male suffrage, annual election of the House of Commons, the secret ballot, equal electoral districts, and the abolition of property qualifications for and the payment of salaries to members of the House of Commons.

For more than a decade, the Chartists fought for the adoption of their program. On three occasions the Charter was presented to Parliament. Petitions with millions of signatures were sent to the House of Commons. Strikes were called, and a newspaper, *The Northern Star*, was published—all to no avail.

The Chartists had more success dealing with local governments, but Chartism failed to cohere as a national movement. It split between those who favored violence and those who wanted to use peaceful tactics to enact reform. Rising prosperity in the wake of a depression in the late 1830s and early 1840s also led many working people to lose interest in the issues Chartism advocated. Nevertheless, as the first large-scale political movement organized by the working class, Chartism provided an inspiration and organizational model for workers throughout Europe who wanted to improve their situation.

FAMILY STRUCTURES AND THE INDUSTRIAL REVOLUTION

HOW DID industrialization affect European families?

It is more difficult to generalize about the European working-class family structure in the age of early industrialism than under the Old Regime. Industrialism developed at different rates across the Continent, and the impact of industrialism cannot be separated from that of migration and urbanization. More is known about the relationships of the new industry to the family in Great Britain than elsewhere, and many British developments foreshadowed those in other countries.

The Family in the Early Factory System

Before the late-eighteenth-century revolution in textile production in England, the individual family involved in textiles was the chief unit of production. The mechanization of weaving led to a major change. The father who became a machine weaver was then employed in a factory. His work was thus separated from his home. Nonetheless, the structure of early English factories allowed the father to preserve certain of his traditional family roles as they had existed before the factory system.

In the domestic system of the family economy, the father and mother had worked with their children in textile production as a family unit. Early factory owners and supervisors permitted the father to employ his wife and children as his assistants. Thus, parental training and discipline could be transferred from the home into the early factory. Despite those accommodations to family life, family members still had to face the new work discipline of the factory setting. Moreover, women assisting their husbands in the factory often did less skilled work than they had in their homes.

A major shift in this family and factory structure began in the mid-1820s in England and had been more or less completed by the mid-1830s. As spinning and weaving were put under one roof, the size of factories and of the machinery grew. These newer machines required fewer skilled operators, but many relatively unskilled attendants. This became the work of unmarried women and children, who would accept lower wages and were less likely than adult men to try to form worker organizations or unions.

Factory wages for the more skilled adult males, however, became sufficiently high to allow some fathers to remove their children from the factory and send them to school. The wives of the skilled operatives also usually no longer worked in the factories. So the original links of the family in the British textile factory that had existed for well over a quarter century largely disappeared.

Concern for Child Labor At this point in the 1830s, workers became concerned about the plight of child laborers because parents were no longer exercising discipline over their own children in the factories. The English Factory Act of 1833 forbade the employment of children under age nine, limited the workday of children aged nine to thirteen to nine hours a day, and required the factory owner to pay for two hours of education a day for these children. The effect was further to divide work and home life.

By the mid-1840s, in the lives of industrial workers, the roles of men as breadwinners and as fathers and husbands had become distinct in the British textile industry. Furthermore, reformers' concerns about the working conditions of women in factories and in mines arose in part from the relatively new view that the place of women was in the home rather than in an industrial or even agrarian workplace.

Changing Economic Role for the Family By the middle of the 1840s, men of the working class in the British textile industry had evolved distinct roles as breadwinners, fathers, and husbands. What took place in Britain was paralleled elsewhere as industrial capitalism and public education spread. The European family ceased to be a unit of production and consumption and became only a consumer. The family did not stop performing as an economic unit, but its members shared wages from different sources rather than work in a home or factory. Sharing wages rather than labor affected the strength of family bonds. Children could find work far from home, for wages could be sent over long distances.

WOMEN IN THE EARLY INDUSTRIAL REVOLUTION

WHAT ROLE did women play in the Industrial Revolution?

The industrial economy eventually took most productive work out of the home and allowed many families to live on the wages of the male spouse. That transformation prepared the way for a new concept of gender-determined roles in the home and in domestic life generally. Women came to be associated with domestic duties or with poorly paid, largely unskilled cottage industries. Men came to be associated almost exclusively with supporting the family. Children were raised to conform to these expected gender patterns.

As textile production became increasingly automated in the nineteenth century, textile factories required fewer skilled workers and more unskilled attendants. To fill these unskilled positions, factory owners turned increasingly to unmarried women and widows who worked for lower wages than men and were less likely to form labor organizations.

Courtesy of the Library of Congress

How would you explain the fact that all of the workers depicted in this image of factory life are young and female?

Opportunities and Exploitation in Employment

Because the early Industrial Revolution had begun in textile production, women and their labor were deeply involved from the start. Women usually worked in all stages of textile production and hand spinning was virtually always a woman's task. At first, when spinning was moved into factories and involved large machines, men often displaced women.

Women in Factories With the next generation of machines in the 1820s, however, unmarried women rapidly became employed in the factories, where they often constituted the majority of workers. Their new jobs, however, often demanded fewer skills than those they had previously exercised in the home production of textiles. There was thus a certain paradox in the impact of the factory on women: It opened many new jobs to them but lowered the level of skills they needed to have.

Moreover, almost always, the women in the factories were young, single women or widows. Upon marriage or perhaps after the birth of the first child, young women usually found their husbands earned enough money for them to leave the factory. Widows might return to factory work because they lacked their husbands' former income.

Work on the Land and in the Home In Britain and elsewhere by midcentury, industrial factory work still accounted for less than half of all employment for women. The largest group of employed women in France continued to work on the land. In England, they were domestic servants. Throughout Western Europe, domestic cottage industries, such as lace making, glove making, garment making, and other kinds of needlework, employed many women. It cannot be overemphasized that all work by women commanded low wages and involved low skills. They had virtually no effective modes to protect themselves from exploitation.

The low wages of female workers in all areas of employment sometimes led them to become prostitutes to supplement their wage income. Such sexual exploitation of women was hardly new to European society, but the particular pressures of the transformation of the economy from one of skilled artisans to that of unskilled factory workers made many women especially vulnerable.

Changing Expectations in the Working-Class Marriage

Moving to cities and entering the wage economy gave women wider opportunities for marriage. Cohabitation before marriage was not uncommon. Parents had less to do with arranging marriages than in the past. Marriage now usually meant a woman would leave the workforce to live on her husband's earnings. Despite these changes, many of the traditional practices associated with the family economy survived into the industrial era. As a young woman came of age, both family needs and her desire to marry still directed what she would do with her life. As in the past, as a young woman she would try to earn enough in wages to give herself a dowry, so she might marry and set up her own household.

Marriage in the wage industrial economy was different in certain respects from marriage in earlier times. Marriage was less an economic partnership. The husband's

wages might well be able to support the entire family. The wage economy and the industrialization separating workplace from home made it difficult for women to combine domestic duties with work. More often than not, the children rather than the wife were sent to work. This may help explain the increase in the number of births within marriages, as children in the wage economy usually were an economic asset. Married women worked outside the home only when family needs, illness, or widowhood forced them to.

In the home, working-class women were by no means idle. Wives were concerned primarily with food and cooking, but they were also often in charge of the family's finances. The role of the mother expanded when the children still living at home became wage earners. She was now providing home support for her entire wage-earning family. The longer period of home life of working children may also have increased and strengthened familial bonds of affection between those children and their hardworking homebound mothers. In all these respects, the culture of the working-class marriage and family tended to imitate the family patterns of the middle and upper classes, whose members had often accepted the view of separate gender spheres set forth by Rousseau and popularized in hundreds of novels, journals, and newspapers.

QUICK REVIEW

Modern Police

- First appeared in early nineteenth century
- Their creation reflected elite fears and anxieties about disorder
- Came to be seen by most Europeans as a positive force

PROBLEMS OF CRIME AND ORDER

HOW DID the establishment of police forces and the reform of prisons change society?

Throughout the nineteenth century, the political and economic elite in Europe were profoundly concerned about social order. The revolutions of the late eighteenth and early nineteenth centuries made them fearful of future disorder and threats to life and property, at the same time as industrialization and urbanization upset traditional social patterns. Throughout the first sixty years of the nineteenth century, crime appears to have increased slowly but steadily before more or less reaching a plateau.

New Police Forces

From the propertied, elite classes, two major views about containing crime and criminals emerged during the nineteenth century: better systems of police and prison reform. The result of these efforts was the triumph in Europe of the idea of a policed society in which a paid, professionally trained group of law-enforcement officers keeps order, protects property and lives, investigates crime, and apprehends offenders. Professional police forces did not really exist until the early nineteenth century. They differed from one country to another in both authority and organization, but their creation proved crucial to the emergence of an orderly European society.

Professional police forces appeared in Paris in 1828. The next year, the British Parliament passed legislation sponsored by Sir Robert Peel (1788–1850) that placed police on London streets. Berlin deployed similar police departments after the Revolution of 1848. Although citizens sometimes viewed police with suspicion, by the end of the century, most Europeans regarded the police as their protectors.

London Policeman Professional police forces did not exist before the early nineteenth century. The London police force was created in 1828.

Peter Newark's Pictures

What urban problems were police forces created to address?

Prison Reform

Before the nineteenth century, European prisons were local jails or state prisons, such as the Bastille. In prisons, inmates lived under wretched conditions. Men, women, and children were housed together. Persons guilty of minor offenses were left in the same room with those guilty of the most serious offenses.

Beginning in the late eighteenth century, the British government sentenced persons convicted of the most serious offenses to transportation. Transportation to the colony of New South Wales in Australia was regarded as an alternative to capital punishment, and the British used it until the mid–nineteenth century, when the colonies began to object. Thereafter, the British government housed long-term prisoners in public works prisons in Britain.

Overview Major Works of Economic and Political Commentary

YEAR	WORK	AUTHOR
1776	*The Wealth of Nations*	Adam Smith
1798	*Essay on the Principle of Population*	Thomas Malthus
1817	*Principles of Political Economy*	David Ricardo
1839	*The Organization of Labor*	Louis Blanc
1845	*The Condition of the Working Class in England*	Friedrich Engels
1848	*The Communist Manifesto*	Karl Marx and Friedrich Engels

By the close of the eighteenth century and in the early nineteenth century, reformers, such as John Howard (1726–1790) and Elizabeth Fry (1780–1845) in England and Charles Lucas (1803–1889) in France, exposed the horrendous conditions in prisons and demanded change. Reform came slowly because of the expense of constructing new prisons and a lack of sympathy for criminals. In the 1840s, however, both the French and the English undertook several bold efforts at prison reform. These efforts would appear to indicate a shift in opinion whereby crime was seen not as an assault on order or on authority but as a mark of a character fault in the criminal. Thereafter, part of the goal of imprisonment was to rehabilitate or transform the prisoner.

Europeans used various prison models originally established in the United States. All these experiments depended on separating prisoners from each other. The chief characteristics of these systems were an individual cell for each prisoner and long periods of separation and silence among prisoners. The point of the system was to induce self-reflection in which the prisoners would think about their crimes and eventually decide to repudiate their criminal tendencies. As time passed, the system became more relaxed because the intense isolation often led to mental collapse.

These attempts to create a police force and to reform prisons illustrate the concern about order and stability by European political and social elites that developed after the French Revolution. On the whole, their efforts succeeded. By the end of the century, an orderly society had been established, and the new police and prisons had no small role in that development.

CLASSICAL ECONOMICS

WHAT WERE the key assumptions of classical economic theory?

Economists whose thought derived largely from Adam Smith's *The Wealth of Nations* (1776) dominated private and public discussions of industrial and commercial policy. Their ideas are often associated with the phrase *laissez-faire* (a French phrase that means roughly "let people do as they please"). Although they thought the government should perform many important functions, they believed the mechanism of the marketplace should govern most economic decisions.

Malthus on Population

The classical economists had complicated and pessimistic ideas about the working class. Thomas Malthus (1766–1834) and David Ricardo (1772–1823), probably the most influential of all these writers, suggested, in effect, that nothing could improve the condition of the working class. Malthus contended that population must eventually outstrip the food supply. Although the human population grows geometrically, the food supply can expand only arithmetically. There was little hope of averting the disaster, in Malthus's opinion, except through late marriage, chastity, and contraception, the last of which he considered a vice.

Ricardo on Wages

In his *Principles of Political Economy* (1817), David Ricardo transformed the concepts of Malthus into the "iron law of wages." If wages were raised, parents would have more children. They, in turn, would enter the labor market, thus expanding the number of workers and lowering wages. As wages fell, working people would produce fewer children. Wages would then rise, and the process would start all over again. Consequently, in the long run, wages would always tend toward a minimum level. These arguments simply supported employers in their natural reluctance to raise wages and also provided strong theoretical support for opposing labor unions.

Thomas Malthus.

Courtesy of the Library of Congress

Government Policies Based on Classical Economics

The working classes of France and Great Britain, needless to say, resented the attitudes of the economists, but the governments embraced them. Louis Philippe (1773–1850) and his minister François Guizot (1787–1874) told the French to go forth and enrich themselves. The July Monarchy (1830–1848) saw the construction of major capital-intensive projects, such as roads, canals, and railways. Little, however, was done about the poverty in the cities and the countryside.

After the Napoleonic wars, Prussian reformers had seen the desirability of abolishing internal tariffs that impeded economic growth. In 1834, all the major German states, except Austria, formed the *Zollverein*, or free trading union. Classical economics had less influence in Germany because of the tradition dating from the enlightened absolutism of state direction of economic development.

Britain was the home of the major classical economists, and their policies were widely accepted. The utilitarian thought of Jeremy Bentham (1748–1832) increased their influence. Although **utilitarianism** did not originate with him, Bentham sought to create codes of scientific law that were founded on the principle of utility, that is, the greatest happiness for the greatest number. The application of reason and utility would remove the legal clutter that prevented justice from being realized. He believed the principle of utility could be applied to other areas of government administration.

utilitarianism Maintained that people should always pursue the course that promotes the greatest happiness for the greatest number.

Bentham gathered round him political disciples who combined his ideas with those of classical economics. In 1834, the reformed House of Commons passed a new Poor Law that followers of Bentham had prepared. This measure established a Poor Law Commission that set out to make poverty the most undesirable of all social situations. Government poor relief was to be disbursed only in workhouses. Life in the workhouse was consciously designed to be more unpleasant than life outside. The law and its administration presupposed that people would not work because they were lazy. The laboring class, not unjustly, regarded the workhouses as new "bastilles."

The second British monument to applied classical economics was the repeal of the Corn Laws in 1846. The Anti-Corn Law League, organized by manufacturers, had sought this goal for more than six years. The League wanted to abolish the tariffs protecting the domestic price of grain. That change would lead to lower food prices, which would then allow lower wages at no real cost to the workers. In turn, the prices on British manufactured goods could also be lowered to strengthen their competitive position in the world market. The actual reason for Sir Robert Peel's repeal of the Corn Laws in 1846 was the Irish famine. Peel had to open British ports to foreign grain to feed the starving Irish.

EARLY SOCIALISM

HOW DID socialism challenge classical economics?

The early socialists generally applauded the new productive capacity of industrialism. They denied, however, that the free market could adequately produce and distribute goods the way the classical economists claimed. Moreover, the socialists thought human society should be organized as a community, rather than merely as a conglomerate of atomistic, selfish individuals.

Utopian Socialism

utopian socialists Early critics of industrialism whose visionary programs often involved plans to establish ideal societies based on noncapitalistic values.

Among the earliest people to define the social question were a group of writers whom their critics called the **utopian socialists**. They were considered utopian because their ideas were often visionary and because they frequently advocated the creation of ideal communities. They were called socialists because they questioned the structures and values of the existing capitalistic framework. In some cases, they actually deserved neither description.

Saint-Simonianism Count Claude Henri de Saint-Simon (1760–1825) was the earliest of the socialist pioneers. Above all else, Saint-Simon believed modern society would require rational management. Private wealth, property, and enterprise should be subject to an administration other than that of its owners. His ideal government would have consisted of a large board of directors organizing and coordinating the activity of individuals and groups to achieve social harmony. Not the *redistribution* of wealth, but its *management* by experts, would alleviate the poverty and social dislocation of the age.

When Saint-Simon died in 1825, he had persuaded only a handful of people his ideas were correct. Nonetheless, Saint-Simonian societies were always centers for lively discussion of advanced social ideals. Some of the earliest debates in France over feminism took place within these societies.

Owenism The major British contributor to the early socialist tradition was Robert Owen (1771–1858), a self-made cotton manufacturer. In his early twenties, Owen became a partner in one of the largest cotton factories in Britain at New Lanark, Scotland. Owen was a firm believer in the environmentalist psychology of the Enlightenment that had flowed from the thought of John Locke. If human beings were placed in the correct surroundings, they and their character could be improved. Moreover, Owen saw no incompatibility between creating a humane industrial environment and making a good profit.

At New Lanark, he put his ideas into practice. Workers were provided with good quarters. Recreational possibilities abounded, and the children received an education. There were several churches, although Owen himself was a notorious freethinker on matters of religion and sex. In the factory itself, rewards were given for good work. His plant made a fine profit. Visitors flocked from all over Europe to see what Owen had done through enlightened management.

Robert Owen, the Scottish industrialist and early socialist, created an ideal industrial community at New Lanark, Scotland. He believed deeply in the power of education and saw that the children of workmen received sound educations.

Eileen Tweedy/Picture Desk, Inc./Kobal Collection

What light does this image shed on Owen's ideas about social order and harmony?

During the 1820s, Owen sold his New Lanark factory and then went to the United States, where he established the community of New Harmony, Indiana. When quarrels among the members led to the community's failure, he refused to give up his reformist causes. He returned to Britain, where he became the moving force behind the organization of the Grand National Union, an attempt to draw all British trade unions into a single body. It collapsed along with other labor organizations during the early 1830s.

Fourierism Charles Fourier (1772–1837) was Owen's French intellectual counterpart. Fourier believed the industrial order ignored the passionate side of human nature. Social discipline ignored all the pleasures that human beings naturally seek. Fourier advocated the construction of communities, called

phalanxes, in which liberated living would replace the boredom and dullness of industrial existence. Agrarian rather than industrial production would predominate in these communities. Sexual activity would be relatively free, and marriage was to be reserved only for later life. Fourier also urged that no person be required to perform the same kind of work for the entire day. People would be both happier and more productive if they moved from one task to another. Through his emphasis on the problem of boredom, Fourier isolated one of the key difficulties of modern economic life.

Saint-Simon, Owen, and Fourier failed to confront the political difficulties their envisioned social transformations would arouse. Other figures paid more attention to the politics of the situation. In 1839, Louis Blanc (1811–1882) published *The Organization of Labor*. Blanc called for political reform that would give the vote to the working class. Once so empowered, workers could use the vote to turn the political processes to their own economic advantage. A state controlled by a working-class electorate would finance workshops to employ the poor. In time, such workshops might replace private enterprise, and industry would be organized to ensure jobs. The state itself could become the great employer of labor.

QUICK REVIEW

Charles Fourier (1772–1837)

- Believed that industrial order ignored the emotional side of human nature
- Advocated the construction of communities called *phalanxes*
- Envisioned agrarian production as the basis of *phalanxes*

Anarchism

Other writers and activists of the 1840s, however, rejected both industry and the dominance of government. These were the **anarchists**. They are usually included in the socialist tradition, although they do not exactly fit there. Some favored programs of violence and terrorism; others were peaceful. Auguste Blanqui (1805–1881) was a major spokesperson for terror. Seeking to abolish both capitalism and the state, Blanqui urged the development of a professional revolutionary vanguard to attack capitalist society.

anarchists Those who opposed any cooperation with industry or government.

Pierre-Joseph Proudhon (1809–1865) represented the other strain of anarchism. He believed that society should be organized on the basis of mutualism, which amounted to a system of small businesses and other cooperative enterprises among which there would be peaceful cooperation and exchanges of goods based on mutual recognition of the labor each area of production required. With such a social system, the state as the protector of property would be unnecessary. Proudhon's ideas later influenced the French labor movement, which was generally less directly political in its activities than the labor movements in Britain and Germany.

Marxism Socialist movement begun by Karl Marx in the mid–nineteenth century that differed from competing socialist views primarily in its claim to a scientific foundation and in its insistence on reform through revolution.

Marxism

The mode of socialist thought that eventually exerted more influence over modern European history than any other was **Marxism**. At midcentury, the ideas of Karl Marx were simply one more contribution to a heady mixture of concepts and programs criticizing the emerging industrial capitalist society. Marxism differed from its competitors in its claims to scientific accuracy, its rejection of liberal reform, its harsh criticism of other contemporary socialist platforms, and its call for revolution, though the character of that revolution was not well defined. Furthermore, Marx set the emergence of the industrial workforce in the context of a world historical development from which he drew sweeping political conclusions.

Karl Marx (1818–1883) was born in Germany in the Prussian Rhineland. Marx's middle-class parents sent him to the University of Berlin, where he became deeply involved in Hegelian philosophy and radical politics. Soon the Prussian authorities drove him from his native land. He lived as an exile, first in Paris, then in Brussels, and finally, after 1849, in London.

Karl Marx's socialist philosophy eventually triumphed over most alternative versions of socialism in Europe, but his monumental work became subject to varying interpretations, criticism, and revisions that continue to this day.

Library of Congress

Should Marx be considered a utopian thinker?

Partnership with Engels In 1844, Marx met Friedrich Engels (1820–1895), another young middle-class German, whose father owned a textile factory in Manchester, England. The next year Engels published *The Condition of the Working Class in England*, which presented a devastating picture of industrial life. Late in 1847, they were asked to write a pamphlet for a newly organized and ultimately short-lived secret Communist League. *The Communist Manifesto*, published in German, appeared early in 1848.

Sources of Marx's Ideas Marx derived the major ideas of the *Manifesto* and of his later work, including *Capital* (vol. 1, 1867), from German Hegelianism, French utopian socialism, and British classical economics. Marx applied to concrete historical, social, and economic developments Hegel's abstract philosophical concept that thought develops from the clash of thesis and antithesis into a new intellectual synthesis. For Marx, the conflict between dominant and subordinate social groups led to the emergence of a new dominant social group. These new social relationships, in turn, generated new discontent, conflict, and development. The French utopian socialists had depicted the problems of capitalist society and had raised the issue of property redistribution. Both Hegel and Saint-Simon led Marx to see society and economic conditions as developing through historical stages. The classical economists had produced the analytical tools for an empirical, scientific examination of the industrial capitalist society. Using the intellectual tools of Hegel, the French utopian socialists, and the British classical economists provided, Marx fashioned a philosophy that gave a special role or function to the new industrial workforce as the single most important driving force of contemporary history.

Revolution Through Class Conflict In *The Communist Manifesto*, Marx and Engels contended that human history must be understood rationally and as a whole. History is the record of humankind's coming to grips with physical nature to produce the goods necessary for survival. That basic productive process determines the structures, values, and ideas of a society. Historically, the organization of the means of production has always involved conflict between the classes that owned and controlled the means of production and the classes that worked for them. That necessary conflict has provided the engine for historical development; it is not an accidental by-product of mismanagement or bad intentions. Thus, piecemeal reforms cannot eliminate the social and economic evils inherent in the very structures of production. To achieve that, a radical social transformation is required. The development of capitalism will make such a revolution inevitable.

In Marx's and Engels's eyes, the class conflict that had characterized previous Western history had become simplified during the early nineteenth century into a struggle between the bourgeoisie and the proletariat, or between the middle class associated with industry and commerce, on the one hand, and the workers, on the other. The character of capitalism itself ensured the sharpening of the struggle. Capitalist production and competition would steadily increase the size of the unpropertied proletariat, at the same time as it resulted in fewer, but larger, capitalist firms. As this ever-expanding body of workers suffered increasingly from the competition among the ever-enlarging firms, Marx contended, they would eventually begin to foment revolution. Finally, they would overthrow the few remaining owners of the means of production. For a time, the workers would organize the means of production through a dictatorship of the proletariat. This would eventually give way to a propertyless and classless communist society. This victory of the proletariat over the bourgeoisie would represent the culmination of human history. For the first time in human history, one group of people would not be oppressing another.

The economic environment of the 1840s had conditioned Marx's analysis. The decade had seen much unemployment and deprivation. During the later part of the century, however, European and American capitalism did not collapse as he had predicted, nor did the middle class become proletarianized. Rather, the industrial system benefited more and more people. Nonetheless, within a generation of the publication of *The Communist Manifesto*, Marxism had captured the imagination of

many socialists, especially in Germany, and large segments of the working class. Marxist doctrines appeared to be based on the empirical evidence of hard economic fact. Marxism's scientific claim helped spread the ideology as science became more influential during the second half of the century. At its core, however, the attraction of the ideology was its utopian vision of ultimate human liberation, no matter how illiberal or authoritarian the governments that embraced the Marxist vision in the twentieth century were.

1848: YEAR OF REVOLUTIONS

WHY DID a series of revolutions erupt across Europe in 1848?

In 1848, a series of liberal and nationalistic revolutions erupted across the Continent. (See Map 21–2, page 532.) No single factor caused this general revolutionary groundswell; rather, similar conditions existed in several countries. Severe food shortages had prevailed since 1846. The commercial and industrial economy was also depressed. Unemployment was widespread. Systems of poor relief were overburdened. These difficulties, added to the wretched living conditions in the cities, heightened the frustration and discontent of the urban artisan and laboring classes.

The dynamic force for change in 1848 originated, however, not with the working classes, but with the political liberals, who were generally drawn from the middle classes. Throughout the Continent, liberals were pushing for their program of a more representative government, civil liberty, and unregulated economic life. To put additional pressure on their governments, they began to appeal for the support of the urban working classes. The latter, however, wanted improved working and economic conditions, rather than a more liberal government. Moreover, their tactics were frequently violent rather than peaceful. The temporary alliance of liberals and workers in several states overthrew or severely shook the old order; then the allies began to fight each other.

Finally, outside France, nationalism was an important common factor in the uprisings. Germans, Hungarians, Italians, Czechs, and smaller national groups in eastern Europe sought to create national states that would reorganize or replace existing political entities. At the same time, various national groups clashed with each other during these revolutions.

The immediate results of the 1848 revolutions were stunning. Yet, without exception, the revolutions failed to establish genuinely liberal or national states. The conservative order proved stronger and more resilient than anyone had expected. The liberals refused to follow political revolution with social reform and thus isolated themselves from the working classes. Once separated from potential mass support, the liberal revolutions became an easy prey for the armies of the reactionary classes.

France: The Second Republic and Louis Napoleon

As had happened twice before, the revolutionary tinder first blazed in Paris. The liberal political opponents of the corrupt regime of Louis Philippe and his minister Guizot organized a series of political banquets. They used these occasions to criticize the government and demand further admission for them and their middle-class supporters to the political process. The poor harvests of 1846 and 1847 and the resulting high food prices and unemployment brought working-class support to the liberal campaign. On February 21, 1848, the government forbade further banquets. On February 22, disgruntled Parisian workers paraded through the streets demanding reform and Guizot's ouster. The next morning the crowds grew, and by afternoon, Guizot had resigned. The crowds erected barricades, and numerous clashes occurred between the citizenry and the municipal guard. On February 24, 1848, Louis Philippe abdicated and fled to England.

MAP 21–2 **Centers of Revolution in 1848–1849** The revolution that toppled the July Monarchy in Paris in 1848 soon spread to Austria and many of the German and Italian states. Yet by the end of 1849, most of these uprisings had been suppressed.

Why would Austria and Germany have provided fertile grounds for the spread of a revolutionary movement that began in France?

The National Assembly and Paris Workers The liberal opposition, led by the poet Alphonse de Lamartine (1790–1869), organized a provisional government. The liberals intended to call an election for an assembly that would write a republican constitution. The various working-class groups in Paris, however, had other ideas: They wanted a social as well as a political revolution. Led by Louis Blanc, they demanded representation in the cabinet. Blanc and two other radical leaders became ministers. Under their pressure, the provisional government organized national workshops to provide work and relief for thousands of unemployed workers.

On Sunday, April 23, an election based on universal male suffrage chose the new National Assembly. The result was a legislature dominated by moderates and conservatives. In the French provinces, many people resented the Paris radicals and were frightened by their ideas. The new conservative National Assembly had little sympathy for the expensive national workshops, which they incorrectly perceived to be socialistic.

Throughout May, government troops and the unemployed workers and artisans of Paris clashed. As a result, the assembly closed the workshops to new entrants and planned to eject many enrolled workers. By late June, barricades again appeared in Paris. On June 24, under orders from the government, General Louis Cavaignac (1802–1857), with troops drawn largely from the conservative countryside, moved to destroy the barricades and quell disturbances. During the next two days, more than four hundred people were killed. Thereafter, troops hunted down another 3,000 persons in street fighting. The drive for social revolution had ended.

Emergence of Louis Napoleon The so-called June Days confirmed the political predominance of conservative property holders in French life. They wanted a state that was safe for small property. Late in 1848, the election for president confirmed this search for social order. The new president was Louis Napoleon Bonaparte (1808–1873), a nephew of the great emperor. After the corruption of Louis Philippe and the turmoil of the early months of the Second Republic, the voters turned to the name of Bonaparte as a source of stability and greatness.

The election of the "Little Napoleon" doomed the Second Republic. Louis Napoleon was dedicated to his own fame rather than to republican institutions. In 1851, the assembly refused to amend the constitution to allow the president to run for reelection. Consequently, on December 2, 1851, the anniversary of the great Napoleon's victory at Austerlitz, Louis Napoleon seized power. Troops dispersed the assembly, and the president called for new elections. More than two hundred people died resisting the coup, and more than 26,000 persons were arrested throughout the country. Almost 10,000 persons who opposed the coup were transported to Algeria.

Yet, in the plebiscite of December 21, 1851, more than 7.5 million voters supported the actions of Louis Napoleon and approved a new constitution that consolidated his power. Only about 600,000 citizens dared to vote against him. A year later, in December 1852, an empire was proclaimed, and Louis Napoleon became Emperor Napoleon III. Again a plebiscite approved the action.

Frenchwomen in 1848 The years between the February Revolution of 1848 and the Napoleonic coup of 1851 saw major feminist activity by Frenchwomen. Especially in Paris, women seized the opportunity of the collapse of the July Monarchy to voice demands for reform of their social conditions. They joined the wide variety of political clubs that emerged in the wake of the revolution. Some of these clubs emphasized women's rights. Some women even tried unsuccessfully to vote in the elections of 1848. Both middle-class and working-class women were involved in these activities. The most radical group, the Vesuvians, demanded full domestic household equality between men and women, the right of women to serve in the military, and similarity in dress for both sexes. They also conducted street demonstrations. The radical character of their demands and actions lost them the support of more moderate women.

Certain Parisian women quickly attempted to use for their own cause the liberal freedoms that suddenly had become available. They organized the *Voix des femmes* (*The Women's Voice*), a daily newspaper that addressed issues of concern to women. The newspaper insisted that improving the lot of men would not necessarily improve the condition of women. They soon organized a society with the same name as the newspaper. Members of the *Voix des femmes* group were relatively conservative feminists. They cooperated with male political groups, and they urged the integrity of the family and fidelity in marriage. They furthermore warmly embraced the maternal role for women but tried to use it to raise the importance of women in society. The emphasis on family and motherhood represented, in part, a defensive strategy to prevent conservative women and men from accusing the advocates of women's rights of seeking to destroy the family and traditional marriage.

The fate of French feminists in 1848 was similar to that of the radical workers. Once the elections were held that spring, the new government expressed no sympathy for their causes. The closing of the national workshops adversely affected women workers as well as men and blocked one outlet that women had used to make their needs known. The conservative crackdown on political clubs closed another arena in which women had participated. Women were soon specifically forbidden to participate in political clubs either by themselves or with men. By 1852, the entire feminist movement that had sprung up in 1848 had been eradicated.

The Habsburg Empire: Nationalism Resisted

The events of February 1848 in Paris immediately reverberated throughout the Habsburg domains. The empire was susceptible to revolutionary challenge on every score. Its government rejected liberal institutions. Its borders cut across national lines. Its society perpetuated serfdom. In 1848, the regime confronted rebellions in Vienna, Prague, Hungary, and Italy. The disturbances that broke out in Germany also threatened Habsburg predominance.

The Vienna Uprising The Habsburg troubles began on March 3, 1848, when Louis Kossuth (1802–1894), a Magyar nationalist and member of the Hungarian diet, attacked Austrian domination, called for the independence of Hungary, and demanded a responsible ministry under the Habsburg dynasty. Ten days later, inspired by Kossuth's speeches, students led a series of disturbances in Vienna. The army failed to restore order. Metternich resigned and fled the country. The feeble-minded Emperor Ferdinand (r. 1835–1848) promised a moderately liberal constitution. Unsatisfied, the radical students then formed democratic clubs to press the revolution further. On May 17, the emperor and the imperial court fled to Innsbruck.

What the Habsburg government most feared was not the urban rebellions, but an uprising of the serfs in the countryside. Consequently, almost immediately after the Vienna uprising, the imperial government emancipated the serfs in much of Austria. The Hungarian diet also abolished serfdom in March 1848. These actions smothered the most serious potential threat to order in the empire.

The Magyar Revolt The Vienna revolt had emboldened the Hungarians. The Magyar leaders of the Hungarian March Revolution were primarily liberals supported by nobles who wanted their aristocratic liberties guaranteed against the central government in Vienna. The Hungarian Diet passed the March Laws, which mandated equality of religion, jury trials, the election of the lower chamber of the Diet, a relatively free press, and payment of

taxes by the nobility. Emperor Ferdinand approved these measures because in the spring of 1848 he could do little else.

The Magyars also hoped to establish a separate Hungarian state within the Habsburg domains. As part of this scheme for a partially independent state, the Hungarians attempted to annex Transylvania, Croatia, and other eastern territories of the Habsburg Empire. That annexation would have brought Romanians, Croatians, and Serbs under Magyar government. These national groups resisted the drive toward Magyarization, especially the imposition on them, for the purposes of the government and administration, of the Hungarian language. The national groups whom the Hungarians were now repressing believed the Habsburgs offered them a better chance to preserve their national or ethnic identity, their languages, and their economic self-interest. In late March, the Vienna government sent Count Joseph Jellachich (1801–1859) to aid the national groups who were rebelling against the rebellious Hungarians. By early September 1848, he was invading Hungary with the support of the national groups who were resisting Magyarization.

Louis Kossuth, a Magyar nationalist, shown here seeking to raise troops to fight for Hungarian independence during the revolutionary disturbances of 1848.

Bildarchiv Preussischer Kulturbesitz

Who were the leaders of the Magyar revolt? What did they want?

Czech Nationalism In mid-March 1848, with Vienna and Budapest in revolt, Czech nationalists demanded that the Czech provinces of Bohemia and Moravia be permitted to constitute an autonomous Slavic state within the empire similar to that just enacted in Hungary. Conflict immediately developed, however, between the Czechs and the Germans living in these regions. The Czechs summoned a congress of Slavs, including Poles, Ruthenians, Czechs, Slovaks, Croats, Slovenes, and Serbs, which met in Prague in early June. Under the leadership of Francis Palacky (1798–1876), this first Pan-Slavic Congress called for the national equality of Slavs within the Habsburg Empire. The manifesto also protested the repression of all Slavic peoples under Habsburg, Hungarian, German, and Ottoman domination.

On June 12, the day the Pan-Slavic Congress closed, a radical insurrection broke out in Prague. General Prince Alfred Windischgraetz (1787–1862), whose wife had been killed by a stray bullet, moved his troops against the uprising. The Prague middle class was happy to see the radicals suppressed, which was finalized by June 17. The Germans in the area approved the smothering of Czech nationalism. The policy of "divide and conquer" had succeeded.

Rebellion in Northern Italy While repelling the Hungarian and Czech bids for autonomy, the Habsburg government also faced war in northern Italy. A revolt against Habsburg domination began in Milan on March 18. King Charles Albert of Piedmont (r. 1831–1849), who wanted to annex Lombardy (the province of which Milan is the capital), aided the rebels. The Austrian forces fared badly until July, when Austrian reinforcements arrived, defeated Piedmont, and suppressed the revolt. For the time being, Austria held its position in northern Italy.

Vienna and Hungary remained to be recaptured. In midsummer, the emperor returned to the capital and the imperial government decided to reassert its control. When a new insurrection occurred in October, the imperial army bombarded Vienna and crushed the revolt. On December 2, Emperor Ferdinand, clearly too feeble to govern, abdicated in favor of his young nephew Francis Joseph (r. 1848–1916). Real power now lay with Prince Felix Schwarzenberg (1800–1852), who intended to use the army with full force.

On January 5, 1849, troops occupied Budapest. By March the triumphant Austrian forces had imposed military rule over Hungary, and the new emperor repudiated the recent constitution. The Magyar nobles attempted one last revolt. In August, Austrian troops, reinforced by 200,000 soldiers that Tsar Nicholas I of Russia (r. 1825–1855) happily furnished, finally crushed the Hungarians. Croatians and other nationalities that had resisted Magyarization welcomed the collapse of the revolt. The imperial Habsburg government survived its gravest internal challenge because of the divisions among its enemies and its own willingness to use military force with a vengeance.

Italy: Republicanism Defeated

The brief war between Piedmont and Austria in 1848 marked only the first stage of the Italian revolution. Many Italians hoped King Charles Albert of Piedmont would drive Austria from the peninsula and thus prepare the way for Italian unification. Liberal and nationalist hopes then shifted to Pope Pius IX (r. 1846–1878) who had a liberal reputation. Nationalists believed a united Italian state might emerge under his leadership.

In Rome, however, as in other cities, political radicalism was on the rise. On November 15, 1848, a democratic radical assassinated Count Pelligrino Rossi (r. 1787–1848), the liberal minister of the Papal States. The next day, popular demonstrations forced the pope to appoint a radical ministry. Shortly thereafter, Pius IX fled to Naples for refuge. In February 1849, the radicals proclaimed the Roman Republic. Republican nationalists from all over Italy, including Giuseppe Mazzini (1805–1872) and Giuseppe Garibaldi (1807–1882), two of the most prominent, flocked to Rome. They hoped to use the new republic as a base of operations to unite the rest of Italy under a republican government.

In March 1849, radicals in Piedmont forced Charles Albert to renew the patriotic war against Austria. After the almost immediate defeat of Piedmont at the Battle of Novara, the king abdicated in favor of his son, Victor Emmanuel II (r. 1849–1878). The defeat meant the Roman Republic must defend itself alone. The troops that attacked Rome and restored the pope came from France. The French wanted to prevent the rise of a strong, unified state on their southern border. By the end of the June, the French were victorious and the Roman Republic had dissolved.

Germany: Liberalism Frustrated

The revolutionary contagion had also spread rapidly through the German states. The most important of these revolutions occurred in Prussia.

Revolution in Prussia By March 15, 1848, large popular disturbances had erupted in Berlin. Frederick William IV (r. 1840–1861) refused to turn his troops on the Berliners and even announced limited reforms. Nevertheless, on March 18, several citizens were killed when troops cleared a square near the palace.

The king called for a Prussian constituent assembly to write a constitution. The next day, as angry Berliners crowded around the palace, Frederick William IV appeared on the balcony to salute the corpses of his slain subjects. He made further concessions and implied that henceforth Prussia would helpe unify Germany. For all practical purposes, the Prussian monarchy had capitulated.

Frederick William IV appointed a cabinet headed by David Hansemann (1790–1864), a widely respected moderate liberal. The Prussian constituent assembly, however, proved to be radical and democratic. As time passed, the king and his conservative supporters decided to ignore the assembly. The liberal ministry resigned and a conservative one replaced it. In April 1849, the assembly was dissolved, and the monarch proclaimed his own constitution. One of its key elements was a system of three-class voting which gave the wealthy disproportionate political power. In the revised Prussian constitution of 1850, the ministry was responsible to the king alone. Moreover, the Prussian army and officer corps swore loyalty directly to the monarch.

The Frankfurt Parliament While Prussia was moving from revolution to reaction, other events were unfolding in Germany as a whole. On May 18, 1848, representatives from all the German states gathered in Saint Paul's Church in Frankfurt to revise the organization of the German Confederation. The Frankfurt Parliament intended to write a moderately liberal constitution for a united Germany. The liberal character of the Frankfurt Parliament alienated both German conservatives and the German working class. The very existence of the parliament, representing as it did a challenge to the existing political order, offended the conservatives. The liberals were too attached to the concept of a free labor market to offer meaningful legislation to workers. This failure marked the beginning of a profound split between German liberals and the German working class. For the rest of the century, German conservatives would be able to play on that division.

The Frankfurt Parliament also floundered on the issue of unification. Members differed over whether to include Austria in a united Germany. The "large German [*grossdeutsch*] solution" favored Austria's inclusion, whereas the "small German [*kleindeutsch*] solution" advocated its exclusion. The latter formula prevailed because Austria rejected the whole notion of German unification. Consequently, the Frankfurt Parliament looked to Prussian, rather than Austrian, leadership.

On March 27, 1849, the parliament produced its constitution. Shortly thereafter, its delegates offered the crown of a united Germany to Frederick William IV of Prussia. He rejected the offer, asserting that kings ruled by the grace of God rather than by the permission of man-made constitutions. On his refusal, the Frankfurt Parliament began to dissolve. Not long afterward, troops drove off the remaining members. German liberals never fully recovered from this defeat.

THE REVOLUTIONARY CRISIS OF 1848 TO 1851

1848	
February 22–24	Abdication of Louis Philippe
March 3	Kossuth demands freedom for Hungary
March 13	Revolution in Vienna
March 15	Habsburg emperor accepts the March Laws
March 18	Frederick William IV promises a constitution; revolution in Milan
March 22	Piedmont declares war on Austria
April 23	Election of the French National Assembly
May 17	Emperor Ferdinand flees Vienna
May 18	Frankfurt Parliament gathers
June 2	Pan-Slavic Congress convenes in Prague
July 24	Austria defeats Piedmont
September 17	General Jellachich invades Hungary
October 31	General Windischgraetz pacifies Vienna
November 16	Revolution in Rome
November 25	Pope Pius IX flees Rome
December 2	Francis Joseph becomes Habsburg emperor
December 10	Louis Napoleon and the Second French Republic
1849	
January 5	General Windischgraetz occupies Budapest
February 2	The Roman Republic proclaimed
March 12	War resumes between Piedmont and Austria
March 23	Piedmont is defeated; Victor Emmanuel II crowned
March 28	German crown offered to Frederick William IV
June 18	Frankfurt Parliament dispersed
July 3	Collapse of the Roman Republic
August 9–13	Austria defeats Hungarian forces
1851	
December 2	Coup d'état of Louis Napoleon

SUMMARY

HOW DID industrialization spread across Europe?

Toward an Industrial Society Multiple factors helped make Britain the early leader in the Industrial Revolution. Textiles were the first industrialized industry. Belgium, France, and Germany were industrializing rapidly by the 1830s. Population growth and urbanization continued; many cities were unable to accommodate the new influx of residents, so slums grew and crime increased. Most peasants had become landowners, but many lacked the capital to use their land effectively. The ease with which people could leave rural land varied, with migration generally more difficult in eastern parts of Europe. Railroads, canals, and improved roads facilitated movement. Many railways were built in the 1830s and 1840s, reflecting this period's emphasis on capital production rather than consumer production. *page 516*

HOW DID industrialization change the European labor force?

The Labor Force The labor experience varied, according to industry and location. In the first half of the nineteenth century, only textile manufacture was fully mechanized and factory based. Skilled artisans made up far more of the nonagricultural workforce than factory workers. Both, however, were proletarianized. Textile workers who resisted factory production were slowly impoverished. Urban artisans were slowly proletarianized, as labor and guild organizations were suppressed for political reasons, and craftwork was standardized for economic reasons. British Chartists provided a model for a large-scale working-class political movement. *page 519*

HOW DID industrialization affect European families?

Family Structures and the Industrial Revolution Industrialization transformed the family from being the chief unit of both production and consumption, to being the chief unit of consumption alone. This occurred slowly and was not completed throughout Europe before the end of the nineteenth century. By the 1830s, work associated with textile machinery had largely been split into skilled work, performed by men who were relatively well paid, and unskilled work, performed by poorly paid unmarried women and the children of poor weavers. Child labor and education laws improved children's working conditions but further separated them from their families. *page 522*

WHAT ROLE did women play in the Industrial Revolution?

Women in the Early Industrial Revolution With industrialization, the gender division of labor spread to the working class. In the 1820s, factory work for women became more widely available but paid less. Wages for men in factories were often enough to support a family; in families where that was not the case, children were more likely to enter the workforce than were wives. Therefore, the women who worked in factories were generally young and single, or widowed. Domestic cottage industries employed many women throughout Europe. In virtually all cases, however, women were poorly paid. Marriage and family life changed too, although slowly. Women's domestic work became more sharply defined. *page 523*

HOW DID the establishment of police forces and the reform of prisons change society?

Problems of Crime and Order Revolutions, industrialization, and urbanization all contributed to a fear of crime. In cities, crime did increase in the early to mid–nineteenth century. To assuage the fears of the propertied elite, prisons were reformed, and police systems were instituted or improved. The existence of a paid, professional, nonpolitical group of law enforcement officers, distinct from the army, was a new development in nineteenth-century Europe. By the end of the century, most Europeans of all classes viewed police favorably. Experimental prisons based on models used in the United States, in which prisoners were separated from each other, were tried in England and France. *page 525*

WHAT WERE the key assumptions of classical economic theory?

Classical Economics Laissez-faire economic theories predominated in this period. Classical economists believed competitive free enterprise was the best path to economic growth. Malthus argued that food supply could not grow as quickly as population; if working-class wages were raised, working-class families would have more children, worsening the situation. Ricardo postulated the "iron law of wages," linking wages and fertility in an even more deterministic and pessimistic way than Malthus. The governments of France, Germany, and Britain all enacted policies based on classical economic theory. *page 526*

HOW DID socialism challenge classical economics?

Early Socialism Socialists believed society could and should be organized as a community. They rejected the classical economists' claim that the free market was the best system. Saint-Simon in France advocated rational management. Owen combined a wholesome environment for employees with a healthy profit for himself at his factory. In the 1840s, anarchists rejected industry and government. Marx believed revolution, not reform, was inevitable. Although some of his predictions had already been disproved by the mid-nineteenth century, his theories proved themselves to be enormously appealing and influential. *page 527*

WHY DID a series of revolutions erupt across Europe in 1848?

1848: Year of Revolutions Revolutions occurred throughout Europe in 1848. All essentially ended in failure. During the revolutions, middle-class liberals, who wanted more representative government, civil liberty, and minimal economic regulations, joined forces with the urban working class, which sought improved working and economic conditions. Nationalists generally hoped to use the revolutions to further their own ends. Conservatives fought back, however, and the middle-class/working-class alliance faltered after the political liberals got what they wanted and refused to support working-class social demands. In France, King Louis Philippe abdicated in February 1848; in the new National Assembly, moderates and conservatives quickly displaced Paris radicals. Napoleon's nephew, Louis Napoleon Bonaparte, was elected president in December, and in 1852 he proclaimed himself emperor. In the Habsburg Empire, Hungary called for independence in March 1848. Serfs were emancipated in Austria and Hungary. The Slavs held their first Pan-Slavic Congress in the summer. Northern Italy revolted against the Habsburgs but was quickly suppressed. In late 1848 and early 1849, revolt spread throughout Italy, and the French sent troops to protect the pope until 1870. In Prussia, Frederick William IV went along with liberal demands at first, then imposed his own reforms on the state. In Germany, attempts to revise the German Confederation failed and led to a long-standing division between German liberals and the working class. *page 531*

REVIEW QUESTIONS

1. What inventions were particularly important in the development of industrialism? What changes did industrialism make in society? What is meant by "the proletarianization of workers"? In what ways did the industrial economy change the working-class family?

2. How did the police change in the nineteenth century? Why were new systems of enforcement instituted? In what ways were prisons improved? How do you account for the reform movement that led to the improvements?

3. How would you define *socialism?* Were Karl Marx's ideas different from those of the socialists?

4. Why did revolutions break out in so many places in 1848? Were circumstances essentially the same or were they different in the various countries? Why did the revolutions fail? What roles did liberals and nationalists play in them? Did they always agree?

KEY TERMS

anarchists (p. 529)
Chartism (p. 522)
Marxism (p. 529)
utilitarianism (p. 527)
utopian socialists (p. 528)

22

The Age of Nation-States

Giuseppe Garibaldi, the charismatic leader, can be seen on the right urging on his troops in the rout of Neapolitan forces at Calatafimi, Sicily, in 1860.

Bildarchiv Preussischer Kulturbesitz

How did Garibaldi's vision of a united Italy differ from that of Cavour?

THE CRIMEAN WAR (1853–1856) *page 542*

WHY WAS the Crimean War fought?

REFORMS IN THE OTTOMAN EMPIRE *page 543*

HOW DID the Ottoman Empire attempt to reform itself?

ITALIAN UNIFICATION *page 544*

HOW DID Italy achieve unification?

GERMAN UNIFICATION *page 547*

HOW DID Bismarck use war as a tool for achieving German unification?

FRANCE: FROM LIBERAL EMPIRE TO THE THIRD REPUBLIC *page 552*

WHAT EVENT led to the establishment of a Third Republic in France?

THE HABSBURG EMPIRE *page 554*

WHY WAS nationalism such a threat to the Habsburg Empire?

RUSSIA: EMANCIPATION AND REVOLUTIONARY STIRRINGS *page 556*

WHY DID reform in Russia fail to produce political stability?

GREAT BRITAIN: TOWARD DEMOCRACY *page 558*

WHAT FORCES led to the expansion of democracy in Great Britain?

Although the revolutions of 1848 collapsed and authoritarian regimes spread across Europe in the early 1850s, many of the objectives of early-nineteenth-century liberals and nationalists had been achieved by 1875. Italy and Germany were each unified under constitutional monarchies. The Habsburg emperor accepted a constitution that recognized the liberties of the Magyars of Hungary. Russia's tsar emancipated the serfs. France again became a republic. Liberalism (even democracy) flourished in Great Britain, and the Ottoman Empire attempted major reforms. Paradoxically, most of this liberal agenda was enacted while conservatives were in power. ■

THE CRIMEAN WAR (1853–1856)

WHY WAS the Crimean War fought?

As has so often been true in modern European history, the impetus for change originated in war. The Crimean War (1853–1856) was rooted in the long-standing desire of Russia to extend its influence over the Ottoman Empire. Two disputes led to the conflict. First, as noted in Chapter 17, the Russians had, since the time of Catherine the Great (r. 1762–1796), been given protective oversight of Orthodox Christians in the Empire, and France had similar oversight of Roman Catholics. In 1851, yielding to French pressure, the Ottoman sultan had assigned care of certain holy places in Palestine to Roman Catholics, angering Russia. Second, in the summer of 1853, the Russians used their right to protect Orthodox Christians in the Ottoman Empire as the pretext to occupy the Ottoman provinces of Moldavia and Wallachia. Shortly thereafter, the Ottoman Empire declared war on Russia.

The Russian government envisioned the eventual breakup of the empire and hoped to extend its influence at Ottoman expense. Both France and Britain, though recognizing the difficulties of the Ottoman government and using it to their own advantage when the opportunity presented itself, opposed Russian expansion in the eastern Mediterranean, where they had extensive naval and commercial interests. On March 28, 1854, France and Britain declared war on Russia in alliance with the Ottomans.

Both sides conducted the conflict ineptly, a fact that became widely known in Western Europe because the Crimean War was the first to be covered by war correspondents and photographers. The ill-equipped and poorly commanded armies became bogged down along the Crimean coast of the Black Sea. In September 1855, after a long siege, the Russian fortress of Sevastopol finally fell to the French and British. Thereafter, both sides moved to end the war.

This painting by Elizabeth Thompson, Lady Butler, portrays the comradeship and suffering of ordinary troops. Completed in 1874 and purchased by Queen Victoria, Butler's work reflects the public's awareness of the horrors of war and the mismanagement by discredited aristocratic army officers.

Lady Elizabeth Thompson Butler (1846–1933), *The Roll Call: Calling the Roll after an Engagement, Crimea* (unframed). The Royal Collection © 2003, Her Majesty Queen Elizabeth II. Photo by SC

How did widespread print reporting change public perceptions of war in the second half of the nineteenth century?

Overview Reforms and Attempts at Reform in the Ottoman Empire

YEAR	REFORM	INTENTION OF REFORM
1839	*Hatt-i Sharif of Gülhane*	A decree calling for reform measures.
1856	*Hatt-i Hümayun*	Rights of non-Muslims were spelled out. It put Jews and Christians on equal footing with Muslims for military service, school admission, and political offices.
1908	*Young Turks*	A military revolution brought up this group of reformist officers. Their decision to ally the empire with the Central Powers led to its defeat.

Peace Settlement and Long-Term Results

In March 1856, a conference in Paris concluded the Treaty of Paris. This treaty required a series of concession from Russia and the image of an invincible Russia that had prevailed across Europe since the close of the Napoleonic Wars was shattered. Also shattered was the Concert of Europe, as a means of dealing with international relations on the Continent. Following the successful repression of the 1848 uprisings, the great powers feared revolution less than they had earlier in the century, and, consequently, they displayed much less reverence for the Vienna settlement. As a result, for about twenty-five years after the Crimean War, European affairs were unstable, producing a period of adventurism in foreign policy. While these events reshaped Western Europe, however, the Ottoman Empire over whose fate the Crimean War had been fought undertook reforms.

REFORMS IN THE OTTOMAN EMPIRE

HOW DID the Ottoman Empire attempt to reform itself?

The short-lived Napoleonic invasion of the Ottoman province of Egypt in 1798–1799 (see Chapter 19) sparked a drive for change in the Ottoman Empire. In 1839, the sultan issued a decree, called the *Hatt-i Sharif of Gülhane*, that attempted to reorganize the empire's administration and military along European lines. This decree opened what became known as the *Tanzimat* (meaning "reorganization") era of the Ottoman Empire, lasting from 1839 to 1876. The reforms liberalized the economy, ended the practice of tax farming, and sought to eliminate corruption. The *Hatt-i Sharif* was particularly remarkable for extending civic equality to Ottoman subjects regardless of their religion. Muslims, Christians, and Jews were now equal before the law. The empire also made it much easier for Muslims to enter into commercial agreements with non-Muslims, both within the empire and from abroad.

Another reform decree isssued in 1856, called the *Hatti-i Hümayun*, spelled out the rights of non-Muslims more explicitly, giving them equal obligations with Muslims for military service and equal opportunity for state employment and admission to state schools. The decree also abolished torture and allowed foreigners to acquire some forms of property. The imperial government took these steps to gain the loyalty of its Christian subjects at a time when nationalism was making increasing inroads among them.

However, putting these reforms into practice proved difficult. In some regions of the empire, especially in Egypt and Tunis, local rulers were virtually independent of Istanbul. They carried out their own modernizing reforms, often working closely with European powers. In the capital itself, power struggles developed between proponents and opponents of reform. Because of these tensions, as well as growing nationalism in various regions, the Ottoman Empire failed to achieve genuine political strength and stability.

The Balkan wars of the late 1870s, which resulted in either the independence of, or Russian or Austrian dominance over, most of the empire's European holdings, demonstrated the inability of the Ottoman Empire to master its own destiny. (See Chapter 26.) The response to these foreign defeats resulted in greater efforts to modernize the army and the economy and to build railways and telegraphs. In 1876, reformers persuaded the sultan to proclaim an Ottoman constitution. The constitution called for a parliament consisting of an elected chamber of deputies and an appointed senate (these met for the first time in 1877) but left the sultan's power mostly intact. Nonetheless, a new sultan soon rejected even these limited steps toward constitutionalism and dismissed the parliament. In 1908, military officers carried out a revolution against the authority, though not the person, of the sultan. Another group of reformist officers, known as the *Young Turks*, came to the fore with another program to modernize the empire. They were still in charge when World War I broke out, and their decision to enter the war on the side of the Central Powers in November 1914 led to the empire's defeat and collapse. (See Chapter 26.)

ITALIAN UNIFICATION

HOW DID Italy achieve unification?

Nationalists had long wanted to unite Italy into a single state. During the first half of the century, however, opinion differed about how to achieve unification.

ROMANTIC REPUBLICANS

After the Congress of Vienna, secret romantic republican societies were founded throughout Italy, the most famous of which was the Carbonari ("charcoal burners"). They were ineffective and, after the failure of nationalist uprisings in Italy in 1831, the leadership of romantic republican nationalism passed to Giuseppe Mazzini (1805–1872). In 1831, he founded the Young Italy Society to drive Austria from the peninsula and establish an Italian republic. During the 1830s and 1840s, Mazzini and his fellow republican Giuseppe Garibaldi (1807–1882) led insurrections. Both were involved in the ill-fated Roman Republic of 1849. Throughout the 1850s, they continued to conduct what amounted to guerrilla warfare.

QUICK REVIEW

Romantic Republicans

- Giuseppe Mazzini (1805–1872)
- Giuseppe Garibaldi (1807–1882)
- Campaigned for Italian unification in the 1830s, 40s, and 50s

At midcentury, "Italy" remained a geographical expression rather than a political entity. Yet by 1860, the Italian peninsula was transformed into a nation-state under a constitutional monarchy. Count Camillo Cavour (1810–1861), the prime minister of Piedmont—no friend of romantic republicanism—made this possible. His method was a force of arms tied to secret diplomacy.

CAVOUR'S POLICY

Piedmont (officially styled the Kingdom of Sardinia), in northwestern Italy, was the most independent state on the peninsula. The Congress of Vienna had restored the kingdom as a buffer between French and Austrian ambitions. As has been seen, during 1848 and 1849, King Charles Albert of Piedmont twice unsuccessfully fought Austria. After the second defeat, he abdicated in favor of his son, Victor Emmanuel I (r. 1849–1878). In 1852, the new monarch chose Cavour as his prime minister.

A cunning statesman, Cavour had begun political life as a conservative but had gradually moved toward a moderately liberal position. He was deeply imbued with the ideas of the Enlightenment, classical economics, and utilitarianism. Cavour was a nationalist of a new breed who had no respect for Mazzini's ideals. A strong monarchist, Cavour rejected republicanism. Economic and material progress, not romantic ideals, required a large, unified state on the Italian peninsula. The prime minister also be-

lieved only French intervention could defeat Austria and unite Italy. The accession of Napoleon III in France seemed to open the way for such aid.

French Sympathies Cavour used the Crimean War to bring Italy into European politics. Piedmont's small but significant participation in the war allowed Cavour to raise the Italian question at the Paris conference. During the rest of the decade, he achieved further international respectability for Piedmont by opposing Mazzini, who was still attempting to lead nationalist uprisings. By 1858, Cavour represented a moderate liberal, monarchist alternative to both republicanism and reactionary absolutism in Italy.

In January 1858, an Italian named Felice Orsini attempted to assassinate Napoleon III. The incident heightened the emperor's interest in the Italian issue. He also saw Piedmont as a potential ally against Austria. In July 1858, Cavour and Napoleon III met at Plombières in southern France. The two men plotted to provoke a war in Italy that would permit them to defeat Austria.

War with Austria In early 1859, tension grew between Austria and Piedmont as Piedmont mobilized its army. On April 22, Austria demanded that Piedmont demobilize. That allowed Piedmont to claim that Austria was provoking a war. France intervened to aid its ally. On June 4, the Austrians were defeated at Magenta, and on June 24 at Solferino. Meanwhile, revolutions had broken out across northern Italy.

With the Austrians in retreat and the new revolutionary regimes calling for union with Piedmont, Napoleon III feared too extensive a Piedmontese victory. On July 11, he concluded peace with Austria at Villafranca. Piedmont received Lombardy, but Venetia remained under Austrian control. Later that summer, Parma, Modena, Tuscany, and the Romagna voted to unite with Piedmont. (See Map 22–1, page 546.)

Garibaldi's Campaign At this point, the forces of romantic republican nationalism compelled Cavour to pursue the complete unification of northern and southern Italy. In May 1860, Garibaldi landed in Sicily, captured Palermo, and prepared to attack the mainland. By September he controlled the city and kingdom of Naples. For more than two decades Garibaldi had hoped to form a republican Italy, but Cavour forestalled him. He rushed Piedmontese troops south to confront Garibaldi. On the way, they conquered the rest of the Papal States except the area around Rome, which French troops saved for the pope. Garibaldi's nationalism won out over his republicanism, and he accepted Piedmontese domination. In late 1860, Naples and Sicily voted to join the Italian kingdom. (See "Compare & Connect: Nineteenth-Century Nationalism: Two Sides" pages 548–549.)

THE NEW ITALIAN STATE

In March 1861, Victor Emmanuel II was proclaimed king of Italy. Three months later Cavour died. The new state more than ever needed his skills, because Piedmont had, in effect, not so much united Italy as conquered it. The republicans resented the treatment of Garibaldi. The clericals were appalled at the conquest of the Papal States. In the south, armed resistance against the imposition of Piedmontese-style administration continued until 1866. The economies and societies of north and south Italy were incompatible. The south was rural, poor, and backward. The north was industrializing, and its economy was increasingly linked to that of the rest of Europe.

The political framework of the united Italy could not overcome these problems. The constitution, which was that promulgated for Piedmont in 1848, provided for a conservative constitutional monarchy. Parliament consisted of two houses: a senate

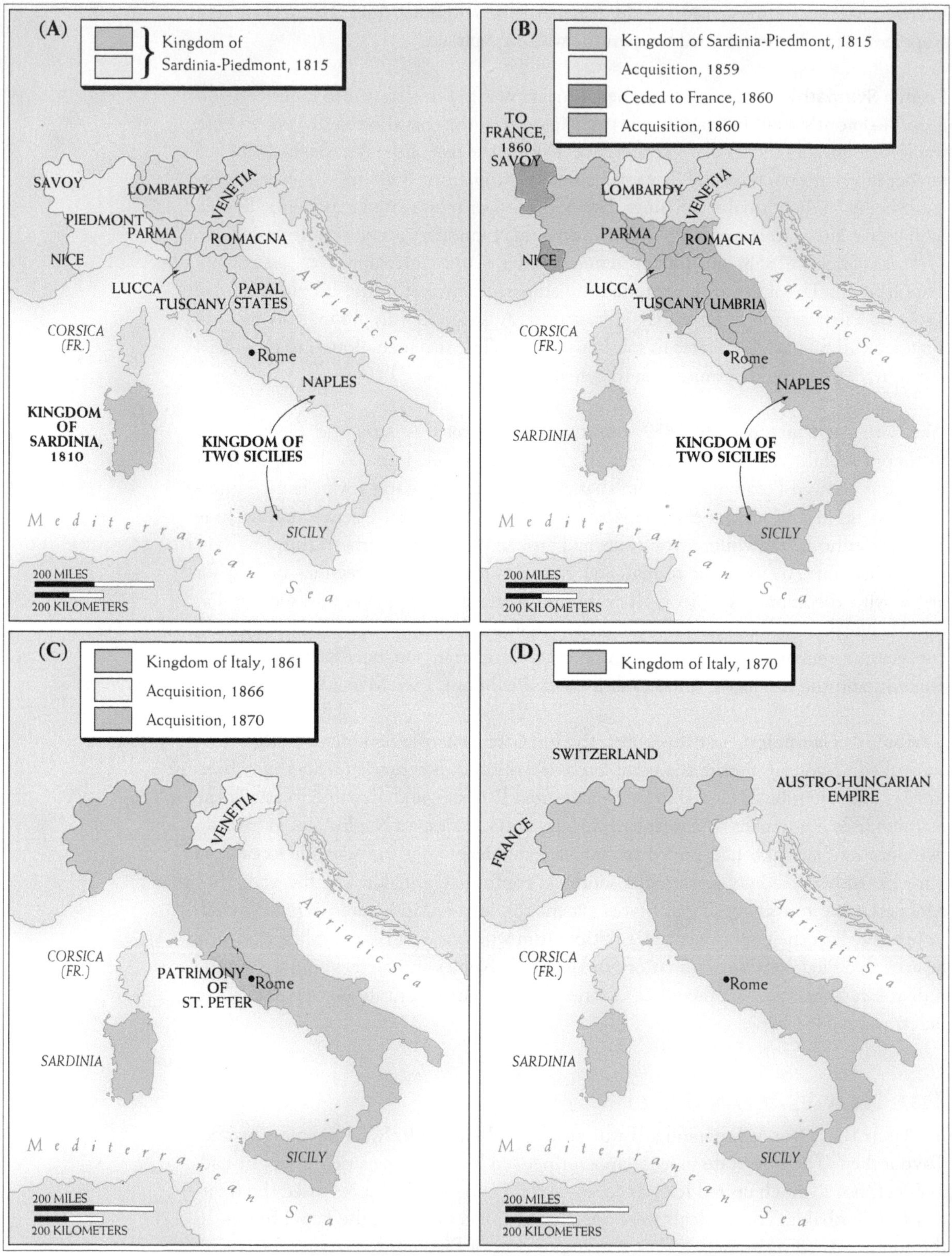

MAP 22–1 **The Unification of Italy** Beginning with the association of Sardinia and Piedmont by the Congress of Vienna in 1815, unification was achieved through the expansion of Piedmont between 1859 and 1870. Both Cavour's statesmanship and the campaigns of ardent nationalists played large roles.

Why was it so difficult to unify Italy?

appointed by the king and a chamber of deputies elected on a narrow franchise. Ministers were responsible to the monarch, not to Parliament. These arrangements did not foster vigorous parliamentary life and Italian politics became a byword for corruption.

Many Italians believed other territories should be added to their nation. The most important of these were Venetia and Rome. The former was gained in 1866 in return for Italy's alliance with Prussia in the Austro-Prussian War. French troops continued to guard Rome and the papacy until the troops were withdrawn during the Franco-Prussian War of 1870. The Italian state then annexed Rome and made it the capital.

QUICK REVIEW

Keys to Italian Unification

- Piedmont's leadership under Count Camillo Cavour
- French assistance
- Victory in war with Austria
- Success of Garibaldi's campaign in the south

GERMAN UNIFICATION

German unification was the most important political development in Europe between 1848 and 1914. (See Map 22–2.) It transformed the balance of economic, military, and international power.

During the 1850s, German unification seemed remote. The political structure of the German-speaking lands was the German Confederation, which had been established at the Congress of Vienna. It was a loose federation of thirty-nine states, the two strongest of which

HOW DID Bismarck use war as a tool for achieving German unification?

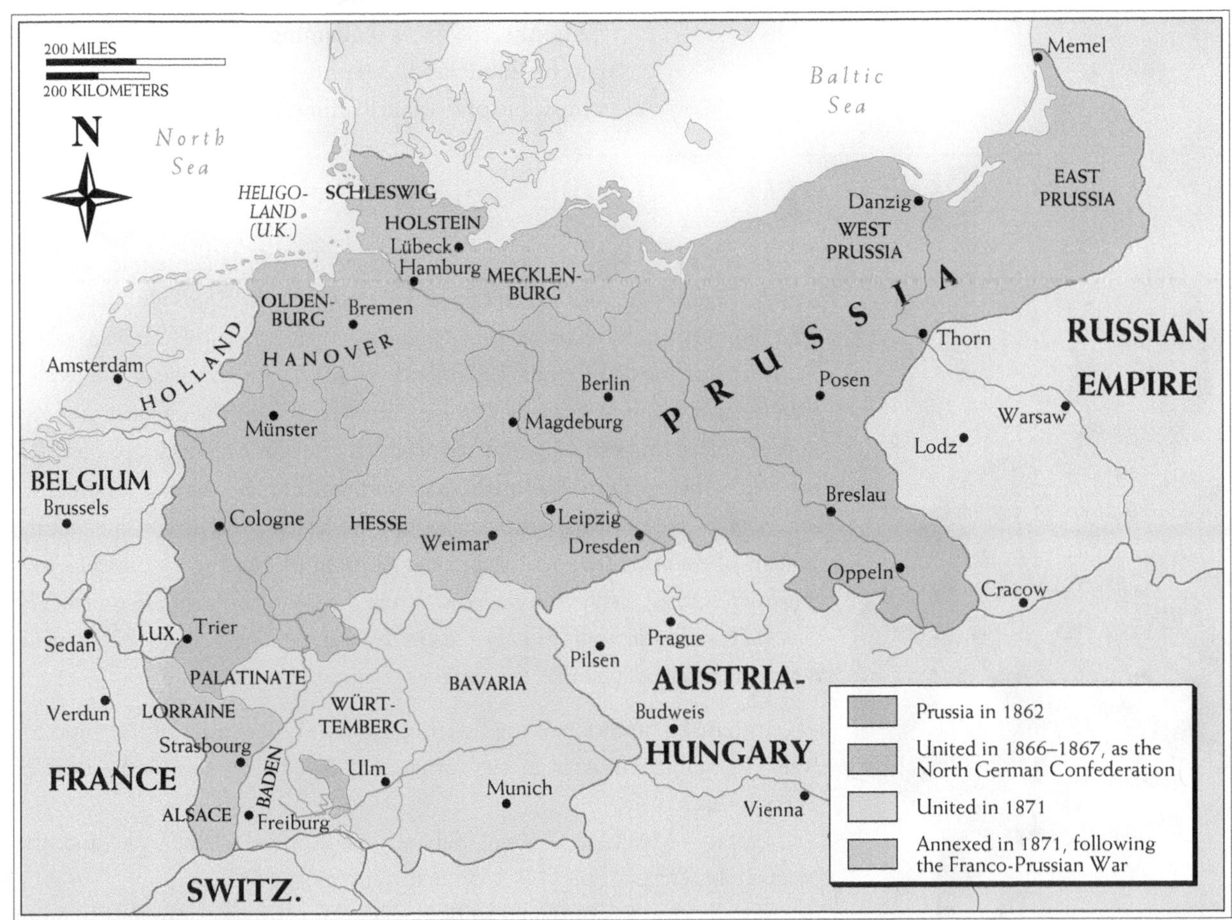

MAP 22–2 **The Unification of Germany** Under Bismarck's leadership, and with the strong support of its royal house, Prussia used diplomatic and military means, on both the German and international stages, to forcibly unify the German states into a strong national entity.

Which neighboring countries were most directly affected by German unification?

COMPARE & CONNECT

NINETEENTH-CENTURY NATIONALISM: TWO SIDES

The second quarter of the nineteenth century witnessed the unification first of Italy and then of Germany. Both processes involved warfare. The Kingdom of Sardinia conquered and united northern Italy, and then Garibaldi led his "Red Shirts" to conquer the south. Prussia united Germany in a series of wars against Denmark, Austria, and France. These two documents illustrate different justifications for the call to military action for unifying each nation. Garibaldi presents his forces as liberators against tyranny. Treitschke makes an argument for the German annexation of Alsace and Lorraine on the grounds of national security and history.

QUESTIONS

1. How does Garibaldi's manifesto turn the war for unification in southern Italy into a popular campaign?
2. How does Garibaldi portray the struggle for unification as a battle against tyranny?
3. On what grounds does Treitschke base the German claim to Alsace and Lorraine?
4. Why does Treitschke contend it is proper to ignore the wishes of the people involved?
5. How could one nationalist, Garibaldi, see his goal as one of popular liberation while another, Treitschke, see his as reclaiming lost regions of a national homeland? Are these two views compatible or distinctly different?

I. GARIBALDI CALLS ITALIANS TO ACT TO UNIFY THEIR NATION

General Giuseppe Garibaldi (1807–1882)

Getty Images, Inc.—Hulton Archive Photos/Museum of the City of New York/Hulton Archive

How might Garibaldi have defined "nation"?

Garibaldi was the most charismatic figure in the drive to Italian unification. He was the leader of guerrilla military forces known as the Red Shirts. In May 1860, after northern Italy had been united under the Kingdom of Sardinia whose monarch was Victor Emmanuel, Garibaldi landed his force of about a thousand men in Sicily and from there they crossed into southern Italy to conquer the kingdom of Naples and make it part of a united Italian state. Garibaldi was himself a republican, but he reconciled himself to supporting Victor Emmanuel. Before leaving Sicily for the mainland, Garibaldi issued this call to arms demanding that the Italians of southern Italy rise against the kingdom of Naples. The various geographical areas he mentions were located from the south northward to Rome. The Tincino River lay in northern Italy and Garibaldi is recalling the participation of his troops in the war that unified the north.

Italians! The Sicilians are fighting against the enemies of Italy and for Italy. To help them with money, arms, and especially men, is the duty of every Italian.

Let the Marches, Umbria, Sabine, the Roman Compagne, and the Neapolitan territory rise, so as to drive the enemy's forces.

If the cities do not offer a sufficient basis for insurrection, let the more resolute throw themselves into the open country. A brave man can always find a weapon. In the name of Heaven, hearken not to the voice of those who cram themselves at well-served tables. Let us arm. Let us fight for our brothers; tomorrow we can fight for ourselves.

A handful of brave men, who have followed me in battles for our country, are advancing with me to the rescue. Italy knows them; they always appear at the hour of danger. Brave and generous companions, they have devoted their lives to their country; they will shed their last drop of blood for it, seeking no other reward than that of a pure conscience.

"Italy and Victor Emmanuel!"—that was our battle-cry when we crossed the Tincino; it will resound into the very depths of Aetna [the volcanic mountain]. As this prophetic battle-cry re-echoes from the hills of Italy to the Tarpeian Mount, the tottering thrones of tyranny will fall to pieces, and the whole country will rise like one man.

Source: "History," *The Annual Register . . .* 1860 (London: F. and J. Rivington, 1861), p. 221 as quoted in Raymond Phineas Stearns, *Pageant of Europe: Sources and Selections from the Renaissance to the Present Day* (New York: Harcourt, Brace and Company, 1948), pp. 583–584.

II. HEINRICH VON TREITSCHKE DEMANDS THE ANNEXATION OF ALSACE AND LORRAINE

The Franco-Prussian War witnessed outbursts of extreme nationalistic rhetoric on both sides. One such voice was that of the German historian Heinrich von Treitschke (1834–1896). In a newspaper article, he demanded the annexation of Alsace and Lorraine from France. He did so even though the population of Alsace wished to remain part of France and German was not the dominant language in the region. He appealed to an earlier time when the region had been German in language and culture, and he asserted that "might makes right" to assure German domination.

The sense of justice to Germany demands the lessening of France. . . .

What is demanded by justice is, at the same time, absolutely necessary for our security. . . .

Every State must seek the guarantees of its own security in itself alone. . . .

In view of our obligation to secure the peace of the world, who will venture to object that the people of Alsace and Lorraine do not want to belong to us? The doctrine of the right of all the branches of the German race to decide on their own destinies, the plausible solution of demagogues without a fatherland, shiver to pieces in presence of the sacred necessity of these great days. These territories are ours by the right of the sword, and we shall dispose of them in virtue of a higher right—the right of the German nation, which will not permit its lost children to remain strangers to the German Empire. We Germans, who know Germany and France, know better than these unfortunates themselves what is good for the people of Alsace. . . . Against their will we shall restore them to their true selves. We have seen with joyful wonder the undying power of the moral forces of history, manifested far too frequently in the immense changes of these days, to place much confidence in the value of a mere popular disinclination. The spirit of a nation lays hold, not only of the generation which lives beside it, but of those who are before and behind it. We appeal from the mistaken wishes of the men who are there today to the wishes of those who were there before them. We appeal to all those strong German men who once stamped the seal of our German nature on the language and manners, the art and the social life of the Upper Rhine. Before the nineteenth century closes, the world will recognize that . . . we were only obeying the dictates of national honor when we made little account of the preferences of the people who live in Alsace today. . . .

At all times the subjection of a German race to France has been an unhealthy thing; today it is an offense against the reason of History—a vassalship of free men to half-educated barbarians. . . .

There is no perfect identity between the political and national frontier of any European country. Not one of the great Powers, and Germany no more than the rest of them, can ever subscribe to the principle that "language alone decides the formation of States." It would be impossible to carry that principle into effect. . . .

The German territory which we demand is ours by nature and by history. . . . In the tempests of the great Revolution the people of Alsace, like all the citizens of France, learned to forget their past. . . .

Most assuredly, the task of reuniting there the broken links between the ages is one of the heaviest that has ever been imposed upon the political forces of our nation. . . .

The people of Alsace are already beginning to doubt the invincibility of their nation, and at all events to divine the mighty growth of the German Empire. Perverse obstinacy, and a thousand French intrigues creeping in the dark, will make every step on the newly conquered soil difficult for us: but our ultimate success is certain, for on our side fights what is stronger than the lying artifices of the stranger—nature herself and the voice of common blood.

Source: From Heinrich von Treitschke, "What We Demand from France" (1870), in Heinrich von Treitschke, *Germany, France, Russia and Islam* (New York: G. P. Putnam's Sons, 1915), pp. 100, 102, 106, 109, 120, 122, 134–135, 153, 158.

by far were Austria and Prussia. Frederick William IV of Prussia had given up thoughts of unification under Prussian leadership. Austria continued to oppose any union that might lessen its influence. Liberal nationalists had not recovered from the humiliations of 1848 and 1849, so they could do little or nothing for unification. What quickly overturned this static situation was a series of domestic political changes and problems within Prussia.

In 1858, Frederick William IV was adjudged insane, and his brother William assumed the regency. William I (r. 1861–1888), who became king in his own right in 1861, was less idealistic than his brother and more of a Prussian patriot. In 1860, his war minister and chief of staff, in an effort to enhance Prussia's military power, proposed to enlarge the army, to increase the number of officers, and to extend the period of conscription from two to three years. The Prussian Parliament, created by the Constitution of 1850, refused to approve the necessary taxes. The liberals, who dominated the body, sought to avoid placing additional power in the hands of the monarchy. For two years, monarch and Parliament were deadlocked.

Bismarck

In September 1862, William I turned for help to the person who, more than any other single individual, shaped the next thirty years of European history: Otto von Bismarck (1815–1898). Bismarck opposed parliamentary government, but not a constitutionalism that preserved a strong monarchy. He understood that Prussia—and later, Germany—must have a strong industrial base. In politics, he was a pragmatist who put more trust in power and action than in ideas.

Upon becoming prime minister in 1862, Bismarck immediately moved against the liberal Parliament. He contended that even without new financial levies, the Prussian constitution permitted the government to carry out its functions on the basis of previously granted taxes. Therefore, taxes could be collected and spent despite the parliamentary refusal to vote them. The army and most of the bureaucracy supported this interpretation of the constitution. In 1863, however, new elections sustained the liberal majority in the Parliament. Bismarck had to find a way to attract popular support away from the liberals and toward the monarchy and the army. He, therefore, set about uniting Germany through the conservative institutions of Prussia. In effect, Bismarck embraced the cause of German nationalism as a strategy to enable Prussian conservatives to outflank Prussian liberals.

The Danish War (1864) Bismarck's vision of a united Germany did not include all German-speaking lands. He intended to exclude Austria from any future united German state. This goal required complex diplomacy.

The Schleswig-Holstein problem gave Bismarck the handle for his policy. The kings of Denmark had longed ruled these two northern duchies, which had never actually become part of Denmark itself. Their populations were a mixture of Germans and Danes. Holstein, where Germans predominated, belonged to the German Confederation. In 1863, the Danish Parliament moved to incorporate both duchies into Denmark. The smaller states of the German Confederation proposed an all-German war to halt this move. Bismarck, however, wanted Prussia to act alone or only in cooperation with Austria. Together, the two large states easily defeated Denmark in 1864.

The Danish defeat increased Bismarck's personal prestige and strengthened his political hand. Over the next two years, he managed to maneuver Austria into war with Prussia. In August 1865, the two powers negotiated the Convention of Gastein, which put Austria in charge of Holstein and Prussia in charge of Schleswig. Bismarck then mended other diplomatic fences. He had gained Russian sympathy in 1863 by supporting Russia's suppression of a Polish revolt, and he persuaded Napoleon III to promise neutrality in an Austro-Prussian conflict. In April 1866, Bismarck promised Italy Venetia if it attacked Austria in support of Prussia when war broke out. Now Bismarck had to provoke his war.

The Austro-Prussian War (1866) Constant Austro-Prussian tensions had arisen over the administration of Schleswig and Holstein. Bismarck ordered the Prussian forces to be as obnoxious as possible to the Austrians. On June 1, 1866, Austria appealed to the German Confederation to intervene in the dispute. Bismarck claimed that this request violated the 1864 alliance and the Convention of Gastein. The Seven Weeks' War, which resulted in the summer of 1866, led to the decisive defeat of Austria. The Treaty of Prague, which ended the conflict on August 23, was lenient toward Austria, which lost only Venetia, but permanently excluded the Austrian Habsburgs from German affairs. Prussia had thus established itself as the only major power among the German states.

The North German Confederation In 1867, Prussia annexed the German states that had supported Austria during the war and deposed their rulers. Under Prussian leadership, all Germany north of the Main River now formed the North German Confederation. Each state retained its own local government, but all military forces were under federal control. The president of the federation was the king of Prussia, represented by his chancellor, Bismarck. A legislature consisted of two houses: a federal council, or *Bundesrat*, composed of members appointed by the governments of the states, and a lower house, or *Reichstag*, chosen by universal male suffrage.

Bismarck embraced a democratic franchise because he sensed that the peasants would vote for conservatives. Moreover, the *Reichstag* had little real power. The constitution of the North German Confederation, which, after 1871, became the constitution of the German Empire, possessed some of the appearances, but none of the substance, of liberalism. Germany was, in effect, a military monarchy.

Bismarck's spectacular successes overwhelmed the liberal opposition in the Prussian Parliament. The liberals were split between those who prized liberalism and those who supported unification. In the end, nationalism proved more attractive. Bismarck had crushed the Prussian liberals by making the monarchy and the army the most popular institutions in the country.

The Franco-Prussian War and the German Empire (1870–1871)

Bismarck now wanted to complete unification by bringing the states of southern Germany into the newly established confederation. Spain gave him the excuse. In 1868, a military coup deposed the corrupt Bourbon queen of Spain, Isabella II (r. 1833–1868). To replace her, the Spaniards chose Prince Leopold of Hohenzollern-Sigmaringen, a Catholic cousin of William I of Prussia. On June 19, 1870, Leopold accepted the Spanish crown with Prussian blessings. Bismarck knew that France would object strongly to a Hohenzollern Spain. On July 12, Leopold's father renounced his son's candidacy for the Spanish throne, fearing the issue would cause war between Prussia and France.

There the matter might have rested had it not been for the impetuosity of the French and the guile of Bismarck. On July 13, the French government instructed their ambassador to Prussia to ask William for assurances he would tolerate no future Spanish candidacy for Leopold. The king refused but said he might take the question under further consideration. Later that day he sent Bismarck, who was in Berlin, a telegram

The proclamation of the German Empire in the Hall of Mirrors at Versailles, January 18, 1871, after the defeat of France in the Franco-Prussian War. Kaiser Wilhelm I is standing at the top of the steps under the flags. Bismarck is in the center in a white uniform.

Bildarchiv Preussischer Kulturbesitz

What was the symbolic importance of holding this ceremony in Versailles?

reporting the substance of the meeting. The peaceful resolution of the controversy had disappointed the chancellor, who desperately wanted a war with France to complete unification. The king's telegram gave him a new opportunity to provoke war. Bismarck released an edited version of the dispatch that made it appear that William had insulted the French ambassador. The idea was to goad France into declaring war.

The French government fell for Bismarck's bait and declared war on July 19. Once the conflict erupted, the southern German states, honoring treaties of 1866, joined Prussia against France, whose defeat was not long in coming. France's defeat was capped with the capitulation of Paris on January 28, 1871.

Ten days earlier, in the Hall of Mirrors at the Palace of Versailles, the German Empire had been proclaimed. The German princes requested William to accept the title of German emperor. The princes remained heads of their respective states within the new empire. Through the peace settlement with France, Germany annexed Alsace and part of Lorraine and forced the French to pay a large indemnity.

QUICK REVIEW

Keys to German Unification

- Victory in the Danish War (1864)
- Victory in the Austro-Prussian War (1866)
- Creation of the North German Federation (1867)
- Victory in the Franco-Prussian War (1870–1871)

Both the fact and the manner of German unification produced long-range effects in Europe. A powerful new state had been created in north central Europe. It was rich in natural resources and talented citizens. Militarily and economically, the German Empire would be far stronger than Prussia had been alone. The unification of Germany was also a blow to European liberalism, because the new state was a conservative creation.

FRANCE: FROM LIBERAL EMPIRE TO THE THIRD REPUBLIC

WHAT EVENTS led to the establishment of a Third Republic in France?

Historians divide the reign of Napoleon III (r. 1852–1870) into the years of the authoritarian empire and those of the liberal empire. The year of division is 1860. After the coup in December 1851, Napoleon III had controlled the legislature, censored the press, and harassed political dissidents. From the late 1850s onward, Napoleon III began to modify his policy. In 1860, he concluded a free-trade treaty with Britain and permitted freer debate in the legislature. By the late 1860s, he had relaxed the press laws and permitted labor unions. In 1870, he allowed the leaders of the moderates in the legislature to form a ministry, and he also agreed to a liberal constitution that made the ministers responsible to the legislature.

Napoleon III's liberal concessions sought to shore up domestic support to compensate for his failures in foreign policy. By 1860, he had lost control of the diplomacy of Italian unification. Between 1861 and 1867, he had supported a disastrous military expedition against Mexico. In 1866, France had watched passively while Bismarck and Prussia reorganized German affairs. The war of 1870 against Germany had been the French government's last and most disastrous attempt to shore up its foreign policy and secure domestic popularity.

The Second Empire, but not the war, came to an inglorious end with the Battle of Sedan in September 1870. The emperor was captured and then allowed to go to England, where he died in 1873. Shortly after news of Sedan reached Paris, a republic was proclaimed and a government of national defense established. Paris itself was soon under Prussian siege, and the government moved to Bordeaux. Paris finally surrendered in January 1871, but France had been ready to sue for peace long before.

THE PARIS COMMUNE

The division between the provinces and Paris became sharper after the fighting with Germany stopped. Monarchists dominated the new National Assembly elected in February. For the time being, the assembly gave executive power to Adolphe Thiers (1797–1877) who negotiated a settlement with Prussia (the Treaty of Frankfurt).

Many Parisians felt betrayed by the monarchist National Assembly. They elected a new municipal government, called the *Paris Commune*, which was formally proclaimed on March 28, 1871. The Commune intended to administer Paris separately from the rest of France. Radicals and socialists of all stripes participated in the Commune. In April, the National Assembly surrounded Paris with an army. On May 8, this army bombarded the city. On May 21, it broke through the city's defenses. During the next seven days, the troops killed about 20,000 inhabitants while the communards shot scores of hostages.

THE THIRD REPUBLIC

The National Assembly backed into a republican form of government against its will. Its monarchist majority was divided in loyalty between the House of Bourbon and the House of Orléans. While the monarchists quarreled among themselves, events marched on. By September 1873, the indemnity had been paid, and the Prussian occupation troops had withdrawn. Thiers was ousted from office and replaced with a president more sympathetic to the monarchist cause, Marshal Patrice MacMahon (1808–1893). In 1875, the National Assembly, still monarchist in sentiment, but unable to find a king, decided to regularize the political system. It adopted a law that provided for a Chamber of Deputies elected by universal male suffrage, a Senate chosen indirectly, and a president elected by the two legislative houses. This rather simple republican system had resulted from the bickering and frustration of the monarchists.

THE DREYFUS AFFAIR

The greatest trauma of the Third Republic occurred over what became known as the *Dreyfus affair*. On December 22, 1894, a French military court found Captain Alfred Dreyfus (1859–1935) guilty of passing secret information to the German army. The evidence against him was flimsy and was later revealed to have been forged. Someone in the officer corps had been passing documents to the Germans, and it suited the army investigators to accuse Dreyfus, who was Jewish. After Dreyfus had been sent to Devil's Island, a notorious prison in French Guiana, however, secrets continued to flow to the German army. In 1896, a new head of French counterintelligence reexamined the Dreyfus file and found evidence of forgery. A different officer was implicated, but a military court acquitted him of all charges.

The prosecution of Captain Alfred Dreyfus, who is shown here standing on the right at his military trial, provoked the most serious crisis of the Third Republic.

Why was the Dreyfus case so divisive? What were its long-term political repercussions?

By then the affair had provoked near-hysterical public debate. The army, the French Catholic Church, political conservatives, and vehemently anti-Semitic newspapers contended that Dreyfus was guilty. In 1898, however, the novelist Émile Zola (1840–1902) published a newspaper article entitled "*J'accuse*" ("I accuse"), in which he contended that the army had denied due process to Dreyfus and had suppressed or forged evidence. Zola was convicted of libel and fled to England to avoid serving a one-year prison sentence.

Zola was only one of numerous liberals, radicals, and socialists who had begun to demand a new trial for Dreyfus. In August 1898, further evidence of forged material came to light. The officer responsible for those forgeries committed suicide in jail, but a new military trial again convicted Dreyfus. The president of France immediately pardoned him, however, and eventually, in 1906, a civilian court set aside the results of both military trials.

The Dreyfus case divided France as no issue had done since the Paris Commune. By its conclusion, the conservatives were on the defensive. They had allowed themselves to persecute an innocent person and to manufacture false evidence against him to protect themselves from disclosure. They had also embraced violent anti-Semitism. On the political left, radicals, republicans, and socialists developed an informal alliance, which outlived the Dreyfus case itself. These groups realized that the political left had to support republican institutions to achieve its goals. Nonetheless, the political, religious, and racial divisions and suspicions growing out of the Dreyfus affair continued to divide the Third Republic until France's defeat by Germany in 1940.

QUICK REVIEW

Captain Alfred Dreyfus (1859–1935)

- December 22, 1894: found guilty of espionage
- Conviction stirred near-hysterical public debate
- 1906: civilian court voids his conviction

THE HABSBURG EMPIRE

WHY WAS nationalism such a threat to the Habsburg Empire?

In the age of national states, liberal institutions, and industrialism, the Habsburg domains remained primarily dynastic, absolutist, and agrarian. The Habsburg response to the revolts of 1848–1849 had been to reassert absolutism. During the 1850s, Emperor Francis Joseph's (r. 1848–1916) ministers attempted to impose a centralized administration on the empire. The system amounted to a military and bureaucratic regime dominated by German-speaking Austrians. Although this system provoked resentment, it eventually floundered because of setbacks in foreign affairs.

Austrian refusal to support Russia during the Crimean War meant the new tsar Alexander II (r. 1855–1881) would no longer help preserve Habsburg rule in Hungary, as Nicholas I had done in 1849. The Austrian defeat in 1859 at the hands of France and Piedmont and the subsequent loss of territory in Italy confirmed the necessity for a new domestic policy. For seven years the emperor, the civil servants, the aristocrats, and the politicians tried to construct a viable system of government.

FORMATION OF THE DUAL MONARCHY

In 1860, Francis Joseph issued the October Diploma, which created a federation among the states and provinces of the empire. There were to be local diets dominated by the landed classes and a single imperial parliament. The Magyar nobility of Hungary, however, rejected the plan.

Consequently, in 1861, the emperor issued the February Patent, which set up an entirely different form of government. It established a bicameral imperial parliament, or *Reichsrat*, with an upper chamber appointed by the emperor and an indirectly elected lower chamber. Again, the Magyars refused to cooperate in a system designed to give political dominance in the empire to German-speaking Austrians. Nevertheless, for six years, the February Patent governed the empire, and it prevailed in Austria proper until 1918. Ministers were responsible to the emperor, not the *Reichsrat*, and civil liberties were not guaranteed. Armies could be levied and taxes raised without parliamentary consent. When the *Reichsrat* was not in session, the emperor could simply rule by decree.

Meanwhile, secret negotiations between the emperor and the Magyars produced no concrete result until the Prussian defeat of Austria in the summer of 1866. Francis

Joseph now had to come to terms with the Magyars. The subsequent Ausgleich, or Compromise, of 1867 transformed the Habsburg Empire into a dual monarchy known as Austria-Hungary. Francis Joseph was crowned king of Hungary in Budapest in 1867. Except for the common monarch, army, and foreign relations, Austria and Hungary became almost wholly separate states. The Compromise reconciled the Magyars to Habsburg rule. They had achieved the free hand they had long wanted in Hungary.

Unrest of Nationalities

The Compromise of 1867 introduced two different principles of political legitimacy into the two sections of the Habsburg Empire. In Hungary, political loyalty was based on nationality because Hungary had been recognized as a distinct part of the monarchy on the basis of nationalism. In the rest of the Habsburg domains, the principle of legitimacy meant dynastic loyalty to the emperor. Many of the other nationalities wished to achieve the same type of settlement that the Hungarians had won, or to govern themselves, or as time went on, to unite with fellow nationals who lived outside the empire. (See Map 22–3.)

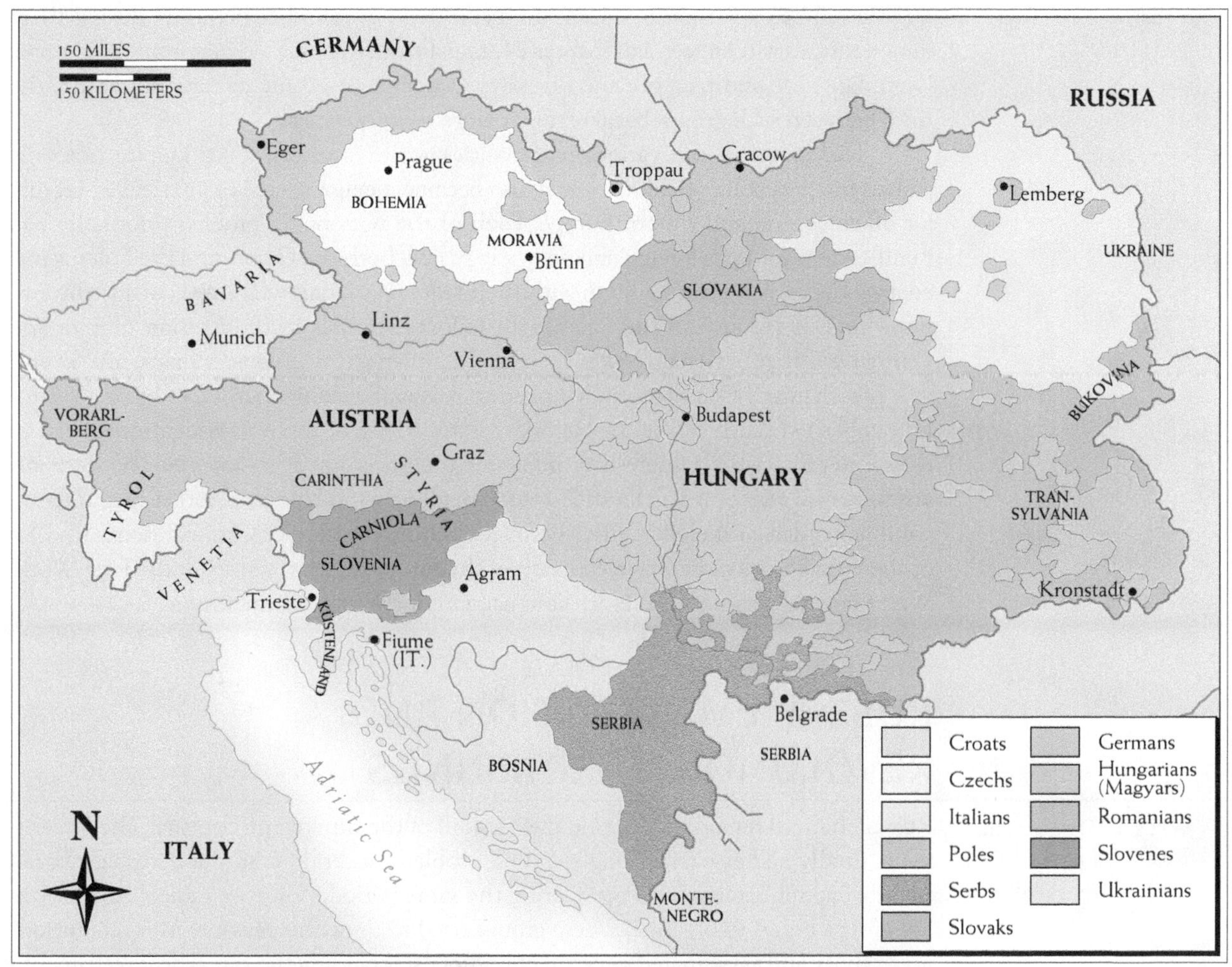

MAP 22–3 Nationalities within the Habsburg Empire The patchwork appearance reflects the unusual problem of the numerous ethnic groups that the Habsburgs could not, of course, meld into a modern national state. Only the Magyars were recognized in 1867, leaving nationalist Czechs, Slovaks, and the others chronically dissatisfied.

Why was ethnic diversity in the Habsburg Empire an impediment to building a strong national state?

Many of these other national groups—including the Czechs, the Ruthenians, the Romanians, and the Croatians—opposed the Compromise of 1867 that, in effect, had permitted the German-speaking Austrians and the Hungarian Magyars to dominate all other nationalities within the empire. The most vocal critics were the Czechs of Bohemia. They favored a policy of "trialism," or triple monarchy, in which the Czechs would have a position similar to that of the Hungarians. In 1871, Francis Joseph was willing to accept this concept. The Magyars, however, vetoed it.

For more than twenty years, generous patronage and posts in the bureaucracy placated the Czechs. By the 1890s, however, Czech nationalism again became more strident. In 1897, Francis Joseph gave the Czechs and the Germans equality of language in various localities. Thereafter, the Germans in the Austrian *Reichsrat* opposed these measures by disrupting Parliament. The Czechs replied in kind. By the turn of the century, this obstructionism had paralyzed parliamentary life. The emperor ruled by imperial decree through the bureaucracy. In effect, by 1914, constitutionalism was a dead letter in Austria.

There is reason to believe nationalism became stronger during the last quarter of the nineteenth century. Language became the single most important factor in defining a nation. The expansion of education made this possible. Furthermore, during these same years, as will be seen in Chapter 24, racial thinking became important in Europe. Once language and race became the ways to define an ethnic or national group, the lines between such groups became much more sharply drawn.

The unrest of the various nationalities within the Habsburg Empire not only caused internal political difficulties; it also became a major source of political instability for all of central and eastern Europe. Each of the nationality problems normally had ramifications for both foreign and domestic policy. Both the Croats and the Poles wanted an independent state in union with their fellow nationals who lived outside the empire—and in the case of the Poles, with fellow nationals in the Russian Empire and Germany. Other national groups, such as Ukrainians, Romanians, Italians, and Bosnians, saw themselves as potentially linked to Russia, Romania, Serbia, Italy, or a yet-to-be established south Slavic, or Yugoslav, state. Many of these nationalities looked to Russia to protect their interests or influence the government in Vienna. The Romanians were also concerned about the Romanian minority in Hungary. Serbia sought to expand its borders to include Serbs who lived within Habsburg or Ottoman territory. Out of these Balkan tensions emerged much of the turmoil that would spark the First World War. Many of the same ethnic tensions account for warfare in the former Yugoslavia.

RUSSIA: EMANCIPATION AND REVOLUTIONARY STIRRINGS

WHY DID reform in Russia fail to produce political stability?

Russia changed remarkably during the last half of the nineteenth century. The government finally addressed the long-standing problem of serfdom and undertook a broad range of administrative reforms. During the same period, however, radical revolutionary groups began to organize. These groups tried to draw the peasants into revolutionary activity and assassinated government officials, including the tsar. The government's response was renewed repression.

Reforms of Alexander II

Russia's defeat in the Crimean War and its humiliation in the Treaty of Paris compelled the government to reconsider its domestic policies. The debacle of the war had made reform both necessary and possible. Alexander II (r. 1855–1881) took advantage of this turn of events to institute the most extensive restructuring of Russian society and administration since Peter the Great. Like Peter, Alexander imposed his reforms from the top.

Abolition of Serfdom In Russia, serfdom had changed little since the eighteenth century, although every other nation on the Continent had abandoned it. In March 1856, at the conclusion of the Crimean War, Alexander II announced his intention to abolish serfdom. He had decided that its abolition was necessary if Russia was to remain a great power. For five years, government commissions wrestled over how to implement the tsar's desire. Finally, in February 1861, despite opposition from the nobility and the landlords, Alexander II ended serfdom.

The actual emancipation law was a disappointment, however, because land did not accompany freedom. Serfs immediately received the personal right to marry without their landlord's permission, as well as the rights to buy and sell property, to sue in court, and to pursue trades. What they did not receive was free title to their land. They had to pay for their land over a period of forty-nine years and would not receive title to the land until the debt was paid. The redemption payments led to almost unending difficulty. Poor harvests made it impossible for many peasants to keep up with the payments, and they fell increasingly behind in their debt. The situation was not remedied until 1906, when, during the widespread revolutionary unrest following the Japanese defeat of Russia in 1905, the government grudgingly completed the process of emancipation by canceling the remaining debts.

Reform of Local Government and the Judicial System The abolition of serfdom required the reorganization of local government and the judicial system. The authority of village communes replaced that of the landlord over the peasant. The nobility were given a larger role in local administration through a system of provincial and county *zemstvos*, or councils, organized in 1864. These councils were to oversee local matters, such as bridge and road repair, education, and agricultural improvement. The *zemstvos*, however, were underfunded, and many of them remained ineffective.

In 1864, Alexander II issued a new statute on the judiciary that for the first time introduced Western European legal principles into Russia. These included equality before the law, impartial hearings, uniform procedures, judicial independence, and trial by jury. The new system was far from perfect. The judges were not genuinely independent, and the tsar could increase as well as reduce sentences. Certain offenses, such as those involving the press, were not tried before a jury. Nonetheless, the new courts were both more efficient and less corrupt than the old system.

Military Reform The government also reformed the army. Russia possessed the largest army on the Continent, but it had floundered badly in the Crimean War. In the 1860s, the army lowered the period of service from twenty-five to fifteen years and relaxed discipline slightly. In 1874, the enlistment period was lowered to six years of active duty and nine years in the reserves. All males were subject to military service after the age of twenty.

Repression in Poland Alexander's reforms became more measured shortly after the Polish Rebellion of 1863. As in 1830, Polish nationalists attempted to overthrow Russian dominance. Once again the Russian army suppressed the rebellion. Alexander II then moved to Russify Poland. Russian law, language, and administration were imposed on all areas of Polish life. Henceforth, until the close of World War I, Poland was treated as merely another Russian province.

As the Polish suppression demonstrated, Alexander II was a reformer only within the limits of his own autocracy. His changes in Russian life failed to create new loyalty to, or gratitude for, the government among his subjects. Consequently, although

Tsar Alexander II (r. 1855–1881) was assassinated on March 1, 1881. The assassins first threw a bomb that wounded several Imperial guards. When the tsar stopped his carriage to see the wounded, the assassins threw a second bomb that killed him.

Bildarchiv Preussischer Kulturbesitz

How did the event depicted here alter the course of Russian history?

Alexander II became known as the Tsar Liberator, he was never popular. After an attempt was made on his life in 1866, Russia increasingly became a police state. This new repression fueled the activity of radical groups within Russia. Their actions, in turn, made the autocracy more reactionary.

Revolutionaries

The initial reforms of Alexander II had raised great hopes among Russian students and intellectuals, but they soon became discontented with the limited character of the reforms. These students formed a revolutionary movement known as *populism*. They sought a social revolution based on the communal life of the Russian peasants. The chief radical society was called *Land and Freedom*.

In the early 1870s, hundreds of young Russian men and women took their revolutionary message into the countryside. They intended to live with the peasants, to gain their trust, and to teach them about the peasant's role in the coming revolution. The bewildered and distrustful peasants turned most of the youths over to the police. In the winter of 1877–1878, almost two hundred students were tried. Most were acquitted or given light sentences, because they had been held for months in preventive detention and because the court believed a display of mercy might lessen public sympathy for the young revolutionaries. The court even suggested the tsar might wish to pardon those students given heavier sentences. The tsar refused and let it be known he favored heavy penalties for all persons involved in revolutionary activity. Thereafter, the revolutionaries decided the tsarist regime must be attacked directly. They adopted a policy of terrorism.

In 1879, Land and Freedom split into two groups. One advocated educating the peasants, and it soon dissolved. The other, known as *The People's Will*, was dedicated to the overthrow of the autocracy. On March 1, 1881, a bomb hurled by a member of The People's Will killed Alexander II. Four men and two women were sentenced to death for the deed. The emergence of such dedicated revolutionary opposition was as much a part of the reign of Alexander II as were his reforms. The limited character of those reforms convinced many Russians that the autocracy could never truly redirect Russian society.

The reign of Alexander III (r. 1881–1894) strengthened that pessimism. Some slight improvements were made to conditions in Russian factories, but Alexander III sought primarily to roll back his father's reforms. In effect, he confirmed all the evils that the revolutionaries saw as inherent in autocratic government. His son, Nicholas II (r. 1894–1917), would discover that autocracy could not survive the pressures of the twentieth century.

GREAT BRITAIN: TOWARD DEMOCRACY

WHAT FORCES led to the expansion of democracy in Great Britain?

While the continental nations became unified and struggled toward internal political restructuring, Great Britain symbolized the confident liberal state. Britain was not without its difficulties and domestic conflicts, but it seemed able to deal with them through its existing political institutions. (See "Encountering the Past: The Arrival of Penny Postage.")

ENCOUNTERING THE PAST

The Arrival of Penny Postage

Communication systems help draw nations together and are essential to the functioning of popular government. Thus, the inexpensive postal system was one of the nineteenth century's more significant innovations, and the British government led the way in its development.

Early postal systems charged by weight and distance to delivery, and the receiver, not the sender, was liable for the cost of delivery. High postage made newspapers expensive and encouraged inventive strategies for avoiding payment. In 1837, an English reformer, Rowland Hill (1795–1879), proposed a simple new system. He suggested low uniform rates for each category of mail (letters, newspapers, etc.) regardless of distance and charged the sender with paying the postage. A system known as the Uniform Penny Post was launched in 1840 and became an instant success. By 1849, it was delivering 329 million items annually. Low cost meant almost everyone could afford to send letters, and the postal service provided a huge number of new jobs in the public sector. In 1874, an international treaty, the Universal Postal Union, guaranteed that postage paid in a sender's nation would assure delivery anywhere in the world.

Hill also proposed the self-adhesive postage stamp—a small receipt pasted to the cover of an item to indicate that delivery costs had been paid. The first stamp bore only the simple legend, "Postage One Penny." Governments soon began to print more elaborate stamps from engraved plates and frequently to alter their design to frustrate forgers. As the number of stamps and postal systems multiplied, the hobby of stamp collecting was born.

With the new British postal system, the volume of mail vastly increased as did the number of postal workers involved in sorting and delivering it.

Image Works/Mary Evans Picture Library Ltd.

How did the development of an inexpensive postal system help bind British communities together?

WHAT POSTAGE innovations did Rowland Hill introduce? What were their effects on society?

The Second Reform Act (1867)

By the early 1860s, most observers realized the franchise would again have to be expanded. In 1866, Lord Russell's Liberal ministry introduced a reform bill that a coalition of traditional Conservatives and antidemocratic Liberals defeated. Russell resigned, and the Conservative Lord Derby (1799–1869) replaced him. A surprise then occurred. The Conservative ministry, led in the House of Commons by Benjamin Disraeli (1804–1881), introduced its own reform bill in 1867. As the debate proceeded, Disraeli accepted one amendment after another and expanded the electorate well beyond the limits the Liberals had earlier proposed. The final measure increased the number of voters from approximately 1,430,000 to 2,470,000. Britain had taken a major step toward democracy.

Disraeli hoped the Conservatives would receive the gratitude of the new voters. Because reform was inevitable, it was best for the Conservatives to enjoy the credit for it. The immediate election of 1868, however, dashed Disraeli's hopes. William Gladstone (1809–1898) became the new prime minister.

In a House of Commons debate, William Ewart Gladstone, standing on the right, is attacking Benjamin Disraeli, who sits with legs crossed and arms folded. Gladstone served in the British Parliament from the 1830s through the 1890s. Four times the Liberal Party prime minister, he was responsible for guiding major reforms through Parliament. Disraeli, regarded as the founder of modern British conservatism, served as prime minister from 1874 to 1880.

Image Works/Mary Evans Picture Library Ltd.

What were the most important political differences between Gladstone and Disraeli?

Gladstone's Great Ministry (1868–1874)

Gladstone's ministry of 1868 to 1874 witnessed the culmination of classical British liberalism. Those institutions that remained the preserve of the aristocracy and the Anglican church were opened to people from other classes and religious denominations. In 1870, competitive examinations for the civil service replaced patronage. In 1871, the purchase of officers' commissions in the army was abolished. The same year, Anglican religious requirements for the faculties of Oxford and Cambridge universities were removed. The Ballot Act of 1872 introduced voting by secret ballot. The most momentous measure of Gladstone's first ministry was the Education Act of 1870. For the first time in British history, the government assumed the responsibility for establishing and running elementary schools.

These reforms were typically liberal. They sought to remove abuses without destroying institutions and to permit all able citizens to compete on the grounds of ability and merit. They tried to avoid the potential danger to a democratic state of an illiterate citizenry. These reforms were also a mode of state building, because they reinforced loyalty to the nation by abolishing sources of discontent.

Disraeli in Office (1874–1880)

The liberal policy of creating popular support for the nation by extending political liberties and reforming abuses had its conservative counterpart in concern for social reform. Disraeli succeeded Gladstone as prime minister in 1874, when the election produced sharp divisions among Liberal Party voters over religion, education, and the sale of alcohol.

Disraeli believed in paternalistic legislation to protect the weak and ease class antagonisms, but he had few specific programs or ideas. The significant social legislation of his ministry stemmed primarily from the efforts of his home secretary, Richard Cross (1823–1914). The Public Health Act of 1875 consolidated previous legislation on sanitation and reaffirmed the duty of the state to interfere with private property to protect health and physical well-being. Through the Artisan Dwelling Act of 1875, the government became actively involved in providing housing for the working class. That same year, in an important symbolic gesture, the Conservative majority in Parliament gave new protection to British trade unions and allowed them to raise picket lines.

The Irish Question

In 1880, a second Gladstone ministry took office after an agricultural depression and an unpopular foreign policy undermined the Conservative government. In 1884, with Conservative cooperation, a third reform act gave the vote to most male farm workers. The major issue of the decade, however, was Ireland. From the late 1860s onward, Irish nationalists had sought to achieve **home rule** for Ireland, by which they meant Irish control of local government.

home rule Government of a country or locality by its own citizens.

During his first ministry, Gladstone addressed the Irish question through two major pieces of legislation. In 1869, he disestablished the Church of Ireland, the Irish branch of the Anglican church. Henceforth, Irish Roman Catholics would not pay taxes to support the hated Protestant church, to which few of the Irish belonged. Second, in 1870, the Liberal ministry sponsored a land act that provided compensation to those Irish tenant farmers who were evicted and loans for those who wished to purchase their land. Throughout the 1870s, the Irish question continued to fester. Land remained the center of the agitation. The organization of the Irish Land League in the late 1870s led to intense agitation and intimidation of landlords, who were often Protestants of English descent. The leader of the Irish movement for a just land settlement and for home rule was Charles Stewart Parnell (1846–1891). In 1881, the second Gladstone ministry passed another Irish land act that strengthened tenant rights. It was accompanied, however, by a Coercion Act to restore law and order to Ireland.

By 1885, Parnell had organized eighty-five Irish members of the House of Commons into a tightly disciplined party. In the election of 1885, the Irish Party emerged holding the balance of power between the English Liberals and Conservatives. In December 1885, Gladstone announced his support of home rule for Ireland. Parnell gave his votes to a Liberal ministry. The home rule issue then split the Liberal Party. In 1886, a group known as the Liberal Unionists joined with the Conservatives to defeat home rule. Gladstone called for a new election, but the Liberals were defeated. They remained divided, and Ireland remained firmly under English administration.

The new Conservative ministry of Lord Salisbury (1830–1903) attempted to reconcile the Irish to British rule through public works and administrative reform. The policy, which was tied to further coercion, had only marginal success. In 1892, Gladstone returned to power. A second Home Rule Bill passed the House of Commons but was defeated in the House of Lords. There the Irish question stood until after the turn of the century. The Conservatives sponsored a land act in 1903 that carried out the final transfer of land to tenant ownership. Ireland became a country of small farms. In 1912, a Liberal ministry passed the third Home Rule Bill. Under the provisions of the House of Lords Act of 1911, which curbed the power of the Lords, the bill had to pass the Commons three times over the Lords' veto to become law. The third passage occurred in the summer of 1914, but the implementation of home rule was suspended for the duration of World War I.

Normal British domestic issues could not be resolved because of the political divisions Ireland created. The split of the Liberal Party proved especially harmful to the cause of further social and political reform. People who could agree about reform could not agree about Ireland, and the Irish problem seemed more important. Because the two traditional parties failed to deal with the social questions by the turn of the century, a newly organized Labour Party began to fill the vacuum.

CONSOLIDATION OF STATES (1854–1900)

1854–1856	The Crimean War
1855	Alexander II becomes tsar
1859	Piedmont and France fight Austria
1860	Garibaldi invades southern Italy
1861	Austria issues the February Patent; Proclamation of the Kingdom of Italy (March 17); Russia abolishes serfdom
1862	Bismarck becomes prime minister of Prussia
1863	Russia suppresses the Polish Rebellion
1864	Danish-Prussian War
1866	Austro-Prussian War; Venetia ceded to Italy
1867	North German Confederation formed; formation of the Dual Monarchy; Hungary and Austria; Britain's Second Reform Act
1868	Gladstone becomes prime minister of Britain
1870	Franco-Prussian War begins (July 19); Third Republic proclaimed in France (September 4); Italian state annexes Rome (October 2)
1871	The German Empire proclaimed (January 18); Paris Commune (March 28–May 28); Treaty of Frankfurt between France and Germany (May 1)
1872	Introduction of the secret ballot in Britain
1874	Disraeli becomes prime minister of Britain
1880	Gladstone's second ministry
1881	Alexander II assassinated; Alexander III succeeds
1884	Britain's Third Reform Act
1886	Lord Salisbury becomes prime minister of Britain
1892	Gladstone's third ministry
1894	Nicholas II becomes tsar

SUMMARY

WHY WAS the Crimean War faught?

The Crimean War (1853–1856) Russia's attempts to expand its influence over the Ottoman Empire resulted in the Crimean War. France and Britain were hardly natural allies of the Ottomans, but because they did not want Russian power to grow in a region where they had extensive naval and commercial interest, they declared war on Russia in March 1854. The war was a debacle for all parties, made all the more embarrassing by the presence of journalists and photographers who recorded the ineptness on all sides. The Russian mistakes were worse than the British and French mistakes, and the March 1856 Treaty of Paris required Russia to give up territories and claims. Russia lost the image of invincibility that the nation had earned by defeating Napoleon. The Concert of Europe, too, was a casualty of the war. *page 542*

HOW DID the Ottoman Empire attempt to reform itself?

Reforms in the Ottoman Empire During the Tanzimat era, the Ottoman Empire underwent significant reforms. Under the *Hatt-i Sharif*, in 1839, and the *Hatt-i Hümayun*, in 1856, the economy was liberalized, corruption reduced, and all Ottoman subjects were granted civic equality regardless of religion. The rights of non-Muslims and foreigners were spelled out. Christian missionaries opened schools and operated printing presses. The imperial government sought to copy European legal and military institutions and the secular values of liberalism. Local leaders undertook their own reforms while tension and opposition prevented the Ottoman Empire from gaining strength and stability. In the late 1870s, the Ottoman Empire lost most of its European holdings in the Balkan wars. In 1876, reformers took even bolder steps, but a backlash set in. The empire collapsed after entering World War I on the side of the Central Powers. *page 543*

HOW DID Italy achieve unification?

Italian Unification Nationalists of various persuasions wanted to unify Italy. The romantic republicans started with secret societies after the Congress of Vienna. Later, Mazzini and Garibaldi publicized the republican cause and mounted guerrilla campaigns. They were opposed by moderate Italians. Count Camillo Cavour rejected republicanism and embraced Enlightenment ideals. He was a monarchist who believed economic ties would foster Italian desire for unification. In 1859, French and Piedmontese forces defeated the Austrians in most of northern Italy; soon thereafter, a large group of Italian provinces united with Piedmont. Meanwhile, Garibaldi was uniting southern Italy by force. The Italian kingdom was created in 1860, under Piedmontese rule. *page 544*

HOW DID Bismarck use war as a tool for achieving German unification?

German Unification Germany was unified under Prussia, and specifically under the conservative guidance of prime minister Otto von Bismarck. Through complex diplomacy, Bismarck joined Austria in war against Denmark in 1864, then turned against Austria in 1866. Prussia won both conflicts, and in the process cut the Habsburgs out of German affairs. In 1867, the North German Confederation was organized under a constitution that looked liberal but kept real power in the hands of the Prussian monarchy. Another complex round of diplomacy and warfare, this time involving the Spanish monarchy and French pride, resulted in an important German victory at the Battle of Sedan in September 1870, and the proclamation of the German Empire in January 1871. *page 547*

WHAT EVENT led to the establishment of a Third Republic in France?

France: From Liberal Empire to the Third Republic Napoleon III began his rule in 1851 as an authoritarian. Around 1860, his rule entered a liberal phase, in which he endorsed free trade, loosened political controls and, in 1870, agreed to a liberal constitution. Although these measures widened his domestic support, his foreign policy continued to be disastrous. The Second Empire ended at the Battle of Sedan in September 1870, when Napoleon III was captured by the Germans. France declared the Third Republic and was ready to sue, but Paris continued to resist Prussian siege until January 1871. The National Assembly was dominated by monarchists, although they could not agree on a monarch. Paris, meanwhile, attempted to govern itself independently under the Paris Commune, but the army surrounded the city in April and invaded in late May. In 1875, the National Assembly created a republican legislative system. The Dreyfus affair in the 1890s presented the Third Republic with its greatest trauma. *page 552*

WHY WAS nationalism such a threat to the Habsburg Empire?

The Habsburg Empire From 1848 until it collapsed, the Habsburg Empire caused problems. Francis Joseph used various mechanisms to attempt to preserve the empire, but in the end he failed. When Austria failed to assist Russia in the Crimean War, it lost a valuable ally. In 1859, Austria was defeated by France and Piedmont. In 1860 and 1861, Francis Joseph attempted to organize the empire's government, but the Magyars resisted. The February Patent of 1861 was the basis of government in Austria proper until World War I. In 1866, Austria was defeated by the Prussians, and in 1867, Francis Joseph compromised with the Magyars to create the dual monarchy, Austria-Hungary. But the Compromise of 1867 fed the hopes of other nationalists, at a time when language and race were being used to draw the boundaries of national and ethnic groups more sharply than ever before. *page 554*

WHY DID reform in Russia fail to produce political stability?

Russia: Emancipation and Revolutionary Stirrings When Alexander II took the throne in Russia in 1855, he set out to impose reforms from the top. He abolished serfdom, but the mechanisms he used for emancipation were a huge disappointment. Local government, the judicial system, and the military were more satisfactorily reformed. But as his reforms failed to earn him new loyalty, and after Polish nationalists rebelled in 1863, Alexander turned increasingly to repression. In the 1870s, students started a revolutionary movement called populism. In 1881, a member of the radical society The People's Will assassinated Alexander II. His son Alexander III ruled more repressively until 1894, when Nicholas II took the throne. *page 556*

WHAT FORCES led to the expansion of democracy in Great Britain?

Great Britain: Toward Democracy Great Britain experienced difficulties and domestic conflicts during this period but was able to deal with them through the political institutions of the liberal state. Conservative Benjamin Disraeli shepherded the Second Reform Act in 1867. William Gladstone was elected prime minister in 1868, and over the next six years access to government institutions was widened to include members of all classes and religions. The paternalistic Disraeli returned to the prime minister's office in 1874 and instituted public health measures, among others. The largest question of the 1880s was Irish home rule. Home rule passed the House of Commons repeatedly but was only able to overcome the veto of the House of Lords in 1914. *page 558*

REVIEW QUESTIONS

1. Why was it so difficult to unify Italy? What were Garibaldi's contributions to Italian unification? What was Otto von Bismarck's plan for unifying Germany? What effect did the unification of Germany have on the rest of Europe?
2. How did France's Second Empire (under Napoleon III) become its Third Republic? What made the Paris Commune a legend throughout Europe? What effect did the Dreyfus affair have on the politics of the Third Republic?
3. What reforms did Tsar Alexander II institute? Can he accurately be called a "visionary" reformer?
4. How did the politics of the British Liberal and Conservative Parties evolve in the period from 1860 to 1890? How did British politicians handle the "Irish question"? Are there similarities between England's situation with Ireland and the Austrian Empire's struggles with its nationalities?

KEY TERMS

home rule (p. 560)

For additional learning resources related to this chapter, please go to **www.myhistorylab.com**

PEARSON myhistorylab

23

The Building of European Supremacy: Society and Politics to World War I

Women Laundry Workers Although new opportunities opened to them in the late nineteenth century, many working-class women, like these women ironing in a laundry, remained in traditional occupations. As the wine bottle suggests, alcoholism was a problem for women as well as men engaged in tedious work. The painting is by Edgar Degas (1834–1917).

How did artists' and writers' depictions of working-class life change in the late nineteenth century?

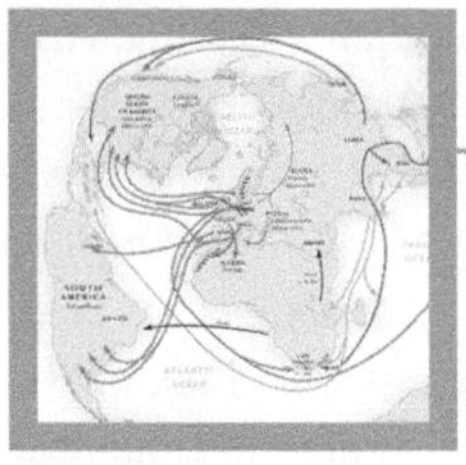

WHY WERE so many Europeans on the move in the late nineteenth century?

HOW DID the second Industrial Revolution transform European life?

WHAT EXPLAINS the prominence of the middle class in late-nineteenth-century Europe?

WHAT FORCES shaped the development of European cities?

WHAT WAS life like for women in late-nineteenth-century Europe?

HOW DID Jewish life in Europe change in the late nineteenth century?

WHAT ROLE did the socialist and labor movements play in late-nineteenth-century politics?

The growth of industrialism between 1860 and 1914 increased Europe's productive capacity to unprecedented levels. As goods and capital flowed out of Europe and across the globe, Europe's political, economic, and social institutions assumed many of their current characteristics. Nation-states with centralized bureaucracies, large electorates, and competing political parties appeared. Huge corporate structures dominated the business world. Labor organized trade unions. The number of white-collar workers increased. Urban life predominated. Socialism became a major political force. Foundations were laid for welfare states and for vast military establishments—and tax burdens increased to support them.

Europeans, confident in their prosperity, failed to realize how dependent they were on the resources and markets of the wider world. Their assumption that European supremacy was natural and enduring was challenged as the twentieth century unfolded.

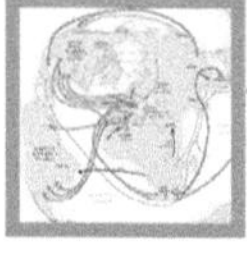

POPULATION TRENDS AND MIGRATION

WHY WERE so many Europeans on the move in the late nineteenth century?

The number of Europeans rose from approximately 266 million in 1850 to 401 million in 1900 and to 447 million in 1910. Thereafter, birth and death rates declined or stabilized in Europe and other developed regions, and population growth began to slow in those areas but not elsewhere. The result has been a persistent demographic differential between the developed and undeveloped world—stable or slowly growing populations in developed countries and large, rapidly growing populations in undeveloped regions—that contributes to the world's present food and resource crisis.

Europe's peoples were on the move in the latter half of the century as never before (see Map 23–1). The midcentury emancipation of peasants lessened the authority of landlords and made legal movement and migration easier. Railways, steamships, and better roads increased mobility. Cheap land and better wages accompanied economic development in Europe, North America, Latin America, and Australia, enticing people to move from regions where they had little prospect of improving their lives to regions that held or seemed to hold opportunity. In Europe itself the main migration continued to be from the countryside into urban areas. Between 1846 and 1932, more than 50 million Europeans left their homelands. The major areas to benefit from this movement were the United States, Canada, Australia, South Africa, Brazil, Algeria, and Argentina. At midcentury, most of the emigrants were from Great Britain (especially Ireland), Germany, and Scandinavia. After 1885, migration from southern and eastern Europe rose. This exodus helped relieve the social and population pressures on the Continent. The outward movement of peoples, in conjunction with Europe's economic and technological superiority, contributed heavily to the Europeanization of the world.

THE SECOND INDUSTRIAL REVOLUTION

HOW DID the second Industrial Revolution transform European life?

During the third quarter of the nineteenth century, the gap that had long existed between British and continental economic development closed. (See Map 23–2, page 568.) In particular, the growth of the German industry was stunning. German steel production surpassed Britain's in 1893 and was nearly twice that of Britain by the outbreak of World War I. This emergence of an industrial Germany was the major fact of European economic and political life at the turn of the century.

NEW INDUSTRIES

Initially, the economic expansion of the third quarter of the century involved the spread of industries similar to those pioneered earlier in Great Britain. In particular, the expansion of railway systems on the Continent spurred economic growth. Thereafter, however, wholly

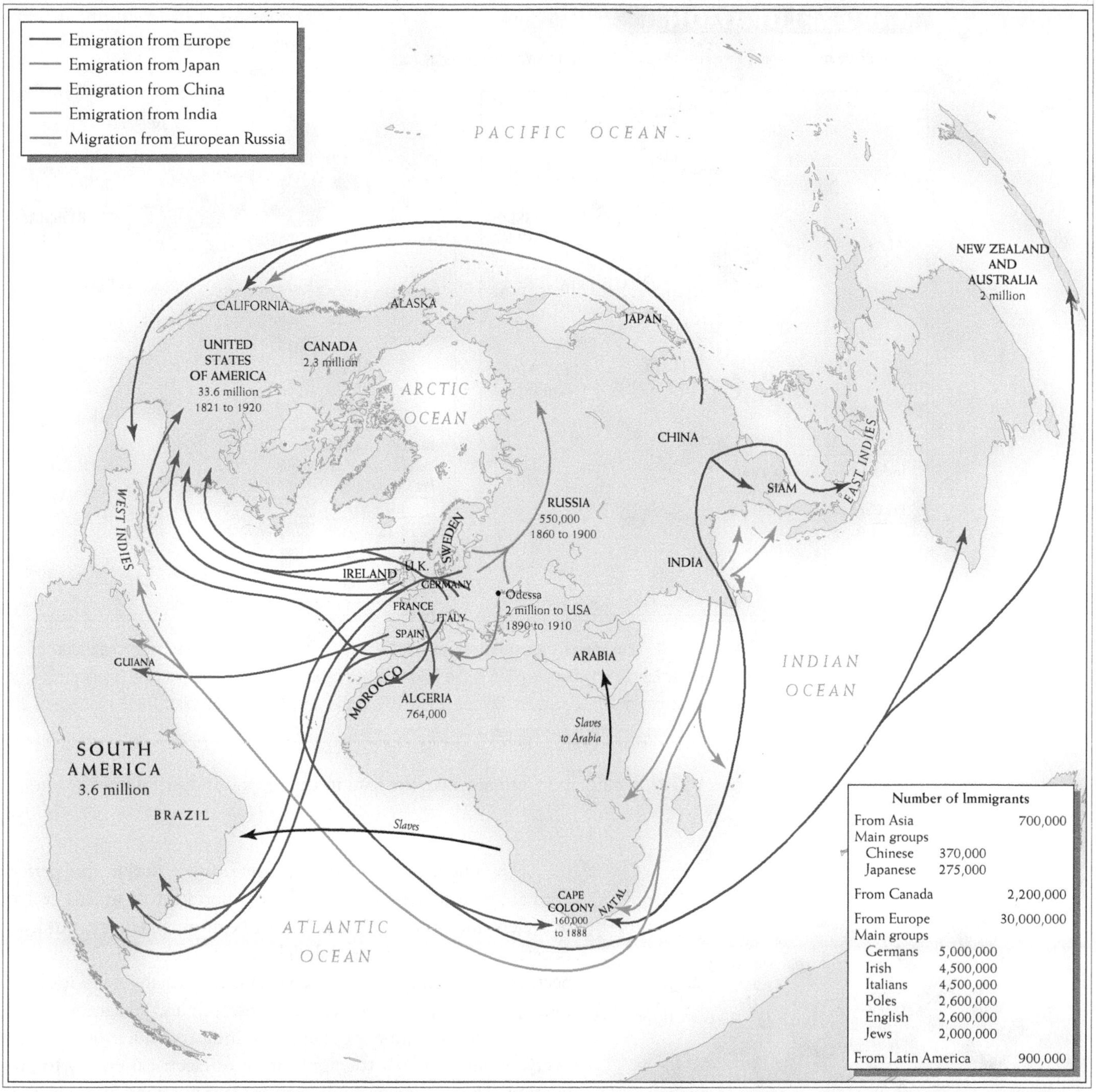

- Emigration from Europe
- Emigration from Japan
- Emigration from China
- Emigration from India
- Migration from European Russia

Number of Immigrants		
From Asia		700,000
Main groups		
Chinese	370,000	
Japanese	275,000	
From Canada		2,200,000
From Europe		30,000,000
Main groups		
Germans	5,000,000	
Irish	4,500,000	
Italians	4,500,000	
Poles	2,600,000	
English	2,600,000	
Jews	2,000,000	
From Latin America		900,000

MAP 23–1 **Patterns of Global Migration, 1840–1900** Emigration was a global process by the late nineteenth century, but more immigrants went to the United States than to all other nations combined.

What changes enabled the migration of millions of people in the late nineteenth century?

new industries emerged. This latter development is usually termed the ***second Industrial Revolution***. The first Industrial Revolution was associated with textiles, steam, and iron; by contrast, the second was associated with steel, chemicals, electricity, and oil.

second Industrial Revolution Started after 1850, it expanded the production of steel, chemicals, electricity, and oil.

In the 1850s, Henry Bessemer (1830–1898), an English engineer, discovered a new process, named after him, for manufacturing steel cheaply in large quantities. In 1860, Great Britain, Belgium, France, and Germany combined produced 125,000 tons of steel. By 1913, the figure had risen to over 32 million tons.

MAP EXPLORATION

Interactive map: To explore this map further, go to www.myhistorylab.com

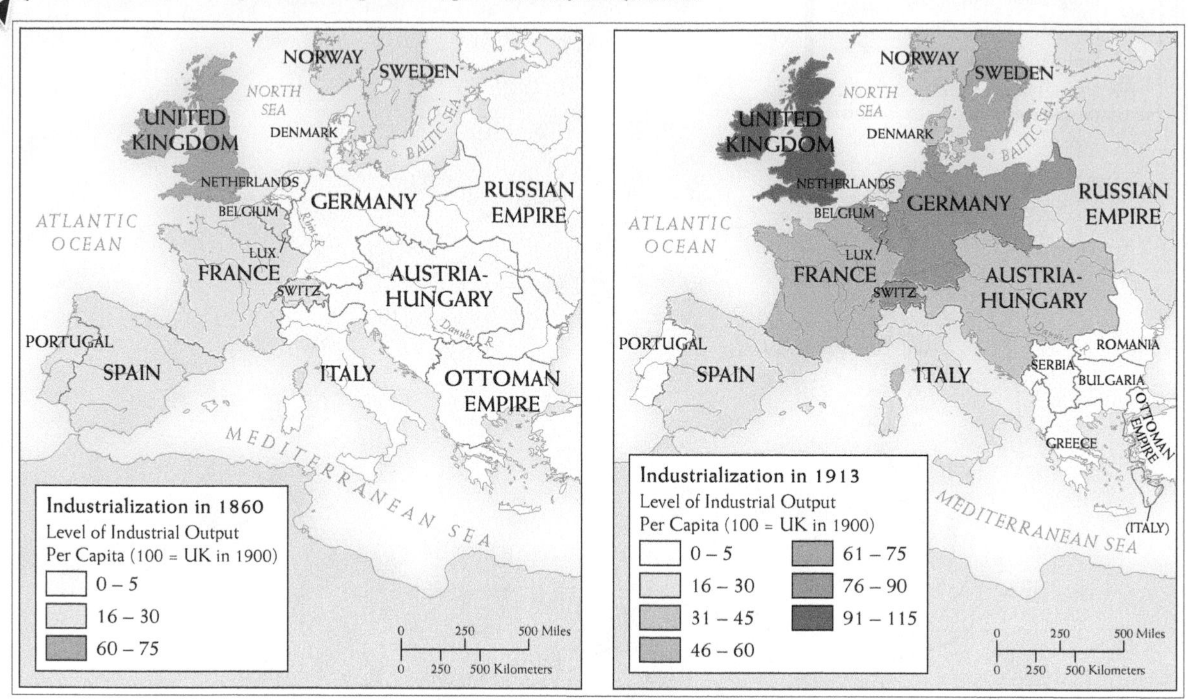

MAP 23–2 **European Industrialization, 1860–1913** In 1860, Britain was far more industrialized than other European countries. But in the following half century, industrial output rose significantly, if unevenly, across much of western Europe, especially in the new German Empire. The Balkan states and the Ottoman Empire, however, remained economically backward.

Why did Britain and Germany take the lead in the second Industrial Revolution?

The invention and commercialization of automobiles soon led to auto races in Europe and North America. Here Henri Fournier, the winner of the 1901 Paris to Berlin Motor Car Race, sits in his winning racing car manufactured by the Paris-based auto firm of Emile and Louis Mors.

Getty Images Inc.— Hulton Archive Photos

What made the widespread availability of automobiles possible?

The chemical industry also came of age during this period. Formal scientific research played an important role in this growth of the chemical industry, marking the beginning of a direct link between science and industrial development. As in so many other aspects of the second Industrial Revolution, Germany was a leader in forging this link, fostering scientific research and education.

The most significant change for industry and, eventually, for everyday life involved the application of electrical energy to production. The first major public power plant was constructed in 1881 in Great Britain. Soon electric poles, lines, and generating stations dotted the European landscape. Homes began to use electric lights. Streetcar and subway systems were electrified.

The internal combustion automobile was invented by the German engineer Gottlieb Daimler (1834–1900) in 1889. France initially took the lead in auto manufacturing, but it was the American, Henry Ford (1863–1947), who later made the automobile accessible to the masses. The automobile industry created a vast new demand for steel and the materials that went into other auto parts and established an ever-growing demand for petroleum products that continues to this day.

Economic Difficulties

Despite the multiplication of new industries, the second half of the nineteenth century was not a period of uninterrupted or smooth economic growth. In the last quarter of the century, economic advance slowed. Bad weather and foreign competition put grave pressures on European agriculture and caused many European peasants to emigrate to other parts of the world.

As new farming regions developed in the United States, Canada, Argentina, Australia, and New Zealand, products from those areas challenged the market for home-produced European agricultural goods. Refrigerated ships could bring meat and dairy products to Europe from all over the world. Grain could be grown more economically on the plains of North America, Argentina, and Ukraine than it could in Western Europe, and railways and steamships made it easy and cheap to ship it across continents and oceans.

Several large banks failed in 1873, and the rate of capital investment slowed. Some industries then entered a two-decade-long period of stagnation that many contemporaries regarded as a depression. Overall, however, the general standard of living in the industrialized nations improved in the second half of the nineteenth century. Yet many workers still lived and labored in abysmal conditions. There were pockets of *unemployment* (a word that was coined during this period), and strikes and other forms of labor unrest were common. These economic difficulties fed the growth of trade unions and socialist political parties.

The new industries produced consumer goods, and expansion in consumer demand brought the economy out of stagnation by the end of the century. (See "Encountering the Past: Bicycles: Transportation, Freedom, and Sport," page 570.) Lower food prices eventually allowed all classes to spend more on consumer goods. Urbanization naturally created larger markets. New forms of retailing and marketing appeared—department stores, chain stores, mail-order catalogs, and advertising—simultaneously stimulating and feeding consumer demand. Imperialism also opened new markets overseas for European consumer goods.

THE MIDDLE CLASSES IN ASCENDANCY

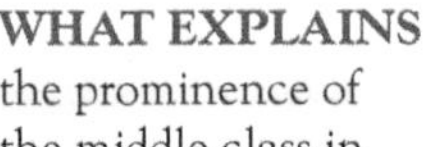

WHAT EXPLAINS the prominence of the middle class in late-nineteenth-century Europe?

The sixty years before World War I were the age of the middle classes. The middle classes became the arbiter of consumer taste and ceased to be a revolutionary group.

Social Distinctions Within the Middle Classes

The middle classes, never perfectly homogeneous, grew increasingly diverse. Their most prosperous members—the owners and managers of great businesses and banks—lived in splendor that rivaled, and sometimes exceeded, that of the aristocracy. Beneath them were the comfortable small entrepreneurs and professional people. Also in this group were the shopkeepers, schoolteachers, librarians, and others who had either a bit of property or a skill derived from education that provided respectable nonmanual employment. Finally, there was a wholly new element—"white-collar workers"—who formed the lower middle class, or ***petite bourgeoisie***. They included secretaries, retail clerks, and lower-level bureaucrats in business and government. They often had working-class origins and might even belong to unions, but they had middle-class aspirations and consciously sought to distance themselves from a lower-class lifestyle.

petite bourgeoisie New lower middle class made up of white-collar workers such as secretaries, retail clerks, and lower-level bureaucrats.

Significant tensions and social anxieties marked relations among the various middle-class groups. Small shopkeepers resented the power of the great capitalists, with their department stores and mail-order catalogs. There is some evidence that the professions

ENCOUNTERING THE PAST

BICYCLES: TRANSPORTATION, FREEDOM, AND SPORT

Bicycles, the first mass-produced affordable machines for individual travel, took Western nations by storm between 1880 and 1900. The unprecedented freedom to travel that they gave men and (significantly) women had an immense impact on society.

The bicycle was invented in Germany about 1817, but the early models were clumsy, dangerous, and uncomfortable. They were made of wood, had to be pushed, and riders could not control their speed. Metal frames, solid rubber tires, and chain drives did not appear until the 1870s. In the 1880s, John Boyd Dunlop, an Irish physician, invented the pneumatic tire and France's Michelin brothers the inner tube. By the 1890s, the modern "safety bicycle" was in mass production.

Bicycles enabled people to commute from homes located farther from their workplaces, and bicycles provided new opportunities for recreation and sport. Special clothing was designed for cyclists. "Bloomers," ample trousers worn under skirts, preserved the modesty of female riders. (Feminists hailed the mobility the bicycle provided as a major contribution to women's liberation.) Cycling clubs appeared in the early twentieth century, and the first travel guides were published for cycling tourists. The Michelin tire company's famous series of *Guides Michelin* was initiated in 1900 to promote cycling—and consumption of tires. Bicycle racing soon became a competitive sport. It was featured in the first modern Olympic Games in 1896, and in 1903, the first Tour de France was held.

The bicycle helped liberate women's lives, but as this poster suggests, it was also associated with glamour and fashion.

Who rode bicycles? What needs did they meet?

WHAT EXPLAINS the bicycle's huge popularity in the late nineteenth century?

were becoming overcrowded. People who had only recently attained a middle-class lifestyle feared losing it in bad economic times. Nonetheless, in the decades immediately before World War I, the middle classes set the values and goals for most of society.

LATE-NINETEENTH-CENTURY URBAN LIFE

WHAT FORCES shaped the development of European cities?

Europe became more urbanized than ever in the latter half of the nineteenth century as migration to the cities continued. The rural migrants to the cities often faced poor housing, social anonymity, and, because they rarely possessed the right kinds of skills, unemployment. People from different ethnic backgrounds found themselves in proximity to one another and had difficulty mixing socially. Competition for jobs generated new varieties of political and social discontent, such as the anti-Semitism directed at the thousands of Russian Jews who had migrated to Western Europe. Indeed, much of the political anti-Semitism of the latter part of the century had its roots in the problems urban migration generated.

The Redesign of Cities

The inward urban migration placed new social and economic demands on already strained city resources and gradually transformed the patterns of urban living. National and municipal governments redesigned the central portions of many large European cities during the second half of the century.

The New Paris The most famous and extensive transformation of a major city occurred in Paris. Like so many other European cities, Paris had expanded from the Middle Ages onward with little or no design or planning. Great public buildings and squalid hovels stood near each other. The Seine River was an open sewer. The streets were narrow, crooked, and crowded. Of more concern to the government of Napoleon III (r. 1852–1870), the city's streets had for sixty years provided battlegrounds for urban insurrections that had threatened or toppled French governments on numerous occasions, most recently in 1848.

Napoleon III personally determined to redesign Paris. He appointed Baron Georges Haussmann (1809–1891), who, as prefect of the Seine from 1853 to 1870, oversaw a vast urban reconstruction program. Whole districts were destroyed to open the way for the broad boulevards and streets that became the hallmark of modern Paris. Much, though by no means all, of the purpose of this street planning was political. The wide vistas not only were beautiful, but they also allowed for the quick deployment of troops to put down riots. The eradication of the many small streets and alleys removed areas where barricades could be, and had been, erected. Urban reconstruction was also political in another sense. It created thousands of government and private sector jobs.

Further rebuilding and redesign occurred under the Third Republic after the destruction that accompanied the suppression of the Commune in 1871. Many department stores, office complexes, and largely middle-class apartment buildings were constructed. The public transportation network was expanded to include mechanical trams, a subway system, and new railroad stations linking the city and the suburbs.

EVENTS IN THE FORMATION OF THE EARLY TWENTIETH CENTURY

1848	Britain's Public Health Act
1851	France's Melun Act
1857	Bessemer steel manufacturing process invented
1864	Meeting of the First International
1869	John Stuart Mill publishes *The Subjection of Women*
1875	German Social Democratic Party founded
1876	Telephone invented
1879	Electric light bulb invented
1882	England's Married Woman's Property Act
1884	Britain's Fabian Society founded
1887	Automobile invented
1889	Establishment of the Second International
1895	Invention of wireless telegraphy
1900	Lenin leaves Russia
1902	Formation of the British Labour Party
1903	British Women's Social and Political Union founded; Lenin creates the Bolsheviks; the Wright brothers begin the age of aviation
1904–1905	Russo-Japanese War
1905	Saint Petersburg's Bloody Sunday; Russia's October Manifesto
1907	Norway, first nation to grant women the vote
1909	Henry Ford begins mass production of automobiles
1910	British suffragettes adopt radical tactics
1911	Stolypin assassinated
1914	World War I begins
1918	Some British women acquire the vote
1918	Constitution of the Weimar Republic gives women the vote
1928	British women acquire same voting rights as men

Development of Suburbs Commercial development, railway construction, and slum clearance displaced many city dwellers and raised urban land values and rents. Consequently, both the middle classes and the working class began to seek housing elsewhere. The middle classes looked for neighborhoods removed from urban congestion. The working class looked for affordable housing. The result, in virtually all countries, was the

Overview Growth of Major European Cities (Figures in Thousands)

	1850	1880	1910
BERLIN	419	1,122	2,071
BIRMINGHAM	233	437	840
FRANKFURT	65	137	415
LONDON	2,685	4,470	7,256
MADRID	281	398	600
MOSCOW	365	748	1,533
PARIS	1,053	2,269	2,888
ROME	175	300	542
SAINT PETERSBURG	485	877	1,962
VIENNA	444	1,104	2,031
WARSAW	160	339	872

development of suburbs surrounding the city proper. These suburbs housed families whose breadwinners worked in the central city or in a factory located within the city limits.

The expansion of railways with cheap workday fares and the introduction of mechanical and, later, electric tramways, as well as subways, allowed tens of thousands of workers from all classes to move daily between the city and the outlying suburbs. For hundreds of thousands of Europeans, home and work became more physically separated than ever before.

Urban Sanitation

The efforts of governments and of the increasingly conservative middle classes to maintain public order after 1848 led to a growing concern with the problems of public health and housing for the poor. A widespread feeling arose that only when the health and housing of the working class were improved would middle-class health also be secure and the political order stable.

Impact of Cholera Concerns with health and housing first manifested themselves as a result of the great cholera epidemics of the 1830s and 1840s. Unlike many other common deadly diseases of the day that touched only the poor, cholera struck all classes, and the middle class demanded a solution. Physicians and sanitary reformers believed that miasmas in the air spread the infections that led to cholera and other diseases. These miasmas, which could be detected by their foul odors, were believed to arise from filth. The way to get rid of the dangerous, foul-smelling air was to clean up the cities.

During the 1840s, many physicians and some government officials began to publicize the dangerous unsanitary conditions associated with overcrowding in cities and with businesses, such as basement slaughterhouses. They closely linked the issues of wretched living conditions and public health. They also argued that sanitary reform would remove the dangers.

New Water and Sewer Systems The proposed solution to the health hazard was cleanliness, to be achieved through new water and sewer systems. These facilities were constructed slowly, usually first in capital cities and then much later in provincial centers. The building of such systems was one of the major health and engineering achievements of the second half of the nineteenth century. Wherever these sanitary facilities were installed, the mortality rate dropped considerably—not because they prevented miasmas, but because they disposed of human waste and provided clean water free of harmful bacteria for people to drink, cook with, and bathe in.

A major feature of the reconstruction of mid-nineteenth-century Paris under the Emperor Napoleon III was a vast new sewer system to provide for drainage in the city. Sewer workmen could travel the length of the structure on small rail cars. Even today tourists still may visit parts of the midcity Paris sewer system.

Nadar/Getty Images

What were the motives behind the reconstruction of Paris?

Expanded Government Involvement in Public Health The concern with public health led to an expansion of governmental power on various levels. In Britain the Public Health Act of 1848, in France the Melun Act of 1851, and various laws in the still-disunited German states, as well as later legislation, introduced new restraints on private life and enterprise. This legislation allowed medical officers and building inspectors to enter homes and businesses in the name of public health. The state could condemn private property for posing health hazards. Private land could be excavated to construct the sewers and water mains required to protect the public. New building regulations restrained the activities of private contractors.

Full acceptance at the close of the century of the bacterial theory of disease associated with the discoveries of Louis Pasteur (1822–1895) in France, Robert Koch (1843–1910) in Germany, and Joseph Lister (1827–1912) in Britain increased public concern about cleanliness. Throughout Europe, issues related to the maintenance of public health and the physical well-being of the population repeatedly opened the way for new modes of government intervention in the lives of citizens.

QUICK REVIEW

Improved Conditions in Cities

- Cholera epidemics spurred action
- New awareness of the value of modern water and sewer systems
- Expanded involvement of government in public health

Housing Reform and Middle-Class Values

The information about working-class living conditions the sanitary reformers revealed also led to heated debates over the housing problem. The wretched dwellings of the poor were themselves a cause of poor sanitation and thus became a newly perceived health hazard. Furthermore, the domestic arrangements of the poor, whose large families might live in a single room without any personal privacy, shocked middle-class reformers and bureaucrats. After the revolutions of 1848, the overcrowding in housing and the social discontent that it generated were also seen to pose a political danger. Middle-class reformers thus turned to housing reform to solve the medical, moral, and political dangers slums posed. Decent housing would foster a good home life, in turn leading to a healthy, moral, and politically stable population.

Private philanthropy made the first attack on the housing problem. Companies operating on low profit margins or making low-interest loans encouraged housing for the poor. Firms such as the German Krupp Armaments concern that sought to ensure a contented, healthy, and stable workforce constructed model housing projects and industrial communities.

By the mid-1880s, the migration into cities had made housing a political issue. Legislation in England in 1885 lowered the interest rates to construct cheap housing, and soon thereafter local governments began public housing projects. In Germany, action on housing came later in the century through the initiative of local municipalities. In 1894, France made inexpensive credit available to construct housing for the poor.

VARIETIES OF LATE-NINETEENTH-CENTURY WOMEN'S EXPERIENCES

WHAT WAS life like for women in late-nineteenth-century Europe?

Late-nineteenth-century women and men led lives that reflected their social rank. Yet, within each rank, the experience of women was distinct from that of men. Women remained, generally speaking, economically dependent and legally inferior, whatever their social class.

WOMEN'S SOCIAL DISABILITIES

In the mid–nineteenth century, virtually all European women faced social and legal disabilities in three areas: property rights, family law, and education. By the close of the century, there had been some improvement in each area.

Women and Property Until the last quarter of the century in most European countries, married women could not own property in their own names, no matter what their social class. Their legal identities were subsumed in their husbands' identities, and they had no independent standing before the law. Because private property and wage earning were the bases of European society, these disabilities put married women at a great disadvantage, limiting their freedom to work, to save, and to move from one location to another.

Reform of women's property rights came slowly. By 1882, Great Britain had passed the Married Woman's Property Act, which allowed married women to own property in their own right. In France, however, a married woman could not even open a savings account in her own name until 1895, and married French women did not gain possession of the wages they earned until 1907. In 1900, Germany allowed women to take jobs without their husbands' permission, but except for her wages, a German husband retained control of most of his wife's property.

Family Law European family law also disadvantaged women. The Napoleonic Code and the remnants of Roman law still in effect made women legal minors throughout Europe. Divorce was difficult everywhere for most of the century. Most nations did not permit divorce by mutual consent. Thereafter, the majority of nations recognized a legal cause for divorce—cruelty or injury—which had to be proved in court. Across Europe, some version of the double standard prevailed whereby husbands' extramarital sexual relations were tolerated to a much greater degree than those of wives. Everywhere, divorce required hearings in court and the presentation of legal proof, making the process expensive and more difficult for women, who did not control their own property.

The authority of husbands also extended to children. A husband could take children away from their mother and give them to someone else to rear. Only a father, in most countries, could permit his daughter to marry. In some countries, he could virtually force his daughter to marry the man of his choice. In cases of divorce and separation, courts normally awarded the husband authority over, and custody of, children, no matter how he had treated them previously.

Until well into the twentieth century, both contraception and abortion were illegal. The law surrounding rape normally worked to the disadvantage of women. Wherever they turned with their problems—whether to physicians or lawyers—women confronted an official or legal world that men almost wholly populated and controlled.

QUICK REVIEW

Family Law

- European family law disadvantaged women
- Divorce was difficult for most of the century
- Husbands were given considerable authority over wives and children
- Contraception and abortion were illegal

Educational Barriers Throughout the nineteenth century, women had less access to education than men had and what was available to them was inferior to that available to men. Not surprisingly, there were many more illiterate women than men.

Women only gradually gained access to secondary and university education during the second half of the nineteenth century and the early twentieth century. Young women on their way to school, the subject of this 1880 English painting, would thus have been a new sight when it was painted.

Sir George Clausen (RA) (1852–1944), *Schoolgirls, Haverstock Hill,* signed and dated 1880, oil on canvas, 20 1/2 X 30 3/8 in. (52 × 77.2 cm), Yale Center for British Art/Paul Mellon Collection, USA/Bridgeman Art Library (B1985.10.1). Courtesy of the Estate of Sir George Clausen

Why do you think the artist included the older working-class woman in the street in this painting?

University and professional education remained reserved for men until at least the third quarter of the century. Moreover, the absence of a system of private or public secondary education for women prevented most of them from gaining the qualifications they needed to enter a university whether or not the university prohibited them. Evidence suggests that educated, professional men feared that admitting women would overcrowd their professions. Women who attended universities and medical schools were sometimes labeled political radicals.

By the turn of the century, some men in the educated elites feared the challenge educated women posed to traditional gender roles in the home and workplace. Restricting women's access to secondary and university education helped bar them from social and economic advancement. Women would benefit only marginally from the expansion of professional employment that occurred during the late nineteenth and early twentieth centuries. Some women did enter the professions, particularly medicine, but their number remained few. Most nations refused to allow women to become lawyers until after World War I.

The few women who pioneered in the professions and on government commissions and school boards or who dispersed birth control information faced social obstacles, humiliation, and often outright bigotry. These women and their male supporters were challenging that clear separation into male and female spheres that had emerged in middle-class European social life during the nineteenth century. Women themselves were often hesitant to support feminist causes or expanded opportunities for females because they had been so thoroughly acculturated into the recently stereotyped roles. Many women, as well as men, saw a real conflict between family responsibilities and feminism.

New Employment Patterns for Women

During the second Industrial Revolution, two major developments affected the economic lives of women. The first was the large-scale expansion in the variety of jobs available to women outside the better-paying learned professions. The second was the withdrawal of many married women from the workforce.

Availability of New Jobs The expansion of governmental bureaucracies, the emergence of corporations and other large businesses, and the vast growth of retail stores opened many new employment opportunities for women. The need for elementary school teachers, usually women, grew as governments adopted compulsory education laws. Women by the thousands became secretaries and clerks for governments and private businesses. Thousands more became shop assistants.

Although these jobs did open new and often better employment opportunities for women, they nonetheless required low-level skills and involved minimal training. They were occupied primarily by unmarried women or widows. Women rarely occupied more prominent positions.

Employers continued to pay women low wages, because they assumed, although they often knew better, that a woman did not need to live on what she herself earned but could expect additional financial support from her father or her husband. Consequently, a woman who did need to support herself independently could seldom find a job that paid an adequate income—or a position that paid as well as one a man who was supporting himself held.

Withdrawal from the Labor Force Most of the women filling the new service positions were young and unmarried. Upon marriage, or certainly after the birth of her first child, a woman normally withdrew from the labor force. This pattern was not new, but it had become significantly more common by the end of the nineteenth century. The kinds of industrial occupations that women had filled in the mid–nineteenth century, especially textile and garment making, were shrinking. Employers in offices and retail stores preferred young, unmarried women whose family responsibilities would not interfere with their work.

The real wages paid to male workers increased during this period, so families had a somewhat reduced need for a second income. Also, thanks to improving health conditions, men lived longer than before, so the death of their husbands was less likely to thrust wives into the workforce. The smaller size of families also lowered the need for

Shown are women working in the London Central Telephone Exchange. The invention of the telephone opened new employment opportunities for women.

Image Works/Mary Evans Picture Library Ltd.

How did technology change women's employment opportunities in the late nineteenth century?

supplementary wages. Working children stayed at home longer and continued to contribute to the family's wage pool.

Finally, the cultural dominance of the middle class established a pattern of social expectations, especially for wives. The more prosperous a working-class family became, the less involved in employment its women were supposed to be. Indeed, the less income-producing work a wife did, the more prosperous and stable the family was considered.

Yet behind these generalities stands the enormous variety of social and economic experiences late-nineteenth-century women actually encountered. As might be expected, the chief determinant of these individual experiences was social class.

QUICK REVIEW

Women's Work

- Opportunities in factories diminished
- Expansion of governmental bureaucracies, large-scale business organizations, and retail stores increased demand for women workers
- Many married women left workforce

Working-Class Women

Although the textile industry and garment making were much less dominant than earlier in the century, they continued to employ many women. The German clothing-making trade illustrates the kind of vulnerable economic situation that women could encounter as a result of their limited skills and the way the trade was organized. A major manufacturer would produce clothing through what was called a *putting-out system*. The manufacturer would purchase the material and then put it out for tailoring. Usually, numerous independently owned, small sweatshops or workers in their homes made the clothing.

In Berlin in 1896, this system employed more than 80,000 garment workers. When business was good and demand strong, employment for these women was high. As the seasons shifted or business slackened, however, less and less work was put out, idling many of them. In effect, the workers who actually sewed the clothing carried much of the risk of the enterprise. Some women did work in clothing factories, but they, too, were subject to layoffs. Furthermore, women in the clothing trade were nearly always in positions less skilled than those of the male tailors or the middlemen who owned the workshops.

The expectation of separate social and economic spheres for men and women and the definition of women's chief work as pertaining to the home contributed mightily to the exploitation of women workers outside the home. Because their wages were regarded merely as supplementing their husbands' wages, they became particularly vulnerable to economic exploitation. Women were nearly always treated as casual workers everywhere in Europe.

Poverty and Prostitution

The economic vulnerability of women and the consequent poverty many of them faced were among the chief causes of prostitution. Every major late-nineteenth-century European city had thousands of prostitutes. Prostitution was, of course, not new. It had always been one way for poor women to find income. In the late nineteenth century, however, it was closely related to the difficulty encountered by indigent women who were trying to make their way in an overcrowded female labor force. On the Continent, prostitution was generally legalized and subject to governmental and municipal regulations that male legislatures and councils passed and male police and physicians enforced. In Britain, prostitution received only minimal regulation.

The most recent studies of prostitution in England emphasize that most prostitutes were active on the streets for only a few years, from their late teens to about age twenty-five. Certain cities—those with large army garrisons or naval bases or those, like London, with large transient populations—attracted prostitutes. Far fewer prostitutes worked in manufacturing towns, where there were more opportunities for steady employment and community life was more stable.

Department stores, such as Bon Marché in Paris, sold wide selections of consumer goods under one roof. These modern stores increased the economic pressure on small traditional merchants who specialized in selling only one kind of good.

Image Works/Mary Evans Picture Library Ltd.

How did department stores embody middle-class values and aspirations?

Women who became prostitutes usually came from families of unskilled workers and had minimal skills and education themselves. Many had been servants. They also often were orphans or came from broken homes. The customers of poor working-class prostitutes were primarily working-class men.

Women of the Middle Class

A vast social gap separated poor working-class women from their middle-class counterparts. As their fathers' and husbands' incomes permitted, middle-class women participated in the vast expansion of consumerism and domestic comfort that marked the late nineteenth and the early twentieth centuries.

The Cult of Domesticity Middle-class women, if at all possible, did not work. More than any other women, they became limited to the roles of wife and mother. As a result, they might enjoy great domestic luxury and comfort, but their lives, talents, ambitions, and opportunities for applying their intelligence were sharply circumscribed.

Middle-class women became, in large measure, the product of a particular understanding of social life. Home life was to be different from the life of business and the marketplace. The home was to be a private place of refuge, a view scores of women's journals across Europe set forth. For middle-class women, the home came to be seen as the center of virtue, children, and the respectable life. Marriages were usually arranged to benefit the family economically. The first child was often born within the first year. Rearing and nurturing her children was a woman's chief task. Her only experience or training was for the role of dutiful daughter, wife, and mother.

Within the home, a middle-class woman largely directed the household. She oversaw virtually all domestic management and child care. She was in charge of the home as a unit of consumption, which is why so much advertising was directed toward women. All this domestic activity, however, occurred within the bounds of the approved middle-class lifestyle that set strict limits on a woman's initiative. In her conspicuous position within the home and family, a woman symbolized first her father's and then her husband's worldly success.

Religious and Charitable Activities The cult of domesticity in France and elsewhere assigned firm religious duties to women, which the Roman Catholic Church strongly supported. Women were expected to attend Mass frequently and assure the religious instruction of their children. They were charged with observing meatless Fridays and participating in religious observances. Prayer was a major part of their daily lives. They internalized those portions of the Christian religion that stressed meekness and passivity. In other countries, religion and religious activities also became part of the expected work of women. This close association between religion and a strict domestic life for women was one reason for later tension between feminism and religious authorities.

Another important role for middle-class women was the administration of charity. Women were considered especially qualified for this work because of their presumed innate spirituality and their capacity to instill domestic and personal discipline. Women were supposed to be particularly interested in the problems of poor women, their families, and their children. By the end of the century, middle-class women seeking to expand their spheres of activity became social workers for the church, for private charities, or for the government. These vocations were a natural extension of the roles society assigned to them.

Sexuality and Family Size Historians have come to realize that the world of the middle-class wife and her family was much more complicated than they once thought. Neither all wives nor their families conformed to the stereotypes. Recent studies suggest that the middle classes of the nineteenth century enjoyed sexual relations within marriage far more than was once thought. Much of the inhibition about sexuality stemmed from the dangers of childbirth, which, in an age of limited sanitation and anesthesia, were widely and rightly feared, rather than from any dislike or disapproval of sex itself.

One of the major changes in this regard during the second half of the century was the acceptance of a small family size among the middle classes. During the last decades of the century, new contraceptive devices became available, which middle-class couples used. One of the chief reasons for the apparently conscious decision of couples to limit their family size was to maintain a relatively high level of material consumption. Fewer children probably meant more attention for each of them, possibly increasing the emotional bonds between mothers and their children.

The Rise of Political Feminism

Plainly, liberal society and its values had neither automatically nor inevitably improved the lot of women. In particular, they did not give women the vote or access to political activity.

Obstacles to Achieving Equality Women were often reluctant to support feminist causes. Political issues relating to gender were only one of several priorities for many women. Some were sensitive to their class and economic interests. Others subordinated feminist political issues to national unity and patriotism. Still others would not support particular feminist organizations because they objected to their tactics. The various social and tactical differences among women often led to sharp divisions within the feminists' own ranks. There were other disagreements about which goals were most important for improving women's legal and social conditions.

Although liberal society and law presented women with many obstacles, they also provided feminists with many of their intellectual and political tools. As early as 1792 in Britain, Mary Wollstonecraft (1759–1797), in *The Vindication of the Rights of Woman*, had applied the revolutionary doctrines of the rights of man to the predicament of the members of her own sex. (See Chapter 17.) John Stuart Mill (1806–1873), together with his wife, Harriet Taylor (1804–1858), extended the logic of liberal freedom to the position of women in *The Subjection of Women* (1869). The arguments for utility and efficiency so dear to middle-class liberals could be used to expose the human and social waste implicit in the inferior role assigned to women.

Furthermore, the socialist criticism of capitalist society often, though by no means always, included a harsh indictment of the social and economic position to which women had been relegated. The earliest statements in support of feminism arose from critics of the existing order who were often people who had unorthodox opinions about sexuality, family life, and property. This hardened resistance to the feminist message, especially on the Continent.

These difficulties prevented continental feminists from raising the massive public support or mounting the large demonstrations that feminists in Britain and the United States could. Everywhere in Europe, however, including Britain, the feminist cause was badly divided over both goals and tactics.

Votes for Women in Britain Europe's most advanced women's movement was in Britain. There, Millicent Fawcett (1847–1929) led the moderate National Union of Women's Suffrage Societies. She believed Parliament would grant women the vote only if it were convinced they would be respectable and responsible in their political activity. Her tactics were those of English liberals.

Emmeline Pankhurst (1858–1928) led a much more radical branch of British feminists. In 1903, Pankhurst and her daughters, Christabel and Sylvia, founded the Women's Social and Political Union. For years they and their followers, known derisively as **suffragettes**, lobbied publicly and privately for extending the vote to women. By 1910, having failed to move the government, they turned to the violent tactics of arson, breaking windows, and sabotage of postal boxes. They marched en masse on Parliament. The Liberal government of Prime Minister Herbert Asquith (1852–1928) imprisoned demonstrators and force-fed those who went on hunger strikes in jail. The government refused to extend the franchise. Only in 1918, and then as a result of their contribution to the war effort in World War I, did British women over age thirty receive the vote. (Men could vote at age twenty-one.)

suffragettes Derisive name for members of the Women's Social and Political Union, who lobbied for votes for women.

Political Feminism on the Continent The contrast between the women's movement in Britain and those in France and Germany shows how advanced the British women's movement was. In France, when Hubertine Auclert (1848–1914) began campaigning for the vote in the 1880s, she stood virtually alone. During the 1890s, several women's organizations emerged. In 1901, the National Council of French Women (CNFF) was organized among upper-middle-class women, but it did not support the vote for women for several years. French Roman Catholic feminists such as Marie Mauguet (1844–1928) supported the franchise. Almost all French feminists, however, rejected violence. Nor were they ever able to organize mass rallies. In 1919, the French Chamber of Deputies passed a bill granting the vote to women, but in 1922, the French Senate defeated the bill. French women did not receive the right to vote until after World War II.

In Germany, feminist awareness and action were even more underdeveloped. In 1894, the Union of German Women's Organizations (BDFK) was founded. By 1902, it

was supporting the right to vote. But its main concern was improving women's social conditions, increasing their access to education, and extending their right to other protections. The BDKF also tried to gain women's admittance to political or civic activity on the municipal level. Its work usually included education, child welfare, charity, and public health. The German Social Democratic Party supported women's suffrage, but the German authorities and German Roman Catholics so disdained the socialists that its support only made suffrage more suspect in their eyes. Women received the vote in Germany only in 1919, under the constitution of the Weimar Republic after the German defeat in war and revolution at home.

JEWISH EMANCIPATION

HOW DID Jewish life in Europe change in the late nineteenth century?

The emancipation of European Jews from the narrow life of the ghetto into a world of equal or nearly equal citizenship and social status was a major accomplishment of political liberalism and had an enduring impact on European life. Emancipation, slow and never fully completed, began in the late eighteenth century and continued throughout the nineteenth. It moved at different paces in different countries.

Differing Degrees of Citizenship

In 1782, Joseph II, the Habsburg emperor, issued a decree that placed the Jews of his empire under more or less the same laws as Christians. In France, the National Assembly recognized Jews as French citizens in 1789. These steps toward political emancipation were always uncertain and were frequently limited or abrogated when rulers or governments changed. Even countries that had given Jews political rights did not permit them to own land and often subjected them to discriminatory taxes. Nonetheless, during the first half of the century, Jews in Western Europe, and to a much lesser extent in central and eastern Europe, began to gain equal or more nearly equal citizenship.

In Russia, and in Poland under Russian rule, the traditional modes of prejudice and discrimination continued unabated until World War I. Russian rule treated Jews as aliens. The government undermined Jewish community life, limited the publication of Jewish books, restricted areas where Jews could live, required Jews to have internal passports to move about the country, banned Jews from many forms of state service, and excluded Jews from many institutions of higher education. The state allowed the police and right-wing nationalist groups to conduct *pogroms*—organized riots—against Jewish neighborhoods and villages.

Because many major financial institutions of nineteenth-century Europe were owned by wealthy Jewish families, anti-Semitic political figures often blamed them for economic hard times. The most famous such family was the Rothschilds, who controlled banks in several countries. The head of the London branch was Lionel Rothschild (1808–1879). He was elected to Parliament several times but was not seated because he would not take the required Christian oath. After the requirement of that oath was abolished in 1858, he sat in Parliament from 1858 to 1874.

Getty Images Inc.— Hulton Archive Photos

What was life like for the majority of European Jews?

Broadened Opportunities

After the revolutions of 1848, European Jews saw a general improvement in their situation that lasted for several decades. Indeed, from about 1850 to 1880, relatively little organized or overt prejudice was expressed against Jews in Western Europe. They entered the professions and other occupations once closed to them. They participated fully in literary and cultural life. They were active in the arts and music. They became leaders in science and education. Jews intermarried freely with non-Jews as legal, secular prohibitions against such marriages were repealed during the last quarter of the century. Outside of Russia, Jewish politicians entered cabinets and served in the highest offices of the state. In Western Europe, including England, France, Italy, Germany, and the Low Countries, the legalized persecution and discrimination that had so haunted Jews in the past seemed to have ended.

That newfound security began to erode during the last two decades of the nineteenth century. Anti-Semitic voices began to be heard in the 1870s, attributing the economic stagnation of the decade to Jewish bankers and financial interests. In the 1880s, organized **anti-Semitism** erupted in Germany, as it did in France at the time of the Dreyfus affair. Most Jewish leaders believed the attacks on Jewish life were merely temporary recurrences of older forms of prejudice; they felt their communities would remain safe under the liberal legal protections that had been extended during the century. That analysis would be proved disastrously wrong in the 1930s and 1940s.

anti-Semitism Hostility toward or prejudice against Jews.

LABOR, SOCIALISM, AND POLITICS TO WORLD WAR I

WHAT ROLE did the socialist and labor movements play in late-nineteenth-century politics?

The late-century industrial expansion further changed the life of the labor force. In all industrializing continental countries, the numbers of the urban proletariat rose. The proportion of artisans and highly skilled workers declined, and for the first time, factory wage earners predominated. The number of unskilled workers in shipping, transportation, and building also grew.

After 1848, European workers stopped rioting in the streets to voice their grievances. They also stopped trying to revive the old paternal guilds and similar institutions. Instead, they turned to new institutions and ideologies. Chief among these were trade unions, democratic political parties, and socialism.

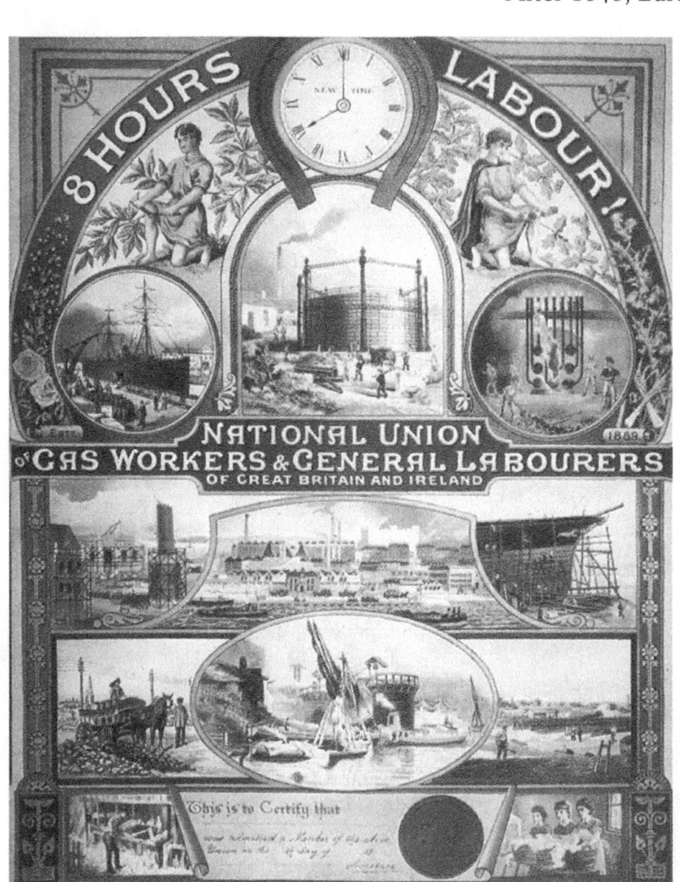

Trade unions continued to grow in late-century Great Britain. The effort to curb the unions eventually led to the formation of the Labour Party. The British unions often had quite elaborate membership certificates, such as this one for the National Union of Gas Workers and General Labourers of Great Britain and Ireland.

The Granger Collection

What role did unions play in late nineteenth-century British politics?

Trade Unionism

Trade unionism came of age when governments extended legal protections to unions during the second half of the century. Unions became fully legal in Great Britain in 1871. In France, the Third French Republic fully legalized unions in 1884. In Germany, unions were permitted to function with little disturbance after 1890. Union participation in the political process was at first marginal. As long as the representatives of the traditional governing classes looked after labor interests, members of the working class rarely sought office themselves.

Unions directed their midcentury organizational efforts toward skilled workers and the immediate improvement of wages and working conditions. By the close of the century, industrial unions for unskilled workers were being organized. Employers intensely opposed these large unions of thousands of workers. Unions frequently had to engage in long strikes to convince employers to accept their demands. Despite union advances, however, and the growth of union membership, most of Europe's labor force was never unionized in this period. What the unions did represent for workers was a new collective form of association to confront economic difficulties and improve security.

Democracy and Political Parties

Except for Russia, all the major European states adopted broad-based, if not perfectly democratic, electoral systems in the late nineteenth century. Great Britain passed its second voting reform act in 1867 and its third in 1884. Bismarck brought universal male suffrage to the German Empire in 1871. The French Chamber of Deputies was democratically elected. The broadened franchise meant politicians could no longer ignore workers, and discontented groups could now voice their grievances and advocate their programs within the institutions of government rather than from the outside.

The advent of democracy brought organized mass political parties like those already in existence in the United States to Europe for the first time. The expansion of the electorate brought into the political process many people whose level of political consciousness, awareness, and interest was low. This electorate had to be organized and taught about power and influence in the liberal democratic state. The organized political party—with its workers, newspapers, offices, social life, and discipline—was the vehicle that mobilized the new voters. The democratization of politics presented the socialists with opportunities and required the traditional ruling classes to vie with the socialists for the support of the new working-class voters.

The major question for late-century socialist parties throughout Europe was whether revolution or democratic reform would improve the life of the working class. This question sharply divided all socialist parties and especially those whose leadership adhered to the intellectual legacy of Karl Marx. The dispute over whether to achieve socialism through revolution or reform sharply shaped socialist thought, party programs, and political behavior and influenced not only socialism but the larger European political arena as well.

QUICK REVIEW

Expanding Democracy

- Great Britain passed second (1867) and third (1884) voting reform acts
- Universal male suffrage in German Empire (1871)
- French Chamber of Deputies democratically elected

Karl Marx and the First International

In 1864, a group of British and French trade unionists founded the International Working Men's Association. Known as the First International, its membership encompassed a vast array of radical political types, including socialists, anarchists, and Polish nationalists. In the inaugural address for the First International, Karl Marx approved workers' and trade unions' efforts to reform the conditions of labor within the existing political and economic processes. In his private writings he often criticized such reformist activity, but these writings were not made public until near the end of the century, years after his death.

The violence involved in the rise and suppression of the Paris Commune (see Chapter 22), which Marx had declared a genuine proletarian uprising, cast a pall over socialism throughout Europe. British trade unionists, who received legal protections in 1871, wanted no connection with the events in Paris. The French authorities used the uprising to suppress socialist activity. Under these pressures, the First International held its last European congress in 1873. It soon transferred its offices to the United States, where it was dissolved in 1876.

The short-lived First International had a disproportionately great impact on the future of European socialism. Throughout the late 1860s, the organization gathered statistics, kept labor groups informed of mutual problems, provided a forum to debate socialist doctrine, and extravagantly proclaimed (and overstated) its own influence over contemporary events. From these debates and activities, Marxism emerged as the single most important strand of socialism. Marx's thought deeply impressed German socialists, who were to establish the most powerful socialist party in Europe, and became the chief vehicle for preserving and developing it. The full development of German socialism, however, also involved the influence of non-Marxist socialists in Great Britain.

Great Britain: Fabianism and Early Welfare Programs

Neither Marxism nor any other form of socialism made significant progress in Great Britain, the most advanced industrial society of the day. There trade unions grew steadily, and their members normally supported Liberal Party candidates. Until 1901, labor's general political activity remained limited. In that year, however, the House of Lords, which also acts as Britain's highest court, through the Taff Vale decision, removed the legal protection previously accorded union funds. The Trades Union Congress responded by launching the Labour Party. In the election of 1906, the fledgling party sent twenty-nine members to Parliament. Their goals as trade unionists, however, did not yet include socialism. In this same period, the British labor movement became more militant. In scores of strikes before the war, workers fought for wages to meet the rising cost of living. The government took a larger role than ever before in mediating these strikes.

British socialism itself remained primarily the preserve of non-Marxist intellectuals. The Fabian Society, founded in 1884, was Britain's most influential socialist group. Many Fabians were civil servants who believed the problems of industry, the expansion of ownership, and the state direction of production could be solved and achieved gradually, peacefully, and democratically. They sought to educate the country about the rational wisdom of socialism. They were particularly interested in modes of collective ownership on the municipal level, the so-called gas-and-water socialism.

The British government and the Liberal and Conservative parties responded slowly to these pressures. In 1903, Joseph Chamberlain (1836–1914) launched his unsuccessful campaign to match foreign tariffs and to finance social reform through higher import duties. The campaign split the Conservative Party. After 1906, the Liberal Party, led by Sir Henry Campbell-Bannerman (1836–1908) and, after 1908, by Herbert Asquith, pursued a two-pronged policy. Fearful of losing seats in Parliament to the new Labour Party, they restored the former protection of the unions. Then, after 1909, with Chancellor of the Exchequer David Lloyd George (1863–1945) as its guiding light, the Liberal ministry undertook a broad program of social legislation that included establishing labor exchanges, regulating certain trades, and passing the National Insurance Act of 1911, which provided unemployment benefits and health care.

The new taxes and social programs meant that in Britain, the home of nineteenth-century liberalism, the state was taking on an expanded role in the life of its citizens. The early welfare legislation was only marginally satisfactory to labor, many of whose members still thought they could gain more from the direct action of strikes.

France: "Opportunism" Rejected

French socialism was a less united and more politically factionalized movement than socialism in other countries. At the turn of the century, Jean Jaurès (1859–1914) and Jules Guesde (1845–1922) led the two major factions of French socialists. Jaurès believed socialists should cooperate with middle-class Radical ministries to ensure the enactment of needed social legislation. Guesde opposed this policy, arguing that socialists could not, with integrity, support a bourgeois cabinet they were theoretically dedicated to overthrowing. The government's response to the Dreyfus affair brought the quarrel to a head. In 1899, seeking to unite all supporters of Dreyfus, Prime Minister René Waldeck-Rousseau (1846–1904) appointed the socialist Alexander Millerand (1859–1943) to the cabinet.

The Second International had been founded in 1889 in a new effort to unify the various national socialist parties and trade unions. By 1904, the Amsterdam Congress of the Second International debated the issue of *opportunism*, as such participation by socialists in cabinets was termed. The Congress condemned opportunism in France and ordered French socialists to form a single party. Jaurès accepted the decision. Thereafter French socialists began to work together, and by 1914, the recently united Socialist Party had become the second largest group in the Chamber of Deputies.

The French labor movement, with deep roots in anarchism, was uninterested in either politics or socialism. French workers usually voted socialist, but the unions themselves, unlike those in Britain, avoided active political participation. The main labor union, Confédération Générale du Travail, founded in 1895, regarded itself as a rival to the socialist parties. Its leaders sought to improve the workers' conditions through direct action, such as general strikes. The strike tactic often conflicted with the socialist belief in aiding labor through state action. Strikes were common in France between 1905 and 1914, and the middle-class Radical ministry used troops to suppress them on more than one occasion.

Germany: Social Democrats and Revisionism

The German Social Democratic Party, or SPD, was founded in 1875. From the beginning, the SPD was divided between those who advocated reform and those who advocated revolution.

Bismarck's Repression of the SPD Twelve years of persecution under Bismarck forged the character of the SPD. The so-called Iron Chancellor used an assassination attempt on Emperor William I (r. 1861–1888) in 1878, in which the socialists were not involved, to steer antisocialist laws through the *Reichstag*. The measures suppressed the organization, meetings, newspapers, and other public activities of the SPD. Thereafter, to remain a socialist meant to remove oneself from the mainstream of respectable German life and possibly to lose one's job. Nonetheless, from the early 1880s onward, the SPD steadily polled more and more votes in elections to the *Reichstag*.

As simple repression failed to wean German workers from socialist loyalties, Bismarck undertook a program of social welfare legislation. In 1883, the German Empire adopted a health insurance measure. The next year the *Reichstag* enacted accident insurance legislation. Finally, in 1889, Bismarck sponsored a plan for old age and disability pensions. These programs, to which both workers and employers contributed, represented a paternalistic, conservative alternative to socialism.

The Erfurt Program After forcing Bismarck's resignation mainly because of differences over foreign policy, Emperor William II (r. 1888–1918) allowed the antisocialist legislation to expire, hoping to build new political support among the working class. Even under the repressive laws, members of the SPD could sit in the *Reichstag*. With the repressive measures lifted, the party needed to decide what attitude to assume toward the German Empire.

The answer came in the Erfurt Program of 1891. In good Marxist fashion, the program declared the imminent doom of capitalism and the necessity of socialist ownership of the means of production. The party intended to pursue these goals through legal political participation rather than by revolutionary activity. So, although in theory the SPD was vehemently hostile to the German Empire, in practice the party functioned within its institutions.

The Debate over Revisionism The dilemma of the SPD, however, generated the most important challenge within the socialist movement to the orthodox Marxist analysis of capitalism and the socialist revolution. The author of this socialist heresy, Eduard Bernstein (1850–1932), had lived in Britain and was familiar with the Fabians. In *Evolutionary Socialism* (1899), he questioned whether Marx and his later orthodox followers had been correct in their pessimistic appraisal of capitalism and the necessity of revolution. For Bernstein, social reform through democratic institutions replaced revolution as the path to a humane socialist society. (See "Compare & Connect: Bernstein and Lenin Debate the Character of Tactics of European Socialism," pages, 590–591.)

Bernstein's doctrines, known as Revisionism, generated heated debate among German socialists, who finally condemned them. Nonetheless, while still calling for revolution, the SPD pursued a course of action similar to what Bernstein advocated. Its trade union members, prospering within the German economy, did not want revolution. Its grassroots members wanted to be patriotic Germans as well as good socialists. Its leaders feared anything that might renew the persecution they had experienced under Bismarck. Consequently, the SPD worked for electoral gains, expansion of its membership, and short-term political and social reform. It prospered and became one of the most important institutions of imperial Germany. Even middle-class Germans voted for it to oppose the illiberal institutions of the empire.

Russia: Industrial Development and the Birth of Bolshevism

In the 1890s, Russia entered the industrial age and confronted many of the problems that the more advanced nations of the Continent had experienced fifty or seventy-five years earlier. Unlike those other countries, Russia had to deal with political discontent and economic development simultaneously. Russian socialism reflected that peculiar situation.

Witte's Program for Industrial Growth Tsar Alexander III (r. 1881–1894) and, after him, Nicholas II (r. 1894–1917) were determined that Russia should become an industrial power. Only by doing so, they believed, could the country maintain its position as a great power. Count Sergei Witte (1849–1915) led Russia into the industrial age. After a career in railways and other private business, he was appointed first minister of communications and then finance minister in 1892. Witte pursued a policy of planned economic development, protective tariffs, high taxes, putting Russia's currency on the gold standard, and efficiency in government and business.

Witte favored heavy industries. Between 1890 and 1904, the Russian railway system grew from 30,596 to 59,616 kilometers. Coal, pig-iron, and steel output rose rapidly. Textile manufacturing continued to expand and was still the single largest industry. The factory system spread extensively.

Industrialism, however, also brought social discontent to Russia, as it had elsewhere. Landowners felt that foreign capitalists were earning too much of the profit. The peasants saw their grain exports and tax payments finance development that did not measurably improve their lives. A small, but significant, industrial proletariat emerged. In 1900, Russia had approximately 3 million factory workers, working and living in poor conditions, with little or no state protection.

Similar social and economic problems arose in the countryside. Russian agriculture had not prospered after the emancipation of the serfs in 1861. The peasants remained burdened with redemption payments for the land they farmed, local taxes, excessive national taxes, and falling grain prices. Peasants did not own their land as individuals, but communally through the *mir*, or village. They farmed the land inefficiently through strip farming or by tilling small plots. Many free peasants with too little land to support their families had to work on large estates owned by nobles or for more prosperous peasant farmers, known as *kulaks*. Between 1860 and 1914, the population of European Russia rose from about 50 million to around 103 million people. Land hunger and discontent spread among the peasants and sparked frequent uprisings in the countryside.

New political developments accompanied economic changes. The Social Revolutionary Party, founded in 1901, opposed industrialism and looked to the communal life of rural Russia as a model for the future. In 1903, the Constitutional Democratic Party, or Cadets, was formed. Modeling themselves on the liberal parties of Western

In this photograph taken in 1895, Lenin sits at the table among a group of other young Russian radicals from Saint Petersburg.

CORBIS/Bettmann

How did Lenin change communist theory to fit Russian circumstances?

Europe, the Cadets wanted a constitutional monarchy under a parliamentary regime with civil liberties and economic progress.

Lenin's Early Thought and Career The situation of Russian socialists differed radically from that of socialists in other major European countries. Russia had no representative institutions and only a small working class. The compromises and accommodations achieved elsewhere were meaningless in Russia, where socialists believed that in both theory and practice they must be revolutionary. The repressive policies of the tsarist regime required the Russian Social Democratic Party, founded in 1898, to function in exile. The party members greatly admired the German Social Democratic Party and adopted its Marxist ideology.

The future leader of the communist revolution, Vladimir Ilyich Ulyanov (1870–1924), who later took the name of Lenin, was the son of a high bureaucrat. In 1893, Lenin moved to Saint Petersburg, where he studied law and was soon drawn to the revolutionary groups among the factory workers. He was arrested in 1895 and exiled to Siberia. In 1900, after his release, Lenin left Russia for the West. He spent most of the next seventeen years in Switzerland.

There, Lenin became deeply involved in the disputes of the exiled Russian Social Democrats. Unlike the backward-looking Social Revolutionaries, the Social Democrats were modernizers who favored industrial development. Looking to Karl Marx's writings, most Russian Social Democrats believed Russia must develop a large proletariat before the Marxist revolution could come. They also hoped to build a mass political party like the German SPD.

Lenin dissented from both these ideas. In *What Is to Be Done?* (1902), he condemned any accommodations, such as those the German SPD practiced. He also criticized trade unionism that settled for short-term reformist gains and rejected the concept of a mass democratic party composed of workers. Instead, he declared that revolutionary consciousness would not arise spontaneously from the working class. Only a small, tightly organized, elite party could possess the proper dedication to revolution and resist penetration by police spies. Lenin thus rejected both the view that revolution was inevitable and that democratic means could achieve revolutionary goals. Lenin substituted the small, professional, nondemocratic revolutionary party for Marx's proletariat as the instrument of revolutionary change. (See ""Compare & Connect: Bernstein and Lenin Debate the Character of Tactics of European Socialism," pages 590–591.)

In 1903, at the London Congress of the Russian Social Democratic Party, Lenin forced a split in the party ranks. He and his followers lost many votes on questions put before the congress, but near its close they mustered a slim majority. Thereafter Lenin's faction assumed the name **Bolsheviks**, meaning "majority," and the other, more moderate, democratic revolutionary faction came to be known as the **Mensheviks**, or "minority."

Bolsheviks ("majority") Lenin's turn-of-the-century socialist Russian faction favoring a party of elite professionals who would provide the working class with centralized leadership.

Mensheviks ("minority") Turn-of-the-century socialist Russian faction that wanted to create a party with a large mass membership (like Germany's SPD).

A fundamental organizational difference had existed between what in 1903 were the two chief factions of the Russian Social Democratic Party. The Mensheviks wanted a party with a mass membership, similar to the German SDP and other Western European socialist parties, which would function democratically. The Bolsheviks intended the party to consist of elite professional revolutionaries who would provide centralized leadership for the working class.

In 1905, Lenin complemented his organizational theory with a program for revolution in Russia. In *Two Tactics of Social Democracy in the Bourgeois-Democratic Revolution*, he urged the socialist revolution to unite the proletariat and the peasantry. Lenin grasped better than any other revolutionary the profound discontent in the Russian countryside. He believed the tsarist government probably could not suppress an alliance of workers and peasants in rebellion.

The Revolution of 1905 and Its Aftermath The quarrels among the exiled Russian socialists and Lenin's doctrines had no immediate influence on events in Russia. Industrialization continued to stir resentment. In 1903, Nicholas II dismissed Witte, hoping to quell the criticism. The next year, in response to conflicts over Manchuria and Korea, Russia went to war against Japan, partly in hopes the conflict would rally public opinion to the tsar. Instead, the Russians lost the war, and the government faced an internal political crisis. The Japanese captured Port Arthur, Russia's naval base on the coast of China, early in 1905. A few days later, on January 22, a Russian Orthodox priest named Father George Gapon led several hundred workers to present a petition to the tsar to improve industrial conditions. As they approached the Winter Palace, troops opened fire, killing approximately forty people and wounding hundreds of others. As word of this massacre spread, and large, angry crowds gathered elsewhere in the city, the military shot more people. The final death toll was approximately two hundred killed and eight hundred wounded. The day, soon known as Bloody Sunday, marked a turning point. Vast numbers of ordinary Russians came to believe they could no longer trust the tsar or his government.

During the next ten months, revolutionary disturbances spread throughout Russia. In early October 1905, strikes broke out in Saint Petersburg, and for all practical purposes, worker groups, called soviets, controlled the city. Nicholas II, who had recalled Witte, issued the October Manifesto, which promised Russia a constitutional government. Early in 1906, Nicholas II announced the creation of a representative body, the Duma, with two chambers. He reserved to himself, however, ministerial appointments, financial policy, and military and foreign affairs. The April elections returned a highly radical group of representatives. The tsar then replaced Witte with P. A. Stolypin (1862–1911), who had little sympathy for parliamentary government. Stolypin persuaded Nicholas to dissolve the Duma. A second assembly was elected in February 1907. Again, cooperation proved impossible, and the tsar dissolved that Duma in June. A third Duma, elected in late 1907 on the basis of a more conservative

On Bloody Sunday, January 22, 1905, troops of Tsar Nicholas II fired on a peaceful procession of workers who sought to present a petition for better working and living conditions at the Winter Palace in St. Petersburg. This event all but destroyed any chance of reconciliation between the tsarist government and the Russian working class.

Bildarchiv Preussischer Kulturbesitz

How did defeat in the Russo-Japanese war contribute to domestic political unrest in Russia?

franchise, proved sufficiently pliable for the tsar and his minister. Thus, within two years of the 1905 Revolution, Nicholas II had recaptured much of the ground he had conceded.

Stolypin set about repressing rebellion, removing some causes of the revolt, and rallying property owners behind the tsarist regime. Early in 1907, special field courts-martial condemned almost seven hundred rebellious peasants to death. Before undertaking this repression, Stolypin, in November 1906, had canceled any redemptive payments that the peasants still owed the government from the emancipation of the serfs in 1861. He took this step to encourage peasants to assume individual proprietorship of the land they farmed and to abandon the communal system of the *mirs*. Combined with a program to instruct peasants on how to farm more efficiently, this policy improved agricultural production. However, many peasant small-holders sold their land and joined the industrial labor force.

The moderate liberals who sat in the Duma approved of the new land measures. They liked the idea of competition and individual property ownership. The Constitutional Democrats wanted a more genuinely parliamentary mode of government, but they compromised out of fear of new revolutionary disturbances. Hatred of Stolypin was still widespread, however, among the country's older conservative groups, and industrial workers remained antagonistic to the tsar. In 1911, Stolypin was assassinated by a Social Revolutionary, who may have been a police agent in the pay of conservatives. Nicholas II found no worthy successor. His government simply muddled along.

Meanwhile, at court, the monk Grigory Efimovich Rasputin (1871?–1916) gained ascendancy with the tsar and his wife because of his alleged power to heal the tsar's hemophilic son Alexis, the heir to the throne, when medicine proved unable to help the boy. The undue influence of this strange, uncouth man, as well as continued social discontent and conservative resistance to any further liberal reforms, undermined the position of the tsar and his government after 1911. Once again, as in 1904, he and his ministers thought that some bold move in foreign policy might bring the regime the popular support it desperately needed.

COMPARE & CONNECT

BERNSTEIN AND LENIN DEBATE THE CHARACTER OF TACTICS OF EUROPEAN SOCIALISM

By the close of the nineteenth century, the European Socialist movement found itself sharply divided over its future goals and tactics. On the one side, some socialists, here represented by Eduard Bernstein, came to reject many of the ideas of Karl Marx, particularly that of a proletarian revolution, and embraced democratic politics as the best way to realize their goals of the improvement of the life of the working class. Others, a minority at the time, represented here by Lenin, rejected democracy and embraced the concept of violent revolution achieved by a small professional elite rather than by a spontaneous proletarian uprising. In the twentieth century after the 1917 Bolshevik Revolution in Russia, those divisions would play themselves out in an enormously hostile conflict between democratic socialist parties in Western Europe and Communists in the Soviet Union and Communist parties in Western Europe dominated by the Soviet Union. (See Chapters 26 and 27.)

QUESTIONS

1. According to Bernstein, what specific predictions in The *Communist Manifesto* failed to materialize?
2. Why is the advance of democracy important to Bernstein's argument? Why does he renounce the concept of a "dictatorship of the proletariat"?
3. What does Lenin mean by "professional revolutionaries"? Why does Russia need such revolutionaries?
4. How does Lenin reconcile his antidemocratic views to the goal of aiding the working class?
5. How could the ideas of both Bernstein and Lenin be seen as departures from Marx's own thinking?

I. EDUARD BERNSTEIN URGES SOCIALISTS TO EMBRACE DEMOCRACY

Eduard Bernstein was responsible for the emergence of Revisionism within the German Social Democratic Party. He was a dedicated socialist who recognized that Marx's Communist Manifesto *(1848) had not predicted the actual future of the European working classes. Bernstein believed the capitalist system would not suddenly collapse and that socialists should change their tactics to achieve democratic political rights and pursue reform instead of revolution.*

Social conditions have not developed to such an acute opposition of things and classes as is depicted in the [Communist] *Manifesto*. . . . The number of members of the possessing classes is today not smaller but larger. The enormous increase of social wealth is not accompanied by a decreasing number of large capitalists but by an increasing number of capitalists of all degrees. . . .

In all advanced countries we see the privileges of the capitalist bourgeoisie yielding step by step to democratic organizations. . . .

The conquest of political power by the working classes, the expropriation of capitalists, are not ends in themselves but only means for the accomplishment of certain aims and endeavours. . . .

Democracy is in principle the suppression of class government, though it is not yet the actual suppression of classes. . . . The right to vote in a democracy makes its members virtually partners in the community, and this virtual partnership must in the end lead to real partnership. . . .

Universal franchise is, from two sides, the alternative to a violent revolution. But universal suffrage is only a part of democracy, although a part which in time must draw the other parts after it as the magnet attracts to itself the scattered portions of iron. It certainly proceeds more slowly than many would wish, but in spite of that it is at work. And social democracy cannot further this work better than by taking its stand unreserved only the theory of democracy—on the ground of universal suffrage with all the consequences resulting therefrom to its tactics. . . .

By the close of the nineteenth century, European socialists had come to doubt whether the industrial proletariat around the world, such as these workers in the United States, would or could actually bring about a revolution as predicted by Marx. Eduard Bernstein thought democratic social change would improve the lot of workers. Lenin believed an elite revolutionary party would produce such radical change.

Courtesy of the Library of Congress

Did late nineteenth-century industrial workers see themselves as a unified political force capable of and committed to bringing about the kind of revolutionary change that socialists advocated?

Is there any sense . . . in maintaining the phrase of the 'dictatorship of the proletariot' at a time when in all possible places representatives of social democracy have placed themselves practically in the arena of Parliamentary work, have declared for the proportional representation of the people, and for direct legislation—all of which is inconsistent with a dictatorship.

The phrase is to-day so antiquated that is is only to be reconciled with reality by stripping the word dictatorship of its actual meaning and attaching to it some kind of weakened interpretation. The whole practical activity of social democracy is directed towards creating circumstances and condition which shall render possible and secure a transition (free from convulsive outbursts) of the modern social order to a higher one.

Source: From Eduard Bernstein, *Evolutionary Socialism: A Criticism and Affirmation*, 1899 (New York: Schocken Books, 1961), pp. xxiv–xxv, xxix, 143–146.

II. LENIN ARGUES FOR THE NECESSITY OF A SECRET AND ELITE PARTY OF PROFESSIONAL REVOLUTIONARIES

Social democratic parties in Western Europe had mass memberships and were generally democratic organizations. In this passage from What Is to Be Done? *(1902), Lenin explains why the autocratic political conditions of Russia demanded a different kind of organization for the Russian Social Democratic Party. Lenin's ideas became the guiding principles of Bolshevik organization. Lenin departed from Marx's own thought by urging the necessity of fulminating revolution rather than waiting for it to occur as a necessary result of the collapse of capitalism.*

I assert that it is far more difficult [for government police] to unearth a dozen wise men than a hundred fools. This position I will defend, no matter how much you instigate the masses against me for my "anti-democratic" views, etc. As I have stated repeatedly, by "wise men," in connection with organization, I mean professional revolutionaries, irrespective of whether they have developed from among students or working men. I assert: (1) that no revolutionary movement can endure without a stable organization of leaders maintaining continuity; (2) that the broader the popular mass drawn spontaneously into the struggle, which forms the basis of the movement and participates in it, the more urgent the need for such an organization, and the more solid this organization must be . . .; (3) that such an organization must consist chiefly of people professionally engaged in revolutionary activity; (4) that in an autocratic state [such as Russia], the more we confine the membership of such an organization to people who are professionally engaged in revolutionary activity and who have been professionally trained in the art of combating the political police, the more difficult will it be to unearth the organization; and (5) the greater will be the number of people from the working class and from other social classes who will be able to join the movement and perform active work in it. . . .

The only serious organization principle for the active workers of our movement should be the strictest secrecy, the strictest selection of members, and the training of professional revolutionaries.

Source: From *Socialist Thought: A Documentary History*, ed. by Albert Fried and Ronald Sanders (Garden City, NY: Anchor Doubleday, 1964), pp. 460, 468.

SUMMARY

WHY WERE so many Europeans on the move in the late nineteenth century?

Population Trends and Migration Europeans made up approximately 20 percent of the world's population around 1900. Soon thereafter, birth and death rates stabilized or declined in developed regions but continued to increase elsewhere. In the second half of the nineteenth century, Europeans emigrated in huge numbers. Many went to the Americas, Australia, and South Africa. At midcentury, most of them came from Great Britain, Germany, and Scandinavia; after 1885, more came from southern and eastern Europe. *page 566*

HOW DID the second Industrial Revolution transform European life?

The Second Industrial Revolution The second Industrial Revolution was dominated by Germany. At the turn of the century, the emergence of an industrial Germany was the most significant aspect of political and economic life in Europe. The steel industry produced over 32 million tons of steel by 1913. The chemical industry depended on scientific research, and Germany was the first country to attempt to facilitate the flow of information between research and industry. Electrical energy was widely applied, and the automobile had been invented. Economic advances slowed in the final quarter of the century, although the standard of living in most industrial nations continued to grow slowly. Unemployment and poverty contributed to the appeal of trade unions and socialist political parties. Consumer goods were an important aspect of the urban lifestyle. *page 566*

WHAT EXPLAINS the prominence of the middle class in late-nineteenth-century Europe?

The Middle Classes in Ascendancy The middle classes set the values and goals for most of society between the middle of the nineteenth century and World War I. In reaction to the 1848 revolutions, the middle classes put aside revolution in favor of preserving their status and possessions. The middle classes diversified: A few families gained wealth exceeding that of the aristocracy; small entrepreneurs and professionals earned enough to purchase private homes, education for their children, and vacations; secretaries, retail workers, and low-level bureaucrats made up the white-collar workers (the *petite bourgeoisie*), who were close to the working class but deliberately adopted middle-class behaviors and consumption patterns. Tensions existed among these middle-class groups. *page 569*

WHAT FORCES shaped the development of European cities?

Late-Nineteenth-Century Urban Life Urbanization increased in the late nineteenth century. Between 1850 and 1910, the population of many major European cities doubled or tripled. There were social, political, economic, environmental, and health consequences of this growth. Governments led the redesign of the central portions of many cities. Parisian streets were widened, for aesthetic and practical reasons. Public works projects created many jobs. Displaced city dwellers often moved to suburbs. Health and housing for the poor came to be seen as prerequisites for safety and security for the middle classes. The cholera epidemics of the early nineteenth century led to concerns in public health and sanitation. Governments gained new powers to intervene in citizens' lives in the name of public health. Working-class housing conditions also became a subject of medical, moral, and political concern to middle-class reformers and bureaucrats. Philanthropies, businesses, and government offered economic incentives to build housing for the poor, trying to create working-class homes and facilitate middle-class family life. *page 570*

WHAT WAS life like for women in late-nineteenth-century Europe?

Varieties of Late-Nineteenth-Century Women's Experiences Like men, women's experiences reflected their class, but women of all ranks faced disabilities in property rights, family law, and education. The degree of disability diminished in the late nineteenth century. Men controlled their wives' property in Europe until late in the century. Family law often required a woman's obedience to her husband; sexual double standards prevailed; divorce was difficult; and contraception and abortion were illegal. Women's education was minimal and inferior. Teaching was one of the few career paths open to women. The second Industrial Revolution opened more jobs to women, but the jobs were often low skilled and almost inevitably low paying. Working-class women often labored in sweatshops that lacked job security; some became prostitutes. Middle-class women were usually wives and mothers and discouraged from employment. The "cult of domesticity" made women and their roles within the home a symbol of the success of their father or husband. Women in Britain ("suffragettes"), France, Germany, and elsewhere lobbied for the right to vote, but nowhere did they gain it until after the turn of the century. *page 574*

HOW DID Jewish life in Europe change in the late nineteenth century?

Jewish Emancipation Political liberalism facilitated the emancipation of European Jews, to varying degrees and at various speeds in different nations. In the late eighteenth century and the first half of the nineteenth century, Jews gained rights approximating those of other citizens in most western European states. In Russia, traditional discrimination persisted. After the revolutions of 1848, the situation for most European Jews improved, with further political and citizenship rights being granted to Jews in most of western Europe. Even Jews in Austria-Hungary gained full legal rights in 1867. Institutionalized prejudice seemed to have dissipated in western Europe, although certainly not in Russia and only sporadically in eastern Europe. Anti-Semitism grew in the 1870s and 1880s, though, largely as a by-product of economic stagnation. Jewish leaders had faith in liberal government structures to protect their rights. *page 581*

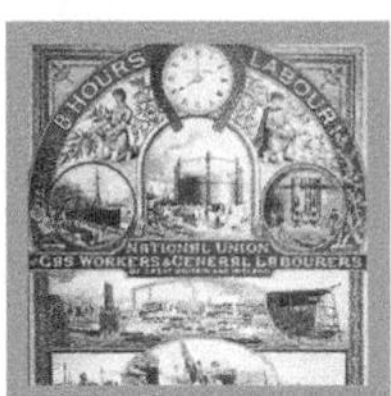

WHAT ROLE did the socialist and labor movements play in late-nineteenth-century politics?

Labor, Socialism, and Politics to World War I With industrial expansion, the size of the urban proletariat grew. New institutions and ideologies had replaced riots as the way by which workers expressed their will. Unions grew in the second half of the century, but most workers were still not unionized. Broader-based political systems everywhere except Russia brought with them organized mass political parties. Socialist parties divided on whether change would come through reform or revolution. Marx publicly endorsed reform. In Great Britain, trade unionism was allied with the Liberal Party and then the Labour Party. The Fabian Society was Britain's most significant socialist group, and it was gradualist and non-Marxist. In France, socialist parties quarreled among themselves; labor unions favored strikes over political participation. The German Social Democratic Party kept Marxist socialism alive through the turn of the century. In Russia, socialism was almost by definition revolutionary. In 1903, Lenin forced a split in the Russian Social Democratic Party over whether the party should strive for mass membership (the "Menshevik" position) or be limited to elite professional revolutionaries (Lenin's "Bolshevik" position). In 1905, Lenin wrote that the proletariat and the peasantry should unite in revolution in Russia. His formula would prove successful in 1917. Meanwhile, the Bloody Sunday massacre of January 1905 led to upheaval. By October 1905, worker groups called soviets controlled Saint Petersburg, and tsar Nicholas II promised constitutional government. By 1907, however, Nicholas II had dissolved two sessions of the Duma, the new representative legislature, and had taken back most of his powers. *page 582*

REVIEW QUESTIONS

1. How was European society transformed by the second Industrial Revolution? What were living conditions like in European cities during the late nineteenth century? Why were European cities redesigned during this period? How were they redesigned?
2. What was the status of European women in the second half of the nineteenth century? Why did they grow discontented with their lot? What tactics did they use in effecting change? What forms did the emancipation of Jews take in the nineteenth century?
3. What was the status of the proletariat in 1860? Had it improved by 1914? What caused the growth in trade unions and organized mass political parties? What were the differences among socialist parties?
4. How important was industrialism in Russia? Were the tsars wise to attempt to modernize their country? How did Lenin's view of socialism differ from that of the socialists in western Europe?

KEY TERMS

anti-Semitism (p. 582)
Bolsheviks (p. 588)
Mensheviks (p. 588)
petite bourgeoisie (p. 569)
second Industrial Revolution (p. 567)
suffragettes (p. 580)

For additional learning resources related to this chapter, please go to **www.myhistorylab.com**

myhistorylab

24

The Birth of Modern European Thought

Darwin's theories about the evolution of humankind from the higher primates aroused enormous controversy. This caricature shows him with a monkey's body holding a mirror to an apelike creature.

National History Museum, London, UK/Bridgeman Art Library

What groups felt most threatened by Darwin's theories? Why?

THE NEW READING PUBLIC *page 596*

WHAT EFFECT did state-financed education have on literacy in late-nineteenth-century Europe?

SCIENCE AT MIDCENTURY *page 597*

WHAT ROLE did science play in the second half of the nineteenth century?

CHRISTIANITY AND THE CHURCH UNDER SIEGE *page 599*

WHAT CHALLENGES did European Christianity face in the late nineteenth century?

TOWARD A TWENTIETH-CENTURY FRAME OF MIND *page 605*

HOW DID developments in art, psychology, and science reflect a profound shift in Western thought?

WOMEN AND MODERN THOUGHT *page 613*

HOW DID women challenge gender stereotypes in the late nineteenth and early twentieth centuries?

The political systems, industrialized economies, and middle-class lifestyles that emerged in the late nineteenth century were accompanied by intellectual developments that shaped a "modern" mind. The new intellectual orientation was rooted in the Enlightenment (which contributed confidence in reason and science and a tolerant, cosmopolitan outlook) and the romantic movement (which fostered respect for feeling, imagination, artistic insight, and the value of individuals). Most of the West's traditional assumptions about nature, religion, and social life were subjected to radical reexamination. As a result, at the turn of the century European intellectuals were more daring than ever before but less certain about where their work might lead. Fading confidence in the reliability of traditional points of view helped some disadvantaged groups, such as women, win liberating social reforms.

THE NEW READING PUBLIC

WHAT EFFECT did state-financed education have on literacy in late-nineteenth-century Europe?

The social context of intellectual life changed in the latter part of the nineteenth century. For the first time in Europe, a mass reading public came into existence as more people than ever before became drawn into the world of print culture.

Advances in Primary Education

Literacy on the Continent improved steadily from the 1860s onward as governments financed education. By 1900, in Britain, France, Belgium, the Netherlands, Germany, and Scandinavia, approximately 85 percent or more of the people could read, but Italy, Spain, Russia, Austria-Hungary, and the Balkans still had illiteracy rates of between 30 and 60 percent.

The new primary education in the basic skills of reading, writing, and elementary arithmetic reflected and generated social change. Both liberals and conservatives regarded such minimal training as necessary for orderly political behavior by the newly enfranchised voters. They also hoped that literacy would create a more productive labor force.

Public education became widespread in Europe during the second half of the nineteenth century and women came to dominate the profession of schoolteaching, especially at the elementary level. This 1905 photograph shows English school-children going through morning drills.

How did public education affect home life for working-class families?

Literacy and its extension, however, soon became a force in its own right. The school-teaching profession grew rapidly in numbers and prestige and, as noted in Chapter 23, became a major area for the employment of women. Having created systems of primary education, the major nations had to give further attention to secondary education by the time of World War I. In another generation, the question would become one of democratic university instruction.

Reading Material for the Mass Audience

The expanding literate population created a vast market for new reading material. The number of newspapers, books, magazines, mail-order catalogs, and libraries grew rapidly. Cheap mass-circulation newspapers enjoyed their first heyday. Such newspapers carried advertising that alerted readers to the new consumer products available through the Second Industrial Revolution. Other publishers produced newspapers with specialized political or religious viewpoints. Probably more people with different ideas could get into print in the late nineteenth century than ever before in European history. In addition, more people could read their ideas than ever before.

Because many of the new readers were only marginally literate and still ignorant about many subjects, the books and journals catering to them were often mediocre. The cheap newspapers prospered on stories of sensational crimes and political scandal and on pages of adver-

Overview Development in Science, Psychology, Sociology, and Fiction

DISCIPLINE	YEAR	DEVELOPMENT
SCIENCE	1830s	Comte's positivism says all knowledge should be knowledge common to the physical sciences
	1859	Darwin's theory of evolution by natural selection disputes creationism
	1895	Roentgen announces the discovery of X-rays
PSYCHOLOGY	1900	Freud, the founder of psychoanalysis, publishes *The Interpretation of Dreams*
	early 1900s	Jung, student of Freud, theorizes that the subconscious is inherited from ancestors
	mid-1900s	Horney and Klein attempt to establish a psychoanalytic basis for feminism
SOCIOLOGY	1850s	Gobineau presents first arguments that race is the major determinant of human history
	1870s	Nationalism becomes a well-organized mass movement equating nationality with race
	1900	Weber traces capitalism to religious doctrines of Puritanism
FICTION	1856	*Madame Bovary* by Flaubert signals the advent of realism
	1870	Verne modernizes popular science fiction
	1920s	Woolf becomes a chief proponent of modernism

tising. Religious journals depended on denominational rivalry. A brisk market existed for pornography. Newspapers with editorials on the front page became major factors in the emerging mass politics. The news could be managed, but in central Europe more often by the government censor than by the publisher.

SCIENCE AT MIDCENTURY

WHAT ROLE did science play in the second half of the nineteenth century?

In about 1850, the basic Newtonian picture of physical nature still prevailed. At midcentury, learned persons regarded the physical world as rational, mechanical, and dependable. Experiment and observation could reveal its laws objectively. Scientific theory purportedly described physical nature as it really existed. Moreover, by 1850, science had a strong institutional life in French and German universities and in new professional societies. (See "Encountering the Past: The Birth of Science Fiction," page 598.)

Comte, Positivism, and the Prestige of Science

During the early nineteenth century, science had continued to establish itself as the model for all human knowledge. The French philosopher Auguste Comte (1798–1857) developed **positivism**, a philosophy of human intellectual development that culminated in science. In *The Positive Philosophy* (1830–1842), Comte argued that human thought had developed in three stages. In the first, or theological, stage, physical nature was explained in terms of the action of divinities or spirits. In the second, or metaphysical, stage, abstract principles were regarded as the operative agencies of nature. In the final, or positive stage, explanations of nature became matters of exact description of phenomena, without recourse to an unobservable operative principle. Physical science had, in Comte's view, entered the positive stage, and similar thinking should penetrate other areas of analysis, including social behavior. He is, thus, generally regarded as the father

positivism Comte's philosophy that all knowledge should be the kind of knowledge common to the physical sciences.

ENCOUNTERING THE PAST

The Birth of Science Fiction

During the Renaissance, Europe's fantasy writers set their stories in exotic foreign lands. In the seventeenth century, the moon became a favorite locale, and during the nineteenth century, authors turned to outer space and the earth's unexplored deep seas and interior. Modern popular science fiction begins with the work of Jules Verne (1828–1905), who wrote serialized stories for magazines. Verne prided himself on scientific accuracy, and he set his tales in his own age—giving his readers a sense of experiencing real adventures. His most enduring novel is Twenty Thousand Leagues under the Sea *(1870), the story of Captain Nemo's submarine* Nautilus. *English author H. G. Wells (1866–1946) helped establish many of the conventions of science fiction.* The Time Machine *(1895) explored the conundrum of time travel.* The Island of Dr. Moreau *(1896) described the consequences of inhuman medical experimentation, and* The War of the Worlds *(1898) raised the possibility of invasion from outer space.*

The stories of Verne and Wells appeared in cheap illustrated magazines with mass circulation and helped establish science fiction as a fixture of popular culture. As new entertainment media appeared (radio, movies, and then television), their works were repeatedly dramatized. A radio play by Orson Wells (1915–1985) in 1938 based on Wells's *The War of the Worlds* was so realistic that many Americans mistook it for a news report of a Martian landing in New Jersey.

Captain Nemo's submarine confronts a giant octopus in Verne's *Twenty Thousand Leagues under the Sea.*

What sort of future did nineteenth-century science fiction writers imagine?

WHY DID science fiction suddenly become popular with the masses in the late nineteenth century? What is the reason for its enduring popularity?

of sociology. Works like Comte's helped convince learned Europeans that all knowledge must resemble scientific knowledge.

From the mid–nineteenth century onward, the links of science to the technology of the Second Industrial Revolution made the general European public aware of science and technology as never before. Writers spoke of a religion of science that would explain all nature without resorting to supernaturalism. Popularizers, such as Thomas Henry Huxley (1825–1895) in Britain and Ernst Haeckel (1834–1919) in Germany, worked to gain government support of scientific research and to include science in the schools and universities.

Darwin's Theory of Natural Selection

In 1859, Charles Darwin (1809–1882) published *On the Origin of Species*, which carried the mechanical interpretation of physical nature into the world of living things. Darwin did not originate the concept of evolution, which had been discussed widely before

he wrote. What he and Alfred Russel Wallace (1823–1913) did, working independently, was to formulate the principle of natural selection, which explained how species had changed or evolved over time. Earlier writers had believed evolution might occur; Darwin and Wallace explained how it could occur.

Drawing on Malthus, the two scientists contended that more living organisms come into existence than can survive in their environment. Those organisms with a marginal advantage in the struggle for existence live long enough to propagate. This principle of survival of the fittest Darwin called **natural selection**. Darwin and Wallace's theory represented the triumph of naturalistic explanation, which removed the idea of purpose from organic nature. Eyes were not made for seeing according to the rational wisdom and purpose of God but had developed mechanistically over time. Thus, the theory of evolution through natural selection not only contradicted the biblical narrative of the Creation but also undermined both the deistic argument for the existence of God from the design of the universe and the whole concept of fixity in nature or the universe at large. The world was a realm of flux. The idea that physical and organic nature might be constantly changing allowed people to believe that society, values, customs, and beliefs should also change.

natural selection Darwin and Wallace's theory that those species with a unique trait that gives them a marginal advantage in the struggle for existence change the nature of their species by reproducing more successfully than their competitors; the fittest survive to pass on their unique characteristics.

In 1871, in *The Descent of Man*, Darwin applied the principle of evolution by natural selection to human beings. Darwin contended that humankind's moral nature and religious sentiments, as well as its physical frame, had developed naturalistically largely in response to the requirements of survival. Neither the origin nor the character of humankind, in Darwin's view, required the existence of a god for their explanation.

Science and Ethics—Social Darwinism

One area in which science came to have a new significance was social thought and ethics. Philosophers applied the concept of the struggle for survival to human social relationships. The phrase "survival of the fittest" predated Darwin and reflected the competitive outlook of classical economics. Darwin's use of the phrase gave it the prestige associated with advanced science.

The most famous advocate of evolutionary ethics was Herbert Spencer (1820–1903), a British philosopher. Spencer, a strong individualist, believed human society progresses through competition. If the weak receive too much protection, the rest of humankind is the loser. The concept could be applied to justify not aiding the poor and the working class or to justify the domination of colonial peoples or to advocate aggressive competition among nations. Evolutionary ethics and similar concepts, all of which are usually termed ***social Darwinism***, often came close to saying that "might makes right."

social Darwinism Darwin and Wallace's theory that those species with a unique trait that gives them a marginal advantage in the struggle for existence change the nature of their species by reproducing more successfully than their competitors; the fittest survive to pass on their unique characteristics.

One of the chief opponents of such thinking was Thomas Henry Huxley, the great defender of Darwin. In 1893, Huxley declared that the physical process of evolution was at odds with human ethical development. The struggle in nature only showed how human beings should not behave. (See "Compare & Connect: The Debate over Social Darwinism," pages 600–601.) Despite Huxley's arguments, the ideas of social Darwinism continued to influence thought and public policy on both sides of the Atlantic.

CHRISTIANITY AND THE CHURCH UNDER SIEGE

WHAT CHALLENGES did European Christianity face in the late nineteenth century?

The nineteenth century was one of the most difficult periods in the history of the organized Christian churches. Many European intellectuals left the faith. The secular, liberal nation-states attacked the influence of the church. The expansion of population and the growth of cities challenged its organizational capacity. Yet during all of this

COMPARE & CONNECT

THE DEBATE OVER SOCIAL DARWINISM

During the late nineteenth and early twentieth centuries, scientists as well as other social commentators debated the question of whether the concept of "survival of the fittest" on which Charles Darwin had based his concept of evolution by natural selection should apply to human society and the competition between nations. Some commentators, such as Herbert Spencer, had advocated generally unbridled economic competition with little or no help to the poor and others who fared badly as a result of such competition. In 1893, T. H. Huxley rejected that view. However, a few years later, Karl Pearson, another distinguished British scientist who supported the idea of evolution, argued that social Darwinism should and did govern the relationships among nations.

QUESTIONS

1. Why does Huxley equate "social progress" with the "ethical process"?
2. In this passage, does Huxley present human society as part of nature or as something that may be separate from nature?
3. How does Pearson connect Darwin's ideas to the concept of human progress?
4. How might Pearson's ideas justify imperial expansion, which will be considered in the next chapter? How could these arguments foster a climate of international violence?
5. How might Huxley's ideas be used to support broadly beneficial social welfare programs enacted to produce national populations healthy enough to compete in the international rivalry envisioned by Pearson?

I. T. H. HUXLEY CRITICIZES EVOLUTIONARY ETHICS

T. H. Huxley (1825–1895) was a British scientist who had been among Darwin's strongest defenders. Huxley, however, became a major critic of social Darwinism, which attempted to deduce ethical principles from evolutionary processes involving struggle in nature. Drawing a strong distinction between the cosmic process of evolution and the social process of ethical development, he argued in Evolution and Ethics *(1893) that human ethical progress occurs through combating the cosmic process.*

Men in society are undoubtedly subject to the cosmic process. As among other animals, multiplication goes on without cessation, and involves severe competition for the means of support. The struggle for existence tends to eliminate those less fitted to adapt themselves to the circumstances of their existence. The strongest, the most self-assertive, tend to tread down the weaker. But the influence of the cosmic process on the evolution of society is the greater the more rudimentary its civilization. Social progress means a checking of the cosmic process at every step and the substitution for it of another, which may be called the ethical process; the end of which is not the survival of those who may happen to be the fittest, in respect of the whole of the conditions which obtain, but of those who are ethically the best.

As I have already urged, the practice of that which is ethically best—what we call goodness or virtue—involves a course of conduct which, in all respects, is opposed to that which leads to success in the cosmic struggle for existence. In place of ruthless self-assertion it demands self-restraint; in place of thrusting aside, or treading down, all competitors, it requires that the individual shall not merely respect, but shall help his fellows; its influence is directed, not so much to the survival of the fittest, as to the fitting of as many as possible to survive. It repudiates the gladiatorial theory of existence.

It is from neglect of these plain considerations that the fanatical individualism of our time attempts to apply the analogy of cosmic nature to society. . . .

Let us understand, once for all, that the ethical progress of society depends, not on imitating the cosmic process, still less in running away from it, but in combating it.

Source: From T. H. Huxley, *Evolution and Ethics* (London: Macmillan & Co., 1893), as quoted in Franklin L. Baumer, *Main Currents of Western Thought: Readings in Western European Intellectual History from the Middle Ages to the Present*, 3rd ed., rev. (New York: Alfred A. Knopf, 1970), pp. 561–562.

Racism was often a by-product of social Darwinist theory. At the turn of the twentieth century, racism permeated many facets of popular life. This ad for Pears' Soap caters to the racist attitudes held by many whites during this time.

Library of Congress/*Colliers*, October 4, 1899

What relationship did this advertisement posit between race and hygiene?

II. SOCIAL DARWINISM AND IMPERIALISM

T. H. Huxley's assault did not end the influence of social Darwinism. Debates about competition among nations for trade, military superiority, and empire dominated much turn-of-the-twentieth-century political thought. The idea of biological competition became applied to nations and races and produced substantial impact on public opinion and among policymakers. In the selection that follows, Karl Pearson (1857–1936), an English scientist, attempts to connect concepts from evolutionary theory—the struggle for survival and the survival of the fittest—to the development of human societies.

History shows me one way, and one way only, in which a state of civilisation has been produced, namely, the struggle of race with race, and the survival of the physically and mentally fitter race. This dependence of progress on the survival of the fitter race, terribly black as it may seem to some of you, gives the struggle for existence its redeeming features; it is the fiery crucible out of which comes the finer metal. You may hope for a time when the sword shall be turned into the ploughshare, when American and German and English traders shall no longer compete in the markets of the world for raw materials, for their food supply, when the white man and the dark shall share the soil between them, and each till it as he lists. But, believe me, when that day comes mankind will no longer progress; there will be nothing to check the fertility of inferior stock; the relentless law of heredity will not be controlled and guided by natural selection. Man will stagnate. . . . The path of progress is strewn with the wreck of nations; traces are everywhere to be seen of the hecatombs of inferior races, and of victims who found not the narrow way to the greater perfection. Yet these dead peoples are, in very truth, the stepping stones on which mankind has arisen to the higher intellectual and deeper emotional life of today.

Source: From Karl Pearson, *National Life from the Standpoint of Science*, 2nd ed. (Cambridge: Cambridge University Press, 1907), pp. 21, 26–27, 64.

turmoil, the Protestant and Catholic churches continued to draw much popular support and personal religious devotion. Nonetheless, what would in the twentieth century become the overwhelmingly secular character of European society, a development that now largely distinguishes Europe from the United States, had its roots in the changes that commenced in the late nineteenth century.

Intellectual Skepticism

The intellectual attack on Christianity challenged its historical credibility, its scientific accuracy, and its morality.

History In 1835, David Friedrich Strauss (1808–1874) published *The Life of Jesus*, in which he questioned whether the Bible provides any genuine historical evidence about Jesus. Strauss argued the story of Jesus is a myth that arose from the particular social and intellectual conditions of first-century Palestine. Other authors also published skeptical examinations of the life of Jesus. During the second half of the century, scholars such as Julius Wellhausen (1844–1918) in Germany, Ernst Renan (1823–1892) in France, and Matthew Arnold (1822–1888) in Great Britain contended that human authors had written and revised the books of the Bible with the problems of Jewish society and politics in mind. This questioning of the historical validity of the Bible caused more literate men and women to lose faith in Christianity than any other single cause.

Science Science also undermined Christianity and faith in the validity of biblical narratives. The geology of Charles Lyell (1797–1875) suggested the earth is much older than the biblical records contend. By looking to natural causes to explain floods, mountains, and valleys, Lyell removed the miraculous hand of God from the physical development of the earth. Darwin's theory cast doubt on the Creation. His ideas and those of other writers suggested that the moral nature of humankind can be explained without appeal to God. Finally, anthropologists, psychologists, and sociologists proposed that religious sentiments are just one more set of natural phenomena.

Morality Other intellectuals questioned the morality of Christianity. The morality of the Old Testament God, his cruelty and unpredictability, did not fit well with the tolerant, rational values of liberals. They also wondered about the morality of the New Testament God, who would sacrifice for his own satisfaction the only perfect being ever to walk the earth. Many of the clergy began to wonder if they could preach doctrines they felt to be immoral. From another direction, writers like Friedrich Nietzsche (1844–1900) in Germany portrayed Christianity as a religion that glorified weakness rather than the strength life required. These skeptical currents created a climate in which Christianity lost much of its intellectual respectability.

The secularism of everyday life proved as harmful to the faith as the direct attacks. This situation was especially prevalent in the cities, which were growing faster than the capacity of the churches to meet the challenge. Whole generations of the urban poor grew up with little or no experience of the church as an institution or of Christianity as a religious faith.

Conflict Between Church and State

The secular states of late-nineteenth-century Europe clashed with both the Protestant and the Roman Catholic churches. The primary area of conflict between the state and the churches was education. Previously, most education in Europe had taken place in church schools. The churches feared that future generations would emerge from the new state-financed schools without any religious teaching. From 1870 through the turn of the century, all the major countries debated religious education.

Great Britain In Great Britain, the Education Act of 1870 provided for state-supported schools run by elected school boards, whereas earlier the government had given small grants to religious schools. The new schools were to be built in areas where the religious denominations did not provide satisfactory education. There was rivalry both between the Anglican church and the state and between the Anglican church and the Nonconformist denominations—that is, those Protestant denominations that were not part of the Church of England. All the churches opposed improvements in education because these increased the costs of church schools. In the Education Act of 1902, the government provided state support for both religious and nonreligious schools but imposed the same educational standards on each.

The conflict between church and state disrupted German politics during the 1870s. This cartoon shows Bismarck and Pope Pius IX attempting to checkmate each other in a game of chess.

Bildarchiv Preussischer Kulturbesitz

Why did Bismarck see the Catholic Church as a threat to the German state?

France The British conflict was calm compared with that in France, which had a dual system of Catholic and public schools. The conservative French Catholic Church and the Third French Republic loathed each other. Between 1878 and 1886, a series of educational laws sponsored by Jules Ferry (1832–1893) replaced religious instruction in the public schools with civic training. The number of public schools was expanded, and members of religious orders could no longer teach in them. After the Dreyfus affair, the French Catholic Church again paid a price for its reactionary politics. The Radical government of Pierre Waldeck-Rousseau (1846–1904), drawn from pro-Dreyfus groups, suppressed the religious orders. In 1905, the Napoleonic Concordat was terminated, and church and state were separated.

Germany and the *Kulturkampf* The most extreme and violent church-state conflict occurred in Germany during the 1870s. At unification, the German Catholic hierarchy wanted freedom for the churches guaranteed in the constitution. Bismarck left the matter to the federal states, but he soon felt the Roman Catholic Church and the Catholic Center Party threatened the unity of the German Empire. In 1870 and 1871, he removed the clergy from overseeing local education in Prussia and set education under state direction. This secularization of education represented the beginning of a concerted attack on the Catholic Church in Germany.

Kulturkampf ("cultural struggle") An extreme church-state conflict waged by Bismarck in Germany during the 1870s in response to a perceived threat to German political unity from the Roman Catholic Church.

The "May Laws" of 1873, which applied to Prussia, but not to the entire German Empire, required priests to be educated in German schools and universities and to pass state examinations. The state could veto the appointments of priests. The legislation abolished the disciplinary power of the pope and the church over the clergy and transferred it to the state. Many of the clergy refused to obey these laws, and by 1876, Bismarck had either arrested or expelled all Catholic bishops from Prussia. In the end, Bismarck's ***Kulturkampf*** ("cultural struggle") against the Catholic Church failed. By the end of the 1870s, he abandoned his attack. He had gained state control of education and civil laws governing marriage only at the price of provoking Catholic resentment against the German state.

QUICK REVIEW

Sites of Conflict

- Britain: quality of education provided by schools sponsored by religious institutions
- France: increasing hostility between conservative clergy and the state
- Germany: Bismarck's *Kulturkampf*

Areas of Religious Revival

The German Catholic resistance to the intrusions of the secular state illustrates the continuing vitality of Christianity during this period of intellectual and political hardship for the church. Across Europe, Christianity showed signs of revival and growth. In effect, the last half of the nineteenth century witnessed the final great effort to Christianize Europe. It was well organized, well led, and well financed. It failed only because the population of Europe had outstripped the resources of the churches. The vitality of the churches accounts, in part, for the intense hostility of their enemies.

The Roman Catholic Church and the Modern World

The most striking feature of Christian religious revival was the resilience of the papacy. In 1864, Pope Pius IX (r. 1846–1878) issued the *Syllabus of Errors*, which set the Catholic Church squarely against contemporary science, philosophy, and politics. In 1869, the pope summoned the First Vatican Council. The next year, through the political manipulations of the pontiff and against opposition from many bishops, the council promulgated the dogma of **papal infallibility** when speaking officially on matters of faith and morals. No earlier pope had asserted such centralized authority within the church. Pius IX and many other Roman Catholics believed the Catholic Church could sustain itself in the modern world of nation-states with large electorates only by centering the authority of the church in the papacy itself.

papal infallibility Assertion that the pope's pronouncements on matters of faith and morals could not be questioned.

Pius IX was succeeded by Leo XIII (r. 1878–1903) who tried to be more accommodating to the modern age. Leo's most important pronouncement on public issues was the encyclical *Rerum Novarum* (1891). In that document, he defended private property, religious education, and religious control of the marriage laws, and he condemned socialism and Marxism, but he also declared that employers should treat their employees justly, pay them proper wages, and permit them to organize labor unions. The pope supported laws to protect workers and urged that modern society be organized in corporate groups that would include people from various classes who would cooperate according to Christian principles. On the basis of Leo XIII's pronouncements, democratic Catholic political parties and Catholic trade unions were founded throughout Europe.

His successor Pius X (r. 1903–1914) hoped to resist modern thought and restore traditional devotional life. Between 1903 and 1907, he condemned Catholic modernism, a movement of modern biblical criticism within the church, and in 1910 he required all priests to take an anti-Modernist oath. The struggle between Catholicism and modern thought was resumed.

Islam and Late-Nineteenth-Century European Thought

The few European thinkers who wrote about Islam in the late nineteenth century discussed it using the same scientific and naturalistic scholarly methods they applied to Christianity and Judaism. In the works of scholars such as the influential French writer Ernest Renan, Islam was, like Judaism, a manifestation of the ancient Semitic mentality, which had given rise to a powerful monotheistic vision. Renan, and sociologists such as Max Weber, also dismissed Islam as a religion and culture incapable of developing science and closed to new ideas.

The European racial and cultural outlooks that denigrated nonwhite peoples and their civilizations were also directed toward the Arab world. European authors who championed white racial superiority looked to India and the Aryan civilization that was supposed to have risen there and later influenced northern European life as the source of Europe's cultural superiority.

Christian missionaries reinforced these anti-Islamic attitudes. They blamed Islam for Arab economic backwardness, for mistreating women, and for condoning slavery. They founded schools and hospitals, hoping these Christian foundations would eventually lead some Muslims to Christianity. Few Muslims converted, but these institutions did educate young Arabs in Western science and medicine, and many of their students became leaders in the Middle East.

Within the Islamic world, and especially in the decaying Ottoman Empire, as political leaders continued to champion Western scientific education and technology, they confronted a variety of responses from religious thinkers. Some of these thinkers sought to combine modern thought with Islam. For example, the Salafi, or the salafiyya movement, believed there was no inherent contradiction between science and Islam. Other Islamic religious leaders simply rejected the West and modern thought. They included the Mahdist movement in Sudan, the Sanussiya in Libya, and the Wahhabi movement in the Arabian peninsula.

QUICK REVIEW

Islam and the West

- European thinkers applied the same scientific critique to Islam as they did to Christianity and Judaism
- European racism shaped attitudes toward Arabs
- Response to Western ideas and technology varied in the Islamic world

TOWARD A TWENTIETH-CENTURY FRAME OF MIND

HOW DID developments in art, psychology, and science reflect a profound shift in Western thought?

The last quarter of the nineteenth century and the first decade of the twentieth century were the crucible of modern Western thought. New concepts challenged the major presuppositions of mid-nineteenth-century science, rationalism, liberalism, and bourgeois morality.

SCIENCE: THE REVOLUTION IN PHYSICS

The changes in the scientific worldview originated within the scientific community itself. By the late 1870s, discontent existed over the excessive realism of midcentury science. In 1883, Ernst Mach (1838–1916) published *The Science of Mechanics*, in which he urged that scientists consider their concepts descriptive not of the physical world, but of the sensations the scientific observer experiences. In line with Mach, the French scientist Henri Poincaré (1854–1912) urged that the theories of scientists be regarded as hypothetical constructs of the human mind rather than as true descriptions of nature. By World War I, few scientists believed they could portray the "truth" about physical reality. Rather, they saw themselves as recording the observations of instruments and as offering useful hypothetical or symbolic models of nature.

X-Rays and Radiation Discoveries in the laboratory paralleled the philosophical challenge to nineteenth-century science. In December 1895, Wilhelm Roentgen (1845–1923) published a paper on his discovery of X-rays, a form of energy that penetrated various opaque materials. In 1896, Henri Becquerel (1852–1908) discovered that uranium emitted a similar form of energy. The next year, J. J. Thomson (1856–1940), at Cambridge University, formulated the theory of the electron. The interior world of the atom had become a new area for human exploration. In 1902, Ernest Rutherford (1871–1937) explained the cause of radiation through the disintegration of the atoms of radioactive materials. Shortly thereafter, he speculated on the immense store of energy present in the atom.

Marie Curie (1869–1934) and Pierre Curie (1859–1906) were two of the most important figures in the advance of physics and chemistry. Marie was born in Poland but worked in France for most of her life. She is credited with the discovery of radium, for which she was awarded the Nobel Prize in Chemistry in 1911.

The Granger Collection, New York.

How did the Curies contribute to the revolution in physics?

Theories of Quantum Energy, Relativity, and Uncertainty The discovery of radioactivity and discontent with the existing mechanical models led to revolutionary theories in physics. In 1900, Max Planck (1858–1947) pioneered the articulation of the quantum theory of energy, according to which energy is a series of discrete quantities, or packets, rather than a continuous stream. In 1905, Albert Einstein (1879–1955) published his first epoch-making papers on relativity in which he contended that time and space exist not separately, but rather as a combined continuum. Moreover, the measurement of time and space depends on the observer as well as on the entities being measured. In 1927, Werner Heisenberg (1901–1976) set forth his uncertainty principle, according to which the behavior of subatomic particles is a matter of statistical probability rather than of exactly determinable cause and effect. The mathematical complexity of twentieth-century physics meant science would rarely again be successfully popularized. At the same time, science, through research, medicine, and technological change, has affected modern life more significantly than any other intellectual activity.

Literature: Realism and Naturalism

Between 1850 and 1914, the moral certainties of middle-class Europeans changed no less radically than their concepts of the physical universe. The realist movement in literature portrayed the hypocrisy, brutality, and the dullness that underlay bourgeois life. The **realist** and **naturalist** writers brought scientific objectivity and observation to their work. The major figures of late-century realism examined the dreary and unseemly side of life without being certain whether a better life was possible. In good Darwinian fashion, they portrayed human beings as subject to the passions, the materialistic determinism, and the pressures of the environment like any other animals. Most of them, however, also saw society itself as perpetuating evil.

realists Authors who tried to describe human behavior with scientific objectivity, rejecting the romantic idealization of nature, poverty, love, and polite society, and portraying the hypocrisy, physical and psychic brutality, and the dullness that underlay bourgeois life.

naturalists Authors who tried to portray nature and human life without sentimentality.

Flaubert and Zola Critics have often considered Gustave Flaubert's (1821–1880) *Madame Bovary* (1857), with its story of colorless provincial life and a woman's hapless search for love in and outside of marriage, as the first genuinely realistic novel. The work portrayed life without heroism, purpose, or even civility.

The author who turned realism into a movement, however, was Émile Zola (1840–1902). He believed absolute physical and psychological determinism ruled human events in the way it did the physical world. Between 1871 and 1893, Zola published twenty novels exploring subjects normally untouched by writers: alcoholism, prostitution, adultery, labor strife. Nothing in his purview received the light of hope or the aura of romance. Although critics faulted his taste and moralists condemned his subject matter, Zola enjoyed a worldwide following. As noted in Chapter 22, he took a leading role in the defense of Captain Dreyfus.

Ibsen and Shaw The Norwegian playwright Henrik Ibsen (1828–1906) carried realism into the dramatic presentation of domestic life. He sought to strip away the illusory mask of middle-class morality. His most famous play is *A Doll's House* (1879). Its chief character, Nora, has a narrow-minded husband who cannot tolerate independence of character or thought on her part. Ibsen's works were controversial. He dared to attack sentimentality, the ideal of the female "angel of the house," and the cloak of respectability that hung so insecurely over the middle-class family. One of Ibsen's greatest champions was the Irish writer George Bernard Shaw (1856–1950), who spent most of his life in England. Shaw defended Ibsen's work and made his own realistic onslaught against romanticism and false respectability.

Realist writers believed it their duty to portray reality and the commonplace. By presenting their audiences with unmentionable subjects, they sought to remove the veneer of hypocrisy that had forbidden such discussion. They hoped to destroy illusions and compel the public to face reality. Few of the realist writers who raised these problems posed solutions to them. They often left their readers unable to sustain old values and uncertain about where to find new ones.

QUICK REVIEW

Leading Realists

- Gustave Flaubert (1821–1880)
- Émile Zola (1840–1902)
- Henrik Ibsen (1828–1906)
- George Bernard Shaw (1856–1950)

Modernism in Literature

From the 1870s onward throughout Europe, a new multifaceted movement, usually called **modernism**, touched all the arts. Like realism, modernism was critical of middle-class society and morality. Modernism, however, was not deeply concerned with social issues. What drove the modernists was a concern for the aesthetic or the beautiful. Across the spectrum of the arts, modernists tried to break the received forms and to create new forms.

modernism Movement of the 1870s criticizing middle-class society and traditional morality.

Among the chief proponents of modernism in England were the members of the Bloomsbury Group, including authors Virginia Woolf (1882–1941) and Leonard Woolf (1880–1969), artists Vanessa Bell (1879–1961) and Duncan Grant (1885–1978), the historian and literary critic Lytton Strachey (1880–1932), and the economist John Maynard Keynes (1883–1946). In both personal practice and theory, the Bloomsbury Group rejected what they regarded as the repressive sexual morality of their parents' generation.

On the Continent, one of the major practitioners of modernism in literature was Marcel Proust (1871–1922). In his seven-volume novel *In Search of Time Past* (*À la Recherche du Temps Perdu*), published between 1913 and 1927, he adopted a stream-of-consciousness format that allowed him to explore his memories. In Germany, Thomas Mann (1875–1955), through a long series of novels, the most famous of which were *Buddenbrooks* (1901) and *The Magic Mountain* (1924), explored both the social experience of middle-class Germans and how they dealt with the intellectual heritage of the nineteenth century. In *Ulysses* (1922), James Joyce (1882–1941), who was born in Ireland but spent much of his life on the Continent, transformed not only the novel, but also the structure of the paragraph.

The Coming of Modern Art

The last quarter of the nineteenth century witnessed a series of new departures in Western art that transformed painting and later sculpture in a revolutionary manner that has continued to the present day.

impressionism Focuses on social life and leisured activities of the urban middle and lower-middle classes, a fascination with light, color, and representation of momentary experience of social life or of landscape.

Impressionism **Impressionism** in European painting arose primarily in Paris. Two major characteristics marked this new style of painting. First, instead of portraying religious, mythological, and historical themes, painters began to depict modern life itself, focusing on the social life and leisure activities of the urban middle and lower-middle classes. Second, many of these artists were fascinated with light, color, and the representation through painting itself of momentary, largely unfocused, visual experience whether of social life or of landscape.

The new paintings of modern life by the impressionists, including Édouard Manet (1837–1883), Claude Monet (1840–1926), Camille Pissaro (1830–1903), Pierre-Auguste Renoir (1841–1919), and Edgar Degas (1834–1917), recorded Parisians attending cafés, dance halls, concerts, picnics, horse races, boating excursions, and beach parties. The backdrop for these works was Paris as it had been reconstructed under Napoleon III (r. 1852–1870) into a city of wide boulevards, parks, and places for middle-class leisure.

Édouard Manet (1832–1883), *A Bar at the Folies-Bergère*, 1882

Oil on canvas, 96 X 130 cm. Signed dated. Courtauld gift 1932. Courtauld Institute Gallery, London

What does this painting suggest about the commercialization of late-nineteenth-century life?

The sites included in these paintings allowed people from different classes to mix socially while pursuing a leisure activity. One such meeting place was the Folies-Bergère, a café/concert hall where patrons could enjoy a variety of popular entertainment, including singers, musicians, dancers, gymnasts, and animal shows. Paris had many such establishments, but the Folies-Bergère was one of the largest and most expensive.

A Sunday on La Grande Jatte, 1884, by Georges Seurat implicitly includes social commentary.

Georges Seurat (French 1859-1891), *A Sunday Afternoon on the Island of La Grande Jatte*. 1884–86. Oil on Canvas. 81 3/4 X 121 1/4 in. (207.5 X 308.1 cm). Helen Birch Bartlett Memorial Collection. 1926.224. Reproduction, The Art Institute of Chicago. Photograph © The Art Institute of Chicago. All Rights Reserved.

What comment was Seurat making on the social life of the Parisian middle class?

Postimpressionism By the 1880s, the impressionists had had an enormous impact on contemporary art. Their work was followed by that of younger artists who drew upon their techniques but also attempted often to relate the achievement of impressionism to earlier artistic traditions. Form and structure rather than the effort to record the impression of the moment played a major role in their work. This later group of artists has been described as ***postimpressionists***. The chief figures associated with postimpressionism are Georges Seurat, Paul Cezanne, Vincent van Gogh, and Paul Gauguin.

postimpressionism Focuses more on form and structure to bring painting of modern life back in touch with earlier artistic traditions.

Georges Seurat (1859–1891) was a young French painter who read extensively in contemporary scientific works about light, color, and vision. These studies led him to a technique of painting known as pointillism whereby the artist applied small dots or points of paint to the canvas. Through this laborious process he hoped to decompose colors into their basic units leaving it to the eye of the viewer to mix those dots into the desired color or shade of color. Seurat is counted among the first postimpressionists because he saw himself bringing the new painting of modern life back into touch with earlier artistic traditions.

Seurat's work implicitly included social commentary, as in his 1884 painting *A Sunday on La Grande Jatte*, situated on the Grande Jatte, an island in the Seine where Parisians would gather on Sundays. A boatman indicates a brooding working-class presence amid the largely middle-class figures, all of whom resemble mechanical mannequins who stand bored and perhaps puzzled by their situation of comfort, leisure, and ease.

In reaction to the impressionists' fascination with light, Paul Cezanne (1839–1906), working largely in isolation, attempted to bring form and solidity back into his paintings of still life and of the landscape of Provence. Displaying a new sensitivity to non-Western peoples and their art, Paul Gauguin (1848–1903) produced works portraying peoples living in the South Pacific. Other artists collected African masks or studied such objects in the anthropological museum in Paris. The art of Africa and of the Pacific gave artists examples of remarkable works that had no relationship to the long-standing Western artistic tradition.

Cubism The single most important new departure in early-twentieth-century Western art was ***cubism***, a term first coined to describe the paintings of Pablo Picasso (1881–1973) and Georges Braque (1882–1963).

cubism Autonomous realm of art with no purpose beyond itself. Includes as many different perspectives, angles, or views of the object as possible.

Beginning in 1907, Picasso and Braque rejected the idea of a painting as constituting a window onto the real world. Rather, they saw painting as an autonomous realm of art itself with no purpose beyond itself. Echoing the art of ancient Egypt, medieval primitives, and Africa, Picasso and Braque represented only two dimensions in their painting. They attempted to include at one time on a single surface as many different perspectives, angles, or views of the object painted as possible. "Reality" was the construction of their experience of multiple perceptions.

Braque's still life *Violin and Palette* (1909 and 1910) represents the cubist determination to present "a new, completely non-illusionistic and non-imitative method of depicting the visual world." Various shapes seem to flow into other shapes. Portions of the violin and of the palette are recognizable, but as shapes, not as objects in and of themselves. The violin appears at one moment from a host of perspectives, but the violin has interest only in its relationship to the other shapes of color in the painting. Throughout the painting Braque is literally taking apart the violin and other objects, so that he and the viewer can analyze them. The elements of the palette, the violin, and the notes of a musical score floating on folded paper tents hold interest and meaning in this painting only because they are in the painting, not because they are imitations of a violin, a palette, or a musical score.

Georges Braque, *Violin and Palette* (*Violon et Palette*), 1909–1910, is representative of the autonomous realm of art itself.

Georges Braque, *Violin and Palette (Violon et Palette)*, 1909–1910. Autumn 1909. Oil on canvas. 91.7l X 42.8 cm (36 1/8 X 16 7/8 inches). Solomon R. Guggenheim Museum, New York, 54.1412. Photograph by Lee B. Ewing © The Solomon R. Guggenheim Foundation, New York.

What were the goals of the cubist painters?

Friedrich Nietzsche and the Revolt Against Reason

During the second half of the century, philosophers began to question the adequacy of rational thinking to address the human situation. No writer better exemplified this new attitude than the German philosopher Friedrich Nietzsche (1844–1900). He was wholly at odds with the values of the age and attacked Christianity, democracy, nationalism, rationality, science, and progress. He sought less to change values than to probe their sources in the human character. He wanted not only to tear away the masks of respectable life, but also to explore how human beings made such masks.

His first important work was *The Birth of Tragedy* (1872) in which he urged that the nonrational aspects of human nature are as important and noble as the rational characteristics. He insisted on the positive function of instinct and ecstasy in human life. In Nietzsche's view, the strength for the heroic life and the highest artistic achievement arises from sources beyond rationality.

In later works, such as the prose poem *Thus Spake Zarathustra* (1883), Nietzsche criticized democracy and Christianity. Both would lead only to the mediocrity of sheepish masses. He announced the death of God and proclaimed the coming of the *Overman* (Übermensch), who would embody heroism and greatness. The term was frequently interpreted as some mode of superman or super race, but such was not Nietzsche's intention. He sought a return to the heroism that he associated with Greek life in the Homeric age.

Two of Nietzsche's most profound works are *Beyond Good and Evil* (1886) and *The Genealogy of Morals* (1887). Nietzsche sought to discover not what is good and what is evil, but the social and psychological sources of the judgment of good and evil. In Nietzsche's view, morality was a human convention that had no independent existence. Christianity, utilitarianism, and middle-class respectability could, in good conscience, be abandoned. Human beings could create a new moral order that would glorify pride, assertiveness, and strength rather than meekness, humility, and weakness.

In his appeal to feelings and emotions and in his questioning of the adequacy of rationalism, Nietzsche drew on the romantic tradition. The kind of creative impulse that earlier romantics had considered the gift of artists Nietzsche saw as the burden of all human beings. The character of the human situation that this philosophy urged on its contemporaries was that of an ever-changing flux in which nothing but change itself was permanent. Human beings had to forge from their own will and determination the values that were to exist in the world.

The Birth of Psychoanalysis

A determination to probe beneath the surface or public appearance united the major figures of late-nineteenth-century science, art, and philosophy. As a result of their theories and discoveries, educated Europeans could never again view the surface of life with complacency or even with much confidence. No intellectual development more exemplified this trend than psychoanalysis through the work of Sigmund Freud (1856–1939).

Development of Freud's Early Theories Freud was born into an Austrian Jewish family that settled in Vienna. In 1886, he opened his medical practice in Vienna, where he lived until the Nazis drove him out in 1938. Freud conducted all his research and writing from the base of his medical practice. His earliest medical interests had been psychic disorders, to which he sought to apply the critical method of science. In late 1885, he studied in Paris with Jean-Martin Charcot (1825–1893), who used hypnosis to treat hysteria.

In the mid-1890s, Freud abandoned hypnosis and allowed his patients to talk freely and spontaneously about themselves. He found that they associated their particular neurotic symptoms with experiences related to earlier experiences, going back to childhood. He also noted that sexual matters were significant in his patients' problems. By 1897, Freud had formulated a theory of infantile sexuality, according to which sexual drives and energy already exist in infants and do not simply emerge at puberty. For Freud, human beings are sexual creatures from birth through adulthood. He also portrayed the little acknowledged matter of sexuality as one of the bases of mental order and disorder.

QUICK REVIEW

Sigmund Freud (1856–1939)

- Founder of psychoanalysis
- Worked in Vienna until he was driven out by the Nazis in 1938
- Focused attention on infantile sexuality
- Emphasized the importance of what happens in the mind below the level of consciousness

Freud's Concern with Dreams During the same decade, Freud also examined the psychic phenomena of dreams. Freud believed the seemingly irrational content of dreams must have a reasonable, scientific explanation. His research led him to reconsider the general nature of the human mind. He concluded that dreams allow unconscious wishes, desires, and drives that had been excluded from everyday conscious life to enjoy freer play in the mind. During the waking hours, the mind represses or censors certain wishes, which are as important to the individual's psychological makeup as conscious thought is. In fact, Freud argued, unconscious drives and desires contribute to conscious behavior. Freud developed these concepts and related them to his idea of infantile sexuality in his most important book *The Interpretation of Dreams*, published in 1900.

id Among Freud's three entities of the mind, the *id* consists of innate, amoral, irrational drives for sexual gratification, aggression, and sensual pleasure.

superego Among Freud's three entities of the mind, the *superego* internalizes the moral imperatives that society and culture impose on the personality.

ego Among Freud's three entities of the mind, the *ego* mediates between the impulsive id and the self-denying superego.

Freud's Later Thought In later books and essays, Freud developed a new model of the internal organization of the mind as an arena of struggle and conflict among three entities: the id, the superego, and the ego. The **id** consists of amoral, irrational, driving instincts for sexual gratification, aggression, and general physical and sensual pleasure. The **superego** embodies the external moral imperatives and expectations imposed on the personality by society and culture. The **ego** mediates between the impulses of the id and the asceticism of the superego and allows the personality to cope with the inner and outer demands of its existence. Consequently, everyday behavior displays the activity of the personality as its inner drives are partially repressed through the ego's coping with external moral expectations, as interpreted by the superego.

It has been a grave misreading of Freud to see him as urging humankind to thrust off all repression. He did indeed believe that excessive repression could lead to a mental disorder, but he also believed civilization and the survival of humankind required some repression of sexuality and aggression. Freud thought the sacrifice and struggle were worthwhile, but he understood the immense sacrifice of instinctual drives required for rational civilized behavior and was pessimistic about the future of civilization in the West.

Divisions in the Psychoanalytic Movement By 1910, Freud had gathered around him a small, but able, group of disciples. Several of his early followers soon moved toward theories of which the master disapproved. The most important of these dissenters was Carl Jung (1875–1961). Jung questioned the primacy of sexual drives in forming personality and in contributing to mental disorder. He also put less faith in reason.

Jung believed the human subconscious contains inherited memories from previous generations. These collective memories, as well as the personal experience of an individual, constitute his or her soul. Jung regarded human beings in the twentieth century as alienated from these useful collective memories. In *Modern Man in Search of a Soul* (1933) and other works, Jung tended toward mysticism and saw positive values in religion. Freud was highly critical of most of Jung's work. If Freud's thought derived primarily from the Enlightenment, Jung's was more dependent on romanticism.

In 1909 Freud and his then-devoted disciple Carl Jung visited Clark University in Worcester, Massachusetts, during Freud's only trip to the United States. Here Freud sits on the right holding a cane; Jung is sitting on the far left.

Archives of the History of American Psychology—The University of Akron. Courtesy Clark University, Special Collections

How did Freud see the relationship between the individual and civilization?

Retreat from Rationalism in Politics

Nineteenth-century liberals and socialists agreed that rational analysis could discern the problems of society and prepare solutions. These thinkers felt that, once given the vote, individuals would behave according to their rational political self-interest. Education would improve the human condition. By 1900, these views had come under attack. Political scientists and sociologists painted politics as frequently irrational. Racial theorists questioned whether rationality and education could affect human society at all.

Weber During this period, however, one major social theorist was impressed by the role of reason in human society. The German sociologist Max Weber (1864–1920) regarded the emergence of rationalism throughout society as the major development of human history. Such rationalization displayed itself in the rise of both scientific knowledge and bureaucratic organization.

Weber saw bureaucratization as the basic feature of modern social life. He used this view to oppose Marx's concept of the development of capitalism as the driving force in modern society. Bureaucratization involved the division of labor as each individual fit into a particular role in much larger organizations. Furthermore, Weber believed that in modern society people derive their own self-images and sense of personal worth from their positions in these organizations. Weber also contended—again, in contrast to Marx—that noneconomic factors might account for major developments in human history. For example, in his best known essay *The Protestant Ethic and the Spirit of Capitalism* (1905), Weber traced much of the rational character of capitalist enterprise to the ascetic religious doctrines of Puritanism.

Theorists of Collective Behavior In his emphasis on the individual and on the dominant role of rationality, Weber differed from many contemporary social scientists, such as Gustave LeBon (1841–1931), Emile Durkheim (1858–1917), and Georges Sorel (1847–1922) in France, Vilfredo Pareto (1848–1923) in Italy, and Graham Wallas (1858–1932) in England. LeBon was a psychologist who explored the activity of crowds and mobs. He believed that crowds behave irrationally. In *Reflections on Violence* (1908), Sorel argued that people do not pursue rationally perceived goals but are led to action by collectively shared ideals. Durkheim and Wallas became deeply interested in the necessity of shared values and activities in a society. Besides playing down the function of reason in society, all these theorists emphasized the role of collective groups in politics rather than that of the individual, formerly championed by liberals.

Racism

racism Belief that some peoples are innately superior to others.

The same tendencies to question or even to deny the constructive activity of reason in human affairs and to sacrifice the individual to the group manifested themselves in theories of race. **Racism** had long existed in Europe. What transformed racial thinking at the end of the century was its association with the biological sciences. The prestige associated with biology and science in general became transferred to racial thinking, whose advocates now claimed to possess a materialistic, scientific basis for their thought.

Gobineau Count Arthur de Gobineau (1816–1882), a reactionary French diplomat, enunciated the first important theory of race as the major determinant of human history. In his four-volume *Essay on the Inequality of the Human Races* (1853–1854), Gobineau claimed the white Aryan race had unwisely intermarried with the inferior yellow and black races, thus diluting the greatness and ability that originally existed in its blood. Gobineau saw no way to reverse this degeneration.

Chamberlain At the close of the century, Houston Stewart Chamberlain (1855–1927), an Englishman who settled in Germany, championed the concept of biological determinism through race but believed that through genetics the human race could be improved and even that a superior race could be developed. Chamberlain was anti-Semitic. He pointed to the Jews as the major enemy of European racial regeneration.

Late-Century Nationalism Racial thinking was one part of a wider late-century movement toward more aggressive nationalism. Previously, nationalism had in general been a movement among European literary figures and liberals. From the 1870s onward, however, nationalism became a movement with mass support, well-financed organizations, and political parties. Nationalists often redefined nationality in terms of race and blood. The new nationalism opposed the internationalism of both liberalism and socialism. The ideal of nationality was used to overcome the pluralism of class, religion, and geography. The nation replaced religion for many secularized people. It sometimes became a secular religion in the hands of state schoolteachers, who were replacing the clergy as the instructors of youth. Nationalism of this aggressive, racist variety became the most powerful ideology of the early twentieth century and would reemerge after the collapse of communism in the 1990s.

Some Europeans also used racial theory to support harsh, condescending treatment of colonial peoples in the late nineteenth and early twentieth centuries. They were convinced that white Europeans were racially superior to the peoples of color whom they governed and that these peoples would always be inferior to them. Similar racial theory also informed attitudes toward peoples of color in the West itself as was the case with the inferiority ascribed to African Americans and Native Americans in the United States.

Anti-Semitism and the Birth of Zionism

Political and racial anti-Semitism, which cast such dark shadows across the twentieth century, developed, in part, from the prevailing atmosphere of racial thought and the retreat from rationality in politics. Since the French Revolution, West European Jews had gradually gained entry into civil life. Popular anti-Semitism, however, survived, with the Jewish community being identified with money and banking interests. During the last third of the century, as finance capitalism changed the economic structure of Europe, many non-Jewish Europeans threatened by the changes became hostile toward the Jewish community.

Anti-Semitic Politics In Vienna, Mayor Karl Lueger (1844–1910) used anti-Semitism as a major attraction for his Christian Socialist Party. In Germany, the ultraconservative Lutheran chaplain Adolf Stoecker (1835–1909) revived anti-Semitism. The Dreyfus affair in France focused a new hatred toward the Jews.

To this ugly atmosphere, racial thought contributed the belief that no matter to what extent Jews assimilated themselves into the culture of their country, their Jewishness—and thus their alleged danger to society—would remain. For racial thinkers, the problem of race was not in the character, but in the blood of the Jew. An important Jewish response to this new, rabid outbreak of anti-Semitism was the launching in 1896 of the **Zionism** movement to found a separate Jewish state. Its founder was the Austro-Hungarian Theodor Herzl (1860–1904).

Zionism Movement based on the theory that if Jews were unacceptable as citizens of European nations, their only safety lay in establishing a nation of their own.

Herzl's Response Herzl was convinced that liberal politics and the institutions of the liberal state could not protect the Jews in Europe or ensure that they would be treated justly. In 1896, Herzl published *The Jewish State*, in which he called for a separate state in which all Jews might be assured of those rights and liberties that they should be enjoying in the liberal states of Europe. Furthermore, Herzl followed the tactics of late-century mass democratic politics by directing his appeal particularly to the poor Jews who lived in the ghettos of Eastern Europe and the slums of Western Europe. The original call to Zionism thus combined a rejection of the anti-Semitism of Europe and a desire to realize some of the ideals of both liberalism and socialism in a state outside Europe.

WOMEN AND MODERN THOUGHT

The ideas that so shook Europe from the publication of *The Origin of Species* through the opening of World War I produced, at best, mixed results for women. Within the often radically new ways of thinking about the world, views of women and their roles in society often remained remarkably unchanged.

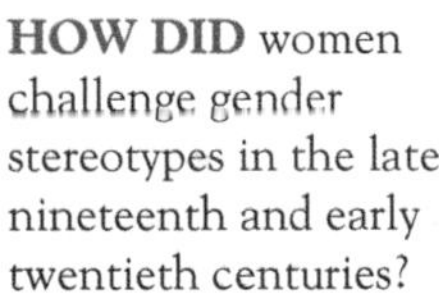

HOW DID women challenge gender stereotypes in the late nineteenth and early twentieth centuries?

ANTIFEMINISM IN LATE-CENTURY THOUGHT

The influence of biology on the thinking of intellectuals during the late nineteenth century and their own interest in the nonrational side of human behavior led many of them to sustain what had become stereotyped views of women. The emphasis on biology, evolution, and reproduction led intellectuals to concentrate on women's mothering role. Their interest in the nonrational led them to reassert the traditional view that feeling and the nurturing instinct are basic to women's nature. Many late-century thinkers and writers of fiction also often displayed fear and hostility toward women, portraying them as creatures susceptible to overwhelming and often destructive feelings and instincts. A genuinely misogynist strain emerged in late-century fiction and painting.

This conservative and hostile perception of women manifested itself in several ways within the scientific community. In London in 1860, the Ethnological Society excluded women from its discussions on the grounds that the subject matter of the customs of primitive peoples was unfit for women and that women were amateurs whose presence would lower the level of the discussion. T. H. Huxley, in public lectures, claimed to have found scientific evidence of the inferiority of women to men. Karl Vogt (1817–1895), a leading German anthropologist, held similar views about the character of women. Darwin would repeat the ideas of both Huxley and Vogt in his *Descent of Man*. Late-Victorian anthropologists tended likewise to assign women, as well as nonwhite races, an inferior place in the human family.

The position of women in Freud's thought is controversial. Critics have claimed that Freud portrayed women as incomplete human beings who might be inevitably destined to unhappy mental lives. He saw the natural destiny of women as motherhood and the rearing of sons as their greatest fulfillment. The first psychoanalysts were trained as medical doctors, and their views of women reflected contemporary medical education, which, like much of the scientific establishment, tended to portray women as inferior. Distinguished women psychoanalysts, such as Karen Horney (1885–1952) and Melanie Klein (1882–1960), would later challenge Freud's views on women, and other writers would try to establish a psychoanalytic basis for feminism. Nonetheless, the psychoanalytic profession would remain dominated by men, as would academic psychology.

The social sciences of the late nineteenth and early twentieth centuries similarly reinforced traditional gender roles. Most major theorists believed that women's role in reproduction and child rearing demanded a social position inferior to men. Virtually all the early sociologists took a conservative view of marriage, the family, child rearing, and divorce.

New Directions in Feminism

The close of the century witnessed a revival of feminist thought in Europe that would grow in the twentieth century. Many women's organizations, as seen in Chapter 23, concentrated on achieving the vote for women, but feminist writers and activists raised other questions as well.

Sexual Morality and the Family In various nations, middle-class women began to challenge the double standard of sexual morality and the traditional male-dominated family. This often meant challenging laws about prostitution.

Between 1864 and 1886, English prostitutes were subject to the Contagious Diseases Acts. The police in certain cities with naval or military bases could require any woman identified as, or suspected of being, a prostitute to undergo an immediate internal medical examination for venereal disease. Those found to have a disease could be confined for months to locked hospitals (women's hospitals for the treatment of venereal diseases) without legal recourse. The law took no action against their male customers.

These laws angered English middle-class women who believed the harsh working conditions and the poverty imposed on so many working-class women were the true causes of prostitution. They framed the issue in the context of their own efforts to prove that women are as human and rational as men and thus properly subject to equal treatment. The Contagious Diseases Acts assumed that women were inferior to men and treated them as less than rational human beings. The laws literally put women's bodies under the control of male customers, male physicians, and male law-enforcement personnel. They denied to poor women the freedoms that all men enjoyed in English society. By 1869, the Ladies' National Association for the Repeal of the Contagious Diseases Acts, a distinctly middle-class organization led by Josephine Butler (1828–1906), began actively to oppose those laws. The group achieved the suspension of the acts in 1883 and their repeal in 1886. Government and police regulation of prostitution roused similar movements in other nations, which adopted the English movement as a model.

The feminist groups that demanded the abolition of laws that punished prostitutes without questioning the behavior of their customers were challenging the double standard and, by extension, the traditional relationship of men and women in marriage. In their view, marriage should be a free union of equals with men and women sharing responsibility for their children. In Germany, the Mothers' Protection League (*Bund für Mutterschutz*) contended that both married and unmarried mothers required the help of the state, including leaves for pregnancy and child care. This radical group emphasized the need to rethink all sexual morality. In Sweden, Ellen Key (1849–1926), in *The Century of the Child* (1900) and *The Renaissance of Motherhood* (1914), maintained that motherhood is so crucial to society that the government, rather than husbands, should support mothers and their children.

Virtually all turn-of-the-century feminists in one way or another supported wider sexual freedom for women, often claiming it would benefit society as well as improve women's lives. Many of the early advocates of contraception had also been influenced by social Darwinism. They hoped that limiting the number of children would allow more healthy and intelligent children to survive.

Women Defining Their Own Lives For many continental feminists, achieving legal and social equality for women would be one step toward transforming Europe from a male-dominated society to one in which both men and women could control their own destinies. Increasingly, feminists would concentrate on freeing and developing women's personalities through better education and government financial support for women engaged in traditional social roles, whether or not they had gained the vote.

Some women also became active within socialist circles. There they argued that the socialist transformation of society should include major reforms for women. Socialist parties usually had all-male leadership. By the close of the century, most male socialist leaders, including Lenin and later Stalin, were intolerant of demands for changes in the family or greater sexual freedom for either men or women. Nonetheless, socialist writings began to include calls for improvements in the economic situation of women that were compatible with more advanced feminist ideals.

It was within literary circles, however, that feminist writers often most clearly articulated the problems that they now understood themselves to face. Virginia Woolf's *A Room of One's Own* (1929) became one of the fundamental texts of twentieth-century feminist literature. In it, she meditated first on the difficulties that women of both brilliance and social standing encountered in being taken seriously as writers and intellectuals. She concluded that a woman who wishes to write requires both a room of her own, meaning a space not dominated by male institutions, and an adequate independent income. Woolf was concerned with more than asserting the right of women to participate in intellectual life, however. Establishing a new stance for feminist writers, she asked whether women, as writers, must imitate men or whether they should bring to their endeavors the separate intellectual and psychological qualities they possessed as women. As she had challenged some of the literary conventions of the traditional novel in her fiction, she challenged some of the accepted notions of feminist thought in *A Room of One's Own* and concluded that male and female writers must actually be able to think as both men and women and share the sensibilities of each. In this sense, she sought to open the whole question of gender definition.

Virginia Woolf, a member of the Bloomsbury Group whose members were the chief proponents of modernism in England.

Hulton Archive Photos/Getty Images, Inc.

What were the goals of the modernist writers?

By World War I, feminism in Europe, fairly or not, had become associated in the popular imagination with challenges to traditional gender roles and sexual morality and with either socialism or political radicalism. So when extremely conservative political movements arose between the world wars, their leaders often emphasized traditional roles for women and traditional ideas about sexual morality. (See Chapter 27.)

SUMMARY

WHAT EFFECT did state-financed education have on literacy in late-nineteenth-century Europe?

The New Reading Public Governments started funding education in the late 1860s. Liberals and conservatives shared the Enlightenment belief that new voters needed more information to exercise their rights properly and thus maintain the political order. By 1900, 85 percent or more of the population of Britain, France, Belgium, the Netherlands, Germany, and Scandinavia could read. (Literacy rates in Italy, Spain, Russia, Austria-Hungary, and the Balkans were about 40 to 70 percent.) This created a mass reading public. New reading material proliferated. Much of it was of low quality, but the sheer numbers of readers allowed an unprecedented popularization of knowledge. *page 596*

WHAT ROLE did science play in the second half of the nineteenth century?

Science at Midcentury In the mid–nineteenth century, many considered science the model for all forms of human understanding. Educated people believed the physical world was rational, mechanical, and predictable and that science described nature as it really was. Comte developed positivism. Sociology is based on his belief that positive knowledge, the kind obtained by physical science, is possible in other areas, including social behavior. Darwin proposed natural selection as the mechanism for evolution. Darwin explained humans as products of the struggle for survival. Philosophers and economists also applied the idea of survival of the fittest to their fields. Spencer wrote of competition as an ethical imperative. Huxley countered that evolution determines only physical development, not moral behavior. *page 597*

WHAT CHALLENGES did European Christianity face in the late nineteenth century?

Christianity and the Church under Siege Protestant and Catholic churches remained popular, despite urban growth that outstripped their capacity, attacks on church influence by the secular nation-state, and a rejection of faith by many European intellectuals. Nineteenth-century historical scholarship challenged the validity of the Bible. Science and moral reasoning also posed challenges to Christian faith. The secular state and the church clashed over many issues, particularly education. In Great Britain, France, and Germany, the government limited religious roles in education. But Christian churches were still strong enough to fight back. Different popes had different ideas about the Catholic Church's best response to modernism, but all aggressively engaged it. The small group of scholars of Islam in Europe applied scientific and naturalistic forms of inquiry to the Islamic faith and the Qur'an. In the Ottoman Empire, political leaders called for Westernized scientific education and technology, but religious leaders had more varied responses to Western ideas. *page 599*

HOW DID developments in art, psychology, and science reflect a profound shift in Western thought?

Toward a Twentieth-Century Frame of Mind At the turn of the century, new ideas of physical reality, human nature, and society challenged the beliefs of earlier science, rationalism, liberalism, and bourgeois morality. New scientific discoveries pointed to the inadequacy of the mechanistic models of the physical world. Einstein's theories of relativity and Heisenberg's uncertainty principle opened the doors to new ways of understanding the material world. Middle-class morality was also thrown into disarray; realist and naturalist authors adopted objective, "scientific" stances. Modernism was critical of bourgeois morality but endorsed an aesthetic ideal of beauty and experimentation with form. In literature and art, modernism was interested in artistic experience for its own sake. Freud's psychoanalysis explored areas of the human mind that had not yet been imagined. He used romanticism and Enlightenment rationality. Weber built a model of social behavior that emphasized noneconomic factors in social development. Racism was used to explain the history and characteristics of large groups. Racial thinking and biological determinism linked with anti-Semitism and aggressive nationalism in a poisonous strand of political theory. The Zionist movement was an important Jewish response to anti-Semitism. *page 605*

HOW DID women challenge gender streotypes in the late nineteenth and early twentieth centuries?

Women and Modern Thought Women's social roles remained largely static. A distinct strain of misogyny became evident in fiction and painting at the end of the nineteenth century. The scientific community, too, held a conservative and hostile view of women. Racial thinking often placed women on a lower plane than men of the same race. Biological thinking led social scientists to reinforce so-called traditional roles for women. Feminist groups worked to gain voting rights for women. They also questioned the double standard of sexual morality and the male domination of the family. Often they approached these issues through challenges to prostitution laws, which punished female prostitutes but not their customers. Some advocated contraception. Others argued that women should be free to develop their personalities; still others joined socialist movements and worked to incorporate a change for the role of women into the socialist agenda. Virginia Woolf articulated a vision of men and women both becoming aware of the full range of identities within each individual. *page 613*

Review Questions

1. What were some of the major changes in scientific outlook that occurred between 1850 and 1914? What advances took place in physics? What was the theory of natural selection proposed by Darwin and Wallace? Why did Christianity come under attack in the late nineteenth century? What form did the attack take?
2. How were changes in society reflected in the literature of the late nineteenth century? What was the significance of the explosion of literacy and literary material? What was literary *realism?* How did literary *modernism* differ from realism?
3. How did Nietzsche and Freud challenge traditional middle-class and religious morality? How do you account for the fear and hostility many late-nineteenth-century intellectuals displayed toward women? What were some of the social and political issues that especially affected women in the late nineteenth and early twentieth centuries? What new directions did feminism take?
4. What forms did racism take in the late nineteenth century? How did it become associated with anti-Semitism? What was Zionism? Why did Herzl develop it?

KEY TERMS

cubism (p. 608)
ego (p. 610)
id (p. 610)
Impressionism (p. 607)
Kulturkampf (p. 603)
modernism (p. 607)
naturalists (p. 606)
natural selection (p. 599)
papal infallibility (p. 604)
positivism (p. 597)
postimpressionism (p. 608)
racism (p. 612)
realists (p. 606)
social Darwinism (p. 599)
superego (p. 610)
Zionism (p. 613)

For additional learning resources related to this chapter, please go to **www.myhistorylab.com**

myhistorylab

25

The Age of Western Imperialism

The global British Empire dominated the nineteenth-century European imperial experience. The empire was popularized in newspapers, books, and novels, as well as in thousands of illustrations and photographs. This illustration seeks to portray the worldwide reach of the British Empire and the varied peoples whom it governed abroad and, at the same time, as seen in the caption, how Great Britain sought to build domestic pride in the imperial achievement. Similar illustrations could be found portraying the empires of France, German, the Netherlands, Belgium, and Russia.

"Citizens of the British Empire, the Greatest Empire the world has ever known . . ." 1911, London Illustrated News. © Mary Evans Picture Library

What relationship did white Britons see between themselves and the peoples of the empire?

HOW DID early modern colonization differ from nineteenth-century Western imperialism?

HOW DID Britain use its economic might to extend its influence around the world?

WHY WAS India such an important part of the British Empire?

WHAT WAS new about the "New Imperialism" and what role did economic motives play in nineteenth-century imperialism?

HOW DID European politics contribute to the "Scramble for Africa"?

HOW DID Russia come to control a vast and diverse Asian empire and what developments facilitated Western penetration and control of Asia?

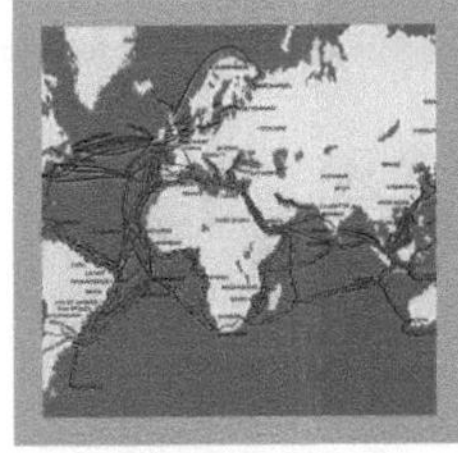

HOW DID technological innovations make nineteenth-century imperialism possible?

WHAT WAS the relationship between missionaries and their home governments?

HOW DID science help imperialism capture the imagination of domestic audiences in Europe?

The half-century between the opening of the American Revolution and the end of the Latin American Wars of Independence (1775–1830) marked the end of the early modern era of European interaction with the wider world that had begun in the late fifteenth century. The second and third quarters of the nineteenth century witnessed the high age of the British Empire. During that time other European nations had fewer interests in the non-Western world. For a variety of reasons, this situation began to change in the 1870s, however, with the dawn of the period historians call the **New Imperialism**. *For the next half-century, until the outbreak of World War I in 1914, European powers brought much of the world under their dominance and direct control. During this period the United States and Japan also first appeared as major players on the world stage.*

New Imperialism The extension in the late nineteenth and early twentieth centuries of Western political and economic dominance to Asia, the Middle East, and Africa.

THE CLOSE OF THE AGE OF EARLY MODERN COLONIZATION

HOW DID early modern colonization differ from nineteenth-century Western imperialism?

The era of early modern European expansion that lasted from the late fifteenth to the late eighteenth centuries had witnessed the encounter, conquest, settlement, and exploitation of the American continents by the Spanish, Portuguese, French, and English, the establishment of modest trading posts by European countries in Africa and Asia, Dutch dominance in the East Indies (modern Indonesia), and British domination of India.

Early European colonial rivalry had occurred primarily within the transatlantic world. By the early eighteenth century, the following patterns of European domination prevailed in the Americas. The Spanish Empire extended from California and Texas to Argentina. The Spanish also claimed Florida. Portugal controlled Brazil. The Dutch, French, Spanish, and British exploited the rich sugar islands of the Caribbean. France loosely controlled the Saint Lawrence and Mississippi River Valleys and the upper Atlantic coast. The British had settled the Atlantic coast from Maine to Georgia.

Between the mid–eighteenth and the early nineteenth centuries, a vast political transformation occurred in these regions. The French lost their North American empire to the British. The American Revolution drove the British from their Atlantic coastal colonies, which became the United States. But thousands of American loyalists fled to Canada, which developed a closer relationship with Britain. Warfare shifted the ownership of the Caribbean islands from one country to another with Haiti by 1804 establishing its independence from France. (See Chapter 20.) In 1803, Napoleon sold the vast Louisiana Territory to the United States. In the 1820s Latin America shook off Spanish and Portuguese control. Except for Canada, the Caribbean islands, and a few toeholds on the coasts of Central and South America, European rule in the Americas had ended. The Monroe Doctrine, which the United States announced in 1823 and the British navy enforced, closed the Americas to European colonialism. The most striking result of these events was the collapse of Spain, Portugal, and France as significant colonial powers.

In contrast to early modern European empires, slavery was absent from those of the nineteenth century. In 1807 Britain had banned the slave trade and had abolished slavery itself in its own colonies in 1833–1834. Thereafter, the British navy worked to close down the slave trade of other nations. Consequently, although economic inequality and forced labor were common in the European empires of the late nineteenth century, the institution of slavery, which had been the chief characteristic of the earlier imperial transatlantic plantation economies, had disappeared.

Roman Catholicism had been the driving religious influence among the early modern transatlantic empires. Almost from the moment Europeans first reached the Americas in the 1490s, Catholic priests, friars, and nuns had worked relentlessly to convert the indigenous peoples of the Caribbean, Latin America, and French Canada. These regions remain overwhelming Catholic. The largely Protestant settlers of the British colonies had been religiously zealous, but their missionary impulse was less strong, and there were fewer indigenous people along the Atlantic seaboard for them to convert. By contrast, during the nineteenth century, evangelical Protestants from Britain and the societies that backed them set the pace for missionary enterprises that other Western nations imitated, including those that sponsored Roman Catholic missions.

THE AGE OF BRITISH IMPERIAL DOMINANCE

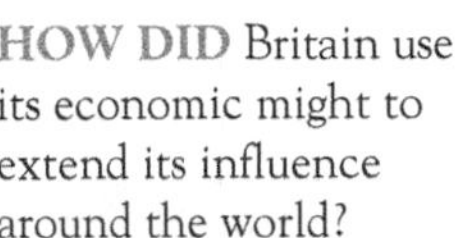

HOW DID Britain use its economic might to extend its influence around the world?

During the first half of the nineteenth century, no one doubted that Great Britain was the single power that could exert its influence virtually around the world. However, until the 1860s and 1870s, except in India and western Canada, Britain did not seek additional territory. Rather, it extended its influence through what historians call the **Imperialism of Free Trade**.

Imperialism of Free Trade The advance of European economic and political interests in the nineteenth century by demanding that non-European nations allow European nations, most particularly Great Britain, to introduce their manufactured goods freely into all nations or to introduce other goods, such as opium into China, that allowed those nations to establish economic influence and to determine the terms of trade.

The Imperialism of Free Trade

Nineteenth-century British imperial economic ideas differed sharply from the mercantilist doctrines that had dominated previous centuries. Mercantile economic doctrine had asserted that a nation measured its wealth in terms of the amount of gold and silver it amassed and that the amount of trade was finite: If one nation's trade increased, another nation's trade had to decrease. But in the 1770s, economic thinkers such as Adam Smith (see Chapter 17) argued that empires would best prosper by abandoning closed imperial systems in favor of free trade, that is, by fostering the exchange of goods across borders and oceans with minimal government regulation and tariff barriers. Free traders argued that this would allow trade to grow upon itself—that the amount of trade was potentially infinite—and would assure consumers the lowest prices.

As a result of the productive energies that the Industrial Revolution of the late eighteenth and early nineteenth centuries unleashed, Britain became "the workshop of the world." It could and did produce more manufactured goods than its population could absorb on its own. Britain was also able to produce those goods, especially consumer goods such as textiles, more cheaply than anyone else. To dominate a foreign market, British merchants needed only the ability to trade without government interference in the form of tariffs, subsidies, or price controls. Until at least the 1870s, free trade alone allowed Britain to dominate economically one region of the world after another without the need to establish a formal colonial administration.

Free trade could and did lead to warfare. The most important example of this concerned the opium trade between British merchants operating out of India and their potential Chinese customers. Europeans and Americans wanted to import Chinese goods, especially tea, silk, and porcelain, in large quantities. With the Chinese uninterested in buying Western manufactured goods, British merchants looked for another product to sell to the Chinese market. They found it in the opium produced in India. The Chinese government resisted the import of opium to prevent addiction among its people.

Between 1839 and 1842 and again between 1856 and 1860, the British went to war to impose a free trade in opium on China. At the conclusion of the first of these Opium Wars, the British gained control of Hong Kong, and forced the Chinese to allow Christian missionaries to operate in China, to open various ports to

Armed Chinese junks were no match for British warships during the first Opium War. The war ended in 1842 with the Treaty of Nanjing.

Picture Desk, Inc./Kobal Collection

Why were the British so determined to import opium into China?

QUICK REVIEW

The Opium Wars

- China resisted British importation of opium into China
- British went to war twice (1839–1842, 1856–1860) to impose free trade in opium in China
- British victories led to broad Chinese trade concessions

British merchants who remained subject to British rather than Chinese law, and to pay substantial reparations. During the Second Opium War, Britain in alliance with France forced the Chinese to allow foreign envoys to establish embassies in Beijing, to open more ports and areas to foreign trade, and to permit Christian missionaries to operate even more freely in China.

British Settler Colonies

During the early nineteenth century, Britain oversaw the settlement and economic development of three regions that had come under its domination in the eighteenth century: Canada, Australia, and New Zealand. The settlement of these lands, which attracted millions of immigrants from Britain and other European nations, resembled the westward movement in the United States during the same period, including conflicts with native peoples.

The British assumed that eventually these regions would have some form of self-government and be a market for British goods. And in fact during the nineteenth century, each of these colonies did establish responsible self-government based on British law and political institutions. The British system of self-government based on an increasingly inclusive franchise was thus transferred to large parts of the world.

INDIA—THE JEWEL IN THE CROWN OF THE BRITISH EMPIRE

WHY WAS India such an important part of the British empire?

Except for Canada, nineteenth-century British colonial interest shifted from the Atlantic world to Asia and the Indian and Pacific Oceans. During the same years that Britain had lost its North American colonies (1775–1783), it had established itself as the ruler of India. The protection of the commercial and military routes to India would be the chief concern of British imperial strategy during the nineteenth century.

In theory until 1857, India was still ruled by the Mughal Empire, which had governed the region since the 1500s. But that empire was only a shadow of its former self. Local rulers, called nawabs or maharajahs, paid little attention to the Mughal emperor who still resided in Delhi, the old imperial capital.

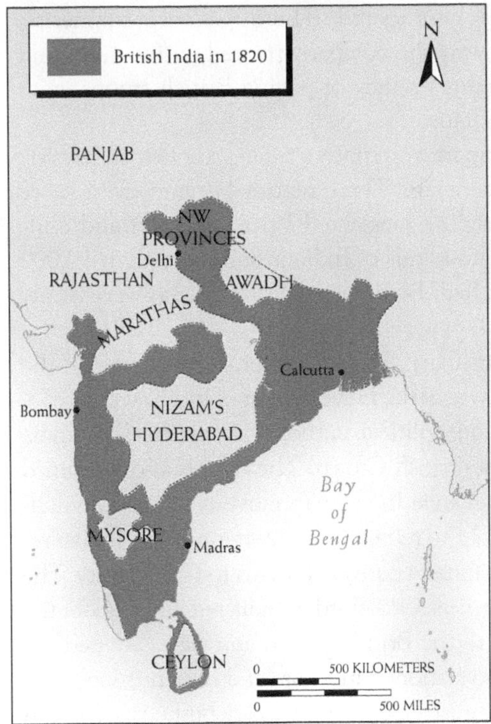

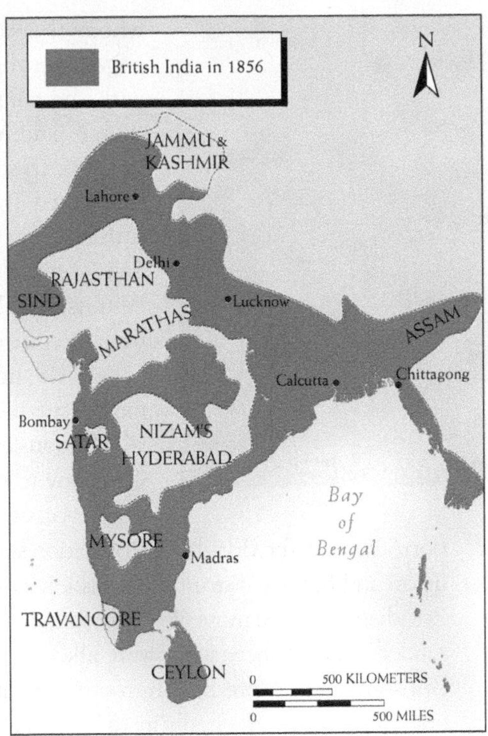

MAP 25–1 **British India, 1820 and 1856.**

What were the key factors in British expansion in India between 1820 and 1856?

Initially the British achieved their domination of India through the East India Company, which was a private company of merchants chartered by Parliament in 1600. In the late eighteenth and early nineteenth centuries, the company expanded its authority across India by warfare and negotiation. By the 1830s, British control over India was essentially complete. The willingness of Indians to defer to British authority rather than accept the dominance of other Indians made British rule possible. Like the Romans, the British had perfected the imperial art of dividing and conquering (see Map 25–1).

The rationale for British rule in India changed over time. The East India Company essentially saw India as a place to make money through economic exploitation. By the early nineteenth century, while still hoping to make India profitable, the British saw themselves as bringing wise administration to a subcontinent where local authority was in disarray. In 1813, Parliament permitted British Christian missionaries to work in India. Their presence meant that for the first time Britons would challenge the religious customs of Indian Hindus and Muslims. Some British administrators began to cooperate with missionaries to bring the "enlightenment" of Western values to India. These and other intrusions suggested that British administrators believed they could raise India to what they considered to be a higher rung on the ladder of civilization.

In 1857, however, India witnessed the most extensive resistance against any European power that occurred in the nineteenth century. The sepoy rebellion or mutiny (Indian troops were called sepoys) was all the more frightening to the British because it occurred within the Indian Army itself. The precipitating cause of the mutiny was the company's introduction of new cartridges for its soldiers' muskets that the sepoys believed (falsely, the cartridges were in fact coated with vegetable oil) were lubricated with pork or beef fat. Soldiers had to bite off the end of the cartridge to use it. This would have offended both Muslims, for whom the pig was unclean, and Hindus, to

The mutinous sepoy cavalry attacking a British infantry division at the Battle of Cawnpore in 1857. Although the uprising was suppressed, it was not easily forgotten. In its aftermath the British reorganized the government of India.

The Granger Collection, New York

What importance might be attached to the contrast between the orderly ranks of British soldiers on the right and the relative disorder of the sepoys on the left?

whom the cow was sacred. There was also simmering anger over the way the company treated native rulers and with the company's policy of paying British troops more than it paid Indians.

With support from native rulers, the British harshly suppressed the rebels. Their tactics became even more ruthless after sepoys massacred British women and children. Tens of thousands of Indians and more than 10,000 Britons were killed. By June 1858, the British were firmly back in control.

The immediate British political response to the mutiny was passage of the Government of India Act in 1858, which transferred political authority from the East India Company to the British Crown. The British also restrained their efforts to change India or to move it "toward civilization." Instead, the British administration sought to refrain from interfering with Indian religion and became distrustful of missionary efforts to convert Indians to Christianity. The British also worked more closely with Indian rulers. One-third of India remained under the rule of Indian princes who swore allegiance to the British Crown and were "advised" by British officials. More British troops were also stationed in India, and Indian troops were not allowed artillery. Finally in 1877, Prime Minister Benjamin Disraeli pushed through an Act of Parliament that declared Queen Victoria (r. 1837–1901) to be Empress of India.

But India remained restive. In 1885, Hindus founded the Indian National Congress with the goals of modernizing Indian life and liberalizing British policy. Muslims organized the Muslim League in 1887, which for a time cooperated with the National Congress but eventually sought an independent Muslim state.

THE "NEW IMPERIALISM," 1870–1914

WHAT WAS new about the "New Imperialism"?

Whereas in the first three quarters of the nineteenth century Britain had largely dominated the world stage, between 1870 and 1914 other Western powers undertook colonial ventures with remarkable results. During this half-century, Western nations including the United States and Japan, which had industrialized and modernized its government and armed forces along Western lines between the 1860s and the 1880s, achieved unprecedented influence and control over the rest of the world and provoked intense colonial rivalries with each other. During this period, imperial expansion went forward with great speed, and empire was regarded as necessary for a great power. Contemporaries at the time and historians have regarded this era as constituting a "New Imperialism" that was different from the imperialism of the early nineteenth century.

Why were the imperial encounters of this era perceived to be "new"? First, they were more intentionally imperial and involved direct political and administrative control of non-Westerners by the Western powers. In a **protectorate** a Western nation placed officials in a foreign state to oversee its government without formally assuming responsibility for administration. In other instances, a European state, the United States, or Japan established "**spheres of influence**" in which it received special commercial and legal privileges in part of an Asian or African state without direct political involvement.

protectorate A non-Western territory administered by a Western nation without formal conquest or annexation, usually a de facto colony.

spheres of influence A region, city, or territory where a non-Western nation exercised informal administrative influence through economic, diplomatic, or military advisors.

Second, the New Imperialism occurred over a relatively brief period and involved an unprecedented number of nations. In addition to the older imperial powers—Britain, France, Russia, the Netherlands, Spain, and Portugal—the newly united Germany and Italy and the Belgian monarchy, which had only existed since 1830, sought to achieve empires as did the United States and Japan.

Third, virtually none of the numerous imperial ventures of this era involved significant numbers of immigrants as settlers. Rather in one way or another over a few decades, Westerners came to govern directly or indirectly vast numbers of non-European peoples. Fourth, during these decades Europeans at home and in colonial settings exhibited a cultural confidence and racial arrogance that marked a departure from previous eras when many persons associated with European empires esteemed indigenous cultures or assumed that these cultures could be raised on the ladder of civilization. Fifth, despite its worldwide scope and especially the establishment of French rule in Indochina, the New Imperialism focused to an unprecedented degree on Africa with the European powers partitioning Africa among themselves. The boundaries they established still determine Africa's political divisions.

Two other points should be noted about the New Imperialism. First, the actual number of Westerners involved in carrying it out was relatively small. Except for soldiers and sailors, only a few thousand administrators, merchants, and missionaries were associated with empire. Second, the empires created by the New Imperialism were short-lived. In most places they lasted less than a century, much shorter than the earlier European empires, which had endured for more than three centuries.

QUICK REVIEW

The New Imperialism

- Intentionally imperial and involved direct political and administrative control of non-Westerners
- Occurred over a brief period of time and involved many Western nations
- Did not involve significant numbers of settlers
- Marked by cultural confidence and racial arrogance

MOTIVES FOR THE NEW IMPERIALISM

WHAT ROLE did economic motives play in nineteenth-century imperialism?

Until the mid–twentieth century, the predominant interpretation of the motives for the New Imperialism was economic. This view originated in a book entitled *Imperialism: A Study* published in 1902 by the English economist and journalist J. A. Hobson (1858–1940). According to Hobson, capitalist economies overproduced, which caused manufacturers, bankers, and financiers, to press governments into imperial ventures to provide new markets for their excess goods and capital. Hobson, who was a radical, but not a Marxist critic of capitalism, believed that European economies should be restructured to make imperialism as he understood it unnecessary.

In 1916 Lenin adopted and modified Hobson's ideas in his book *Imperialism: The Highest Stage of Capitalism*. Lenin argued that competition inevitably eliminates inefficient capitalists and therefore leads to monopoly. Powerful industrial and financial capitalists soon run out of profitable investments in their own countries and persuade their governments to gain colonies in "less developed" countries. Here they can find higher profits, new markets for their products, and safe sources of raw materials. For Lenin, as we saw in Chapter 23, capitalism could not be reformed. Revolution was needed.

The history of the Western imperial advance, as we will see in subsequent sections of this chapter, does not support the theories of Hobson and Lenin. European powers did invest considerable capital abroad and did seek markets, but not in a way that fits the Hobson-Lenin model. Britain, for example, made heavier investments abroad before 1875, when it was not actively acquiring new colonies than during the next two decades when it was expanding its empire. Only a small percentage of British and European overseas investments, moreover, went to their new colonies. Most capital went into other European countries or to older, well-established states like the United States and Argentina and to the settler colonies of Canada, Australia, and New Zealand. Even when Western countries did invest in new colonies, they often did not invest in their own colonies.

The facts are equally discouraging for those who try to explain the New Imperialism by emphasizing the need for markets and raw materials. While some European businesspeople and politicians hoped that colonial expansion would cure the great depression of 1873 to 1896, few colonies were important markets for the great imperial nations. All these states were forced to rely on areas that they did not control as sources of vital raw materials. It is not even clear that control of the new colonies was particularly profitable, though Britain, to be sure, benefited greatly from its rule of India, a rule, however, established long before the New Imperialism. Economics certainly played a part, but a full understanding of the New Imperialism requires a search for other motives.

It is now clear that many motives beyond economic ones influenced the imperial policies of each of the major European nations. Three stand out.

First, after 1870, many political leaders came to believe that the possession of colonies or of imperial influence was an important and even necessary characteristic of a great European power. Here they were clearly following the British example. By the 1880s French politicians believed that colonies could compensate for France's loss of prestige and territory in the Franco-Prussian War of 1870–1871. Similar motives drove Russia's advance into Asia following its defeat in the Crimean War (1854–1856). As a result, vast French and Russian empires were created. Two newly created European states also embraced imperial ventures: Italy believed it must secure colonies to prove that it was a great power, but did so with only modest success; Germany created a more significant, if short-lived, empire. The United States at the time of the Spanish-American War in 1898 also came to believe that possession of colonies was essential to its world status. So did Japan, which became a major imperial power in Asia, acquiring Taiwan in 1895 after defeating China and annexing the independent kingdom of Korea in 1910.

Second, much of the territorial acquisitions associated with the New Imperialism as well as subsequent Western involvement in the Middle East arose in direct response to the power vacuums that the decay of the Ottoman Empire created (see Chapter 22). Throughout the nineteenth century, the Ottoman government in Istanbul slowly but steadily lost province after province to Western powers or nationalist revolts. Ottoman decay gave rise to grave and long-lasting problems. The demise of Ottoman authority in the Balkans created the conflicts that provided the immediate cause for the outbreak of World War I, and the turmoil that has characterized much of the Middle East since 1945 originated in the collapse of Ottoman power in that area. The painfully slow collapse of the Ottoman Empire also brought the West into an unprecedented encounter with Islam.

Third, the geopolitical assumptions of European statesmen led them to deeper and deeper involvements from the eastern Mediterranean to Africa. European powers often intruded into other regions of the world to protect what they regarded as their strategic interest and then had to decide what to do with those regions when faced with the necessity of administering them.

THE PARTITION OF AFRICA

HOW DID European politics contribute to the "Scramble for Africa"?

For almost fifty years inter-European rivalries played out in regions far away from Europe itself and nowhere more intensely than in Africa. During the so-called "Scramble for Africa," which occurred between the late 1870s and about 1912, the European powers sought to maximize their strategic control of African territory, markets, and raw materials. Motivated by intense competition, the imperial powers eventually divided almost all the continent among themselves (see Maps 25–2 and 25–3, on page 630).

The European partition of Africa was not based on a universal policy, and each power acquired and administered its new possessions in different ways. Their goals, however, were the same: to gain control, or at least dominance, through diplomacy or force and then either to place Europeans directly in charge of administering the territories or to compel local rulers to accept European "advisors" who would exercise real authority.

MAP EXPLORATION

Interactive map: To explore this map further, go to www.myhistorylab.com

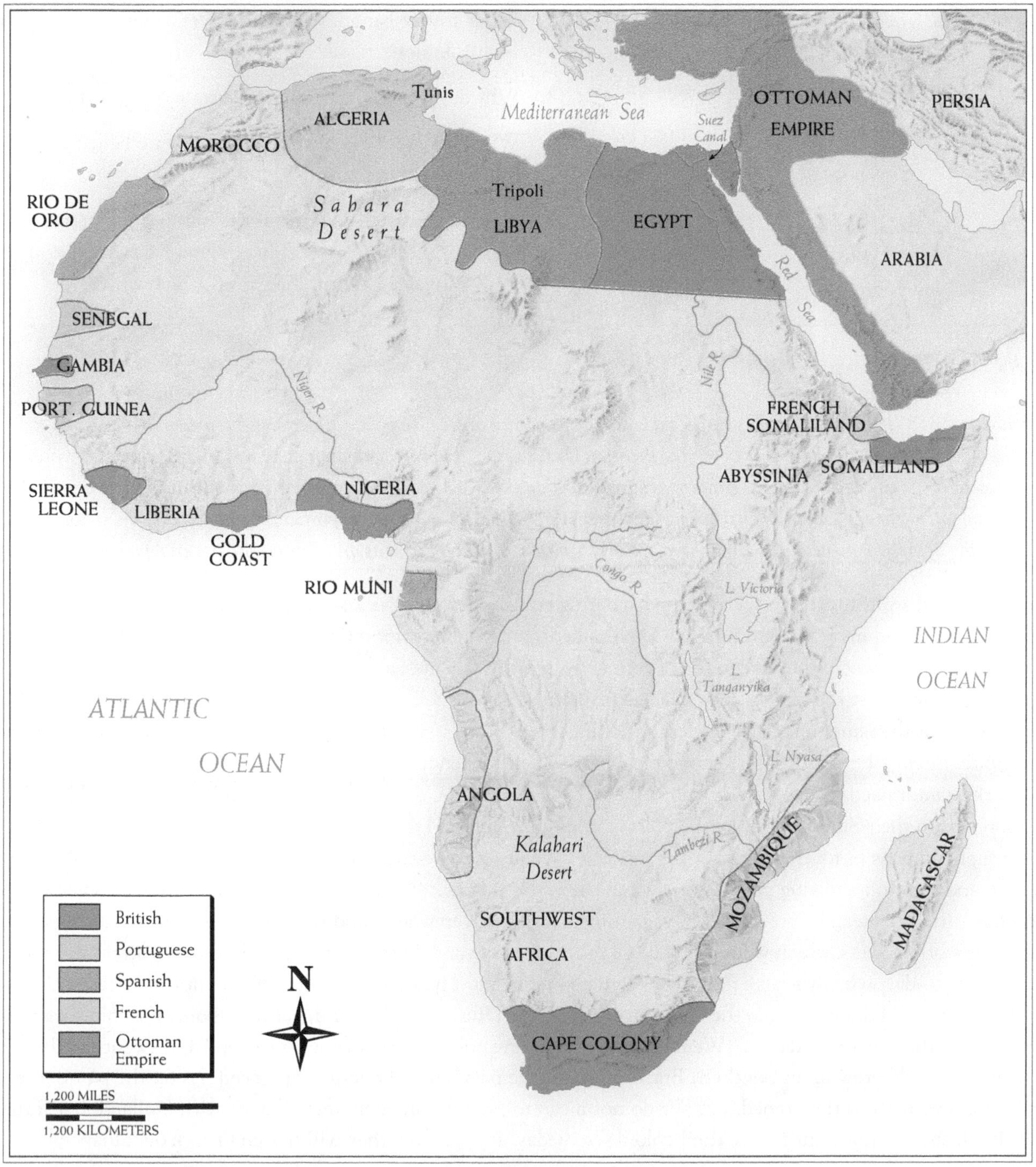

MAP 25–2 **Imperial Expansion in Africa to 1880** Until the 1880s, few European countries held colonies in Africa, mostly on its fringes.

For what purposes did European countries control parts of Africa before 1880?

COMPARE & CONNECT

TWO VIEWS OF TURN-OF-THE-TWENTIETH-CENTURY IMPERIAL EXPANSION

Throughout the age of the most active European expansion, political and popular opinion was divided over whether imperialism was desirable and morally right for the major European powers. Gustav Schmoller, a German political economist, sets forth the argument in favor of imperial expansion about 1900; four years later, the French socialist novelist Anatole France attacked imperialism.

QUESTIONS

1. What are the characteristics that Schmoller ascribes to other contemporary imperial powers?
2. What are the benefits Schmoller sees arising from colonies?
3. Why does France equate imperialism with barbarism?
4. Why does France believe that virtually no benefits result from imperialism?
5. How could writers looking at the European imperial enterprise come to such different conclusions about it? What values inform the views of each writer?

I. GUSTAV SCHMOLLER MAKES THE CASE FOR GERMAN IMPERIAL EXPANSION

Gustav Schmoller (1838–1917) was a highly respected German economist and active political figure who served in the Prussian Privy Council and as a member of the Upper Chamber in the Prussian Diet. He was a strong German nationalist. In this lecture from around the turn of the century Schmoller presents Germany as surrounded on the world scene by aggressive imperial powers. He argues that Germany must imitate them and create its own strong navy and overseas empire. Note the importance he attached to the victory of the United States in the Spanish-American War and the manner in which he portrays Spain as an unsuccessful imperial power.

In various States, arrogant, reckless, cold-blooded daring bullies, men who possess the morals of a captain of pirates. . . push themselves more and more forward into the Government. . . . We must not forget that it is in the freest States, England and North America, where the tendencies of conquest, Imperial schemes, and hatred against new economic competitors are growing up amongst the masses. The leaders of these agitations are great speculators, who have the morals of a pirate, and who are at the same time party leaders and Ministers of State. . . . The conquest of Cuba and the Philippines by the United States alters their political and economical basis. Their tendency to exclude Europe from the North and South American markets must needs lead to new great conflicts. . . . These bullies, these pirates and speculators *à la* Cecil Rhodes, act like poison within their State. They buy the press, corrupt ministers and the aristocracy, and bring on wars for the benefit of a bankrupt company or for the gain of filthy lucre. . . . We mean to extend our trade and industries far enough to enable us to live and sustain a growing population. We mean to defend our colonies, and, if possible, to acquire somewhere agricultural colonies. We mean to prevent extravagant mercantilism everywhere, and to prevent the division of the earth among the three world powers, which would exclude all other countries and destroy their trade. In order to attain this modest gain we require to-day so badly a large fleet. The German Empire must become the centre of a coalition of States, chiefly in order to be able to hold the balance in the death-struggle between Russia and England, but that is only possible if we possess a stronger fleet than that of today. . . . We must wish that at any price a German country, peopled by twenty to thirty7 million Germans, should grow up in Southern Brazil. Without the possibility of energetic proceedings on the part of Germany our future over there is threatened. . . . We do not mean to press for an economic alliance with Holland, but if the Dutch are wise, if they do not want to lose their colonies someday, as Spain did, they will hasten to seek our alliance.

Source: Gustav Schmoller lecture of about 1900, quoted in J. Ellis Barker, *Modern Germany: Her Political and Economic Problems, Her Foreign and Domestic Policy, Her Ambitions, and the Causes of Her Success*, 2nd ed. (London: Smith, Elder, & Co., 1907), pp. 139–140.

II. ANATOLE FRANCE DENOUNCES IMPERIALISM

Anatole France (1844–1924) was a famous late-century French novelist who was also active in the French socialist movement. Many socialists across Europe criticized the imperial ventures of their governments. In this passage France provides both a moral and a utilitarian critique of French imperialism around the world. He associates it with ambitious military figures, greedy businessmen, and corrupt politicians. He also contends that it brings nothing of value to France. Critiques of similar character appeared among other liberal, socialist, and radical politicians and political commentators across Europe and also in the United State. Criticism of imperialism of this character would continue until the close of the colonial age during the last quarter of the twentieth century. Notice that like Schmoller, France see imperialism as something now characterizing all the major powers.

Arrival in Saigon of Paul Beau (1857–1927), governor general of Indo-China 1902–1907, from "Le Petit Journal," November 1902.

Private Collection/The Bridgeman Art Library International

Does the encounter depicted in this illustration seem friendly or hostile? Why?

Imperialism is the most recent form of barbarism, the end of the line for civilization. I do not distinguish between the two terms—imperialism and barbarism—for they mean the same thing.

We Frenchmen, a thrifty people, who see to it that we have no more children than we are able to support easily, careful of adventuring into foreign lands, we Frenchmen who hardly ever leave our own gardens, for what in the world do we need colonies? What can we do with them? What are the benefits for us? It has cost Franc much in lives and money so that the Congo, Cochinchina, Annam, Tonkin, Guinea, and Madagascar may be able to buy cotton from Manchester, liquors from Danzig, and wine from Hamburg. For the last seventy years France has attacked and persecuted the Arabs so that Algeria might be inhabited by Italians and Spaniards!

The French people get nothing from the colonial lands of Africa and Asia. But their government finds it profitable. Through colonial conquest the military people get promotions, pensions, and awards, in addition to the glory gained by quelling the natives. Shipowners, army contractors, and shady politicians prosper. The ignorant mob is flattered because it believes that an overseas empire will make the British and Germans green with envy.

Will this colonial madness never end? I know well that nations are not reasonable. Considering their composition, it would be strange, indeed, if they were. But sometimes they know instinctively what is bad for them. Through long and bitter experience they will come to see the mistakes they have made. And, one day, they will realize that colonies bring only danger and ruin.

Source: Anatole France, "The Colonial Folly," (1904), as quoted in Louis L. Snyder, *The Imperialism Reader: Documents and Readings on Modern Expansionism* (New York: D. Van Nostrand Company, Inc., 1962), pp. 155–156.

MAP EXPLORATION

Interactive map: To explore this map further, go to www.myhistorylab.com

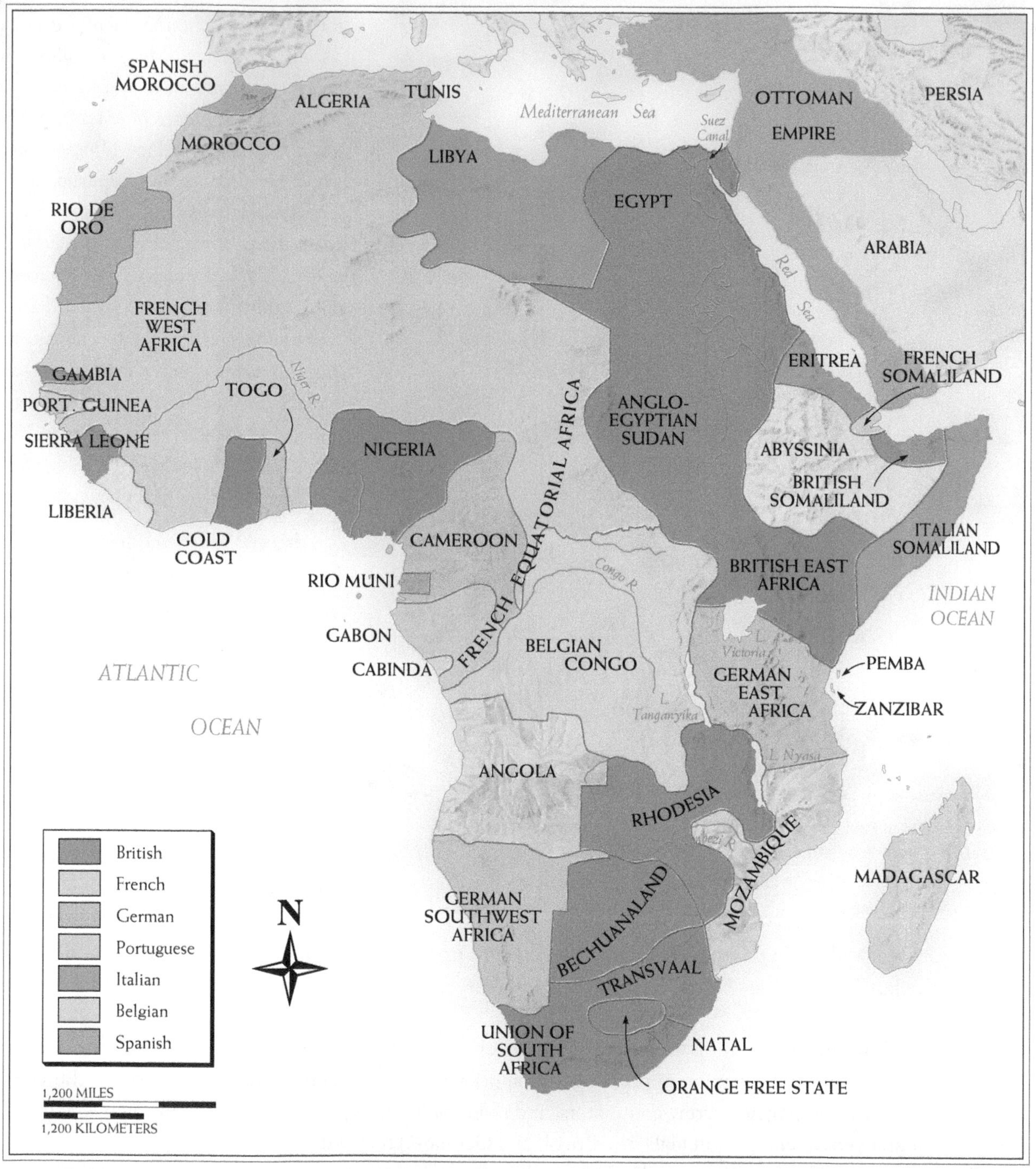

MAP 25–3 **Partition of Africa, 1880–1914** Before 1880, the European presence in Africa was largely the remains of early exploration by old imperialists and did not penetrate the heart of the continent. By 1914, the occupying powers included most large European states; only Liberia and Abyssinia remained independent.

Which European country had the most African colonies?

ALGERIA, TUNISIA, MOROCCO, AND LIBYA

France left the Congress of Vienna in 1815 with only a few small colonies and trading posts. For a time French popular opinion seems to have resisted further colonial ventures. Then in 1830, as we saw in Chapter 20, the government of Charles X (r. 1824–1830) literally in its last days launched a military expedition against Algiers. Following the Revolution of 1830, which deposed Charles, France did not pull back from Algeria. French governments saw Algeria's fertile coastal regions as providing the land for a settler colony. By 1871 more than 275, 000 French settlers were living there. Over the decades, France pushed beyond the coast into the Sahara Desert where its forces established their authority over various nomadic Muslim peoples. The French came to regard Algeria as an integral part of France.

In 1881–1882, the French also established a protectorate over Tunisia, which was nominally a province of the Ottoman Empire, and then between 1901 and 1912, set up another protectorate in Morocco. In both Tunisia and Morocco, the French retained the local rulers as puppet monarchs.

Italy, having failed to conquer Ethiopia in 1896, seized Libya from Turkey in 1911–1912, establishing its most important colony. These French and Italian colonial advances in North Africa demonstrated the profound weakness of the Ottoman Empire. Thus by the outbreak of World War I, all of North Africa lay under some form of European control. In each of these cases a Western power dominated a largely Muslim population.

EGYPT AND BRITISH STRATEGIC CONCERN ABOUT THE UPPER NILE

Egypt, the richest and most populous region of North Africa, came under European domination as a result of political stagnation and economic collapse. Like Tunisia, Egypt was a semi-independent province of the Ottoman Empire under the hereditary rule of a Muslim dynasty. After the failed Napoleonic invasion in 1798, the Khedives, as these rulers were titled, had tried to modernize Egypt by building new harbors, roads, and a modern army. Egypt also sought to expand its rule into the Sudan. To pay for these projects, the Khedives borrowed money from European creditors. To earn the money to repay these loans, they forced farmers to plant cash crops, particularly cotton, which could be sold on the international market. The Egyptian economy and government revenue rose and fell with the price of cotton. Ultimately, the Egyptian government became utterly dependent on European creditors for new loans at exorbitant rates of interest. The construction of the Suez Canal was the final blow to Egypt's finances.

Linking Asia and Europe, the Suez Canal, opened in 1869, was a major engineering achievement. It also became a major international waterway benefiting all maritime states by reducing the distance from London to Bombay by half.

Bibliothèque des Arts Decoratifs, Paris, France/The Bridgeman Art Library International

What benefits, if any, did the people of Egypt get from the opening of the Suez Canal?

The Suez Canal was opened in 1869. Built by French engineers with European capital, it was one of the most remarkable engineering feats of the day. The canal connected the Mediterranean to the Red Sea, which meant that ships from Europe no longer had to sail around Africa to reach Asia. The canal increased the speed of international contacts and, by reducing shipping costs, made many goods on the world market more affordable. Yet the tangible benefits to Egypt itself were not immediately clear. By 1875, the Khedive was bankrupt. Egypt's European creditors were taking more than 50 percent of Egyptian revenue each year to repay their loans, and they forced the Egyptian government to increase taxes to raise more revenue. This provoked a nationalist rebellion, and in 1881, the Egyptian army took over the government to defend Egypt from foreign exploitation. In 1882 Britain sent a fleet and army to Egypt that easily defeated the Egyptians and established seventy years of British supremacy in the country.

Egypt was never an official part of the British Empire. The Khedives continued to reign, but a small number of British officials dominated the Egyptian administration. Britain's primary goal in Egypt was political and military stability. Egypt had to repay its debts, and Britain was to retain control of the Suez Canal. The British built a naval base at Alexandria and installed a large garrison in Cairo. They established municipal governments that were responsible for taxation and public services and further expanded cotton cultivation. They also prevented the Egyptians from establishing a textile industry that would compete with Britain's own mills.

Economically, this meant that while the Egyptian economy grew and tax revenues increased, per capita income actually declined among Egyptians, most of whom were peasants who owned little or no land. Politically, it led to the growth of Egyptian nationalism, to Islamic militancy, and to demands that the British leave Egypt.

The British occupation of Egypt quickly drew Britain even deeper into Africa along the Nile. Control of the upper Nile had been understood to be essential to the security of Egypt since ancient times. The collapse of the Khedive's authority in Cairo in 1881 had led to a similar collapse of Egyptian authority in the Sudan. The Sudan remained in turmoil until 1898 when an Anglo-Egyptian army under General Sir Herbert, later Lord, Kitchener (1850–1916) conquered it in a remarkably violent campaign during which 11,000 Sudanese troops were killed and 16,000 wounded by modern weaponry in a single battle at Omdurman. The British lost only 48 men in the battle.

The battle of Omdurman, fought on September 2, 1898, demonstrated the capacity of European forces armed with the most modern weapons—in this case, a British army composed of British, Egyptian, and Sudanese troops, commanded by Major General Sir Horatio Kitchener, to decimate a vast Sudanese force armed with less advanced weapons. In the battle, which occurred near Khartoum, the British encircled the Sudanese forces. Approximately 10,000 African warriors were killed, while British losses numbered 48 men. Contrary to the image on this contemporary print, the British forces wore khaki rather than red uniforms.

Picture Desk, Inc./Kobal Collection

How did this battle demonstrate the power of Western military technology?

The British determination to secure the upper Nile and the Sudan led to one of the major crises of the imperial age. Although the French had refused to participate when British forces invaded Egypt in 1882, they retained large investments there and still hoped to influence Egyptian affairs by controlling the upper Nile. In the summer of

1898, a small French military force from West Africa reached the upper Nile at an unimportant location called Fashoda. As Kitchener's forces moved south, he confronted the French. War seemed possible until Paris ordered the French to withdraw. Instead of fighting, France and Britain eventually resolved their imperial rivalries. France acquiesced in Britain's domination of Egypt, and Britain agreed to support French ambitions in Morocco. The peaceful resolution of the Fashoda incident and other imperial disputes was essential to the formation of the loose alliance called the Anglo-French Entente in 1904 and to the two countries fighting as allies in World War I.

West Africa

France could surrender hope of dominating Egypt because it already controlled much of sub-Saharan Africa. West Africa, in particular, was a key area for French imperialism. In 1895 French West Africa included 12 million inhabitants and was eight times larger than France itself.

The British had four West African colonies: Sierra Leone, which was originally a home for freed slaves, Gambia, the Gold Coast (now Ghana), and Nigeria, the largest and most populous black African colony that any European power possessed. British slavers had worked on the Nigerian coast during the eighteenth century, and Britain had moved steadily into the Nigerian interior since the 1840s seeking to establish trade and acquire tropical products, especially palm oil and cotton. Over time the British established protectorates over the Muslim emirates in northern Nigeria and direct control over other areas. In 1914, they combined all these territories into a single administrative unit, which they called the colony of Nigeria. To prevent indigenous resistance, British officials ran the country through local rulers, a policy known as indirect rule.

The Belgian Congo

Perhaps the most remarkable story in the European Scramble for Africa was the acquisition of the Belgian Congo. As a young monarch, King Leopold II of Belgium (r. 1865–1909) had become determined that Belgium, despite its small territory, must acquire colonies. The Belgian government, however, had no interest in colonies. So despite being a constitutional monarch, Leopold used his own wealth and political guile to realize his colonial ambitions. He did so under the guise of humanitarian concern for Africans. In 1876, he gathered explorers, geographers, and antislavery reformers in Brussels and formed the International African Association. He then recruited the English-born journalist and explorer Henry Morton Stanley (1841–1904) to undertake an expedition into the Congo. Between 1879 and 1884, he explored the Congo and on Leopold's behalf made "treaties" with African rulers who had no idea what they were signing. Leopold then won diplomatic recognition for those treaties and for his own allegedly humanitarian efforts in the region. Leopold, thus, personally became the ruler of an African domain that was over seventy times the size of Belgium.

Although Leopold cultivated the image of a humanitarian ruler by sponsoring antislavery conferences and manipulating public relations, his goal in the Congo was brutal economic exploitation. Leopold's administrators used slave labor, intimidation, torture, mutilation, and mass murder to extract rubber and ivory from what became known as the Congo Free State. Eventually, Leopold's crimes were exposed, and he formally turned the Congo over to Belgium in 1908, the year before he died.

German Empire in Africa

The German chancellor Otto von Bismarck appears to have pursued an imperial policy, however briefly, from coldly political motives and with only modest enthusiasm. In 1884 and 1885, Germany declared protectorates over South-West Africa (today the country of Namibia), Togoland, and the Cameroons in West Africa, and Tanganyika in East Africa. Bismarck acquired colonies chiefly to improve Germany's diplomatic position in Europe and to divert France into colonial expansion and away from hostility to Germany. He also used German colonial activities in Africa to pressure the British to be reasonable about European affairs.

Bismarck had used Leopold II's efforts in the Congo to call the Berlin Conference in 1884 (not to be confused with the Congress of Berlin, which sought to settle the Eastern Question in 1879). At the Berlin Conference the major European powers decided on what amounted to the formal partition of Africa. By 1890 almost all the continent had been parceled out.

Germany's proved to be the shortest lived of any of the European colonial ventures. German imperialism involved few Germans and produced no significant economic returns. At the end of World War I, the Allies stripped Germany of its colonial holdings. This meant that Germany was the only major West European state not drawn into the struggles of decolonization after World War II. But the German entry into the arena of imperial competition did contribute to the tensions that led to World War I (see Chapter 26).

Genocide in South-West Africa The German Empire lasted for only about three decades, but in that time German administrators carried out a major atrocity against indigenous peoples in German South-West Africa. In 1904 the Herero people in the colony revolted, and the Germans decided to take severe action. They announced that the Hereros had to leave their land, and the German commander General Lothar von Trotha authorized the killing of all male Hereros and driving their women and children into the desert. Herero prisoners were placed in concentration camps where the death rates from disease were high although the Germans ran the camps with meticulous bureaucratic attention to detail. A United Nations report in 1985 concluded that by the time the Germans suppressed the revolt in 1908, 80 percent of the Herero population had died.

Great Trek The migration by Boer (Dutch) farmers during the 1830s and 1840s from regions around Cape Town into the eastern and northeastern regions of South Africa that ultimately resulted in the founding of the Orange Free State and Transvaal.

Diamond mining in South Africa took off in the late 1860s. By 1880 Kimberly, the biggest mine in the region, had 30,000 people, second only to Cape Town. Whites, such as these diamond sorters, monopolized the well-paid, skilled jobs.

National Archives of South Africa

How did the discovery of gold and gems in South Africa lead to conflict in the region?

Southern Africa

Except for coastal Algeria, only South Africa had attracted large numbers of European settlers. The Dutch had begun to settle there in the mid-1600s. By 1800, Cape Town had become an important port for ships on their way to Asia. During the Napoleonic Wars the British captured Cape Town from the Dutch. Soon thereafter, British settlers began to arrive, and British economic and cultural influence soon predominated on the Cape.

Not surprisingly, the Dutch resented British control. During the 1830s and 1840s, the Boers or Afrikaners, as the descendants of the Dutch were known, undertook the **Great Trek** during which they moved north and east of the Cape. This migration became the key moment in the forging of Afrikaner national consciousness. They founded states outside British control that would become Natal, Transvaal, and the Orange Free State.

In 1886 gold was discovered in the Transvaal, and 50,000 miners rushed to Johannesburg. There were now more non-Boer white settlers in the

Transvaal than Boers, but the government refused to allow non-Boers the right to vote. Tensions mounted between Britain and the Boers over the region and, in 1899, war broke out. Although the British finally won this Boer War in 1902, they were surprised by the strength of Boer resistance. When the Boers resorted to guerilla tactics, the British gathered Boer women and children into what they called **concentration camps** where many died from disease and exposure.

In 1910, the British combined the colonies in South Africa into a confederation whose constitution guaranteed the rule of the European minority over the majority black and nonwhite population. Africans and people of mixed race whom the British referred to as "colored" were forbidden to own land, denied the right to vote, and excluded from positions of power. To preserve their political power and economic privileges, the white elite of South Africa eventually enforced a policy of racial **apartheid**—"separateness"—that turned the country into a totally segregated land until the 1990s. The result was decades of oppression, racial tensions, and economic exploitation.

concentration camps Camps first established by Great Britain in South Africa during the Boer War to incarcerate noncombatant civilians; later camps established for political prisoners and other persons deemed dangerous to the state in the Soviet Union and Nazi Germany. The term is now primarily associated with the camps established by the Nazis during the Holocaust.

apartheid (a-PAR-tid) An official policy of segregation, assignment of peoples to distinct regions, and other forms of social, political, and economic discrimination based on race associated primarily with South Africa.

RUSSIAN EXPANSION IN MAINLAND ASIA

HOW DID Russia come to control a vast and diverse Asian empire?

The British presence in India was intimately related to Russian expansion across mainland Asia in the nineteenth century, which eventually brought huge territories and millions of people of a variety of ethnicities and religions under tsarist rule.

During the early eighteenth century, the tsars had consolidated their control around the Baltic Sea. Catherine the Great (r. 1762–1796) had gained much of southern Ukraine and opened the regions around the Black Sea to Russian control at the cost of Ottoman influence. The partitions of Poland had extended Russian authority toward the west (see Chapter 17). During the nineteenth century the Russian government would look to the east where no major state could oppose its advance and where the weakness of the Ottoman Empire and China worked to Russian advantage.

Even during the eighteenth century, the tsarist government had ruled extremely diverse groups of people who were not Russian by language, religion, or cultural heritage. The Russians had generally approached these peoples in a pragmatic way, tolerating their religions and recognizing their social elites. What the Russian government sought was those elites' loyalty to the tsar rather than conformity to Russian language, the Orthodox Church, or Russian culture.

Beginning in the late eighteenth century, however, the tsarist government began to regard the nomadic societies or communities who lived in the mountainous regions to the south and east as *inorodtsy*, meaning "foreign." Moreover, the government drew upon the Enlightenment four-stage theory of social development, discussed in Chapter 17, to distinguish sedentary peoples as superior to those who lived as hunters, gatherers, fishermen, or nomads. One of the purposes thereafter of Russian expansion was, like that of early Victorian British administrators in India, to raise these people

EXPANSION OF EUROPEAN POWER AND THE NEW IMPERIALISM

1869	Suez Canal completed
1875	Britain gains control of the Suez Canal
1879–1884	Leopold II establishes his personal rule in the Congo
1882	France controls Tunisia
1880s	Britain establishes protectorate over Egypt
1884–1885	Germany establishes protectorate over Southwest Africa (Namibia), Togoland, the Cameroons, and East Africa (Tanzania)
1895	Japan seizes Taiwan from China
1898	Spanish-American War: United States acquires Puerto Rico, Philippines, and Guam, annexes Hawaiian Islands, and establishes virtual protectorate over Cuba
1899	United States proposes Open Door Policy in Far East
1899–1902	Boer War in South Africa
1908	Belgium takes over the Congo from Leopold II
1905–1912	France establishes protectorate over Morocco
1910	Japan annexes Korea
1912	Italy conquers Libya from Turkey

Though the Russians largely subdued the Caucasus region by the 1860s—with a Muslim separatist movement led by Imam Shamil put down only after decades of struggle—the many ethnic groups of this rugged mountain region remained largely autonomous until well into the twentieth century. This photograph, most likely taken around 1890, shows a group of chain-clad warriors from the Khevsureti region of Georgia (which had been incorporated into the Russian Empire early in the nineteenth century). With their primitive firearms, swords, and shields, these fighting men may appear like no match for mechanized firepower, but in reality the people of this region remained largely free of governmental authority until well into the twentieth century.

Courtesy of the Library of Congress

What challenges did Russia's ethnic diversity pose for the Russian Empire?

on the ladder of civilization. Russian governors would henceforth rarely, if ever, consider conquered peoples to be their social or cultural equals.

The nineteenth century saw Russia extend its authority in three distinct areas of mainland Asia. The first was in the Transcaucasus. This expansion came at the cost of Persia and the Ottoman Empire, both of which by nineteenth-century standards had become weak states. But Russia never securely incorporated these regions into the Russian Empire because their aristocratic elites were not willing to be co-opted. By the late nineteenth century, nationalistic unrest was rising among Georgians, Armenians, and Azerbaijainis. The Russians were also only modestly successful in subjugating the Muslim peoples living in the Caucasus regions of Chechnya, Dagestan, and Circassia.

The second prong of Russian imperial advance occurred in the vast steppes of Central Asia where various nomadic peoples lived. The most important of these were Kazakhs who remained nomadic even under Russian rule until Stalin forced them onto collective farms in the 1930s (see Chapter 27).

The final area of Russian imperial conquest occurred in southern Middle Asia from the 1860s to the 1880s. This is the region of present-day Uzbekistan, Turkistan, and the areas bordering Afghanistan, all of which are primarily Muslim. Expansion in this area followed Russia's defeat in the Crimean War and sought to demonstrate that Russia could still exert imperial influence in Asia and counter the British presence in India. The Russian-British rivalry over these regions sometimes brought Russia and Britain to the edge of war until the early twentieth century when both powers became concerned about German influence in the Ottoman Empire. The Anglo-Russian Convention of 1907 ended their Central Asian rivalry and gave each power spheres of influence in Persia. Like the settlement of colonial claims between Britain and France, the end of this particular imperial contest also opened the way for Britain and Russia to become allies against Germany during World War I.

WESTERN POWERS IN ASIA

WHAT DEVELOPMENTS facilitated Western penetration and control of Asia?

France in Asia

While merchants had established the British interest in India and South Asia, French interest in Indochina arose because of the activity of Roman Catholic missionaries. French missionaries gained ground in Indochina and elsewhere in Asia in the 1830s and 1840s. Persecution soon followed. In 1856, Napoleon III (r. 1852–1870) sent forces to Vietnam to protect the missionaries and give France a base from which the French navy could operate in the Far East and French commerce could expand in Asia. By the 1880s, France controlled all of Vietnam and had made Cambodia a protectorate. In 1896, Laos also became a French protectorate. Missionary work continued throughout Indochina, especially in Vietnam where Catholics became and remain a significant minority.

The United States Actions in Asia and the Pacific

In 1853, a United States naval squadron under Commodore Matthew C. Perry (1794–1858) arrived in Japanese waters to open Japanese markets to American goods. In 1867, American interest in the Pacific again manifested itself when the United States bought Alaska from Russia. For the next twenty-five years, the United States assumed a fairly passive role in foreign affairs, but it had established its presence in the Pacific.

Cuba's revolt against Spain in the 1890s ended this passivity and provided the impetus for the creation of an American Empire. Sympathy for the Cuban cause, investments on the island, the desire for Cuban sugar, and concern over Cuba's strategic importance all helped drive the United States to fight Spain.

Victory in the brief Spanish-American War of 1898 brought the United States an informal protectorate over Cuba, and the annexation of Puerto Rico ended four hundred years of Spanish rule in the Western Hemisphere. The United States also forced Spain to sell it the Philippines and Guam, while Germany bought the other Spanish islands in the Pacific. The United States and Germany divided Samoa between them. In 1898 the United States also annexed Hawaii, five years after an American-backed coup had overthrown the native Hawaiian monarchy. This burst of activity made the United States an imperial power.

The Boxer Rebellion

By the close of the nineteenth century, the Qing Dynasty, which had ruled China since 1644, was in a state of near collapse, and its decay both enabled Western penetration and was exacerbated by it. The United States feared that the European powers and Japan would soon carve up China and close its lucrative markets and investment opportunities to American interests. In 1899, to prevent this, the United States proposed the Open Door Policy, which was designed to prevent formal foreign annexations of Chinese territory and to allow businesspeople from all nations to

In 1900 an international force composed of troops drawn from Austria-Hungary, the French Third Republic, the German Empire, Italy, Japan, Russia, Great Britain, and the United States invaded China to put down the Boxer Rebellion, which had endangered Western missionaries and Western interests in China. In August 1900 these forces occupied Beijing. This contemporary print presents the image of a romanticized heroic assault by these foreign troops.

Courtesy of the Library of Congress

Who were the Boxers and what did they want?

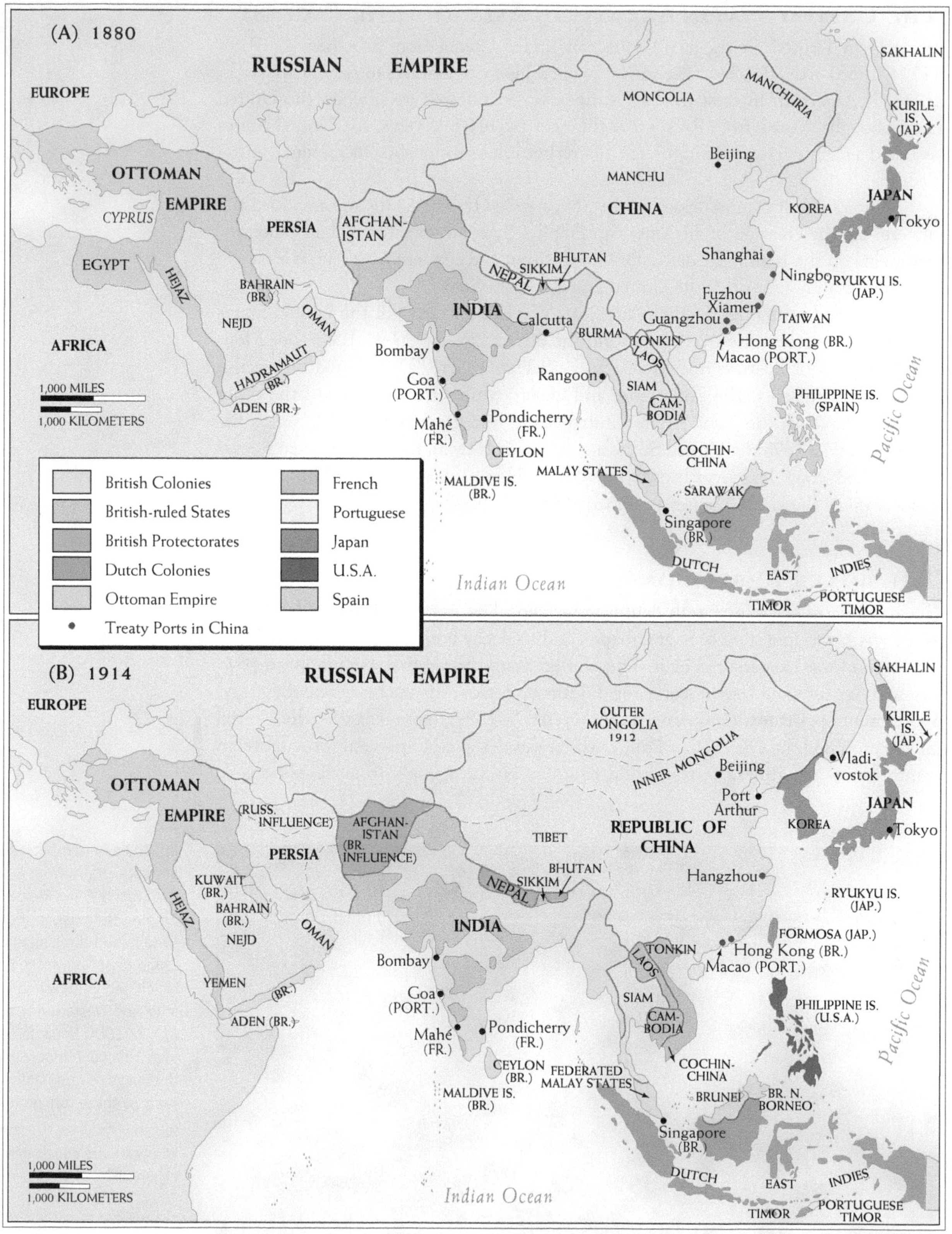

MAP 25–4 Asia, 1880–1914 As in Africa, the decades before World War I saw imperialism spread widely and rapidly in Asia. Two new powers, Japan and the United States, joined the British, French, and Dutch in extending control both to islands and to the mainland and in exploiting an enfeebled China.

Why did the emergence of Japan as a great power frighten European nations?

trade in China on equal terms. Although all the powers except Russia eventually agreed to this policy in principle, they nonetheless carved out spheres of influence in China, and France, Britain, Germany, and Russia established naval bases on the Chinese coast (see Map 25–4).

Although the Qing government was too feeble to resist Western bullying, hatred of foreigners and resentment at their presence were strong. From late 1899 through the autumn of 1901, a Chinese group called The Righteous and Harmonious Society of Fists, better known in the West as the Boxers, attempted to resist the Western incursions. The Boxers, who were supported by a faction at the Qing court, hated missionaries whom they saw as agents of the imperial powers and killed thousands of their Chinese converts.

For the imperial powers, the key moment in the Boxer Rebellion was the attacks on the foreign diplomatic missions in Beijing, which lasted off and on for three months in 1900 until an international army occupied the Chinese capital in August 1900. For the second time in less than half a century, Western troops had seized Beijing. In September 1901, the Chinese government agreed to execute officials who had helped the Boxers and pay large reparations to the Western powers and Japan.

TOOLS OF IMPERIALISM

HOW DID technological innovations make nineteenth-century imperialism possible?

The domination that Europe and peoples of European descent came to exert over the entire globe by 1900 was based on distinct and temporary technological advantages, what one historian called the "tools of empire." These tools gave Westerners the capacity to conquer and dominate vast areas of the world. (See "Encountering the Past: Submarine Cables," page 640.)

STEAMBOATS

Robert Fulton, an American, had invented the steamboat in 1807. By the 1830s, steam power enabled warships to penetrate the inland rivers and shallow coastal waters of Asia and Africa, giving rise to the projection of Western power that became known as "gunboat diplomacy." By the late 1820s, steamboats were being constructed of iron. In the nineteenth century, such boats carried European goods and European arms to assure trade in those goods up rivers around the world. It was almost impossible for local rulers and officials to defend themselves against iron warships.

Western steamboats were particularly effective along the vast rivers of Asia. The presence of gunboats on a river beside a city usually assured European merchants, and especially for many decades British merchants, access to the local markets. Iron steamboats, including some of the largest built to that date, assured British success against China in the first Opium War.

CONQUEST OF TROPICAL DISEASES

Tropical diseases often proved more of an obstacle to European conquest than African or Asian armed forces. For centuries diseases, especially malaria, had prevented Europeans from penetrating deep into the forests of sub-Saharan Africa. To move inland and increase their profits from commerce, especially after the formal end of the slave trade in the early nineteenth century, Europeans had to find a way around the malaria problem. The solution was quinine. Quinine pills made possible the rapid exploration and eventual partition of Africa. Moreover, the demand for quinine transformed its area of production. Originally cinchona bark had been grown in Peru. By the late

ENCOUNTERING THE PAST

SUBMARINE CABLES

Underwater telegraphic cables were among the important inventions of the mid–nineteenth century utilizing the then new electrical technology. Submarine cables amazed people of that era and the early twentieth century much as the Internet does today. These cables also allowed for unprecedented international communication.

The first submarine cable was laid between Great Britain and France in 1850, and the first transatlantic cable was installed successfully in 1866. Thereafter, to a remarkable extent, made evident by the accompanying world map of the early twentieth century, the imperial strategic, military concerns of the British government determined the pattern of the installation of these cables of the Eastern Associated Telegraph Companies founded in 1872. It was a case of imperial expansion determining the application of an exciting new technology using electricity. The route of the original Eastern cable of 1872 traced the coast of Western Europe, then across the Mediterranean through the Red Sea into the Indian Ocean to India, then overland in India, then eastward underwater to northern Australia and Hong Kong. By 1922, as seen in the map, cables linked all the areas of the British Empire acquired in the previous half-century as well as the important markets for British trade in Latin America. The company oversaw approximately 130,000 miles of cable. These submarine cables thus reflected late-nineteenth-century British imperial expansion and also provided essential communication allowing the empire to function economically, politically, and militarily.

In 1922 the Eastern Associated Telegraph Companies of Great Britain published a celebratory fiftieth-anniversary volume. It opened by declaring, "On the world's oceans, surrounded by forests of vegetation, faintly reflected in the waving seaweeds of shallow shores, amidst the haunts of creatures which never see the light of the sun, where the skeletons of the wrecked ships of today and yesterday loom like phantom far and near, lie the great submarine ropes with which man has encircled the earth. Through the dark underworld of the sea, across submerged continents, and over valleys, plains and mountains, trodden in an ageless past by the forerunners of mankind, these electrified ropes carry the messages of man to man." Eastern Associated Telegraph described its cables as "the nervous system of the civilized world" and boasted, "There is hardly any spot in the more developed parts of the British Empire and of the world which cannot speedily be reached by a message marked 'via Eastern.'"

Fifty Years of "Via Eastern": A Souvenir and Record of the Celebrations in Connection with the Jubilee of the Eastern Associated Telegraph Companies MXMXII (privately printed, 1922), pp. 13, 16.

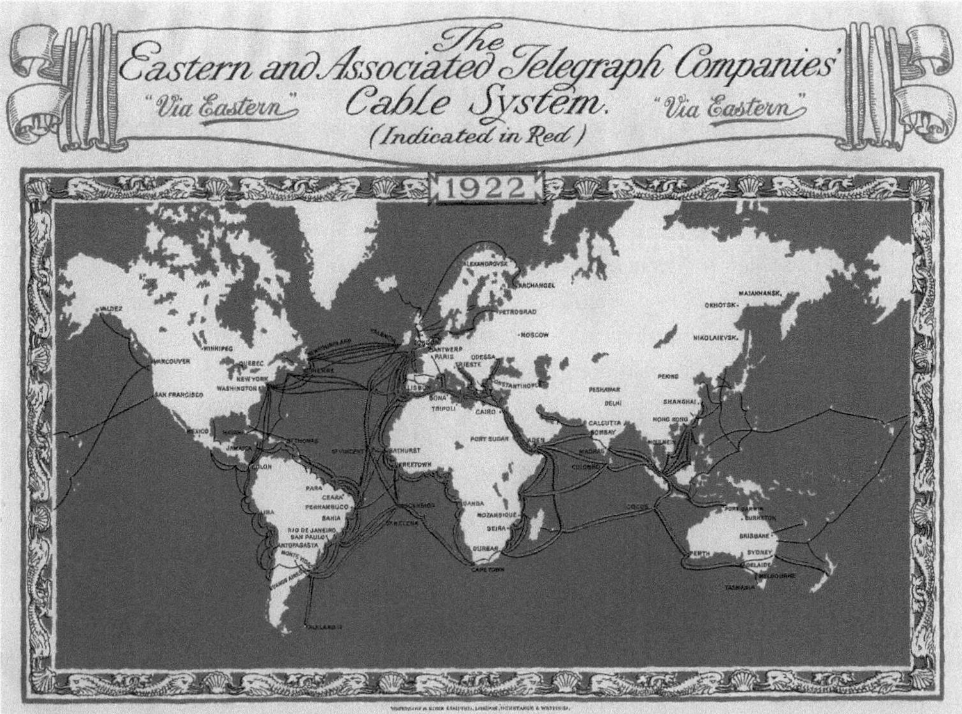

HOW DID the deployment of undersea telegraph cables facilitate the imperial campaign?

Overview The Tools of Imperialism

STEAMBOATS	• Steam power enabled warships to penetrate inland rivers and shallow coastal waters of Asia and Africa • Advent of ironclad warships gave rise to "gunboat diplomacy" • Steamboats particularly effective along the vast rivers of Asia
CONQUEST OF TROPICAL DISEASES	• Tropical diseases often an obstacle to European conquest • Malaria prevented exploitation of inland sub-Saharan Africa • Use of quinine to prevent malaria made the "Scramble for Africa" possible
FIREARMS	• Improved firearms gave Europeans an overwhelming military advantage over non-Western peoples • Advances were made in weapons, bullets, and gunpowder • Technological advances culminated in the invention of the machine gun

nineteenth century, its chief regions of cultivation were Dutch plantations in the East Indies and British plantations in India.

FIREARMS

During the nineteenth century, vast and momentous changes occurred in the technology of Western firearms. These changes gave Western nations an overwhelming advantage over non-Western peoples.

The rifle was improved, so that bullets would spin more rapidly and move in a straighter direction. Early in the century, Thomas Shaw invented the percussion cap for bullets. Unlike the earlier flintlock rifles, the percussion caps could easily be used in wet weather. The design of bullets themselves changed to allow greater speed and precision. By the mid-1850s, the British had adopted the Enfield rifle, which incorporated all the new technologies and was manufactured with interchangeable parts. The invention of the breechloader in the 1860s brought still greater distance and precision in firepower for both rifles and artillery. Later in the century, smokeless gunpowder and repeating mechanisms further enhanced accuracy and firepower.

All these technological changes were incorporated into the development of the machine gun. By 1900, the machine gun had become arguably the single most important weapon in colonial warfare and accounted for the deaths of tens of thousands of non-European peoples. Europeans also used dum-dum bullets, which exploded inside a wound, against native peoples when they would not use them against other Europeans.

THE MISSIONARY FACTOR

WHAT WAS the relationship between missionaries and their home governments?

The modern Western missionary movement, which continues to the present day, originated in Great Britain in the late eighteenth century as a direct outgrowth of the rise of evangelical Christianity. Evangelicalism, which influenced Protestant communities from Central Europe to the United States, emphasized the authority of the Bible, the importance of a personal conversion experience, and the duty to spread the Gospel. By

Women played a prominent role as teachers in the Western foreign missionary effort. Miss Emily Hartwell was a turn-of-the-century, American-born Protestant missionary to the Foochow Mission in Fuzhou Shi, China. Here, in a photo from the missionary magazine *Light and Life,* she is pictured with one of her Bible classes composed of Chinese women. Her letters home spoke of the disadvantages of women in Chinese culture.

Courtesy of the Library of Congress

What explains the surge of missionary activity in the late nineteenth century?

the close of the eighteenth century, small groups of Evangelicals began to be active in the non-Western world. Roman Catholics later copied these early Protestant missionary efforts. The result of this widespread nineteenth-century missionary campaign was the establishment of large Christian communities in Africa and Asia, which today thrive and continue to expand.

Evangelical Protestant Missionaries

The chief moving forces in the British missionary movement were the Baptist Missionary Society, the London Missionary Society, the Edinburgh and Glasgow Missionary Societies, and the Church [of England] Missionary Society, all founded in the 1790s. American Protestant missionary societies soon followed. Initially the missionary societies, who often competed with each other along denominational lines, floundered and attracted little support, but by the mid-1820s, they were firmly established and growing enterprises. By 1900, British missionary societies employed approximately 10,000 missionaries.

German Protestants also embraced the missionary impulse. The earliest German societies such as the Leipzig Mission, founded in 1836, devoted their efforts to India. The Rhenish Missionary Society, founded 1828, established itself in East Africa and supported German colonial claims there in the 1880s. As early as 1833, the Berlin Missionary Society sent missionaries to South Africa; by 1869, it was also working to China.

Roman Catholic Missionary Advance

The nineteenth-century French Roman Catholic missionary effort was also enormous. It reflected the resurgence of the Catholic Church in France in the decades following the French Revolution and Napoleon. The Society for the Propagation of the Faith, the largest French missionary society, was founded in 1822. By the 1860s, it had over a million members. Its earliest missionaries went to China and Vietnam. Over time, however, French Catholic missionaries worked on every continent, including the islands of the Pacific.

Tensions Between Missionaries and Imperial Administrators

The mission societies and their missionaries had a complex relationship with their home governments. Missionary work did not necessarily support imperial missions. Missionaries from both Europe and America often settled in regions their governments did not control, and missionary societies often employed missionaries who came from a country other than the one sponsoring their mission. Nonetheless, the missionaries did develop many links with Western governments. The British missionary movement often saw the expansion of the British Empire as opening the way for the spread of the Gospel. They saw the spread of Western commerce as both financially beneficial for missions and as opening up new areas for the missionary enterprise. Missionaries and advocates of free trade imperialism thus could have a mutually supportive relationship. This relationship softened toward the close of the century when the missionary societies defined themselves more strictly in terms of the spiritual mission of bearing witness to the Gospel.

Colonial administrators frequently resisted the introduction of missionaries into their territories for fear the missionaries would prove a destabilizing force as they challenged traditional religions and cultural values. Missionaries might defend the rights of native peoples against official imperial policy or commercial interests' efforts to increase their profits. In the settlement colonies missionaries often clashed with the settlers who wanted to prevent native peoples from gaining the skills that would enable them to compete with whites. Colonial officials were also concerned about conflicts between Christian converts from different denominations. Some missionaries also tried to change the modes of worship that an earlier generation of missionaries had introduced and persecuted converts who refused to conform. Furthermore, missionaries frequently educated persons from the lower levels of society who might resent colonial rule and the authority of native elites. The Christian vision of equality before God could, though it did not always, undermine the hierarchies of colonial authority.

But even when colonial officials disliked them, missionaries nonetheless provided much of the educational infrastructure of imperialism particularly in India. At the village level their schools provided instruction in the local languages and English. Missionaries also established institutions of higher education. Later in the century, missionaries founded women's colleges. These colleges trained primarily members of the Indian elite, both Hindu and Muslim. As missionary groups became more directly associated with education, the number of women missionaries in India grew, and by the early twentieth century, most missionaries there were women.

The relationship of French Roman Catholic missionaries to imperialism was complicated because the governments of the Third Republic in France were usually anticlerical after the 1870s. Yet although the republican government often clashed with the Catholic Church in France, it frequently supported missionary activity abroad as a way of extending French national interests. In some cases the government in Paris or local colonial administrators encouraged French missionary activity to make native peoples sympathetic to French rule or to block the advance of other European powers. By teaching the French language, French missionaries also made it easier for French commercial interests to operate in a territory.

By 1900, approximately 58,000 French priests, religious brothers, and nuns were involved in the missionary enterprise. Like their British and German counterparts, French missionaries also often experienced tense relations with colonial administrators. Sometimes the colonial government pressed the **civilizing mission** through secular physicians, teachers, and agricultural consultants to counter the religious influence of missionaries. At the same time, however, the success of the French Catholic missionary effort meant that colonial officials in Vietnam and parts of Africa and the

civilizing mission The concept that Western nations could bring advanced science and economic development to non-Western parts of the world that justified imperial administration.

Pacific had to deal with large numbers of native Roman Catholics who supported and admired the missionaries. Yet by the early twentieth century, French missionaries increasingly saw their role as not only winning converts, but as also molding native cultures in the image of France.

However sympathetic missionaries might become to indigenous peoples, they remained spokespersons for Western civilization. Because missionaries wished to convert indigenous peoples to Western Christianity, they implicitly shared with colonial officials the general cultural assumption of the superiority of things Western. Even when missionaries were not formal agents of empire, they introduced Western cultural values, manners, and outlooks. While colonial governments might be associated with more advanced military and transportation technology, missionaries might be associated with more advanced medicine or agriculture in the hospitals and mission stations they ran. And missionaries, like colonial officials, generally assumed that native peoples were inferior to Westerners. While a few missionaries by 1900 believed that Christians and persons of other religions could learn from each other, most missionaries, regarded non-Christians simply as heathens. That outlook, like the attitudes of secular administrators, generated its own sets of reactions.

Missionaries and Indigenous Religious Movements

Just as the presence of colonial administrations during the nineteenth century gave rise to various nationalist movements or movements that promoted the rights and interests of native peoples, the missionary activities gave rise to Asian and African religious movements that challenged the dominance of Western missionaries. The founding of new African and Asian Christian churches occurred as a result of the rejection of the racial and cultural assumptions of Western missionaries and as a means of reconciling Christianity with long-standing cultural practices, such as polygamy in Africa. The most important fact about the independent churches of Africa was that their leaders were African. For example, in 1888 David Brown Vincent established the Native Baptist Church in Lagos, Nigeria, after leaving the American-founded Baptist Church there. Not long thereafter, in South Africa Mangena Makone broke with the Methodists to found the Ethiopian Church. In Kenya, Christian members of the Kikuyu tribe split with the Church of Scotland Mission. In the early twentieth century, Christian Pentecostal groups arose among African Christians, as did other churches associated with gifts of healing or prophecy.

In summary, how may one describe the interrelationship of the missionary movement and colonialism? First, it was dynamic and changed during the nineteenth century as missionary goals and sensibilities changed from one generation to another. Second, the missionary movement spawned an enormous amount of printed publicity in the form of newspaper and journal articles, missionary society publications, and missionary narratives and autobiographies. These materials publicized the vision of empire and raised interest in the West about the non-Western world. They also strongly influenced popular culture at a time when the churches were more influential than they are today, especially in Europe. Third, the missionary societies and the churches with which they were associated became skilled at pressuring their governments. Initially they directed their efforts toward permitting and protecting missionary activities. By the early twentieth century, however, many missionaries were supporting native peoples in their opposition to colonial authorities. Fourth, the religious effects of the missions were a two-way street. While Westerners brought Christianity to Africa and Asia, by 1900, non-Western Christians were beginning to move Christianity away from its dominance by Europeans and Americans. This

QUICK REVIEW

The Missionary Movement

- Changed over the course of the nineteenth century
- Helped publicize the vision of empire and stirred interest in non-Western peoples and places
- Missionary societies and associated churches were skilled at pressuring governments
- Had an impact on Christianity in both the Western and non-Western worlds
- Made Christianity a true world religion for the first time

process is still going on today. Finally, the missionary movement of the nineteenth century made Christianity a genuinely worldwide religion for the first time. The spread of Christianity like the development of self-government in the British settler colonies was thus one of the major elements of the extension of Western civilization around the globe.

SCIENCE AND IMPERIALISM

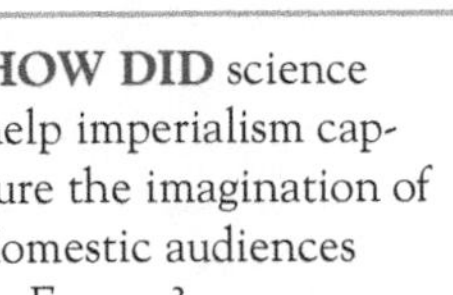

HOW DID science help imperialism capture the imagination of domestic audiences in Europe?

The early modern European encounter with the non-Western world from the fifteenth-century voyages of discovery onward had been associated with the expansion of natural knowledge. The same would be true of Western imperialism in the nineteenth and early twentieth centuries. Geography was an expanding scientific discipline in the nineteenth century. Explorers wrote of their discoveries and adventures in Africa and Asia. Some explorers, such as the Scottish Presbyterian David Livingstone (1813–1873) and the French Jesuit Armand David (1829–1900), were also missionaries. Explorers portrayed themselves as pioneers who opened wild and savage spaces for commerce, religion, and ultimately civilization. Consequently, scientific and geographical societies generally supported their nations' imperialist goals and saw their research as benefiting from it.

Four areas of scientific research deserve particular mention because they demonstrate how imperialism could filter into the wider European culture and capture the imagination of domestic audiences who never set foot outside Europe. These are botany, zoology, medicine, and anthropology.

Botany

Botany was the nineteenth-century colonial science par excellence, reflecting and nurturing the vast expansion of agriculture around the globe. This expansion brought millions of acres of new land under cultivation in the Americas, Australia, New Zealand, and Algeria. Colonial officials and Western investors also forced or induced colonial peoples, mainly in the tropics, to grow cash crops, such as coffee, sugar, tea, rubber, jute, cotton, bananas, and cocoa, for export to Europe.

European botanists were intensely interested in the plants they might discover abroad. Their interest ranged from the discovery of previously unknown specimens through the development of new crops that would improve agriculture. Changes in taste like the spread of tea and coffee drinking and in technology like the demand for rubber for bicycle and motorcar tires could create demands for colonial agricultural products.

Gardens such as the Royal Botanical Garden at Kew, near London, and the *Jardin des Plantes* at Paris also allowed the general public to encounter a soft and inviting side of empire. Visitors could experience different parts of the empire in a pleasant setting as they strolled along flowerbeds, under trees, or through greenhouses. These gardens and the new products and foods that Europeans and Americans consumed persuaded them that empire was part of the general progress of the age, which they associated with science.

The gardens with their research staffs also were devices for transforming economies. The same spirit of agricultural improvement that had begun in Britain in the eighteenth century was carried throughout the empire. Botanists worked as economic innovators to achieve intercontinental transfers of plants to secure products for their home countries and to develop colonial economies.

As plant commodities fell in value in one part of the British Empire, British administrators and merchants would contact Kew Garden for suggestions of other profitable crops. The botanists thus profited from empire by establishing themselves as the experts for the economic development of colonies after they had been annexed or after the crops that had once supported them were no longer profitable. Planters associations in the European colonies also established their own experimental stations to improve existing crops or develop new ones for cultivation.

Zoology

In the eighteenth century, some European monarchs, such as the Habsburg emperors in Vienna and the French kings in Paris, had established collections of exotic animals. In the nineteenth century, zoos and zoological gardens were founded in major European and American cities. These zoos displayed animals from around the world that expeditions acquired from the regions that European imperialism was penetrating.

Other scientists would collect specimens of animals, particularly birds, which they killed and brought back from the colonies to Europe to be placed in natural history museums. These museums became increasingly popular in the late nineteenth century.

Medicine

Medical science was an integral part of the imperial enterprise on several different levels. As already noted, Westerners had to overcome various tropical diseases, especially malaria, that prevented them from surviving in the tropics. But Western medicine also became a fundamental feature of the civilizing mission of colonial administrators and missionaries, many of whom were physicians. The spread of Western medicine justified colonial rule and helped win converts. The primary diseases that Western doctors sought to battle in the tropical colonies were yellow fever, sleeping sickness, small pox, hookworms, and leprosy.

Missionaries had pioneered the introduction of Western medicine into the colonial setting. Some missionaries thought they could convert native peoples to Christianity by first demonstrating the power of Western medicine. Physicians and medical researchers sought to win government financial support by demonstrating that modern medicine could cure the endemic diseases that ravaged colonial peoples. Among the most influential colonial medical institutions were the Pasteur Institutes, named after Louis Pasteur (1822–1895), the French scientist who had found a cure for rabies and other diseases.

In general in the colonial world, Western science became a vehicle for what is often termed *cultural imperialism*. Medical advances allowed Western penetration of the tropics and then underpinned Western cultural and political domination. European medical institutions controlled research in the colonies. Westerners seldom had respect for Asian and African medical personnel no matter how well they were trained. Yet there is no question that Western medicine either eradicated or lessened the impact of diseases that had ravaged the non-Western world for centuries and, especially in the twentieth century, extended the life span and physical well-being of colonial or former colonial peoples.

Anthropology

In the late nineteenth century, the study of non-Western peoples became associated with the science of anthropology. Anthropological societies were founded in Paris (1859), London (1863), and Berlin (1870). The leaders of these new societies were convinced of the multiple origins of the races of humankind (a theory termed *polygenesis*) and of the inherent inequality of races. Polygenesis was one of many scientific theories that supported a hierarchy of unequal races at the top of which Westerners always placed the white races.

Peoples from colonized nations were transported to various world's fairs and similar exhibitions during the late nineteenth and early twentieth centuries. They constituted living exhibitions, where they were expected to portray "native customs" or the like. Here at the St. Louis World's Fair of 1904, African Pygmies demonstrated beheading. In this and other similar examples, native peoples were frequently presented in demeaning roles that filled the expectations of spectators to see "exotic" behavior. Such performances and exhibitions served to convince the Western spectators of the superiority of their civilization over that of the peoples living in the colonized world.

Courtesy of the Library of Congress

What light does this image shed on late nineteenth-century views of non-Western peoples?

Many anthropologists believed that such factors as skull type determined human character. Paul Broca (1824–1880), a French physician who specialized in the brain, measured the skulls of human beings from different races and assigned them intellectual capacity on the basis of brain size. Other European and American scientists followed his lead. Anthropologists who studied colonial societies carried these ideas with them.

Anthropology as a social science infused with racial thinking (see Chapter 24) had become organized in Western Europe on the eve of the Scramble for Africa. Anthropologists from then through the Second World War rode the wave of imperial enthusiasm. In fact, however, colonial officials rarely sought anthropologists' advice. Instead, anthropologists influenced imperial policies through their books, lectures, and university classes. European and American readers and students were invariably told that non-Western peoples were inferior, that their economies were underdeveloped, that their societies were corrupt, decadent, or primitive, and that their religions were dangerous and false. All this proved the need for Western administration and control.

Many of these same attitudes informed the creation of the great anthropological museums in Europe and the United States. These museums, which were very popular, often presented artifacts of African and Asian culture that explorers or other travelers or researchers had brought home. These exhibitions, like the botanical gardens, zoos, and museums of natural history, introduced Western audiences to what they considered to be the exotic features and otherness of non-Western peoples and cultures.

The idea of museums or zoos to display exotic creatures was also extended to human beings in both Europe and the United States. Showmen such as the American P. T. Barnum would exhibit Africans, Asians, and Native Americans. Carl Hagenbeck, a German, brought Polynesians, Sudanese, and Inuits from Canada to live in "native villages" in the Hamburg Zoo. In the thirty years before World War I, the Paris zoo staged over twenty-five such exhibitions. At World's Fairs, millions of Europeans and Americans paid to view native peoples.

QUICK REVIEW

Anthropology and Imperialism

- Study of non-Western peoples became associated with the science of anthropology
- Racial thinking shaped much of anthropology
- Anthropological museums reflected racial thinking and reinforced its place in the popular imagination

SUMMARY

HOW DID early modern colonization differ from nineteenth-century Western imperialism?

The Close of the Age of Early Modern Colonization The era of early modern European expansion lasted from the late fifteenth to the late eighteenth centuries. Between the mid–eighteenth and the early nineteenth centuries, a vast political transformation occurred in the colonized transatlantic world. The French lost their North American empire and the British were driven from their Atlantic coastal colonies. In the 1820s Latin America shook off Spanish and Portuguese control. The most striking result of these events was the collapse of Spain, Portugal, and France as significant colonial powers. *page 620*

HOW DID Britain use its economic might to extend its influence around the world?

The Age of British Imperial Dominance Until at least the 1870s, free trade alone allowed Britain to dominate economically one region of the world after another without the need to establish a formal colonial administration. Free trade could and did lead to warfare, the most important example being the Opium Wars between Britain and China. During the early nineteenth century, Britain oversaw the settlement and economic development of Canada, Australia, and New Zealand. *page 621*

WHY WAS India such an important part of the British Empire?

India—The Jewel in the Crown of the British Empire Initially the British achieved their domination of India through the East India Company. By the 1830s, British control over India was essentially complete. The sepoy rebellion or mutiny of 1857 precipitated the passage of the Government of India Act in 1858, which transferred political authority from the East India Company to the British Crown. The late nineteenth century saw the formation of the Indian National Congress and the Muslim League. *page 622*

WHAT WAS new about the "New Imperialism"?

The "New Imperialism," 1870–1914 Between 1870 and 1914, Western nations including the United States and Japan achieved unprecedented influence and control over the rest of the world and provoked intense colonial rivalries with each other. The "New Imperialism" involved direct political and administrative control of non-Westerners by the Western powers, occurred over a relatively brief period and involved an unprecedented number of nations, did not involve significant numbers of immigrants as settlers, exhibited a new cultural confidence and racial arrogance, and focused to an unprecedented degree on Africa. *page 624*

WHAT ROLE did economic motives play in nineteenth-century imperialism?

Motives for the New Imperialism Until the mid–twentieth century, the predominant interpretation of the motives for the New Imperialism was economic. However, many motives beyond economic ones influenced the imperial policies of each of the major European nations. First, after 1870, many political leaders came to believe that the possession of colonies or of imperial influence was an important and even necessary characteristic of a great European power. Second, much of the territorial acquisitions associated with the New Imperialism arose in direct response to the power vacuums that the decay of the Ottoman Empire created. Third, the geopolitical assumptions of European statesmen led them to deeper and deeper involvements from the eastern Mediterranean to Africa. *page 625*

HOW DID European politics contribute to the "Scramble for Africa"?

The Partition of Africa During the so-called "Scramble for Africa," which occurred between the late 1870s and about 1912, the European powers sought to maximize their strategic control of African territory, markets, and raw materials, eventually dividing almost all the continent among themselves. France came to see Algeria as part of France and controlled much of sub-Saharan Africa. Political stagnation and economic collapse paved the way for British domination of Egypt. King Leopold II of Belgium's rule of the Congo was one of brutal economic exploitation. German imperialism in Africa was motivated primarily by European diplomatic concerns. The British and the Boers competed for control of South Africa. *page 626*

HOW DID Russia come to control a vast and diverse Asian empire?

Russian Expansion in Mainland Asia Russian expansion across mainland Asia in the nineteenth century brought huge territories and millions of people of a variety of ethnicities and religions under tsarist rule. Beginning in the late eighteenth century, the tsarist government began to regard the nomadic societies or communities under its domination as foreign and inferior. The nineteenth century saw Russia extend its authority in the Transcaucasus, the steppes of Central Asia, and southern Middle Asia. *page 635*

WHAT DEVELOPMENTS facilitated Western penetration and control of Asia?

Western Powers in Asia Roman Catholic missionaries spearheaded French involvement in Indonesia. The United States established its interest in the Pacific and gained an empire as a result of victory in the Spanish-American war. By the close of the nineteenth century, the Qing Dynasty of China was in a state of near collapse. The Open Door policy of the United States was meant to prevent China's partition by European powers. Resentment of Western interference and domination led to the Boxer Rebellion. *page 636*

HOW DID technological innovations make nineteenth-century imperialism possible?

Tools of Imperialism The domination that Europe and peoples of European descent came to exert over the entire globe by 1900 was based on distinct and temporary technological advantages. Key among them were ironclad steam-powered warships, advances in the prevention of tropical diseases, and superior firearms. *page 639*

WHAT WAS the relationship between missionaries and their home government?

The Missionary Factor The modern Western missionary movement originated in Great Britain in the late eighteenth century as a direct outgrowth of the rise of evangelical Christianity. Roman Catholics later copied Protestant missionary efforts. The mission societies and their missionaries had a complex relationship with their home governments and tensions sometimes arose. Missionaries provided much of the educational infrastructure of imperialism. Missionaries shared with colonial officials the general cultural assumption of the superiority of things Western. Missionary activities gave rise to Asian and African religious movements that challenged the dominance of Western missionaries. *page 641*

HOW DID science help imperialism capture the imagination of domestic audiences in Europe?

Science and Imperialism Western imperialism in the nineteenth and early twentieth centuries was associated with the expansion of natural knowledge. Developments in botany, zoology, medicine, and anthropology demonstrate how imperialism could filter into the wider European culture and capture the imagination of domestic audiences. *page 645*

REVIEW QUESTIONS

1. How did European imperial interests shift geographically in the nineteenth century? How was free trade related to the expansion of European influence around the globe?
2. What was the New Imperialism? How was it different from free-trade imperialism? Why was Britain the dominant world power until the late nineteenth century? What were the Opium Wars?
3. How did the British come to dominate India? What were the causes of the Indian rebellion of 1857? How did British rule in India change after the rebellion? Why was India so important to Britain?
4. Why was Algeria the most important part of the French Empire? What parts of the Ottoman Empire fell under European rule between the 1880s and 1914? Why did Britain come to dominate Egypt? Why did Germany and Italy acquire colonies? Why did Leopold II build an empire in the Congo? What was the "Scramble for Africa"?
5. What were the "tools of imperialism"? Why was quinine so important for the spread of empires? What technological improvements enabled Western powers to dominate so much of the non-Western world? Why were the new colonial empires so short lived?
6. Why did Western missionary efforts expand in the nineteenth century? Why was the relationship between Western missionaries and colonial officials so complicated? Why did Africans want to found their own churches? How has the spread of Christianity in the non-Western world affected the Christian churches?
7. How did Westerners justify imperialism? What was the civilizing mission? What sciences were most associated with the New Imperialism? What role did racism play in the New Imperialism?

KEY TERMS

apartheid (p. 635)
civilizing mission (p. 643)
concentration camps (p. 635)
Great Trek (p. 634)
Imperialism of Free Trade (p. 621)
New Imperialism (p. 620)
protectorate (p. 324)
spheres of influence (p. 624)

For additional learning resources related to this chapter, please go to **www.myhistorylab.com**

PEARSON myhistorylab

26

Alliances, War, and a Troubled Peace

World War I produced unprecedented destruction and loss of life. Rather than a war of rapid movement, much combat occurred along stationary trenches dug in both western and eastern Europe. Here, Austro-Hungarian troops fight from trenches on the eastern front wearing gas masks. The use of poison gas was one of the innovations of the war and was generally condemned after the war.

National Archives and Records Administration

How did the reality of combat during World War I differ from public expectations at the beginning of the war?

EMERGENCE OF THE GERMAN EMPIRE AND THE ALLIANCE SYSTEMS (1873–1890) *page 652*

WHY DID the alliance system fail?

WORLD WAR I *page 656*

HOW DID conflict in the Balkans lead to the outbreak of general war in Europe?

THE RUSSIAN REVOLUTION *page 666*

WHAT FACTORS made the rise of the Bolsheviks to power in Russia possible?

THE END OF WORLD WAR I *page 668*

WHAT WERE the immediate consequences of the end of World War I?

THE SETTLEMENT AT PARIS *page 670*

WHAT WERE the key weaknesses of the Paris peace settlement?

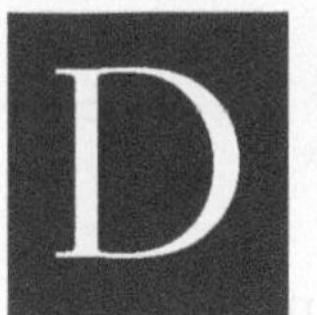

During the second half of the nineteenth century, Europe wielded unprecedented worldwide influence. Europe's dominance created a single world economy that might have increased general prosperity, but competition among the great powers led instead to a terrible war that undermined Europe's strength and global influence. The peace settlement that followed humiliated Germany and provoked its desire for revenge. The United States also made the fateful decision to withdraw into disdainful isolation from world affairs. ■

EMERGENCE OF THE GERMAN EMPIRE AND THE ALLIANCE SYSTEMS (1873–1890)

WHY DID the alliance system fail?

Prussia's victories over Austria and France and its creation of a large, powerful German Empire in 1871 revolutionized European diplomacy. A vast new political unit had united the majority of Germans to form a nation of great and growing population, wealth, industrial capacity, and military power. Its sudden appearance created new problems and upset the balance of power that the Congress of Vienna had forged. Britain and Russia retained their positions, although the Crimean War had weakened the latter. Austria, however, had been severely weakened, and the forces of nationalism threatened it with disintegration. The Franco-Prussian War and the German annexation of Alsace-Lorraine badly damaged French power and prestige.

Bismarck and the young Kaiser William II meet in 1888. The two disagreed over many issues, and in 1890 William dismissed the aged chancellor.

German Information Center

How did the dismissal of Bismarck contribute to heightened international tension?

BISMARCK'S LEADERSHIP

Until 1890, Bismarck continued to guide German policy. After 1871, he insisted Germany was a satisfied power and wanted no further territorial gains, and he meant it. He tried to assuage French resentment by pursuing friendly relations and by supporting French colonial aspirations. He also prepared for the worst. If France could not be conciliated, it must be isolated. Bismarck sought to prevent an alliance between France and any other European power—especially Austria or Russia—that would threaten Germany with a war on two fronts.

War in the Balkans Bismarck's first move was to establish the Three Emperors' League in 1873, which brought together Germany, Austria, and Russia. The league soon collapsed over Austro-Russian rivalry in the Balkans that arose from the Russo-Turkish War that broke out in 1877. Ottoman weakness encouraged Serbia and Montenegro to come to the aid of their fellow Slavs in Bosnia and Herzegovina when they revolted against Turkish rule. Soon the rebellion spread to Bulgaria.

Then Russia entered the fray and turned it into a major international crisis. The Russians hoped to pursue their traditional policy of expansion at Ottoman expense and especially to achieve their most cherished goal: control of Constantinople and the Dardanelles. Russian intervention also reflected the influence of the Pan-Slavic movement, which sought to unite all the Slavic peoples, even those under Austrian or Ottoman rule, under the protection of Holy Mother Russia.

The Ottoman Empire was soon forced to sue for peace. Under the Treaty of San Stefano of March 1878, the Slavic states in the Balkans were freed of Ottoman rule, and Russia itself obtained territory and a large monetary indemnity. The settlement, however, alarmed the other great powers. Austria feared that the Slavic victory and the increase in Russian influence in the Balkans would threaten its own Balkan provinces. The British were alarmed both by the effect of the Russian victory on the European balance of power and by the possibility of Russian control of the Dardanelles, which would make Russia a Mediterranean power and threaten Britain's control of the Suez Canal.

The Congress of Berlin Britain and Austria forced Russia to agree to an international conference at which the other great powers would review the provisions of San Stefano. The resulting Congress of Berlin met in June and July 1878 under the presidency of Bismarck. The choice of site and presiding officer was a clear recognition of Germany's new importance and of Bismarck's claim that Germany wanted no new territory and sought to preserve the peace.

The decisions of the congress were a blow to Russian ambitions. Bulgaria, a Russian client, was reduced in size by two-thirds and deprived of access to the Aegean Sea. Austria-Hungary was given Bosnia and Herzegovina to "occupy and administer," although those provinces remained formally under Ottoman rule. Britain received Cyprus, and France was encouraged to occupy Tunisia. These territories were compensation for the gains that Russia was permitted to keep. Germany asked for nothing but still earned Russian resentment. The Three Emperors' League was dead. Moreover, the south Slavic states of Serbia and Montenegro resented the Austrian occupation of Bosnia and Herzegovina, as did many of the natives of those provinces. The south Slavic question, no less than the estrangement between Russia and Germany, was a threat to the peace of Europe.

QUICK REVIEW

Congress of Berlin (1878)

- Convened to review the terms of the Treaty of San Stefano between Russia and the Ottoman Empire
- Bismarck acted as the impartial arbiter
- Russian concessions created animosity in Russia against Germany

German Alliances with Russia and Austria With Russia alienated, Bismarck concluded a secret treaty with Austria in 1879. This Dual Alliance provided that Germany and Austria would come to each other's aid if Russia attacked either of them. If another country attacked one of them, each promised at least to maintain neutrality.

Bismarck believed that monarchical, reactionary Russia would not seek an alliance either with republican, revolutionary France or with increasingly democratic Britain. In fact, he expected the Austro-German negotiations to frighten Russia into seeking closer relations with Germany, and he was right. By 1881, he had renewed the Three Emperors' League on a firmer basis.

The Triple Alliance In 1882, Italy, ambitious for colonial expansion and angered by the French occupation of Tunisia, asked to join the Dual Alliance. Bismarck's policy was now a complete success. He was allied with three of the great powers and friendly with the other, Great Britain, which held aloof from all alliances. France was isolated and no threat. Bismarck's diplomacy was a great achievement, but an even greater challenge was to maintain this complicated system of secret alliances in the face of the continuing rivalries among Germany's allies. Despite a war in 1885 between Serbia and Bulgaria that again estranged Austria and Russia, Bismarck succeeded.

Although the Three Emperors' League lapsed, the Triple Alliance (Germany, Austria, and Italy) was renewed for another five years. To restore German relations with Russia, Bismarck negotiated the Reinsurance Treaty of 1887, in which both powers promised to remain neutral if either was attacked. All seemed smooth, but a change in the German monarchy upset Bismarck's arrangements. In 1888, William II

QUICK REVIEW

The Triple Alliance

- Germany and Austria formed the Dual Alliance in 1879
- Italy joined the alliance in 1882 forming the Triple Alliance
- The Triple Alliance and friendly relations between Germany and Great Britain isolated France

(r. 1888–1918) came to the German throne. He was twenty-nine years old, ambitious, and impetuous. Like many Germans of his generation, William II was filled with a sense of Germany's destiny as the leading power of Europe. He wanted recognition of at least equality with Britain. To achieve a "place in the sun," he and his contemporaries wanted a navy and colonies like Britain's. These aims, of course, ran counter to Bismarck's limited continental policy. In 1890, William used a disagreement over domestic policy to dismiss Bismarck.

Forging the Triple Entente (1890–1907)

Franco-Russian Alliance Almost immediately after Bismarck's retirement, his system of alliances collapsed. His successor, General Leo von Caprivi (1831–1899), refused the Russian request to renew the Reinsurance Treaty, in part because he felt incompetent to continue Bismarck's complicated policy and in part because he wished to draw Germany closer to Britain, but Britain remained aloof, and Russia was alienated.

Political isolation and the need for foreign capital drove the Russians toward France. The French, who were even more isolated, encouraged their investors to pour capital into Russia if such investment would help produce security against Germany. In 1894, France and Russia signed a defensive alliance against Germany.

Britain and Germany Britain now became the key to the international situation. Colonial rivalries pitted the British against the Russians in Central Asia and against the French in Africa. (See Chapter 25.) Traditionally, Britain had also opposed Russian control of Constantinople and the Dardanelles and French control of the Low Countries. There was no reason to think Britain would soon become friendly to its traditional rivals or abandon its accustomed friendliness toward the Germans. Yet within a decade of William II's accession, Germany had become the enemy in British minds.

William II admired Britain's colonial empire and mighty fleet. At first, Germany tried to win the British over to the Triple Alliance, but when Britain clung to its "splendid isolation," German policy changed. The idea was to demonstrate Germany's worth as an ally by withdrawing support and even making trouble for Britain. In Africa, the Germans blocked British attempts to build a railroad from Cape Town to Cairo. They also openly sympathized with the Boers of South Africa in their resistance to British expansion. In 1896, William congratulated Paul Kruger (1825–1904), president of the Boer Transvaal Republic, for repulsing a British raid "without having to appeal to friendly powers [i.e., Germany] for assistance." (See Chapter 25.)

In 1898, William began to realize his dream of a German navy with the passage of a naval law providing for the construction of nineteen battleships. In 1900, a second law doubled that figure. The architect of the new navy was Admiral Alfred von Tirpitz (1849–1930), who openly proclaimed that Germany's naval policy was aimed at Britain. The naval policy was a failure. Its main results were to waste German resources and to begin a great naval race with Britain. Eventually, the threat the German navy posed so antagonized and alarmed British opinion that the British abandoned their traditional policies of avoiding alliances.

The Entente Cordiale The first breach in Britain's isolation came in 1902, when it concluded an alliance with Japan to defend British interests in the Far East against Russia. Next, Britain abandoned its traditional antagonism toward France and in 1904

concluded a series of agreements with the French, collectively called the Entente Cordiale. It was not a formal treaty and had no military provisions, but it settled all outstanding colonial differences between the two nations. In particular, Britain gave France a free hand in Morocco in return for French recognition of British control over Egypt. The Entente Cordiale was a long step toward aligning the British with Germany's great potential enemy.

Britain's new relationship with France was surprising, but in 1904, hardly anyone believed the British whale and the Russian bear would ever come together. The Russo-Japanese War of 1904–1905 made such a development seem even less likely, because Britain was allied with Russia's enemy, but Britain had behaved with restraint, and their unexpected defeat, which also led to the Russian Revolution of 1905, humiliated the Russians. Although the revolution was put down, it weakened Russia and reduced British apprehensions about Russian power. The British also became concerned that Russia might again drift into the German orbit.

The First Moroccan Crisis At this point, Germany decided to test the new understanding between Britain and France. In March 1905, Emperor William II landed at Tangier, made a speech in favor of Moroccan independence, and by implication asserted Germany's right to participate in Morocco's destiny. This speech was a challenge to France.

The Germans demanded an international conference to show their power more dramatically. The conference met in 1906 at Algeciras in Spain. Austria sided with its German ally, but Spain, which also had claims in Morocco, Italy, Russia, and the United States, voted with Britain and France. The Germans had overplayed their hand, receiving trivial concessions, and the French position in Morocco was confirmed. German bullying had, moreover, driven Britain and France closer together. By 1914, French and British military and naval plans were so mutually dependent that the two countries were effectively, if not formally, allies.

QUICK REVIEW

First Moroccan Crisis

- March 1905: William II implies Germany has a role in furthering Moroccan independence
- Germany hoped to weaken relationship between France and Great Britain
- 1906: Conference in Algeciras confirms France's claims in Morocco

British Agreement with Russia Britain's fear of Germany's growing naval power, its concern over German ambitions in the Near East, and its closer relations with France made it desirable for Britain to become more friendly with France's ally, Russia. With French support, in 1907 the British concluded an agreement with Russia much like the Entente Cordiale with France. It settled Russo-British quarrels in Central Asia and opened the door for wider cooperation. The Triple Entente, an informal, but powerful, association of Britain, France, and Russia, was now ranged against the Triple Alliance. Italy was an unreliable ally, however, which meant two great land powers and Great Britain encircled Germany and Austria-Hungary.

William II and his ministers had turned Bismarck's nightmare of the prospect of a two-front war with France and Russia into a reality. They had made it more horrible by adding Britain to their foes. The equilibrium that Bismarck had worked so hard to achieve was destroyed. Britain would no longer support Austria in restraining Russian ambitions in the Balkans. Germany, increasingly alarmed by a sense of being encircled, was less willing to restrain the Austrians for fear of alienating them, too.

Bismarck had built his alliance system to maintain peace, but the new alliance increased the risk of war and made the Balkans a likely spot for it to break out. Bismarck's diplomacy had left France isolated and impotent. The new arrangement associated France with the two greatest powers in Europe besides Germany. The Germans could rely only on Austria, and Austria's troubles made it less likely to provide aid than to need it.

WORLD WAR I

HOW DID conflict in the Balkans lead to the outbreak of general war in Europe?

The Road to War (1908–1914)

The weak Ottoman Empire still controlled the central strip of the Balkan Peninsula running west from Constantinople to the Adriatic. North and south of it were the independent states of Romania, Serbia, Montenegro, and Greece, as well as Bulgaria, technically still part of the empire, but legally autonomous and practically independent. The Austro-Hungarian Empire included Croatia and Slovenia and, since 1878, had "occupied and administered" Bosnia and Herzegovina.

Except for the Greeks and the Romanians, most of the inhabitants of the Balkans spoke variants of the same Slavic language and felt a cultural and historical kinship with one another. For centuries Austrians, Hungarians, or Turks had ruled them, and the nationalism that characterized late-nineteenth-century Europe made many of them eager for independence. The more radical among them longed for a union of the south Slavic, or Yugoslav, peoples in a single nation with Serbia at its center.

In 1908, a group of modernizing reformers called the Young Turks seized power in the Ottoman Empire. Their actions threatened to breathe new life into the empire and to interfere with the plans of the European jackals to pounce on the Ottoman corpse. These events brought on the first of a series of Balkan crises that would eventually lead to war.

The Bosnian Crisis In 1908, the Austrian and Russian governments decided to act quickly before Turkey became strong enough to resist. They struck a bargain in which Russia agreed to support the Austrian annexation of Bosnia and Herzegovina in return for Austrian backing for opening the Dardanelles to Russian warships.

Austria, however, declared the annexation before the Russians could act. The British and French, eager for the favor of the Young Turks, refused to agree to the Russian demand to open the Dardanelles. The Russians were humiliated and furious, but too weak to do anything but protest. The Austrian annexation of Bosnia enraged Russia's "little brothers," the Serbs.

Germany had not been warned in advance of Austria's plans and was unhappy because the action threatened its relations with Russia and Turkey. Germany felt so dependent on the Dual Alliance, however, that it nevertheless assured Austria of its support. It was a dangerous precedent. Also, the failure of Britain and France to support Russia strained the Triple Entente. This made it harder for them to oppose Russian interests in the future if they were to keep Russian friendship.

The Second Moroccan Crisis The second Moroccan crisis, in 1911, emphasized the French and British need for mutual support. When France sent an army to Morocco, Germany took the opportunity to "protect German interests" there as a means to extort colonial concessions in the French Congo. To add force to their demands, the Germans sent the gunboat *Panther* to the Moroccan port of Agadir, purportedly to protect German citizens there. Once again, as in 1905, the Germans went too far. The *Panther*'s visit to Agadir provoked a strong reaction in Britain. For some time Anglo-German relations had been growing worse, chiefly because the naval race had intensified. The British wrongly believed the Germans meant to turn Agadir into a naval base on the Atlantic. The crisis passed, but Britain drew closer to France. The British made plans to send an expeditionary force to defend France in case Germany attacked, and the British and French navies agreed to cooperate. Without any formal treaty, the German naval construction and the Agadir crisis had turned the Entente Cordiale into a de facto alliance.

QUICK REVIEW

Second Moroccan Crisis

- 1911: France sends an army to Morocco and Germany sends gunboat to Moroccan port of Agadir
- British overreaction leads to naval arms race between Germany and Britain
- Chief effects of the crisis were to increase suspicion between Germany and Britain and to draw France and Britain closer together

War in the Balkans The second Moroccan crisis also provoked another crisis in the Balkans. Italy sought to gain colonies and to take its place among the great powers. It wanted Libya and feared that the recognition of the French protectorate in Morocco would encourage France to move into Libya also. So, in 1911, Italy attacked the Ottoman Empire to preempt the French and forced Turkey to cede Libya and the Dodecanese Islands in the Aegean. The Italian victory encouraged the Balkan states to try their luck. In 1912, Bulgaria, Greece, Montenegro, and Serbia jointly attacked the Ottoman Empire and won easily. After this First Balkan War, the victors fell out among themselves over the division of Macedonia, and in 1913 a Second Balkan War erupted. This time, Turkey and Romania joined Serbia and Greece against Bulgaria and stripped away much of what the Bulgarians had gained in 1878 and 1912.

After the First Balkan War, the alarmed Austrians were determined to limit Serbian gains and especially to prevent the Serbs from gaining a port on the Adriatic. This policy meant keeping Serbia out of Albania, but the Russians backed the Serbs, and tensions mounted. An international conference sponsored by Britain in early 1913 resolved the dispute in Austria's favor and called for an independent principality of Albania. The Serbs, however, defied the powers and continued to occupy parts of Albania. Finally, in October 1913, Austria issued an ultimatum, and Serbia withdrew its forces from Albania.

The lessons learned from this crisis of 1913 influenced behavior in the final crisis in 1914. As in 1908, the Russians had been embarrassed by their passivity; and their allies were more reluctant to restrain them again. The Austrians were embarrassed by the results of accepting an international conference and were determined not to do it again. They had gotten better results from threatening to use force; they and their German allies did not miss the lesson.

The Austrian archduke Francis Ferdinand and his wife photographed in Sarajevo on June 28, 1914. Later in the day the royal couple were assassinated by young revolutionaries trained and supplied in Serbia, igniting the crisis that led to World War I.

Brown Brothers

What made the archduke Francis Ferdinand a target for a terrorist attack?

Moments after the assassination the Austrian police captured one of the assassins.

Brown Brothers

Who were the archduke Francis Ferdinand's assassins and what did they hope to achieve?

Sarajevo and the Outbreak of War (June–August 1914)

The Assassination On June 28, 1914, a nineteen-year-old Serbian nationalist shot and killed Archduke Francis Ferdinand, heir to the Austrian throne, and his wife as they drove in an open car through the Bosnian capital of Sarajevo. The chief of intelligence of the Serbian army's general staff had helped plan and prepare the crime. Though his role was not known at the time, it was generally believed throughout Europe that Serbian officials were involved.

Germany and Austria's Response News of the assassination produced outrage everywhere in Europe except in Serbia. To those Austrians who had long favored an attack on Serbia, the opportunity seemed irresistible. Count Leopold von Berchtold (1863–1942), the Austro-Hungarian foreign minister, felt the need for strong action, but he knew German support would be required in the likely event that Russia should intervene to protect Serbia. Moreover, only German support could persuade the Hungarians to accept a war. The question of peace or war against Serbia, therefore, had to be answered in Berlin.

William II and Chancellor Theobald von Bethmann-Hollweg (1856–1921) readily promised German support for an attack on Serbia. It has often been said that they gave the Austrians a "blank check," but their message was more specific than that. They urged the Austrians to move swiftly while the other powers were still angry at Serbia. They also made the Austrians feel they would view a failure to act as evidence of Austria-Hungary's weakness and uselessness as an ally. Therefore, the Austrians never wavered in their determination to make war on Serbia. They hoped, with the protection of Germany, to fight Serbia alone, but they were prepared to risk a general European conflict. The Germans also knew they risked a general war, but they too hoped to "localize" the fight between Austria and Serbia.

Unfortunately, the calculations proved to be incorrect. Bethmann-Hollweg hoped the Austrians would strike swiftly and present the powers with a fait accompli while the outrage of the assassination was still fresh, and he hoped German support would deter Russia. Failing that, he was prepared for a continental war against France and Russia. This policy, though, depended on British neutrality, and the German chancellor convinced himself the British would stand aloof.

The Austrians, however, were slow to act. They did not even deliver their deliberately unacceptable ultimatum to Serbia until July 23, when the general hostility toward Serbia had begun to subside. Serbia further embarrassed the Austrians by returning so soft and conciliatory an answer that even the mercurial German emperor thought it removed all reason for war, but the Austrians were determined not to turn back. (See "Compare & Connect: The Outbreak of World War I," pages 660–661.) On July 28, they declared war on Serbia, even though the army would not be ready to attack until mid-August.

The Triple Entente's Response The Russians, previously so often forced to back off, responded angrily to the Austrian demands on Serbia and ordered partial mobilization, against Austria only. This policy was militarily impossible, but its intention was to put diplomatic pressure on Austria to refrain from attacking Serbia. Mobilization of any kind, however, was a dangerous weapon because it was generally understood to be equivalent to an act of war. In fact, only Germany's war plan made mobilization the first and irrevocable start of a war. It required a quick victory in the west before the Russians were ready to act. Even partial Russian mobilization seemed to jeopardize this plan and put Germany in great danger. From this point on, the general staff pressed for German mobilization and war. Their claim of military necessity soon became irresistible.

France and Britain were not eager for war. France's president and prime minister were on their way back from a long-planned state visit to Russia when the crisis flared on July 23. In their absence and without consulting his government, the French ambassador to Russia gave the Russians the same assurances of support that Germany had given Austria. The British worked hard to resolve the crisis by traditional means: a conference of the powers. Austria, still smarting from its humiliation after the London Conference of 1913, would not hear of it. The Germans privately supported the Austrians but publicly took on a conciliatory tone to placate the British.

On July 30, Austria ordered mobilization against Russia. Bethmann-Hollweg resisted the enormous pressure to mobilize, not because he hoped to avoid war, but because he wanted Russia to mobilize against Germany first and appear to be the aggressor. Only in that way could he win the support of the German nation for war, especially the backing of pacifist Social Democrats. His luck was good for a change. The news of Russian general mobilization came only minutes before Germany would have mobilized in any case. Germany then declared war on Russia on August 1. The Schlieffen Plan went into effect. The Germans occupied Luxembourg on August 2 and invaded Belgium, which resisted, on August 3—the same day Germany declared war on France. The invasion of Belgium violated the treaty of 1839 in which the British had joined the other

Overview Relative Strengths of Combatants in World War I

	POPULATION (TOTAL)	SOLDIERS POTENTIALLY AVAILABLE	MILITARY EXPENDITURES (1913–1914)
GREAT BRITAIN	45,000,000	711,000	$250,000,000
FRANCE	40,000,000	1,250,000	$185,000,000
ITALY	35,000,000	750,000	$50,000,000
RUSSIA	164,000,000	1,200,000	$335,000,000
BELGIUM	7,500,000	180,000	$13,750,000
ROMANIA	7,500,000	420,000	$15,000,000
GREECE	5,000,000	120,000	$3,750,000
SERBIA	5,000,000	195,000	$5,250,000
MONTENEGRO	500,000		
UNITED STATES	92,000,000	150,000	$150,000,000
GERMANY	65,000,000	2,200,000	$300,000,000
AUSTRIA-HUNGARY	50,000,000	810,000	$110,000,000
OTTOMAN EMPIRE	20,000,000	360,000	$40,000,000
BULGARIA	4,500,000	340,000	$5,500,000

powers in guaranteeing Belgian neutrality. This factor undermined sentiment in Britain for neutrality and united the nation against Germany, which then invaded France. On August 4, Britain declared war on Germany. The Great War had begun.

STRATEGIES AND STALEMATE: 1914–1917

Throughout Europe, jubilation greeted the outbreak of war. After years of crises and resentments, war came as a release of tension. The popular press had increased public awareness of, and interest in, foreign affairs and had fanned the flames of patriotism.

Both sides expected to take the offensive, force a battle on favorable ground, and win a quick victory. The Triple Entente powers—or the Allies, as they called themselves—held superiority in numbers and financial resources, as well as command of the sea. Germany and Austria, the Central Powers, had the advantages of possessing internal lines of communication and having launched their attack first.

Germany's war plan was based on ideas developed by Count Alfred von Schlieffen (1833–1913), chief of the German general staff from 1891 to 1906. It aimed to outflank the French frontier defenses by sweeping through Belgium to the Channel and then wheeling to the south and east to envelop the French and crush them against the German

COMPARE & CONNECT

THE OUTBREAK OF WORLD WAR I

In the century between the Congress of Vienna and the events at Sarajevo, Europe had overcome one crisis after another without recourse to a major war. Yet the assassination of the Archduke Francis Ferdinand, heir to the Austro-Hungarian Empire, in a Bosnian town on June 28, 1914, produced a crisis that led to a general and catastrophic war. It is interesting to focus attention on the crisis of July 1914 and to trace the steps that turned a Balkan incident into a major disaster. Austria's ultimatum to Serbia and the answer of the Serbians were critical events in bringing on the war.

QUESTIONS

1. Which of the demands were the most difficult for the Serbians to meet?
2. Why did the Austrians fix so short a time for response?
3. Which demands did the Serbians fail to grant? Why?
4. Was the Austrian immediate declaration of war justified?

I. THE AUSTRIAN ULTIMATUM

On the afternoon of July 23, after an investigation of the assassination of the Archduke Franz Ferdinand at Sarajevo, the Austrians presented a list of demands to Serbia, and the Serbs were given forty-eight hours to reply. The Austrian ambassador to Belgrade was instructed to leave the country and break off diplomatic relations unless the demands were met without reservations. The Serbians knew that some officials of the Serbian government took part in the plot.

THE RESULTS BROUGHT OUT by the inquiry no longer permit the Imperial and Royal Government to maintain the attitude of patient tolerance which it has observed for years toward those agitations which center at Belgrade and are spread thence into the territories of the Monarchy. Instead, these results impose upon the Imperial and Royal Government the obligation to put an end to those intrigues, which constitute a standing menace to the peace of the Monarchy.

In order to attain this end, the Imperial and Royal Government finds itself compelled to demand that the Serbian Government give official assurance that it will condemn the propaganda directed against Austria-Hungary, that is to say, the whole body of the efforts whose ultimate object it is to separate from the Monarchy territories that belong to it; and that it will obligate itself to suppress with all the means at its command this criminal and terroristic propaganda. . . .

1. to suppress every publication which shall incite to hatred and contempt the Monarchy, and the general tendency of which shall be directed against the territorial integrity of the latter;
2. to proceed at once to the dissolution of the Narodna Odbrana, [a Serbian nationalist propaganda and paramilitary organization] confiscate all of its means of propaganda, and in the same manner to proceed against the other unions and associations in Serbia which occupy themselves with propaganda against Austria-Hungary; the Royal Government will take such measures as are necessary to make sure that the dissolved associations may not continue their activities under other names in other forms;

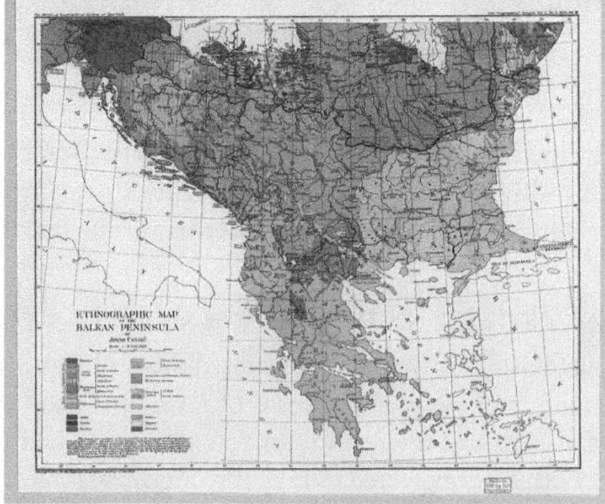

This ethnographic map of the Balkan peninsula, made by a Serbian nationalist named Jovan Cvijić in 1918, served as inspiration for the campaign of ethnic cleansing that would devastate the region once known as Yugoslavia.
Library of Congress

Why were the Balkans a focal point of international conflict?

3. to eliminate without delay from public instruction in Serbia, everything, whether connected with the teaching corps or with the methods of teaching, that serves or may serve to nourish the propaganda against Austria-Hungary;
4. to remove from the military and administrative service in general all officers and officials who have been guilty of carrying on the propaganda against Austria-Hungary, whose names the Imperial and Royal Government reserve the right to make known to the Royal Government . . . ;
5. to agree to the cooperation in Serbia of the organs of the Imperial Royal Government in the suppression of the subversive movement directed against the integrity of the Monarchy;
6. to institute a judicial inquiry against every participant in the conspiracy of the twenty-eighth of June who may be found in Serbian territory; the organs of the Imperial and Royal Government delegated for this purpose will take part in the proceedings held for this purpose;
7. to undertake with all haste the arrest of Major Voislav Tankositch and of one Milan Ciganovitch, a Serbian official, who have been compromised the results of the inquiry; . . .
10. to inform the Imperial and Royal Government without delay of the execution of the measures comprised in the foregoing points.

The Imperial and Royal Government awaits the reply of the Royal Government by Saturday, the twenty-fifth instant, at 6 P.M., at the latest.

Source: "The Austrian Ultimatum," in *Outbreak of the World War; German Documents Collected by Karl Kautsky and ed. by Max Montgelas and Walther Schucking*, trans. by the Carnegie Endowment for International Peace. Division of International Law, Supplement I (1924). (New York: Oxford University Press, 1924), pp. 604–605.

II. THE SERBIAN RESPONSE

The reply of the Serbians was remarkably reasonable. In his first reaction to it, the German Kaiser said: "AFTER READING OVER THE SERBIAN REPLY, which I received this morning, I am convinced that on the whole the wishes of the Danube Monarchy have been acceded to. The few reservations that Serbia makes in regard to individual points could, according to my opinion, be settled by negotiation. But it contains the announcement orbi et urbi of a capitulation of the most humiliating kind, and as a result, every cause for war falls to the ground." But it was not unconditional acceptance of the ultimatum.

THE ROYAL SERVIAN GOVERNMENT have received the communication of the Imperial and Royal Government of the 10th instant, and are convinced that their reply will remove any misunderstanding which may threaten to impair the good neighbourly relations between the Austro-Hungarian Monarchy and the Kingdom of Servia. . . .

The Royal Government have been pained and surprised at the statements, according to which members of the Kingdom of Servia are supposed to have participated in the preparations for the crime committed at Serajevo; the Royal Government expected to be invited to collaborate in an investigation of all that concerns this crime, and they were ready, in order to prove the entire correctness of their attitude, to take measures against any persons concerning whom representations were made to them. Falling in, therefore, with the desire of the Imperial and Royal Government, they are prepared to hand over for trial any Servian subject, without regard to his situation or rank, of whose complicity in the crime of Serajevo proofs are forthcoming, and more especially they undertake to cause to be published on the first page of the "Journal officiel," on the date of the 13th (26th) July, the following declaration:—

The Royal Government of Servia condemn all propaganda which may be directed against Austria-Hungary, that is to say, all such tendencies as aim at ultimately detaching from the Austro-Hungarian Monarchy territories which form part thereof and they sincerely deplore the baneful consequences of these criminal movements. The Royal Government regret that, according to the communication from the Imperial and Royal Government, certain Servian officers and officials should have taken part in the above-mentioned propaganda and thus compromised the good neighbourly relations to which the Royal Servian Government was solemnly engaged by the declaration of the 31st March, 1909, which

(continued)

declaration disapproves and repudiates all idea or attempt at interference with the destiny of the inhabitants of any part whatsoever of Austria-Hungary, and they consider it their duty formally to warn the officers, officials, and entire population of the kingdom that henceforth they will take the most rigorous steps against all such persons as are guilty of such acts, to prevent and to repress which they will use their utmost endeavour. . . .

The Royal Government further undertake:—

1. To introduce at the first regular convocation of the Skuptchina a provision into the press law providing for the most severe punishment of incitement to hatred or contempt of the Austro-Hungarian Monarchy, and for taking action against any publication the general tendency of which is directed against the territorial integrity of Austria-Hungary. . . .
2. The Royal Government will accept the demand of the Imperial and Royal Government, and will dissolve the "Narodna Odbrana" Society and every other society which may be directing its efforts against Austria-Hungary.
3. The Royal Servian Government undertake to remove without delay from their public educational establishments in Servia all that serves or could serve to foment propaganda against Austria-Hungary, whenever the Imperial and Royal Government furnish them with facts and proofs of this propaganda.
4. The Royal Government also agree to remove from military service all such persons as the judicial enquiry may have proved to be guilty of acts directed against the integrity of the territory of the Austro-Hungarian Monarchy, and they expect the Imperial and Royal Government to communicate to them at a later date the names and the acts of these officers and officials for the purposes of the proceedings which are to be taken against them.
5. The Royal Government must confess that they do not clearly grasp the meaning or the scope of the demand made by the Imperial and Royal Government that Servia shall undertake to accept the collaboration of the organs of the Imperial and Royal Government upon their territory, but they declare that they will admit such collaboration as agrees with the principle of international law, with criminal procedure, and with good neighbourly relations.
6. It goes without saying that the Royal Government consider it their duty to open an enquiry against all such persons as are, or eventually may be, implicated in the plot of the 15th June, and who happen to be within the territory of the kingdom. As regards the participation in this enquiry of Austro-Hungarian agents or authorities appointed for this purpose by the Imperial and Royal Government, the Royal Government cannot accept such an arrangement, as it would be a violation of the Constitution and of the law of criminal procedure; nevertheless, in concrete cases communications as to the results of the investigation in question might be given to the Austro-Hungarian agents.
7. The Royal Government proceeded, on the very evening of the delivery of the note, to arrest Commandant Voislav Tankossitch. As regards Milan Ziganovitch, who is a subject of the Austro-Hungarian Monarchy and who, up to the 15th June was employed (on probation) by the directorate of railways, it has not yet been possible to arrest him. . . .
10. The Royal Government will inform the Imperial and Royal Government the execution of the measures comprised under the above heads, in so far as this has not already been done by the present note, as soon as each measure has been ordered and carried out.

If the Imperial and Royal Government are not satisfied with this reply, the Servian Government, considering that it is not to the common interest to precipitate the solution of this question, are ready, as always, to accept a pacific understanding, either by referring this question to the decision of the International Tribunal of The Hague, or to the Great Powers which took part in the drawing up of the declaration made by the Servian Government on the 18th (31st) March 1909.

Belgrade, July 12 (25), 1914

Source: "Serbia's Answer to Ultimatum," from *British Diplomatic Correspondence in Collected Diplomatic Documents Relating to the Outbreak of the European War*, No. 39 (H. M. Stationary Off: 1915), pp. 31–37.

fortresses in Lorraine. In the east, the Germans planned to stand on the defensive against Russia until France had been crushed, a task they thought would take only six weeks.

The apparent risk, besides the violation of Belgian neutrality and the consequent alienation of Britain, lay in weakening the German defenses against a direct attack across the frontier. The true danger was that the German striking force on the right through Belgium would not be powerful enough to make the swift progress vital to success. In the end, for reasons still debated, the plan failed by a narrow margin.

The War in the West The French had also put their faith in the offensive, but with less reason than the Germans. They underestimated the numbers and effectiveness of the German reserves and overestimated what the courage and spirit of their own troops could achieve. The French offensive on Germany's western frontier failed totally. This defeat probably was preferable to a partial success, because it released troops for use against the main German army. As a result, the French and the British were able to stop the German advance on Paris at the Battle of the Marne in September 1914. (See Map 26–1 and Map 26–2, page 664.)

MAP 26–1 World War I in Europe Despite the importance of military action in the Far East, in the Arab world, and at sea, the main theaters of activity in World War I were in the European areas.

Which European countries saw the most military action in World War I?

MAP EXPLORATION

Interactive map: To explore this map further, go to www.myhistorylab.com

MAP 26–2 **The Western Front, 1914–1918** This map shows the crucial western front in detail.

What factors made the war on the western front one of position rather than of movement?

Thereafter, the nature of the war in the west became one of position instead of movement. Both sides dug in behind a wall of trenches protected by barbed wire that stretched from the North Sea to Switzerland. Strategically placed machine-gun nests made assaults difficult and dangerous. Both sides, nonetheless, attempted massive attacks preceded by artillery bombardments of unprecedented and horrible force and duration. Still, the defense was always able to recover and to bring up reserves fast enough to prevent a breakthrough.

Assaults that cost hundreds of thousands of lives produced advances of only hundreds of yards. Even poison gas proved ineffective. In 1916, the British introduced the tank, which eventually proved to be the answer to the machine gun. The Allied command was slow to understand this, however, and until the end of the war, defense was supreme. For three years after its establishment, the western front moved only a few miles in either direction.

The War in the East In the east, the war began auspiciously for the Allies. The Russians advanced into Austrian territory and inflicted heavy casualties, but Russian incompetence and German energy soon reversed the situation. In 1915, the Central Powers pressed their advantage in the east and drove into the Baltic states and Russian Poland, inflicting more than 2 million casualties in a single year.

As the battle lines hardened, both sides sought new allies. Turkey (because of its hostility to Russia) and Bulgaria (the enemy of Serbia) joined the Central Powers. Both sides bid for Italian support with promises of the spoils of victory. Because the Austrians held what the Italians wanted most, the Allies could promise more. In a secret treaty of 1915, they agreed to deliver to Italy after victory most of *Italia irredenta* (i.e., the South Tyrol, Trieste, and some of the Dalmatian Islands), plus colonies in Africa and a share of the Turkish Empire. By the spring of 1915, Italy was engaging Austrian armies. Romania joined the Allies in 1916 but was quickly defeated and driven from the war.

In the Far East, Japan honored its alliance with Britain and entered the war. The Japanese quickly overran the German colonies in China and the Pacific and used the opportunity to put pressure on China. Both sides also appealed to nationalistic sentiment in areas the enemy held. The Germans supported nationalist movements among the Irish, the Flemings in Belgium, and the Poles and Ukrainians under Russian rule. They even tried to persuade the Turks to lead a Muslim uprising against the British in Egypt and India, and against the French and Italians in North Africa. The Allies made the same appeals with greater success. They sponsored movements of national autonomy for the Czechs, the Slovaks, the south Slavs, and againt the Poles who were under Austrian rule. They also favored a movement of Arab independence from Turkey.

In 1915, the Allies tried to break the deadlock on the western front by going around it. The idea came chiefly from Winston Churchill (1874–1965), first lord of the British admiralty. He proposed to attack the Dardanelles and capture Constantinople. This policy supposedly would knock Turkey from the war, bring help to the Balkan front, and ease communications with Russia. The success of Churchill's plan depended on timing, speed, and daring leadership, but all of these were lacking. Worse, the execution of the attack was inept and overly cautious. Before the campaign was abandoned, the Allies lost almost 150,000 men and diverted three times that number from more useful occupations.

British tanks moving toward the Battle of Cambrai in Flanders late in 1917. Tanks were impervious to machine-gun fire. Had they been used in great numbers, they might have broken the stalemate in the west.

Bildarchiv Preussischer Kulturbesitz

How did tanks change the nature of the fighting on the western front?

Return to the West Both sides turned back to the west in 1916. General Erich von Falkenhayn (1861–1922), who had succeeded Moltke in September 1914, attacked the French stronghold of Verdun. The French held Verdun with comparatively few men and inflicted almost as many casualties as they suffered. The commander of Verdun, Henri Pétain (1856–1951), became a national hero, and "They shall not pass" became a slogan of national defiance.

The Allies tried to end the impasse by launching a major offensive along the River Somme in July. Aided by a Russian attack in the east that drew off some German strength and by an enormous artillery bombardment, they hoped at last to break through. Once again, the defense was superior. Enormous casualties on both sides brought no result. The war on land dragged on with no end in sight.

The War at Sea As the war continued, control of the sea became more important. The British imposed a strict blockade meant to starve out the enemy. The Germans responded with submarine warfare meant to destroy British shipping and starve the British. They declared the waters around the British Isles a war zone, where even neutral ships would not be safe. Both policies were unwelcome to neutrals, and especially to the United States, which conducted extensive trade in the Atlantic. Yet the sinking of neutral ships by German submarines was both more dramatic and more offensive than the British blockade.

In May 1915, a German submarine torpedoed the British liner *Lusitania.* Among the 1,200 who drowned were 118 Americans. President Woodrow Wilson (1856–1924) warned Germany that a repetition would have grave consequences; the Germans desisted for the time being, rather than further anger the United States.

America Enters the War In December 1916, President Woodrow Wilson intervened to try to bring about a negotiated peace. Neither side, however, was willing to renounce war aims that its opponent found acceptable. The war seemed likely to continue until one or both sides reached exhaustion. Two events early in 1917 changed the situation radically. First, on February 1, the Germans announced the resumption of unrestricted submarine warfare, which led the United States to break off diplomatic relations and to declare war on Germany on April 6. Second, in March 1917 a revolution in Russia overthrew the tsarist government.

The use of poison gas (by both sides) during the First World War and its dreadful effects—blinding, asphyxiation, burned lungs—came to symbolize the horrors of modern war. This painting shows a group of British soldiers being guided to the rear after they were blinded by mustard gas on the western front.

John Singer Sargent, *Gassed*, 1918–1919. Imperial War Museum, London

How did the horrors of World War I shape political opinion in the post-war era?

THE RUSSIAN REVOLUTION

WHAT FACTORS made the rise of the Bolsheviks to power in Russia possible?

No political faction planned or led the March 1917 Revolution in Russia. It was the result of the collapse of the monarchy's ability to govern. Nicholas II was weak and incompetent and suspected of being under the domination of his German wife and the insidious peasant faith healer Rasputin, whom a group of Russian noblemen assassinated in 1916. Military and domestic failures produced massive casualties, widespread hunger, strikes by workers, and disorganization in the army. The peasant discontent that had plagued the countryside before 1914 did not subside during the conflict. In 1915, the tsar took personal command of the armies on the German front, which kept him away from the capital. In his absence, corrupt and incompetent ministers increasingly discredited the government even in the eyes of conservative monarchists. All political factions in the Duma, Russia's parliament, were discontented.

The Provisional Government

In early March 1917, strikes and worker demonstrations erupted in Petrograd, as Saint Petersburg had been renamed. The ill-disciplined troops in the city refused to fire on the demonstrators. The tsar abdicated on March 15. The government of Russia fell into the hands of members of the Duma, who soon formed a provisional government composed chiefly of Constitutional Democrats (Cadets) with Western sympathies.

At the same time, the various socialist groups, including both Social Revolutionaries and Social Democrats of the Menshevik wing, began to organize soviets, councils of workers and soldiers. Initially, they allowed the provisional government to function without actually supporting it, but they became estranged when the Cadets failed to control the army or to purge "reactionaries" from the government.

In this climate, the provisional government decided to remain loyal to Russia's alliances and continue the war. The provisional government thus accepted tsarist foreign

Petrograd Munitions Workers demonstrating in 1917.

Ria-Novosti/Sovfoto/Eastfoto

What was the relationship between World War I and political upheaval in Russia?

policy and associated itself with the main source of domestic suffering and discontent. The collapse of the last Russian offensive in the summer of 1917 sealed its fate. Disillusionment with the war, shortages of food and other necessities at home, and the peasants' demands for land reform undermined the government. This occurred even after the moderate socialist Alexander Kerensky (1881–1970) became prime minister. Moreover, discipline in the army had disintegrated.

Lenin and the Bolsheviks

Ever since April, the Bolshevik wing of the Social Democratic Party had been working against the provisional government. The Germans, in their most successful attempt at subversion, had rushed the brilliant Bolshevik leader V. I. Lenin (1870–1924) in a sealed train from his exile in Switzerland across Germany to Petrograd. They hoped he would cause trouble for the revolutionary government.

Lenin saw the opportunity to achieve the political alliance of workers and peasants he had discussed before the war. In speech after speech, he hammered away on the theme of peace, bread, and land. The Bolsheviks demanded that all political power go to the soviets, which they controlled. The failure of the summer offensive encouraged them to attempt a coup, but the effort was a failure. Lenin fled to Finland, and his chief collaborator, Leon Trotsky (1879–1940), was imprisoned.

The failure of a right-wing countercoup gave the Bolsheviks another chance. Trotsky, released from prison, led the powerful Petrograd soviet. Lenin returned in October and insisted to his doubting colleagues that the time was ripe to take power. Trotsky organized the coup that took place on November 6 and concluded with an armed assault on the provisional government. The Bolsheviks, almost as much to their own astonishment as to that of the rest of the world, had come to rule Russia.

The Communist Dictatorship

The victors moved to fulfill their promises and to assure their own security. The provisional government had decreed an election for late November to select a Constituent Assembly. The Social Revolutionaries won a large majority over the Bolsheviks. When the assembly gathered in January, it met for only a day before the Red Army, controlled by the Bolsheviks, dispersed it. In November and January, the Bolshevik government nationalized the land and turned it over to its peasant proprietors. Factory workers were put in charge of their plants. The state seized banks and repudiated the debt of the tsarist government. Property of the church reverted to the state.

The Bolshevik government also took Russia out of the war, which they believed benefited only capitalism. They signed an armistice with Germany in December 1917 and in March 1918 accepted the Treaty of Brest-Litovsk, by which Russia yielded Poland, Finland, the Baltic states, and Ukraine. Some territory in the Transcaucasus region went to Turkey. The Bolsheviks also agreed to pay a heavy war indemnity. These terms were a high price to pay for peace, but Lenin had no choice. Russia was incapable of renewing the war effort, and the Bolsheviks needed time to impose their rule.

The new Bolshevik government met major domestic resistance. Civil war erupted between Red Russians, who supported the revolution, and White Russians, who opposed it. In the summer of 1918, the Bolsheviks murdered the tsar and his family. Loyal army officers continued to fight the revolution and received aid from Allied armies. Under the leadership of Trotsky, however, the Red Army eventually overcame the domestic opposition. By 1921, Lenin and his supporters were in firm control.

THE END OF WORLD WAR I

WHAT WERE the immediate consequences of the end of World War I?

The collapse of Russia and the Treaty of Brest-Litovsk were the zenith of German success. The Germans controlled eastern Europe and its resources, especially food, and by 1918 they were free to concentrate their forces on the western front. These developments would probably have been decisive without American intervention. Still, American troops would not arrive in significant numbers for about a year, and both sides tried to win the war in 1917.

An Allied attempt to break through in the west failed disastrously. The Austrians, supported by the Germans, defeated the Italians at Caporetto and threatened to overrun northern Italy, until they were checked with the aid of Allied troops. The deadlock continued, but time was running out for the Central Powers.

Germany's Last Offensive

In March 1918, the Germans decided to gamble everything on one last offensive. The German army reached the Marne again but got no farther. They had no more reserves, and the entire nation was exhausted. In contrast, the arrival of American troops in ever-increasing numbers bolstered the Allies. An Allied counteroffensive proved irresistible. As the exhausted Austrians collapsed in Italy, and Bulgaria and Turkey dropped out of the war, the German high command knew the end was imminent.

Ludendorff was determined to make peace before the German army was thoroughly defeated in the field and to make civilians responsible for ending the war. For some time, he had been the effective ruler of Germany under the aegis of the emperor. He now allowed a new government to be established on democratic principles and to seek peace immediately. The new government, under Prince Max of Baden, asked for peace on the basis of the **Fourteen Points** that President Wilson had declared as the American war aims. These were idealistic principles, including self-determination for nationalities, open diplomacy, freedom of the seas, disarmament, and the establishment of the League of Nations to keep the peace.

Fourteen Points President Woodrow Wilson's idealistic principles articulated as America's goals in World War I, including self-determination for nationalities, open diplomacy, freedom of the seas, disarmament, and establishment of the League of Nations to keep the peace.

Women Munitions Workers in England. World War I demanded more from the civilian populations than had previous wars, resulting in important social changes. The demands of the munitions industries and a shortage of men (so many of whom were in uniform) brought many women out of traditional roles at home and into factories and other war-related work.

Getty Images Inc.—Hulton Archive Photos

What were the consequences of World War I for British society?

THE ARMISTICE

The disintegration of the German army forced William II to abdicate on November 9, 1918. The majority branch of the Social Democratic Party proclaimed a republic to prevent their radical Leninist wing from setting up a soviet government. Two days later, this republican, socialist-led government signed the armistice that ended the war by accepting German defeat. The German people were, in general, unaware their army had been defeated and was crumbling. Many of them came to believe Germany had not been defeated but had been tricked by the enemy and betrayed—even stabbed in the back—by republicans and socialists at home.

The Great War, as contemporaries called it, lasted more than four years, doing terrible damage. Battle casualties alone counted more than 4 million dead and 8.3 million wounded among the Central Powers and 5.4 million dead and 7 million wounded from their opponents, and millions of civilians died from the war and causes arising from it. Among the casualties also were the German, Austro-Hungarian, Russian, and Turkish Empires. The American intervention in 1917 thrust the United States into European affairs with a vengeance, and the collapse of the Russian autocracy brought the Bolshevik revolution and the reality of a great communist state. Disappointment, resentment, and economic dislocations caused by the war brought various forms of fascism to Italy, Germany, and other countries. The comfortable nineteenth-century assumptions of inevitable progress based on reason, science and technology, individual freedom, democracy, and free enterprise gave way in many places to cynicism, nihilism, dictatorship, statism, official racism, and class warfare. It is widely agreed that the First World War was the mother of the Second and to most of the horrors of the rest of the century.

These kinds of changes affected the colonial peoples the European powers ruled, and overseas empires would never again be as secure as they had seemed before the war. Europe was no longer the center of the world, free to interfere when it wished or to ignore the rest of the world if it chose. The memory of that war lived on to shake the nerve of the victorious Western powers as they faced the new conditions of the postwar world.

SIGNIFICANT DATES FROM THE ERA CULMINATING IN WORLD WAR I

1871	Creation of the German Empire
1873	The Three Emperors' League
1875	The Russo-Turkish War
1879	The Dual Alliance (Germany and Austria)
1882	The Triple Alliance (Germany, Austria, and Italy)
1888	William II becomes the German emperor (kaiser)
1890	Bismarck is dismissed
1894	The Franco-Russian alliance
1898	Germany begins to build a battleship navy
1899–1902	Boer War
1902	The British alliance with Japan
1904	The Entente Cordiale (Britain and France)
1904–1905	The Russo-Japanese War
1905	The first Moroccan crisis
1908–1909	The Bosnian crisis
1911	The second Moroccan crisis
1912–1913	The First and Second Balkan Wars
1914	(August) Germans attack in the West; (August–September) First Battle of the Marne; (September) Battles of Tannenberg and the Masurian Lakes
1915	(April) Dardanelles campaign; (May) Germans sink British ship *Lusitania*
1916	(February) Germans attack Verdun; (May–June) Battle of Jutland
1917	(February) Germans declare unrestricted submarine warfare; (March) Russian Revolution; (April) United States enters war; (November) Bolsheviks seize power
1918	(March) Treaty of Brest-Litovsk; German offensive in the West; (November) Armistice

THE END OF THE OTTOMAN EMPIRE

At the outbreak of World War I in August 1914, the Ottoman Empire was neutral, but many military officers, the so-called Young Turks who had taken control of the Ottoman government in 1909, were pro-German. After hesitating for three months, the Turks decided to enter the war on the German side in November 1914. This decision ultimately brought about the end of the Ottoman Empire. Early victories gave way to defeat after defeat at the hands of the Russians and the British. By October 30, 1918, Turkey was out of the war. In November, an Allied fleet sailed into the harbor of Constantinople and landed troops who occupied the city.

The peace treaty signed in Paris in 1920 between Turkey and the Allies dismembered the Ottoman Empire, placing large parts of it, particularly the areas Arabs inhabited, under the control of Britain and France. In Mesopotamia the British created the state of Iraq, which, along with Palestine, became British mandates. Syria and Lebanon became French mandates. (**Mandates** were territories that were legally administered under the auspices of the League of Nations, but were in effect ruled as colonies.) A Greek invasion of the Turkish homeland in Anatolia in 1919 provoked a nationalist reaction, bringing the young general Mustafa Kemal (1881–1938), who later took the name Ataturk, meaning "Father of the Turks," to power. He drove the Greeks out of Anatolia and compelled the victorious powers to make a new arrangement sealed by the treaty of Lausanne in 1923. Ataturk abolished the Ottoman sultanate and deposed the last caliph. The new Republic of Turkey abandoned most of the old Ottoman Empire but became fully independent of control by the European powers and sovereign in its Anatolian homeland. Under Ataturk and his successors, Turkey, although its population was overwhelmingly Muslim, became a secular state and a force for stability in the region.

mandates Territories under the aegis of the League of Nations but actually ruled as a colonies.

The Arab portions of the old empire, however, were a different story. Divided into a collection of artificial states that had no historical reality, governed or dominated as client regimes by the British and French, they were relatively quiet during the 1920s and 1930s. The weakening of Britain and France during and after the Second World War, however, and their subsequent abandonment of control in the Middle East would create problems in the latter part of the century.

THE SETTLEMENT AT PARIS

WHAT WERE the key weaknesses of the Paris peace settlement?

The representatives of the victorious states gathered at Versailles and other Parisian suburbs in the first half of 1919. Wilson speaking for the United States, David Lloyd George (1863–1945) for Britain, Georges Clemenceau (1841–1929) for France, and Vittorio Emanuele Orlando (1860–1952) for Italy made up the Big Four. Japan also had an important part in the discussions.

Obstacles the Peacemakers Faced

The negotiators at Paris in 1919 represented constitutional, generally democratic governments, and public opinion had become a mighty force. Though there were secret sessions, the conference often worked in the full glare of publicity. Nationalism had become almost a secular religion, and Europe's many ethnic groups could not be relied on to remain quiet while the great powers distributed them on the map. Moreover, propaganda and especially the intervention of Woodrow Wilson had transformed World War I into a moral crusade to achieve a peace that would be just as well as secure. (See "Encountering the Past: War Propaganda and the Movies," page 672) The Fourteen Points set forth the right of nationalities to self-determination as an absolute value, but in fact no one could draw the map of Europe to match ethnic groups perfectly with their homelands. All these elements made compromise difficult. Wilson's idealism, moreover, came into conflict with the more practical war aims of the victorious powers and with many of the secret treaties that had been made before and during the war.

The continuing national goals of the victors presented further obstacles to an idealistic "peace without victors." France was painfully conscious of its numerical inferiority to Germany and of the low birthrate that would keep it inferior. So France was naturally eager to weaken Germany permanently and preserve French superiority. Italy continued to seek *Italia irredenta*, Britain looked to its imperial interests, and Japan pursued its own advantage in Asia. The United States insisted on freedom of the seas, which favored American commerce, and on its right to maintain the Monroe Doctrine.

Finally, the peacemakers of 1919 faced a world still in turmoil. The greatest immediate threat appeared to be the spread of Bolshevism. While civil war distracted Lenin and his colleagues, the Allies landed small armies in Russia to help overthrow the Bolshevik regime. The revolution seemed likely to spread as communist governments were established in Bavaria and Hungary. A communist uprising led by the "Spartacus group" had to be suppressed in Berlin. The worried Allies even allowed an army of German volunteers to fight the Bolsheviks in the Baltic states.

The Peace

The Paris settlement consisted of five separate treaties between the victors and the defeated powers. Formal sessions began on January 18, 1919, and the last treaty

The Allies promoted Arab efforts to secure independence from Turkey in an effort to remove Turkey from the war. Delegates to the peace conference of 1919 in Paris included British colonel T. E. Lawrence, who helped lead the rebellion, and representatives from the Middle Eastern region. Prince Feisal, the third son of King Hussein, stands in the foreground of this picture; Colonel T. E. Lawrence is in the middle row, second from the right; and Brigadier General Nuri Pasha Said of Baghdad is second from the left.

CORBIS/Bettmann

How did the settlements reached after World War I contribute to future unrest in the Middle East?

"The Big Four" attending the Paris peace conference in 1919: Vittorio Orlande, premier of Italy; David Lloyd George, prime minister of Great Britain; Georges Clemenceau, premier of France, and Woodrow Wilson, president of the United States (l. to r.).

National Archives and Records Administration

What were the goals of the "Big Four" at the peace conference that followed World War I?

ENCOUNTERING THE PAST

War Propaganda and the Movies—Charlie Chaplin

The huge expenditure of life and treasure required to conduct the war would not have been tolerated by the masses had governments on both sides not used propaganda to convince their people of its necessity. Propagandists demonized opponents and represented the homefront as totally committed to a noble, even holy, cause. The propagandists of World War I initially relied on newspaper articles and pamphlets to get their message across, but they soon developed powerful visual media—posters, cartoons, caricatures, and (by the middle war years) films. These were equally effective with persons of every age, class, and level of education, and they had great emotional impact.

Movies graphically represented the enemy as horrible or ridiculous and one's own people as noble, brave, and self-sacrificing. Both sides in the Great War produced films that were immensely popular with their people. The Germans considered films so important as morale boosters that they issued special rations of scarce fuel to theaters to keep them functioning through the brutal winter of 1917–1918. Germany did not, however, produce an actor of the status of the British-American comedian Charlie Chaplin (1889–1977). Chaplin came to America in 1914 to work in vaudeville, and he was a noted film star by the time the war broke out. His most famous character was a tragi-comic tramp figure who had many adventures in many movies. Chaplin's major wartime success was *Shoulder Arms* (1918), a farce in which a lone American soldier single-handedly captures a unit of bumbling Germans and the kaiser himself.

Charlie Chaplin in *Shoulder Arms.*

What new forms of propaganda were used during World War I?

WHAT IS the purpose of military propaganda? Can films hurt as well as help war efforts?

was signed on August 10, 1920. (See Map 26–3.) Wilson arrived in Europe to unprecedented popular acclaim. Liberals and idealists expected a new kind of international order achieved in a new and better way, but they were soon disillusioned. "Open covenants openly arrived at" soon gave way to closed sessions in which Wilson, Clemenceau, and Lloyd George made arrangements that seemed cynical to outsiders.

The notion of "a peace without victors" became a mockery when the Soviet Union (as Russia was now called) and Germany were excluded from the peace conference. The principle of national self-determination was violated many times and was unavoidable. Still, their exclusion from decisions angered the diplomats from the small nations. The undeserved adulation accorded Wilson on his arrival gradually turned into equally undeserved scorn. He had not abandoned his ideals lightly but had merely given way to the irresistible force of reality.

MAP 26–3 **World War I Peace Settlement in Europe and the Middle East** The map of central and eastern Europe, as well as that of the Middle East, underwent drastic revision after World War I. The enormous territorial losses suffered by Germany, Austria-Hungary, the Ottoman Empire, Bulgaria, and Russia were the other side of the coin represented by gains for France, Italy, Greece, and Romania and by the appearance or reappearance of at least eight new independent states from Finland in the north to Yugoslavia in the south. The mandate system for former Ottoman territories outside Turkey proper laid foundations for several new, mostly Arab, states in the Middle East. In Africa, the mandate system placed the former German colonies under British, French, and South African rule.

How did the peace settlement affect the territorial makeup of Europe?

The League of Nations Wilson could make unpalatable concessions without abandoning his ideals because he put great faith in a new instrument for peace and justice: the League of Nations. Its covenant was an essential part of the peace treaty. The league was to be not an international government, but a body of sovereign states that agreed to pursue common policies and to consult in the common interest, especially when war threatened. The members promised to submit differences among themselves to arbitration, an international court, or the League Council. The league was unlikely to be effective, however, because it had no armed forces at its disposal. Furthermore, any action required the unanimous consent of its council, consisting permanently of Britain, France, Italy, the United States, and Japan, as well as four other states that had temporary seats. The Covenant of the League bound its members to "respect and preserve" the territorial integrity of all its members; this was generally seen as a device to ensure the security of the victorious powers. The exclusion of Germany and the Soviet Union from the League Assembly further undermined its claim to evenhandedness.

Germany In the West, the main territorial issue was the fate of Germany. The French wanted to set the Rhineland up as a separate buffer state, but Lloyd George and Wilson would not permit it. Still, they could not ignore France's need for protection against a resurgent Germany. France received Alsace-Lorraine and the right to work the coal mines of the Saar for fifteen years. Germany west of the Rhine and fifty kilometers east of it was to be a demilitarized zone. Allied troops could stay on the west bank for fifteen years. The treaty also provided that Britain and the United States would help France if Germany attacked it. Such an attack was made more unlikely by the permanent disarmament of Germany. As long as these provisions were observed, France would be safe.

The East The settlement in the East reflected the collapse of the great defeated empires that had ruled it for centuries. Germany lost part of Silesia, and East Prussia was cut off from the rest of Germany by a corridor carved out to give the revived state of Poland access to the sea. The Austro-Hungarian Empire disappeared entirely, giving way to five small successor states. Most of its German-speaking people were gathered in the Republic of Austria, cut off from the Germans of Bohemia and forbidden to unite with Germany.

The Magyars were left with the much reduced kingdom of Hungary. The Czechs of Bohemia and Moravia joined with the Slovaks and Ruthenians to the east to form Czechoslovakia, and this new state included several million unhappy Germans plus Poles, Magyars, and Ukrainians. The southern Slavs were united in the Kingdom of Serbs, Croats, and Slovenes, or Yugoslavia. Italy gained Trentino, which included tens of thousands of German speakers, and the port of Trieste. Romania was enlarged by receiving Transylvania from Hungary and Bessarabia from Russia. Bulgaria lost territory to Greece and Yugoslavia. Russia lost vast territories in the west. Finland, Estonia, Latvia, and Lithuania became independent states, and most of Poland was carved out of formerly Russian soil.

Reparations Perhaps the most debated part of the peace settlement dealt with reparations for the damage Germany did during the war. Before the armistice, the Germans promised to pay compensation "for all damages done to the civilian population of the Allies and their property." The Americans judged the amount would be between $15 billion and $25 billion and that Germany would be able to pay that amount. France and Britain, however, who worried about repaying their war debts to the United States, were eager to have Germany pay the full cost of the war, including pensions to survivors and dependents.

There was general agreement that Germany could not afford to pay such a huge sum, whatever it might be, and the conference did not specify an amount. In the meantime, Germany was to pay $5 billion annually until 1921. At that time, a final figure would be set, which Germany would have to pay in thirty years.

To justify these huge reparation payments, the Allies inserted the notorious war guilt clause (Clause 231) into the treaty in which German aggression was identified as the sole cause of the war. The Germans, of course, did not believe they were solely responsible for the war and bitterly resented the charge. They had lost territories containing badly needed natural resources. Yet they were presented with an astronomical and apparently unlimited reparations bill. To add insult to injury, they were required to admit to a war guilt they did not feel.

Finally, to heap insult upon insult, they were required to accept the entire treaty as the victors wrote it, without negotiation. There was no choice. The Social Democrats and the Catholic Center Party formed a new government, and their representatives signed the treaty. These parties formed the backbone of the Weimar government that ruled Germany until 1933. They never overcame the stigma of having accepted the Treaty of Versailles.

World War I and Colonial Empires

The First World War and the peace settlement introduced numerous changes and transformations into the European colonial world.

Redistribution of Colonies into Mandates The rivalries over empire that had predated the outbreak of the war and that had contributed so mightily to prewar tensions continued throughout the conflict. The war opened the possibility for whoever won it to expand their empires at the cost of the defeated powers. As a result, the single most important imperial consequence of World War I was Germany being stripped of its colonies and the Ottoman Empire of regions it had formerly governed.

The Covenant of the League of Nations established mandates within these former colonies and regions. These mandates located in the Middle East, Africa, and the Pacific were placed under the "tutelage" of one of the great powers under League of Nations supervision and encouraged to advance toward independence. Britain and France became the chief mandate administrators and were consequently drawn more deeply into new regions of the world, most particularly, the Middle East. In effect, the mandates became colonies of the administering powers. Some mandates, most notably Iraq, became independent between the wars. Other mandates became independent often with considerable conflict from the closing years of World War II through the third quarter of the twentieth century. These latter mandates included Palestine, Syria, Lebanon, Transjordan, Tanganyka, Kamerun, Southwest Africa, and German New Guinea to mention only some of the major areas.

Colonial Participation Colonial peoples themselves had played a significant role in the First World War. Germany itself did not call upon troops from its colonies. The war led Britain and France, however, to view their empires in new ways as sources of military as well as economic support. The French government recruited tens of thousands of Algerians into its armed forces and over 150,000 West Africans. It is estimated that more than 2.5 million British colonial troops participated in the war. The presence of so many non-European troops on the European continent even before the arrival of U.S. troops was one of the factors that made the war a genuinely world conflict.

What Europeans had learned from the wartime experience was the value of their colonies in terms of troops to be recruited and natural resources to be devoted to the war effort, and they tended to seek ways to draw them into closer relations. In this respect, the years after the war were in some respects the period of most extensive direct colonial involvement by Great Britain and France and the ongoing desire for empire on the part of Italy. When the Second World War broke out, both nations would encounter much more nationalist resistance, which following the war would culminate in decolonization. (See Chapter 29.)

Impact of the Peace Settlement on Future Colonial Relations Many native colonial leaders in Africa and Asia had supported the allied war effort in the hope that their peoples would be rewarded with greater independence and better economic relations with Europe. These hopes were dashed at the peace conference and in the years thereafter. These colonial leaders had hoped they might be allowed to put their case for independence or major administrative reform before the conference, and they had been denied that opportunity. Their disappointment led them over the years to reject engagement with the existing international order and to move in various new directions of disruptive and ultimately successful national anticolonialism.

The European powers themselves had directly contributed to these developments in another fashion. They had sought to stir nationalist uprisings in the lands of their opponents. Here the most significant effort took place among Arab peoples governed by the Ottoman Empire, which had sided with Germany. The British led Arab nationalist groups to believe that they might achieve independence in the wake of an allied victory. T. E. Lawrence, later known popularly as Lawrence of Arabia, led much of this effort on behalf of the British. For their part the Germans had attempted to stir unrest in northern Africa.

A glance at the new map of the post–World War I world could give the impression that the old imperial nations, especially Britain and France, were more powerful than ever, but that impression would be superficial and misleading. The great Western European powers had paid an enormous price in lives, money, and will for their victory in the war. Colonial peoples pressed for the rights that the West proclaimed as universal but denied to their colonies, and some influential minorities in the countries that ruled those colonies sympathized with colonial aspirations for independence. Tension between colonies and their ruling nations was a cause of serious instability in the world the Paris treaties of 1919 created.

Evaluating the Peace

Few peace settlements have undergone more severe attacks than the one negotiated in Paris in 1919. It was natural that the defeated powers should object to it, but the peace soon came under bitter criticism in the victorious countries as well. Many of the French objected that the treaty tied French security to promises of aid from the unreliable Anglo-Saxon countries. In England and the United States, a wave of bitter criticism arose in liberal quarters because the treaty seemed to violate the idealistic and liberal aims that the Western leaders had professed.

The Economic Consequences of the Peace The most influential economic critic of the treaty was John Maynard Keynes (1883–1946). His book *The Economic Consequences of the Peace* (1920) was a scathing attack, especially on reparations and the other economic aspects of the peace. Keynes argued that the Treaty of Versailles was both immoral and unworkable. He argued it would bring economic ruin and war to Europe unless it was repudiated.

Keynes's argument had a great effect on the British, who were already suspicious of France and glad of an excuse to withdraw from continental affairs. The decent and respectable position came to be one that supported revision of the treaty in favor of Germany. In the United States, the book fed the traditional tendency toward isolationism and gave powerful weapons to Wilson's enemies. Wilson's own political mistakes helped prevent American ratification of the treaty. Thus, America was out of the League of Nations and not bound to defend France. Britain, therefore, was also free from its obligation to France. France was left to protect itself without adequate means to do so for long.

Many of the attacks on the Treaty of Versailles are unjustified. Germany was neither dismembered nor ruined. Reparations could be and were scaled down. Until the great world depression of the 1930s, the Germans recovered prosperity. Complaints against the peace should also be measured against the peace that the victorious Germans had imposed on Russia at Brest-Litovsk and their plans for a European settlement if they had won. Both were far more severe than anything enacted at Versailles. The attempt to achieve self-determination for nationalities was less than perfect, but it was the best effort Europe had ever made to do so.

Divisive New Boundaries and Tariff Walls The peace, nevertheless, was unsatisfactory in important ways. The elimination of the Austro-Hungarian Empire, however inevitable, created serious problems. Economically, it was disastrous. New borders and tariff walls separated raw materials from manufacturing areas and producers from their markets. In hard times, this separation created friction and hostility that aggravated other quarrels the peace treaties also created. Poland contained unhappy German, Lithuanian, and Ukrainian minorities, and Czechoslovakia and Yugoslavia were collections of nationalities that did not find it easy to live together. Territorial disputes in Eastern Europe promoted further tension.

Moreover, the peace rested on a victory that Germany did not admit. The Germans felt cheated rather than defeated. The high moral principles the Allies proclaimed undercut the validity of the peace, for it plainly fell far short of those principles.

Failure to Accept Reality Finally, the great weakness of the peace was its failure to accept reality. Germany and Russia must inevitably play an important part in European affairs, yet the settlement and the League of Nations excluded them. Given the many discontented parties, the peace was not self-enforcing, yet no satisfactory machinery to enforce it was established. The League of Nations was never a serious force for this purpose. It was left to France, with no guarantee of support from Britain and no hope of help from the United States, to defend the new arrangements. Finland, the Baltic states, Poland, Romania, Czechoslovakia, and Yugoslavia were expected to be a barrier to the westward expansion of Russian communism and to help deter a revival of German power. Most of these states, however, would have to rely on France in case of danger, and France was simply not strong enough to protect them if Germany revived.

The tragedy of the Treaty of Versailles was that it was neither conciliatory enough to remove the desire for revision, even at the cost of war, nor harsh enough to make another war impossible. The only hope for a lasting peace was that Germany would remain disarmed while the more obnoxious clauses of the peace treaty were revised. Such a policy required continued attention to the problem, unity among the victors, and farsighted leadership, but none of these was consistently present during the next two decades.

Summary

WHY DID the alliance system fail?

Emergence of the German Empire and the Alliance Systems (1873–1890) From 1871 until his dismissal by Kaiser William II in 1890, Bismarck acted as an "honest broker" for peace in Europe. He entered Germany into multiple alliances, some of them secret, in a successful effort to maintain a balance of power in Europe. Bismarck's system of alliances collapsed soon after he left office. Caprivi's incompetence and Kaiser William II's arrogance made an enemy of Britain, which proceeded to enter relationships with France and Russia, creating the Triple Entente. Germany's Triple Alliance (with Austria and Italy) was weak and unstable by comparison. *page 652*

HOW DID conflict in the Balkans lead to the outbreak of general war in Europe?

World War I The 1908 Bosnian crisis, the second Moroccan crisis in 1911, and the First and Second Balkan Wars solidified Europe's alliances and antagonisms and left many of the powers believing they could not afford to repeat various "mistakes" they had made in facing these crises. When the heir to the Austrian throne was assassinated in Sarajevo, Bosnia, Austria was determined to go to war with Serbia. As the crisis dragged on throughout the summer, all the other European powers came to feel they must go to war. Both the Triple Entente (Britain, France, and Russia) and the Central Powers (essentially, Austria and Germany) had reasonable expectations of quick victory. Both sides bungled their strategies, and neither side understood how to take the offensive against machine guns. The land war dragged on with massive casualties and minimal results. On the sea, Germany's fleet served little purpose except, eventually, to help bring the United States into the war against the Central Powers. U.S. entry into the war came only after the Russian Revolution had overthrown the tsar. *page 656*

WHAT FACTORS made the rise of the Bolshrviks to power in Russia possible?

The Russian Revolution The government of Nicholas II was incapable of managing a viable war effort. Nicholas II tried to deal with widespread discontent by adjourning parliament (the Duma) and ruling alone, but that strategy also failed. On March 15, 1917, Russia's last tsar abdicated. The Duma reconvened and formed a provisional government; the provisional government continued the war against Germany. Socialist factions formed *soviets*, councils of workers and soldiers; they did not support the provisional government. The Bolsheviks worked against the provisional government. The Germans helped Lenin get from his Swiss exile to Petrograd. The Bolsheviks attempted a coup in the summer of 1917. In November 1917, a second Bolshevik coup took control. The Bolsheviks nationalized land, factories, banks, and church property; they repudiated the tsarist government's debt; and they withdrew from the war. The Treaty of Brest-Litovsk imposed harsh terms on Russia, but Lenin had to sign. It took the Bolsheviks until 1921 to overcome domestic resistance and a civil war against the White Russians. *page 666*

WHAT WERE the immediate consequences of the end of World War I?

The End of World War I German victory on the eastern front was balanced by the U.S. entry into the war. Germany's last offensive was a fiasco. Kaiser William II abdicated on November 9, 1918, and a republican, socialist-led government signed the armistice on November 11. Most Germans, however, had been prevented from learning the extent of the German army's losses, so the terms of the peace settlement came as an unpleasant surprise; later, the political myth that leftists at home had betrayed the nation became a rallying cry for the right. The Great War was over, at a cost of millions of soldiers' lives and millions of civilians' lives. Europe was transformed forever: The German, Austro-Hungarian, Russian, and Ottoman Empires were all dissolved; the United States became a factor in European affairs; and the nineteenth-century belief in the inevitability of progress was shattered. The Ottoman Empire was dismembered by a treaty between Turkey and the Allies in 1920. Britain and France controlled swaths of the Arab world; Ataturk established the independent republic of Turkey in 1923. *page 668*

WHAT WERE the key weaknesses of the Paris peace settlement?

The Settlement at Paris The Treaty of Versailles was a failure because it was not mild enough to win long-term acceptance by all parties, but it was also not harsh enough to make another war impossible. The victorious Big Four represented constitutional democracies and had to respond to public opinion. In Europe, nationalism reached the status of a secular religion, and Wilson's Fourteen Points had raised unrealistically idealistic expectations; a comprehensive resolution of Europe's nationalist controversies was impossible. Previous agreements and secret treaties could not all be honored and were sometimes mutually exclusive. All the powers feared the spread of communism; France in particular feared a rearmed Germany. The League of Nations was meant to remedy the inevitable shortcomings of the peace settlement, but it had no military power to back claims; when the United States failed to ratify the treaty, it also destroyed the league's viability. The most problematic aspect of the treaty was the harshness of its terms toward Germany. The exclusion of Russia from the settlement and the League of Nations reflected a Big Four failure to face realities of European politics. *page 670*

REVIEW QUESTIONS

1. To what areas of the world did Europe extend its power after 1870? How did the New Imperialism (after 1870) compare with previous imperialistic movements? What role in the world did Bismarck envision for the new Germany after 1871? What was Bismarck's attitude toward colonies?
2. Why, at the turn of the century, did Britain abandon its policy of "splendid isolation"? How did developments in the Balkans lead to the outbreak of World War I? Did Germany want a general war?
3. Why did Germany lose World War I? What were the benefits and drawbacks of the Treaty of Versailles? Could it have secured lasting peace in Europe?
4. How did Lenin establish the Bolsheviks in control of Russia? What role did Trotsky play?

KEY TERMS

Fourteen Points (p. 668)

mandate (p. 670)

For additional learning resources related to this chapter, please go to **www.myhistorylab.com**

PEARSON myhistorylab

27

The Interwar Years: The Challenge of Dictators and Depression

Poster concerning the First Five-Year Plan (1928–1932) with a photograph of Joseph Stalin (1879–1953). The poster declares: "By the end of the Five-Year Plan, the basis of the USSR's collectivization must be completed."

1932 (color litho) by Klutchis (fl. 1932). Deutsches Plakat Museum, Essen, Germany/Archives Charmet/The Bridgeman Art Library

How did Soviet economic policy under Stalin change Soviet society?

During the two decades that followed the Paris settlement, Europe saw bold experiments in politics and economic life. Two broad sets of factors accounted for these experiments. First, the war, the Russian Revolution, and the peace treaty had transformed the political face of Europe. New political regimes had emerged in the wake of the collapse of the monarchies of Germany, Austria-Hungary, and Russia. These new governments immediately faced the problems of postwar reconstruction, economic dislocation, and nationalistic resentment. Most of these nations also included large groups who questioned the legitimacy of their governments. All the governments and societies of both Western and Eastern Europe believed themselves profoundly threatened by the Soviet Union.

Second, beginning in the early twenties, economic dislocations that led to the economic downturn that became known as the Great Depression began to spread across the world. The Great Depression itself, which began in 1929, was the most severe downturn capitalist economies had ever experienced. Business and political leaders despaired over the market's seeming inability to resolve the crisis. Marxists and, indeed, many other observers thought the final downfall of capitalism was at hand.

European voters looked for new ways out of the doldrums, and politicians sought to escape the pressures that the depression had brought on them. One result of the fight for economic security was the establishment of the Nazi dictatorship in Germany. Another was the piecemeal construction of what became known as the mixed economy; that is, governments became directly involved in making economic decisions alongside business and labor. In both cases, most of the political and economic guidelines of nineteenth-century liberalism were abandoned, and so were decency and civility in political life. Authoritarianism and aggression were not the inescapable destiny of Europe. They emerged from the failure to secure alternative modes of democratic political life and stable international relations and from the inability to achieve long-term economic prosperity. ■

AFTER VERSAILLES: DEMANDS FOR REVISION AND ENFORCEMENT

WHY DID the Paris settlement fail to bring peace and prosperity to Europe?

The Paris settlement fostered both resentments and discontent. Those resentments counted among the chief political factors in Europe for the next two decades. Germany had been humiliated. The arrangements for reparations led to endless haggling over payments. Many national groups in the successor states of the Austro-Hungarian Empire felt that their rights to self-determination had been violated or ignored. There were strident demands for further border adjustments because significant national minorities, particularly Germans and Magyars, resided outside the national boundaries drawn in Paris. On the other side, the victorious powers, especially France, often believed that the provisions of the treaties were being inadequately enforced. Consequently, throughout the 1920s and into the 1930s, demands either to revise or to enforce the Paris treaties contributed to domestic political turmoil across the Continent.

TOWARD THE GREAT DEPRESSION IN EUROPE

WHAT KEY factors combined to produce the Great Depression?

Along with the move toward political experimentation and the demands for revision of the new international order, there was a widespread yearning to return to the economic prosperity of the prewar years. Unfortunately, during the Great War, Europeans had turned the military and industrial power that they had created during the previous

TABLE 27–1 Total Casualties in the First World War

Country	Dead	Wounded	Total Killed as a Percentage of Population (%)
FRANCE	1,398,000	2,000,000	3.4
BELGIUM	38,000	44,700	0.5
ITALY	578,000	947,000	1.6
BRITISH EMPIRE	921,000	2,090,000	1.7
ROMANIA	250,000	120,000	3.3
SERBIA	278,000	133,000	5.7
GREECE	26,000	21,000	0.5
RUSSIA	1,811,000	1,450,000	1.1
BULGARIA	88,000	152,000	1.9
GERMANY	2,037,000	4,207,000	3.0
AUSTRIA-HUNGARY	1,100,000	3,620,000	1.9
TURKEY	804,000	400,000	3.7
UNITED STATES	114,000	206,000	0.1

Source: Niall Ferguson, *The Pity of War* (New York: Basic Books, 1998).

century against themselves. What had been "normal" in economic and social life before 1914 could not be reestablished.

The casualties from the war numbered in the millions. (See Table 27–1.) This represented not only a waste of human life and talent, but also the loss of producers and consumers.

Three factors originating in the 1920s combined to bring about the intense severity and the extended length of the **Great Depression**. First, a financial crisis stemmed directly from the war and the peace settlement. To this was added a crisis in the production and distribution of goods in the world market. Finally, both of these difficulties became worse than they might have been because no major Western European country or the United States provided strong, responsible economic leadership that might have resulted in some form of cooperation to face the challenge of the depression.

Great Depression A prolonged worldwide economic downturn that began in 1929 with the collapse of the New York Stock Exchange.

Financial Tailspin

As one of the chief victors in the war, France was determined to collect reparations from Germany for the destruction the war had caused in northern France. The United States was no less determined that its allies repay the money it had lent them during the war. The European allies also owed debts to each other. German reparations were to provide the means of repaying all these debts. Most of the money that the Allies collected from each other also went to the United States.

The quest for payment of German reparations caused one of the major diplomatic crises of the 1920s; that crisis itself resulted in further economic upheaval. In early 1923, the Allies—France in particular—declared Germany to be in technical default of its reparation payments. On January 11, to ensure receipt of the hard-won reparations, French and Belgian troops occupied the Ruhr mining and manufacturing district.

The French invasion of the German Ruhr began a crisis that brought strikes and rampant inflation in Germany. Here French troops have commandeered a German locomotive during one of the strikes.

UPI/Corbis/BETTMANN

What explains France's aggressive policy toward Germany in the years following the war?

The **Weimar Republic** ordered passive resistance that amounted to a general strike in Germany's largest industrial region. Confronted with this tactic, the French sent technicians and engineers to run the German mines and railroads. France got its way. The Germans paid, but its victory cost France dearly. The British were alienated by the French heavy-handedness and took no part in the occupation. The cost of the Ruhr occupation, moreover, vastly increased French as well as German inflation and damaged the French economy.

The political and economic turmoil of the Ruhr invasion led to international attempts to ease the German payment of reparations. At the same time, American investment capital was pouring into Europe. However, by 1928 this investment decreased as American money became diverted into the booming New York stock market. The crash of Wall Street in October 1929—the result of virtually unregulated financial speculation—saw the loss of large amounts of money. Credit sharply contracted in the United States as numerous banks failed. Thereafter, little American capital was available for investment in Europe.

Weimar Republic German republic that came to power in 1918 embodying the hopes of German liberals.

As American credit for Europe began to run out, a major financial crisis struck the Continent. U.S. president Herbert Hoover (1874–1964) announced in June 1931 a one-year moratorium on all payments of international debts. The Hoover moratorium was a prelude to the end of reparations. The Lausanne Conference in the summer of 1932 brought, in effect, the era of reparations to a close. The next year the debts owed to the United States were settled either through small token payments or simply through default.

Problems in Agricultural Commodities

In the 1920s the market demand for European goods shrank, leaving much of the Continent's productive capacity idle or underused. This problem originated both within and outside Europe. In both instances the difficulty arose from agriculture. Vast increases in the quantity of grain farmers around the world produced led to record low prices. Although this helped consumers, it decreased the income of European farmers. At the same time, higher industrial wages raised the cost of the industrial goods that farmers or peasants used. These problems were especially acute in central and eastern Europe and increased farmers' disillusionment with liberal politics.

Outside Europe similar problems affected other producers of agricultural commodities, such as coffee, sugar, and wheat. As supply outstripped demand, the prices they received for their products plummeted. The people who produced these goods in underdeveloped nations could no longer make enough money to buy goods from industrial Europe. As world credit collapsed, the economic position of these commodity producers worsened.

The results of the collapse in the agricultural sector of the world economy and the financial turmoil were stagnation and depression for European industry. Coal, iron, and textiles had depended largely on international markets. Unemployment spread from these industries to those producing consumer goods. The policies of reduced spending with which the governments confronted the Depression further weakened domestic demand. By the early 1930s the Depression was feeding on itself.

Depression and Government Policy in Britain and France

The depression did not mean absolute economic decline or total unemployment. But the economic downturn spread potential as well as actual insecurity. People in nearly all walks of life feared the loss of their economic security. The depression also frustrated normal social and economic expectations. Even the employed often seemed to make no progress, and their anxieties created a major source of discontent.

The governments of the late 1920s and the early 1930s were not well suited in either structure or ideology to confront these problems. The electorates demanded action. The governments' responses depended largely on the severity of the depression in a particular country and on the self-confidence of the nation's political system.

Great Britain and France, which because of their vast empires commanded very large economies, undertook moderate political experiments. Under the pressure of the depression and at the urging of King George V (r. 1910–1936), the Labour prime minister Ramsay MacDonald (1866–1937) organized a National Government, which was a coalition of the Labour, Conservative, and Liberal Parties.

The 1920s also saw the establishment of an independent Irish state. On Easter Monday in April 1916, a nationalist uprising occurred in Dublin. The British suppressed the rising but made martyrs of its leaders by executing several of them. Leadership of the nationalist cause quickly shifted from the Irish Party in Parliament to the extremist Sinn Fein, or "Ourselves Alone," movement. On January 21, 1919, they declared Irish independence. Thereafter a civil war broke out between the military wing of Sinn Fein, which became the Irish Republican Army (IRA), and the British army. The conflict ended with a treaty in December 1921, which established the Irish Free State as one of the dominions in the British Commonwealth. The six, predominately Protestant, counties of Ulster, or Northern Ireland, were permitted to remain part of what was now called

Overview Capitalist, Fascist, and Communist Economic Systems

CAPITALISM	• Private ownership of the means of production • Personal profit can be acquired through investment of capital • Limited government intervention in the economy • Free market, based on supply and demand
FASCISM	• Seeks to steer a course between socialism and a liberal laissez-faire system • Corporatism organizes major industries as syndicates of labor and management • Subsidized shipping and protective tariffs are among efforts to become self-sufficient
COMMUNISM	• Central planning sets goals for production and coordinates manufacturing • Focuses on development of heavy industries and infrastructure, not consumer goods • Strictly controlled labor force

the United Kingdom of Great Britain and Northern Ireland, with provisions for home rule. In the 1920s and 1930s, the Free State gradually severed its ties to Britain and declared itself an independent republic in 1949.

Popular Front A government of all left-wing parties that took power in France in 1936 to enact social and economic reforms.

The most important French interwar political experiment was the **Popular Front** Ministry, which came to office in 1936. It was composed of Socialists, Radicals, and Communists. Despite fierce resistance from business and conservative groups, the Popular Front enacted major social and economic reforms, but its parliamentary support gradually faded until its final collapse in October 1938.

THE SOVIET EXPERIMENT

WHAT WAS the relationship between politics and economics in the early decades of the Soviet Union?

The consolidation of the Bolshevik Revolution in Russia established the most extensive and durable of all twentieth-century authoritarian governments. The Communist Party of the Soviet Union retained power from 1917 until the end of 1991, and its presence influenced the political history of Europe and much of the rest of the world, as did no other single factor. (See "Compare & Connect: The Soviets and the Nazis Confront the Issues of Women and the Family," pages 702–703.)

WAR COMMUNISM

Within the Soviet Union the Red Army under the organizational genius of Leon Trotsky (1879–1940) had suppressed internal and foreign military opposition to the new government during the civil war that raged from 1918 to 1920. Within months of the revolution, a new secret police, known as *Cheka*, appeared. Political and economic administration became highly centralized. All major decisions flowed from the top in a nondemocratic manner. Under the economic policy of **"War Communism,"** the revolutionary government confiscated and then operated the banks, the transport facilities, and heavy industry. The state also forcibly requisitioned grain and shipped it from the countryside to feed the army and the urban workers. The Bolsheviks used the need to fight the civil war as justification for suppressing any resistance to these economic policies.

War Communism The economic policy adopted by the Bolsheviks during the Russian Civil War to seize the banks, heavy industry, railroads, and grain.

War Communism helped the Red Army defeat its opponents. The policy, however, generated domestic opposition to the Bolsheviks, who in 1920 numbered only about 600,000. The alliance of workers and peasants forged in 1917 by the Bolsheviks' slogan of "Peace, Bread, and Land" had begun to dissolve. Many Russians were no longer willing to make the sacrifices demanded by the central party bureaucrats. In 1920 and 1921 serious strikes occurred. Peasants were discontented and resisted the requisition of grain. In March 1921 the sailors mutinied at the Kronstadt naval base on the Baltic. The Red Army crushed the rebellion with grave loss of life. Also, by late 1920 it had become clear that revolution was not going to sweep across the rest of Europe.

THE NEW ECONOMIC POLICY

New Economic Policy (NEP) A limited revival of capitalism, especially in light industry and agriculture, introduced by Lenin in 1921 to repair the damage inflicted on the Russian economy by the civil war and War Communism.

Under these difficult conditions Lenin made a strategic retreat. In March 1921, following the Kronstadt mutiny, he outlined the **New Economic Policy**, or NEP. Apart from banking, heavy industry, transportation, and international commerce, considerable private economic enterprise was allowed. In particular, peasants could farm for a profit. They would pay taxes like other citizens, but they could sell their surplus grain on the open market. The NEP was consistent with Lenin's earlier conviction that the Russian peasantry held the key to the success of the revolution. After 1921 the countryside did

become more stable, and a secure food supply seemed assured for the cities. Similar free enterprise flourished within light industry and the domestic retail trade. By 1927 industrial production had reached its 1913 level. The revolution seemed to have transformed Russia into a land of small farms and privately owned shops and businesses.

Anxiety over the spread of the Bolshevik revolution was a fundamental factor of European politics during the 1920s and 1930s. Images like this Soviet portrait of Lenin as a heroic revolutionary conjured fears among people in the rest of Europe of a political force determined to overturn their social, political, and economic institutions.

Bildarchiv Preussischer Kulturbesitz

What was this image meant to convey about Lenin's role in the Russian Revolution?

THE THIRD INTERNATIONAL

The onset and consolidation of the Bolshevik revolution in Russia was a transforming event for the history of socialism as well as for Russia and international affairs. In the West, before the war, as discussed in Chapter 23, social democratic parties had regarded the Russian Bolsheviks as eccentric, politically marginal Marxist extremists. The Bolshevik victory forced West European social democrats to rethink their position within the world of international socialism. For their part, the Bolsheviks intended to establish themselves as the international leaders of Marxism and regarded reformist social democrats as enemies and rivals.

In 1919, the Soviet communists founded the Third International of the European socialist movement, better known as the *Comintern*. The Comintern worked to make the Bolshevik model of socialism, as Lenin had developed it, the rule for all socialist parties outside the Soviet Union. In 1920, the Comintern imposed its Twenty-one Conditions on any socialist party that wished to join it. These conditions included acknowledging Moscow's leadership, rejecting reformist or revisionist socialism, repudiating previous socialist leaders, and adopting the Communist Party name. The decision whether to accept these conditions split every major European socialist party. As a result, separate communist and social democratic parties emerged in most countries and fought each other more intensely than they fought either capitalism or conservative political parties.

These Comintern polices and the resulting divisions of the socialist parties directly affected the rise of the fascists and the Nazis in Western Europe. It is difficult to overestimate the fears that Soviet political rhetoric and Communist Party activity aroused in Europe during the 1920s and 1930s. Conservative and right-wing political groups manipulated and exaggerated these fears. The presence of separate communist parties in Western Europe meant that right-wing politicians always had a convenient target they could justly accuse of seeking to overthrow the government and to impose Soviet-style political, social, and economic systems in their nations. Furthermore, right-wing politicians also accused the democratic socialists of supporting policies that might facilitate a communist takeover. The divisions between Communists and democratic socialists also meant that right-wing political movements rarely had to confront a united left.

Stalin Versus Trotsky

The NEP had caused sharp disputes within the Politburo, the highest governing committee of the Communist Party. These frictions increased as Lenin's firm hand disappeared. In 1922 he suffered a stroke and never again dominated party affairs; in 1924 he died. In the ensuing power vacuum, an intense struggle for leadership of the party commenced. Two factions emerged. One was led by Trotsky; the other by Joseph Stalin (1879–1953), who had become general secretary of the party in 1922.

Trotsky, speaking for what became known as the left wing, urged rapid industrialization and looked to voluntary collectivization of farming by poor peasants as a means of increasing agricultural production. He further argued that the revolution in Russia could succeed only if new revolutions took place elsewhere. A right-wing faction led by Stalin opposed Trotsky. In the mid-1920s this group pressed for the continuation of Lenin's NEP and relatively slow industrialization.

In 1924 Stalin enunciated, in opposition to Trotsky, the doctrine of "socialism in one country." He urged that socialism could be achieved in Russia alone. Russian success did not depend on the fate of the revolution elsewhere. Stalin thus nationalized the previously international scope of the Marxist revolution. He cunningly used the apparatus of the party and his control over its Central Committee to edge out Trotsky and his supporters. By 1927 Trotsky had been removed from all his offices, ousted from the party, and exiled to Siberia. In 1929 he was expelled from Russia and eventually moved to Mexico, where he was murdered in 1940 by one of Stalin's agents. With the removal of Trotsky, Stalin was firmly in control of the Soviet state.

QUICK REVIEW

Stalin's Rise to Power

- Sided with the opposition to Trotsky in the 1920s
- Used control of the Central Committee to marginalize Trotsky and his supporters
- Emerged from struggle with Trotsky with unchallenged control of the Soviet state

The Decision for Rapid Industrialization

In 1927 the Party Congress decided to push for rapid industrialization, a sharp departure from the NEP and a rejection of the pockets of relatively free-market operations within the larger Soviet economy. Stalin's goal was to have the Soviet Union overtake the productive capacity of its enemies, the capitalist nations. This policy required the rapid construction of heavy industries, such as iron, steel, and machine-tool making, building electricity-generating stations, and manufacturing tractors. Stalin's organizational vehicle for industrialization was a series of five-year plans, starting in 1928. The State Planning Commission, or *Gosplan*, set goals for production in every area of economic life and attempted to organize the economy to meet them. The task of coordinating all facets of production was immensely complicated and enormous economic disruption occurred as the *Gosplan* built power plants and steel mills and increased the output of mines. The plans consistently favored capital projects over the production of consumer goods. The number of centralized agencies and ministries involved in planning soared, and they often competed with each other.

The rapid expansion of the industrial base created the first genuinely large factory labor force in what had been Russia. Workers were recruited from the countryside and from the urban unemployed. New cities and industrial districts in existing cities arose. Most workers were crowded into shoddy buildings with inadequate sanitation, living space, and nourishment. The results, however, were impressive. Soviet industrial production rose approximately 400 percent between 1928 and 1940. Industries that had never existed in Russia challenged their foreign counterparts. Hundreds of thousands of people populated new industrial cities. The social and human cost of this effort had, however, been appalling.

Magnitogorsk was a city that became a monument to Stalin's drive toward rapid industrialization. Located in the Ural Mountains near a vast supply of iron ore, the city became the site of major iron and steel production. It was one of the new industrial cities founded under the Five-Year Plans designed to challenge the capitalist production of the Western nations.

National Archives and Records Administration

Why was the creation of heavy industry so important to Stalin?

The Collectivization of Agriculture

Agricultural productivity had always been a core problem for the emerging Soviet economy. Under the NEP, the government purchased a certain amount of grain at prices it set itself. The rest of the grain was then supposed to be sold at market prices, which were higher than the government-set prices. Many peasant farmers of all degrees of wealth tried to circumvent this system, often by keeping grain off the market in hopes that its price would rise. The scarcity of consumer goods available for purchase in the countryside also encouraged hoarding. With little to buy from what they earned by selling their grain, farmers had little incentive to sell it. In 1928 and 1929, as a result of peasants hoarding their grains for better prices, the Soviet government confronted shortfalls of grain on the market and the prospect of food shortages in the cities and social unrest.

Stalin therefore decided to reverse the agricultural policies of the NEP. Stalin decided that Soviet agriculture must be collectivized to produce enough grain for domestic food and foreign export. **Collectivization**—the replacement of private peasant farms with huge state-run and state-owned farms called collectives—would also put the Communist Party firmly in control of the farm sector of the economy and free up peasant labor to work in the expanding industrial sector. To carry out this policy, Stalin portrayed the *kulaks*, the small group of relatively prosperous peasants, as the fundamental cause of the agricultural problems.

Collectivization The bedrock of Stalinist agriculture, which forced Russian peasants to give up their private farms and work as members of collectives, large agricultural units controlled by the state.

Stalin used intimidation and propaganda to support his drive to collectivize Soviet agriculture. Communist Party agitators led groups of peasants, such as these shown above, to demand the seizure of the farms worked by the better-off and more successful farmers known as *kulaks*.

AP/Wide World Photos

Who resisted collectivization? Why?

Party officials with troops at their command carried out the initial campaign of dekulakization and collectivization. Usually they would seek first to remove *kulaks* from a village while confiscating their land and would then attempt to coerce the remaining peasants into organizing a collective farm. Enormous turmoil and violence resulted. Peasants who resisted were killed outright. Others starved to death on their own farms when all the grain that they had produced was seized. Over 2 million peasants were forcibly removed from their homes and deported to distant areas of the Soviet Union or to prison camps where many died from disease, exposure, and malnutrition. Much of the violence of collectivization occurred in Ukraine, where Stalin used the process not only to restructure agricultural production but also to crush any vestiges of Ukrainian nationalism, and many millions of lives were lost as a result.

By 1937, over 90 percent of Soviet grain production had been collectivized. At the cost of millions of peasant lives, Stalin and the Communist Party had won the battle of the grain fields, but they had not solved the problem of producing enough food. That difficulty would plague the Soviet Union until its collapse in 1991 and remains a problem for its successor states.

QUICK REVIEW

Collectivization

- 1929: Stalin orders collectivization of Soviet agriculture
- Stalin responded to resistance by targeting *kulaks* for elimination
- Collectivization failed to solve the Soviet Union's food supply problem

THE PURGES

In 1933, with turmoil in the countryside and economic dislocation caused by industrialization, Stalin and others in the central Soviet bureaucracy began to fear they were losing control of the country and the party apparatus and that effective rivals to their power and policies might emerge. These apprehensions were largely a figment of Stalin's own paranoia and lust for power, but they resulted in the **Great Purges**.

Great Purges The arrests, trials, Communist Party expulsions, and executions—beginning with the assassination of Politburo member Sergei Kirov in December 1934—that mainly targeted party officials and reached its climax from 1936 to 1938.

The pretext for the onset of the purges was the assassination on December 1, 1934, of Sergei Kirov (1888–1934), the popular party chief of Leningrad and a member of the Politburo. In the wake of the shooting, thousands of people were arrested, and still more were expelled from the party and sent to labor camps. Today, many scholars believe that Stalin himself authorized Kirov's assassination because he was afraid of him. The available documentary evidence does not allow us to know for sure whether Stalin was involved, but he quickly used Kirov's death for his own purposes.

The purges that took place immediately after Kirov's death were just the beginning of a larger and longer process. Between 1936 and 1938, a series of spectacular show trials were held in Moscow. Former high Soviet leaders, including members of the Politburo, publicly confessed to political crimes and were convicted and executed. Other lower-level party members were tried in private and shot. Hundreds of thousands, perhaps millions, of ordinary Soviet citizens received no trial at all and were either executed or deported to slave labor camps where many died. Within the party itself, thousands of members were expelled, and applicants for membership were removed from the rolls. After the civilian party members and leaders had been purged, the prosecutors turned against the government bureaucracy and the Soviet army and navy, convicting and executing thousands of officials and officers, including heroes of the civil war. The exact number of executions, imprisonments, interrogations, and expulsions is unknown, but ran well into the millions. While the purges went on, no one in the Soviet Union, except Stalin himself, was safe.

The rational explanations of the purges—to the extent that mass murder can ever be rationally explained—probably lie in two directions. First, over the several years the purges lasted, different portions of the party leadership moved against others. Initially, Stalin and the central Moscow leadership used the purges to settle old scores and to discipline and gain more control over lower levels of the party in the far-flung regions of the Soviet Union. In addition to increasing Stalin's authority, these central bureaucratic groups wanted to eliminate any opposition to their own positions or policies. By 1937, however, Stalin seems to have become distrustful of the central party elite, his own supporters, and began to find or pretend to find enemies within its ranks. Moreover, by that date, local communist groups were allowed to designate their own victims with little direction from Moscow. Thereafter, a self-destructive cascade of accusations, imprisonments, and executions occurred throughout the party and within its highest levels.

Second, no matter how much tension and rivalry there were among the different levels and regions of the Communist Party, Stalin's primary motive in the purges was almost certainly fear for his own power and a ruthless determination to preserve and increase it. In effect, the purges created a new Communist Party that was absolutely subservient and loyal to Stalin. New, younger recruits replaced the party members who were executed or expelled. The newcomers knew little about old Russia or the ideals of the original Bolsheviks. They had not been loyal to Lenin, Trotsky, or any other Soviet leader, except Stalin himself.

The internal difficulties collectivization and industrialization and his worries about internal opposition caused led Stalin to make an important shift in foreign policy. In 1934, he began to fear the nation might be left isolated against aggression by Nazi Germany. The Soviet Union was not yet strong enough to withstand such an attack. So that year he ordered the Comintern to permit communist parties in other countries to cooperate with noncommunist parties against Nazism and fascism. This reversed the Comintern policy Lenin established as part of the Twenty-one Conditions in 1919. The new Stalinist policy allowed the Popular Front government in France to come to power.

THE FASCIST EXPERIMENT IN ITALY

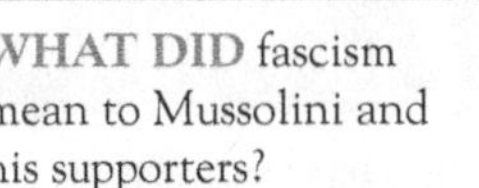

WHAT DID fascism mean to Mussolini and his supporters?

The first authoritarian political experiment in Western Europe that arose in part from fears of the spread of Bolshevism beyond the Soviet Union occurred in Italy. The general term *fascist*, which has been used to describe the various right-wing dictatorships that arose between the wars, was derived from the Italian Fascist movement of Benito Mussolini (1883–1945).

fascism System of extreme right-wing dictatorial government.

While scholars still dispute the exact meaning of ***fascism*** as a political term, the governments regarded as fascist were antidemocratic, anti-Marxist, antiparliamentary, and frequently anti-Semitic. They wanted to overcome the class conflict of Marxism and the party conflict of liberalism by consolidating the various groups and classes within the nation for great national purposes. Fascist governments were usually single-party dictatorships characterized by terrorism against, and police surveillance of, both opponents and the general citizenry. These dictatorships were rooted in the base of mass political parties.

The Rise of Mussolini

The Italian *Fasci di Combattimento* ("Band of Combat") was founded in 1919 in Milan. Most of its members were war veterans who felt that the sacrifices Italy had made in World War I had not been rewarded at the Paris conference. They feared socialism, inflation, and labor unrest. In 1919, their leader or ***Duce***, Benito Mussolini, was just another Italian politician. His *Fasci* organization was one of many small political groups in a country characterized by such entities. As a politician, Mussolini was an opportunist par excellence. He could change his ideas and principles to suit every new occasion. Action for him was always more important than thought or rational justification. His one real rule was political survival.

Duce (DO-chay) Meaning "leader." Mussolini's title as head of the Fascist Party.

Postwar Italian politics was a muddle. Many Italians were dissatisfied with the parliamentary system as it then existed. They felt that Italy had emerged from the war as less than a victorious nation, had not been treated as a great power at the peace conference, and had not received the rewards it deserved. Between 1919 and 1921 Italy was also wracked by social turmoil. Numerous industrial strikes occurred, and workers occupied factories. Peasants seized uncultivated land from large estates. Parliamentary and constitutional government seemed incapable of dealing with this unrest.

Benito Mussolini became famous for bombastic public speeches delivered in settings surrounded by his fascist followers and military supporters.

AP Wide World Photos

How did Mussolini use public spectacles to shape his public image?

Initially, Mussolini was uncertain which way the political winds were blowing. He first supported the factory occupations and land seizures. Never one to be concerned with consistency, however, he soon reversed himself. He had discovered that many upper- and middle-class Italians who were hurt by inflation and who feared the loss of their property had no sympathy for the workers or the peasants. They wanted order rather than some vague social justice that might harm their own interests. Consequently, Mussolini and his Fascists took direct action in the face of the government's inaction. They formed local squads who terrorized Socialists. They attacked strikers and farm workers and protected strikebreakers. Conservative land and factory owners were grateful to the terrorists. The officers of the law simply ignored these crimes. By early 1922 the Fascists controlled local government in many parts of northern Italy.

In 1921 Mussolini and thirty-four of his followers had been elected to the Chamber of Deputies. Their importance grew as the local Fascists gained more direct power. The Fascist movement now had hundreds of thousands of supporters. In October 1922 the Fascists, dressed in their characteristic black shirts, began a march on Rome. Intimidated, King Victor Emmanuel III (r. 1900–1946) refused to authorize using the army against the marchers. No other single decision so ensured a Fascist seizure of power. The cabinet resigned in protest. On October 29, the monarch telegraphed Mussolini in Milan and asked him to become prime minister.

QUICK REVIEW

Mussolini's Rise to Power

- Motivated by the desire for power rather than by ideology
- Postwar political and economic turmoil provided environment for rise of fascists
- October 1922: Black Shirts march on Rome intimidates king into asking Mussolini to become prime minister

The Fascists in Power

Mussolini had not really expected to be appointed prime minister. He moved cautiously to consolidate his power. He succeeded because of the impotence of his rivals, his effective use of his office, his power over the masses, and his sheer ruthlessness. On November 23, 1922, the king and Parliament granted Mussolini dictatorial authority for one year to bring order to the lower levels of the government. Wherever possible, Mussolini appointed Fascists to office. Late in 1924, at Mussolini's behest, Parliament changed the election law. Previously parties had been represented in the Chamber of Deputies in proportion to the popular vote cast for them. According to the new election law, the party that gained the largest popular vote (with a minimum of at least 25 percent) received two-thirds of the seats in the chamber. Coalition government, with all its compromises and hesitations, would no longer be necessary. In the election of 1924 the Fascists won a great victory and complete control of the Chamber of Deputies. They used that majority to end legitimate parliamentary life. A series of laws passed in 1925 and 1926 permitted Mussolini, in effect, to rule by decree. In 1926 all other political parties were dissolved, and Italy was transformed into a single-party, dictatorial state.

The Italian dictator made one important domestic departure that brought him significant political dividends. Through the Lateran Accord he signed with the Vatican in February 1929, the Roman Catholic Church and the Italian state made peace with each other. Ever since the armies of Italian unification had seized papal lands in the 1860s, the church had been hostile to the state. The agreement of 1929 recognized the pope as the temporal ruler of the ministate of Vatican City. The Italian government agreed to pay an indemnity to the papacy for confiscated land. The state also recognized Catholicism as the religion of the nation, exempted church property from taxes, and allowed church law to govern marriage. The Lateran Accord brought further respectability to Mussolini's authoritarian regime.

GERMAN DEMOCRACY AND DICTATORSHIP

WHY DID democracy fail to thrive in postwar Germany?

The Weimar Republic

The Weimar Republic was born from the defeat of the imperial army, the revolution of 1918 against the Hohenzollerns, and the hopes of German Liberals and Social Democrats. Its name derived from the city in which its constitution was written and promulgated in August 1919. While the constitution was being debated, the republic, headed by the Social Democrats, accepted the humiliating terms of the Versailles Treaty. Although its officials had signed only under the threat of an Allied invasion, the republic was nevertheless permanently associated with the national disgrace and the economic burdens of the treaty. In Germany, more than in other countries, the desire to revise the treaty was closely related to a desire to change the mode of domestic government.

In 1923, Germany suffered from cataclysmic inflation. Paper money became worthless and people used it as fuel for kitchen stoves.

Library of Congress

What were the consequences of hyperinflation in Germany?

The new government suffered major and minor humiliations as well as considerable economic instability. In March 1920, the right-wing Kapp Putsch, or armed insurrection, erupted in Berlin. Led by a conservative civil servant and supported by army officers, the attempted coup failed, but only after government officials had fled the city and workers had carried out a general strike. In the same month, strikes took place in the Ruhr mining district. The government sent in troops. Such extremism from both the left and the right would haunt the republic for all its days. In May 1921, the Allies presented a reparations bill for 132 billion gold marks. The German Republican government accepted this preposterous demand only after new Allied threats of occupation. Throughout the early 1920s there were numerous assassinations or attempted assassinations of important Republican leaders. Violence was the hallmark of the first five years of the republic.

Invasion of the Ruhr and Inflation Inflation brought on the major crisis of this period. The financing of the war and continued postwar deficit spending generated an immense rise in prices. Consequently, the value of German currency fell. By early 1921 the German mark traded against the American dollar at a ratio of 64 to 1, compared with a ratio of 4.2 to 1 in 1914. The German financial community contended that the value of the currency could not be stabilized until the reparations issue had been solved. In the meantime, the printing presses kept pouring forth paper money, which was used to redeem government bonds as they fell due.

The French invasion of the Ruhr in January 1923, to secure the payment of reparations, and the German response of passive economic resistance produced cataclysmic inflation. The Weimar government paid subsidies to the Ruhr labor force, who had laid down their tools. Unemployment soon spread from the Ruhr to other parts of the country, creating a new drain on the treasury and also reducing tax revenues. The printing presses by this point had difficulty providing enough paper currency to keep up with the daily rise in prices. Money was literally not worth the paper it was printed on.

Middle-class savings, pensions, and insurance policies were wiped out, as were investments in government bonds. Simultaneously, debts and mortgages could not be paid off. To the middle and lower-middle classes, the inflation was another trauma coming hard on the heels of the military defeat and the peace treaty. Only when the social and economic upheaval of these months is grasped can one understand the German desire for order and security at almost any cost.

Hitler's Early Career Late in 1923 Adolf Hitler (1889–1945) made his first significant appearance on the German political scene. The son of a minor Austrian customs official, he had gone to Vienna, where his hopes of gaining admission to an elite art school were soon dashed. Hitler absorbed the rabid German nationalism and extreme anti-Semitism that flourished in Vienna. He came to hate Marxism, which he associated with Jews. During World War I Hitler fought in the German army, was wounded, rose to the rank of corporal, and won the Iron Cross for bravery. The war gave him his first sense of purpose.

After the conflict, Hitler settled in Munich. He soon became associated with a small nationalistic, anti-Semitic political party that in 1920 adopted the name of National Socialist German Workers Party, better known simply as the **Nazis**. It issued a platform, or program, of Twenty-Five Points. Among other things, this platform called for the repudiation of the Versailles Treaty, the unification of Austria and Germany, the exclusion of Jews from German citizenship, agrarian reform, the prohibition of land speculation, the confiscation of war profits, state administration of the giant cartels, and the replacement of department stores with small retail shops.

Nazis Members of the National Socialist German Workers' Party that formed in 1920 and supported a mythical Aryan race alleged to be the source of the purest German lineage.

The "socialism" that Hitler and the Nazis had in mind was not state ownership of the means of production, but the subordination of all economic enterprise to the welfare of the nation. It often implied protection for small economic enterprises. Increasingly, the Nazis discovered their party appealed to virtually any economic group that was at risk and under pressure. They often tailored their messages to the particular local problems these groups confronted in different parts of Germany. The Nazis also found considerable support among war veterans, who faced economic and social displacement in Weimar society.

Soon after the promulgation of the Twenty-Five Points, the storm troopers, or **SA** *(Sturm Abteilung)*, were organized under the leadership of Captain Ernst Roehm (1887–1934). The storm troopers were the chief Nazi instrument for terror and intimidation before the party controlled the government. They were a law unto themselves. The organization constituted a means of preserving military discipline and values outside the small army permitted by the Paris settlement. The existence of such a private party army and of a similar one run by the Communists was a sign of the potential for violence in the Weimar Republic and the widespread contempt for the law and the institutions of the republic.

SA The Nazi parliamentary forces, or storm troopers.

The social and economic turmoil following the French occupation of the Ruhr and the German inflation gave the fledgling party an opportunity for direct action against the Weimar Republic, which seemed incapable of providing military or economic security. By this time, because of his immense oratorical skills and organizational abilities, Hitler personally dominated the Nazi Party. As he established his dominance within the party, he clearly had the model of Mussolini in mind and spoke of the Italian dictator's accomplishments in glowing terms. In late 1923, with the memory of Mussolini's march on Rome still fresh, Hitler attempted to seize power by force.

On November 9, 1923, Hitler and a band of followers, accompanied by General Erich Ludendorff (1865–1937), attempted an unsuccessful putsch from a beer hall in Munich. When the local authorities crushed the rising, sixteen Nazis were killed. Hitler and Ludendorff were arrested and tried for treason. The general was acquitted. Hitler used the trial to make himself into a national figure. He condemned the republic, the Versailles Treaty, the Jews, and the weakened condition of his adopted country. He was convicted and sentenced to five years in prison. He actually spent

MAP EXPLORATION

Interactive map: To explore this map further, go to www.myhistorylab.com

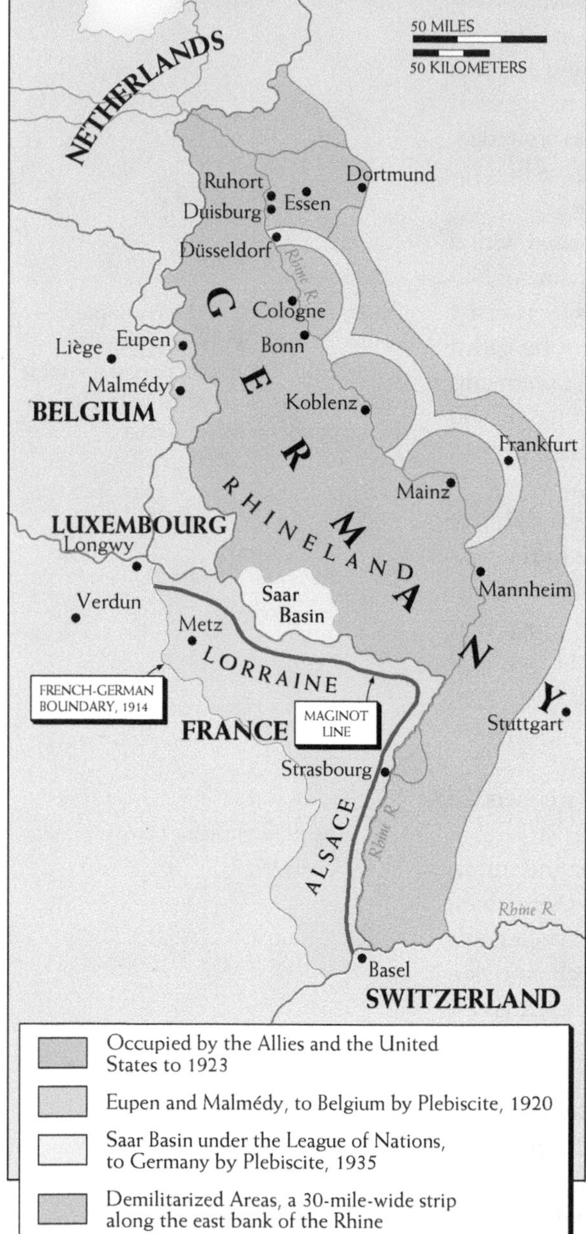

MAP 27–1 **Germany's Western Frontier** The French-Belgian-German border area between the two world wars was sensitive. Despite efforts to restrain tensions, there were persistent difficulties related to the Ruhr, Rhineland, Saar, and Eupen-Malmédy regions that required strong defenses.

Why were the territorial divisions between France, Germany, and Belgium unsatisfactory?

only a few months in jail before being paroled. During this time, he dictated ***Mein Kampf*** ("My Struggle"), from which he eventually made a good deal of money. In this book, not taken seriously enough at the time, he outlined key political views from which he never swerved, including a fierce racial anti-Semitism, opposition to Bolshevism, which he associated with Jews, and a conviction that Germany must expand eastward into Poland and Ukraine to achieve greater "living space." Such expansion assumed the resurgence of German military might. In effect, Hitler transferred the foreign policy goals and racial outlooks previously associated with German overseas imperialism to the politics of central and eastern Europe. The natural targets of implementing these ideas would be Jews, the successor states of eastern Europe, the Soviet Union, and any groups within Germany that opposed Hitler's vision of national unity and purpose.

During his imprisonment, Hitler reached two other decisions. First, it appears that this was the moment when he came to see himself as the leader who could transform Germany from a position of weakness to strength. Second, he decided that he and the party must pursue power by legal means, but as Hitler emerged from his imprisonment, he was still a regional politician (albeit one who was transforming himself into a national figure).

The Stresemann Years The officials of the republic were attempting to repair the damage from the inflation. Gustav Stresemann (1878–1929) was responsible primarily for reconstruction of the republic and for its achievement of a sense of self-confidence. Stresemann abandoned the policy of passive resistance in the Ruhr. The country simply could not afford it. Then, with the aid of banker Hjalmar Schacht (1877–1970), he introduced a new German currency. The rate of exchange was 1 trillion of the old German marks for one new Rentenmark. Stresemann also moved against challenges from both the left and the right. He supported the crushing of both Hitler's abortive putsch and smaller Communist disturbances. In late November 1923, after four months as chancellor, he resigned to become foreign minister, a post he held until his death in 1929. In that office he continued to influence the affairs of the republic.

In 1924 the Weimar Republic and the Allies renegotiated the reparation payments. The Dawes Plan lowered the annual payments and allowed them to fluctuate according to the fortunes of the German economy. The last French troops left the Ruhr in 1925 (see Map 27–1). The same year, Field Marshal Paul von Hindenburg (1847–1934), a military hero and a conservative monarchist, was elected president of the republic. This conservatism was in line with the prosperity of the latter 1920s. Foreign capital flowed into Germany, and employment, which had been poor throughout most of the postwar years, improved smartly. Giant industrial combines spread. The prosperity helped to establish broader acceptance and appreciation of the republic.

In foreign affairs, Stresemann pursued a conciliatory course. He fulfilled the provisions of the Versailles Treaty even as he attempted to revise it by diplomacy. He was willing to accept the set-

tlement in the west but was a determined, if sometimes secret, revisionist in the east. He aimed to recover German-speaking territories lost to Poland and Czechoslovakia and possibly to unite with Austria, chiefly by diplomatic means. The first step, however, was to achieve respectability and economic recovery. That goal required a policy of accommodation and "fulfillment," for the moment at least.

Mein Kampf (*My Struggle*) Strategy dictated by Adolf Hitler during his period of imprisonment in 1923 outlining his political views.

Locarno These developments gave rise to the Locarno Agreements of October 1925. The spirit of conciliation led foreign ministers Austen Chamberlain (1863–1937) for Britain and Aristide Briand (1862–1932) for France to accept Stresemann's proposal for a fresh start. France and Germany both accepted the western frontier established at Versailles as legitimate. Britain and Italy agreed to intervene against the aggressor if either side violated the frontier or if Germany sent troops into the demilitarized Rhineland. Significantly, no such agreement was made about Germany's eastern frontier, but the Germans made treaties of arbitration with Poland and Czechoslovakia, and France strengthened its ties with those countries. France supported German membership in the League of Nations and agreed to withdraw its occupation troops from the Rhineland in 1930, five years earlier than specified at Versailles.

The Locarno Agreements brought new hope to Europe. The spirit of Locarno was carried even further when the leading European states, Japan, and the United States signed the Kellogg-Briand Pact in 1928, renouncing "war as an instrument of national policy." The joy and optimism were not justified. France had merely recognized its inability to coerce Germany without help. Britain had shown its unwillingness to uphold the settlement in the east. Germany was not reconciled to the eastern settlement. It maintained clandestine military connections with the Soviet Union and planned to continue to press for revision.

In both France and Germany, moreover, the conciliatory politicians represented only a part of the nation. In Germany especially, most people continued to reject Versailles and regarded Locarno as only an extension of it. When the Dawes Plan ran out in 1929, it was replaced by the Young Plan, which lowered the reparation payments, put a term on how long they must be made, and removed Germany entirely from outside supervision and control. The intensity of the outcry in Germany against the continuation of any reparations showed how far the Germans were from accepting their situation. Despite these problems, war was by no means inevitable. Europe, aided by American loans, was returning to prosperity. German leaders like Stresemann would certainly have continued to press for change, but there is little reason to think that they would have resorted to force, much less to a general war. Continued prosperity and diplomatic success might have won the loyalty of the German people for the Weimar Republic and moderate revisionism, but the Great Depression of the 1930s brought new forces to power.

Depression and Political Deadlock

The outflow of foreign, and especially American, capital from Germany that began in 1928 undermined the economic prosperity of the Weimar Republic. The resulting economic crisis brought parliamentary government to a halt. In 1928 a coalition of center parties and the Social Democrats governed. All went reasonably well until the depression struck. Then the coalition partners differed sharply on economic policy. The Social Democrats refused to reduce social and unemployment insurance. The more conservative parties, remembering the inflation of 1923, insisted on a balanced budget. The coalition dissolved in March 1930. To resolve the parliamentary deadlock in the ***Reichstag***, President von Hindenburg appointed Heinrich Brüning (1885–1970) as chancellor. Lacking a majority in the *Reichstag*, the new chancellor governed through

Reichstag (RIKES-stahg) The German parliament, which existed in various forms, until 1945.

emergency presidential decrees, as authorized by Article 48 of the constitution. Party divisions prevented the *Reichstag* from overriding the decrees. The Weimar Republic had become a presidential dictatorship.

German unemployment rose from 2,258,000 in March 1930 to over 6,000,000 in March 1932. The economic downturn and the parliamentary deadlock worked to the advantage of the more extreme political parties. In the election of 1928, the Nazis had won only 12 seats in the *Reichstag*, and the Communists had won 54 seats. Two years later, after the election of 1930, the Nazis held 107 seats and the Communists 77.

The power of the Nazis in the streets was also on the rise. The unemployment fed thousands of men into the storm troopers, which had 100,000 members in 1930 and almost 1 million in 1933. The SA freely and viciously attacked Communists and Social Democrats. For the Nazis, politics meant the capture of power through terror and intimidation as well as through elections. Nazi rallies resembled secular religious revivals. The Nazis paraded through the streets and the countryside. They gained powerful supporters and sympathizers among businessmen, military officers, and newspaper owners. Some intellectuals were also sympathetic. The Nazis transformed this discipline and enthusiasm born of economic despair and nationalistic frustration into impressive electoral results.

Hitler Comes to Power

For two years Brüning continued to govern with the backing of Hindenburg. In 1932 the eighty-three-year-old president stood for reelection. Hitler ran against him and forced a runoff. The Nazi leader garnered 30.1 percent of the vote in the first election and 36.8 percent in the second. Although Hindenburg was returned to office, the vote convinced him that Brüning had lost the confidence of conservative German voters. In May 1932 he dismissed Brüning and appointed Franz von Papen (1878–1969) in his place. The new chancellor was one of a small group of extremely conservative advisers on whom the aged Hindenburg had become dependent.

Papen and the circle around the president wanted to draw the Nazis into cooperation with them without giving Hitler effective power. The government needed the popular support on the right that only the Nazis seemed able to generate. The Hindenburg circle decided to convince Hitler that the Nazis could not come to power on their own. Papen removed the ban on Nazi meetings that Brüning had imposed and then called a *Reichstag* election for July 1932. The Nazis won 230 seats and polled 37.2 percent of the vote. Hitler would only enter the Cabinet if he were made chancellor. Hindenburg refused. Another election was called in November, partly to wear down the Nazis' financial resources. The Nazis won only 196 seats, and their percentage of the popular vote dipped to 33.1 percent. The advisers around Hindenburg still refused to appoint Hitler to office.

In early December 1932 Papen resigned, and General Kurt von Schleicher (1882–1934) became chancellor. Schleicher decided to try and fashion a broad-based coalition of conservative groups and trade unionists. The prospect of such a coalition, including groups from the political left, frightened the Hindenburg circle even more than the prospect of Hitler. Consequently, they persuaded Hindenburg to appoint Hitler chancellor. To control him and to see that he did little mischief, Papen was named vice chancellor, and other traditional conservatives were appointed to the cabinet. On January 30, 1933, Adolf Hitler became the chancellor of Germany. It is important to emphasize that this outcome had not been inevitable. Hitler did not come to office on the tide of history, but through the blunders of conservative German politicians who hated the Weimar Republic and its rejection of traditional German political elites and who feared the domestic political turmoil the depression had spawned.

ENCOUNTERING THE PAST

CINEMA OF THE POLITICAL LEFT AND RIGHT

Before television, cinema was the most powerful medium for political propaganda, and brilliant directors served authoritarian regimes of both the left and the right. Sergei Eisenstein (1898–1948) made films for the Soviet Union that, despite their propagandistic content, are acknowledged masterpieces. The Battleship Potemkin, *his most famous work, depicts a mutiny aboard a warship during the Russian Revolution. It portrays the working class as the hero of the story and of history itself. Two other historical epics,* Alexander Nevsky *(a medieval Russian prince who defeated German invaders) and* Ivan the Terrible *(a sixteenth-century despotic tsar), managed remarkably to meet the highest artistic standards and promote reflection on contemporary events—all while pleasing Stalin.*

Nazi Germany's great artistic resource was a female documentary filmmaker, Leni Riefenstahl (1902–2003). After the Nazis took power in 1933, Hitler commissioned her to make documentaries extolling his Third Reich. She produced two dazzling films: *Triumph of the Will* (1934), a record of a Nazi Party rally, and *Olympia* (1938), based on the Olympic Games held in Berlin in 1936. Her innovative, dramatic techniques made her films classics of twentieth-century cinema—and made them perfect vehicles for conveying the theatricality of the Nazi regime. Despite the support her films gave Hitler, she defended herself as a "pure" artist who (as some scientists have also argued) cannot be held responsible for the use others made of her work.

Leni Riefenstahl films the 1936 Olympic Games in Berlin with Hitler on the reviewing stand.

How did Riefenstahl's films promote Nazi ideology?

WHY WERE authoritarian regimes so interested in the cinema? Are artists ethically responsible for the effects of their art?

Hitler had forged a rigidly disciplined party structure and had mastered the techniques of mass politics and propaganda. (See "Encountering the Past: Cinema of the Political Left and Right.") He understood how to touch the raw social and political nerves of the electorate. His support appears to have come from across the social spectrum and not, as historians once thought, just from the lower middle class. Pockets of resistance appeared among Roman Catholic voters in the countryside and small towns. Otherwise, support for Hitler was particularly strong among groups such as farmers, war veterans, and the young, whom the insecurity of the 1920s and the depression of the early 1930s had badly hurt. Hitler promised them security against communists and socialists, effective government in place of the petty politics of the other parties, and a strong, restored, purposeful Germany.

QUICK REVIEW

Hitler's Rise to Power

- January 30, 1933: in an effort to hold onto power, Hindenburg appoints Hitler chancellor
- Hitler obtained office legally
- Successfully appealed to broad spectrum of German society

HITLER'S CONSOLIDATION OF POWER

Once in office, Hitler consolidated his control with almost lightning speed. This process had three facets: the capture of full legal authority, the crushing of alternative political groups, and the purging of rivals within the Nazi Party itself. On February 27, 1933, a mentally ill Dutch Communist set fire to the *Reichstag* building in Berlin. The Nazis quickly turned the incident to their own advantage by claiming that the fire proved the existence

The *Reichstag* fire in 1933 provided Hitler with an excuse to consolidate his power.

Bildarchiv Preussischer Kulturbesitz

How did Hitler use the *Reichstag* fire to advance his political agenda?

of an immediate Communist threat against the government. To the public, it seemed plausible that the Communists might attempt some action against the state now that the Nazis were in power. Under Article 48, Hitler issued an Emergency Decree suspending civil liberties and proceeded to arrest Communists or alleged Communists. This decree remained in force as long as Hitler ruled Germany.

In early March another *Reichstag* election took place. The Nazis still received only 43.9 percent of the vote. However, the arrest of the newly elected Communist deputies and the political fear aroused by the fire meant that Hitler could control the *Reichstag*. On March 23, 1933, the *Reichstag* passed an Enabling Act that permitted Hitler to rule by decree. Thereafter, there were no legal limits on his exercise of power.

In a series of complex moves, Hitler outlawed or undermined various German institutions that might have served as rallying points for opposition. In early May 1933, the offices, banks, and newspapers of the free trade unions were seized, and their leaders arrested. In late June and early July, the other German political parties were outlawed. By July 14, 1933, the National Socialists were the only legal party in Germany. During the same months the Nazis had taken control of the governments of the individual federal states in Germany. By the close of 1933, all major institutions of potential opposition had been eliminated.

The final element in Hitler's personal consolidation of power involved the Nazi Party itself. By late 1933 the SA consisted of approximately 1 million active members and a larger number of reserves. The commander of this party army was Ernst Roehm, a possible rival to Hitler himself. The German army officer corps, on whom Hitler depended to rebuild the national army, was jealous of the SA. Consequently, to protect his own position and to shore up support with the regular army, on June 30, 1934, Hitler ordered the murder of key SA officers, including Roehm. The German army, which was the only institution in the nation that might have prevented the murders, did nothing. A month later, on August 2, 1934, President Hindenburg died. Thereafter, the offices of chancellor and president were combined. Hitler was now the ***Führer***, or sole ruler of Germany and of the Nazi Party.

Führer (FYOOR-er) Meaning "leader." The title taken by Hitler when he became dictator of Germany.

Anti-Semitism and the Police State

Terror and intimidation had helped propel the Nazis to office. As Hitler consolidated his power, he oversaw the organization of a police state. The chief vehicle of police surveillance was the **SS** (*Schutzstaffel*), or security units, commanded by Heinrich Himmler (1900–1945). In 1933, the SS had approximately 52,000 members. It was the instrument that carried out the blood purges of the party in 1934. By 1936 Himmler had become head of all police matters in Germany.

SS The chief security units of the Nazi state.

Nazi Attack on the Jews The police character of the Nazi regime was all-pervasive, but the people who most consistently experienced its terror were the German Jews.

Anti-Semitism had been a key plank of the Nazi program—anti-Semitism based on biological racial theories stemming from late-nineteenth-century thought rather than from religious discrimination. Before World War II the Nazi attack on the Jews went through three stages of increasing intensity. In 1933, shortly after assuming power, the Nazis excluded Jews from the civil service. For a time they also attempted to enforce boycotts of Jewish shops and businesses. The boycotts won relatively little public support. Then in 1935, a series of measures known as the Nuremberg Laws robbed German Jews of their citizenship. The professions and the major occupations were closed to those defined as Jews. Marriage and sexual intercourse between Jews and non-Jews were prohibited. Legal exclusion and humiliation of the Jews became the order of the day.

The persecution of the Jews increased again in 1938. Business careers were forbidden. In November 1938, under orders from the Nazi Party, thousands of Jewish stores and synagogues were burned or otherwise destroyed. The Jewish community itself had to pay for the damage that occurred on this ***Kristallnacht*** ("Night of Smashed Glass") because the government confiscated the insurance money. In many other ways, large and petty, the German Jews were harassed. This persecution allowed the Nazis to inculcate the rest of the population with the concept of a master race of pure German "Aryans" and also to display their own contempt for civil liberties.

Anti-Jewish Policies Soon after seizing power, the Nazi government began harassing German Jewish businesses. Non-Jewish German citizens were urged not to buy merchandise from shops owned by Jews.

Art Resource/Bildarchiv Preussischer Kulturbesitz

Why was anti-Semitism such an important part of Nazi policy?

The Final Solution After the war broke out, Hitler decided in 1942 to destroy the Jews in Europe. It is thought that over 6 million Jews, mostly from eastern European nations, died as a result of that staggering decision, unprecedented in its scope and implementation. This subject will be more fully treated in the next chapter.

Racial Ideology and the Lives of Women

Hitler and other Nazis were less interested in increasing the national population, which was Mussolini's policy in Italy, than in producing racially pure Germans. In their role as mothers, German women had the special task of preserving racial purity and giving birth to pure Germans who were healthy in mind and body. Nazi journalists often compared the role of women in childbirth to that of men in battle. Each served the state in particular social and gender roles. In both cases, the good of the nation was more important than that of the individual. (See "Compare & Connect: The Soviets and the Nazis Confront the Issues of Women and the Family," pages 702–703.)

Kristallnacht (KRIS-tahl-NAHKT) Meaning "crystal night" because of the broken glass that littered German streets after the looting and destruction of Jewish homes, businesses, and synagogues across Germany on the orders of the Nazi Party in November 1938.

Nazi policy favored motherhood only for those whom its adherents regarded as racially fit for it. As early as late 1933, the government raised the issue of what kind of persons were fit to bear children for the nation. This policy disapproved of fostering motherhood among those people Nazi racism condemned—particularly the Jews, but also Slavs and Gypsies. During the mass executions of Jews in the Holocaust, Jewish women were specifically targeted for death, in part to prevent them from bearing a new generation.

Nazi theorists also discriminated between the healthy and unhealthy, the desirable and undesirable, in the German population itself. The government sought to prevent "undesirables" from reproducing, a policy that led to both the sterilization and death of many women, often because of an alleged mental "degeneracy." Some pregnant women were forced to have abortions. The Nazis' population policy was, in effect, one of selective breeding, or antenatalism, that profoundly affected the lives of women.

COMPARE & CONNECT

THE SOVIETS AND THE NAZIS CONFRONT THE ISSUES OF WOMEN AND THE FAMILY

Both the Soviet and Nazi dictatorships intruded deeply into the private lives of their citizens. Some Communist writers in the Soviet Union imagined utopian changes to traditional family life and traditional roles for women. In Germany, the state imposed policies on women that would make their roles of wives and mothers serve the larger political and ideological goals of the Nazi Party. Different and opposed as were these policies of the two dictatorships, both challenged the social roles of women that were emerging in Western Europe and in the United States.

QUESTIONS

1. Why did Kollontai see the restructuring of the family as essential to the establishment of a new kind of Communist society? Would these changes make people loyal to that society?
2. What are the social tasks Hitler assigns to women? How does he attempt to subordinate the lives of women to the supremacy of the state?
3. Why was the present and future role of women such an important topic for both the Communist and the Nazi governments?

I. A COMMUNIST WOMAN DEMANDS A NEW FAMILY LIFE

While Lenin sought to consolidate the Bolshevik Revolution against internal and external enemies, there existed within the young Soviet Union a vast utopian impulse to change and reform virtually every social institution that had existed before the revolution or those Communists associated with capitalist society. Alexandra Kollontai (1872–1952) was a spokesperson of the extreme political left within the early Soviet Union. There had been much speculation on how the end of bourgeois society might change the structure of the family and the position of women. In this passage written in 1920, Kollontai states one of the most radically utopian visions of this change. During the years immediately after the revolution, extreme rumors circulated in both Europe and America about sexual and family experimentation in the Soviet Union. Statements such as this fostered such rumors. Kollontai herself later became a supporter of Stalin and a Soviet diplomat.

There is no escaping the fact: the old type of family has seen its day. It is not the fault of the Communist State, it is the result of the changed conditions of life. The family is ceasing to be a necessity of the State, as it was in the past; on the contrary, it is worse than useless, since it needlessly holds back the female workers from more productive and far more serious work. . . . But on the ruins of the former family we shall soon see a new form rising which will involve altogether different relations between men and women, and which will be a union of affection and comradeship, a union of two equal members of the Communist society, both of them free, both of them independent, both of them workers. No more domestic "servitude" of women. No more inequality within the family. No more fear on the part of the woman lest she remain without support or aid with little ones in her arms if her husband should desert her. The woman in the Communist city no longer depends on her husband but on her work. It is not her husband but her robust arms which will support her. There will be no more anxiety as to the fate of her children. The State of the Workers will assume responsibility for these. Marriage will be purified of all its material elements, of all money calculations, which constitute a hideous blemish on family life in our days. . . .

The woman who is called upon to struggle in the great cause of the liberation of the workers—such a woman should know that in the new State there will be no more room for such petty divisions as were formerly understood: "These are my own children, to them I owe all my maternal solicitude, all my affection; those are your children, my neighbour's children; I am not concerned with them. I have enough to do with my own." Henceforth the worker-mother, who is conscious of her social function, will rise to a point where she no longer differentiates between yours and mine; she must remember that there are henceforth only our children, those of the Communist State, the common possession of all the workers.

The Worker's State has need of a new form of relation between the sexes. The narrow and exclusive affection of the mother for her own children must expand until it embraces all the children of the great proletarian family. In place of the indissoluble marriage based on the servitude of woman, we shall see rise the free union, fortified by the love and mutual respect of the two members of the Workers' State, equal in their rights and in their obligations. In place of the individual and egotistic family there will arise a great universal family of workers, in which all the workers, men and women, will be, above all, workers, comrades.

Source: From Alexandra Kollontai, *Communism and the Family*, as reprinted in *The Family in the USSR*, ed. and trans. by Rudolph Schlesinger (London: Routledge and Kegan Paul, 1949), pp. 67–69. Reprinted by permission.

This Soviet poster illustrates the role of women in communist society as key players in industrial and agricultural development and progress. This differs greatly from the traditional role assigned to women in Nazi ideology.

Corbis/Bettmann © Swim Inc./CORBIS

What role did Soviet propaganda imagine for women in communist society?

II. HITLER REJECTS THE EMANCIPATION OF WOMEN

According to Nazi ideology, women's place was in the home producing and rearing children and supporting their husbands. In this speech, Hitler urges this view of the role of women. He uses anti-Semitism to discredit those writers who had urged the emancipation of women from their traditional roles and occupations. Hitler returns here to the "separate spheres" concept of the relationship of men and women. His traditional view of women was directed against views that were associated with the Soviet experiment during the interwar years. Contrast this Nazi outlook on women and the family with the Bolshevik position described by Alexandra Kollontai in the previous document. Ironically, once World War II began, the Nazi leadership demanded that women leave the home and work in factories to support the war effort.

The slogan "Emancipation of women" was invented by Jewish intellectuals and its content was formed by the same spirit. In the really good times of German life the German woman had no need to emancipate herself. She possessed exactly what nature had necessarily given her to administer and preserve; just as the man in his good times had no need to fear that he would be ousted from his position in relation to the woman. . . .

If the man's world is said to be the State, his struggle, his readiness to devote his powers to the service of the community, then it may perhaps be said that the woman's is a smaller world. For her world is her husband, her family, her children, and her home. But what would become of the greater world if there were no one to tend and care for the smaller one? How could the greater world survive if there were no one to make the cares of the smaller world the content of their lives? No, the greater world is built on the foundation of this smaller world. This great world cannot survive if the smaller world is not stable. Providence has entrusted to the woman the cares of that world which is her very own, and only on the basis of this smaller world can the man's world be formed and built up. The two worlds are not antagonistic. They complement each other, they belong together just as man and woman belong together.

We do not consider it correct for the woman to interfere in the world of the man, in his main sphere. We consider it natural if these two worlds remain distinct. To the one belongs the strength of feeling, the strength of the soul. To the other belongs the strength of vision, of toughness, of decision, and of the willingness to act. In the one case this strength demands the willingness of the woman to risk her life to preserve this important cell and to multiply it, and in the other case it demands from the man the readiness to safeguard life. . . .

So our women's movement is for us not something which inscribes on its banner as its programme the fight against men, but something which has as its programme the common fight together with men. For the new National Socialist national community acquires a firm basis precisely because we have gained the trust of millions of women as fanatical fellow-combatants, women who have fought for the common life in the service of the common task of preserving life. . . .

Whereas previously the programmes of the liberal, intellectualist women's movements contained many points, the programme of our National Socialist Women's movement has in reality but one single point, and that point is the child, that tiny creature which must be born and grow strong and which alone gives meaning to the whole life-struggle.

Source: From J. Noakes and G. Pridham, eds., *Nazism, 1919–1945*, Vol. 2, *State, Economy and Society, 1933–39: A Documentary Reader*, Exeter Studies in History No. 8 (Exeter, England: University of Exeter Press, 1984), pp. 449–450.

Young women among an enthusiastic crowd extend the Nazi salute at a party rally in 1938. Nazi ideology encouraged women to favor traditional domestic roles over employment in the workplace and to bear many children. The onset of the war, however, forced the government to recruit women workers.
Bildarchiv Preussischer Kulturbesitz

What appeal might the Nazis have had for German women?

To support motherhood among those whom they believed should have children, the Nazis provided loans to encourage early marriage, tax breaks for families with children, and child allowances. In this respect, Nazi legislation resembled that passed elsewhere in Europe during the decade. The subsidies and other family payments were sent to husbands rather than wives, to make married fatherhood seem preferable to bachelorhood. Furthermore, these policies were administered on the premise that only racially and physically desirable children received support.

Although Nazi ideology emphasized motherhood, in 1930 the party vowed to protect the jobs of working women, and the number of women working in Germany rose steadily under the Nazi regime. The Nazis recognized that in the midst of the depression many women needed to work, but the party urged them to pursue employment that was "natural" to their character as women. Such employment included agricultural labor, teaching, nursing, social service, and domestic service. The Nazis also intended women to be educators of the young. In that role, whether as mothers or as members of the serving professions, women became special protectors of German cultural values.

Nazi Economic Policy

Besides consolidating political authority and pursuing anti-Semitic policies, Hitler still had to confront the Great Depression. German unemployment had helped propel him to power. The Nazis attacked this problem with a success that astonished and frightened Europe. By 1936, while the rest of the European economy remained stagnant, the specter of unemployment and other difficulties associated with the Great Depression no longer haunted Germany.

This success was perhaps the most important reason Germans supported his tyrannical regime. Behind the direction of both business and labor stood the Nazi terror and police. The Nazi economic experiment proved that, by sacrificing all political and civil liberty, destroying a free trade-union movement, limiting the private exercise of capital, and ignoring consumer satisfaction, a government could achieve full employment to prepare for war and aggression.

Nazi economic policies supported private property and private capitalism but subordinated all significant economic enterprise and decisions about prices and investment to the goals of the state. Hitler reversed the deflationary policy of the cabinets that had preceded him. He instituted a massive program of public works and vast military spending. From the earliest years of the Nazi regime, government spending and other economic policies served to pursue the cause of rearmament. The government built canals, reclaimed land, and constructed an extensive highway system with clear military uses. It also sent unemployed workers back to farms if they had originally come from them. Other laborers were not permitted to change jobs without official permission.

In 1935, the renunciation of the military provisions of the Versailles treaty led to open rearmament and military expansion with little opposition, as explained in Chapter 28. These measures essentially restored full employment. In 1936, Hitler instructed Hermann Göring (1893–1946), who had headed the air force since 1933, to undertake a four-year plan to prepare the army and the economy for war.

TRIALS OF THE SUCCESSOR STATES IN EASTERN EUROPE

WHAT SHARED challenges faced the successor states in eastern Europe?

It had been an article of faith among nineteenth-century liberals sympathetic to nationalism that only good could flow from the demise of Austria-Hungary, the restoration of Poland, and the establishment of nation-states throughout eastern Europe. These new states were to embody the principle of national self-determination and to provide a buffer against the westward spread of Bolshevism. They were, however, in trouble from the beginning.

Economic and Ethnic Pressures

All the new states faced immense postwar economic difficulties. None of them possessed the kind of strong economy that nation-states such as France and Germany had developed in the nineteenth century. Indeed, political independence disrupted the previous economic relationships that each of them had developed as part of one of the prewar empires. None of the new states was financially independent; except for Czechoslovakia, all of them depended on foreign loans to finance economic development. Nationalistic antagonisms often prevented these states from trading with each other, and as a consequence, most became highly dependent on trade with Germany. The successor states of eastern Europe were poor and overwhelmingly rural nations in an industrialized world. The depression hit them especially hard, because they had to import finished goods for which they paid with agricultural exports whose value was falling sharply.

Finally, throughout eastern Europe, the collapse of the old German, Russian, and Austrian empires allowed various ethnic groups—large and small—to pursue nationalistic goals unchecked by any great power or central political authority. The major social and political groups in these countries were generally unwilling to make compromises lest they undermine their nationalist identity and independence. Each state included minority groups that wanted to be independent or to become part of a different nation in the region. Again, except for Czechoslovakia, all these states succumbed to some form of domestic authoritarian government.

Poland: Democracy to Military Rule

The nation whose postwar fortunes probably most disappointed liberal Europeans was Poland. For more than a hundred years, the country had been erased from the map. (See Chapter 17.) When the country was restored in 1919, nationalism proved an insufficient bond to overcome political disagreements stemming from class differences, diverse economic interests, and regionalism. Furthermore, large Ukrainian, Jewish, Lithuanian, and German minorities distrusted the Polish government and resented attempts to force them to adopt Polish culture. The new Poland had been constructed from portions governed by Germany, Russia, and Austria for over a century. Each of those regions of partitioned Poland had different administrative systems and laws, different economies, and different degrees of experience with electoral institutions. A host of small political parties bedeviled the new Polish Parliament, and the executive was weak. In 1926, Marshal Josef Pilsudski (1867–1935) carried out a military coup. Thereafter, he ruled, in effect, personally until his death, when the government passed into the hands of a group of his military followers. The government became increasingly anti-Semitic, and non-Polish minorities suffered various forms of discrimination.

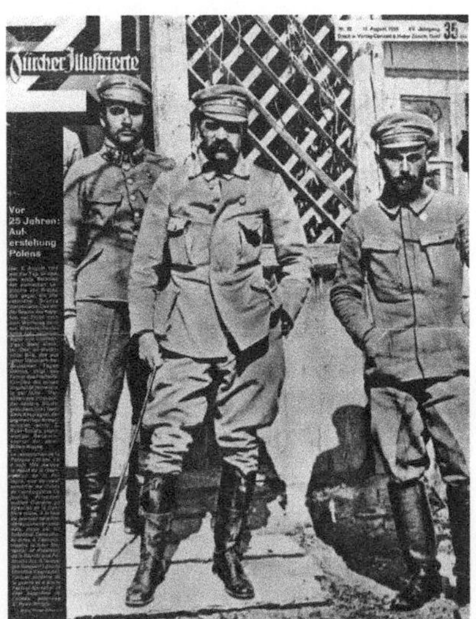

Marshal Josef Pilsudski governed Poland from 1926 to 1935.

Hulton Archive/Getty Images

Czechoslovakia: A Viable Democratic Experiment

Only one central European successor state escaped the fate of self-imposed authoritarian government. Czechoslovakia possessed a strong industrial base, a substantial middle class, and a tradition of liberal values. After the war, the new government had broken up large estates in favor of small peasant holdings. In the person of Thomas Masaryk (1850–1937), the nation possessed a gifted leader of immense integrity and fairness. The country had a real chance of becoming a viable modern nation-state.

There were, however, tensions between the Czechs and the Slovaks, who were poorer and more rural. Moreover, other non-Czech national groups, including Poles, Magyars, Ukrainians, and especially the Germans of the Sudetenland, which the Paris settlement had placed within Czech borders, resented being part of Czechoslovakia. The parliamentary regime might have been able to work through these problems, but extreme German nationalists in the Sudetenland looked to Hitler, who wanted to expand into eastern Europe, for help. In 1938, at Munich, the great powers first divided liberal Czechoslovakia to appease Hitler's aggressive instincts and then watched passively in early 1939 as he occupied much of the country, gave parts to Poland and Hungary, and manipulated a Slovak puppet state.

Hungary: Turn to Authoritarianism

Hungary was one of the defeated powers of World War I. In that defeat, it achieved its long-desired separation from Austria, but at a high political and economic price. In Hungary during 1919, Bela Kun (1885–1937), a communist, established a short-lived Hungarian Soviet Republic, which received socialist support. The Allies authorized an invasion by Romanian troops to remove the communist danger. The Hungarian landowners then established Admiral Miklós Horthy (1868–1957) as regent for the Habsburg monarch who could not return to his throne—a position Horthy held until 1944. After the collapse of the Kun government, thousands of Hungarians were either executed or imprisoned.

The Hungarians also deeply resented the territory Hungary had lost in the Paris settlement. The largely agrarian Hungarian economy suffered from a general stagnation. During the 1920s, the effective ruler of Hungary was Count Stephen Bethlen (1874–1947). He presided over a government that was parliamentary in form, but aristocratic in character. In 1932, he was succeeded by General Julius Gömbös (1886–1936), who pursued anti-Semitic policies and rigged elections. After his death in 1936, anti-Semitism lingered in Hungarian politics.

Austria: Political Turmoil and Nazi Occupation

Austria's situation was little better than that of the other successor states. A quarter of the 8 million Austrians lived in Vienna. Viable economic life was almost impossible, and the Paris settlement forbade union with Germany. Throughout the 1920s, the leftist Social Democrats and the conservative Christian Socialists contended for power. Both groups employed small armies to terrorize their opponents and to impress their followers.

In 1933, the Christian Socialist Engelbert Dollfuss (1892–1934) became chancellor. He tried to steer a course between the Austrian Social Democrats and the German Nazis, who had surfaced in Austria. In 1934, he outlawed all political parties except the Christian Socialists, the agrarians, and the paramilitary groups that composed his own Fatherland Front. He used troops against the Social Democrats but was murdered later that year during an unsuccessful Nazi coup. His successor, Kurt von Schuschnigg (1897–1977), presided over Austria until Hitler annexed it in 1938.

Southeastern Europe: Royal Dictatorships

In southeastern Europe, revision of the arrangements in the Paris settlement was less of an issue. Parliamentary government floundered there nevertheless. Yugoslavia had been founded by the Corfu Agreement of 1917 and was known as the Kingdom of the Serbs, Croats, and Slovenes until 1929. Throughout the interwar period, the Serbs dominated the government and were opposed by the Croats. The two groups clashed violently, but the Serbs had the advantage of having had an independent state with an army prior to World War I, whereas the Croats and Slovenes had been part of the Austro-Hungarian Empire. The Croats generally were Roman Catholic, better educated, and accustomed to reasonably incorrupt government administration. The Serbs were Orthodox, less well educated, and considered corrupt administrators by the Croats. Furthermore, although each group predominated in certain areas of the country, each had isolated enclaves in other parts of the nation. Bosnia-Herzegovina, in addition to Serbs and Croats, had a significant Muslim population. The Slovenes, Muslims, Albanians, and other small national groups often played the Serbs and the Croats against each other. All the political parties except the small Communist Party represented a particular ethnic group rather than the nation of Yugoslavia. The violent clash of nationalities eventually led to a royal dictatorship in 1929 under King Alexander I (r. 1921–1934), himself a Serb. He outlawed political parties and jailed popular politicians. Alexander was assassinated in 1934, but the authoritarian government continued under a regency for his son.

Other royal dictatorships were imposed elsewhere in the Balkans: in Romania by King Carol II (r. 1930–1940) and in Bulgaria by King Boris III (r. 1918–1943). They regarded their own illiberal regimes as preventing the seizure of power by more extreme antiparliamentary movements and as quieting the discontent of the varied nationalities within their borders. In Greece, the parliamentary monarchy floundered amid military coups and calls for a republic. In 1936, General John Metaxas (1871–1941) instituted a dictatorship under King George II (r. 1935–1947) that, for the time being, ended parliamentary life in Greece.

MAJOR POLITICAL EVENTS OF THE 1920S AND 1930S

1919, August	Constitution of the Weimar Republic promulgated
1920	Kapp Putsch in Berlin
1921, March	Kronstadt mutiny leads Lenin to initiate his New Economic Policy
1922, October	Fascist march on Rome leads to Mussolini's assumption of power
1923, January	France invades the Ruhr
November	Hitler's Beer Hall Putsch
1924	Death of Lenin
1925	Locarno Agreements
1928	Kellogg-Briand Pact; first Five-Year Plan launched in USSR
1929, January	Trotsky expelled from USSR
February	Lateran Accord between the Vatican and the Italian state
October	New York stock market crash
November	Bukharin expelled from his offices in the Soviet Union; Stalin's central position thus affirmed
1930, March	Brüning government begins in Germany; Stalin calls for moderation in his policy of agricultural collectivization because of "dizziness from success"
September	Nazis capture 107 seats in German *Reichstag*
1931, August	National Government formed in Britain
1932, March 13	Hindenberg defeats Hitler for German presidency
May 31	Franz von Papen forms German cabinet
July 31	German *Reichstag* election
November 6	German *Reichstag* election
December 2	Kurt von Schleicher forms German cabinet
1933, January 30	Hitler made German chancellor
February 27	*Reichstag* fire
March 5	*Reichstag* election
March 23	Enabling Act consolidates Nazi power
1934, June 30	Blood purge of the Nazi Party
August 2	Death of Hindenburg
December 1	Assassination of Kirov leads to the beginning of Stalin's purges
1936, May	Popular Front government in France
July–August	Most famous of public purge trials in Russia

SUMMARY

WHY DID the Paris settlement fail to bring peace and prosperity to Europe?

After Versailles: Demands for Revision and Enforcement The Paris settlement fostered both resentments and discontent. Germany had been humiliated. The arrangements for reparations led to endless haggling over payments. There were strident demands for further border adjustments because significant national minorities resided outside the national boundaries drawn in Paris. The victorious powers, especially France, often believed that the provisions of the treaties were being inadequately enforced. *page 682*

WHAT KEY factors combined to produce the Great Depression?

Toward the Great Depression in Europe The severity and length of the Great Depression have three interrelated causes: the financial crisis caused by the Great War and the Paris peace settlement; the global crisis in the production and distribution of goods, especially after 1929; and the failure of the Western European and U.S. governments to respond appropriately to these conditions. The Allies depended on payments from Germany to subsidize their economies and pay their own debts to the United States; the German economy, in turn, had become dependent on U.S. private investment in the mid-1920s. When the U.S. stock market collapsed in 1929, U.S. loans to Europe dried up, and the German economy nearly collapsed. Meanwhile, production and trade faced their own difficulties, including agricultural overproduction; farmers could no longer afford to purchase industrial products, so the manufacture of consumer goods stagnated. This led to a reduction in demand for coal, iron, and textiles, crippling those industries as well. Under the pressure of the depression, Britain's Labour prime minister Ramsay MacDonald (1866–1937) organized a National Government, which was a coalition of the Labour, Conservative, and Liberal Parties. The 1920s also saw the establishment of an independent Irish state. The most important French interwar political experiment was the Popular Front Ministry, which came to office in 1936. It was composed of Socialists, Radicals, and Communists. *page 682*

WHAT WAS the relationship between politics and economics in the early decades of the Soviet Union?

The Soviet Experiment Trotsky led the Red Army to victory over the White Russians. Lenin and the Bolsheviks imposed centralized control over almost all aspects of life, but workers, peasants, and soldiers were all expressing strong discontent by 1921. Lenin responded with the New Economic Policy. In 1922, Lenin suffered a stroke. Trotsky and Stalin competed for control of the party; Stalin won. Comintern policy split Europe's socialist parties, allowing the rise of conservative and right-wing groups. Stalin implemented a plan for rapid industrialization, which led to tremendous economic growth through the 1930s but cost millions of lives. Starting in 1928, a succession of five-year plans set production goals, and the State Planning Commission organized the economy to meet those goals. Meanwhile, in 1929, Stalin had ordered the collectivization of agriculture, so production could be increased under state control and restive peasants could be transformed into obedient industrial laborers in the new factories. Stalin retained his grip on power through the Great Purges and the "show trials" of the mid to late 1930s. *page 686*

WHAT DID fascism mean to Mussolini and his supporters?

The Fascist Experiment in Italy Mussolini's fascist movement was the first to gain power in Western Europe in response to fears of the spread of Bolshevism. Fascist movements opposed more than they stood for, but all were nationalistic and based on mass political parties. In October 1922, after he and his followers had marched on Rome, Mussolini was legally appointed prime minister. By 1926, he had made Italy into a single-party dictatorship. He used propaganda to build a cult of personality. He used violence and terror to consolidate power; he also made peace between the Italian state and the Vatican with the Lateran Accord in 1929. *page 691*

WHY DID democracy fail to thrive in postwar Germany?

German Democracy and Dictatorship The Social Democratic leadership of the Weimar Republic was unfairly blamed for accepting the terms of the Versailles Treaty, when in fact the Allies had offered no choice in the matter. All political groups in Germany wanted to revise the treaty, although they all disagreed about how and to what extent to do so. The enlightened Weimar constitution carried the seeds of its own destruction, because it allowed its liberal institutions to be overthrown. Extremism from both the left and the right, often accompanied by violence, threatened the republic throughout its existence. In the late 1920s, the Nazis were visible on the Weimar political scene but had little influence. In the early 1930s, unemployment soared—as did membership in the Nazi Storm Troopers

(SA). President von Hindenburg appointed Hitler chancellor of Germany in January 1933, hoping to control him. But Hitler consolidated his power by capturing full legal authority, crushing alternative political groups, and purging the Nazi Party of rivals. In March 1933, the Enabling Act allowed Hitler to rule by decree. By the end of 1933, the Nazis had disabled all institutions that might oppose Hitler. Through violence and intimidation, the Nazis created a terrorist police state. The Nuremberg Laws and *Kristallnacht* marked the escalation of official anti-Semitism, which culminated in the Final Solution. Nazi racial ideology encouraged or discouraged women to reproduce, depending on their ethnic and health characteristics, and women were given responsibilities in transmitting the approved culture. Hitler's economic policies achieved great successes. Rearmament and other war preparations spurred economic growth. *page 693*

WHAT SHARED challenges faced the successor states in eastern Europe?

Trials of the Successor States in Eastern Europe Parliamentary governments floundered in most of the eastern European states set up after the dissolution of the Austro-Hungarian Empire. They lacked the economic base and the history of the gradual expansion of liberal democracy that helped provide stability in Great Britain and France. The new states were not financially independent; they were poor and rural nations in an industrialized world. Each state had at least one minority ethnic group living within its new borders. With the exception of Czechoslovakia, all wound up under authoritarian rule. Poland particularly disappointed European liberals, because its recreation had been a celebrated cause among them. *page 705*

REVIEW QUESTIONS

1. What caused the Great Depression? Why was it more severe and why did it last longer than previous economic downturns? Could it have been avoided?
2. How did Stalin achieve supreme power in the Soviet Union? Why did he decide that Russia had to industrialize rapidly? Why did this require the collectivization of agriculture? Was the policy a success? How did it affect the Russian people? Why did Stalin carry out the Great Purges?
3. Why was Italy dissatisfied and unstable after World War I? How did Mussolini achieve power? What were the characteristics of the Fascist state?
4. Why did the Weimar Republic collapse in Germany? How did Hitler come to power? Which groups in Germany supported Hitler and why were they pro-Nazi? How did he consolidate his power? Why was anti-Semitism central to Nazi policy?
5. What characteristics did the authoritarian regimes in the Soviet Union, Italy, and Germany have in common? What role did terror play in each?
6. Why did liberal democracy fail in the successor states of eastern Europe?

KEY TERMS

collectivization (p. 689)
Duce (p. 692)
fascism (p. 692)
Führer (p. 700)
Great Depression (p. 683)
Great Purges (p. 690)
Kristallnacht (p. 701)
Mein Kampf (p. 697)
Nazis (p. 695)
New Economic Policy (NEP) (p. 686)
Popular Front (p. 684)
Reichstag (p. 697)
SA (p. 695)
SS (p. 700)
War Communism (p. 686)
Weimar Republic (p. 682)

28

World War II

In August 1945, the United States exploded atomic bombs on the Japanese cities of Hiroshima and Nagasaki. A week later Japan surrendered. Without the bombs, the United States would almost certainly have had to invade Japan, and tens of thousands of Americans would have been killed. Still, the decision to use the bomb remains controversial.

What led to the decision to use atomic bombs against Japan?

POLAND

Idealistic survivors of the First World War hoped it would be "the war to end all wars," but only twenty years after its conclusion a second and even more terrible global conflict erupted. In Europe and Asia, democracies fought for their lives against militaristic, nationalistic, authoritarian, and totalitarian states. Their victory did not establish world peace but marked the start of an era of Cold War during which the European states were subordinated to the Soviet Union and the United States. ■

AGAIN THE ROAD TO WAR (1933–1939)

HOW DID World War I sow the seeds of World War II?

Nationalism and attention to the social question, along with party discipline, had been the sources of Nazi success. They continued to influence Hitler's foreign policy after he became chancellor in January 1933. Moreover, the Nazi destruction of the Weimar constitution and of political opposition meant that Hitler himself totally dominated German foreign policy. Consequently, it is important to know what his goals were and how he planned to achieve them.

HITLER'S GOALS

From the first expression of his goals in a book written in jail, *Mein Kampf* (*My Struggle*), to his last days in the underground bunker in Berlin where he killed himself, Hitler's racial theories and goals were at the center of his thought. He meant to bring the entire German people—the *Volk*—understood as a racial group, together into a single nation.

The new Germany would include all the Germanic parts of the old Habsburg Empire, including Austria. This virile and growing nation would need more space to live, or ***Lebensraum***, that would be taken from the Slavs, who, according to Nazi theory, were a lesser race, fit only for servitude. The removal of the Jews, another inferior race according to Nazi theory, would purify the new Germany. The plans required the conquest of Poland and Ukraine as the primary areas for German settlement and for providing badly needed food. Neither *Mein Kampf* nor later statements of policy were blueprints for action. Rather, Hitler was a brilliant improviser who exploited opportunities as they arose. He never lost sight of his goal, however, which would almost certainly require a major war.

Lebensraum German for "living space."

Germany Rearms When Hitler came to power, Germany was far too weak to permit a direct approach to reach his aims. The first problem he set out to resolve was to shake off the fetters of Versailles and to make Germany a formidable military power. In October 1933, Germany withdrew from an international disarmament conference and also from the League of Nations. These acts alarmed the French but were merely symbolic. In January 1934, Germany signed a nonaggression pact with Poland that was of greater concern to France, for it undermined France's chief means of containing the Germans. At last, in March 1935, Hitler formally renounced the disarmament provisions of the Versailles treaty with the formation of a German air force, and soon he reinstated conscription, which aimed at an army of half a million men.

The League of Nations Fails Growing evidence that the League of Nations could not keep the peace and that collective security was a myth made Hitler's path easier. In September 1931, Japan occupied Manchuria. China appealed to the League of Nations. The league dispatched a commission under a British diplomat, the earl of Lytton (1876–1951). The *Lytton Report* condemned the Japanese for resorting to force, but the powers were unwilling to impose sanctions. Japan withdrew from the League and kept control of Manchuria.

When Hitler announced his decision to rearm Germany, the League formally condemned that action, but it took no steps to prevent it. Hitler had taken a major step toward his goal without provoking serious opposition. Italy's expansionist ambitions in Africa, however, soon brought it into conflict with the Western powers.

Italy Attacks Ethiopia

In October 1935, Mussolini, using a border incident as an excuse, attacked Ethiopia. This attack made the impotence of the League of Nations and the timidity of the Allies clear. The League of Nations condemned Italian aggression and, for the first time, voted economic sanctions. It imposed an arms embargo that limited loans and credits to, and imports from, Italy. To avoid alienating Mussolini, however, Britain and France refused to embargo oil, the one economic sanction that could have prevented Italian victory. Even more important, Britain allowed Italian troops and munitions to reach Ethiopia through the Suez Canal. The results of this policy were disastrous. The League of Nations and collective security were discredited, and Mussolini was still alienated. He now turned to Germany, and by November 1, 1936, he spoke publicly of a Rome-Berlin **Axis**.

Axis Forces (opposed to the Allies) joined together in Europe, including Germany and Italy, before and during World War II.

Remilitarization of the Rhineland

The Ethiopian affair also convinced Hitler that the Western powers were too timid to oppose him forcefully. On March 7, 1936, he took his greatest risk yet, sending a small armed force into the demilitarized Rhineland. This was a breach not only of the Versailles treaty, but also of the Locarno Agreements of 1925—agreements Germany had made voluntarily. It also removed a crucial element of French security. Yet neither France nor Britain did anything but register a feeble protest with the League of Nations. British opinion would not permit support for France, and the French would not act alone. Internal division and a military doctrine that stressed defense and shunned the offensive paralyzed them. A growing pacifism further weakened both countries.

A Germany that was rapidly rearming and had a defensible western frontier presented a completely new problem to the Western powers. Their response was the policy of **appeasement**, based on the assumption that Germany had real grievances and that Hitler's goals were limited and ultimately acceptable. They set out to negotiate and make concessions before a crisis could lead to war.

appeasement Allied policy of making concessions to Germany based on the belief that Germany's grievances were real and Hitler's goals limited.

Behind this approach was the universal dread of another war. Memories of the horrors of the last war were still vivid, and the prospect of aerial bombardment made the thought of a new war even more terrifying. A firmer policy, moreover, would have required rapid rearmament. British leaders especially were reluctant to pursue this path because of the expense and the widespread belief that the arms race had been a major cause of the last war.

The Spanish Civil War

The Spanish Civil War, which broke out in July 1936, made the new European alignment that found the Western democracies on one side and the fascist states on the other clearer. In 1931, the monarchy had collapsed, and Spain became a democratic republic. The new government followed a program of moderate reform that antagonized landowners, the Catholic Church, nationalists, and conservatives without satisfying the demands of peasants, workers, Catalán separatists, or radicals. Elections in February 1936 brought to power a Spanish Popular Front government ranging from republicans of the left to communists and anarchists. The losers, especially the Falangists, the Spanish fascists, would not accept defeat at the polls. In July, General Francisco Franco (1892–1975) led an army from Spanish Morocco against the republic.

This poster supports General Francisco Franco's Nationalists in the bloody Spanish Civil War, which lasted almost three years and claimed hundreds of thousands of lives.

Courtesy of the Library of Congress

How did the Spanish Civil War come to be seen as a war of contending ideologies?

Thus began the Spanish Civil War, which lasted almost three years, cost hundreds of thousands of lives, and provided a training ground for World War II. Germany and Italy supported Franco with troops, airplanes, and supplies. The Soviet Union sent equipment and advisers to the republicans. Liberals and leftists from Europe and America volunteered to fight in the republican ranks against fascism.

The civil war, fought on blatantly ideological lines, profoundly affected world politics. It brought Germany and Italy closer together, leading to the Rome-Berlin Axis Pact in 1936. Japan joined the Axis powers in the Anti-Comintern Pact, ostensibly directed against international communism, but really a new and powerful diplomatic alliance. Western Europe, especially France, had a great interest in preventing Spain from falling into the hands of a fascist regime closely allied with Germany and Italy. Appeasement reigned, however. Although international law permitted the sale of weapons and munitions to the legitimate republican government, France and Britain forbade the export of war materials to either side, and the United States passed new neutrality legislation to the same end. When Barcelona fell to Franco early in 1939, the fascists had won effective control of Spain.

Austria and Czechoslovakia

Hitler made good use of his new friendship with Mussolini. He had always planned to annex his native Austria. In 1934, the Nazi Party in Austria assassinated the prime minister and tried to seize power. Mussolini had not yet allied with Hitler and was suspicious of German intentions. He quickly moved an army to the Austrian border, thus preventing German intervention and causing the coup to fail.

In 1938, the new diplomatic situation encouraged Hitler to try again. On March 13, Austrian chancellor Kurt von Schuschnigg (1897–1977) announced a plebiscite for March 13, in which the Austrian people themselves could decide whether to unite with Germany. To forestall the plebiscite, Hitler sent his army into Austria on March 12. To his relief, Mussolini did not object, and Hitler rode to Vienna amid the cheers of his Austrian sympathizers.

Anschluss Union of Germany and Austria.

The ***Anschluss***, or union of Germany and Austria, was another clear violation of Versailles. The treaty, however, was now a dead letter, and the West remained passive. The *Anschluss* had great strategic significance, however, because Germany now surrounded Czechoslovakia, one of the bulwarks of French security, on three sides.

Czechoslovakia contained about 3.5 million Germans who lived in the Sudetenland, near the German border. These Germans had belonged to the dominant nationality group in the old Austro-Hungarian Empire and resented their new minority position. Supported by Hitler and led by Konrad Henlein (1898–1945), they made ever-increasing demands for privileges and autonomy within the Czech state. The Czechs made concessions, but Hitler really wanted to destroy Czechoslovakia.

On September 12, 1938, Hitler made a provocative speech at the Nuremberg Nazi Party rally. His rhetoric led to rioting in the Sudetenland, and the Czechs declared martial law. German intervention seemed imminent. British prime minister Neville Chamberlain (1869–1940) made three flights to Germany between September 15 and September 29 in an attempt to appease Hitler at Czech expense and thus to avoid war. At Hitler's mountain retreat, Berchtesgaden, on September 15, Chamberlain accepted the separation of the Sudetenland from Czechoslovakia, and he and the French premier, Edouard Daladier (1884–1970), forced the Czechs to agree by threatening to abandon them if they did not. A week later, Chamberlain flew yet again to

MAP EXPLORATION

Interactive map: To explore this map further, go to www.myhistorylab.com

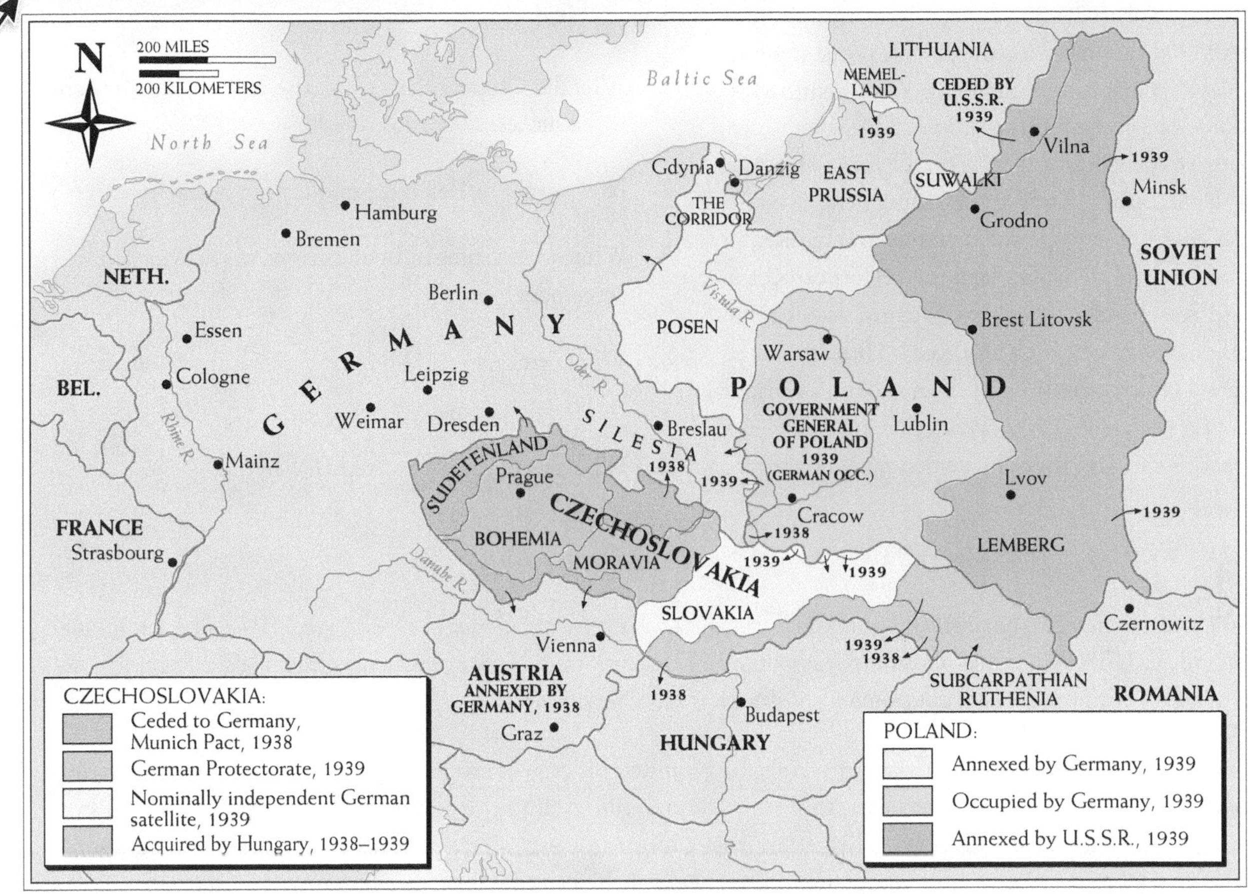

MAP 28–1 **Partitions of Czechoslovakia and Poland, 1938–1939** The immediate background of World War II is found in the complex international drama unfolding on Germany's eastern frontier in 1938 and 1939. Germany's expansion inevitably meant the victimization of Austria, Czechoslovakia, and Poland. With the failure of the Western powers' appeasement policy and the signing of a German-Soviet pact, the stage for the war was set.

How did appeasement ultimately lead to war?

Germany, only to find that Hitler had raised his demands. He wanted cession of the Sudetenland in three days and immediate occupation by the German army.

Munich

Chamberlain returned to England, and France and Britain prepared for war. At Chamberlain's request and at the last moment, Mussolini proposed a conference of Germany, Italy, France, and Britain. It met on September 29 in Munich. Hitler received almost everything he had demanded. (See Map 28–1.) The Sudetenland, the key to Czech security, became part of Germany, thus depriving the Czechs of any chance of self-defense. In return, Hitler agreed to spare the rest of Czechoslovakia.

Even in the short run, the appeasement of Hitler at Munich was a failure. Czechoslovakia did not survive. Soon Poland and Hungary tore more territory from it, and the Slovaks demanded a state of their own. Finally, on March 15, 1939, Hitler broke his promise and occupied Prague, putting an end to the Czech state and to illusions that his only goal was to restore Germans to the Reich. (See "Compare & Connect: The Munich Settlement," pages 716–717.)

QUICK REVIEW

The Occupation of the Sudetenland

- May 1938: Czechs mobilize their army in response to rumors of German invasion
- September 1938: Neville Chamberlain forces Czechs to separate the Sudetenland from Czechoslovakia
- September 29, 1938: Sudetenland is given to Germany at Munich conference

COMPARE & CONNECT

THE MUNICH SETTLEMENT

On September 29–30, 1938, Germany's dictator Adolf Hitler met with the British prime minister Neville Chamberlain, Italy's dictator Benito Mussolini, and France's prime minister Edouard Daladier to settle the fate of Czechoslovakia. The Czechs were not permitted to take part. It was the height of the Western democracies' effort to appease the dictators and resulted in the partition of Czechoslovakia, and the region called the Sudetenland was handed over to Germany, leaving the Czechs without a viable defense. Although Hitler promised to stop there, he took over the rest of the country without firing a shot on March 15, 1939. The following documents present opposite views on the achievement at Munich.

QUESTIONS

1. Why did Chamberlain think the meeting at Munich was a success for Britain?
2. How would he defend his policy of appeasement?
3. What were Churchill's objections to the Munich agreement?
4. What critique would he make of the appeasement policy?
5. Who do you think was right? Why?

I. CHAMBERLAIN'S EVALUATION

The following is an account of Chamberlain's return to England the day after the conference. He was greeted like a hero at the airport by a big crowd. Later that day he stood outside Number 10 Downing Street where again he read from the document and declared that he had brought back "peace with honour. I believe it is peace for our time."

Various shots of Mrs Chamberlain waving and shaking hands with crowds around Downing Street who are offering their support. M/S as Chamberlain's aeroplane finishes its return journey after the conference, taxis and comes to a stop at Heston. M/S of newsreel cameras filming his return from a roof at the aerodrome. M/S as Chamberlain emerges smiling from the door of a British Airways aeroplane to the cheers of the crowd. He shakes hands with a man waiting for him. L/S of crowds watching.

C/U as he makes a speech on the airfield — "The settlement of the Czech problem, which has now been achieved, is, in my view only the prelude to a larger settlement in which all Europe may find peace" (people cheer at this). "This morning I had another talk with the German Chancellor Herr Hitler and here is the paper which bears his name upon it as well as mine." (He holds paper up and waves it about, people cheer again.) "Some of you perhaps have already heard what it contains, but I would just like to read it to you." (He reads — 'We, the German Fuhrer and Chancellor and the British Prime Minister, have had a further meeting today and are agreed in recognising that the question of Anglo-German relations is of the first importance for the two countries, and for Europe. We regard the agreement signed last night and the Anglo-German naval agreement, as symbolic of the desire of our two peoples never to go to war with one another again' (everyone cheers). 'We are resolved that the method of consultation shall be the method adopted' (lots of "hear hears") 'to deal with any other questions that may concern our two countries, and we are determined to continue our efforts to remove possible sources of difference and thus to contribute to assure the peace of Europe.'" Everyone cheers and someone shouts "three cheers for Chamberlain" which they all do as he walks away and gets into the car. Everyone waves as he drives away.

Various shots as his car drives through the crowds to Buckingham Palace, people wave as he passes. M/S as King George VI and Queen Elizabeth (later the Queen Mother) come out onto the balcony of the palace with Neville Chamberlain and his wife. L/S as they wave and crowds wave back. L/S of cars and people blocking the street outside the palace.

Source: British Pathe.com Peace Four Power Conference 983.14.

Agreement at Munich On September 29–30, 1938, Hitler met with the leaders of Britain and France at Munich to decide the fate of Czechoslovakia. The Allied leaders abandoned the small democratic nation in a vain attempt to appease Hitler and avoid war. From left to right in the foreground: British Prime Minister Neville Chamberlain, French Prime Minister Edouard Daladier, Adolf Hitler, Benito Mussolini, and Italian Minister of Foreign Affairs (and Mussolini's son-in-law), Count Ciano.

National Archives and Records Administration

What did Chamberlain hope to accomplish at Munich?

II. CHURCHILL'S RESPONSE TO MUNICH

In the parliamentary debate that followed the Munich conference at the end of September 1938, Winston Churchill was one of the few critics of what had been accomplished. In the following selections from his speech, he expresses his concerns.

I will begin by saying what everybody would like to ignore or forget but which must nevertheless be stated, namely, that we have sustained a total and unmitigated defeat, and that France has suffered even more than we have . . . .

We really must not waste time after all this long debate upon the difference between the positions reached at Berchtesgaden, at Godesberg and at Munich. They can be very simply epitomized if the House will permit me to vary the metaphor. One pound was demanded at the pistol's point. When it was given, £2 were demanded at the pistol's point. Finally, the dictator consented to take £1 17s. 6d. and the rest in promises of good will for the future. . . .

All is over. Silent, mournful, abandoned, broken, Czechoslovakia recedes into the darkness. She has suffered in every respect by her association with the Western democracies and with the League of Nations, of which she has always been an obedient servant. . . .

We have been reduced in these five years from a position of security so overwhelming and so unchallengeable that we never cared to think about it. We have been reduced from a position where the very word "war" was considered one which could be used only by persons qualifying for a lunatic asylum. We have been reduced from a position of safety and power—power to do good, power to be generous to a beaten foe, power to make terms with Germany, power to give her proper redress for her grievances, power to stop her arming if we chose, power to take any step in strength or mercy or justice which we thought right—reduced in five years from a position safe and unchallenged to where we stand now. . . .

The responsibility must rest with those who have had the undisputed control of our political affairs. They neither prevented Germany from rearming, nor did they rearm ourselves in time. They quarreled with Italy without saving Ethiopia. They exploited and discredited the vast institution of the League of Nations and they neglected to make alliances and combinations which might have repaired previous errors, and thus they left us in the hour of trial without adequate national defense or effective international security. . . .

We are in the presence of a disaster of the first magnitude which has befallen Great Britain and France. Do not let us blind ourselves to that. It must now be accepted that all the countries of Central and Eastern Europe will make the best terms they can with the triumphant Nazi power. The system of alliances in Central Europe upon which France has relied for her safety has been swept away, and I can see no means by which it can be reconstituted. The road down the Danube Valley to the Black Sea, the road which leads as far as Turkey, has been opened.

Source: "Churchill's Response to Munich" from Winston S. Churchill, *Blood, Sweat, and Tears* (New York: G. P. Putnam's Sons, 1941), pp. 55–56, 58, 60–61.

Poland was the next target of German expansion. In the spring of 1939, the Germans put pressure on Poland to restore the formerly German city of Danzig and to allow a railroad and a highway through the Polish Corridor to connect East Prussia with the rest of Germany. When the Poles would not yield, the usual propaganda campaign began, and the pressure mounted. On March 31, Chamberlain announced a Franco-British guarantee of Polish independence. Hitler appears to have expected to fight a war with Poland, but not with the Western allies, for he did not take their guarantee seriously. Moreover, France and Britain had no means to get effective help to the Poles. The French, still dominated by the defensive mentality of the Maginot Line, had no intention of attacking Germany. The only way to defend Poland was to bring Russia into the alliance against Hitler, but a Russian alliance posed many problems. Each side was profoundly suspicious of the other. The French and the British were hostile to communism, and since Stalin's purge of the Red Army, they were skeptical of the military value of a Russian alliance. Besides, the Russians could not help Poland without being given the right to enter Poland and Romania. Both nations, suspicious of Russian intentions—and with good reason—refused to grant these rights. As a result, Western negotiations for an alliance with Russia made little progress.

The Nazi-Soviet Pact

The Russians had at least equally good reason to hesitate. They resented being left out of the Munich agreement. The low priority that the West gave to negotiations with Russia, compared with the urgency with which Britain and France dealt with Hitler, annoyed them. The Russians feared, rightly, that the Western powers meant them to bear the burden of the war against Germany. As a result, they opened negotiations with Hitler, and on August 23, 1939, the world was shocked to learn of a Nazi-Soviet nonaggression pact. The secret provisions of the pact, which were easily guessed and soon carried out, divided Poland between the two powers and allowed Russia to occupy the Baltic states and to take Bessarabia from Romania.

The Nazi-Soviet pact sealed the fate of Poland, and the Franco-British commitment guaranteed a general war. On September 1, 1939, the Germans invaded Poland. Two days later, Britain and France declared war on Germany. World War II had begun.

WORLD WAR II (1939–1945)

IN WHAT ways was World War II a "total" war?

World War II was truly global. Fighting took place in Europe, North Africa, and Asia, on the Atlantic and the Pacific Oceans, and in the Northern and Southern Hemispheres. The demand for the fullest exploitation of material and human resources for increased production, the use of blockades, and the intensive bombing of civilian targets made the war of 1939 even more "total"—that is, comprehensive and intense—than that of 1914.

The German Conquest of Europe

The German attack on Poland produced swift success. The new style of "lightning warfare," or *blitzkrieg*, employed fast-moving, massed armored columns supported by airpower. The speed of the German victory astonished the Russians, who hastened to collect their share of the booty before Hitler could deprive them of it.

On September 17, Russia invaded Poland from the east, dividing the country with the Germans. The Red Army then occupied the encircled Baltic countries of Estonia, Latvia, and Lithuania. In June 1940, the Russians forced Romania to cede Bessarabia. In November 1939, the Russians invaded Finland, but the Finns resisted fiercely for six months. Although they were finally worn down and compelled to yield territory and bases to Russia, the Finns remained independent.

Until the spring of 1940, the western front was quiet. The French remained behind the Maginot Line. Britain rearmed hastily, and the British navy blockaded Germany. Cynics in the West called it the phony war, or *Sitzkrieg*, but Hitler shattered the stillness in the spring of 1940. In April, the Germans invaded Denmark and Norway. A month later, a combined land and air attack struck Belgium, the Netherlands, and Luxembourg.

The British and French armies in Belgium were forced to flee to the English Channel to seek escape on the beaches of Dunkirk. The heroic efforts of hundreds of Britons manning small boats saved more than 200,000 British and 100,000 French soldiers. Casualties, however, were high, and valuable equipment was abandoned.

The Maginot Line ran from Switzerland to the Belgian frontier. Until 1936, the French had expected the Belgians to continue the fortifications along their German border. After Hitler remilitarized the Rhineland without opposition, the Belgians lost faith in their French alliance and proclaimed their neutrality, leaving the Maginot Line exposed on its left flank. Hitler's swift advance through Belgium, therefore, circumvented France's main line of defense.

The French army collapsed. Mussolini, eager to claim the spoils of victory when he thought it was safe to do so, invaded southern France on June 10. Less than a week later, the new French government, under the ancient hero of Verdun, Marshal Henri Philippe Pétain (1856–1951), asked for an armistice.

The Battle of Britain

If there was any chance the British would consider coming to terms with Germany after the fall of France, it disappeared when Winston Churchill (1874–1965) replaced Chamberlain as prime minister in May 1940. Churchill had been an early and forceful critic of Hitler, the Nazis, and the policy of appeasement. His skill as a speaker and a writer enabled him to inspire the British people with his own courage and determination and to undertake what seemed a hopeless fight. Hitler and his allies, including the Soviet Union, controlled all of Europe. Japan was having its way in Asia. The United States was neutral, dominated by isolationist sentiment, and determined to avoid involvement outside the Western Hemisphere.

One of Churchill's greatest achievements was establishing a close relationship with the American president Franklin D. Roosevelt (1882–1945). Roosevelt found ways to help the British despite strong political opposition. In 1940 and 1941, before the United States was at war, America sent military supplies, traded badly needed warships for leases on British naval bases, and even convoyed ships across the Atlantic to help the British survive.

As weeks passed and Britain remained defiant, Hitler was forced to contemplate an invasion, and that required control of the air. The first strikes by the German air force (**Luftwaffe**), directed against the airfields and fighter planes in southeast England, began in August 1940. In early September, however, seeking revenge for some British bombing raids on German cities, the Luftwaffe switched its main attacks to London. For two months, it bombed London every night. Much of the city was destroyed, and about 15,000 people were killed. Far from shattering British morale, however, the bombings united the British people and made them more resolute.

Luftwaffe The German air force.

The Royal Air Force (RAF) inflicted heavy losses on the Luftwaffe. Aided by the newly developed radar and excellent communications, the British Spitfire and Hurricane fighter planes destroyed more than twice as many enemy planes as the RAF lost. Hitler had lost the Battle of Britain in the air and was forced to abandon his plans for invasion.

The German Attack on Russia

The defeat of Russia and the conquest of the Ukraine to provide *Lebensraum*, or "living space," for the German people had always been a major goal for Hitler. In December 1940, even while the bombing of England continued, he ordered his generals to prepare to invade Russia by May 15, 1941. (See Map 28–2.)

MAP 28–2 **Axis Europe, 1941** On the eve of the German invasion of the Soviet Union, a German-Italian Axis bestrode most of Europe by annexation, occupation, or alliance—from Norway and Finland in the north to Greece in the south, and from Poland to France. Britain, the Soviet Union, a number of insurgent groups, and, finally, America, had before them the long struggle of conquering this "fortress Europe" of the Axis.

Given the diversity of cultures within the Axis, what were its prospects for maintaining order and stability in Europe over the long term?

Operation Barbarossa, the code name for the invasion of Russia, was aimed to destroy Russia before winter could set in. Success depended, in part, on an early start, but here Hitler's Italian alliance proved costly. Mussolini's invasion of France was a fiasco, even though the Germans were simultaneously crushing the main French forces. Hitler did not allow Mussolini to annex French territory in Europe or North Africa. Mussolini instead attacked the British in Egypt and drove them back some sixty miles. Encouraged by this success, he also invaded Greece from his base in Albania (which he had seized in 1939).

In North Africa, however, the British counterattacked and invaded Libya. The Greeks themselves pushed into Albania. In March 1941, the British sent help to the Greeks, and Hitler was forced to divert his attention to the Balkans and Africa. General Erwin Rommel (1891–1944) went to Africa and soon drove the British back into Egypt. In the Balkans, the German army swiftly occupied Yugoslavia and crushed Greek resistance. The price, however, was a delay of six weeks that would prove costly the following winter in the Russian campaign.

Operation Barbarossa was launched against Russia on June 22, 1941, and it almost succeeded. Despite their deep suspicion of Germany, the Russians were taken quite by surprise. By November, the German army stood at the gates of Leningrad, on the outskirts of Moscow, and on the Don River. Yet the Germans could not deliver the final blow. In August, they delayed their advance while Hitler decided strategy. The German general staff wanted to take Moscow before winter. Hitler, however, diverted a significant force to the south. By the time he was ready to return to the offensive near Moscow, it was too late. Winter devastated the German army, which was not equipped to face it. In November and December, the Russians counterattacked. The *blitzkrieg* had turned into a war of attrition, and the Germans began to have nightmares of duplicating Napoleon's retreat.

QUICK REVIEW

Operation Barbarossa

- June 22, 1941: surprise invasion of Soviet Union by Germany (Operation Barbarossa) launched
- Germany advanced rapidly in the early stages of the campaign
- German failure to deliver a decisive blow delayed victory until winter set in, turning the tide in the Soviets' favor

Hitler's Plans for Europe

Hitler often spoke of the "new order" that he meant to impose after he had established his **Third Reich** (Empire) throughout Europe. If his organization of Germany before the war is a proper guide, he had no single plan of government but relied on intuition and pragmatism. His organization of a conquered Europe had the same patchwork characteristics. Some conquered territory was annexed to Germany, some was not annexed but administered directly by German officials, and other lands were nominally autonomous but ruled by puppet governments.

Third Reich Hitler's Nazi regime.

Hitler's regime was probably unmatched in history for carefully planned terror and inhumanity. His plan of giving *Lebensraum* to the Germans was to be accomplished at the expense of people he deemed to be inferior. Hitler established colonies of Germans in parts of Poland, driving the local people from their land and employing them as cheap, virtually slave, labor. He had similar plans on an even greater scale for Russia.

Hitler's long-range plans included germanization as well as colonization. In lands people racially akin to the Germans inhabited, like the Scandinavian countries, the Netherlands, and Switzerland, the German nation would absorb the natives. Hitler even had plans to adopt selected people from the lesser races into the master race. For example, the Nazis planned to bring half a million Ukrainian girls to Germany as servants and find German husbands for them.

Hitler regarded the conquered lands as a source of plunder. From Eastern Europe, he removed everything useful, including entire industries. In Russia and Poland, the Germans simply confiscated the land itself. In the West, the conquered countries had to support the occupying army at a rate several times above the real cost. The Germans used the profits to buy up everything desirable, stripping the conquered peoples of most necessities.

Japan and the United States Enter the War

The U.S. government might not have overcome isolationist sentiment and entered the war in the Atlantic if war had not been thrust on America in the Pacific. Since the Japanese conquest of Manchuria in 1931, American policy toward Japan had been suspicious and unfriendly. The outbreak of the war in Europe emboldened the Japanese to accelerate their drive to dominate Asia. They allied themselves with Germany and Italy, made a treaty of neutrality with the Soviet Union, and forced defeated France to give them bases in Indochina. They also continued their war in China and planned to gain control of Malaya and the East Indies (Indonesia) at the expense of beleaguered Britain and the conquered Netherlands. The only barrier to Japanese expansion was the United States.

The Americans had temporized, unwilling to cut off vital supplies of oil and other materials for fear of provoking a Japanese attack on Southeast Asia and the East Indies. The Japanese occupation of Indochina in July 1941 changed that policy, which had already begun to stiffen. The United States froze Japanese assets and cut off oil supplies; the British and Dutch did the same. Japanese plans for expansion could not continue without the conquest of the Indonesian oil fields and Malayan rubber and tin.

QUICK REVIEW

The Path to War

- 1931: Japan conquers Manchuria
- July 1941: in response to Japanese occupation of Indonesia, the United States freezes Japanese assets and cuts off oil shipments
- December 7, 1941: Japan launches a surprise attack on Pearl Harbor

In October, a war faction led by General Hideki Tojo (1885–1948) took power in Japan and decided to risk a war rather than yield. On Sunday morning, December 7, 1941, Japan launched an air attack on Pearl Harbor, Hawaii, the chief American naval base in the Pacific. The attack destroyed much of the American fleet and many airplanes. The American capacity to wage war in the Pacific was negated for the time being. The next day, the United States and Britain declared war on Japan. Three days later, Germany and Italy declared war on the United States.

The Tide Turns

The Japanese swiftly captured Guam, Wake Island, and the Philippine Islands. By the spring of 1942, they had conquered Hong Kong, Malaya, Burma, and the Dutch East Indies. They controlled the southwest Pacific as far as New Guinea and were poised for an attack on Australia. It seemed that nothing could stop them.

The successful Japanese attack on the American base at Pearl Harbor in Hawaii on December 7, 1941, together with simultaneous attacks on other Pacific bases, brought the United States into war against the Axis powers. This picture shows the battleships USS *West Virginia* and USS *Tennessee* in flames as a small boat rescues a man from the water.

U.S. Army Photo

How did the news of the attack on Pearl Harbor change American public opinion?

In 1942, the Germans also advanced deeper into Russia, while in Africa Rommel drove the British back into Egypt until they stopped him at El Alamein, only seventy miles from Alexandria. Relations between the democracies and their Soviet ally were not close. German submarine warfare was threatening British supplies. The Allies were being thrown back on every front, and the future looked bleak.

The first good news for the Allied cause in the Pacific came in the spring of 1942. A naval battle in the Coral Sea sank many Japanese ships and gave security to Australia. A month later, the United States defeated the Japanese in a fierce air and naval battle off Midway Island. This victory blunted the chance of another assault on Hawaii and did enough damage to halt the Japanese advance. Soon American marines landed on Guadalcanal in the Solomon Islands and began to reverse the momentum of the war. The war in the Pacific was far from over, but the check to Japan allowed the Allies to concentrate their efforts on Europe.

In 1942, American preparation and production were inadequate to invade Europe. Not until 1944 were conditions right for the invasion, but in the meantime other developments forecast the doom of the Axis. (See "Encountering the Past: Rosie the Riveter and American Women in the War Effort, page 724.")

In the battle of Stalingrad, Russian troops contested every street and building. Although the city was all but destroyed in the fighting and Russian casualties were enormous, the German army in the east never recovered from the defeat it suffered there.

Hulton Archives/Getty Images, Inc.

What made Stalingrad such an important turning point in the war?

Allied Landings in Africa, Sicily, and Italy In November 1942, an Allied force landed in French North Africa. Even before that landing, after stopping Rommel at El Alamein, British field marshal Bernard Montgomery (1887–1976) had begun a drive to the west. Now, the Americans pushed eastward through Morocco and Algeria. The two armies caught the German army between them in Tunisia and crushed it. The Allies now controlled the Mediterranean and could attack southern Europe.

In July and August 1943, the Allies took Sicily. A coup toppled Mussolini, but the Germans occupied Italy. The Allies landed in Italy, and Marshal Pietro Badoglio (1871–1956), the leader of the new Italian government, declared war on Germany. The Germans there resisted fiercely, but the need to defend Italy weakened the Germans on other fronts.

Battle of Stalingrad The Russian campaign became especially demanding. In the summer of 1942, the Germans resumed the offensive on all fronts but were unable to get far except in the south. (See Map 28–3, page 725.) Their goal was the oil fields near the Caspian Sea. Stalingrad, on the Volga, was a key point on the flank of the German army in the south. The Battle of Stalingrad raged for months with unexampled ferocity. The Russians lost more men in this one battle than the Americans lost in combat during the entire war, but their heroic defense prevailed.

Stalingrad marked the turning point of the Russian campaign. Thereafter, the Americans provided material help. Even more importantly, increased production from their own industry allowed the Russians to gain and keep the offensive. As the Germans' resources dwindled, the Russians inexorably advanced westward.

Strategic Bombing In 1943, the Allies also gained ground in production and logistics. The industrial might of the United States began to come into full force, and new technology and tactics reduced the submarine menace.

In the same year, the American and British air forces began a series of massive bombardments of Germany by night and day. By 1945, the Allies could bomb at will. Concentrated attacks on industrial targets, especially communication centers and oil refineries, did extensive damage and helped shorten the war. Terror bombing of the civilian population was carried out too, but with no useful result. The bombardment of Dresden in February 1945 was especially savage and destructive. Whatever else it accomplished, the aerial war over Germany took a heavy toll on the German air force and diverted German resources from other military purposes.

Allied troops landed in Normandy on D-day, June 6, 1944.

Courtesy of the Library of Congress

How did American economic power make D-day possible?

The Defeat of Nazi Germany

On June 6, 1944 ("D-day"), American, British, and Canadian troops landed in force on the coast of Normandy. The "second

ENCOUNTERING THE PAST

Rosie the Riveter and American Women in the War Effort

The huge productive capacity of American industry was essential to Allied victory in the war, and American women helped sustain it. Before the start of the war and despite the unprecedented number of women the Great Depression had forced to seek employment, society was still hostile to the idea of women working outside their homes. World War II changed that. The workforce lost millions of men to the military, and women were needed to take their places.

Factories proliferated to produce the vast amounts of equipment needed for the war, and they eagerly recruited workers from groups they had previously spurned: African Americans from the rural south and women. President Roosevelt in a speech in October 1942 observed, "In some communities employers dislike to hire women. In others they are reluctant to hire Negroes. We can no longer afford to indulge such prejudice."

For some women, patriotism was more important than pay. Their jobs provided them with a way to support their male friends and relatives on the battlefield. A popular song told the story of "Rosie the Riveter," a young woman who made aircraft to protect her Marine boyfriend. A painting by Norman Rockwell for the cover of the *Saturday Evening Post* depicted her holding her rivet gun and resting her foot on a copy of Hitler's *Mein Kampf.*

Rosie the Riveter was one of the best known symbols of the U.S. war effort in World War II.

What contribution did American women make to the war effort?

HOW DID the war change attitudes about the place of women and minorities in American society?

front" was opened. The German defense was strong, but the Allies established a beachhead and then broke out of it. In mid-August, the Allies also landed in southern France. By the beginning of September, France had been liberated.

The Battle of the Bulge All went smoothly until December, when the Germans launched a counterattack in Belgium and Luxembourg through the Ardennes Forest. Because the Germans pushed forward into the Allied line, this was called the Battle of the Bulge. Although the Allies suffered heavy losses, the Bulge was the last gasp for the Germans in the West. The Allies crossed the Rhine in March 1945, and German resistance crumbled.

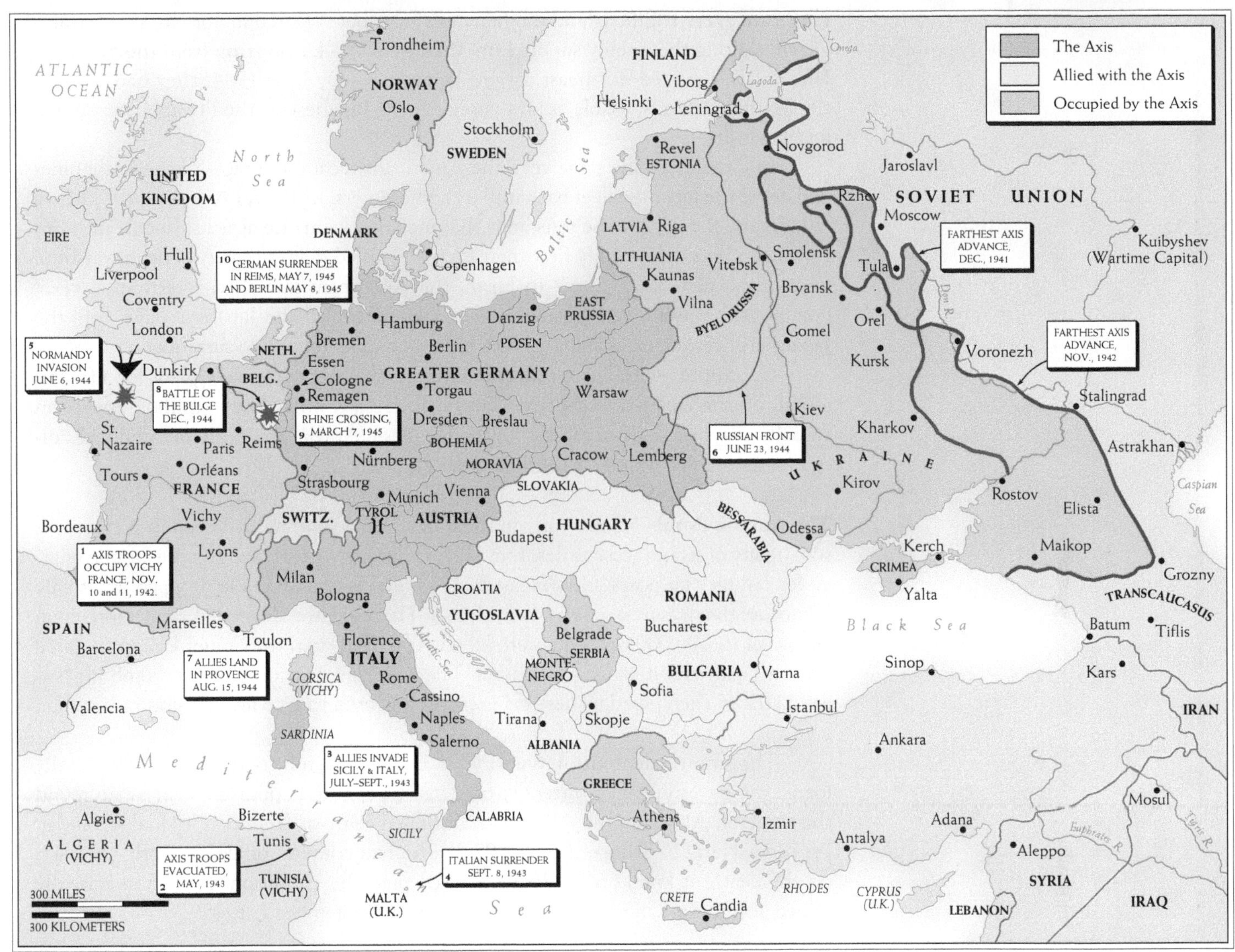

MAP 28–3 **Defeat of the Axis in Europe, 1942–1945** Here are some of the major steps in the progress toward Allied victory against Axis Europe. From the south through Italy, the west through France, and the east through Russia, the Allies gradually conquered the Continent to bring the war in Europe to a close.

On which of these three fronts—southern, western, or eastern—was World War II fought the longest?

The Capture of Berlin By March 1945, the Russians were near Berlin. Because the Allies insisted on unconditional surrender, the Germans fought on until May. Hitler committed suicide in an underground bunker in Berlin on April 30, 1945. The Russians occupied Berlin by agreement with their Western allies. The Third Reich lasted only a dozen years instead of the thousand Hitler had predicted.

QUICK REVIEW

Key Battles in Europe

- June 6, 1944 (D-day): Allied forces land in Normandy
- December 1944: Germans inflict heavy losses at the Battle of the Bulge but fail to halt Allies' advance
- May 1945: Soviet troops capture Berlin

Fall of the Japanese Empire

The war in Europe ended on May 8, 1945, and by then, victory over Japan was also in sight.

Americans Recapture the Pacific Islands In 1943, the American forces, still small in number, began a campaign of "island hopping." They did not try to recapture every Pacific island the Japanese held, but selected major bases and strategic sites along the enemy supply line. (See Map 28–4.) Starting from the Solomon Islands, they moved northeast toward Japan itself. By June 1944, they had reached the Mariana Islands, usable as bases to bomb the Japanese in the Philippines, China, and Japan itself.

In October of the same year, the Americans recaptured most of the Philippines and drove the Japanese fleet back into its home waters. In 1945, Iwo Jima and Okinawa fell, despite fierce Japanese resistance that included kamikaze attacks, suicide missions in which pilots deliberately flew their explosive-filled planes into American warships. From these new bases, closer to Japan, the Americans launched a terrible wave of bombings that destroyed Japanese industry and disabled the Japanese navy. Still the Japanese government, dominated by a military clique, refused to surrender.

Confronted with Japan's determination, the Americans made plans for a frontal assault on the Japanese homeland. They calculated it might cost a million American casualties and even greater losses for the Japanese. At this point, science and technology presented the Americans with another choice.

The Atomic Bomb Since early in the war, a secret program had been in progress. Its staff, many of whom were exiles from Hitler's Europe, was working to use atomic energy for military purposes. On August 6, 1945, an American plane dropped an atomic bomb on the Japanese city of Hiroshima. The city was destroyed, and more than 70,000 of its 200,000 residents were killed. Two days later, the Soviet Union declared war on Japan and invaded Manchuria. The next day, a second atomic bomb hit Nagasaki. Even then, the Japanese cabinet was prepared to face an invasion rather than give up.

The unprecedented intervention of Emperor Hirohito (r. 1926–1989) finally forced the government to surrender on August 14 on the condition that Japan retain the emperor. Although the Allies had continued to insist on unconditional surrender, President Harry S. Truman (1884–1972), who had come to office on April 12, 1945, on the death of Franklin D. Roosevelt, accepted the condition. Peace was formally signed aboard the USS *Missouri* in Tokyo Bay on September 2, 1945.

The Cost of War

World War II was the most terrible war in history. Military deaths are estimated at some 15 million, and at least as many civilians were killed. If we include deaths linked indirectly to the war, from disease, hunger, and other causes, the number of victims might reach 40 million. Most of Europe and large parts of Asia were devastated. Yet the end of so terrible a war brought little opportunity to relax. The dawn of the atomic age made people conscious that another major war might extinguish humanity. Everything depended on concluding a stable peace, but even as the fighting ended, conflicts among the victors made the prospects of a lasting peace doubtful.

RACISM AND THE HOLOCAUST

WHAT WAS the Holocaust?

The most horrible aspect of the Nazi rule in Europe arose not from military or economic necessity but from the inhumanity and brutality inherent in Hitler's racial doctrines. These were applied to several groups of people in Eastern Europe.

Hitler considered the Slavs *Untermenschen*, subhuman creatures like beasts who need not be treated as people. In parts of Poland, the upper and professional classes

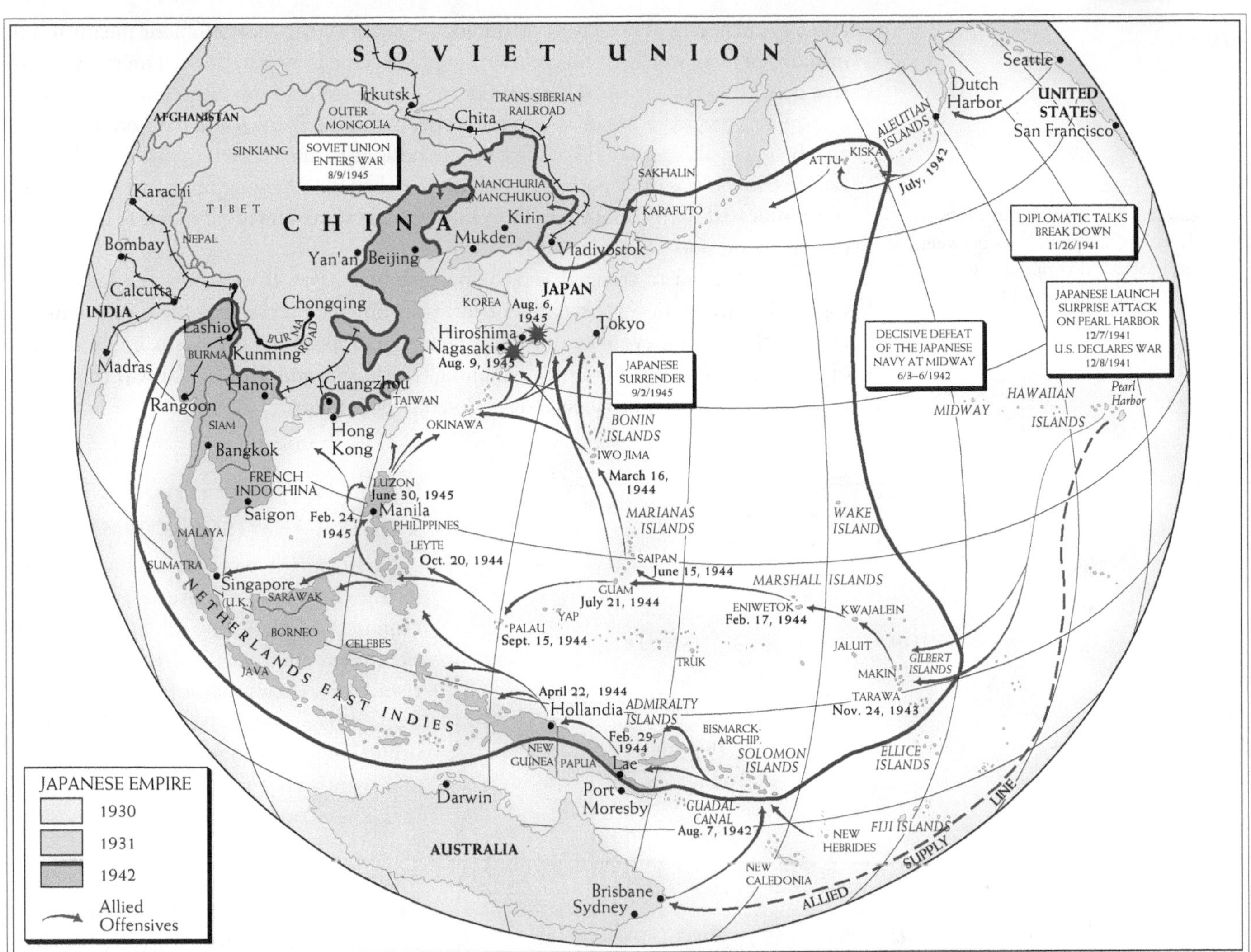

MAP 28–4 World War II in the Pacific As in Europe, the Pacific war involved Allied recapture of areas that had been quickly taken earlier by the enemy. The enormous area represented by the map shows the initial expansion of Japanese holdings to cover half the Pacific and its islands, as well as huge sections of eastern Asia, and the long struggle to push the Japanese back to their homeland and defeat them.

Could the territories that Japan seized at the start of the war have become a coherent empire?

were entirely removed—jailed, deported, or killed. Schools and churches were closed. The Nazis limited marriage to keep down the Polish birthrate and imposed harsh living conditions.

In Russia, things were even worse. Hitler spoke of his Russian campaign as a war of extermination. Heinrich Himmler (1900–1945), head of Hitler's elite SS formations, planned to eliminate 30 million Slavs to make room for Germans; he formed extermination squads for this purpose. Six million Russian prisoners of war and deported civilians may have died under Nazi rule.

Hitler, however, had envisioned a special fate for the Jews. He meant to make all Europe *Judenrein*, or "free of Jews." The Nazis built extermination camps in Germany and Poland and used the latest technology to achieve the most efficient means to kill millions of men, women, and children simply because they were Jews. The most extensive destruction occurred in Eastern Europe and Russia, but the Nazis and their collaborators in occupied areas of Western Europe, including France, the Netherlands, Italy, and Belgium, also deported Jews from these nations to almost certain death in the east. Before the war was over, perhaps 6 million Jews had died in what has come to be called the **Holocaust**. Only about a million European Jews remained alive, most of them in pitiable condition. (See Map 28–5.)

Holocaust The Nazi extermination of millions of European Jews between 1940 and 1945. Also called the "final solution to the Jewish problem."

It is difficult to comprehend the massive Nazi effort to eradicate the Jews of Europe. This destruction took different forms in different regions of the Continent. To explore this central event of twentieth-century European history, we examine the fate of the Polish Jewish community, which before the Second World War was the largest in Europe, consisting of 10 percent of Poland's population.

MAP 28–5 **The Holocaust** The Nazi policy of ethnic cleansing—targeting Jews, Gypsies, political dissidents, and "social deviants"—began with imprisoning them in concentration camps, but by 1943 the *Endlösung*, or *Final Solution*, called for the systematic extermination of "undesirables."

How important were the logistics of rail transportation to the Final Solution?

The Destruction of the Polish Jewish Community

A large Jewish community had dwelled within Poland for centuries, often in a climate of religious and cultural anti-Semitism. As a result of this anti-Semitism, Polish Jews had long lived in their own villages and later in their own urban neighborhoods. After the late-eighteenth-century partitions of Poland and the Congress of Vienna, most of Poland came under Russian rule. Through the policy of Official Nationalism (see Chapter 21), the nineteenth-century tsars identified loyalty to their government with membership in the Russian Orthodox Church. Jews were subject to a wide variety of discriminatory legislation. Polish Jews did not experience any of the forms of Jewish emancipation that occurred in Western Europe. (See Chapter 24.)

Language, food, dress, and place of residence as well as religion distinguished Jews from the rest of the Polish population, almost all of whom were Roman Catholics. Many Polish Jews also moved to cities, and Jews were regarded as an urban people in a predominantly rural nation. Moreover, Jews were among the poorest people in Poland, often working as self-employed merchants, peddlers, and craftspeople, or in industries, such as textiles, clothing, and paper, that other Poles identified as Jewish-dominated. Few Polish Jews belonged to trade unions. These conditions made them vulnerable during the economic turmoil of the 1920s and especially of the 1930s.

Polish Anti-Semitism Between the Wars

Discrimination against Jews existed throughout the culture and politics of interwar Poland. During those years, the Polish government, supported by spokesmen for the Polish Roman Catholic Church, pursued policies that were anti-Semitic. The Polish government nationalized the matches, salt, tobacco, and alcohol industries and then enacted legislation that discriminated against hiring Jews for these government monopolies. Other laws made it difficult for Jews to observe the Sabbath while keeping their jobs. Regulations requiring businesses to be closed on Sunday meant Jewish shops had to close two days of the week. By the late 1930s, as ethnic nationalism became stronger, the government required businesses to display their owners' names prominently, which made it easy for people to avoid Jewish shops.

Whatever active anti-Semitism existed in Poland before the German invasion of 1939, it was the Nazis who tried to destroy the Polish Jewish community and Jewish communities elsewhere in Europe that fell under German control. In that respect, the Holocaust constitutes an event driven by German policy within the larger event of the Second World War.

World War II resulted in the near total destruction of the Jews of Europe, victims of the Holocaust spawned by Hitler's racial theories of the superiority and inferiority of particular ethnic groups. Hitler placed special emphasis on the need to exterminate the Jews, to whom he attributed particular wickedness. This picture shows Hungarian Jewish women, after "disinfection" and head shaving, marching to the concentration or death camp at Auschwitz-Birkenau, Poland.

Library of Congress/Photo by Bernhard Walter; source: National Archives and Records Administration

What did the German public know about the Holocaust prior to the end of World War II?

The Nazi Assault on the Jews of Poland

The joint German-Soviet invasion of Poland brought millions of Jews under either German or Soviet authority. By late autumn 1939, the Germans had begun to move against Polish Jews. The Nazi government first thought it might herd virtually all the Jews of occupied Europe into the Lublin region of Poland. By early 1940, the Nazis decided to move as many Jews as possible into ghettos, where they would be separated from the rest of the Polish population. The largest ghettos were Lodz and Warsaw, each of which had populations of several hundred thousand. The Nazis moved Jews from all over Poland and, eventually, other occupied regions by rail into these ghettos and then sealed them off with police guards and walls. Jewish councils, which were torn between responsibility to their communities and the need to respond to German orders, administered the ghettos. The Nazis confiscated and sold the personal property and businesses of the Jews who were herded into the ghettos. Jewish laborers were sent out to work as contract labor while their families remained in the ghettos. By 1941, the Polish Jews had lost their civic standing and property. They had been located in segregated communities within Poland where disease was rampant and the food supply meager. Approximately 20 percent of the population of both the Lodz and Warsaw ghettos died of disease and malnourishment.

The German invasion of the Soviet Union in June 1941 made the situation of Jews in Poland even worse. The advancing German forces killed tens of thousands of Jews in the Soviet Union during 1941 and hundreds of thousands more the next year. During the second half of 1941, the Nazi government decided to exterminate the Jews of Europe. From late 1941 through 1944, the Germans transported Jews from the ghettos by rail to death camps in Poland, including Kulmhof, Belzen, Sobibor, Treblinka, Birkenau, and Auschwitz. In these camps, Jews were systematically killed in gas chambers.

By 1945, approximately 90 percent of the pre-1939 Jewish population of Poland had been destroyed. The tiny minority of Polish Jews who had survived faced bitter anti-Semitism under the postwar Soviet-dominated government. Many immigrated to Israel, leaving only a few thousand Jews within the borders of a nation where they had numbered in the millions and where they had created a rich religious, cultural, and political community. The largest Jewish community in Europe had virtually ceased to exist.

Explanations of the Holocaust

As interest in the Holocaust has grown since the 1960s, so has debate about its character and meaning. Was it a unique event of unprecedented and unparalleled evil, or was it one specific instance of a more general human wickedness that has found expression throughout history? Are its roots to be found in flaws in human nature as a whole, or are they unique to the experience of the West or, perhaps, to the German people?

Perhaps we should think of the problem from the standpoint of two questions: Why were the Jews the main target of Hitler's policy of extermination? How was it possible to carry out such a vast mass murder? Surely, an essential part of an answer to the first question is the persistence of anti-Semitism in Christianity and Western culture, from the Church Fathers to Luther and to the teachings of churches in modern times. Some would combine this religious and historical anti-Semitism with the coming of the Enlightenment and the social sciences, which gave rise to pseudoscientific racial theories that lent a new twist to the old hatred of the Jews. Pseudoscientific racism appears to have been the most powerful influence on Hitler, but it could not have found widespread support without deeply rooted religious and social anti-Semitism.

As to how it was possible to murder 6 million people, part of the answer must lie in the parochial nationalism that arose during and after the French Revolution. For many people, nationalism divided the world into one's fellow nationals and all others. It encouraged, excused, and even justified terrible and violent acts performed on behalf of one's homeland. Another part of the answer may derive from the utopian visions also unleashed by some Enlightenment writers, who promised to achieve perfect societies through social engineering, regardless of the human cost. To this were added the scientific and technological advances that gave the modern state new power to command its people, to persuade them to obey by controlling the media of propaganda, and to enforce its will with efficient brutality. All of these permitted the creation of a totalitarian state that, for the first time in history, could conduct mass murder on the scale of the Holocaust.

These questions and their possible answers are but suggestions meant to encourage further and deeper thought in what will surely be a continuing debate among scholars and the general public.

THE DOMESTIC FRONTS

WHAT IMPACT did World War II have on European society?

World War II represented an effort at total war by all the belligerents. One result was the carnage that occurred during the fighting. Another was an unprecedented organization of civilians on the home fronts. Each domestic effort and experience was different, but few escaped the impact of the conflict. Everywhere there were shortages, propaganda campaigns, and new political developments.

Germany: From Apparent Victory to Defeat

Hitler had expected to defeat all his enemies by rapid strokes, or *blitzkriegs*. Such campaigns would have required little change in Germany's society and economy. During the first two years of the war, in fact, Hitler demanded few sacrifices from the German people. Germany's failure to quickly overwhelm the Soviet Union changed everything. Food was no longer available from the east in needed quantities, Germany had to mobilize for total war, and the government demanded major sacrifices.

A great expansion of the army and of military production began in 1942. The government sought the cooperation of major German businesses to increase wartime production. Between 1942 and late 1944, the output of military products tripled. As the war went on, more men were drafted from industry into the army, and military production suffered. As the manufacture of armaments replaced the production of consumer goods, shortages of everyday products became serious. Food rationing began in April 1942, and shortages were severe until the Nazi government seized more food from occupied Europe.

By 1943, labor shortages became severe. The Nazis required German teenagers and retired men to work in the factories, and many women joined them. To achieve total mobilization, the Germans closed retail businesses, raised the age of eligibility of women for compulsory service, shifted non-German domestic workers to wartime industry, moved artists and entertainers into military service, closed theaters, and reduced such basic public services as mail and railways. Finally, the Nazis compelled thousands of non-Germans to do forced labor in Germany.

Hitler assigned women a special place in the war effort. The celebration of motherhood continued, with an emphasis on women who were the mothers of important military figures. Films portrayed ordinary women who became brave and patriotic during the war and remained faithful to their husbands who were at the front. Women were shown as mothers and wives who sent their sons and husbands off to war. The government pictured other wartime activities of women as the natural fulfillment of their maternal roles. Finally, by their faithful chastity, German women were protecting racial purity. They were not to marry or to have sex with non-Germans.

Propaganda minister Josef Goebbels (1897–1945) used both radio and films to boost the Nazi cause. Movies of the collapse of Poland, Belgium, Holland, and France showed German military might. Throughout the conquered territories, the Nazis used the same mass media to frighten inhabitants about the possible consequences of an Allied victory. Later in the war, Goebbels broadcast exaggerated claims of Nazi victories. As the German armies were checked on the battlefield, especially in Russia, propaganda became a substitute for victory. To stiffen German resolve, propaganda now aimed to frighten Germans about the consequences of defeat.

After May 1943, when the Allies began their major bombing offensive over Germany, the German people had much to fear. The bombing devastated one German city after another but did not undermine German morale. The bombing may even have increased German resistance by seeming to confirm the regime's propaganda about the ruthlessness of Germany's opponents.

The war brought great changes to Germany, but what transformed the country most was the experience of physical destruction, invasion, and occupation. Hitler and the Nazis had brought Germany to such a complete and disastrous defeat that only a new kind of state with new political structures could emerge.

France: Defeat, Collaboration, and Resistance

The terms of the 1940 armistice between France, under Pétain, and Germany, signed June 22, allowed the Germans to occupy more than half of France, including the Atlantic and English Channel coasts. Marshal Pétain set up a dictatorial regime at the resort city of Vichy and collaborated with the Germans in hopes of preserving as much autonomy as possible.

Some of the collaborators believed the Germans were sure to win the war and wanted to be on the victorious side. A few sympathized with Nazi ideas and plans.

Many conservatives regarded the French defeat as a judgment on what they saw as the corrupt, secularized, liberal Third Republic. Most of the French were not active collaborators but were demoralized by defeat and German power.

Many conservatives and extreme rightists saw in the Vichy government a way to reshape the French national character and to halt the decadence they associated with political and religious liberalism. The Roman Catholic clergy, which had lost power and influence under the Third Republic, gained status under Vichy. The church supported Pétain, and his government restored religious instruction in the state schools, increased financial support for Catholic schools, and supported the church's positions on social issues.

The Vichy regime also encouraged an intense, chauvinistic nationalism. It exploited prejudice against foreigners working in France and fostered resentment even against French men and women whom it regarded as not genuinely "French," especially French Jews. Even before Germany undertook Hitler's "final solution" in 1942, the French had begun to remove Jews from positions of influence in government, education, and publishing. The Vichy government had no part in the German policies that culminated in the deportation of French Jews to the extermination camps of Eastern Europe, but it made no protest, and its own anti-Semitic policies made the whole process easier to carry out.

Some French men and women, notably General Charles de Gaulle (1890–1969), fled to Britain after the defeat of France. There they organized the French National Committee of Liberation, or "Free French." From London, they broadcast hope and defiance to their compatriots in France. Serious internal resistance to the German occupiers and the Vichy government, however, began to develop only late in 1942. Fear of German retaliation deterred many. Others disliked the violence that resistance to a powerful ruthless nation inevitably entailed. As long as it appeared the Germans would win the war, moreover, resistance seemed imprudent and futile. For these reasons, the organized Resistance never attracted more than 5 percent of the adult French population.

By early 1944, the tide of battle had shifted. The Allies seemed sure to win, and the Vichy government would clearly not survive; only then did a large-scale active movement of resistance assert itself. From Algiers on August 9, 1944, the Committee of National Liberation declared the authority of Vichy illegitimate. French soldiers joined in the liberation of Paris and established a government for Free France. On October 21, 1945, France voted to end the Third Republic and adopted a new constitution as the basis of the Fourth Republic. The French people had experienced defeat, disgrace, deprivation, and suffering. Hostility and quarrels over who had done what during the occupation and under Vichy divided them for decades.

Great Britain: Organization for Victory

On May 22, 1940, the British Parliament gave the government emergency powers. Together with others already in effect, this measure allowed the government to institute compulsory military service, rationing, and economic controls.

To deal with the crisis, all British political parties joined in a national government under Winston Churchill. Churchill and the British war cabinet moved as quickly as possible to mobilize the nation. The demand for more planes and other armaments inspired a campaign to reclaim scrap metal. Wrought-iron fences, kitchen pots and pans, and every conceivable metal object were collected for the war effort. This was only one successful example of the many ways the civilian population enthusiastically engaged in the struggle.

By the end of 1941, British production had already surpassed Germany's. To meet the heavy demands on the labor force, factory hours were extended, and many women joined the workforce. Unemployment disappeared, and the working classes had more money to spend than they had enjoyed for many years. To avoid inflation caused by increased demand for an inadequate supply of consumer goods, savings were encouraged, and taxes were raised to absorb the excess purchasing power.

The "blitz" air attacks in 1940–1941 were the most immediate and dramatic experience of the war for the British people. The German air raids killed thousands of people and left many others homeless. Once the bombing began, many families removed their children to the countryside. The government issued gas masks to thousands of city dwellers, who were frequently compelled to take shelter from the bombs in the London subways.

Fires destroy a commercial dock in London, England, during the German air raids. Despite many casualties and widespread devastation, the German bombing of London did not break British morale or prevent the city from functioning.

British Information Services

How did strategic bombing impact the course of the war?

The British made many sacrifices. Transportation facilities were strained simply from carrying enough coal to heat homes and run factories. Food and clothing for civilians were scarce and strictly rationed. Every scrap of land was farmed, increasing the productive portion by almost 4 million acres. Gasoline was scarce, and private vehicles almost vanished.

The British established their own propaganda machine to influence the Continent. The British Broadcasting Company (BBC) sent programs to every country in Europe in the local language to encourage resistance to the Nazis. At home, the government used the radio to unify the nation. Soldiers at the front heard the same programs their families did at home.

Strangely, for the broad mass of the population, the standard of living improved during the war. The general health of the nation also improved, for reasons that are still not clear. These improvements should not be exaggerated, but they did occur, and many connected them with the active involvement of the government in the economy and in the lives of the citizens. This wartime experience may have contributed to the Labour Party's victory in 1945; many feared a return to Conservative Party rule would also mean a return to the economic problems and unemployment of the 1930s.

The Soviet Union: "The Great Patriotic War"

The war against Germany came as a great surprise to Stalin and the Soviet Union. The German attack violated the 1939 pact with Hitler and put the government of the Soviet Union on the defensive militarily and politically. It showed the failure of Stalin's foreign policy and the ineptness of his preparation for war. Within days, German troops occupied much of the western Soviet Union. The communist government feared that Soviet citizens in the occupied zones—many of whom were not ethnic Russians—might welcome the Germans as liberators.

No nation suffered more during World War II than the Soviet Union. Perhaps as many as 16 million people were killed, and vast numbers of Soviet troops were taken prisoner. Hundreds of cities and towns and well over half of the industrial and transportation facilities of the country were devastated. From 1942, thousands of Soviet prisoners worked in German factories as forced labor. The Germans also seized grain, mineral resources, and oil from the Soviet Union.

Stalin conducted the war as the virtual chief of the armed forces, and the State Committee for Defense provided strong central coordination. When the war began, millions of citizens entered the army, but the army itself did not grow in influence at the expense of the state and the Communist Party—that is, of Stalin. As the war continued, however, the army gained more freedom of action, and eventually the generals were no longer subservient to party commissars. The power of Stalin and the nature of Soviet government and society, however, still sharply limited the army.

Soviet propaganda was different from that of other nations. Because the Soviet government distrusted the loyalty of its citizens, it confiscated radios to prevent the people from listening to German or British propaganda. In cities, the government broadcast to the people over loudspeakers in place of radios. During the war, Soviet propaganda emphasized Russian patriotism rather than traditional Marxist themes that stressed class conflict. The struggle against the Germans was called "The Great Patriotic War."

Within occupied portions of the western Soviet Union, an active resistance movement harassed the Germans. The swiftness of the German invasion had stranded thousands of Soviet troops behind German lines. Some escaped and carried on guerrilla warfare behind enemy lines. Stalin supported partisan forces in lands the enemy held for two reasons: He wanted to cause as much difficulty as possible for the Germans, and Soviet-sponsored resistance reminded the peasants that the Soviet government had not disappeared. Stalin feared the peasants' hatred of the communist government and collectivization might lead them to collaborate with the invaders. When the Soviet army moved westward, it incorporated the partisans into the regular army.

As its armies reclaimed the occupied areas and then moved across Eastern and Central Europe, the Soviet Union established itself as a world power second only to the United States. Stalin had entered the war a reluctant belligerent, but he emerged a major victor. In that respect, the war and the extraordinary patriotic effort and sacrifice it generated consolidated the power of Stalin and the party more effectively than the political and social policies of the previous decade.

PREPARATIONS FOR PEACE

HOW DID the Allies prepare for a postwar Europe?

The split between the Soviet Union and its wartime allies should cause no surprise. As the self-proclaimed center of world communism, the Soviet Union was openly dedicated to the overthrow of the capitalist nations. The Soviets muted this message, however, when the occasion demanded. On the other side, the Western allies were no less open about their hostility to communism and its chief purveyor, the Soviet Union.

Nonetheless, the need to cooperate against a common enemy and strenuous propaganda efforts helped improve Western feeling toward the Soviet ally. Still, Stalin remained suspicious and critical of the Western war effort, and Churchill was determined to contain the Soviet advance into Europe. Roosevelt perhaps had been more hopeful that the Allies could continue to work together after the war, but even he was losing faith by 1945. Differences in historical development and ideology, as well as traditional conflicts over political power and influence, soon dashed hopes of a mutually satisfactory peace settlement and continued cooperation to uphold it.

THE ATLANTIC CHARTER

In August 1941, even before the Americans were at war, Roosevelt and Churchill met on a ship off Newfoundland and agreed to the Atlantic Charter. This broad set of principles in the spirit of Wilson's Fourteen Points provided a theoretical basis for the peace they sought. When Russia and the United States joined Britain in the war, the three powers entered a purely military alliance in January 1942, leaving all political questions aside. The first political conference was the meeting of foreign ministers in Moscow in October 1943. The ministers reaffirmed earlier agreements to fight on until the enemy surrendered unconditionally and to continue cooperating after the war in a united-nations organization.

Tehran: Agreement on a Second Front

The first meeting of the leaders of the "Big Three" (the USSR, Britain, and the United States) took place at Tehran, the capital of Iran, in 1943. Western promises to open a second front in France the next summer (1944) and Stalin's agreement to fight Japan when Germany was defeated created an atmosphere of goodwill in which to discuss a postwar settlement. Stalin wanted to retain what he had gained in his pact with Hitler and to dismember Germany. Roosevelt and Churchill were conciliatory but made no firm commitments.

The most important decision was the one that chose Europe's west coast as the main point of attack instead of the Mediterranean. That meant, in retrospect, that Soviet forces would occupy Eastern Europe and control its destiny. At Tehran in 1943, the Western allies did not foresee this clearly, for the Russians were still fighting deep within their own frontiers, and military considerations were paramount.

Churchill and Stalin By 1944, the situation had changed. In August, Soviet armies were before Warsaw, which had revolted against the Germans in expectation of liberation, but the Russians halted and turned south into the Balkans, allowing the Germans to annihilate the Poles. The Russians gained control of Romania, Bulgaria, and Hungary, advances that centuries of expansionist tsars had only dreamed of achieving. Alarmed by these developments, Churchill went to Moscow and met with Stalin in October. They agreed to share power in the Balkans on the basis of Soviet predominance in Romania and Bulgaria, Western predominance in Greece, and equality of influence in Yugoslavia and Hungary. These agreements were not enforceable without American approval, and the Americans were hostile to such un-Wilsonian devices as "spheres of influence."

Germany The three powers easily agreed on Germany—its disarmament, de-Nazification, and division into four zones of occupation by France and the Big Three. Churchill, however, began to balk at Stalin's demand for $20 billion in reparations as well as forced labor from all the zones, with Russia to get half of everything. These matters festered and caused dissension in the future.

Eastern Europe The settlement of Eastern Europe was equally thorny. Everyone agreed the Soviet Union deserved to have friendly neighboring governments, but the West insisted they also be autonomous and democratic. The Western leaders, particularly Churchill, were not eager to see Russia dominate Eastern Europe. They were also, especially Roosevelt, committed to democracy and self-determination.

SIGNIFICANT DATES FROM THE ERA CULMINATING IN WORLD WAR II

1919	(June) The Versailles Treaty
1931	(Spring) Onset of the Great Depression in Europe
1933	(January) Hitler comes to power
1935	(March) Hitler renounces disarmament; (October) Mussolini attacks Ethiopia
1936	(March) Germany remilitarizes the Rhineland; (July) Outbreak of the Spanish Civil War; (October) Formation of the Rome-Berlin Axis
1938	(March) *Anschluss* with Austria; (September) Munich Conference; Partition of Czechoslovakia
1939	(August) The Nazi-Soviet pact; (September) Germany and the Soviet Union invade Poland; Britain and France declare war on Germany; (November) The Soviet Union invades Finland
1940	(April) Germany invades Denmark and Norway; (May) Germany invades Belgium, the Netherlands, Luxembourg, and France; (June) Fall of France; (August) Battle of Britain begins
1941	(June) Germany invades the Soviet Union; (July) Japan takes Indochina; (December) Japan attacks Pearl Harbor; United States enters the war
1942	(June) Battle of Midway
1942	(November) Battle of Stalingrad begins; Allies land in North Africa
1943	(February–August) Allies take Sicily, land in Italy
1944	(June) Allies land in Normandy
1945	(May) Germany surrenders; (August) Atomic bombs dropped on Hiroshima and Nagasaki; (September) Japan surrenders

In February 1945, Churchill, Roosevelt, and Stalin met at Yalta in the Crimea to plan for the organization of Europe after the end of the war. The Big Three are seated. Standing behind President Roosevelt is Admiral William D. Leahy. Behind the prime minister are Admiral Sir Andrew Cunningham and Air Marshal Portal.

U.S. Army Photograph

What were the goals of the "Big Three" at Yalta?

Stalin, however, knew that independent, freely elected governments in Poland, Hungary, and Romania would not be friendly to Russia. He had already established a puppet government in Poland in competition with the Polish government-in-exile in London. Under pressure from the Western leaders, however, he agreed to include some Poles friendly to the West in it. He also signed a Declaration on Liberated Europe, promising self-determination and free democratic elections.

Stalin may have been eager to avoid conflict before the war with Germany was over. He was always afraid the Allies would make a separate peace with Germany and betray him, and he probably thought it worth endorsing some hollow principles as the price of continued harmony. In any case, he wasted little time violating these agreements.

Yalta

The next meeting of the Big Three was at Yalta in Crimea in February 1945. The Western armies had not yet crossed the Rhine, but the Soviet army was within a hundred miles of Berlin. The war with Japan continued, and no atomic explosion had yet taken place. Roosevelt, faced with a prospective invasion of Japan and heavy losses, was eager to bring the Russians into the Pacific war as soon as possible. As a true Wilsonian, he also suspected Churchill's determination to maintain the British Empire and Britain's colonial advantages. The Americans thought Churchill's plan to set up British spheres of influence in Europe would encourage the Russians to do the same and would lead to friction and war. To encourage Russian participation in the war against Japan, Roosevelt and Churchill made extensive concessions to Russia, ceding the Soviets Sakhalin and the Kurile Islands, and accommodating some of their desires in Korea and in Manchuria.

Again in the tradition of Wilson, Roosevelt emphasized a united-nations organization: "Through the United Nations, he hoped to achieve a self-enforcing peace settlement that would not require American troops, as well as an open world without spheres of influence in which American enterprise could work freely." Soviet agreement on these points seemed worth concessions elsewhere.

POTSDAM

The Big Three met for the last time in the Berlin suburb of Potsdam in July 1945. Much had changed since the previous conference. Germany had been defeated, and news of the successful explosion of an atomic weapon reached the American president during the meetings. The cast of characters was also different: President Truman replaced the deceased Roosevelt, and Clement Attlee (1883–1967), leader of the Labour Party that had just won a general election, replaced Churchill as Britain's spokesperson during the conference. Previous agreements were reaffirmed, but progress on undecided questions was slow.

Russia's western frontier was moved far into what had been Poland and included most of German East Prussia. In compensation, Poland was allowed "temporary administration" over the rest of East Prussia and Germany east of the Oder-Neisse River, a condition that became permanent. In effect, Poland was moved about a hundred miles west, at the expense of Germany, to accommodate the Soviet Union. The Allies agreed to divide Germany into occupation zones until the final peace treaty was signed. Germany remained divided until 1990.

A Council of Foreign Ministers was established to draft peace treaties for Germany's allies. Growing disagreements made the job difficult, and Italy, Romania, Hungary, Bulgaria, and Finland did not sign treaties until February 1947. The Russians were dissatisfied with the treaty that the United States made with Japan in 1951 and signed their own agreements with the Japanese in 1956. These disagreements were foreshadowed at Potsdam.

Overview Negotiations Among the Allies

AUGUST 1941	Churchill and Roosevelt meet off Newfoundland to sign Atlantic Charter.	Provides basis for the alliance between Britain and the United States.
OCTOBER 1943	American, British, and Soviet foreign ministers meet in Moscow.	Allies reaffirm to fight until the enemy surrenders and to continue cooperating after the war.
NOVEMBER 1943	Churchill, Roosevelt, and Stalin meet at Tehran.	Britain and the United States agree to open a second front in France; Stalin promises to join war in Japan after Germany is defeated, and Allied offensive begins on Europe's west coast.
OCTOBER 1944	Churchill meets with Stalin in Moscow.	Agree to share power in the Balkans, with Soviet predominance in Romania and Bulgaria, Western predominance in Greece, and equality of influence in Yugoslavia and Hungary.
FEBRUARY 1945	Churchill, Roosevelt, and Stalin meet at Yalta.	Concessions are made to Stalin concerning the settlement of Eastern Europe.
JULY 1945	Attlee, Stalin, and Truman meet at Potsdam.	Polish border moved a hundred miles west to accommodate the Soviet Union; Germany divided into occupational zones; and a Council of Foreign Ministers is established to draft peace treaties for Germany's allies.

Summary

HOW DID World War I sow the seeds of World War II?

Again the Road to War (1933–1939) Hitler and the Nazi Party came to power in Germany through relentless discipline. They were consistent in their nationalism, in their attention to social and economic anxieties faced by Germans, and in their insistence that all of Germany's problems flowed from the Paris peace settlement. Hitler's racial theories and his goal of uniting all German people into one nation drove Nazi Germany's foreign policy. Germany started rebuilding its military in the mid-1930s. Neither the Allies nor the League of Nations took steps to oppose German rearmament. In 1936, Hitler remilitarized the Rhineland; the Western powers responded with appeasement. The 1938 *Anschluss* unified Germany and Austria. Hitler's next target was Czechoslovakia. The British prime minister worked hard to avoid the inevitable, but his policy of appeasing Hitler not only failed to save Czechoslovakia but also earned him history's disapprobation for further encouraging Hitler's aggression. Hitler occupied Prague in 1939. Chamberlain announced Britain and France would guarantee the independence of the country that Germany intended to dismember next, Poland. In August 1939, Germany and the Soviet Union signed the nonaggression pact that allowed them to divide Poland between themselves; on September 1, 1939, Germans invaded Poland; and on September 3, Britain and France declared war on Germany. *page 712*

IN WHAT ways was World War II a "total" war?

World War II (1939–1945) World War II was global, and for the combatants in Europe it was total: Civilians died in numbers equal to soldiers, and all aspects of economic, social, and political life were shaped by the war. In June 1940, the Germans occupied France. Churchill, the newly elected prime minister in Britain, was all that stood between Hitler and continental domination. The Luftwaffe's nightly bombing raids on London in the fall of 1940 were Hitler's first significant wartime blunder: They resulted in substantial losses for the Luftwaffe and stiffened British resistance. Operation Barbarossa was his second. The Germans were defeated by the Russian winter and by the heroism of Stalin's army in the Battle of Stalingrad. Hitler intended for his Third Reich to germanize, colonize, and plunder the rest of Europe. His hopes for keeping the United States out of the war were dashed when Japan bombed Pearl Harbor on December 7, 1941. The United States waited until it was on its way to victory in the Pacific before turning to the war in North Africa, and then Europe. In 1943, the United States and Britain began a massive aerial bombardment campaign against Germany. D-day, June 6, 1944, marked the beginning of the Allied land offensive in France, which resulted in the fall of Berlin in May and Allied victory in Europe. Japan fought on until Emperor Hirohito forced the government to surrender in August 1945, after the United States had dropped atomic bombs on Hiroshima and Nagasaki. *page 718*

WHAT WAS the Holocaust?

Racism and the Holocaust Hitler's racial doctrines resulted in brutality against Jews, Slavs, and other peoples. Approximately 6 million Jews were killed in the Holocaust. Jews made up 10 percent of Poland's prewar population, mostly poor and living in separate communities. The government, church, and society in general were anti-Semitic. Nonetheless, Polish Jews were numerous and included many religious, cultural, and political leaders; they were a prime target for the Nazis. In early 1940, Nazis relocated many Polish Jews to sealed ghettos, where 20 percent of the population died of disease and malnourishment. When Germany invaded the Soviet Union in 1941, Nazi propaganda connected Jews and Bolsheviks, and soon the Nazis adopted the policy of exterminating Jews. By 1945, 90 percent of Poland's pre-1939 population of Jews had been killed. *page 726*

WHAT IMPACT did World War II have on European society?

The Domestic Fronts On the home front, civilians were organized for war to a greater extent than in any previous conflict. In Germany, the economy was redirected to wartime production. Consumer goods became scarce. Women were given many roles in the German war effort. Nazi propaganda permeated society, and there was virtually no popular resistance. Much of Germany's physical and political infrastructure was destroyed by the end of the war. In France, the Vichy government was supported by the church and conservatives. All of Britain's political parties had joined in a national government under Churchill. For most of the population, the standard of living improved during the war, leading some to conclude that active government involvement in the society was a positive force. The Great Patriotic War was most destructive in the Soviet Union, where 16 million people were killed. Stalin won further centralization of authority, and the Soviet Union emerged from the war as a great power, second only to the United States. *page 730*

HOW DID the Allies prepare for a postwar Europe?

Preparations for Peace The fundamental differences between the Soviet Union and the other Allies had been dormant during the fight against Nazi Germany, but they reemerged with a vengeance as soon as the war was over. In 1941, Roosevelt and Churchill had agreed on the Atlantic Charter. The Big Three had entered a purely military alliance in January 1942. At the first meeting between Roosevelt, Churchill, and Stalin, in Tehran in 1943, the three agreed the United States and Britain would open the second front against Germany from the Atlantic coast; this had far-reaching consequences for the geography of the postwar Soviet sphere of influence. By the time the Big Three met again, in February 1945 at Yalta, the situation on the ground was far different. The Soviet Army occupied much of Eastern Europe already. Churchill and Roosevelt ceded much to Stalin; Roosevelt also pressed for a united-nations organization that would help ensure the eventual peace. The final Big Three meeting, at Potsdam in July 1945, gave Russia much of Poland, and Poland a sizable piece of Germany. The seeds of future dissension were sown. *page 734*

REVIEW QUESTIONS

1. What were Hitler's foreign policy aims? Why did Britain and France adopt a policy of appeasement? Did it buy the West valuable time to prepare for war?
2. How was Hitler able to defeat France so easily in 1940? Why was his air war against Britain a failure? Why did he invade Russia? Why did the invasion ultimately fail?
3. Why did Japan attack the United States at Pearl Harbor? What was the significance of American intervention in the war? Did President Truman make the right decision when he ordered the atomic bombs dropped on Japan?
4. What impact did World War II have on the civilian population of Europe? What impact did the "Great Patriotic War" have on the people of the Soviet Union? What was Hitler's "final solution" for Europe's Jewish population?

KEY TERMS

Anschluss (p. 714)
appeasement (p. 713)
Axis (p. 713)
Holocaust (p. 728)
Lebensraum (p. 712)
Luftwaffe (p. 719)
Third Reich (p. 721)

For additional learning resources related to this chapter, please go to **www.myhistorylab.com**

PEARSON myhistorylab

29

The Cold War Era, Decolonization, and the Emergence of a New Europe

A statue of Queen Victoria is removed from the front of the Supreme Court building in Georgetown, former capital of the British colony of Guyana, in February 1970, in preparation for the transition to independence. Decolonization represented as dramatic a transition in world political relations as had the establishment of European empires in the nineteenth-century Victorian age.

What was the relationship between Britain and its former colonies after decolonization?

THE EMERGENCE OF THE COLD WAR *page 742*

WHAT WERE the origins of the Cold War?

THE KHRUSHCHEV ERA IN THE SOVIET UNION AND LATER COLD WAR CONFRONTATIONS *page 749*

HOW DID the Berlin Wall and the Cuban Missile Crisis strain relations between the United States and the Soviet Union?

THE BREZHNEV ERA *page 752*

WHAT IMPACT did Brezhnev have on the Soviet Union and Eastern Europe?

DECOLONIZATION: THE EUROPEAN RETREAT FROM EMPIRE *page 754*

HOW DID World War II serve as a catalyst for decolonization?

THE TURMOIL OF FRENCH DECOLONIZATION *page 756*

WHY WAS France so reluctant to decolonize?

THE COLLAPSE OF EUROPEAN COMMUNISM *page 759*

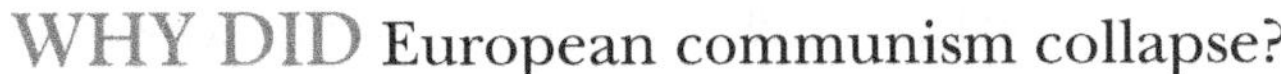

WHY DID European communism collapse?

THE COLLAPSE OF YUGOSLAVIA AND CIVIL WAR *page 765*

HOW DID ethnic tensions lead to civil war in Yugoslavia?

PUTIN AND THE RESURGENCE OF RUSSIA *page 767*

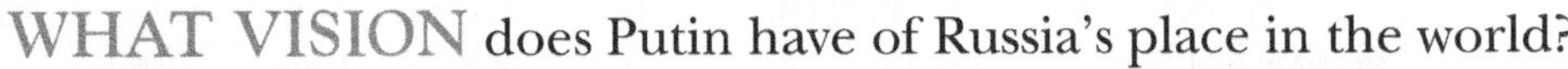

WHAT VISION does Putin have of Russia's place in the world?

THE RISE OF RADICAL POLITICAL ISLAMISM *page 768*

WHAT FORCES gave rise to radical political Islamism?

A TRANSFORMED WEST *page 772*

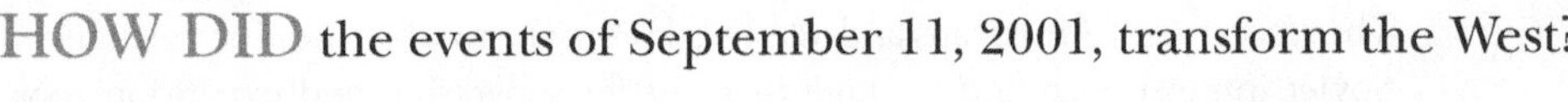

HOW DID the events of September 11, 2001, transform the West?

Cold War Period between the end of World War II (1945) and the collapse of the Soviet Union (1991) in which U.S. and Soviet relations were tense, seemingly moments away from actual war at any time during these years.

Since the end of World War II, two often interrelated sets of international political relationships shaped world events: the **Cold War** *between the United States and the Soviet Union and the process of decolonization, whereby the peoples of lands dominated by European nations and later by the United States rejected that domination.*

From 1945 until the collapse of communist regimes in Eastern Europe between 1989 and 1991, the simmering conflict of the Cold War dominated global politics and threatened the peace of Europe. Decolonization rapidly became enmeshed with the Cold War, as the rivalry of the two nuclear-armed superpowers expanded into a contest for dominance in the postcolonial world, aggravating local conflicts on every continent.

Since the collapse of the Soviet Union in 1991, the United States has remained the world's single superpower. Symbolically identified as embodying modern values of Western civilization, the United States has replaced Europe as the object of anti-Western resistance. A notable result of this new situation is the clash between the United States and radical political Islamism. As the era of European and American colonial dominance came to an end, the reciprocal nature of the relationship between the West and the rest of the global community has intensified. ■

THE EMERGENCE OF THE COLD WAR

WHAT WERE the origins of the Cold War?

The tense relationship between the United States and the Soviet Union began in the closing months of World War II. In part, the coldness between the Allies arose from the mutual feeling that each had violated previous agreements. The Russians were plainly asserting permanent control of Poland and Romania under puppet communist governments. The United States was taking a harder line about German reparation payments to the Soviet Union. In retrospect, however, it appears unlikely that friendlier styles on either side could have avoided a split that arose from basic differences of ideology and interest.

The Americans made no attempt to roll back Soviet power where it existed at the close of World War II. In less than a year from the war's end, the Americans had reduced their forces in Europe from 3.5 million to 500,000. The speed of the withdrawal reflected domestic pressure to "get the boys home" but was also fully in accord with America's peacetime plans and goals, which included support for self-determination, autonomy, and democracy in the political sphere, and free trade, freedom of the seas, no barriers to investment, and an Open Door policy in the economic sphere. As the strongest, richest nation in the world—the one with the greatest industrial base and the strongest currency—the United States would benefit handsomely from an international order based on such goals.

Although postwar American hostility to colonial empires created tensions with France and Britain, the main conflict lay with the Soviet Union. The growth in France and Italy of large popular communist parties taking orders from Moscow led the Americans to believe that Stalin was engaged in a worldwide plot to subvert capitalism and democracy. From the Soviet perspective, extending the borders of the USSR and dominating the formerly independent successor states of Eastern Europe would provide needed security and compensate for the fearful losses the Soviet people had endured in the war. The Soviets could thus see American resistance to their expansion as a threat to their security and their legitimate aims.

CONTAINMENT IN AMERICAN FOREIGN POLICY

containment American foreign policy strategy (beginning in 1947) for countering the communist threat and resisting the spread of Soviet influence.

The resistance of Americans and Western Europeans to what they increasingly perceived as Soviet intransigence and communist plans for subversion and expansion took a clearer form in 1947. The American policy became known as one of **containment**, the purpose of which was to resist the extension of Soviet expansion and influence in the expectation that eventually the Soviet Union would collapse from internal pressures and the burdens of its foreign oppression. This strategy, which American policymakers devised in the late 1940s, would direct the broad outlines of American foreign policy for the next four decades, until the Soviet Union did collapse from exactly such pressures. Containment marked a major departure in American foreign policy and transformed the international situation during the second half of the twentieth century. The execution of the policy led the United States to enter overseas alliances, to make formal and informal commitments of support to regimes around the world it perceived as being anticommunist, to undertake enormous military expenditures, and to send large amounts of money abroad. (See "Compare & Connect: The Soviet Union and the United States Draw the Lines of the Cold War," pages 744–745.)

The Truman Doctrine Since 1944, civil war had been raging in Greece between the royalist government restored by Britain and insurgents supported by the communist countries, chiefly Yugoslavia. In 1947, Britain informed the United States it could no longer financially support its Greek allies. On March 12, President Truman asked Congress to provide funds to support Greece and Turkey and Congress complied. In a speech to Congress that gave these actions much broader significance, the president set forth what came to be called the Truman Doctrine. He advocated a policy of support for "free people who are resisting attempted subjugation by armed minorities or by outside pressures," by implication, anywhere in the world.

The Marshall Plan American aid to Greece and Turkey took the form of military equipment and advisers. For Western Europe, where postwar poverty and hunger fueled the menacing growth of communist parties, the Americans devised the European Recovery Program. Named the **Marshall Plan** after George C. Marshall (1880–1959), the secretary of state who introduced it, this program provided broad economic aid to European states on the sole condition that they work together for their mutual benefit. The Marshall Plan restored prosperity to Western Europe and set the stage for Europe's unprecedented postwar economic growth.

Marshall Plan The U.S. European Recovery Program introduced by George C. Marshall, American secretary of state, whereby America provided extensive economic aid to the European states, conditional only on their working together for their mutual benefit.

Following the declaration of the Truman Doctrine and the announcement of the Marshall Plan, the Soviet Union defined a new era of conflict between the United States and itself. (See "Compare & Connect: The Soviet Union and the United States Draw the Lines of the Cold War," pages 744–745.)

Soviet Domination of Eastern Europe

Stalin may have seen containment as a renewed Western attempt to isolate and encircle the USSR. In the autumn of 1947, Stalin called a meeting in Warsaw of all communist parties from around the globe. There they organized the Communist Information Bureau (Cominform), a revival of the old Comintern, dedicated to spreading revolutionary communism throughout the world. In Western Europe the establishment of the Cominform officially ended the era of the popular front during which communists had cooperated with noncommunist parties.

During the late 1940s, the Soviet Union required the subject governments in Eastern Europe to impose Stalinist policies, including one-party political systems, close military cooperation with the Soviet Union, the collectivization of agriculture, Communist Party domination of education, and attacks on the churches. Longtime Communist Party officials were purged and condemned in show trials like those that had taken place in Moscow during the late 1930s. The catalyst for this harsh tightening probably was the success of Marshal Josip (Broz) Tito (1892–1980), the leader of communist Yugoslavia, in freeing his country from Soviet domination. Stalin wanted to prevent other Eastern European states from following the Yugoslav example.

COMPARE & CONNECT

THE SOVIET UNION AND THE UNITED STATES DRAW THE LINES OF THE COLD WAR

Between 1945 and 1950, the lines between the United States and the Soviet Union that became known as the Cold War were drawn. Each country quickly came to define the other as its principal enemy on the world scene. These two documents illustrate the manner in which each nation set its conflict with the other into a larger framework of ideological and political rivalry. Much of the rhetoric of these two documents would characterize the Cold War from its inception until the collapse of the Soviet Union.

QUESTIONS

1. How did the Cominform use the terms "democratic" and "imperialist" to its advantage?
2. Why did it see the Marshall Plan as an act of aggression?
3. How did the National Security Council characterize Soviet policy?
4. What were the goals of containment?
5. Why did the Council urge that the Soviet Union always be given opportunity to save face and to back down with dignity?
6. How does each document indicate that both the Soviet Union and the United States regarded their tensions and conflict as part of a wider global political scene?

I. THE COMINFORM DEFINES CONFLICT BETWEEN THE SOVIET UNION AND THE UNITED STATES

In 1947, under the leadership of the Soviet Union, the leaders of the Soviet and East European Communist Parties formed the Communist Information Bureau, which became known as the Cominform. It was organized in the wake of the Truman Doctrine and Marshall Plan. In September 1947, the Communist Parties constituting the Cominform issued a statement that set forth their view of the emerging conflict between the Soviet bloc and the United States. In doing so, they not only attacked the United States, but also the democratic socialist parties of Western Europe which the Soviet Union had seen as an enemy since the days of Lenin.

Fundamental changes have taken place in the international situation as a result of the Second World War and in the post-war period.

These changes are characterized by a new disposition of the basic political forces operating in the world arena, by a change in the relations among the victor states in the Second World War, and their realignment.

.... The Soviet Union and the other democratic countries regarded as their basic war aims the restoration and consolidation of democratic order in Europe, the eradication of fascism and the prevention of the possibility of new aggression on the part of Germany, and the establishment of a lasting all-round cooperation among the nations of Europe. The United States of America, and Britain in agreement with them, set themselves another aim in the war: to rid themselves of competitors on the markets (Germany and Japan) and to establish their dominant position. . . .

Thus two camps were formed—the imperialist and anti-democratic camp having as its basic aim the establishment of world domination of American imperialism and the smashing of democracy, and the anti-imperialist and democratic camp having as its basic aim the undermining of imperialism, the consolidation of democracy, and the eradication of the remnants of fascism. . . .

. . . the imperialist camp and its leading force, the United States, are displaying particularly aggressive activity. . . . The Truman-Marshall Plan is only a constituent part . . . of the general plan for the policy of global expansion pursued by the United States in all parts of the World. . . .

To frustrate the plan of imperialist aggression the efforts of all the democratic anti-imperialist forces of Europe are necessary. The right-wing Socialists are traitors to this cause. . . . and primarily the French Socialists and the British Labourites. . . by their servility and sycophancy are helping American capital to achieve its aims, provoking it to resort to extortion and impelling their own countries on to a path of vassal-like dependence on the United States of America.

This imposes a special task on the Communist Parties. They must take into their hands the banner of defense of the national independence and sovereignty of their countries. . . .

The principle danger for the working class today lies in underestimating their own strength and overestimating the strength of the imperialist camp.

Source: United States Senate, 81st Congress, 1st Session, Document No. 48, *North Atlantic Treaty: Documents Relating to the North Atlantic Treaty* (Washington, DC: U.S. Government Printing Office, 1949), pp. 117–120 as quoted in Katharine J. Lualdi, *Sources of the Making of the West: Peoples and Culture* (Boston: Bedford/St. Martin's, 2009), 2, pp. 248–250.

The Allied airlift in action during the Berlin Blockade, which took place from June 1948 until Stalin lifted it in May 1949. Every day during the blockade Western planes supplied the city.

Art Resource/Bildarchiv Preussischer Kulturbesitz

What led to the Soviet blockade of Berlin?

II. THE UNITED STATES NATIONAL SECURITY COUNCIL PROPOSES TO CONTAIN THE SOVIET UNION

In response to the domination of Eastern Europe by Communist Parties dominated by the Soviet Union and the occupation of these nations by Soviet troops, the United States government in 1950 adopted a policy of "containment" of the Soviet Union. This policy had been debated for many months and had for all practical purposes been in effect since the declaration of the Truman Doctrine in 1947. It was formally set forth after a period of implementation in what became known as the National Security Council Paper 68, arguably the most important statement of American foreign policy of the mid–twentieth century. The paper presented the Soviet Union as a nation determined to pursue an expansionist foreign policy and ideological struggle and as a long-term solution to that challenge proposed a policy of containing the influence of the Soviet Union diplomatically and militarily.

The fundamental design of those who control the Soviet Union and the international communist movement is to retain and solidify their absolute power, first in the Soviet Union and second in the areas now under their control. . . .

The design, therefore, calls for the complete subversion or forcible destruction of the machinery of government and structure of society in the countries of the non-Soviet world and their replacement by an apparatus and structure subservient to and controlled from the Kremlin. . . .

Our overall policy at the present time may be described as one designed to foster a world environment in which the American system can survive and flourish. It therefore rejects the concept of isolation and affirms the necessity of our positive participation in the world community.

This broad intention embraces two subsidiary policies. One is a policy which we would probably pursue even if there were no Soviet threat. It is a policy of attempting to develop a healthy international community. The other is the policy of "containing" the Soviet system. . . .

As for the policy of "containment," it is one which seeks by all means short of war to (1) block further expansion of Soviet power, (2) expose the falsities of Soviet pretensions, (3) induce a retraction of the Kremlin's control and influence, and (4) in general, so foster the seeds of destruction within the Soviet system that the Kremlin is brought at least to the point of modifying its behavior to conform to generally accepted international standards. . . .

One of the most important ingredients of power is military strength. . . . Without superior aggregate military strength . . . a policy of "containment"—which is in effect a policy of calculated and gradual coercion—is no more than a policy of bluff.

At the same time, it is essential to the successful conduct of a policy of "containment" that we always leave open the possibility of negotiation with the USSR . . .

In "containment" it is desirable to exert pressure in a fashion which will avoid so far as possible directly challenging Soviet prestige, to keep open the possibility for the USSR to retreat before pressure with a minimum loss of face and to secure political advantage from the failure of the Kremlin to yield or take advantage of the openings we leave it.

Source: National Security Council, Paper Number 68, *Foreign Relations of the United States* (Washington, DC: U.S. Government Printing Office, 1977), Sections: III, IV, VI. as cited on www.seattleu.edu/artsci/history/us1945/docs/nsc68-1.htm

The Postwar Division of Germany

Soviet actions increased the determination of the United States to go ahead with its own arrangements in Germany.

Disagreements over Germany During the war, the Allies had never decided how to treat Germany after its defeat. At first they all agreed it should be dismembered, but they differed on how. By the time of Yalta, Churchill had come to fear Russian control of Eastern and central Europe and began to oppose dismemberment.

The Allies also differed on economic policy. The Russians swiftly dismantled German industry in the eastern zone, but the Americans acted differently in the western zone. They concluded that if they followed the Soviet policy, the United States would have to support Germany economically for the foreseeable future. It would also cause chaos and open the way for communism. They preferred, therefore, to try to make Germany self-sufficient, and this meant restoring, rather than destroying, its industrial capacity. To the Soviets, the restoration of a powerful industrial Germany, even in the western zone only, was frightening. The same difference of approach hampered agreement on reparations. The Soviets claimed the right to the industrial equipment in all the zones, and the Americans resisted their demands.

Berlin Blockade When the Western powers agreed to go forward with a separate constitution for the western sectors of Germany in February 1948, the Soviets walked out of the joint Allied Control Commission. In the summer of that year, the Western powers issued a new currency in their zone. All four powers governed Berlin, though it was well within the Soviet zone. The Soviets chose to seal the city off by closing all railroads and highways that led from Berlin to West Germany. Their purpose was to drive the Western powers out of Berlin.

The Western allies responded to the Berlin blockade by airlifting supplies to the city for almost a year. In May 1949, the Russians were forced to reopen access to Berlin. The incident, however, was decisive. It increased tensions and suspicions between the opponents and hastened the separation of Germany into two states. West Germany formally became the German Federal Republic in September 1949, and the eastern region became the German Democratic Republic a month later.

NATO and the Warsaw Pact

Meanwhile, the nations of Western Europe had been drawing closer together. The Marshall Plan encouraged international cooperation. In March 1948, Belgium, the Netherlands, Luxembourg, France, and Britain signed the Treaty of Brussels, providing for cooperation in economic and military matters. In April 1949, these nations joined with Italy, Denmark, Norway, Portugal, and Iceland to sign a treaty with Canada and the United States that formed the North Atlantic Treaty Organization (**NATO**), which committed its members to mutual assistance if any of them was attacked. The NATO treaty transformed the West into a bloc. A few years later, West Germany, Greece, and Turkey joined the alliance. For the first time in history, the United States was committed to defend allies outside the Western Hemisphere.

NATO North Atlantic Treaty Organization, a mutual defense pact.

A series of bilateral treaties providing for close ties and mutual assistance in case of attack governed Soviet relations with the states of Eastern Europe. In 1949, these states formed the Council of Mutual Assistance (COMECON) to integrate their economies. Unlike the NATO states, the Soviets directly dominated the Eastern alliance system through local communist parties controlled from Moscow and the presence of the Red Army. The **Warsaw Pact** of May 1955, which included Albania, Bulgaria, Czechoslovakia, East Germany, Hungary, Poland, Romania, and the Soviet

Warsaw Pact Mutual defense agreement among Albania, Bulgaria, Czechoslovakia, East Germany, Hungary, Poland, Romania, and the Soviet Union.

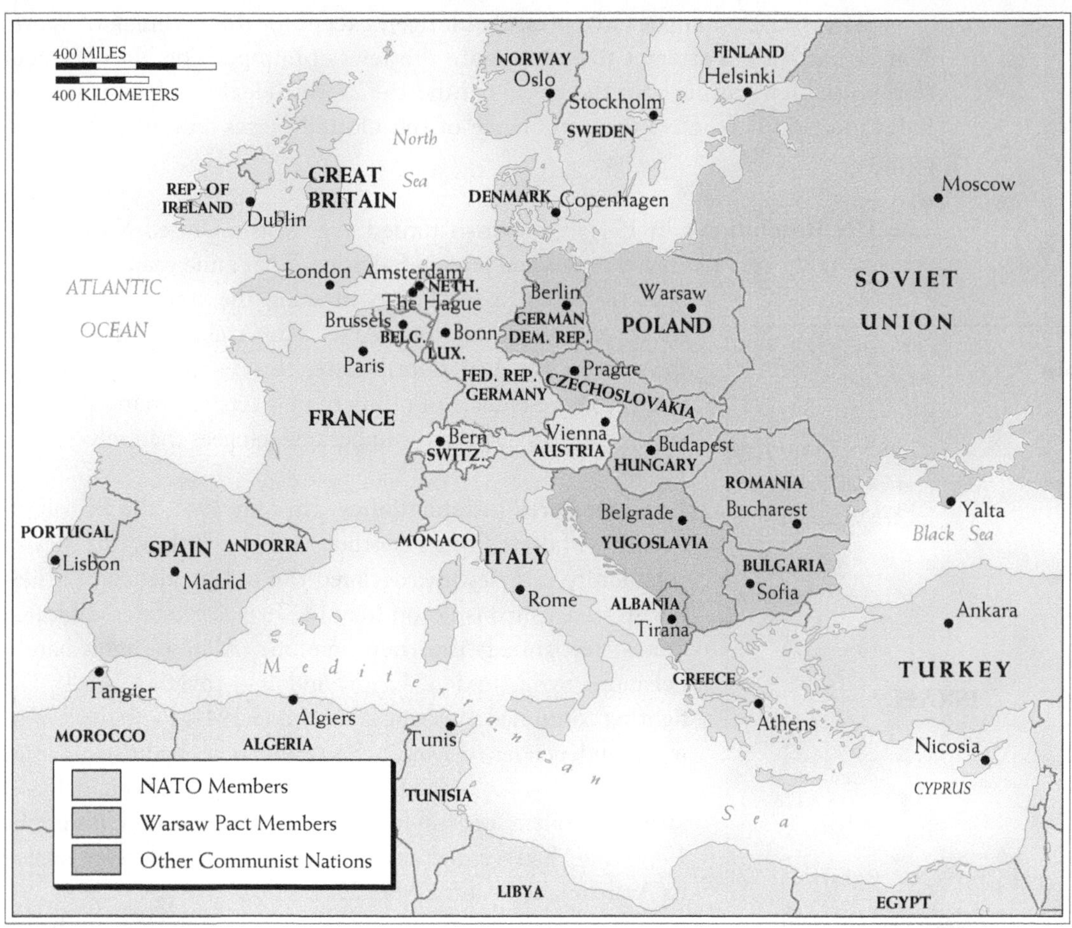

MAP 29–1 Major Cold War European Alliance Systems The North Atlantic Treaty Organization, which includes both Canada and the United States, stretches as far east as Turkey. By contrast, the Warsaw Pact nations were the contiguous communist states of Eastern Europe, with the Soviet Union, of course, as the dominant member.

Territorially, was NATO or the Warsaw Pact the stronger alliance?

Union, gave formal recognition to this system. Europe was divided into two unfriendly blocs. The Cold War had taken firm shape in Europe. (See Map 29–1.)

The Creation of the State of Israel

The strategic interests of the United States and the Soviet Union would not, however, permit the Cold War to be limited to the European continent. One of the areas of ongoing regional conflict that became a major point of Cold War rivalry was the Middle East.

British Balfour Declaration The modern state of Israel was the achievement of the world Zionist movement, founded in 1897 by Theodor Herzl (see Chapter 24) and later led by Chaim Weizmann (1874–1952). In 1917, during World War I, Arthur Balfour (1846–1930), the British foreign secretary, declared that Britain favored establishing a national home for the Jewish people in Palestine, which was then under Ottoman rule. Between the wars, thousands of Jews, mainly from Europe, immigrated to what had become British-ruled Palestine. Arabs already living in Palestine considered the Jewish settlers intruders, and violent conflicts ensued. The British tried, but failed, to mediate these clashes.

This situation might have prevailed longer, except for the outbreak of World War II and Hitler's attempt to exterminate the Jews of Europe. The Nazi persecution united Jews throughout the world behind the Zionist ideal of a Jewish state in Palestine, and it touched the conscience of the United States and other Western powers.

The UN Resolution In 1947, the British turned over to the United Nations the problem of the relationship of Arabs and Jews in Palestine. That same year, the United Nations passed a resolution dividing the territory into two states, one Jewish and one Arab. The Arabs in Palestine and the surrounding Arab states resisted this resolution. Not unnaturally, they resented the influx of new settlers. Many Palestinian Arabs were displaced and became refugees themselves.

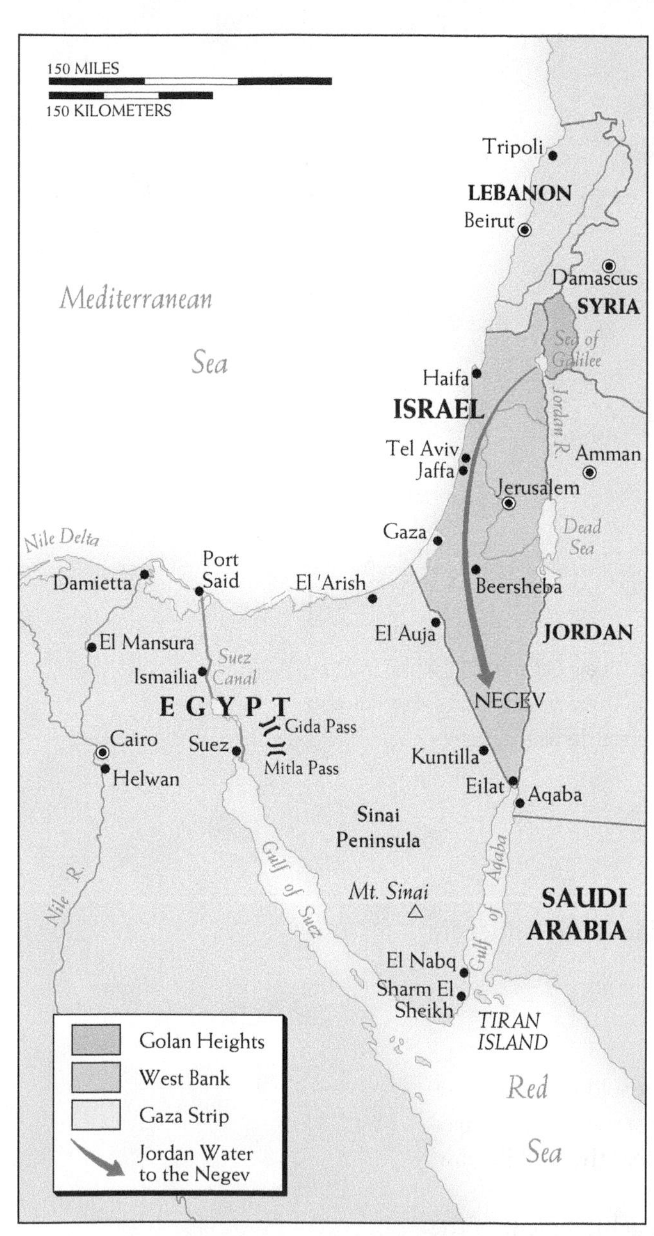

MAP 29–2 **Israel and Its Neighbors in 1949** The territories gained by Israel in 1949 did not secure peace in the region. In fact, the disposition of those lands and the Arab refugees who live there have constituted the core of the region's unresolved problems to the present day.

What challenges does Israel face in terms of territory and self-defense?

Israel Declares Independence In May 1948, the British officially withdrew from Palestine, and the Yishuv, the Jewish community in Palestine, declared the independence of a new Jewish state called *Israel* on May 14. Two days later, the United States recognized the new nation. Almost immediately, Lebanon, Syria, Jordan, Egypt, and Iraq invaded Israel. The fighting continued throughout 1948 and 1949. By the end of its war of independence against the Arabs, Israel had expanded its borders beyond the limits the United Nations had originally set forth. Jerusalem was divided between Jordan and Israel. By 1949, Israel had secured its existence, but not the acceptance of its Arab neighbors. (See Map 29–2.)

The Arab-Israeli conflict would inevitably draw in the superpowers. Both the United States and the Soviet Union believed they had major strategic and economic interests in the region. By 1949, the United States had established itself as a firm ally of Israel. Gradually, the Soviet Union began to furnish aid to the Arab nations. The bipolar tensions that had settled over Europe were thus transferred to the Middle East.

The Korean War

Between 1910 and 1945, Japan, as an Asian colonial power, had occupied and exploited the formerly independent kingdom of Korea, but at the close of World War II, the United States and the Soviet Union expelled the Japanese and divided Korea into two parts along the thirty-eighth parallel of latitude. Korea was supposed to be reunited. By 1948, however, two separate states had emerged: the Democratic People's Republic of Korea in the north, supported by the Soviet Union, and the Republic of Korea in the south, supported by the United States.

In late June 1950, after border clashes, North Korea invaded South Korea across the thirty-eighth parallel. The United States intervened, at first unilaterally and then under the authority of a UN resolution. For the United States, the point of the Korean conflict was to contain the spread and halt the aggression of communism.

Late in 1950, the Chinese, responding to the approach of UN forces near their border, sent troops to support North Korea. The American forces had to retreat. The U.S. policymakers believed, mistakenly, that the Chinese, who, since 1949, had been under the communist government of Mao Zedong (1893–1976), were simply Soviet puppets. Accordingly, the Americans viewed the movement of Chinese troops into Korea as another example of communist pressure against a noncommunist state, similar to what had previously happened in Europe. On June 16, 1953, the Eisenhower administration concluded an armistice ending the Korean War and restoring the border near the thirty-eighth parallel. Thousands of American troops, however, are still stationed in Korea.

The formation of NATO and the Korean conflict capped the first round of the Cold War. In 1953, Stalin's death and the armistice in Korea fostered hopes that international tensions might ease. In early 1955, Soviet occupation forces left Austria after that nation accepted neutral status. Later that year, the leaders of France, Great Britain, the Soviet Union, and the United States held a summit conference in Geneva. Nuclear weapons and the future of a divided Germany were the chief items on the agenda. Despite public displays of friendliness, the meeting produced few substantial agreements, and the Cold War soon resumed.

THE KHRUSHCHEV ERA IN THE SOVIET UNION

WHAT WERE the three crises of 1956, and how did they affect world order?

Many Russians had hoped the end of World War II would signal a reduction in the scope of the police state and a redirection of the economy away from heavy industry to consumer products. They were disappointed. Stalin did little or nothing to modify the character of the regime he had created. If anything, his determination to centralize his authority and a desire to undertake a new wave of internal purges continued until his death on March 6, 1953.

For a time, no single leader replaced Stalin. Rather, the *presidium* (the renamed Politburo) pursued a policy of collective leadership. Gradually, however, power and influence began to devolve on Nikita Khrushchev (1894–1971), who had been named party secretary in 1953. Three years later, he became premier. Khrushchev's rise ended collective leadership, but he never commanded the extraordinary powers of Stalin.

Khrushchev's Domestic Policies

The Khrushchev era, which lasted until the autumn of 1964, witnessed a retreat from Stalinism, though not from authoritarianism. Khrushchev sought to reform the Soviet system but to maintain the dominance of the Communist Party. Intellectuals were somewhat freer to express their opinions. Khrushchev also made modest efforts to meet the demand for more consumer goods and decentralize economic planning. In agriculture, he removed many of the more restrictive regulations on private cultivation and sought to expand the area available for growing wheat.

The Secret Speech of 1956 In February 1956, at the Twentieth Congress of the Communist Party, Khrushchev gave a secret speech (later published outside the Soviet Union) in which he denounced Stalin and his crimes against socialist justice during the purges of the 1930s. The speech stunned party circles, but it also opened the way for genuine, if limited, internal criticism of the Soviet government and for many of the changes in intellectual and economic life cited earlier. Khrushchev's speech, however, had repercussions well beyond the borders of the Soviet Union. Communist leaders in

Eastern Europe took it as a signal that they could govern with greater leeway than before and retreat from Stalinist policies. Indeed, Khrushchev's speech was simply the first of a number of extraordinary events in 1956.

The Three Crises of 1956

The Suez Intervention In July 1956, President Gamal Abdel Nasser (1918–1970) of Egypt nationalized the Suez Canal. Great Britain and France who had controlled the private company that had run the canal feared that this action would close the canal to their supplies of oil in the Persian Gulf. In October 1956, war broke out between Egypt and Israel. The British and French seized the opportunity to intervene militarily; however, the United States refused to support their action. The Soviet Union protested vehemently. The Anglo-French forces had to be withdrawn, and Egypt retained control of the canal.

The Suez intervention proved that without the support of the United States the nations of Western Europe could no longer impose their will on the rest of the world. It also appeared that the United States and the Soviet Union had restrained their allies from undertaking actions that might result in a wider conflict. The fact that neither of the superpowers wanted war constrained both Egypt and the Anglo-French forces.

Polish Efforts Toward Independent Action The autumn of 1956 also saw important developments in Eastern Europe that demonstrated similar limitations on independent action among the Soviet bloc nations. When the prime minister of Poland died, the Polish Communist Party leaders refused to replace him with Moscow's nominee. In the end, Wladyslaw Gomulka (1905–1982) emerged as the new Communist leader of Poland. He was the choice of the Poles, and he proved acceptable to the Soviets because he promised continued economic and military cooperation, and particularly because he continued Polish membership in the Warsaw Pact. Within those limits he halted the collectivization of Polish agriculture and improved relations with the Polish Roman Catholic Church.

QUICK REVIEW

Polish-Soviet Relations

- 1956: Wladyslaw Gomulka comes to power in Poland
- Gomulka confirmed Poland's membership in Warsaw Pact, promised an end to collectivization, and improved relations with the Catholic Church
- Compromise prompted Hungary to seek greater autonomy

The Hungarian Uprising Hungary provided the third trouble spot for the Soviet Union. In late October, demonstrations of sympathy for the Poles in Budapest led to street fighting. The Hungarian communists installed a new ministry headed by former premier Imre Nagy (1896–1958). Nagy was a Communist who sought a more independent position for Hungary. He went much further in his demands than Gomulka, calling for the removal of Soviet troops, the ultimate neutralization of Hungary, and for Hungarian withdrawal from the Warsaw Pact. These demands were wholly unacceptable to the Soviet Union. In early November, Soviet troops invaded Hungary; deposed Nagy, who was later executed; and imposed Janos Kadar (1912–1989) as premier.

LATER COLD WAR CONFRONTATIONS

HOW DID the Berlin Wall and the Cuban missile crisis strain relations between the United States and the Soviet Union?

After 1956, the Soviet Union began to talk about "peaceful coexistence" with the United States. By 1959, tensions had relaxed sufficiently for Western leaders to visit Moscow and for Khrushchev to tour the United States. A summit meeting was scheduled for May 1960, and President Eisenhower was to go to Moscow. Just before the Paris Summit Conference, the Soviet Union shot down an American U-2 aircraft that was flying reconnaissance over Soviet territory. Khrushchev demanded an apology from Eisenhower for this air surveillance. Eisenhower accepted full responsibility for the surveillance policy but refused to apologize publicly. Khrushchev then refused to take part in the summit conference.

The Soviets did not scuttle the summit meeting on the eve of its opening simply because of the American spy flights. They had long been aware of these flights and had other reasons for protesting them when they did. By 1960, the communist world itself had split between the Soviets and the Chinese, who were portraying the Russians as lacking revolutionary zeal. Destroying the summit was, in part, a way to demonstrate the Soviet Union's hard-line attitude toward the capitalist world.

The Berlin Wall

The aborted Paris conference opened the most difficult period of the Cold War. Throughout 1961, thousands of refugees from East Germany crossed the border into West Berlin. This outflow of people embarrassed East Germany, hurt its economy, and demonstrated the Soviet Union's inability to control Eastern Europe. Consequently, in August 1961, the East Germans, with Soviet support, erected a concrete wall along the border between East and West Berlin, separating the two parts of the city. Despite speeches and symbolic support from the West, the wall halted the flow of refugees and brought the U.S. commitment to West Germany into doubt.

The Cuban Missile Crisis

The most dangerous days of the Cold War occurred during the Cuban missile crisis of 1962. In 1957, Fidel Castro (b. 1926) launched an insurgency in Cuba, which toppled the dictatorship of Flugencio Batista (1901–1973) on New Year's Day of 1959. Thereafter Castro established a communist government, and Cuba became an ally of the Soviet Union. These events caused enormous concern within the United States.

QUICK REVIEW

The Cuban Missile Crisis

- 1959: Fidel Castro comes to power as a result of the Cuban revolution
- 1962: Khrushchev orders construction of missile bases in Cuba
- Tense negotiations resulted in the Soviets backing down and removing the missiles

In 1962, the Soviet Union secretly began to place nuclear missiles in Cuba. In response, the American government, under President John F. Kennedy (1917–1963), blockaded Cuba, halted the shipment of new missiles, and demanded the removal of existing installations. After a tense week, during which nuclear war seemed a real possibility, the Soviets backed down, and the crisis ended. This adventurism in foreign policy undermined Khrushchev's credibility in the ruling circles of the Soviet Union and caused other non-European communist regimes to question the Soviet commitment to their security and survival. It also increased the influence of the People's Republic of China in communist circles and convinced Soviet military leaders of the need to strengthen their forces, so that they would be as strong as, or stronger than, those of the United States in any future confrontation.

If the Cuban missile crisis had led to war, the United States could have launched missiles over Europe or from European bases into the Soviet Union. The crisis thus threatened Europe directly, but it was the last major Cold War confrontation to do so. In 1963, the United States and the Soviet Union concluded a nuclear test ban treaty. This agreement marked the beginning of a lessening in the overt tensions between the two powers.

Cuban Missile Crisis of 1962. The American ambassador to the United Nations displayed photographs to persuade the world of the threat to the United States less than one hundred miles from its own shores.

How did the Cuban missile crisis raise Cold War tensions?

THE BREZHNEV ERA

WHAT IMPACT did Brezhnev have on the Soviet Union and Eastern Europe?

By 1964, many in the Soviet Communist Party had concluded that Khrushchev had tried to do too much too soon and had done it poorly. On October 16, 1964, Khrushchev was forced to resign. He was replaced by Alexei Kosygin (1904–1980) as premier and Leonid Brezhnev (1906–1982) as party secretary. Brezhnev eventually emerged as the dominant figure.

1968: The Invasion of Czechoslovakia

In 1968, during what became known as the Prague Spring, the government of Czechoslovakia, under Alexander Dubcek (1921–1992), began to experiment with a more liberal communism. In the summer of 1968, the Soviet government and its allies in the Warsaw Pact sent troops into Czechoslovakia and replaced Dubcek with communist leaders more to its own liking.

Brezhnev Doctrine Asserted the right of the Soviet Union to intervene in domestic politics of communist countries.

At the time of the invasion, Soviet party chairman Brezhnev, in what came to be termed the ***Brezhnev Doctrine***, declared the right of the Soviet Union to interfere in the domestic politics of other communist countries. No further direct Soviet interventions occurred in Eastern Europe after 1968, yet the invasion of Czechoslovakia showed that any attempt at a greater liberalization could trigger Soviet military repression.

The United States and *Détente*

détente Relaxation of tensions between the United States and Soviet Union that involved increased trade and reduced deployment of strategic arms.

Foreign policy under Brezhnev combined attempts to reach an accommodation with the United States with continued efforts to expand Soviet influence and maintain Soviet leadership of the communist movement.

Under President Richard Nixon (1969–1974), the United States began a policy of ***détente*** with the Soviet Union, and the two countries concluded agreements on trade and on reducing strategic arms. Despite these agreements, Soviet spending on defense, and particularly on its navy, grew, damaging the consumer sectors of the economy.

During Gerald Ford's presidency (1974–1977), both the United States and the Soviet Union along with other European nations signed the Helsinki Accords. The accords recognized the Soviet sphere of influence in Eastern Europe, but they also recognized the human rights of the signers' citizens, which every government, including the Soviet Union, agreed to protect. President Jimmy Carter (1977–1981), a strong advocate of human rights, sought to induce the Soviet Union to comply with this commitment, a policy that cooled relations between the two countries.

Throughout this period of *détente*, in addition to its military presence in Eastern Europe, the Soviet Union pursued an activist foreign policy around the world. During the 1970s, it financed Cuban military intervention in Angola, Mozambique, and Ethiopia. Soviet funds flowed to the Sandinista forces in Nicaragua and to Vietnam, which permitted the So-

In the summer of 1968, Soviet tanks rolled into Czechoslovakia, ending that country's experiment in liberalized communism. This picture shows defiant flag-waving Czechs on a truck rolling past a Soviet tank in the immediate aftermath of the invasion.

Hulton Archive Photos/Getty Images, Inc.

Why did the leaders of the Soviet Union think it was so important to suppress liberalization in Soviet Bloc countries?

viets to use naval bases after North Vietnam conquered the south in 1975. The Soviet Union also provided funds and weapons to various Arab governments for use against Israel. By the early 1980s, the Soviet Union possessed the largest armed force in the world and had achieved virtual nuclear parity with the United States.

QUICK REVIEW

Détente

- Brezhnev sought accommodation with the United States while continuing to extend Soviet influence
- Brezhnev and President Nixon agreed to a policy of *détente* that increased trade and reduced deployment of strategic arms
- 1975: United States and Soviet Union signed the Helsinki Accords

The Invasion of Afghanistan

It was at this moment of great military strength in 1979 that the Brezhnev government decided to invade Afghanistan, a strategic decision of enormous long-range consequences for the future of the Soviet Union as well as the United States. The invasion brought a sharp response from the United States. The U.S. Senate refused to ratify a second Strategic Arms Limitation agreement that President Carter had signed earlier that year. The United States also embargoed grain shipments to the Soviet Union, boycotted the 1980 Olympic Games in Moscow, and sent aid to the Afghan rebels through various third parties, as did Pakistan, Saudi Arabia, and other Islamic nations. The U.S. Central Intelligence Agency became directly involved with the Afghan resistance forces, some of whom were radical Muslims. China, which felt threatened by the invasion, also helped the rebels.

Eventually, the Soviet forces bogged down in Afghanistan and could not defeat their guerrilla enemies. At first, few Soviets knew about the problems in Afghanistan, but during the 1980s, the military failure became common knowledge in the Soviet Union. Although the Afghan war did not make daily headline news in the Western press, it sapped Soviet strength for ten years and demoralized the Soviet Union not unlike the way the Vietnam conflict did the United States.

Communism and Solidarity in Poland

Events in Poland commencing in 1980—a time when the Soviet government was becoming increasingly rigidified and involved in Afghanistan—challenged both the authority of the Polish Communist Party and the influence of the Soviet Union.

In 1978, the election of Karol Wojtyla, cardinal archbishop of Kraków, as Pope John Paul II (d. 2005) proved important for Polish resistance to communist control and Soviet domination. An outspoken Polish opponent of communism now occupied a position of authority and enormous public visibility well beyond the reach of Soviet or communist control. The new pope visited his homeland in 1979 and received a tumultuous welcome.

In July 1980, the Polish government raised meat prices, leading to hundreds of protest strikes across the country. On August 14, workers occupied the Lenin shipyard at Gdansk on the Baltic coast. The strike soon spread to other shipyards, transport facilities, and factories connected with the shipbuilding industry. The strikers, led by Lech Walesa (b. 1944), refused to negotiate through any of the government-controlled unions. The Gdansk strike ended on August 31 after the government promised the workers the right to organize an independent union called Solidarity. In September, the head of the Polish Communist Party was replaced, the Polish courts recognized Solidarity as an independent union, and the state-controlled radio broadcast a Roman Catholic mass for the first time in thirty years. The summer of 1981 saw events that were no less remarkable occur within the Polish Communist Party itself. For the first time in any European communist state, secret elections for the party congress were permitted with real choices among the candidates.

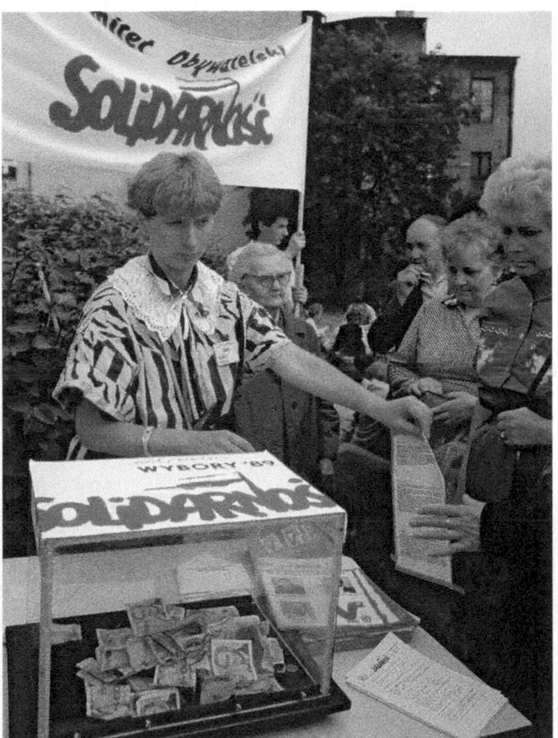

The Polish trade union "Solidarity" in 1989 successfully forced the Polish communist government to hold free elections. In June of that year, Solidarity, whose members here are collecting funds for their campaign, won overwhelmingly.

Bernard Bisson/CORBIS/Bettmann

Why did Poland's government find it so hard to defeat Solidarity?

This extraordinary Polish experiment, however, ended abruptly. In 1981, General Wojciech Jaruzelski (b. 1923) became head of the Polish Communist Party, and the army imposed martial law in December. The leaders of Solidarity were arrested. Martial law remained in effect until late in 1983, but the Polish Communist Party could not solve Poland's major economic problems.

Relations with the Reagan Administration

Early in the administration of President Ronald Reagan (1981–1989), the United States relaxed its grain embargo on the Soviet Union and placed less emphasis on human rights. At the same time, however, Reagan intensified Cold War rhetoric, famously describing the Soviet Union as an "evil empire." More importantly, the Reagan administration increased U.S. military spending, slowed arms limitation negotiations, deployed a new missile system in Europe, and proposed the Strategic Defense Initiative (dubbed "Star Wars" by the press), involving a high-technology space-based defense against nuclear attack. Star Wars and the Reagan defense spending forced the Soviet Union to increase its own defense spending when it could ill afford to do so and contributed to the economic problems that helped bring about its collapse.

DECOLONIZATION: THE EUROPEAN RETREAT FROM EMPIRE

HOW DID World War II serve as a catalyst for decolonization?

At the founding of the United Nations in 1945, approximately one-third of the population of the world was subject to the government of colonial powers. Since that time, more than eighty of those then non-self-governing territories have been admitted to UN membership as independent states. (See Map 29–3.)

The catalyst for this transformation was World War II. The war drew the military forces of the colonial powers back to Europe. The Japanese overran European possessions in East Asia and demonstrated thus that the European presence there might not be permanent. After the dislocations of the war came the immediate postwar European economic collapse, which left the European colonial powers less able to afford to maintain their military and administrative positions abroad. Consequently, in less than a century after the great nineteenth-century drive toward empire, European imperialists found themselves in retreat around the globe.

The liberal-democratic war aims of the Allies had also undermined colonialism. It was difficult to fight against tyranny in Europe while maintaining colonial dominance abroad. The United States opposed the continuation of the colonial empires. This policy was, in part, a matter of principle, but it also recognized that both the political and economic interests of the United States were more likely to prosper in a decolonized world. The founding of the United Nations also assured the presence of an international body opposed to colonialism.

The Cold War complicated the process of decolonization. Both the United States and the Soviet Union opposed the old colonial empires, but both also worried about the potential alignment of the new nations and moved to create spheres of influence and, in some cases, alliances with the newly independent states. Certain nations, such as India, fiercely pursued policies of neutrality in hopes of receiving aid and support from both sides.

Decolonization was a worldwide event lasting throughout the second half of the twentieth century and beyond. The two largest colonial empires were the British and the French. Their retreat from empire produced the most far-reaching repercussions not only in former colonial nations, but also in both Europe and the United States.

MAP EXPLORATION

Interactive map: To explore this map further, go to www.myhistorylab.com

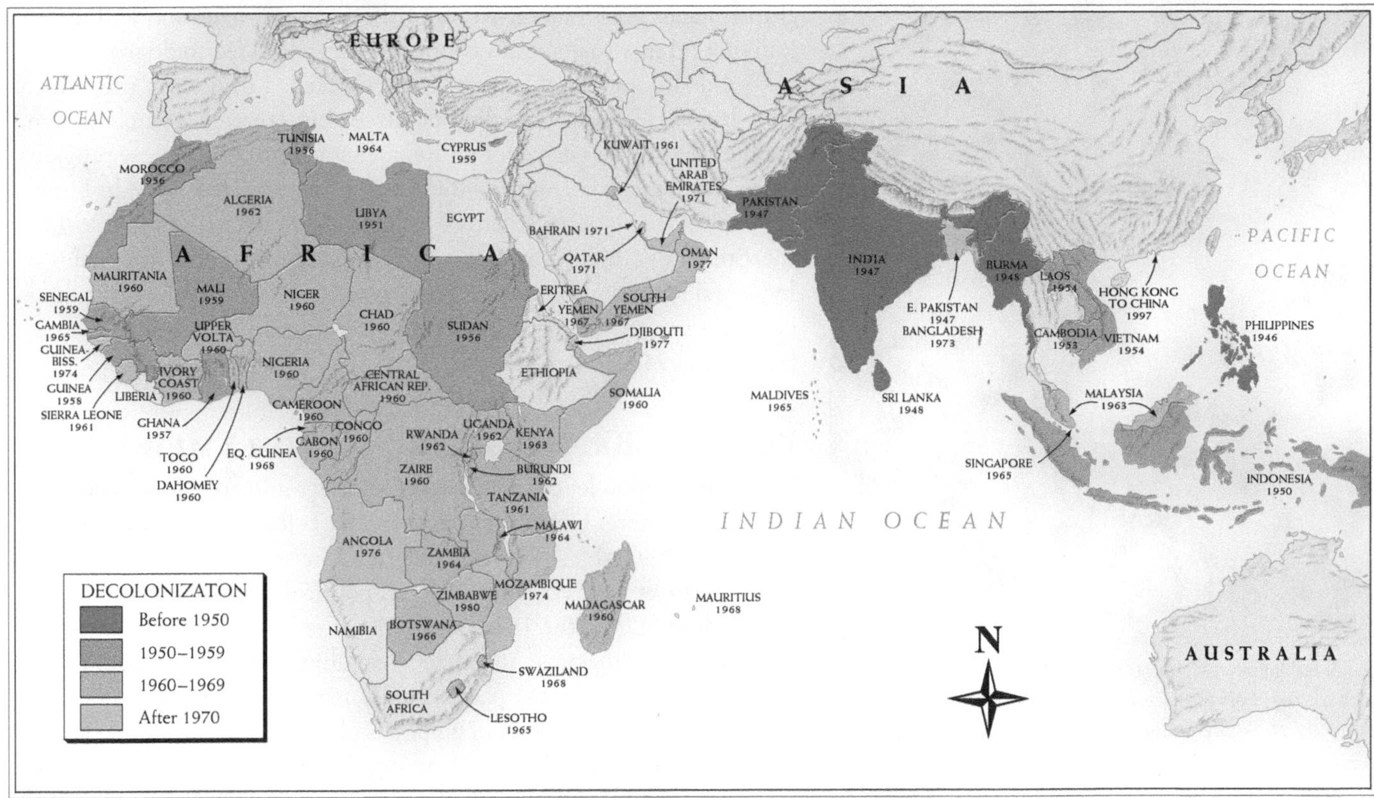

MAP 29–3 Decolonization Since World War II The Western powers' rapid retreat from imperialism after World War II is graphically shown on this outline map covering half the globe—from West Africa to the Southwest Pacific.

What patterns are noticeable about the time when South Asian, Southeast Asian, and African countries gained their independence?

INDIA

As early as 1885, politically active Hindu Indians founded the Indian National Congress with the goals of modernizing Indian life and liberalizing British policy. Muslims organized the Muslim League in 1887, which for a time cooperated with the National Congress but eventually sought an independent Muslim nation. After World War I, the Indian nationalist movement grew steadily in strength, in part because of British blunders, but more importantly because remarkable leaders pursued effective strategies.

Chief among these leaders was Mohandas Gandhi (1869–1948), who had studied law in Britain and there began to encounter the ideas of liberal Western thinkers, including the American Henry David Thoreau (1817–1862) from whom he learned the concept of passive resistance. In 1893 Ghandi went to South Africa where for over twenty years he worked on behalf of Indian immigrants. Gandhi returned to India in 1915 and soon distinguished himself as a leader of Indian nationalism by his insistence on religious toleration. From the 1920s to the mid-1940s, he inspired a growing movement of passive resistance to British rule in India. In 1930, he lead a famous march to break the British salt monopoly by collecting salt from the sea. He was repeatedly arrested and jailed by the British authorities. To embarrass the British during these

Ghandi led Indian resistance to British colonial rule. Part of his appeal was the simplicity of his life and dress.

How did Ghandi use the celebration of traditional Indian culture in his fight for Indian independence?

imprisonments and to gain worldwide publicity, he undertook long protest fasts during which he nearly died. In 1942, during World War II, Gandhi called on the British Government to leave India. In 1947, the British Labor government, weary of the incessant agitation and uncertain of its ability to maintain control in India, decided to do so.

Gandhi and the Congress Party succeeded in forcing the British from India. However, they did not succeed in creating a single nation. Parallel to Gandhi's drive for an India characterized by diverse religions living in mutual toleration, the Muslim League led by Ali Jinnah (1876–1948) sought a distinctly Muslim state. What occurred in 1947 as the British left India was a partition of the country into the states of India and Pakistan. Intense sectarian warfare and hundreds of thousands of deaths marked the partition. A Hindu extremist assassinated Gandhi himself in 1948.

Further British Retreat from Empire

The British surrender of India marked the beginning of a long, steady retreat from empire. Generally speaking, the British accepted the loss of empire as inevitable. British decolonization sought first to maintain whatever links were economically and politically possible without conflict. Indeed, during the 1940s and 1950s, the British undertook various development programs in their remaining Asian, African, and Caribbean colonies. These investments paradoxically made the British government and public more aware of the actual costs of empire and may have led both to accept more easily the end of empire. Second, throughout decolonization the British hoped to oversee the creation of institutions in their former colonies that would assure representative self-government once they had departed.

In 1948, Burma and Sri Lanka (formerly Ceylon) became independent. As already observed, the formation of the state of Israel and Arab nationalist movements forced Britain to withdraw from Palestine. During the 1950s, the British tried, belatedly, to prepare their tropical colonies for self-government. Ghana (formerly the Gold Coast) and Nigeria—which became self-governing in 1957 and 1960, respectively—were the major examples of planned decolonization. In other areas, such as Cyprus, Kenya, and Aden (now part of Yemen), the British withdrew under the pressure of militant nationalist movements. In many areas, violence between the British and the forces demanding independence hastened this retreat.

The development of these former colonies in the second half of the twentieth century has followed two distinct paths. In general, political instability and poverty have characterized the history of the independent states in Africa. By contrast, Asia has been an area of overall political stability and remarkable economic growth, challenging the economies of both the United States and Western Europe.

THE TURMOIL OF FRENCH DECOLONIZATION

WHY WAS France so reluctant to decolonize?

Although the British retreat from empire involved violence, at no point did the British "make a stand." Such was not the case with France. Having been defeated by the Nazis and then liberated by the allied forces, France believed it must reassert its position as a great power. This determination led it into two disastrous attempts to maintain its colonial empire, in Algeria and Vietnam.

France and Algeria

Over the decades, as France consolidated and extended its position in Algeria, French soldiers and hundreds of thousands of Europeans from France and other Mediterranean countries settled there, primarily in the cities and on small farms. By the close of World War I, approximately 20 percent of the population was of European descent. Collectively these immigrants were termed the *pieds noirs* (meaning "black feet," a derogatory term). The voting structure was set up to give the French settlers as large a voice as the majority Arab Muslim population. Algerian Muslims were not given posts in the administration. Shortly after World War I, the French extended the rights of full French citizenship to Algerian Muslims who had fought in the war, who were literate in French, or who owned land, but this rewarded only a few thousand of them.

In May 1945, during celebrations of the Allied victory in World War II, a violent clash broke out at Sétif between Muslims and French settlers. Matters rapidly got out of hand, and people on both sides were killed, but the French repressed the Muslims with a considerable loss of life. The incident robbed the French administration of legitimacy and marked the beginning of conscious Algerian nationalism. To placate Muslim opinion, in 1947, the French established a structure for limited political representation of the Muslim population and undertook economic reforms. Not unsurprisingly, these steps proved ineffective.

Algerian nationalists soon founded the National Liberation Front (FLN). In late 1954, insurrections and soon open civil war broke out in Algeria as the FLN undertook highly effective guerrilla warfare. Thereafter a war lasting until 1962 ground on between the Algerian nationalists and the French. Both sides committed atrocities; hundreds of thousands of Algerians were killed. The war divided France itself with many French citizens, often of left-wing political opinion, objecting to the war, and the French military, still smarting from its defeats in World War II and in Indochina, determined to fight on. The presence of more than 1 million European settlers in Algeria, who saw any settlement with the nationalists as a betrayal, exacerbated the situation. The French government itself became paralyzed and lost control of the army. There was fear of civil war in France itself or of a military takeover. In Algeria, violence was spreading.

In the midst of this turmoil, General Charles de Gaulle (1890–1970), who had led the Free French forces during World War II and had briefly governed France immediately after the war, reentered French political life largely at the urging of the military. His condition for taking office was the end of the Fourth Republic and the promulgation of a new constitution, which enhanced the power of the president and created the Fifth Republic. The voters ratified this, and de Gaulle became president of France in December 1958. He then undertook a long strategic retreat from Algeria. The process was neither peaceful nor easy. In 1962, however, de Gaulle held a referendum in Algeria on independence, which passed overwhelmingly. Algeria became independent on July 3, 1962.

France and Vietnam

In its push for empire, France had occupied Indochina (which contained Laos, Cambodia, and Vietnam) between 1857 and 1893. By 1930, Ho Chi Minh (1892–1969) had turned a nationalist movement against French colonial rule into the Indochina Communist Party, which the French, for a time, succeeded in suppressing. World War II, however, provided new opportunities for Ho Chi Minh and other nationalists as they fought both the Japanese who occupied Indochina in 1941 and the pro-Vichy French colonial administration that collaborated with the Japanese until 1945. The war thus established Ho Chi Minh as a major anticolonial, nationalist leader.

In September 1945, Ho Chi Minh declared the independence of Vietnam under the Viet Minh, a coalition of nationalists that the communists soon dominated. By 1947, a full-fledged civil war had erupted in Vietnam. (Cambodia and, to a lesser extent, Laos remained quiescent under pro-French or neutralist monarchies.)

Until 1949, the United States displayed minimal concern about the Indochina war. The establishment of the Communist People's Republic of China that year dramatically changed the U.S. outlook. The United States now saw the French colonial war against Ho Chi Minh as an integral part of the Cold War conflict. The U.S. support for France in southeast Asia also served to gain French support for the establishment of NATO. Even though the United States supported the French effort in Vietnam financially, it was not prepared, despite divisions among policymakers, to intervene militarily. In the spring of 1954, during an international conference in Geneva on the future of Vietnam, the French military stronghold of Dien Bien Phu fell to Viet Minh forces after a prolonged siege. France lost the will to continue the struggle, which had become increasingly unpopular with the French people.

By late June, a complicated and unsatisfactory peace accord divided Vietnam at the seventeenth parallel of latitude. North of the parallel, centered in Hanoi, the Viet Minh were in charge; below it, centered in Saigon, the French were in charge. This was to be a temporary border. By 1956, elections were to be held to reunify the country. In effect, the conference attempted to transform a military conflict into a political one.

Vietnam Drawn into the Cold War

Unhappy with these arrangements, the United States, in September 1954, formed the Southeast Asia Treaty Organization (SEATO), a collective security agreement that somewhat resembled the European NATO alliance, but without the integration of military forces or inclusion of all states in the region. Its membership consisted of the United States, Great Britain, France, Australia, New Zealand, Thailand, Pakistan, and the Philippines.

U.S. Troops Engaged in Combat in Vietnam At the war's peak, more than 500,000 American troops were stationed in South Vietnam. The United States struggled in Vietnam for more than a decade, seriously threatening its commitment to Western Europe.

U.S. Army Photo

What led to the escalation of American involvement in Vietnam?

In 1955, French troops began to withdraw from South Vietnam. As they left, the various Vietnamese political groups began to fight for power among themselves. The United States stepped into the turmoil in Vietnam with military and economic aid. Among the Vietnamese politicians, it chose to support was Ngo Dinh Diem (1901–1963). In October 1955, Diem established a Republic of Vietnam in the territory for which the Geneva conference had made France responsible. Diem announced that the Geneva agreements would not bind his newly established government and that elections would not be held in 1956. The American government, which had not signed the Geneva documents, supported his position.

In 1960, the National Liberation Front was founded, with the goals of overthrowing Diem, unifying the country, reforming the economy, and ousting the Americans. It was anticolonial, nationalist, and communist. Its military arm was called the Viet Cong and was aided by the government of North Vietnam. Diem, a Roman Catholic, also faced mounting criticism from Buddhists and the army. His response to these pressures was further repression and dependence on an ever-smaller group of advisers.

Direct United States Involvement

The Eisenhower and Kennedy administrations continued to support Diem while demanding reforms in his government. The American military presence grew from about 600 advisers in early 1961 to more than 16,000 troops in late 1963. The political situation in Vietnam became increasingly unstable. On November 1, 1963, an army coup in which the United States was deeply involved overthrew and murdered Diem. The United States hoped a new government in South Vietnam would generate popular support. Thereafter, the United States sought to find a leader who could fulfill that hope. It finally settled on Nguyen Van Thieu (1923–2001), who governed South Vietnam from 1966 to 1975.

President Kennedy was assassinated on November 22, 1963. His successor, Lyndon Johnson (1963–1969), vastly expanded the commitment to South Vietnam. In August 1964, after an attack on an American ship in the Gulf of Tonkin, Johnson authorized the first bombing of North Vietnam. In February 1965, major bombing attacks began. They continued, with only brief pauses, until early in 1973. The land war grew until more than 500,000 Americans were stationed in South Vietnam.

In 1969, President Richard Nixon began a policy known as *Vietnamization*, which involved the gradual withdrawal of American troops from Vietnam while the South Vietnamese army took over the full military effort. Peace negotiations had begun in Paris in the spring of 1968, but a cease-fire was not finally arranged until January 1973. American troops left South Vietnam, and North Vietnam released its American prisoners of war. On April 30, 1975, Saigon (renamed Ho Chi Minh City) fell to the Viet Cong and the North Vietnamese army. Vietnam was finally united. (See Map 29–4.)

The U.S. intervention in Vietnam, which grew out of a power vacuum left by French decolonization, affected the entire Western world. For a decade after the Cuban missile crisis, Vietnam largely diverted the attention of the United States from Europe. American prestige suffered, and the U.S. policy in Southeast Asia made many Europeans question the wisdom of the American government and its commitment to Western Europe. Within the United States, the Vietnam conflict produced enormous divisions and debates over American involvement in the rest of the world that persist to the present day.

MAP EXPLORATION

Interactive map: To explore this map further, go to www.myhistorylab.com

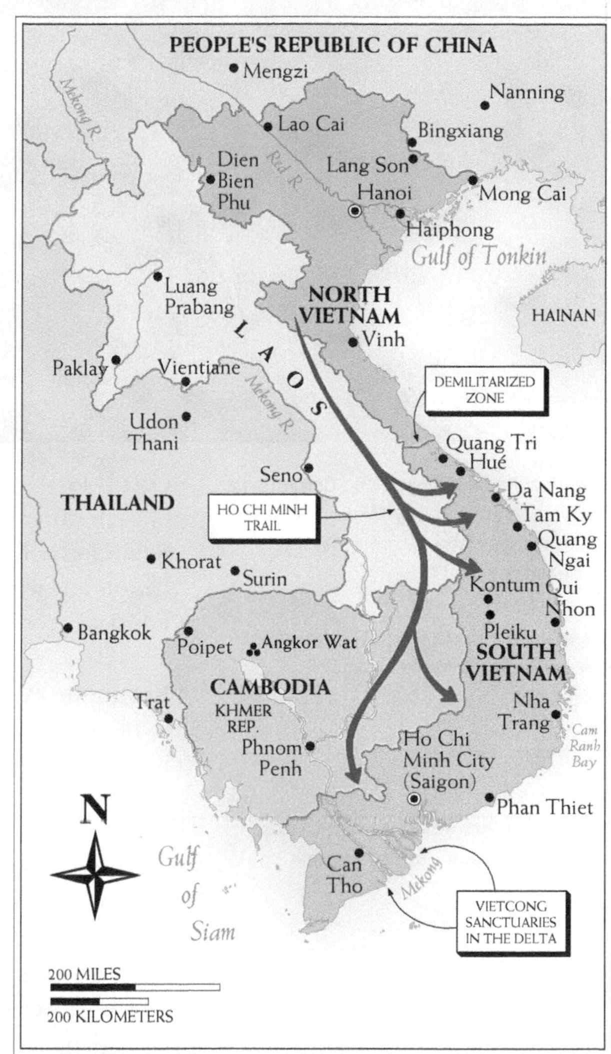

MAP 29–4 Vietnam and Its Southeast Asian Neighbors The map identifies important locations associated with the war in Vietnam.

How did the Ho Chi Minh Trail affect the outcome of the war?

THE COLLAPSE OF EUROPEAN COMMUNISM

WHY DID European communism collapse?

The withdrawal of Soviet influence from Eastern Europe and the internal collapse of the Soviet Union are the most important European historical events of the second half of the twentieth century. Many of the factors leading to the Soviet collapse remain murky, but here is a relatively clear narrative of what occurred.

Under Brezhnev, who governed from 1964 to 1982, the Soviet government became markedly more repressive at home, suggesting a return to Stalinist policies. This internal repression gave rise to a dissident movement. Certain Soviet citizens dared to criticize the regime in public and accused the government of violating the human

President Ronald Reagan and Communist Party general secretary Mikhail Gorbachev confer at a summit meeting in December 1987.

AP Wide World Photos

What made it possible for Gorbachev and Reagan to find common ground?

rights provision of the 1975 Helsinki Accords. The Soviet government responded with further repression, placing some opponents in psychiatric hospitals and others under what amounted to house arrest. During the same period the structures of the Communist Party became both rigidified and corrupt, which increasingly demoralized younger Soviet bureaucrats and party members.

Gorbachev Attempts to Reform the Soviet Union

Although economic stagnation, party corruption, and the lingering Afghan war had long been undermining Soviet authority, what brought these forces to a head and began the dramatic collapse of the Soviet Empire was the accession to power of Mikhail S. Gorbachev (b. 1931) in 1985 after both of Brezhnev's two immediate successors, Yuri Andropov (1914–1984) and Konstantin Chernenko (1911–1985), died within thirteen months of each other. In what proved to be the last great attempt to reform the Soviet system, Gorbachev immediately began the most remarkable changes that the Soviet Union had witnessed since the 1920s. (See "Encountering the Past: Rock Music and Political Protest.")

Economic *Perestroika* Gorbachev's primary goal was to revive the Russian economy to raise the country's standard of living. Initially, he and his supporters, most of whom he had appointed himself, challenged traditional party and bureaucratic management of the Soviet government and economy. Under the policy of ***perestroika***, or "restructuring," they reduced the size and importance of the centralized economic ministries.

perestroika ("restructuring") Means by which Gorbachev wished to raise his country's standard of living.

By early 1990, in a clear abandonment of traditional Marxist ideology, Gorbachev began to advocate private ownership of property and liberalization of the economy toward free market mechanisms. Despite many organizational changes, the Soviet economy remained stagnate and even declined. The failure of Gorbachev's economic policies affected his political policies. To some extent, he pursued bold political reform because he failed to achieve economic progress.

Glasnost Gorbachev allowed an extraordinary public discussion and criticism of Soviet history and Soviet Communist Party policy. This development was termed ***glasnost***, or openness. Workers were permitted to criticize party officials and the economic plans of the party and the government. Censorship was relaxed and free expression encouraged. Dissidents were released from prison. In the summer of 1988, Gorbachev presided over a party congress that witnessed full debates.

glasnost ("openness") Gorbachev's policy of opening the way for unprecedented public discussion and criticism of Soviet history and the Communist Party. Censorship was relaxed and dissidents were released from prison.

Gorbachev soon applied *perestroika* to the political arena. In 1988, a new constitution permitted openly contested elections. After real political campaigning—a new experience for the Soviet Union—the Congress of People's Deputies was elected in 1989. After lively debate, the Supreme Soviet, another elected body—although one the Communist Party dominated—formally elected Gorbachev president in 1989.

The policy of open discussion allowed national minorities within the Soviet Union to demand political autonomy. Throughout its history, the Soviet Union had remained a vast empire of subject peoples. *Glasnost* quickly brought to the foreground the discontent of all such peoples. Gorbachev proved inept in addressing these ethnic complaints. He badly underestimated the unrest that internal national discontent could generate.

ENCOUNTERING THE PAST

ROCK MUSIC AND POLITICAL PROTEST

The political scene in many parts of the modern world has been powerfully influenced by the rock music pioneered in the United States in the 1950s by African American, working-class, and folk musicians. In America it served as a vehicle for protesting the Vietnam War and for demanding civil rights. Europeans also took it up and set their own stamp on it. Britain's Beatles were the most successful of the early European rock bands, but the lyrics of their songs were minimally political.

The Russian rock group "Dynamic" performs in Moscow in 1987.

R. Podemi/TASS/Sovfoto/Eastfoto

How did *glasnost* change Soviet society?

Rock music acquired its hard edge as social commentary in the 1970s with the appearance of punk rock groups with provocative names such as the Sex Pistols. Pluralistic Western societies took its antiestablishment message in stride, but in Eastern Europe and the Soviet Union, it was literally revolutionary. During the 1970s and 1980s, it offered social and political critics a major outlet. Rock stars were celebrated for their personal heroism in openly attacking communist governments, and their music expressed and spread the disaffection that contributed to the collapse of communist regimes throughout Eastern Europe.

WHAT IS the source of the mass appeal of rock music? Why did it become antiestablishment? How did it undermine communism?

1989: REVOLUTION IN EASTERN EUROPE

Solidarity Reemerges in Poland In the early 1980s, Poland's government relaxed martial law, and it eventually released all the Solidarity prisoners, although Jaruzelski remained president. In 1988, new strikes surprised even the leaders of Solidarity. This time, the communist government could not reimpose control. After consultations between the government and Solidarity, the union was legalized. Lech Walesa again took center stage, as a kind of mediator between the government and the more independent elements of the trade union movement he had founded.

Jaruzelski began some political reforms with the tacit consent of the Soviet Union. When free elections were held in 1989, the communists lost overwhelmingly to Solidarity candidates. Late in the summer, Jaruzelski, unable to find a communist who could forge a majority coalition in parliament, turned to Solidarity and appointed the first noncommunist prime minister of Poland since 1945. Gorbachev expressly approved the appointment.

German youth breach the Berlin Wall in November 1989, an act that days earlier would have been unthinkable and deadly; the breach of the wall was the most symbolic moment in the collapse of European communism.

R. Bossu/Sygma/CORBIS

Why did communism in Eastern Europe collapse so rapidly?

Toward Hungarian Independence Throughout 1989, as these events unfolded within Poland, one Soviet-dominated state after another in Eastern Europe moved toward independence. Early in the year, the Hungarian government opened its border with Austria, permitting free travel between the two countries. This breach in the Iron Curtain immediately led thousands of East Germans to move through Hungary and Austria to West Germany. The Hungarian Communist Party changed its name to the Socialist Party, permitted other parties to engage openly in politics, and promised free elections by October.

German Reunification In the autumn of 1989, popular demonstrations erupted in East German cities. Adding to the pressure, Gorbachev told the leaders of the East German Communist Party that the Soviet Union would not use force to support them. In November 1989, in one of the most emotional moments in European history since 1945, the government of East Germany ordered the opening of the Berlin Wall. That week, tens of thousands of East Berliners crossed into West Berlin to celebrate, to visit their families, and to shop with money the West German government gave them. Shortly thereafter, free travel began between East and West Germany.

Within days of these dramatic events, West Germany and the other Western nations faced the issue of German reunification. Helmut Kohl (b. 1930), the chancellor of West Germany, became the leading force in moving toward full unification. Late in 1989, the European Economic Community accepted, in principle, the unification of Germany. By February 1990, some form of reunification had become a forgone conclusion, accepted by the United States, the Soviet Union, Great Britain, and France.

The Velvet Revolution in Czechoslovakia Revolution in Czechoslovakia rapidly followed the breach of the Berlin Wall. The popular new Czech leader who led the forces against the party was Václav Havel (b. 1936), a playwright of international standing whom the communist government had imprisoned. In December 1989, Havel's group, known as Civic Forum, forced Gustav Husak (b. 1913), who had been president of Czechoslovakia since 1968, to resign. On December 28, 1989, Alexander Dubcek became chairman of the parliament, and the next day, Havel was elected president.

Violent Revolution in Romania The only revolution of 1989 that involved significant violence occurred in Romania. There, in mid-December, the forces of President Nicolae Ceausescu (1918–1989), who had governed without opposition since 1965, fired on crowds that were protesting conditions in the country. By December 22, Bucharest was in full revolt. Ceausescu and his wife attempted to flee, but were captured, secretly tried, and shot on December 25.

The Soviet Stance on Revolutionary Developments None of the revolutions of 1989 could have taken place unless the Soviet Union had refused to intervene militarily, in contrast to 1956 and 1968. For the first time since the end of World War II, Eastern Europeans could shape their own political destiny without the fear of Soviet military intervention. Once they realized the Soviets would not act, thousands of ordinary citizens took to the streets to denounce Communist Party domination and assert their desire for democracy. The major question facing the Soviet Union became the peaceful withdrawal of its troops from Eastern Europe. The haphazard nature of that withdrawal and the general poverty to which those troops returned were other factors undermining the Soviet armed forces.

The Collapse of the Soviet Union

Gorbachev clearly believed, as his behavior toward Eastern Europe in 1989 showed, that the Soviet Union could no longer afford to support communist governments in that region or intervene to uphold their authority while seeking to restructure its own economy. He also had concluded that the Communist Party in the Soviet Union must restructure itself and its relationship to the Soviet state and society.

Renunciation of Communist Political Monopoly In early 1990, Gorbachev formally proposed to the Central Committee of the Soviet Communist Party that the party abandon its monopoly of power. After intense debate, the committee abandoned the Leninist position that only a single elite party could act as the vanguard of the revolution and forge a new Soviet society.

New Political Forces Gorbachev confronted challenges from three major political forces by 1990. One consisted of those groups—considered conservative in the Soviet context—whose members wanted to preserve the influence of the Communist Party and the Soviet army. The country's economic stagnation and political and social turmoil deeply disturbed them. They appeared to control significant groups in the economy and society. During late 1990 and early 1991, Gorbachev, who himself seems to have been disturbed by the nation's turmoil, began to appoint members of these factions to key positions in the government. In other words, he seemed to be making a strategic retreat.

Gorbachev initiated these moves because he was now facing opposition from a second group—those who wanted much more extensive and rapid change. Their leading spokesman was Boris Yeltsin (1931–2007). He and his supporters wanted to move quickly to a market economy and a more democratic government. In 1990, he was elected president of the Russian Republic, the largest and most important of the Soviet Union's constituent republics. In the new political climate, that position gave him a firm political base from which to challenge Gorbachev's authority and increase his own.

The third force that came into play from 1989 onward was growing regional unrest in some of the republics of the Soviet Union. Initially, the greatest unrest came from the three Baltic republics

SIGNIFICANT DATES FROM THE ERA OF THE COLD WAR

1945	Yalta Conference; founding of the United Nations
1946	Churchill's Iron Curtain speech
1947	(March) Truman Doctrine; (June) announcement of Marshall Plan
1948	Communist takeovers in Czechoslovakia and Hungary; State of Israel proclaimed
1948–1949	Berlin Blockade
1949	NATO founded; East and West Germany emerge as separate states
1950–1953	Korean conflict
1953	Death of Stalin
1955	Warsaw Pact founded; Austria established as a neutral state
1956	(February) Khrushchev's secret speech denouncing Stalin; (October) Suez crisis and the Hungarian uprising
1957	*Sputnik* launched
1961	Berlin Wall erected
1962	Cuban missile crisis
1963	Test Ban Treaty (Soviet Union and the United States)
1964	Gulf of Tonkin Resolution; America in Vietnam
1967	Six Days' War, Arab-Israeli conflict
1968	Soviet invasion of Czechoslovakia
1972	Strategic Arms Limitation Treaty
1973	Yom Kippur War
1975	Saigon falls to North Vietnam; Helsinki Accords
1978	Camp David Accords
1979	Soviet invasion of Afghanistan
1981	Solidarity founded in Poland
1982	Israel invades Lebanon; death of Brezhnev
1985	Israel withdraws from Lebanon
1987	Arab uprising on the West Bank commences
1988	PLO accepts Israel's right to exist
1993	Israel and PLO agree to phase out self-rule in the West Bank and Gaza
1995	Israeli prime minister Rabin assassinated

of Estonia, Latvia, and Lithuania, which had been independent states until 1940 when the Soviet Union had occupied them in accord with secret provisions of the Soviet-German nonaggression pact of 1939. In these republics, many local communist leaders began to see themselves as national leaders rather than as party stalwarts.

During 1989 and 1990, the parliaments of the Baltic republics tried to decrease Soviet control, and Lithuania actually declared independence. Gorbachev used military force to resist these moves. Discontent also arose in the Soviet Islamic republics in Central Asia and the Caucasus. Riots broke out in Azerbaijan and Tajikistan, where the army was used as a police force against Soviet citizens. Throughout 1990 and 1991, Gorbachev sought to negotiate new constitutional arrangements between the republics and the central government. His failure to effect such arrangements may have been the single most important reason for the rapid collapse of the Soviet Union.

The August 1991 Coup The turning point in all these events came in August 1991, when the conservative forces that Gorbachev had brought into the government attempted a coup. Troops occupied Moscow, and Gorbachev was placed under house arrest while on vacation in the Crimea. The day of the coup, Boris Yeltsin climbed on a tank in front of the Russian Parliament building to denounce the coup and ask the world for help to maintain the Soviet Union's movement toward democracy.

Within two days, the coup collapsed and a humiliated Gorbachev returned to Moscow. From that point on, Yeltsin steadily became the dominant political figure in the nation. The Communist Party, compromised by its participation in the coup, collapsed as a political force. The constitutional arrangements between the central government and the individual republics were revised. In December 1991, the Soviet Union ceased to exist, Gorbachev left office, and the Commonwealth of Independent States came into being. (See Map 29–5.)

The Yeltsin Decade

Boris Yeltsin emerged as the strongest leader within the new commonwealth. As president of Russia, he was head of the largest and most powerful of the new states. His popularity was high both in Russia and in the commonwealth in 1992, but within a year, he faced serious economic and political problems. The Russian Parliament, most of whose members were former communists, opposed Yeltsin personally and his policies of economic and political reform. In September 1993, Yeltsin suspended parliament, which responded by deposing him. Parliament leaders tried to incite popular uprisings against Yeltsin in Moscow. The military, however, backed Yeltsin, and he surrounded the parliament building with troops and tanks. On October 4, 1993, after pro-parliament rioters rampaged through Moscow, Yeltsin ordered the tanks to attack the parliament building, crushing the opposition.

These actions consolidated Yeltsin's authority. The major Western powers, deeply concerned by the turmoil in Russia, supported him. In December 1993, Russians voted for a new parliament and approved a new constitution. By 1994, the central government found itself at war in the Islamic province of Chechnya in the Caucasus. Under Yeltsin, Russian forces held off a rebel victory, but the war reached no clear conclusion.

During the mid-1990s, to dismantle the Soviet state and economy, former state-owned industries were privatized. This complicated process involved much corruption and opportunism by individuals determined to profit from the emerging economic organization. One result was the creation of a small group of enormously wealthy individuals, whom the press dubbed "the oligarchs." While these people amassed vast wealth, the general Russian economy remained stagnant. The economic downturn contributed

MAP 29–5 **The Commonwealth of Independent States** In December 1991, the Soviet Union broke up into its fifteen constituent republics. Eleven of these were loosely joined in the Commonwealth of Independent States. Also shown is the autonomous region of Chechnya, which has waged two bloody wars with Russia in the last decade.

What does the breakup of the Soviet Union say about nationalism in the modern era?

to further political unrest. In the face of these problems and in declining health, Yeltsin resigned the presidency in a dramatic gesture just as the new century opened. His hand-picked successor was Vladimir Putin (b. 1952), a relatively unknown figure at the time. Putin would lead the Russian Federation in new economic and political directions. Before considering Putin's role, it is necessary to examine the events that occurred during the 1990s in southeastern Europe.

THE COLLAPSE OF YUGOSLAVIA AND CIVIL WAR

HOW DID ethnic tensions lead to civil war in Yugoslavia?

Yugoslavia was created after World War I. Its borders included seven major national groups—Serbs, Croats, Slovenes, Montenegrins, Macedonians, Bosnians, and Albanians—among whom there have been ethnic disputes for centuries. The Croats and Slovenes are Roman Catholic and use the Latin alphabet. The Serbs, Montenegrins, and Macedonians are Eastern Orthodox and use the Cyrillic alphabet. The Bosnians and

Albanians are mostly Muslims. Most members of each group reside in a region with which they are associated historically—Serbia, Croatia, Slovenia, Montenegro, Macedonia, Bosnia-Herzegovina, and Kosovo—and these regions constituted individual republics or autonomous areas within Yugoslavia. Many Serbs, however, lived outside Serbia proper.

Tito (1892–1980) had acted independently of Stalin in the late 1940s and pursued his own foreign policy. To mute ethnic differences, he encouraged a cult of personality around himself and instituted complex political power sharing among these different groups. After his death, economic difficulties undermined the authority of the central government, and Yugoslavia gradually dissolved into civil war.

In the late 1980s, the old ethnic differences came to the foreground again in Yugoslav politics. Nationalist leaders—most notably Slobodan Milosevic (b. 1941–2006) in Serbia and Franjo Tudjman (b. 1922) in Croatia—gained authority. During the summer of 1990, in the wake of the changes in the former Soviet bloc nations, Slovenia and Croatia declared independence from the central Yugoslav government, and several European nations, including, most importantly, Germany, immediately granted them recognition. The full European community soon did likewise.

From this point on, violence escalated. Serbia—concerned about Serbs living in Croatia and about the loss of lands and resources there—was determined to maintain a unitary Yugoslav state that it would dominate. Croatia was equally determined to secure independence. By June 1991, full-fledged war had erupted between the two republics.

The conflict took a new turn in 1992 when Croatian and Serbian forces determined to divide Bosnia-Herzegovina. The Muslims in Bosnia—who had lived alongside Serbs and Croats for generations—soon became crushed between the opposing forces. The Serbs in particular, pursuing a policy called "ethnic cleansing," a euphemism redolent of some of the worst horrors of World War II, killed or forcibly removed many Bosnian Muslims.

More than any other single event, the unremitting bombardment of Sarajevo, the capital of Bosnia-Herzegovina, brought the violence of the Yugoslav civil war to the attention of the world. The United Nations attempted unsuccessfully to mediate the conflict and imposed sanctions that had little affect. Early in 1994, however, a shell exploded in the marketplace in Sarajevo, killing dozens of people. Thereafter, NATO forced the Serbs to withdraw their artillery from around Sarajevo.

Destruction of Sarajevo An elderly parishioner walks through the ruins of St. Mary's Roman Catholic Church in Sarajevo. The church was destroyed by Serb shelling in May 1992.

Reuters/CORBIS/ Bettmann

Why did the fall of communism lead to civil war in Yugoslavia?

The events of the civil war came to a head in 1995 when NATO forces carried out strategic air strikes. Later that year, under the leadership of the United States, the leaders of the warring forces negotiated a peace agreement in Dayton, Ohio. The agreement was of great complexity but recognized an independent Bosnia. NATO troops, including those from the United States, have enforced the terms of the agreement.

Toward the end of the 1990s, Serbian aggression against ethnic Albanians in the province of Kosovo again drew NATO into Yugoslav affairs. For months, the world watched the Serbian military deport Albanians from Kosovo where Albanians constituted a majority of the population. There were many casualties, atrocities, and deaths. Early in 1999, NATO again carried out an air campaign and sent troops into Kosovo to safeguard the ethnic Albanians. In 2000, a revolution overthrew Slobodan Milosevic.

The disintegration of the former Yugoslavia took still another important turn in February 2008 when Kosovo with its Albanian majority population declared its independence from Serbia. The United States, a majority of the nations composing the European Union, and all Kosovo's neighbors except Serbia have recognized the independence of Kosovo. The Russian Federation, a longtime supporter of Serbia, immediately and strongly condemned the independence of Kosovo. The issue of Kosovo's independence, as will be seen in the next section, led to Russian military actions in the region of the Black Sea later in 2008.

PUTIN AND THE RESURGENCE OF RUSSIA

WHAT VISION does Putin have of Russia's place in the world?

Vladimir Putin, who had become president of the Russian Federation in 2000, immediately moved to establish his position as a national and nationalistic leader of the federation. He vigorously renewed the war against the rebels in Chechnya, which resulted in heavy casualties and enormous destruction there, but also strengthened Putin's political support in Russia itself. By the middle of the decade, however, Russian forces had clearly established the upper hand over the Chechen rebels and the drive toward independence was firmly checked at a very high cost in lives on both sides.

In the wake of the Chechen war and as part of his determination that the central government will dominate Russia's economy and political life, Putin has sought to diminish local autonomy and centralize power in his own hands. The central government has also moved against leading oligarchs and other businessmen with some being imprisoned. Putin used the attacks on these enormously wealthy and economically powerful figures to generate support from the broad Russian public who regard the oligarchs as thieves and one of the causes of the economic hardship of the 1990s. Putin also imprisoned political critics and opponents and moved against independent newspapers and television stations as well.

During Putin's presidency the Russian economy genuinely began to improve. Foreign debts were paid. The Russian ruble came to be regarded as a serious currency. Many more consumer goods were available. Much of this relative prosperity was the result of the oil resources available to the Russian Federation and the rising price of oil on the world market. Under Putin a clear trade-off occurred between political freedom and economic and political stability. In 2008 Putin left the elected presidency at the end of his second four-year term, turning the office over to his own handpicked successor Dmitri Medvedev (b. 1965). At the same time, however, Putin assumed the office of prime minister and clearly remained the chief political figure in the country.

Putin both as president and now prime minister has been determined to use the nation's economic recovery and new wealth to allow Russia to reassert its position as a major power on both the regional and world scene. After the terrorist attacks on the United States in September 2001, Putin supported the American assault on Afghanistan, largely because the Russian government was afraid that Islamic extremism would spread beyond Chechnya to other regions in Russia and to the largely Muslim nations that bordered Russia in Central Asia and the Caucasus. This period of cooperation proved short-lived. Putin became one of the leading voices against the American-led invasion of Iraq and has continued to criticize American policy in the region. Putin has also been sharply critical of the ongoing expansion of NATO, which has embraced nations directly bordering the Russian Federation. His government continued to attempt to exert influence in various of the new nations, such as the former Soviet republics of Ukraine and Georgia, that came into existence with the collapse of the former Soviet Union.

The aftermath of an attack by a Russian warplane on an apartment block in Gori, Georgia, during the conflict in South Ossetia in August 2008. Here a Georgian man cradles the body of a relative killed during the bombing, which killed at least five people.

Gleb Garanich/Corbis/Reuters America LLC

How has the world responded to Russia's aggressive foreign policy during the Putin era?

This determination to assert Russian domination over recently independent nations once part of the former Soviet Union dramatically displayed itself in August 2008. That month troops of the Russian Federation invaded the republic of Georgia. What had provoked this attack was Georgia's having shortly before sent troops into South Ossetia. Russian troops first drove the Georgians out of South Ossetia and then continued into Georgia itself. South Ossetia itself a part of the former Soviet Union had been divided into regions dominated by Russia and Georgia. Georgia sought to assert further influence only to be immediately and overwhelmingly blocked by Russian forces. Russia eventually withdrew after a cease-fire but had succeeded in demonstrating its power in the region and in creating potential instability in postwar Georgia.

The Russian invasion of Georgia marked a new departure in post-Soviet Russian foreign policy and a resurgence of Russian international influence following the collapse of the Soviet Union nearly twenty years earlier. During that period both the European Union and NATO had moved to expand their memberships by expanding into Eastern Europe and into regions previously dominated by or part of the former Soviet Union. Discussions had taken place about the possibility of bringing both Ukraine and Georgia into NATO. The United States had indicated support for such inclusion. Putin and other leaders of the Russian Federation had witnessed the manner in which various regions of the former Yugoslavia, most recently Kosovo in February 2008, had broken away from Serbia and established their own independence. The Russia Federation feared the example of Kosovo and the international recognition its independence had achieved might serve as a pattern for potential break-away regions in the Russian Federation. It also feared encirclement by NATO member nations where the United States might locate military bases. The action taken against Georgia served to demonstrate the ability of the Russian Federation to take military action on its borders and to give warning to other nations in the region of its capacity to intervene. At the same time the absence of any effective resistance to Russian actions in Georgia from either the United States or the European Union nations raised doubts about the capacity of either to influence events in the region of the Black Sea. Moreover, the action also demonstrated Russian willingness to take advantage of American involvement in Iraq and Afghanistan to reassert its potential authority in those regions it has dominated since the wars of Catherine the Great in the eighteenth century.

In late 2008 another question suddenly confronted Russia. As one element in the worldwide financial crisis, commodity prices dropped sharply. These included the price of oil on the world market. It remains to be seen whether Russia will be able to maintain its economic growth and political resurgence in the face of dropping income from the sale of oil, which had financed its new international influence during the past decade.

THE RISE OF RADICAL POLITICAL ISLAMISM

WHAT FORCES gave rise to radical political Islamism?

On September 11, 2001, Islamic terrorists attacked the United States, crashing hijacked civilian domestic aircraft into the twin towers of the World Trade Center in New York City, the Pentagon in Washington, D.C., and a Pennsylvania field with a vast loss of life and property. These events and those flowing from them have not only

transformed American foreign policy toward the Middle East but have also changed European relations with the United States.

In retrospect, we can see that those attacks were the result of forces that had been affecting not only the United States but also the Western world for at least a half century. The end of the Cold War has been succeeded by a new political world in which both the United States and the nations of Europe, including the Russian Federation, are endangered by terrorist attacks from nongovernmental or non-state-based organizations. These groups are guided by ideologies in the Islamic world that have filled a political and ideological vacuum left by the end of the Cold War.

Radical Islamism is the term scholars use to describe an interpretation of Islam that came to have a significant impact in the Muslim world during the decades of decolonization. It is only one—and by no means the most popular—interpretation of Islam. The ideas informing radical Islamism extend back to the 1930s and resistance to British rule in Egypt, but for many years, those had little impact on the politics of the Middle East.

Arab Nationalism

Radical Islamism arose primarily in reaction to the secular Arab nationalism that developed in countries like Egypt and Syria in the 1920s and 1930s. Although Arab and other Middle Eastern nationalists, like nineteenth-century modernizers in the Ottoman Empire, believed that the path to independence and strength lay in adopting the technology and imitating the political institutions of the West, these advocates of radical Islamism wanted to reject Western ideas and create a society based on a rigorous interpretation of Islam and its teachings. (See Chapter 22.)

In the wake of World War II, many of the foremost leaders of Arab nationalism against Western direct and indirect dominance, such as Gamal Abdul Nasser of Egypt, were sympathetic to socialism or to the Soviet Union. Because socialism and communism were Western ideologies, left-leaning Arab nationalism was no less Western in its orientation than were nationalists friendly to the United States. Moreover, Soviet communism was overtly atheistic and hence doubly offensive to devout Arab Muslims.

Arab governments defining themselves according to the values of nationalism worked out arrangements with local Muslim authorities. For example, the Saudi royal family turned over its educational system to adherents of a rigorist, puritanical form of Islam called *Wahhabism* while modernizing the country's infrastructure. The Egyptian government attempted to play different Islamic groups off against one another. These governments retained the support of prosperous, devout middle-class Muslims while doing little about the plight of the poor. In general, Muslim religious leaders were hostile to the Soviet Union and its influence in the Islamic world.

The Iranian Revolution

The Iranian Revolution of 1979 transformed the Middle East. The Ayatollah Ruhollah Khomeini (1902–1989) managed to unite both the middle and lower classes of a major Middle Eastern nation to overthrow a repressive but a modernizing government that had long cooperated with the United States. Iran's revolutionary government was a theocracy; that is, there was no separation of religion and government or, in European terms, of church and state. The Iranian constitution gave the clergy the final say in all matters.

By challenging the Westernization of Iranian society, the Iranian Revolution shocked the world. It also challenged the largely secular presuppositions of Arab nationalists in states such as Egypt, Saudi Arabia, and Algeria that had failed to satisfy

Overview The Rise of Radical Political Islamism

1979	Iranian Revolution
1979	Russian invasion of Afghanistan
1981	Assassination of President Anwar Sadat
1991	Persian Gulf War
1993	Bombing of the World Trade Center in New York City
1996	Bombing of U.S. army barracks in Saudi Arabia
1998	Bombing of U.S. embassies in East Africa
2000	Bombing of USS *Cole* in the Yemeni port of Aden
2001	September 11 terrorist attacks on American soil

the needs of their own underclasses. In the mid-twentieth century, Arabs and other Middle Eastern peoples had turned to nationalism in reaction against European colonial powers. Those who grew up under nationalist leadership and still found themselves politically and economically disadvantaged, however, reacted against nationalism. The Iranian Revolution, which many thought would spread throughout the Islamic world, attracted them.

The Iranian Revolution both embodied and emboldened the forces of what is commonly called Islamic *fundamentalism* but is more correctly termed Islamic or Muslim *reformism*. This is the belief that a reformed or pure Islam must be established in the contemporary world. Most adherents of this point of view would emphasize personal piety and religious practice. However, a minority wish to see their states strictly governed the way Iran purports to be by Islamic law or the Shari'a. (In fact, the Iranian clergy made numerous compromises to the practical demands of everyday government and the oil industry.)

The conservative Arab governments feared the Iranian Revolution would challenge their legitimacy. They consequently began to pay much more attention to their own religious authorities and cracked down on radical reformist or fundamentalist Muslims. In Egypt, such actions followed the assassination in 1981 of President Anwar Sadat (b. 1918) by a member of the Muslim Brotherhood.

Afghanistan and Radical Islamism

The Russian invasion of Afghanistan of 1979, discussed earlier in this chapter, introduced a major new component into this already complicated picture, illustrating the convergence of Cold War and Islamist politics. The Soviet Union sought to impose a communist, and hence both Western and atheist, government in Afghanistan. Muslim religious authorities declared ***jihad***, literally meaning "a struggle" but commonly interpreted as a religious war, against the Soviet Union. The Afghan resistance to the Soviets thus became simultaneously nationalistic, universalistic, and religious.

jihad A struggle; interpreted as a call for religious war.

Thousands of Muslims, mostly fundamentalist in outlook, arrived in Afghanistan from across the Islamic world to oust the Soviets and their Afghan puppets. Conservative Arab states and the United States supported this effort, which succeeded when all Soviet forces withdrew in 1989. The conservative Arab states saw the Afghan war as an opportunity both to resist Soviet influence and to divert the energies of their own religious extremists. The United States saw the Afghan war as another round in the Cold War. The militant Muslim fundamentalists saw it as a religious struggle against an impious Western power.

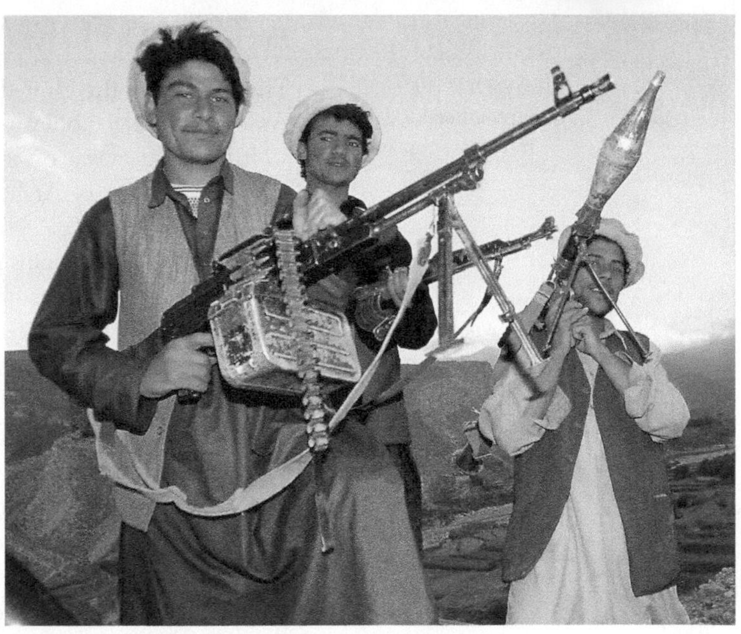

Taliban fighters brandish machine-guns and rocket launchers near the Tora Bora mountains in Afghanistan, the site of a major battle with U.S. forces in late 2001.

Knut Mueller/Das Fotoarchiv/Peter Arnold, Inc.

What makes Afghanistan so attractive to terrorist organizations?

The Taliban and Al Qaeda The Soviet withdrawal created a power vacuum in Afghanistan that lasted almost a decade. By 1998, however, rigorist Muslims known as the *Taliban* had seized control of the country. They imposed their own version of Islamic law, which involved strict regimentation of women and public executions, floggings, and mutilations for criminal, religious, and moral offenses. The Taliban also allowed groups of Muslim terrorists known as *Al Qaeda*, which means "Base," to establish training camps in their country. The terrorists who attacked the United States on September 11, 2001, came from these camps.

The ideology of these groups had emerged over several decades from different regions of the Islamic world but had been inculcated in Pakistan. The Pakistani government had long assigned considerable control over education to Islamic schools, or *madrasas*, that taught reformed Islam, rejection of liberal and nationalist secular values, intolerance toward non-Muslims, repudiation of Western culture, hostility to Israel, and hatred of the United States.

***Jihad* Against the United States** Once the *jihad* against the Soviet Union had succeeded, radical Muslims, largely educated in these Pakistani schools, turned their attention to the United States, the other great Western power. The event that brought about this redirection was the Persian Gulf War of 1991. The occasion for that conflict was the invasion of Kuwait by Iraq, under Saddam Hussein (1937–2006). The conservative Arab governments, most importantly Saudi Arabia, not only supported the United States but also permitted it to construct military bases on their territory. Islamic extremists who had fought in Afghanistan, one of whom was Osama Bin Laden (b. 1957), saw the establishment of U.S. bases in Saudi Arabia, which was the home of the prophet Muhammed and contained Islam's two holiest cities, Mecca and Medina, as a new invasion by Western Crusaders. The bases added a new grievance to the already long list of radical Muslim complaints against the United States.

The United States became a target because of its secular public morality, its international wealth and power, its military strength, its ongoing support for Israel, and its adherence to the UN sanctions imposed on Iraq after the Gulf War. Certain Muslim religious authorities declared a *jihad* against the United States, thus transforming opposition to American policies and culture into a religious war. Through the 1990s, terrorist attacks were directed against targets in or associated with the United States. These included bombings of the World Trade Center in New York City in 1993, of a U.S. army barracks in Saudi Arabia in 1996, of U.S. embassies in East Africa in 1998, and of the USS *Cole* in the Yemeni port of Aden in 2000. These attacks resulted in a considerable loss of life.

A TRANSFORMED WEST

HOW DID the events of September 11, 2001, transform the West?

The attacks on the United States on September 11, 2001, transformed and redirected American foreign policy into what the administration of President George W. Bush (b. 1946) termed "a war on terrorism." In late 2001, the United States attacked the Taliban government of Afghanistan, rapidly overthrowing it. The defeat of the Taliban destroyed Al Qaeda's Afghan bases but not its leadership, which survived, although it was dispersed and remains in hiding. By 2008, there was evidence that the Taliban had regrouped and again become active.

Following the Afghan campaign, the Bush administration set forth a policy of preemptive strikes and intervention against potential enemies of the United States. The administration argued that the danger of weapons of mass destruction developed by governments such as that of Iraq falling into the hands of international terrorist organizations posed so severe a danger to the security of the United States that the nation could not wait to respond to an attack but must take preemptive action. This argument, which aroused controversy both at home and abroad, marked a major departure from previous United States foreign policy. It is a direct result of the attacks on the United States that occurred on September 11.

In 2002, the Bush administration turned its attention to Saddam Hussein's government in Iraq. Since the defeat of Iraq in 1991 by an international coalition led by the United States, Saddam Hussein, contrary to widespread expectations, had remained in power and had continued to oppress his own people. Throughout the 1990s, the Iraqi government had also resisted the work of United Nations inspectors charged with discovering and destroying weapons of mass destruction found in Iraq or facilities capable of manufacturing such weapons. The Iraqis eventually expelled the United Nations inspectors in 1998, and the United Nations was unable to reinsert them for almost five years.

In the wake of the September 11, 2001, attacks the Bush administration determined to overthrow Saddam Hussein and remove any threat from supposed Iraqi weapons of mass destruction. In late 2002 and early 2003, the United States and British governments sought to obtain passage of United Nations Security Council resolutions that would require Iraq to disarm on its own or to be disarmed by military force. Nonetheless, the United States and Great Britain, backed by token forces or other support from over thirty other nations, invaded Iraq in late March 2003. After three weeks of fighting, the Iraqi army and with it the government of Saddam Hussein collapsed. The announced goals of the invasion, in addition to toppling the Iraqi regime, were to destroy Iraq's capacity to manufacture or deploy weapons of mass destruction and to bring consensual government to the Iraqi people. The latter goal has remained elusive as Iraq has been violently split by deadly internal political conflict.

The invasion of Iraq was undertaken in the face of considerable opposition from France, Germany, and Russia. It also provoked large antiwar demonstrations in the United States and throughout the world. Both the war and the diplomatic difficulties preceding it disrupted the long-standing Atlantic alliance. Moreover, French and German opposition to the war created strains within Europe and particularly within NATO and the European Union, as other European governments either strongly supported or opposed the United States and Britain. As a result, the war in Iraq marked a new and divisive era in relations between the United States and Europe, and between the United States and the rest of the world.

Once the invasion of Iraq had been carried out and the occupation commenced, Al Qaeda terrorists struck in Europe itself. On March 11, 2004, at least 190 people were killed in train bombings in Madrid, Spain. The terrorist attack occurred just before the Spanish election. The Spanish government, which had supported the American invasion of Iraq, unexpectedly lost the election. The new government then soon

On July 7, 2005, a series of bombs rocked the London transport system with the loss of over fifty lives. This photo shows the remains of a London bus on which a suicide bomber took more than a dozen lives near Russell Square, London.

Sion Touhig/CORBIS/Bettmann

How do Europeans and Americans differ in their views on the best ways to combat terrorism?

withdrew Spanish troops from Iraq. The Madrid bombings were the largest act of terrorism against civilians in Europe since World War II. The attack demonstrated that terrorist attacks can directly influence European political processes.

The Iraq War and the bloody insurgency that followed generated enormous controversy. The coalition forces found no weapons of mass destruction in Iraq. Government commissions in the United States and Britain have criticized the intelligence information used to justify the invasion. In 2004, however, President Bush was reelected. In March 2005, thousands of Iraqis braved threats to vote in the first meaningful election held in Iraq since the 1950s; in October 2005, they voted to ratify a new constitution. In 2006, Saddam Hussein was tried and executed for crimes against humanity. Meanwhile, in May 2005, the British government of Prime Minister Tony Blair was also reelected, though with a much reduced parliamentary majority. However, on July 7, 2005, terrorist bombings struck the London bus and subway system with a considerable loss of life. Once more, as in Spain, terrorism struck a major European city. The British government, unlike the Spanish, continued to retain its armed forces in Iraq.

The Iraq war, which has witnessed the death of more than 4,000 American troops and thousands of Iraqis, continued to cause controversy in the United States and between the United States and its NATO allies. However, in early 2007, the Bush administration increased the number of troops committed to Iraq. The purpose of the increase in troops, called "the surge" in the press, was to bring about greater internal stability in the country and most particularly in Baghdad. Over the months the level of violence did subside. By 2008, the United States under the Bush administration and the Iraq government were negotiating the future status of American troops in Iraq with the goal of significantly reducing their numbers in upcoming years. Somewhat surprisingly, issues of the economy more than those of Middle East involvement dominated the 2008 U.S. presidential campaign. Early in 2009 after assuming the presidency, President Barack Obama undertook a policy to establish an orderly withdrawal of most American combat troops from Iraq by the late summer of 2010.

SUMMARY

WHAT WERE the origins of the Cold War?

The Emergence of the Cold War The Cold War was based on the fundamental opposition between the ideologies of the Soviet Union and the Western democracies. An "Iron Curtain" separated Western Europe from the satellite states of the USSR. Germany was divided, and in 1949, most nations of Western Europe joined the United States, Canada, and the island states of the Atlantic to form NATO. The Soviet Union responded in 1955 with the Warsaw Pact. Israel's independence in 1948, and the Arab response, brought the Cold War to the Middle East. The Korean conflict (1950–1953) was motivated by the West's policy of containing the spread of communism. *page 742*

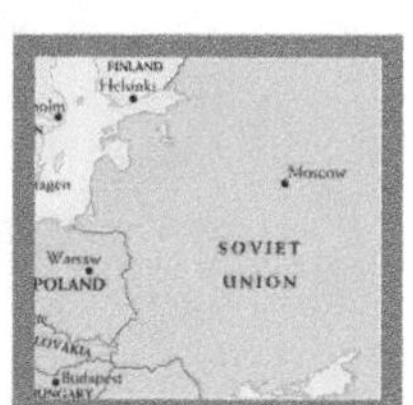

WHAT WERE the three crises of 1956, and how did they affect world order?

The Khrushchev Era in the Soviet Union Stalin strengthened his hold over the Soviet Union during World War II. Nikhita Khrushchev, who succeeded him in 1953, was less powerful. He allowed more intellectual and economic freedom but preserved the Communist Party's dominance. In 1956, the war that followed Egyptian president Nasser's nationalization of the Suez Canal prompted the United States to curtail intervention by the Western European powers in affairs beyond Europe. The USSR permitted modest political reforms in Poland, as long as Poland remained a member of the Warsaw Pact, but in Hungary, it toppled an independent communist government. *page 749*

HOW DID the Berlin Wall and the Cuban missile crisis strain relations between the United States and the Soviet Union?

Later Cold War Confrontations Tensions continued to simmer between the United States and the USSR in the late 1950s. In August 1961 the Berlin Wall was erected, and in 1966 the Cuban missile crisis brought the Cold War to the Americas. In 1968 the USSR invaded Czechoslovakia to suppress the Prague Spring. *page 750*

WHAT IMPACT did Brezhnev have on the Soviet Union and Eastern Europe?

The Brezhnev Era Brezhnev led the Soviet Union from 1964 to 1982. In 1968 the USSR invaded Czechoslovakia to suppress the Prague Spring in the last major Soviet military action in Europe of the Cold War. The Helsinki Accords recognized the Soviet sphere of influence in Eastern Europe but protected human rights. By the early 1980s, Soviet armed forces were the largest in the world, and the USSR's nuclear arsenal nearly equaled that of the United States. The Soviet invasion of Afghanistan in 1979 sapped much of that strength. In July 1980, a shipyard workers' strike at Gdansk in Poland created Solidarity, an independent union. The Soviets responded by increasing their own military spending, a tactic that accelerated the end of the regime. *page 752*

HOW DID World War II serve as a catalyst for decolonization?

Decolonization: The European Retreat from Empire World War II accelerated the decolonization process. Mohandas Gandhi utilized Western liberal ideas and the passive resistance strategy of Henry David Thoreau to gain Indian independence in 1947. Britain generally succeeded in establishing representative self-governments in its former colonies. *page 754*

WHY WAS France so reluctant to decolonize?

The Turmoil of French Decolonization France ended its colonial era more slowly and painfully than did Britain. In Algeria, nationalists demanded civic equality and fought a civil war until 1962, when a referendum ordered by President Charles de Gaulle approved Algerian independence. In Vietnam, Ho Chi Minh fought for independence from France, but in 1955, when the French began to withdraw from South Vietnam, the United States entered the Vietnam War. Many Europeans, Americans, and others questioned U.S. motives and goals. *page 756*

WHY DID European communism collapse?

The Collapse of European Communism Gorbachev took power in 1985 and attempted to reform the Soviet system, but his reforms set off a cascade of consequences. Revolutions swept Eastern Europe in 1989. Poland elected a Solidarity government, Hungary opened its borders with Austria and promised free elections, and East Germany opened the Berlin Wall. By late 1990, Gorbachev had allied with conservatives, and Yeltsin became the spokesman for a rival group that wanted to move quickly to a market economy and greater democratization. Gorbachev left office, and on December 25, 1991, the Commonwealth of Independent States replaced the Soviet Union, with Boris Yeltsin as president of the Russian Federation. *page 759*

HOW DID ethnic tensions lead to civil war in Yugoslavia?

The Collapse of Yugoslavia and Civil War Yugoslavia was created after World War I. Its major national groups have been involved in ethnic disputes for centuries. After Tito's death in 1980, Yugoslavia gradually dissolved into civil war. By June 1991, full-fledged war had erupted between Serbia and Croatia. Bosnian Muslims were caught between the two sides. The Serbs in particular killed or forcibly removed many Bosnian Muslims. The intervention of NATO forces led to the negotiation of a peace agreement in Dayton, Ohio, in 1995. Toward the end of the 1990s, Serbian aggression against ethnic Albanians in the province of Kosovo again drew NATO into Yugoslav affairs. In 2008, Kosovo with its Albanian majority population declared its independence from Serbia. *page 765*

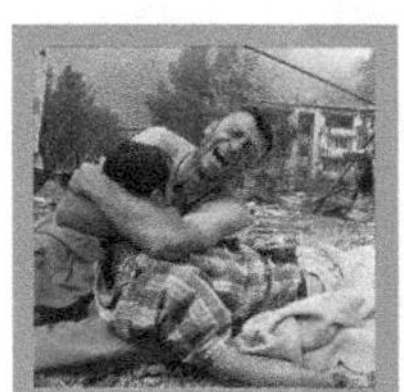

WHAT VISION does Putin have of Russia's place in the world?

Putin and the Resurgence of Russia Vladimir Putin, who had become president of the Russian Federation in 2000, sought to diminish local autonomy and centralize power in his own hands. Putin also imprisoned political critics and opponents and moved against independent newspapers and television stations as well. During Putin's presidency the Russian economy genuinely began to improve, largely as the result of rising oil prices on the world market. Putin has been determined to use Russia's economic recovery and new wealth to allow Russia to reassert its position as a major power on both the regional and world scene. The 2008 Russian invasion of Georgia marked a new departure in post-Soviet Russian foreign policy. *page 767*

WHAT FORCES gave rise to radical political Islamism?

The Rise of Radical Political Islamism Radical Islamism is a reaction to early-twentieth-century Arab secular nationalism. Most nationalist leaders of Muslim countries satisfied their religious critics by giving them some control over social institutions, but the Iranian Revolution of 1979 subjected a major state to Islamist domination. Afghanistan in 1998 was taken over by the Muslim-led Taliban, and radical Pakistani-educated Muslims targeted the United States after the 1991 Persian Gulf War, which they saw as an assault on the Muslim Holy Land. *page 768*

HOW DID the events of September 11, 2001, transform the West?

A Transformed West Terrorist attacks, incuding those of September 11, 2001, targeted the United States for its military and economic strength and its Western values. The U.S. military response against Afghanistan was widely supported by Europe, but only Great Britain supported the Bush administration's actions against Iraq. Despite lack of support by the United Nations, the invasion of Iraq succeeded in removing the government of Saddam Hussein after only three weeks of fighting. The Iraq War and the bloody insurgency that followed generated enormous controversy. In early 2007, the Bush administration increased the number of troops committed to Iraq. By 2008, the United States under the Bush administration and the Iraq government were negotiating the future status of American troops in Iraq with the goal of significantly reducing their numbers in upcoming years. Issues of the economy more than those of Middle East involvement dominated the 2008 U.S. presidential campaign. *page 772*

REVIEW QUESTIONS

1. How did Europe come to be dominated by the United States and the Soviet Union after 1945? How would you define the policy of containment? What were some of the global events in the period from 1945 to 1982 that were influenced by this American policy?
2. Why did the nations of Europe give up their empires? How did the United States become involved in Vietnam?
3. What internal political pressures did the Soviet Union experience in the 1970s and early 1980s? How did Gorbachev's reforms contribute to the collapse of the Soviet Union?
4. What were the major events in Eastern Europe that contributed to the collapse of communism? What was Poland's role in this process?
5. How has radical political Islamism developed? How has it been affected by the invasion of Afghanistan and recent military conflicts in the Middle East?

KEY TERMS

Brezhnev Doctrine (p. 752)
Cold War (p. 742)
containment (p. 742)
détente (p. 752)
glasnost (p. 760)
jihad (p. 770)
Marshall Plan (p. 743)
NATO (p. 746)
perestroika (p. 760)
Warsaw Pact (p. 746)

For additional learning resources related to this chapter, please go to **www.myhistorylab.com**

myhistorylab

30

The West at the Dawn of the Twenty-First Century

The most important accomplishment of the European Community was the launching on January 1, 1999, of the euro, a single monetary unit that replaced the national currencies of most of its member nations. In Frankfurt, Germany, people crowded around a symbol of the new currency. The world financial crisis that commenced in 2008 has placed many internal pressures on the European Community and upon its currency.

AP Wide World Photos

Why was the establishment of the euro such an important step on the road to European unification?

THE TWENTIETH-CENTURY MOVEMENT OF PEOPLES *page 778*

HOW HAS migration changed the face of Europe?

TOWARD A WELFARE STATE SOCIETY *page 780*

WHAT EFFECT did the Great Depression and World War II have on the way Europeans viewed the role of government in social and economic life?

NEW PATTERNS IN WORK AND EXPECTATIONS OF WOMEN *page 784*

HOW DID the status of women in business, politics, and the professions change in Europe in the second half of the twentieth century?

TRANSFORMATIONS IN KNOWLEDGE AND CULTURE *page 786*

HOW WAS cultural and intellectual life transformed in Europe during the twentieth century?

ART SINCE WORLD WAR II *page 790*

HOW DID the Cold War shape Western art in the second half of the twentieth century?

THE CHRISTIAN HERITAGE *page 791*

HOW HAS the Christian heritage of the West been affected by events of the twentieth century?

LATE-TWENTIETH-CENTURY TECHNOLOGY: THE ARRIVAL OF THE COMPUTER *page 793*

WHAT IMPACT has the computer had on twentieth-century society?

THE CHALLENGES OF EUROPEAN UNIFICATION *page 794*

WHAT LED to Western European unification following World War II?

NEW AMERICAN LEADERSHIP AND FINANCIAL CRISIS *page 797*

WHY MIGHT 2008 prove to be a turning point in the relationship between the United States and Europe?

During the second half of the twentieth century, the Cold War influenced life in the West—for individuals as well as states. It closed vast areas to travel and sealed off most of Eastern Europe from the era's material and technological advances. It did not, however, impede the developments that remarkably transformed the Western European countries and the United States. They achieved unprecedented prosperity and technological progress. Europe also took unprecedented steps toward economic cooperation and political union. ■

THE TWENTIETH-CENTURY MOVEMENT OF PEOPLES

HOW HAS migration changed the face of Europe?

In the twentieth century, the movement of peoples transformed European society and the character of many European communities. The most pervasive trend in this movement of peoples was the continuing shift from the countryside to the cities. Today, except for Albania, at least one-third of the population of every European nation lives in large cities. In Western Europe, city dwellers are approximately 75 percent of the population.

Other vast forced movements of peoples by governments, however, were little discussed during the Cold War. During the century, millions of Germans, Hungarians, Poles, Ukrainians, Bulgarians, Serbs, Finns, Chechens, Armenians, Greeks, Turks, Balts, and Bosnian Muslims were displaced. These forced displacements transformed parts of Europe. Stalin literally moved whole nationalities from one area of the Soviet Union to another and killed millions of people in the process. The Nazis first displaced the Jews and then sought to exterminate them. Throughout Eastern Europe, cities that once had large Jewish populations and a vibrant Jewish religious and cultural life lost any Jewish presence. The displacement of Germans from Eastern Europe back into Germany immediately after World War II transformed cities that had been German into places almost wholly populated by Czechs, Poles, or Russians.

Displacement Through War

World War II created a vast refugee problem. An estimated 46 million people were displaced in central and Eastern Europe and the Soviet Union alone between 1938 and 1948. Many cities in Germany and in central and Eastern Europe had been bombed or overrun by invading armies. The Nazis had moved hundreds of thousands of foreign workers into Germany as slave laborers. Millions more were prisoners of war. Some of these people returned to their homeland willingly; others, particularly Soviet prisoners fearful of being executed by Stalin, had to be forced to go back, and many were executed. Hundreds of thousands of Baltic, Polish, and Yugoslav prisoners found asylum in Western Europe.

Changes in political borders after the war also uprooted many people. For example, Poland, Czechoslovakia, and Hungary forcibly expelled millions of ethnic Germans from their territories to Germany. In another case of forced migration, hundreds of thousands of Poles were transferred to within Poland's new borders from territory the Soviet Union annexed. Other minorities, such as Ukrainians in Poland and Italians on the Yugoslav coast, were driven into their ethnic homelands.

External and Internal Migration

Between 1945 and 1960, approximately half a million Europeans left Europe each year. In the second half of the nineteenth century, most immigrants were from rural areas. After World War II, they often included educated city dwellers. Immediately after the war, some governments encouraged migration because they were afraid that, as in the 1930s, their economies would not be able to provide adequate employment for all their citizens.

Decolonization in the postwar period led many European colonials to return to Europe from overseas. Decolonization also led non-European inhabitants of the former colonies to migrate to Europe. Great Britain, for example, received thousands of immigrants from its former colonies in the Caribbean, Africa, and the Indian subcontinent. France received many immigrants from its empire in Africa, Indochina, and the Arab world. This influx has proved to be a long-term source of social tension and conflict. In Britain, racial tensions were high during the 1980s. France faced similar difficulties, which contributed to the emergence of the National Front, an extreme right-wing group led by Jean-Marie Le Pen (b. 1928) that sought to exploit the resentment many working-class voters felt toward North African immigrants. Similar pressures have arisen in Germany, Austria, Italy, the Netherlands, and even Denmark. Such tension did not result only from immigration from Africa and Asia; internal European migration—from the Balkans, Turkey, and the former Soviet Union, often of people in search of jobs—also changed the social and economic face of the Continent and led to a backlash. In recent years, internal immigration within the European Union has seen the movement of significant numbers of people. However, the growing Muslim presence in Europe has produced some of the most serious ethnic and political tensions.

The New Muslim Population

Until recently most Europeans paid little direct attention to Islam as a domestic matter. That indifference began to change in the 1960s and had dissolved by the end of the twentieth century as a sizable Muslim population settled in Europe. This highly diverse immigrant community had become an issue in Europe even before the events of September 11, 2001.

The immigration of Muslims into Europe, and particularly Western Europe, arose from two chief sources: European economic growth and decolonization. As the economies of Western Europe began to recover in the quarter century after World War II, a labor shortage developed. To fill this demand, Western Europe imported laborers, many of whom came from Muslim nations. For example, Turkish "guest workers" were invited to move to West Germany—on a temporary basis, it was presumed—in the 1960s, and Britain welcomed Pakistanis. The aftermath of decolonization and the quest for a better life led Muslims from East Africa and the Indian subcontinent to settle in Great Britain. The Algerian war brought many Muslims to France. Today there are approximately 1.3 million Muslims in Great Britain, 3.2 million in Germany, and 4.2 million in France.

These Muslim immigrant communities share certain social and religious characteristics. Originally, many Muslims came to Europe expecting they would eventually return to their homes, an expectation their host countries shared. Moreover, except for Great Britain, where all immigrants from the Commonwealth may vote immediately upon settling there, European governments made it difficult for Muslim, or any other, immigrants to take part in civic life. The Muslim communities have, therefore, generally remained unassimilated and self-contained. This apartness has

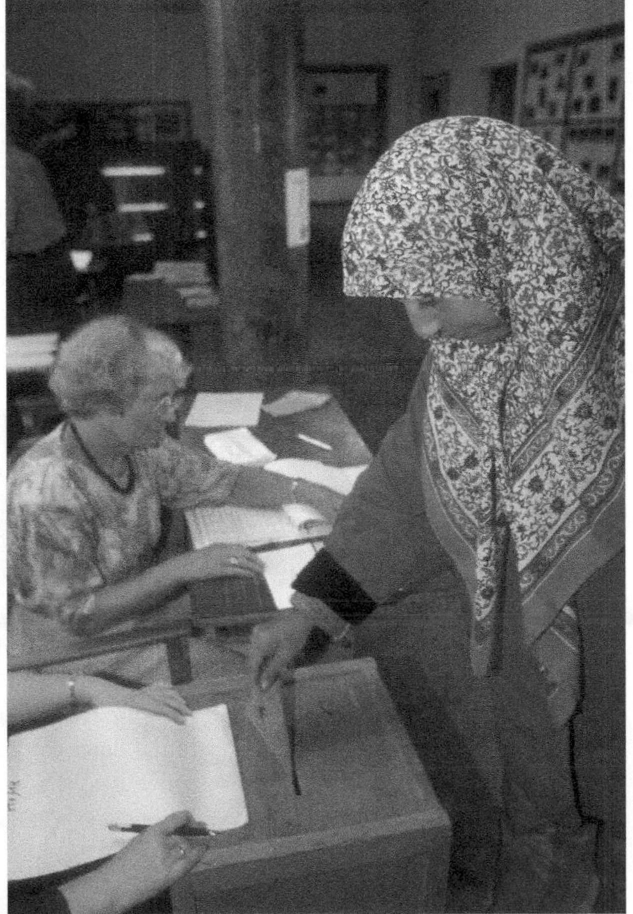

A Muslim woman wearing a traditional headscarf in Hamburg, Germany, votes in the Bundestag elections. The presence of foreign-born Muslims whose labor is necessary for the prosperity of the European economy is an important issue in contemporary Europe. Many of these Muslims live in self-contained communities.

Peter Arnold, Inc.

What is the relationship between Muslim communities in Europe and the larger societies of which they are a part?

provided internal community support for Muslim immigrants but has also prevented them from fully engaging with the societies in which they live.

Yet the world around these communities has changed. Many of the largely unskilled jobs that the immigrants originally filled have disappeared. Most of the Muslim immigrants to Europe, unlike many who have settled in the United States and Canada, were neither highly skilled nor professionally educated. As a result, they and their adult children who may have grown up in Europe find it difficult to get jobs in the modern service economy. Furthermore, as European economic growth has slowed, European Muslims have become the target of politicians, such as Le Pen in France, who seek to blame the immigrants for a host of problems from crime to unemployment.

The radicalization of parts of the Islamic world has also touched the Muslim communities in Europe. The July 7, 2005, suicide bombings in London were carried out by four young Muslims, three of whom had been born in the United Kingdom and one in Jamaica. By contrast, the French government has exerted more control over its Muslim population. However, that policy appeared to have failed badly when in the autumn of 2005 immigrant youth, largely Muslim, carried out riots in various parts of France. These were the most serious civil disturbances in France since 1968. There have also been sharp disputes in France over attempts by the government to forbide young Muslim women from wearing headscarves while attending secular government schools.

Nonetheless, European Muslims are not a homogeneous group. They come from different countries, have different class backgrounds, and espouse different Islamic traditions. At the same time, these Muslim communities, so often now marked by deep poverty and unemployment, have become a major concern for European social workers, who disagree among themselves about how their governments should respond to them. What has become clear, however, is that European governments cannot regard their Muslim populations as passive communities; rather European governments and societies must engage them as a permanent fact in the life of early-twenty-first-century Europe.

European Population Trends

During the past quarter century, the population of Europe, measured in terms of the European birthrate, has stabilized in a manner that has deeply disturbed many observers. Europeans are having so few children that they are no longer replacing themselves. There is no consensus on why the European birthrate has declined. One reason often cited is that women are postponing having children until later in their childbearing years.

This falling birthrate means that Europe will face the prospect of an aging population. The energy and drive that youth can provide may shift to the other side of the Atlantic. An aging population is unlikely to give rise to economic innovation. The internal European market, now larger than the internal American market, will shrink. In contrast to the late nineteenth century (see Chapter 23), Europe itself will have fewer Europeans, and Europe's share of the world's population will also decline.

TOWARD A WELFARE STATE SOCIETY

WHAT EFFECT did the Great Depression and World War II have on the way Europeans viewed the role of government in social and economic life?

During the decades spanning the Cold War, the U.S. involvement in Vietnam, and the Soviet domination of Eastern Europe, the nations of Western Europe achieved unprecedented economic prosperity and maintained or inaugurated independent, liberal democratic governments. Most of them also confronted problems associated with decolonization and with maintaining economic growth. The Great Depression had shown that democracy requires a social and economic base, as well as a political structure. Most Europeans came to believe that government ought to ensure economic prosperity and social security.

Christian Democratic Parties

Except for the British Labour Party, the vehicles of the new postwar politics were not, as might have been expected, the democratic socialist parties. Outside Scandinavia, those parties generally did not prosper after the onset of the Cold War. Both communists and conservatives opposed them. Rather, various **Christian democratic parties**, usually leading coalition governments, introduced the new policies.

Christian democratic parties Post–World War II political parties that, although predominately Roman Catholic, welcomed non-Catholic members and fought for democracy, social reform, and economic growth.

These parties were a major new feature of postwar politics. They were largely Roman Catholic in leadership and membership. Until the 1930s, Catholic parties had been conservative and had protected the social, political, and educational interests of the church. The postwar Christian democratic parties of Germany, France, Austria, and Italy, however, were progressive and welcomed non-Catholic members. Democracy, social reform, economic growth, and anticommunism were their hallmarks.

The most immediate postwar domestic problems included not only those the physical damage of the conflict created, but often also those that had existed in 1939. The war, however, opened new opportunities to solve those prewar difficulties.

The Creation of Welfare States

The Great Depression, the rise of authoritarian states in the wake of economic dislocation and mass unemployment, and World War II, which involved more people in a war effort than ever before, changed how many Europeans thought about social welfare. Governments began to spend more on social welfare than they did on the military. This reallocation of funds was a reaction to the state violence of the first half of the century and was possible because the NATO defense umbrella, which the United States primarily staffed and funded, protected Western Europe.

The modern European welfare state was broadly similar across the Continent. Before World War II, except in Scandinavia, the two basic models for social legislation were the German and the British. In both the German and British systems, workers were insured only against the risks from disease, injury on the job, and old age. Unemployment was assumed to be only a short-term problem and often one that workers brought on themselves. People higher up in the social structure could look out for themselves and did not need government help.

After World War II, the concept emerged that social insurance against predictable risks was a social right and should be available to all citizens. Paradoxically, making coverage universal appealed to conservatives as well as socialists. If medical care, old-age pensions, and other benefits were available to all, they would not become a device to redistribute income from one part of the population to another.

The first major European nation to begin to create a welfare state was Britain, in 1945–1951 under the Labour Party ministry of Clement Attlee (1883–1967). The most important element of this early legislation was the creation of the National Health Service. France and Germany did not adopt similar health care legislation until the 1970s, because their governments initially refused to make coverage universal.

The spread of welfare legislation (including unemployment insurance) within Western Europe was related to both the Cold War and domestic political and economic policy. The communist states of Eastern Europe were promising their people social security as well as full employment. The capitalist states came to believe they had to provide similar security for their people, but, in fact, the social security of the communist states was often more rhetoric than reality.

QUICK REVIEW

The Welfare State

- Great Britain was the first European nation to create a welfare state
- France and Germany followed Britain's lead in the 1970s
- European attitudes toward the welfare state have fluctuated with the European economy

COMPARE & CONNECT

MARGARET THATCHER AND TONY BLAIR DEBATE GOVERNMENT'S SOCIAL RESPONSIBILITY FOR WELFARE

Toward the close of the twentieth century, and the turn of the twenty-first century, many of the assumptions that had informed the creation of mid-twentieth-century European welfare states came under criticism and redefinition. Nowhere was the debate sharper than in the United Kingdom where the modern welfare state had essentially been invented through social policies enacted in the aftermath of World War II. Margaret Thatcher's government raised serious questions about the role of government in society. By the turn of the century, even the British Labour Party led by Tony Blair had come to modify its own understanding of government social responsibility.

QUESTIONS

1. How and why does Thatcher contend that there is no such thing as society? How does she emphasize the reciprocal character of social relationships?
2. How does Thatcher argue in favor of personal and private charity to aid persons in need? Does she criticize all government aid to citizens?
3. How is it clear in Blair's speech that he is trying to lead a traditional party of the left toward a new understanding of government social responsibility?
4. What does Blair portray as duties of government? How does he seek to mesh government help for individuals with still assigning responsibility to the individuals receiving that help?
5. Though Thatcher and Blair differ in their views of policy, what social and political values do they share despite those differences?

I. MARGARET THATCHER ASSERTS THE NEED FOR INDIVIDUAL RESPONSIBILITY

No single European political figure so challenged and criticized the assumptions of the welfare state and of state intervention in general than Margaret Thatcher, British prime minister from 1979 to 1990. Known as the "Iron Lady," Mrs. Thatcher repeatedly demanded that people take individual responsibility rather than rely on state-sponsored support. Yet her administration did not dismantle the key structures of the British welfare state. The discussion below is from an interview by Mrs. Thatcher in October 1987.

I think we have gone through a period when too many children and people have been given to understand "I have a problem, it is the Government's job to cope with it!" or "I have a problem, I will go and get a grant to cope with it!" "I am homeless, the Government must house me!" and so they are casting their problems on society and who is society? There is no such thing! There are individual men and women . . . there are families and no government can do anything except through people and people look to themselves first. It is our duty to look after ourselves and then also to help look after our neighbour and life is a reciprocal business and people have got the entitlements too much in mind without the obligations, because there is no such thing as an entitlement unless someone has first met an obligation and it is, I think, one of the tragedies in which many of the benefits we give, which were meant to reassure people that if they were sick or ill there was a safety net and there was help, that many of the benefits which were meant to help people who were unfortunate—"It is all right. We joined together and we have these insurance schemes to look after it." That was the objective . . . But it went too far. If children have a problem, it is society that is at fault. There is no such thing as society. There is living tapestry of men and women and people and the beauty of that tapestry and the quality of our lives will depend upon how much each of us is prepared to take responsibility for ourselves and each of us prepared to turn round and help by our own efforts those who are unfortunate.

Source: This extract derives from a transcript of the original interview rather than the published text. Reprinted with permission from margaretthatcher.org, the official Web site of the Margaret Thatcher Foundation.

Despite the ongoing debate among political leaders on the merits of government programs in Britain, these programs continue to be popular. This 1998 celebration commemorates fifty years of the British National Health Service (NHS).

What accounts for continuing public support for social welfare programs in Britain?

II. TONY BLAIR SEEKS TO REDEFINE THE BRITISH WELFARE STATE

Tony Blair (b. 1953) served as Labour Party prime minister of the United Kingdom from 1997 to 2007. During his time in office he championed what he termed "New Labour" and sought to redefine the British welfare state while still preserving many of its most basic outlines. In June 2002, he outlined his new understanding of the character of the welfare state and its role in promoting individual responsibility. In many respects his view of welfare and government social responsibility had been influenced by Margaret Thatcher's attack on earlier understandings of welfare and government social responsibility.

In welfare, for too long, the right had let social division and chronic unemployment grow; the left argued for rights but were weak on responsibilities. We believe passionately in giving people the chance to get off benefit and into work. . . .

It's right for them, for the country, for society. But with the chance, comes a responsibility on the individual — to take the chance, to make something of their lives and use their ability and potential to the full. . . .

We must give the unemployed youth the skills to find a job; give the single mother the childcare she needs to go out and work; give the middle-aged man on a disability benefit the support and confidence to go back into the office.

And we must not only lift people out of poverty. We must transform their horizons, aspirations and hopes as well — through helping people get the skills they need for better jobs, and through giving them chance to save and build up a nest egg.

Only in this way will we drive up social mobility, the great force for equality in dynamic market economies.

To do all that, ours has to be an enabling welfare state — one which helps people to help themselves. . . .

Government has a responsibility to provide real opportunities for individuals to gain skills and to get into work that pays. But individuals also have a responsibility to grasp those opportunities.

We are now seeing the beginnings of a sea-change in how people view our welfare state. There is growing public support for a welfare state that tackles poverty at its source; that gets people into work; that offers people hope — in exchange for a commitment to help themselves. . . .

This is a welfare state which reflects all our responsibilities: the responsibility we have to engage actively with the jobless to provide them with opportunities; their responsibility to engage actively with us and take those opportunities. . . .

All of our reforms have the same underlying principles — opportunity, fairness and mutual responsibility. We want to give people the chance to fulfill their potential. We want to raise people's expectations and their self-belief, by giving them the tools to help themselves.

Source: Tony Blair, June 10, 2002, as made available at www.guardian.co.uk/society/2002/jun/10/socialexclusion.politics1

Margaret Thatcher, a shopkeeper's daughter who became the first female prime minister of Great Britain, served in that office from May 1979 through November 1990. Known as the "Iron Lady" of British politics, she led the Conservative Party to three electoral victories and carried out extensive restructuring of the British government and economy.

AP Wide World Photos

Why did Thatcher attempt to roll back Britain's welfare state?

Resistance to the Expansion of the Welfare State

Western European attitudes toward the welfare state have reflected three periods that have marked economic life since the end of the war. The first period was one of reconstruction from 1945 through the early 1950s. It was followed by the second period—almost twenty-five years of generally steady and expanding economic growth. The third period brought first an era of inflation in the late 1970s and then one of relatively low growth and high unemployment from the 1990s to the present. During each of the first two periods, a general conviction existed, based on Keynesian economics, that the foundation of economic policy was government involvement in a mixed economy. From the late 1970s, more people came to believe the market should be allowed to regulate itself and that government should be less involved in, though not completely withdraw from, the economy.

The most influential political figure in reasserting the importance of markets and resisting the power of labor unions was Margaret Thatcher (b. 1925) of the British Conservative Party who served as prime minister from 1979 to 1990. She cut taxes and sought to curb inflation. She and her party were determined to roll back many of the socialist policies that Britain had enacted since the war. Her administration privatized many industries that Labour Party governments had nationalized. She also curbed the power of the trade unions in a series of bitter and often violent confrontations. Although her administration roused enormous controversy, she was able to push these policies through Parliament. Furthermore, over time the British Labour Party under the leadership of Tony Blair (b. 1953) itself largely came to accept what was at the time known as the Thatcher Revolution. (See "Compare & Connect: Margaret Thatcher and Tony Blair Debate the Government Social Responsibility for Welfare," pages 782–783.)

While Thatcher redirected the British economy, the government-furnished welfare services now found across continental Europe began to encounter resistance. The funding on which they are based assumed a growing population and low unemployment, conditions that no longer exist. As the proportion of the population consuming the services of the welfare state—the sick, the injured, the unemployed, and the elderly—increases relative to the number of able-bodied workers who pay for them, the costs of those services have risen.

The general growth of confidence in the ability of market forces rather than government intervention to sustain social cohesion has also spread in the past twenty-five years and has raised questions about the existing welfare structures. Governments across the Continent, including those normally associated with left-of-center politics, such as the British Labour Party and the German Social Democratic Party, have limited further growth of the welfare state and have reduced benefits.

NEW PATTERNS IN WORK AND EXPECTATIONS OF WOMEN

HOW DID the status of women in business, politics, and the professions change in Europe in the second half of the twentieth century?

Since World War II, the work patterns and social expectations of European women have changed enormously. In all social ranks, women have begun to assume larger economic and political roles. More women have entered the "learned professions," and more are filling major managerial positions than ever before in European history. Yet certain more or less traditional patterns continue to describe the position of women in both family and economic life.

Feminism

Simone de Beauvoir, here with her companion, the philosopher Jean-Paul Sartre, was the major feminist writer in postwar Europe.

Keystone_Paris/ Getty Images Inc./Hulton Archive Photos

How has European feminism changed in the decades since World War II?

Since World War II, European feminism, although less highly organized than in America, has set forth a new agenda. The most influential postwar work on women's issues was Simone de Beauvoir's (1908–1986) *The Second Sex*, published in 1949. In that work, de Beauvoir explored the difference being a woman had made in her life. She and other European feminists argued that, at all levels, European women experienced distinct social and economic disadvantages. Divorce and family laws, for example, favored men. European feminists also called attention to the social problems that women faced, including spousal abuse.

In contrast to earlier feminism, recent feminism has been less a political movement pressing for specific rights than a social movement offering a broader critique of European culture. An emphasis on women controlling their own lives may be the most important element of recent European feminism. Whereas in the past feminists sought and, in significant measure, gained legal and civil equality with men, they are now pursuing personal independence and issues that are particular to women. In this sense, feminism is an important manifestation of the critical tradition in Western culture.

More Married Women in the Workforce

One of the patterns that seemed firmly established in 1900 has reversed itself. The number of married women in the workforce has risen sharply. Both middle-class and working-class married women have sought jobs outside the home. Some factories changed their work shifts to accommodate the needs of married women. Consumer conveniences and improvements in health care also made it easier for married women to enter the workforce by reducing the demands child care made on their time. At the same time, all surveys indicate that the need to provide care for their children is the most important difficulty women face in the workplace. This situation is a main reason why so many women remain in part-time employment.

In the twentieth century, children were no longer expected to contribute substantially to family income. They now spend more than a decade in compulsory education. When families need more income than one worker can provide, both parents work, bringing many married women with children into the workforce. Such financial necessity led many married women back to work. Evidence also suggests that married women began to work to escape the boredom of housework and to enjoy the companionship of other adult workers.

New Work Patterns

The work pattern of European women was far more consistent in the twentieth century than it was in the nineteenth century. Single women enter the workforce after their schooling and continue to work after marriage. They may stop working to care for their young children, but they return to work when the children begin school. Several factors created this new pattern, but women's increasing life expectancy is one of the most important.

When women died relatively young, child rearing filled a large proportion of their lives. As a longer life span has shortened that proportion, women throughout the West are seeking ways to lead satisfying lives after their children have grown. Decisions about when to have children and how many also shaped the late-twentieth-century work pattern for women. Many women have begun to limit the number of children they bear or to forgo childbearing and child rearing altogether. The age at which women have decided to bear children has risen, to the early twenties in Eastern Europe and to the late twenties in Western Europe. In urban areas, women have fewer children and have them later in life than rural women do. These various personal decisions leave many years free to develop careers and stay in the workforce.

Women in the New Eastern Europe

Many paradoxes surround the situation of Eastern European women now that communists no longer govern the region. Under communism, women generally enjoyed social equality, as well as a broad spectrum of government-financed benefits. Most women worked in these societies. No significant women's movements existed, however, because communist governments regarded them with suspicion, as they did all independent associations.

The new governments of the region are free but have shown little concern with women's issues. Indeed, the economic difficulties the new governments face may endanger their funding of health and welfare programs that benefit women and children. Moreover, the high proportion of women in the workforce could leave them more vulnerable than men to the region's economic troubles. Women may be laid off before men and hired later than men for lower pay.

TRANSFORMATIONS IN KNOWLEDGE AND CULTURE

HOW WAS cultural and intellectual life transformed in Europe during the twentieth century?

Knowledge and culture in Europe were rapidly transformed in the twentieth century. Institutions of higher education enrolled a larger and more diverse student body, making knowledge more widely available than ever before. Also, movements such as existentialism challenged traditional intellectual attitudes. Environmental concerns also raised new issues. Throughout this ferment, representatives of the Christian faith tried to keep their religion relevant.

Communism and Western Europe

Until the final decade of the twentieth century, Western Europe had large, organized communist parties, as well as groups of intellectuals sympathetic to communism.

The Intellectuals During the 1930s, as liberal democracies floundered in the face of the Great Depression and as right-wing regimes spread across the Continent, many people saw communism as a vehicle for protecting humane and even liberal values. European university students were often affiliated with the Communist Party. During the late 1920s and the 1930s, communism became a substitute religion for some Europeans.

Four events proved crucial to the intellectuals' disillusionment: the great Soviet public purge trials of the late 1930s, the Spanish Civil War (1936–1939), the Nazi-Soviet pact of 1939, and the Soviet invasion of Hungary in 1956. Yet disillusionment with the Soviet Union or with Stalin did not always mean disillusionment with Marxism or with radical socialist criticisms of European society. Some writers and social critics looked to the establishment of alternative communist governments based on non-Soviet models. During the decade after World War II, Yugoslavia provided such an example. Beginning in the late 1950s, radical students and a few intellectuals found inspiration in the Chinese Revolution. Other groups hoped a European Marxist system would develop. The thinking of non-Soviet communists became important to Western European communist parties, such as the Italian Communist Party, that hoped to gain office democratically.

Another way to accommodate Marxism within mid-twentieth-century European thought was to redefine the basic message of Marx himself. During the 1930s, many of Marx's previously unprinted essays were published. These books and articles, written

before the *Communist Manifesto* of 1848, are abstract and philosophical. They make the "young Marx" appear to belong more nearly to the humanist than to the revolutionary tradition of European thought. They allowed some people to consider themselves sympathetic to Marxism without also seeing themselves as revolutionaries or supporters of the Soviet Union. With the collapse of the communist governments of Eastern Europe and the Soviet Union, what influence Marxism will continue to have on European intellectual life in the future is unclear.

QUICK REVIEW

Factors Leading to Disillusionment with Communism and the Soviet Union

- Purges of the 1930s
- Spanish Civil War
- Alliance between Russia and Germany in 1939
- Soviet invasion of Hungary in 1956

EXISTENTIALISM

The intellectual movement that perhaps best captured the predicament and mood of mid-twentieth-century European culture was **existentialism**. Existentialism was badly divided; most of the philosophers associated with it disagreed with each other on major issues. The movement represented, in part, a continuation of the revolt against reason that began in the nineteenth century.

existentialism Philosophy that maintains that human beings are compelled to formulate their own ethical values and cannot depend on traditional religion, rational philosophy, intuition, or social customs for ethical guidance.

Roots in Nietzsche and Kierkegaard Friedrich Nietzsche (1844–1900), discussed in Chapter 24, was a major forerunner of existentialism. Another was the Danish writer Søren Kierkegaard (1813–1855), who received little attention until after World War I. He maintained that the truth of Christianity could be grasped only in the lives of those who faced extreme situations, not in creeds, doctrines, and church structures. Kierkegaard also criticized Hegelian philosophy and, by implication, all academic rational philosophy. Philosophy's failure, he felt, was the attempt to contain life and human experience within abstract categories. Kierkegaard spurned this faith in the power of mere reason.

The intellectual and ethical crisis of World War I brought Kierkegaard's thought to the foreground and also created new interest in Nietzsche's critique of reason. The war led many people to doubt whether human beings were actually in control of their own destiny. Its destructiveness challenged faith in human rationality and improvement. Indeed, the war's most terrible weapons—poison gas, machine guns, submarines, high explosives—were the products of rational technology.

Questioning of Rationalism Existentialist thought thrived in this climate and received further support from the trauma of World War II. The major existential writers included the Germans Martin Heidegger (1889–1976) and Karl Jaspers (1883–1969) and the French Jean-Paul Sartre (1905–1980) and Albert Camus (1913–1960). Although they frequently disagreed with each other, they all, in one way or another, questioned the primacy of reason and scientific understanding as ways to come to grips with the human situation.

The Romantic writers of the early nineteenth century had also questioned the primacy of reason, but their criticisms were much less radical than those of the existentialists. The Romantics emphasized the imagination and intuition, but the existentialists dwelled primarily on the extremes of human experience. Death, fear, and anxiety provided their themes.

According to the existentialists, human beings are compelled to formulate their own ethical values and cannot depend on traditional religion, rational philosophy, intuition, or social customs for ethical guidance. The opportunity and need to define values endow humans with a dreadful freedom.

European intellectuals were attracted to communism and existentialism before and just after World War II, but in the 1960s, the turmoil over Vietnam and the youth rebellion brought other intellectual and social issues to the fore. Even before the collapse of communism, these had begun to redirect European intellectual interests.

In 1968 a student rebellion in Paris threatened to bring down the government of Charles de Gaulle. This was only one example of the explosion of student activity that rocked the West in the late 1960s.

© Bettmann/CORBIS

What role did universities play in the social upheaval of the 1960s?

Expansion of the University Population and Student Rebellion

As rapid changes in communications technology vastly expanded access to information, more Europeans received some form of university education. In 1900, only a few thousand people were enrolled in universities in any major European country. By 2000, that figure had risen to hundreds of thousands, although university education is still less common in Europe than in the United States. Higher education is now available to people from a variety of social and economic backgrounds, and, for the first time, to women.

One of the most striking and unexpected results of this rising post–World War II population of students and intellectuals was the student rebellion of the 1960s. Student uprisings began in the early 1960s in the United States and grew with opposition to the war in Vietnam. The student rebellion then spread into Europe and other parts of the world. It was almost always associated with a radical political critique of the United States, although Eastern European students resented the Soviet Union even more. The movement was generally antimilitarist. Students also questioned middle-class values and traditional sexual mores and family life.

The student movement peaked in 1968, when American students demonstrated forcibly against U.S. involvement in Vietnam. In the same year, students at the Sorbonne in Paris almost brought down the government of Charles de Gaulle, and in Czechoslovakia, students were in the forefront of the liberal socialist experiment.

By the early 1970s, the era of student rebellion seemed to have passed. Students remained active in European movements against nuclear weapons and particularly against the placement of American nuclear weapons in Germany and elsewhere in Europe. From the mid-1970s, however, although often remaining political radicals, they generally abandoned the disruptive protests that had marked the 1960s.

The Americanization of Europe

During the past half century, through the Marshall Plan, the leadership of NATO, the stationing of huge military bases, student exchanges, popular culture, and tourism, the United States has exerted enormous influence on Europe, especially Western Europe. The word *Americanization*, an often pejorative term in European publications, refers, in part, to this economic and military influence but also to concerns about cultural loss. Many Europeans feel that American popular entertainment, companies, and business methods threaten to extinguish Europe's unique qualities. Many American firms now have European branches. Shopping centers and supermarkets, first pioneered in America, are displacing neighborhood markets in European cities. American television programs, movies, computer games, and rock and rap music are readily available. Furthermore, as Europe moves toward greater economic cooperation, English has become the common language of business, technology, and even some academic fields—and it is American English, not British. (See "Encountering the Past: Toys from Europe Conquer the United States.")

A Consumer Society

Although European economies came under pressure during the 1990s and experienced high levels of unemployment, the consumer sector has expanded to an extraordinary degree during most of the last half century.

The consumer orientation of the Western European economy emerged as one of the most important characteristics differentiating it from Eastern Europe. Those differences produced political results. In the Soviet Union and the nations it dominated in Eastern Europe, economic planning overwhelmingly favored capital investment and military production. These nations produced inadequate food for their people and few

ENCOUNTERING THE PAST

TOYS FROM EUROPE CONQUER THE UNITED STATES

Europeans often complain about American influences on their culture, but European products have also shaped life in America. At least one European toy, the LEGO building block, has had an effect on childhood comparable to that of the American Disney Corporation's cartoon characters.

In 1932, Ole Kirk Christiansen founded a company in Denmark to manufacture household goods and wooden toys. The toys did so well that in 1934 the company adopted the name LEGO (from Danish, *Leg godt*, "Play well"). The first LEGO building block sets were produced in 1955. The ingenious interlocking design of the LEGO block allowed children to build all kinds of things, and the sets were a hit when they went on sale in the United States in 1961. Subsequent editions were improved by the addition of new forms (such as wheels) that allowed children even freer range for their imaginations.

In 1968, the LEGO Company followed the lead of the Disney organization and began to open amusement parks with rides that resembled large LEGO toys. By the 1990s, it had become the largest toy manufacturer in Europe, and LEGO blocks were established as staples of popular culture. Museums now house structures made from them, and contests are held at which their builders compete. Some management gurus have even urged business executives to play with LEGO blocks to clarify their thinking.

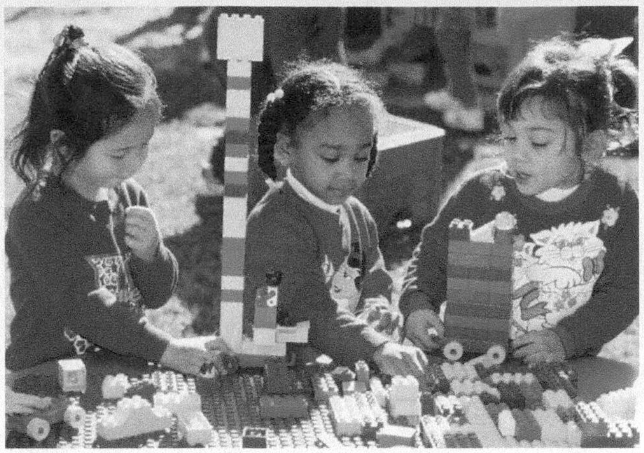

Children across the world play with LEGO toys.

Tom Prettyman/PhotoEdit Inc.

Why do so many Europeans fear Americanization?

WHY HAS the influence of LEGO on America been less controversial than that of American fast-food chains on Europe?

consumer goods. By contrast, by the early 1950s, Western Europeans enjoyed an excellent food supply that has continued to improve. Western Europe has enjoyed a similar expansion of consumer goods and services.

This vast expansion of consumerism, which, as we noted in Chapter 15, began in the eighteenth century, became a defining characteristic of Western Europe in the late twentieth century. It stood in marked contrast to the consumer shortages in Eastern Europe. Yet through even the limited number of radios, televisions, movies, and videos available to them, people in the East grew increasingly aware of the discrepancy between their lifestyle and that of the West. They associated Western consumerism with democratic governments, free societies, and economic policies that favored the free market and limited government planning. Thus, the expansion of consumerism in the West, which many intellectuals and moralists deplored, helped generate the discontent that brought down communism in Eastern Europe and the Soviet Union.

QUICK REVIEW

Western Europe's Consumer Society

- Western Europe's economy emphasized consumer goods in the second half of the twentieth century
- Soviet bloc economies focused on capital investments and the military
- Discrepancy in Western and Eastern European standards of living caused resentment in the East

ENVIRONMENTALISM

After World War II, shortages of consumer goods created a demand that fueled postwar economic reconstruction and growth into the 1950s and 1960s. In those expansive times, public debate about the ethics of economic expansion and efficiency and their effects on the environment was muted. Concerns about pollution began to grow in the

1970s, and by the 1980s, environmentalists had developed real political clout. Among the most important environmental groups were the German Greens. The Greens formed a political party in 1979 that immediately became an electoral force.

Several developments lay behind this new concern for the environment. The Arab oil embargo of 1973–1974 pressed home two messages to the industrialized West: Natural resources are limited, and foreign, potentially hostile, countries control critical resources. By the 1970s, too, the environmental consequences of three decades of economic expansion were becoming increasingly apparent. Finally, long-standing worries about nuclear weapons merged with concerns about their environmental effects, strengthening antinuclear groups and generating opposition to the placement of nuclear weapons in Europe.

Green movement Made up, in part, of members from the radical student groups of the 1960s, this movement was anticapitalistic, peace oriented, in opposition of nuclear arms, and condemned business for producing pollution. Unlike earlier student groups, though, the Greens opted to compete in the electoral process.

The German **Green movement** originated among radical student groups in the late 1960s. Like them, it was anticapitalist, blaming business for pollution. The Greens and other European environmental groups were also strongly antinuclear. Unlike the students of the 1960s, the Greens avoided violence and mass demonstrations, seeking instead to become a significant political presence through the electoral process.

The 1986 disaster at the Chernobyl nuclear reactor in the Soviet Union heightened concern about environmental issues and raised questions that no European government could ignore. The Soviet government had to confront casualties at the site and relocate tens of thousands of people. Radioactive fallout spread across Europe. Environmentalists had always contended that their issues transcended national borders. The Chernobyl fire proved them right.

After Chernobyl, European governments, East and West, began to respond to environmental concerns. Economic and political integration opens the possibility of transnational cooperation on environmental matters. As the European Economic Community solidifies, it and its member nations will likely impose more environmental regulations on business and industry. The nations of Eastern Europe have been forced to face the cleanup of vast areas of industrial development polluted during the communist era and to try to combine environmental protection with economic growth.

ART SINCE WORLD WAR II

HOW DID the Cold War shape Western art in the second half of the twentieth century?

It is impossible to cover even briefly the expansive and varied world of Western art since the end of World War II. However, we can note how both the Cold War and the memory of the horrors of the Second World War influenced Western art.

CULTURAL DIVISIONS AND THE COLD WAR

Although they may seem like products from different centuries, the Soviet painter Tatjiana Yablonskaya's (b. 1917) sun-strewn *Bread* (1949) and the American Jackson Pollock's (1912–1956) dizzyingly abstract *One* (Number 31, 1950) were painted only one year apart. The stark differences between these two works mirror the cultural divisions of the early Cold War.

socialist realism Doctrine of Soviet art and literature that sought to create figurative, traditional, optimistic, and easily intelligible scenes of a bold socialist future of prosperity and solidarity.

Bread, measuring over six feet high and twelve feet wide, is a monumental example of **socialist realism**. Established, on Stalin's orders, as the official doctrine of Soviet art and literature in 1934, socialist realism sought to create optimistic and easily intelligible scenes of a bold socialist future, in which prosperity and solidarity would reign.

The looping skeins of paint in *One* (Number 31, 1950)—on display at the Museum of Modern Art in New York—may seem completely different from the kind of "realistic" propaganda visible in *Bread*, but Pollock's painting is in fact a central document of postwar American cultural life. Flinging paint from sticks and brushes onto his floor-bound canvas, Pollock freed his lines from representing any figure or outline. In the politically charged atmosphere of the early Cold War, critics saw Pollock's exuberant "drip" paintings as the embodiment of American cultural freedom and celebrated the

Wyoming-born Pollock as a kind of artist cowboy. As skeptical as many viewers might have been about the merits of abstract art, many people in the West saw it as the antithesis of socialist, realist totalitarianism.

Indeed, New York City—not Paris—emerged as the international center of modern art after World War II, a position it retains today. Just as American political and economic structures became models for the postwar redevelopment of Western Europe, so did American cultural developments. By the time Pollock's first posthumous retrospective toured Europe in 1958, much European painting resembled an elegant imitation of his frenetic lines.

Tatjiana Yablonskaya, *Bread,* 1949.
Ria Novosti/Sovfoto/Eastfoto
Why were paintings such as this one favored by Soviet leaders in the years after World War II?

Yablonskaya and Pollock together illustrate the two central poles of twentieth-century art: realism and abstraction. Although artistic style is no longer as closely associated with political programs as it once was, these two poles still frame the work of countless artists today.

Memory of the Holocaust

The British sculptor Rachel Whiteread (b. 1963) is one of the leading artists of today's Europe. Her work illustrates how European art is breaking out of the modernist contours that were set at the beginning of the twentieth century. On one hand, Whiteread's art returns to what seem like familiar forms; on the other, it forces us to view these forms in ways that are as new to us as cubism was to the public in its day.

Whiteread's *Nameless Library* in Vienna commemorates the thousands of Austrian Jews killed in the Nazi Holocaust.
© Reuters NewMedia Inc./CORBIS
What does this monument tell us about the ongoing cost of the Holocaust?

Whiteread's work is associated with minimalism in contemporary art. This movement, which originated in architecture and interior design, seeks to remove from the object being portrayed as many features as possible while retaining the object's form and the viewer's interest. Minimalist art aims to be as understated as possible.

Whiteread's most important public work is *Nameless Library,* the Judenplatz Holocaust Memorial in Vienna, which commemorates the deaths of 65,000 Austrian Jews under the Nazis. This memorial, which resembles a vast haunting tomb, is cast in concrete and embodies the outline of books whose spines are turned inward, thus remaining forever unread and as unopenable as the library's huge concrete doors are. Whiteread has said the molded, unopened books, which have been compared to the ghost of a library, symbolize the loss both of Jewish contributions to culture and of Jewish lives in the Holocaust.

THE CHRISTIAN HERITAGE

HOW HAS the Christian heritage of the West been affected by events of the twentieth century?

In most ways, Christianity in Europe continued to be as hard-pressed during the twentieth century as it had been in the late nineteenth. Material prosperity, political ideologies, environmentalism, gender politics, and simple indifference have replaced religious faith for many people. Still, despite the loss of much of their popular support and legal privileges and the low rates of church attendance, the European Christian churches continue to exercise social and political influence.

In Western Europe, religious affiliation provided much of the initial basis for the Christian Democratic parties. The churches have also raised critical questions about colonialism, nuclear weapons, human rights, war, and other issues. Consequently, even in this most secular of ages, Christian churches have influenced state and society.

Neo-Orthodoxy

Liberal theologians of the nineteenth century often softened the concept of sin and portrayed human nature as close to the divine. The horror of World War I destroyed that optimistic faith. Many Europeans felt that evil had stalked the Continent.

The most important Christian response to World War I appeared in the theology of Karl Barth (1886–1968). Barth portrayed God as wholly other than, and different

from, humankind. In a sense, Barth was returning to the Reformation theology of Luther, but the work of Kierkegaard had profoundly influenced his reading of the reformer. Like the Danish writer, Barth regarded the lived experience of men and women as the best testimony to the truth of Luther's theology.

This view challenged much nineteenth-century writing about human nature. Barth's theology, which came to be known as neo-Orthodoxy, proved influential throughout the West in the wake of new disasters and suffering.

Liberal Theology

Neo-Orthodoxy did not, however, sweep away liberal theology, which had a strong advocate in Paul Tillich (1886–1965). This German-American theologian tended to regard religion as a human, rather than a divine, phenomenon. Whereas Barth saw God as dwelling outside humankind, Tillich believed that evidence of the divine had to be sought in human nature and human culture. Other liberal theologians, such as Rudolf Bultmann (1884–1976), continued to work on the problems of naturalism and supernaturalism that had troubled earlier writers. Another liberal Christian writer from Britain, C. S. Lewis (1878–1963), attracted millions of readers during and after World War II.

Roman Catholic Reform

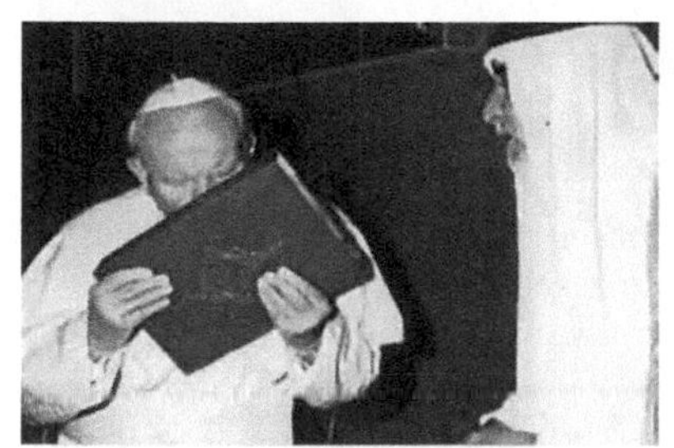

Pope John Paul II kisses a copy of the Qu'ran. Pope John Paul II and his successor, Pope Benedict XVI, made an effort to reach out to other religions and cultures.

National Archives and Records Administration

Among Christian denominations, the most significant postwar changes have been in the Roman Catholic Church. In 1959, Pope John XXIII (r. 1958–1963) summoned the Twenty-First Ecumenical Council (the Emperor Constantine had called the first council in the fourth century), which came to be called Vatican II. The council finished its work in 1965 under John's successor, Pope Paul VI (r. 1963–1978). Among many changes in Catholic liturgy the council introduced, Mass was now celebrated in the vernacular languages rather than in Latin. The council also encouraged freer relations with other Christian denominations, fostered a new spirit toward Judaism, and gave more power to bishops. In recognition of the growing importance to the church of the world outside Europe and North America, Pope Paul appointed several cardinals from the former colonial nations, transforming the church into a truly world body.

In contrast to these liberal changes, however, Pope Paul and his successors have firmly upheld the celibacy of priests, maintained the church's prohibition on contraception and abortion, and opposed moves to open the priesthood to women. The church's unyielding stand on clerical celibacy has caused many men to leave the priesthood and many men and women to leave religious orders. The laity has widely ignored the prohibition on contraception.

Elected in 1978, John Paul II (1920–2005), the former Karol Wojtyla, archbishop of Kraków in Poland, pursued a three-pronged policy during his long pontificate. First, he maintained traditionalist doctrine, stressing the authority of the papacy and attempting to limit doctrinal and liturgical experimentation. Second, taking a firm stand against communism, he supported the spirit of freedom in Eastern Europe that brought down the communist regimes. Third, John Paul II encouraged the growth of the church in the non-Western world, stressing the need for social justice, but limiting the political activity of priests.

The pope's concern for the expansion of Roman Catholicism beyond Europe and North America recognized and encouraged what appears to be a transformation in Christianity as a world religion. Whereas in Europe Christian observance whether Roman Catholic, Protestant, or Orthodox had declined sharply during the twentieth century, Christianity has grown rapidly and fervently in Africa and Latin America. Observers estimate that within a few years, over half of the world's Christians will live in those two continents.

QUICK REVIEW

Pope John Paul II

- 1978: Karol Wojtyla, archbishop of Cracow, becomes Pope John Paul II
- Defended traditional doctrines, stressed papal authority, and opposed doctrinal and liturgical experimentation
- Worked hard to promote church in non-Western nations

LATE-TWENTIETH-CENTURY TECHNOLOGY: THE ARRIVAL OF THE COMPUTER

WHAT IMPACT has the computer had on twentieth-century society?

During the twentieth century, technology crossed international borders the way popular culture did. As with other areas of European life and society, American technology had an unprecedented impact on the Continent. It seems certain that no single American technological achievement of the twentieth century will so influence Western life on both sides of the Atlantic, as well as throughout the rest of the world, as the computer.

THE DEMAND FOR CALCULATING MACHINES

Starting in the late nineteenth century, the governments of the consolidating nation-states of Europe and of the United States confronted new administrative tasks that involved collecting and organizing vast amounts of data about national censuses, tax collection, economic statistics, and the administration of pensions and welfare legislation. During the same years, private businesses sought calculating machinery to handle and organize growing amounts of economic and business data. Such machines became technologically possible through the development of complex circuitry for electricity, the most versatile mode of energy in human history. Moreover, inventions that were dependent on electricity, including the telephone, the telegraph, underwater cables, and the wireless, created a new communications industry that in and of itself also required the organization of large databases of customer information to deliver their services. By the late 1920s, companies like National Cash Register, Remington Rand, and International Business Machines Corporation (IBM) had begun to manufacture such business machinery.

The earliest computers were very large. Here in a 1946 photograph J. Presper Eckert and J. W. Mauchly stand by the Electronic Numerical Integrator and Computer (ENIAC), which was dedicated at the University of Pennsylvania Moore School of Electrical Engineering.
CORBIS/Bettmann

What role did governments play in the development of computers in the twentieth century?

EARLY COMPUTER TECHNOLOGY

As has happened so often in history, warfare was the chief catalyst of change. After World War I and during World War II, the major powers developed new weapons that required exact mathematical ballistic calculations to effectively strike targets with bombs delivered by aircraft or long-range guns.

The first machine genuinely recognizable as a modern digital computer was the Electronic Numerical Integrator and Computer (ENIAC), built and designed at Moore Laboratories of the University of Pennsylvania and put into use by the U.S. Army in 1946 for ballistics calculation. Further computer engineering occurred at the Institute for Advanced Research in Princeton, New Jersey, in laboratories at the Massachusetts Institute of Technology, and in other laboratories the U.S. government and private businesses, especially IBM, ran. The other primary sites for computer development were laboratories in Britain.

THE DEVELOPMENT OF DESKTOP COMPUTERS

During the 1950s, the **transistor** revolutionized electronics, permitting a miniaturization of circuitry that made vacuum tubes obsolete and allowed computers to become smaller. Yet computers still had to be programmed with difficult computer languages by persons expertly trained to use them.

transistor Miniaturized electronics circuitry making the vacuum tube obsolete.

By the late 1960s, however, two innovations transformed computing technology. First, control of the computer was transferred to a bitmap covering the screen of a computer monitor. The mouse, invented in 1964, eased the movement of the cursor around the computer screen. Second, engineers at the Intel Corporation—then a California start-up company—invented the microchip, which became the heart of all future computers.

The bitmap on the screen, operated through the mouse, in effect embedded complicated computer language in the machine, hidden from the user, who simply manipulated images on the screen with the mouse. Almost anyone could thus learn to operate computers. At the same time, the tiny microchip, itself a miniature computer or microprocessor, permitted computer technology to abandon the mainframe and move to still smaller computers. By the mid-1980s, for a relatively modest cost (and one that has continued to drop), individuals had available for their own personal use in their offices or homes computers with far more power than the old mainframes. Computers became objects of everyday life and, by being so, began to transform everyday life itself. Nonetheless, the chief contemporary users of computers remain governments followed by the telephone industry, banking and finance, automobile operation, and airline reservation systems.

Despite the potential democratizing character of computer technology, the computer revolution has also introduced new concepts of "haves" and "have-nots" to societies around the world. Whether in poor school districts in the United States or in poor countries of the former Soviet bloc, students who graduate without computer skills will have difficulty making their way in the world's rapidly computerizing economy. Some commentators also fear that boys are more likely than girls to receive technological training in computers. Nations whose governments and businesses become networked into the world of computers will prosper more fully than those whose access to computer technology is deficient. In that regard, the possession of computers and the ability to use them will probably determine future economic competition, just as they have determined recent military competition.

THE CHALLENGES OF EUROPEAN UNIFICATION

WHAT LED to Western European unification following World War II?

The unprecedented steps toward economic cooperation and unity Western European nations took during the second half of the twentieth century were the single most important European success story of that era.

Postwar Cooperation

The mid-twentieth-century Western European movement toward unity could have occurred in at least three ways: politically, militarily, or economically. Economic cooperation, unlike military and political cooperation, involved little or no immediate loss of sovereignty by the participating nations. Furthermore, it brought material benefits to all the states involved, increasing popular support for their governments. Moreover, the administration of the Marshall Plan and the organization of NATO gave the countries involved new experience in working with each other and demonstrated the productivity and efficiency that mutual cooperation could achieve.

The first effort toward economic cooperation was the formation of the European Coal and Steel Community in 1951 by France, West Germany, Italy, and the Benelux countries (Belgium, the Netherlands, and Luxembourg). The community both benefited from and contributed to the immense growth of material production in Western Europe during this period. Its success reduced the suspicions of government and business groups about coordination and economic integration.

The European Economic Community

It took more than the prosperity of the European Coal and Steel Community to draw European leaders toward further unity, however. The unsuccessful Suez intervention of 1956 and the resulting diplomatic isolation of France and Britain persuaded many Europeans that only by acting together could they significantly influence the United States and the Soviet Union or control their own national and regional destinies. So, in 1957, through the Treaty of Rome, the six members of the Coal and Steel Community agreed to form a new organization: the **European Economic Community (EEC)**. The members of the Common Market, as the EEC was soon known, sought to achieve the eventual elimination of tariffs, a free flow of capital and labor, and similar wage and social benefits in all their countries.

European Economic Community (EEC) European nations as members of the "Common Market" pledging to eliminate tariffs, guarantee unimpeded flow of capital and labor, and establish uniform wage scales and social benefits.

The Common Market achieved stunning success during its early years. By 1968, well ahead of schedule, the six members had abolished all tariffs among themselves. Trade and labor migration among the members grew steadily. Moreover, nonmember states began to copy the EEC and, later, to seek to join it. In 1973, Great Britain, Ireland, and Denmark became members. Throughout the late 1970s, however, and into the 1980s, momentum for expanding EEC membership slowed. Norway and Sweden, with relatively strong economies, declined to join. Although in 1982, Spain, Portugal, and Greece applied for membership and were eventually admitted, sharp disagreements and a sense of stagnation within the EEC continued.

The European Union

In 1988, the leaders of the EEC reached an important decision. By 1992, the EEC was to be a virtual free-trade zone with no trade barriers or other restrictive trade policies among its members. In 1991, the Treaty of Maastricht made a series of specific proposals that led to a unified EEC currency (the euro) and a strong central bank. The treaty was submitted to referendums in several European states. Denmark initially rejected it, and it passed only narrowly in France and Great Britain, making clear that it needed wider popular support. When the treaty finally took effect in November 1993, the EEC was renamed the **European Union**. Throughout the 1990s, the Union's influence grew. Its most notable achievement was the launching in early 1999 of the **euro**, which by 2002 had become the common currency in twelve of the member nations. In May 2004, the European Union added ten new nations raising the total number of members to twenty-five. (See Map 30–1.)

European Union Formerly the European Economic Community (EEC), renamed in 1993.

euro Launched in 1999 by the EU, a single currency circulating in most of Western Europe.

Discord over the Union

The 2004 expansion of the European Union may mark for some time the high point of European integration. During that year the leaders of the member nations adopted a new constitutional treaty for the Union. This treaty, generally known as the **European Constitution**, was a long, detailed, and highly complicated document involving a bill of rights

European Constitution Treaty that would transfer considerable decision-making authority from governments of the individual states to the Union's central institutions.

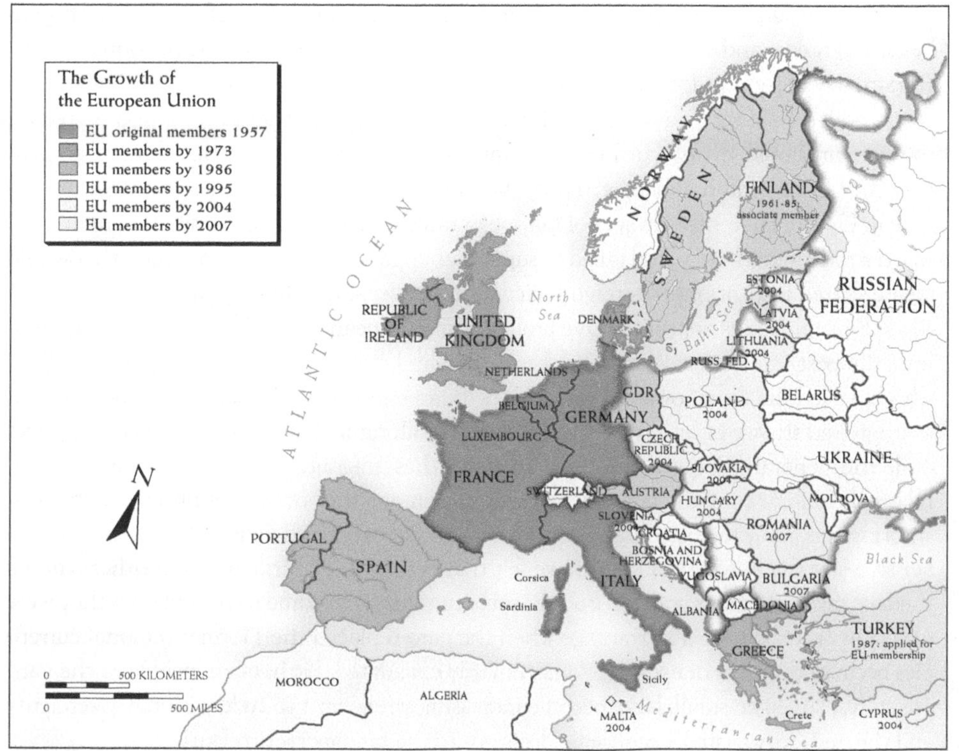

MAP 30–1 The Growth of the European Union This map traces the growth of membership in the European Union from its founding in 1957 through the introduction of its newest members in 2007. Note that Turkey, though having applied for membership, has not yet been admitted.

Given the political, social, historical, and demographic differences among its member states, how successful will EU enlargement and integration be?

Overview Steps Toward European Unification

EUROPEAN COAL AND STEEL COMMUNITY	• Formed in 1951 by France, West Germany, Italy, Belgium, the Netherlands, and Luxembourg • Benefited from and contributed to the growth of material production in postwar Western Europe
EUROPEAN ECONOMIC COMMUNITY (EEC)	• Formed in 1957 by members of the Coal and Steel Community • Also known as the Common Market • Sought to achieve the elimination of tariffs, free flow of capital and labor, and similar wage and social benefits in member countries • Membership expanded in the 1970s and 1980s to include Great Britain, Ireland, Denmark, Spain, Portugal, and Greece
EUROPEAN UNION (EU)	• Replaced EEC in 1993 when the Treaty of Maastricht (1991) took effect • European common currency, the euro, launched in 1999 • Ten new members added in 2004 bringing total number of members to twenty-five
EUROPEAN CONSTITUTION	• Adopted by the leaders of EU nations in 2004 • Would have transferred considerable authority from member states to central institutions of the EU • Failure of voters to ratify the Constitution in many members states has slowed movement toward greater European unity

On Friday, May 27, 2005, two days before the vote on France's referendum on the EU constitution, a woman stands between a "yes" and a "no" campaign poster in a street of Rennes, western France.

AP Wide World Photos

Why has public opinion in Europe turned against the European Constitution?

and complex economic and political agreements among all the member states. It would have transferred considerable decision-making authority from the governments of the individual states to the central institutions of the European Union, many of which are located in Brussels, Luxembourg, and Strasbourg. To become effective, all the member states had to ratify the constitution either by their parliaments or through national referendums.

To the surprise of many in the European elite, in the spring of 2005, referendums held in France and the Netherlands heavily defeated the new constitutional treaty. Britain, where support for further European integration was lukewarm at best, immediately postponed holding its own referendum. Public opinion in other nations also soured on the constitutional treaty. Furthermore, immediately after these events, discord erupted over the Union's internal budget. These events marked an unprecedented crisis for the European Union and for the project of European integration. A similar crisis erupted in 2008 when a referendum in Ireland failed to support changes in the European Union that would create shared institutions of foreign policy formulation and military policy.

Several factors appear to have brought the European Union to this pass. First, for at least the past fifteen years, a gap has been growing between the European political elites, who have led the drive toward unity, and the European voting public. The former have either ignored the latter or have moved the project along with only narrow majorities. Second, the general Western European economy has stagnated for the last decade with relatively high rates of unemployment, especially among the young. Voting against the constitution was a way to voice discontent with this situation. Third, many of the smaller member states of the European Union have felt that France and Germany have either ignored them or taken them for granted. Fourth, some nations have come to believe that they were placed at an economic disadvantage when the euro replaced their former national currencies because the rates of exchange were unfairly calculated. Fifth, many people in the various states, large and small, have become increasingly reluctant to cede national sovereignty and the authority to make economic decisions to the bureaucracy in Brussels.

Finally, another large issue has informed the internal skeptics of the current European Union. Over the past several years, the leaders of the major member states have grown more favorable to the eventual admission of Turkey as a member state. If Turkey were admitted, Europe would have to integrate into the Union a state whose population is larger and much poorer than that of any other member state. Furthermore, although the Turkish government has long been seen as adamantly secular, the Turkish people are overwhelmingly Muslim. This "Islamic factor" has become increasingly controversial among those Europeans who, whether they are religiously observant or not, believe European culture to be Christian, and among those secular Europeans who are deeply concerned about the political, economic, and social implications of the Continent's already significant Muslim population.

It seems inconceivable that the effort to unify in Europe will either halt or be reversed. At the present time, however, it also seems certain that all future developments will move much more slowly and will require increasingly complicated negotiations. Moreover, the future of the European Union has become enmeshed in often bitter and divisive debates within the member states over social policies, the future of their economies, and what role the state should play in economic affairs.

NEW AMERICAN LEADERSHIP AND FINANCIAL CRISIS

WHY MIGHT 2008 prove to be a turning point in the relationship between the United States and Europe?

Much of the first decade of the twenty-first century witnessed considerable strain between the new post–Soviet Union Europe and the United States. The events leading up to the U.S. Iraq invasion in 2003 and the violence occurring since that invasion caused considerable strain between the United States and Europe, especially in terms of popular opinion. Europeans through their press and to some extent through their governments voiced much criticism over what they regarded as unilateral action by the United States in its foreign policy.

Three events in 2008 may have begun to change this situation and possibly to lessen those tensions. The first was the Russian invasion of Georgia discussed in Chapter 29. The United States and the European Union agreed in condemning that action. Second, the American presidential election of 2008 saw the strong victory of Barack Obama, the Democratic Party candidate. Obama is the first African American to be elected to the presidency. He ran on a platform critical of the Iraq invasion and American unilateralism. Even though he also voiced strong support for the war in Afghanistan, Obama has generated enormous popular support across Europe. Third, during the second half of 2008 a major international financial crisis potentially of the dimensions of that of the 1930s overwhelmed the American, transatlantic, and world economies. The crisis originated in the United States mortgage market where numerous major banks found themselves holding mortgages that could not be paid. Several major financial institutions in the United States failed as did some banks in Europe. The United States and some European governments intervened deeply in areas of the economy where they had previously generally refrained from intervening. Stock markets around the world lost a third or more of their value. The interconnectedness of world markets demonstrated itself as never before with financial panic displaying itself around the globe.

The financial crisis and its broad fallout even more than the wars in Iraq and Afghanistan will be the major issues confronting the new Obama administration. The financial problems even more than matters of traditional and foreign policy may for the next several years determine the relationship of the United States and Europe and hence the role of the West in the world.

Barack Obama shakes hands with supporters in Berlin, Germany, on July 24, 2008, following a speech he gave before a crowd of tens of thousands at the Victory Column in Tiergarten Park.

Reuters/Jim Young/Landov Media

What explains Barack Obama's extraordinary popularity in Europe?

Summary

HOW HAS migration changed the face of Europe?

The Twentieth-Century Movement of Peoples Significant numbers of people relocated in Europe during the twentieth century. Millions of Europeans also emigrated, European colonials returned from overseas, and non-European peoples migrated to the former colonial powers. Europe's immigrant Muslim communities are often segregated, poorly assimilated, and discriminated against. The declining European birthrate will undoubtedly have profound consequences for future developments. *page 778*

WHAT EFFECT did the Great Depression and World War II have on the way Europeans viewed the role of government in social and economic life?

Toward a Welfare State Society After World War II, most Western European nations endorsed principles of liberal democracy, and many Europeans wanted their governments to take responsibility for ensuring prosperity and social security. Christian democratic parties took the lead in introducing new policies. A Labour Party ministry introduced universal health care in Britain in 1945, and welfare legislation spread across Western Europe. Through the postwar reconstruction period and the quarter century that followed many Europeans endorsed government management of the economy. Since then, confidence in free markets has grown, and some social welfare programs have been scaled back. Margaret Thatcher was the foremost proponent of a freer market economy. *page 780*

HOW DID the status of women in business, politics, and the professions change in Europe in the second half of the twentieth century?

New Patterns in Work and Expectations of Women Gender inequality persists in Europe, despite expanding economic and political roles for women. Recent feminism has focused on helping women as individuals take control of their lives. European women now have fewer children and more time to develop careers. Women in Eastern Europe are adapting to free-market, democratic systems. *page 784*

HOW WAS cultural and intellectual life transformed in Europe during the twentieth century?

Transformations in Knowledge and Culture Most Western European intellectuals have become disillusioned with Soviet communism. Interest in existentialism, a philosophy that questions rationalism, has been encouraged by distrust of the pride in rational achievement that has produced so much suffering and warfare. Social concerns prompted student rebellions in the 1960s, and the economic and military influence of the United States has threatened European culture. *page 786*

HOW DID the Cold War shape Western art in the second half of the twentieth century?

Art Since World War II The Second World War and the Cold War influenced art in the twentieth century. Socialist realism was the dominant official form of art in the Soviet Union and communist bloc, while abstract art, like that of Jackson Pollock, reflected postwar cultural freedom in the West. Minimalist art returns to familiar forms while it compels new ways of viewing the objects being portrayed. *page 790*

HOW HAS the Christian heritage of the West been affected by events of the twentieth century?

The Christian Heritage Christian churches have continued to be influential even in an increasingly secularized Europe. The Roman Catholic Church changed significantly under Pope John XXIII, but subsequent papacies have been more traditionalist and have furthered the spread of Christianity as a world religion. *page 791*

WHAT IMPACT has the computer had on twentieth-century society?

Late-Twentieth-Century Technology: The Arrival of the Computer Most of the development work for computers was done in the United States and Britain. Calculating machines started to become available in the 1920s. The U.S. Army used the first digital computer, ENIAC, for ballistics computations starting in 1946. By the 1980s, desktop computers were becoming everyday objects. *page 793*

WHAT LED to Western European unification following World War II?

The Challenges of European Unification Economic unification was easier for European nations than military or political union. In 1951 six nations formed the European Coal and Steel Community, which in 1957 became the European Economic Community or the Common Market. In 1973 membership was increased, and in 1998 the EEC created a free-trade zone. In 1999 a common currency was decreed, and the EEC was renamed the European Union. Its euro became the currency of most of Western Europe in 2001. In 2004, the European Union admitted ten more member nations, but discord spread over the details of a constitution designed to regulate relations among members. *page 794*

WHY MIGHT 2008 prove to be a turning point in the relationship between the United States and Europe?

New American Leadership and Financial Crisis Much of the first decade of the twenty-first century witnessed considerable strain between the new post–Soviet Union Europe and the United States. Three events in 2008 may have begun to change this situation and possibly to lessen those tensions: the Russian invasion of Georgia, the election of Barack Obama to the American presidency, and the emergence of a major international financial crisis. The financial crisis may for the next several years determine the relationship of the United States and Europe and hence the role of the West in the world. *page 797*

REVIEW QUESTIONS

1. How did migration affect twentieth-century social life in Europe? In what ways was Europe "Americanized" in the second half of the century?
2. How and why did European attitudes toward the welfare state and free-market economics change from the end of World War II to the dawn of the twenty-first century?
3. How did women's social and economic roles change in the second half of the twentieth century? What problems have new patterns of work created for women?
4. How did the pursuit and diffusion of knowledge change during the twentieth century? In what sense was existentialism a response to the crises of the twentieth century?
5. What kind of artistic styles arose in the mid– and late-twentieth century and how did World War II and the Cold War influence those styles?
6. How did Western Christian theology develop in the twentieth century? What changes are computers most likely to bring?
7. How did the nations of Western Europe move toward economic and political unity? What challenges face further European integration?

KEY TERMS

Christian democratic parties (p. 781)
euro (p. 795)
European Constitution (p. 795)
European Economic Community (EEC) (p. 794)
European Union (p. 795)
existentialism (p. 787)
Green movement (p. 790)
socialist realism (p. 790)
transistor (p. 793)

For additional learning resources related to this chapter, please go to **www.myhistorylab.com**

myhistorylab

Academy School founded by Plato in Athens to train statesmen and citizens.

Acropolis At the center of the city of Athens, the most famous example of a citadel.

Act of Supremacy Act of 1534 proclaiming Henry VIII "the only supreme head on earth of the Church of England."

agape Common meal, or "love feast," that was the central ritual of the church in early Christianity.

agora Place for markets and political assemblies.

Ahura Mazda The chief deity of Zoroastrianism, the native religion of Persia. Ahura Mazda is the creator of the world, the source of light, and the embodiment of good.

Albigensians Heretical sect that advocated a simple, pious way of life following the example set by Jesus and the Apostles, but rejecting key Christian doctrines.

Anabaptists ("rebaptizers") The most important of several groups of Protestants forming more radical organizations that sought a more rapid and thorough restoration of the "primitive Christianity" described in the New Testament.

anarchists Those who opposed any cooperation with industry or government.

Anschluss Union of Germany and Austria.

anti-Semitism Prejudice against Jews often displayed through hostility.

apartheid (a-PAR-tid) An official policy of segregation, assignment of peoples to distinct regions, and other forms of social, political, and economic discrimination based on race associated primarily with South Africa.

appeasement Allied policy of making concessions to Germany based on the belief that Germany's grievances were real and Hitler's goals limited.

Aramaic Semitic language spoken widely throughout the Middle East in antiquity.

Areopagus Council heading Athens's government comprised of a group of nobles that annually chose the city's nine *archons*, the magistrates who administered the *polis*.

arete The highest virtue in Homeric society: the manliness, courage, and excellence that equipped a hero to acquire and defend honor.

Arianism Belief that Christ was the first of God the Father's creations and the being through whom the Father created all other things.

aristocratic resurgence Eighteenth-century resurgence of nobles that mantained the exclusiveness of noble rank, made it difficult to obtain, reserved powerful posts to nobles, and protected nobles from taxation.

Attica Region (about 1,000 square miles) that Athens dominated.

Augsburg Confession Moderate Protestant creed endorsed by the Schmalkaldic League (a defensive alliance of Lutherans).

Augustus ("revered") Name by which the Senate hailed Octavian for his restoration of the republic.

Avignon Papacy Period from 1309 to 1377 when the papal court was situated in Avignon, France, and gained a reputation for greed and worldly corruption.

Axis Forces (opposed to the Allies) joined together in Europe, including Germany and Italy, before and during World War II.

banalities Monopolies maintained by landowners giving them the right to demand that tenants pay to grind all their grain in the landowner's mill and bake all their bread in his oven.

baroque Artistic and architectural styles that were naturalistic rather than idealized to involve observer on an emotional level through dramatic portrayals.

Beguines Sisterhoods of pious, self-supporting single women.

Black Death Virulent plague that struck in Sicily in 1347 and spread through Europe. It discolored the bodies of its victims. By the early fifteenth century, the plague may have reduced the population of Western Europe by two-fifths.

Bolsheviks ("majority") Lenin's turn-of-the-century Russian faction favoring a party of elite professionals who would provide the working class with centralized leadership.

boyars Wealthy landowners among the freemen in late medieval Russia.

Brezhnev Doctrine Asserted the right of the Soviet Union to intervene in domestic politics of communist countries.

Bronze Age (3100–1200 B.C.E.) Began with the increasing importance of metal that also ended the Stone Ages.

Caesaropapism Emperor acting as if he were pope as well as caesar.

caliphate Office of the leader of the Muslim community.

categorical imperative Kant's view that all human beings possess an innate sense of moral duty, an inner command to act in every situation as one would have other people act in that same situation.

catholic ("universal") As in "universal" majority of Christians.

censors Men of unimpeachable reputation, chosen to carry the responsibility for enrolling, keeping track of, and determining the status and tax liability of each citizen.

Chartism The London Working Men's Association's 1838 proposal for political reform featuring the Six Points.

Christian democratic parties Post–World War II parties that welcomed non-Catholic members and fought for democracy, social reform, and economic growth.

civilization Stage in the evolution of organized society that has among its characteristics urbanism, long-distance trade, writing systems, and accelerated technological and social development.

civilizing mission The concept that Western nations could bring advanced science and economic development to non-Western parts of the world that justified imperial administration.

clientage The custom in ancient Rome whereby men became supporters of more powerful men in return for legal and physical protection and economic benefits.

Cold War Period between the end of World War II (1945) and the collapse of the Soviet Union (1991) in which U.S. and Soviet relations were tense, seemingly moments away from actual war at any time during these years.

collectivization The bedrock of Stalinist agriculture, which forced Russian peasants to give up their private farms and work as members of collectives, large agricultural units controlled by the state.

coloni Tenant farmers who were bound to the lands they worked.

concentration camps Camps first established by Great Britain in South Africa during the Boer War to incarcerate noncombatant civilians; later, camps established for political prisoners and other persons deemed dangerous to the state in the Soviet Union and Nazi Germany. The term is now primarily associated with the camps established by the Nazis during the Holocaust.

condottieri Military brokers from whom one could hire a mercenary army.

Congregationalists The more extreme Puritans who believed every congregation ought to be autonomous, a law unto itself controlled by neither bishops nor presbyterian assemblies.

conquistadores "Conquerors."

conservatism Form of political thought that, in mid-nineteenth-century Europe, promoted legitimate monarchies, landed aristocracies, and established churches.

Consulate A republican facade for one-man government by Napoleon.

consuls Elected magistrates from patrician families chosen annually to lead the army, oversee the state religion, and sit as judges.

containment American foreign policy strategy (beginning in 1947) for countering the communist threat and resisting the spread of Soviet influence.

Convention The newly elected French body that met on September 21, 1792, whose first act was to declare France a republic—a nation governed by an elected assembly without a king.

Counter-Reformation A reorganization of the Catholic Church that equipped it to meet the challenges posed by the Protestant Reformation.

Creole Merchants, landowners, and professional people of Spanish descent.

Crusades Campaigns authorized by the church to combat heresies and rival faiths.

cubism Autonomous realm of art with no purpose beyond itself. Includes as many different perspectives, angles, or views of the object as possible.

culture Way of life invented by a group and passed on by teaching.

cuneiform Developed by the Sumerians as the very first writing system ever used, it used several thousand characters, some of which stood for words and some for sounds.

deism The *philosophes'* theology. A rational religion, a faith without fanaticism and intolerance that acknowledged the sovereign authority of reason.

Delian League Pact joined in 478 B.C.E. by Athenians and other Greeks to continue the war with Persia.

détente Relaxation of tensions between the United States and Soviet Union that involved increased trade and reduced deployment of strategic arms.

"divine right of kings" The belief that God appoints kings and that kings are accountable only to God for how they use their power.

domestic system of textile production Means by which urban merchants obtained their wares. They bought wool or other unfinished fiber for distribution to peasant workers who took it home, spun it into thread, wove it into cloth, and returned the finished product to the merchants for sale.

Duce (DO-chay) Meaning "leader." Mussolini's title as head of the Fascist Party.

ego Among Freud's three entities of the mind, the *ego* mediates between the impulsive id and the self-denying superego.

émigrés French aristocrats and enemies of the revolution who fled to countries on France's borders and set up bases for counterrevolutionary activities.

empiricism The use of experiment and observation derived from sensory evidence to construct scientific theory or philosophy of knowledge.

encomienda Legal grant of the right to the labor of a specific number of Indians for a particular period of time. This was used as a Spanish strategy for exploiting the labor of the natives.

Enlightenment The eighteenth-century movement led by the *philosophes* that held that change and reform were both desirable through the application of reason and science.

Epicureans People who believed the proper pursuit of humankind is undisturbed withdrawal from the world.

equestrians Men rich enough to qualify for cavalry service.

Estates General Assembly of representatives from France's propertied classes.

Etruscans A people of central Italy who exerted the most powerful external influence on the early Romans. Etruscan kings ruled Rome until 509 B.C.E.

Eucharist ("thanksgiving") Celebration of the Lord's Supper in which bread and wine were blessed and consumed.

euro Launched in 1999 by the EU, a single currency circulating in most of Western Europe.

European Constitution Treaty that would transfer considerable decision-making authority from governments of the individual states to the European Union's central institutions.

European Economic Community (EEC) European nations as members of the "Common Market" pledging to eliminate tariffs, guarantee unimpeded flow of capital and labor, and establish uniform wage scales and social benefits.

European Union (EU) Formerly the European Economic Community (EEC), renamed in 1993.

existentialism Maintains that the human condition is greater than the sum of its parts and can only be grouped as whole.

fascism System of extreme right-wing dictatorial government.

fiefs ("lands") Granted to cavalry men to fund their equipment and service.

Fourteen Points President Woodrow Wilson's idealistic principles articulated as America's goals in World War I, including self-determination for nationalities, open diplomacy, freedom of the seas, disarmament, and establishment of a league of nations to keep the peace.

Fronde Widespread rebellions in France between 1649 and 1652 (named after a slingshot used by street ruffians) aimed at reversing the drift toward absolute monarchy and preserving local autonomy.

Führer (FYOOR-er) Meaning "leader." The title taken by Hitler when he became dictator of Germany.

Gallican Liberties The French Roman Catholic Church's ecclesiastical independence of papal authority in Rome.

Gaul Area that is now modern France.

ghettos Separate districts in cities and entire villages in the countryside where Jews lived apart from Christians in eighteenth-century Europe.

glasnost ("openness") Gorbachev's policy of opening the way for unprecedented public discussion and criticism of Soviet history and the Communist Party. Censorship was relaxed and dissidents were released from prison.

"Glorious Revolution" Parliament's bloodless 1688 declaration of a vacant throne and proclamation that William and Mary were its heirs.

Golden Bull Arrangements agreed to by the Holy Roman Emperor and the major German territorial rulers in 1356 that helped stabilize Germany.

Great Depression A prolonged worldwide economic downturn that began in 1929 with the collapse of the New York Stock Exchange.

Great Purges The arrests, trials, Communist Party expulsions, and executions—beginning with the assassination of Politburo member Sergei Kirov in December 1934—that mainly targeted Party officials and reached its climax from 1936 to 1938.

Great Trek The migration by Boer (Dutch) farmers during the 1830s and 1840s from regions around Cape Town into the eastern and northeastern regions of South Africa that ultimately resulted in the founding of the Orange Free State and Transvaal.

Green movement Made up, in part, of members from the radical student groups of the 1960s, this movement was anticapitalistic, peace oriented, in opposition of nuclear arms, and condemned business for producing pollution. Unlike earlier student groups, though, the Greens opted to compete in the electoral process.

guild An association of merchants or craftsmen that offered protection to its members and set rules for their work and products.

hacienda Large landed estate that characterized most Spanish colonies.

Hegira Forced flight of Muhammad and his followers to Medina, 240 miles north of Mecca. This event marks the beginning of the Islamic calendar.

Hellenistic Term that describes the cosmopolitan civilization, established under the Macedonians, that combined aspects of Greek and Middle Eastern cultures.

Helots Slaves to the Spartans that revolted and nearly destroyed Sparta in 650 B.C.E.

heretics "Takers" of contrary positions, namely in Christianity.

hieroglyphs ("sacred carving") Greek name for Egyptian writing. The writing was often used to engrave holy texts on monuments.

Holocaust The Nazi extermination of millions of European Jews between 1940 and 1945. Also called the "final solution to the Jewish problem."

Holy Roman Empire The domain of the German monarchs who revived the use of the Roman imperial title during the Middle Ages.

home rule Government of a country or locality by its own citizens.

hoplite A true infantry soldier who began to dominate the battlefield in the late eighth century B.C.E.

Homo sapiens Our own species, which dates back roughly 200,000 years.

hubris Arrogance produced by excessive wealth or good fortune.

Huguenots French Protestants, named after Besançon Hugues, the leader of the revolt that won Geneva its freedom at that time.

humanitas Wide-ranging intellectual curiosity and habits of critical thinking that are the goals of liberal education.

iconoclasm Opposition to the use of images in Christian worship.

id Among Freud's three entities of the mind, the *id* consists of innate, amoral, irrational drives for sexual gratification, aggression, and sensual pleasure.

Iliad Homer's poem narrates a dispute between Agamemnon the king and his warrior Achilles, whose honor is wounded and then avenged.

imperator "Commander in chief."

imperialism The extension of a nation's authority over other nations or areas through conquest or political or economic hegemony.

Imperialism of Free Trade The advance of European economic and political interests in the nineteenth century by demanding that non-European nations allow European nations, most particularly Great Britain, to introduce their manufactured goods freely into all nations or to introduce other goods, such as opium into China, that allowed those nations to establish economic influence and to determine the terms of trade.

imperium Right held by a Roman king to enforce commands by fines, arrests, and corporal and capital punishment.

impressionism Focuses on social life and leisured activities of the urban middle and lower-middle classes; a fascination with light, color, and representation of momentary experience of social life or of landscape.

indulgence Remission of the obligation to perform a "work of satisfaction" for a sin.

Industrial Revolution Term coined by early-nineteenth-century observers to describe the changes that the spreading use of powered machinery made in society and economics.

Inquisition Formal ecclesiastical court dedicated to discovering and punishing heresy.

Intolerable Acts Series of laws passed by Parliament in 1774 that closed the port of Boston, reorganized the government of Massachusetts, quartered soldiers in private homes, and transferred trials of customs officials accused of crimes to England.

Ionia Western coast of Asia Minor.

Islam New religion appearing in Arabia in the sixth century in response to the work of the Prophet Muhammad.

Jacobins The best organized of the political clubs, they embraced the most radical of the Enlightenment's political theories, and they wanted a republic, not a constitutional monarchy.

Jacquerie (From "Jacques Bonhomme," a peasant caricature) Name given to the series of bloody rebellions that desperate French peasants waged beginning in 1358.

Jansenism Appearing in the 1630s, it followed the teachings of St. Augustine, who stressed the role divine grace played in human salvation.

jihad A struggle; interpreted as a call for religious war.

Junkers (Prussian nobles) They were allowed to demand absolute obedience from the serfs on their estates in exchange for their support of the Hohenzollerns.

jus gentium Law of all peoples as opposed to the law that reflected only Roman practice.

jus naturale Law of nature that enshrined the principles of divine reason that Cicero and the Stoics believed governed the universe.

Ka'ba One of Arabia's holiest shrines located in Mecca, the birthplace of Muhammad.

Keynesian economics Economic theories and programs ascribed to John M. Keynes and his followers advocating government monetary and fiscal policies that increase employment and spending.

Kristallnacht (KRIS-tahl-NAHKT) Meaning "crystal night" because of the broken glass that littered German streets after the looting and destruction of Jewish homes, businesses, and synagogues across Germany on the orders of the Nazi Party in November 1938.

Kulturkampf ("cultural struggle") An extreme church-state conflict waged by Bismarck in Germany during the 1870s in response to a perceived threat to German political unity from the Roman Catholic Church.

laissez-faire Policy of noninterference, especially the policy of government noninterference in economic affairs or business.

latifundia Great estates that produced capital-intensive cash crops for the international market.

Latium Region located in present-day Italy that included the small town of Rome.

Lebensraum German for "living space."

levée en masse Order for total military mobilization of both men and property.

liberal arts The medieval university program that consisted of the *trivium* (TRI-vee-um): grammar, rhetoric, and logic, and the *quadrivium* (qua-DRI-vee-um): arithmetic, geometry, astronomy, and music.

Lower Egypt The Nile's one-hundred-mile deep, triangularly shaped delta.

Luftwaffe The German air force.

Lyceum School founded by Aristotle in Athens that focused on the gathering and analysis of data from all fields of knowledge.

Magna Carta ("Great Charter") Document spelling out limitations on royal authority agreed to by John in 1215. It created foundation for modern English law.

mandate Territory under the aegis of the League of Nations but actually ruled as a colony.

mannerism Reaction against the simplicity, symmetry, and idealism of High Renaissance art. It made room for the strange, even the abnormal, and gave free reign to the subjectivity of the artist. The name reflects a tendency by artists to employ "mannered" ("affected") techniques—distortions that expressed individual perceptions and feelings.

manor A self-sufficient rural community that was a fundamental institution of medieval life.

Marshall Plan The U.S. European Recovery Program introduced by George C. Marshall, American secretary of state, whereby America provided extensive economic aid to the European states, conditional only on their working together for their mutual benefit.

Marxism Socialist movement begun by Karl Marx in the mid–nineteenth century that differed from competing socialist views primarily in its claim to a scientific foundation and in its insistence on reform through revolution.

Mein Kampf (*My Struggle*) Strategy dictated by Adolf Hitler during his period of imprisonment in 1923 outlining his political views.

Mensheviks ("minority") Turn-of-the-century Russian faction that wanted to create a party with a large mass membership (like Germany's SPD).

mercantilism Economic theory in which governments heavily regulated trade and promoted empires in order to increase national wealth.

Methodism Movement begun in England by John Wesley, an Oxford-educated Anglican priest, the first major religion to embody romanticism. It emphasized religion as a "method" for living more than a set of doctrines.

millets Communities of the officially recognized religions that governed portions of the Ottoman Empire.

Minoan Civilization of Crete (2100–1150 B.C.E.), and the Aegean's first civilization, named for a legendary king on the island.

modernism Movement of the 1870s criticizing middle-class society and traditional morality.

Monophysites Believers in a single, immortal nature of Christ; not both eternal God and mortal man in one and the same person.

monotheism Having faith in a single God.

Mycenaean Civilization occupying mainland Greece during the Late Helladic era (1580–1150 B.C.E.).

nationalism The belief that the people who share an ethnic identity (language, culture, and history) should also be recognized as having a right to a government and political identity of their own.

NATO North Atlantic Treaty Organization, a mutual defense pact.

natural selection Darwin and Wallace's theory that those species with a unique trait that gives them a marginal advantage in the struggle for existence change the nature of their species by reproducing more successfully than their competitors; the fittest survive to pass on their unique characteristics.

naturalists Authors who tried to portray nature and human life without sentimentality.

Nazis Members of the National Socialist German Workers' Party that formed in 1920 and supported a mythical Aryan race alleged to be the source of the purest German lineage.

neo-Gothic Style that idealized nature and portrayed it in all its power.

neoclassicism Style that embodied a return to figurative and architectural models drawn from the Renaissance and the ancient world.

Neolithic "New Stone" Age, dating back 10,000 years to when people living in some parts of the Middle East made advances in the production of stone tools and shifted from hunting and gathering to agriculture.

New Economic Policy (NEP) A limited revival of capitalism, especially in light industry and agriculture, introduced by Lenin in 1921 to repair the damage inflicted on the Russian economy by the Civil War and war communism.

New Imperialism The extension in the late nineteenth and early twentieth centuries of Western political and economic dominance to Asia, the Middle East, and Africa.

nomes Egyptian districts ruled by regional governors who were called nomarchs.

Odyssey Homer's epic poem that tells of the wanderings of the hero Odysseus.

oikos The Greek household, always headed by a male.

Old Regime Eighteenth-century era marked by absolutist monarchies, agrarian economies, tradition, hierarchy, corporateness, and privilege.

optimates ("the best men") Opponents of Tiberius and defenders of the traditional prerogatives of the Senate.

orthodox ("correct") As in "correct" faith in Christianity.

Ottoman Empire The authority Istanbul's Ottoman Turkish sultan exercised over the Balkans, the Middle East, and North Africa from the end of the Middle Ages to World War I.

Paleolithic Greek for "old stone"; the earliest period in cultural development that began with the first use of stone tools about a million years ago and continued until about 10,000 B.C.E.

Panhellenic (All Greek) Sense of cultural identity that all Greeks felt in common with one other.

papal infallibility Assertion that the pope's pronouncements on matters of faith and morals could not be questioned.

Papal States Central part of Italy where Pope Stephen II became the secular ruler when confirmed by the Franks in 755.

parlements Regional courts allowed considerable latitude by Louis XIV to deal with local issues.

parliamentary monarchy English rule by a monarch with some parliamentary guidance or input.

patricians Upper class of Roman families that originally monopolized all political authority. Only they could serve as priests, senators, and magistrates.

Peloponnesian Wars Series of wars between Athens and Sparta beginning in 460 B.C.E.

Peloponnesus Southern half of the Greek peninsula.

perestroika ("restructuring") Means by which Gorbachev wished to raise his country's standard of living.

petite bourgeoisie New lower-middle class made up of white- collar workers such as secretaries, retail clerks, and lower-level bureaucrats.

phalanx Tight military formation of men eight or more ranks deep.

pharaoh The god-kings of ancient Egypt.

Pharisee Member of a Jewish sect known for strict adherence to the Jewish law.

Phoenicians Seafaring people (Canaanites and Syrians) who scattered trading colonies from one end of the Mediterranean to the other.

plebeians Commoner class of Roman families, usually families of small farmers, laborers, and artisans who were early clients of the patricians.

political absolutism Government by a ruler with absolute authority.

politique Ruler or person in a position of power who puts the success and well-being of his or her state above all else.

polytheists Name given those who workship many gods and/or goddesses.

Popular Front A government of all left-wing parties that took power in France in 1936 to enact social and economic reforms.

populares Politicians who followed Tiberius's example of politics and governing.

positivism Comte's philosophy that all knowledge should be the kind of knowledge common to the physical sciences.

postimpressionism Focuses more on form and structure to bring painting of modern life back in touch with earlier artistic traditions.

Pragmatic Sanction Document recognizing Charles VI's daughter Maria Theresa as his heir.

Presbyterians Puritans who favored a national church of semiautonomous congregations governed by representative presbyteries.

proconsulships Extension of terms for consuls who had important work to finish.

protectorate A non-Western territory administered by a Western nation without formal conquest or annexation, usually a de facto colony.

Ptolemaic system Astronomical theory, named after Greek astronomer Ptolemy, that assumed Earth was the center point of a ball-shaped universe composed of concentric layers of rotating crystalline spheres to which the heavenly bodies were attached.

Puritans English Protestants who wanted simpler forms of church ceremony and strictness and gravity in personal behavior.

Qur'an Sacred book comprised of a collection of the revealed texts that God had chosen Muhammad to convey.

racism Belief that some peoples are innately superior to others.

realists Authors who tried to describe human behavior with scientific objectivity, rejecting the Romantic idealization of nature, poverty, love, and polite society, and portraying the hypocrisy, physical and psychic brutality, and the dullness that underlay bourgeois life.

regular clergy Those clergy living under a *regula*, the rule of a monastic order.

Reichstag (RIKES-stahg) The German parliament, which existed in various forms, until 1945.

Reign of Terror Extreme measures employed by the French government in an effort to protect the revolution.

rococo Style that embraced lavish, often lighthearted decoration with an emphasis on pastel colors and the play of light.

romanticism Reaction against the rationalism and scientism of the Enlightenment, insisting on the importance of human feelings, intuition, and imagination as supplements for reason in the human quest to understand the world.

SA The Nazi parliamentary forces, or storm troopers.

sans-culottes Parisians (shopkeepers, artisans, wage earners, and factory workers who had been ignored by the Old Regime) who, along with radical Jacobins, began the second revolution in France.

Scholasticism Method of study associated with the medieval university.

scientific revolution The emergence in the sixteenth century of rational and empirical methods of research that challenged traditional thought and promoted the rise of science and technology.

second Industrial Revolution Started after 1850, it expanded the production of steel, chemicals, electricity, and oil.

secular clergy Clergy, such as bishops and priests, who lived and worked among the laity in the *saeculum* ("world").

Sejm Central legislative body to which the Polish nobles belonged.

September Massacres The execution ordered by the Paris Commune of approximately 1,200 aristocrats, priests, and common criminals who, because they were being held in city jails, were assumed to be counterrevolutionaries.

serf Peasant bound to the land he worked.

Shi'a The "party" of Ali. They believed Ali and his descendants were Muhammad's only rightful successors.

social Darwinism Spencer's argument (coming close to claiming that might makes right) used to justify neglect of the poor and the working class, exploitation of colonial peoples, and aggressive competition among nations.

socialist realism Doctrine of Soviet art and literature that sought to create figurative, traditional, optimistic, and easily intelligible scenes of a bold socialist future of prosperity and solidarity.

Sophists Professional teachers who emerged in Greece in the mid–fifth century B.C.E. who were paid to teach techniques of rhetoric, dialectic, and argumentation.

spheres of influence A region, city, or territory where a non-Western nation exercised informal administrative influence through economic, diplomatic, or military advisers.

spinning jenny Invented by James Hargreaves in 1765, this machine spun sixteen spindles of thread simultaneously.

SS The chief security units of the Nazi state.

Stoics People who sought freedom from passion and harmony with nature.

***studia humanitas* (humanism)** Scholarship of the Renaissance that championed the study of Latin and Greek classics and Christian church fathers as an end in itself and as a guide to reforming society. Some claim it is an un-Christian philosophy emphasizing human dignity, individualism, and secular values.

Sturm und Drang ("Storm and Stress") Movement in German romantic literature that emphasized feeling and emotion.

suffragettes Derisive name for members of the Women's Social and Political Union, who lobbied for votes for women.

Sunnis Followers of the *sunna*, "tradition." They emphasize loyalty to the fundamental principles of Islam.

superego Among Freud's three entities of the mind, the *superego* internalizes the moral imperatives that society and culture impose on the personality.

symposium A men's drinking party at the center of aristocratic social life in archaic Greece.

Table of Ranks Issued by Peter the Great to draw nobles into state service, it made rank in the bureaucracy or military, not lineage, the determinant of an individual's social status.

tabula rasa (a blank page) John Locke's *An Essay Concerning Human Understanding* (1690) theorized that at birth the human mind is a tabula rasa.

taille The direct tax on the French peasantry.

ten lost tribes Israelites who were scattered and lost to history when the northern kingdom of Israel fell to the Assyrians in 722 B.C.E.

tetrarchy Coalition of four men, each of whom was responsible for a different part of the empire, established by Diocletian.

Thermidorian Reaction Tempering of revolutionary fervor that led to the establishment of a new constitutional regime.

Third Estate Members of the commercial and professional middle classes, or everyone but the clergy (the First Estate) and the nobility (the Second Estate).

Third Reich Hitler's regime of Nazis.

three-field system Developed by medieval farmers, a system in which three fields were utilized during different growing seasons to limit the amount of nonproductive plowing and to restore soil fertility through crop rotation.

transistor Miniaturized electronics circuitry making the vacuum tube obsolete.

transubstantiation Christian doctrine which holds that, at the moment of priestly consecration, the bread and wine of the Lord's Supper become the body and blood of Christ.

tribunes Officials elected by the plebeian tribal assembly given the power to protect plebeians from abuse by patrician magistrates.

ulema ("Persons with correct knowledge") Scholarly elite leading Islam.

Upper Egypt Narrow valley extending 650 miles from Aswan to the border of Lower Egypt.

utilitarianism Maintained that people should always pursue the course that promotes the greatest happiness for the greatest number.

utopian socialists Early critics of industrialism whose visionary programs often involved plans to establish ideal societies based on noncapitalistic values.

vassal A person granted an estate or cash payments in return for rendering services to a lord.

Vulgate Latin translation of the Bible that became the standard text for the Catholic Church.

War Communism The economic policy adopted by the Bolsheviks during the Russian Civil War to seize the banks, heavy industry, railroads, and grain.

Warsaw Pact Mutual defense agreement among Albania, Bulgaria, Czechoslovakia, East Germany, Hungary, Poland, Romania, and the Soviet Union.

water frame Invented in 1769 by Richard Arkwright, this water-powered device produced a 100 percent cotton fabric rather than the standard earlier blend of cotton and linen.

Weimar Republic German republic that came to power in 1918 embodying the hopes of German liberals.

Zionism Movement based on the theory that if Jews were unacceptable as citizens of European nations, their only safety lay in establishing a nation of their own.

Chapter 1

C. ALDRED, *The Egyptians* (1998). Probably the best one-volume history of the subject.

P. BRIANT, *From Cyrus to Alexander: A History of the Persian Empire* (2002). A scholarly account of ancient Persia with greater knowledge of the Persian evidence than is usual.

T. BRYCE, *The Kingdom of the Hittites* (1998). A fine new account.

M. EHRENBERG, *Women in Prehistory* (1989). Discusses the role of women in early times.

B. M. FAGAN, *People of the Earth: An Introduction to World Prehistory*, 11th ed. (2003). A narrative account of human prehistory up to the earliest civilizations.

W. W. HALLO AND W. K. SIMPSON, *The Ancient Near East: A History*, rev. ed. (1998). A fine survey of Egyptian and Mesopotamian history.

A. KAMM, *The Israelites: An Introduction* (1999). A brief, excellent, and accessible account.

R. MATTHEWS, *Archaeology of Mesopotamia: Theories and Approaches* (2003). A fascinating investigation of the theories, methods, approaches, and history of Mesopotamian archaeology from its origins in the nineteenth century up to the present day.

J. B. PRITCHARD, ED., *Ancient Near Eastern Texts Relating to the Old Testament* (1969). A good collection of documents in translation with useful introductory material.

R. RUDGLEY, *The Lost Civilizations of the Stone Age* (1999). A bold new interpretation that claims that many elements of civilization were already present in the Stone Age.

H. W. F. SAGGS, *Babylonians* (1995). A general account of ancient Mesopotamia by an expert scholar.

I. SHAW, ED., *The Oxford History of Ancient Egypt* (2000). An up-to-date survey by leading scholars.

W. K. SIMPSON ET AL., *The Literature of Ancient Egypt: An Anthology of Stories, Instructions, Stelae, Autobiographies, and Poetry* (2003). A fine collection of writings from ancient Egypt.

D. C. SNELL, *Life in the Ancient Near East, 3100–332* B.C.E. (1997). A social history with emphasis on culture and daily life.

Chapter 2

E. K. ANHALT, *Solon the Singer* (1993). A fine study of the Athenian poet-politician.

W. BURKERT, *The Orientalizing Revolution: Near Eastern Influence on Greek Culture in the Early Archaic Age* (1992). A study of the Eastern impact on Greek literature and religion from 750 to 650 B.C.E.

J. CHADWICK, *The Mycenaean World* (1976). A readable account by an author who helped decipher Mycenaean writing.

R. DREWS, *The Coming of the Greeks* (1988). A fine study of the arrival of the Greeks as part of the movement of Indo-European peoples.

J. V. A. FINE, *The Ancient Greeks* (1983). An excellent survey that discusses historical problems and the evidence that gives rise to them.

M. I. FINLEY, *World of Odysseus*, rev. ed. (1965). A fascinating attempt to reconstruct Homeric society.

V. D. HANSON, *The Other Greeks* (1995). A revolutionary account of the invention of the family farm by the Greeks and the central role of agrarianism in shaping the Greek city-state.

V. D. HANSON, *The Western Way of War* (1989). A brilliant and lively discussion of the rise and character of the *hoplite* phalanx and its influence on Greek society.

J. M. HURWIT, *The Art and Culture of Early Greece* (1985). A fascinating study of the art of early Greece in its literary and cultural context.

W. K. LACEY, *The Family in Ancient Greece* (1984). A valuable survey of family life in ancient Greece.

P. B. MANVILLE, *The Origins of Citizenship in Ancient Athens* (1990). An examination of the origins of citizenship in the time of Solon of Athens.

J. F. MCGLEW, *Tyranny and Political Culture in Ancient Greece* (1993). A study of tyranny and its effect on Greek political tradition.

S. G. MILLER, *Ancient Greek Athletics* (2004). The best available account.

R. OSBORNE, *Greece in the Making, 1200–479 B.C.* (1996). An up-to-date, well-illustrated account of early Greek history.

S. PRICE, *Religions of the Ancient Greeks* (1999). A valuable survey from early times through the fifth century B.C.E.

R. SALLARES, *The Ecology of the Ancient Greek World* (1991). A valuable study of the Greeks and their environment.

D. M. SCHAPS, *Economic Rights of Women in Ancient Greece* (1981). Exploration of the economic conditions of ordinary free Greek women.

B. STRAUSS, *The Battle of Salamis: The Naval Encounter That Saved Greece—and Western Civilization* (2004). A lively account of the great Persian invasion of Greece.

C. G. THOMAS AND C. CONANT, *Citadel to City-State: The Transformation of Greece, 1200–700 B.C.E.* (1999). A good account of Greece's emergence from the Dark Ages into the world of the *polis*.

H. VAN WEES, *Greek Warfare: Myths and Realities* (2004). An account of Greek fighting that challenges traditional understandings.

Chapter 3

J. BUCKLER, *Aegean Greece in the Fourth Century BC* (2003). A political, diplomatic, and military history of the Aegean Greeks of the fourth century B.C.E.

W. BURKERT, *Greek Religion* (1985). A fine general study.

P. CARTLEDGE, *Alexander the Great: The Hunt for a New Past* (2004). A learned and lively biography.

P. CARTLEDGE, *Spartan Reflections* (2001). A collection of valuable essays by a leading scholar of ancient Sparta.

G. CAWKWELL, *Philip of Macedon* (1978). A brief but learned account of Philip's career.

Y. GARLAN, *Slavery in Ancient Greece* (1988). An up-to-date survey.

R. GARLAND, *Daily Life of the Ancient Greeks* (1998). A good account of the way the Greeks lived.

P. GREEN, *From Alexander to Actium* (1990). A brilliant synthesis of the Hellenistic period.

P. GREEN, *The Greco-Persian War* (1996). A lively account by a fine scholar with a keen feeling for the terrain.

E. S. GRUEN, *Heritage and Hellenism: The Reinvention of Jewish Tradition* (1998). A fine account of the interaction beteween Jews and Greeks in Hellenistic times.

C. D. HAMILTON, *Agesilaus and the Failure of Spartan Hegemony* (1991). An excellent biography of the king who was the central figure in Sparta during its domination in the fourth century B.C.E.

R. JUST, *Women in Athenian Law and Life* (1988). A good study of the place of women in Athenian life.

D. KAGAN, *The Peloponnesian War* (2003). An analytic narrative of the great war between Athens and Sparta.

D. KAGAN, *Pericles of Athens and the Birth of Athenian Democracy* (1991). An account of the life and times of the great Athenian statesman.

B. M. W. KNOX, *The Heroic Temper: Studies in Sophoclean Tragedy* (1964). A brilliant analysis of tragic heroism.

D. M. LEWIS, *Sparta and Persia* (1977). A valuable discussion of relations between Sparta and Persia in the fifth and fourth centuries B.C.E.

C. B. PATTERSON, *The Family in Greek History* (1998). An interesting interpretation of the relationship between family and state in ancient Greece.

J. J. POLLITT, *Art and Experience in Classical Greece* (1972). A scholarly and entertaining study of the relationship between art and history in Classical Greece, with excellent illustrations.

J. J. POLLITT, *Art in the Hellenistic Age* (1986). An extraordinary analysis that places the art in its historical and intellectual context.

R. W. SHARPLES, *Stoics, Epicureans, and Sceptics. An Introduction to Hellenistic Philosophy* (1996). A brief and useful introduction.

B. S. STRAUSS, *Athens after the Peloponnesian War* (1987). An excellent discussion of Athens's recovery and of the nature of Athenian society and politics in the fourth century B.C.E.

I. WORTHINGTON, *Demosthenes, Statesman and Orator* (2000). A useful collection of essays on the career and importance of the Athenian political leader.

Chapter 4

G. BARKER AND T. RASMUSSEN, *The Etruscans* (2000). A valuable new study of a mysterious people.

R. BAUMANN, *Women and Politics in Ancient Rome* (1995). A study of the role of women in Roman public life.

A. H. BERNSTEIN, *Tiberius Sempronius Gracchus: Tradition and Apostasy* (1978). An interpretation of Tiberius's place in Roman politics.

T. J. CORNELL, *The Beginnings of Rome: Italy and Rome from the Bronze Age to the Punic Wars* (1995). A fine new study of early Rome.

T. CORNELL AND J. MATTHEWS, *Atlas of the Roman World* (1982). Presents a comprehensive view of the Roman world in its physical and cultural setting.

J-M. DAVID, *The Roman Conquest of Italy* (1997). A good analysis of how Rome united Italy.

E. S. GRUEN, *The Hellenistic World and the Coming of Rome* (1984). A new interpretation of Rome's conquest of the eastern Mediterranean.

W. V. HARRIS, *War and Imperialism in Republican Rome, 327–70 B.C.E.* (1975). An analysis of Roman attitudes and intentions concerning imperial expansion and war.

T. HOLLAND, *Rubicon: The Last Years of the Roman Republic* (2004). A lively account of the fall of the republic.

S. LANCEL, *Carthage, A History* (1995). A good account of Rome's great competitor.

H. MOURITSEN, *Plebs and Politics in the Late Roman Republic* (2001). A new study of Roman republican politics and the place of the common people in them.

J. POWELL AND J. PATTERSON, *Cicero the Advocate* (2004). A careful study of the Roman statesman's legal career.

H. H. SCULLARD, *A History of the Roman World 753–146 B.C.E.*, 4th ed. (1980). An unusually fine narrative history with useful critical notes.

Chapter 5

W. BALL, *Rome in the East* (2000). A study of the eastern parts of the empire and how they interacted with the West.

A. A. BARRETT, *Livia: First Lady of Imperial Rome* (2004). Biography of Augustus's powerful and controversial wife.

P. BROWN, *The Rise of Western Christendom: Triumph and Diversity, 200–1000*, 2nd ed. (2003). A vivid picture of the spread of Christianity by a master of the field.

A. FERRILL, *The Fall of the Roman Empire, The Military Explanation* (1986). An interpretation that emphasizes the decline in the quality of the Roman army.

K. GALINSKY, *Augustan Culture* (1996). A work that integrates art, literature, and politics.

E. GIBBON, *The History of the Decline and Fall of the Roman Empire*, 2nd ed. 7 vols., ed. by J. B. Bury (1909–1914). A masterwork of the English language.

D. JOHNSTON, *Roman Law in Context* (2000). Places Rome's law in the context of its economy and society.

D. KAGAN, ED., *The End of the Roman Empire: Decline or Transformation?*, 3rd ed. (1992). A collection of essays on the problems of the decline and fall of the Roman Empire.

C. KELLY, *Ruling the Later Roman Empire* (2004). A study of the complexities of Roman government in the last centuries of the empire.

J. LENDON, *Empire of Honour: The Art of Government in the Roman World* (1997). A brilliant study that reveals how an aristocratic code of honor led the upper classes to cooperate in Roman rule.

R. W. MATHISON, *Roman Aristocrats in Barbarian Gaul: Strategies for Survival* (1993). An unusual slant on the late empire.

S. MATTERN, *Rome and the Enemy: Imperial Strategy in the Principate* (1999). A study of Rome's foreign and imperial policy under the Principate.

F. G. B. MILLAR, *The Emperor in the Roman World, 31 B.C.–A.D. 337* (1977). A study of Roman imperial government.

H. M. D. PARKER, *A History of the Roman World from A.D. 138 to 337* (1969). A good survey.

D. S. POTTER, *The Roman Empire at Bay: A.D. 180–395* (2004). An account of the challenges to Rome in the third and fourth centuries and how the Romans tried to meet them.

M. I. ROSTOVTZEFF, *Social and Economic History of the Roman Empire*, 2nd ed. (1957). A masterpiece whose main thesis is much disputed.

V. RUDICH, *Political Dissidence under Nero, The Price of Dissimulation* (1993). A brilliant exposition of the lives and thoughts of political dissidents in the early empire.

G. E. M. DE STE. CROIX, *The Class Struggle in the Ancient World* (1981). An ambitious interpretation of all of classical civilization from a Marxist perspective.

R. SYME, *The Roman Revolution* (1960). A brilliant study of Augustus, his supporters, and their rise to power.

Chapter 6

K. ARMSTRONG, *Muhammad: A Biography of the Prophet* (1992). Substantial popular biography.

G. BARRACLOUGH, *The Origins of Modern Germany* (1963). Originally published in 1946 and still the best survey of medieval Germany.

R. BARTLETT, *The Making of Europe* (1993). How migration and colonization created Europe.

G. W. BOWERSOCK ET AL., *Interpreting Late Antiquity: Essays on the Postclassical World* (2001). Introductory essays presenting a unified interpretation of the centuries between 250 C.E. and 800 C.E.

P. BROWN, *Augustine of Hippo: A Biography* (1967). Late antiquity seen through the biography of its greatest Christian thinker.

P. BROWN ET AL., EDS., *The Rise of Western Christendom: Triumph and Diversity* (1997). Sweeping, detailed summary.

VIRGINIA BURRUS, ED., *A Peoples' History of Christianity, II* (2005). Substantial and accessible.

R. COLLINS, *Charlemagne* (1998). Latest biography.

J. W. CURRIER, *Clovis, King of the Franks* (1997). Biography of founder of first Frankish dynasty.

F. L. GANSHOF, *Feudalism* (1964). The most profound brief analysis of the subject.

P. GODMAN ET AL., EDS., *Charlemagne's Heir: New Perspectives on Louis the Pious (814–40)* (1990). Latest research on the king whose divided kingdom set the boundaries of modern Europe.

S. GUTHRIE, *Arab Social Life in the Middle Ages* (1995). How Arab society holds itself together.

A. HOURANI, *A History of the Arab Peoples* (1991). Comprehensive with overviews of the origins and early history of Islam.

B. LEWIS, *The Middle East: A Brief History of the Last 2,000 Years* (1995). An authoritative overview.

R. MCKITTERICK, ED., *Carolingian Culture: Emulation and Innovation* (1994). The culture from which Western Europe was born.

R. J. MORRISSEY, *Charlemagne and France: A 1000 Years of Mythology* (2002). The European argument over who owns Charlemagne.

J. J. NORRIS, *Byzantium: The Decline and Fall* (1995). The final volume in an essential three-volume history of Byzantium.

P. RICHE, *The Carolingians: A Family Who Forged Europe* (1993). Readable account of the dynasty from start to finish.

P. SAWYER, *Kings and Vikings: Scandinavia and Europe A.D. 700–1100* (1994). Raiding Vikings and their impact on Europe.

W. WALTHER, *Woman in Islam* (1981). One hour spent with this book teaches more about the social import of Islam than days spent with others.

Chapter 7

J. W. BALDWIN, *The Government of Philip Augustus* (1986). The standard work.

S. FLANAGAN, *Hildegard of Bingen, 1098–1179: A Visionary Life* (1998). Latest biography of a powerful religious woman.

S. D. GOITEIN, *Letters of Medieval Jewish Traders* (1973). Rare first-person accounts.

E. M. HALLAM, *Capetian France 987–1328* (1980). Good on politics and heretics.

J. C. HOLT, *Magna Carta*, 2nd ed. (1992). Succeeding generations interpret the famous document.

K. LEYSER, *Medieval Germany and Its Neighbors, 900–1250* (1982). Basic and authoritative.

H. E. MAYER, *The Crusades,* trans. by John Gilligham (1972). The best one-volume account.

W. MELCZER, *The Pilgrim's Guide to Santiago de Compostela* (1993). Do's and dont's, and what the medieval pilgrim might expect along the way.

C. MORIARITY, ED., *The Voice of the Middle Ages: In Personal Letters, 1100–1500* (1989). Rare first-person accounts.

J. B. MORRALL, *Political Thought in Medieval Times* (1962). Readable, elucidating account.

J. RICHARD, *Saint Louis: Crusader King of France* (1992). Biography of Louis IX and an exploration of the mental, political, and religious world of the thirteenth century.

J. RILEY-SMITH, *The Oxford Illustrated History of the Crusades* (1995). Sweeping account.

C. TYERMAN, *Fighting for Christendom* (2004). Brief and accessible.

Chapter 8

E. AMT, ED., *Women's Lives in Medieval Europe: A Sourcebook* (1993). Outstanding collection of sources.

P. ARIES, *Centuries of Childhood: A Social History of Family Life* (1962). Influential pioneer effort on the subject.

J. W. BALDWIN, *The Scholastic Culture of the Middle Ages: 1000–1300* (1971). Good brief synthesis.

M. BLACK, *The Medieval Cookbook* (1992). Dishing it up in the Middle Ages.

M. T. CLANCHY, *Abelard: A Medieval Life* (1998). The biography of the famous philosopher and seducer of Héloïse.

L. GRANE, *Peter Abelard: Philosophy and Christianity in the Middle Ages* (1970). Places Abelard in his philosophieal and theological context.

B. A. HANAWALT, *Growing Up in Medieval London* (1993). Positive portrayal of parental and societal treatment of children.

D. HERLIHY, *Women, Family, and Society in Medieval Europe: Historical Essays, 1978–91* (1995). A major historian's collected essays.

A. HOPKINS, *Knights* (1990). Europe's warriors and models.

D. KRUEGER, ED., *Byzantine Christianity* (2006).

E. MALE, *The Gothic Image: Religious Art in France in the Thirteenth Century* (1913). An enduring classic.

L. DE MAUSE, ED., *The History of Childhood* (1974). Substantial essays on the inner as well as the material lives of children.

R. I. MOORE, *The Formation of a Persecuting Society: Power and Deviance in Western Europe, 950–1250* (1987). A sympathetic look at heresy and dissent.

J. T. NOONAN, *Contraception: A History of Its Treatment by the Catholic Theologians and Canonists* (1967). Fascinating account of medieval theologians' take on sex.

S. OZMENT, *Ancestors: The Loving Family in Old Europe* (2001). A sympathetic look at families past.

S. SHAHAR, *The Fourth Estate: A History of Women in the Middle Ages* (1983). A comprehensive survey, making clear the great variety of women's work.

Chapter 9

C. ALLMAND, *The Hundred Years' War: England and France at War, c. 1300–c. 1450* (1988). Overview of the war's development and consequences.

P. R. BACKSCHEIDER ET AL., EDS., *A Journal of the Plague Year* (1992). The Black Death at ground level.

R. BARBER, ED., *The Pastons: Letters of a Family in the War of the Roses* (1984). Rare revelations of English family life in an age of crisis.

E. H. GILLETT ET AL., *Life and Times of John Huss: The Bohemian Reformation of the Fifteenth Century* (2001). The latest biography.

J. HUIZINGA, *The Waning of the Middle Ages: A Study of the Forms of Life, Thought, and Art in France and the Netherlands in the Dawn of the Renaissance* (1924). Exaggerated, but engrossing study of mentality at the end of the Middle Ages.

P. KAHN ET AL., *Secret History of the Mongols: The Origins of Ghingis Kahn* (1998). Introduction to the greatest Mongol ruler.

S. OZMENT, *The Age of Reform, 1250–1550* (1980). Highlights of late medieval intellectual and religious history.

E. PERROY, *The Hundred Years' War,* trans. by W. B. Wells (1965). Still the most comprehensive one-volume account.

M. SPINKA, *John Huss's Concept of the Church* (1966). Lucid account of Hussite theology.

W. R. TRASK, ED./TRANS., *Joan of Arc in Her Own Words* (1996). Joan's interrogation and self-defense.

P. ZIEGLER, *The Black Death* (1969). Highly readable account.

Chapter 10

D. ABULAFIA, *The Discovery of Mankind: Atlantic Encounters in the Age of Columbus* (2008). Emphasizes contact between peoples in its exploration of European colonization of the Americas.

L. B. ALBERTI, *The Family in Renaissance Florence,* trans. by R. N. Watkins (1962). A contemporary humanist, who never married, explains how a family should behave.

K. ATCHITY, ED., *The Renaissance Reader* (1996). The Renaissance in its own words.

H. BARON, *The Crisis of the Early Italian Renaissance,* vols. 1 and 2 (1966). A major work on the civic dimension of Italian humanism.

G. A. BRUCKER, *Giovanni and Lusanna: Love and Marriage in Renaissance Florence* (1986). Love in the Renaissance shown to be more Bergman than Fellini.

J. BURCKHARDT, *The Civilization of the Renaissance in Italy* (1958). Modern edition of an old nineteenth-century classic that still has as many defenders as detractors.

R. E. CONRAD, *Children of God's Fire: A Documentary History of Black Slavery in Brazil* (1983). Not for the squeamish.

L. HANKE, *Bartholomé de Las Casas: An Interpretation of His Life and Writings* (1951). Biography of the great Dominican critic of Spanish exploitation of Native Americans.

J. HANKINS, *Plato in the Renaissance* (1992). A magisterial study of how Plato was read and interpreted by Renaissance scholars.

D. HERLIHY AND C. KLAPISCH-ZUBER, *Tuscans and Their Families* (1985). Important work based on unique demographic data that give the reader a new appreciation of quantitative history.

J. C. HUTCHISON, *Albrecht Dürer: A Biography* (1990). A solid biography of the German artist.

L. MARTINES, *Power and Imagination: City States in Renaissance Italy* (1980). Stimulating account of cultural and political history.

S. E. MORRISON, *Admiral of the Ocean Sea: A Life of Christopher Columbus* (1946). Still the best Columbus read.

E. PANOFSKY, *Meaning in the Visual Arts* (1955). Eloquent treatment of Renaissance art.

J. H. PARRY, *The Age of Reconnaissance* (1964). A comprehensive account of exploration in the years 1450 to 1650.

I. A. RICHTER, ED., *The Notebooks of Leonardo da Vinci* (1985). The master in his own words.

A. WHEATCROFT, *The Habsburgs* (1995). The dynasty that ruled the center of late medieval and early modern Europe.

C. C. WILLARD, *Christine de Pizan* (1984). Demonstration of what an educated woman could accomplish in the Renaissance.

Chapter 11

H. BLOOM, *Shakespeare: The Invention of the Human* (1998). An analysis of the greatest writer in the English language.

T. A. BRADY, JR., ED., *Handbook of European History: Late Middle Ages, Renaissance, Reformation* (1995). Essays summarizing recent research on aspects of the Reformation.

P. COLLINSON, *The Reformation* (2004). Portrays the Reformation as creating religious pluralism and civil liberty despite itself.

E. DUFFY, *The Stripping of the Altars: Traditional Religion in England, 1400–1580* (1992). Strongest of recent arguments that popular piety survived the Reformation in England.

M. DURAN, *Cervantes* (1974). Detailed biography.

B. S. GREGORY, *Salvation at Stake: Christian Martyrdom in Early Modern Europe* (1999). Massive, enthralling study of religion.

R. HOULBROOKE, *English Family Life, 1450–1716. An Anthology from Diaries* (1988). A rich collection of documents illustrating family relationships.

J. C. HUTCHISON, *Albrecht Dürer: A Biography* (1990). An art historian chronicles both the life and work of the artist.

H. JEDIN, *A History of the Council of Trent*, vols. 1 and 2 (1957–1961). Still the gold standard.

P. JOHNSTON AND R. W. SCRIBNER, *The Reformation in Germany and Switzerland* (1993). Reformation from the bottom up.

D. MACCOLLOCH, *The Reformation* (2004). Finds old Catholics and non-Protestant Evangelicals to be the forerunners of modern religion.

H. A. OBERMAN, *Luther: Man between God and the Devil* (1989). Perhaps the best account of Luther's life, by a Dutch master.

J. O'MALLEY, *The First Jesuits* (1993). Detailed account of the creation of the Society of Jesus and its original purposes.

S. OZMENT, *The Age of Reform, 1250–1550: An Intellectual and Religious History of Late Medieval and Reformation Europe* (1980). A broad survey of major religious ideas and beliefs.

B. ROBERTS, *Through the Keyhole: Dutch Child-Rearing Practices in the 17th and 18th Centuries* (1998). A study of three elite families.

Q. SKINNER, *The Foundations of Modern Political Thought II: The Age of Reformation* (1978). A comprehensive survey that treats every political thinker and tract.

D. STARKEY, *Elizabeth: The Struggle for the Throne* (2000). Details the early years of Elizabeth's life.

L. STONE, *The Family, Sex, and Marriage in England 1500–1800* (1977). Controversial, but enduring in many respects.

G. STRAUSS, ED. AND TRANS., *Manifestations of Discontent in Germany on the Eve of the Reformation* (1971). Rich collection of both rural and urban sources.

F. WENDEL, *Calvin: The Origins and Development of His Religious Thought*, trans. by P. Mairet (1963). The best treatment of Calvin's theology.

H. WUNDER, *He Is the Sun, She Is the Moon: A History of Women in Early Modern Germany* (1998). A model of gender history.

Chapter 12

F. BRAUDEL, *The Mediterranean and the Mediterranean World in the Age of Philip the Second*, vols. 1 and 2 (1976). Widely acclaimed "big picture" by a master historian.

N. Z. DAVIS, *Society and Culture in Early Modern France* (1975). Essays on popular culture.

R. DUNN, *The Age of Religious Wars, 1559–1689* (1979). Excellent brief survey of every major conflict.

J. H. FRANKLIN, ED. AND TRANS., *Constitutionalism and Resistance in the Sixteenth Century: Three Treatises by Hotman, Beza, and Mornay* (1969). Three defenders of the right to resist tyranny.

J. GUY, *Tudor England* (1990). The standard history and a good synthesis of recent scholarship.

D. LOADES, *Mary Tudor* (1989). Authoritative and good storytelling.

G. MATTINGLY, *The Armada* (1959). A masterpiece resembling a novel in style.

J. E. NEALE, *The Age of Catherine de Médicis* (1962). Short, concise summary.

A. SOMAN, ED., *The Massacre of St. Bartholomew's Day: Reappraisals and Documents* (1974). Essays from an international symposium on the anniversary of the massacre.

C. WEDGWOOD, *William the Silent* (1944). Eloquent political biography of William of Orange.

A. B. WEIR, *The Life of Elizabeth I* (1998). Detailed portrayal of a successful ruler.

J. WORMALD, *Mary, Queen of Scots: A Study in Failure* (1991). Mary portrayed as out of touch with her country and her times.

Chapter 13

W. BEIK, *Louis XIV and Absolutism: A Brief Study with Documents* (2000). An excellent collection by a major scholar of absolutism.

T. Blanning, *The Pursuit of Glory: Europe 1648–1815* (2007). The best recent synthesis of the emergence of the modern European state system.

J. BREWER, *The Sinews of Power: War, Money and the English State, 1688–1783* (1989). An important study of the financial basis of English power.

P. BURKE, *The Fabrication of Louis XIV* (1992). Examines how Louis XIV used art to forge his public image.

C. CLARK, *The Rise and Downfall of Prussia 1600–1947* (2006). A stunning survey.

R. CUST, *Charles I* (2007). The definitive biography.

P. COLLINSON, *The Religion of Protestants: The Church in English Society, 1559–1625* (1982). Remains the best introduction to Puritanism.

N. DAVIS, *God's Playground: A History of Poland: The Origins to 1795* (2005). The recent revision of a classic survey.

J. DE VRIES AND A. VAN DER WOUDE, *The First Modern Economy* (1997). Compares Holland to other European nations.

P. G. DWYER, *The Rise of Prussia 1700–1830* (2002). An excellent collection of essays.

S. FAROQHI, *The Ottoman Empire and the World Around It* (2006). Emphasizes the various interactions of the empire with both Asian and European powers.

R. I. FROST, *The Northern Wars: War, State and Society in Northeastern Europe, 1558–1721* (2000) A survey of an often neglected subject.

D. GOFFMAN, *The Ottoman Empire and Early Modern Europe* (2002). An accessible introduction to a complex subject.

T. HARRIS, *Restoration: Charles II and His Kingdom, 1660–1685* (2006). A major exploration of the tumultuous years of the restoration of the English monarchy after the civil war.

L. HUGHES, *Russia in the Age of Peter the Great* (2000). A major overview of the history and society of Peter's time.

C. IMBER, *The Ottoman Empire, 1300–1650: The Structure of Power* (2003). A sweeping analysis based on a broad range of sources.

C. J. INGRAO, *The Habsburg Monarchy, 1618–1815* (2000). The best recent survey.

J. I. ISRAEL, *The Dutch Republic: Its Rise, Greatness, and Fall, 1477–1806* (1995). The major work of the subject.

M. KISHLANSKY, *A Monarchy Transformed: Britain, 1603–1714* (1996). An important overview.

J. A. LYNN, *The Wars of Louis XIV* (1999). The best recent treatment.

J. LUKOWSKI AND H. ZAWADZKI, *A Concise History of Poland* (2006). A straightforward survey.

D. MCKAY, *The Great Elector: Frederick William of Brandenburg–Prussia* (2001). An account of the origins of Prussian power.

P. K. MONOD, *The Power of Kings: Monarchy and Religion in Europe, 1589–1715* (1999). An important and innovative examination of the roots of royal authority as early modern Europe became modern Europe.

G. PARKER, *The Military Revolution: Military Innovation and the Rise of the West (1500–1800)* (1988). A classic work on the impact of military matters on the emergence of centralized monarchies.

H. PHILLIPS, *Church and Culture in Seventeenth-Century France* (1997). A clear examination of the major religious issues confronting France and their relationship to the larger culture.

S. PINCUS, *England's Glorious Revolution 1688–1689: A Brief History with Documents* (2005). A useful collection by an outstanding historian of the subject.

G. TREASURE, *Louis XIV* (2001). The best, most accessible recent study.

Chapter 14

R. ASHCRAFT, *Revolutionary Politics and Locke's Two Treatises of Government* (1986). A major study emphasizing the radical side of Locke's thought.

J. BARRY, M. HESTER, AND G. ROBERTS, EDS., *Witchcraft in Early Modern Europe: Studies in Culture and Belief* (1998). A collection of recent essays.

M. BIAGIOLI, *Galileo Courtier: The Practice of Science in the Culture of Absolutism* (1993). A major revisionist work.

J. A. CONNER, *Kepler's Witch: An Astronomer's Discovery of Cosmic Order Amid Religious War, Political Intrigue, and the Heresy Trial of His Mother*

(2005). Fascinating account of Kepler's effort to vindicate his mother against charges of witchcraft.

P. DEAR, *Revolutionizing the Sciences: European Knowledge and Its Ambitions, 1500–1700* (2001). A broad-ranging study of both the ideas and institutions of the new science.

M. FEINGOLD, *The Newtonian Moment: Isaac Newton and the Making of Modern Culture* (2004). A superb, well-illustrated volume.

S. GAUKROGER, *The Emergence of a Scientific Culture: Science and the Shaping of Modernity* (2007). A challenging book exploring the differing understanding of natural knowledge in early modern European culture.

S. GAUKROGER, *Francis Bacon and the Transformation of Early-Modern Philosophy* (2001). An excellent, accessible introduction.

J. GLEIK, *Isaac Newton* (2003). Highly accessible to the general reader.

I. HARRIS, *The Mind of John Locke: A Study of Political Theory in Its Intellectual Setting* (1994). The most comprehensive recent treatment.

J. L. HEILBRON, *The Sun in the Church: Cathedrals as Solar Observatories* (2000). Explores uses made of Roman Catholic cathedrals to make astronomical observations.

K. J. HOWELL, *God's Two Books: Copernican Cosmology and Biblical Interpretation in Early Modern Science* (2002). The clearest discussion of this important subject.

L. JARDINE, *Ingenious Pursuits: Building the Scientific Revolution* (1999). A lively exploration of the interface of personalities, new knowledge, and English society.

A. C. KORS AND E. PETERS, EDS., *European Witchcraft, 1100–1700* (1972). Classics of witch belief.

T. S. KUHN, *The Copernican Revolution: Planetary Astronomy in the Development of Western Thought* (1957). Remains the classic work.

B. LEVACK, *The Witch Hunt in Early Modern Europe* (1986). Lucid survey.

P. MACHAMER, ED., *The Cambridge Companion to Galileo* (1998). Essays that aid the understanding of the entire spectrum of the new science.

J. MARSHALL, *John Locke, Toleration and Early Enlightenment Culture* (2006). A magisterial and challenging survey of the background of seventeenth-century arguments for and against toleration.

J. R. MARTIN, *Baroque* (1977). A classic introduction to baroque art.

M. OSLER, *Rethinking the Scientific Revolution* (2000). A collection of revisionist essays particularly exploring issues of the interrelationship of the new science and religion.

R. POPKIN, *The History of Scepticism: From Savonarola to Bayle* (2003). A classic study of the fear of loss of intellectual certainty.

L. PYENSON AND S. SHEETS-PYENSON, *Servants of Nature: A History of Scientific Institutions, Enterprises, and Sensibilities* (1999). A history of the settings in which the creation and diffusion of scientific knowledge have occurred.

J. REPCHECK, *Copernicus' Secret: How the Scientific Revolution Began* (2007). A highly accessible biography of Copernicus.

L. SCHIEBINGER, *The Mind Has No Sex? Women in the Origins of Modern Science* (1989). A major study of the subject.

S. SHAPIN, *The Scientific Revolution* (1996). A readable brief introduction.

W. R. SHEA AND M. ARTIGAS, *Galileo in Rome: The Rise and Fall of a Troublesome Genius* (2003). Argues that Galileo in part brought about his own condemnation.

T. SORELL, *The Cambridge Companion to Hobbes* (1994). Excellent essays on the major themes of Hobbes's thought.

Chapter 15

J. BLUM, *Lord and Peasant in Russia from the Ninth to the Nineteenth Century* (1961). Remains a classic discussion.

J. BURNET, *Gender, Work and Wages in Industrial Revolution Britain* (2008). A major revisionist study of the wage structure for work by men and women.

P. M. DEANE, *The First Industrial Revolution* (1999). A well-balanced and systematic treatment.

P. EARLE, *The Making of the English Middle Class: Business, Community, and Family Life in London, 1660–1730* (1989). The most careful study of the subject.

M. W. FLINN, *The European Demographic System, 1500–1820* (1981). Remains a major summary.

E. HOBSBAWM, *Industry and Empire: The Birth of the Industrial Revolution* (1999). A survey by a major historian of the subject.

K. HONEYMAN, *Women, Gender and Industrialization in England, 1700–1850* (2000). Emphasizes how certain work or economic roles became associated with either men or women.

O. H. HUFTON, *The Poor of Eighteenth-Century France, 1750–1789* (1975). A brilliant study of poverty and the family economy.

A. KAHAN, *The Plow, the Hammer, and the Knout: An Economic History of Eighteenth-Century Russia* (1985). An extensive and detailed treatment.

D. I. KERTZER AND M. BARBAGLI, *The History of the European Family: Family Life in Early Modern Times, 1500–1709* (2001). Broad-ranging essays covering the entire Continent.

S. KING AND G. TIMMONS, *Making Sense of the Industrial Revolution: English Economy and Society, 1700–1850* (2001). Examines the Industrial Revolution through the social institutions that brought it about and were changed by it.

F. E. MANUEL, *The Broken Staff: Judaism Through Christian Eyes* (1992). An important discussion of Christian interpretations of Judaism.

K. MORGAN, *The Birth of Industrial Britain: Social Change, 1750–1850* (2004). A useful brief overview.

M. OVERTON, *Agricultural Revolution in England: The Transformation of the Agrarian Economy, 1500–1850* (1996). A highly accessible treatment.

J. R. RUFF, *Violence in Early Modern Europe 1500–1800* (2001). An excellent survey of an important and disturbing topic.

P. STEARNS, *The Industrial Revolution in World History* (2007). A broad interpretive account.

D. VALENZE, *The First Industrial Woman* (1995). An elegant, penetrating volume.

E. A. WRIGLEY, *Continuity, Chance and Change: The Character of the Industrial Revolution in England* (1994). A major conceptual reassessment.

Chapter 16

F. ANDERSON, *Crucible of War: The Seven Years' War and the Fate of Empire in British North America, 1754–1766* (2001). A splendid narrative account.

B. BAILYN, *The Ideological Origins of the American Revolution* (1992). An important work illustrating the role of English radical thought in the perceptions of the colonists.

C. A. BAYLY, *Imperial Meridian: The British Empire and the World, 1780–1830* (1989). A major study of the empire after the loss of America.

I. BERLIN, *Many Thousands Gone: The First Two Centuries of Slavery in North America* (1998). The most extensive recent treatment emphasizing the differences in the slave economy during different decades.

R. BLACKBURN, *The Making of New World Slavery from the Baroque to the Modern, 1492–1800* (1997). An extraordinary work.

M. A. BURKHOLDER AND L. L. JOHNSON, *Colonial Latin America* (2004). A standard synthesis.

L. COLLEY, *Britons: Forging the Nation, 1707–1837* (1992). Important discussions of the recovery from the loss of America.

D. B. DAVIS, *Inhuman Bondage: The Rise and Fall of Slavery in the New World* (2006). A splendid overview by a leading scholar.

D. B. DAVIS, *The Problem of Slavery in the Age of Revolution, 1770–1823* (1975). A major work on both European and American history.

J. ELLIOTT, *Empires of the Atlantic: Britain and Spain in America 1492–1830* (2006). A brilliant and accessible comparative history.

J. J. ELLIS, *His Excellency: George Washington* (2004). A biography that explores the entire era of the American Revolution.

R. HARMS, *The Diligent: A Voyage through the Worlds of the Slave Trade* (2002). A powerful narrative of the voyage of a French slave trader.

H. S. KLEIN, *The Atlantic Slave Trade* (1999). A succinct synthesis based on recent literature.

P. LANGFORD, *A Polite and Commercial People: England, 1717–1783* (1989). An excellent survey covering social history, politics, the overseas wars, and the American Revolution.

P. MAIER, *American Scripture: Making the Declaration of Independence* (1997). Replaces previous works on the subject.

A. PAGDEN, *Lords of All the World: Ideologies of Empire in Spain, Britain, and France, 1492–1830* (1995). One of the few comparative studies of the empires during this period.

M. REDIKER, *The Slave Ship: A Human History* (2007). An exploration of the harrowing experience of slave transportation across the Atlantic.

M. REDIKER, *Villains of All Nations: Atlantic Pirates in the Golden Age* (2008). A serious historical treatment of the subject.

J. THORNTON, *Africa and the Africans in the Making of the Atlantic World, 1400–1800*, 2nd ed. (1998). A discussion of the role of Africans in the emergence of the transatlantic economy.

J. WINIK, *The Great Upheaval: America and the Birth of the Modern World, 1788–1800* (2007). Sets the founding of the American republic in a transatlantic political context.

G. S. WOOD, *The American Revolution: A History* (2002). A major interpretation.

Chapter 17

D. D. BIEN, *The Calas Affair: Persecution, Toleration, and Heresy in Eighteenth-Century Toulouse* (1960). The standard treatment of the famous case.

T. C. W. BLANNING, *The Culture of Power and the Power of Culture: Old Regime Europe 1660–1789* (2002). A remarkable synthesis of the interaction of political power and culture in France, Prussia, and Austria.

P. BLOOM, *Enlightening the World: Encyclopedie, The Book That Changed the Course of History* (2005). A lively, accessible introduction.

J. BUCHAN, *Crowded with Genius: The Scottish Enlightenment* (2003). A lively, accessible introduction.

L. DAMROSCH, *Rousseau: Restless Genius* (2007). The best recent biography.

I. DE MADARIAGA, *Russia in the Age of Catherine the Great* (1981). The best discussion in English.

S. FEINER, *The Jewish Enlightenment* (2002). An extensive, challenging pan-European treatment of the subject.

P. GAY, *The Enlightenment: An Interpretation*, 2 vols. (1966, 1969). A classic.

D. GOODMAN, *The Republic of Letters: A Cultural History of the French Enlightenment* (1994). Concentrates on the role of salons.

C. HESSE, *The Other Enlightenment: How French Women Became Modern* (2004). Explores the manner in which French women authors created their own sphere of thought and cultural actiavity.

J. ISRAEL, *Enlightenment Contested: Philosophy, Modernity, and the Emancipation of Man 1670–1752* (2006). A challenging major revisionist history of the subject.

J. I. ISRAEL, *Radical Enlightenment: Philosophy and the Making of Modernity* (2001). A controversial account of the most radical strains of thought in Enlightenment culture.

C. A. KORS, *Encyclopedia of the Enlightenment* (2002). A major reference work on all of the chief intellectual themes of the era.

J. P. LEDONNE, *The Russian Empire and the World, 1700–1917* (1996). Explores the major reasons for Russian expansion from the eighteenth to the early twentieth centuries.

G. MACDONAGH, *Frederick the Great* (2001). A thoughtful and accessible biography.

D. MACMAHON, *Enemies of the Enlightenment: The French Counter-Enlightenment and the Making of Modernity* (2001). A fine exploration of French writers critical of the *philosophes*.

J. V. H. MELTON, *The Rise of the Public in Enlightenment Europe* (2001). Explores the social basis of print culture with an excellent bibliography.

S. MUTHU, *Enlightenment Against Empire* (2003). A challenging volume covering the critique of the empire.

R. PEASON, *Voltaire Almighty: A Life in Pursuit of Freedom* (2005). An accessible biography

R. PORTER, *The Creation of the Modern World: The Untold Story of the British Enlightenment* (2000). Seeks to shift the center of the Enlightenment from France to England.

P. RILEY, *The Cambridge Companion to Rousseau* (2001). Excellent accessible essays by major scholars.

E. ROTHCHILD, *Economic Sentiments: Adam Smith, Condorcet, and the Enlightenment* (2001). A sensitive account of Smith's thought and its relationship to the social questions of the day.

J. SHEEHAN, *The Enlightenment Bible* (2007). Explores the Enlightenment treatment of the Bible.

S. SMITH, *Spinoza, Liberalism, and the Question of Jewish Identity* (1997). A clear introduction to a challenging thinker.

A. M. WILSON, *Diderot* (1972). A splendid biography of the person behind the *Encyclopedia* and other major Enlightenment publications.

L. WOLFF, *Inventing Eastern Europe: The Map of Civilization on the Mind of the Enlightenment* (1994). A remarkable study of how Enlightenment writers recast the understanding of this part of the Continent.

Chapter 18

D. ANDRESS, *The Terror: The Merciless War for Freedom in Revolutionary France* (2006). The best recent survey of the reign of terror.

N. ASTON, *Christianity and Revolutionary Europe c. 1750–1830* (2002). Continent-wide survey of the impact of revolution on religion.

T. C. BLANNING, *The Revolutionary Wars, 1787–1802* (1996). Essential for understanding the role of the army and the revolution.

S. DESAN, *The Family on Trial in Revolutionary France* (2004). An important analysis of how the revolution impacted French domestic life.

W. DOYLE, *The Oxford History of the French Revolution* (2003). A broad, complex narrative with an excellent bibliography.

A. FORREST, *Revolutionary Paris, the Provinces and the French Revolution* (2004). A clear presentation of the tensions between the center of the revolution and the provinces.

C. HAYDEN AND W. DOYLE, EDS., *Robespierre* (1999). Essays evaluating Robespierre's ideas, career, and reputation.

P. HIGONNET, *Goodness beyond Virtue: Jacobins During the French Revolution* (1998). An outstanding work that clearly relates political values to political actions.

D. JORDON, *The King's Trial: Louis XVI vs. the French Revolution* (1979). A gripping account of the event.

E. KENNEDY, *A Cultural History of the French Revolution* (1989). An important examination of the role of the arts, schools, clubs, and intellectual institutions.

S. E. MELZER AND L. W. RABINE, EDS., *Rebel Daughters: Women and the French Revolution* (1997). Essays exploring the role and image of women in the revolution.

S. NEELY, *A Concise History of the French Revolution* (2008). The best of the numerous brief accounts.

C. C. O'BRIEN, *The Great Melody: A Thematic Biography of Edmund Burke* (1992). A deeply thoughtful biography

R. R. PALMER, *The Age of Democratic Revolution: A Political History of Europe and America, 1760–1800*, 2 vols. (1959, 1964). Still an impressive survey of the political turmoil in the transatlantic world.

M. PRICE, *The Road from Versailles: Louis XVI, Marie Antoinette, and the Fall of the French Monarchy* (2004). A lively narrative that brings the personalities of the king and queen into focus.

R. SCURR, *Fatal Purity: Robespierre and the French Revolution* (2007). A compelling analysis of a personality long difficult to understand.

T. TACKETT, *Becoming a Revolutionary: The Deputies of the French National Assembly and the Emergence of a Revolutionary Culture (1789–1790)* (1996). The best study of the early months of the revolution.

Chapter 19

M. H. ABRAMS, *The Mirror and the Lamp: Romantic Theory and the Critical Tradition* (1958). A classic on romantic literary theory.

E. BEHLER, *German Romantic Literary Theory* (1993). A clear introduction to a difficult subject.

D. BELL, *The First Total War: Napoleon's Europe and the Birth of Warfare as We Know It* (2007). A consideration of the Napoleonic conflicts and the culture of warfare.

G. E. BENTLEY, *The Stranger from Paradise: A Biography of William Blake* (2001). Now the standard work.

N. BOYLE, *Goethe* (2001). A challenging two-volume biography.
M. BROERS, *Europe under Napoleon 1799–1815* (2002). Examines the subject from the standpoint of those Napoleon conquered.
T. CHAPMAN, *Congress of Vienna: Origins, Processes, and Results* (1998). A clear introduction to the major issues.
P. DWYER, *Napoleon: The Path to Power, 1769–1799* (2008). A major study of the subject.
P. DWYER, *Talleyrand* (2002). A useful account of his diplomatic influence.
S. ENGLUND, *Napoleon: A Political Life* (2004). A thoughtful recent biography.
C. ESDAILE, *The Peninsular War: A New History* (2003). A narrative of the Napoleonic wars in Spain.
A. FORREST, *Napoleon's Men: The Soldiers of the Revolution and Empire* (2002). An examination of the troops rather than their commander.
H. HONOUR, *Romanticism* (1979). Still the best introduction to romantic art, well illustrated.
F. KAGAN, *The End of the Old Order: Napoleon and Europe, 1801–1805* (2006). A masterful narrative.
S. KÖRNER, *Kant* (1955). A classic brief, clear introduction.
J. LUSVASS, *Napoleon on the Art of War* (2001). A collection of Napoleon's own writings.
J. J. MCGANN AND J. SODERHOLM, EDS., *Byron and Romanticism* (2002). Essays on the poet who most embodied romantic qualities to the people of his time.
R. MUIR, *Tactics and the Experience of Battle in the Age of Napoleon* (1998). A splendid account of troops in battle.
T. PINKARD, *Hegel: A Biography* (2000). A long but accessible study.
N. ROE, *Romanticism: An Oxford Guide* (2005). A series of informative essays.
P. W. SCHROEDER, *The Transformation of European Politics, 1763–1848* (1994). A major synthesis of the diplomatic history of the period, emphasizing the new departures of the Congress of Vienna.
I. WOLOCH, *Napoleon and His Collaborators: The Making of a Dictatorship* (2001). A key study by one of the major scholars of the subject.
A. ZAMOYSKI, *Rites of Peace: The Fall of Napoleon and the Congress of Vienna* (2007). A lively analysis and narrative.

Chapter 20

B. ANDERSON, *Imagined Communities*, rev. ed. (2006). An influential and controversial discussion of nationalism.
M. S. BELL, *Toussaint Louverture: A Biography* (2007). An outstanding new biography.
M. BERDAHL, *The Politics of the Prussian Nobility: The Development of a Conservative Ideology, 1770–1848* (1988). A major examination of German conservative outlooks.
A. BRIGGS, *The Making of Modern England* (1959). Classic survey of English history during the first half of the nineteenth century.
A. CRAITU, *Liberalism under Siege: The Political Thought of the French Doctrinaires* (2003). An outstanding study of early-nineteenth-century French liberalism.
M. F. CROSS AND D. WILLIAMS, EDS., *French Experience from Republic to Monarchy, 1792–1824: New Dawns in Politics, Knowledge and Culture* (2000). Essays on French culture from the revolution through the restoration.
D. DAKIN, *The Struggle for Greek Independence* (1973). An excellent explanation of the Greek independence question.
L. DUBOIS, *Avengers of the New World: The Story of the Haitian Revolution* (2004). An analytic narrative likely to replace others.
E. J. EVANS, *Britain Before the Reform Act: Politics and Society, 1815–1832* (2008). Explores the forces that resisted and pressed for reform.
W. FORTESCUE, *Revolution and Counter-Revolution in France, 1815–1852* (2002). A helpful brief survey.
E. GELLNER, *Nations and Nationalism* (1983). A classic theoretical work.
L. GREENFELD, *Nationalism: Five Roads to Modernity* (1992). A major comparative study.
R. HARVEY, *Liberators: Latin America's Struggle for Independence* (2002). An excellent, lively treatment.
E. J. HOBSBAWM, *Nations and Nationalism since 1780: Programme, Myth, Reality*, rev. ed. (1992). Emphasizes intellectual factors.
C. JELAVICH AND B. JELAVICH, *The Establishment of the Balkan National States, 1804–1920* (1987). A standard survey.
G. A. KELLY, *The Humane Comedy: Constant, Tocqueville, and French Liberalism* (2007). The best introduction to the subject.
M. B. LEVINGER, *Enlightened Nationalism: The Transformation of Prussian Political Culture, 1806–1848* (2002). A clear and expansive coverview on the most recent scholarship.
J. LYNCH, *Simon Bolivar: A Life* (2006). Now the standard biography.
C. A. MACARTNEY, *The Habsburg Empire, 1790–1918* (1971). Remains an important survey.
N. V. RIASANOVSKY, *Nicholas I and Official Nationality in Russia, 1825–1855* (1959). Remains a lucid discussion of the conservative ideology that made Russia the major opponent of liberalism.
J. SHEEHAN, *German History, 1770–1866* (1989). A long work that is now the best available survey of the subject.
A. SKED, *Metternich and Austria: An Evaluation* (2008). A thoughtful restoration of Metternich to the position of leading diplomat of his age.
A. B. ULAM, *Russia's Failed Revolutionaries* (1981). Contains a useful discussion of the Decembrists as a background for other nineteenth-century Russian revolutionary activity.
B. WILSON, *The Making of Victorian Values: Decency and Dissent in Britain: 1789–1837* (2007). A very lively overview of the cultural factors shaping early-nineteenth-century British society.

Chapter 21

B. S. ANDERSON AND J. P. ZINSSER, *A History of Their Own: Women in Europe from Prehistory to the Present*, vol. 2 (1988). A wide-ranging survey.
I. BERLIN, *Karl Marx: His Life and Environment*, 4th ed. (1996). A classic introduction.
R. B. CARLISLE, *The Proffered Crown: Saint-Simonianism and the Doctrine of Hope* (1987). The best treatment of the broad social doctrines of Saint-Simonianism.
J. COFFIN, *The Politics of Women's Work* (1996). Examines the subject in France.
I. DEAK, *The Lawful Revolution: Louis Kossuth and the Hungarians, 1848–1849* (1979). The most significant study of the topic in English.
R. J. EVANS, *The Revolutions in Europe, 1848–1849: From Reform to Reaction* (2002). A series of essays by major expterts.
J. F. C. HARRISON, *Quest for the New Moral World: Robert Owen and the Owenites in Britain and America* (1969). The standard work.
D. I. KERTZER AND M. BARBAGLI, EDS., *Family Life in the Long Nineteenth Century, 1789–1913: The History of the European Family* (2002). Wide-ranging collection of essays.
K. KOLAKOWSKI, *Main Currents of Marxism: Its Rise, Growth, and Dissolution*, 3 vols. (1978). A classic, comprehensive survey.
D. LANDES, *The Unbound Prometheus: Technological Change and Industrial Development in Western Europe from 1750 to the Present* (1969). Classic one-volume treatment of technological development in a broad social and economic context.
H. PERKIN, *The Origins of Modern English Society, 1780–1880* (1969). A provocative attempt to look at the society as a whole.
J. D. RANDERS-PEHRSON, *Germans and the Revolution of 1848–1849* (2001). An exhaustive treatment of the subject.
W. H. SEWELL, JR., *Work and Revolution in France: The Language of Labor from the Old Regime to 1848* (1980). A fine analysis of French artisans.
J. SPERBER, *The European Revolution, 1841–1851* (2005). An excellent synthesis.
E. P. THOMPSON, *The Making of the English Working Class* (1964). A classic work.
F. WHEEN, *Karl Marx: A Life* (2001). An accessible work that emphasizes the contradictions in Marx's career and personality.

D. WINCH, *Riches and Poverty: An Intellectual History of Political Economy in Britain, 1750–1834* (1996). A superb survey from Adam Smith through Thomas Malthus.

Chapter 22

V. AKSAN, *Ottoman Wars, 1700–1870: An Empire Besieged* (2007). Explores the impact of war on the weakening of the Ottoman Empire.

R. ALDOUS, *The Lion and the Unicorn: Gladstone vs. Disraeli* (2008). An accessible volume tracing the great political rivalry of the mid-Victorian age.

I. T. BEREND, *History Derailed: Central and Eastern Europe in the Long Nineteenth Century* (2003). The best one-volume treatment of the complexities of this region.

P. BEW, *Ireland: The Politics of Enmity 1789–2006* (2007). A major, new, outstanding survey of the sweep of modern Irish history.

E. F. BIAGINI, *British Democracy and Irish Nationalism 1876–1906* (2007). Explores impact of the Irish question on British political structures themselves.

D. BLACKBOURN, *The Long Nineteenth Century: A History of Germany, 1780–1918* (1998). An outstanding survey.

R. BLAKE, *Disraeli* (1967). Remains the best biography.

J. BREUILLY, *Austria, Prussia and Germany, 1806–1871* (2002). Examines the complex relations of these states leading up to German unification.

C. CLARK, *Iron Kingdom: The Rise and Downfall of Prussia, 1600–1947* (2006). Now the standard survey.

M. CLARK, *The Italian Risorgimento* (1998). A brief overview.

R. B. EDGERTON, *Death or Glory: The Legacy of the Crimean War* (2000). Multifaceted study of a mismanaged war that transformed European politics.

C. J. EICHNER, *Surmounting the Barricades: Women in the Paris Commune* (2004). Explores the impact of women's journalism and organizing in the Commune and wider radical political tradition.

B. EKLOF AND J. BUSHNELL, *Russia's Great Reforms, 1855–1881* (1994). A clear analysis.

M. A. HANIOGLU, *A Brief History of the Late Ottoman Empire* (2008). An accessible introduction.

R. KEE, *The Green Flag: A History of Irish Nationalism* (2001). A lively, accessible account.

D. LANGEWIESCHE, *Liberalism in Germany* (1999). A broad survey that is particularly good on the problems unification caused for German Liberals.

H. C. G. MATTHEW, *Gladstone, 1809–1898* (1998). A superb biography.

D. MOON, *Abolition of Serfdom in Russia: 1762–1907* (2001). Analysis with docments.

W. G. MOSS, *Russia in the Age of Alexander II, Tolstoy and Dostoyevsky* (2002). Emphaises the cultural background.

N. M. NAIMARK, *Terrorists and Social Democrats: The Russian Revolutionary Movement under Alexander III* (1983). Useful discussion of a complicated subject.

P. G. NORD, *The Republican Moment: Struggles for Democracy in Nineteenth-Century France* (1996). A major examination of nineteenth-century French political culture.

J. PARRY, *The Politics of Patriotism: English Liberalism, National Identity and Europe, 1830–1886* (2006). An excellent overview of English Liberalism and how its values determined mid-Victorian relations with the Continent.

J. P. PARRY, *The Rise and Fall of Liberal Government in Victorian Britain* (1994). An outstanding study.

O. PFLANZE, *Bismarck and the Development of Germany*, 3 vols. (1990). A major biography and history of Germany for the period.

R. PRICE, *The French Second Empire: An Anatomy of Political Power* (2001). This volume along with the following title are the most comprehensive recent study.

R. PRICE, *People and Politics in France, 1848–1870* (2004). Examines the rise of Louis Napoleon Bonaparte and his use of political power.

E. RADZINSKY, *Alexander II: The Last Great Tsar* (2005). An accessible biography.

L. RIALL, *Garibaldi: Invention of a Hero* (2007). An exploration of a nationalist hero's reputation in his own day and later.

A. SCIROCCO, *Garibaldi: Citizen of the World: A Biography* (2007). An admiring account.

D. SHAFER, *The Paris Commune: French Politics, Culture, and Society at the Crossroads of the Revolutionary Tradition and Revolutionary Socialism* (2005). Excellent in relating the Commune to previous and later revolutionary traditions.

A. SKED, *Decline and Fall of the Habsburg Empire 1815–1918* (2001). A major, accessible survey of a difficult subject.

D. M. SMITH, *Cavour* (1984). An excellent biography.

Chapter 23

A. ASCHER, *P. A. Stolypin: The Search for Stability in Late Imperial Russia* (2000). A broad-ranging biography based on extensive research.

P. BIRNBAUM, *Jewish Destinies: Citizenship, State, and Community in Modern France* (2000). Explores the subject from the French Revolution to the present.

T. W. CLYMAN AND J. VOWLES, *Russia through Women's Eyes: Autobiographies from Tsarist Russia* (1996). A splendid collection of relatively brief memoirs.

G. CROSSICK AND S. JAUMAIN, EDS., *Cathedrals of Consumption: The European Department Store, 1850–1939* (1999). Essays on the development of a new mode of distribution of consumer goods.

D. ELLENSON, *After Emancipation: Jewish Religious Responses to Modernity* (2004). A volume that explores numerous examples of this response across Europe.

A. GEIFMAN, *Thou Shalt Kill: Revolutionary Terrorism in Russia, 1894–1917* (1993). An examination of political violence in late imperial Russia.

R. F. HAMILTON, *Marxism, Revisionism, and Leninism: Explication, Assessment, and Commentary* (2000). A contribution by a historically minded sociologist.

J. HARSIN, *Policing Prostitution in Nineteenth-Century Paris* (1985). A major study of this significant subject in French social history.

G. HIMMELFARB, *Poverty and Compassion: The Moral Imagination of the Late Victorians* (1991). The best examination of late Victorian social thought.

E. HOBSBAWM, *The Age of Empire, 1875–1914* (1987). A stimulating survey that covers cultural as well as political developments.

S. S. HOLTON, *Feminism and Democracy: Women's Suffrage and Reform Politics in Britain, 1900–1918* (1986). An excellent treatment of the subject.

T. HOPPEN, *The Mid-Victorian Generation, 1846–1886* (1998). The most extensive treatment of the subject.

S. KOVIN, *Slumming: Sexual and Social Politics in Victorian London* (2004). Explores the complexities of the extension of charity and social services in late Victorian London.

M. MALIA, *Russia under Western Eyes: From the Bronze Horseman to the Lenin Mausoleum* (2000). A brilliant work on how Western intellectuals understood Russia.

E. D. RAPPAPORT, *Shopping for Pleasure: Women in the Making of London's West End* (2001). A study of the rise of department stores in London.

H. ROGGER, *Jewish Policies and Right-Wing Politics in Imperial Russia* (1986). A learned examination of Russian anti-Semitism.

M. L. ROZENBLIT, *The Jews of Vienna, 1867–1914: Assimilation and Identity* (1983). Covers the cultural, economic, and political life of Viennese Jews.

R. SERVICE, *Lenin: A Biography* (2002). Based on new sources and will no doubt become the standard biography.

D. SORKIN, *The Transformation of German Jewry, 1780–1840* (1987). An examination of Jewish emancipation in Germany.

G. P. STEENSON, *Not One Man! Not One Penny!: German Social Democracy, 1863–1914* (1999). An extensive survey.

N. STONE, *Europe Transformed* (1984). A sweeping survey that emphasizes the difficulties of late-nineteenth-century liberalism.

A. THORPE, *A History of the British Labour Party* (2001). From its inception to the twenty-first century.

J. R. WALKOWITZ, *Prostitution and Victorian Society: Women, Class, and the State* (1980). A work of great insight and sensitivity.

Chapter 24

C. ALLEN, *The Human Christ: The Search for the Historical Jesus* (1998). A broad survey of the issue for the past two centuries.

M. D. BIDDIS, *Father of Racist Ideology: The Social and Political Thought of Count Gobineau* (1970). Sets the subject in the more general context of nineteenth-century thought.

P. BOWLER, *Evolution: The History of an Idea* (2003). An outstanding survey.

J. BROWNE, *Charles Darwin*, 2 vols. (1995, 2002). A stunning biography.

J. BURROW, *The Crisis of Reason: European Thought, 1848–1914* (2000). The best overview available.

F. J. COPPA, *The Modern Papacy since 1789* (1999). A straightforward survey.

F. J. COPPA, *Politics and Papacy in the Modern World* (2008). A broad-ranging exploration.

B. DENVIR, *Post-Impressionism* (1992). A brief introduction.

M. FRANCIS, *Herbert Spence and the Invention of Modern Life* (2007). Now the standard biography.

P. GAY, *Modernism: The Lure of Heresy* (2007). A broad interdisciplinary exploration.

R. HARRIS, *Lourdes: Body and Soul in a Secular Age* (1999). A sensitive discussion of Lourdes in its religious and cultural contexts.

R. HELMSTADTER, ED., *Freedom and Religion in the Nineteenth Century* (1997). Major essays on the relationship of church and state.

J. HODGE AND G. RADICK, *The Cambridge Companion to Darwin* (2003). A far-ranging collection of essays with a good bibliography.

A. HOURANI, *Arab Thought in the Liberal Age 1789–1939* (1967). A classic account, clearly written and accessible to the nonspecialist.

J. KÖHLER, *Zarathustra's Secret: The Interior Life of Friedrich Nietzsche* (2002). A controversial new biography.

W. LACQUEUR, *A History of Zionism* (2003). The most extensive one-volume treatment.

M. LEVENSON, *The Cambridge Companion to Modernism* (1999). Excellent essays on a wide range of subjects.

B. LIGHTMAN, *Victorian Popularizers of Science: Designing Nature for New Audiences* (2007). A study that adds numerous new dimensions to the subject.

G. MAKARI, *Revolution in Mind: The Creation of Psychoanalysis* (2008). A major, multidimensional survey.

A. PAIS, *Subtle Is the Lord: The Science and Life of Albert Einstein* (1983). The most accessible biography.

P. G. J. PULZER, *The Rise of Political Anti-Semitism in Germany and Austria* (1989). A sound discussion of anti-Semitism and central European politics.

F. QUINN, *The Sum of All Heresies: The Image of Islam in Western Thought* (2008). An interesting and clear overview of this important subject.

R. ROSENBLUM, *Cubism and 20th Century Art* (2001). A well-informed introduction.

C. E. SCHORSKE, *Fin de Siècle Vienna: Politics and Culture* (1980). Classic essays on the creative intellectual climate of Vienna.

W. SMITH, *Politics and the Sciences of Culture in Germany, 1840–1920* (1991). A major survey of the interaction between science and the social sciences.

F. M. TURNER, *Contesting Cultural Authority: Essays in Victorian Intellectual Life* (1993). Explorations in issues relating to Victorian science and religion.

D. VITAL, *A People Apart: The Jews in Europe 1789–1939* (1999). A broad and deeply researched volume.

A. N. WILSON, *God's Funeral* (1999). Explores the thinkers who contributed to religious doubt during the nineteenth and twentieth centuries.

Chapter 25

M. ADAS, *Machines as the Measure of Men: Science, Technology, and Ideologies of Western Dominance* (1989). The best single volume on racial thinking and technological advances as forming ideologies of European colonial dominance.

R. ALDRICH, *Greater France: A History of French Overseas Expansion* (1996). Remains the best overview.

C. BAYLY, *Imperial Meridian: The British Empire and the World: 1780–1830* (1989). Places the British expansion in India into larger imperial contexts.

D. BROWER, *Turkestan and the Fate of the Russian Empire* (2003). A concise treatment of a case study in Russian imperialism in Asia.

A. BURTON, *Burdens of History: British Feminists, Indian Women, and Imperial Culture, 1865–1915* (1994). Explores the relationship of women in Britain's Indian empire.

A. CONKLIN, *A Mission to Civilize: The Republican Idea of Empire in France and West Africa, 1895–1930* (2000). An in-depth analysis of a case history of the civilizing mission.

F. COOPER AND A. L. STOLER, EDS., *Tensions of Empire: Colonial Cultures in a Bourgeois World* (1997). Explores difficulties of accommodating ideas and realities of empire to domestic middle-class values and outlooks.

J. COX, *Imperial Fault Lines: Christianity and Colonial Power in India, 1818–1940* (2002). The best treatment of British missionaries in India.

J. P. DAUGHTON, *An Empire Divided: Religion, Republicanism, and the Making of French Colonialism, 1880–1914* (2008). A superb discussion of the interaction of religion, empire, and domestic French politics.

N. P. DIRKS, *The Scandal of Empire: India and the Creation of Imperial Britain* (2006). An elegant study of the interaction of British political sensibilities and the emergence of the British empire in India.

R. DRAYTON, *Nature's Government: Science, Imperial Britain, and the "Improvement" of the World* (2000). The best volume on the relationship of science and imperialism.

M. H. EDNEY, *Mapping an Empire: The Geograhical Constuction of British India, 1765–1843* (1997). Discusses how the science of cartography contributed to the British domination of India.

N. ETHERINGTON, ED., *Misions and Empire* (2005). An excellent collection of essays.

D. HEADRICK, *The Tools of Empire: Technology and European Imperialism in the Nineteenth Century* (1981). Remains an important work of analysis.

A. HOCHSCHILD, *King Leopold's Ghost: A Study of Greed, Terror, and Heroism in Colonial Africa* (1999). A well-informed account of a tragedy.

I. HULL, *Absolute Destruction: Military Culture and the Practices of War in Imperial Germany* (2006). Excellent account of destructive German actions in East Africa.

R. HYAM, *Britain's Imperial Century 1815–1914: A Study of Empire and Expansion* (2002). The single best one-volume analysis.

T. JEAL, *Livingstone* (2001). This and the following title recount the lives of the two persons most associated in the popular mind with the exploration of Africa.

T. JEAL, *Stanley: The Impossible Life of Africa's Greatest Explorer* (2008). A fascinating portrait of the famous explorer.

A. KAPPELLER, *The Russian Empire: A Multiethnic History* (2001). A straightforward overview that is very clear on the concepts behind Russian expansionist policy.

D. C. LIEVAN, *The Russian Empire and Its Rivals* (2001). Explores the imperial side of Russian government.

K. E. MEYER AND S. B. BRYSA, *Tournament of Shadows: The Great Game and the Race for Empire in Central Asia* (1999). A lively account of the conflict between Great Britain and Russia.

W. J. MOMMSEN, *Theories of Imperialism* (1980). A study of the debate on the meaning of imperialism.

M. A. OSBORNE, *Nature, the Exotic, and the Science of French Colonialism* (1994). Explores the impact of French horticultural gardens and imperialism.

B. PORTER, *The Absent-Minded Imperialists: Empire, Society, and Culture in Britain* (2006). Discusses the relatively few people actually involved in Britain imperialism and how imperialism often had a low profile in the British Isles.

B. PORTER, *The Lion's Share: A Short History of British Imperialism, 1850–2004* (2004). A lively narrative.

L. PYENSON, *Civilizing Mission: Exact Sciences and French Overseas Expansion, 1830–1940* (1993). A major work of the history of both science and imperialism.

R. ROBINSON, J. GALLAGHER, AND A. DENNY, *Africa and the Victorians: The Official Mind of Imperialism* (2000). A classic analysis that continues to bear rereading.

P. J. TUCK, *French Catholic Missionaries and the Politics of Imperialism in Vietnam, 1857–1914* (1987). Includes both narrative and documents.

H. L. WESSELING, *Divide and Rule: The Partition of Africa, 1889–1914* (1996). A clear narrative and analysis of a complicated topic.

H. L. WESSELING, *The European Colonial Empires: 1815–1919* (2004). The best recent overview of the entire nineteenth-century European colonial ventures.

E. R. WOLF, *Europe and the People Without History* (1990). A classic, highly critical account.

A. ZIMMERMAN, *Anthropology and Antihumanism in Imperial Germany* (2001). Discusses the manner in which anthropology in conjunction with imperialism challenged humanistic ideas in German intellectual life.

Chapter 26

L. ALBERTINI, *The Origins of the War of 1914*, 3 vols. (1952, 1957). Discursive, but invaluable.

V. R. BERGHAHN, *Germany and the Approach of War in 1914* (1973). Stresses the importance of Germany's naval program.

S. B. FAY, *The Origins of the World War*, 2 vols. (1928). The best and most influential of the revisionist accounts.

N. FERGUSON, *The Pity of War* (1999). An analytic study of the First World War with controversial interpretations, especially of why it began and why it ended.

O. FIGES, *A People's Tragedy: The Russian Revolution: 1891–1924* (1998). The best recent analytic narrrative.

F. FISCHER, *Germany's Aims in the First World War* (1967). An influential interpretation that stirred an enormous controversy by emphasizing Germany's role in bringing on the war.

D. FROMKIN, *Europe's Last Summer: Who Started the Great War in 1914?* (2004). A lively and readable account of the outbreak of the war based on the latest scholarship.

D. FROMKIN, *A Peace to End All Peace: The Fall of the Ottoman Empire and the Creation of the Modern Middle East* (1989). A well-informed narrative of a complicated process.

R. F. HAMILTON AND H. H. HERWIG, *The Origins of World War I* (2003). An extensive collection of recent essays examining the subject from a number of differing perspectives.

H. HERWIG, *The First World War: Germany and Austria, 1914–18* (1997). A fine study of the war from the losers' perspective.

J. N. HORNE, *Labour at War: France and Britain, 1914–1918* (1991). Examines a major issue on the home fronts.

J. JOLL, *The Origins of the First World War* (2006). Most recent revision of a classic study.

J. KEEGAN, *The First World War* (1999). A vivid and readable narrative.

P. KENNEDY, *The Rise of the Anglo-German Antagonism, 1860–1914* (1980). An unusual and thorough analysis of the political, economic, and cultural roots of important diplomatic developments.

D. C. B. LIEVEN, *Russia and the Origins of the First World War* (1983). A good account of the forces that shaped Russian policy.

M. MACMILLAN, *Paris 1919: Six Months That Changed the World* (2003). The most extensive recent treatment.

E. MANELA, *The Wilsonian Moment: Self Determination and the International Origins of Anticolonial Nationalism* (2007). A major exploration of how Wilson's foreign policy at Versailles raised colonial expectations and revolts in Egypt, India, China, and Korea.

A. MOMBAUER, *The Origins of the First World War: Controversies and Consensus* (2002). A discussion and evaluation of historians' shifting views regarding the responsibility for the outbreak of the war.

Z. STEINER, *Britain and the Origins of the First World War* (2003). A perceptive and informed account of British foreign policy before the war.

D. STEVENSON, *Cataclysm: The First World War as Political Tragedy* (2004). Analyzes the bankruptcy of reason that precipitated the war and kept it going.

N. STONE, *The Eastern Front 1917–1917* (2004). A study of the often neglected region of the war.

H. STRACHAN, *The First World War* (2004). A one-volume version of the massive three-volume magisterial account now underway.

S. R. WILLIAMSON, Jr., *Austria-Hungary and the Origins of the First World War* (1991). A valuable study of a complex subject.

Chapter 27

L. AHAMED, *Lords of Finance: The Bankers Who Broke the World* (2009). A lively narrative of the banking collapse leading to the Great Depression.

W. S. ALLEN, *The Nazi Seizure of Power: The Experience of a Single German Town, 1930–1935*, rev. ed. (1984). A classic treatment of Nazism in a microcosmic setting.

A. APPLEBAUM, *Gulag: A History* (2003). A superbly readable account of Stalin's system of persecution and resulting prison camps.

I. T. BEREND, *Decades of Crisis: Central and Eastern Europe before World War II* (2001). The best recent survey of the subject.

R. J. BOSWORTH, *Mussolini* (2002). A major new biography.

R. J. BOSWORTH, *Mussolini's Italy: Life Under the Fascist Dictatorship, 1915–1945* (2007). A broad-based study of both fascist politics and the impact of those politics on Italian life.

M. BURLEIGH AND W. WIPPERMAN, *The Racial State: Germany 1933–1945* (1991). Emphasizes the manner in which racial theory influenced numerous areas of policy.

I. DEUTSCHER, *The Prophet Armed* (1954), *The Prophet Unarmed* (1959), and *The Prophet Outcast* (1963). Remains the major biography of Trotsky.

B. A. ENGEL AND A. POSADSKAYA-VANDERBECK, *A Revolution of Their Own: Voices of Women in Soviet History* (1998). Long interviews and autobiographical recollections by women who lived through the Soviet era.

R. EVANS, *The Coming of the Third Reich* (2004) and *The Third Reich in Power, 1933–1939* (2005). Superb narratives.

G. FELDMAN, *The Great Disorder: Politics, Economics, and Society in the German Inflation, 1914–1924* (1993). The best work on the subject.

S. FITZPATRICK, *Stalin's Peasants: Resistance and Survival in the Russian Village After Collectivization* (1994). A pioneering study.

F. FURET, *The Passing of an Illusion: The Idea of Communism in the Twentieth Century* (1995). A brilliant account of how communism shaped politics and thought outside the Soviet Union.

R. GELLATELY, *Lenin, Stalin, and Hitler: The Age of Social Catastrophe* (2007). A major new study of the Soviet and Nazi dictatorships.

R. GELLATELY AND N. STOLTZFUS, *Social Outsiders in Nazi Germany* (2001). Important essays on Nazi treatment of groups the party regarded as undesirables.

J. A. GETTY AND O. V. NAUMOV, *The Road to Terror: Stalin and the Self-Destruction of the Bolsheviks, 1932–1939* (1999). A remarkable collection of documents and commentary on Stalin's purges.

R. HAMILTON, *Who Voted for Hitler?* (1982). An examination of voting patterns and sources of Nazi support.

J. JACKSON, *The Popular Front in France: Defending Democracy, 1934–1938* (1988). An extensive treatment.

P. KENEZ, *The Birth of the Propaganda State: Soviet Methods of Mass Mobilization, 1917–1929* (1985). An examination of the manner in which the Communist government inculcated popular support.

B. KENT, *The Spoils of War: The Politics, Economics, and Diplomacy of Reparations, 1918–1932* (1993). A comprehensive account of the intricacies of the reparations problem of the 1920s.

I. KERSHAW, *Hitler*, 2 vols. (2001). Replaces all previous biographies.

C. KINDLEBERGER, *The World in Depression, 1929–1939* (1986). A classic, accessible analysis.

B. LINCOLN, *Red Victory: A History of the Russian Civil War* (1989). An excellent narrative account.

M. MCAULEY, *Bread and Justice: State and Society in Petrograd, 1917–1922* (1991). A study that examines the impact of the Russian Revolution and Leninist policies on a major Russian city.

R. McKibbin, *Classes and Cultures: England, 1918–1951* (2000). Viewing the era through the lens of class.

R. Pipes, *The Unknown Lenin: From the Secret Archives* (1996). A collection of previously unpublished documents that indicated the repressive character of Lenin's government.

P. Pulzer, *Jews and the German State: The Political History of a Minority, 1848–1933* (1992). A detailed history by a major historian of European minorities.

R. Service, *Stalin: A Biography* (2005). The strongest of a host of recent biographical studies.

J. Stephenson, *Women in Nazi Germany* (2001). Analysis with documents.

A. Tooze, *The Wages of Destruction: The Making and Breaking of the Nazi Economy* (2006). A wide-ranging, accessible study of the politics and ideology behind Nazi economic policy.

E. Weber, *The Hollow Years: France in the 1930s* (1995). Examines France between the wars.

L. Yahil, *The Holocaust: The Fate of European Jewry, 1932–1945* (1990). A major study of this fundamental subject in twentieth-century history.

Chapter 28

O. Bartov, *Mirrors of Destruction: War, Genocide, and Modern Identity* (2000). Remarkably penetrating essays.

A. Beevor, *The Spanish Civil War* (2001). Particularly strong on the political issues.

R. S. Botwinick, *A History of the Holocaust*, 2nd ed. (2002). A brief but useful account of the causes, character, and results of the Holocaust.

C. Browning, *The Origins of the Final Solution: The Evolution of the Nazi Jewish Policy* (2004). The story of how Hitler's policy developed from discrimination to annihilation.

W. S. Churchill, *The Second World War*, 6 vols. (1948–1954). The memoirs of the great British leader.

A. Crozier, *The Causes of the Second World War* (1997). An examination of what brought on the war.

J. C. Fest, *Hitler* (2002). Probably the best Hitler biography.

R. B. Frank, *Downfall: The End of the Imperial Japanese Empire* (1998). A thorough, well-documented account of the last months of the Japanese Empire and why it surrendered.

J. L. Gaddis, *We Now Know: Rethinking Cold War History* (1998). A fine account of the early Cold War using new evidence emerging since the collapse of the Soviet Union.

J. L. Gaddis, P. H. Gordon, and E. May, eds., *Cold War Statesmen Confront the Bomb: Nuclear Diplomacy since 1945* (1999). Essays on the effect of atomic and nuclear weapons on diplomacy since World War II.

M. Gilbert, *The Holocaust: A History of the Jews of Europe during the Second World War* (1985). The best and most comprehensive treatment.

M. Hastings, *The Second World War: A World in Flames* (2004). A fine account by a leading student of contemporary warfare.

A. Iriye, *Pearl Harbor and the Coming of the Pacific War* (1999). Essays on how the Pacific war came about, including a selection of documents.

J. Keegan, *The Second World War* (1990). A lively and penetrating account by a master military historian.

W. F. Kimball, *Forged in War: Roosevelt, Churchill, and the Second World War* (1998). A study of the collaboration between the two great leaders of the West.

M. Knox, *Common Destiny, Dictatorship, Foreign Policy, and War in Fascist Italy and Nazi Germany* (2000). A brilliant comparison between the two dictatorships.

M. Knox, *Mussolini Unleashed* (1982). An outstanding study of fascist Italy in World War II.

S. Marks, *The Illusion of Peace* (1976). A good discussion of European international relations in the 1920s and early 1930s.

W. Murray, *The Change in the European Balance of Power 1938–1939* (1984). A brilliant study of the relationship among strategy, foreign policy, economics, and domestic politics.

W. Murray and A. R. Millett, *A War to Be Won: Fighting the Second World War* (2000). A splendid account of military operations.

P. Neville, *Hitler and Appeasement: The British Attempt to Prevent the Second World War* (2005). A defense of the British appeasers of Hitler.

R. Overy, *Why the Allies Won* (1997). An analysis of the reasons for the Allied victory with emphasis on technology.

N. Rich, *Hitler's War Aims*, 2 vols. (1973–1974). The best study of the subject in English.

D. Vital, *A People Apart: The Jews in Europe, 1789–1939* (1999). A major survey with excellent discussions of the interwar period.

R. Wade, *The Russian Revolution, 1917* (2000). A fine account that includes political and social history.

G. L. Weinberg, *A World at Arms: A Global History of World War II* (1994). An excellent narrative.

Chapter 29

A. Ahmed, *Discovering Islam. Making Sense of Muslim History and Society*, rev. ed (2003). An excellent and readable overview of Islamic–Western relations.

C. Bayly, *Forgotten Wars: Freedom and Revolution in Southeast Asia* (2007). An important volume on decolonization by a master historian of the region.

R. Betts, *France and Decolonization* (1991). Explores the complexities of the French case.

A. Brown, *The Gorbachev Factor* (1996). Reflections by a thoughtful observer.

C. Elkins, *Imperial Reckoning: The Untold Story of Britain's Gulag in Kenya* (2005). A study of the violence involved in Britain's eventual departure from Kenya.

M. Ellman and V. Kontorovich, *The Disintegration of the Soviet Economic System* (1992). An overview of the economic strains in the Soviet Union during the 1980s.

G. Fuller, *The Future of Political Islam* (2003). A good overview of Islamist ideology by a former CIA staff member.

J. L. Gaddis, *The United States and the Origins of the Cold War, 1941–1947* (1992). A major discussion.

M. Glenny, *The Balkans, 1804–1999: Nationalism, War and the Great Powers* (1999). A lively narrative by a well-informed journalist.

D. Halberstam, *The Coldest Winter: America and the Korean War* (2007). A superb narrative by a gifted journalist.

M. I. Goldman, *Petrostate: Putin, Power, and the New Russia* (2008). A thoughtful, but critical analysis.

W. Hitchcock, *Struggle for Europe: The Turbulent History of a Divided Continent, 1945–2002* (2003). The best overall narrative now available.

A. Horne, *A Savage War of Peace: Algeria 1954–1962* (1987). A now dated but still classic narrative.

R. Hyam, *Britain's Declining Empire: The Road to Decolonization, 1918–1968* (2007). The best one-volume treatment.

T. Judah, *The Serbs: History, Myth and the Destruction of Yugoslavia* (1997). A clear overview of a complex event.

J. Keay, *Sowing the Wind: The Seeds of Conflict in the Middle East* (2003). A thoughtful account.

N. R. Keddie, *Modern Iran: Roots and Results of Revolution* (2003). Chapters 6–12 focus on Iran from 1941 through the 1978 revolution.

J. Keep, *Last of the Empires: A History of the Soviet Union, 1945–1991* (1995, 2007). An outstanding one-volume survey.

G. Kepel, *Jihad: The Trail of Political Islam* (2002). An extensive treatment by a leading French scholar.

Y. Khan, *The Great Partition: The Making of India and Pakistan* (2008). An important recent study of a difficult issue.

P. Khanna, *The Second World: Empires and Influence in the New Global Order* (2008). A volume that seeks to provide a broad global analysis of recent events.

W. R. Louis, *Ends of British Imperialism: The Scramble for Empire, Suez, and Decolonization* (2007). A major study that captures the intensity and passions of the events.

R. Mann, *A Grand Delusion: America's Descent into Vietnam* (2001). The best recent narrative.

K. E. MEYER AND S. B. BRYSAC, *Kingmakers: The Invention of the Modern Middle East* (2008). A lively narrative of the past two centuries of British and then American influence in the Middle East.

D. E. MURPHY, S. A. KONDRASHEV, AND G. BAILEY, *Battleground Berlin: CIA vs. KGB in the Cold War* (1997). One of the best of a vast literature on Cold War espionage.

W. E. ODOM, *The Collapse of the Soviet Military* (1999). A study more wide ranging than the title suggests.

M. OREN, *Power, Faith, and Fantasy: America in the Middle East: 1776 to the Present* (2007). A thoughtful, balanced analysis.

B. PAREKH, *Gandhi: A Very Short Introduction* (2001). A useful introduction to Gandhi's ideas.

T. R. REID, *The United States of Europe: The New Superpower and the End of American Supremacy* (2004). A journalist's exploration of the impact of the European Union on American policy.

T. SHEPARD, *The Invention of Decolonization: The Algerian War and the Remaking of France* (2008). Explores the impact of the Algerian War on French politics.

L. SHEVTSOVA, *Russia—Lost in Transition: The Yeltsin and Putin Legacies* (2007). A major analysis and meditation on the past two decades.

J. SPRINGHALL, *Decolonization since 1945: The Collapse of European Empires* (2001). Systematic treatment of each major former colony.

B. STANLEY, *Missions, Nationalism, and the End of Empire* (2003). Discusses the often ignored role of Christian missions and decolonization.

M. THOMAS, *The French Empire Between the Wars: Imperialism, Politics and Society* (2005). Useful background to postwar decolonization.

M. VIORST, *In the Shadow of the Prophet: The Struggle for the Soul of Islam* (2001). Explores the divisions in contemporary Islam.

L. WRIGHT, *The Looming Tower: Al Qaeda and the Road to 9/11* (2007). A compelling narrative.

Chapter 30

G. AMBROSIUS AND W. H. HUBBARD, *A Social and Economic History of Twentieth-Century Europe* (1989). An excellent one-volume treatment of the subject.

B. S. ANDERSON AND J. P. ZINSSER, *A History of Their Own: Women in Europe from Prehistory to the Present*, vol. 2 (1988). A broad-ranging survey.

G. BOCK AND P. THANE, EDS., *Maternity and Gender Politics: Women and the Rise of the European Welfare States, 1880s–1950s* (1991). Explores the emergence of welfare legislation.

E. BRAMWELL, *Ecology in the 20th Century: A History* (1989). Traces the environmental movement to its late-nineteenth-century origins.

P. E. CERUZZI, *A History of Modern Computing* (2003). A comprehensive survey.

S. COLLINSON, *Beyond Borders: West European Migration Policy and the 21st Century* (1993). Explores a major contemporary European social issue.

R. CROSSMAN, ED., *The God That Failed* (1949). Classic essays by former communist intellectuals.

D. DINAN, *Europe Recast: A History of the European Union* (2004). A major overview.

C. FINK, P. GASERT, AND D. JUNKER, *1968: The World Transformed* (1998). The best collection of essays on a momentous year.

B. GRAHAM, *Modern Europe: Place, Culture, Identity* (1998). Thoughtful essays on the future of Europe by a group of geographers.

H. S. HUGHES, *Sophisticated Rebels: The Political Culture of European Dissent, 1968–1987* (1988). Thoughtful essays on recent cultural critics.

P. JENKINS, *Mrs. Thatcher's Revolution: The Ending of the Socialist Era* (1988). The best work on the subject.

P. JENKINS, *The Next Christendom: The Coming of Global Christianity* (2002). A provocative analysis.

T. JUDT, *Past Imperfect: French Intellectuals, 1944–1956* (1992). An important study of French intellectuals and communism.

T. JUDT, *Postwar: A History of Europe Since 1945* (2005). The most recent authoritative overview.

R. MALTBY, ED., *Passing Parade: A History of Popular Culture in the Twentieth Century* (1989). Essays on a topic just beginning to receive scholarly attention.

R. MARRUS, *The Unwanted: European Refugees in the 20th Century* (1985). An important work on a disturbing subject.

D. MEYER, *Sex and Power: The Rise of Women in America, Russia, Sweden, and Italy* (1987). A lively, useful survey.

N. NAIMARK, *Fires of Hatred: Ethnic Cleansing in Twentieth-Century Europe* (2002). A remarkably sensitive treatment of a tragic subject.

M. POSTER, *Existential Marxism in Postwar France* (1975). An excellent and clear work.

H. ROWLEY, *Tête-á-Tête: Simone de Beauvoir and Jean-Paul Sartre* (2005). A highly critical joint biography.

S. STRASSER, C. MCGOVERN, AND M. JUDT, *Getting and Spending: European and American Consumer Societies in the Twentieth Century* (1998). An extensive collection of comparative essays.

F. THEBAUD, ED., *A History of Women in the West*, vol. 5: *Toward a Cultural Identity in the Twentieth Century* (1994). A collection of wide-ranging essays of the highest quality.

INDEX

S